Cosima Wagner's *Diaries*

Cosima Wagner's
DIARIES

VOLUME II
1878-1883

Edited and Annotated by
Martin Gregor-Dellin and Dietrich Mack

Translated and with an Introduction, Postscript,
and Additional Notes by Geoffrey Skelton

COLLINS
St James's Place, London
1980

William Collins Sons & Co Ltd
London · Glasgow · Sydney · Auckland
Toronto · Johannesburg

First published in the UK 1980
Copyright © 1977 by R. Piper & Co. Verlag
English translation © 1980 by Geoffrey Skelton
and Harcourt Brace Jovanovich, Inc.

ISBN 0 00 216189 3

Set in Monotype Garamond
Made and Printed in Great Britain by
William Collins Sons & Co Ltd, Glasgow

Contents

List of Illustrations

Orchestra pit of the Bayreuth festival theater during rehearsals for *Parsifal*, 1882
  Drawing in India ink by Josef Greif

Cap for the Knights of the Grail, "designed by R. in hasty fury (jumping up in the midst of supper)."

The Baptism, *Parsifal*, Act III, 1882

Amalie Materna as Kundry, 1882

Heinrich Gudehus as Parsifal, 1882

Siena Cathedral

Temple of the Grail in *Parsifal*
  Scene painting by Paul von Joukowsky

Parsifal, Act III, final scene, 1882
  Woodcut after a drawing by Ludwig Bechstein

Palazzo Vendramin, Venice. The Wagners' quarters were in the rear wing.

Teatro La Fenice, Venice

Richard Wagner while playing the piano, Palazzo Vendramin, February 12, 1883
  Pencil drawing by Paul von Joukowsky

Franz Liszt, 1884

Richard Wagner
  Death mask

All photographs were supplied by Dr. Dietrich Mack, Bayreuth.

Introduction

Volume II of Cosima Wagner's Diaries covers the last five years of
Richard Wagner's life and ends on the eve of his death on February 13,
1883, in Venice. After finishing her final entry, on February 12, Cosima
closed her Diaries forever. Her professed aim in writing them had been
to provide her five children with a full account of the life and character
of Richard Wagner. This task was completed with his death, and in the
forty-seven years of life which remained to her she kept no further
diary.

At the centre of this second volume stands *Parsifal,* Wagner's last
musical work, which he staged at his festival theatre in Bayreuth in
1882. On the literary side there were a few essays and articles written
for and published in his own periodical, the *Bayreuther Blätter;* the final
installment of his autobiography, *Mein Leben,* bringing it up to his
summons to Munich by King Ludwig II of Bavaria in 1864; and a
short account of the performance of his youthful Symphony in C
Major, which he conducted at the Teatro La Fenice in Venice on
December 24, 1882, in honor of Cosima's forty-fifth birthday. This
was virtually his only appearance as a conductor during these years,
though he did, anonymously and without premeditation, take the
baton from Hermann Levi at the last performance of *Parsifal,* on August
29, 1882, to conduct the final scene himself.

Consequently this second volume has less to record in the way of
external events than Volume I, which covered nine years as opposed
to five, yet the two books are almost exactly the same in length. The
main reason for this is clearly that, with the five children older (ranging
in age from nine to eighteen in 1878), Cosima had more time to devote
to her Diaries. She gives fuller accounts of Wagner's conversations
and describes family life—much of it spent away from Wahnfried in
long visits to Italy and Sicily—in much greater detail. However,
though their habits become increasingly reclusive, the outside world
continues to intrude, and the important figures who featured so largely
in the previous years—Bismarck, King Ludwig, Liszt, Hans von Bülow,
etc.—make frequent appearances in these pages. Judith Gautier, the
last of Wagner's so-called loves, is, on the other hand, all but ignored
entirely. That, of course, is not surprising, since Cosima was avowedly
writing her Diaries for her children. Still, what *is* recorded of Judith
is perhaps in its very reticence revealing.

The day-to-day account of the composing of *Parsifal* is particularly fascinating for the insight it gives, both into the work itself and into Wagner's composition methods in general. On the personal level, the picture is more often a sad one, as we watch a physically declining genius move gradually toward his grave. But, for all the melancholy, there are still many flashes of the sturdy resilience and humour which, so faithfully recorded by Cosima in her Diaries, have now shown this extraordinary man in a new and more human light than ever before.

The biographical background to the Diaries was provided in the introduction to the first volume and therefore requires no repetition here. However, in order to enable readers to refresh their memories about the events preceding this second volume, a detailed chronology is provided at the back of this book, covering the full period of the Diaries. Also at the back will be found a postscript describing what happened after Wagner's death to Cosima, her family, and others featured prominently in the Diaries.

For ease of understanding it might be helpful to repeat and even add to the various nicknames under which Cosima's children are referred to: Daniela (her name now spelled thus by Cosima, not "Daniella," as in Volume I): Loulou, Lulu, Lusch, Luschchen; Blandine: Boni, Bonichen, Bonus, Ponsch; Isolde: Loldi, Loldchen; Eva: Evi, Evchen; Siegfried: Fidi, Fidichen, Fidchen, Fidel, Friedel.

In preparing this second volume, the German editors had to contend with a number of passages which had been blocked out in the original, handwritten notebooks. The quality of the ink used in these operations leaves no doubt that they were performed at some later date, but by whom is an unsolved question. As the editors point out, apart from Cosima herself, who can be presumed not to have looked again at them after her husband's death, only three people saw the Diaries— Wagner's biographer, Carl Friedrich Glasenapp; Cosima's biographer, Richard Count Du Moulin Eckart; and Cosima's daughter Eva, wife of the British-born writer Houston Stewart Chamberlain. It was to Eva that Cosima entrusted the Diaries in 1908, and from the time Glasenapp returned them in 1910 until her own death in 1942, Eva did not let them out of her sight.

With the help of various chemical processes the German editors succeeded in bringing most of the obliterated passages back to light, and they are now included in the text with an identification. It is easy to see why certain slightly derogatory references to the editor of the *Bayreuther Blätter,* Hans von Wolzogen, were blocked out, since he remained alive and active in Bayreuth until 1938. The deletions of passages concerning Cosima's father, Franz Liszt, were probably due to feelings of family piety. Other excisions—critical remarks concerning Bismarck and the German state—may have been made, the German editors speculate, during the National Socialist era, during which (in 1935) Eva decided that on her death the Diaries should pass to the town of Bayreuth. If, in this case, the intention had been to avoid casting doubt on Wagner's German patriotism and his devotion to his country's leaders, the editing was clumsily done: many of Wagner's remarks about Bismarck that were *not* obliterated are at least as critical as those that were.

Another feature of this second volume is the large number of additions Cosima made to her text, not only in the margins surrounding her entries, but also often on later pages, in which case she usually referred them with a sign back to their proper place in the text. Since she wrote her entries not regularly each day, but sometimes in batches of several days at a time, relying on jottings in a smaller notebook, there seems no reason to read any particular significance into these marginal additions, and in my translation I have, for the sake of easier reading, incorporated them into the main text without comment, except when they do not fit naturally into the context; in such cases I have enclosed them in brackets and identified them.

In all other matters I have followed in this second volume the presentation methods I defined in my introduction to the first. In this volume, too, the text is complete, except for a very few passages which defy intelligible translation, and in all such cases the omission is indicated. The explanatory notes differ in many instances from those provided in the German edition, reflecting the different requirements of Anglo-Saxon readers.

In making this translation I have been much indebted to my wife, Gertrude, who checked every word of it and whose help in divining Cosima's probable meaning in her obscurer moments has been of inestimable value to me. I also owe gratitude to Mr H. B. Mallalieu, who prepared the index to the second volume and assisted me with the compilation of the chronology, to the German editors for help in solving specific textual problems and to Helen Wolff and Anne T. Zaroff for much advice and assistance in preparing this English edition of the Diaries.

Geoffrey Skelton

The Diaries

1878

[*This volume starts with page 179 of the ninth notebook of the Diaries. Between the pages lies a telegram from Franz Liszt in Budapest, dated December 27, 1877, reading:* "*Parsifal* just received; speechless with gratitude, with heart and soul, your Liszt."]

Tuesday, January 1 "The sinful world is keeping me busy," says R. — He is working today, as every day, and says laughingly that I must have told everyone to spare him, since nobody is bringing him any bad news. We drive out to the Feustels' and the mayor's. In the evening [Dante's] *Divina commedia*. Very nice letter from the King's new secretary, to which R. replies cordially.

Wednesday, January 2 R. works and makes me happy at lunch with the remark, "I am enjoying my life tremendously, I am immersing myself more and more in my world of spirits, the whole day is taken up with their rhythms and fluctuations," etc. "I am a lucky man," he tells me in the evening. Oh, God, oh, heavens, what have I done to deserve the happiness of seeing him so contented? — From Count Apponyi a *wonderful* letter about *Parsifal*, which Richard calls *sublime*. A very trying one for me from Hans [von Bülow], which I answer at once. Herr von W[olzogen] reads us his circular letter, written in R.'s name to the local Wagner Societies. In the evening the *Divina commedia* and the 8th Symphony, of whose concluding movement R. says that for him it is the finest thing B[eethoven] ever produced, a celebration of life and all that it means, divine! — To end the day he plays and sings to me "*Die sündige Welt*"—how overwhelming it is, how incomparably beautiful! What can one possibly say? . . .

Thursday, January 3 R. working! He does not feel entirely well, has a curious taste of sour milk in his mouth which will not go away; I hope it is nothing, but I am worried. At lunch he tells us how he asked his mother for money to buy his first music paper, in order to copy out "*Lützow's wilde Jagd*". She gave him the money grudgingly at first, but was then quite moved when she saw his first notes! — The news coming to Herr von W[olzogen] from all quarters concerning the organization of the Society of Patrons sounds quite good. — I spend the morning arranging the library. In the evening the history of the

Arabs once more, since R. feels too worn out to read the *Divina commedia*.

Friday, January 4   R. dreamed that I was in tears and embraced him, because he was ill! It makes us laugh that this was the best dream he could think up for himself! He works, is feeling well again, tells us at lunch how as a child he once swindled the parson out of ¾ of his confession money, having spent it on cream puffs! When he fell out with his mother, he pretended he wanted to go to confession, and was then given the money! — A walk with him in the palace gardens. Then he goes to work again; when I come down to see him, he says, "You come right on a middle voice, a difficult middle voice!" In the evening the *Divina commedia* again; despite his admiration for the poet, he feels great repugnance for the subject of the poet's imagination. As we go off to bed, he says he is having difficulty in baking life's daily bread. — Yesterday a very nice letter (reply) from the King's new secretary. — Yesterday, too, Herr v. Wolzogen read us his circular, written in R.'s name to the local Societies.

Saturday, January 5   Once again R. dreamed the thoughts which gave me a sleepless night! . . . He works and, around noon, calls me in order to play me the conclusion of the entrance [of the Knights of the Grail] and Titurel's wonderfully melancholic appeal. "I have spoiled things for the spa orchestras," he says with a laugh; "my entrance ends without suffering!" I am still overwhelmed by my impressions, while he, seeming to be swimming in his element, enlivens our lunch table with his high spirits. He gives me the *"Schmerzensblatt"!* — I then tell him how this morning Herr v. W. and I began to arrange the library; then we discuss Herr v. W.'s work with the patrons. "It was time," says R., "that I was allowed for once to write a work under such good auspices." At 7 o'clock I leave him to take Lusch to her first ball, returning home at 3:30 A.M.! . . . I decide to make up for the boredom of this most frivolous of duties by not showing any signs of weariness at home, and on

Sunday, January 6   I get up at my usual time. R. tells me that he waited up for me until 1:30 A.M.! . . . Very early in the morning I felt his hand groping to see that I was there. During the evening he had read an article by Pohl with the W[olzogen]s and had looked through his *"Fantasie"* again. Today he works on his essay for the [*Bayreuther*] *Blätter,* which will soon be published. He told me that, if he had not invited Herr v. W. to settle here, nothing would have induced him to say a single word more. I arrange the library with Herr v. W. At lunch R. says, "I propose a toast—nobody will guess to what." We ask him. "Today is the first performance of *Die Walküre* in Schwerin!" He talks very indignantly about this affair, which really is iniquitous.

He paid Herr Hill 7,000 marks, and as a reward for releasing him they demand *Die Walküre*—but R. had only meant the right to perform it! . . . I do not remember how we came to speak of the Venetians, but R. said, "Excellent statesmen, but completely heartless human beings: nothing can be more alien to what one calls religion than a state." — In the evening, the history of the Arabs, an unpoetical, unsympathetic, yet noble people. Nice letter from friend Schuré about *Parsifal*. R. takes pleasure in the ideas and the nice drawings in the *Fliegende Blätter,* he says it is still a truly German periodical.

Monday, January 7   Coming from his bath, R. says to me: "You are quite right—we should have slaves" (I declared recently that slaves had been happier than the present-day proletariat), "but who should be the first slave? Ross or Georg?" We laugh heartily. — I continue arranging the books with Herr v. W., and we finish the first section. R. works on his essay. When I told R. yesterday that if he was not in the mood to write it, he should drop it, he replied, "Oh, I can't be such a weakling." I: "The weakness which is creating *Parsifal*." He: "What comes pouring out of one's soul can't be described as work." — I spoke to Herr v. W. about the Society of Patrons, and afterward R. says to me: "You turn my life into a real blessing. — When shall we go down to our graves?" "Whenever you like," I reply! In the evening scenes from [Shakespeare's] *Coriolanus*.

Tuesday, January 8   R. finishes his article for the B[ayreuther] *Blätter.* He is well and in good spirits. I have to pay some calls with Lusch, R. comes to meet me, an old lady sees him by the school and calls out to him, "Your dear wife went that way." He turns into the road to find me, but since I am paying a call, he has to wait a while, and I come upon him with Dr. Landgraf, gaping at the moon, as he says! Cheerful walk home with him. In the evening he reads us his introduction; he says, "I give little, but I spare nothing, either." After that, continue with *Coriolanus*. Hans sends me his letters to Herr Scnff; dismal impression . . .

Wednesday, January 9   R. returns to work! At lunch, recalling Rossini's *Moses,* he says, "I'm now making my two Pharaohs sing their duet." I continue arranging books with Herr v. W. — An aunt of his has sent 100 marks for the Society of Patrons. Walk with R. Unfortunately when we return home he is vexed about his C Major Overture and decides not to publish it. In the evening the history of the Arabs and *Coriolanus*.

Thursday, January 10   Skating for the children, R.'s cold weather has arrived! Last night we dreamed more or less the same thing—that I was arranging concerts for somebody and R. was jealous. We laugh. "We are now enjoying the happiest time of our lives," he said yesterday evening. At lunch he announces, "My Pharaohs are locked in battle," and tells me I will be amazed to see what he has done with the words *"zu diesem Amt verdammt zu sein"* ["to be condemned to this office"]. With R. and the children on the ice. — Correcting the proofs of the [*Siegfried*] *Idyll;* R. says, "It is my favorite composition." — In the evening the history of the Arabs and then the conclusion of *Coriolanus.* — Never before has the scene between the women and C. had such an overwhelming effect on me! I can hardly contain my emotion. One must acknowledge that one can never really know these works: they are inexhaustible. And to hear them read by R.! . . .

Friday, January 11 R. works. Before lunch he tells me things are going so well for him that he intends to compose *Die Sieger* immediately after *Parsifal,* in order to prolong his condition. I teased him for talking as if things did not always go well for him. Cheerful mood. Lovely winter weather. The children on the ice, we with them. In the evening the history of the Arabs. R. does not take as much pleasure in it as at the first reading. I tell him the reason is that he is such a productive reader, he conjures up a vivid picture and believes it is the author who has created it, and then he is astonished not to find it again! — After our friends have left, we remain together talking intimately about *Parsifal.* — R. speaks of the perplexity with which P[arsifal] listens to Amf[ortas]'s complaints; his mysterious, unconscious gestures of fellow suffering, which comes out into the open with Kundry's kiss and only then becomes clear to him.

Saturday, January 12 Around lunchtime R. plays me what he has composed of "Amfortas's Lament"; the modulation on the words *"nach ihm"* ["after him"] occupied him the whole morning; talking about it at lunch, he says, "I sit there, looking at your portrait, [*illegible word*], I am an idiotic composer, it's all such an effort." — Very cold weather. Worry about Fidi, whose room has become damp; we move him to the nursery. In the evening the history of the Arabs. Then R. sings us some of the recitatives from [Spohr's] *Jessonda,* in which the "interchange of feeling" and similar absurdities make us laugh a lot. "Such things never occur with French composers," says R.

Sunday, January 13 "A son has arrived"—R. remembers his happiness when Vreneli spoke these words to him! Yesterday evening, thinking about various dates in his life, R. felt he had made a mistake in his biography, and that it was only the stillness of the Asyl garden which felt in his memory like a Good Friday, it had not been Good Friday in fact. — In the evening R. says he will have to rewrite everything he wrote during the morning. He was looking for a certain key, and mechanical modulation is something he finds impossible! "I'm a fine musician," he says with a laugh, adding that it is only when he is working without reflection that he finds what he wants—if he starts to consider how to transpose a theme into another key, he gets confused! — He sings us Titurel and the beginning of Amfortas. . . . Impossible after that to pick up something like the history of the Arabs! . . . We gradually drift into conversation. A nice letter has arrived from the King, and it is read aloud. Herr v. W. tells us of all sorts of good things he has experienced in connection with the Society of P[atrons]; the Academic Society in Vienna is behaving very well again and has sent 200 florins. A Herr Kürschner, who prepares statistics for all the theater periodicals, writes declaring his utter devotion to Bayreuth! A *"Juge"* ["judge"] wishes the *Blätter* to be sent to him. All of them touching signs! . . . Herr Hill writes about *Die Walküre* in Schwerin; R., however, is ignoring this production entirely, and he deposits unopened on Hans Wolzogen's desk a letter in which the latter's father is presumably offering a royalty payment. The conductor Schmitt has written to me, but R. asks me not to reply.

Monday, January 14 Letters of all kinds. R. inscribes the pages *"Eulalia"!* Everything that has gone awry is now called "Eulalia," after an anecdote in the *Fl[iegende] Blätter!* R. says laughingly that future generations will think it refers to a secret love! Fidi not quite well, which causes us concern. In the afternoon I have a conversation with Herr Feustel, and he requests me to ask the King to approve payment of royalties by the Munich theater. I thank friend Feustel very cordially for entrusting this to me and sparing R. at this time. R. comes to fetch me, and I return home with him. Two lean cows remind him of Pharaoh's dream, which keeps him occupied the whole way home. — Conversed in the evening, then two "songs from Hell."

Tuesday, January 15 Our friend Wolzogen works out the membership statistics of the Society of Patrons, according to which we possess about 11,000 marks! In the evening he reads us his memorandum for the *Blätter,* which, apart from a few stylistic blemishes, is excellent. — Dismay over a letter from Hans with an enclosure; R.'s letter deliberately misinterpreted! . . . I reply to Hans that it would indeed have been better to remain silent—but from the very start! . . . R. has been working: "No more Eulalia," he says! — I suggested to Herr Feustel that the royalties from *Die Walküre* in Schwerin be put toward the deficit. — Talked about *Die Walküre,* the performances of which seem fated to bring us sorrow! . . . In the evening R. plays us the "Grail March" and sings "Amfortas's Lament." — He seems to me to be in a somewhat bad mood; I fear it is due to financial worries.

Wednesday, January 16 Library again. R. works meanwhile, he did not have a very good night, but he does not feel unwell. Without his knowledge I write to the King, begging him to give orders that royalties be paid on R.'s works to help wipe out the deficit. — A Spaniard, Herr Marsillach, announces the publication of his book and asks for an autograph as a motto. R. writes it. — Today during his afternoon rest he had a sad dream: someone was singing on the water, I said I did not care for it, then we got nearer, and it was Fidi, who, still singing, sank beneath the water, saying, "Adieu, Papa, adieu, Mama"! — In the evening *The Spaniards.*

Thursday, January 17 R. works. I am occupied with accounts and the library. R. goes for a walk in the afternoon, returns home in good spirits, and does some work. In the evening the history of the Arabs. After that [Schiller's] *Don Carlos,* the scene between the Queen and Posa, moves us profoundly—we pity people who no longer respond to it.

Friday, January 18 Nice letter from H[err] Glasenapp in Riga about *Parsifal.* R. works, then tells me he has never thought up anything as "terrific" as this work, it gets better and better! . . . Yesterday we had to laugh heartily over a letter from our good Lesimple, who declares that Herr Lindau has been won over, is delighted with *Parsifal!* — In the evening R. says, "I have got Amfortas to shut his mouth." — When our friends have gone, he plays me the wonderful fulfillment of the prophecy following Amfortas's last words. — A man in Olmütz (named Mandelblüh!) sends suggestions for altering the chorus of the Valkyries to make it sound better! . . . R. plays through his Sonata in A Major and decides not to publish it, either; he says the *"Fantasie"* is more him, this could be by one of Spohr's pupils.

Saturday, January 19 R. works, tells me that the hardest part now lies ahead; in the evening he informs me that he has made the knights join in on the words *"harre sein"* ["await him"], otherwise the boys' voices would have gone too low: "That was a good idea I had." — He goes out in the afternoon, in the evening he is upset that I should feel obliged to fetch Lulu from a ball, where she is with friends; to see me under an obligation toward anyone but himself offends him. I feel sad and can only hope that a kind guardian angel will soon relieve me of this task.

Sunday, January 20 Everything evenly balanced: love and the blessings of work. In the evening R. improvises the Communion service in the way he has now designed it: "The percussion will accompany the singing, like a faint earth tremor." — R. looked through Berlioz's scores of the *Requiem* and *Te Deum* and laughed over the many instructions they contain for the percussion players, etc., etc.; he said it reminded him of a theater director setting straight the wigs of his actors; the uproar on the *"rex tremendae majestatis"* made him laugh heartily. He goes for a short walk in the palace gardens.

I am delighted with his appearance in the evening: "I feel so well," he tells me with shining eyes. I am filled with both bliss and apprehension—oh, this mortal life! R. says, "Fidi looks at me the way Parsifal looks on the Grail, in a wonder of amazement."

Monday, January 21 R. dreamed of a complete break between us. "What is the good of knowing that inside us we belong entirely to each other," he exclaims, "when something like this is still possible?" — When I ask him how he can ever dream such things: "Well, our dear Lord is not selective when he wants to wake us up—or, rather, he *is* selective, and chooses the most hideous thing he can think of, knowing he can no longer scare me much with the failure of one of my operas." — R. had to get up very early! However, he managed to work and is utterly filled with his glorious work. He thinks he will not allow Titurel to speak again after the rites. "A modulation" causes him difficulties in the afternoon and, as he is going off to sleep, I hear him cry aloud, "It must be A flat, G flat, F." — A curious interruption in our sublime life is provided by the visit of the opera director Angelo Neumann from Leipzig and Israel. He has come for the *Ring* but would also like to have *Parsifal!* Coaxes R. out of half the royalties for the subscription quota—in short, is just what such gentlemen always are. R. says he has nothing against his coming, insofar as it shows they still need him—and we need money, so agreement is reached!

Tuesday, January 22 Around lunchtime R. calls me and says he has something to show me; he plays and sings to me the heavenly scene of the uncovering of the Grail! As tender and exalted as Salvation itself! The words "*Wein und Brot des letzten Mahles*" ["wine and bread of the Last Supper"] sound like an ancient saga told by angels. . . . "But I won't let the old man appear again," R. says; "he would remind me too much of that old gondolier in Venice who always butted in when others were singing." Stormy weather, no sun, but no cold, either. In the evening finished the history of the Arabs. Then the Falstaff scenes in *Henry IV Part I*. R. says the scene with the carriers and Gadshill is one of those he admires most of all. "That is real closeness to Nature, for the life of the common people is Nature." — A man sends us a paper about the Nibelungs; R. says, "I've only got to hear the syllable *Ni* now to take to my heels."

Wednesday, January 23 R. says, "We are living like gods," although he again had a disturbed night. In the evening he says to me, "You will laugh!," and he shows me the part of Titurel, whom he has brought in again after all. In the morning we discussed the scenery for the Temple of the Grail, and I suggest a basilica, two naves leading through pillars to doors hidden behind them. In the evening R. plays and sings to us the most glorious scenes ever to have been written and set to music!

Thursday, January 24   R. still disturbed at night . . . But he works with enjoyment. At lunch he tells me, "I shall alter the words *'den Erlöser, den ihr preist'* ["the Redeemer whom you praise"] into *'Liebes-Geist, der euch speist'* ["spirit of love which feeds you"], for *'den ihr preist'* is flat, is there just for the sake of the rhyme." Our final words yesterday had to do with the Godhead; I: "I must believe in it—my unworthiness and my happiness lead me to believe." He: "The first part, your unworthiness, you can cross out; Godhead is Nature, the will which seeks salvation and, to quote Darwin, selects the strongest to bring this salvation about." — At lunch admired once again the objectivity of Shakespeare's genius; Henry V, hero and model, thoroughly unsympathetic. His Lancaster instinct makes him feel he should appear better than he is, and he leads a wild life purposely, as it were, in order to make an impression. The ending [of *Henry V*] with its marriage scene incredible in its veracity. — If only R. could sleep well again at night! — We ate alone together upstairs, both lunch and supper. We start W[alter] Scott's *The Heart of Midlothian* and find much enjoyment in it. R. tells me of the alteration in his text, now fixed. When I wish him a very good night, he says he is all contentment now, and little disturbances do not affect him.

Friday, January 25   Again ate alone upstairs with R. "I shall soon have my *monsieurs* shuffling off to the 'Radetzky March,'" he says with a laugh. Another blissful day of love and work, oblivious of the world. In the evening our noble W. Scott again gives us the utmost enjoyment.

Saturday, January 26   Work with the children, hearing the sacred sounds! R. is still preoccupied when he comes to lunch, and in the evening he sings to me *"Selig in Liebe, selig im Glauben"* ["Blessed in love, blessed in faith"]. "Oh, that's beautiful!" he cries, "exactly as I wanted it." And it *is* beautiful! How can I describe these feelings which send shivers through me? How express this wish to die, this apprehension about his well-being, this blessing and trembling, this pleading and thanking? Our life is now even more blissful, ecstatic, than it was in Tribschen! . . . Only the knowledge that R.'s foot is giving him pain and preventing his walking much casts a shadow over my feelings— and a large one, alas! — In the evening W. Scott.

Sunday, January 27   R. got no sleep after 3:30 A.M. and had digestion troubles. . . . He works still, and thus I hover between bliss and apprehension! — Rumors of peace in the East; we are hoping for a serious and definitive solution to this problem, after all the terrible sufferings it has caused.

Monday, January 28   Herr v. Hülsen has forbidden the theater managers in Kassel, Wiesbaden, Hanover to produce anything not previously approved by him!! . . . The German Reich! R. feels tired, I beg him from my heart not to overwork, and all day long he says with a laugh, "I'm not permitted to compose." — Friend Standhartner reports that Hans [Richter] has made up for his remissness and that *Rheingold* is a big success in Vienna—which we doubt, insofar as we have received no telegrams about it. Friend Feustel reports that he has found everything progressing well in Munich, and it therefore seems that my letter had a not unfavorable effect on the King. The proofs of the periodical have arrived, and R. is working. So everything is nice and pleasant, but my feelings of apprehension persist—when one has been used to difficulties, one takes only a painful delight in happiness; what is happiness but complete disassociation from life and the world, a premonition of death, and indeed a longing for it? I am filled with horror at the thought of a life in which he would not be there to show me the way, to bring me salvation—even our simple "good night," a momentary separation, conjures up this vision and makes me shudder. Oh, this mortal life! . . .

Tuesday, January 29 R. had a good night, that is, he got up only once. But to my eyes he looks run down. On the penciled sketches is written "January 29, '78"—they are finished. R. shows me the voice which breathes the words "*selig im Glauben*" once again after Parsifal has been repulsed by Gurnemanz. I said to R. that, just like the imperceptible change and the unfelt development within Parsifal himself, this music develops, changes, hovers—one is wrapped up and borne along by it as if by magic; light gives way to dark as in the colors of clouds at sunset, and all one feels is a constant, unchanging sense of spiritual well-being as one is borne along by it. . . . And what is the world doing for *him?* The W. Society in Berlin is having a commemoration day! In this chasm which divides him from the world I lay all my love, my poor, infinite love, filled with sacrificial longings! —

Wednesday, January 30 When I say to R. in the morning that it is at any rate a good thing the French no longer have a say in foreign affairs, he replies, "But what have we to show, we Germans?" He recalls the behavior of the people and of the princes toward him, how none of them are following him, supporting him; after carrying through the festival in spite of all difficulties, what does he now get but silence? — In the evening R. inks in his work after writing a few letters, among them one to Herr Pollini, saying he should present *Rheingold* at the same time as *Walküre* and not after it. In the evening W. Scott. — R. looks in on me when he returns from his walk and says, "You are a gift from Heaven; it's because of you that I believe in God!" —

Thursday, January 31 R. had a somewhat disturbed night, he awakes with a headache, but it subsides, he works, and in the evening he shows me the ink sketch of the conclusion of the first act. "Now thank we all our God" is my prayer! We spend the evening in reminiscences of Tribschen, my joining him there, the subsequent arrival of the two elder children, Fidi's birth—lost in blissful thoughts. Only when I am alone does my apprehension return; R.'s foot prevents his taking walks, and that in turn upsets his digestive processes. He tells me it is nothing, that on the whole he feels very well, but how, once beset by it, can one banish worry?

Friday, February 1 R. had a good night, and I hear him practicing the final words of Gurnemanz. For me this is like sunshine. But today unfortunately we have a housewarming lunch with the Wolzogens, who yesterday moved into their apartment, and in the evening a reception here, our sacrificial offering for living in Bayreuth. Both disagreeable for R., though he endures them with great kindness and amiability. — Annoying letters: from the conductor Eckert, who is unwilling to take the refusal of *Die Walküre* seriously, and from Herr Voltz: these gentlemen want to take over *Der Ring des Nibelungen,* too! The conductor Abt writes to Batz: "*Cosima* has written to me to say . . ." For this "Cosima" R. gives Herr Voltz a deserved rebuke; and to Herr Eckert he writes that though his letter may have contained a joke, it was by no means meant as a joke.

Saturday, February 2 R. slept well, but he feels tired. Splendid letter to me from the King, he is approving royalties as a means of wiping out the deficit. And this news I am able to bring R.! — The King's letter is very beautiful. R. jokes and calls me his *Jeanie,* who looks after him; we are really delighted, particularly since the solution comes from R.'s earnings (royalties on his works). In the evening W. Scott with our friends the Wolzogens.

Sunday, February 3 I write to the King to thank him. For some time now R. has been reading with great enjoyment Turgenev's *Sportsman's Sketches,* which I recommended to him, and he tells us about them at lunch. His foot is paining him, which distresses me deeply. In the evening we finish *The Heart of Midlothian* with great satisfaction. "A great writer, the crown of a civilized period, a great master," says R. — Before that he played me the scene between Gurnemanz and the squires, the entrance of Amfortas, his words to Kundry—oh, how beautiful it all is, how singularly moving! — All sorts of silly things are being said about *Parsifal,* I gather from H. v. W.; someone thinks it is like an *auto,* other Christian people deplore Klingsor's maidens, many are shocked by the "gooseherd"—oh, dear! . . .

Monday, February 4 R. says that when he is not composing he does not feel well, then thinks his life is too good! In the evening we go through *What Is German?,* to be rewritten perhaps for the second issue of the periodical. R. feels he can only tell the truth without reserve, and I agree with him that the proper thing for us is either truthfulness or silence. I should prefer to remain silent, R., too, but the engagement of Herr v. W. and the periodical in consequence of that oblige us to speak—so then, in God's name, the truth! . . . "It is this stupid theater I have hung around my neck which makes all this necessary," R. says; "otherwise I could be enjoying the quietest and most pleasant of lives."

Tuesday–Wednesday, February 5–6   The contract with Munich has arrived; it will be discussed tomorrow. All sorts of domestic things to occupy me. — R. has had sent to him *The Trumpeter of Säckingen* (60th reprinting) and also the symphony by Brahms which has been performed with tremendous success in Vienna and Leipzig. After reading it through, he says: "One can't really wonder that such things get written; there is nothing in it, but the public cheers! As far as they are concerned, Beethoven and the great poets have lived in vain." R. finds the formlessness of *The Trumpeter* distasteful, rather like a student, pipe in mouth. The symphony, with all its triviality blown up by orchestral effects, its tremolando theme which might have come from the introduction to a Strauss waltz, we find utterly shocking. — R. has written to our friend Schuré asking him to send some tobacco, and he adds the remark that, if only he had opted for Germany, what could he not say to the Germans, how he could reproach them for their meanness, whereas in France he is nothing! — After the Brahms symphony, a chapter of Scott's *The Presbyterians.* Copies of the *Idyll* arrive. —

Thursday, February 7   R. tells me he has started work again, I helped him to it! A little gift (a tablecloth with roses), which I presented to him to celebrate the conclusion of the first act, has given him pleasure. Better than anyone else he can take delight in the smallest of things. Klingsor will be very brutal, he says—"brooding, as you can imagine." — He has also got Kundry's cry. — In the afternoon a conference with Feustel about the contract with Munich, in which a few points will have to be changed. Arrival of the *Bayreuther Blätter,* orthopedic consultation with Frau Dr. Herz, then the Pope dying, the Russians in Constantinople, and trouble brewing in France, Gambetta and Roscher accusing each other of the disaster of 1870! Quite a lot for Saint Richard's Day—but in Wahnfried all is peace and happiness. R. is delighted with the *Idyll,* he says again that it is his favorite composition, and he sends it to my father "with Cosel's permission."

Friday, February 8   R. works, I have all kinds of things to arrange and put away, much fighting with the dragon. R. sketches out a canon for a domestic symphony, then he writes to the King, describing our life in Tribschen at the time of the *Idyll,* which he sends to the King as a gift, saying that he is now enjoying the happiest days of his life. His words move me deeply, and I pray we may be granted a prolongation of them. In the evening we read *The Presbyterians* with growing pleasure.

Saturday, February 9 R. did not have an entirely good night, but it was disturbed only by silly dreams, not bad ones; yesterday, too, he woke up, laughing loudly, and told me that somewhere outside Paris he had been seeking the way to a house in which *Rothschild* lived, and had suddenly found himself in an avenue of cows (like a terrace of sphinxes), and these had been very smelly! Unable to find his way, he had asked someone where the house was. "Between Blasewitz and Pilnitz," the other said. "*Non, non, pas Pilnitz, c'est la maison de Roth-schild.*" "*Ah, Ferrières.*" "*Mais non, je sprecherai . . .*"—and in his vexation at not having said "*je vous dirai*" or "*parlerai,*" he had woken up! This mixture of words in French and places in Saxony together with Rothschild made him and us laugh heartily. — But his foot is still painful and hinders his walking, it worries me deeply, and I do not know what to do. In the evening I take Lusch to a ball at the President's house, leave her there in the care of a friend, return home after an hour, and find R. playing [Mozart's] G Minor Symphony with Herr Seidl. In Herr Tappert's *Mus[ik]zeitung* there was a report of a performance of this symphony at the Hochschule, and T. had added the remark "There is not much in it." — This dismissive comment makes R. indignant. He says of the themes of the first and second movements, "They should be set in diamonds," and adds that Beethoven had lived on them in his early works. Distress over our friends and their rash judgments, based on ignorance. To rid ourselves of this we read W. Scott. — Every evening, every tranquil night is a seal on a blissful day!

Sunday, February 10 R. tells me he is now clear about his prelude. At lunch he again talks about the G Minor Symphony with the utmost admiration. He goes out, but only for a short while and with slow steps, on account of his poor foot. In the evening W. Scott; also Haydn's *Military* Symphony—"All our music is based on these works." Report of a defensive and offensive alliance between Russia and Turkey; unexpected and perhaps wise, but how must the people, who shed their blood, feel about it? How can heroism continue to live in a nation when its people are forced to see everything, however tragical, as a comedy? . . .

Monday, February 11 R. revises *What Is German?* for the *Bayreuther Blätter.* He awoke with a headache. The sky remains gray, in the past four months it has cleared only for my birthday and at Candlemas. In their concert the students of Jena gave, as they tell us, the first public performance of the *Siegfried Idyll*. W. Scott in the evening.

Tuesday, February 12 The grief I was fearing has not passed me by; it has come upon me from outside. May God help me! . . . Oh, sorrow, my old companion, come back and dwell within me; we know each other well—how long wilt thou stay with me this time, most loyal and dependable of friends? Purify me, make me worthy of thee, I shall not flee from thee—but when wilt thou bring me thy brother? . . . Splendid weather, R. is able to go out a while, but not much, on account of his foot. W. Scott in the evening. The scenes in the castle of Tillietudlem rather too prolonged.

Wednesday, February 13 R. has a headache and cannot work; he is reading *A Sportsman's Sketches* with growing enjoyment. We go for a walk in the palace gardens, the weather is splendid, the children skate on the ice. In the evening W. Scott.

Thursday, February 14 R. tells me that three mornings ago he saw a spider in his dressing room and, with thoughts of "dire warning," shooed it away; this morning he found it drowned in the bath! We laugh and recall that spiders have been his messengers fairly often. — A man in Rostock sends us an article about *Die Walküre* in Schwerin, written with much good will and some correctness, though with gross blunders in it—for example, though the "Magic Fire" was so beautifully artistic here, they would prefer to see actual flames before their eyes! — Bad political news, the British are reported to have forced the Dardanelles, which suggests an alliance with Austria! If that happens, France will not remain idle, and then we shall have a general war on our hands! Speaking about it, R. says, "Hardly has Prof. Haase been paid off when my royalties go up in smoke, for it will be the end of Austria." I observed that Herr von Hülsen would then become master in Vienna as well. Letter from Herr Rudolphi, the theater manager in Brunswick. R. replies, advising him against producing the *Ring*. In the evening I take Lusch to a ball, hand her over to a friend there, and return home at 8:30 to find R. playing *Parsifal* with Herr Seidl. They start again for me, singing and playing the first act up to Gurnemanz's great narration. In distant places the ambiguous, noisy success of his works, here in tranquillity the unfolding and blossoming of this divine flower. May Heaven grant us this tranquillity a little longer! I pray and pray, calling on God for help. How well I know that all my sufferings are deserved, I know it and bear it in silence with a heavy heart. Prayer and work! — In my absence the children begged, through Fidi, to be allowed to listen to *Parsifal*, saying it is so beautiful!

Friday, February 15 R. somewhat run down, he suffers with me, and we resolve to take no notice of anything, but just to concentrate on our happiness. He is reading Lichtenberg with much enjoyment;

his deeper philosophical nature and education make him far superior to the French moralists. At lunch R. relates to us his dream about a performance of *Die M[eister]singer* which was very bad—almost all the members of the orchestra left, and it was more spoken than sung. In the afternoon he goes for a little walk, in the evening W. Scott. Morton's rescue seems to us a little too noble, but afterward R. says the humane purpose of these works is to show how, amid all the terrible happenings, the better side of the individual characters triumphs. If just the horrors, such as this meeting of the Covenanters, were described, it would be unbearable. I do the reading, since my eyes are somewhat better, and R. says I read the story in a tone of regret at all these terrible happenings. The confusion in the insurgents' camp, the sense of panic remind R. of the Dresden rebellion, the episode in Freiberg, and how one can be deceived by an apparent victory into telling oneself that, when it is all over, a new world will begin.

Saturday, February 16 R. asks me whether I am cheerful, for only then does his ideal world exist for him, only then can he work. This helps to dispel all the clouds, I see my sad thoughts dispersing like patches of fog, and though weariness remains, it is of a gentle nature. R. is working! He is delighted with the F he has given Klingsor at the start, and he also shows me the surging movement he has placed beneath Klingsor's somber and mysterious melody. I go out to attend to purchases for R.'s birthday, he comes to meet me with friend Gross, and we walk home together in thick fog with Marke and Brange. In the evening W. Scott, whom I read aloud; R. says it seems as if Lichtenberg must have based all his definitions of a good novelist on W. Scott. How splendid the conversation between Claverhouse and Morton! The [*illegible word*] things, however, unfortunately always rather trivial. — Before we begin our reading we hear issuing from the *salon* the beginning of the "Holy Grail March"—Loldi is playing it and adding a kind of upper voice to it; this pleases R. very much, and it is truly very moving—"the best testimony to my work," says R. — Some ridiculous newspaper reports, such as the engagement of Herr Glatz in Paris for 40,000 francs. Then a Prussian deputy who declared in a public debate that such a law could not be made *ex ungue leone* [from the lion's claws]—what he meant to say was "off the cuff." Then a report that for the approaching wedding Eckert's new torch dance would be made up of themes from *Die Msinger,* particularly *"Am stillen Herd."* One of our friends read us the article on *Parsifal,* which says W. cannot be reproached for not having remained loyal to the legend. We inquire which legend is meant. Much nonsense.

Sunday, February 17 Eva's birthday; I celebrate it first of all with the children in a rehearsal of the May Festival. R. works. At 1 o'clock the presentation of gifts, with the *Msinger* melody, merry lunch, sunshine; in the evening we finish *The Presbyterians,* regretting the obtrusiveness of the "educated" lovers' episode. But before that *Parsifal,* our friend Seidl playing, R. singing—indescribable delight! — When I thank R. for letting me be present at what he calls his studies with Seidl, he chides me and says, "When I see your eyes fixed on me, you could coax the very last note out of me."

Monday, February 18 R. works in the garden, Fidi sings Klingsor's motive, which pleases R. very much. Lovely sunshine. R. and I go for a walk in the palace gardens, but since it is very wet and muddy, we just walk in a circle on the green meadow beside the parade ground, thinking of the Elysian fields and of Achilles, who preferred being a laborer on earth to dwelling in bliss in the shades! — In the evening read Lichtenberg with much, much enjoyment. The aphorisms on philosophy and religion are splendid: he is a true forerunner of Schopenhauer.

Tuesday, February 19 Again R. did not have a very good night, and his foot is still very painful; there is nowhere here to buy good boots. Then he works, and tells me he has reached the "*Höllenrose*" ["rose of hell"]. I am not well, and we lunch together upstairs. "Who is Titurel?" he asks me. I reflect. "Wotan," he says. "After his renunciation of the world he is granted salvation, the greatest of possessions is entrusted to his care, and now he is guarding it like a mortal god"—a lovely thought! I say that Wotan's name ought to be reflected in the name Titurel, and he replies, "Titurel, the little Titus, Titus the symbol of royal standing and power, Wotan the God-King." Nice letter from my father about the *Idyll,* "this flower of a thousand petals"; when he speaks of it as "the cult of the family," we are struck by the phrase, and R. says he ought to have called it "the blessings of a happy love"! Bismarck's peaceful statement—it is a good thing that it is Germany which is now permitted to preach peace, and Germany will without a doubt always be just and straightforward—but we do not like the reference to "training in the right methods," it gives the impression of a bluff mockery of ideality. A telegram from Gothenburg. In the evening Lichtenberg's essay on Captain Cook.

Wednesday, February 20 R. did not have a good night, but he goes to his work. This morning he sang to me "*Fal-parsi, Parsifal.*" — He says that during the night he sang the *Idyll,* up to the entrance of the theme on the cello, then he fell asleep; waking up again, he sang it from the point at which he had fallen asleep to the end. I love the days when one of us is not feeling well; we eat by ourselves, and it is always like a little celebration—yesterday we drank to the 2nd act! Talking about the oboe, R. calls it a naïvely tragical instrument. — He tells me that in his speech Bismarck spoke of dueling bouts and likened Germany to an honest broker! A sad speech, though certainly in a worthy cause. Pope Leo XIII (Cardinal Pecci) has been elected; he is said to be one of the implacables. No reading in the evening. Memories of Tribschen, our good Vreneli, a rare example of her class.

Thursday, February 21   R. had a better night; he works—we are still laughing about the "cult of the family"—the "wildly despairing lovers" turning into a family! says R. — [*Here the following sentence has been erased:* "He reads to me what he wrote before his walk, the conclusion of *What Is German?*, the irony of which gives us much delight." *See February 22.*] Letter from Herr Rudolphi, again with "*selbstredend*" ["self-evident"], the favorite word nowadays! — He persists in wanting to present the *Nibelungen*. In the evening *Parsifal!*

Friday, February 22   R. does no composing but works out the conclusion of *What Is German?* and reads it to me before lunch. Spring-like weather, I walk to the theater in order to make some preparations for the festival. R. goes for quite a long walk along the road to Konradsreuth. In the evening *Parsifal* with Herr Seidl; R. sings, and we enjoy some splendid, blessed hours such as no public performance could ever provide. — Poor Frau Materna is asking to be released, because of press persecution since her appearance at Bayreuth! — R. talks of a symphony he intends to dedicate to Fidi, another theme for it occurred to him today, and he says it would be as merry and friendly as the boy himself! — To have discovered and declared that a generous and pure heart is greater than all genius—this is something for which R. praises Schopenhauer particularly.

Saturday, February 23   R. working, I with the children. After lunch R. comes back to Mozart, and particularly *Die Zauberflöte;* he says that certain things in it marked a turning point in the history of art; Sarastro introduced dignity of spirit in place of conventional dignity. — Certain things in Mozart will and can never be excelled, he says. With the children to the theater in the afternoon, another dress rehearsal. In the evening read Bismarck's speech in its entirety. R. finds it clear and sensible, but not great; he deplores the constant adulation of the press, and the conclusion with Andrássy he says is like a comedy, like the buffoons and the clowns who always put on a show for the audience, while the audience shouts "Bravo." It is as if Bismarck were thinking to himself, "If I can only reduce the press to silence, then I can deal with the Reichstag," says R., who is of the opinion that Russia should have been given maximum support. The arrangement of the *Idyll* arrives and is played by R. and friend Seidl. This wonderfully delicate work now thrown out into the raw world, which is so alien to us! . . . R. says with a laugh that what distinguishes him from today's composers and gives them such a great advantage over him is that he cannot compose anything without inspiration, whereas they can: a great advantage.

Sunday, February 24   R. is well and works, I to the theater with the 3 youngest. Hasty homecoming, R. shows me the new Court theater in Dresden, for which we cannot raise much enthusiasm. We laugh over the opening of this large building, so out of proportion to the size of the population, with *Iphigenie, Tasso,* and *Minna von Barnhelm,* as also over the wedding opera in Berlin: [*La*] *Clemenza di Tito!* R. says *Dido abbandonata* by Marshal Kalb would have been better! In the evening *Parsifal.* Getting to know this wonderful work brings happiness and bliss. R. tells me that I have it in black and white that my coming into his life has made him happy—now he is able to get on with it and work! I take leave of this book with feelings of gratitude toward life, with ardent love, with faith, and with hope!
[*End of the ninth notebook of the Diaries. The tenth begins:* "Dedicated to my Siegfried—from its fleeting strokes may he deduce and recognize the great love to which he owes his existence!"]

Monday, February 25   R. works, is vexed about the "duet" he now has to compose. He reads a pamphlet about the Jews, an extract from a newspaper, the *Deutsche Reichspost,* which the author has sent him and which reveals some not very pleasant statistical facts. I walk with the children up to the theater, on account of costumes. In the evening begin [Scott's] *Waverley.* The founder here is starting work on the bell for *Parsifal.* —

Tuesday, February 26   R. works; in a very nice letter he has written to my father he says, "I am composing now all day long, like Raff or Brahms." He is in a splendid mood, his eyes radiate joy, kindness, and cheerfulness. Many stupidities about the *Idyll;* someone sees the "Forest Murmurs" in it without the "*sung dialogue*" of Fafner and Siegfried, another says there is no motive from *Siegfried* in it! — In the evening *Waverley,* after again walking secretly to the theater with the children. Much enjoyment from this beautiful and serene book. Then R. is in the mood for music and takes up Haydn's *Bear* Symphony, great delight in the final movement; then he shows friend Seidl the Andante of Haydn's G Major Symphony and says it is one of the loveliest things ever written; and how wonderful it sounds! — Continuing to talk about music, he says there are few things in music which completely satisfy one's longing; the Adagio from the 9th Symphony is one of them—that could go on as long as it pleased, it is like a Sabbath, complete rest, it relaxes all one's limbs! — But much belongs to what he calls cold music—quintets, trios, concertos, duets—music in which "the notes never pierce one like a dagger, the sweet compulsion is never felt"—for example, Beethoven's B-flat Major Symphony, for which one has to be in the right mood. The Scherzo is splendid, he says, but in the Adagio he always feels like saying, *"Yes, I know,"* and the theme of the first movement does not appeal to him. On the other hand, the F Major never fails to affect him. In this connection I remark that the difference between the two works is the difference between a play by Schiller and a play by Shakespeare. — We talk again about the pamphlet on the Jews—R. says that the 1813 uprising, so misinterpreted by the ruling princes and thus crushed, was as much a disaster for Germany as the 30 Years' War.

Wednesday, February 27 R. slept well and is working, I do the same with the children and preparations. R. goes out with the dogs. In the evening continued *Waverley* with great enjoyment. R. tells us of a deplorable session in the Reichstag on the question of the tobacco monopoly—more *dueling bouts.* — Letter from the wife of the Master of the Household [in Schwerin]—they want only to know R.'s terms for the whole of the *Ring des N.,* and R. decides to hold his great rage in check and give vent to it only if Berlin ever shows a desire for the *Ring.* For the wedding festivities in Berlin they have painted a backcloth with a seated audience for the entry of Titus, this consisting of the Emperor and his Court! Also a curtain showing the palaces of Oldenburg and Meiningen—such is art in the capital of the German Reich!

Thursday, February 28 R. again had a bad night, but he works and, as he tells me, reaches the *"Teufelsbraut"* ["the devil's bride"]. While he is taking his rest, I practice the *Idyll* with indescribable emotion, he comes in quietly and listens. When I notice his presence, he tells me that he wrote down the first theme in Starnberg (during my visit there): "Oh, yes, we know where it all started." From the garden, where he is walking around, he calls out to me that these are the loveliest days of our lives. He then calls me again to listen to a blackbird in a bush singing—the *Idyll!* The little bird is singing shyly still, but very touchingly. Returning from his walk, R. tells me he would like to show me a passage in Lichtenberg which pleased him greatly, in which he talks of man and wife and says how helpful it is for the husband when he can complain to his fellow sufferer—only a wife can be a man's friend. R. reads Schemann's preface to his anthology of his [Wagner's] writings about the great masters of music and regrets the author's inability to understand why he does not respect Schumann, in whose music he can discern not a single melody and whom he knowingly regards as a very fragile talent; when he does produce a theme, it is a Beethovenian one: "How there can be Schumann devotees I cannot imagine." Delight in Fidi's good looks and kindness of heart. — In the evening *Parsifal,* "Amfortas's Lament" and the songs in the Temple of the Grail. Like the Grail itself R.'s face lights up as he sings, while the sounds penetrate to my heart, wonderfully uplifting!

Friday, March 1 R. works, he had a better night. I have some domestic difficulties to contend with, but it can all be borne cheerfully when R. is well. News from Vienna that *Das Rheingold* is a great success, bringing full houses; we find this difficult to explain; memories of Jauner, "head over heels," as R. calls him, always in a fever of excitement and never knowing what is going on! . . . In the evening *Waverley*, also looked at some new songs by R. Franz, finding little in them to enjoy. The debates in the Reichstag more and more deplorable.

Saturday, March 2 At breakfast R. told me that he had been reflecting on our whole life together, the torment of our separations, he had no idea how we had managed to bear it. "If we don't thank Heaven every day for our having come as far as we have, we ought to be thrashed," he says, laughing. I tell him I know why I love God and am grateful to him. R.: "Yes, not the God who created the world, but the one who leads us out of it." In spite of the bad weather these last two days, R. goes out of doors. — Herr Kipke in Leipzig informs us that bankruptcy proceedings have been started against poor Herr Fritzsch. Of R.'s collected writings 1,500 copies have been sold, 700 still remain; Herr K. wants R. Schott's Söhne to buy them for 12,000 marks, and R. suggests it to Herr Strecker. — Herr Seitz Junior, the painter, has turned down my request for some sketches for the *Parsifal* costumes, which I wanted for R.'s birthday. — *Waverley* in the evening. — Comparison between Alberich and Klingsor; R. tells me that he once felt every sympathy for Alberich, who represents the ugly person's longing for beauty. In Alberich the naïveté of the non-Christian world, in Klingsor the peculiar quality which Christianity brought into the world; just like the Jesuits, he does not believe in goodness, and this is his strength but at the same time his downfall, for through the ages *one* good man does occasionally emerge! — R. gives me an extract from the *V[ossische] Zeitung* to read regarding the Bismarck legend; it says he is supposed to have very great plans but is held back by Court officials, scheming ladies in waiting; but nobody at all knows or has seen anything of these great ideas. R. compares him with Robespierre, to the extent that the latter had people beheaded right and left, and when there was nobody left to stand in his way, he could think up nothing better than to proclaim *"la vertu."* The clumsy organization of the German Reich, the destruction of the small states, the failure, in order to help them adapt to the new organization, to look into the damage done, the petty lies—a university in Strassburg, a memorial in the Harz, etc. All of this is regrettable, for despite everything

Bismarck is still one of the most significant men in our history. —

Sunday, March 3 Arrival of our amiable friend Frau v. Schleinitz, who intends to spend a few days near us. Much chatting about a world which seems ever stranger to us. In the evening *Waverley,* not much to enjoy about the Highlanders. A very good article by a Herr Löffler on the legend of Mimir and its connection with the *Ring des Nibelungen.* Loldi unwell.

Monday, March 4 R. well, working cheerfully, although he wishes the "duet" were already behind him—he is looking forward to the third act. The greater part of the day devoted to our charming friend. In the evening *Parsifal,* up to the arrival of the "pure fool."

Tuesday, March 5 Work with the children; our friend with us at lunch, as friendly and charming as ever, really nice weather, we go for a little walk. In the evening the second part of *Parsifal* . . .

Wednesday, March 6 R. and I resume the discussion we began yesterday evening; R. describes [Raphael's] *Sistine Madonna* as the most consummate work of art, precisely on account of its fine restraint; the very fact that it contains so few figures makes R. feel that as a work of art it is more significant than Titian's *Ascension,* which all but transgresses the boundaries. The *Sistine Madonna* stands in the same relationship to the *Ascension* as the C Minor Symphony (first movement) to the *Eroica.* — R. is very interested in his symphony, which Seidl is copying out from the orchestral parts; R. says it could have been written by a young composer between the first and second symphonies of Beethoven. But in the evening he is dismayed by the second theme. R. works, I visit our friend, and she joins us again in the evening. The first scene of [Shakespeare's] *Henry IV Part Two,* read aloud by R. He is lost in admiration for its greatness and individuality, the immediacy of history in the poet's imagination as displayed in the conference with the Archbishop of York. Letter from Schwerin, they agree to R.'s terms for *Der Ring des Nibelungen,* which makes R. remark that Berlin will now be surrounded on all sides, as *Plevna* was: Hamburg, Schwerin, Brunswick, Leipzig, Vienna, Munich are all doing the *Ring.* — The only curious thing is that Schwerin is not yet including *Die Walküre* in the contract, a point which R. is having put right by our Wolzogen.

Thursday, March 7 R. works; lunch with our friend. All the reports she brings us of the outside world contain little to give us pleasure: "brutality and servility," socialist machinations (she has given me Lassalle's *Une Page d'amour* to read!), etc. — R. continues to read Lichtenberg, with ever-increasing enjoyment. Of certain passages he said yesterday, laughing, "That could have been taken from my collected writings." In the evening conversation with our friend, then some music—the Prelude to Act III of *Die Msinger:* "At that time I was a lonely man," says R. "I no longer need such consolation." Memories of the performance of *Die Meistersinger* in Munich: "The loveliest experience of my artistic life—it was virtually perfect." Then R. plays the C-sharp Minor Prelude from [Bach's] *48 Preludes and Fugues.* An indescribable impression—it echoes within us like the quiet lament of a sphinx, or vanishing gods, or Nature before the creation of mankind! R. says he has been composing it himself ever since his childhood, but he is not sure whether he plays it properly. The sonata, he says, brought shallowness to this original form of prelude and fugue; it was [Carl] Philipp Emanuel [Bach] who introduced this Italianate style, and all instrumental music since then has sounded like a concert, a Court concert, when compared with this revelation. And just think what Bach himself looked like, with his half-blind, anxious eyes, like Beethoven; musicians are like that, curious creatures! . . . Before that R. played various Italian themes, from Bellini's *I Capuleti ed i Montecchi, La Straniera,* and *Norma,* and said: "For all the poverty of invention, there is real passion and feeling there, and the right singer has only to get up and sing it for it to win all hearts. I have learned things from them which Messrs. Brahms & Co. have never learned, and they can be seen in my melodies." After playing the C-sharp Minor Prelude, he observes, with reference to the Italian melodies whose peculiar passion we have just acknowledged, "That is *pour le monde,* but this (the Prelude) is the world itself." Second issue of the *Bayreuther Blätter,* very good. Mimi has given me an essay by Renan, "*La Poésie des races celtiques,*" which is another curious example of the superficial, poetically sentimental way in which even the most significant Frenchmen treat scientific subjects; what most clearly shines forth is his ignorance of the German character, but it is readable and entertaining, as long as one is aware of what is incorrect in it.

Friday, March 8 Snow squalls, R. somewhat worn out, but he works all the same. Our friend to lunch, and also again in the evening. R. sings Amfortas, but with some reluctance, he says he does not wish to do any more singing like this. Affectionate parting from our friend.

Saturday, March 9 Snow flurries and stormy weather, also weariness and neuralgia for me. R., however, is fairly well, and very cheerful. In the evening we return to our usual occupation; we read *Waverley,* agreeing that in it the great novelist, then still a beginner, spreads himself somewhat thin in many places, and he uses dialogue for things which would perhaps be better narrated. — R. in excellent spirits, he very humorously enlarges upon the present fashions for men and describes his struggles doing up buttons. As we are laughing heartily, he says to Seidl, "Yes, Seidl, you won't always have such an entertaining companion at your side!" — Nice letter from the King. — To conclude the evening R. plays the beginning of [Weber's] *Euryanthe* Overture, and we are both lost in admiration for the radiant beauty, integrity, chivalrous nobility against which the tender femininity is displayed. R. feels that a German theater should be opened with this work, rather than with *Fidelio,* which is much more conventional and cold. As we are going to bed, he once again thinks of Weber, and says, "I feel so closely akin to him; maybe that is because my childhood was associated with him." — At lunch R. says he has discovered the years of his life to be 96, he has added 1878 together—18 and 78! — He finds the *Fl. Blätter* very enjoyable.

Sunday, March 10 I feel really indisposed; perhaps the break in my usual daily routine is to blame. R. is very tired and languid, but he says he has had a good inspiration and has "cast Klingsor down." — He goes for a walk to the Rollwenzel tavern. — I have to write to friend Heckel, who appears to have been brought into a state of complete confusion by his theater management. R. again recalls the performance of *Die Msinger* and the fine behavior of the King on that occasion. In the afternoon R. and Hans Wolzogen set the whole of culture to rights, as he puts it. In the evening we read *Waverley;* R. says he greatly admires novelists: this art form is as incomprehensible to him as perhaps his scores are to others.

Monday, March 11 R. remarks that I again have my "melancholy, eager look," which means that I am completely restored, and indeed the sweet habit of existence has me in its grip again! My work with the children and nothing to disturb my close life with R. — He says to me, "My maidens come rushing in with wild gesticulations, like children whose toys have been taken away; without anger." — Yesterday evening the children were reading aloud, and R. was captivated by the sight of Fidi's fair head as he listened: "We must be glad that we lived to hear these children's voices," he says. He recalled his own childhood, running around the Plauen estate, for him the embodiment of all romance; then he told us about a prank at his school, the Nikolai-Schule, when during the absence of the teacher he jumped on the podium to imitate him and, in opening the desk, broke it; given away by one of his fellow pupils, he started to lie, declaring that something had been passing by, all the pupils had gone to the window, and, since there was no other place from which he could see, he had jumped on the podium; after all kinds of dire threats (suspension from school, sending him home), the teachers were astounded by his vivid imagination, and they merely told him to be less eloquent in future! — I asked him (yesterday) whether he still needed the ink sketches of the first act of *P.*: "No, for I'm such a dolt that I can't transpose; I always go by the sound and never by abstract knowledge. Perhaps that has sometimes been my salvation, keeping me from writing down something just because, according to this or that relationship, it ought to be so." — Today there are no sounds of music in the house, he feels he must write something for the *Blätter:* "I am afraid of Porges, and my pencilings have just reached a point where I can break off. After these furious affairs it will be strange for me to have to compose nothing but pleasantnesses. Maybe I won't succeed." Regarding his article, he says he enjoys writing it, but one always has too much to say. He tells me he has read in a newspaper that musicians who have heard some of *Parsifal* are saying it is even more beautiful than *Lohengrin:* "Certainly it should be like *Lohengrin* but, with the help of a few 'swannishnesses,' even more beautiful." — I go out and, on my return, find R. in the garden, he had been with friend Seidl, looking at his symphony, and now has some doubts whether he will publish it. (At lunch he sang something from Mozart's *Don Giovanni,* "*Vivan le femmine, viva il buon vino,*" praising it and delighting in the charm of Mozart's genius: "He died too young, had to work in too much of a rush. He would still have had a lot to show the world.") — We wandered in the garden, finding much to delight us even now, a fat blackbird on the wall. In the evening *Waverley,* fine scene with the Pretender. When mention is made of the Highlanders' crawling, R. says, "I know all about that; it is not unlike the time I crossed the border in Riga." He tells me, "When *you* are reading, all these people seem like angels and spirits, not a trace of treachery in them." We end this day in tender intimacy, with a full sense of our happiness, oblivious of the world, immersed in each other. — Nothing can disturb us as long as we are together—not even the eternally gray skies! We talk of Italy, but only for a very short visit. I tell R. that he would miss his familiar contacts with the people—his only contact with the outside world; we should never escape our feelings of remoteness; but we intend, toward the end of winter (February, March), to spend some time in the South, or at any rate we talk about it, though not very urgently.

Tuesday, March 12 Last night I wrote an article for the *Blätter.* R. laughs: "We're always doing the same thing." He works on his, while I give the children their lessons. He comes to lunch in a very cheerful mood: "I've now got into my stride and only hope that nothing comes to disturb me." In the afternoon I read some of Goethe's *Zahme Xenien* with great enjoyment. R. could find no proper afternoon rest and soon went out into the garden. Before supper in the evening he reads aloud to me and the W[olzogen]s his article, "*Modern,*" which is truly unique. Before beginning, he says, "Such things ought not to be read aloud, the sound doesn't matter, they're for the eye."

Several applications for the Society of Patrons, mainly from Riga! — In the evening *Waverley,* the hero reminds one in character and outlook of W[ilhelm] Meister. Splendid episode with Waverley's dying tenant. — The melancholy of having stepped outside the world of law and order to follow one's own inclinations is very clearly revealed at the outset of the action, without being given direct expression. — Another lovely day brought to an end. Oh, may the children retain their memories of this life, and may they form a shield for them against the vulgar world! — The Pretender's single cannon reminds R. of the three little cannons a manufacturer sent the revolutionaries in Dresden, and with what cheers they received these artillery weapons which were designed only to fire joyous salutes! — After reading, R. plays me a melody with two different turns: "Which is better?" — "I prefer the first one." "I know what I shall do," he exclaims later as he is undressing. "What?" "I shall use them both."

Wednesday, March 13   R. had a good night and goes to his work; he tells me he is satisfied with what he has done, although, at the time he wrote it, he had not been fully satisfied. The "Grail" returns, Amfortas is healed. I to the theater with the children. R. goes out in the garden for a while to walk. In the evening our friend Count Du Moulin, announcing 27 members—our little Society is growing. — "It is as impossible to write music without melody," R. says in the course of the conversation, "as to speak without thoughts: melody is musical thought." Many amusing examples of the poor and threadbare melodies in Meyerbeer, strung together from bar to bar with an oom-pah-pah accompaniment. As a contrast R. sings Don Ottavio's aria and says, "There, that is melody, there one is confronted with a real person." (R. also spoke in recent days with the greatest admiration of Haydn's *Sieben Worte,* saying it was deeply moving.) — In the evening R. says to me: "Everybody is astonished that I look so well; that after things and experiences that would have killed anyone else I am now writing a new work. Where do I find the strength, when after *Tristan* nobody thought I would ever write another note? From the fact that I am borne along on your love!" — Letter from the King's secretary, saying they intend to put the matter in order. Contract from Brunswick. Friend Heckel is now also asking for the *Ring.* In the evening we went through the Prelude to *Parsifal,* friend Seidl played it, and R. had to spend much time talking about the tempo, which S. took too slowly, or, rather, incorrectly. R. says that tempo cannot be written down, every piece has its own way of being played; of course there are pieces, he says, in which the tempo must be taken with tremendous sharpness and precision, but one must know which they are, and that must be learned from the composer. That is why he had wanted to found a school, "where I should have vexed myself to death every day," he added. Herr S. then plays the entrance of the knights into the Temple of the Grail, and R. is pleased when our good Count joins in to play the upper voice. "That's what I like," he says, "people who can do things." — We recall that in Tribschen I had always taken over Loge's "tingling delight" when R. was playing "Siegfried's Journey to the Rhine." Talking about this violin figuration, R. speaks of the violin figuration he wrote in Paris for Tannhäuser's staggering exit, and how Gaspérini called it *"le beau désordre."*

Thursday, March 14 R. had a bad night with terrible dreams, he wanted to play the Bach Prelude and it had to be done on chopped meat, there was none available, Fidi was suddenly missing, whisperings, forebodings, a scream, awakening. "Then I start yodeling," laughs R. "Can our dear Lord find nothing better to do than torment a poor genius like me?!" — Letter to me from Herr Glasenapp, which I put in the corner cupboard along with the monographs of Ludw. Geyer and Adolph Wagner, it is again full of items of family news; very touching, also, on account of its final words regarding *Parsifal*. However, R. says, "I had very few thoughts on the German people while I was writing it, but I understand what he means: feelings like that are always slumbering inside one." Around lunchtime R. plays me the introduction to the 2nd act, Klingsor's approach and the raging of sin; it is glorious. After lunch R. returns to the difficulties of tempo. In the morning he talked about Beethoven's early sonatas and their youthful beauty. During an incredible snowstorm in the afternoon, I walk up to the theater with the children, to see about costumes. Then with friend Gross; the contract from Munich here, a few points unacceptable. Returning home, I find R. in the *salon* between the first movement of his symphony and the sketches; he greets me with the words "I have just composed a trio for the Scherzo of my symphony," and he plays it to me. I: "It's a veritable composing factory here!" Laughter! He inquires about the contract, insists on the repayment of my 32,000 marks from the proceeds of *Parsifal,* which hurts me very much, and deeply, but I let it pass, so as not to spoil R.'s splendidly cheerful spirits. Several times today R. says, "Now I have got into my stride." When I tell him about my lessons, that I gave a "lecture" on Demetrius Poliorcetes, he says, "Greek history ends up just like the *Iliad,* all these people are like Homer's heroes, but they cover an enormous field." — At lunch friend Wolzogen remarks that the linen drapers Israel have supplied us with many actors. — R. is still reading Lichtenberg and quotes a lot from him—the growing pains of books, for example, and the irony of Lord Chesterfield; R. hopes to have achieved this tone of mild irony in his essay, *"Modern."* — *Waverley* in the evening. — To conclude the evening downstairs R. plays me the opening of his symphony, truly magnificent. R. says one can see in it the overpowering influence of Beethoven's works, as far as a young man of 20 can know and understand them, and, dismayed as it were by the impressions of the latter, he had attempted to link onto the 2nd Symphony. The way Mendelssohn tried to ignore it by having it disappear was very curious: "This symphony was certainly an unpleasant surprise to him." Talked in the evening about V[ictor] Hugo. "To the extent that the French can be poets, he is a poet." R. places his *Notre Dame* above *Les Misérables,* if only because of its love and knowledge of old Paris, which was quite unknown to the French before him; its influence extended as far as the *Mousquetaires.* — Before our affectionate parting for the night, which cannot in fact part us, I tell R. that Gl[asenapp] had been seeking "Minna and Klara" in spirit at the performance of *Rienzi* in Riga. "Oh, yes, I have left a lot of people behind." "Do you miss any of them?" "No. The worry over losing something I have learned only since living with you."

Friday, March 15 R. had a better night; at breakfast he reads Tappert's newspaper and finds all kinds of wrong things in it about *Parsifal*—even the "choruses" are praised! "Why can I never be left in peace to write a work in tranquillity for ourselves alone?" — He works and says he is more satisfied with what he has written in pencil than he had expected to be. After lunch we go out together; he laughs over his "fresh and stormy gait" when with me; if he had been alone, he says, he would just have slouched along, hands behind his back. At the Wolzogens' we find the contract from Schwerin, now in order— and so this unpleasant episode has also been resolved. On our return home R. writes to Herr v. Wolzogen Senior and then does some more work in ink. In the evening *Waverley;* the way the hero spends his lonely hours with his tenant reminds R. of Magdala: "Not regret at what had happened—I didn't feel that—but a feeling of having got myself into an absurd situation." Our interest in the book grows ever greater: "You could have gone on reading it for hours and I should have listened." — To conclude the evening he plays the melody from the Andante of his symphony, which I like very much; I tell him so. "Yes, that's why I still believe I stole it from somewhere, though I knew very little at that time." — At lunch he talked about Mozart, how he had earned nothing from *Die Zauberflöte* and how after J[oseph] II's death no prince, no nobleman had bothered himself about Mozart, in spite of *Figaro* and all the other things. "Yes, our princes have always behaved splendidly! Mozart got 800 florins, and Jommelli 3,000 ducats!" — After lunch he says he is nervous about the great scene between Kundry and Pars.; he has already done several things in this style, among others the Venus scene; Mozart only once did a scene such as the appearance of the Commendatore, and it is impossible to imagine that he would have done something similar a second time. — At supper we talk about the German language; he says Lessing did not really know it, Goethe had instinctively come much closer; Lessing wanted to set up a German language along the lines of French and English. He quotes Lichtenberg's saying that one would be amazed how much there is in a word if only one thought about it. After Kunersdorf Frederick the Great wrote his resignation in German. Regret on my part that neither Goethe, Schiller, nor Kleist treated the Seven Years' War in an epic manner. R. says they were already too much occupied with form and with foreign cultures. Recently R. said, "I almost wish Goethe had written nothing except *Faust,* so splendid is it!" (He had just quoted "From time to time I like to see the old boy," etc.)

Saturday, March 16 R. did not have a very good night, he had to get up once; he tells me his dream: "I was with Pope Pius IX; he received me in a friendly way, in a sort of office, but then he suddenly said, 'You are supposed to be a very bad man, a heretic.' I: 'There are such things as libels.' 'No, no, I know. You are Russian?' 'Oh, then you mean Rubinstein.' 'Perhaps. Is his name Richard?' 'Oh, then you do mean me, but you know how the newspapers lie.' 'Yes, I do know that, and I see from your face that you are an honest man.' " After that they said nothing but nice things to each other, and R. thought to himself, "Oh, Lord, you'll have to kiss his hand now." — He did so. Cordial parting, exchanging "humble servants" with the very impressive-looking Pope, who accompanied him to the door and then, from a lighted chapel into which he had withdrawn and whose door stood open, looked around at R., and nodded when R., on his way out, looked around again. — At breakfast reminiscences of our Italian journey; concerning Verona R. says, "It is a sign of vigorous life in a city when monuments such as those of the Scaligeri are set up in narrow alleys and corners." — R. works and comes in cheerful mood to give me the *Fl. Blätter,* which he finds very entertaining. "It is a truly German periodical," he says. Downstairs he finds a composition, "*Durch Kampf zum Sieg*" ["Through Battle to Victory"], which he calls "*Durch Dampf zum Bier*" ["Through Steam to Beer"]. He sings bits from it; astonishment over its amateurishness: "People have learned nothing from me," says R. — A report on the *Idyll:* "I ought to be pleased when something sensible is said about it, not on account of the praise, but that there is somebody who knows how to listen to such things." In the afternoon R. goes for a walk, far beyond the Sophienberg, as he tells me, trying to find us. I had gone to the theater with the children for a rehearsal and consequently could not go to meet him. He works but is interrupted; annoyance over this, and late in the evening I express regret for not having kept it from him: "Yes, when somebody comes and you are not there, I howl like Wana for Brange." He had previously told us that he wanted to take the little dog with him on his walk; at first she had been frightened to go past the railings into the street, then she complained when he left, so he returned and took her with him, but when she saw Brange chasing across the fields the little creature began to whine and howl! — Read *Waverley,* great delight in the old Baron, R. thinks him one of the most successful of W. Sc.'s characters. — I do not know why I am so beset this evening by gloomy fears, everything startles my heart, R.'s room, everything. When R. said, "With what different feelings will our children cross this hall!" (he meant less weighty feelings), I felt a shudder go through me. Oh, happiness—too heavy a crown for a human head! How uncertainly it bears thee! But in the tender embrace which a moment ago preceded our final words to each other before parting, my fears vanish; God in His Heaven will not desert me! . . . This afternoon R. spoke of a thought which sometimes strikes him and which could drive him mad: the possibility of a child's falling seriously ill and its life being in danger. — At supper the nastiness of people toward my father: "He is living now like his own shadow," R. says. How few people recognize that he opened the way for R.! "Well, what Liszt can do we can surely do, too." And without Liszt, R. says, "I cannot imagine what would have happened to my things—possibly I should be moldering beside Reissiger and his *Schiffbruch der Medusa.*" The same for all the rest of my father's experiences, with Joachim, Raff, etc., "for he was able to do far more for others than I could." — Contract with Brunswick signed.

Sunday, March 17   R. had a tolerable night, though with one frightening dream about me: "Minna no longer suffices when the aim is to give me a fright—they need you for that," he says with a laugh. He works and reaches "*Verfluchtes Weib, was frägst du dies.*" Friend Heckel is not able to accept the terms but would like very much to have *Die Walküre.* R. writes to him saying he would gladly give him personally the whole of the *Ring* for nothing, but he would not make the Mannheim theater a present of a single cent. At lunch R. laughs over their imagining they could cast *Die Walküre* properly. "I ought to advise them to do *Tristan und Isolde,* for at least they've got a good flute player." R. goes out and then works again until suppertime. We finish *Waverley;* R. thinks the court scene splendid; it is fine of W. Scott to sacrifice the people whose exaltation does have a tinge of corruption in it. — Talking of various themes which have occurred to him, R. says, "It's all just playing around, not the right thing at all." Of the experience with H[eckel] R. says, "One mustn't get involved with people without education—they don't understand what one is saying." — Baron Bradwardine is R.'s favorite, I love such people. The whole thing is splendid, a vanishing era, a quite different one emerging. If only we had something like that, a similar picture of the Diadochi! — I tell R. how much I enjoy reading *Wolfdietrich* to the girls, he agrees with me and praises Simrock's work very highly, saying he took from the ancient language everything that was necessary and understandable. "How, after such works, can something like *The Trumpeter of S[äckingen]* became popular in such a sloppy version?" The German language, he says, is now the only one which, as J. Grimm says, can be studied physiologically, not just in order to speak it or to read the classical writers (in contrast to French, English, and Italian). —

Monday, March 18 R. had a good night; at breakfast he shows me a hymn written by Prof. Minckwitz in his honor. He works, but at lunch complains of having felt cold, and I cannot describe the concern with which I searched that dear countenance to see whether it showed any traces of indisposition! But Heaven remains merciful to me, he does not become unwell, goes walking in the garden, and continues to work in ink on his penciled sketches in the evening. Friend Wolzogen brings the cheerful news that the Emperor of Brazil has sent 15 marks through his ambassador in Berlin! — The pension the Emperor recently granted Herr J. Schmidt leads us to the little book written against him by Lassalle. Herr Gottschall is being given a title for his services to literature. R. was pleased with the portrait of Leisewitz in the *Ill[ustrirte] Zeit[ung]*; he likes his pigtail: "There is something cultivated, careful about it, it reminds one slightly of the Greeks; we run around like savages, even in our dress suits!" — At supper much merriment over the collapse of our school and the curious people we should have had here for it, Hey and his 13 children—"and he always takes his nurse around with him," says R. — Began the biography of Schopenhauer, skipping all Gwinner's comments, but everything by Sch. himself deeply moving. When, as we say good night, I express my great delight that R. is looking so well, he says, "Yes, when I hear people talking about the jubilee of some 60-year-old, I have to laugh over the way I feel—but that is due to you and your love!" — How to express in words my happiness, such blessings?

Tuesday, March 19 "I had a quite *convenable* night," R. replies in the style of Frederick the Great (echoes of yesterday's reading) when I ask him. — I mention the beauty and splendor of the *Idyll*. R. says: "I should like to write many more things like that. No one feels gratitude for the daemonic things: did anyone take notice of Hill's Alberich?"

Yesterday he said he always thought of Hill in connection with Klingsor. Talking about the orchestra for the *Idyll* and his pleasure in writing things of this kind, R. moves on to quartets and says: "It is a peculiar thing about quartets: the four instruments have at times to assume a role similar to a piano, stepping in for others; the cello, having just played low notes, must start singing right up high, and that takes away its beautiful repose and evenness, it sounds in some way hurried, uncertain, and the themes don't divide and separate. I should very much like to score the first movement of Beethoven's E-flat Major Quartet, for instance, for an orchestra more or less the same as that for the *Idyll*. You would see how the themes would stand out, how something played on the horns would become clearer, whereas even in the best performance so much is lost, things are not separated out." — Talked again about Sch[openhauer], how fortunate it was that he learned Latin and Greek so late in life, but how remarkable that he then mastered them so completely. — After embracing me, R. goes off to his work singing, bells are ringing, I hear my children laughing, I enjoy then one of those moments of bliss in which the poor heart struggles for expression and finds it solely in tears! — Lunch alone with R., he eats something cold, he has done a lot of work downstairs, but he looks well and is cheerful. "You are all things," he says to me when I show my pleasure, "you are the whole of Wahnfried, and I am your Wahnfritz." — Curious telegram from friend Heckel! . . . Friend Gross comes in the afternoon and unfortunately mentions the Munich contract; I beg R. just to get on with his work, and he then sends the card [*not discovered*] in to me; I answer it at once with a "yes" and ask Gross to instruct his father[-in-law] accordingly. Splendid letter from my father about the *Idyll,* once again; inimitable quotation from *Faust.* "What an artist he is!" says R., deeply touched. And the quotation is indeed perfect in all particulars. — R. very upset by the little—the very little—he has heard about the contract. Friend Feustel arrives with extremely unpleasant accounts of the King's position, it is being said that a trustee will have to be appointed to control his affairs, but nobody dares take the responsibility for such an act. Feustel and the mayor are to go to Munich tomorrow. — In the evening a gathering here in honor of Feustel. — R. brought me the first pencil sketches of the 2nd act. — R. told me recently that he owes the "yes" in Parsifal and Kundry's dialogue (Act I) to the children's conversations here—that importantly eager "yes"! — After the gathering R. comes up to me, rather worn out. Everything that disturbs his routine disagrees with him. "I am sorry for my poor maidens, whom I must now make sing," he says as he is getting into bed. "I feel as if I were drunk," he said at supper, "and it is only in a state of drunkenness that one can look upon this world; to look at it straight is impossible." "Did Fidi bring you the kiss I gave him for you? He was quite astounded by its violence. 'Silly boy,' I told him, 'that's for Mama.' " (Fidi had taken him my "yes" to his decision.) "I shall sing nothing now except the *Idyll*."

Wednesday, March 20   R. has a slight headache from yesterday, also a little nosebleed, but he works. At lunch he is very absorbed: "I shall have to start a new page, for everything has got to be *Shipka'd*." All day long he is absorbed, but we celebrate Boni's birthday in cheerful style. "Then and now!" I say to R.! . . . Since he lunches with me upstairs, we drink Boni's health from the gallery upstairs, while the children clink glasses in the hall below. In the evening Eva reads a Grimm fairy tale, "The Girl Who Had No Hands." R. says, "That she was turned out is common enough, but that she did not want to stay in her father's house after her hands were chopped off is a very significant feature." — In the evening I read aloud from Schop.'s biography, everything about him from his earliest youth is profound and significant. We decide to let Fidi read *only* Schop. as his introduction to philosophy, then after him Plato and Kant. — The painters Böcklin and Seitz Junior decline to make me scenery and costume sketches for *Parsifal*. The architect Sitte demands to hear the music first. Oh, Germany! — Friend W. comes to see R., who tells me, "When you are not there, I have no idea what to say to people, everything seems to me either unimportant or repugnant."

Thursday, March 21   R. had a tolerable night, the first part at any rate very peaceful; he complains about the sunless skies, it really is always gray outside. At breakfast he recalls that friend Seidl asked him about the tempo of the Adagio in the *Pastoral*: "Adagio! They don't know the difference between andante and adagio, they drag movements which ought to flow and ruin them that way. What on earth do they learn in Leipzig, Vienna, and all the other places where Seidl was?" Spanish biography, a Dutch account of R.'s life! — At lunch R. says that "*Mirregni*" is now in order. "Mirregni" is the song Loldi composed two years ago in honor of the dog Marke; yesterday I said to R., when he was humming to himself something from the 2nd act, that he was singing "Mirregni"; he laughed, and the name stuck. "Incidentally, I shall compose your 'Mirregni' once again, Loldi, particularly with that nice echo." — Newspapers from Australia, which gives R. a chance to talk about the British: "A curious people, our present-day Vikings, and their faces—so limited, yet so assured, so resourceful and prudent." — Talking about Parsifal's arrival in the garden, he says: "Ah, yes, music! What could ever replace it? When he appears up there and his theme is heard—in spoken drama this pause would be impossible. The eloquent pause—that is the province of music." Talking about Lichtenberg, he says he finds it difficult on the whole to read such isolated thoughts strung together, the time comes when he no longer really knows what he is reading; one needs a context, order, a plan, a drama. "In the end I watch them as if they were fleas, waiting for one of them to bite." In reading them one just looks for the witticism. Even Ottilie's diary in *Elective Affinities:* "I was always glad to reach the end of it." — R. goes to see the W.'s and afterward tells me that a disgruntled man, won over again by *What Is German?,* has joined the Society of Patrons. — After his walk R. works, but first he answers friend Heckel's letter, dispelling his curious delusion that he, R., had looked upon his appointment as a victory for the cause. How few friends have any real idea of what goes on in R.'s mind! — Good letter from Feustel, R. says, "Let's wait and see." In the evening with friend W., went through Herr Porges's article. R. finds the beginning (religion as a link between art and public) not bad, but what follows is such that R. decides to write to the author asking him to shorten his opus. I come to realize during the reading that these people have no separate inner life of their own, no real experience of good and evil, which is why everything they say is shallow and indefinite; people who lead an inner life and are aware of it (never mind how important or petty the outward circumstances) *must* affirm Schopenhauer's philosophy. — R. also has much to say about language. [*A sentence about the meaning of certain German words omitted.*] — He laughs at the term "reformer" being applied to him: "I have reformed nothing. The expression fits Luther, but I have just cultivated seeds already there." In our final colloquy in the evening all our outside experiences are forgotten, we speak only of ourselves or of things; today, for example, of what used to be looked upon as a necessity—that every finale "should be a sort of frenzy, a drunken hotchpotch of suffering and joy; I provided my share of that in *Rienzi.*" "*Die Msinger,*" I say, "is also unique in this respect—the conclusion of the first act, for example."

Friday, March 22   R. says the sky is like a blow on the nerves. It is and remains gray. A batch of songs sent to him provokes R. into an indictment of lyric poetry; he does not believe the poets, he finds such things repulsive in our present world, these musical love laments, the singers with their lovelorn expressions. Goethe went back to the style of folk poetry, he says, also he wanted to get whatever he wrote about off his mind, and such things are all right when you are young. He thinks *Elective Affinities* the finest thing besides *Faust* that Goethe ever wrote; we discussed several things in it: "Oh, this Charlotte!" "It's already 30 years since the March days, and I have to keep on asking myself what happened during that time and tell myself, 'Ah, that was in the '50s, the '60s.' " At lunch R. is somewhat out of humor, he wanted to let me hear the beginning of the 2nd act, and friend S. was not ready in time. But by coffeetime he is cheerful again, though his walk did not do him much good: vexation with the dogs even made him spit up some blood. With indescribable concern I leave him to himself, so that he can have complete rest; I give my history lesson, wondering all the time how he is, and experience the bliss of being greeted by him, completely recovered, with the words "Here comes the slender doe!" — At supper, reports that in Prussia no ministers are to be found—the result of successful intrigues or of these utterly depraved times? . . . R. sings the finale of Beethoven's Violin Sonata Opus [*left blank*] and once again praises the beauty and uniqueness of these youthful works: "One finds the beginnings of them in Mozart, but here this kind of melody forms the basis—in Mozart there are too many frills." — The biography of Schopenhauer, regret that it was written by a man as little qualified as Dr. Gwinner: "That's what happens to all our great men." I express to R. my joy at seeing him well again; awareness of our happiness. "We are quite alone in this world," says R., "not another kindred soul," and he adds: "It is not very pretty, this world. What keeps me alive, if not your love?" And so we lay ourselves down to rest.

Saturday, March 23 R. had a good night; in the morning he thinks of *Tr. und Is.* and says: "How did I ever achieve the rapture of the 2nd act? I know, it was through seeing Schröder-D. as Romeo, and it isn't so silly to have a woman in that role, for these little runts of men, and particularly tenors, can never do those lovely wild embraces; it would have to be a brother and sister, specially trained for it by their father, as the Marchisios were trained." — Yesterday evening he said, "I had looked forward to my Flower Maidens, now they are proving difficult, too." He asked me what they should wear on their first appearance: "Perhaps something suggesting flower stems, and then they might decorate themselves with petals." — Snowfall. R. is very exasperated by the weather and these skies and tells me we really must always spend a part of the winter in Italy, where we should at least have an interesting city. But in the afternoon he goes through the 2nd act of *Parsifal* with friend S. Oh, what does one care then about the lack of sunshine, about difficulties and cares—how unimportant and petty they all seem! — I can scarcely express my emotion with an embrace—how, then, for you, my children, in words? The whole world of sin writhes and laments, sighs and laughs in these sounds, how frail Kundry's resistance, her initial "I will not," how frail even her rebellion, how overpowering her laugh of desire! And Parsifal's appearance, childlike, heroic, victorious, radiantly pure and strong as steel as he resists all their pressure! "They could not catch him, unlike Siegfried," says R., "the fly was too large." R. rests for a while, but he cannot sleep. He is also pleased with his work, which is unparalleled— even compared with Erda's awakening, Alberich's curse! . . . In the evening the Schopenhauer biog.; his sister's letters very beautiful and tender, "perhaps rather too much preoccupation with herself," R. feels. But Schopenhauer's letters to the business manager in Danzig quite splendid, they thoroughly delight R. with their truthfulness, their acute understanding, their wit, and their passion. . . . When our friends have left, we remain a little while together, R. and I. "Let us not forget the times when such things had their beginning," R. replies to my stammering enthusiasm.

Sunday, March 24 [*Between the pages of this entry, which was incorrectly dated March 26, is a sheet of paper bearing the words:* "March 26, taken in the night / Seidlitz powder / bicarbonate of soda / valerian 1 / valerian 2 / Karlsbad salt / castor oil / red wine / opium."] R. did not have a very good night. But he is cheerful at breakfast, and we talk again about Sch.'s letters; R. is pleased that he once revealed a similar streak of firmness toward Schott: "One feels so annoyed that these people always take one to be a fool." While undressing last night he sang something from *Figaro* (last act, the scene between Figaro and Susanna, when F. has recognized her beneath her mask), and he tells me he usually sings this when he is undressing, particularly the arabesque which early interrupts the melody: "Oh, it's glorious! But it belongs to one particular style and time; it is the masque, and it couldn't be done more fittingly." — Recently we spoke of Herr v. Hülsen. " 'You are—a senator'—that's what one should say to him," R. observes. — R. works. Snow flurries, but sunshine between, "Loge's flakes" fall on us gently, as in a dream, during our walk, happy feelings as we part, he to talk business with friend Wolzogen, I to read with the children, and he says, embracing me, "This cannot pass!" — Friend Wolzogen informs him that the significant Jewish voice, a rabbi from Bucovina, is a quasi-papal authority named Fried-mann; R. finds the German name and the importance Israel attaches to German culture very remarkable. — Minister shortage in Berlin! — R. says, "If somebody of power and rank were now to reproach Bismarck proudly for his mistakes, what would he say in reply?" . . . In the evening R. feels the desire to play the graceful second theme of [Beethoven's] F Major Symphony, he plays a part of the finale in the piano-duet arrangement. Continued with the Schop. biography; the episode with the seamstress, it reminds one of Beethoven's relationship with his housekeeper—a sad world that shows a genius in such a light! — During a pause in our reading R. says: "Creation is everything; fame is like an oyster shell. I find no pleasure in my things except in the moment of creation. Take the scene between Klingsor and Kundry, for instance—I have no wish to go through it again, it is all strange to me already." — In parting I tell R. that Schopenhauer was after all not entirely right about happiness: there is such a thing. "Yes," says R. with a smile, "but we are just a very small exception and almost unique—you can't build universal rules on that." He also said, "I am in the 3rd phase of my life; in the first, people from other times, like Bierey, still figured; the second was horrible, Meyerbeer, Mendelssohn."

Monday, March 25 R. had to get up during the night; I am alarmed because he is now drinking more cognac than he used to, and I tell him so. — Dear God, everything alarms me now; recently he complained of pressure above his left eye. But he works and is cheerful at lunch. I go out while it is snowing gently; when I return home, I find him playing the end of the *Pastoral* in the arrangement for piano duet. After that we go through the first scene of the 2nd act again. "What would I have to be in order to be worthy of you?" "Quiet, quiet, you see we are still having inspirations, and you are the personification of all inspirations!" — In the evening he laughs at my remark that the difference between him and the other musicians of today is that they can work without inspiration, but he cannot: "And so I am a bungler compared with them." Friend Heckel is in fact accepting *Die Walküre!* Herr Lesimple is also asking for it. In the evening Schop., the episode with the seamstress provides a terrible, tragicomic picture of the *life* of a genius! . . . Over coffee R. tells me he is now writing words for his maidens, and it reminds him of the time when he wrote words for the ending of the 2nd act of *Die Msinger;* also in *Lohengrin* (1st finale) he thought of the music first and then worked out a text for the chorus.

Tuesday, March 26 Spoke a lot about Schop. in the morning, his miserable life in Berlin, magnificent the 12 years of endurance. R. goes off to his "street girls"; he says, "They're giving me a lot of trouble," but yesterday he was pleased that he had now written over a half of his work, I tell him to me it seems like magic. The mayor comes to see me and brings the revised contract; he says the secretary does not have the slightest doubt that the King will sign it. R. goes walking in the garden, I to the theater with Boni to see about costumes. R. continues working on his text and says he will have 18 maidens, no more. No one in the audience will take any notice of the text, he says, but the singers sing differently and feel like individuals if they do not just have to sing senseless repetitions in chorus, and this adds

to the general effect, as, for instance, with the song of the Valkyries. —
Yesterday I asked him whether he was contented. "Infinitely," he
replied. This answer, and the emphatic way he spoke it, flooded me
with a feeling of well-being, and with the memory of it I passed blissfully in the evening from waking to sleeping; he was resting quietly
beside me, his "infinitely" stirred in my heart; all my sorrows seemed
like departed spirits which would never return, and I enjoyed my
moment of exaltation! . . . At supper he spoke of an earthquake in
Lima, during which petroleum lamps fell over and caused an explosion.
"So it's no longer an act of God," he says with a laugh, "but an act of
civilization." I: "But how can these people burn petroleum?" He:
"You mean, in earthquakes they should at least burn oil lamps!" — He
has got a lot of pleasure from Lichtenberg; he quotes to us his thoughts
about starving people in India and in our country [*an illegible word*],
talents for earth or Heaven—stupidities in the depiction of the planetary
system. — Read the Schopenh. biography, then the "By the Brook"
movement of the *Pastoral,* played by R. as a piano duet with friend
Seidl, glorious, tender impression. "It is not at all too long," says R.

Wednesday, March 27   R. had a good night; he tells me at breakfast
that he has half a mind to send for the Munich machinist, in order to
ensure that the dragon and the fight are done properly in Munich, but
then he would want the newspapers to report that he had arranged it.
The dragon should come from below, he says; only its head should be
seen, and then its tail when Siegfried, springing down, fights with it. —
We remember with pleasure all the things we have carried out and
arranged, the production of the *Ring* just one episode among the rest.
Before that R. said to me, "We are now enjoying the fruits, not of
resignation, but of the desires, all the striving of our natures." — He
feels the wish to buy more land for the garden, then he would no
longer need to go outside his own home. At lunch R. comes to fetch
me with the words "*Nenn 'ich Euch schön, dünkt Euch das recht*" ["If I
call you beautiful, does that seem right to you?"]—he has just reached
this point. At lunch he talks about the Greek lyric poets, whom he is
now reading, the preface by [*left blank*] interests him, particularly in
connection with the oracles and the significance the poets attached to
rhyme, also the fact that people wrote in verse at all. "That was new
to me," he says. In the afternoon he writes to Herr v. Perfall about the
dragon. Reading Sch. biography, in the middle of it he exclaims,
"A mistake, it will be A-flat major!" A break in our reading, he goes
into the garden, comes back, and says he has seen the carriage with its
shafts turned completely toward the east. "What does the donkey
mean with this pointing toward the east? . . . Maybe that after *Parsifal*
I am to compose *Die Sieger.*" — Sch.'s letter to the Danish Academy

reminds him of his letter to Bismarck (1873), and he asks me if I have it; I fetch it, we read it and are astonished that it was never answered. — I found it an oppressive day, in reply to my inquiry about the condition of our friend Pusinelli I learned from his daughter that his life is despaired of! I do not tell R. this. In the evening R. thinks of friend Sulzer and resolves to send him a copy of *Parsifal.*

Thursday, March 28 In the morning R. said to me: "In my bath I thought of the Japanese ministers, who have to slit open their own bellies. That can't be easy; it would be better to let someone else do it." — Then he sang me a theme: "The Andante of your symphony," I say—and then he suddenly asks me about Pusinelli; as so often before, he puts my thoughts into words; I have to tell him the truth. Silence.— He goes to his work; my telling him to write down the theme distracted him, he says, and now he also has the finale. He plays it. "What key shall I write my symphony in?" he asks me. "When *Parsifal* has been composed, I shall write nine symphonies, the ninth with choruses: 'O Pain, thou spark of hellish darkness, knocks and blows are all thou gav'st us, and a foe besmeared with mud.'" — Yesterday, when R. asked me for the letter and I had to search for the folder in the darkness, I decided to consider it a good omen if I found it at once among all the other things; I was successful, and R. was delighted with my methodicalness. "You are splendid," he says. I confess my foolishness to him. "No faith without superstition," and in his kindness he indulges my superstitious nonsense about the light! . . . Oh, how kind he is! . . . After his siesta he comes to me and sings "*Bravo bravissimo, bravo bravissimo, Figaro*" and says he is always singing this to himself nowadays. He leaves me, singing it anew. I call after him, "Your love is necessary to me." "No, it is *I* who need *you!*" — In the evening he writes to his friend Sulzer, sending him *Parsifal;* he ends his letter, "There is such a thing as happiness, and we know how to appreciate it"! He says to me, "I enjoy telling Sulzer things like that." — Sch. biog., R. tells of the Hungarian refugee Bizonfy, who confided his situation to Sch., whereupon the latter advised him to beg the Emperor for an amnesty, "which he was reluctant to do." — Our discussion of Sch.'s way of expressing himself reminds me of R., and how I share Sch.'s feeling that every conversation with another person leaves a disturbing echo! My only wish is to be left unmolested with R., living by and for ourselves. He tells me that during his walk he was searching around for a theme for a scherzo, until he began to feel how absurd it all was, for the symphonic form was obsolete, done with. Marke made him laugh during his walk. R. had shut him up, but he escaped through the fences of three other gardens, and finally through the fence of the palace gardens, and

hopped madly around R. — R. took great delight in his unspoiled
animal nature. Late in the evening he goes walking in the garden, and
I immerse myself in my thoughts, wandering through our dear rooms,
in my happiness and unworthiness! — Friend Wol. tells us that the
Grand Duke of Meckl[enburg] has sent 900 marks for the Society.
Regarding the *"Bravo bravissimo, Figaro"* theme he says, "What could
taste right after the drastic dynamic effect of that? With Mozart's
Figaro that didn't matter."

Friday, March 29 R. had a somewhat troubled night. At least,
troubled dreams in the early morning: that friend W. had wanted to
assault me, because I had told R. that the former was attempting to
force him out of the *B. Blätter,* and R. challenged him on it! — Conversation about Sch. and the splendors of Indian wisdom, as reflected
in the saying about badness and mediocrity. "Now we haven't even got
mediocrity, under which I should put Schumann, Hölderlin; so we
have to promote badness to that position, like assigning the King of
W[ürttemberg] to the second class of violinists." Yesterday R. expressed
his astonishment that, although he was so famous, people still tended
to read what was written about him, rather than what he himself
wrote; this was true even of the Jewish pamphlet. "I have been sitting
at the piano for two hours," he tells me, he is somewhat tired. Arrival
of the 6,000 marks from Schwerin, we take them to the banker Gross,
who receives us with the words "My joys know no ending," meaning
the constant flow of subscriptions to the Society of Patrons. — Walking
in our garden, we catch sight of the first crocuses, a touching moment.
As we return home through the palace gardens, he says: "It does not
say much for Schopenhauer that he did not pay more attention to my
Ring des Nibelungen. I know no other work in which the breaking of a
will (and what a will, which delighted in the creation of a world!) is
shown as being accomplished through the individual strength of a
proud nature *without the intervention of a higher grace,* as it is in Wotan.
Almost obliterated by the separation from Brünnhilde, this will rears
up once again, bursts into flame in the meeting with Siegfried, flickers
in the dispatching of Waltraute, until we see it entirely extinguished
at the end in Valhalla." At supper he returns to this and says: "I am
convinced Sch. would have been annoyed that I discovered this before
I knew about his philosophy—I, a political refugee, the indefensibility
of whose theories had been proved by his disciple Kossak on the basis
of his philosophy, since my music is supposed to have no melody. But
it was not very nice. It's the way Goethe treated Kleist, whom he
should have acclaimed, as Schumann acclaimed Brahms—but that
only seems to happen among donkeys." — We finish the biography.
R. then plays something from the Overture to *Die Feen,* which has just

arrived in piano arrangement. — We laugh at Sch.'s mistaken beliefs, for instance, that De Sanctis was his disciple. "One should never yield to such mistaken beliefs," R. says, "and then one can be truly happy." I tell R. that I believe him to be the only person who has really absorbed Sch.'s philosophy into his thinking. "Most people," he says, "want to do something with philosophy, as with religion, even redeem themselves; I can't become saintly all at once, but at least a bit more just."

Saturday, March 30 Again R. had to get out of bed around 4 o'clock and had a disturbed night. . . . Thinking of his overture, he says: "How this idea of fairies and fairyland introduces superficiality into one's imagination! The glittering ballet costumes and the splendor, which can only be taken from real life, produce nothing worth while. What is the origin of it?" I ask whether it might not perhaps be a remnant of the houris. — Discussion about Fidi—whether he is not too sensitive. R. feels this need be no obstacle to energy of character. "Must he be a hooligan?" People who possess only energy, without this sensitivity, are sinister, inhibited characters, he says. The Greek lyric poets remind him of Nietzsche's "extraordinary" outpourings about these very poems. Yesterday evening he could clearly recall Kügelgen, who drew a portrait of Sch. in his youth, his murder and the name of the murderer and his accomplices: "How strong these youthful impressions on one's memory are!" We also spoke yesterday evening about the various methods of execution. Of beheading, he said he had thought how brutal, how barbaric it was suddenly to cut off the head of a woman like Mary Stuart; here, too, the Greeks had discovered a better way with their cup of hemlock. He is satisfied with his work, yet feels oppressed; we go for a walk together, taking the two dogs, warm sunshine. R. thinks of Ajax, how he carried Patroclus from the battlefield on his sturdy shoulders, I suggest that we read the *Iliad,* and he says, "Yes, that is something completely different from Dante, and we have a very good translation." On our return home he says to me, "You will be astonished to see how Parsifal's theme appears in the third act, to describe the long journey he has made—for that is necessary." In the evening he writes to the King and mentions the following notice in the *Musik[alische] Zeitung.* [*Enclosed between the pages is a clipping which looks like a footnote to a lecture by Wilhelm Heinrich Riehl, a German writer on music; it appears that Riehl had compared Beethoven's music with that of Haydn, remarking that "the most modern musicians prefer to play on the fiddle things which can only be expressed in words"; the paper says in criticism of Riehl that "one should not deal with things one dislikes because one does not understand them."*] R. says to the King that people never learn, for the same director who earns good money with R.'s operas in his theater allows such lectures to be

given by Riehl in the music school. — In the evening the Overture to
Die Feen and the lovely Andante from his symphony; the Overture
does not please R., he finds it too dramatic and says it is just well
orchestrated; but he is very happy with the Andante, which he says
has character and melody; thoughts of Mendels[sohn]'s malice in
connection with it. When we are alone, R. and I play the first half of
the *Idyll* as a piano duet, then to rest. R. mentions the *eos krokopeplos,
eos rhododaktylos* [dawn's saffron mantle, dawn's rosy fingers] in the
springtime; going off to his afternoon rest, he embraced me and said:
"Lord, when I sit there in the mornings and work and know that you
do not begrudge me rest and comfort, I find it hard to believe that I
could be doing something else, writing an article or whatever. It
needs a complete reversal of one's nature to do it. But it is probably a
good thing that one does." — And so now this lovely day comes to
an end; when I showed delight in the countryside on our walk, R.
said, "You are so modest in your desires!" Ah, I wish for nothing,
nothing but that he should feel well—everything, everything I find
right and good if it helps him. He urged himself to walk erect, saying
one is always inclined to stoop, particularly when reflecting on something.

Sunday, March 31   R. very languid in the morning, and I, God knows
why, completely worn out; R. reproaches me for not looking after
myself enough, for working too much with the children, he says I
should copy him. I: "Oh, with you it is completely different, you are
creating something." He: "Well, I'm not such a pretty creation myself,
that is your doing." — How soon, however, am I completely recovered; R. fetches me for lunch and says, "Do you know how Kundry
calls to Parsifal?" He sings me the phrase, so piercingly tender, with
which she names him: "It is the first time his name is spoken, and thus
his mother had called him! Only music can do that." "And only your
music," I add. At lunch he tells us stories from the *Oberf[ränkische]
Zeitung* supplement: "How I love people who fight against the will!"
Telegram from Hamburg. R. goes for a walk, a stone breaker joins
him: "You are without your wife today, yesterday she was with you."
He talks about his job. — R. complains of the feelings of oppression
besetting him. In the evening R. sings a theme from a Mozart quartet
which he finds uniquely graceful and beautiful, but unfortunately it
soon gives way to banality: "That is what we owe to Beethoven, that
he did away with the bridging passages, in him everything is part of
the melody." He sings us Beethoven's splendid songs to words by
Gellert; the first in particular moves me to tears. "They were among the
decisive impressions of my youth," R. says. — He bemoans the fact
that Weber always felt obliged to introduce a hunters' chorus, an aria

of expectant waiting. At lunch he sings something from *Tristan,* and I tell him it had been in my mind in the morning. "Things went badly for me with this," he says, "my first Italian opera for an audience of mulattoes; my model was *Romeo and Juliet* — nothing but duets!" . . . In the evening he starts chiding me again and says, "You would like to use yourself all up, so that nothing is left." I, laughing: "Well, yes, that's true." "Then you'd see what a fine mess I should become." Just before going off to bed he remembers the little dog he bought in Meudon for 3 francs; he did not know what to call it, told M. Jadin it raised no associations in his mind. "Call it 3 francs," said his landlord.

Monday, April 1 R. had a good night, except that his wife Minna again made a nuisance of herself: "But I have learned to be suitably rude now." He performs all kinds of April Fools' jokes with the children at lunch, much to his amusement. Various house and garden problems for me! — R. goes for a walk but complains of the weather, which is very windy; the forecasts for April are bad! — A construction worker greets him: "Good day, master." — In the afternoon R. finishes his letter to the King, in which he talks of the talented theater manager His Excellency Baron P[erfall] and of his fellow knight Brahms! — In the evening he goes through [Spontini's] *Olimpie* Overture with Herr Seidl, who does not know it: "Splendid stuff," says R., "I can actually see the Diadochi filing in. It stands somewhere between Gluck and Rossini, quite remarkable—it has an entirely Gluckian structure and a passion for cadences such as no one showed before Rossini, except Cherubini. But it has character, one is aware of a proud fellow who will stand no nonsense, wears all his medals on his chest. One can see what a difference self-assurance makes, how unmistakably dramatic it all is when one compares it with Brahms, for instance." — Of Cherubini's works he praises the *Lodoiska* Overture and in *Médée* the entrance of the dominant, which he felt in his youth to be like the sun coming out. — A discourse on the un-German nature of rhyme and its impracticability in music produces from him a remark about the trochees in *The Trump[eter] of S[äckingen]:* "That is just a dirty joke." Regarding the Diadochi he says: "Alexander was after all too great for epic poetry, his deeds during those 10 years too tremendous. I once sketched out a drama called *Alex.,* the first act was the murder of Clitus, the second the decision to withdraw from Asia, the third his death; writers nowadays usually select the burning of Persepolis, Thais with the torch—the lyrical elements! I also sketched the third act of an *Achilles* and a *Barbarossa*" (to this he linked his remarks about verse). — He then, in his wonderful way, reads us the first canto of the *Iliad,* with overpowering effect. "There one can start thinking again about the author problem," he says. He finds Voss's

April 2, 1878

translation very good but regrets that in his use of German he had not yet progressed beyond Lessing: words like *"Palast"* ["palace"], etc., disturb him. He remarks on the fact that the sense of a line is often transferred to another, which shows the illusory nature of verse. — After that several things from Bach's *48 Preludes and Fugues,* and R. cannot praise highly enough the remarkable singing quality of the figurations. — After our friends have gone R. and I once more talk about the beauties of the first canto of the *Iliad.* I tell him I was particularly struck by the way H[omer], dealing with the human quality in a woman's needs, has made the insult to her honor a particularly sensitive point, and I was reminded of Loge's conclusion that nobody is prepared to sacrifice love.

Tuesday, April 2 R. woke up with a loud cry. "Spirits, phantoms; they were playing D, F sharp, A on the Geneva F-sharp harmonica, but it came out as G sharp, G, E, and I knew who they were." He goes to sleep again, I remain awake and at dawn hear a sweet little bird singing. R. works and is looking forward to what he has to do, for he is now working out the theme he wrote down some time ago. At noon I receive from Marie Pusinelli the news of the death of our dear friend. I decide not to give R. the news until the end of the evening; I order wreaths and conceal my feelings from R., who is enjoying the springlike weather. We go for a walk together, delight in the birds, particularly a splendid finch which R. points out to me. In the evening he works out what he sketched in the morning and shows me with much enjoyment the transition to gentleness: "It had to pass from turbulence to tenderness." At supper an unkind fate decrees that Herr Stern send me a reply, which I was not expecting. R. opens the telegram. Silence. He gets up and goes out, comes back after a little while; I at once start to read a further installment of Herr Porges's article; earnest discussion. Friend W. reads his article on Schemann's collected works. Present-day art, present-day theater leads R. to the performance of *Le Baruffe Chiozzotte* which he once saw; we read Goethe's description of the play. An article by Herr Lindau, mentioned by W., about the unfortunate effect of our classical writers on the theater, the need to form a link with Molière: "As if we possessed a society for which and from which we could work!" I said to R. He: "Yes, we can succeed only with the truly ideal, for then we speak to the souls that feel the need for this ideal." Our friends leave: "Let's go straight to bed," says R. On the stairs I ask, "You understood the telegram?" He: "Oh!" We prepare for sleep; in bed he says, "He was a small man but a great heart, an unflinchingly great heart, which helped him to understand everything, and that was the reason for his happy career."

Wednesday, April 3 R. slept tolerably. "You poor little woman," he says to me, "what a lot of worries you have, problems you conceal from me!" At breakfast: "Just keep flourishing, we also want to set an example of perseverance, to die without noticing it—in fact, to the world we are already dead!" "Nobody perhaps held so closely, so loyally and steadfastly to me as P[usinelli]; he showed only love for me, pleasure in helping me, sorrow over my sad life." He relates how pleasant and congenial the Pusinelli home in Dresden had been to him, he had often been there with Minna. He does not work; writes to Frau P. — At midday he receives the Munich theater representative whom he had asked to come to discuss the serpent question. They have in fact constructed a winged dragon, which makes R. ask why, if it could fly, it has laboriously to crawl up, and anyway it is nowhere called a dragon, but a *serpent*. His report of the interview reminds him of Brandt and the "agonizing patience" he displayed on that occasion, and how this then turned into arrogance. He tells friend Seidl of the death of his friend. He showers praise on him, tells of his initial shy approaches. "A friendly fate ordained that we not meet too often, for the differences of our natures might perhaps have caused friction; as it was, only the real core, that which really mattered, showed. It is comforting and sad at the same time—but what in life is not sad?" He remarks what a strange effect such a blow has on one; even if one tries to banish the thought of it, it still affects one physically, he feels a terrible weight lying on him. — During a snow flurry I thought of our friend's death, and then the sun came out, as if to say that it is now all over and everything has resumed its wonted path. — R. goes for a walk. Yesterday he told me that he wished the *broom*like would turn into bloomlike, meaning that the leafless trees would put on their green again. He returns home and, still incapable of work, reads V. Hugo's *Histoire d'un crime*. "You know I like reading stories about crime, and to have one like this, written by so superb a comedian!" He is very amused at the frivolity of the plot on the one hand and the clumsy theatrical earnestness on the other. Today is Saint Richard's Day, I give him a little Japanese box; when I go in to him, he tells me he has just been studying my photographs and thinks the middle one, taken in London, is the best, the clearest. "Oh, you are such a good creature, and more than that!" he says. Then he tells me how the dogs caused him trouble during his walk, Brange went rushing far away, little Wana lost her way in a field and started howling, the older ones showed no concern for the little dog, he went to fetch her, and as he picked her up, a theme for a symphony suddenly came into his mind. "Look, there it is, written down. It seems to me very good, but possibly it's worthless." "On such trivialities the mind depends," he exclaims, "the brain blowing bubbles and playing!" — We do no reading in the evening. R. talks of his experiences with Herr Schmitt the singing teacher, who is now writing articles attacking R. in the papers.

Thursday, April 4 R. says, "Shall I go back to my maidens?" "*Im Lenz pflückt uns der Meister*" ["In spring the master plucks us"], he says, and then, "Just keep flourishing, do nothing, be Madame Kling-sor, wander in the garden." He works. "I am having trouble with the German language, I find it downright repugnant, I shall change a lot," he says to me at lunch. A walk with him in the palace gardens; much merriment over Hugo's book; the Romans and Lacedaemonians mere prattlers in comparison! — A catalogue of R.'s works by E. Kastner, many things incorrect and useless. — In the evening extracts from *Der Freischütz* and *Euryanthe,* much of it played through with delight. Second canto of the *Iliad.* "I have found a transition," he tells me as the evening ends. We go through our troubles in Munich. — "Yes, when I get melancholy and think, 'When will all these vexations come to an end?,' I comfort myself with the thought that we have a mission to perform and must live forever; I could still do much to help, if I were asked." In the palace gardens, getting to his feet, he says, "Walking erect in this world is not worth the trouble." — A singer here wants to sing "*L'Attente,*" unbelievably bad translations! "*Storch, lass im Teich dein Gewürm!*"—unsingable.

Friday, April 5 R. had a good night. He complained yesterday of the oppressive effect of the constantly gray skies; we resolve to spend three months each year, from January to the middle of April, in Florence: "I shall then write a symphony a year." As he embraces me before leaving me after breakfast, he says, "You are the most beautiful of all." — Around lunchtime he calls me and plays me "*Komm', holder Knabe*" from his sketches, that most enchanting of scenes. Yesterday he said, "In the first act I was very sparing of sensuous intervals, but now I am going back to my old paintpot." — A *Deutsche Revue* (the title alone makes him laugh!) asks him for his recollections, he tells friend F[eustel] to reply saying he has no recollections, except of bad newspaper articles. — We decide not to go out, the skies are still gray; yesterday he said during our walk: "Why do the birds sing so much? They don't worry about how the heavens look, they just sing as children laugh, without cause!" — At the end of Herr Kastner's catalogue ("Laborious work, unlaboriously done") is printed an article by R. on the ballet *Gräfin Egmont.* R. is not pleased, since he did not wish to acknowledge the article, which was a sort of concession to prevailing circumstances. — R. went out after all. In the evening he says gaily that Herr v. Hülsen is giving as few performances of his works as possible, being too stupid, like an ox one can take to a certain point, but then it gets angry and refuses to go farther. We think of Javert in [Hugo's] *Les Misérables,* and I say to R., "Hülsen may yet go mad over the *Ring* and throw himself into the water." — Read [Scott's] *Ivanhoe.* Some schoolteachers from Dillingen in Swabia have joined the Society of Patrons. — R. complains of not having played his maidens well enough to me! . . .

Saturday, April 6 R. had a good night; he works. "I have found a transition," he exclaimed yesterday. He goes to his work after we talked at breakfast about the Crown Prince, his lack of interest, and wondered whether his wife might do something. — "I shall never forget how, when he told Marie D[önhoff] that he would have to do something for Bayreuth, she replied with such childish simplicity, 'Oh, no, Fritz.' " — At lunch Frl. Olden, a young and already celebrated singer! Strange, long-forgotten association. — Around 3 o'clock to the theater with the children, costume fitting, home around 6 o'clock to find R. amusing himself with V. H[ugo]; he says to me: "After the 1848 revolution I told myself it would never be possible for a publication by Heine to cause a stir again, but then a few years later I myself was reading his *Romanzero;* during the war with France we said it would never again be possible for events in Paris to interest us as they did then, it was over; and now I am getting so much entertainment from this book, looking forward to every page of it!" "Everything Bismarck does is an imitation of N[apoleon] III. And everything in Paris has character." At 7 o'clock to the amateur concert to hear Frl. Olden—great disappointment, not to say dismay, over the present state of theatrical art. Indescribable tempi, *"L'Attente"* too hurried, the splendid *"Mignonne"* garbled, Agathe's aria without feeling, merely scamped. And this lady already has an engagement worth 24,000 marks! "For such was my school intended; but it's very doubtful whether I would even have accepted her." — The program included the *Danse macabre* by Saint-Saëns, which is at present all the rage in Germany, and R. is amused when I say this work is like a Berlioz *Panaritium.* Home in merry mood: "I'll never be caught again," R. exclaims. "Yet it has its advantages—it makes us see even more clearly how happy we are. — No, I don't want anything more to do with the world, the most we will do is hurl our bulls into it through the *B. Blätter.*" "Who would have the nerve to deny that we are living in a time of appalling decadence?"

Sunday, April 7 "Recall the pledges that we plighted, recall the love we bear between us, recall the earth where we are one." With these words R. releases me after breakfast. "I did not need the hypothesis of Christianity," he adds after a while, "as Laplace did not need the hypothesis of God, to express the negation of the will in the *Ring.*" —

We come back to the subject of Frl. O[lden]; a letter of recommendation
from her teacher makes him thoroughly indignant, and he intends to
send her a rude answer. Frl. Götz's opinion, mentioned in the letter,
that Frl. Olden would be particularly suited to Kundry, brings from
R. the remark: "That reminds me of my mother, who once wrote to
my sister Klara, 'The baritone in Nuremberg has drunk himself to
death—that would be just in your husband's line.'" R. works. He
goes out in the afternoon; in the evening we read *Ivanhoe.*

Monday, April 8 Deep sorrow, caused by Lulu! . . . A telegram
announcing my father's arrival; at 11 o'clock he is here, much to our
joy. — Discussed many things in mutual sympathy and concord. — R.
takes the contract with Munich to the mayor for signature.

Tuesday, April 9 R. says to me in the morning: "Your father, you,
and I seem to me like survivors of a vanished species, such as the
mammoth. Apart from these, there has been no single contact in my
life which did not end with a horrible disappointment. And when I
think of our theater! That will become a mere subsidiary of Munich."
I: "Oh, no, for Fidi will be there." "He will want to enjoy his life,
and that makes one selfish." R. works. Toward evening he receives a
wonderfully touching letter from Frau Pusinelli, which profoundly
moves him. — Of Saint-Saëns and the *Danse macabre* R. says, "The
donkey doesn't even know how a cock crows; on the dominant; he
makes it yodel." After his walk R. comes to me, and when I ask him
how things are going, he says: "Oh, very well, I know now that I
shall not compose *Parsifal,* God preserve me from that! Oh, that
scene between Kundry and Parsifal! I had a look at his cry—compared
with that, Tristan's curse is a mere joke." "Then you must quickly
think up another work for the Society of Patrons." — In the evening
my father was kind enough to play us some of his recent compositions.
— As R. and I prepare for bed, various episodes from Hugo's *Crime*
come into our minds, and we cannot stop laughing—certainly no
comedy could be quite so diverting. Good news of the Society of
Patrons, every day brings new subscriptions. Only one Israelite (from
Kassel) has withdrawn, since he finds himself unable to reconcile the
article "*Modern*" with his convictions. Schoolteachers, officers, all
kinds of small fry are joining.

Wednesday, April 10 Loldi's birthday, but we postpone the celebrations. R. works. He receives a touching letter in Italian (from
Rossano) written by the son of a man who had been here at the festival
and who has now died. Fidi has a sore throat, I hope nothing serious.
In the evening my father plays us "*Jeux d'eau*" and "*Anges gardiens*"—R.
says, "A dreamy, melancholy existence in the Villa d'Este, there

he extols the cypresses, the angelus bells, the fountains—I like that."

Thursday, April 11 R. works on his article for the *Blätter*—still no spring! Our good mayor dines with us. In the evening a game of whist, a curious sight in Wahnfried, R. says it will still be haunting it 100 years hence. — At lunch R. gets indignant, because a Colonel S. describes Balzac as superficial, Gutzkow as deep and fundamental. Afterward he is annoyed with his indignation: "I never consider the people with whom I am talking, I see everything *sub species aeterni.*" — He spoke up splendidly for Balzac.

Friday, April 12 R. works out his article; at lunch he says he will write it, but to him it is only the time spent on his true work which is really sacred, even if a day's work produces just a single modulation or turn. In the afternoon he goes out, in the evening *Parsifal* for my father, from the entrance into the Temple onward. A most remarkable, unforgettable sight, R. and my father, the greatness of life, the greatness of withdrawal from it! — After my father has gone, R. speaks G[oethe]'s lines from *Faust:*

> "*Man kann nicht stets das Fremde meiden,*
> *Das Gute liegt oft gar zu fern;*
> *Ein echter deutscher Mann kann keinen Franzmann leiden,*
> *Doch seine Weine trinkt er gern.*"

He admires the lengthening of the third line and says: "What feeling for rhythm that shows! In the excitement of the moment it must be spoken very quickly, following the more sober preceding line. But this line is always spoken with a senselessly solemn accentuation."

Saturday, April 13 R. finishes his article and reads it to us in the evening; the work has tired him and he does not feel entirely well, he complains of lumbago. Although Baron Seydlitz, who happens to be here on a visit, says that he looks ever younger, I feel some concern.

Sunday, April 14 R. had a good night, but his aches have not yet gone. However, he returns to his "maidens" and says he believes I will like them. Fine spring day, I walk slowly with my father in the palace gardens, and suddenly we meet R., striding along with the 2 dogs as he returns from the Students' Wood; merry greetings; R., as he goes, cries out to my father, "I can't be cross with you, since you gave birth to your daughter for me." In the evening my father again plays us several of his compositions. Some of it does not appeal to R., and this arouses feelings of embarrassment in him, but he takes great pains to show my father only his love and admiration. — It is wonderful and touching to see how these two such fundamentally different natures, who have taken such divergent paths, respect, understand, and protect each other, and that is one more jewel in the crown of my happiness. [*Added in margin:* " 'Have you still got a body?' R. says to me today, embracing me."]

Monday, April 15   R. works, though not yet free of his ailments. He also goes out, but he sends for the doctor, who does not seem to be alarmed. In the evening a double game of whist, my father with Bayreuth friends at one table, R., I, friend Seidl, and Lulu at the other, R. doing the teaching. It makes us laugh a lot, this *grazioso* table! R. joins in everything in so amiable a manner, even something as unaccustomed as this.

Tuesday, April 16   R. very upset by the 2nd volume of V. Hugo, finding the massacre horrible, the people who after it could still go on amusing themselves incomprehensible. The fact that such a man as N. III could also do some good things shows the wretchedness of all politics. We think of our good friend Pusinelli and his excellent family: "I do not believe that there are people as good as these among my enemies," R. says. — Yesterday he went to Wolzogen in order to alter two words in his article—instead of "then he received from the minister," "then the minister obtained for him." Regret that Heyse, who had a sense of form, has been "spoiled" by the theater. R. works and is pleased with his "*Du—Tor,*" which he sings to me frequently. In the evening my father plays us the *Album-Sonate,* in which R. finds little to enjoy: "Though the '*Albumblatt für Betty Schott*' is also artificial, it is nevertheless better." — I ask my father to play something for R. from the *48 Preludes and Fugues,* which he does, playing the [*left blank*], to the amazement and delight of us all. Friend Feustel approaches my father regarding capital for the deficit, which, it seems, is not easy to raise at 5%; I beg my father, who is reluctant to touch his investments, only to do so if we are unable to raise the necessary loan elsewhere.

Wednesday, April 17   In the morning R. recalls the circumstances that surrounded Fidi's birth and, continuing from that, says how curious it is that the births of extraordinary people were always connected with torments—Parsifal, Tristan, Apollo, Perseus—it was as if divine grace always found expression in anger, like Wotan's behavior toward the Wälsungen. — When he releases me, he says: "Now I must go to my dear old primeval woman." Departure of my father, whom I accompany as far as Neuenmarkt. R. goes for a walk and works; complains humorously about his problem with the *choreography,* says it will turn out like the so-called street-brawl scene in *Die Meistersinger.* Delight in the birds at coffeetime. In the evening, coming back to the German language, he says the spirit of the language does not allow one to express oneself just in short sentences, the art lies in being clear and definite within the *encapsulated* structure of German. — Then he tells us how ridiculous it is that, having just been composing his *Parsifal,* he should find such things as the cadenza of Princess Elvira's first aria in *La Muette de Portici* coming into his mind as he was "putting on his trousers and shoes"!

Maundy Thursday, April 18 To church with Bonus. (R. works.) Not a proper service, Communion only for a few, in the silence of the empty church I read Tauler's sermons with great edification. *Non sum!* How dearly I should like, following this saintly man, to make that my motto! And to possess "a brightly burning mind amid deep silence"! — In the afternoon I go with friend Wolzogen through some of the articles for the *B. Blätter,* and it is the lack of clarity and sloppiness of style which I have most often to point out. In the evening conversation with friend Heckel, who has been here on a visit for the past two days. It is true that in the last quarter Herr v. Hülsen put on *Lohengrin* and *Tannhäuser* only once—these performances, however, being full to bursting and sold out. R. does not feel entirely well. "I do nothing else in this world except love you," R. says to me as we bid each other good night.

Good Friday, April 19 All day yesterday I heard singing inside me "*Wein und Brot des letzten Mahles wandelt einst der Herr des Grales,*" and R., when I tell him this, plays it to me at the end of the day. That it is his art which found the note for the mystery of faith which possesses me, and that the wordless fervor of my soul sings through him—oh, what bliss, what grace! — In the afternoon went to church with the three younger ones; in my childhood I heard that every wish expressed at 3 o'clock, the time of the death of our Lord, would be granted; today I asked that my light be extinguished at the same moment as R.'s, that we might die united; I begged the little birds to ask with me, I asked through their song, through the faces of the little blossoms, through the buds on the trees, through the blessings of the cross, through the tones of the organ, through the prayers of the poor, through my repentance and my pain—oh, might I be heard? Whom did I ask, who is to grant it? Oh, wish so strong, hast thou the strength? Oh, thou will so almighty, become pure and worthy of the highest grace! — All the mortal longing and pain which through the ages has lit and transfigured the sacred picture of the Redeemer—through all this I beg this boon! — A blessed day, a day of innocence, everything is singing, spreading its perfume, sending forth its shoots; from the little house next door the sound of "Wotan's Farewell" wafts across to me in my peaceful surroundings, and Parsifal's gentle sadness encloses me! — We go out together, R. and I, the hills in beautiful color, serene and mild conversation; Good Friday! R. feels that even on the northern slopes of Spain the blossoms must have been more luxuriant, the fields and meadows here must replace them for us with their tender green. — R. also talks about V. Hugo, whom he calls "a grandiose fool." — In the evening Frau Materna with her husband, many reminiscences of the festival. — I tell R. that I have made a prayer, and he looks at me, long, lovingly, and with deep understanding—ah, he knows what it is I have to ask!

Saturday, April 20 R. works. The Maternas at lunch, also in the evening with Dr. Schemann. R. has a slight cold and, however sincerely he delights in the South German temperament of our good singer, he nevertheless grows tired; our intimate talks are suspended, and the whole conversation takes a different turn.

Sunday, April 21 R. works. At lunch friend Richter, very well and goodhearted; he brings me the happy news that Makart wants to do the sketches for the costumes and bring them here in time for the 22nd. But in the afternoon R. does not feel well; he lies down and reads Hugo, while Richter and Seidl play *Parsifal* downstairs. A melancholy day and evening for me; all friendliness from the outside world seems a burden when one is inwardly dreary.

Monday, April 22 R. coughs all night, but he is cheerful in the morning. A manuscript that arrives in the mail (*Odysseus* by M. Wesendonck) causes some embarrassment. "A proper fiasco," R. says with a laugh, "but it has its good side—it will be seen later how exaggerated all those blatherings of mine were." — He finds the ending of the V. Hugo book downright despicable, says it is in their inability to see anything besides themselves that the French fall down: the ending spoils the whole book. — R. remains in his room, I alone look in on him from time to time: "You best of all men!" "You're wrong, you are the best of all women." "Oh, you good man!" — "What you mean is: Oh, you lucky man!" — He is reading Renan's *Evangiles*. In the evening he comes downstairs to say goodbye to Frau Materna. He is feeling worn out and agitated. Everything that upsets our daily routine is bad for him. When I visited him he was talking to himself: "Gentlemen, that would not look well." He was imagining a curtain call after *Parsifal* and laughed at his own reply.

Tuesday, April 23 R. had a tolerable night, though he had a very absurd dream about Major Müller, who was courting me so energetically that he drew my attention to it; I was quite annoyed over the prospect and at last, when the disagreeable man became importunate, hit him over the head with a roll of music I had in my hands. We discuss the things that disturb our life. "You are always ready to make sacrifices," R. says to me; "if we are talking about kindness, then only you deserve mention." When I object he says, "The only sacrifice I make is that for your sake I continue to work for this evil world." —

The Ezra Apocalypse and Clement of Rome's *Epistle* bring him back once more to the wretchedness of the church: "I repeat, the three greatest scandals are the Sultan in C[onstantinople], the Pope in Rome, and Hülsen in Berlin," he says with a laugh. We also laugh over how Renan depicts Jesus and describes the Gospel According to Saint Matthew, in a very modern way, entirely from the viewpoint of present-day Paris society; if Christ were to appear to him, R. feels, he would say, "*Au plaisir de vous revoir*" ["Pleased to see you again"] — We also laugh about Hugo, who always uses the German word for "department," as if it were something very mysterious, and portrays the people in this "*Abteilung*" at the Battle of Sedan as if they were paid assassins! — R. stays home all day; in the evening we read C. Frantz's letter in reply to the challenge made to him in *What Is German?*. We were alone, and very happy to be that way! — Much in C. Fr. makes one wonder, but it is always well considered; R. says, "Just as one begins to think he is blathering, a thought always emerges." — Referring to our reading, R. says, "All that remains for us is to give each other pleasure."

Wednesday, April 24 R. is woken during the night by Marke's barking, he tells me he has just dreamed that he was reciting Shakespeare in English in England and was amazed at how sure he was: "What inspiration does for one!" he said to himself. "But all the same I shall have to ask my wife." — R. works and tells me that he will have finished the maidens' scene by the end of the month; he will then give it to me to read before singing it to me. We are glad that we are alone for our dessert. Went walking in the garden with R.; many spring problems beside our spring joys! But we shall bear them all serenely "for the sake of our love." In the evening we return at last to our Jew in Ashby; much entertainment from it. Heartfelt enjoyment of the tranquil life now restored to us.

Thursday, April 25 R. had a good night; he looks forward to his work, and that is pleasure enough for me amid all kinds of little worries! — At noon arrival of a new book by friend Nietzsche— feelings of apprehension after a short glance through it; R. feels he would be doing the author a favor, for which the latter would one day thank him, if he did not read it. It seems to me to contain much inner rage and sullenness, and R. laughs heartily when I say that Voltaire, here so acclaimed, would less than any other man have understood *The Birth of Tragedy*. A wet day. Inspection of the small theater; R. goes out for a while, then works again in the afternoon. Friend Wolzogen reads me some things for the *Blätter*. In the evening *Ivanhoe*. And later in the evening the full tide of our love!

Friday, April 26 Though R. slept well, he still feels somewhat tired; he works, however, and at lunch is very cheerful at having come so far (with his maidens). After lunch he says to me, "Because it gives you pleasure to see me well, I feel well, for love of you." — R. is now reading Renan's *The Apostles:* "They are so attractively put together, these books," he says with a smile. In the evening *Ivanhoe,* with great enjoyment. But R. is slightly indisposed, something like a cold, his eyes hurt. If only my worry did not at once assume such great proportions! When I am with him everything is all right, but then I am overcome by an indescribable longing for death!

Saturday, April 27 R. was already awake at 5 o'clock, at lunchtime he shows me the scene, almost completed *in ink,* and he plays the theme, the enchanting theme, to the children. I with the children to the schoolhouse for rehearsals. — R. not entirely well, but still working and enjoying his work; only he says he dare not think of the performance: "When I hear, for instance, that Vogl is already saying he will sing Parsifal, my blood boils." Firm resolve not to read friend Nietzsche's book, which seems at first glance to be strangely perverse. — In the evening *Ivanhoe,* then amused ourselves with some things from Marschner's *Templer.* Yesterday R. praised *La Dame Blanche,* calling it a unique work, incomparable in its way.

Sunday, April 28 R. had a good night. Ah, that is what I need! — I become quite superstitious when he lacks anything; yesterday his eyes were somewhat inflamed, and that was enough to put me in torments, even the fact that he had a little rash on his leg disquieted me. But he is cheerful, and at lunchtime he shows me the completed Flower Maidens' scene. Joyful spirits during the meal as a result. After lunch he talks of continuing his article, dealing with what is bad, the folklike quality which is allied to genius, the mediocre, what it is that distinguishes the "bad" from the sublime. I quote examples—Gozzi bad, Goldoni mediocre, Rossini bad, Brahms, Schumann mediocre—and appear to have understood R. He says he will only indicate the theme, and others can work it out in detail. The military band today played some dreadful things: "Even Haydn was coarse now and again, but it has all changed so greatly, there is no longer any sensitive coarseness." — A walk in the afternoon; the W.'s, the children, and I wait for R. in Birken, he comes with the three dogs, the children, catching sight of him from afar, run to meet him; in the beautiful air to the Students' Wood, a complete caravanserai—festival of the Flower Maidens, the green meadow blooming, the children reveling, the young birch trees bursting into bud among the dark firs, the sun smiling down on dark and light, the dogs running wild, "Brange-Kundry, passionate, mysterious," gets lost, finds us again, renewed rejoicing, the birds try to tempt us into the woods: "Stay here, stay here," says one of them to me as we walk along the edge, heading for home; and above the field, lost in the blueness, a lark flutters, intoxicating the heart. "It is like the scent of violets," says R., plucking the little flower for me. We return home filled with happiness, and it is *he* whom I have to thank for all this light, this air, these sounds, this greeting from both Heaven and earth: "We shall enjoy many more such days," says R., "with one good work behind us, and another before us"!

Monday, April 29 R. had a good night and was not wearied by our long walk. — We find it hard not to speak now and again about friend N.'s sad book, although both of us can only surmise its contents from a few passages, rather than really know it! — R. is reading Renan's *The Apostles* and is pleased with the remark that the Gospel According to Saint Matthew was the first book to be written in a popular style. — At breakfast he says that, if he were to present anything here after *Parsifal,* it would be *Tristan* and *Die Msinger,* but he doubts whether he could find a singer for Tristan; he says he wants to make some alterations in the 3rd act, also in the 2nd: "I don't know what devil it was that drove me to produce such stuff—it was the music, which came welling like that out of the subject." — How little words contributed to the drama, he told us recently, he saw from the fact that in London he had understood hardly any of Jefferson's words but had been able to follow everything, had not been bored for an instant. "It's characters one wants, not speeches." I study the Flower Maidens' scene, this splendid, incomparable scene, about which R. said to me, "Yes, I am rather proud of it." In the afternoon a rehearsal with the children while R. is resting, then I drive with R. to the Waldhütte: lovely hours! [*Pressed between this page and the next are a few dried stalks of forget-me-not.*] R. remarks that the absence of a large river is responsible for our countryside here being so remote, so like Paradise. Where there is a large river there is also activity, here it is idyllic. The cuckoo greets us as we turn into the woods; he calls 24 times in a row; we listen blissfully! The sky not as clear as yesterday, but a fine day nevertheless. — In the evening *Ivanhoe,* unfortunately we become only too conscious of certain weaknesses in this beautiful work, as, for instance, the long stretches of dialogue, Rebecca and Ivanhoe's arguing about chivalrous honor even in the most terrible situations, and the short, but still too long, conversation when the Templar fetches Rebecca. — After our friends have gone, R. recalls our old and difficult times in Munich: "How did I manage to put up with it?"

Tuesday, April 30 R. had a good night. N.'s pitiful book makes him exclaim to me, "We shall remain true to each other." He works; the good news from Leipzig about *Rheingold* and *Walküre* pleases him. I visit friend Gross, to find out how things stand with the capital loan. He tells me it had almost been settled when a jurist (the 4th J.!) frightened off the bank. He says the King insists that R. no longer have to worry about it; Herr Bürkel has done as much as he can, but he cannot very well show his face in a bank, for then it would be spread around that the King was getting into debt—he, B., had only recently had to reply to some malicious articles in the *Fr[änkische] Zeit[ung]* entitled "The King of Bavaria and His Debts." — In the evening R. feels severe pain in his leg, the physician discovers a furuncle and orders complete rest. To see him flat on his back robs me of all my strength, and when, as he frequently does, he sings to me "*Sostegno e gloria dell'umanità*" ["Support and glory of humanity"], I have to tell him this *gloria* does not amount to much, for when he is not shining, everything in and around me dies!

Wednesday, May 1 R. slept well but still has his ailment and has to stay in bed. A sore trial! All the same, he works and writes the conclusion of his "Public and Popularity" article. He then manages to drag himself into the garden and sits down on a bench, from which he calls to me. I struggle hard to show him a cheerfulness I no longer feel, but it returns to me as I sit with R. on the steps outside the *salon* and we watch and listen to a blackbird; the greenery of the trees delights him, and the church towers can be seen through a faint mist. In the evening, *Ivanhoe. The uncle* (as the children call Seidl) returns home from Leipzig and gives us good reports of Schelper, but bad ones of the production, music and action never together. "None of them has any idea of what the main thing in my works is," R. says. — "Good night, Paradeta," he calls out to me.

Thursday, May 2 His furuncle is getting bigger, and he is certainly in pain, even if his splendid spirits remain the same; he laughs about his ailment, says that the grass seed which has not arrived (much to his annoyance) has taken root in his leg! At lunchtime he plays me Kundry's first words, "*Parsifal, fal-parsi*," to my unutterable delight. — Music rehearsal with the children, R. lying down upstairs! — In the evening an article by Hans Herrig, with whom we have been out of touch for some considerable time, "Wagner and Literature," very good; we decide to ask him to contribute to the *B. Bl.* Before that friend W. read me a charming letter from the Spaniard. These signs from the outside world affect me in a very curious way; everything to do with fame makes me feel melancholy; it seems to me like the shadow cast by the light—which I have here before my eyes—through the body of the world. I tell R. about my feelings, and he says it is because nothing outside is genuine; perhaps I just feel like this because *he* is indisposed.

Friday, May 3 The trouble will still take several days to clear up!

But R. works in spite of it. We hold a music rehearsal. On my return I find the tenor Herr Jäger in Wahnfried; he sings to R. "Lohengrin's Narration," with a good voice but all the mistakes in delivery usual in German opera houses. R. then sings it to him with that noble simplicity which allows the soul to speak directly to us. After our guests have gone, R. having put on an amiable front in spite of his pain, he reads to me the conclusion of his article, and we decide that it needs an additional ending. R. now writes such articles with reluctance and is glad not to have anything more to do for the *Bayreuther Blätter* until July. We also read Herr Löffler on Kundry. —

Saturday, May 4 R. had a tolerable night, but his ailment is taking a long time to clear up, and even spring is now proving a burden to him, since he cannot enjoy it properly. He is still working, however. — I hold a rehearsal with the children in the schoolhouse. During that time R. writes to Dr. Jauner and to friend Richter, saying he would like them here to study *Siegfried*. As a result of coaching, friend Seidl tells me, Herr Jäger is turning out very well. — Conversation about R.'s experiences in the theater, he says he has always got along well with orchestral players and singers, but never with conductors, managers, stage directors, etc. — Restored to each other again, we discuss our "lengthy past"—14 years! "The second period of your life, the third of mine." I: "I did not live at all before." He, jokingly: "And all I did was compose." — Lulu is causing me concern.

Sunday, May 5 R.'s leg getting more painful . . . I to the studio to have Fidi photographed in his suits. R. lifts a weight off me with regard to Lulu! — The capital loan still causing difficulties. And so "spring's behest" is by no means blessed just now as far as we are concerned, even though, through all our troubles, R. remains cheerful and communicative. For instance, he reads me a passage from the end of Renan's *Apostles* which pleases him greatly, to the effect that in a nobler state of humanity the capabilities of religion would also be strengthened. — The "cuckoo's eggs laid in our nest," as R. calls them, are proving troublesome.

Monday, May 6 Eva also photographed. But in spite of all these activities which I enjoy so much, since they are connected with the 22nd, my outlook is *very gloomy,* for R.'s leg grows increasingly painful, and he looks very run down. — The children wheel him to the summerhouse, for the first time; high above us joy continues to hover, though the ground remains in darkness—for R. is so cheerful, and we have only to be together two seconds for all disagreeable thoughts to fly out of the window. In the evening I read the first act of *Die Perlenschnur,* with great satisfaction.

Tuesday, May 7 Much cheerful talk with R., who jokes about his ailment: "My beloved has a furuncle" to the strains of "My beloved lies wounded." — He dreamed that he had presented his theater to Fidi, who sold it for one mark in order to buy some paper; but the purchaser gave him only 50 pfennigs, and Fidi asked for another 50 pfennigs for paper. "You bad boy, you have sold the theater!" R. works in spite of his furuncle and great vexations caused by Lulu. With all his usual kindness R. helps me put things right, and when he praises my sense of justness which smooths out the difficulties, I tell him that the justness stems from him. In the evening the sweet fragrance of the Indian sagarika. R. says the reason he will never carry out his Indian project is that he does not know the names of the flowers, and these are an integral part of the subject. (With Loldi in the morning to the photographer's.)

Wednesday, May 8 R.'s ailment still not cured, but the doctor encourages no complaints, telling us we can be glad that this carbuncle is such a superficial and insignificant one. R. works. I with Loldi again to the photographer's. — Now Königsberg also wants to do *Rheingold* and *Walküre*—Herr von Hülsen will soon be ringed around by the *Ring!* — At lunch I have to rebuke Lulu sharply. — R. writes to Herr von Loën, suggesting that instead of royalties the Grand Duke might grant him a small pension until 30 years after his death. In this way he could circumvent Messrs. Voltz and Batz. "This would be for one of my 130 daughters," R. says with a laugh. In the evening we begin [Scott's] *Kenilworth*. R. revises his article, but without any pleasure, says he has nothing more to say to anybody. At supper much merriment over the way I get entangled in my own lies; R. declares that I must have been ordering a trumpet serenade for him from the military band!

Thursday, May 9 R.'s leg still very painful, but the core seems to be loosening. He works; maternal cares caused him trouble! — Friend Wolzogen reads to me his excellent "Fight with the Dragon." In the evening the curious Herr Schmeitzner, I feel we would do better to print our little periodical here! When this strange man talks of various publishing tricks and manipulations, I feel like exclaiming, "God help me, I'd sooner be a cobbler!," all the more so since he and his publishing firm have not produced even one pair of good shoes—he tells us everything he has done has failed! . . . Much laughter with R. about it after they have all left Wahnfried. Strong forebodings, light thrown on Nietzsche by R. (Daniel's birthday.)

Friday, May 10 During the night our poor lonely deer cried so piteously! I felt this sound would never end and would echo inside me to all eternity. This lament, the terrible lament of sin, this cry, the fearful cry of desire! Desire, sin—how they resound in the silent night and fill one with pity for the poor beast, its call of nature piercing my heart! — R.'s carbuncle bursting at last, but he still cannot walk; however, he remains in good spirits and is working. But Vienna is causing him great vexation; he had written saying that it was precisely for Siegfried at the Imperial Opera that he wished to coach Herr Jäger, who is proving to be a sterling character. Herr Jauner writes that Herr Glatz has already been engaged for this role. We remember our experiences with Glatz, and R. is hurt by Richter's having "treacherously" made the engagement without saying anything to him about it. R. very affected; we are alone in the *salon,* he goes to the piano, plays Kundry's narration up to "*sie bettete dich auf weichen Moosen*" ["she laid thee down on soft mosses"], and once again we are in Heaven, the evil world banished. We then go out on the steps in front of the *salon,* a beautiful sunset has given way to a splendid evening, the moon is shining, stars twinkling; one of them falls, and I am ready with my wish: the Good Friday wish.

Saturday, May 11   Fidi shed 3 eyelashes, I blew them away and was again permitted to state a wish! Glorious day, R.'s ailment clearing up, but he cannot yet go out. We hold a rehearsal in the schoolhouse, the children very good and charming throughout. In the evening *Kenilworth.*

Sunday, May 12   When I take Bonichen to the photographer's this morning, we hear that shots have been fired at the German Emperor. Discussing all the possible motives with R., I feel that penury is the only convincing one: to commit suicide rather than starve, but beforehand to get some sort of satisfaction through a mad act of revenge against the person one might regard as the symbol of our society. A horrible deed, yet the condition which brought it about more horrible still! — R. in general not very well, somewhat languid. We read *Kenilworth* in the evening.

Monday, May 13   Loldchen in bed, always the problem child! A curious episode causes us much merriment. Returning home from my birthday preparations, I find R. in not such a good mood as usual, and I take the opportunity to disclose to him a domestic trouble with which I would not otherwise have bothered him, for fear of spoiling his good mood; he is so absent-minded, however, that he simply— for the first time in his life—offers his hand to the girl about whom I have been earnestly complaining, thus contravening my intention of dismissal, etc. When I explain the situation to him, he chides himself for his incredible absent-mindedness, but I have to laugh heartily, and everything dissolves, as always with us, in great merriment! In the evening R. rehearses with Herr Jäger, I also had a rehearsal with the children; when we returned home, I found R. exhausted and out of

humor, all the wretchedness of the theatrical world coming back to
him. . . . Oh, solitude! In the evening reading, but before that more
about the attempted assassination; everybody indignant, but nobody
shocked at belonging to a society in which penury is rampant. Fine
description of the state of mind of Robsart the father in *Kenilworth,*
the projected hunt on which he turns his back in silence.

Tuesday, May 14 Mime rehearsal with the children. R. got a letter
from Herr Neumann in Leipzig, he has received an invitation from
Paris to give performances there but has "flatly refused." Performances
are also desired in Berlin, in the Viktoria Theater, and R. agrees—a
curious state of affairs. — Since I am tired, R. puts the W.'s off, and
we spend the evening alone, to our great contentment! R. plays to me
Herzeleide's distress, her anxiety, her death. . . . Then we read some
curious articles which have been sent to R.: an attack on *Kladderadatsch*
and an appeal for Christianity. — R. feels it is a very bad thing to
deprive the people of their religion, and he quotes the noble words of
the *Wandsbecker Bote* on Christianity. — He is pleased with Renan's
Saint Paul, and he reads to me with his splendid delivery the First
Epistle to the Corinthians in Luther's translation. The evening passes
blissfully; every annoyance arising from the outside world is banished,
illusion finds peace, and we conclude the day in love! . . .

Wednesday, May 15 Rehearsal with the children. At lunchtime R.
complains of making things too difficult for himself with his "composing." Josef Rubinstein on a visit, has lunch with us, and R. observes,
"Jews like him behave quite differently from us Germans, they know
the world belongs to them, we are *déshérités* [outcasts of fortune]!" —
In the afternoon I am with R. in the summerhouse, delight in the
blackbirds, one very fat one flew past us: "It knew you were there." —
Wandering in the garden with R. in a mood of blissful tranquillity.
In the evening Herr Rub. plays his piano arrangement, "The Awakening of Brünnhilde," and it gives us great delight to hear these sounds
again. R. says he enjoys its joyful pagan flavor and adds, "How
different from *Parsifal!*" — After that the Prelude to *Parsif.* and the
piano-duet arrangement of the lively Overture to *Die Feen.* R. says it is
well orchestrated, he was always good at orchestration.

Thursday, May 16 R. still happy with his reading of Renan's *Saint
Paul,* but he tells me in the morning that he always feels the need to
consult Luther's translations; for someone who has been brought
up a German its language is so familiar, and he prefers to look up the
Luther text, rather than the Greek. R. works—only 4 lines of text,
he tells us, but very remarkable ones! — In the afternoon a rehearsal,
which proves something of a strain on me, so that I have no voice left
in the evening, which is no help in conversation. R. somewhat agitated;

says he wanted to make music this afternoon, but Herr R. had gone off suddenly. So now in the evening we go through the glorious scenes of the 2nd act, and I should have been full of bliss if I had not had the feeling that R. was not at ease. It is remarkable with what confidence Herr R. plays something so new to him; indeed, he can even sing the text straight off at the same time. "What coldness that requires," says R., "what presence of mind!" R. praises an article by Prof. Holtzendorff, who seizes the occasion of Vera Sassulich's trial in Russia to expound present-day legal procedures.

Friday, May 17 My voice still gone. R. reads to me a nice letter from his friend Sulzer, with which is enclosed a curious poem. R. works; I spend the day in my room; R. tells me he has recomposed a whole passage. In the evening he reads Renan's *Saint Paul* to me, he now wants to read the complete series of these books; I recommend them all except for *The Life of Jesus;* his talent is insufficient for the Saviour.

Saturday, May 18 Still unwell, I have to observe the lovely weather from my room. Late last night R. received the good Russian Sorokumovski, who, before starting on his voyage around the world, wishes to make a small contribution to our cause; a childish character— after placing R. above all the monarchs in the world, he then compares R. with Humboldt, kisses his hand repeatedly, talks about the performances in Leipzig, saying R. was expected there: "No, my friend, if I have been obliged to give up such things here, it is not for the purpose of attending other performances and having myself serenaded by the municipal brass band!" — When the good man visits me, he tells me he has deposited 10,000 marks with Feustel for the patrons' fund! — The theater director in Cologne still wants to begin with *Walküre;* R. refuses permission. In the evening Dr. Eiser from Frankfurt, also coming from Leipzig; he tells us about the Society in Fr[ankfurt] and begs pardon for continuing to present such concerts, etc., but he knows no other way of getting people to participate. R. laughs and says, "Yes, I understand, you have to create animal warmth with the music." Speaking of the performances in Leipzig, Dr. E. says he asked himself whether the composer would be pleased that they were taking place, and he had answered himself in the affirmative. R. says that, having been left in the lurch as he was here, he must approve of the *Ring*'s being done as often as possible, but he has no wish to see it. Departure of our good friends. R. then reads to me from *The Antichrist.*

Sunday, May 19 Much coughing, not a good night. But R. slept well, and though awaiting my recovery with considerable impatience, he is nevertheless well! He works. Yesterday he told me he feared he was tiring, the rewriting was a torment to him, and he was still not satisfied;

he would take it as far as the kiss, then break off. "Do that," say I. "Yes, but on the other hand, my zeal is boundless." "What a lot of things come into his mind with this kiss!" R. says. "She was trying too hard." As I am wandering up and down in my room (around lunchtime), he gently parts the curtains and says to me, "It will be all right." He had interrupted his work to bring me this consolation. In the evening he goes through the Flower Maidens' scene with friend Seidl, and this gives us quite a different pleasure from the recent occasion, when the undoubtedly very gifted musician from Israel played the same thing to us with such tingling fluency, his eyes darting everywhere, as if engaged in a business deal! — Before this delight I had been reading Tauler, with infinite delight, edification, and indeed consolation: the advice he gives one—always to imagine Christ present in everything one does—has a powerful effect on me; to have that mild, suffering countenance in one's mind at all times—I feel one might do that, and how much good it would do one, how completely it would banish all evil, all *will power!* — An evening of conversation for the sake of the others. They soon depart, and R. then comes to my bedside for a short while; conversation about Tauler, then memories of our life, how I fell asleep when I was carrying Fidi, and he read Schopenhauer to me!

Monday, May 20 Much laughter about the *tableau vivant* his father Geyer arranged for R.'s mother's birthday: Councilor Georgi, a stout elderly man, lying on her bed drinking coffee, the children grouped around, as they always did, a female singer dressed as an officer, news from town. I am told that Fidi has caught a cold; my great annoyance over this restores my voice. R. works; but he has resolved not to compose more than four lines at a time, since he finds it very exhausting; I can see that when he comes down to lunch. A curious newspaper report, inspired by Herr von Hülsen, about the failure of *Tristan* and *Meistersinger,* the lack of "drawing power" in the *Ring des Nibelungen* except for *Walküre;* all this does not help to raise his spirits. The writer of the piece, who intercedes in R.'s behalf, does this in such a peculiarly Semitic way that R. says to me in the evening: "Oh, if only we could shut out the world entirely! You and I, we are living in a desert." — The only thing that can restore us is to shake it all off and think only of each other; today R. took me into the palace gardens to see the elderberry blossoms, and, already half asleep, I hear his dear voice exclaiming to me, "You are everything to me."

Tuesday, May 21 When, as again today, R. calls me his "soul," I feel like swooning, dying, or cherishing forever the blissful moment. But life rolls on—we are not permitted for long to dwell on the heights! To you, my Siegfried, I bequeath these moments: you will possess them fully, my bliss will be for you an experience free of all clouds, whereas I myself must still struggle with worries and fears! The skies open on my little preparations, and just as I am about to write in this diary, R. comes in, saying he has had to break off, he finds his work too exhausting. Then, showing his leg to the barber, he catches sight of an inflamed spot on it: another carbuncle perhaps? . . . Now I call on the divine countenance to appear to me, so that I may not complain, but bear it all serenely. Take my happiness, my darling child, and raise it high—you receive it freed of all care! — Dress rehearsal without Siegfried, since he is hoarse. In the evening *Kenilworth*. "You are everything to me," R. whispers to me as I am going off to sleep; I am unable to reply, yet hear this blessing which accompanies me toward the night.

Wednesday, May 22 The day of days! We wake up at the same time, R. and I, to the sound of bells: "I congratulate myself for having you," says R. I can say nothing at all, for not even the tenderest of embraces can express what death alone would enable me to say to him. Letter from the King, delivered by a messenger; R. goes off to thank him for it, and during this time we set up our little festival in the hall. We begin it at 11 o'clock, the good children, in a mood of utter dedication, perform their tasks exactly as I instructed them, the pantomime makes a sublime impression, and not for a moment does their earnestness waver. Many, many tears. "It is the loveliest experience of my life!" R. exclaims. "What is all care compared with such a moment? Oh, what a lovely death it would have been if I had fallen asleep at the end of this celebration!" He asks to be left alone for a while. A lovely, blissful day! "Children, I saw you today in a completely different light!" R. says to the little ones, and to me, "They all came from your womb— that one sees at times like this." — Then much joking, tales of the winter rehearsals, not a day passing by since the New Year without my doing something for this dear day, my winter blessings. During a pause following the performance R. went into the garden and saw the new carriage, he got in, sent for me, and then we were pulled all over the Wahnfried grounds in it, by the Wolzogens, Seidl, the children, Mrs. Cooper, and the servants! — Many telegrams, among them one from Herr von Hülsen which causes some surprise; many touching signs of devotion. Walk with R. in the palace gardens, we wander around like blessed spirits, then go off to drink beer with the children and the Wolzogens. Some friends in the evening, *Parsifal* (the first act, from the entrance into the Temple to the end) puts the last sublime crown on a blissful day.

Thursday, May 23 R. wishes to keep the little theater standing and to have a repeat performance today, for he says his emotion had made him miss much, and he now wants to enjoy it artistically. Siegfried, still somewhat hoarse, is put to bed, so as to be ready for the great moment. The second performance is also successful, and in place of yesterday's tears and sobs we have cheers and merriment at the end. R. even takes pleasure in my little stage, says he loves such conventions; he says he had frequently wondered from where the children made their entrances, and he would now appoint me his stage director! [*Added in margin:* "Fidi somewhat hoarse, in bed for part of the day, we hear a noise, rush in, it is nothing: 'When one is entirely happy, one is also truly unhappy,' R. says. — Oh, these anxieties! . . ."] Reading in the evening. R. has written to Prof. Overbeck, thanking him for his nice letter; in it he mentions N. and says meaningfully that he hopes Nietzsche will one day thank him for not having read his book. — R. thanks Herr v. H[ülsen] for his telegram. — Herr Neumann writes that the Leipzig authorities have denied permission for performances in Berlin. It is being said that the Emperor sent for Herr v. Hülsen and complained about having a work such as the *Ring* presented in the Viktoria Theater; it is possible that pressure may be put on the Leipzig authorities, and now reports say that the stage of the Berlin opera house is to be rebuilt! — Herr v. Loën has written in connection with the suggested pension, saying that over 30 years R.'s works have brought in only 30,000 thalers! Curious indeed.

Friday, May 24   Farewell to our festival! The theater is pulled down, the costumes returned to the festival theater, a little section of our lives concluded. "Remember it," R. tells the children. Then we talked a lot about the theater in general: in the 16th century it worked excellently well to have Greeks and Romans played in the contemporary costumes of those days, and it was still possible even in the 18th century, but just imagine playing Hamlet or Lear in our present-day clothing, with uniforms and redingotes! One need say no more. — The repressive laws against the socialists, now being put forward by the government on Bismarck's special recommendation, appear to be very childish and unimaginative—the idea of making special laws for a special category of people! . . . In the evening R. brings up the whole subject of Hülsen's attitude toward him, which shows that it is only by dint of circumstance that anything has ever been achieved in Berlin; and it is still the same: if the *Ring* is to be performed there, it will be due solely to pressure! No reading in the evening. Before supper R. expressed delight in the garden, the house, gazing from his *salon* upon the fine, luxuriant greenery, a lovely sight.

Saturday, May 25   R. did not have a very good night, but he is in good spirits, and he works out his last penciled sketches in ink. In the afternoon he reads to me the very spirited pages from Renan's

Antichrist on the Jews; he is referring solely to the Jews who have remained Jewish and, says R., "quite overlooks the main point that Jews can never really become anything else." — The Reichstag has thrown out the government's bill, Bennigsen is reported to have spoken sensibly, but without getting to the heart of the matter—he was close to it, says R., when he spoke about our school, but then he did not do it, and nor did anyone else. — More applications for membership in the Society of Patrons. Unpleasantnesses with the publishers. Continued reading *Kenilworth;* the crude way in which the draught is offered to the heroine vexes "the artist" in R.

Sunday, May 26 R. works and is feeling well; I write all kinds of letters, after committing to paper the scenario of our little festival. R. remembers this performance with delight: "I could have eaten the children up in my gratitude and emotion," he says. Wonderful letter to me from our friend Glasenapp, with touching enclosures. In the afternoon a walk with R., many adventures with the three dogs, merriment. In the evening *Kenilworth*. — A curious feeling of apprehension has had me in its grip these last few days—oh, this mortal life! . . .

Monday, May 27 R. had a good night and is in good spirits. Nice letter from the King, regretting that R. should have felt obliged, as it were, to write to him on the 22nd through his messenger. (The King deplores the consequences of 1869–1870!) R. replies at once, sending him the scenario of the May Festival, then does some work. "I am so well that I feel like composing," he says. At lunch we decide against our projected outing, but over coffee R. looks at the sky and resolves on it again; christening of the carriage with the children, "Uncle" Seidl, and both of us; to the Waldhütte. Splendid mood of gaiety, the new carriage (a birthday gift) fills R. with utter delight, he takes pleasure in us, the children, the countryside, the people (a man offers the children beer from his mug), the woods. Rest on a rock, listening to the cuckoo, the liveliest and most cheerful of spirits, even my new English hat, bought to celebrate R.'s birthday, pleases him: "You look like a Roman patrician's lady from the first centuries who has just embraced Christianity but still retains her old habits." — The children recite their May Festival in the carriage. "Keep that fast in your memory," R. exclaims to them, "and may life never strip this act of dedication from you. They all showed that they came from your womb," he adds, turning to me, "and are different from others. All of them are a part of our happiness." Looking at Fidi, he says, "I should be fifteen years younger." In the evening we read the enclosures from our incomparable friend Glasenapp; the article "Bellini" pleases even R. himself, and he finds the letter from Uncle Adolph very interesting.

Of his article on German opera he says, "That was pretty bold: I knew nothing of Gluck, and *Euryanthe* I knew only from one bad performance." Even in his most excessive assertions I can always recognize the great feeling for truth, the fight against all hypocrisy, the receptive feeling and sharp eye for dramatic significance, in whatever form it may show itself, and the fight against the undramatic, however lovely it might otherwise be. We exclaim with a laugh, "If only Schopenhauer had read this article about Bellini!" "Yes," says R., "then he would have consigned Kossak to the scrap heap." As we are preparing for bed we go once more through the whole splendid day. "It's a never-ending joy, this carriage," says R., and "You are to thank for every day I remain alive." Thus he brings this blissful day to a close.

I forgot to note down that after the enclosures R. felt the need, as he put it, for someone really great, and he read to us the first act of *Macbeth*. "Beside that everything else is child's play," he says at the end, after we have once again been shattered by its power, which impresses one anew at each encounter. The way Macbeth, the simple, rough soldier, is at once totally consumed after seeing the apparition, nothing left of him but a single thought, the mutual distrust between him and Banquo; and then all the subsidiary factors, from the accounts of the witches to the significant feature of Duncan's melancholy over his disappointed trust in Cawdor, expressed in the very moment in which he once again places his trust wrongly. The whole daemonic nature of life set before one's eyes, naked, beyond all deception. "Everyone before him and after him is condemned to silence," says R.

Tuesday, May 28   R. had a good night, and we are glad that we had our merry drive yesterday, for the weather today is cloudy and close. I start work again with the children. R. is once more filling in his sketches in ink, and when I go downstairs to greet him, around lunchtime, he plays me Parsifal's sorrowful outburst on hearing of his mother's death, so sorrowful and so tender that Herzeleide's whole nature is revealed before one's eyes. In the afternoon R. does some more work and plays to me Kundry's words of consolation. I have become immersed in [Dante's] *Divina commedia* and tell R. of the wonderful impression it is making on me. "Oh," says R., "nobody can be held responsible for his own time, and the horrible scenes are transcended by the poet's genius." I tell him that even the horrible scenes do not put me off, they seem to me curiously dreamlike, and I never lose my feeling of being on earth; these physical torments are almost easier to bear than the spiritual strife of *Macbeth,* for example. — In the evening we read *Kenilworth;* the description of the feast provokes an outburst from R.: "I cannot bear these Renaissance masquerades!

The Romans were better at it, they had criminals sent to Rome from all the provinces and staged a real comedy, that is to say, killed them. But these parades, etc., stem from the Latin world, which still dominates us entirely. The Greeks were different." R. wanted to amuse himself by sending Prof. Nietzsche a telegram of congratulations on Voltaire's birthday, but I advise him against it and recommend silence here, as in many other things. When our friends, who were joined by the Jägers, have gone, we feel how much we need to be alone together. . . . A Dr. Franz from Zabern informs us touchingly of the success of a concert in support of the Society of Patrons and sends us 80 marks.

Wednesday, May 29 R. had a good night, and he tells me he would like to take up his composing again: "Life is treating me so well now that I consider it my downright duty to work, and the only work analogous to my state is creative work. That is my favorite activity, the one which does me most good; though of course there are feelings which are more important." — I work with the children and write in detail to friend Glasenapp, expressing my gratitude. In the afternoon I meet R. at the Wolzogens' and am able to tell him the news, just received from Feustel, that the bank in Gera has advanced the sum needed to cover the deficit. I return home with R., the mean and vicious face of a common man in the street upsets him. He works until supper and afterward reads to me, Lusch, and friend Seidl two acts of *Macbeth,* with indescribable effect. R. is also of my opinion that in *Macbeth* the English language is particularly true to itself, that the word "Hail," for instance, sounds completely different from *"Heil,"* hoarse and daemonic. "Yes, that's also something for a fan-waving audience!" he exclaims. "How genius invariably shoots far beyond the target! It gives me downright joy to see how impossible Shakespeare is, too. Of course the main thing is the shattering effect, not the artistic pleasure of savoring every detail, as we are doing here—just as in my works it is not necessary for the audience to recognize the many-sidedness of the music." — When we are left alone in the *salon* we become immersed in each other. "Oh, my treasure, you bring out all the good in me—and then there will be nothing left but the bad!" "My only one." "No, you are the only one!" When we part after a silent embrace, R. exclaims, "Oh, if people only knew how sufficient unto each other we are!"

Thursday, May 30 R. had a good night, and we start another day in good spirits, separating, he to go to his work and I to my children. — Ascension Day brings us the military band, and when themes from *Das Rheingold* are heard the eyes of my good children begin to shine, I judge them happy and favored, him content, and my happiness seems almost too great to bear—a feeling of apprehension oppresses my heart. Is this the ghost of former sufferings, foreboding of gloomy days ahead, or just the raw gray sky, which is so out of keeping with my feelings of gratitude? I do not know—bliss without rest, the crowning of life, this is love. . . . R. has returned to his pencil sketches, and his mind is still full, as he says when he comes down to lunch. Over coffee he comes back to Prof. Nietzsche and his book, which seems to him so insignificant, whereas the feelings which gave rise to it are so evil. Herr v. W. comes to read me an excellent article by Glasenapp about nations and national art; R. does not stay for the reading, he says he cannot listen to panegyrics about himself—only when he is able to forget completely that he is being talked about can he take pleasure in good ideas. Afterward, music—the heavenly Flower Maidens' scene, in which R. has conjured up for all time spring and its longing, its sweet complaint. And in the middle of it Kundry's cry, like a mortal soul suddenly giving voice to its suffering and its loving amid the innocence of Nature. Recently R. said to me, "Herzeleide dies very simply; she dies like a twig on a tree." He feels that in certain places he would like to hear the orchestra at once, to write a few things in orchestral score from the start. This would help him, just as he had written the Prelude to *Das Rheingold* straight out in full score; the sound of the horns—in certain places, he says, he absolutely needs to hear it. — At supper the repressive measures against the socialists produce sad laughter: what a restricted outlook these measures show! — Read *Kenilworth* and, despite many very fine features, found much of it wearisome, giving us the impression almost that even W. Scott sometimes wrote according to the size of his paper!

Friday, May 31   R. had a bad night with wild dreams: his bedroom was separated from mine by several other rooms, next to his a tavern, from which noisy people closely overlooked his bed; he went to search for me, found me at last in my bed; an ugly old Polish count was sitting beside it, courting me, and I seemed to have no objection, while to R. I had pretended I was ill; then near my room the sounds of a tavern, which woke him up! "Then I said to myself: '*Bon, je sais ce que c'est,*' " he tells me, quoting one of his favorite popular expressions from [Hugo's] *Histoire d'un crime.* " '*Je sais ce que c'est*—I must wake up, apply poultices, etc.' " — R. works. A light lunch with friend Feustel is responsible for R.'s drinking more wine than he is used to, and it upsets him; he has a headache. A lengthy rest in the summerhouse and short strolls do him good; he finishes *The Antichrist.* Coming back to Voltaire, he remarks on the superficiality which induced this great intellect to reject Christ, yet to uphold Jehovah. While he is reading R[enan], I read the *Purgatorio* and then tell him episodes from it. In the evening *Kenilworth,* embarrassing moments, for the writer seems almost to be spinning it out rather too long, but the scene of Elizabeth's anger is magnificent. At lunch friend Feustel says he voted against the government's repressive proposals with a heavy heart, whereupon R.: "Reaction is always a bad thing; we possess a very unconsidered piece of legislation and are now paying the consequences." The leaders of the [socialist] movement are no doubt muddled people and perhaps intriguers as well, but the movement itself belongs to the future, all the more so since we can think of no better ways of stopping it than taking foolish repressive measures. N[apoleon] III had at least understood his business enough to make his people rich and create jobs for them. But what do we do? We found a Prussian empire with Berlin as its capital! It is the same with the struggle against Rome— there, too, just police measures, nothing that leaves the German spirit room to breathe. It is hopeless. Now the German Emperor is calling for more Christianity, and the most innocent meetings of the socialists, in which the deputies want, for example, just to report to their electors, are banned by the police! . . .

Saturday, June 1 R. did not have a very good night, and he read friend W.'s pamphlet on language. In the morning he asks me whether I have thought about Fidi's birthday: "He was born in what is really the German May," he said yesterday. He works and, as he tells me, produces seven or eight bars. "What I have let myself in for!" he frequently exclaims. "It goes far beyond *Tristan,* though I showed enough of the sufferings of love in the third act of that." — We take the children to the agricultural show; the cocks in particular fascinate R., he remembers how at the livestock exhibition in Paris (during the sixties) he had dearly wanted to buy a cock priced at 800 francs, though he had barely a cent to his name: "I thought if I owned that bird I should really feel like somebody." A cock with a splendid wig reminds him of Berlioz, with its violent nervous movements; the disheveled wig of another reminds him of Beethoven's tousled hair; the din of the crowing amuses him vastly, and he wishes he had a poultry yard like that. He also enjoys the cows and the bulls, and after an hour we leave the little exhibition greatly pleased and go for a short walk in the palace gardens. R. returns home, while I accompany Lusch into town; then I go home and we chat until suppertime, just as if we had not seen each other for ages, I delighting in his healthy appearance and his nearness. In the evening we finish *Kenilworth,* then R. reads me various scenes from Schiller's *Maria Stuart* (the Queen's council, L[eicester] and Mortimer). The scene between Elizabeth and Mortimer strikes us as somewhat too drastic, and the short exchange of words between M. and Leicester at the end of their conversation seems rather artificial, for it is not all that brief, being stretched out in iambic pentameter. But the elegance of the language strikes one again and again; R. remarks how different it is from the elegance of Shakespeare's language, in which the peculiar nobility of expression is brought about by the forcefulness of the characters, whereas in Schiller it is really a Court language, a lofty convention. Today, through the kind offices of Marie Schleinitz, I received a photograph of Lenbach's portrait of R. The expression in it appeals to me greatly—that tender, earnest, transcendent, kind expression which, as I look, becomes radiant. But the children do not like this "sad picture," in which to them he looks so old and glum; they see their father as cheerful, youthful, amiable, and indeed radiant cheerfulness is a prominent feature of his character. R. observes that here the artist has sacrificed everything for the sake of a single expression, or, rather, he has exaggerated everything—age, weariness—to convey the single impression of transcendence just as in the profile portrait he exaggerated the sharpness of the features in order to create an impression of boldness; he says it is not a restful picture, such as the great painters can conjure up. He feels it is too morose.

Sunday, June 2   R. did not have a good night, I beg him not to work, and he decides on an outing. We set off with the children and the Wolzogens for Creussen in serene and happy spirits; the little town pleases us, it looks so pretty when we go for a walk along the highway and look back at it—"just like an old etching." We settle ourselves in a lush meadow, the children pick flowers, and we enjoy each moment as it comes. Fidi's tales of his "thirteen boys" amuse us vastly. While walking with R. along the Creussen highway, I say how pleased I am that the *active days* are past. "Yes, clumsy old London was a good ending." At the inn, drinking beer and milk, we have to agree with R. that such simple bourgeois pleasures are the best. Pretty homeward journey in the evening sunshine, we are glad to have made the acquaintance of this district; for the first time we have a feeling of being at home, R. and I, "with everyone and everything," he says. Our gay and peaceful day ends horribly with the news that another attempt has been made on the Emperor's life! [*Inserted between the pages is a special edition of the* Bayreuther Tagblatt *dated June 2, 1878; see notes.*] This can be a nail in the Emperor's coffin; it may also cloud his mind, rob him of all spontaneity. And the consequences! R. thinks it must have been a Social Democrat who, enraged by the police measures, wished to show how matters really stand. The state, organized solely for the protection of the propertied classes, and now universal suffrage on top of it. These assassination attempts seem to me so un-German, as if the whole German nation has become a stranger to itself. With much effort we succeed in diverting our thoughts in other directions, reading some letters from Sch[openhauer] to Frauenstädt in which, fascinat-ingly intermingled, one finds a great and kind sympathy, a violent dissatisfaction with the inadequacy of his talent, eagerness to implant his teachings, and a frenzy for truth. —

Monday, June 3 R. dreamed that I was his sister and it was his task to guard my honor. He again had a disturbed night, he read the *Tagblatt (Nachtblatt,* he adds jokingly!) and applied a poultice. But he works and is in good and lively spirits when he fetches me for lunch. We read the news about the Emperor's condition and the "Nibelung" (Nobiling). R. observes that he would not object if the socialists were suppressed altogether, but the means used must be the right ones. He would like to see a day of repentance proclaimed, so that the whole nation might reflect! In the name "Social Democrat" he objects to the "Democrat," says it is absurd to build a political party on such strivings. We fear all the nonsense which is now being talked in circles close to the Emperor. The situation in Germany is terribly sad; it is as if everything were sinking, like the new ship *Kurfürst,* which through incompetent handling was involved in a collision in which more than 200 people were drowned. "One spendthrift the less," a woman is said to have remarked, regretting that the attempt on the Emperor's life had failed—a terrible saying! The rage of penury, deriving nothing from all the money spent. In the evening R. sang something from *Tristan* and said, "This *Tristan* has a color all its own, it is mauve, a sort of lilac." From news received in the evening we learn that the latest assassin is a Catholic and a reader of *Germania,* which confirms my suspicions, for I see the Catholic party as the only one that possesses fanaticism and the quality so lacking in our world, faith; probably socialism has been put forward just to divert attention. R. says jokingly: "A good thing that the *Bayreuther Blätter* was not found on him, or worse still *The Destiny of Opera,* which might be interpreted as a hint to assassinate Hülsen. But what is the Emperor to do? After Hödel he called for more Christianity, now after Nobiling he will have to have religion prohibited." Much enjoyment in the evening from Schopenhauer's letters. Sitting at his feet, I tell him that I still believe in God; something all-embracing, powerfully guiding, beyond all grasping or envisaging: "Thanks be to thee!" was the prayer I have just uttered. Let me call it the highest need, which wished to set an example in which later generations could take delight. As we went to the summerhouse today, R. was pleased with our little wood, which he said was all he required, and above all the four acacias, which have established themselves well and look beautiful; I thought of them as they will be in distant times and spoke a greeting, with the wish that my children, when they look upon them, will remember this moment of joy. Went out with R. after coffee and bought a telephone for Fidi; we have great fun in the evening trying it out, and R. says with feeling, "There is something uncanny about it, but there was a time, when I was separated from my companion, when it would have been a great consolation to have been able to hear each other's voices." [*Added in margin:* "He, with a sense of his worthiness, may see it thus; I, in the knowledge of my unworthiness, must give thanks eternally!"] As we are returning from our walk through the palace gardens, we meet the minister Herr Pfeufer, who gets an acquaintance to introduce him and then reminds me of the last time we saw each other; it was in December 1865, at a banquet during which he was summoned from my side by a deputation which told him that a demonstration against R. was to take place that evening outside the royal residence; but he did not say anything to me about it at the time. I remember this lunch very well, as also my conversation with the Minister of Police and my immediate visit to R.'s house, where I witnessed the arrival of Herr v. Lutz, who asked R. in the King's name to leave Bavaria! . . .

Tuesday, June 4 R. again had a very bad night; we went to bed at eleven thirty, he had to get up first at one thirty and then again at four thirty, when he went downstairs to walk around the house; toward 6 o'clock he comes back to me, and despite the torments which caused his restlessness, he makes a pleasant reply to my greeting, and soon I hear him laughing loudly over our friend Hagen, who has suddenly written to friend W. from Lucerne, saying that a terrible intrigue is being woven against him by his "four-dimensional" enemies. Oddly enough, two unknown people recently inquired by postcard where Herr v. Hagen was now living. — Cheerful breakfast, with memories of Sch.'s letters. R. says: "I appear quite early on. Kossak turned him against me by applying his philosophy against my principles, and on top of that, my democratic outlook." I: "And the dedication to Feuerbach." — R.: "That never meant anything to me, or led me astray." — I discover a resemblance between Sch. and Beethoven. "Yes," says R., "the belief in himself, the sharpness." — At lunch on Sunday R. again praised *La Juive* highly; then he spoke about Schumann and said, "No dedicated artist or poet goes mad, and it is no credit to Kleist that he committed suicide, for it is precisely this which marks out the artist—that through all torments he retains the serene capacity to observe." — This morning R. says, "No good star is watching over Bismarck's creation." We try to remember how the convocation of princes presided over by the Emperor of Austria came about, and we ask ourselves whether it had been right for Prussia to refuse the invitation and then immediately afterward to fall upon Denmark, along with Austria. — At lunch we at last forget the dismal subject, we talk about Sch.'s letters, and R. emphasizes the value to Sch. of his little fortune: "Not to have to work for money! I work for money." I: "Oh, no!" R.: "No, I don't work for money, but I suffer for it." He rests a little, and then we go for a walk in the palace gardens; the weather is close; as we are passing a tree, a woodpecker leaves its place and flies to one side: "Here come those people," says R., speaking for the bird, "I mustn't let them see there's something good here." And, speaking for other birds who do not allow themselves to be disturbed by us: "Oh, it's them—not him." R. goes to change, I write to friend Klindworth, who has touched me very much with his memories of Tribschen. (This morning I read in my diary the pages R. wrote for me while I was bringing Siegfried into the world! Deep emotion, tears run down my cheeks in my sweet melancholy.) R. sends for me: "I'm about to start." The scene between Parsifal and Kundry, up to the cry of the former: "Amfortas!" Indescribably moving! "A moment of daemonic absorption," R. calls the bars which accompany Kundry's kiss and in which the fatal motive of love's longing, creeping like poison through the blood, makes a shattering effect. This, along with the tenderly sorrowful sounds of Herzeleide, the majestic way in which Kundry proclaims her liberation from the pressure of remorse— all these things, so richly and variously laid out, so ravishing and so painful, form a whole of unfathomable beauty and nobility. Oh, the wonderful man! — R. sees a resemblance between Wotan and Kundry: both long for salvation and both rebel against it, Kundry in the scene with P., Wotan with Siegfried. — The sublime impression is soon scattered to the winds by the news from the outside world. The Emperor lies in a fever from his wounds, the would-be murderer (incidentally, a Protestant, so all the suspicions were wrong) has died, also the coachman, the innkeeper mutilated—all horribly cruel. [*Inserted between the pages is a newspaper clipping dated June 3, recording the details mentioned above.*] We take refuge in reading and gradually cheer ourselves up with Schopenhauer's letters, which are magnificent! To end with, R. plays the joyful, popular tune from [Beethoven's] *Battle of Vittoria* and exclaims, "This is folk art—a superb thing!"

Wednesday, June 5 R. had a good night. He thinks of his good friend Pusinelli and how pleased he would have been with *Parsifal*. Memories of all our other good old friends—Standhartner, Math[ilde] Maier, A. Frommann, M. Meysenbug, Sulzer. Then he cries: "Shall I fetch the midwife? Do you want to bring down your blankets?" . . . R. works. He says he has found a transition, and at coffeetime he jumps up and plays this deeply moving passage. "It leads into the vision of Amfortas, abbreviated: everything of course rushes headlong through Parsifal's memory." At lunch we feel a desire for news of the Emperor, but there is nothing new. The sight of Siegfried's handsome, cheerful, good face, which gives his father such pleasure, starts a detailed discussion about the boy's education; I remark that, if I were well off, I should try to engage Glasenapp to carry out this task, along with Wolzogen. "Yes," says R., "it would have to be somebody with a great love for me who, for the sake of this love, would feel the urge to turn the nice boy into a respectable man." — "Now Cologne has accepted my conditions—so we may still become rich! It is very curious—it must be that other things don't draw. People will think I've given all the other composers some magic potion in order to keep them from producing anything worth having." — He goes for a short walk, and after reading Plutarch's life of Pericles with the older children upstairs, I go down to him. He is sitting at the Italian table and reading the article on God in Voltaire's *Dictionnaire philosophique;* the very first sentence reminds him of Schopenhauer, but then he says one can see in what poor shape philosophy was before the arrival of Kant. First, however, as I entered, he greets me with the words "I have had a brain wave, a composing whim," and, after speaking of V., he gets up and plays me a theme, which he intends to give to Kundry. "You can see, of course, how much can be developed from it." I tell him I am downright grateful that Kundry is to be given some "accents" of this kind, for so far only the melancholy tenderness of Herzeleide and the awesomeness of amorous desire have shown through. "Yes," says R., "one has to be very careful here, the emotional element must always be kept terribly noble. All the same," he adds jokingly, "for the sake of the house, for Fidi's birthday, one can perhaps make a slight concession." — At supper he tells us that he also read the article on Cromwell in V. with much enjoyment, and indeed he laughed aloud over the description of the twice-won battle (*"cite Moïse, Gédéon, Josué"*). Friend Wolzogen's pamphlet on language pleases him greatly. "That's the way to sing your own praises!" he remarks with a laugh. "But I can say in my own defense that it is other people's thoughts which please me, not their praise." — Continued reading Schopenhauer; but the reading does not give us undiluted pleasure, however unique these letters; when we are alone, R. says to me: "This man might almost be called scurrilous. I wonder whether among the Greeks people did not show up better—Sophocles, for example? The only ones who look truly great in the face of the world are the saints!" — Friend Feustel has discovered a lawyer in Dresden who will now look after R.'s rights in connection with the Court theater.

Thursday, June 6 At 4 A.M. R. goes into the *orange salon,* and from there he once more watches the sunrise and listens to the birds; in the garden he sees a deer nibbling blades of grass through the fence; and when two pigeons fly over it with a rustle of wings, it pulls its head back in alarm, as if it had done something wrong! Then he comes in to me. When we part, we exchange congratulations on our son. "He is such a handsome boy." Presentation of gifts at two o'clock, before lunch. R. begins the toast gaily, but toward the end he becomes serious, and Fidi's expression changes nicely in tune with his. Nice letter from the King, who pleases R. by remarking how different his birthday was this year from last year! No work for the children, so a little leisure for me. At R.'s request I write to friend Schuré, asking him to reply in our *Blätter* to R.'s letter. R. works, although he says he is feeling lazy! In the afternoon he goes out, while I, somewhat tired, read Dante and receive friend Wolzogen, who reads to me his re-written—and excellent—article on the "stage-dedication festival," as well as some other things, among them a lecture on the *Völu-Spa* (which is the way R. wants it spelled) and something by a Herr Schlemm about dignity and pride and Kundry's curse; I advise combining these, since R. is portrayed as P[arsifal], like him carrying his lance, his ideal, undefiled through the labyrinth. Then I hurry down to R., who is reading Voltaire on Christianity, without much enjoyment in spite of all its wit. Blissful chat with R. — In the evening, before going off to sleep, R. again recalls the May Festival: "It was splendid! The way these children moved and looked!" — The 9-year-old volunteer! He said good night to Fidi in the evening with tender earnestness and was again touched by his expression. In the evening Schopenhauer's letters, much enjoyment from them; incredible wit and liveliness, yet in spite of it his astonishing delusion that he could change the world, hence the eagerness with which he sought recognition; a delusion which blinded him to the significance of someone like R. R. feels that he addressed himself only to minds open to reason, so that his liberating doctrine should not go unrecognized, and for that reason had found "the noise of battle" not unwelcome. No trace of vanity in his self-knowledge. — Late in the evening went walking with R. in the garden. At friend Seidl's window, sang "Harlequin, thou must perish!" — I ask him where he got this funny little duet, and he says: from his first wife, who was "full of popular songs."

Friday, June 7 The walk did R. good. He slept through the entire night. Cheerful breakfast, with a squabble over whose walk it was—mine or his! He works, and along with his sounds I hear a blackbird; I pack for Lulu, who is about to start on her journey. After lunch I make some purchases. I walk in spirit with R. along the St.-Georgen-Allee, as if it were 40 years ago, and admire the lovely situation of the town, loveliest of all perhaps from there. Returning, I find that R. has come out to look for me; he sits down on the bench to the right of the house, I likewise. "Nowhere can be lovelier than here," R. exclaims. "Just look at that sea of various greens! There can't be anything like that in the gardens of Italy, where the foliage is dark and there is none of the serenity we have here. But," he adds in the next moment, "I should like to see the road from Naples to Sorrento now—it must be splendid." Over coffee the subject of Fidi's education again; no sacrifice to be spared; our main task. — Then thoughts of a letter to the King of Bavaria, to get him to intervene in the political situation. We listen to a blackbird which is sitting and singing on the branch above the roof of the newly built Wolzogen house. "It will miss that branch. 'My branch has vanished,' " he calls out in the manner of the Flower Maidens! The bird continues its song, and R. sets words to it—"Not yet coming, *still* not?"—and observes, "The tone is lowered for the question—the lower it sinks, the more urgent the question." Silence, then suddenly R.: "Never, never, never will I have anything more to do with outside productions—they are detrimental to truth. That *Tristan* in Berlin, for example, when I had to praise Eckert." Complaining letter to friend W. from the Viennese academicians, saying the performances of *Rheingold, Walküre, Tannhäuser* are getting worse and worse; could one not put a stop to them? — The singer they have chosen for Wotan, Scaria, was described by R., when he saw him as the King in *Lohengrin,* as "an out-of-work butcher." Seeing Fidi approach in his best suit reminds me of Daniel in his first commnnion clothes, I can still see his beautiful glistening eyes, and I have to weep. R. notices it as my tears are drying and asks me why; I tell him. "You had nobler figures around you in your childhood than I did—your father, your mother, your brother, your sister." We embrace, and then R. asks, "Which of the W.'s will live in the upper story of the house?" I: "You mean, who will see our kisses?" He laughs: "Yes, our friends or their family." — We part in laughter, to come together again at supper. Fairly good news of the Emperor; we read an article by O. Beta about the assailant, Nobiling. Some Schopenhauer letters, and to end the evening R. and I again go for a walk in the garden. This day, too, ends in a hymn of love; as we come in from the garden, R. observes, speaking of former times, "Things could have started happening, but nothing did happen; if it had not been for my unruly pine tree, everything would have remained nice and quiet." — The pine tree, which made us laugh aloud, was a reference to something said yesterday: when I was going up the stairs ahead of R., he said, "You are so slender—you are my palm tree." I: "But the palm tree is dreaming of the fir tree." R., laughing: "Well, what I previously had was a pine tree." R. has a fancy, *after 46 years,* to perform his symphony again, either in Prague, where it was first played privately, or in Leipzig, where first in public. Tappert's citation of the story of the apostles in connection with Herr v. Hülsen amuses R. He looks it up in the Bible.

Saturday, June 8 R. had a good night. He sings the andante theme from the Adagio of [Beethoven's] 9th Symphony and says, "That is really a dance, a theme for a minuet, and so with this andante the structure of the Adagio is nicely variegated." Then from *Figaro* he sings "*Perdona Signora*": "It's like flowing honey, this melody of Mozart's," he says. "If only in performances one did not have to put up with those wretched singers—the Count, some dressed-up brat as Cherubino, a vulgar Susanna! The performances I had in mind for my school would have been in Italian, French operas such as *La Dame Blanche* in French. These language studies would have done something to counteract the singer's vulgarity." — When we separate to go to our daily work, he jokes, "Your father would be disgusted at the time it takes us to do things!" R. does some work and then decides on an outing to the Sophienberg, which we then carry out in the gayest of spirits. A woman who was here today carried the barrel of beer up for us. R. gives her 2 marks afterward; she looks at him very earnestly, gives him her hand, and wishes us a happy time "for thinking of the day." — The scurrying of the children, who run up and down the hill like messengers, delights him: "Ten horses couldn't drag me away from here." — Much joking *lamento:* not enough tobacco in his box; before that, *ham*-stitches—"I've eaten too much ham, that's why I got stitches." "Uncle" Seidl taps the barrel. Home at 8:30, Fidi's memory of the "rough mountaintop" on the Sophienberg makes R. laugh. In the evening some Sch. letters. The Emperor's condition satisfactory; but Bismarck "*en colère*" ["enraged"], as R. puts it, threatening to dissolve the Reichstag if it does not accept the laws. On top of that a conference of three gout sufferers! Even Moltke mentions in the Reichstag the dismal possibility of the army's marching against the people! . . . The head of the Church Council talks sensibly about the state's atonement, to which the *A.A.Z.* adds a mocking exclamation point! — The Emperor in the simplicity of his character truly great. — In the evening, while we are simultaneously discussing various things and forgetting everything else, R. exclaims to me, "You are all I have, but you are also the only one." And later: "Set wigs of million curls upon your heads—all this" (he means his work) "seems to me like a wig, though I haven't set it on myself—it has been set on me."

Sunday, June 9 R. slept well; at breakfast he shows me in the *Illustrirte Zeitung* some etchings in the style of the old Dutch masters, which give him great pleasure: "You can search for a long time in literature before finding anything to equal that—Shakespeare, *Faust*, Dante, *Don Quixote*, and that's all. How far below the painters of his time does

Ariosto stand! He is a sort of Makart." "Vegetation of figures and colors." An audience given by the Emperor to the Moroccan legation produces from R. the exclamation: "If they would only wear at least coats over that uniform! What do they look like (our princes)?" — He works and says at lunch that one passage caused him much trouble until he decided to transpose it—"Stupid fellow, not D minor, it must be C minor!"—and then everything was all right. He says he will be glad, when he stops for his cure, not to have to do it in a mood of dissatisfaction, leaving an uncompleted passage. — (Our poor friend Hagen seems to be insane. Nietzsche's book is causing our friends a lot of embarrassment.) — At lunch, when talking about this transposition, R. comes to the subject of Bach's fugues, in most of which there is hardly ever a modulation: "It is like a cosmic system, which moves according to eternal laws, without feeling; the sorrows of the world are indeed reflected in it, but not in the same way as in other music." Similarly, he says, he has used only one strong modulation in the *Parsifal* Prelude. Regarding Kundry's "*die Liebe lerne kennen*" ["learn to understand the love"], he says he has not given it a *Tristan* flavor, as when Isolde speaks of Frau Minne [Lady Love]: "It is quite different." Gay lunch with anecdotes about Frederick the Great told by R., among them one which was new to him concerning a man whom he put under house arrest and who tried to escape by pretending to have a toothache; in the end he was obliged to have a good tooth pulled: "Now tell me, have you been lying to me?" The Renz Circus is preparing a Rhinemaidens' scene and a "Ride of the Valkyries"! In the afternoon R. sits with me on the bench and enjoys the greenery which the curving hills of our countryside spread in varying shades before his eyes. The fountain brings to his mind the savage force of water, which a dam or even a faucet can tame: "This is what gave Goethe his ideas on culture, that is fine." A swallow flies over our heads: "What a beautiful creature! It has some of the qualities of a bat—it is the daytime bat." Oh, how we enjoy these hours! In the evening, when he gets a bit heated, he says, "I have drunk too much beer, and then I become quarrelsome and overly touchy, like R. Schumann." — A crucifix I saw yesterday at Dr. Berr's, by a master of the Veit Stoss school, made a very deep impression on me, and today I still find myself thinking about its facial expression and gestures whenever some painful or selfish emotion stirs in me. Of [Weber's] *Invitation to the Dance* R. says: "If only people understood how to perform it! In Paris, where Berlioz orchestrated it, they did all the usual *pas* [steps]. But it is a full-blooded love display: following the tender glances and gestures, the first approaches, the man proudly shows what he is. It is unique."

Monday, June 10   R. slept well, but he is not yet starting on his cure. Today I tell Fidi about Achilles and Homer and show him the drawings by Carstens. A picture of Juliet in the *I[llustrirte] Z[eitung]* does not at all displease me, but R. says, "I cannot imagine Juliet ever meditating— just seeking, watching." — Yesterday R. spoke of the difference between England and Germany; there it is at least feasible that party leaders such as Gladstone now and Cobden previously should voice their opinions clearly to the government and gather a number of people with similar views around them; here such a thing is not feasible—all we can offer is a weakling like Bennigsen and a few Jews. — R. works. In the afternoon, when I go down to join him, he has written to Mama Lehmann, demanding news of her daughters—he had missed a greeting from them on the 22nd. Telegram to Vogl, singing Siegfried: "If in the last act you should find that your wife has gone to sleep, wake her up and give her my kind regards." We stroll about the garden; R. tells me of Renan's *Life of Jesus,* which does not displease him; among other things he feels that he has depicted the idea of God the Father very well. — Then the second act, up to the last kiss! The beauty of some of the themes one appreciates only after frequent listening, the first few times one is much too moved by it all, the artistic delight comes only retrospectively, and in growing measure. — R. is in an agitated state and would prefer to spend the evening alone with me, and when I am obliged to leave the room for odd moments, I find a sultry atmosphere downstairs on my return. "As pants the hart for cooling streams," he tells me, "so do I pant for you."

Tuesday, June 11   R. had a bad night, he had to get out of bed at 12:30 and again at 3:30, he goes into my sitting room and is amused by the 3 dogs, who come out of the kennel one after another like a platoon and go for a walk on the terrace. Conversation about the Schop. letters, which we finished yesterday, R. deploring the mistaken ideas about the dissemination of his philosophy; R. goes on with it and says: "These donkeys who do not believe in God and who think that such figures as Jesus of N. or a great creative genius move according to the ordinary processes of Nature! They cannot understand that what prevails here is a special urge, a noble need which in the end produces something good. But one must not think in this connection of the old Jewish God." — I ask him to write about this, for in his one essay on the subject he had dealt only with the relationship of religion to the state. "So you want me to start writing again? You do it—you understand pretty well what I mean." "Yes, I understand, but you must do the writing." "All right, but not until after *Parsifal* and the biography, and then there are the symphonies, too: you're to get one on each birthday." After purchasing some things for D[aniela]'s departure,

I find R. in the garden, and we spend in chat one of those loveliest of hours to which I cry, "Oh, stay a while, you are so fair!" The dismal news of wholesale prison sentences of 5 to 10 years for lese majesty, which offers the prospect in five years' time of a terrible generation of human beings, leads us in the evening to the subject of Egmont and his discussion with Alba, in which "these things are talked about in such human terms, not at all political." R. reads it to us; unthinkable that nowadays anyone would even listen to such noble language. "What trivialities a similar conversation between the Emperor and Bismarck would produce!" The collections being made for the families of the *Kurfürst* victims also arouse R.'s indignation: "With all the funds that have been approved, the taxes that have been paid, for the state not to give its aid!" — Before supper he informs me that he has just written down a theme "with a rising fifth"; he plays it to me, it is full of noble melancholy, tragic. Then he reads to me the fine pages in Renan (p. 73 onward) about the unification of Jesus with God. R. develops this subject further in his mind, calling this God which dwells within us "the inborn antidote to the will"—not at all the Faustian God, who can set nothing in motion outwardly; with our God one does not sell oneself to the Devil. Since R. is coughing a little, I am once again deeply concerned. Apart from this, I do not see suffering as an enemy; almost everywhere I look I see the sign of the cross, in the window frames, in the cornices, in the trees—everywhere it rises up before me, exhorting, consoling, but within me all courage fails when such worries assail me. They rage within me like a furnace, and then, alas, God speaks no more!

Wednesday, June 12 R.'s night was not completely undisturbed, but he managed not to get out of bed. He begins his cure (Marienbad waters) and intends to interrupt his work, he has got as far as "*O Qual der Liebe*" ["Oh, pang of love"]. He talks about the subject which is now occupying him and remarks how through this God characters such as the Maid of Orleans and Parsifal were deprived forever of sensual urges by a great impression made on them in their adolescent years. He believes that in this way Christianity could be preached to the world with renewed purity and truth; all the material for its elucidation can be found in Schop. We then laugh about the Schopenhauerian "donkeys" Humboldt (R. says he, too, has never been able to read *Cosmos* to the end) and Helmholtz—"that's how he always seemed to me." When I tell him I can never understand how certain people can find enjoyment in certain books, such as the *History of Materialism,* for instance, he says, "Basically they are ignoramuses who think that knowledge comes with a bang." R. says goodbye to Loulou: "She looked at me exactly as her father used to." Tender and melancholy

parting from my child, who is going to her relations in England. —
But my thoughts are dominated by my concern that R. get well. At
supper R. sings the melody from the wedding chorus in [Cherubini's]
Médée and observes what power this unique composer achieved through
his command of proportions, as for example in the Credo of the *Mass
in D Minor,* which is magnificent; Cherubini, he says, occupies a place
of his own, for he wrote solidly, cleanly, whereas in Spontini, for
instance, there were already too many frills. — A visit in the evening
from our poor friend Hagen, who, in reply to my calm questioning,
seriously maintains that a 4th-dimensional being is upsetting his mind.
R. tries to convince him that everything happens inside us and there
are no attacks from outside, but I fear it is in vain. "I have nice supporters," R. says with a laugh. "I should have liked to see Hagen and
Nietzsche going for a walk together!"

Thursday, June 13   R. was restless and had to get up again at 1 A.M.
He is continuing with his cure and talks much with me about the
divinity within us. We go for a walk together as far as the Students'
Wood, taking pleasure in each other and in Nature: "A wood like this,
however small, lies somehow outside the world—it is as if one has
come to a border." (The pale-pink roses in our garden also delighted
him with their "suppressed fire.") And on our homeward journey we
are accompanied intoxicatingly by larksong. Our splendid friend
Glasenapp has procured for me the score of the *Egmont* music written
in R.'s hand; it arrived today. The death of the King of Hanover
produces from R. the joke: "The King of Prussia is shot and the King
of Hanover dies—that is a *qui pro quo.*" The little ones rather naughty,
R. very solemn, not to say strict, gives Fidi his first box on the ear,
Loldi quite beside herself. Tender reconciliation! . . .

Friday, June 14   R. slept better, rose very early, went for a walk
with the children; after that a rest for him and for me and Boni's
examination in church; she passes it satisfactorily. In the afternoon R.
decides on a drive to the forester's lodge at Ottmannsreuth, splendid
picnic on a mossy bank in the woods after a nice walk. It reminds R.
of Don Quixote with the shepherds, when, divested of all absurdity,
he appears literally like a savior. R. feels so well and enjoys these hours
so much that they remain in my memory twinkling like stars. In the
woods R. reads to us with emotion a report on the Emperor's condition. Yesterday R. spoke to us about Sch.'s resemblance to Beethoven,
saying they had in common an unconditional truthfulness and belief
in themselves, undisturbed by the man-of-the-world considerations
we see in Goethe: "One can imagine nothing more bizarre than Goethe
and Beeth. together, let alone as room neighbors." In the evening
strolled with R. in the garden, then to bed at 9 o'clock on account of

his cure, after reading the new *B. Bl.* together and rejoicing at how well Constantin Frantz's letter matches outward events. — R.'s amusement over a nice and very originally phrased letter from my father to Herr Kastner.

Saturday, June 15 A huge thunderstorm woke R. up and he had to resort to a poultice, in spite of our walks and the fact that we had spent the whole day out of doors. . . . He has a talk with Blandine about the meaning of confession and Communion and shows her the whole essence of Christianity in them, avowal and salvation. I to confession with the dear child; deep emotion. Tauler preserves within me the mood to which the act transports my dear child. When we return home, R. tells us of a brewery assistant who, having fallen into the brew, now lies dying; his master was not prepared to keep him nor the hospital to take him in, and his father did not want him. I beg R. to bring him to our house; R. sends someone to the surgeon Schnappauf, who informs him that the poor young man has been taken forcibly to his father's house, where he cannot be nursed; R. arranges that, if he can still be moved, he is to be taken to the hospital at his expense. — "How can one wonder at all the murder and pillage?" R. says. "We're heading for a kind of Hussite War." Cold and raw weather. R. spends much time reading Renan's *Life of Jesus,* and reads bits of it aloud to me in the evening; he (Richard) believes that Christianity can still be rescued for future ages and that up till now it has only experienced its barbarian epochs. — "The barometer shows R. W., Richard Wagner, rain and wind." This makes me sorry because of R.'s cure, and he is also troubled by his foot.

Sunday, June 16 Blandine's Communion! R. embraces me. "You have a lot to do, but the blessing is with you." — It comes from him, and, when I see my good, earnest girl walk around the altar, I think to myself that no preliminary training could have prepared her so well, plowed her soul so thoroughly for the seed, as living in the sight of *his* image! I ask R. not to come to church, but he appears in time for the sacred act. "There is a lot to be learned from it," he says when we return home, "and it is always the human beings who dismay one at such times, the brutal human beings for whom nevertheless Jesus came to earth." "Just in front of you was a face which really did look brutal!" "I should like to demand of our dear parsons that they remove their spectacles on such occasions. What do they need spectacles for? And it takes away all their dignity." "Spectacles to see the word of God!" he says again later. R. deplores the wafer, would prefer a loaf of bread to be broken and distributed. — The 40 years of which Tauler speaks have already struck for me, today with all my soul I submerged myself, forgot the "harsh murmur" of mortal souls, or thought of them as better than myself. My thanks to you, my dear child, you have given me more than I have given you! I made you the gift of this sad life, you have given me this hour. Blessings on you all! — A quiet day, R. reads Renan, smiling over certain expressions, I sit beside him reading Dante, and we exchange impressions of our reading. Early to bed. — R. is pleased that in *Parsifal* he has not depicted the action of the service in the Temple, but has concentrated everything into the blessing of the Grail. — During the service the sounds of *Parsifal* echoed within me and accompanied my child.

Monday, June 17 Still raw and overcast weather, but R. rises early, drinks his waters, and takes his walk. Afterward he lies down again, then spends his morning reading; the character of the divine human being is becoming ever clearer and deeper in his mind; the difference between Jesus and the saints is the difference between the revealer and the receivers. He will write splendidly about it. After lunch R. recalled our meeting in Reichenhall, our parting, "you with your eyes always lowered." Discussion about love relationships. If they are not every-thing, if they do not lead either to death or to union, there is always something absurd about them, he said. After lunch yesterday he delighted me with the remark that, when Boni walked past the altar with such beautiful earnestness, he had been reminded of how as Evening she had walked past his portrait. He found renewed pleasure in our simple church and the upper altar picture in particular; "The Saviour ascending to Heaven in a shroud, transfigured—this is a very beautiful symbol." — The Christ on the Mount of Olives beneath it seems to him to have his hair too nicely curled. Dwelling on this theme (yesterday), he recalls our Communion together, and how beautifully our friend Dittmar spoke the words "He approaches," how stirring he was, and how well he looked even when moving around busily. Then he goes on to speak about the great moment, "so terribly stirring," of Peter's recognition of Christ. For me his words are a lovely extension of the divine service, and yesterday I hardly ceased praying! — Today, when I go walking in the garden with R., I speak to him of Tauler and tell him my feeling that, just as poets see their characters from the outside, so saints must experience the emotions of their hearts as forms perceptible to the eye. R. would very much like to read a history of present-day Christian sects. Drive to the Fantaisie, which R. much enjoys; on our return friend Seidl tells us about the performance of *Siegfried* in Munich, which, to judge by his report, must have been thoroughly bad—they have gone out of their way, it seems, to do everything differently from Bayreuth. "I don't want to hear a word about it," R. exclaims, and "What a curious fate these works have had!" In the evening R. reads Renan to me. — In the newspaper a never-ending stream of arrests for lese majesty! . . . A dismal story. Baron Staff tells me that in Lower Franconia they are *praying for the welfare of France!*

Tuesday, June 18   R. did not have a bad night, but it was also not completely undisturbed; however, he arranged an outing to Berneck. At breakfast he tells me briefly his thoughts for the 3rd "Public and Popularity" article: art is dished out by professors, distorted by academies, as religion is by the church. In the morning he finishes Renan's *Life of Jesus* and is in complete agreement with his interpretation, also with his description of the Roman Empire and the mediocrity to which we are now irretrievably devoted. We have lunch at 12 o'clock and at 1:30 drive to Berneck with the children and the Wolzogens, by way of Goldkronach. Much delight in the countryside; when, in Berneck, we pass by a narrow bridge, R. says it belongs in one of his most frightening dreams, a bridge like that and more and more people crowding onto it (last night he dreamed of a mass of people who forced their way into his room; though he did not know them, each one had individual features). Merry supper in lovely sunshine in the Molkengarten opposite the ruins, after R. and I had gone for a long walk in the woods. On the beautiful homeward journey via Bindlach we see Bayreuth lying bathed in sunshine before us, dominated by the theater—"The lookout tower," says R. — He recalls his impressions in 1835, how the coachman told him the town's name, how the broad avenues had impressed him, and the whole town struck him as a place "where things were happening." R., very content with the outing, makes me happy by looking so well. He draws our attention to a man standing upright on a hay wagon, contrasting boldly on the green heap against the blue sky; when he takes a staff in his hand, R. says, "Now the cart looks like a ship." I think of *The Artwork of the Future* and R.'s dreams for the people.

Wednesday, June 19   When I ask R. how he slept, he replies, "Excellently!" He gets up at 6 o'clock, goes, as he says, "*wherever I won't meet the Dauphin,*" walks for two hours in the palace gardens, and returns home for breakfast, during which he talks to me at length about Christ and Christianity: "If the world were truly Christian, it would virtually cease to exist." — The poor brewery assistant has died: an incident of shocking heartlessness. R. has read Renan's *Caliban* and thinks it very childish, about which he is really sorry. Friend Wolzogen reads some articles aloud to me, R. laughs at our conventicle. In the evening on the balcony with R.; delight in the blackbirds, a male bird comes frequently to my feeding ledge and sings, R. says, "I am really sorry that he hasn't yet found himself a mate." — At lunch he talked about the sins of the princes; turning to me, he says,

"And you have utterly spoiled Barbarossa for me with your Arnold of Brescia."

Thursday, June 20 R.'s sleep was not entirely undisturbed, but he rises early, drinks his waters, and goes into the palace gardens with the children. I sing the beautiful coda to one of the variations in the *Eroica:* "Ah, that is the original basic melody," he says; much about the execution, which Beethoven has not marked legato for the oboe, though we visualize this passage as entirely legato. He reads the *Bhagavad-Gita* in a French translation, having decided on it after a long search through the library. At lunch he places on Fidi's plate the menu of his christening lunch, which Vreneli has sent him; many memories and much talk about those days. Drive with our friends to the Waldhütte. Friend C[yriax] says R. is looking very well, and during our walk he does indeed behave as if he were the youngest among us. R.'s gaiety astonishes him. Long rest in the woods, R. talks about Buddhism, compares it with Christianity. (He laughs later, exclaiming, "*Tat tvam* asini"!) Home fairly late. In the evening vexation for R. with the royalty accounts from Hamburg.

Friday, June 21 R. had a very bad night, horrid dreams, congestions, an error of diet no doubt the cause. He does not drink his waters. He visits my class, where everything is going well, the children very good; then he goes to the summerhouse, reads the *Bhagavad-Gita,* and then reads to me a fragment from it which I feel could have been written by him: he, too, is quiet in deed, active in repose; he, too, creates free from desire. It seems to me that these sages kept a closer contact with the thread of life than the mystics, though these move me more: the former are sages, the latter saints, as I see it. In the afternoon R. reads to me first the joke about N., with much laughter, and then the beginning of the *Bhagavad-Gita*. "How advanced they were!" he exclaims. "The Greeks in their philosophy were always bound by the law of cause and effect, they always saw things materialistically. Here, in the law of reason, one finds all those things which guide a great general, often without his knowledge. And what a conception it is!" — R. writes a few lines to Frau Materna, recalling her great zeal; in the morning he thought of his sister Klara, "the singing soul," as he was singing something from *Euryanthe*—he had often heard her singing it. — A thundery afternoon, R. is glad, content to remain indoors. Anniversary of my arrival in Starnberg, memories of that event, also of the first performance of *Die Meistersinger:* "Then we staged something else." At supper he rescues a spider, "out of self-interest," as he says; he then recalls the "class" (the children and I): "Ah, that was a spider at night." — Walk with R. in the garden, pleasure in our home. Early to bed.

Saturday, June 22 R. slept well, he goes walking in the palace gardens with the children; Loldi, holding Marke on the lead, is suddenly dragged away when he catches sight of a cat, R. laughingly tells me at breakfast; then he recalls Catulle Mendès, wishes he could make up for not having received him, also recompense Belloni and Giacomelli for their services to him. "Oh, what useless years those were! A waste of my energies—I could have done my work in Zurich until the summons came from the King." I: "It's a terrible thing to say, but I can scarcely regret it, for perhaps we might not then have found each other." R.: "Oh, yes, we would have come together, and I would have run away with you, to Greece or somewhere." Returning to this in the afternoon, I tell him those years had been a sort of labyrinth, into which, like Parsifal, he had been lured by an evil curse, but inwardly he had never lost his way, he had preserved his ideals pure and intact, as P. had his lance. "I have remained true to my law," he answers, referring to the *Bhagavad-Gita.* In the course of the conversation he also said, "One must assume that Kundry's curse loses its power when she awakes, and this awakening attracts Parsifal, all kinds of mysterious relationships like that." To which I: "The wicked world was the Kundry's curse which lured you into the labyrinth." — R. decides on a drive to Berneck, in order to satisfy his longing to follow the path beside the brook to its end. He rests with the *Bhagavad-Gita,* I have all sorts of things to attend to, the house, the children, reports from W. and Feustel (the bank again wants a guarantor). At lunch R. relates the curious dream with which he awoke from the "twilight" of his morning sleep: he was waiting in the *salon* for the carriage he had ordered when suddenly a hearse appeared before the door from the *salon* into the garden. "Why this? It is much too early!" he exclaimed, and woke up. The shape and color of the carriage for our outing was responsible for this dream, which he was hesitant at first to impart to me. I tell R. of the joy I felt in discussing the 2nd act of *Parsifal* with friend Wolzogen, how after Kundry's overwhelming *"Ich will nicht"* ["I will not"] she is overcome by the will to live, and this seemingly strong "will not" comes to nothing; her laughter when Parsifal first appears, then the knights, and Klingsor, now fully master of the situation, giving voice to the triumphant joy of dominion as he gazes on P.! As we ascend the hill, he says, "I should like to start composing again, since it gives you so much joy, I should like to go on working." Then he sings a succession of *endings* to themes from *Parsifal,* as, for instance, to the scene between Klings. and Kund. I: "For concert use, I suppose?!" While, to spare the horses, we are walking up to the crest of the hill, R. quotes *Faust:* "Had I the strength of but two horses—then she will *not* be mine, without a question mark." A threatening thunderstorm passes over, chased away by the Wagner luck, a W. sun shines down on us. In the liveliest of spirits, alternating between the noble tones of the *Bhagavad-Gita* and jokes about all and sundry ("I was born about two of the clock in the afternoon with something of a wet shirt," he says, misquoting Falstaff, in order to make excuses for drinking a non-cure glass of brandy), imparting happiness through his very presence, enchanting me with his words, he wanders with me along the lovely path beside the brook, as far as the tower and back, amid the scent of those *lilacs* which so charmed Hans Sachs! (We stick to the name "lilac.") We have supper in the Molkengarten and then return home (children and friends welcoming us and making us happy). But his foot is hurting him; in a kiss which I press on it in the evening I lay the whole humility of my love and my fervent wish for his recovery. — He talked of Cosimo de' Medici as compared with Pericles: "Exhumation from the age of decadence, however gifted C. may have been—same relationship as that of Louis XIV to Augustus. The aristocracy has done very little." And all the splendid things he says end in a declaration of our love. "How glad we are," he says, "that we discover ever more and more in each other," and thus we slip into sleep. Oh, children, may my happiness become yours!

Sunday, June 23 [*Incorrectly dated June 24. Added in margin:* "Regarding Christ, for whom God was the positive element within the heart, while the intervening world was just the evil there, the conflict with God. R. writes to C. Frantz to thank him for his letter."] Midsummer Day, *Meistersinger* day! R. slept well, seven hours without interruption! In the palace gardens with children and dogs. Told me many amusing things about it. Discussion regarding Lusch; R. concerned that she make a good marriage; I tell him that I have no worries, whoever lives in his house is blessed by fortune, and the rest will turn out all right. Then he recalls our good Frau Materna and her "energy"—how, when she had to sing beside that "boy with a plum in his mouth" (in the third act of *Siegfried*), she did not allow herself to be led astray. We also talk about the fact that no rich man could be found to promote the festival performances; R. observes that they are all Jews, or, if they are not, they keep their distance, frightened off by the press. At lunch R. says, "To my sorrow I must state that the *Bhagavad-Gita* is becoming very childish; a downright grotesque hocus-pocus when, as Vishnu, he reveals himself as an *être suprême* [supreme being]." In the evening R. talks about the time of the awakening of sensual feelings in a youth, and how important it is then to guide him toward an ideal. — The Congress has begun by safeguarding the position of the Jews in Rumania, friend Wolzogen tells us. "I don't want to hear anything more about that," R. exclaims, and, when it is mentioned that the prospects look warlike, "Let them butcher one another, I thirst for downfall, destruction, anything but having to go through another pleasure like that of 1870." R. says that the Pope has changed beyond all recognition and intends to abdicate. Thunderstorm; I write to Secretary B[ürkel] regarding decorations, R. starts to read *"Le Lotus de la bonne Loi"* and, when I come downstairs, he tells me I should read just the first few pages: "Just like the Gospels, isn't it?" he cries, as we laugh loudly together over the jumble of names, numbers, etc. A little *Meistersinger,* distress over Seidl, who is completely ignorant. "Always starting again from scratch," R. exclaims. A walk in the garden. R. shows me how he takes his spa walk.

Monday, June 24 Today is Midsummer Day! R. up once in the night, but on the whole slept well. Solemn exhortation to Fidi from me, no punishment, I try to awake his sense of pride; R. fears he is too soft. Fidi good; also a good letter from Lulu in England. An Israelite in Cologne, Herr Seligmann, is providing the necessary funds for the production of the *Ring* there. — R. continues after all to read the *B-G* and discovers some more good things, the bad only intermittent. He took great delight in the portrait of the actor Eckhoff in the *I. Z.:* "It's good to see Germans with such faces." When we part after lunch, R. to take a rest, he says to me in tender jest, "So we can agree about one or two things at least!" I: "If you will permit me to be one with you." He: "Oh! . . . And she is surprised that I look so well, and doesn't know where it comes from!" . . . After this embrace I ask myself whether life smiles on such moments of happiness between us. Blackbirds calling and answering lull my heart to peace again, and daily work resumes its course. R. reads some of Nietzsche's latest book and is astonished by its pretentious ordinariness. "I can understand why Rée's company is more congenial to him than mine." And when I remark that to judge by this book N.'s earlier ones were just reflections of something else, they did not come from within, he says, "And now they are Rée-flections!"

Tuesday, June 25 R. had a good night; he goes for a walk in the palace gardens with children and dogs and then takes a rest with Prof. Nietzsche's book, the trivial contents of which thoroughly disgust him. He tells me of the insolent tone in which Disraeli is speaking in Berlin, and Germany has to put up with it! Outing to the Sophienberg, somewhat exhausting, but pleasant all the same; the hilly country like motionless waves before our eyes, and R. remarks how glad one is to be amid so much prettiness; a flock of geese looks from above like a "moving silver ribbon," and the differing greens of meadow and valley are a feast to the eye. The absurd melody of the chorus from *Tancredi,* "Tancred has gone," accompanies our ascent

(R. was reminded of it by W.'s remark that he had been reading the Voltaire-Goethe *Tancred*); but no music on the descent, since we disperse across the meadows. "The wisest gives way," says R., when two carriages meet, "but nobody is foolish enough to want to be the wisest." Late arrival home.

(Over coffee in the summerhouse R. quotes *"Nimm den Eid"* ["Take my oath"] and recalls the feeling of satisfaction which then imbues Fricka with dignity; no one, he says, has ever said a word to him about Wotan's inner resolve, and how this is brought about by his having to acknowledge that everything is his own work, all are his creatures, and he can no longer deceive himself about it.) [*Added in margin:* "During our drive Wolz. spoke about an article entitled 'From Beethoven to Brahms' and signed D. A. S. We wonder who this D. A. S. may be. 'Da Dvam *Asini*,' says R. with a laugh."] In the evening, when we reflect that, though the world is becoming increasingly alien to us, we feel increasingly close to each other, our thoughts move to my father, who is also completely withdrawn from the world but has not consciously bid it farewell—hence his melancholy and our serenity!

Wednesday, June 26 R. woke up just once, from a ghostly dream in which he was frightened by his double; I was worried during the night that he might have caught cold, but he is, thank goodness, well, and takes his spa walk with the children; then he continues reading Prof. N. I place open on his desk the 21st canto of Dante's *Purgatorio,* which enchanted me yesterday with its interplay of dream and reality; the images it conjured up in me of the dreamlike quality of our thoughts also please R., but he feels it is all too far away from us in time, too remote, and this spoils the effect of the poem, since we cannot accustom ourselves to all these punished heathens: in what a completely different way does *Faust* move us, he says, though he adds that *Faust* is equally remote from our railroad age. For me these shadowy times, to which we stand in the same relation as D[ante] to Vergil, have an added fascination and a sublime horror; one is astonished to feel so attracted toward, indeed so much at home in, so alien a world. The sudden death of Obernitz, whom we knew, produces from R. the remark: "I feel a downright cosmic figure among all these dead people and the dead who refuse to lie down." But one's impressions become blunted, the good O., for example, had never dared express his opinion of R. to Princess B[ismarck]. "No more about the outside world, I find it horrible." He feels sad that he has not left any pupils behind him. During the morning, as he sat in the summerhouse, he had been assailed by thoughts of his isolation in the world, and, watching our groom cutting the grass with a scythe [*Sense*], he had wondered,

"When shall I be crying, 'Senzi, Senzi'?" Fidi's nursemaid was called Creszenz, and when he wanted anything from her he called out, "Senzi, Senzi." Saddened by these associations with death, I ask R., "Are you content with life?" "Not with *this* life, but with *life*, yes," he replies. Miss Cartwright tells him that in England money is everything, and the money is all in the hands of the Jews. Bism. is said to have forbidden the election of Bennigsen and Lasker; R. laughs about Lasker and says, "He will soon find out what it costs to attack a Jew [*a few words based on untranslatable word play omitted*]." — We listen to the blackbirds, which never stop singing, and I say I shall miss their singing. "Then I shall begin," he says, "summer will do the composing. I am now thinking of the 3rd act, I don't like thinking of the 2nd." In the evening I stroll in the garden with R., he shows me the roses he particularly likes (I shall dry them) and regrets that the growers now seem to favor the unroselike colors. In the evening we read a little about poor N. ("it does me no great honor to be praised by such a one"), and I read aloud to R. the scene with the Khan in the *Wandsbecker Bote;* his "Surely he understands what he is saying" amuses R.

Thursday, June 27   R. awoken by a troublesome dream, the importunities of a former acquaintance: "God, what will Cosima think?" In the palace gardens with the children, I tidy the house, then give the children lessons while R. writes to Dr. Jauner, asking for a report on his earnings and complaining of negligence in the production of *Rheingold,* also that it has on occasion been performed after *Walküre.* He also writes to Dr. Ernst in Cologne, who is really "in earnest" about his [*Ring*] performances and would like, afterward, to take his production to Berlin. Also to the publisher Fritzsch, who has asked for a composition: he says he cannot supply one, but he mentions a possible performance of his symphony in the Euterpe in the coming winter, on its 46th anniversary. Recently he told me that he felt like composing all sorts of things into it, from *Parsifal, Götterdämmerung,* etc. "I am writing letters again," R. says. "I think my final hour must be approaching." The death of the Queen of Spain arouses melancholy feelings, and we are haunted by the thought that it was an unnatural death. "Well, Spain!" says R. "Immediately after that comes Munich and then Vienna, if you are looking for a vulnerable spot!" — Friend Gross visits me to say that he is standing security for the loan, whereupon I beg him to let me take it on. Nobody, he says, is willing to lend even a single cent to the King or the theater management. (I do not tell R. this, in order not to alarm him.) "Look down, O gracious one," he whispers to me as we part in the afternoon. — "You are the gracious one," I reply, and continue with this theme in my thoughts! —

Nice drive to the Eremitage after supper, the sun gleaming gold through the cheerful green of the trees, what could be lovelier? Tender farewell to this day and also to R. in the evening. "Just wait, you'll see what an explosion (of creativity) there's going to be!" I: "Just keep well and cheerful, then I shall be happy." Thus our parting, and I wish I could hold fast forever every word from his lips, every glance! — (At supper R. spoke of the Emperor's condition: not yet ready for a parade, he had said, "You see how one's whole imagination is captured by these things." And: "Terrible thoughts take possession of one; it is as if an injustice that has been committed were seeking vengeance—to have dispossessed three princes simply because my minister talked me into it!" Tappert has written a witty review about Bülow's compositions, performed in Erfurt. Letter to friend Wolzogen from Prof. Bernays, who says he does not dare to write about *Die M[eister]s[inger]*. "So he says," we remark amid smiles, quoting the anecdote. — N.'s book provokes R. into saying playfully, "Oh, art and religion are just what is left in human beings of the monkey's tail, the remains of an ancient culture!" He also talks about the patience of a genius, which others notice only when now and again it turns into impatience; and about teasing, which R. explains as a kindhearted wish to conceal one's superiority and thus to teach. "Actually," R. adds with a laugh, "genius is simply envy."

Friday, June 28 R. got up once but was on the whole content with his night's sleep; in the morning he brings me some pretty material for a negligee which he has had sent for me. He rests, reads N., while I am giving the children their lessons. After lunch R. says: "If the French republic continues to give itself airs as it is doing, it will be a bad omen for the monarchy in Europe. For belief in it is already shattered." In the evening a drive to the Fantaisie.

Saturday, June 29 R. dreamed of a reception in Vienna to which his friends had also invited Herr Hanslick; but when the latter approached R., he exclaimed, "I don't want anything to do with such a miserable fellow as you." "That's true," a voice behind him said, whereupon R. woke up, very tired still. His cure is proving a strain to him, he complains of buzzing in the ears. I am sorry that while taking it he is reading N.'s bad book, although he maintains that this is not affecting him. R. is having a jacket made for himself out of the same material as my negligee, and I am very pleased about it; he asked me "whether it would be proper." — The enclosed witticism from my father [*not found*] gives him much pleasure. "That is priceless," he says, "one can say of your father that he is free" (alluding to N.)—"imperturbable in the zigzag of his life." Still referring to the book, whose ending he reads to me in almost lyrical tones, R. says, "To be blind and not to believe in anything inside one—that is bad." Nice drive to the zoological gardens, a new sight in our pretty countryside.

Sunday, June 30　Again R. woke up in the night and had to get out of bed; he feels tired and would prefer to give up his cure. But at lunch he is again fresh and cheerful. He has sent for a hairdresser for me and wants my blonde hair to be brought out; I would prefer to keep my gray hairs, but if he wants it thus, I shall also be happy; he wants me to have it done in an Apollo knot and intends to study etchings of the ancient Greeks! At lunch discussion of the children's journey to Dresden (Loldi and Fidi) to have their teeth seen to. R. talks about his former homes there, one of them on Moritzstrasse, where the "Kasserl" had hung; he says his father had hung a Kasperl, a large metal puppet, on the door of the dining room, to scare him off if he tried to creep into the room when forbidden; it had successfully scared him off. And of the other apartment in Judenhof: an armorer named Voigt lived below them, and he had once made a sword, intended as a Christmas present for R., dance on a red leather strap before his eyes, before immediately hiding it again. He recalls his father with some emotion. Then our conversation moves to the concert in Leipzig where we met and were so merry together in spite of all our misfortunes: "We were always smiling amid tears." When we part in the afternoon, he exclaims, "Oh, gods, feast your eyes on this blessed couple!" Then, when we meet again in the afternoon and stroll around the garden, we recall the time when *Die Msinger* was being written, also that day in the Schiff when R. played to me the end of the 2nd act of *Siegfried*. "Oh, it was a time of discontent, and something tremendous had to come along to restore my urge to create." [*Added in margin:* " 'Oh, my one and only one!' R.: 'You get things muddled, like your datives and accusatives: that is you.' — 'How can you be so good to me?' — 'Why shouldn't I be? You get lovelier every day.' "] Then R. says to me: "You will have a bit of peace and quiet when the children are all grown up. That is what you lack—*a morning philosophy.*" Much laughter about that. In the evening we read some of Voltaire's prose writings ("*Réponse à un docteur allemand*") and discover in them, as Herwegh once remarked to R., a source of much of Heine's wit.

Monday, July 1　R. up once, the cure does not seem to be helping him at all; my main fear is that his cheerfulness is deceiving me—Ah, life, life, borne on wings, woven from love, how painful are thy thorns! In the morning R. places the little aromatic lamp which "Kundry" gave him on the 22nd in my dressing room, thereby bringing me his fragrant greeting! The two children leave with the Wolzogens. R. at the station after all, though this kind of parting upsets him, particularly the waiting around after the goodbyes. In the afternoon, while I am walking in the garden with R., the conductor Levi (who was expected) comes to join us; he has realized that no good production of the *Ring* is possible outside Bayreuth. R. complains about the trend of wanting to do it differently from the way he did it here. — In the morning I read [Schiller's] *Wilhelm Tell* with Boni and, worried at the way this splendid work is jeopardized by its iambic pentameter, which makes the words of the sentries guarding the governor's hat, for example, seem so unnatural, I tell R. that I should like to see *Die Msinger* compared with *Tell,* purely in relation to the language, with the music left entirely aside. All the time I felt tempted, I said, to skip the verse in order not to lose the children's sympathy and attention. R. says, "How curious—when I was thinking today about Levi's visit, there came into my mind the verse 'Today is Simon and Judah, the lake is wild and wants its sacrifices.' " We laugh. — He got a nice letter from Constant. Frantz, whose article in the *Bayr. Blätter* seems to have caused bad blood; Levi mentions it, and Tappert has written to friend W. that many people intend to protest. "All the better," says R. "Those who are not with us are at liberty to go." The publisher Schmeitzner really has printed extracts from N.'s book as a supplement to the *B. Blätter.* Herr L[evi] feels that a man like N. is too good for that, and R. laughs over the *qui pro quo.* Much talk about tempi, R. feels it is "impossible to mark them."

Tuesday, July 2 R. still having to get up once! But he takes his morning walks. He misses Fidi and Loldi. For me still no "morning philosophy"—a new governess to settle in, lessons, visit from Herr Levi (who touches R. by saying that, as a Jew, he is *a walking anachronism*). R. tells him that, if the Catholics consider themselves superior to the Protestants, the Jews are the most superior of all, being the eldest. Conversation about the 4th dimension of space, Mr. Slade, expelled by the police, not a fraud. R. says he can understand the ecstasy of martyrs, and he believes in their visions. "Farewell, you strange man," he says to L. as the latter leaves us. — R. de des on A. Thierry's *Les Récits mér* for his morning reading and reads it with enjoyment; for the afternoon Voltaire's *Pucelle,* which, however, he gives up in disgust. A visit from the Glasenapps. Concern about W., whose family circumstances in his run-down state of health alarm us (his mother-in-law and two sisters-in-law have arrived here).

Wednesday, July 3 R. is tired, but when he woke up in the early morning, he had just had some funny dreams; when, later, on his 2nd awakening, I asked about them, he had forgotten, could only remember that we had been together and had laughed over comical things. — Concerned thoughts exchanged about friend W. — The Glasenapps at lunch; R. gives his opinion on Russia, how he had wished it to be victorious, but the very stupid way in which this war had been waged and the heroism of Osman Pasha had lured him away from the one side and aroused his sympathies for the other. The assassination attempt on Emperor W., he says, was connected with the dispossession of the King of Hanover, all of it involuntary: "These are the concealed underground threads," but those who live by faith must not undermine this faith, for then one is left with only the army for support. Of Charles V, R. says the fact that he abdicated was to his credit. Conversation about Riga leads us to the subject of Dorn and R.'s frightful experiences with him! — I drive out to the Fantaisie to see our friends' family. Return and reunion is always a homecoming and a rediscovery! . . . R. reads his "Public and Popularity" articles, because he wants now to get down to the final installment, so as to be able to resume *Parsifal* on August 1: "I shall then finish composing in time for your birthday." Herr Renz writes asking for permission to present the "Ride of the Valkyries" in his circus, R. gives his permission in a splendid letter. In the evening our friends the Gl.'s; he brings me a little book containing a puppet play, *Delila,* by L. Geyer, and R. remembers having seen it produced in his home! — Friend Gross also comes, and tells us among other things that the King of B[avaria] is now allowed to go out only with a police escort; the instructions have come from Berlin, and the King finds it very unpleasant, he says. R. observes that they are trying by this means to enforce consent to the laws. — In the evening R. comes back to N[ietzsche]; it is not so easy to ignore, R. feels: the circle is too small for one not to keep coming back to the same experiences.

Thursday, July 4 H. Ixora—R. poured into my bath a bottle of Indian perfume which had been sent to him to try and which is called Ixoras. — R. says that in *Jessonda* there is a god Ixora, the name had always amused him. "Thou who comest from on high, who all woes and sorrows stillest, who, for twofold misery, hearts with twofold balsam fillest"—thus does my soul call out to him! My night was a troubled one, heavy thoughts weighed me down, and it seemed that my poor brain, overtired, would cease to serve me. Gloomy weather, no birds singing—that was probably the cause. Then in the early morning there comes from R.'s room a wondrous fair melody, and daytime and nighttime spirits are banished! "A theme for a quartet for you": with these words R. comes into my room, and after breakfast we part with an embrace, "the day's blessing," as R. calls it; for me it is blessed indeed! — At noon return of the children. Many things for me to arrange, which earns me R.'s sweet and affectionate chiding. The news that Hans is well came to me like an echo of the theme, as if all my blessings stem from this morning greeting. R. goes to see the Jägers, whose home pleases him; he then takes them all—J[äger], W[olzogen], Gl[asenapp]—to Angermann's; since it starts to rain heavily, I send Georg there with an umbrella; when R. sees him, he cries, "Here comes my wife!" [*Added in margin:* "R. says with a laugh, 'I shall compose the scene between Kundry and Parsifal as a canon, to be sung first singly and then together.' "] In the evening he reads to me the first two scenes of *Götz,* the fine excitement of the man of action, the eagerness for booty in the enthusiastic outburst of Brother Martin, these enchant us with their truth and vividness; and how fortunate that it is written in prose! Also, at my request, he reads *Euphrosyne* to me, first according to the meter, which makes it almost nonsensical, then according to the sense, which we find more moving; but we regret the hexameters and the Hermes, R. even Antigone and Polyxena, though I am less disturbed by them, since here they seem to me like theatrical sisters, being welcomed by Euphrosyne. — As I part from R. in the evening, I tell him that his melody will not leave my mind. "Yes, such things occur to one during sleepless nights: the early bird gets the first canons."

Friday, July 5 Raw weather; but R. goes for a walk with the children and tells me about a blackbird which warbles its call twice with trumpetlike clarity, and another, a wheatear, which endlessly twitters and then all at once breaks off. Herr Cyriax sends all kinds of things; R.: "I like people who make presents to my wife, but who are in fact just going along with my secret intentions!" . . . He reads the *Récits mérovingiens* with enjoyment. I speak earnestly to friend W. He brings a letter from Herr Tappert, who is going through a very bad time. When I tell R. this, he decides to send him 500 marks as an advance payment for newspaper articles. After lunch R. says, "If I were rich, nobody would ever hear a note of *Parsifal;* I should bequeath it to Fidi, so that he could give it out as his own work and draw royalties on it till 30 years after his death." "I have continued the canon," he tells me. "I have found a very pretty turn. Later I shall write only such things, they don't have to be in 4 movements, and I shall ask Lachner for his formula for suites; I have a whole host of similar ideas which I haven't yet used. I shall also find time to write a play, *Luther's Wedding,* in prose." In connection with the newspaper article R. says to me, "Now you can sing '*O Richard, ô mon roi! tous les juifs l'abandonnent*' ['Oh, Richard, oh, my King, all the Jews are abandoning him']." We go to see friend Feustel to settle the Tap[pert] matter. F. says the Emperor has now recovered and asks R. whether he would like to express his pleasure in writing. R.: "Oh, the Emperor would just ask himself: 'What does he want? Ah, he has that deficit, he needs money!' " We walk home through the palace gardens, and R. points out his blackbird and the wheatear, which are both singing again. In the evening R. takes up [Spontini's] *Olimpie* again, the Overture to which he likes very much. He tells me about his dream: that Beethoven had wanted to do some work on *Fidelio* and had run through a wall— "It's always something either too ridiculous or bad, just to wake one up."

Saturday, July 6 R. interrupts his cure today, the weather is raw. However, he is looking well, and I go in good spirits to my work with house and children, also a little correspondence. Friend Feustel's speech to his supporters brings R. back to the subject of the socialists, whom F. has described as easy to master. That they certainly are, says R., for the moment, but they will keep coming back; one should not be giving them votes in the Reichstag, but, rather, considering the problems, investigating the basic principles, and doing something to relieve the need. But they are all stupid, and the socialists themselves are both crude and stupid, for all they really want is to gain control of the state in order to impose impossible conditions. In this connection R. recalls Herr v. Trützschler (shot in Baden), who, when R. once mentioned the state, replied: "I recognize no state, I recognize only society." R. goes off to his afternoon rest; as he leaves me, after figuring out that he would have to be 94 when I achieved my father's present age, he says: "I shall stay with you. — But what shall we do with our lives? — Console each other." — With friend Glasenapp I start the catalogue of the corner bureau (manuscripts), at 6 o'clock go for a walk with R., in our garden, then in the palace gardens. On our return we start a conversation about *Don Giovanni* and the new version of the text, which R. considers unfortunate; he observes that these works, as Semper once said about theaters, cannot be too baroque in style; of course *Don Giovanni* is a divine, an incomparable work, but it is that because it opened up vistas from a certain definite popular basis; to take these vistas as the starting point would be to destroy it, to make its lightness and informality incredible and turn it into something stiff and boring; he had been thinking only today about Don G.'s joke with Leporello, when he squeezes his fingers to see whether he will betray him—in a word, it is *opera giocosa*. — Supper with the Glasenapps, and afterward R. deals with the subject of the Jews, which he says nobody cares to notice, either out of fear or out of apathy. Either the Jews possess a past, he says, in which case they are connected with the Talmud, or they are finished: "How can such a person love my works, and what does it matter to me whether he loves them or not?" But whatever the Jews may be, the main blame lies with the Germans. "What are we?" he cries indignantly. "There's not a single statesman who asks himself this question. They play with us as if we were sparrows, and the first point the Congress reaches agreement on is the emancipation of the Jews in Rumania; they let Bessarabia go, and all else besides, but the Jews are saved! Oh . . . !"

Sunday, July 7   R. goes for a walk in spite of the overcast skies; at breakfast he looks at me: "You are so complete, and everything around you so incomplete! . . . I was just trying to recall the lines from *Götterdämmerung,* but they lie wrapped in a cheerful mist." We recall the lines, and then R. sings the *Idyll:* "A son has arrived!" — We invoke a blessing on the day, and work begins. For R., who is still looking very well at lunchtime, the day proves tiring, alas! — Friend W. tells us about the Congress dinner given by Herr Bleichröder, who has really been organizing everything; when I laugh over the Bleich-röder coat of arms being displayed everywhere, R. says, "Alas, I can no longer laugh about it." — Some anonymous person, signing him-self in a postscript as "warning Erda," complains of R.'s misuse of his genius to campaign against the Jews—he should leave state and empire to politicians such as Bismarck! — After lunch R. looks through the French piano score of *La Muette de Portici* to find the blackbird's call; he finds it at the beginning of the market chorus in D major and tells us that the blackbird in the palace gardens sang it three times in succession. — Then he talks about the Gospels, praises Renan, says that Strauss entirely missed the point, either such studies must set out to show that the subject lacked content, or they must recognize the content and describe it; that is what Renan has done. And anyone who does not in times of sorrow—say, when a child has died—open the Gospels again and feel uplifted by the spirit that breathes through them is not worth much. A short walk with the Glasenapps in the afternoon, thundery rain, in the summerhouse R. talks very movingly about a theft in Riga; some articles of clothing belonging to Minna were stolen, and the maid (Lieschen), horror-stricken, at once accused her lover, who was arrested. The police told R. that, if the stolen articles were worth more than one hundred roubles, the accused man would be sent to Siberia. R. put the value as low as possible, but he could not save the man, since he was a recidivist, and he had to look on as the man was brought in with shaved head and dressed in prison garb, already condemned to Siberia. A terrible sight, and he had then and there sworn never to prosecute anyone again; he could not bear to think of it even now. "I said to myself," he adds, "*si jamais on m'y reprend*" ["may I never be caught like that again"]. R. amazes Gl. with his memory for the streets and names in Riga. — Coming back to Bleich-röder, he says, "They can now regard themselves as Germans, like that Negro who proudly showed the card on which the Spanish government had given him the right to regard himself as a white man." — Returning home from the summerhouse, he spits up a little blood, talking has tired him; I suppress my concern but go to him in his room: "The world does bad things to me, but in return I have you—be glad that it is so, for otherwise you would not mean so much." I: "Then I would sooner mean nothing." — The blood has only come from his throat, but he looks worn out. At supper, talk about Bakunin, "whom one could call the personification of Russia's future," "a wild, noble fellow."

Monday, July 8   Night disturbed by constant furious barking of the dogs; at lunch I amuse R. by reminding him that, after pacifying the dogs from the window, he got irritably back into bed, saying, "I shall stop paying tax on Putz." — Still some blood—no walk; some business letters, vexation over the lawyer in Dresden. I continue the catalogue with Herr Glasenapp. Various things from the past read through with deep emotion. R. worn out—avoidance of any conversation. — This restores him, he is enjoying the French book. Friend Wolzogen reads me an article by Dr. Eiser about Sch[openhauer] and R., very nice. Spent a cozy evening entirely alone with R., chatting intimately, memories, children's future, joys, griefs, and worries, all transfigured through conversation! Also talked about Alcibiades and Socrates.

Tuesday, July 9   R. slept tolerably well, but the unfavorable weather causes him to stop his cure; he dreamed that during a meal I sat down on a raised chair, my former mother-in-law, Frau v. Bülow, to one side, while he had to go to a place right at the end of the table, which astonished him. At lunch he says, "Now I know what you meant by it: you wanted to live like Saint Radegunde, to ornament and bedeck the table for your lover, but to possess nothing yourself." — The weather clears up, we drive out to the Waldhütte. During the drive we admire Eva's beauty, then R. recalls Tribschen, our drive to the Grütli. "Those were sublime and blessed times," he says. The air is pleasant and fresh, and we enjoy a nice evening. On our return home we go straight to bed.

Wednesday, July 10   R. did not have a bad night, but unfortunately the weather is wretched, overcast sky, rain, and the house is cold. R. suffers very much from it. I catalogue the manuscripts with friend Glasenapp, a beloved and refreshing occupation for me. When I tell R. about it, he says, "You foolish girl!" When I tell him I have been reading some of his letters to the King, he says, "Oh, those don't sound very good, but it wasn't I who set the tone." R. also begins to feel better, and he writes a very lively and funny letter to Malwida [von Meysenbug], declaring that, since all present-day musicians are Schumannians, Beethoven really lived in vain. But unfortunately his mood does not persist, and even such nice people as Gl. prove a burden to him. When we are alone his cheerfulness always returns, in spite of his not feeling well. After supper we go for a walk, first of all in the garden, then in the palace gardens, where we are surrounded by swarms of fireflies, thoughts of *Die Msinger:* "Here comes one to greet you," R. calls out to me. He tells me the story of Saint Radegunde from the *Récits mérovingiens,* which he says has given him "a very good idea of those times." — On our return home R. reads me something from the second part of the *Nibelungenlied* in the Simrock translation, which we find rather pedestrian. Regarding iambics, R. says, "The trouble is that they force one to be too long, not too short." He says the Schlegel translations are for him a fine monument to the German language.

Thursday, July 11 R. had a peaceful night, he dreamed that he had cut his finger with a razor and had to withdraw the knife carefully in order not to lose the whole finger! — He looks run down, and I can scarcely imagine a harder battle than that I fought to hide my concern. But I succeeded at breakfast, he conjures up a picture of a party of all our best friends together, all so shy and ill at ease, particularly our good Germans, like C. Frantz, etc. I laugh and say I am beginning to understand better and better the custom of having a court jester in cases where one is obliged to maintain a sort of court or party system. He laughs, and since I have come to the table in a brightly colored dress, which he likes, he says that at any rate the Harlequin costume is there. — As we part in the morning, he says to me, "Let us cling tight to each other, become more and more united." — The gloomy weather always arouses in him lively thoughts of a stay in Italy. At lunch he informs us of various denunciations, and since we happen to have some new pickled herrings, which he enjoys, he exclaims, "I fear *Matjes* crimes"—Middle High German abbreviation for "majesty"! Friend Glasenapp and I finish the catalogue, then to R. Speaking of his library, he says he is not at all obsessed with books, and now that he has his collection, he will not buy any more. In the evening he first of all played "for the children" the Andante from [Beethoven's] A Major Symphony, to my indescribable delight, then for *us* the Prelude to *Parsifal;* he complains of the realistic, abstract nature of the piano, on which one always has to strike the notes, and I felt this must be particularly distracting for him in the Prelude to *Parsifal.* In the evening he sends for all our friends, Herr Jäger is to sing something from *Siegfried;* he sings the "Forging and Hammering Songs," friend Seidl again getting the tempi wrong—that is to say, after the first 'Nothung, Nothung," which must be very broad, he drags it out as if it were narrative: "Then the melody gets lost," says R.; and in the "Hammering Songs" he is too fast. — R. plays the American march with him as a piano duet, and this recalls to me the fate of the two marches, the "*Kaisermarsch*" and the "Centennial March," and the consequent difference between them. Then R. takes out [Halévy's] *La Juive* and shows us how good dramatically are the "*Je suis chrétien*" ["I am a Christian"] and Recha's following words, which are so disjointed. When we say good night, R. uses such expressions to me, says such glorious things, that I do not dare write them down here—indeed, I hardly dare preserve them in my heart! — "What am I saying," he concluded, "when I call you my one and only? That still implies some sort of comparison! . . ."

Friday, July 12 Sky still overcast and R. with a headache: "But it will be all right," he says, "*ça ira, ça ira, j'aimerai toujours ma Cosima*" ["it will be all right, I shall always love my Cosima"]. Discussing at lunch the performance in Leipzig and the division of *Götterdäm.* into an introduction and three acts, he decides after all to leave it as it is and just to make some cuts—almost the whole of the Norns' scene and a large part of the scene between Waltraute and Brünnhilde. He does this because he knows that, when badly performed, they are bound to be incomprehensible, and he would rather not sacrifice the transition to the "Journey to the Rhine," which he knows to be effective; he would have to do this if the introduction were to be separated from the first act. Even here [in Bayreuth] the Norns' scene and the Br.-Walt. scene proved unsuccessful, he says, so how much more likely are they to fail in an ordinary theater. [*Added in margin of the following page, but presumably with reference to the foregoing:* "Indescribable melancholy about this scene! This work also now cast aside and disfigured—and he himself has to take a hand in it!" *Added in margin on the present page:* " 'Come, *extinguisher* of bitter sorrows,' he says, turning from the sky to the *Tagblatt*."] — Glance at the barometer: "It can't do anything but rise." Walk with R. in the palace gardens, pleasure in the birds in our garden, R. observes the individuality in each one's song; a cold wind is blowing strongly. In the evening friend Gross, conversation about the Congress, R. very indignant over its decisions, says the Jews are again pulling the strings. He alone retains the faculty of reacting indignantly in all spheres of life; among other things he tells us about the boy whom a gentleman here struck on the back of the neck for throwing a stone at his dog; the boy, who lost consciousness, died three days later. The doctor declared that it was not manslaughter, the boy died of an internal ailment. That's what humanitarianism means now, he says—never take anything seriously. R. also brings along an extract from the Hödel trial to read to me, saying it is remarkable in its beastliness. I find it reprehensible that such horrible things should be made public—what is happening to reverence, that most necessary religion? — The children have been watching some tightrope walkers, their account produces from R.

some anecdotes about tightrope walkers, who made such an impression
on him in Eisleben during his childhood: for instance, one of them
wheeled his old mother along the rope in a wheelbarrow, and she,
suddenly losing her nerve, called out loudly to him, "Let me roll
down!" Then two others who, meeting on the rope above the river
Danube, had not considered in advance what they would do, and had
got out of this embarrassing situation by somersaulting over each
other. "I firmly believed what people said, that they had not decided
what to do when they met, and it made a great impression on me," R.
says. Squabble about happiness as the day ends: "I am so very happy."
"No, I am."

Saturday, July 13   R. had quite a tolerable night. "At night one has
to fight off demons, in the day donkeys and blockheads." When we
separate, he says to me: "I was thinking early this morning what it is
that a man of genius needs, independence protected by love. Your
father, Beethoven, all these untamed fellows, they wanted just the
independence." I: "They were none of them poets." R.: "That's true,
musicians are only half-tamed creatures." — Around lunchtime he
comes to my room and shows me the travel adventures of Herr Will
and Frau Vorstel, which he had been rereading with much emotion
and merriment. He is very amused by the "mandarin," and now he
praises me—oh, dear!—and in such high-flown terms that I am almost
consumed by melancholy. Talking at lunch about the bust of myself,
I say I should feel pretentious, giving away the full-size one, and that
is why I should like reductions of it; he replies, "Where my bust stands,
yours can, too." I: "Oh, that is something different." "Not at all,
there have been lots of composers, but cosimers are rare." The *J.
Zeitung*, which prints a picture of a Renaissance ball in Weimar in
connection with the Grand Duke's jubilee, provokes R. into expressing his utter disgust for mummeries of this kind. After lunch he
again enjoins friend Seidl to study tempi, not to drag the adagios, not
to rush the allegros. He cites the Andante in the A Major Symphony,
for which Beethoven stipulated a very quick tempo; when the second
theme is introduced, the tempo must be broadened, but at the end the
march rhythm must be retained, and it is quite a different thing whether
one is playing a theme for the first time or repeating it. "But it is only
the composer who can teach people that, which is why I wanted to
set up my school, to teach it, for example, through Weber's overtures.
But that brings us back to the Reich!" . . . I do not know what brought
him to the Julierberg, but he reminds me that it was on this mountain
that he visualized Wotan and Fricka: "There, where all is silence, one
imagines the beings who rule there, unaffected by the passage of time."
The name Julierberg brings us to the Romans: "That was a true city

system, city against city, until one city at last dominated all the other cities and formed a state. The ancient Germans, on the other hand, used a tribal system." He compared the Frankish, the Merovingian tribes with the Pelopidae and other Greek tribes; naïve cruelty, one must not underestimate the influence of Christianity, he says. Arrival in the afternoon of our nice Fr[anziska] Ritter, sad accounts of the family. R.'s earnest and sympathetic expression as Franziska was speaking took up the whole of my attention—something of this expression, though only a little, is reflected in the photograph of Lenbach's portrait. Resolve at all costs to help this man who was once so helpful to R. To the Jägers' in the evening; Herr Jäger sings a passage from *Siegfried,* from "*Mein Vöglein schwebte mir fort*" to the end, much of it to R.'s great satisfaction, R. as the Wanderer wonderfully gripping. A nice evening, the only thing that vexes R. the way the audience remained seated in silence after a performance such as Jäger gave: "If only at least they had risen to their feet!" Merry walk home through the palace gardens. — Once more to have heard *Siegfried!* . . .

Sunday, July 14 The rare instance of going out in the evening did R. much good, he slept well. At 3 o'clock we gave our farewell banquet for Herr Jäger and Herr Seidl, who are going to Leipzig; a gay little celebration, R. proposes a toast to friend Glasenapp, "who brings the dead to life and kills off the living by writing biographies!" Somebody says it is being rumored that R. is writing a march for King Humbert. "Yes," he replies, "for King Humbug" . . . Walk in the palace gardens with the entire company; above all the fate of Ritter discussed with friend Gross—whether it would be possible to find them a position here, R. and I determined to help them. In the evening, when we are alone with our relations, our conversation is confined almost exclusively to this subject. R. delighted with my appearance, I should like to be as lovely as light and imbued with all the talents, since it is for his sake!

Monday, July 15 R. has received strange telegrams from Herr v. Hagen. "The demons are envious of us," he says, "they cannot bear to see our joy in each other and in the children, every minute some such matter intervenes." R. tells how in his childhood he always spoke of "Glücklich [Happy] van Beethoven." Today another letter from Secretary Bürkel, saying that the King prefers the Munich stage decorations to ours here, and he also wishes the *Ring* not to be given anywhere in its entirety before Munich. Friend Seidl leaves our house, to help in Leipzig with the rehearsals of *Siegfried* and *Götterdämmerung.* R. writes at length to the King about the present German Reich, with reference to the article by C. Frantz. He also speaks of the fate of his *Ring* and tries to avert a similar one for *Parsifal.* A sketch for

Rheingold, sent by the King, produces from R. the remark written on the following card: [*not found*]. In the evening conversation turns once again to the decisions of the Congress and the terrible denunciations; R. has marked in red the almost unbelievable story about the painter Piloty. A disgrace for Germany is what he calls the Congress decisions, which have brought from the Israelites a petition of thanks addressed to the Reich Chancellor! — He talks continually of India and Indian culture, compared with which we are barbarians, for what relationship do great poetic works such as *Faust* bear to their own times, and how can our dogmas be compared with the dogma of reincarnation? He talks with continual fire, although he frequently complains to me that he finds talking difficult, as if his voice were strained.

Tuesday, July 16 R. slept well and resolved to work on his article; at lunch he tells me that he could not get into the mood. I write letters, among others to the King's secretary. In the afternoon a drive with R. and the children. Raw weather, but in the Eremitage we are sheltered, and the walk gives us pleasure in spite of the sad sight of completely frostbitten trees [?], which R. points out to me; the view from one of the heights over St. Johannis and the hills is wonderful and heartily delights us. In the evening our friends Gl. and the W.'s. Franziska made her departure today, we very much hope we shall be able to help these good people. A long letter from poor E. Hagen induces R. to write to his mother. C. Frantz has sent us a nice article on socialism, written in a popular but nonetheless cultivated style.

Wednesday, July 17 A fine day at last, after perpetual cold! The *Bayreuther Blätter* arrives, and R. is pleased with the articles by Gl. and by W., regretting only some repetitions in "The Fight with the Dragon." Lunch with the Gl.'s, looked at the caricatures by Kietz, the words beneath the King of Hanover were written by R. — R. comes up to my room in the afternoon, Herr Jauner has sent him a nice signet, which he earmarked for him during the festival; R. thanks him with friendly gaiety. I know of nobody who is so appreciative of small attentions as R. In the evening R. sups with me in the little gray room, lovely sunset, his shining eyes are turned to the heavens, sun to sun: "How little one is conscious of one's individuality!" he exclaims. "How could one otherwise feel at home in the universe? If one tells oneself that in a few years all this will end, how can one delight in it? Yet one does delight in it, because individuality means nothing." — To take my mind off my indisposition I have gone back to Balzac's novel, which I like more than almost anything else; even its exclusively Catholic character seems to me justified; it provides the firm framework indispensable to any work of art; the thoroughgoing praise R. recently bestowed on this great writer suggested it to me. In the evening R.

reads to me from this novel, *Le Curé de village*—the scene in which Véronique's servants tell her in their own way about the life of "Farrabesche," and their peasant speech make us laugh heartily. "What a gifted man he is!" R. exclaims in the middle of his reading. He reads it to me with complete fluency.

Thursday, July 18   In the morning R. says to me, "Oh, yes, it was on the Brünig that I promised you the *Tristan* march and all the other marches." I: "You have done much more than you promised." He: "Yes, I didn't promise *Parsifal*." He works on his article and tells me that he wants to continue with it, so as not to have to think any more about the *Bayreuth. Bl.* for some time. He is glad that we are having lunch alone together upstairs, says it is like on our travels. When he came in he was complaining of pains in his chest, but then he grew increasingly cheerful, and suddenly he said with a laugh: "Pigtails! How funny that human beings should feel the need to replace their vanished tails in that way!" — As he left me, he said, "Do you know that sometimes, when I have a musical thought, I catch myself with my mouth set just like Beethoven's in his death mask?" — We have supper on the balcony, just the two of us, the happiest of existences. R. watches the sunset, I his face; he talks about the birds, for whom these woods, these green variations, are the earth, on which they suddenly swoop down. He talks of his letters to the King, saying that posterity, if it ever came to know of them, would not understand the tone in which they were written. I: "You have idealized every situation in which you found yourself." He: "I feel a great longing one day to reveal the awful truth about them." He returns to the set mouth and says: "I demonstrated it to you quite wrong, the lower lip should not be thrust forward, it is a grimace of clenched teeth, of keeping silent." I: "Probably peculiar to musicians." He: "Yes, very often, when I am in the grip of some musical idea, I fall asleep like this; it is a sort of enforced silence, from which the sound then emerges." Afterward R. goes for a walk in the palace gardens with the children. They saw fireflies and asked about them; telling me about it, R. says: "What is one telling them when one says it is phosphorus? It's like all our science today and its significance in life." Then I read aloud Lulu's letter—to him who is my support, my adviser in all things! He then goes away, and I stay behind to complete my notebook. Attempt to rescue with roses a butterfly which is fluttering around the lamp. In vain, alas! — The light kills, the rose just smells sweet. (He wrote to Herr v. Hagen.)

Friday, July 19   R. did not have a very good night, something upset his stomach. He wanders out onto the balcony, contemplates the stars. He sleeps soundly from 3 to 7 o'clock. At lunch he expresses satisfaction with his article. After coffee, when we part, he to take his afternoon rest, we hear sounds of *Das Rheingold* being played by the military band. I: "What happiness to hear these sounds, if only in this form!" "They are very heathen sounds, as direct as Nature, no sensibility, no hypocrisy in them." I: "Yes, it was religion which introduced hypocrisy." He: "Say, rather, the *-isms,* Catholicism, Judaism, etc." We go our separate ways: "My familiar spirit, known to me long before my life began," he says to me; I am filled with a nameless feeling, a desire to live *only* in him, to have no cares, no feelings apart from him: it is an overwhelming yearning to be worthy of him, and indescribable grief at not being that—nothing, nothing stirring within me but this single feeling! . . . He reads Strauss's *Life of Jesus* and finds it on the whole better than he expected, except that "by God they always mean the Jewish creator of the world, and do not admit that here it is a manifestation of the divine principle." We drive to the Eremitage with our friends the Glasenapps and the Wolzogens, after I have made some arrangements; after a long walk along the river Main we come to the lower basin, "Wagnerian luck" holds, the sun shines through for the first time and then stays loyal to us by setting beautifully; a table has been set for us under the trees lining the big lawn, and beautiful flowers decorate it, a spirit of gaiety, the lovely artistic setting pleases us, and we are glad that we have been permitted to eat our meal here, rather than in the restaurant garden. R. looks well, his dear countenance is full of vitality, he talks about the Greek theater, saying that in art everything must start out from a convention. Tieck's production of *A Midsummer Night's Dream* was very good, he says, a lively intelligence always makes a good impression. He believes that in his own theater he did more or less the right thing, given the present cultural conditions. Reminiscences of Moscow—when R. refused a second concert, the members of the orchestra asked if they might *at least* have a rehearsal. Very cheerful journey home, the children following behind in a one-horse carriage. Then R. says goodbye to the Glasenapps. We remain a few more moments together, he and I, he is so kind, satisfied with everything, says it all went off successfully. To the G.'s he says, "You see, things are now going well with me."

Saturday, July 20 R. satisfied with his night's sleep, he woke up and got out of bed just once. Letters from the Ritters, the good people are happy at the thought of coming to Bayreuth. I take leave of the loyal Glasenapps. When I was looking through some papers with him yesterday, I came upon the original theme for *"Sangst du nicht, dein Wissen"*; I tell R. that the present one (meant at first for Buddha) pleases me far more. "Yes," he says, "I couldn't do it then, though I felt it; at the time it had to be completed for Weimar, and I found working repugnant." The first really fine day, we drive out in the evening to the Fantaisie. Boni is causing me concern, R. wonderfully kind with his sympathy and help, he speaks to Boni.

Sunday, July 21   Much work in the house, my worry about my child has upset me, and according to R. I had a very restless night; but under his protecting hand I succeed, with thoughts of him, in dispelling all evil effects, and we gain for ourselves another very cheerful day. After the lively Frau Jäger and the W.'s have dined with us, we go to Frau J.'s apartment (in the old palace) with the children to watch a company of tightrope walkers. The spacious square, the people in their Sunday best in the sunset glow, the characteristic houses, and on top of that the great skill of the performers, make a merry scene. "How boring we would find a show like this in Berlin or any other great city!" says R. "In the Prater in Vienna, for instance." I did not watch when the younger son walked up the rope right to the roof, boldly and easily, as I was told. It is not the danger that makes me afraid, but a curious feeling of watching my brother fight for his miserable existence with just such an inner application of courage and presence of mind. All the pity of it overcomes me, and I cannot watch. R. is highly delighted with the skill and assurance of one of the men, and, responding to my persuasions, he goes up to him at the end with the children, to make a substantial extra contribution to the collection; I am told the young man behaved with uncommon courtesy when he did so. R. looked at him for a long while and said, "You have great talent." "How much more pleasure," I said to R., "does one get from giving a little bit more than one intended to such people, than from paying for a box in some theater or other!" A lot of talk, too, about the plucky boy who calmly allowed himself to be carried by the tightrope walker along the rope. I cannot remember when a show gave us so much pleasure as a whole, it has no place at all in our present times. In the morning R. worked without interruption on his article and found enjoyment in it; he says that he is taking on Nietzsche in it, but in such a way that a reader who is not fully in the know will not notice.

Monday, July 22   Great but welcome heat, R. busy, as he says, with theology. At lunch a dismal occurrence; Fidi behaves badly toward his father; the dreadful thought that he might prove unworthy of him takes possession of me, and this thought, instead of being turned against myself in resigned acknowledgment of original sin, turns inside me against my child, and I hit him, so violently that it causes bruises. No words, not even my sobs, can express the horror I feel about myself—oh, fortunate people who lived in times when one could atone! In this instance, as always, R. heavenly toward me. But, alas, no kindness could help me here, and with dread I ask myself what demon constantly lurks in one to cause a normally calm person thus to lose all sense of proportion. It was the first time—will it be the last? I am afraid, and in my desperation I struggle to regain the self-control which is habitual to me. It is not life I now fear, I think, and it is also not death or other people, but *myself!* . . . We drive out to the Waldhütte, returning via the Fantaisie, all the children well and very good. Oh, God, R. said to me that I am noble in all things, yet I must hate myself so!

Tuesday, July 23 A heavy night, and I find it all but impossible to reply to R.'s cheerful morning greeting, I feel like hiding timidly away—alas, to be so unworthy of him! I part from him in tears, and only the thought that this welling remorse, which disturbs his tranquillity, is also an evil luxury, makes me take a grip on myself. I work with the children; we receive our good Frau Jäger, and in the afternoon R. reads me his splendid concluding article. A nice letter from the Knights of the Grail gives him pleasure, and we drive with the children to the Bürgerreuth; first of all we visit the theater and take great delight in it. R. regards the furniture with amusement. "My God, these chairs, these mirrors! And nobody actually owns them." I: "Yes, it is probably the only property without an owner." Then, however, a sad look back on the performances; very emphatically he exclaims: "I should not like to go through all that again! It was all wrong! . . . All the activity kept me going and allowed me to overlook the bad things at the time, but I should not like to go through it again." All the same, we are glad that the theater is there, beneath the trees it looks like an eternal sunset, and it pleases us in its simple polychromy. — A lovely warm evening, R.'s kindness and merriness always shining forth anew—oh, if only I had the strength and the worthiness to erect for him the monument he deserves, the glory of Beatrice as woven by Dante would melt into nothingness! He has raised his own eternal monument in the memory of mankind; what I should like to do is to ensure that through me my children will come to know him, so that, when we are no more, they will love him like a god. Oh, if only I might succeed in this—that they may become good people, noble and pure, honoring him, proud in his memory, superior beings because of the strength of their love for him! . . . When Frau J. told us that they had read the whole of *Faust* in order, R. said, connecting her remark with Gounod's *Faust,* "To start with you said to yourself '*rien, rien,*' then '*tiens, tiens*'!"

Wednesday, July 24 R. slept well, he sets to work on the revision of his article. Chance played into his hands the paper on which I stood security with my property for the sum borrowed from the Gera bank, it causes him concern, but I am able to dispel his worries. I work with the children more busily than ever before. An unfortunate farmer writes to R.; so many people turn to him as if he were a god! In the afternoon R. points out to me on the lawn a tea rose which, as he says, "is as seductive in effect as some sweet poison." I: "Yes, it is rather like the melody of your Flower Maidens." Then he leads me to a pink rose and says, "Here the scent is like something which eludes you when you try to get near it." In the evening anxiety about Fidi; first a cold bath, too long, then too long a walk, he cannot sleep, but my stroking at last sends him off. R. calms me down. Discussion with R. about Tauler's three enemies of mankind: the Devil, the world, and the flesh. Under Devil R. will admit only malice, pleasure in the misfortune of others; I see it as something which suddenly takes possession of us, makes us quite unrecognizable, destroys our whole nature (ambition in Macbeth, jealousy in women). R. talks with restrained anger about Nietzsche's assumption of our failure here, and the inference he draws that we no longer reflect the needs of our time, whereas in fact the attempt has never been made, for the very reason that those in need of it are poor and helpless. — During such prolonged discussions R. and I as if swimming in a broad river; I happy only when I open my whole heart to him, so that he can enlighten and uplift it! . . . R. observes that it is only while working that he must be alone: "Of course even then you are utterly with and in me, but I cannot allow you to approach me in person."

Thursday, July 25 Fidi is not at all ill; but R. and I spent a restless night, R. up from 2 to 6, goes downstairs, reads *Faust* in my room; but despite the disturbance he starts the day in good spirits and does some more work on his revision. He has given up Strauss—too dry and boring—the Ginnungagap of boredom! Referring to his article, he says, "I shall look forward to the theologians' letters." Invited by friend W. to write something about architecture, Herr Reichensperger rather comically says, among other things, "In fact I support the Catholic party." — We decide to take no account of party affiliations on condition that no party views are expressed by party members in articles written for us. A poem attacking the Jews, written in a very repulsive form, pleases R. only to the extent that it suggests the emergence of some sort of popular feeling in this direction. He says, "Better barbaric than this present attitude." — He reads *Le Curé de village* with enjoyment and renewed admiration for Balzac, wonders whether Balzac would not have found him quite unacceptable. I: "Not at all, if he had only heard something from your works and seen you." — Pleasure in Fidi's good health, the night before last R. had seen him fall, and he recalled his dream anxiously when he heard that Fidi's bath had upset him. In the afternoon, while R. is working on his revision, I read *Opera and Drama*. Afterward he plays something from *Parsifal,* Kundry's *"Ich bin müde,"* then reads to us (myself and the W.'s) his article, which is no more an article than the *"Kaisermarsch"* is a march! "Salvation to the savior," I say to R., "that is the motto for this concluding article." "You are bold, my little woman," he replies. He intends to make some alterations in the proofs—regarding Christ's return to earth, for instance, he says his words are somewhat colorless, for he had wanted to avoid being emotional or ironic (with regard to what the theologians have made of Christ, and his assertion that the second coming of Christ can be hoped for only when they have put an end to their confusions). Young Herr Plüddemann here, R. very gay and friendly: "You are off to St. Gallen (as musical director), and I go empty-handed!" Herr Pl. talks about E. T. A. Hoffmann, and R. says that Herr Fischer, the chorus master, who had known Hoffmann, maintained that R. resembled Hoffmann in appearance, or, rather, had reminded him of him; R. observes that this does not surprise him. In the evening some more talk with R. about his article; this is theology, such as Dante discerned and felt it in the characteristics of Beatrice but could not express in words. R. thinks he will do no more writing.

Friday, July 26 R. had a good night, and in the morning I again hear sounds of *Parsifal*. Oh, how blissful I feel! . . . But we have been deprived entirely of our summer, today it is again continually wet and cold. R. said yesterday (Thursday) that he had been looking in the encyclopedia for *Schwanzknochen* [coccyx] and had found Schumann instead! "My God, he, too, has now been dead for 22 years!" R. tells us at lunch that in the morning he had vacillated between Paul and Vir*ginie* (mentioned in *Le Curé de village*) and Parsifal and Kun*dry*. He is enjoying the novel. Over coffee discussion about *Die Jungfrau* [*von Orleans*], which I am reading with Blandine, its weakness the idea that it is necessary to apportion *blame*. R. says, "The temptation of love was impossible here, but through it Schiller showed that he knew what the public wanted." Joan is also not sufficiently naïve, he says, it jars to hear her speaking about the tender shepherdess, but that lies in the nature of dramatic writing: "He did become something of a theatrical writer," R. says. The Montgomery scene is embarrassing, the poet's noble design too apparent, and the scenes between Dunois and La Hire about their love are also disagreeable; but as a whole it is touchingly exalted. R. tells me that in his youth the ending, with Joan in chains, her liberation, then the victory, her death, the recovery of the flag to serve as her shroud—all this had moved him indescribably. Of the short dialogue between La Hire and Dunois he says: "That is a coccyx, a leftover from French tragedy, where there always had to be a love interest, like that between Achilles and Iphigenia. This was something the French missed in my *Rienzi*, though I did also have a coccyx in it." — In the afternoon he reads Balzac and admires his gift for identifying himself in such detail with some apparently insignificant character; in this respect, he says, Balz. was superior to W. Scott (yesterday we were talking about Emperor Maximilian, and R. observed that he could have done with a W. Scott). To be written about in summary fashion makes one feel so insignificant: out of his professor before and during the class, for example, Balzac would have made a complete novel. At lunch we tried to remember whether in *Egmont* Goethe described sleep as "sweet," and what word he then used for the habit of life; it could not have been "violent," R. feels, and it is something very delicate we are here talking about. — The correspondence between Goethe and [Marianne] Willemer does not interest R.: "As if people knew nothing of Goethe except his relations with women!" — He attempts to play some of *Parsifal* but has forgotten almost all of it: "As a musician I'm not worth the price of a mongrel!" he says with a laugh. — In the evening we talked again about his article. He: "Yes, Schop. and others have already spoken about the misfortune that Christianity was propped up on Judaism, but nobody has yet said, 'That is God!'" — Reports of the stupid things singers are doing with the role of Tannhäuser in imitation of Niemann, to the delight of audiences, provokes from R. the sorrowful exclamation "And I cannot speak the truth." —

Saturday, July 27   R. slept well. In the morning he gives me the single hairs from his eyebrows which had grown too long above his left eye, and I am carrying them around with me. The fact that he has hardly any eyebrows seems to me to show the complete absence of animality in his nature. — When I tell him that I have written to my father to explain my failure to visit him, since my presence here is necessary for R.'s tranquillity, he says, "Yes, when one misses someone it is impossible to work." R. is working! The discovery of the orchestral sketch for the new scene in *Tannhäuser* recalls to R. the time when he was composing it: "It was my best time in Paris, I forgot all the misery around me. But of course it is different now, when I no longer work to forget, but to give you pleasure." He tells me he must give up reading the Balzac novel in the afternoon, it absorbs him too much and disturbs his necessary morning tranquillity. After I have given the children their lessons I read the correspondence between Marianne Willemer and Goethe; a gracious and modest person, and some very pretty play-acting! R. says, "They were all of them painters—" Passion banished, a friendly, melancholy, yet serene calmness. — Went for a walk with R.; took Fidi to swimming school, and R. goes in with him to keep an eye on him. At lunch R. mentioned the difficult point at which he has had to take up work again; when I acknowledge the difficulty, he says to me, "But it will all get finished one day." Dull weather, but we were able to have our coffee in the summerhouse; as we part for our afternoon rest, R. says with a laugh, "Your father would be cross with us again." "Why?" "Well, because we are so fond of each other!" Radiant, serene, he recalls his dismal past. — But the heavens outside are overcast, and R. feels worn out by his walk. In the evening reading manuscripts for the *B. Blätter,* without much enjoyment. R. talks in disgust about Nietzsche's denial of inspiration as shown by the Beethoven sketchbooks; it would be better, he says, if such sketches were not published—as if the search for a form for a particular inspiration were a denial of its existence! I observe how even in the most modest realms of thought this process is reflected: yesterday I had clearly discerned a parallel between W. Scott and Balzac—that the former saw an apparition before him and gave it shape, without analyzing its psychological motives, whereas the latter took the apparition apart and examined it atom by atom, through which process it came together as a whole; what I could not possibly express well in words had been as clear as day in my mind, and if I had to express it, my task would be with the help of hard work to reproduce this lightning-flash vision. Played through some chorales in the evening; R. prefers the stark form of Luther's *"Ein' feste Burg"* to any of its later arrangements, even the one by Bach. He finds the modernization of old German songs distasteful. Herr Plüddemann played us one such. The difficulties of party connections emerged during this visit, and R. found himself misled into declaring in Anger-mann's that he had need of nobody, and that the Society of Patrons hindered more than it helped him. A sharp remark from our friend Schuré brings R. to the saddest, most grievous of experiences. We describe to the Wolz.'s our doubts about the sweet habit of life, and when we read the passage, R. says to me, "Suddenly I feel offended by the prose here; we both feel the same about iambic pentameter, and yet here, at this moment, I find prose disagreeable."

Sunday, July 28 R. had a good night. At breakfast we talked about Italians, Arabs, and the fact that the quality of genius seems to be connected with the highest possible freedom in the limbs of a body; all a great statesman needs to do is to think up ways of stimulating Germany's limbs, making them independent. — The quality of genius is past and gone, R. feels, he is disgusted with "the triviality of the jokes—Bismarck's student jokes as well as the Crown Prince's subaltern ones." — He goes off to work, and at lunchtime he comes to me, crying, "Eureka!" What happiness in these words! Since our friends are with us at table, I cannot question him further, but as we part after coffee he says, "I have found it, it is very moving—you will see, I say nothing more." At lunch friend W. talks of a state of ferment against Israel. R. laughs: "Is our *Bayreuther Blätter* responsible for that?" In the evening we are rather tired, as always when we are kept from being together. Several times during the day, when we were unable to talk to each other, R. sang to me, "*Sostegno e gloria d[ell]'umanità!*" Loldi unwell, worry; worry, too, about Boni, but of a different kind. Continual rain.

Monday, July 29 Worry kept me awake, R.'s quiet rest consoled me. He sings, "*Einsam bin ich, nicht allein*" ["I am lonely, not alone"], and thinks of Rosalie, who could not sing it well, however, because her voice was too thin. From this pretty melody, which still delights him, R. goes on to recall other things, dismal ones: how "bad" Minna had been to utilize her meeting with R. in Dresden just to go with him to the law courts and take out a maintenance order against the Einsiedels on behalf of Nathalie. R. says he cannot understand how he came to put his signature to it, he had not given the matter any thought, but it must look very strange. I: "Anyone can see you did it out of kindness." Minna's lack of tenderness shocks R. even now, whereas at the time, and after she had betrayed him, his kindness made him overlook it, as it were. — At breakfast we also talk about the civilizing influence of religions, Christianity and Buddhism, and I wonder "whether these are addressing themselves to the will or only to the appearance, like the other line of thought." R.: "Surely to the will via the appearance." "Then why is their influence so different from that in the other line of thought—for example, in morality?" R. laughs: "I cannot tell you that straight off at 9 o'clock in the morning; we shall have to think about it later." We switch to merry chat: "I like my beautiful Chinese girl and the two humanely resigned Chinese men stirring their tea" (on his breakfast cup). He works; I to my sick little daughter, the lower bones of her spine are too prominent; I read her stories from *The Arabian Nights,* then finish reading *Götz* with Boni. At lunch an article by Dr. Schemann about the *Parsifal* of both Wolfram [von Eschenbach] and R. brings us to the subject of the poem. I remark I do not understand what is meant by the "idea" said to underlie it, and R. agrees with me; he says they ought to draw attention to W[olfram] as a storyteller in the style of Ariosto or even Byron, and not eternally bring up the old fairy tale of his profundity. In the afternoon Eva also ill, heart palpitations and stitches. Both girls very individual, each in her own way. Coming up to Loldi, R. exclaims, "Ah, the little Cosima!" — R. takes Fidi to the baths, enjoys what he calls his first paternal act, dries the boy off, and takes care that he does not catch cold. — Over coffee I saw him suddenly contemplative, with tears in his eyes, preoccupied;

when he then resumed conversation, I asked him what he had been thinking of previously; he told me he had been thinking of a musical passage, whether he should keep it going so long. That was inspiration —and I saw it! — At supper he talks a lot about old age, says that having seen the Norwegian fjords 40 years ago makes him feel like a ghost. The many people he has outlived, and then the extreme youthfulness of the children—"Shall I live to see the girls as young women?" —aroused these thoughts in this eternally young being, thoughts which I tease away with the remark that I am much older than he. We spend the evening alone in great contentment, reading the end of Götz's memoirs. When I tell R. that with the children I cannot recapture my first impression of the play, he says, "To do that we should have to be in Tribschen and read it together." I: "And for that it needs your voice." He has been writing letters to Herr Neumann and to Seidl, then reading Balzac with great interest, even the irrigation affair interests him, it is only the long descriptions of places and houses he does not care for. — Amid never-ending declarations of love we say good night! A butterfly wing, found in the garden, reminds me of what R. once said about a drawing of some wonderful animals: "What would we know of form and line were it not for the existence of such creatures?"

Tuesday, July 30 R. slept well. "Our evening alone together did me good," he says. The girls somewhat better; I repress my worried thoughts about the elder ones. — At breakfast R. mentions the four most original characters literature has given the world: Hamlet, Falstaff, Don Quixote, and Sancho. He works; at lunch we decide on a drive, but the sky soon clouds over again and we give up the idea. R. reads Balzac and writes to his lawyer in Dresden; he says that, by refusing to allow a note of his to be played there, he wants to find out who can hold out longer, he or the Court theater. In this letter he gives himself another ten years of life, which makes me shudder! — They are maintaining in Dresden that, when he was a conductor there, he was under obligation to write operas for the theater! . . . Toward evening Loldi very unwell, running a temperature; the doctor says reassuringly that it is just a slight intermittent fever; I spend a part of the evening with her and then take her into my bed; R. muddles us up, says, "The large one and the small one."

Wednesday, July 31 My little girl did not sleep, but R. had a good night. The doctor calls Loldi's condition a slight attack of rheumatic fever. I overcome my concern and weariness sufficiently to be able to discuss with R. in detail religion and music and their direct influence over the will; when I tell R. I should like to see this more clearly expressed than it has been by Sch., he says, "Then do it; here is ink, a pen, paper; I'll write it down for you, dictate it to me." This leads us to *Die Msinger,* he is pleased with the poem, the invention it reveals. "Music and religion are directed at the will, but since compassion is aroused, the individual is raised above himself to the species level, and to this extent the world is equivalent to God." — I stay at my daughter's bedside; R. "bungles around," as he puts it, having found the ending of the novel so absorbing. He teases me all day long, says I ought to be wearing a hair shirt—he himself disdains the *austérités,* prefers oysters [*Austern*]. I tell him that through him I have been made healthy for all eternity. Not just healthy—no, if there has come into me a single spark of kindness or any other quality which people treasure or gods bless, then it has sprung from him and will return to him in the blessings of love! Bad, raw weather, but my little girl is looking better; I sit beside her and read *Opera and Drama,* R. plays some music, I write to Hans about the future of the two elder girls. Profound discussion with R. about original sin, the transgression of love which Sieglinde is made to realize; then about Véronique, whose "*Non*" in reply to the placatory bishop R. finds splendid; in the morning we talked about the women in the final part of *W[ilhelm] Meister['s Lehrjahre]*; as R. laughingly says, "the happiness of discovering that Therese was the child of a frivolous relationship and can now be rescued from her milk pails!" "Everything as if sketched in pencil." In the evening R. goes into the garden and soon calls me out to see the starry sky flickering gloriously above us; the Milky Way, surrounded by other stars, stretches over our house like a benediction, the Wain looks as if it is being drawn along in triumph: "In Dante the nine Muses point to it," I tell R. A cornucopia of blessings shines down on us. R.: "I no longer have a wish to address to the stars." I: "But I have one." — Back indoors, talking about being happy, R. says, "Either I am, or I can never become so." — He talks about the impossibility of geniuses' emerging from the world in its present state, then about our children, so loving and so loved! . . . We bid each other good night with indescribable feelings of belonging together.

Thursday, August 1 R. says laughingly that he comes to offer me my breakfast on ashes, and we embark gaily on this day, on which Heaven shines dimly! Loldi is very much better; R. works, but he does not seem fully satisfied, says a violin passage—"I am working for Wilhelmj"—is bothering him, he has already written so many of them! — A visit from the conductor Levi, by no means unpleasant, and, as R. says, in his Jewish way he is very touching. R. with him to Angermann's, I meant to arrange a rendezvous with R. in the palace gardens, but the awful weather restrained me—this summer truly "the winter of our discontent"! R. reads Barante's *Ducs de Bourgogne* and is very pleased with the depiction of Joan of Arc. He finds the anonymous story of Bluebeard and the virgin an excellent theme: "I should like to suggest it to some Frenchman as a subject." In the evening conversation turns to the unending denunciations, regret that a stop is not put to them from above. To end with, R. plays the Prelude to *Parsifal;* long since we last heard it, renewed impression! — He says he would not dare give the "*Nehmet hin*" theme to a single instrument, an oboe or a clarinet, for he could not trust present-day instrumentalists to play it with the proper feeling, in the way the clarinetist, for instance, whom Weber had trained, and who had still been active in R.'s time, had played the theme from *Preciosa*. I permit myself to remark that I, too, feel that his orchestra has a different significance and that individual effort, left entirely to the singer, has no place in it as in Weber, and also in the Beethoven symphonies. He agrees with me. As always when guests have been with us, our return to being alone together makes us cheerful and blissful!

Friday, August 2 R. had a good night and tells me the dream he had about two lambs, crouched curiously on top of each other on a ewe's back. "That will bring good luck." At breakfast he laughs heartily over Strauss's expression that "*history does not know what to do with*" a Jesus without sin. He is much amused by the absurd association of history with this phenomenon, and the way of expressing it. He works, and beforehand reads the *Ducs de Bourgogne,* in speaking of which he says to me, "In history it is all the same, reverses or victories, until some great personality comes along, then it becomes absorbing." I say goodbye to Herr Levi, whose feelings toward us arouse complete sympathy. Speaking of the *B. Bl.,* R. said to Herr Levi, "I am interested only in complete truthfulness, I seek no quarrel with anybody, but I shall state my opinion of everything that comes into my mind, sparing nobody." We talk a lot with R. about the attitude of the Israelites to mystical matters, closed doors; then, talking about his own relations with his contemporaries, R. says, "I admit that I no longer wish to sit in an attic and starve—history is not worth that much to me." He opens the glass door, the wind whistles, summer is gone. And the starlings are flying home, we see a whole flock of these returning migrants and watch them. He laughs: "A bad climate, and all this for an artistic ideal!" . . . Then we part, after he has told me, "The only thing I still wish is that you become stronger and I get rid of some of my ailments, then things will become even better and nicer between us, and we shall attain a state of complete ironic happiness." He means by this that we shall look serenely on our complete detachment from the world. — In the afternoon Herr Kellermann, sent by my father at R.'s request to act as piano teacher and copier of scores. A pleasant person with

refined features, already bearing the traces of life's hardships. "We must fatten him up," says R., who thinks he must be a descendant of the Spanish occupation during the Thirty Years' War, since he does not look at all like one's idea of a native of Nuremberg, "and at that time no one could be certain of his birth." — A walk with R., an east wind brings us a clear sky, but, says R., there's a world's ending in store, since the barometer is falling at the same time. I: "That will be the completion of *Parsifal*." We speak also about my last conversation with Herr Levi. He does not seem fully to understand *Parsifal*, and I tell him that R.'s article theoretically bears almost the same relationship to the poem as his words on music (the *loving* woman) and on drama (the man) in *Opera and Drama* bear to Brünnhilde and Siegfried. Through this R. comes to Nietzsche, of whom he says: "That bad person has taken everything from me, even the weapons with which he now attacks me. How sad that he should be so perverse —so clever, yet at the same time so shallow!" In the evening R. goes through Palestrina's *Stabat Mater,* which has just been published, in order to show it to me; it makes a fine impression, but R. feels that if one were to compare it with the painting of that period—a Titian, for instance—one would have to call it a beginning. I now say farewell to this notebook, in which, I believe, I have been more detailed than in the others. For whom am I writing them? Will they give Siegfried what I intended—a portrait of his dear adored father, for whom no love, no admiration is too great? . . . I do not know, and yet I will continue to *"far tesoro"* ["make a treasure trove"] of my memories, even if only for myself!
[*End of the tenth notebook of the Diaries; the eleventh begins:* "In his honor, since all happiness has come from him. Every thought, every heartbeat is his! Dead in all else but to live in him!—" *At the top of the page:* "Begun on August 4, 1878."]

Saturday, August 3 R. had a good night, he goes off to his work. I busy myself with the children and various domestic matters. R. oppressed by the sultry weather, he does so need a blue sky. [*Added in margin:* "Blackbird silence!"] In the afternoon he continues inking in. A young man in Freising writes suggesting that, in order to restore his reputation, R. give a concert for the starving people of China. He would like to see R. freed from slander, and not, like "the great Tilly," pursued by it after his death! — In the evening Baron Seydlitz with wife and mother, the last of whom has not seen R. for 30 years and finds him looking healthier and younger! — An indescribable pleasure for me. R. says, "I shall really live to be very old." When these people have gone, R. tells me that, as he walked past our grave, he imagined to himself how the other would feel when one of us died: to linger on alone for a long time would surely be impossible now. God, who has so far been so gracious to us, will surely remain gracious to us at the end! Thought of past times, of Hans! . . .

Sunday, August 4   "The bells are calling you again," R. says to me at breakfast, "but you have no duties to perform now!" Talk about the function of the German aristocracy—R. would like to see the idea of it revived; then about religion and monasteries on hilltops: "Come unto me, all ye that are heavy laden," the Sermon on the Mount; the monks, who would not be bound by any vows and who would have withdrawn from the world, not in their youth but in their maturity, would descend from the mountains, to share all sufferings and always to stand up for justice. I speak to him about the beauty of his chorus for the Knights of the Grail, and how the theme of the bells, which interrupts their song and at the same time answers it, as it were, gives me the impression of a cheering multitude. At that R. laughs again and says, "Don Quixote is really an offshoot of the Knights of the Grail, the splendid fellow!" "You understand how to help me," he tells me. "All my friends thought I was beyond help, that I would never work again, but you knew I could be helped, and came to my aid." When I leave him he says, "Shall we found a monastery?" I: "There would have to be a place in it for me—even if only as a serving maid." He: "And Fidi as a serving boy." — Small lunch party with the Seydlitzes and the W.'s, after which R. to his afternoon rest and I with friend Wolzogen, who reads to me his article about Valhalla, then to Fidi, who is suddenly unwell. R. goes out with friend W.; on his return he calls me out to show me the rainbow, which is forming an arch between the W. house and our own; he is quite content with his walk, "pleased with the town of Bayreuth"; a conversation with an Israelite piano teacher particularly amuses him, since the man said he tried to recognize the orchestral conductor in him by looking for the "strongly Semitic" outward appearance of which he had been told! In the evening we talk about *Opera and Drama,* I tell R. of the tremendous impression this book makes on me, but I feel one would have to have some very clear ideas of Spontini, Weber, Berlioz to understand it; also, with an expression such as the "hidebound surroundings of Paris," for example, one would need to have experienced the stiffness, poverty of imagination, and conventionality of the French in order to appreciate how brilliantly right this expression is. R. agrees and says these three books, *Opera and Drama, Art and Revolution,* and *The Artwork of the Future,* are his most significant works. We are so blissful at being alone together in the evening, since we feel separated for all eternity when people are with us, even only a few of our best friends.

Monday, August 5　R. had a good night, and Fidi is somewhat better, R. reads the proofs of his article. Friend Klindworth pays us a visit, he brings with him the good news that Hans is looking and feeling very much better. . . . A merry meal, reminiscences exchanged between R. and Klindworth about Manchester Street, where Kl. was living in London. Five students from Leipzig come to pay homage, and Baron Seydlitz wishes us a fateful turn in our affairs! Drive to Emtmannsberg, the road too bad and too long, we turn back and have our picnic in the summerhouse, to the great amusement of the children. [*Added in margin:* "When something is said about the assassination attempt, R. tells a lady that the Emperor, in order to do Bismarck a favor, shot himself, so that B. could then take measures against the Liberals."] — Later on R., Kl., and I begin to talk about Hans; R. still remembers those letters to Senff and is surprised that no one bears him a grudge for them; when he mentions my father, and I reply that the reason for this is probably that my father owes him a debt of gratitude, R. misunderstands my remark and becomes bitter, thinking I am referring to our own position. When we are alone, I explain that I meant this in an artistic sense; R. at once understands and, in order to account for his annoyance, says that always, when someone comes between us, it brings on a sort of paroxysm inside him.

Tuesday, August 6　R. has a slight cold, but he settles down to work and announces joyfully that he has overcome the main difficulty. We walk up and down, then in the *salon;* when I laughingly reproach him for having compared me with "Jungfer Züss" in my conversation with Herr Levi, he says: "Oh, that is my salvation, this ability to convert the most serious of things into nonsense in a flash—it has always kept me from going over the brink. Thus, for example, in the midst of my composing today, I almost wrote down in my composition sketch, 'Now comes Mamsell Kundry.' " — In the afternoon I go through the first act of *Parsifal* with friend Kl., after which R. plays to me what he wrote today (and has already filled out in ink): it is *terribly* beautiful! R. says to me, "With Amfortas it is the pain of languishing, here it is the whole strength of vitality which responds to this ecstasy." — R. again goes to swimming school with Fidi but is very dissatisfied with the way he is being taught. A Herr Glagau has sent us a pamphlet about National Liberalism and reaction; R. considers it good, not tied to any particular party. "Things are stirring," he says. A visit from our six friends in the evening; Kl. plays some Chopin, which R. enjoys. Then at last alone together again. — When our friend was reluctant to fold his hands for grace at lunch today, R. reproached him with self-consciousness and spoke splendidly and at length about religion, saying how this trivial cult of atheism is to blame for the loss of reverence and the fact that in religion people now see nothing more than just the Jewish God.

Wednesday, August 7   R. had a good night's rest and does some work; I busy with the children, correspondence with Hans concerning Daniella, and household books! — At lunch and during the afternoon, reminiscences of the festival performances, how fantastic it all appeared from the outside, the moments that turned out well, the frustrations (Richter's tempi). "As far as honor and glory were concerned, it was incredible," R. says, "and people must think me mad for not being satisfied with it." — He also tells Kl. about his "Never again" when, in the concluding scene, after Siegfried's body had been removed, he saw that yet again Richter had not understood him. We also talked about Hans and his sad experiences in America; concern that he might again be overworking. Having now finished the story of Joan of Arc, R. lays the *Ducs de Bourgogne* aside. In the evening a conversation about the death penalty, R. explains his views on this to Kl.— the false humanitarianism, the way of covering things up, which is the result of the community's bad conscience. Then music, a ballade by Chopin and Beethoven's E Major Sonata. R. says laughingly today, "I am a mixture between Hamlet and Don Quixote."

Thursday, August 8   R. slept well and goes to work; while working, as he tells me, he was somewhat disturbed by the "banging," the thunderstorm was "like an old man in a rage hurling everything about." Talking to Kl. about his experiences in St. Petersburg, he says that the Prelude to *Lohengrin* was played so beautifully that, standing at the head of this orchestra of 140 players, he had a sort of Joan of Arc vision. — Then he talks of the marriages of most of his friends, and laughs: "They are all donkeys, except for me!" — Friend Wolz. comes and reads to me an article by Dr. Schemann, which astonishes us with its mixture of ideas, some sloppily and inaccurately expressed, some very good, and some rather perverse! — R. goes for a walk with our friends, and after that a part of the first act of *Parsifal;* at Amfortas's words to Kundry R. says, "More languid, with calm deliberation: he loves another, whose name also begins with *C.*" In the evening reminiscences: Berlioz in Paris and in London, then the *Tannhäuser* business, many good experiences, but the Germans always bad—for example, when R. wrote in his account of the production that the Jockey Club was to blame for the scandal, the German newspaper in Paris observed that others had been there as well; whereupon R. wrote to the editor, saying he was willing to concede that the Germans, his fellow countrymen, were also partly to blame. In the evening R. says to me regarding *Parsifal:* "I sometimes have my doubts about the whole thing, whether it is not nonsense, a complete failure; but I can see the coming and going (during Gurnemanz's narration) and know how it ought to be." "Whatever you do, don't think of the production" is then his constant exhortation.

Friday, August 9   R. somewhat run down, he has pains in his chest and a slight hemorrhage. I implore him not to work, and try to ensure that he talk as little as possible; in the evening friend Klindworth plays us a Chopin prelude, which gives R. great pleasure. My entry today will be short, for the whole day's effort consisted in taking good care of R. It was the playing of the new page the day before yesterday, and of the first act yesterday, which put such a strain on him. Any contact with others is too much for him, he says with a laugh: "I must retire with you to Paris—there one is not molested." Herr Glagau's pamphlet has interested him. Socialists and Catholic party are said to be in alliance, and R. thinks many people who can no longer go along with National Liberalism and Bismarckism have sought refuge beneath the Catholic party banner.

Saturday, August 10   R. wakes up with a protesting "Oh, no!"; he dreamed that I had gone away. He is still very run down, and the doctor, whom I sent for, says he should not exert himself, and so this day, too, is restricted to care and quietness. I talk to Kl. about Hans and the children, then I give lessons, write letters, listen to the rest of Schemann's article, and long for his recovery! — Departure of friend Kl. —

Sunday, August 11   R. still very weak; we enjoin silence and keep strictly to ourselves. R. reads: he has taken up the *Ducs de Bourgogne* again, with Charles the Bold. He has had another look at his clarinet solo, he tells me, and is pleased with it. I pay some calls, during which I hear news of the general situation. The Emperor is said to be looking very downcast, in a way that has never been observed before; the elections have turned out badly, and the government has little idea what to do about the black-red-gold International. — We spend the evening in quiet and gentle conversation and go off to bed at 10 o'clock. Talking about the *Ducs de Bour.*, R. remarks how differently one gets to know the characters in Shakespeare, and we read the scene in R[ichard] III, which always seems new to us, where the King comes to Lady Grey [Queen Elizabeth] and her relatives in the palace; the energy and wit, the power of the language make a direct impact, as if it were all happening before one's eyes.

Monday, August 12   R. had a good night, but he still feels weak and complains of stabbing pains in his heart, he says it is like a clock in which something is blocked up, but the doctors will not allow that there is anything wrong with his heart. Nice, original letter from the King. Although he is so run down, R. goes to his work and begins to feel better as the day proceeds. We go for a walk together in the garden, he inspects the new aviary (I tell him that, like Faust, he is in his element creating external things); then we have our "beer session" in the garden, feeling happy and content. "This is what we always wanted," he says. "From now on I shall only invite people along when we stop appreciating how happy we are." — The children with us off and on, climbing (Loldi in particular) fearlessly on the beams of the aviary, and in the end they bring me a spider ("at night brings delight"), R. admires the delicacy of its legs. — I talk a lot with R. about *Opera and Drama*, he opens the book and, reading a point in it, recognizes with pleasure the unity of his whole life and work. — In the *Ducs de Bourgogne* he takes great enjoyment in a speech by Louis XI to his generals before a battle; he reads it to me and says, "This fellow was a true Shakespearean character." — In the evening *Boni* reads Glagau's pamphlet to us; my left eye is refusing to function. The description of the various parties very good, sharp and witty observation.

Tuesday, August 13 R. slept well, but his catarrhal condition (slight bronchitis) has still not quite cleared up. He works all the same, and we spend a happy time drinking coffee in the summerhouse. "Here, here, beloved, let us stay," says R. An English illustrated periodical with pictures of Bristol reminds us that R. once thought of hiding himself away with me there. A play called *Garrick in Bristol,* seen in Dresden, gave him such a good impression of the ancient town. Today is an anniversary of the festival, friend Wolzogen sends us some nice roses and some nice words; otherwise all is still, nobody has remembered the day, and we feel genuinely happy in our solitude. We go to see our friend, who is unfortunately not well, and silently celebrate the occasion; a raw wind is blowing, and R. feels run down; he should never leave Wahnfried, he feels. — In the evening Boni continues reading us the pamphlet. "Evil things I there espy."

Wednesday, August 14 R. dreamed that he introduced a ballet into the Kundry scene, including a bolero; that he wanted to play something to his wife Minna, who, on hearing the accompaniment, opened her eyes wide in astonishment and said it was from *La Muette,* whereupon he: "That is just the accompaniment, stupid, now listen to the melody!" He works, and I have my hands full with housekeeping books, children, etc. — Still wretched weather, rain and wind, drafts everywhere; *Kindschy* is behaving badly, says R., who frequently tells the story of the pastry cook in Leipzig who on Sundays, when the weather would not clear, used to throw his doughnuts toward the sky with the words "Eat them yourself!" — In the afternoon, while I am writing to Lusch, R. plays some music downstairs, and he tells me afterward he was working on Kundry; Brange came in, and that made him feel

"Kundryesque." In the evening finished Herr Glagau's pamphlet; a terrible picture of conditions in our country; R. says that now at last he knows what became of those French billions. Concern over friend W.'s health, R. writes reassuringly to his wife, urging caution. In the evening R. takes a little notebook out of the drawer of his desk: "These are my recipes, so to speak."

Thursday, August 15   R. had a good night and laughs with me over a scene in the *Ducs de Bourgogne* which amused him greatly, namely, the scene in which Charles the Bold is expecting the King's crown, and Frederick III, to avoid giving it to him, departs secretly for Cologne in the early morning on a ship. Then he talks about "old" Jehovah in the burning bush, "like old Ziethen." — Cheered by our morning conversation, we go each to our own work, but unfortunately guests soon tear us away from it. The presence of Herr Sucher, the conductor in Leipzig, and his wife obliges R. to make conversation, and about things he now finds disagreeable; then the change of diet for our meal—in short, it all has a bad effect on him, and after his afternoon rest he comes to me looking worn out. "Everything one hears about the outside world only upsets one," he says. He tells me he has written to Zumpe. "Zumpe and Wolzogen are the two opposite poles of which I am the center—they know nothing about each other." Of the conductor Sucher: "He is a typical *Musikant,* a brand of persons who do not really belong to me. Brendel was right when he said once that present-day musicians (your father and I) differ from all previous ones by possessing intellectual faces; intellectuality is not a quality of musicians." — "Lucky that the self is divided, that both of me can be with you," he adds, "for otherwise there is nobody with whom one can talk." Letter from our dear Frau Materna, R. praises her as the only one who is warm and natural. Recently he said that, if all else failed, he would engage her for Kundry after all. Delight in the children, in Fidi's sketchbook (towns: *Wankel, Ruheborn,* etc.), in the names they give to the workmen building the aviary; one of them, who stretched himself out on a bundle of brushwood and covered his head, they have named the Sleeping Beauty, for instance. In the evening Boni reads to us from *Opera and Drama,* which I find more and more absorbing; the words on Ariosto, on Iphigenia, and the comparison with Beethoven's symphonic form are utterly superb; perhaps not quite easy to grasp for those who cannot distinguish between a work of art and an artistic phenomenon. R. shares my pleasure. "It is all an idea," he says, "and I can remember with what passion I wrote it. It is a protracted duologue, with Sulzer, for example, to whom I wanted to clarify all the things which had become clear and definite to me in the course of our conversation. No possibility of dividing it into paragraphs, for this reason alone." — A lovely evening, exchanging such impressions and thoughts.

Friday, August 16   R. did not have a good night, he got up and read the *Ducs de Bourgogne;* this the usual result of having guests; we discuss whether he gave himself indigestion. "Oh, it is everything together," he says, "the fact that one drinks more, above all the conversations with people who mean nothing to one." He tells me about the sophisms which friend Feustel in his capacity of Reichstag deputy has now learned and got into the habit of using, for example, about the denunciations and how nothing can be done about them; how the world now consists of similar attitudes which are certainly sophisms. I tell R. in reply that his violence of expression, for which he is so often admonished, is for me just a sign of his instinct for recognizing the world's falsehoods, and that he often, unconsciously, does not listen to others because he does not wish the truth to be obscured—and it almost always is imperiled on such occasions. For as a rule nobody is more forbearing, more willing to listen to others, than he—indeed, when he trusts in another's integrity, he has often enough taken hollow phrases to be genuine opinions and has defended them, even against the facts. His violence is his "Get thee behind me, Satan," for even to listen would be to make a pact with falsehood and destroy his holy indignation. — R. eats nothing at lunch. Afterward, as we are conversing alone together, he points to a bleak sky and says, "I wouldn't care about *Kindschy,* either, if only there were no other people on earth and we were always alone together like this." But he also says to me, "I should like to hear Berlioz's *Les Troyens,* that quiet '*Italie, Italie*' chorus —do you know why I say this?" I: "I suppose you mean we should go to Italy?" Today we drew up a plan for Fidi's future reading. *Philosophy:* Schopenhauer. *Religion:* Eckhart, Tauler. *Art:* R. Wagner. *Natural history:* Darwin. *History:* Greeks, Romans, English. *Novels:* W. Scott, Balzac. Frenchmen, Italians (Machiavelli). Otherwise all minds of the top grade (but *only* these): Goethe, Schiller, Dante, Calderón, Shakespeare, Homer, Aeschylus, Sophocles. No German historians, R. says, "I have read Ranke's *Reformation,* and I felt as if I had a piece of blotting paper in front of me, on which one can see just a few individual letters; it is all so hazy." Arrival of the *B. Blätter* with the splendid 3rd installment of "Public and Popularity." Nice letter to me from Kl. with sad comments on the present *Tannhäuser* in Munich. — R. spends a very quiet day; I go for a walk in the garden when the sky clears, delighting in our pretty home; a rose, wonderfully graceful and fragrant, regards me with regal mildness, and the rosy clouds glowing above me seem like a reflection of its beauty. As the sun bids farewell in golden glory, indescribable emotions stir within me and come together in a humble prayer. . . . Denial of life—if Christianity can be a religion on this account, not so the church, which, through the contradiction of being of the world and against the world, must needs become an organized hypocrisy. True, nondenominational Christianity calls to us from life itself, and all who suffer hear the call! — R. comes to join me, asks what the dogs will think, seeing me wandering all on my own: "They must have been quarreling." — But he soon leaves me, and in the evening has to eat very abstemiously. — Boni reads to us a leaflet sent from Bern, also dealing, in remarkably cultured language, with present conditions, which it describes as "depraved." Then a few pages of *Opera and Drama*. We feel peculiarly sad about the news brought us by the children that the graceful and daring young tightrope walker to whom R. recently spoke a few friendly words here fell from the rope in Regensburg and is now dead. — R. thinks the authorities should forbid these performances. — When R. complains of his upset stomach, I blame myself for having lost the moral courage I once possessed and not warning him off. "So," says R., "I have destroyed you utterly, molded you entirely anew?" I: "I hope so." —

Saturday, August 17 I got up during the night, in the belief that R. was also up, but he was still in bed, and I had the pleasure of smiling with him over my concern. He slept tolerably well, and we begin the day in amiable mood, in spite of *Kindschy,* who again threw things around last night and today is blowing! "Oh, how lucky I am that I got you!" R. says. "Or, rather, that you existed, for the getting was not so easy." I: "You forget that I exist only because of you." [*Added in margin:* "When I chanced to look yesterday at a book now being used by the children and found in it some very melancholy thoughts written down by me in French about 18 years ago, I felt perhaps more clearly than ever before that it is through him that I have lived and am living."] R.: "Oh, rot, there were others existing at the same time as me." — "But it is nice that we have children, they belong to it, they are the seal on it." Yesterday he was pleased with Fidi's meditative expression: "Perhaps there's not much behind it yet, but it shows his propensities." In connection with *Opera and Drama,* for an assessment of which I have drawn up a little plan, I told R. I should like to see a plan prepared for the *B. Blätter,* in which the basic idea we have received from him might be applied to all spheres—school, house, theater, all the arts; and R. agrees with me. — He is pleased with the simplification of the gods' serving staff in the *Ring,* made clear to him through Herr v. W.'s article "Valhalla." When he leaves me I am glad to see how well he looks. "Yes," he says, "it's sorrow that drags one down," and, with that sudden change from seriousness to humor which is so characteristic of him, he adds with a laugh, "A peach does less damage than deep sorrow"—for the day before yesterday he had eaten a peach. The play of his eyes when this sudden change of mood takes place is wonderful—humor breaks through the melancholy of his expression like a flash of lightning through thundery clouds. He works; when he tells me that he is making slow progress, I observe that his happiness is responsible, and he agrees. — After lunch I visit friend Wolzogen and return home concerned about his health. There is happiness only in Wahnfried; I tell R. that on my return I asked the governess, "Have you seen my husband?" and she replied, "Yes, and he asked me, 'Have you seen my wife?' " R. compares returning to Wahnfried with reaching the sheltering cliffs of Norway. In the evening we read the horrible details of Hödel's execution. R. intends to express his thoughts on capital punishment in the *Blätter.* Three of the Pringsheims have announced their resignation from the Society!

Sunday, August 18 A good night and a nice day; R. tells me a story from the *Ducs* which has amused him—about Emperor Fr. III relating the fable of the bear. He says that Fidi's voice frequently sounds to him like a drop of water falling into water, so full is it. He says he dreamed that Fidi already had a beard, something like Glasenapp's. Splendid weather, R. resolves on a drive, and we set out at 4 o'clock; delight in the air, the sky, our being alone together, above all in the stillness of the woods. "All this talk with strangers, even with friends— it is just a waste of time, an empty nothing, I can literally feel it here in my breast!" As we pass by a stone, I say, "One must let it lie," and this leads R. to thoughts of the beauties of *Faust* and "its quiet, refined humor; when R[ichard] III says, 'Let it strike,' it's not the same kind of humor." — Meeting with a chamber-music player named Thiele, who played under R.'s direction 30 years ago; since R. praises him, I ask whether he became a concertmaster. "Oh, no," R. says, "they always appoint those from outside, it must be someone famous, and you can't become that by staying in one spot." — We drive home via the Fantaisie, and Frau Jäger, who also happens to be at the Waldhütte, remarks that our carriage looks like a summer pavilion— and it is true that we are in the gayest of spirits. "The pressure is vanishing," R. says of his chest, and he is looking splendid. He talks about Christianity and Buddhism, how Christ could not have approached his people with visions of eternity, which the Indians grasped so easily; he chose *the kingdom of Heaven,* which is yours if you are good, and no expression could be better than that, so vague and at the same time so certain. Again it is Renan to whom R. owes this view of his. Then, goodness knows by what leap of imagination, he comes to "The King of Thule," in which, as he jokingly says, a "point" is lacking; Goethe provided a picture, but no happening; he will not accept that the dying mistress could have given the King a cup, but then he decides that this gives it its heathen air, remarking that she probably thought to herself, "This fellow never stops drinking," and so gave him something to remember her by! I observe that it is all left vague in a folklike way. It reminds R. of a poem called "The Song of the Swan," which his sister Rosalie had also thought not quite right: a hunter, tired of life, threw himself into the water, was rescued by a swan, but now, having regained his taste for life, has always to be expecting the swan, summoning him to death. Then he remembers that when, after a concert in Leipzig given by Frau Schröder's daughter Wilhelmine, he had played the Venusberg theme at the Brockhauses', Mendelssohn had asked eagerly, "What is that?" R.: "Do you think I am going to reveal it to you?," and Mendelssohn immediately sat down and played it himself. — In the evening R. reads to me the passage in *Opera and Drama* about Antigone; when I express to him my admiration for this work, R. says, "I was completely obsessed with it at the time, I could not have composed a single note of music, so absorbed was I in it." Our poor friend Nietzsche seems to have got quite a lot of his ideas on humanity from it.

Monday, August 19   R. slept well. Cheerful breakfast with all kinds of talk about Beethoven's quartets, the tempo markings, and many other things I cannot note down here. Of his present reading he says, "The whole of history is after all nothing but a repetition of 'Reynard the Fox,' until a great and noble man comes along," but he takes great pleasure in Louis XI, in whom he discovers certain features which remind him of Frederick the Great. Our coffeetime in the afternoon consists of nothing but anecdotes from this history book and is very lively. — A week has passed since I last wrote in my diary—I must try to remember: on the evening of the Monday my friend Luise Voss arrived, to my great delight, and spent the morning of Tuesday the 20th with me, again manifesting to me her great sympathy. In the afternoon of Tuesday the 20th my father arrived, looking better than I have seen him for years; cheerful and talkative, a delight both for R. and for me. Much intimate chat.

Wednesday, August 21   In the morning R. enlarges on my father's unique aristocratic personality, everything about him refined, princely, grand, yet at the same time full of artistic genius. The children given a holiday, but R. works; I show some signs of tiredness; Frau v. M[eyendorff] arrives from Weimar. In the evening my father plays a "*Fantaisie*" by Herr v. Bronsart, and R. and I admire the kind indulgence with which he judges such weak products.

Thursday, August 22   For me somewhat distracted life, R., however, works on undisturbed, he tells me I shall see in what a completely different way the Parsifal theme emerges. He is in very good spirits and shows nothing but delight over my father. He tells him, among other things, that he will from now on read only French books, for German books are like an unstraightened bedroom, one stumbles here over a bootjack, there over a pair of stockings, and so on. At lunch my father enlarges upon the hunting fanfare in *Tannhäuser,* its beauty, originality. R. says it is worth the trouble of writing things for him. Then R. plays the fanfare from *Euryanthe,* which he loves very much and prides himself "on playing particularly well!" At supper much talk about Berlioz and his nastiness toward my father. The evening spent in chat.

Friday, August 23　R. did not have a good night, he spends the morning writing to the King for his birthday. In the afternoon he plays *"Komm', holder Knabe"* from *Parsifal,* this captivates my father at once, R. fetches the manuscript, and then the whole second act up to the kiss is gone through, R. thrilled by the fascination the divine work exerts on my father and radiating genius, greatness, kindness!

Saturday, August 24　R. somewhat run down, his chest hurts him when he sings; my father is also ill, even has to take to his bed. I keep him company, read him the article on Cromwell in Voltaire's *Diction-naire,* and later amuse R. by saying that Bismarck ought to appear in the German Reichstag like C. in the English parliament—with a clock.

Sunday, August 25　Our wedding day! The children congratulate us nicely, Loldi gives us a water color which she painted under the guidance of Frl. Schinkel, Wolzogen's aunt, and R. reflects at length on how things were, how they might have been. "That time in Zurich (1858)," he says, "I should have taken you off to Venice with me, I was finished with my wife, your relationship with Hans was not yet formed, and you had no children; but I was as stupid as Tristan, and you were that silly goose Isolde. We would have remained in Italy, and everything would have made sense!" — In the afternoon we drive out to the Eremitage, which pleases my father, too. (Friend Wolzogen sent some nice roses with a nice note.)

Monday, August 26　Departure of Frau v. Meyendorff. R. works: [Kundry's] *"Ich sah ihn und lachte."* — In the afternoon we go through the 2nd act again, to my father's utmost admiration. R. says to me, "I am content, I have been successful with you again." My rapture is the tear which flows in bliss at this revelation. After supper a game of whist between Father, Richard, and me!

Tuesday, August 27　R. had a good night and he works; I go to the station to meet our dear friend Malwida [von Meysenbug], and her visit is a great joy to us. In the gayest fashion R. teases her about her socialism. In the evening we go through my father's *Dante* Symphony,

that is to say, he plays it to us, and, after he has left, R. talks about
this highly poetic conception, how beautifully he has avoided all
suspicion of mere musical scene-painting, a trap into which Berlioz
would certainly have fallen; how beautiful the feeling in the *Purgatorio*
section—one does not know whether it is contrition or hope which
does not dare, as it were, to raise its head there; how beautiful the
fugato! But there is no public for it now, he adds; education is necessary,
to understand it one must have some idea of Dante and also a knowledge
of Catholicism. My father's indescribable modesty about his works
touches R. very much—he says with splendid high spirits that he has
himself "stolen" so much from the symphonic poems. . . .

Wednesday, August 28   R. slept well and works. At lunch with friend
Feustel he has a discussion about the law on the socialists, which our
friend thinks a good one. After lunch R. tells me he has found a
melody which pleased him very much, but it was too broad for
Kundry's words; he was considering writing new words for it when
suddenly a counter-melody occurred to him, and thus he now has what
he wanted: the orchestra would get the broad melody, which here
expresses the emotions, while she has the theme for her hurried
words. — An alarming letter from K. Klindworth, who tells me Hans
is again in danger of losing all his savings! — Difficulty in controlling
my fears. — Wrote very seriously to Lulu. Arrival of the chickens,
peacocks, pheasants, etc., the surprise R. had prepared for me, as he
says; since the aviary is not yet finished, they cannot yet be seen, but I
hear one of them giving the trombone call from the second act of
Lohengrin! In its fear it also literally spoke—cried, "Ow! Ow!" Children
on the roof of the chicken house, singing, "Oh, how happy I am in
the evening," as R. and I and my father pass by. In the evening the
Wolzogens and Frau Jäger, my father plays us Beethoven's E Major
Sonata and his own *Orpheus*. Beautiful impressions. R. again praises
the noble poetic conception in *Orpheus*.

Thursday, August 29   R. still well and working in the best of spirits;
at lunch he sings the theme which he jokingly mentioned a few days
ago, after hearing the *Dante* [Symphony], when he said he had stolen
much from my father; R. calls his symphonic poems *un repaire des
voleurs* [a thieves' den], which makes us laugh heartily. All sorts of
things are being told us about the chickens, the children declare that
one of the cocks sang something from the *Siegfried Idyll!* . . . In the
afternoon went through some of *Parsifal* (1st act), and in the evening
certainly the most original whist game imaginable—my father, Richard,
and I, and Malwida as onlooker; R. bubbling over with wit, high
spirits, and friendliness, the very epitome of Nature's serenity, in-

domitable strength, and creative urge; my father mild and amiable, like a reflection of its melancholy! —

Friday, August 30 R. decrees breakfast in front of the chicken house! The birds are enthroned, children, guests, and we spend a happy morning of celebration in mild weather. When the "two geniuses" have left us, I stroll through the garden with Malwida, and she goes into raptures about R., saying she has at last seen an example of an incomparable old age; she tells me it is I who created this happiness, without me there would have been no festival, no Bayreuth; I listen to her with a thankful heart and remind her of my life's transgression, which enabled me to live for him alone and in him to find my salvation, and that it was from this all the blessings have sprung. Comparison between my father and R.'s essence and being. Concern over Fidi, he looks pale and, as R. says, "peaky." — In the evening a game of whist, this time with Malwida, after my father has played us several of Chopin's preludes, which please R. very much. [*Added in margin here but perhaps referring to the following day:* "In the evening R. spoke with great antipathy about Rome, saying all the monuments there bore witness to infamous and enslaved human beings, from the Roman emperors to the Jesuit churches and cardinals' palaces. Different in Florence, Genoa, Venice."] (In the afternoon we were with the Wolzogens, my father played his *Dante* Symphony to them.)

Saturday, August 31 Departure of my father, the leave-taking unfortunately much disturbed for R. by torment at the station: the delayed train, the noise, it was all a torture to him; on top of that four lovely pigeons which he ordered have flown away. But in spite of these vexations we had a nice outing with the children to the Fantaisie, where we ordered our lunch for the following day. But in the evening the sad mood returned. He made up his mind not to talk and did not even say good night, but in bed he took my hand, weeping, and kissed it. —

Sunday, September 1 Having been depressed by R.'s mood, I have to reproach myself severely for not being able to respond at once to his cheerfulness today, thereby causing him sorrow; but soon everything between us was again what it always is and must be, and, after having breakfast in the summerhouse, we drive out to the Fantaisie, where we have lunch. The somewhat raw day and delay over the meal prevents our carrying out our plan of going to the Waldhütte, and we return straight home, to spend the evening in conversation with our dear Malwida, with whom we feel more at ease and in tune than with anybody else in the world.

Monday, September 2 R. slept well and works again today after two days' break (in order to accompany my father he also interrupted his work on Saturday); he comes to lunch very cheerful, and when, on returning from paying some calls with Malwida, I go to greet him, I find him preoccupied, searching; I withdraw, and presently hear him improvising. The pigeons have been recaptured, R. very pleased about it. — Also Fidi is looking better. At supper R. declares how necessary it is for him to be absolutely alone when he is working, he does not want even those dearest to him near him, though he much likes to gaze, for example, at my portrait. (Resumption of my work with the children.)

Tuesday, September 3   Nice letter from the King; R. working ("*bist du Erlöser*"). In the morning he showed me a page of musical notes: "My catch from yesterday," he said. At lunch conversation about the Austrian advance into Bosnia, which seems like rashness on Andrássy's part. Malwida tells us that almost everywhere a general conflagration is expected as a result of the Congress decisions! Long letter of advice to Loulou! — We take a pleasant walk to Birken, a conversation about the mountains reminds R. of Hoffmann's story "*Die Bergwerke von Falun*," and in his wonderful way he reads us this work, the poetical conception of which he finds superb; some weaknesses of style are in our opinion far outweighed by the beauty of its design. R. feels it must have been influenced by Tieck's "*Runenberg*."

Wednesday, September 4   Nice morning, R., after a good night's sleep, orders the horses, and in splendid weather, after he has done some work in the morning, we drive out to the Waldhütte. I had the feeling that I had never seen R. looking so radiantly well; with him in indescribable high spirits and the children in constant fits of laughter, we reach the woods in the most glorious sunshine; we leave the carriage for a while outside the Waldhütte and, at R.'s instigation, take a path which is delightful but which necessitates some climbing; soon R. is no longer looking so well, he becomes silent, I am beset by feelings of gloom, and in a mood as melancholy as it had earlier been carefree we return home as night begins to fall. The rising moon sparsely illuminates the countryside which had previously seemed to me so cheerful, now so sorrowful! R. is monosyllabic, but back home he tells me that he suddenly felt the stabbing pains in his chest again and spat up a little blood. Then he remembered that the doctor had advised him against walking uphill. — A letter to me from Herr Levi provides material for discussion in the evening. R. speaks of religion as it is regarded by most people: they believe in it as if it were a sort of magic, as if the Pope had the means of getting us to Heaven one way or another. He reads aloud, to our great amusement, a passage in which L[ouis] XI said he did not wish people to pray for the salvation of his soul—only for the health of his body.

Thursday, September 5 During the night I noticed that R. was no longer lying beside me, I got up to look for him and found him sitting in his workroom, reading the *Ducs de Bourgogne;* he told me he had congestions. In the morning he told me the dream which had woken him up: more and more people were forcing their way into his house, among them Klindworth, and finally Nietzsche, who said a lot of malicious things to him and poured scorn on the melody of the "Pilgrims' Chorus" in *Tannhäuser,* that is to say, sang a lampoon on it. R. said to him, "I suppose you treat me like this because I am un-armed?" — I inquired through a window what was the matter, and in order not to alarm me, he told me that Nietzsche was reading his new poem to him; then the uneasy magnitude of his distress woke him up. All day long he looks run down, but he does a little work (he tells me I will be amazed by the simplicity of "*sein Blick*"). Various vexatious matters from Leipzig and Hamburg: the director in H. indignant that R. does not profess unreserved confidence in his conductor. The Leipzig director now seems unwilling to engage Herr Jäger; in short, as R. says, the outside world brings him nothing but vexation; and, which strikes him as saddest of all, he gets no pleasure from thinking of the performance of *Parsifal.* Better perhaps not to perform it at all? . . . In the evening he is still very run down; he asks Malwida to describe to us the building housing the international exposition, and she does so, praising its brilliance and magnificence. R. remarks in this connection, "To have nothing at all to do with this whole civilization whose most prominent expression is Paris, to be entirely strange to it!" — Separated for the night; fervent prayers for R.'s good health. He looks run down.

Friday, September 6 R. had a tolerable night, though he did get up once and is still somewhat languid. Reverting to the subject of the impression made by the international-exposition building, I observe that the fact the French have succeeded so well without Emperor N. is the best proof that people do not need princes. Then R., speaking of the German princes, says, "They do harm with their lack of usefulness, for they could be of infinite use, and their not being so is harmful." He works; at lunch he looks somewhat better, he tells me his dream, in which he saw a spider on my neck and shooed it away. We return to the subject of princes, R. remarks how usurpers left their sons with the necessity of performing great deeds, and their rule soon came to an end (the Lancastrians and Philip of Macedonia and Alexander); a legitimate prince, he says, does not have this need, whereas N. III had always to perform tricks like a buffoon. We tell Malwida about the May Festival, and R. says it was something unique, never to be re-peated, like the *Idyll* on the staircase. — Over coffee we read a biography

of R. in a musical encyclopedia, written by a Herr Musiol, and are
delighted with the correctness of his judgment on *Opera and Drama*.
A nice warm day, which does R. good. He still enjoys the garden and
once again loses himself in making Arabian-style construction plans:
he would like to turn the forecourt, where the King's bust stands,
into a conservatory with a glass roof and palm trees, he already sees it
in his mind. But in the afternoon he says, "I have given up my construction plan." Before that he had laughingly quoted Dr. Wille, who
once remarked, when N. III's buildings were being praised, "All
disagreeable tyrants used to build." — He talks a lot, among other
things of a journey to Naples in the winter, for he has decided in
favor of a stay amid natural surroundings, rather than in "picture-
gallery cities." — I wish it for the sake of his health and as recuperation
from his exhausting work. Today he composes "*Und ob mich Gott und
Welt verstösst, in dir entsündigt sein und erlöst.*" — In the afternoon visit
from friend W., who tells us Bismarck's latest saying—that he cannot
go along with the Catholic church, *it has nothing to offer*—which indeed
amuses us greatly. After R. has joined us for a while, I beg him to
leave us and just to read (*Ducs de Bourgogne*), and he does so. Toward
evening he calls us to have some beer with him, takes great delight in
the children, who have harnessed the two dogs to a cart. After that
rest again, and reading. A Herr Hacker in Würzburg sends us a book
about some aspect of Goethe, with a nice letter; R. says, "If only
people would look not so much at the insides of the poets, but a little
around themselves!" In the evening our friends the Jägers; R. at first
in rather poor spirits, but he soon cheers up and talks about two
popular figures in Dresden some time ago, Peter Kroll and Jungfer
Sternickel, and how once, returning from school with Ottilie, he had
come upon Peter Kroll in his curious clothes and three-cornered hat,
being followed by all the street crowds of Dresden; the children were
looking on in silent alarm, as if watching a ghost, and then he shouted
at them, "Well (using a swear word), don't you have tongues in your
heads?" — He liked being the butt of scandal. Then we talked about
the peculiar secret tribunal now active in Russia, three more people
have been murdered, and in the hand of one of them was found his
death sentence, in his heart the dagger— When, before going to bed,
R. adjusts Fidi's blankets, Fidi says softly in his sleep, "Now I shall
scratch you," which makes R. laugh heartily.

Saturday, September 7 R. slept well; he drinks his Ems water,
complains a little still about pressure in his chest, but seems somewhat
better. Talk in the morning about all sorts of things, about Nietzsche—
how from this corm we raised a flower, but the corm itself remains an
ugly thing. About quickness in the uptake, which is what makes for

genius and gives a man power over others; he gives as an example Nap. I at the Battle of Arcole, which he describes to me. After this conversation he gets up, comes to my bed, embraces me tenderly, calling me his "slender happiness," and goes off to his work saying, "I am an outrageously lucky man," and adding with a laugh, "You must not be cross that we are so fond of each other." At lunch he tells us that in fact he began the morning with a nap, after which he felt terribly heavy, but gradually the weight lifted and he was able to work. But earlier he told me that never again would he compose such passionate scenes as the one he now has in front of him, he had already sworn that while working on *Tristan*. Over coffee we come once again to the curious scenes in Russia, to the energy and the seriousness they call for. He tells us Bakunin's views on Russia—that the only way would be to introduce socialism there without the Proudhon theories, since a community already existed among the people there; when Malwida says that many things have altered since the abolition of serfdom, that individualism has become widespread, R. says, "Yes, civilization always moves in that direction, makes property its goal." — R. goes off for his afternoon rest; when he comes down again, another consignment of birds has arrived; even if he is aware that his grand way of ordering things is almost always abused, nevertheless these new arrivals cause much merriment, "Berlioz" and "the doctor" very unusual and comic, the pigeons with their hoods very pretty to look at. In the evening he writes a new album leaf for Frau Neumann, "Only he who has never learned to fear will forge Nothung anew." Then in his wonderful way he plays to Malwida and me music from *Euryanthe* (3rd act) and recalls [Wilhelmine] Schröder-Devrient's exclamation of joy, her radiant expression as she sang it—he could never play it fast enough for her liking, and yet her enunciation utterly clear. — These sounds ring out as chaste as Diana's love for Endymion. But R. forbids me to praise his playing so much! . . .

Sunday, September 8 A restless night. Soon after going to bed R. gets up, plays the piano; with the first note he plays I see before me great glowing roses, the theme reminds me of one he played me one morning as a movement for a quartet; a short while afterward I get up and go to him, he is reading, says he has written something down, that today Orpheus is more favorable to us than Morpheus; moonlight means a misty night! In the morning R. still feels tight in the chest, but he works; at lunch he complains of stabbing pains in his heart, rheumatism, but nonetheless—and on this very subject—he goes into the most extravagant of high spirits, and my battle then consists, alas, in trying to follow suit while tortured by worry. Letter from Baron Perfall, expressing regret that R. would certainly not accept an invitation to attend the performance of *Götterdämmerung* in Munich, and making a suggestion that he come to Bayreuth with a painter to talk about the decorations for *Parsifal!* After lunch, as we are walking out to the summerhouse, R. goes to the piano and plays a theme, which I guess to belong to the words *"in Ewigkeit wärst du verdammt mit mir."* "I am already past that," says R., "but the motive is used there, too. It is *'die Labung, die dein Leiden endet,'* etc., then comes *'ein andres,'* and then I call on my waistcoat pocket for aid." He takes from it and shows me the piece of paper on which he wrote down the theme yesterday. Then he complains about his task, says the duet in *Die Walküre* was a real treat in comparison, and in *Tristan* there had also been the bliss of the pangs of yearning, but here there is only the savage pain of love. — The topic of conversation—that for a good marriage (indeed for any relationship) equality of intelligence is the main requirement, much more important than identity of character, which is indeed not a good thing—leads him to Minna, the gradual emergence of whose bad qualities was certainly due to her limited intelligence; by nature she had been goodhearted, energetic, and helpful, but then she became mistrustful because of her inability to follow R. He does not admit that she was pretty, as is generally maintained, but says that he told the wise, elderly actress Frl. Hacker, who tried to warn him off Minna, "Nothing means more to me than my poodle, my watch (he had just bought himself a silver watch), and Minna Planer." — After his afternoon rest R. goes out for a while, but only as far as Frau Jäger's, and when he returns he has to change completely, so hot has it made him, and he is still feeling his pains. . . . With Malwida he goes off into reminiscences of Paris, particularly the animals, Fips and Papo! — He recalls his dreadful sense of desolation when Fips died, his feeling of utter homelessness. "Now, my dear wife," he concludes, "the home has been found, and children in plenty!" At my request he plays the Prelude to Act III of *Die Msinger* and Bach's Prelude in E-flat Minor (No. 8), which he plays so incomparably. He is happy about *Die Msinger,* recalls the lovely production ("the prettiest" of its kind he has ever known), and he goes off to bed in cheerful mood—I with anxiety! Delight in Loldi, who today again gives me evidence of her great and tender heart.

Monday, September 9 R. had a good night, but his pains have not gone away, despite the rubdowns. He works; the overpoweringly sultry atmosphere is discharged in a thunderstorm which plunges us almost back into night, about which R. cracks many jokes. He is not looking too bad, though not as I should like to see him. Before his work he reads an article by C. Frantz which has been sent to him (about the law on socialism); he finds it excellent and cannot find words too drastic to express his indignation over the "stupidity" of these measures. In the afternoon he goes for a walk, then he writes his reply to Baron Perfall, making it as firm as he can. "My God," he complains, "the thought of having to talk to such people about the decorations for my *Parsifal!*," but then he changes direction: "I feel the way the Protestants do about Hell—perhaps it won't be so bad after all." In the evening he reads to us C. Frantz's excellent article, which leads to a prolonged discussion about the dismal leadership in Germany. Despite these gloomy observations, we are overcome by tremendous high spirits when we find ourselves alone together and say good night; of course it always stems from him, but I get dragged along: "Let's thank God that we can hardly kiss each other today for laughing!"

Tuesday, September 10   Again a wretched night for R.; he gets up, reads Herr Lipiner's book about the revival of religious ideas, his own "Public and Popularity" essay, which pleases him very much with the concentration of its arguments, and the beginning of Louis XI's reign in Barante. In the morning he tells me the terrible dream which woke him up: we were on a journey, and he called to me that the bedroom contained a double bed, whereupon I: "You can sleep in it alone." Hurt, he asked me whether something had offended me. I: "It's not impossible," whereupon he went into my room, where I had set up a sort of bed for myself; then my [step]sister Claire [Charnacé] came in, also scornful in her manner toward him; he was reminded of a dream of his in which increasing numbers of people gathered to mock him—"Still more of them will be coming"—and then he woke up: "Thank God, here she is lying quietly beside me." Then in his mind he saw clearly a picture of our meeting in Basel (1867) and the difficulties I had gone through there: "How well it has turned out after all!" he says. Despite this wild bad night he is cheerful—as I should be, too, if worry did not ravage me! . . . At lunch we receive a nephew of Malwida's whom she has not seen for 28 years, steward to Prince Reuss; he is a very pleasant man, and R. in his eloquent way describes to him the duties of the aristocracy, the duty of a prince to preserve by association the nation's ideal possessions. In the evening a small gathering of friends, R. very gay and friendly.

Wednesday, September 11   R. had quite a good night, getting up only once, around 2 o'clock (he had another bad dream about me: "Minna no longer suffices," he says, "to wake me up"). He works. At lunch he talks about *W. Meister*, says that in the opening parts it spreads itself out like sunshine breaking through the morning mists. He says he had always wished he could find himself a girl like Philine: "I was a curiously stiff young fellow," he adds. In the afternoon he writes to the King, sends him the etching with the remark that he has never looked so bad-tempered in his life—so perhaps he had just looked like that in London! In the evening my Polish friend, whom we call "the Hussite woman," a fanatical, strange person; R. in his charming way digs up all his memories of Poland. — A lot, too, about conditions in Russia, R. says he cannot stand conspiracies. — Then he plays the march of the Knights of the Grail. — Lovely moonlight.

Thursday, September 12 R. slept well, he jokes with me about my "Hussite" friend, with whom I spend a lovely morning walking to the theater and then to the Fantaisie; the feeling I have of being at home when I gaze on these hills, though it is only a short while since I first came here, seems to me to stem from the fact that R. has built his theater here, that our children will live here, that our grave is here. R. goes out for a while, then he works in ink, then tries out the new, long-desired pencil whose lead, when mixed with water, turns into ink and becomes indelible. In the evening my Polish friend and the Wolzogens; friend W. always brings along all sorts of sadly comic tales about the German Reich—that, for example, two Protestant churches in Berlin have become insolvent and have been turned into beer halls, in which the vergers are employed as waiters; and that to encourage the fine arts a sculptor has been commissioned to make an Alexander studying the map of India. R. thinks this is a dig at Tsar Alexander of Russia, but I tell him these people are not as witty as all that—it is only *he* who is so inventive. He says laughingly about the critical situation in the East, "I'll send them my Berlioz, he'll soon restore order there." The thoroughly boring evening ends very amusingly, with R., Malwida, and I waxing hysterical over the miseries we endured!

Friday, September 13 Again the sky overcast for part of the day; but I take the Hussite woman for a drive, and she visits us in the evening. Alas, nothing fits in well with our present life, everything that tears away from our sweet habit of being alone together has a bad effect. At lunch R. still very gay, relates amusingly how he once sang *"Les Deux Grenadiers"* in Adam Czartoryski's house and crept away from the astonished gathering of genteel people like a drenched poodle. But this mood does not last long; I had reserved his *salon* for his own solitary use and took my friends into the lilac *salon,* but the children and the governess behave tactlessly and disturb him, he, too goodhearted to send them away, suffers very much and at last loses patience. We stay up late, to calm him down with reading, but I in deep concern, feeling I am failing in my duty if I cannot avert such things! Oh, if only they would leave us alone! . . .

Saturday, September 14 R. did not have a good night, but he works. — Friend Standhartner yesterday announced a visit, he is coming from the international exposition in Paris, and since he wrote in French, R. says, "*Il s'est* exposé *lui-même comme ami de Wagner, et en cette qualité il était en effet assez* exposé là-bas" ["He has *exposed* himself as a friend of Wagner, and in that capacity was truly *exposed there*"]. — As always when he jokes in French he makes use of the best and most original of expressions. Over our afternoon coffee we come to talk of the election of women to Parliament, and R. promises to read us in the evening C. Frantz's chapter on this question; he does so, and we are all astonished by the fine, clear language, the depth and originality of the thinking. Then R. recalls his essay "A Happy Evening," the joyousness of the last movement of the 7th Symphony having suddenly come so clearly into his mind! —

Sunday, September 15 R. had a good night, at any rate he did not have to get up; he works, and in the afternoon, after showing me the card on which he had written it down, he plays me something I believe he called a melisma—to me it seemed a fascinating theme. "I wonder if you will recognize the expression," he says, and I reply, "The *Jesus Christ* of Dürer in Nuremberg, isn't it?" He: "Yes!" . . . Beautiful day; after waiting in vain at the station for friend Standhartner, we drive to the Eremitage. Looked at the *Saint Hubert* of Dürer in Fidi's room: "We have some lovely things," says R., "this and the Genelli." From looking at these things there arise within me over-whelming feelings, as if I were in a dream, and they lead to a vision of the Saviour on the cross! I hold melancholy at bay as best I can, and in the evening put into a kiss on R.'s foot all the pain, fervor, and joy of overcoming! . . . After our walk R. invites R. and me to have some beer with him; in the evening, at my request, he reads to us his wonderful "A Happy Evening," then the splendid "The Artist and the Public" and "The Virtuoso and the Artist." The hours pass as in a dream, one would like to hold them back, and yet one is so happy for them to continue. R. is also pleased with his youthful works: "It was spring, I was starting work on *Der Fl. Holländer,* left Paris for Meudon, that was the mood I was in." The new work he did in Tribschen also pleases him, but at the same time saddens him, for—"the conditions have remained the same."

Monday, September 16 R. slept well, we once again discuss his article "The Artist and the Public," and he says, "Yes, I could not have written it quite like that in Paris at that time, I felt it all, was no longer to be moved, but could express it only fleetingly; so one sees how the writer, when he is in the midst of things, produces nothing worth while, the dramatist only when he looks at his subject from afar." He spoke of the singers in Paris who had talent (referring to *Don Giovanni*), even his brother Albert could have learned something from them, but not the present-day singers. When Malwida remarks that one constantly returns to the school, to the need to train singers, he says, "It's not the training but the finding that would be difficult." Concern that his *Parsifal* is getting involved in the deficit arrangements: "If I were 20 years younger, I should do it only with singers I had trained for the task, and only in front of an audience which had made this possible." — But he works nevertheless! Arrival of our friend Standhartner; very dear and precious to us. The present position to which rashness has brought Austria is discussed in sorrow. In the afternoon, as I am writing to friend Glasenapp, who has sent me photographs of the houses in Riga and Magdeburg, I hear R. talking in great excitement down below in the garden; I look out and see an unknown figure; shortly afterward R. comes up and tells me that a Protestant parson with a traveling bag had spoken to him, asking when he might talk with him; R., having first looked him in the face and remarked that he did not care to be accosted in this way, invited him to walk with him. First of all the man asked him to defend the interests of the church, then he asked him not to write anything else offensive to morality. "What do you mean?" "Well, the mermaids, for instance." R.: "You are a very silly man; according to that, trees, birds, and the whole of Nature would be immoral." He: "You listen only to flatterers, you do not want to hear the truth." R. is good enough to give him a copy of *Parsifal:* "In this you will see that I am more Christian than you are." He: "That we shall know when we stand at God's right hand." R.: "Or at the Devil's left," and with these words he dismissed the importunate man. As R. says, he feels annoyed with himself, rather than with the man, for not having simply sent him away. In the evening conversation with our friend, memories of Cornelius; R. can never forget how Cornelius once said to him, as if it were something quite natural, that R. always dropped his friends, whereas R. observes sadly that it was always they who gave him up when he expected more from them than they were able to achieve; thus it was with Herwegh, with Baumgartner, with Cornelius, Weissheimer, Ritter, etc. Friend Standhartner tells us about the policemen in Gastein who surround the German Emperor in masses, and if somebody has a hand in his pocket when the Emperor or Bismarck passes by, he is politely requested to take it out! Of the present dismal political events R. says sadly, "Oh, one must just leave off worrying about them." Then he plays bits of *Parsifal,* the Prelude and part of the Flower Maidens. . . .

Tuesday, September 17   R. had a good night, but at 4 o'clock he got up and took some "Pompeius Magnus" (magnesia) as a precautionary measure; he still laughs when he thinks of that parson. Then he asks me, "How are you feeling today?" I: "Very well." "Then I have hopes of bringing off Kundry's speech." With an embrace, during which it goes to my heart to see in his eyes all his guileless kindness, we go our separate ways. He works; at lunch he starts to talk about the strange parson and says he has heard that the man is attending an ecclesiastical conference here to further Christian ideas: "Perhaps they wanted me to compose something like 'Beware of *fat women*'!" We laugh heartily over this merry nonsense. After lunch, when our friends praise the practical design of our house, R. tells us about his construction plans from the years around '52. In the evening some serious construction plans had again to be discussed, and in between came a walk with Standhartner and the dogs, which brought him a *hunting sermon* and an indisposition on Fidi's part, which caused us *terrible and prolonged* anxiety. His room is pronounced unhealthy; at once R. starts on thoughts, complete in the smallest detail, of extending the outbuildings. — In the evening our friends the W.'s and the Jägers; after that, departure of our friend Standhartner, whose very pleasant visit did us good.

Wednesday, September 18 R. had a good night, I a very restless one; when I led the dogs to the railings for R. yesterday, I found him looking very white, his lips pale, and all evening he seemed to me run down; on top of that Fidi's illness and the searing worry that he might not prove worthy of his father! But this time the flood of wild thoughts gives way to resignation, I behold His gaze, and calm covers my raging till sleep comes. — In the morning discussed the question of the private tutor and the apartment. Fidi is somewhat better. Work with the children. R. also works, and he plays to me "*Lass mich dich Göttlichen lieben*," in which by means of the Flower Maidens' theme he allows us divinely to feel, beyond the wild words, the sweet omnipotence of love's yearning. — Over coffee R. brings up a subject we discussed yesterday, my experience of which, he says, has shown him things in a new light, namely, the Catholic church and its realism, how in its eyes all fervor and faith are worth nothing unless one is a Catholic. — After R.'s afternoon rest we stroll in the garden, sit down in front of the still-fascinating aviary, Brange always at R.'s feet. Friend W. brings news of the continuing debate in the Reichstag, R. finds Bismarck's speech pitiful—that he was happy to have Lassalle as a neighboring landowner, this jocular tone in such a matter, and then his eternal complaints about illness! R. finds all this disgusting, and he feels the King ought to say to Bismarck, "Either we dismiss the Parliament you address in such terms, or I dismiss you." — Later R. works in ink, then plays and sings to me the passage from "*Ja, diese Stimme*" to "*Ha! dieser Kuss*." Indescribable feelings possess me, which I express to him in an embrace; it is only late in the evening, when he again comes back to the Reichstag, that I tell him I have no interest in this wasteland, I can hear only *Parsifal*. R. says, "It is very remarkable, I have never before gone so far; my *'ein andres ist's'* almost goes beyond what is permissible as far as didacticism is concerned, but you will see!"

Thursday, September 19   When R. groaned during the night, I stroked and fondled him, so that he awoke gently and then quietly went to sleep again. At breakfast a look at the houses in Riga, he shows me where Robber always lay; gay memories of the Duna bridge and the Schwarzhäupterhaus. Then *Parsifal* again: "The way he immediately wants to start converting people," he says with a laugh, "when he has only just seen the light himself!" Yesterday evening he was pleased with Parsifal as a character, said he had correctly indicated the things which a noble impression in adolescent years produces, overturning the natural instincts; this is the pattern in all the saints: "With the Saviour himself it was predestined, so to speak, in his mother's womb." Over coffee he tells me about the house on Schmiedegasse with windows opening onto the courtyard: "It was there I believed I no longer had a wife." He recalls compassionately how wretched she had looked. He talks (in the evening) very movingly about the curse of being born without means, then he reads to us from Gfrörer some strange Israelite statements about God. In the afternoon he goes to work, he shows me the *laughter,* then I go away, return through the room again, he complains of his bad luck, that just when he wants to wipe his pen he loses it, but he is cheerful and looks so well and splendid that it is a comfort and a pleasure to see; in the evening, when, as today, he lays his hand on the sofa, that dear, splendid hand, and his eyes shine and his dear voice rings out, my heart rejoices! — To Malwida, dressed in blue, he says, "You look like your pencil." Herr Köhler gives us a manuscript!

Friday, September 20   R. is rubbed down with olive oil and alcohol liniment; I tell him they represent the two sides of his nature, gentleness and fire. When I did this for him yesterday evening he said, "*Cosa stravagante*—but Rossini could never have composed you." Then we talk about *Wilhelm Meister's Wanderjahre,* how splendid of Goethe to have recognized organized handicrafts, colonization, and religion as the three poles of modern life; R. says in regard to this that it is a pity it does not emerge clearly enough, is depicted too vaguely. — At 4 o'clock Daniella arrives home; much emotion, but also much gaiety, the dear child has experienced a great deal. In the evening a Herr Lipiner, with whom we immediately have a very far-reaching discussion on religious matters, arising from the articles by Prof. Lagarde; R. thinks I am right in wanting to protest against all constructional arguments in this sphere. The specifically Israelite aspects of the interpretation—of Luther, for instance—are very noticeable here. R. tells me in the evening that he would like once more to describe very clearly the special qualities of a saint, in the way he has now come to see them.

Saturday, September 21 R. had a good night and goes to his work; I listen with Malwida to a reading of part of Herr Lipiner's "Renatus" and am amazed at its aberrations. At lunch R. says he has crossed out everything he did yesterday. When we meet in the afternoon he tells me, "It must be in ¾ time." Then, when I tell him my impressions of today's reading, he says, "One should regard it as the vision of a starving man," thereby correctly indicating the standpoint to be adopted here, so that I at once resolve to listen to the continuation of the reading in a different spirit. — In the evening we take up an essay by Prof. Dühring about the universities, very correct in its views but not very well written and not suitable for our *Blätter;* R. wants it to be printed separately, and he would then draw attention to it himself in the *Blätter.* He laughs: "On the one hand so many books, on the other so many professors—whereas universities only made sense when books were rare!" The attached telegram gives him pleasure. [*Headed* "Leipzig, September 21," *it reads:* "Holy Ghost descends on Unger, first act just completed, tremendous applause, five curtain calls, everyone amazed—Seidl." *The reference is to a performance of* Siegfried.] When no telegram comes about the 2nd act, R. pretends he has received bad news and goes "weeping" to Malwida's door to lament, thus bringing the evening to an end in great merriment. R. and I still find time to express our surprise and pleasure at the popularity of this gigantic work: in Munich *Götterdämmerung* is reported to have aroused frenetic applause.

Sunday, September 22 I return to our final topic of last night and tell R. how splendid it is that the *Ring* in particular should make such an impact, for it was to create this work that he had been sent into the world. "Not at all; it was to marry you," and, turning things around in his humorous way, he adds: "That's why you had to go and marry Bülow! The Lord did to you what Lüttichau did to me over the decorations for *Tannhäuser*—started off with a refusal, to enhance the value of the thing." — Pleased with having all the children here together, he says, "They are our riches." He goes to work, still complaining of his "*laziness*"; I listen in patience and sympathy to "Renatus." With regard to Israel, R. says it is when it is well behaved that it really becomes alarming. In the evening R. is in the most splendid high spirits, even his most dismal of experiences he describes gaily. Of an opera called *Nero* he inquires, "Is that a watchdog?," and of *Messalina* he wants to know whether many *mésalliances* occur in it! He complains with indescribable humor that now, when he has to compose Kundry, nothing comes into his head but cheerful themes for symphonies. Then he speaks of the canon, in which each singer has to follow the other, the first gets annoyed and growls a bit, then continues, only to get annoyed again when the others follow him. He says he will call his symphonies "symphonic dialogues," for he would not compose four movements in the old style; but theme and countertheme one must have, and allow these to speak to each other. There is nothing of that kind in the whole of Brahms's symphony, he says. Then he tells us about the lean Brahms who had corrected instrumental parts for him in Vienna, and whom he then rediscovered "fattened up" by fame. He says he has often sung to himself themes from Mendelssohn but found it impossible to do the same with Schumann, whereas with Brahms he had really begun to doubt his musical receptivity till his pleasure in Sgambati showed him he was still capable of taking things in. R. goes through Handel's *Alexander's Feast;* the skip in particular pleases him, and he says Handel was the Rossini of his time. He tells Herr L. that attention must now be drawn to his theoretical writings.

Monday, September 23   R. had a good night and is pleased with the telegrams from Leipzig. [*Attached are two telegrams, from Seidl and Neumann, describing the enthusiastic reception of* Siegfried *and* Götterdämmerung, *and also a newspaper clipping containing a letter from R. W. to Neumann. See notes.*] He then works, and he looks so well, he is also full of joy, spreading good cheer around. It is my great triumph and inner rejoicing that this splendid spirit feels so unconstrained, pouring its blessings over us without stint! When we are eating Karlsbad wafers at lunch, R. says, "This is the sort of thing my Knights of the Grail will get. I can't give them bread and butter, or they will start digging in and not want to leave." Yesterday, complaining of the difficulties Kundry is causing him, he exclaimed humorously, "And there are still the others to come, with their lances—oh, it's horrible!" In the afternoon he goes for a walk in beautiful sunshine. "Where have I been?" he says on his return. "At Mime's place." By this he means in Angermann's vaults, looked after by his brother. He says that before his beer he asked for some bread and sat down under the trees, a kitten came up to him and held its tail high up in the air for joy when he gave it some bread; he had enjoyed a few moments of great contentment and could see me sitting there with the children. — After telling me this, he comes to his *Parsifal* and says: "Oh, I hate the thought of all those costumes and grease paint! When I think that characters like Kundry will now have to be dressed up, those dreadful artists' balls immediately spring into my mind. Having created the invisible orchestra, I now feel like inventing the invisible theater! And the inaudible orchestra," he adds, concluding his dismal reflections in humorous vein.

He would like to put things off for one more year, he said this morning after his work, for there is no escaping a production. In the evening Herr Lipiner, who involves R. in a discussion about socialism; R. stresses that the power of this movement can only lie in destruction, constructive ideas are always childish, and everything always comes back to human beings as they are and always have been. All the same one must go on working without hope—he himself is an example of that with his *Parsifal*. To expect much, he says, from tobacco monopolies and other organizations of that sort is foolish, he would be thankful if there were still enough strength left in our society to destroy what exists, but one could see from the Commune in Paris how pitifully and with what effort this process of destruction is accomplished; and even then one could not talk about art, a period of complete barbarism would have to follow, and he would willingly sacrifice both himself and his works for it; but only a tremendous sense of purpose and fanaticism would achieve anything, all else is just fooling around; and besides, people always forget the farmer, the peasant, who is conservative by nature. He speaks of these things with great warmth and excitement, rejecting everything that is petty, or too optimistic.

Tuesday, September 24 But then R. had a bad night, he got out of bed three times, and even in the early hours he was unable to get any real rest. He also complains that he is being plagued by melodies from *Le Postillon de Longjumeau*—however, they are gay ones! He goes to his work, and despite his restless night and the bad weather, he is cheerful again at lunch, and as kind as ever. We go for a stroll in the garden in the afternoon, discussing the peculiarities of Israel, of which we have again become so clearly aware. In the evening the Feustel family, the W.'s, and Frau Jäger, R. performs in his inimitable way two ballades by Loewe, "Edward" and "*Die Hexen*," then, along with Frau Jäger, "*Wenn mir dein Auge strahlt*"—always divine, whether solemn or joking. Lusch plays the piano for us and shows decided progress. After the visitors have gone, R., Malwida, and I remain together in intimate conversation.

Wednesday, September 25 R. slept well, without interruption, and went to his work, he is satisfied with what he has done, but says it was very little. He again brings up the subject of socialism—how everything hangs on the question of property, and that is precisely what is now needed, to interest the poor in property. During the late afternoon he gets very heated with Herr Lipiner about Schopenhauer, since Herr Lipiner claims to detect illogicalities in the great philosopher. But soon after he has gone away, R. repents of his violence and goes to Malwida to say a few friendly words to the bewildered man; however, he has already left. In the evening we read the *B. Blätter,* friend Wolzogen's article on the festival theater excellent; Herr Löffler, on the other hand, very unsuccessful with the "world inheritance"; this lack of simplicity in grasping even the smallest things! Now the *Ring* is supposed to represent *downfall through materialism!* Herr Kulke the Wagnerian argues like Herr Lipiner the Schopenhauerian, accusing the poet of making a mistake! — After that R. reads to us the discussion between Gregory of Tours, Priscus, and Chilperic in Thierry's *Récits mérovingiens*—a delicious scene, charmingly told; R. is always saying how much he enjoys reading these French books, how grateful he is to Renan for making the subject of the Gospel so vivid to him.

Thursday, September 26 Splendid to listen to R.'s summary of Sch.'s philosophy! This morning he gave me another short account of it, while expressing disgust with people who profess to understand him and then accuse him of illogicalities. A letter from Hans determines that Lulu should not travel to Rome with Malwida, but remain here with us. R. works, and then amuses us, on the subject of writing French, by telling us that he writes to the *parfumeur* in Paris under the name of M. Bernard Schnappauf, Ochsengasse. He feels he would almost prefer to thank Herr Marsillach in French, rather than in German. Over coffee, discussion of Fidi's future, we resolve to have him trained as a surgeon, so that he may become a useful and beneficent person here in the place where his father brought a glorious ideal into being; he must of course provide aid without charging for it, thereby earning himself the right to live independently of the world and, if possible, to represent his father's ideas. He will not attend any schools, so that nothing will disturb his image of his father, and he will be able to enjoy to the full the blessings of his youth. He must also get to know everything about his country and feel himself a part of it. R. returns to Goethe, saying he had not seen the point about the casket until he had experienced in Lucerne being beside himself with pity and behaving like a madman because he could not help; reluctance must be overcome by constantly keeping the ideal nature of one's task in mind, for the whole will rebels against such study. He tells very movingly the story of a saint who at first refused to suck out a plague sore, but then, calling upon God, she had done so, and afterward she had maintained that nothing had ever tasted so good as this horrible substance swallowed in ecstasy. In the afternoon friend W. with some news of the patrons: a student from Strassburg is prepared to champion Wagner's Germany against Bismarck's Germany, and the little village of Pössneck is represented by all its top people (only the night watchman missing). R. works in the afternoon, and in the evening we read Herr Letamendi's letter in the *Bayr. Blätter* with real delight; R. finds everything in it—the whole form, images, thoughts, outlook, language—exemplary, and he is so pleased with it that he writes a lengthy letter to Herr Marsillach about it. The little masterpiece reminds him of Cervantes's prefaces, and he compares it with a deep sigh to our German products, devoid of both form and content. This brings him to the relationship between Germans and Spaniards, much more evident than that between Germans and Italians, in whom painting has swallowed everything—he does not believe an Italian could have written such a letter.

Friday, September 27   R. had a restless night, the letter to Marsillach was a strain on him. He dreamed of a clarinet which played by itself. But he goes to his work and becomes so cheerful that he sings the "What delight does travel bring" aria from [Boieldieu's] *Jean de Paris,* then says this is really what Kundry ought to sing, mockingly, when she sets Parsifal out on the wrong path. Saying farewell to Malwida after coffee, he says, "God preserve you, Malwida, you are now—emancipated!" But in the afternoon, when I return from a lengthy walk with M., I find him in a bad mood, he is not feeling well and has pains in his chest, and I regret having left the house. He feels disgusted with the world and is particularly vexed with Seidl, who has not written to him; all the same, he writes to Herr Neumann, asking him to engage Seidl. Herr Glatz already cast aside in Vienna, attempt to get Herr Jäger taken on there. In the evening he says we must go to Spain, to Barcelona, Seville, Granada: "I can see the children arriving in Spain," he says with a laugh. The *Fl[iegende] Blätter* helps cheer R. up, and at last, toward the end of the evening, he sits down at the piano and plays *Tristan,* the 2nd act up to the arrival of Marke; he plays it so beautifully, in a way so far transcending the ordinary bounds of beauty, that I feel I am hearing the sounds which will make me blessed in death. — "What luxuriating!" says R., adding with a laugh, "Just the thing for Berlin and Niemann." — "This work goes beyond all the others: *Götterdämmerung* is a tragedy of Fate, but what is the love scene in *Die Walküre* compared to this obsession with death?" "All this we have experienced," he said earlier. "Oh, you poor woman! You remember my youthful ballad about the swan who saves the youth who wants to drown himself? You are this swan which caught me and held me." — Immediately after he stopped playing, he wanted to talk about other things, but in my state of deep emotion I could neither hear, understand, nor say anything at all; and so I do not remember what he said, though I know it was something serious.

Saturday, September 28   R. had a good night, he tells me that he has ordered the Bulwer [Lytton] novels for Lusch, and he talks again about the impression they made on him, how in *Eugene Aram* he had found it almost impossible to believe in the murder. He works. Around two o'clock arrival of Herr Kellermann, "*l'homme du caveau,*" as R. calls him, typical of the wretched times of today. At the conservatory he was paid 1,200 marks by Herr Stern; when he said he was leaving, the latter offered him 5,000! Before that he had delivered newspapers in order to be able to complete his studies, and was glad when he was ill, for then he did not need to eat! He went to Berlin to learn about acoustics from Helmholtz, and was thus inspired by all the best human motives, but all he discovered there was hunger and exploitation of his willingness to work. His father is a professor of natural science in Nuremberg. A very decent and lively person who, let us hope, will find salvation here—yet how many there are, people of the best character and ideals who fall by the wayside! . . . R. does some work in the afternoon but is vexed by the lack of precision in so many people, whereas he himself is always so scrupulously punctual and exact! In the evening he plays the third act of *Tristan*. When I voice my wonder that he could have completed this miracle in a hotel room, with not a soul to look after or care for him, he says: "Yes, people have no idea how divorced from experience and reality these things happen, and how long one is nourished by one's youth! It is true I sometimes felt inclined in my disgust to throw everything into the gutter, and in fact I eventually did so, unwilling as I was to do any more work; but when the German Emperor exclaims, 'How deeply Wagner must have been in love at that time,' it is really quite ridiculous. — If that were so, I should now be writing *Parsifal* on account of my connections with the Christian church, and you would be Kundry! No, I just felt the need to go to the very limit musically, as if I had been writing a symphony." When, later on, I tell R. how much I regret not having been with him earlier, always, he says, "Yes, I was born too soon." Then he adds with a laugh: "I ought to have come under the influence of Mendelssohn and Meyerbeer! No, Weber was a blessing to me." Recently he was beside himself with delight over the "*Jungfernkranz*" chorus [in *Der Freischütz*]: "It is supposed to be a Silesian folk song," he said, "but the way the words 'green and lovely,' that exclamation of ecstasy, emerge from the simple phrase 'We bind for thee'—that is typical Weber!" Then he laughs at the thought that Polish Jews would soon be enjoying the *Ring* in Leipzig (at the fair!): "Well, one of them was my entire audience for *Das Liebesverbot.*" A chorale by J. S. Bach, sent by Herr Levi, astonishes us with the boldness of its modulations, but R. does not quite trust the "*many* beauties," for Bach "was after all a cantor and was writing all day long. The *48 Preludes and Fugues* and the motets—those are the pearls."

Sunday, September 29   Again a disturbed night for R., but he works, and before going off to work he says as he embraces me: "As long as

all is well between us! But I don't think anything could ever *not* be
well between us." Shortly before one o'clock he fetches me for lunch
and seems to me to be looking pale, which deeply worries me—worse
than that, it stands like a specter between life and myself. But our
lunch is not sad. Herr Kellermann is questioned by R., and various
new details are added to the dismal picture we have of life in the world
outside. After lunch a walk with Malw., on our way home I see R.
standing motionless some distance away, he had recognized us from
afar and was standing waiting; we return home with him, and then he
continues his walk and afterward works. In the evening the children
sing (folk songs), R. accompanying them, and then young Brandt, with
whom we go through our experiences, pleasant as well as painful. R.
says he allows no outsider the right to condemn the [*Ring*] production,
which as a whole was so beautiful and beyond compare: "But among
ourselves we must acknowledge that much was not as it should have
been; for example, the meadow of the gods before Valhalla not free
enough, too restricted by the steps; Erda's cave reminiscent of a door
in the usual sort of fantastic comedy show; the steam transformation to
Nibelheim—there should have been *shafts* in it, a backcloth which
could have been drawn up lengthways, showing these shafts and now
and again a fiery glow; then the mountaintop was too high—I shall
alter that one day, when I produce *Die Walküre* in Heaven at the right
hand of God, and the old fellow and I are watching it—the acting area
too narrow, so that the fight was spoiled and Wotan's storming in a
failure; in *Siegfried,* steps again, and not enough room for the fight;
and steps also hindering Brünnhilde's struggles, too little room for the
Rhinemaidens, and the water sweeping over the funeral pyre, and the
hall of the Gibichungs not impressive enough. Then the costumes bad,
almost all of them. And so it turned out that this production, as far as
the conception was concerned, was on the whole extraordinary, wrong
in only a few details." R. talks of his suffering at the time, the patience
with which he kept silent about it all!

Monday, September 30   R. again did not have a good night, had taken
medicine. He shows me a piece of paper on which he wrote down his
work for today. Animated by my having my breakfast beside him in
bed, he tells me about Lord Chatham, chained to his bed in a cold room
by gout, being visited by another lord who, unable to stand the cold,
lay down on the neighboring bed; they began to argue and were
discovered lying side by side, quarreling violently. Today I have a
sorrow to contend with: "As long as all is well between us," R. said
yesterday forebodingly, and I was unthinking enough not to understand him fully; today I learn that R. does not quite believe that I
begrudge him nothing, nothing at all. However, even the tears this

causes me are selfish; in the same way that from the depths of my soul I begrudge him nothing, would gladly for his sake live in penury, so, too, I do not begrudge myself my pain; after lunch I wander far through the meadows beneath the Birken and regain my spirits, even to the extent of blessing my pain, the most hurtful of all, for I know that there is not a single one among his wishes and inclinations which draw from me even an expression of surprise—may he be blessed in all he does, by everyone and everything, even my pain! I beg him to forgive my tears, he does not want to hear of it, but his tender embrace and his smiling gaze allow me to forgive them myself. Then R. works, and at supper tells me he had been looking for the "*Erlösung biete ich auch dir*" passage but had then closed the piano, telling himself he must wait for inspiration, "for this fellow mustn't speak like a preacher, it must all arise out of his emotions." At supper Herr Kellermann tells us something about conditions in Berlin, the senseless construction projects there, a railway through the whole city, for instance, a canal system going uphill, the poor craftsmen whose tools are pawned, a picture filled with horror and misery. Afterward Herr Kellermann plays us a Beethoven sonata (the *Pastorale*), and we are astonished at his incorrectness; R. then shortly explains to him the style of this work, "a forerunner of the *Pastoral* Symphony," and how simply it should be played, with as few accents as possible and no fixed tempo. He fears that the new school is bringing excess even to things like this, which will be ruined in consequence. — In the evening R. tells me how beautiful I looked as I turned the pages, and how he enjoyed watching me—ah, if only I had all the beauty in the world to lay at his feet!

Tuesday, October 1   Again a bad night for R.; he believes the beer he drinks while working just before supper is the cause, and he frequently determines to give it up. "The house in the morning seems dead to me when not filled with the sounds of your music." He reads Lecky and tells me some things about the attitude of the Romans toward their slaves. October starts very roughly: "We shall have to give up all thoughts of summer now—even of autumn." — Talking of Haeckel's theories, R. is led to Kant's and Laplace's theories of the origin of the world, and he also speaks about the Indian "breath" (an image he much admires), which would form with the ending of the world and is the same thing as what humans understand by desire. Compared with such a myth the whole Jewish mythology is just hack work. "The more I examine history," he says, "the worse I find it," meaning this world. — After lunch letters from Leipzig, excellent account of the performances from friend Seidl. R. asks me to go for a walk with him, he says solitary walks are quite productive, but today he does not wish to meditate. When we reach the entrance to the little terrace on the right of the house which leads through the garden to the railings, R. asks me: "Have you experienced that—that you sometimes see images? Today I saw you, that is to say, just your forehead and eyes; I couldn't conjure up the lower part, for conscious will is no use in this case, it's likely to bring you just the face of some blackamoor instead of what you're looking for. You gazed at me with such a wonderful expression, and then I fell sound asleep." I strolled with him through the palace gardens, first talking about Lecky's book, then I tell him about Plutarch's life of Lycurgus, which I am reading to the children. Then *Tristan,* and R. talks again of his need at that time to push himself to the limit musically, since in the *Nibelungen* the requirements of the drama frequently forced him to restrict the musical expression. We recall the *da capo* in the extract from *Tristan* in London: "That was funny," says R. "The English are dour, but not reserved." Over our beer we continue talking, and R. tells me he does not feel like working, he wants to come to grips with the book about religious sects, and, as if making excuses to himself, he says, "I shall have completed the first two acts within a year; to compose three acts one after another like that—" I interrupt him: "—is not possible." R. decorates my room. During supper recently we talk about gratitude, and R. mentions how intolerable a human being finds it to be grateful (and gives gods as an example) when he is not bound by love. I know that R.—perhaps alone among the people I know—has always loved to express gratitude and has the greatness not to be afraid of accepting it. Perhaps because inside himself he knows how to repay it with interest. — In the evening all sorts of information about poisons from Herr Kellermann, who is well versed in natural science. R. mentions his mother's death, serenely transfigured, with a vision of the Redeemer. My brother saw Saints Peter and Paul and said he would prepare our places for us. In the evening, at my request, R. plays the Prelude to *Parsifal* and the boys' song, "*Wein und Brot des letzten Mahles.*" He speaks of the simplicity of the Prelude: "It is just a few contrasted themes."

Wednesday, October 2   At last R. had a good night. When I embrace him after breakfast, he says, "That is it, that is my image, the look that came back to me." He works. Our conversation leads us to modern surgery, its boldness and frequent foolhardiness. R. tells me about his friend Anders's broken leg, and how a doctor deliberately broke the knee of someone with a bad leg, and how in consequence he was cured. He goes for a walk (but when I am strolling in the garden I hear him playing the piano), and then continues to work in the evening. When Herr Kellermann mentions the poet Wolff, R. recalls his "Pied Piper of Hamelin" and praises him, in spite of some affectations in the careless modern manner; with regard to the same poet's "Till Eulenspiegel," he says the name Till is the same as Tell. When I ask him whether Schiller was thinking of the word's meaning when he wrote, "If I were prudent, I should not be Tell," R. says he does not know, and he adds, "If I were a blockhead, I should not be Wagner, for all the Wagners are people of great and special genius, as one can see from *Faust*." After supper we come to talk about his Beethoven story, and he recalls in amusement that his sister O[ttilie] had known Reichardt, and the anecdote about the X had been told him by Schindler's sister, a singer in Magdeburg. In the evening [Tieck's] *Der gestiefelte Kater,* which R.'s manner of reading transforms into unparalleled delight. He says there is no longer a public like the one held up to ridicule in it. Referring to the King, he says it is true one has to treat all princes as if they were madmen, avoiding this and that subject in conversation with them. My enjoyment in the way he read this splendid work lasts a long time; what pleases him about it is what he calls its Aristophanic flavor.

Thursday, October 3 Not a good night for R., he believes drinking beer is the reason for it; despite these disturbances our breakfast is cheerful and, along with the evening (second to the evening), the nicest time of the day. After I have told him of a tale in *The Arabian Nights* which I am now reading with Fidi, he embraces me: "My Allah and my all!" — Today I hear no musical sounds, and at lunch R. tells me with a laugh, "I am now writing for Wolzogen, like Kant for Lampe." — During a lovely sunset we stroll across the Birk to the little wood, a lovely walk which does R. good, but unfortunately on our homecoming he has the annoyance of finding that despite his recommendation Herr Rudolphi is not engaging our friend Seidl. R. then at once recommends him to Vienna. In the evening we finish *Der Gest. Kater;* before that R. sings some melodies from *Preziosa* and recalls the performance in Munich, also a concert in Basel at which the "Ocean" aria from *Oberon* was sung and he burst into tears—so affected is he by the touching sounds, the idealistic naturalness of Weber's music. He then speaks about the death of Klärchen [in Beethoven's music to Goethe's *Egmont*] and plays the three chords which for him represent necessity, the extraterrestrial.

Friday, October 4 Last night he slept well; in a dream he heard Fidi singing a song about me—I had gone away! After breakfast yesterday he said, "Oh, yes, we shall stick together." Friend Glasenapp has sent a play by L. Geyer, *Das Erntefest,* and some reviews of it. R. smiles at our zeal and observes, "If only we had reports like this about Shakespeare!" I: "That would not be so important!" At lunch he is vexed by Fidi's indisposition; but he himself immediately takes the sting out of his vexation by saying in the same breath that he is vexed. When

Herr K[ellermann] said over coffee that it was remarkable how dogs always knew what mood their masters were in, R. said he felt like sending at once for Marke and Brange to make an experiment. Dr. Jauner pleases him by saying yes to Seidl. In the evening Baron Seydlitz. R. quotes something from Lecky's book which pleased him—that the number of crimes has diminished, but cases of depravity have on the other hand increased. Since Herr K. left Schumann's *Nachtstücke* behind, R. plays the first piece, to the astonishment of us all over such superficiality; he adds, "But I am speaking out of envy!" — Our conversation touches on Jean Paul, for whom R. has no great liking, but he quotes one thing he finds a good observation—about the husband whose wife walks ahead of him and who is suddenly horrified by her way of walking.

Saturday, October 5 Again R. did not sleep well, and again he thinks the beer he drank is to blame. He is affected when he is told in his bath that *Runa* has left, she is going to Aschaffenburg—she really was an unusual person, and we should have liked to keep her. Glorious weather, R. works on his article, tells us he is now on Calderón and must be careful not to go into too much detail, thus having to say to himself, like Polonius, "By the mass, I was about to say something." We drive in the most wonderful weather to the Eremitage, the children in front with the four dogs, a proper procession. Along the journey R. tells me in great indignation about the attached news item and says that with our German Reich we are now— [*Sentence incomplete; an attached newspaper clipping reads:* "Political Roundup, Bayreuth, October 5: The American ambassador in Berlin, Bayard Taylor, has warned his fellow countrymen against visits in Germany, saying that, above all, they should never under any circumstances engage in political conversation if they wish to avoid unpleasantness. How can one reconcile this fact, so humiliating to us, with the claim, so often heard, that we are the most respected nation in the world?"] Merry homecoming; R. goes to his work (completion in ink) and when I go to him in the evening, he says I have come just in time for the kiss ("*war es mein Kuss, der dich hellsichtig machte*"). — In the evening he begins to read *Das Erntefest* but breaks off, saying he does not care for its style (the Dresden style of Kotzebue). He asks Herr K. to play the Overture to [Spohr's] *Jessonda* with him, then plays several other things from this opera; the scene between the two Brahmans leads to Mozart's immortal duologue between Tamino and the Priest—what a gulf divides the two scenes, what aristocracy, what fire, what dramatic force in the latter! I wish everybody could hear R. play them. — Herr K.'s mediocre sight-reading makes us remark on the deleterious influence of present-day piano playing, how all the young people, bewitched by my father's personality, want to acquire what he was literally born with, and spend all their time practicing.

Sunday, October 6 R. slept tolerably well; we return to our conversation of yesterday, and he says, "Yes, great genius destroys minor talents." In connection with something or other he quotes, "This Falstaff has much virtue and an accursed wink," and says he is so filled with admiration for such things that he feels downright annoyed when he reads Shakespeare out loud and every little thing is not received with acclamation; I tell him that in comparison to Sh. all other poetry seems to me like Renaissance sculpture against that of ancient Greece. At lunch he is extraordinarily gay (at the start he suddenly gets up to write something down), sings us all sorts of things from [Donizetti's] *La Favorita,* [Rossini's *Guillaume*] *Tell,* etc., in order to show us Duprez's mannerisms, also praises the text of *La Favorita,* which is very touching. Over coffee he speaks about the curiousness of the musical profession and how he has been reproached for the eternal $\frac{4}{4}$ time in *Lohengrin:* "I have in fact used $\frac{3}{4}$ time in both *Tannhäuser* and *L.,* but only where it is needed, in the 'Pilgrims' Chorus,' in the prayer before the duel; but otherwise the art lies in one's ability to stick to *oratio directa* and not to tell oneself: Now I must make a change, just for change's sake." Musicians are in fact very petty people who don't know what is important, he says, but then, on the other hand, someone like Mozart comes along, who was like a child but never did anything silly. [*Added in margin:* "A few days ago R. spoke in the most affecting way about the Weber ceremony in Dresden and how successfully he had arranged it: he said it was one of the loveliest moments he had ever experienced. He ended by saying that when [Wilhelmine] Schröder-Devrient came out of the chapel with the laurel wreath, he and she 'exchanged a curious look.' "] After lunch, after he has rested, R. and I walk with the children and dogs to Angermann's cellars outside the town, a very merry procession in Faustian mood (the walk) over fields and meadows. Since Herr Angermann is not there, R. goes to meet him, walks and walks until he in fact reaches the tavern in town, wants then to ride back in a cab with the landlord and Brange, Brange uncontrollable, determined to get out, jumps over the horse, R. then gets out, too, retraces the whole long journey to us on foot, but is in the gayest of spirits. We sit beneath the trees in the same place he sat some time ago telling himself, "You must come back here with your little woman." Walk home by moonlight past the churchyard in the same animated procession, with the children calling, the dogs barking (Brange kills a cat), delight in Bayreuth, the trees in the palace gardens, R. feels at home, and so so I; a splendid day, and evening, too, I am filled with unutterable gratitude for R.'s bubbling spirits. When the children gather around R. at the piano in the evening and he plays them the tarantella from *La Muette [de Portici]*, I think of the time when we shall no longer be here and these memories will live on inside them, and thus I enjoy the experience directly and at the same time in a transfigured way. R. relates many things from his childhood, how he brought home some rabbits and put them in a drawer; then how he heard Weber conducting an opera, *Die Bürgschaft,* by Mayer (the same man who [in *Der Freischütz*] played Kaspar and threw himself down flat in front of Samiel, in a way R. always tried to imitate); with his extraordinary memory [*added in margin:* "recently he told the whole story of Goldmark's *Die Königin von Saba,* and I was astonished, as I always am when he talks about some experience and invariably reveals his memory for the essence of it"] he tells us all about this opera, the quartet at the end of the first act, the gloating tyrant, the people bidding their farewells: "I didn't like that, but in the wedding in the 2nd act, the brooding, melancholy friend leaning against a pillar—that I did like." Then he talks about *Der Freischütz,* which he had watched Weber conduct from the actor's box: "I should like to have seen myself!" It was Samiel above all who gripped him, and he was constantly whistling or trying to whistle the devil's whistle. [*Added in margin:* "Concern about Fidi."] After that—and I do not remember what led to it—he reads aloud Aristophanes's *Frogs,* up to the end of the second scene, and when I ask whether these plays were performed in the large theaters, he says he cannot imagine it himself, but one knows next to nothing about the theater of that time. Then yet more music—from *Jessonda!* R. remarks on its peculiar silliness, in spite of many fine passages. He says this kind of silliness so disgusted him in Marschner, at the time he was orchestrating *Tannhäuser,* that he asked Reissinger to take over *Templer und Jüdin* ("in which the whole orchestra plays throughout"), which he was supposed to conduct—though he was well aware of its finer features. A lovely end to a lovely day!

Monday, October 7 R. slept well, our conversation leads him to his feelings of shame vis-à-vis C. Frantz and Schuré, both of whom saw—the one through knowledge, the other by instinct—what would become of the German Reich under Prussian leadership; but he shows no bitterness, and he wishes me "a blessed day, nice things to do and thoughts of me" in a tone of voice which is a blessing in itself! — He seems to be working on his article, for I hear no music. (Yesterday he told us how curiously his themes were linked with certain places— for example, with "*der Glaube lebt, die Taube schwebt*" he always saw the palace gardens and their surroundings.) A letter from Dr. Jauner explains something of the situation in Vienna. In the afternoon R. takes a long walk in the direction of the theater, he returns looking well and goes to his work (*Parsifal*); unfortunately he is interrupted by supper, which he has now fixed for 7 o'clock, and he is quite vexed; I, too, am very concerned, for such things can be avoided. But gradually he recovers, and goes through passages in the early Beethoven sonatas with Herr Kellermann; astonishment over his ignorance and incapability; great compassion for the poor man, whom the world seems already to have broken. After he has left the room, R. goes out into the garden and watches him, unperceived, through the window: he is writing a letter, stops, wipes his brow, sadly shakes his head. R. is moved and goes in to him. "I am not good enough for you, maestro," the poor man says. "You are not good enough for yourself, my friend, forget all the runs and leaps, take out one piano score after another and get to know them all." — R. tells us this touching story illustrating his kindness and an unkind fate. "Your father's personality has caused a lot of trouble: these young people want to imitate something that cannot be imitated, and because of it they miss all the music." Malwida brings us the news that the splendid convent of *San Onofrio* is available for renting: "But *sans* oven," says R. with a laugh, "I'm not going there!" Then, more seriously, he says that Rome does not attract him, nor do its people, who look "so sinister and treacherous" and remind him of *certain people* in Bohemia. After the Beethov. sonatas Herr K.— to make up for it, as it were—plays one of the *Soirées de Vienne,* very pretty. R. pantomimed to it, imagining the couples who might be dancing to it, Hohenlohe and wife, the Dönhoffs, Standhartners, Richters, Jauners—it made us laugh a lot. "Where does your father get it from? I also had my *Soirées de Zurich.*" — When the three of us are alone, he takes up *Othello* and reads aloud the scene with Iago— "Ha, I like not that"—with shattering effect. "Yes," says R., "and what gave him that idea? He had read the mandate, and now he can see it in no other way but that. There one sees how stupid it is to assume that a writer creates out of his own life—one cannot describe a passion in which one is or has been involved."

Tuesday, October 8 He got up once during the night, read some pages in Lecky about the philosophy of Zeno and Epicurus. But he does not seem unwell, makes jokes, saying all women are worthless, "except for one!" Talked again about *Othello,* as if we had been reading it for the first time. Around lunchtime I thank him for the perfume, saying I should like to use it; he says he has put a drop of rose essence in it, and that gives it "its mystical, dark, profound quality"! [*Enclosed between the pages a used envelope on which is drawn a hand and the instruction "Try this!" in Wagner's handwriting. Added in margin:* "I find a little bottle of *Duchesse* on my table. The hand was pointing to the bottle."] — He does not feel entirely well; when I try to treat it lightly, he laughs:

"I shall die on you—you'll see!" The pains are like rheumatic ones in the region of his heart, but they come from abdominal troubles. After lunch R. talks again about Shakespeare, some remarks about the behavior of the children lead to observations on life, and R. recalls King Henry IV's words on the book of Fate: "What philosophical axioms Sh. illuminates just through his observation and vividness of expression! Like, for instance, Othello's remark that we 'can call these delicate creatures ours, and not their appetites.' " Othello's "O misery!" as Iago goes on talking, which shows that he is becoming aware of a cruel world hitherto unimagined—R. also mentioned that shattering cry of pain this morning. R. and I take our walk today up to the theater, the sky is overcast, but the lovely view delights, indeed surprises us. The imposing building gains an ever-increasing power over me. R. arrives home rather tired, we were not allowed to complete our walk undisturbed and by ourselves. [*Added in margin:* "In the evening R. plays the first scene of the Paris version [of *Tannhäuser*]." *Added on the following page, and possibly with reference to this (but see note):* "In the evening R. spoke of the performances and said he would not find it possible to reproach the singers, and that is why he broke off his account. Thoughts of Schnorr in *Tannhäuser;* referring to his death, R. said, 'Terrible!' and added that no death since had made any impression on him."] In the evening we talk a lot about animals, R. recalls Rüpel and Robber, and how the former lay for 11 hours in the stagecoach without being noticed.

Wednesday, October 9   R. got up once and took something which, he says, helped him. Our morning hour is again quite splendid today, we talk about the peculiarities of German humor, how traces of it can be found in the heroic epics, but no longer in the same way in *Faust,* since that contains more irony. I mention the *Odyssey,* and R. agrees with me, recalling with delight both the humor and rashness of O. in taunting Polyphemus as his ship is in danger of being sunk by the rocks the giant hurled. In the afternoon R. goes for a walk, then works on *Parsifal* by lamplight ("*Lachte, lachte*"); he is satisfied with his work, and we are rewarded by a merry supper and a nice evening. R. mentions the action of Gloster in *H. VI,* how he goes to walk around the quadrangle of the palace and then returns; and he feels that this must have been mentioned in some chronicle; I ask him if he does not think the action was Shakespeare's own invention: "It was certainly typical of Shakespeare to notice it and make use of it." At my request R. plays the two finales of *Le Nozze di Figaro,* and this abundance of spirit, inventiveness, and wit in the musical flow delights and astounds us. "That is true mastery," says R., and he points out how even the imperfect cadences, which have an unpleasant effect in the symphonies, are so right here, since they are part of the action, as it were, expressing the tumult and general disorder, until somebody is at last allowed to speak. Nothing differs more from the play *Le Mariage de Figaro* than the opera *Le Nozze di Figaro,* he says, it is the most striking example of how music cannot help transfiguring things and revealing their basic innocence. The Count has accents like Ferdinand in [Schiller's] *Kabale und Liebe,* the cunning, the treachery, it is all pure, and the excellently constructed play can only be helped by music. But the Italian language is essential, and Italians can no longer sing it! "Alas, a dead world," R. sighs. We found great enjoyment in our engagement with this noble, luxuriant genius. Before that R. sang to us "*Les Deux Grenadiers,*" which we have just received and which I like very much. He laughed when he saw the picture by Kietz! The skies were gray all day, the yellow crowns of the trees melancholy against this dreary background; all the same we were cheerful and gay as if safe in port from sorrow; he was well! In the evening R. writes to Richter! — Of a rather silly English lady R. says, "She is an *educated blockhead!*" — Regarding Frau Vogl's leap into the funeral pyre, R. observes that he has in fact included it in his stage directions, and it is a part of the action, but if the audience's attention is going to be drawn to it, he would prefer to cut it out.

Thursday, October 10　Twenty-five years ago today I saw R. for the first time! I put on his table the "litanies" I wrote in memory of that day. At breakfast, before he finds them, we talk more about *Figaro,* and how poor and thin M.'s successors, such as Spontini and Cherubini, are in comparison. The *opera buffa* form gave full scope to his genius, whereas the *opera seria* produced stiffness. At lunchtime he comes to me and says, to my bliss, that when he read my litany he felt quite intoxicated, quite unable either to work or to read, he fell into a sound and gentle sleep from which he rose as if born anew. He reads me a splendid extract from a letter by Seneca about death (quoted by Lecky) and says how much to be preferred are the ideas of the ancient world to those of the church today, whose power is rooted in the fear of death, or, rather, the life after death. We eat alone together in the children's *salon* and lose ourselves in memories—Blandine, Daniel, the two old governesses, *Siegfrieds Tod,* Marie Hohenlohe, Princess C[arolyne], all of it so melancholy and all so sweetly transfigured by our happiness! When Malwida comes up with the children, R. cries out to her, "We are celebrating our 25th anniversary, our silver wedding!" Then he goes off for his rest, and I also lie down. He goes for a walk, and when I awake, I see a reflection of the most golden of sunsets! R.'s spirit shines down on me, pouring blessings! He himself comes to greet me before settling down to work, and, to crown this blissful day, Vreneli sends me photographs of Tribschen and the Schweizerhof, and friend Cyriax writes to say he has discovered the Horseshoe Tavern! A 70-year-old house, the only one still standing, in the City [of London]! . . . R. is satisfied with his work (Kundry's curse); he eats downstairs with the children and comes up to me with two slices of bread and butter, which he has prepared for me. He wants to talk about the "litany," asks me whether Malw. knows anything about it; I shake my head. He: "If I had done something like that, I should have told everyone." Then he takes up *Hamlet* to remind himself of Polonius, and reads the scene with Reynaldo, then all the following scenes up to the players' performance. Oh, could I but describe his expression, the pale, radiant face beneath the noble, arching forehead, recapture the life of melancholy, kindness, humor welling up from within him! Its equal would be seen only in the work he is reading, which hits one like a living experience, in which one is constantly discovering new facets. R. says it is like a criminal case in court, human conduct which one has to decipher: "This is how people are, now learn to understand them." He says he no longer wants to talk about Shakespeare. After the reading he goes out onto the balcony of the children's *salon,* enjoying the evening lit by glorious moonlight, the garden, our home: "What need to seek further? What is a Palazzo Colonna to us? It is all cold, has nothing to tell us." As we part, I utter my request: that he might also want what alone I wish for! "Things are too good for me," he exclaims as he gets into bed, then adds with a laugh, "Of course, if it weren't so, I should keep my mouth shut!"

Friday, October 11 He had a good night and is feeling quite well, the pleasure of having worked well was responsible for his nice rest; he tells me he will soon be finished with the 2nd act. Then he talks about his treatment of the orchestra in *Parsifal,* saying that in the *Nibelungen* he did not have the singers for the orchestra, he had sometimes put them on too elevated a cothurnus, and they had not been able to dominate the orchestra; the singer should be like a single instrument, like a clarinet—[Amalie] Materna, for example, in the scene with Waltraute. When I say that it was precisely in this scene that the balance seemed to me so wonderful, he says, "I am talking about the passionate scenes—I just did not have singers who could dominate." — Thinking of friend Seidl working as a coach, he says: "It will be quite good for him. I started in Würzburg with Paer's *Camilla* and found the wide pages difficult, but I soon learned my way about." Then he enumerates Auber's comic operas and says there is something witty in each of them. He comes to fetch me before lunch and reads me his article, which he calls a proper school essay, "such an effusion"; it is splendid. (Recently he said, "I don't know how Wolz. does it—he always produces such a lot of manuscript pages, whereas mine look like nothing at all.") He says I am to blame, because once, when he was enlarging upon my father, I told him he ought to write it down. Over coffee I read the King's letter to him, very nice. R. says with a laugh, "I shall now have to write an even better one—I can't even show my letters to my wife: it would be a downright insult!" When I ask him whether he loves me, he replies, "My whole life, work, and being tell you that." When I speak to R. about experiments now being made in Strassburg on dogs, involving the removal of the cerebrum, and Malwida explains the reason for them, R. gives her a terrible look, his face white, his head thrown back, and expresses his repugnance for such senseless crimes, which will never bring people any nearer to the nature of things. He goes out in the afternoon, I to meet him, golden rays of sunshine on the yellow leaves, a mild radiance, reminding me of him. Happy meeting in the market place. I tell him I have been thinking over what he says in his article about immortality, that that which is contemporary in a work (its mortality) deprives it of the possibility of gaining a living immortality; then, when its immortal significance is understood and recognized, it can never establish itself fully. "A melancholy state of affairs!" R. replies. — He works, and before supper shows me that the 2nd act is finished! Blessings on this glorious child of sorrow! I tell R. that I feel he is not showing nearly enough joy in this event. — Conversation on all kinds of subjects, among other things the sin against the Holy Ghost, which leads R. to read us something from the book on religious sects, but we find it rather boring and laugh at our tormenting ourselves with it. More thoughts in the evening about the 10th (this was the day on which the 2nd act was in fact completed, but R. says he would have overtired himself if he had written it down then). "You were Isolde," R. says. "You married Marke, with the difference that in this case Marke was the nephew—a curious relationship."

Saturday, October 12   R. had a good night, he dreamed in the early morning that he urged Georg to awake Herr Kellermann, who did not want to get up—"and all the time it was myself," he says with a laugh, "who should have been woken up." He also dreamed that I went away by myself. Lusch's birthday. R. says he is worried about her, but I repeat to him that in his home everyone flourishes and is blessed, and I have nothing but confidence in him. Nice celebrations; R. plays something from the *Holländer* in honor of Lulu (she is called *Senta*), and at lunch he is bubbling over with high spirits, we hardly stop laughing. He then goes out—quite a long way, as far as Konradsreuth. Somewhat tired, he lies down on his couch in the *salon* and reads the book on religious sects; the personality of Zinzendorf interests him very much, he recognizes in the colony of Brethren his own Knights of the Grail, and in the evening he reads aloud various passages connected with it.

Sunday, October 13 R. had a somewhat disturbed night, but in the morning he feels reasonably well, he promises to tell me when the 2nd act is finished, and at 12 o'clock he does so. . . . How to find words for this happiness? In the evening R. says that if anybody had come in and seen us, he would have taken us for a couple of lunatics, I "gobbling up the notes, sometimes helping, guessing," he "playing furiously." But it is my pride and joy that I was really able to follow him, and it was all revealed to me! . . . In the afternoon R. goes for a walk and, when I come upon him, he is lying on the couch beneath the palm. In the evening he plays the Andante from Mozart's D Major Symphony, truly glorious, he observes that it would flow even more smoothly with an orchestra. We stay up quite late together. Mention of Marie Hohenlohe, he says that what made her outburst against him such a sore spot was that it took place at a time when things were going well for him. "In earlier times," he adds with his usual mildness, "she would perhaps not have fought it out to the finish." Then he smiles: "But all these people should not be probed into too deeply, they are much too trivial." "So I can still compose?" he says to me, when I go on feeling the urge to speak to him about the 2nd act but am unable to say a word! — In the evening he says very emphatically that he does not wish to stage *Parsifal,* he would like to pay back the money to the Society members and have nothing to do with singers and orchestra, and above all not with the management of the Munich theater.

Monday, October 14 R. did not have a very good night; he got up once and read Lecky (on Marcus Aurelius). Departure of Malwida, who is going south! — In the morning R. plays *Parsifal,* he says that yesterday he played his thumbs sore for me! Outside everything is gray and yellow, start of the long winter. R. goes out and brings in the China rose, which he calls "the true German rose": these obliging plants touch him very much with their constant blooming, "as long as the cold is not too intense." R. goes out of doors in the afternoon, laughs over the dogs, from whom he cannot get away either by cunning or by threats, but who suddenly forget him and leave him when they catch sight of a large cat, so he is able to get away alone. In the evening I bring down *Opera and Drama,* which I want to continue, and the remark about the horse Xanthos leads R. to read aloud the passage in the *Iliad.* R. then observes that I am restoring his own appetite for his writings. Delight in our existence: "But we must not be disturbed when we are together.'

Tuesday, October 15 R. had a good night. — When we part after the morning hour, he tells me he often asks himself whether I am real, whether I am not a dream! Before lunch he writes his letter to the King and reads it to me. I am overcome by a very curious, indescribable feeling when at the end I read R.'s words that his soul belongs for all eternity to him (the King); it pierces my heart like a serpent's tooth, and I am uncertain what it is I want. I do not want it to be just a phrase, but also not a truth, and even if it were within my power, I should not wish it unwritten, for whatever he does is rightly done. But all the same I suffer, and I disappear, in order to hide my suffering; as always it is the rapturous acceptance of my pain, my passionate welcoming of it, that comes to my aid: greetings, greetings, guest, how gladly I offer you shelter! Cheerfully relaxed, I can then return to his presence and, cleansed, feel myself worthy of being at his side. But how strangely I am affected when R., over our after-lunch coffee, tells me I am wearing my Catholic expression—this is how he jokingly describes a look of exaltation he claims sometimes to see in me. He goes for his rest, and I have some purchases to make in town. I return through the palace gardens, and my thoughts are dispersed as I contemplate the tree-lined paths, overlaid by a fragrant veil of mist, so that in the distance, at the end of the paths, I have the illusion of a curious sunset; there is no outward sun, but instead the earth sends forth its gold; my delight is muted, and my heart is radiant with love. I find R. at his desk, he had been looking for me in Eysser's, arrived five minutes after I left. He is still writing to Herr Jauner about Jäger, and, referring to Richter's telegram, he says with a laugh, "What a good thing it is to have telegraphed 'Letter follows'—then everything can be considered settled." — In the evening read *Opera and Drama;* R. feels Wolzogen should seek out and supply the examples for everything.

Wednesday, October 16 A bad night! R. frequently out of bed, reads Lecky (whom he is enjoying very much), has such a vivid impression of the blows Bakunin had to endure that he feels he himself has received them. In the morning we wonder whether it was a tough partridge he ate in the evening which so upset him, or the reading of *Opera and Drama,* or a very evil-smelling ointment he put on his sore thumb. We both had breakfast in bed and, as always, this first morning hour is cheerful in spite of the bad night. R. is gathering strength for the 3rd act; around lunchtime he comes in, bringing me several "curious bits of paper," some of them from *Tristan.* I ask him to keep them all and give them to me at Christmas, and now I have the joy of already knowing about these precious papers, though I have not yet looked through them. In spite of not having slept in the afternoon, either, R. goes out and attends to some business affairs with friend Gross, during which as always he shows himself to be the soundest businessman of all, for he discovers quite a large error in the Leipzig accounts. We listen to the children singing in Lulu's room; I have the feeling that I shall not live to see Siegfried grow up, and with these poor pages I should like to leave him at least a hint of my existence, so that he may know how much I loved his father, and so that his life's aim may be to show himself worthy of his father. — In the evening R. reads "A Pilgrimage to Beeth." to Lusch and Bonus; before that I read an article by Herr Lipiner about "Art and Revolution" which does not please us. If only people would still start with the words "Once upon a time there were a king and a queen"—that is to say, write simply about the subject under discussion! Talk about the socialists, led astray by their Israelite leaders, always against industry, never against trade!

Thursday, October 17 R. slept well, and after our morning conversation, which concerns Lecky, Mozart, and the German Reich, he leaves me with the words, echoing Frederick the Great, "Now I am going to collect *fuyards* [refugees]." He means all the musical ideas which he has hastily written down; he told me yesterday that most of all he would like to write some symphonies, gay and cheerful works in which he would not venture at all far, but he feels a real need to give vent to this side of himself. He is also thinking of revising Senta's ballade, the beginning of which he finds is quite properly like a folk song, but not characteristic of *Der Holländer*. Over our after-lunch coffee he sings to me a theme with words: "*Dem Morgen nach der Weihnacht*" ["On the morning after Christmas"]. I also heard sounds in the morning which I could imagine to be the beginning of the Prelude. Went out with the children, R. fetches me from the Wolzogens'. He then writes a few words to Herr Lipiner, asking him first of all to discuss the work pragmatically and then, when he has put his readers in the requisite mood, to bring in his philosophical ideas. He also writes to Herr Tappert, inviting him to write for the *Blätter*. In the evening R. reads to me and the two elder girls "Death in Paris," which I find deeply moving, for after all it is a part of R.'s own nature, described by him. Very profound, indeed bitter feelings about my unworthiness, the nearer I come to grasping his character and my happiness. When the children have left, R. remarks that the conception of art as we understand it is in fact a completely new one, never known before. I: "It was you who put forward this definition, before you it was only Schiller who had any inkling of the idea of an artist as a high priest." "And that is why they can't stand him, either," says R. Then he says that, should one wish to name anything that shows the complete detachment of music, its power, of which up till now nobody has had the slightest idea, then he would cite the fugato in the first movement of the 9th Symphony. We also talked of Schopenhauer's wonderful definition of music and Heaven knows what else in the joyful excitement of being alone together!

Friday, October 18 R. slept well, he tells me, but he had to get up once during the early hours. At breakfast he talks about his symphonies, how one might perhaps do something in this form of music if one did not feel obliged to compose in four movements, and if one shaped the motives—first, second, return to the first—into movements. Then much about the German Reich, with much melancholy! "And so we are agreed," says R., half in fun but half in earnest, "that it is done for." "As I said, I am ashamed that so many people have proved me wrong, and knew that a Pomeranian *Junker* would never understand German culture." [*Added in margin:* "—not exactly in those words, lost his composure."] He goes to his work, and when he calls me to lunch he says he now knows exactly how things should be, he must not introduce anything isolatedly, it must all be in context; and so his prelude to the 3rd act will introduce the theme of Titurel's funeral, just as in the prelude to the 1st act he brought in the song of the Knights of the Grail. There is no place, he says, for a big "independent affair" depicting Parsifal's wanderings. After lunch some further newspaper reports about the laws on denunciation and on socialism provoke from R. the remark: "That led to Austria's downfall, and now we are doing just what Austria did: landlords are obliged to give the names of their guests!" — Then he tells me that the English newspapers are declaring openly that Prince Bismarck is no good at domestic affairs. Much talk about German workers emigrating. Walk with R., the children, and the dogs between the poplars to Konradsreuth, autumnal atmosphere, a bat flitting above the fields, but feelings of contentment inside us; R. laughs: "We in Bayreuth! With the children!" He deals with some business matters in the evening, and after supper we read some works by Leopardi which Malwida has sent us. To start with, however, there is a certain amount of prejudice to overcome: R. does not care for poems, the first, "To Italy," does not grip him, and the first dialogue seems trivial; yet another has no appeal at all, and we soon abandon the story of mankind; but the dialogue between Tristan and a friend dispels all misgivings; on reading one sentence, R. gets up and writes a note about "then" and "now": "Strong characters with a limited outlook, now weak characters with a wider outlook, which is harmful for that very reason." At the conclusion of it R. says, "Now we have got to know him." We then read "Plotinus and Porphyrios," and R. declares this to be the best thing ever written about suicide; he is full of admiration for the fine, clear-cut classical form of this dialogue. We also enjoy "Ruysch and the Mummies," and certain isolated thoughts. At the conclusion he says, "Yes, I know it all, and it is above all the disgust which one feels most deeply; but I never think of it; there is one thing they knew nothing about." Then he talks about our being together here on this earth. What is suffering, distress, compared with this moment? To hear from his own lips that it is our love—and not the joy of creating—which makes him forget this misery! I, poor blissful mortal that I am, take leave of this day in a frenzy of delight—what life or death could prevail against this? . . . When he calls suicide the highest affirmation of the will, I: "Oh, don't say that, for I don't want to live without you." He: "That is something different." — He explains that L[eopardi] fled before an outbreak of cholera; thus, "one wants to decide for oneself, and not leave the power over our death to some brute force."

Saturday, October 19 Yesterday was so lovely that I could have died in the intoxication of my soul, and yet R. had a bad night! . . . It was only midnight when he first got up and did some reading (Lecky), then again at 2 o'clock, and so throughout the night. He had a prophetic dream about a flue which collapsed in the kitchen, and the completely blackened bathroom had to be cleaned by Ross; afterward, in the early morning, he heard the chimneysweep at work; then he pulled a large and long white tooth from his mouth and admired it, but then was troubled by a broken tooth cutting his tongue. I appear at lunch looking wintry in a black velvet dress, which pleases him. How many nice, good, kind things he says to me, what an image he conjures up of me in my unworthiness! He does not look too run down, despite his bad night. In the morning, when I begged him not to work, he said, "You know I never force myself to work; if it comes, then that's all right." At lunch he tells me, "Perhaps I shall end by gobbling up the whole *Romeo and Juliet* march for Titurel." He says with a laugh: "I am now composing nothing but funeral marches! People will say, 'Is Amfortas dead?' 'No, Titurel!' 'Oh, yes, that fellow back there in the alcove.'" We laugh over the triviality of the public, and R. says, "They must have it in black and white—whatever happens, no surprises!" He goes for a walk, a very long one, as he tells me on his return, adding that his foot is now better. May he receive all the blessings Heaven and earth can bestow! (Today at breakfast he came back to that sentence about "now" and "then," pleased that history provides him with proof of his conviction—for example, the former and the present-day Italy—for when one bases one's ideas merely on one's own experiences, one runs the risk of deceiving oneself. A reproduction of a picture by Doré showing the retreat of the 10,000— arrival at the sea—gives him great pleasure; he says he likes such pictures, and, looking at it, he remembers Doré with pleasure. We spoke of the absurdities of the literary life, deciding that Leopardi certainly suffered from a sense of being such a useless creature. Goethe had this feeling, and so does my father—but not Schiller, who was content with the prospect of producing a few good pieces every year. — His walk took him to the Students' Wood, and he returned along the highway past the powder magazine; he says the atmosphere reminded him of Berlioz's "*Scène aux champs,*" and he talks of Berlioz's curious outward relationship with Nature. I observe that it was like Klingsor and his power over it. "Yes," says R., "he did not recognize its soul, but he listened to its sounds and captured its scenic atmosphere." In the evening read some more of L.'s dialogues, though with less enjoyment (R. puts in first place "Plotinus and Porphyrios," which we read yesterday). R. says Leopardi was a personality of pathological interest, and to be understood only as such. It seems to me that he could not have known the main source of happiness, which is enthusiasm, arising either from art or from love, and this was the cause of his unhappiness. He did not know Shakespeare, Beethoven, Goethe, R. Wagner. R. feels also that Latin antiquity must have an oppressive effect on an Italian. We Germans are luckier, he says, our origins lie in ourselves, and we can delude ourselves that we are able to bring our past back to life; and also we have no civilization behind us.

Sunday, October 20   R. had a good night! — In the morning we talk about Catholicism and how impossible it is to reach agreement with the Catholics: the subject came up because of a reply by our friend W. in the *Schlesische Zeitung*. "Christ and the Gospels will live forever," R. says, but with the founding of the church and the interpolations in the Gospels everything was spoiled, for the first Christians saw the second coming of Christ as an abolition of the world, an end to earthly existence. Then R. says we ought to write some dialogues together, for instance, a pessimist and an optimist on the present situation in Germany, but he says he wants to be the "stupid" one. I heard no sounds of music in the morning, and at lunch he tells me he ought to have two drawers always open for scraps of paper, one for music, the other for prose, for the *B. Blätter*. He brings all kinds of mail to the table, among it a very nice letter from the Spaniard Marsillach. After lunch he describes the remark by Windthorst—"We are the conservatives, you (the Conservatives) are reactionaries, because you want to upset the existing order"—as an excellent one. He regrets that W[indthorst] is unable, on account of his party, to speak openly. "A bad business," R. says again, with reference to the dethronement of the German princes. At lunch he says with a laugh that no doubt our Society would look very suspicious to Bismarck, and they would confiscate our funds; like the Roman emperors, they feared nothing so much as secret organizations. In the afternoon R. and I go out, calling on Wolzogen, whose article, "The Stage Dedication Play," pleases R. very much, though he remarks to me that W. goes too far in calling Parsifal a reflection of the Redeemer: "I didn't give the Redeemer a thought when I wrote it." — In the evening Herr K. tells us of the uses to which the Niagara Falls are being put; R. replies, "Our good Lord must be clutching his head in exasperation." — Then he reads the first act of *Die Meistersinger* to me and the girls. Shared memories! Impossible to believe it was ten years ago! "Though we, you and I, haven't altered at all." I tell him that only the 4 years before that had seemed long, in spite of the flashes of joy which lit them up, but since the decision life has flown by. — Before the reading he played Auber's summons to the meeting in the market place and found great enjoyment in it; altogether he thinks frequently of Auber, particularly his genius in writing for the trumpet. This leads him to the Prussian trumpet, which lacks a D, and now the whole of Germany has been obliged to adopt it: "It is supposed to sound a signal over a long distance," he adds, more as an explanation than as a consolation. Toward the end of the evening he plays the finale of *Die Zauberflöte,* "where the sun went the other way," and exclaims: "Oh, how beautiful that sounds! How beautiful these sopranos can be!" . . . When we are alone, we read bits from Porges's article in the *B. Bl.* R. says he read the whole thing today, but he cannot remember a word of it, his mind had wandered to all sorts of other things. Certain expressions, such as "the crisis is *established* in a human being," cause us great merriment, and R. says, "The best one can say is that he gives us things which other people before him have said ten times better."

Monday, October 21 R. woke up once during the night and got up, but he soon calmed down, got back into bed, and slept soundly. I tell him in the morning that I prayed for his rest. "To whom?" "I don't know, I just knew that I inwardly wished and pleaded for your rest." "Yes, if anybody could understand these mysteries—" And that brings us jokingly back to Porges! In a dream he saw some large birds with no eyes in their sockets. — But in the morning he woke up cheerful and sang quite an assortment of melodies, my father's "Loreley," "*Am stillen Herd,*" then jokingly challenged me to sing him *one single* melody by Schumann. . . . Then he exclaims: "A melody! What a heavenly thing that is, wrapping everything in purity, ennobling it! When one hears something like that, one has the feeling that nothing ever existed before, as if everything is now beginning to breathe for the first time." He then sings the melody of the Countess's second aria in *Figaro:* "There is nothing there to see, nothing to grasp hold of, yet it goes beyond everything, even the graceful gestures of the most exalted moments, which are what come nearest to melody." — When he takes leave of me, he embraces me and says: "Everything is all right! So it was and so it will be!" We go to our work, I hear the sounds of music again! When R. fetches me for lunch, he says, "Now I am writing something which should sound like nothing, nothing at all, Robert Schumann, but there must be method in it—the theme of the march would have been much too definite." His eye is hurting him, he sprayed something in it; when I ask him about it later, he says: "Already better. It's just that I have to make a great fuss, then I'm ashamed of myself, and it's all right." Over coffee, while I am saying something or other, he exclaims, "That's it—it must be shifted half a bar, held back half a bar." All the time he is noting things down, a musical or some other idea, but if he were to carry a notebook around with him, he says, and think to himself, "Today you must write something down," without a doubt nothing would occur to him. He tells me that again today a theme came to him with which he can do nothing—his room is full of such scraps. Drinking his coffee, he looks at the Wolzogen house and praises it as a kind of creative act in itself. After his afternoon rest we go there together, and then he suggests that I go with him to Angermann's. I say, "With pleasure," and we carry through our "adventure" in merry mood. R. leads me into the empty "notabilities' room," very odd, "Oh, that's the real thing," we sit down opposite each other, and a very gay mood takes possession of us, a mood which not even Frau Angermann's chatter (she greets me as *Frau Meister*") can disturb. The dogs are also with us. After a little while we walk home, still accompanied by heavy rain. R. writes a letter to friend Feustel about raising our friend Wolzogen's salary. — Over coffee we again talk about the peculiar calm and security legitimacy imparts to princes—R. observes that this is what the Roman emperors lacked, and that to some extent explains their excesses. — Yesterday he came back again to his music of mourning for the men who fell in the war, and said he would make use of the Prussian piccolos in it. In the evening I read to R. part of Luther's letter "To the Aristocracy of the German Nation," with great interest and admiration. R. agrees with me when I say a similar sort of letter should now be written about the Israelites to— well, to whom? R. compares our present aristocrats with those of Luther's time: "One has only to look at the way they dressed," he says with a laugh. I observe jokingly that in this case the letter should be addressed to the socialists. — *He* is the only person I know whose heart beats so powerfully with compassionate anger: what L[uther] was for religion, so is he for art, but he is the only one, much more "unified" with his work than even Luther was. We look at the pictures of the "phonomotor" in the I[*llustrirte*] Z[*eitung*], and R. sets it aside jokingly: "You are my phonomotor." I go to bed with great worry on my mind, for it looks to me as if R.'s stomach is very swollen; my worry gnaws at me, and after R. has gently fallen asleep, I take refuge in prayer, call upon the kind and gracious fate which raised me so high, praise it, and implore it for mercy, mercy!

Tuesday, October 22　R. went off to sleep with the words that he was feeling increasingly better and I should not worry; he greets the new day cheerfully with the words "Whether it annoys you or not, I slept completely undisturbed." At breakfast, referring to our reading of yesterday, he says, "We must get down to our letter." Then he observes that on no account should one be put off by the sometimes curious expressions in it but should always try to grasp L[uther]'s larger meaning. The misfortune of Protestantism, he says, is theology—the interpolations in the Gospels made an exegesis necessary. He praises L.'s quotations and says of the apostles, "They were, after all, the only people who called a spade a spade." — At lunch we drink my father's health, after R. has written a telegram in Latin—"*Magnificat anima nostra, Patrem optimum Franciscum. Richardum Cosima cum familia.*" R. clinks glasses with me a second time, saying, "Things are better than they were." Over coffee R. tells me that he has found something, only a few bars, but they contain a lot; these early-hour dawnings produce the best results, he says. He cannot play it to me. When I express my regret, he says, "But I will write it down for you." I try to stop him, telling him he is not supposed to write immediately after lunch: "For whom should I do it if not for you? *Pour l'éternité,* perhaps?" he says with a laugh. He writes it down and plays it, I recognize the lance theme, and with it the sinister figure of Klingsor and Parsifal's motive, though in some way impeded. One feels and in one's mind sees him entangled in the labyrinth, holding the spear on high. R. says one good thing about it is that the lance theme ends chromatically, full of melancholy, whereas P.'s motive is fresh and bold; he praises contrapuntal form, which provides so many possibilities. He goes for his afternoon rest, and afterward I find him unfortunately much annoyed by the gate leading to the Wolzogens' house, which has been positioned asymmetrically. He takes a walk with the children along the highway to Konradsreuth, autumnal atmosphere, Berlioz, says R.! But his vexation has affected him, he looks worn out and is again spitting a little blood, and, with a sword in my heart, I continue reading him Luther's letter to the aristocracy; the reading gives him pleasure, and he scolds me for my worrying. Memories of earlier times; his visit to Berlin, our meeting in Leipzig, I in mourning, he says it was all so transfigured, so dreamlike, I amiable throughout, not high-spirited but serene. "We were so happy at being together." I: "Yes, everything else was like Weissheimer's music at the concert, which I did not take in at all; only *Tannhäuser* and *Die Meistersinger* remained in my mind."

Wednesday, October 23 R. slept well, and so I myself feel all the better when he tells me over our after-lunch coffee that I will see how he continues to improve. In this connection I remark that he is the only person I know who is able to be happy desiring nothing, neither fame nor power, nothing from outside, he leads a completely inner life. "If you count yourself as part of this inner life, then you are right; Fate had to bring me this gift, and then I wanted nothing else." — The promulgation of the socialism law for $2\frac{1}{2}$ years ensures that one no longer has any desire to look ahead. A socialist newspaper is printing some articles on *Art and Revolution;* R. says, "They come somewhat late." — The weather is very wet; *the lemures* are working here, that is to say, a canal is being dug around the house to dry it out; we think of *Faust,* the splendor of its poetry! A rainy day, no walk, R. just for a short while in the garden, drafts a telegram to Herr Jauner about Jäger, writes to Herr Lesimple about performances in Brussels. We spend the evening in the gold chamber, since in the *salon* preparations are going on for autumn and winter; contemplation of the pictures, which have been taken down; R. finds mine too superficial, the soul is lacking. — Continued reading Luther; the quotation of his last word in the socialist newspaper, in combination with the newspaper's narrow-minded judgment, its lack of understanding, exercises R.'s mind greatly: "It is like having cold water thrown over one," he says, "it teaches one a lesson."

Thursday, October 24 R. had a good night, and at 5:30, when he wakes up, he tells me that he has already been composing in his thoughts. At breakfast he comes back to Luther's final assessment of things and the present world's assessment of him: "How tragic and sublime it is!" Later he says jokingly that when, in the rarest of circumstances, the world brings forth a great man, it has always looked upon him with astonishment, just as Rausch, our gardener, looks at his seeds when they come up! . . . But before that he mentioned how the princes accepted Luther's teachings in order to further their own interests, how the peasants had distorted them, how he had to admit that for such people the Pope was just about right, and how he himself is now judged. "And the world imagines it learns something from its great men!" (It was to this he linked his joke.) "And Christ, too, although on his cross he stands high above all such things—he would surely have thought, when he saw his work, 'The Roman *Imperator* is just about right for all of you.' — And now these awful consistorial councilors as Luther's successors!" Even the world figures who seemed the best were bad—Marcus Aurelius, for example, who persecuted the Christians most of all (this he said yesterday, talking about the princes). To all of this he linked our wish not to stage *Parsifal.* When I support him in this, he says, "You and I, we set our sights on the highest heights," which makes us laugh heartily—as always, even the most melancholy of observations cannot spoil our joy in being together! We have our afternoon coffee in my room, R. talks about the sad strains he will now have to compose; they must not contain a single ray of light, he says, for that could lead one far astray. Parsifal's sad wanderings, which must lead up to the situation on Monsalvat. — Telegram saying that Herr Jäger has been engaged for *Siegfried* in Vienna, which pleases R. — In the afternoon (toward evening) he presents me with the manuscript of *Opera and Drama!* And also, seven letters to Uhlig, sent to him by Elsa Uhlig with a very nice accompanying note. We read the letters in the evening, talk about many past events, and then he plays to me some of the gloomy strains, and we end the day happy and uplifted.

Friday, October 25 R. did not have a good night; in the early hours he had a curious dream: he had performed something, and was about to descend from the platform on which he had done this when some wild animals, attracted there by him, appeared; they licked his hand, but at the same time bit him and stopped him from going farther, while I was pleased that the animals were paying homage to him in this way. Telling me this dream, R. says, "So you think animals are particularly fond of me?" I: "Yes, you are closer to Nature than most other people." Despite his bad night he goes to his work, saying to me, "It is a curious life one leads with these figures, a sort of ghostly life." I start my day with the most melancholy of reading material; Glasenapp has sent me a copy of R.'s letters to Damrosch! Oh, God, how to avert this hatred for, and these wicked feelings against, people who suddenly appear before one's eyes? . . . With work; the children help—may I be as useful to them as they are to me! I am able to conceal my feelings from R., but, curiously, Daniel comes into my mind, I talk of him, saying that, if he had lived, things would perhaps have been different for him and R. — R. says I bore the loss of them both in remarkable silence: I believe it is only with him that I can talk about them. — R. writes to Herr Jauner about Jäger. Pleasing news that Hans's concert in Berlin, consisting of Beethoven's last five sonatas, was very successful; R. says it is quite incredible. — In the evening I say to R. that I told Malwida in a letter that we must be very thankful for having found this patch of earth here for ourselves and our children: it would be a crime to think of Italy. He says I am right, and in reward the heavens today pour rain in buckets over us! And bad weather depresses R. In the evening we look through a nice book, written by a Dutchman, *Voltaire musicien;* it is accompanied by a very nice letter. — R. gets Herr Kellermann to explain electricity to him, and feels less and less desire to concern himself with science. R. says: "I wonder when they will discover something to extract ore from its underground shafts? — And whom would the socialists send down for it? Probably the princes and the aristocrats." After that we finish Luther's letters, with the same feelings.

Saturday, October 26 Again a bad night for R. He got up at 2 o'clock and read Lecky. When I am unable to hide my concern he comforts me, saying he is really all right: "Though if I were alone or had a *méchante* [wicked] wife, I should not be all right." Yesterday he suddenly quoted "A wonder must it be when two souls love" and, recalling the curious previous behavior of certain people, said, "And when it happens, they look away." Recently, when he read the letters, he said that people had actually sinned against him, having realized how much he could bear. — At lunch he looks worn out, he tells me he always literally experiences the moods which he is composing! — In Prussia they are now confiscating newspapers, R., indignant, says, "Forbid is all they can do, they never think of anything else." And more about Luther: "He is a link in the great chain." — In the afternoon he goes to see Herr Gross with the accounts from Vienna. At supper he is looking quite well again! He says that in the Berlin newspapers Herr von Hülsen is again dishing up the old fairy tales about *Die Walküre*. R. then asks us what we would like to hear, and I ask for *Tannhäuser;* he plays us (Lusch, Boni, and me) the finale of the 2nd act and the beginning of the third, up to the appearance of Tannhäuser, and we weep, the children and I—those hot, blissful tears whose falling signals a liberation! R. jokes about our emotion, but I tell him this work will never be surpassed. He says of Wolfram that he is a truly German character, "Italians and Frenchmen have too much *chaleur de coeur* [hot blood]," he adds with a laugh. Today it seems to me particularly beautiful, the way in which Wolfram's noble, gentle male feelings are transformed into a symbol, as it were, through his greeting to the evening star. — R. is glad that he shortened the Prelude: "That was foolish, all that recitative." Then he says he can imagine how bored a modern audience, "the Jews," would be with "Elisabeth's Prayer." He recalls Mitterwurzer with great appreciation, I recall and tell the children about the occasion 22 years ago when I saw this work for the first time. Now I am delighted and touched by the children's emotion, and I send a message of remembrance to a grave, for Blandine was with me at that performance. When I say to R. that, now that Herr J[äger] and Frau Materna are in Vienna, they could perform *Tristan und Isolde,* R. says, "It would give me no pleasure—let it rest till my Garrick comes along." —

Sunday, October 27 R. had a good night. When I tell him how pleased I am, he says a stimulation such as he experienced last night did him good, and he would enjoy playing his works to us. "Now I want to come to grips with the prelude to the third act" is practically his first word today. — While we are still in bed he tells me of a conversation between Meyerbeer and Benedict in Boulogne; they had been talking about a "distinguished" talent, and when B. said that the *gants jaunes* had been active in support, M. observed that nowadays one ought really to say *gants blancs,* since yellow gloves were out of fashion. R. has never forgotten it. He comes back to the idea of taking the children to Munich to see *Tannhäuser,* but incognito; he thinks that nobody would recognize him anyway. I say, "Like in Zurich." There, he feels, several generations have grown up since he last appeared publicly, it was only at the beginning of his time there that he used to see people. "Everywhere," he says with a laugh, "my life has ended up in a dead end." After embracing me, he leaves me with the words "Well, the semiquavers must be attended to." "I go without emotion to my emotional sufferings." — When I tell him how much I like the *Gradus ad parnassum,* he says, "Yes, it is like strong coffee" (which he now prefers to tea in the morning), "and there is something about this continuity (like Bach's C Major Prelude, for instance) which one never tires of pursuing, just as one can go on watching a river forever." He laughs when I say, "On the other hand, a theme which advances on one like an individual and destroys the fundamental unity, if it is not in itself very significant—that is not at all pleasant." He is amused by the word "pleasant." We also talk of the chorale Herr Levi has sent us; it starts with a frightful dissonance, and R. says it reminds him of Duprez, to whom Berlioz once gave something quite horrible with the words "*Cela doit vous plaire*" ["This ought to please you"]. — We spoke of the costumes in *Kabale und Liebe* (he recently read the "Put it with the others" scene, which he once saw played in mixed costumes, the President, Wurm, Ferdinand in modern dress, Marshal Kalb, Miller, and his wife in rococo dress), and of the difficulty of finding the proper costumes for nonhistorical dramas. We have outgrown this play, he says, for we are no longer stirred by patriotic feelings: "The Jew is an entirely new creature," and he can no longer identify himself with it. He works, but is unfortunately run down—that is to say, he looks run down when he comes to see me—for at lunch he is in the gayest of moods, bubbling over with scintillating wit. Friend Wolzogen visits us, and we discuss our Society's affairs in great good humor. The wet weather and the complete lack of sunshine oppress him, and we feel like borrowing *Die Zauberflöte*'s sun! — We spend the evening alone in conversation and, following our discussion, go through various

passages in Beeth.'s last quartets. Beforehand we read a bit of Herr
v.d. Straeten's *Voltaire musicien,* but without much enjoyment. "By
music they understand something completely different," says R. (He
has written to Prague, which also wants to do the *Ring.*)

Monday, October 28 "Tolerably well," R. replies when I asked him
how he had slept. Our breakfast conversation is cheerful and harmonious, he goes to his work and tells me, when he comes to fetch me
for lunch, "Tomorrow I shall play something to you." — Over coffee
we talk about my mother and the bitter experiences she went through,
then about mine 10 years ago in October. I don't know how one
manages to survive such things: a kind fate must have been watching
over me! R. speaks of his "raging worry," which induced him to send
Claire to me. — R. goes out for a little while, I have some things to
attend to; when we meet again, he asks me to come up, since he wishes
to play something to me and wants my advice. He then plays the
prelude to me and shows me the many pages of his preliminary sketches,
among them the song for Titurel's funeral. "To improvise like that,
get inspirations—that is not difficult—my difficulty always lies in
restraining myself." Here he has succeeded wonderfully in making his
theme stand out against a background of elemental sorrow, and one
feels completely at home. Noticing my emotion, R. says, "So it is
good—I am glad." He then tells me that Princess Auguste once
compared *Rienzi* to a rich embroidery. I say that is true of *Rienzi,* it is
like a cloak of gold brocade with flowers, but not of the other works. —
In the evening he reads to us the 2nd act of *Die Meistersinger,* to our
great, great joy. And with the words "Another lovely day!" I part
from him at the first station, as he calls it, to meet him again immediately at the next!

Tuesday, October 29 A dream I tell R. amuses him so much that I
will tell it here, as he himself told it to the children at lunch. An
actress playing Minna von Barnhelm was addressed by one of the
other characters on stage as Frl. von *Birn*helm; she tried to keep a
straight face, but when she saw the laughter spreading, she showed her
annoyance; the actor she was addressing replied that it was not at his
mistake that everyone was laughing, but at her hairstyle—blonde in
the middle, brunette at the sides. More or less thus, for no dream can
be told quite as it was. — R. says he has composed two bars, but they
are very important ones, an addition in the middle of the prelude: they
had occupied his mind the minute he awoke in the morning. The
skies still overcast, but R. goes for a walk. In the evening he reads us
the 3rd act of *Die Meistersinger.* (Today received [a picture of] R.'s
wedding house.)

Wednesday, October 30 "Take heed only of the eternal, not the transient"—that was R.'s parting word to me today. He works, and after lunch gaily tells me his dream: Minna and he had been together; she was unpleasant. He: "You know we're separated," whereupon she gave him such a sorrowful look that he felt stricken. Then he thought of his position at the Grand Opera, from which he was drawing 6,000 francs annually; he could not very well show his face there, but he decided to ask Nuitter to fetch the money and send it to Minna. Then he went into a tavern for some cognac, could not find any at once, the people upset, then unpleasant, he replied, then lost courage when things threatened to become dangerous, whereupon he awoke. He had to get up twice in the night, and he read Lecky about the influence of Christianity on the position of slaves. — After lunch he goes out, I do some shopping, and we meet on our way home; he says, "I'm saying nothing, but there's something I want to change, though not at once." I beg him not to do it, to remember the quintet in *Die Ms.,* which he thought bad until he played it to me, I was moved to tears, and he then kept it. — Then he tells me (somewhat later, when we part after our meeting) that the [Good Friday] meadow will be in D major, in $\frac{3}{4}$ time. — In the evening he plays the piano with Lusch, who does very well, sight-reading the three marches. Before that he played all sorts of things to the five children, who settled down beneath the piano—the greeting to the King of S[axony], and the songs *"Mignonne"* and *"Dors";* when I express my continued pleasure in them, particularly *"Mignonne,"* he asks me whether I think they would make the same impression in a Paris *salon;* people there were too heartless to appreciate such idealized images (I had told him that I saw in them that quality of tender, smiling resignation which is also characteristic of the French). Then he recalls [Pauline] Viardot, who had discerned enough in the songs to remark on them, but she did not then sing them: that shows what she was like, he says. A lovely evening, which I can see living on in the girls' memory.

Thursday, October 31 R. slept well; we talk about the marches (yesterday he felt bitter about the fate of the *"Kaisermarsch"!*); he said how strange—that is to say, how new—all these things seemed to him: he looked upon them now with complete objectivity. I ask him whether that does not happen with everything one writes—letters, for instance. He agrees, observing that it is as if one were always play acting. R. in his kindness today writes to friend Seidl, though the latter has not written at all, to inform him of the progress of negotiations with Trieste and Brunswick. — Yesterday he intended to read more Luther, but one cannot spend too much time with it, he feels. Then, still at breakfast, we discuss, first, the meadow (which will be "a pastoral," he says with a laugh), then a visit one day to Spain. R.

feels a great antipathy toward visiting any town in Germany, says he cannot think of one he would enjoy seeing again. — At lunch (after his work) he asks Eva where she would prefer to go, to Barcelona or Heinrichsreuth. "Where do we leave the ship?" "In Eurigsroda!" he says with a laugh. A very nice letter from Mimi Schl. shows us clearly how little the outside world now means to us. "How many people we have outlived!" R. says, then complains that he has never met any truly free people—"at best only eccentrics." In the afternoon I walk to the Rollwenzel tavern with my own and the little Staff children plus the 3 dogs—a company of 12. R. comes to meet us on our return and we walk into town, after offloading the children and the dogs—he to Angermann's, I to the Jäger children, temporarily orphaned. He finds me at the confectioner's, we return home, and he goes to his work; he stays with it until eight o'clock and is afterward preoccupied. We spend the evening alone (after playing, as yesterday, to the children sitting beneath the piano—bits from *Die Walküre* and "*Ach, du lieber Augustin*" with a pompous introduction). He plays the prelude to me; it is very much altered, even more gloomy! It begins like the lament of an extinguished star, after which one discerns, like gestures, Parsifal's arduous wanderings and Kundry's pleas for salvation. [*Added in margin:* "That is to say, not the lament, but the sounds of extinction, out of which lamenting emerges. — 'My preludes must all be elemental, not dramatic like the *Leonore* Overtures, for that makes the drama superfluous.' "] It seems as if none of this could be sung—only the "elemental" quality can be felt here, as R. does indeed emphasize. "People will say," he remarks jokingly, "that if Amfortas had seen the vision of the Grail and heard the lament, he could have carried out the task of salvation as well as Parsifal!" "But just as a professional task," say I, "and if Parsifal had listened to Kundry, she would have laughed, and then everything would have been all right, too!" — Lengthy discussion about this new miracle.

Friday, November 1 Everything exacts its price—R. had a bad night and had to get up twice! He read Lecky and discovered, he tells me, that the Christian reliance on alms had ruined countries such as Spain and Italy. Strangely, France had managed to avoid such excesses, being a country in which a certain common sense prevails generally, but this means that it possesses neither the Catholics' great productivity nor the Protestants' urge for freedom. — As I, returning from my bath, sit down to breakfast with him, he says: "I was just thinking that it is only since I have been with you that I have had the feeling of a home; when I furnished a place and made it comfortable previously, as, for example, in Zurich, I always had a bad conscience, so to speak, as if I knew that it would not last, that everything would soon break up.

That shows how unsound much of my life was." But with how much more justice can I declare that it was he who made a home for me! . . . I then tell him about one of our cocks, whose melancholy call today reminded me of the beginning of his prelude. R. says he knows what I mean and it is true: it is the diminished fifth which sounds so peculiar, he would call this his cock theme. Then he tells me of a green material with which he has turned his chair into an "arbor." "But then I am obliged to compose such dismal things," he says with a laugh. "People will think I must have written such stuff in an attic, starving and freezing!" We go our separate ways laughing. More houses from our good friend Glasenapp! Even R. takes pleasure in them, particularly the Knevels house. At lunch he relates his dream to me and the children: Lenbach was giving a party for us, and then I was sitting with Lenbach in a sort of office, and this annoyed R. Over coffee he exclaims, "When I think of Vienna, how lonely I always was there!" He tells me of a walk he took with Friederike Meyer to Sperl, having in his memory the merry bustle of Vienna in the years around 1830, when old Strauss was still alive and he first got to know it; but by this time it had become melancholy and dreary, nobody there but "a few Jews with good-for-nothing women," and all so dull! — Some shopping for me, after which, as always, a gay reunion with R. In the evening he shows me Tappert's periodical, and when I tell him that musical periodicals make me almost sadder than ordinary newspapers, he replies, "Yes, because they affect us more closely—it's like the resemblance between apes and men." R. and I then go with the 3 little ones to welcome the Wolzogens with champagne in their new house; the idea came from R., and he laughs at my readiness to comply, which reminds him of that wheelbarrow in Frankfurt: "That's how one should be!" he exclaims. The wheelbarrow has become for me the celestial Wain, in which he bears me on and on toward our spiritual home. Returning from the W.'s, we have coffee, then he plays first of all the Alla Marcia movement of [Beethoven's] A Minor Quartet (R. wanted to show me what a "fraud" the *Marches of B.* are—they have just been advertised in an arrangement for piano duet by Kirchner); then he plays the following movement as a piano duet with me, amid much laughter at our clumsiness. — Then we talk about God. I say that for me my fate represents God, omnipotence and benevolence: when it is revealed in that form, one cannot do otherwise than believe. He then talks at length of the manifestation of divinity, something divorced entirely from time and space, which he says can be compared with electricity. "I must write another article about God," he says with a laugh. Then he tells me what Lecky has to say about the insane behavior of the ascetics in the 4th century, and ends, as so often before, with jokes about the "excise."

"True through and through!" he exclaims to me as we return from the W.'s—oh, how was it possible that I be permitted to become the agent of his glory?!

Saturday, November 2 All Souls' Day! Not a good night for either of us and when, in the early hours, we want to rest, the noise of the chimneysweep! Cheerful breakfast all the same—goodness knows how it is possible! I send the children to lay a wreath on the grave of our friend Dittmar. And in the afternoon go for a walk with them in the chilly sunshine. R. rests, but he has done some work, in spite of his tiredness. He also goes out in the palace gardens with the dogs, delights as I did in the moonlight and the ever-recurring feeling of being at home; I tell him about my many excursions, and he laughs at my report of my activities. In the evening he gets Lusch to play the "*Huldigungsmarsch*" with Herr Kellermann as a piano duet. Reminiscences of the fate of this march—its dismal performance in the garden of the Munich Residenz, the King at a window, no members of the public present, a dull and cold November day. The "*Kaisermarsch*" also "scattered to the winds," not to speak of the "Centennial"—"*in front of Grant!*" — When Lusch has gone, the quotation "You match the spirit that you comprehend" brings us to the "efflorescence" of Goethe's genius in his youth, for which no praise can be too high. And what a happy circumstance that he was permitted to finish the work— his life in between was like Parsifal's wanderings in the labyrinth. — R. reads me passages from Lecky about asceticism: he is particularly struck by the sentence saying that during the first two centuries love was put in the forefront, during the 3rd and 4th centuries chastity, and that is what led to the excesses of cruelty. He enjoys reading the English writers, he says, for at the present time they have the clearest and most manly view of things. Great weariness.

Sunday, November 3 Very good night, cheerful awakening, and at breakfast continuation of the conversation about the chapter in Lecky; we decide that the excesses to which the insistence on chastity led constituted a terrible feature; they were due to the impossibility of realizing something felt to lie deep within the human character, the desire to set oneself outside Nature and yet to go on living. Over our afternoon coffee we talk about Blandine, her fate, her strange marriage. Yesterday I was reflecting on Daniel, how he would have blossomed into life in R.'s company: for him, too, all barriers would have fallen, and in his devotion to R. he would have found the source of a new life. In the afternoon R., returning from his walk, shows me a little notebook, telling me that this is how things are. R. vexed in the early evening by the way people talk about the new law; he points to the picture of Bismarck in the *Illustrirte Zeitung*, copied from the statue:

"This is what our present German statesmen look like," he declares to all supporters of the new law. In the evening a reception at Wahn-fried, a Frl. Chiorni sings something from *Le Nozze di Figaro* very nicely, then *Lohengrin* ("Elsa's Dream" and the monologue from the 2nd act), not very enjoyable in Italian. R. writes in the lady's album: "Long breath—fine soul." He accompanies Susanna's aria so beauti-fully that I feel all piano players could learn something from him; there are certain virtuoso skills which we find increasingly unenjoyable, I tell R. that such techniques give me the impression of tendrils, sucking life out of the stem, and he says, "Yes, they are parasites." When the evening ends and we are upstairs, he returns to Susanna's aria, and he cannot find words to describe his delight in its beauty of feeling; when we are lying in bed he talks also of the later passage, the *"Contessa, perdono,"* how glorious it all is! He says he would like to have had Mozart as his contemporary. I: "Shakespeare would have suited you better." He laughs, saying it is difficult to imagine such things.

Monday, November 4   A good night, but R. still feels tired. He tells me that he regards one of our guests, Councilor Kraussold, as a good omen, the councilor is over 70 and still very sturdy. It seems odd to me when R. says such things, for he gives the impression of having nothing to do with age! Very gloomy November day, plenty of rain. Over coffee we read some words in the *Dresdner Nachrichten* about the Trocadéro in Paris, ending with a comparison with our festival theater—short, but full of nice feeling. R. somewhat weary in the evening, but we chat away the time together in such a lively way that it makes us laugh. On this occasion we were exchanging impressions of German painting (Schnorr, Kalbeck, Cornelius), and remarking how soon these great impressions faded into nothing (though R. still likes some things by Cornelius—the picture of the downfall of Troy and the picture of the Nibelungs). "When I saw the first large painting," R. says, "that was enough for me—its clumsiness reminded me of Pecht and Kietz, I felt as if I were standing between them." When I say that literature has not produced any similar illusions, R. says maybe not in us, but in others. We agree that, if there had been anything genuine in this artistic movement (of Schnorr's in Dresden at that time), *Tannhäuser,* for example, ought to have been hailed by it as a fulfillment of all its desires! Our conversation then leads us to the King of Bavaria, his defection from our ideal—how sad, how terrible that was: "I had found my monarch, and this is what came of it! Now I have to ask the King of Prussia and the Crown Prince for what *he* failed to do for me." Penultimate conversation in the evening (at the 2nd station) about perfumes, R. speaks of the melancholy in essence of roses, even if it does not reproduce the scent of roses; he is pleased

that Plato places fragrance among the aesthetic pleasures which do not
arise from necessity, but which come to us as a pure gift. — Before we
go to bed, R. describes to me the present situation in Europe and
observes that war may now break out on account of the Bulgarians.

Tuesday, November 5   A good night for R., and he works. At lunch
friend Wolzogen with his entire family; R. very cheerful and kind; we
discuss the "Knights of the Grail," who have sent us an outline of
their ideas. "They are not much to look at, something like the early
Christians, and their catacombs are in the Orlando. But a beginning
must be made, and though I cannot say I expected it to be like this—
and have indeed to keep silent about it—I must all the same admit they
are on the right path; however, it would look very ridiculous were I to
give them my blessing!" — He goes for a short walk, and in the
evening reads the French text of *Fernand Cortez,* amused and astonished
by what our neighbors consider to be poetry: *"les ardeurs légitimes"*
["legitimate ardors"] amuses him greatly, particularly the final word!
He criticizes the opera's "childish barbarism," also Spontini's recitatives and the lines endlessly repeated, then exclaims: "How great
Mozart is in comparison! Not only with his predecessors, but with his
successors, too." — Then he loses himself in reflections on fame, what
it means when it is possible for people today to hold up Mozart against
him: "Oh, it is tragic! Everything is tragic!" — Before reading this
libretto he received and answered a letter from friend Standh. At tea,
standing by his writing desk, he suddenly sings, "How lovely is my
tunic!" I took this to refer to *Parsifal,* but no, he has ordered a carpet
for my room; then he jokingly gets vexed with himself for having told
me! — When the children have gone he discusses the similarity between
the present world situation and the fall of the Roman Empire, when
national virtues also ceased to flourish, Christianity having torn down
the national barriers; now the Jews are completing this work. "At
best," says R., "I anticipate a return to a kind of state of Nature, for
the Jews will also meet their doom." The present crisis in England
suggests to him that the socialist movement will perhaps start from
there, "for we Germans don't take the initiative in anything." He tells
me that Lecky did not understand Joan of Arc, he just thought she
was mad: "A man like that has no place in our church." — Herr von
Perfall sends a telegram asking whether he might send along *his*
painters, R. says in his reply they will be welcome, but premature. To
conclude the evening he plays passages from Act I of *P.,* and in two
places I join in, in a duet—with much stumbling, but very great
delight. I bid farewell to this day, too, with melancholy: "I should
like to die." R.: "And I to live." "I could call the 3rd act of *Parsifal*
'The Sleeping Beauty,' since she is found in a thornbush." I: "Löffler

would understand that at once." — He tells me that St[andhartner] was pleased with his clear, straightforward letter.

Wednesday, November 6   R. had a good night; he dreamed that he was floating in the air; he was in a kind of boardinghouse in Paris, but the company there turned out to be unpleasant, and he floated ironically away. — He leaves me with the words "*Nulla dies sine linea,*" saying this is the way he earns his happiness! [*A few words of untranslatable word play omitted.*] At lunch he tells the girls they ought to have learned to play stringed instruments, for then we should have had a quartet, and he recalls a Mme Christiani in a red velvet dress, who played the cello; this memory takes him back to Berlin at the time of the *Rienzi* production, and to a *soirée* at the home of poor Gaillard to which this lady came wearing a tiara and a velvet dress, carrying her cello; it was quite unsuitable, for the surroundings were so dismal and dreary: "We didn't even have the money to advertise the piano scores, and it was so cold, everyone so miserable!" The day before he said that with Meyerbeer and Redern he was like the hare between the two hedgehogs! — R. has a slight cold, but he takes a walk. After supper we go through *Fernand Cortez* on the piano and are truly astonished by the clutter of trivialities, everything really just an excuse for ballet. After that a discussion with friend Wolzogen on the present situation— everyone is too compromised ever to be able to speak the truth about Israel, because the bankers have now become identified with the idea of property, and everyone's head reels at the thought that he might not be able to turn himself from a poor man into a rich one. — That teachers in Prussia are now not to be given a bonus, but instead the 2nd examination is being dispensed with—this makes one shake one's head and smile sadly. An old party dress which R. once gave me and which I have turned into a dressing gown pleases R. a great deal: it is such a joy to dress myself up for him—how rewarded I feel by his gay appreciation!

Thursday, November 7   R. had a restful night, but he has a heavy cold and a headache. We talk about my father, whose failure to reply to our letter has a curious effect on us. "There is one thing I can definitely say to your father," R. remarks, "and that is that I am now under a better influence than he—he can't deny that now!" Some women seem unable to realize that happiness in dealing with a man of genius lies in seeing this blossom in its own individual way; they want to be Beatrices, whereas I want to be Dante, to be molded entirely by him, my ego destroyed, myself wholly absorbed in him. When he comes to fetch me for lunch, he says he has pulled everything apart, whereupon I quote to him the French proverb, "*Château démoli est à moitié reconstruit*" ["A demolished castle is half rebuilt"]. At lunch he says he would like to write some marches, even if only funeral marches for ladies: one of them would turn out very ecclesiastical, the other "subaltern"; we soon get his meaning and laugh heartily. "Oh, no," he continues, "I wish for nobody's death, my enemies, as far as I am concerned, can live as long as they like, but there are some specters in this world who are thoroughly superfluous." — Today he does not go out, because of his cold, but he writes letters, including one to the producer in Prague. The projected Indus railway interests R. very much, he says: "When one thinks of the difficulties Alexander encountered in his campaign there, and now sees these activities, one feels really astounded, as previously by the Pacific railway." He thinks I am becoming fatter and regrets that I did not look as I now do when my father was here. I tell him I am only well when I am alone with him, for then I feel purified of original sin, and that benefits me physically as well. At lunch he told us several legends from Lecky about the saints; he said he would soon overtake me in this respect, but one ought not to pay too much attention to the details, for it was all so pedantic that it aroused one's disgust. There had been only one saint who included animals in his compassion and who felt what he, R., has always felt—that for an animal there is no element of reconciliation in suffering, whereas a human being can always overcome it through cognition. He is very impressed by Renan's statement about our present times: that human functions could persist for a while without faith, just as an animal could still continue to live after its brain was removed, but the situation could not last long. In the evening he takes out *As You Like It* to look up the passage on animals when Jaques is being discussed, and he reads all Jaques's scenes to us and also Touchstone's, to our continual amazement. He points out how the princes in Shakes. always dwell on the theme of justice, as the Duke does here when he reminds Jaques of his former life. Then he says that costume in Sh. is still similar to ours, yet idealized; impossible to play this comedy in frock coats. And thus the evening passes in talk about the impact of the sublime; a general review of R.'s past life enables me to remark on the extent to which idealism is the source of his kindness and consideration; he has always seen through everything, I say, but he could never bear to admit it; he preferred to seek excuses or extenuating circumstances even for weaknesses of the very worst kind. He says, however, that the people who declared that he was no longer productive were right: if we had not come together, this would really have been so. — He recalled Betz and Niemann and felt a desire to write to them, for what they did here was truly extraordinary, he said, beginning with their participation in the stone-laying ceremony. He also meant to write to Otto Wesendonck, who had also behaved well formerly.

Friday, November 8 R. slept well in spite of his cold. At breakfast, when he returns to the subject of Renan and I tell him I cannot imagine any of the present famous German writers being able to formulate such thoughts, he says, "They are too difficult, too much concerned with 'progress.' " But then he adds, "Nietzsche could have done it." I tell him that Nietzsche has requested that the *Blätter* not be sent to him. "I'm glad he has taken it to heart," R. says. At lunchtime a telegram about the dress rehearsal. [*Inserted here a telegram from Vienna dated November 7:* "Dress rehearsal successfully completed. Jäger in good voice till end and excellent. Best prospects for performance. Regards, Richter, Seidl."] After lunch I tell R. that, in the course of my lessons with the children, my reflections on the Semper theater and the Dionysian theater in Athens led me to thank Fate that the project was never carried out in that cold building on the banks of the Isar, complete with ballrooms and royal box. Instead, it remains an ideal, pure and eternal, and Athens remains the past. The people who served Fate in this matter had not for that reason been any less reprehensible, I say, but Fate itself was kind. R. agrees with me, and we go on to discuss how nothing is absolute, everything is always conditioned by time and circumstance. I say this is why I do not like to see monuments erected, huge things aimed straight at eternity, all they suggest to me is accumulation and imitation; the Gothic church should be banished from the city, mystery plays in the courtyards, Shakespeare's plays done on his stage, the *Ring* in our "barracks"— an eternal reproach and an eternal symbol. "That is a very tragic view," R. says quietly, and continues reflectively: "One sees to what extent everything depends on individuals when one thinks, for example, of how Luther was influenced by Saint Paul. One might say that the whole of Christianity has been dependent on the personality of Saint Paul, and Luther allowed himself to be guided entirely by him; as we, too, are guided by the wonderful revelation of Christ, by the few frightened apostles of limited intelligence and the senile Saint John who passed the revelation on to us." — Watching me as I listen to him, he says, "Are you putting on your gemmish expression again?" He explains what he means: "Like an engraved gem." [*A few words based on word play omitted.*] In the morning, when we were talking about Renan's ideas and then the Germans, he said he was glad all the same that he had gone through the war with feelings of joy, and not with the feelings he has now. — In the evening he brought back from Angermann's, where he went for a glass of beer, a copy of *Der Sammler,* to read to me some anecdotes about Bismarck. "He's a stout fellow, and pretty remarkable for a Prussian."

Saturday, November 9 R. disturbed by the night light, which was burning poorly, but he is in good shape all the same. When he comes from his bath he plays something on the piano which seems to me to be connected with Kundry's awakening. He is a bit vexed over the visit of the Munich painters, fixed for today, since, as he tells me, he has just got everything nicely prepared and would have been able to do some composing. At 12 noon we receive the two gentlemen, discussion about the scenery for *Parsifal!* Both with their heads full of frills and vistas, R. alone putting his finger on what would be right here; he says the cupola should not be visible, only the architrave supporting it. When they have gone, R. asks me: "Did you look at Döll? There's complete dissipation for you." When I say I did not think much of Herr Jank, either: "Oh, the utter viciousness, disloyalty, wickedness of them all!" It was both curious and sad to see these creatures who once treated R. so badly, now standing embarrassed and humble before him! "No one is uninteresting when one looks at him closely," R. says. When they spoke about the "perseverance" R. showed during the festival, which won him the admiration of all, R. said solemnly, "It was thanks to the application of the artists, which was extraordinary, all of them arriving at the right time, arranging their guest appearances to fit in—that's something no Excellency could achieve." — R. does not go out of doors today, and I am not very well, so he drinks his tea upstairs in my room and reads me some extracts from Dr. Busch's book; he very much likes the story of the cigars, and especially the expression "malicious impotence" as applied to Varnhagen, but the assessment of N. III does not seem very thorough: the "sentimental, foolish, ignorant" may be correct, but there appears to have been more in him than that. R. is very interested in a picture of two natives of Nukaivan; he tells me about the downfall of this handsome, uncultivated race—one could imagine Heracles springing from such a stock, but such types have disappeared with cities and civilization. We have no barbarians left to bring new blood to our world, he says; if it had not been for them the Roman Empire in the West would have gone the same way as the empire in the East; we are collapsing in the same way, and the Jews will become our natural masters. The crisis will occur with the dissolution of the armies, and then the Anglo-American complex will assume dominance. Afterward I read to R. Herr Lipiner's article on *Art and Rev[olution]*, and we find little in it to please us; R. is completely disgusted. —

Sunday, November 10 R. got out of bed only once: "I wanted to make a note of my dream, to tell it to you exactly, but now it's all gone." Telegrams from Vienna, the first of them from Herr Lip[iner]! The others come later; and so *Siegfried* has now conquered this stage! R. thinks it all the more remarkable since this is just a sort of intermezzo, the real tragedy is *Götterdämmerung*. Lunch alone together in the children's *salon,* we toast, firstly, Luther (in St. Perey), then Schiller (in champagne), and R. recalls our meals at Les Artichauts, where, "though all around us the skies were gray," I could be cheerfully relaxed. I do not know why the thought of death should come to me at lunchtime, but I remark that I had heard that a dying person usually speaks an acquired, foreign language—and I was afraid I should speak in French. R.: "Oh, rubbish, we mean to commit euthanasia, we shall both nod off on a chair, asking each other, 'What is going on?,' and then we shall be dead!" He tells me he has just reached the point where Kundry is arranging her hair: "I shall set it in a pleasant Rosenfeld style—or should I, rather, do it like Frau Ziegel (the very dignified ladies' hairdresser here)? But she will let out a little cry of alarm when she sees where she is." A little later he says, "Shall I use triplets or quadruplets for my figure?" Friend Wolz. comes to see us, Lipiner is discussed and condemned by R., his right eye flashing fire, his left inwardly contemplative. He quotes Lecky, whom he likes very much (yesterday he said he knew of no German writer whose books he wished to read), on the mendacious and slanderous nature of church literature. [*Added in margin:* " 'France is now a true idyll,' R. jokes."] Before that he said, "Shakespeare and *Don Quixote*—it's to them we always have to return." He adds with a laugh, "We can smash up the whole library." I: "But take out *Faust* as well." "Yes, but not the Court celebration and Helen. The marriage of Helen and Faust—it's a good idea, but no more than that." "I suppose you prefer Touchstone and Audrey," I say jokingly, and he laughs at the thought of this marriage, considering how she treats him. Returning to the second part of *Faust,* he says one must go straight from the "Classical Walpurgis Night" to the scene where Mephisto takes off his seven-league boots, and from there to the end—that is the way to read it. — The meeting with Count Du Moulin at Angermann's leads R. to the subject of his relations with Munich and the Society of Patrons: "Only a large legacy could rescue me from their clutches." Then he adds: "And then I should be really miserable, for I have nobody, no singers, no conductors, no producers—I tremble at the thought that my little Fricke might not live to a ripe old age. It really is miserable! A legacy would also spoil Italy for me. The best thing would be for me to give these people their money back, but I am scared of the King and of Wolzogen." — In the afternoon he reads me Lecky on Catholicism and says, "I come more and more to the conclusion that its continued existence is a scandal." A glorious sunset lit up the skies today, R. went for a walk and told me the moon came up golden, like a sun, and he asked himself: "Where would you rather be now than here? In Berlin, perhaps, beside the Victory Column?!" In the evening R. reads to us excerpts from the Busch book in the newspaper; in connection with the judgment on Thiers he exclaims earnestly: "Oh, my friends, he did great things for his people." He then summarizes his opinion of Bismarck, particularly in connection with the passage on the Jews: "Great superficiality! He sees the world through the eyes of a diplomat and cannot recognize a significant personality, only the miserable creatures with whom he has to deal." When I emphasize his peculiar religious beliefs, R. says, "He is a man of the people and is guided by popular instinct, reflection is foreign to him; he creates German unity but doesn't know what it is." As we are reading these excerpts with enjoyment, R. says, "Any detailed account of any individual is interesting, I am interested in Bismarck here as I would be in a Shakespeare character; if someone gave me a photographically exact representation of our Georg, I should be captivated by him, too." — After our friends (Wolz., Du M.) have gone and R. has stressed that he does not want any recruiting done for the Society and that everything must be left to find its own course, we talk about his triumph with Jäger in Vienna. I tell him I have one particular superstition—that if we retire into ourselves, live only in and for ourselves, we shall succeed in the outside world in a way we would certainly not succeed if we joined in directly; and I also believe that things will turn out well for the children if they live a completely inward life along with us and we seek no advantages for them outside. R. agrees with me; we imagine what would have happened if we had gone to Vienna with Jäger, how difficult things would have been, how unsatisfying for him; "For everything remains what it always was," says R. "Set wigs of million curls upon your head, and there you are, the wig of million curls, and the situation remains what it always was." — Sad feelings about Herr Kellermann: "They are all specialists nowadays," R. says with a sigh. — Once again we think of Luther and Schiller: "All ideas of Germany are just a dream which one links to individuals like them and to characteristics something like theirs, but one tends to exaggerate them: it all happens just in one's own head." "But it is true that they could not have been born anywhere except Germany," I observe.

Monday, November 11   R. had a good night, and we chat about all sorts of things, beginning with "the wise Englishman Lecky," from him to the "universal pest," the Catholic church, then to the theme of the variations in Beeth.'s E Major Sonata, which all pianists love to play and which has consequently become something of a trial for R., wonderful as it is. Gaily, but with deep, deep tenderness, we part, and I am writing the last lines in this book to the sounds of his music! . . . Just as no painter has ever succeeded, even through exaggeration, in conveying his look, or his mouth, in the same way I ask myself whether I can ever succeed here in giving my Siegfried even a faint reflection of his true nature. I am trying, but how, poor creature that I am, can I hope to succeed? . . . Yet perhaps these pages will bring back to him the impressions he himself received from his father. — Yesterday R. expressed his regret that he could not yet take Siegfried in hand, that this was still a woman's job; he said one could not come close to children just with clear explanations and answers to questions. [*End of the eleventh notebook of the Diaries. The twelfth begins:* "Will they be of any use, these pages? . . . Will they be able to give you, my Siegfried, a picture of your father? I do not know. But remember one thing when you glance through them—that your mother has tried, amid the exertions and worries of the daily round, in the happiness and bliss of love, to preserve for you something which is eternal and ultimately had to be! November 25, 1878, while supervising a dancing lesson."] Speaking the name Corelli in the French way, R. says that what chiefly annoys him about the French is their habit of pronouncing every word as if it were French, and never putting themselves to the trouble of imagining how other nations see things. At coffeetime a telegram from Vienna, which he answers. He then sings the scene of Tamino's parting from Pamina in *Die Zauberflöte.* "It is so pure," he exclaims. "Why couldn't any of the blockheads who followed Mozart declaim as beautifully as he did? Winter, for instance, in his *Opferfest,* and so on." He told me that after breakfast he never felt very well, and that he usually fell into a deathlike sleep, from which he always awoke refreshed. "When I am dozing off, I usually see—today, for instance—your eyes, the Catholic ones, then the big, big, very solemn ones, and then I try to recall the Catholic look." — Returning to the variations in the E Major Sonata, R. says that Beeth. loved this form and gave himself a treat in the *33 V.;* he, R., cannot do it. I observe that he could if he wanted to. R.: "No, you have to have it all at your fingertips, you must be able to improvise on the instrument." Speaking of the sonata itself, he says it is much too easy for pianists who wish to make an impression with it, and Kl[indworth] and others always reminded him of Bottom: "I have enough wit to serve my own turn." This morning he quoted a verse from Marschner's *Vampyr,* which led him to German musicians, so rough, so coarse, but with a certain feeling for pathos: much of *Der Vampyr* sounds as if it is from *Der Dorfbarbier,* he says. — In the afternoon he goes for a walk and returns vexed with the weather, which is gray and damp: "I would sooner be in Moscow. Anywhere but out of doors." In the evening he plays the piano for a while, his songs "*Stehe still*" and "*Der Tannenbaum,*" the "*Albumblatt für Betty Schott,*" and a Bach prelude.

"I like Bach better than myself," he says with a laugh. "This music one really can call sublime! It always reminds me of old cathedrals, it is like the voice of the thing-in-itself; in comparison, the sensitive and the sentimental seem trivial; in Beeth. everything is dramatic. I sometimes feel I don't want to hear anything more by Beeth.—I know the five sonatas. But Bach I should like to be able to play for myself."

Tuesday, November 12 R. had a good night, but also a sad dream: I ran away with my father, so swiftly that he could not catch up with me; Kellermann blocked his path, saying I was already far away; in the evening I returned, very serious and silent, R. sad, but the beds full of watering cans and old metal! . . . "How many generations have I outlived!" he says. "When I think of Tausig and Cornelius, who entered my life so late, and Mendelssohn, already 30 years dead, and it seems only 5 years ago." He describes how Schumann was introduced and played his "ABEGG Variations"—"full of ornaments, something I hated at that time." — Then he sings the C Major Overture: "I should like to play it for you one day: it's impossible to take it too fast, one shouldn't really know what is going on, it must sound completely mad, for the theme is not of sufficient significance, though I can see what induced him to select these sequences; it has to sound completely mad." He also starts singing one of the Gellert-Beethov. songs ("*Vom Tode*"), and when I praise it he says with a laugh, "But it's asking a lot of anybody to sing it." — He comes upstairs to fetch me, sits down beside me, and suddenly laughs about Gurnemanz's herbs and roots: "He sounds so cross, so disgruntled." Then he became a bit impatient and said, "If you only knew!" And soon I do know, for when I enter the *salon*, I see a magnificent Persian carpet for my room lying there! . . . He had been in correspondence with Standhartner about it, and now he sends off a telegram of thanks, signed "He and she." — At lunch he sings a number of Viennese songs to the children, and over coffee we enjoy the carpet, which R. compares to a panther, saying it has the velvet sheen of a panther. He is gradually coming to appreciate my taste, he says: "Just a little while longer I shall go on wanting pretty colors and patterns, but when I am 70 I shall turn Siberian." Then he says I should not give him presents at Christmas, and he wants to put off my birthday to coincide with his, which we will celebrate together; I willingly agree to this nice idea, but he takes it back, saying: "No, no, it's foolish." When I try to insist, he says, "One shouldn't try to pin down every idea that flits through one's mind." Before our evening meal I discover him at his desk, beginning the 3rd act in ink! Jesting at table, he says, "Children, behave yourselves: it is so easy, as you can see from me!" — Talking about Fidi, he recalls the "foolish hanging of thy nether lip," and he reads us Falstaff scenes. He goes out for a while, returns, and says: "A spasm! If you can break its rhythm it goes away—that's the way I used to stop hiccups, and it's the way one can overcome all bad impulses, by just once not giving in to them." — Mozart again, and this time in connection with Beeth.'s *"Du wirst mir alle Ruhe rauben"*: he says Mozart did similar things much better. He also plays me the oboe entrance in Donna Anna's aria: "Such melancholy sweetness!" "I am the last of the Mozartians," he concludes his reflections. Then chance leads him to Lessing, and he reads to me the conversation about John's will and two of the replies to Goeze; much pleasure in their acuity and elegance: "What wit there is in such a brain!" says R. — When I return to him in the evening, after the *first station of parting,* he says as if to himself, "Noble spirit, thou gavest me everything," and then continues to reflect on the relationship of God to the world, how difficult it is to describe; mortals always think of it historically, in terms of time and space, and what emerges is something external. When I observe that Goethe expressed it best of all, he says, "Yes, in *Faust,* Part Two; the curious form of that remarkable book makes it seem a kind of Gospel." Then the foolishly hanging nether lip again: "How he sees these things!" he says. "Such a man comes once and never again."

Wednesday, November 13 He dreamed about lakes, I am reminded of scenes that took place at lakesides! In spite of his cold he is well and cheerful, a letter yesterday from Herr Lip. provokes him to say he is willing to be taken anywhere as long as it is not where he might "meet the Dauphin" (Lipiner). Returning to our reading from yesterday he says: "That is the curse of Christianity, all this clinging to the Old Testament, such a name: Ephraim! It shows how predominant the Old Testament was, in the beginning presumably in order to impart more authority to the new religion. But it can't all be explained by that: there are such things as simple universal pests. I suppose we must accept that another 1,000 years will be needed to cleanse the Revelation of the Old Testament." — A little later he says: "The transformation scene, painted by that tippler Döll—what do you think of that? And Jank, who looks like a valet mixing a drop of poison for his master." — Friend Wolzogen's birthday, Fidi proposes the toast. — R. goes for a walk, says on his return that he feels unwell but observes, when I express concern, that it doesn't need to be shouted at once from the rooftops. — We meet in the dining room, he comes in singing "The mighty Fritz was very small" and says: "What can a Jew make of something like that, which is a sort of folk song for us, and of the way the people saw their great man for themselves in a foreign civilization? Who is better entitled to tell that to the Jews than the Prussians? And so I should like to declare to the Reichstag." He works, in the evening as well. After supper he again talks about Bach, saying, "In him you find all the seeds which later flourished in so fertile a soil as Beethoven's imagination; much of what Bach wrote down was done unconsciously, as if in a dream; my 'unending melody' is predestined in it." He wishes he could play the piano well enough to perform Bach for himself. Then he goes through the introduction to the first movement of [Beethoven's] A Major Symphony and exclaims, "Oh, to have such an inspiration, such an inspiration!" [*Added in margin:* "R. would like to have an orchestra."] — We continue with Lessing (*Anti-Goeze*).

Thursday, November 14 R. had a good night and, after a joyful embrace following a conversation about all kinds of things, we go off to our work. His lasts long, and we eat rather late. After lunch he goes to the piano to play to me Parsifal's arrival, noble and melancholy: "This is only approximate, these are just more or less ink blots," he observes. We talk about our position (in a business sense), and R. decides on 1880 as the year for performance: "Either I stick to that year and am then completely free after the performance—for if anything crops up it will be behind my back—or I put off the performance, pay off the deficit to the King out of my income, and give the patrons their money back. What I want now is to complete the composition, without thinking of either performance or nonperformance." Snow flurries prevent R.'s going out of doors, he works during the afternoon as well and plays to us (the W.'s are present) the prelude to the third act, now written out in ink. Friend W. calls it seeking the Grail, protecting the spear; I am astonished how R. found it possible to present with such concision a motive which is clearly designed for expansion; just the core of the idea, but this done with such intensity that one has the feeling of being able to develop it oneself. Then he tells us that during the afternoon he reread Shakespeare in English and felt an utter repugnance for the English language—he would never succeed in learning it. In vindication I point out the advantages of Shakespeare in English, vividness and precision, whereas in German it is all nobler, more elegant, even more poetic; I give the witches' scene as an example. R. agrees with me, and we go through *Macbeth*, in English and German; but how swiftly is all linguistic curiosity dispersed by the strength of its impact! R. says one must always be able to *see* what is going on, how facial expressions change, the person becoming different through his impressions. We also speak of the great artistry in letting the witches start the play and then reappear; R. says, "One then wonders, not who they are, but what they will say." Later we come again to speak of the fact that the greatest of poets was obliged to write in such a language; also that Goethe made use of

Latin-French words for purposes of irony, which is splendid, but not indicative of a harmonious culture. "Only Luther was German," R. says, and comes back to this unique man, his influence, his work, and his concern for the people; it is all very well now, he says, to criticize the catechism. Such words as "reputation" (Cassio: I have lost my reputation)—how abstract and conventional, how much finer is "*Ruf*"! That is no obstacle, of course, to a genius, but it is to culture. Lecky also leads R. to the subject of the peculiar bigotry of the English, the way in which certain evils cannot be cured because no one is permitted to talk about them by name. Much, much more about cultural matters, always returning to the conclusion that the only true art these days is music. We also talk about the Jews. R. assumes that the present financial calamity in England is also the work of the Israelites (Beaconsfield). It should not be presumed, he says, that these people, who are so separated from us by their religion, have any right to make our laws: "But why blame the Jews? It is we who lack all feeling for our own identity, all sense of honor."

Friday, November 15 R. had a good night, and he goes to his work; at lunchtime he fetches me and says he has a riddle for the children: What animals are always having picnics? Hens, because they *picken* [peck] and *nicken* [nod] at the same time! Lovely sunny day, R. goes for a walk; after the "panther" has been laid in my room, I arrange the "butterfly," to R.'s surprise and delight. We continue our conversation from yesterday about the English language and Shakespeare; R. says Italian was undoubtedly more suited to Dante's genius than English to Shakespeare's. In the evening we read *Anti-Goeze* (after taking much delight in the children, particularly in Fidi's intelligence, with R. playing "*Kunigunde und Eduard*" to them with ornamental flourishes). But we think we shall not be able to continue it: "The main point is never discussed, the root never touched on," R. says. "I must admit that Renan was the first to have got a *bit* closer to the point, but only a bit, he didn't recognize God, either." "It may be that our present-day criticism will succeed in showing Christ in a pure light, for how much in the Gospels has still to be abstracted!" "I shall really have to put my theology in writing one day," he says, half jestingly, half in earnest—or, rather, changing from earnestness to jest.

Saturday, November 16 Ten years ago today I came to join R. We celebrate the day in our thoughts; we go through all our memories, virtually all the details of our life together, and if R. invokes blessings on me, how much more must I bless him, who has given me everything, everything! As we go upstairs after lunch, R. says, "And we have been blessed." It is true: everything has prospered, children and works! —

"How quickly these years have passed!" R. says. He recalls that I was very solemn when I first arrived—like Kundry, I had had only one wish, to serve, to serve! . . . A lovely day, wonderful sunset, rose-colored clouds, a lovely feeling of being at home here; Tribschen a dream, this the reality, but also ideal, sheltered from the world. — R. thought of the concerts in London, the departure, at the end, of the well-dressed ladies with their trains—"like a lot of erlkings"; of his saying something they did not understand to three ladies who were going out while the music was still playing! . . . Then (in '55) how, before starting the *Water Carrier* Overture, he tried to wait until all the departing people had really gone, and how they stopped in alarm and then applauded at the end—but great consternation among the concert managers! He says artists there are regarded as mere domestics, and when someone comes along with a feeling for the dignity of the occasion, everybody gets worked up. (It was of the *Msinger* quintet in London (1877) that R. said, "It sounded like *Der Dorfbarbier*"!) — At coffeetime he sang "*Drei Knäblein fein jung und weise,*" admiring the way Mozart constructed his melody on this text: "He never composed anything foolish," he says. — In the evening utter absorption in old times, so many sufferings. How good it was of Fate to have removed him from Munich in '65, R. says, for it precipitated a decision; how fortunate that Hans was just as he was, R. also observes, for otherwise we should either have been destroyed by his nobleness, or made by his baseness to look despicable in each other's eyes. He sends for half a bottle of champagne, we drink to our life together, which has become happier and happier. "Except that I am too old," R. observes. "I should be 15 years younger." I: "Why?" "So that it could last longer." I tell him that this was the only thing I have contributed, my little bit of youth, and that is already somewhat old! — Alone after this wallowing in reminiscences, I see in my mind once more my parting from Hans, my stay in Augsburg with the two girls, embarking on the ship, the stars, which Loldi noticed, the single light illuminating the dense black night in my heart as I watched over the children in the ship and gazed rigidly and numbly into the unveiled countenance of my destiny. That night was the womb of all my blessings, annihilating all pretense— a holy night, awesome in its acknowledgment of original sin, the silent prophet of love's redeeming power!

Sunday, November 17 I was concerned that R., disturbed by our wallowing in reminiscences of happiness and suffering, might not sleep well, but my blessings did not abandon me, he slept peacefully and well, bathed with Fidi, and at breakfast is well and cheerful. He comes to lunch late, held up by his work. He tells me that he has just composed "*Kar-Freitag*" [Good Friday], which he has accented differently from its usual form: "It ought in fact to be '*Klag-Freitag*' ['mourning Friday']." I beg him to call it so. He: "It's not a good thing to put oneself forward simultaneously as a poet and a philologist— that would draw attention to it." I ask him whether he cannot let Gurnemanz say "*Klag-Freitag*" at the first mention, then subsequently "*Es ist Karfreitags-Zauber*" ["That is Good Friday's wonder"]. He agrees. A letter from the lawyer in Dresden vexes him, for a proposal which R. himself is now unwilling to accept has been turned down by the King. In the evening R. plays the *Eroica* (1st movement) with Lusch, then our conversation leads us by chance to the legend of Geneviève of Brabant. (Loldi read something about Marie Antoinette, and R. was reminded of his sisters, Ottilie and Klara, how they had wept over the story of Geneviève and sworn to each other that they were not weeping.) We wonder about the ending, and I first of all read aloud (from Simrock) the last version, then the one before this. I am unutterably moved by it, and when my tears interrupt my reading, R. says, "The ancient world knew nothing like this." We deplore the additions attributable to the monk's imagination, such as the crucifix in the sky, etc., and come to the corrupt imagination of the modern writers (Tieck, Hebbel, Schumann), who turn Golo into an "interesting" character, whereas he is quite simply a monster! When R. tells me the story of a female saint who swore an oath of chastity with her husband and spoke smilingly to him in death, I tell him that it is the *human* saints who touch me, those who turned their backs on life because of some terrible experience, and not those who never lived at all; I contrast his Elisabeth with Geneviève. This day, too, ends in tears of emotion and love. "Everything comes together in you," R. says to me, and I lay at his feet everything that moves my soul, for he is my salvation, my shield, my support!

Monday, November 18 R. slept well. At breakfast we talk again about Saint Geneviève and the corrupt manner in which the modern poets have treated this story. Yesterday he took pleasure in the language of the *Volksbücher,* which, for all their Latin elegance, give a clear idea of the way the people told this story among themselves. At lunch he says to me with a sigh that the work confronting him now is "too difficult— it is all so significant," and he adds with a laugh, "*Si jamais on m'y reprend*" ["I hope nobody ever takes me up on it"]! We go for a walk together in the palace gardens, where R.'s "strategy" enables us to walk for an hour without going twice along the same path. Letter from Herr Jauner, begging pardon for the "cuts" and requesting a few lines, which R. writes in a very friendly tone, assuring him that 10 years ago nobody, including R. himself, would ever have dreamed of the possibility of *Siegfried*'s being performed in Vienna. As far as the cuts are concerned, he says—all right, as long as he does not have to make them or listen to them! In the evening our friend Wol., who tells us that "*Kar*" is not a Hebrew, but an old German word meaning "care" or "lament," which pleases us. R. told me late in the evening that Wolz.'s future here was still exercising him: "I don't yet see my way clear." He himself would be best pleased if the theater were to burn to the ground and he would no longer have to bother his head about it all! However, W. has based his existence on the future of the *idea,* and this puts him under an obligation. R. plays [Beethoven's] F Major Symphony with Lusch and is indignant at the arrangers and publishers of these works; here, for instance, the *sforzato,* which in the trio is marked only in the accompanying voices, is placed above the leading voice as well; he tells us how in Dresden his tempo for this minuet movement at first upset the audience, then won it over completely, for it is precisely the nuance provided by this *sf.* in the trio which gives it individuality, and that cannot be brought out if it is played too fast. Before this he went through the final movement of the Ninth Symphony, and he regrets that my father did not take the liberty of giving the accompaniment to the voices, which Beeth. wrote for double basses, to the middle range, like the cellos, for that is how Beethoven had meant it, though he had written it otherwise: "I should not hesitate to do it," he says. We then talk about Schumann's *Genoveva.* R. says that even the coarse laughter of the servants in it was taken from Auber's *Gustave III.* This coarseness had once angered him in that work, too, but at least Auber had some excuse for it; here, however, when the Countess's servants find their beloved mistress in such a condition and—instead of showing horror—laugh! But R. feels he would lay himself open to all sorts of misunderstandings if he were to give his real opinion of this work (he also mentions the ridiculous figure of the witch, who is meant to be daemonic). He says even the Society of Patrons is now too widely based for that.

Tuesday, November 19 R. had a good night. When I return from my bath to breakfast, he tells me he has just been thinking that the French manner of being obliging to everybody (the shop assistants in the big stores are the type he has in mind) gives them the appearance of being slaves—quite different from the manners and habits of the English, for example. It reflects the attitude and services the ancient Romans demanded of their slaves. . . . R. did some work, but complained at lunch about his task: "I should like to be writing symphonies, in which I could write down ideas as they come into my mind, for I have no lack of ideas." Over coffee he says to me, "I should return to the old symphonic form, one movement with an andante in the middle; since Beeth. one can no longer write symphonies in four movements, for they just look like imitations—if, for example, one were to write such extended scherzos." We discuss whether any inner connection exists among the movements of the Beeth. symphonies. "Yes and no," says R., when I tell him I do not like to hear individual movements played out of context. "The connections would be loose ones, though of course Beeth. knew what he was doing when he added this movement rather than that; and the styles of the various periods also give the works a certain unity." In the A Major Symphony R. says he can never help thinking of a Dionysian ceremony: "I could actually draw the pictures it arouses in me; but of course, if one were to do that, one would immediately see how widely one had diverged from the music, how alien these drawings would seem, even though the music inspired them." He feels that Goethe attempted to do something similar in the "Classical Walpurgis Night." — R. goes for a short walk, then works again and shows me his page: across his sketch, which concerns Kundry, is written a furious "bad"—"I thought it downright stupid"— and over it is then inscribed the approved alteration. In the evening a very dismal drama, *Phryne,* leads R. to the subject of characters who talk endlessly in plays: "In Shakespeare, speech, however detailed, is always action." He then goes through all the dramatists since Goethe and Schiller—a dismal review! Of Schlegel and Tieck he says, "They knew all about the theater, but they couldn't write for it." R. also blames Goethe to some extent for introducing this speechifying to the stage. — Herr Levi informs us very nicely of the coming performance in M[unich], and Herr Viaresi informs us of the "triumph" of *Tann-häuser* in Trieste, with a request for a few words, which R. sends by telegram. "I am becoming too famous," R. says with a laugh. — Various chapters in Lecky bring R. back again and again to the Roman church and the "scandal" of our present times' being unable to cope with it. Then he says, "How can I possibly write for the *Bayr. Bl.* when out of consideration for the King and your father I am unable to state my opinion of the Catholic church, for example, and I ought to mention it in my projected article, 'Shall We Hope?' I can also say nothing more about the Jews (a contributor has asked whether he might attack Levi, which is hardly possible), or about musicians like Schumann, etc., whom frankly speaking I consider too insignificant. So I can say nothing at all, for the only value of my words lies in their unsparing truth, and this I can no longer express." —

Wednesday, November 20 R. had a good night, and, returning to yesterday's conversation and to an earlier proposal, he says he will draw up lists of themes for the *Blätter* and give a rough outline of his ideas on them, and the other contributors can then fill them out; for example, on the uselessness of the music schools, demonstrated by the poor published editions, poor arrangements, the decline of military bands. "But the whole trouble is," R. observes, "to whom is one speaking?" "A school ought to be founded here for the preservation of my works, for I have created a new style." But the next thought is always: Who will teach in it? . . . Fine weather. R. has done some work, after first reading Lecky as usual; he imparts to me some excerpts from this very stimulating book; today he spoke with horror about the territory of the Pontine Marshes (yesterday my Greek lesson caused him to expatiate on this subject, in his inimitable way). Then about my father: R. says he would prefer to see him writing symphonies than a *Via crucis* or a *Seven Sacraments* ("He should give us Hell as the first sacrament"). Much about my mother and father; all the noble stature of R.'s noble outlook is conveyed in his opinion of my father's attitude toward Lola Montez, and his own repugnance toward it. "The girl likes you," my father said to him at the time, "you are the only man who doesn't pay court to her." "I didn't even notice her," R. said. And he exclaims, "To wound another heart for the sake of so cold a relationship!" . . . He goes for a walk, far, far beyond the Students' Wood, and returns home via the powder magazine; he is tired, in no mood for work: "I shall finish this act, too, one day." "I have no fears about that!" say I, laughing. In the evening a small party, a singer, Frl. Lango, sings all kinds of things, not exactly to our edification. But one thing remains from such disruptions: the pleasure of being alone together again. Since we feel this pleasure particularly keenly today, R. talks about his Starnberg poem. "That gives the proper picture," he says, "I felt the need to turn it into a picture, to give it a poetic form." "We ought to print it," he adds in his kind, ironic, joking way. From this he goes on to *Tristan* and says in the second act he wanted to do just that, to describe happiness, the feeling that there are no more barriers and all else is forgotten, and the desire to perpetuate this condition through death. "How lovely it is that this happiness of total oblivion can only be felt by two alone!" he says, and with these words we go off to sleep.

Thursday, November 21   A curiously restless day; the night was also somewhat disturbed for R., but he does some work. Then an annoying though comical intermezzo with the amateur society, followed by a visit from Herr Josef Rubinstein, who seems exactly the same as he was years ago, that is to say, unmistakably ill! The eventful day is crowned by two young men from Nuremberg, who sing things from *Tannhäuser* more or less as Lauermann would have sung them. But one memory remains: the *Idyll*, which Herr R. played quite nicely in his own very good arrangement. Again, however, R. exclaims, "I won't leave a single person behind who understands my tempo!" He then tells me he is proud of the *Idyll,* it gave him great pleasure today, and so did the children, who were listening. After laughing at several curious things that happened during the day, R. says, "There is no one, not a single soul, whose visit we really look forward to: we are very much alone."

Friday, November 22 "How did you sleep after your nightmarish day?" R. asks me in the morning, and says that he had to get up once. All the same, much merriment about amateur-concert muddles, Nuremberg experiences, Israelite bothers (R. said yesterday, "If ever I were to write again about the Jews, I should say I have nothing against them, it is just that they descended on us Germans too soon, we were not yet steady enough to absorb them"). He tells me his dream: that someone in his presence made an assassination attempt on N. III, but the dagger went wide, and when N. (who had a terribly long nose) started "butchering" children, he, R., "bolted." The recent attempt on the King of Italy's life probably put this into R.'s mind. R. has now finished Lecky, and on my recommendation begins my father's *Chopin* (published in French by Breitkopf und H[ärtel]). But at lunch he tells me it must have been written by *Vulpius* (Princess Carolyne), and such descriptions (of simplicity, for example) and such a flowery style are repugnant to him. At lunch he mentions Saint-Saëns's *Danse macabre* and explains why this work is so trivial compared with similar compositions by my father and by Berlioz. Cheerful lunch; R. says to me afterward, "When I have finished *Parsifal* I intend to compose only what comes into my mind, no more according to plan; all I want is to live happily with you and the children, whose company means more to me than any other." He says he had wanted to call me in order to play something to me, but in the end had decided against it; he says I could never imagine the state he is in when he is working, how he enjoys fiddling about with a ribbon, a curtain, a coverlet—it is impossible for him to have a book nearby. I now have two dancing lessons to supervise daily with the children, R. comes along in the afternoon and has fun with them; then he does some more work. At supper an Orsini-like bomb incident in Florence brings the conversation to princes, how they now seem to be becoming more and more superfluous in the eyes of the people, for "they consist of nothing but fear and cowardice; they send others to represent them, whereas one expects princes to appear in person, show initiative." Herr Rubinstein visits us in the evening; he recommends to us an Indian drama, *Rise of the Moon of Intellect.* When he remarks that in Indian literature it is very difficult to get to the root of the matter, I reply that with any subject one approaches one must in my opinion never lose sight of its relative nature, its position in time and space—nothing is absolute. R. agrees with me and talks of Christianity, in what a bad manner it was handed down to us: the Revelation is not bound to any law or any nationality, and yet it has come through. — Herr Ru. plays the American march to us, and does so quite splendidly, whereas the *Idyll,* which he did not study with R., continues to some extent to elude him. R. takes pleasure in the march and thinks that one day only the Americans will understand his meaning: "This is music of the future, too!" he says with a laugh and a sigh. Reminiscences of *Tristan u. Is.* in Berlin, the time of the Americans. A pleasant evening, though we are always left with a strange agitated feeling of exhaustion when other people come between us. When we are alone again upstairs, R. sings *"froh wie seine Sonnen"* ["joyful as his suns"] from the Ninth Symphony and points out that at this point the tenor becomes nothing more than the accompaniment to the march, as if he were becoming absorbed into the procession. But, he says, only a great artist can grasp this and sing it accordingly: "Schnorr could have done it."

Saturday, November 23   R. had a good night and goes to his work but is unfortunately interrupted by a misunderstanding concerning dancing lesson and mealtime. As a result he is somewhat preoccupied at lunch. He tells me that he has given up *Chopin*—it was undoubtedly "by Vulpius." This then leads us to the literary activities of women, who seem to find so much difficulty in recognizing their proper place in this field. R. says the occupation seems to be connected with a certain morbid condition peculiar to them, a sort of unsatisfied desire to please; they then put on blue stockings in order to dominate through the intellect. He works again in the afternoon. In the evening he astonishes me once more with the peculiarly daemonic way in which he touches on all the things which confuse and trouble human beings without realizing or guessing it—as today with Herr Kellermann. Frau Jäger, returning from Vienna, can tell us nothing either new or pleasurable, though it is also not the reverse. But how happy we are when once again all is still around us! R. brings out his cherished, sacred pages and plays and sings to me—never again will these words and this music be sung in such a manner! "I love Gurnemanz," he says, and how can one help loving him? . . . How utterly is all sorrow, all worry, all tiredness dispelled! Parsifal's approach, his noble, mournful serenity when he realizes where he is, Gurnemanz's fervent greeting to the spear, so filled with wonder—how unearthly and yet how human it all is! My beloved son, let me make you a gift of this evening—may you relive it as you read these poor pages! And may I tell you its crowning glory—and will it make you think your mother vain? . . . It happened like this. When, discussing with your father some arrangements for the greenhouse, I said that we had no sunshine for our camellias and the buds were falling off, he replied, "It is true we have no sunshine," then, embracing me, "but I have my sunshine at all times of the day, however gray it is outside!" Oh, my Siegfried, could you but know what miracles occur in my heart when such sunlit words shine on it! Over them my eyes close, slumber enfolds the wondrous blossom of love!

Sunday, November 24 R. did not have an entirely good night. "*It*" threatened to wake him, and he dreamed that he was to be put in prison for debt, was summoned before a court where all sorts of people scoffed at him and declared that he had also behaved badly toward *Wolnsky;* he, R., hit on the idea of asking me to give him the property received from my father; then Fidi came to see him, sent by me to say I wanted nothing more to do with R., he had behaved too badly and I would put up with anything rather than these perpetual shocks and scandals—then R. woke up! . . . But all the same he does not feel unwell. He laughs, saying Goethe had been quite right to declare that, if he had known how many good things had been written before his time, he would never have taken up his pen—and how handsome of him to make this admission! — Then he talks about Greek tragedy and says it must be due to a misunderstanding that people have assumed each actor was accompanied by a flute player, it is unthinkable—probably the musicians stood in the orchestra. — R. works; at lunch he tells me he has written eight bars which are exquisite, particularly the last two; but he must always keep it very simple—he told me recently that he could never be too simple. In the afternoon we go for a walk together in the palace gardens after I read some of the *Odyssey* to the children, and this is then the subject of our conversation in the misty dusk. In the evening Fidi asks him to play either something from *Die Walküre* or the Andante from the A Major Symphony; R. plays the latter with Lulu, and when the children have gone, R. reads to me the "Classical Walpurgis Night," to our very great delight.

Monday, November 25 R. slept only fairly well, but he works and chides me fondly for also working, saying laughingly, "If Bardolph saved Falstaff so much in torches, you save me just as much in teachers!" — I had told him of my pleasure in Freytag, who has written such a good portrait of Luther that I need only to read it to the children to feel confident that they will have a proper understanding of the great man. (R.'s dream, which he told me over our afternoon coffee, was that he had been standing with some other people among abysses and ravines, and then in a hall where someone cried out, "The only person who can help us now is a ruler of genius." R. agreed with him, and it seemed that by this means the ravines were to be bridged.) A useless Parisian hat causes us to remark on the impossibility of getting a broad-brimmed hat from France ("All they make is little chignon caps," says R.), and he exclaims, "That is a sign of the barbaric times in which we live, that we get the French to supply our costumes." R. works in the afternoon, while I stroll in the garden beneath the stars after the 2nd dancing lesson, filled with gratitude for my fate! — In the evening we take up Disraeli's *Tancred;* the beginning strikes us as quite vapid, and R. tells me to skip wherever possible; but the scene between Montacute and his father interests us, and R. says he is looking forward to seeing how the author develops this; summarizing his attitude toward the Jews, he says, "Here at any rate they have been emancipated a generation too soon." — Later in the evening R. says to me upstairs, "Today I worked out a monologue on the cello for Kundry's awakening by Gurnemanz." He has started to ink in the first penciled pages.

Tuesday, November 26   R. had a very bad night, I am sure because he again drank some beer yesterday while working. . . . He spent part of the night out of bed, and laughs as he tells me that he took up *Chopin* again and was put off completely by its exaggerated style. "I was just thinking how the peculiarity of the French lies in their gaiety and friendliness, their wit, and I remembered Champfleury and his father— and then all this exaggeration, all these descriptions! That is Russian. And then all those quotations in Polish—who speaks Polish except for the Poles? Well, perhaps a Russian police agent." [*Added in margin:* "R. says that two of his friends sought to make an impression on him with the same phrase: 'At last something one can praise with full cheeks.' They were Uhlig, talking about a Volkmann trio, and Laube, about König's *Die hohe Braut.*"] He then talks about the bad German habit of speaking in superlatives, "something we learned from Goethe, who wrote certain words, omitting the article, for reasons of brevity." Then: "I am really curious to see what Israelchen [Disraeli] will do, how he will reveal his positive side. It is always difficult to reconcile oneself with the world after criticizing it. What sophistries will he use to show us that revelation is only possible if we all recognize the God on Mount Sinai? But I can understand why such a man appealed to the Queen and the dissatisfied Tories." "The poison he gave them must have been very refined," he said yesterday. — After lunch he goes for a little walk in the garden; he has done some work but is tired after his bad night. At lunch he again laughed over *Chopin* and all the declamatory passages in it; he says that Goethe, when he is quoted, is made to look like a peasant boy! He is referred to, he says, as "*l'Olympiste.*" I: "*L'Olympien.*" "*Olympiste* would be Curtius, I suppose." I: "Yes, that is his difference from Zeus." — We tell the children the anecdote about the "*accident et malheur*" of N. III, which R. likes so much. At lunch he says, "The downfall of a civilization is only a matter of time, like the completion of *Parsifal!*" After lunch we talk about what R. intends to read next—probably Darwin again, and he says with a sigh: "Oh, only Beethoven can give one true pleasure. That is what is divine about music: that it shows us everything in a mirror image, and yet it is entirely us, the attention of every nerve is held by it—it is the loveliest of delusions!" He speaks of the mazurka he saw danced in Leipzig: "It gave the impression (as they filed past) of a flock of birds, crows or swallows, moving along, and the movements were so free, so natural, so spontaneously rhythmic—nothing artificial as in our dances." He says it was really beautiful. — My morning reading to the children (Lysander) provides the topic for our conversation, and R. says he must catch up on the historians who supplied the material for Plutarch, he knows only the greatest of them. Then news of socialist excesses in Italy, police reprisals—all this calls for an inquiry to find out whether the Jesuits are involved. R. thinks it is possible (there is talk of the Pope's being poisoned), and he exclaims, "The way we have, in our present civilization, of looking to the police for salvation!" "How sad it is," he sighs, "not only having nothing to be pleased about, but also being unable to do anything about it—one just talks in a vacuum." Earlier he said, "If ever I perpetrate such nonsense again, I shall link it to Disraeli, it is always a good thing when one can call on someone in such an important position." R. in a run-down condition all day, he does go outdoors for a while, but it does not help particularly, and he is not looking well when he sits down beside me in the hall after the dancing lesson. When I question him about it, he says: "Oh, it's only that I always live by extremes. It must make things tiresome, but also perhaps pleasant, for the people who live with me; it's either utter dejection or else this *gaieté du cerveau*—there's no other term for it." — In the evening Disraeli, less significant than in that one conversation, and, as R. says, the whole thing so unsettled because of its message. Conveying messages always fails in art, however good the intention (R. quotes Heinse's *Die seligen Inseln* as an example). — Warm weather, R. sees some little blackbirds and finches emerging: "Poor creatures," he thinks, "you'll soon have to be looking for a hiding place."

Wednesday, November 27 R. had a better night, he only had to get up once, had all sorts of dreams about travel, in which Fidi played a prominent role. Coming back to Dis[raeli], he says, "What we read yesterday interested me far less than that single conversation," then he gets heated about the assumption that Jesus was a Jew; it has not been proved, he says, and Jesus spoke Syriac-Chaldaean: "Not until all churches have vanished will we find the Redeemer, from whom we are separated by Judaism. But his ideas are not easy to grasp; God as the ending of the universe—that does not allow for a cult, though perhaps monasteries, in which people of similar beliefs could find a refuge and from which they could influence the world, from the solitary state—but within the world itself it is not possible." We have to laugh over Disraeli's glorification of the Jews: "I have an idea what he is getting at," says R., "racial purity and great men; that ruling genius I dreamed about—only the Jews could produce him." Yesterday R. called himself a "tattooed savage"! (He remembered yesterday having seen coattails tugged in the House of Lords: Lord Melbourne was the object of it.) We talk about Rudolstadt, and R. recalls his apartment there; it had a couch stuffed with down, so soft that he has never forgotten it. Around lunchtime I go to R., who first shows me something sent to him by a manufacturer of steel pens: "I like being given presents." Then he tells me he has written something he is pleased with: "I'll play it to you." We go into his room, and he plays me Parsifal's reply to Gurnemanz's question where he has come from. . . . R. says he did not sing or play it well, having had to start over again. But what does that matter when one's whole soul dissolves in bliss? — Springlike weather, sunshine, warmth. R. says he does not care for such unseasonal pleasures, one cannot enjoy them when one knows everything will soon be overtaken by death. R. works in the afternoon following his walk, and in the evening we continue reading Disraeli. He becomes wilder and wilder in his assertions, and everything not to the point is so superficial and vapid. We poor Germans are very badly treated. — R. tells friend Wolz. he is not going to write his retrospective article about the festival: he cannot exonerate the Reich, and so he would prefer to keep silent. As far as the artists were concerned, he would mention only the good things. — He chooses a minuet from *Armide* as a change from the one from *Don Giovanni*. In the latter he praises the way Mozart captures the note of Spanish dignity, how with the repetition of certain notes he hints at a certain conventionality of behavior, showing it is being danced in Spain!

Thursday, November 28 Smiling meadows! . . . R. thinks of them with delight and looks back over the years; I think there were fifteen, but he: "No, I am reckoning from 1857—we could soon have been celebrating our silver wedding anniversary!" I: "And been spared much misery and suffering." "Yes, my God! But who ever asks me? People build theaters without asking me, they get married without asking me!" he exclaims in a jokingly grumbling manner. "My meeting with you on November 28, 1863, was the expression of my weariness with the world." The "smiling meadow" I have spread across his piano pleases him, and at lunchtime he calls me and shows me his room, saying my portrait now rises up like a lotus flower from a pond. "I

have also written something good," he says, "not much, but good." —
What delight there is in decorating the home of his ideals a little in
accordance with his inclinations! He must be able to immerse himself
completely in his dreams there; recently he said he must not be able to
see the garden paths, which lead outward—that is too definite, it
disturbs concentration. In Tribschen his windows overlooked the
mountains, and that was not quite the same thing. A lovely, mild,
glorious day, the sun shining. I go for a long walk, R. comes with the
dogs to meet me and conduct me home. He does some work. Over
supper he recalls the former glory of Nuremberg, with its 100,000
inhabitants ("no town should have more"), and its present state,
also the ravages left behind by the 30 Years' War. After supper Disraeli,
the appearance of the angel on Mount Sinai: "No doubt Disraeli is
now ashamed of this book." He also laughs at the way God's appearance on Sinai is regarded as such a positive thing. During our reading
we skip all the fictional parts in order to confine ourselves to the
message. ("For that can't be taken lightly, he is the Prime Minister of
England and has the whole Eastern world in his pocket." During our
walk R. said, "I find it embarrassing to keep coming back to the
subject of the Jews, but one can't avoid it when one is thinking of the
future.") — The *Faust* Overture, which R. plays with Josef Rubinstein
as a piano duet. They then talk about his symphony, with which he is
pleased; he says it is perhaps not uninteresting to observe in it what
effect the works of Beethoven, at that time still inaccurately known,
had on a young man. "I also enjoyed putting my contrapuntal studies to
some use—there are some strettos in it, real diabolical stuff." He also
talks about his uncompleted symphony in E major, saying that, as
far as he knew, nobody had yet written a symphony in E. At supper he
praised Mendelssohn's *Calm Sea* [*and Prosperous Voyage* Overture]:
"In general he had a good sense of the orchestra." After playing the
Faust O., he talks about execution, saying that nobody nowadays
knows how to play a mordent, whether it is there to introduce the
following note or intended to replace this note. Then about singers'
breathing. Example: [Amalie] Materna ("the good creature, she learned
it from me")—he quotes the passage in *Die Walküre* ("*Der mir in's
Herz diese Liebe gehaucht*") which she sang in a single breath, whereas
Hill, despite R., who sang it to him, took a new breath at each of the
places indicated in the following by a stroke: "*Wie | aus der Ferne |
längst | vergangner Zeiten | spricht dieses | Mädchens | Bild zu mir.*" R.
recalls having told Frau Dustmann how she should breathe in Donna
Anna's aria, that is to say, he told her she should sing the bar leading
up to the recapitulation of the theme and the theme itself in a single
breath. He goes through this aria, delighting once more in both it and

the accompaniment of the two oboes. R. reveals his opinion that everything in Mozart is song by exclaiming, "The whole Andante of the C Major Symphony is an aria—I should like to put words to it and find a voice like Catalani's to sing it." To end the evening R. plays his prelude to the third act and Gurnemanz's words up to the awakening of Kundry. Later, when we are alone, our whole being becomes immersed in love, and R., crowning mine with his, cries, "What are words to us?" Deep in my heart I feel the unutterable mystery of the blessings bestowed on us. . . .

Friday, November 29 R. slept well; this was not so yesterday, he read *Chopin* for an hour, still quite amused by its extravagant style! I do not remember why our talk today led us to Mazzini, but R. says: "I never cared for him, even his name displeases me, and I have never heard anything but phrases from him: '*Dio e popolo*' ['For God and the people']. I wonder what he would have done without N. III!" . . . He works, and at lunch looks well and cheerful. The sky is overcast: "What do I care for the sun outside? I have my sun inside," he exclaims to me, to my bliss. Over coffee he tells me about his work: "Sometimes it is just a few bars which hold one up terribly, till one can introduce the key one needs in such a way that it is not noticeable. For more and more I shy away from anything with a startling or blatant effect; then at least four or five possibilities occur to me before I find the one which makes the transition smoothly; I set traps for myself, commit all sorts of stupidities before I discover it." I say it must be something like the way great painters such as Titian and Leonardo [da Vinci] chose colors to avoid crude contrasts. "Oh," he says, "painters are fortunate, they have so much time, but you are right, it is something like Titian's coloring I am seeking." Then he mentions Mozart and the aria played yesterday: "The poor fellow, with his broad nose and a mouth (so it's said) literally like a pig's snout, he had a real feeling for beauty! I'm only now learning to appreciate him fully. What aristocracy, what beauty there is in this aria! If only he had not added the ritornello! The allegro is already bad enough, though it just about passes—but that ending! It shows how everything in him was just instinct, not that he couldn't do it any other way." — R. goes out for a walk, then does some work. In the evening, before supper, he calls me to look at the "meadow," now laid out nicely in folds! Then a merry supper, which I unfortunately cannot describe exactly as it was, R. joking with the children, warming us all with his divine humor. Afterward we finish Disraeli's novel: we had expected more talent, it peters out in trivialities, and even its message is significant only because it is spoken by England's subsequent Premier. — Friend W. tells us that the proposed reintroduction of the law against profiteers was just a mockery, and the government is keeping quiet about it. He relates that on the occasion of the Emperor's reception a minor state of emergency is to be declared. R. observes that the Emperor seems now to have become somewhat childish. I: "It would have been better if he had died in France." R.: "Such people never die in France!" He goes on to say that in connection with this French war he is reminded of Weber's experience in Prague, when no one cared to show any enthusiasm. Instead: "H.E. Field Marshal Schwarzenberg has with humble obedience won the battle for H.M. the Emperor"! So also in this case: if one showed one's respect and admiration for the officers, one appeared to be meddling in matters which did not concern one. Moltke, he says, is like a kind of engineer: if there is another war, he will be pleased. This last war was like an arithmetic problem correctly solved. "What is the use," R. exclaims sorrowfully, "when there is no principle involved to inspire people?" "Just how little popular feeling was concerned in it," I say, "we saw in what happened to the '*Kaisermarsch.*'" [*Added in margin:* " 'That I, too, have had to lose my sympathy for the army!' R. said with sad composure."] — "Oh, it is terrible," he exclaims sorrowfully. "What on earth can I say when I ask: 'Shall We Hope?' I shall only give offense everywhere." — Friend W. tells us that in Herr Busch's book it is reported, with reference to the imperial crown, that the Emperor said, "With it Herr Lasker gave me a pleasant surprise." R. says, "That was his profound instinct speaking: it was the Jews who created the imperial crown." These sad thoughts disappear, and we converse together, R. and I, more tranquilly. As the evening draws to an end he says, "That is what is so bad about your company—I no longer enjoy consorting with others." He then adds, in his merry way, "I used to enjoy consorting so much!" I laugh: "That is some comfort to me for the badness of my company." R., seriously: "My sole urge was always to throw off everything. When I left Zurich, for example, I felt, despite the loss of my peace, glad to have left it all behind me." . . .

Saturday, November 30   R. had a good night. He goes off to work and comes at lunchtime to fetch me. After lunch he says: "I can prove mathematically that I am the happiest man on earth! It is hard to sustain my pessimism—you have turned me into an optimist." The reasons for his pessimism are soon discovered. "I have not yet struggled quite free, magic still guides my footsteps," R. says, recalling his connections with Munich. "If only the King would get rid of people like Perfall!" When I tell him he is the only person I know who is capable of happiness, since he has no vain desires, he says, "Yes, but it is precisely this capacity that all my friends denied me; and what an unfair judgment it was, after the sad and pitiful life I had been leading!" He recalls my mother and her remark when Minna, in her anxiety to please, spoke ironically about the pile of cushions on his sofa in Zurich: "*Pas un de trop*" ["Not one too many"]. "I was pleased by that," he says, "and I thought to myself, 'I must get hold of this woman's daughter'!" — Then we speak of my father, who cannot feel at home here with us, though he ought to be glad of our happiness. . . . Dancing lesson for me, R. goes for a walk, then does some work. In the evening we begin Walter Scott's *Life of Napoleon;* R. quotes Heine's criticism of it and talks about the discredit into which it subsequently fell. But he says he himself finds it as interesting as a criminal case. R. is pleased by the sublime and mysterious fact that he has not had to rearrange or alter a single word in P[*arsifal*], melody and words fit throughout—what he wrote down in the prelude contains all he needs, and it all unfolds like a flower from its bud. When he tells me this, I say nobody would ever believe that the melody in *Die Msinger* was invented, not for the words "*scheint mir nicht der Rechte*," but at first for the Overture. "Yes," he says, "that Overture was one of my most remarkable inspirations."

Sunday, December 1   R. slept well and does some work. Over coffee after lunch he tells me: "When *Parsifal* is finished, I shall cast an eye over the world and see what its attitude is likely to be to such a work. But now I don't want to think of it." He complains how little attention is paid to a sense of beauty, "in which I regard myself as Mozart's successor"—for example, the way Brünnhilde talks of Siegmund to Wotan in *Die Walküre*. When I point out that the emotional feelings of the listener at this point prevent his having much regard for the consummate form: "That's what the works are for, they are there and can be studied." — R. stresses the fact that the Jews have been amalgamated with us at least 50 years too soon: "We must first be something ourselves. The damage now is frightful." "I wish a Byron would emerge among us, to describe and castigate our society! But he would have to be a prince, and, above all, immensely rich." Reflecting on Germany's inability to produce a Byron, he says, "Prince Pückler had something of the right qualities, he was elegant and irked by our wretched conditions, but he had no ideas to inspire him, no greatness." We then come to the conclusion that it was not the poet Byron who so impressed Goethe, but the man. — R. goes for a walk, as always now in the palace gardens, for which he has discovered a new measurement (five times lengthways), then he does some work. Our Friedel very full of fun at supper, demonstrates his geographical knowledge. Today we do not continue with Nap., instead R. reads me the conclusion of the "Walpurgis Night," the part in which Thales reappears with Homunculus; we are entranced by its humor: "This is the only way to deal with such things." The Euripidean Helena, however, does not much interest him—only the idea, not the execution. On the other hand, the scene between Proteus, Thales, and Homunculus, the "peevish" Nereus and the whole remarkable mixture of emotion and humor, send him off into joyous laughter and admiring exclamations. But we have to laugh at the idea of trying to depict all this on stage. When he is reading the passage with the sirens, he says, "Here comes Rossini!" — But after the reading R. looks very tired. R. amused us vastly during one of these evenings by admitting his interest in the novel in the *Tagblatt—Alexa,* a criminal case which excites his curiosity: "It is very poor," he says with a laugh.

Monday, December 2 R. is not well, he did not have a good night. He works, but at lunch he looks very preoccupied, and over coffee he reverts to the subject of producing *Parsifal* here. He says the only way in which he could be helped would be by having the deficit taken off his back, thus freeing him from Munich. I tell him that, even if this did not happen, we could still give the Society of Patrons their money back and implore the King not to have *Parsifal* produced in Munich. R. says, "I should like to produce it only when we, you and I, feel we want to." — R. goes for a walk and then works persistently, delaying supper; I am concerned about him, but fight against my fears as much as I can. Fidi again very lively, R. says, "Oh, how I enjoy sitting with you among the children—this is my real triumph." Then he laughs: "But what a pity General Muck is leaving without marrying Daniela!" —a reference to some foolish town gossip, to which, however, he links his theory that a man should be 20 years older than his wife, otherwise he would find himself in his second childhood. The children say: "Like you and Mama." R.: "I am too old, but we are a special case, and anyway everyone must do as he thinks fit." I quote Goethe's (Orphic) words and, since R. does not remember them, read the passage to him; over Ananke he becomes pensive and thinks of his fate as an artist—the obligation he is under to produce *Parsifal*—and his countenance, which normally radiates joy during his conversations with us, becomes clouded and gloomy. He talks of his New Year's article, "Shall We Hope?," to which question he will answer, "Let us hope," but both question and answer must be very precisely formulated—he cannot write mere phrases, he says. — I should prefer silence, but I do not say so. — We pass on to W. Scott and read about the siege of Toulon; R. tells me that in Eisleben (at the age of 7) he dreamed, after reading about this siege in Bredow's history book, that he was standing somewhere in Toulon and seeing all the corpses and other horrors! —

Tuesday, December 3 Again a bad night . . . I do not know how I can bear my worry and overcome it. Despite his fatigue he does some work. When I fetch him for lunch he says, "I have just been thinking of you and saying to myself, 'I simply had to live with her, there was no help for it.' " But at table he is very absorbed, and over coffee he says, "I must have unlimited time for *Parsifal*." — He sleeps in the afternoon longer than usual, then we stroll in the garden and afterward go together to visit our neighbors the Staffs. After the visit R. writes a few letters, but he feels run down—"*heavy*," he says. He plays the first movement of the *Pastoral* with Lusch, then I read aloud some of W. Scott's *Life of N.*, without much enjoyment for either of us. He says it was Thiers who described the battles most vividly. "We are drinking wine already drunk," R. says, making a play on G.'s words, which he says only Goethe could have written. As we are going up to bed we pass by the little Buddha: "I shan't compose you," says R. "How could one make anything of such a fellow in a blue cap?"

Wednesday, December 4 Bad night; when I ask R. at about 4:30 A.M. how he is, he laughs: "All right, I am awake, it's just a pity that it's still night." I have the feeling that his work is wearing him out, he says variants occur to him during the night, "though they are usually not much use," but also thoughts of the Society of Patrons and "Shall We Hope?" "What fifths I have been writing today—they are tremendous!" But gaiety is utterly beyond me, all my efforts are devoted to concealing my concern from him. When I beg him to take good care of himself, he says, "Oh, we shall live to a ripe old age: Fate did not bring us together without some purpose in mind." — "And I can still be of great use, even if people think I am finished and can do no more, just by being alive." Earlier he had talked of Chopin's phrase, "I shall not die like a pig," which he dislikes greatly, observing what a wretched light it threw on the rest of his life; it made him think of his own death (our death), which will be different! — He reads to me a page from *Chopin* about love relationships at the time of the breach with Mme Sand—they were indeed very curious. — This morning he thought about the French, with some sympathy for their present position, and says it would be remarkable all the same if common sense, so outstanding a quality among certain classes in France, the "*concierge* spirit," were to prevail. Paris would, of course, always remain the world's bazaar, but we must not forget that it was a Frenchman, Renan, who wrote the best book about the things which interest us. — He reflects on the English and says the way they write poems about "glorious and victorious" makes him laugh, for that is not their way, even if they are efficient soldiers. At lunch much about the Battle of Leipzig, also the Battle of Waterloo, the Prussian spirit, youth—all of it vanished! R. also describes to us the Battle of Sedan. — Yesterday, while listening to *Hungaria,* which Lusch was playing, R. said: "Your father is much more of a musician than I am. I could never write anything like that, even my marches aim at something quite different."

We are amused by Princess W[ittgenstein]'s interpretations of my father's works, but then R. says, "Those are all distortions, worldly distortions, one shouldn't take any notice of them." — R. does not go for a walk today, but just to the Wolzogens' house. He does some work and in the evening no longer looks so worn out. He is pleased by the news that our friend Sulzer is taking over the leadership of the socialists: "We could do with a man like that in Germany," he says. "The effort will surely be, not against possessions, but in favor of possessions for everybody." R. tells us about people being expelled from Berlin, women among them. So it is true—they are preparing at one and the same time illuminations and emergency measures for the Emperor. — Busch's book has arrived, I read some of it aloud, and R. is pleased by everything in it that has to do with practical life, for example, the Chancellor forbidding Herr Busch the noisy talk about strategy. He is also amused by the nuns with their lorgnettes: "That is modern life." In the afternoon my hopes that R.'s health is improving give me a peculiar sense of well-being; as I watch the snow falling, I lose myself in thoughts of the future and praise Fate for my existence. ("*Ich grolle nicht*" ["I do not complain"]—this line, recalled to mind in some connection or other, leads R. to the unpleasant and unfitting aspects of lyric poetry. Something like Goethe's "*Zueignung*" ["Dedication"], in which a picture of the whole of life is conveyed in tranquillity, is quite different, he says.)

Thursday, December 5 R. got up once, but otherwise, he says, the night was tolerable. During the night he started Turgenev's *Virgin Soil*. I tell him that I had heard him sighing deeply—had he been having sorrowful thoughts? "Probably just my general situation," he says, "or some particular grievance!" — Speaking last night about the "Classical Walpurgis Night" he said that it always seems to him to grow shorter, he had imagined Nereus and the Nereids to be much longer; the humor in it becomes ever more apparent. On the other hand, the quotation from "Ideals" (in *Chopin*), activity which never tires, struck him as curious; why this in verse, when it is prose? Schiller could at times be terribly didactic. — In the afternoon he is unable to sleep, which worries me a lot; he goes for a walk in the palace gardens. At supper he has only tea with some eggs. I read to him from Busch's book, and much of it interests him; his [Bismarck's] sturdy, energetic, fearless, and naïve character, untrammeled by any sort of prejudice, comes through everywhere, and R. says he must completely dominate his surroundings with his freedom of outlook, but there is never any sign of an idea, and also no idealism in his attitude toward things, his opinion of W[ilhelm] Tell deplorable. — I say good night to R. with a heart full of apprehension.

Friday, December 6 Fidi ill for the past three days! R. again had no sleep, he got up during the night and read three chapters of the Turgenev book, in which one passage made him laugh out loud; he reads to me this very funny scene, in which the athletic *diacre,* wishing to say something friendly, makes such a loud noise that everyone is startled. — I implore R. not to work, and he promises me not to. — He looks worn out, and only the fact that he has not lost his appetite gives me some comfort; but he does not sleep in the afternoon, either, "in spite of the *Tagblatt.*" — Over coffee he comes back to Bismarck's judgment on *W. Tell:* "As if the intention were to depict a *hero!*" And then he goes on, in his inimitable way, about the folk instinct which finds expression in this figure, who steels himself to the terrible deed, placing his faith in God, yet at the same time resolving on murder in a dark, unconscious way—not like a hero, hand on heart, but like a prowling wild beast which has to be destroyed. When R. says these splendid things, I observe that he should mention them in his next article, since the people themselves are just as little understood as Tell. R. replies, "I have already made a note of it." He stays indoors and reads *Virgin Soil,* which he finds interesting.

But again he did not rest in the afternoon, and he looks nervous. How difficult to control one's worry, how inefficient I am becoming in everything! I have to ask W. to answer a letter for me! In the evening I read some more Busch to R., and in the end he decides that the language of our greatest man is very vulgar—like tavern talk! —

Saturday, December 7 R.'s night was not a good one. . . . He slept well and gently at first, but then he woke up, got out of bed, read something, lay down again, fell asleep but had spasms in his arms and legs; I took his hand in both of mine and with my pressure fought against his cramp! And truly it subsided, and I had the joy of watching over his sleep, for a few hours at least. What thoughts flooded into my mind as I did so! I sought to settle the children's entire future. Beforehand, a dream had comforted me: a star fell, I uttered the wish that is the only one I now have, the stars fell from the sky, and soon the whole square and the street (somewhat similar to Lindau) were full of stars; rain falling like a blessing. No wonder I was amazed when R. told me at lunchtime today he had had a dream: I came to him full of joy, telling him I had got a letter from Hans, and everything was arranged with regard to the children—and so once again he dreamed what was in my thoughts! — R. agrees with me that such a night seems like something from the distant past. But he feels rather better. He asks for tea, calls tea Catholicism, coffee Protestantism, tea is more elegant. The violin for dancing amuses him: "That's what is meant by improvisation, when there is no melody in it." But then during one exercise he thinks he can discern the theme of the big *Leonore* Overture. I do not re-member what makes me think of the words "Yes, who in his heart's sure keeping counts but one true soul his own" and to say, "Beethoven never possessed one!" "Few ever do. Goethe did not, either, he stopped searching because he did not think it possible, instead he turned to research and the pleasures of his intellect." When he embraces me before we part for our daily duties, he says, "There is only one soul on this earth, and I possess it." He does not work but reads a little, and he looks better when he comes up to my room for lunch. Fidi also had a bad night, which casts a slight shadow over our mood, but, since there is no danger, our spirits gradually become as lively as ever. Of politicians, referring to Bismarck, R. says, "Basically they all harbor a cynical pessimism which is made to look to others like optimism. Since he (B.) has the entire strength of Germany at his disposal, he really might have looked a little deeper" (yesterday he said, "Rome once had people like B. in masses"); "he is not an *ideologist*." "Nap. III cherished an idea—the unification of the Latin races under one scepter—but there was no strength left in the Latin races." With regard to this letter he says, "It does squeeze everything together so." I say I should like to read the American one. "Yes," he says, "that is something for which the strength of this nation was preserved, as it were." — I then tell him about K[arl] Ritter's *König Roderich,* signs of talent, but mixed with a corrupt, and apparently deliberate, negligence in language. R. then speaks about Ritter as an individual, his great gifts, his facility for music—"and that is not a good thing: one should have to exert oneself with music—there are not many Mozarts about." — Then about his collected writings, how few people are buying them: "I must be completely despised in those bourgeois circles which buy expensive books, completely despised. But what a remarkable time that was, when Cotta knew he could do good business with Goethe's writings! The press spoils everything nowadays." He comes to Balzac, his grandiose pessimism—in *Pierrette,* for instance, in which even posterity is unjust. He laughs: "If we had a necromancer, there are all sorts of people we could conjure up." Then he adds: "Though really we should have nothing to say to each other. I should have had nothing to say to Schopenhauer." When I tell him I believe B[alzac] would have under-stood him, in spite of being a Frenchman, R. doubts it and says again, "We should have nothing to say to each other." — He is pleased with *Virgin Soil* and says it could have been written by Balzac. I observe laughingly that it is now always he who reads the French books, and I the German. He goes for a walk; the air has become keener, and I hope it will do him good. In the evening he drinks his glass of grog upstairs with me in the gray room; I have arranged it so that it will please him a bit and raise his spirits; he talks of his rose hill (the meadow), which still gives him pleasure. Then I read Busch to him, little enjoyment!

Sunday, December 8 A still worse night, practically no sleep, three hours of reading, then some walking and, as soon as he gets back into bed, spasms! . . . I rack my brains over what we should do—perhaps travel? . . . Wonderful how fresh he remains in spite of it all; before lunch he goes for a walk, and he has a good appetite. He talks about *Virgin Soil*, which is very well observed. I tell him it seems to me that people here no longer observe things, they just exploit them, and he thinks I am right, says he will make use of it, deck himself out in my feathers! This leads us to the peacock, which has just "called out like an Alpine trumpeter." — Dr. Landgraf refuses to see anything alarming in R.'s condition. R. makes a laughing remark about Turg[enev]'s tender consideration for Mme Viardot, in that he never calls the Jews by name but always talks of "*les marchands.*" "Incidentally, it was very impressive the way she got so heated about my Jewish pamphlet," R. said yesterday. He is not well, has to put up with some vexation over supper, and Herr Busch's book is not of a kind to cheer him up. To bed with feelings of concern! —

Monday, December 9 My concern was not mistaken, he did not have a good night. We change our daily routine so that R. can go out for a while before lunch. — In the morning R. comes to the subject of original sin, saying, with reference to Nietzsche's assertion that all are innocent, that this is correct as regards *operare,* but the sin lies in existence itself, the will to live, and the God without sin is the one for whom life is a sacrifice, and his life in consequence becomes a revelation. — Arrival of blankets from Vienna! Ordered by R. as a "belated gift for N[ovember] 28." I, touched and overemotional, succumb to indescribable sadness when I am alone and gaze out on the snow-covered earth. Lusch is ill, Fidi again unwell, sleepless nights, worrisome thoughts—and now a joy! The poor spirit breaks down and cries out for peace. But the cry is choked back, and when R. remarks at lunchtime that I am not looking well, control is restored. Of Busch's book R. says he would be ashamed to show it to foreigners. He talks about his "friend" Schmitt, saying the latter is now attacking him in the newspapers! "I have had fine friends" (thinking of K. Ritter, Nietzsche, etc.), "and one is always aware that the external enemies see through the hollowness of such relationships, however glowing at the outset, and rejoice." — From L.'s indisposition R. comes to talk about the girls and says how greatly he was touched, back in the summer, when he had been cross with the children and Loldi, lying in her bed, had pressed him to her; he had felt her little breasts against him, and this revelation of maidenliness had touched him like an intimation of Fate.

Tuesday, December 10　Not a very good night for R., he got up once, but he does not complain in the morning, wants to do some work, which worries me, but "I don't deserve my happiness otherwise." At lunch he asks whether in his *Faust* Symphony Berlioz let the Walpurgis Night, the "gliding and gleaming" of the witches, escape him: "If so, he was very silly." He says *Roméo et Juliette* is the work of a bungler, in spite of Berlioz's great talent, and if "the stuttering Count" (Du Moulin) had put such a thing in front of him, he would have received a proper dressing down. R. goes for a walk and says, "When I whistle for the dogs, they just say 'Fiddlesticks.'" He recommends Turgenev's *Virgin Soil* quite strongly to me, says it aroused very peculiar feelings in him because he himself had been through these revolutionary experiences, the lack of contact with the people. — "Then," he says, "a genuine love, a happy marriage, who knows anything about that?" . . . "Young writers nowadays use their powers to denigrate what was formerly held in high regard—but they don't know the reality." — In the evening friend W. sends over an article in the *Nat[ionale] Z[eitung]* about the law against profiteers, very pretentious rubbish quoting Disraeli's *Tancred*. Not worth bothering about. R. gives me great pleasure by playing his funeral music for Weber's reburial; we then talk about this Weberian melody, its purity and chastity; every time I think of it, I see before my eyes a blossoming virgin, lovely in her modesty, whereas with Beethoven I receive no vision at all: he is just everywhere, like the great god Pan. R. agrees with me, saying it is like contrasting Shakespeare with Schiller. R. loses himself in memories of this ceremony, "the most successful of my whole life." After that we play the *Idyll* as a piano duet. We go upstairs in happy, indeed very cheerful, spirits, and when I tell R. I intend to send Glasenapp the stuffed pheasant, he says hardly does a *malheur* occur in Wahnfried but Glasenapp must be made a present of it, stuffed!

Wednesday, December 11　R. again had to get up once. All the same, he is cheerful and does not complain about these nightly disturbances. He goes for a walk in the morning, and this seems to do him good. As always much merriment at lunch! Of Fidi he says, "We two no longer pay any attention to each other, because we both crack jokes." R. remarks, "Fidi must have a tremendous itch in his brain." And it is true, the dear boy has all kinds of nice ideas which I should much like to write down here, if I did not regard myself as being in the service of another. — When we let our Putz into the dining room and he dances around the table, R. remembers Robber in Boulogne who once, in his joy when R. encountered him, ran three times around the great square

with the shops, like a mad thing—the huge creature looked so extraordinary! R. begins his "Retrospect" of the Bayreuth festival. In the
evening we tell friend Wolzogen our impressions of Busch's book, the
coarseness it reveals, and R. says that today he was in Angermann's and
saw such a handsome, distinguished, and candid-looking officer; he
asked himself: "But what is it for? What use is made of such men? All
the people at the top are such pitiful creatures." He praises Turgenev's
book and says at times it really moved him. — Then he once again
plays the Weber funeral music and speaks of the effect Weber had on
him: "He was my begetter, it was he who aroused my passion for
music. He revealed to me what wind instruments can do—for instance,
the entrance of a clarinet, what an effect that can make. I wish someone
could have seen me as a child when I watched *Der Freischütz* being
performed in the small, old theater under Weber's direction. It is a
true blessing to have received in childhood such an impression of one
of God's chosen spirits." — From here to *Tristan;* I had asked for the
Prelude to *Parsifal,* but R. said he would prefer to play *Tr.* He goes
through the love scene and, when this is concluded, exclaims: "What
extraordinary stuff it is! To imagine that as a repertory opera—it's
too absurd! It can never become popular." I dispute this, saying that
it was above all *T. und I.* which won him his true supporters, and that
it is precisely this spun-out musical evocation of love which provides
people with the magic they unconsciously seek in the theater. "Yes,"
says R., "in a first-rate performance of it." Then he says: "This shows
a pair of lovers aglow at the height of sin; they do not confess it to
each other, but they feel there is only one escape—through death;
first they ask each other, 'How did it come about, when we loved each
other from the start, that we parted?' Then she does not wish to contemplate the death he has resolved on for them, until he persuades her,
and both then find their highest happiness in this decision. Who can
follow all that?" I maintain that everyone who has ever been in love,
even if it was a false or foolish love, must have felt the tragedy of love
and of life, and will respond to the magic; he will feel increasingly
liberated from his burdens, transformed by inner impressions which,
slumbering inside him, now awake to enlighten him. R. laughs and
says, "I must tell you what Meyerbeer replied to me when I expressed
to him my feeling that the staging of the bathing girls' scene (in *Les
Huguenots*) did not match the music: 'Maybe, Herr Wagner, but not
everyone has as much imagination as you.'" I say that Wotan's sufferings are much less easily understandable, his farewell to Brünnhilde
undoubtedly only made so for most people through the music. R. says I
am quite right, and that is what he himself thought at first; also the
music, even if he did take it to the utmost limits, always remains

melodious. Later, when we are already upstairs, he says he had felt the urge to express himself symphonically for once, and that led to *Tristan*.

Thursday, December 12 R. had a tolerable night, he got up only once. He is now working on his article; he says it is actually absurd to say anything more about the festival, but he wants to do it for Wolzogen's sake. I am now reading Turgenev's book on his recommendation, and with great interest, too; we talk a lot about it. In the evening Herr R[ubinstein] here again, R. plays the *Idyll* with him as a piano duet, quite wonderful. Afterward he enlarges upon the piano scores, which are intended only as intelligent indications, and one must take care not to break the melodic line by putting in all the middle voices, but try always to provide the outlines. — In the evening, when we are alone, R. wants to know why, "when really we want to stay silent, Fate insists on turning us both into downright chatterers!" — He talked a lot with Herr R. about all sorts of things—Raff and Hellmesberger and [Amalie] Materna. Regarding the *Idyll* he says: "I ought not to have published it. Everything one publishes is cast before swine, but now and again a blind hen comes along and finds the pearl." — (During the afternoon he wrote to Frl. Uhlig.) When we are upstairs, R. says of the *Idyll*, "It is the only work of mine which comes straight from my life; I could write a program for it down to the last *t*."

Friday, December 13 R. *had a good night!* "I ought to sacrifice a cock," he says. "Poor Berlioz, whose head is still plucked bare—he looks like the monk in the rose garden." — We come to the subject of chronicles, he used to own the chronicles of the city of Cologne, in rhyme, and he liked them; he does not know the chronicles of the emperors, but feels they should provide the foundation for the language used in dramas dealing with those times. Two days ago, when I told him about the curious language in K. Ritter's drama, he pointed out how much wiser Goethe had been to use doggerel verse in *Faust*. R. says he wonders whether the tremendous popular element in Goethe has been sufficiently appreciated. — Fine wintry weather. R. goes for a walk before lunch, the children go skating. At lunch spoke about the novel; R. says, "I feel as if I have known such people, and this move-ment, which is really nothing at all but nevertheless upsets the charac-ters." In the evening R. asks me to read the book aloud from the point I have reached. Concerning the revolutionary matters in it, he says: "I was almost at the point of hawking pamphlets myself! And when I think of all the things I told Minna, such as that the movement was being built up somewhere else, and that it was bound to happen that people like me would be needed, and that I should be appointed secretary of the provisional government. I had to put it to her in the form of a *permanent appointment,* and at the same time humbug myself.

But all the same I could not agree with your father when he said to me curtly in Weimar, 'Admit you've been foolish.' " When it comes up in conversation that the Emperor is now so well that he intends to take part again in a hunt, R. says, "Yes, that's all they can think of." And a little later he says, "I was on the point of writing a witty remark— 'Biarritz was after all nothing more than tossing a fox in a blanket'— but I won't do it." — At the conclusion of our reading he says to me, "It often occurs to a man that women are much better than he is, that a woman is much more of a whole than he; for a man, a woman is an episode"—he looks at me and adds, "I am not talking about us now"— "but for a woman the man is everything, and when the thing for which a man gives up a woman turns out to be nothing, he must feel very contemptible." At the first stage of saying good night he remarks, "Don't call up a Solomin!" I: "I hope your feelings for me are not the same as Nezhdanov's." He, laughing: "It would be a bit late to start that." Much merriment.

Saturday, December 14 R. slept well, though he woke very early. Toward noon he complains of tightness in his chest ("I have a mouse scurrying about in my heart, lungs, and liver," he says at lunch; though he means it as a joke, it gnaws at my heart). He went out for a walk in the palace gardens, it is very cold—is this advisable? — He has done some work on his "Retrospect" and says that, though only creative work can satisfy him, nevertheless he finds pleasure in the artistic form which can be given to a descriptive account such as this. This is why he is working on it slowly, he adds; he will neither complain nor accuse, nor will he use any bitter expressions. When we meet again, he returning from Angermann's, where he had an appointment with friend W., and I from making a few odd purchases, such divine words escape his lips that I do not dare write them down. And even if I did dare write the words, how could I convey the soul behind them which turned them to searing flame in my heart? . . . I hardly dare even think of it, and yet cannot stop thinking of it—oh, thou earthly bliss of love, so immense, so timid, I can only cherish thee and, concealing thy treasures in the depths of my soul, appear to forget thee! — In the evening the W.'s come, and R. tells me his young friend told him that his family had settled in Bayreuth 200 years ago (a Frl. Ruckdeschel was mentioned who had written the funeral ode for a Wolzogen; R. says one still finds these genuine old German names in the small towns, and remarks laughingly that this poetess must certainly have been an ancestress of the present schoolmaster Ruckdeschel—the family had a pedantic streak). R. says he spoke appreciatively of Wolzogen and how retiring he is, the way in which, looking neither to right nor to left, he has retired from the world to subordinate himself to a single person.

He also tells me, "W. and I decided that Schopenhauer and Goethe were quite right about melody, and, however absurd Goethe's desire to see his Helena set to music by Rossini might seem, his instinct had been right to a certain extent." This all arose in connection with an article by friend Pohl in which Schumann is mentioned. With regard to him, R. says: "As if a genius says to himself, 'This is the direction I shall take, this is what I mean to do!' It's inspiration he needs, melodies. In Schumann there is not a single melody, and that's why I place Schubert so high above him." He then talks once more of the great impression Turgenev's novel made on him, and also of his "Retrospect": he is vexed at feeling shy now about mentioning the Jews, "just out of consideration for three or four of them," and then, in his usual manner of changing rapidly from annoyance to joking, he exclaims, "Davidsohn gave me a cigar holder!" In the afternoon he had already mentioned the delight he gets from working out his article, his delight in form, and he goes on about it in the evening. During the afternoon he was very preoccupied (I spoke a certain name, and he asked me for the name of Count Magnis, whom he is mentioning in his article; it had nothing to do with what I had said), and I begged him urgently not to do any work. He enjoyed it, he replied. In the morning he told me that by the end of the year he would have reached Parsifal's anointment, and then the rest would follow. When I tell him I am looking forward to Titurel's funeral, he says, "That is already finished —as good as finished." Before that he said, "I shall still one day write my mourning music for the fallen, and its motto will be 'My captain, I am dying for Germany.'" (Words spoken by a dying soldier in 1870.) — Over coffee discussed whether we might ask the King to replace Perfall with someone like Prince Liechtenstein. — Final resolve: always to let things go the way they want to go—and go bad in the process. —

To conclude the evening he takes out Bach's *48 Preludes and Fugues* and plays several of them. "That is music," he exclaims after one of the preludes, "music *eo ipso*." — "He is totally unique," he exclaims after another, "and what accents it has! He knew all about those, though there are no markings, no *sforzati*." R. considers the *48 Preludes and Fugues* to be the quintessence of Bach. — When we are lying beside each other in bed, I whisper the words "Oh, sink down, night of love!" R.: "Nobody has ever commented on my identifying the highest enjoyment of love with obliviousness of the world." Here there is oblivion, and the world is abolished.

Sunday, December 15 "Poor old dear, dear Odysseus . . . Odysseus, adieu!" Thus I hear R. speaking in compassionate tones during the night; at the time he cannot remember why, and in the morning, when

I tell him about it again, he says, "Yes, that was really a very pleasant encounter." We recall that yesterday at lunch he mentioned Laertes and said, "A very odd fellow, letting the suitors ruin his kingdom and not bothering his head about anything!" He had been reminded of Laertes by our gardener, Rausch. We had also talked about my reading the *Odyssey* to the children, and the dream could have arisen out of that. In the night, when I told R. about it, he said, "At any rate better than dreaming of a woman I loved more than you!" In the morning he cannot remember this, either. — We talk about the book *Odysseus, the God of Spring,* which vexed me at first, since it seems to destroy the personal relationships, but is nevertheless very good; Elpenor and all the women, Calypso, Circe—"there is something solicitous, withdrawn about them," says R., "and Laertes is the embodiment of winter."

(Another curious thing during the night, when I tell him about his dream and he answers me, still half asleep, he also says in an undertone, as if to himself, "Oh, these philologists, when they approach the problem of Homer, so uncertain of themselves, splitting hairs—wretched fellows.") — In the morning he works on his article, and says that he wrote about the King today, very noble. Yesterday he observed, "I have not mentioned you, though in the interests of truth I really should." He says he has featured Mimi very prominently. (Yesterday evening he came to the subject of Auber and said he was glad that in his article he had presented him as such a significant figure, particularly with regard to *La Muette*—Spontini was a bungler by comparison. What that had really been was a sigh of relief from the people, once the Napoleonic oppression was lifted, but a sigh that led to nothing. "A heartless fellow, Auber, but a genius." — Then about the laboriousness of all revolutions.) — When I tell him that I have finished Turgenev's book, he discusses it with me in detail and says (regarding Sipniagin), "I realized from this book that the Russian aristocrats did at least go to the trouble of giving themselves certain airs; here they don't even do that—they're just vulgar." — (Yesterday he spoke very disgustedly about the Grand Duchess of Baden—not that she is vulgar, but that she is one of those treacherous people who appear to take an interest in something but do nothing to prove it: "A block off the old chip," he concludes with a laugh.) Heavy snowfall, delight in it, R. says, "It's like an ornament, like lace, with rain it's just needles." He does go for a walk in the afternoon, and to Angermann's, but he again feels tightness in his chest and has no desire to eat. The "Rheingold," sent by Herr Albert, did not agree with him. "I feel like dying," he says to the children, and when a shadow passes across my face, he says with a laugh: "That's just to frighten them, so they'll be good. That's what I always did with the Mrazécks—I threatened them with my death, then they left me in peace." It was not the joke, but the fact that he was unwell that troubled me! In the evening friend Wolz., Josef R., and Herr Kellermann. R. talked about his overture in C major, in $\frac{6}{8}$ time, which he regrets having lost; he says it was not all that bad, and it contained the *Holl.* chord (interrupted cadence). Herr Kellermann plays a polonaise by my father, which R. finds very good: "It is quite worthy of the Chopin ones." — J. R. first of all plays organ fugues by Bach (A minor, C minor), very well—"a little overdramatized," says R., but he enjoys them greatly—then a Prelude in F-sharp Minor (No. 13) from the *48 Preludes and Fugues;* since this reminds us of *Die Msinger* ("continuation of Bach"), R. takes out the collection of pieces from *Die Msinger,* and with these brings the evening to a splendid close. But he says, "This work was more or less cast to the sw——; it brought me nothing." I feel that with all such works it is as with *Hamlet;* recently R. and I laughed at the way people (in this case Turgenev) talk of a Hamlet-like character, a Russian Hamlet, as if this figure had been real, not something created by a poet; and so will it be with his Sachs and his Siegfried; they will be regarded as real people and for that very reason will not be judged aesthetically. To end the evening he reads to us his "Retrospect," or, rather, the first pages of it, so simple in its truth, so true in its simplicity. If only his health were better! . . .

Monday, December 16   R. did not sleep badly, but he had an ugly dream in the early morning: I had propped a clasp knife on my nose and was in a sarcastic mood. He does not look too tired. The "Retrospect" has inevitably left a mood of heaviness behind. "What the story tells," R. exclaims, "one can see from our leaders, the Emperor, the princes, Bismarck." Yesterday evening he said, "The princes are entirely to blame." Of Bismarck he says, "A bad man." [*This last sentence obliterated in ink by an unknown hand.*] I observe that C. Frantz was not far wrong with his "Pomeranian *Junker.*" "He certainly was not. — What does a *Junker* of that sort know about Germany?" [*This last sentence obliterated in ink by an unknown hand.*] — When R. laughed about his piano playing yesterday, I said to him, "And yet now I can really listen to nobody except you." He laughs and says, "It's my magic," and points to his leathery thumb (which is a bit rough). The falling snow, silent, thick, and pure, invites one to seek a still, cozy refuge. — Oh, gleaming white peace, protect and warm my poor heart, consumed by love, full of sprouting worries and fears, that death may appear to it like springtime! . . .

After lunch, at which R. has little appetite, I ask him how he feels. "Bursting with health," he answers. — He is still going out of doors twice a day. In the evening a dance at Wahnfried! Ten young officers and ten girls. R. orders the polonaise to be danced from the hall into his *salon,* where he plays for it, while Herr Kellermann, not noticing, continues playing in my room. The rest of the music is played by "Memel and Schwemel," as R. calls our two fiddlers. — He sticks photographs in my album, until I ask him to do no more, but to wait until the collection is complete. Looking at A. Müller's house, which has just been drawn for me and in which he lived on the fifth floor, he says, "On my first Sunday I gazed out of the window and heard a child say, '*D' Rhchhill isch us*' ('Church is over'), and I thought to myself, 'Look out, things will start happening.'"

Tuesday, December 17   A rather stormy night, R. managed in the end to get some sleep, which relieved me of my worry that I might have demanded too much of him with such an evening. But so great is my happiness at seeing him at last get some rest that my own sleeplessness has left no fatigue behind. At lunch R. speaks of his utter unwillingness to say anything more, for he has already said it all; he tells me he has just been reading his essay *Actors and Singers* and sees how thoroughly he has already dealt with the connection between art and performance, with Shakespeare, with Schiller. And all for nothing. "The whole nation is bad," he exclaims, "from top to bottom." — He says he regrets having summoned Wolz. here—the *Blätter* will have to cease publication, we can find no contributors, he himself has nothing more to say. I tell him that, even if the *Blätter* were to cease publication, W. would still be glad to have come here, in order to be living near him. He admits this is so, and the conversation passes on to the artists, whom he, R., has always regarded as his sole support, the only source of power still available to him—yet to what uses is it now being put! . . . When I tell him I should like to be rich so that we could stage *Parsifal* just for ourselves and the King, R. says with a sigh, "That's a nice thought." He tells me about the Emperor's speeches and says: "Who drove out the princes? When did the German people ever even think of driving out its princes? And the man who says this has himself dethroned three princes from the oldest families! And nobody said a word about it. Indeed, if anyone had tried, he would have been accused of treason." . . . At lunch R. made Lusch happy by remarking that in her dancing she moved well and showed a good, confident manner. R. rests for a while and then goes to Angermann's. On his return he tells me that the Israelite Karpeles was the only one to remember that today is Beethoven's birthday! . . . He says he got absorbed with Josef Rub. in a conversation about Catholicism; then he noticed that other people were listening and thought to himself that Angermann's was probably not the right place for such topics. In the evening, when friend W. and R. visit us, I repeat what the paper hanger said to me today about the sad state of industry in Germany:

everywhere complaints that we are being oppressed. R. returns to the Emperor's speeches. "In order to go hunting he starts doing a bit of ruling again! And he recommends as much religion as possible." He describes with heart-rending indignation the neglect of German interests: "They introduce the gold standard," he exclaims, "we lose our silver and have to buy foreign gold! They make a coin which does not correspond to any other; we have free trade, while all other nations have protective tariffs. It is really disgraceful! And we Germans just look on, nobody says a word, though it is as clear as daylight—nothing but servility and fear. It serves us right, too—it is our punishment for the way we are, for our gloating, our indolence. Börne was quite right when he compared the Germans with a crocodile, which one can kick as much as one pleases, nothing has any effect." — I say we should stop discussing this sad theme, it is too dismal. When I hear R. talking like this, see his pained and angry expression, it takes my breath away. Turning to the piano, he concluded the conversation: " 'Shall We Hope?'—the last thing I shall write, and I shall give it the motto, 'We do not hope, but we should like to.' " We move on to Bach, start the *48 Preludes and Fugues* from the beginning and play the first six. R. gives Herr R. directions; after the first he says the remarkable thing about these works is that one can interpret them in different ways— this first prelude, for instance, sentimentally *à la* Gounod or fast and vigorous in organ style. I ask Herr R. to note down at once in pencil everything that R. says, but he does not seem able to do it properly, and so all I can say about the Fugue in D Major is that he calls it the "Mayor" and says the figuration should arouse a feeling of trepidation; the countertheme he calls the "Mayoress," and to the concluding bars he sings the words "My will has been done." The sixth fugue, in D minor, is the one he finds most wonderful: "Nothing can surpass that. It does not look worked out. What a command he has over his means of expression, using them just as his inspiration demands! And in those times, imagine—the time of Frederick the Great's father and his smokers' gatherings!" — He talks about Bach's fate, his return from a journey to find his wife already dead and buried, and in this connection recalls Rancé, the founder of the Trappist order. — Afterward he declares that these preludes and fugues and the motets are probably the most consummate of Bach's works; as regards the *complete* Passion, he cannot say whether it should be considered their equal, but—he adds—it was performed in church, by the congregation, and that is how it should be. — Then we reminisce about Switzerland, about Lucerne, the beauty of the surroundings, the Richter episodes (also at table), with much merriment. R. says a French *"marchand d'habits"* ["clothier"] is now living in Tribschen, and we laugh afterward because on account of Rubin. he fell back on Turgenev's capers. — He also talked about his ascent of the Faulhorn, which he made in bad weather, but he had the reward of being able to watch an eagle for a long time. I had quoted a line from the Indian play *The Rise of the Moon of Intellect* which had impressed itself on my mind through its profundity: "The world, disunited in itself, is united with God." R. says, "That is quite true, but it is not so easy to understand or to explain." —

Wednesday, December 18 R. had a good night. . . . We return to the subject of Bach, and he says that in his youth he was prompted by the works of E. T. A. Hoffmann to look into these compositions, searching for mysticism, but all he had really felt was boredom. He introduced this remark by exclaiming, "How necessary education is in all things!" He works on his "Retrospect," then he goes for a walk before lunch in intense cold. He tells me he would like to make music again, and since we are talking about Fidi, who is uncommonly bright, R. says, "Wait and see, when I have completed the score of *Parsifal* with much *amore,* I shall occupy myself with the education of my boy." He also goes out in the afternoon, to Angermann's, but this outing does not seem to agree with him; he complains of tightness in the chest, says jokingly that he has hardening of the arteries, but this joke takes my breath away. — In the evening Bach again, but this time I do not really hear the music, my thoughts are too far away. But I hear R.'s words about it. Of the 7th prelude (E-flat Major) he says: "That is Wotan—it (and especially the first 9 bars) must be played wildly. The ensuing fugue is the pacification, the good wife who dresses nicely, calms her husband down." Of the 8th prelude R. says, "I play that in a more moonlit way, never allowing the twilight to lift." The following fugue R. considers the most remarkable of all; he says it is extraordinarily elaborate, yet so full of feeling: "What strettos and augmentations it has—and what accents!" For him, he says, it is the quintessence of fugue, as fugues in his own album, which he regrets having lost, would clearly have shown. — And when today's six have been played he exclaims, "That is music in its true essence; everything we compose is applied music—a rondo by Hummel, for instance, is Bach diluted so-and-so many times, in the way one dilutes essence of roses so-and-so many times to obtain the familiar fragrance." "To give continuity to a dance melody—that is what he has succeeded in doing here; later one used figurations to isolate, to link." — He explains to the children (Lusch and Boni) what a fugue is. Then he says, "Let us now play some applied Bach," and takes out the piano-duet arrangement of the *Ms.* Prelude; then, since his fingers are not working well, he asks Herr R. to play it solo; he does it very nicely, but for me R.'s participation is priceless, irreplaceable, for he sets the tempo. Right away, for instance, Herr R. played the first theme too broadly. R. says, "It is tempo which gives a performance its soul"—and how difficult it is to learn! He tells us that he once made a precise study of it, that they rehearsed the *Eroica* in Leipzig with a double-bass player, Pögner, also that the F Major once went well with Richter. — Infinite delight in *Die Meistersinger*. "And I, stupid fellow that I am," R. exclaims, "had on my return from France to throw it away on such a miserable nation as the Germans! Well, they haven't yet heard the last of it from me." . . .

Thursday, December 19   R. had a somewhat restless night, but on the whole not a bad one; he talked in his sleep about military music. For me the night brought back worry in a terrible form—oh, once Siegfried is set on the right path, to die blissfully with him—from the appearance to the actuality! . . . I feel how remote I am now from the birth which seems to be my own—all the rest of life's trials and all its petty troubles scarcely affect me any more, just one thing dominates my entire existence, and it is only by force that I maintain the appearance of calm. — R. has finished his "Retrospect" today. He goes in bright sunshine for a walk in the palace gardens, where the children are skating, except for Evchen, who is indisposed. R. spent some time at Eva's bedside and came away very touched by the child, who, though restless and unable to sleep, was bearing it all patiently. He says he cannot stand seeing the children ill: "They are usually so beautiful when they are suffering." Over dessert R. tells me of a letter from Frl. Uhlig in reply to the dispatch of the laurel wreath; this letter so upsets R. that he cannot rest in the afternoon. At six o'clock he reads to us (W. and me) his "Retrospect," which gives me great delight; I congratulate him on the idea of the tablet, which has saved him from having to mention everyone by name and hand out compliments right and left. Herr Neumann has invited R. to conduct a concert in Leipzig in support of the pension fund. In the evening a Frl. Steinbach from Vienna sings to us R.'s *"Träume"* and my father's *"Es muss ein Wunderbares sein"*; R. instructs her how to sing the former, with long-sustained breathing, and the resulting performance is at once different, so very, very different. — After that Herr R. plays us three preludes and fugues; R. says of the theme of the 13th fugue that it is like the proclamation of a gospel; in general, he advises Herr Ru. not to emphasize the middle voices too strongly, so that the melody may stand out nicely. — Then R. goes through Mozart's E-flat Major Symphony with Herr Rub. and gives him directions for its execution—for example, to play the second third in the Adagio with some emphasis: this gives significance to the whole theme, whereas it usually sounds rather trivial. R. takes great delight in this symphony and says: "So many ideas, so many accents! Though these things are perhaps not completely satisfying as works of art, there is always delight to be taken from communing with the spirit which shines through them." — R. tells us that, when he was alone in Angermann's, the barmaid came up to him and said it was terrible that *Alexa* was going on so long and that she did not slam the door shut today. R. agrees with her. We laugh heartily at the people's concern over this story.

Friday, December 20 R. had a good night, but he complains of tightness on the left side. The doctor denies any suggestion of a lung or heart ailment. Yesterday R. received a calendar from our printer Bonfantini; he looks up his birthday and sees that it falls on Ascension Day: "So I shall probably also ascend to Heaven then." When, toward evening, he says something similar in front of Wolz. and I tell him he is wrong to do so, he jokes: "It's to keep you all respectful"—no, he said that on some previous occasion—"It's to keep your sympathies aroused!" — Sounds of music in Wahnfried again, and when R. parts from me around noon, he says: "I have been playing the last pages of *Parsifal*. I've never heard any music like it. But I need an awful lot of time!" He adds, "It moved me very much." At lunch we discuss the affair of the Würzburg student. [*Enclosed in the Diaries are two newspaper clippings. One deals with a student in Würzburg who, having drunk too much, taunted the military guard, was arrested, and, on the way to the police station, tried to escape, whereupon he was shot dead by the police sergeant (a Prussian); the case caused a considerable public outcry. The other clipping concerns a worker in Berlin who asked a policeman to arrest him, since he had neither work nor food; when the policeman refused, the worker shouted a treasonable remark in order to provoke his arrest. On this clipping Cosima has written:* "Told to us by R."] R. says the sergeant need only have read Busch's book, where there is talk of nothing else but shooting people down. He says it is a matter of behaving as if we were in a state of war, but everything is like that nowadays in our country; he does not defend the student's conduct, and undoubtedly discipline is now very good in the army, but this was treating a person as if he were cattle. — Talking of *Parsifal*, R. says, "The longer one lives, the longer one has to live—I need a great deal of time." At supper we talk about old times, the sojourn in Biebrich, the pipe that smoked, the servant girl Lieschen, for whom he spoke up when she was falsely accused of something or other, and who, though completely exonerated, still kept on weeping: "Just think, if I hadn't found such a good master, and how many don't find them—" she said. Then his landlord Frickhäfner, "the hypochondriac," who was always quarreling with his old housekeeper and one day shouted to her over the banisters, "You're as stupid as an owl!," whereupon R., who happened to be there, called up, "You mean as rude as an owl!" An unpleasant incident with Herr Kellermann, who goes off to practice for the amateur concert instead of staying for the talk on Bach's fugues. R., very annoyed, tells him his piano playing there is not worth a jot, whereas here he might learn something. Herr K. goes, but R. is very agitated; as he says, he can never tell a person the truth calmly and unconcernedly, and that is why he prefers to avoid such encounters. Now he is sorry about it, or, rather, he is upset, and much time passes before we can settle down to Bach's *48 Preludes and Fugues.* R. describes the 17th fugue as a dance, and traces a few steps to the first bars, then says it is freer in form, already approaching the sonata. Prelude 18 enchants and moves one, and its fugue R. calls a fairy tale told by the grandmother in the *Edda.* The theme is expressive of complete resignation, and he sings some words to it, which end, "And so it then must be." In the 19th prelude he laughs over the fifths and says, "Bach wrote those deliberately, saying, 'People know what a musician I am, and they know that when I write something like this, I do it on purpose, for the sake of the idea.'" Concerning the 20th fugue, he says Bach must first have thought of it in four voices, then arranged it for the piano. It is such things, he says, that brought Bach into disrepute and caused his teacher Weinlig to refuse to have anything to do with him. — Referring to one of the fugues between nos. 16 and 20, R. says it is curious how Bach sometimes reeled off the most significant themes as if on a spinning wheel, "he does not make anything of them." — Then, to our great enjoyment, Mozart's C Major Symphony (not the *Jupiter*), which R. recalls having heard played as entr'acte music amid the bangings of students who wanted the play to begin.

Saturday, December 21 R. got up once during the night but was on the whole not dissatisfied with it. At lunch I notice, however, that he is very absorbed. He tells me he has been going through his manuscript: I did not yet know Gurnemanz's joy when he recognizes the spear. "He howls for joy, and the fifths I've got there, you'll be amazed!" . . . R. is touchingly kind to Herr K., and Herr Jäger comes for coffee, telling us quite a lot about Vienna. — R. puts off the Bach evening, saying he wants to be alone. Things are again brewing inside him, arousing my fears: may this terrible inner process not prove a strain on him! He says: "All I want now is to finish *Parsifal,* then everything will be all right. Let's hope it won't be a success and people won't insist on founding my school for me, for then I should be lost." Previously he told me that he had read *Actors and Singers,* and "I was vexed that I should be expected to say anything beyond that." — In the evening we are all by ourselves, R. and I. "Oh, how much good it does me not to feel cramped!" he says. "All talk with other people is an affectation." Each of us takes a volume by Goethe (*Xenien*), and we take turns reading to each other; R. is particularly amused by "Oh, were I but rid in my halls of Isis and Osiris." After I read to R. Goethe's poems about Indian idols, he says how natural it seems to him to regard animals as divine, how noble they appear in comparison with human beings, and more beautiful, too. "The human being with all his reason is just like that dog with many heads! . . . Only in very rare cases can speech express the soul, and so silence is much nobler." A very cheerful, quiet evening, and R. looks well when we part.

Sunday, December 22 R. slept tolerably well. He regrets that he will no longer hear the melancholy fiddling, for today is the final dancing lesson. [*Added in margin:* "That was yesterday, it was yesterday when the Robber and the Little Doll played their fiddles for the last time!"] Arrival of friend Seidl (Herr Jäger arrived yesterday). All the reports on Vienna are dismal, and I wish none of it reached R.'s ears. But Seidl pleases us with his simple and truthful nature and his correct judgment. Arrival of the pictures from Munich, memories; regarding the house on Briennerstrasse R. says: "It looked for a while as if that would last, as if things would be all right—but no, it was horrible! The only places where life was peaceful and happy were Tribschen, the Dammallee, the Fantaisie, and here. I am glad that I have you so quietly all to myself." — Bach in the evening. Of the Prelude in B Major (No. 23) R. says, "This is full of hope, spring must be coming after all." The 24th prelude he thinks should be taken "like a heartfelt lament"; he says he would like to hear it sung by someone like Catalini, with words—one would see what an impression that would make. He advises Rubinstein always to bring out the melodic line very clearly and says he feels almost like writing words for it himself. I observe that the text would have to be religious, a kind of offertory, and he agrees. He wants the ensuing fugue taken broadly, then gradually quickening. "These pieces are riddles," he says, "one must look at them, follow the melody; he has really lavished melody on them." — After this Herr R. plays us one of his "Pictures," and finally we hear *Die Msinger,* the concluding passages of the 2nd and 3rd acts. Divine impressions, Sachs radiating nobility, dispassionateness. I wish I could describe R.'s countenance when he is playing such things, his eyes opened wide, his gaze ranging ever farther, his brow illumined!

Monday, December 23 R. did not sleep too badly, but he complains of tightness in the chest and looks run down. He did too much yesterday. — But at lunch R. is cheerful, though talking tires him; he laughs a great deal over the story of the death of the conductor Proch, who, shortly before his demise, read in a newspaper that he was dying: "Now I don't know whether I should drink my coffee or not," he said, and a few hours later he was dead! (R. asks whether he perhaps died of a "proken" heart.) He says at lunch, "It is really curious that both the *Pommerania* and the *Grosser Kurfürst* had to sink.") We spend all day alone together, and a curious thing happens: looking for something upstairs in the Parnassus room, I catch sight of a volume of Hoffmann's life and think to myself that R. might perhaps like to glance through it. When I go downstairs, R. tells me that he has just been reading Hoffmann's biography. I: "How is that possible? It is upstairs." R.: "No, downstairs, it is on my table, at any rate the 2nd volume, which is what I read." Our thoughts, dreams, desires, so interwoven that every moment seems like an intimation of eternity! — In the evening I read to R. from the biography and note in it that it was his uncle who visited Hoffmann; then, when the overture in celebration of victory is mentioned, R. says, "I played that as a piano duet with my uncle, I can still remember the allies embracing." He also mentions the name Hoffmann assumed for it. —

Tuesday, December 24 R. had a bad night, but an absurd dream amuses him: his niece Johanna wanted to sing Brünnhilde, but she could not, and she draped herself in a long robe made of our bedroom-curtain material, trying to compensate for her inadequate singing with striking gestures, and looking all the time at R. — Christmas activities. R. says at lunch that he had yet another dream, that "the Robber" (one of the fiddlers who played for the elder girls' dancing lesson in the morning; the second fiddler the children called "the Little Doll") was playing something from *Parsifal* downstairs. R. does not look too worn out at lunch, and in the evening, after the distribution of presents, he is in very high spirits; he tells me that in the palace gardens Jäger fell down in the snow; he was taken to Stützer's tavern and Schnappauf was sent for, but it was nothing, and afterward Wolz., Seidl, Jäger, Rubinstein, and he formed a Serapion Pact. We go to bed early, R. observing that yesterday's reading about the death of Hoffmann had not been a good preparation for the previous night. But he is looking well. The Christmas tree is pushed to one side and the children clear away their things, for there is to be a party in Wahnfried tomorrow evening.

Wednesday, December 25 Oh, that one has nothing but words, words! This threadbare language for such joys, such bliss! I feel reluctant to write about it, there is no one to whom I wish to tell what happened today. . . . The pen slipped from my fingers, I now take it up again [*noted at foot of page:* "Friday the 27th"] to preserve for my children what has perhaps not stamped itself sharply enough on their memories. Early in the morning I hear some rustling and think to myself that preparations are being made for the evening, since R. has promised me a party this evening, and last night they had to clear the presents away. Then Siegfried comes skipping into the room and says softly, "Mama, Papa wants you to know that the Robber is playing something from *Parsifal*," and then—the Prelude begins, really begins, and is played to the end, while my heart reels in bliss! . . .

And then R. comes to my bed, asks me not to weep or expire, jokes gaily, undresses and gets into bed, breakfasts again with me (he had already breakfasted with Lusch at 7 o'clock), and talks and talks. The orchestra from Meiningen is here, he says, there is to be a house concert this evening, the Fugal Overture, the F Major Symphony; yesterday there were two rehearsals, morning and afternoon, and all those things—the dream about the Robber, Jäger's fall, the Serapion Pact—were fibs! But the rehearsals cured him, he greatly enjoyed them. He went to the first feeling languid after his bad night, but with the Fugal Overture it was all forgotten. He crept home very slowly (he did not want to order a carriage, lest he attract my attention with the sound of its wheels), and when Brange saw him wrapped up in furs, she almost tore him to bits, wanting to get the fur off him, as if she thought something must have happened to him. What can I say to all this? I hold in my hands the baton with which he has just been conducting, and the fan which he gave me along with other lovely things, and do not know whether to utter cries of joy or to expire. Death alone could express my feelings, life can scarcely contain them, and so I remain silent, silent, hearing as if from the farthest reaches of Heaven things no mortal being—not even you, my Siegfried—can be allowed to hear from my lips. . . .

At eleven o'clock rehearsal in Wahnfried! Introduction to the Fugal Overture, which, so curiously unsuited to the Josefstädter Theater, R. explains to me by saying that Beethoven probably thought of it as a suburban people's theater, and had imagined, and described in the introduction, Emperor Joseph, the people's friend, who wanted to drive out the Jesuits, whereupon popular acclamation, delirium! . . . After the Overture, the *Idyll* and *Egmont,* and the Andante and Presto from the A Major—this for the children, since Siegfried so loves the Andante. After the rehearsal some construction work in Wahnfried, so that the musicians can have an entrance of their own (work was already started on this yesterday, but secretly, during the evening, and done as if by magic!). Incredible the effect R. has on this by no means very significant orchestra! He himself laughs when, after the rehearsal, he catches sight of a violin case belonging to one of the musicians: "That is Fr.'s magic violin—it plays wrong all by itself." At lunch, when I express my emotion at his having orchestrated the Prelude, he says, "Yes, I was always thinking, 'Surely she must some time notice that I am not progressing beyond those first few bars of Act III?' "

Nothing but revelations at lunchtime! Also much about music, about Beethoven's orchestration, but in him the ideas are so powerful that he triumphs over everything. The evening begins at seven o'clock. — Program: 1st part: *"Zur Weihe des Hauses"* Overture (Beethoven), F Major Symphony. Intermission. — 2nd part: *Idyll,* Andante and Presto from the A Major Symphony, *Egmont* Overture. Long intermission, supper, Prelude to *Parsifal!* — With each bar of each work I feel like exclaiming, "Oh, stay a while, you are so fair!" From no performance ever before have I received such an impression, never! The players, as if transformed by magic, scatter sparks of divinity all around them; it is as if all the themes are being turned to flesh and blood, they approach us like individual people, and even the auditorium looks transfigured. At each intermission R. retires alone, but I am permitted to make sure that he is well; only after the *Egmont* Overture does he have a little headache, but a bit of nourishment restores him. To me it seems that these glorious works have been cleansed of all profanation, of the disparagement inflicted on them by poor, everyday performances; they appear to me like Kundry redeemed by Parsifal; and, as if the ideas themselves were conscious of this, each theme seems to greet the master by displaying all its radiance, gentle or powerful. He and Beethoven! . . . But the evening performance of the Prelude is not like the morning one, when I was all prayer and ecstasy; this time I hear the Redeemer's call to salvation, addressed to an unheeding world, a call so sad, so sorrowful, so fervent, I see his countenance and the gaze which fell on Kundry—I recognize the wilderness across which this call resounds, and the awful recognition fills me with bliss! There stands he who has called forth these wonders, and he loves me. He loves me! —

Richard was by no means displeased when Councilor Kraussold, overwhelmed by his impression of *Parsifal,* spoke a few words and called for a cheer; in his speech he touched me with his reference to me: "she who has no desire to live for an instant without her Richard." — All took their leave silently, solemn in their exaltation. R. stays up with me and Seidl, and we talk—if talking is the right word for a series of exclamations followed by silence! But R. enlarges splendidly upon the *Egmont* Overture and its connection with the play: it is something quite different, he says, and yet all of it is inspired by the play; so beautiful, says R., the figure of the hero at the end, after all the preceding fears in his behalf. Otherwise it is all Klärchen! — We part when R. becomes really tired, only to find, upstairs, that we cannot part! — He is pleased with the white dress he gave me, about which he was involved in a lengthy correspondence. . . .

Thursday, December 26   R. had a very good night—this blessing to crown my happiness! Discussed the glorious performance in detail. How beautifully the clarinet played in the trio of the minuet movement of the F Major! Then R. says that Fidi, to whom he had each time thrown his cap for safekeeping, had looked magnificent, resembling his father Geyer. I: "Father Geyer must surely have been your father." R.: "I don't believe that." "Then why the resemblance?" R.: "My mother loved him at the time—elective affinities." — We eat out today at Lieutenant Colonel Schäffer's, but R. is very tired there; on his behalf I beg that he may be allowed to leave, but he stays seated and by the end of the meal looks somewhat better. As we are riding home, he says, "Yes, we must not leave Wahnfried too often." We then look at the room which has now really become his music room; the magic still pervades it. Everything—the relationship of the orchestra to the room, the acoustics, the choice of works and order of their playing, the number of people present—it was all just right, successful in all respects; and even the present disorder is not disturbing—it reminds us of what has been! In the evening I put on the "Marajah," as R. calls another dress he gave me after giving all the measurements to Steckner in Leipzig and bringing into being a very rich, fantastic, and extremely becoming article of clothing. He is very pleased with it. Talked a lot about music and the concert. How everything, everything, lies in the nature of genius; it is not even the correct tempo which makes the difference, but the power which a genius has over his fellow beings. — We talk away the evening in the lilac *salon*. R. says my dress is like the one Alexander wore after defeating Darius.

Friday, December 27   R. had a good night, and I had the happiness of watching over his sleep and, in my pleasure at doing so, of becoming meditative and forming the only desire within my soul into a prayer. There can be no more vain striving, no worldly sorrow can disturb me, for only love now breathes within me. Merry breakfast with R., he tells me once again how the rehearsal cured him, he had had some trouble with the Prelude to *Parsifal* (they had played it at twice the proper speed in Meiningen, because the conductor had not known how to indicate the rhythm of one passage, like Lachner on a previous occasion with the *Tannhäuser* Overture), but everything had been in order with the Overture. — Departure of Seidl, a good and industrious person. — Lunch with the children, R. asks them what they liked best: *Parsifal* and the Beethoven Andante. R. said yesterday again that he would perhaps amuse himself by orchestrating some things afresh. — In the evening alone with Herr R. (before that R. writes to Herr Förster concerning the engagement of Seidl). Our conversation ends with a very animated description of the evils the Jews have brought on us Germans. R. says that he personally has had some very good friends among the Jews, but their emancipation and equality, granted before we Germans had come to anything, had been ruinous. He considers Germany to be finished. And this worries him, for there were signs to suggest this might happen. The Germans have been exploited and ridiculed by the Jews, and abroad they are hated. So they have become indolent, besotted, wanting to do everything as the Jews do; their faith and loyalty have been undermined. Certainly much of the blame lay with the governments. But it was all ordained by Fate. He, R., has no hope left. — Before that we talked about the influence of impressions on the senses—of music, for instance, on hearing—and, arising out of that, the remark Prof. Haeckel is supposed to have made that R.'s music has changed the hearing of the present generation. R. plays "*Lass mich sterben*" from *Tristan* and says that many people were perplexed when they heard this for the first time. Most of them could hear no melody—but if melody were to be grasped through the intellect, then he (R.) was willing to admit that the senses might change accordingly. The body says, "I look after all the functions, but the perceptions I leave to you, the intellect." R. also tells us of his dream, in which he saw his sister Klara passing by with her husband, and behind them a long line of people, like Banquo's descendants; it had strangely touched him.

Saturday, December 28 R. had a bad night, the animated discussion about the Jews was a strain on him; he praises Rubinstein's manner and serious outlook, "but he should keep his mouth shut about the Jews, as I once said of Pohl about his wife." — At lunch our Nibelungen copyist with his young wife, telling us dismal things about Mannheim— if only these good people would leave us in peace in our Wahnfried, not keep telling us about the outside world, which we wish so much to forget! — R. tells me of a dream he had during the night of Thursday to Friday, which until now he preferred not to mention to me: he entered the town as if coming from the Fantaisie, intending to come to us, but on the way met Seidl, wearing a mourning band and accompanied by a large crowd; Seidl told him it was a funeral and attempted to hold him back; R., struggling to force his way through, exclaimed furiously, "It concerns me most of all." — Once more I see how my thoughts are turned into R.'s dreams: I prayed fervently for a blessed death, and he receives the vision! . . . In the evening we are alone and enjoy being so; Eva reads to us the saga of the trumpeter's castle, which R. had often inquired about without being able to find it, and which means much to me because my brother once lived in the trumpeter's castle. When the children have left, I remain alone with R., and the hours flow past in peaceful happiness until, in the hour of parting, love's bliss floods us with its rays!

Notes

The overwhelming impression which has been dominating my thoughts for days made me incapable of reporting well, but I did not wish to break the thread of my description; hence this appendix to the various days:

Tuesday the 24th　After my morning's work (distributing presents) I sink down somewhat wearily into my chair, and in my usual way of restoring myself by taking up a book at random, I alight on Leopardi's poem "To Aspasia"; his description of beauty and the effect it has on him, Leopardi, brings my thoughts straight back to R., who recently said that beauty means little to him when no soulful gaze shines through it—that is the peculiar thing about it. How different from others is R. in all things! Immersed in these reflections, I saw his cherished image within my soul and returned to my work refreshed. — R. laughs over his illness, says it is *overproduction* (the Emperor's word for the troubles of German industry). The days are longer by a cock's crow—this expression pleases R. — At lunch yesterday he suddenly quoted MacMahon's words, *"Des cuirassiers, il n'y en a plus"* ["There are no longer any cuirassiers"], and he goes on, *"Des Allemands* [Germans], *il n'y en a plus!"*

Wednesday the 25th　The presents R. piled up in my room: the Marajah—the swan dress—the Roxane—the enamel costume—the Jardinière, five in all, each more beautiful than the last. A fan of eagle's down. A bouquet, which in the evening adorns his podium—silk stockings—shoes for each dress, all of it thought out, ordered, and obtained by him! . . . This for the appearance; for the pleasures of reality, however: the orchestral sketches of *Das Liebesverbot* and *Die Walküre* (since the first page was rather smudged, he wrote it out again), the Prelude to *Parsifal!* . . . Before the rehearsal, R. had difficulties: all the servants were away (Christmas Day) and could not help, Miss Murchison gone to church, having her furs carried there and back, so R., Lusch, Fidi, and Seidl had to arrange the chairs themselves! . . . When R. in great annoyance, particularly with Miss Murchison and the transport of her furs, is telling me all about it, he exclaims, "Peter, my fan!," which then causes the greatest merriment amid all the vexation. Another characteristic episode also amuses us: when, after completing his report, he "furiously" looks to see what the servants are doing, he catches sight of Rausch bringing in a barrel of beer: "Yes, beer!" R. cries out in a rage, "Beer! As long as you've got your beer!" A few moments later Georg comes in with a glass of beer on a tray: "The master called for some beer?" Behind all that rage Rausch saw nothing except thirst and a desire for beer!

Before the concert begins, R. says a few words, he explains the significance of the day, and then the Overture. Before the *Idyll* he asks me loudly whether he should read the poem; with a movement of my head I beg him not to. Before *Egmont* he says, "In honor of the army, since Egmont was beheaded by soldiers." High-spirited remarks tumble from his lips, and his eyes radiate enthusiasm. His inspiration transforms all the poor spirits assembled there as if by magic, and it is as if we were taking part in an act of creation! More than the works themselves, it is the way in which he performed them that lingers in my memory. R. tells me how blissful the members of the orchestra had been, how transfigured, when he taught them at rehearsal how to play the minuet and trio of the symphony. — He had first of all intended to play the *Freischütz* Overture but later abandoned the idea, and we agree that, like everything else, this was the right decision, for it would not have been in keeping with the mood. —

Parsifal Prelude: *Ecce homo!* . . .

Thursday the 26th I will note down only one extra thing for today: Lt. Col. Sch[effer] tells us that, if one has not called on a citizen here, and then at some encounter wishes to clink glasses with him, he will pull his glass away. R. says: "That is perhaps not a bad characteristic of the Germans, bourgeois pride. A Jew would clink glasses with you at once, whether you have called on him or not. But everything in our country now looks so petty and ridiculous."

Friday the 27th R. tells me he has looked through the Mendelssohn overtures, which I put among his Christmas presents; the *Calm Sea* pleases him, he was a fine musician. — In the evening we discuss the trait in Hoffmann's character which led him to seek refuge in the tavern after insipid, so-called intellectual gatherings, and when I say I can understand it, R. reads to us the passage about Ludwig Devrient in his essay *Actors and Singers*. R. gets indignant about the customs regulations, that is, about the irresponsible way in which Bismarck says, "I made a mistake, now we must do it differently," yet retains the same people and still listens to their advice. He says of Beeth.'s symphonies: "There are not many such works, and if anybody put an orchestra at my disposal, I should soon be finished with it, for the works are few." When Herr Rubinstein says the Greeks did not recognize blue, R. says: "Or, rather, where we see only a single color, they saw all sorts of nuances—they saw much more than we do." — We had some squabbling among the servants, which R. tried to smooth out himself, but in vain. When I then persuade the cook to beg his pardon, R. says to me: "Oh, she is a genius, she is like an animal, won't listen to reason. She's just as much a genius as Beethoven."

Sunday, December 29   R. had a good night, but he cannot do much talking, it is a strain on him. "Only Bayreuth and Wahnfried are fit for us"—with this paraphrase of Mephisto's words about day and night being fit for human beings he concludes the conversation in which we decide how dead the world has become for us, and that there is nowhere we can go without changing our natures. Yesterday evening we looked at pictures of scholars in an English book about the geologist Murchison. R. remarks: "What an advantage they have over us! They look so proud, so intelligent, if indeed also somewhat foolish, but one can see they don't work for money." Curious faces, curious deportment. The faces in the 2nd volume less interesting than the first, "bad and modern," says R., there are now the beards he so much hates, and also some Jews among them! — R. does not go out, we spend the evening talking and looking through the *Illustrirte* and various other things. We begin Calderón's *El verdadero dios Pan* but are soon put off by its cold manner of dismissing the deepest mysteries with displays of reason; we shall certainly never take up the *autos* again.

Monday, December 30   R. had a good night, which leads to a gentle and harmonious breakfast time. He devotes the morning to a fine letter to the King, which he reads to me after lunch. In the morning he said to me: "The press! The fact that one has made this word the symbol for writing reveals the spirit behind it. It is not the setting of the type which has become the symbol, but the clumsy object one runs over it." He reflects on an alteration in his relationship with the Society of Patrons, and on a few words to introduce Wolzogen's work on the German language, which he is now reading. A quotation from Schopenhauer amuses him greatly: "The lion takes a taste of me." — We invite friend Wolzogen over for the evening and spend the time in conversation; but I notice that R. is somewhat tired, I see it in his speech.

Tuesday, December 31   Not a good night for R. . . . He writes his "introduction" and reads it to me; I then also read parts of the Wolzogen manuscript, and in the evening, while the children are casting lead and the candles on the tree are burning again, together we go through the points which struck me. — R. did not go out today, either, and when we are not working, our conversation continually returns to the divine concert. We part around eleven o'clock, but we do not immediately go to sleep; each of us hears the bells, without remarking on them—everything in my soul changes into a blessing upon Richard and thanks! . . .

1879

Wednesday, January 1   Who could describe the feelings with which I wish R. good fortune today, at the conclusion of a year we were permitted to spend entirely at Wahnfried, unseparated, in which *Parsifal* came nearer to completion and a significant part of R.'s burden was lifted from his shoulders? Though it was late before he fell asleep, he had a tolerable night. He reads the shorter writings of Plutarch, which friend Wolzogen gave him for Christmas, and is enjoying them. I start to file away the papers for 1878 (while the children are dismantling the Christmas tree) and receive calls, one of which, from Dr. Landgraf, gives me much pleasure. He says that R. seemed to him like a god, and none of the many pictures of him he has seen conveys anything of the expression on his face while conducting: his spirit passes into the others like an electric current! — At lunch we talk about the dogma of palingenesis (Loldi said she believed in reincarnation), and R. tells the story of the virtuous prince who was blinded: Buddha explained that he had once blinded antelopes. — How beautifully does this relate suffering to justice! And how pitiful in comparison our Jewish doctrine of sin! — Springlike weather, sunshine; I go out of doors with indescribable emotions, look at the birds in the poultry yard which give R. so much pleasure (particularly the peacock); R. rests for a while, then goes to call on Councilor Kraussold, who does not really understand the purpose of his visit, paid by R. in recognition of the evening of the 25th. Returning home, R. settles down to work—on *Parsifal!* I have told him that I no longer wish to hear any music except *Parsifal,* played by him. . . . Before that, returning from his walk, he says to me, "I have been performing rose miracles in your room." In the morning he placed on my bureau a little bottle of "Extract Richard Wagner," which he brewed himself, and in the afternoon he pours a few drops of rose essence on my bouquet. In the evening we celebrate the "octave" of the concert with my "white robe" and with memories. Such joys are not ephemeral, my feelings are borne upward to Heaven as if on wings, all earthly things are forgotten, and all that remains in my heart apart from love is the desire to be and to do good. — R. spoke a lot about Beethoven—how rarely he modulates, and how his teacher Weinlig had told him to what great extent his novelty lay in rhythm. Referring to the overture: "The jest of a creator, playing with the world." Much about the symphony, too. As we part, R. says: "Oh, the way you looked at me that time in Zurich (1858)! I really was like Tristan, so modest; then I was told by K. Ritter that you both wanted to throw yourselves in the lake, and I became totally confused." Over our after-lunch coffee he spoke of the dissolute companions with whom he spent his youth, and said it would not be necessary for Fidi to go through that—he has been rescued by the spirit of music, just as he himself, when that took possession of him, was liberated from all vulgarity. (After supper I have to write to Paris regarding a dress which took his fancy in the fashion journal; we have to laugh heartily when he says, "If one is *wise,* one grasps such opportunities.")

Thursday, January 2 R. had quite a good night; at breakfast he tells me many things from Plutarch, whose shorter writings he is now reading: Dionysius the Younger's reply concerning Plato, etc., and he says, "They were so complete, those ancients!" — I organize papers with friend Wolzogen, the tree is pushed to one side, and before we go to lunch, R. plays me what he has done today in ink: "*Wirkte dies der heilige Tag,*" the suggestion of the meadow, so heavenly in its twilight! "It must be nothing definite, just a slight haze—oh, how beautiful syncopes are, what lightness of movement they impart!" . . . One magic is followed by another, and the new year begins for me today. At lunch R. tells us anecdotes from Plutarch—Porus, Antigonus, Demetrios, the whole thing splendid. As we are having our coffee, he remembers his early life in Paris, his visit to the singer Dupont, so difficult to find in his country house, only then to have "*Mignonne*" refused! And so home. "And how did Minna react?" "Oh, I suppose she bought radishes or something; she was sorry for me." — Heavy snow flurries, which please R., for he can stay indoors and work. The Wolzogens in the evening; R. goes through his "Language" with him and exhorts him always to maintain a tone of dignity, never to make use of "un-German" language, even in fun. Talking about Plutarch leads him to Droysen's *History of Hellenism,* which he praises highly. — When we are alone again, he plays to me what he was working on today, Parsifal's entrance and the removal of his armor. — Fairest of blessings, final consecration of a blessed day!

Friday, January 3 R. slept well, at any rate toward the end of the night. I sent up a grateful prayer when I heard him breathing in quiet slumber beside me after he had awakened in agitation from a nasty dream. We talk about music, and R. remarks how beautiful, indeed powerful, flutes can sometimes sound—in the Prelude to *Parsifal,* for instance. Then he comes back to the *Calm Sea* Overture and observes, "One might say that he had *a good ear* for landscape." When I say it seems to me that Weber led the way for him, and in Weber it all sounds so different—as if one were hearing the beating of a human heart, so to speak—he replies, "Oh, yes, undoubtedly." He then reflects on Mendelssohn's personality, says the same thing happened to him as to certain apes who, so gifted when young, become stupid as their strength increases. "I saw him (M.) after his marriage, and he looked so fat, so unpleasant—an unsavory fellow!" R. does a little work. At lunch it is again Plutarch who fills our conversation with lovely glimpses of the ancient world. Over coffee R. tells me his dream, and I have to weep over it. We, the children and I, and particularly Lulu, threw him out of the house, and he had a kind of bad conscience, reacted in a cowardly way, and just said to Lulu, "If only you knew how unjust you are being!" — R. laughs at my grief and says that whatever it is that is trying to wake him up always chooses the most horrible means. . . . Herr Rubinstein comes in the evening; R. has given him a task to do, and he speaks of the *sculptural* quality in Beethoven, saying this is the true sign of his work, even more than the rhythmical quality stressed by Weinlig; he tries to explain this quality to Herr R., and says with regard to the instrumentation, "It is quite superb in Beethoven, the groupings and so on, only now and again he misjudges the strength of various instruments, and if one tries to redress the balance a little one is doing him a service." — Today, around noon, he comes up to my room singing, "My *Parsifal* will be good." —

Saturday, January 4 Again R. did not have a good night, but there were no alarming episodes, and after breakfast he greets me with the verse "My wife comes from her bath, and life resumes its normal path!" But all day long he does not feel well, and he does no work, reading Plutarch and also the *Fl. Blätter* instead. In the evening I read some of Wolzogen's "German Language" to him, and we mark places where the style does not seem very good. I do not know why, but late in the evening he says: "Oh, I shall show these gentlemen! I would close all the universities on the spot—and then seek ways and means of enabling significant men to teach." — R. somewhat annoyed at the nonarrival of the advance from Mannheim. A few days ago, referring to the release of the *Ring* to the theaters, he likened himself to a faithful dog who defended the basket of meat from other dogs for a long while, but in the end, assailed on all sides, fell on it himself and ate it up! . . .

Sunday, January 5 R. had a good night, and he works today, after talking a lot with me about Fidi, who had just taken a bath with him.

Joy over the boy's good, sunny character. Today R. and I have lunch in the home of our neighbor Baroness Staff. R. looks well, and I hope that this deviation from our normal routine will not harm him. It is true that he was unable to work afterward, and I, too, remain somewhat distracted. It has a magic of its own this life of ours in Wahnfried, but the secret of its success is that one must yield to it entirely and never abandon it, even for an instant; the mood is not so easily restored. — R. reads Plutarch and tells us admiringly of Agesilaus's reply: "If one is always prudent, one has no need of courage." — "How sad it is to have constantly to exclaim that all these things no longer concern one," says R. as we are talking about present conditions; the Chancellor is said to be threatening again to resign unless protective tariffs are accepted, yet at the same time he wants to introduce indirect taxation, in order, as R. says, to gain a power for himself for which he will not have to answer: "Our present calamity is seen just as an opportunity for extending his power; they have no feeling for the people." We have discovered many unpleasant things about Herr Kellermann. A difficult situation for us.

Monday, January 6   R. had a good night and now intends to get on with the composition—up till now he has only been inking in his penciled sketches. Cheerful breakfast! When I tell him my only wish is that this year be as good as the last, he says, "It will be even better; *Parsifal* will be completed, and then I won't bother myself about anything at all." R. does not go out today, and we spend the evening alone together, after having had a great deal of fun with the children at supper. We go through friend Wolzogen's "Language" and discuss once more the distasteful subject of K[ellermann]: "The fact that I have put up with this poor creature for so long shows how happy I am with you and the children."

Tuesday, January 7   R. had a good night, and as we embrace before parting, he says, "Now I'm going to prepare for your next birthday!" He intends to start sketching today, he spent yesterday collecting his thoughts. At lunchtime he comes to tell me that he has composed 8 bars. — A visit we receive at coffeetime gives him an opportunity to state his views on our modern laws: one has only to mention the Jews, he says, and one is all but stoned. R. goes for a walk in the afternoon and feels well after it. He is reading Xenophon's *Memorabilia* with great enjoyment, and he reads to us the page on which Charicles begs Socrates to leave the cowherds in peace. — A very curious, amicable difference of opinion occurred today between R. and me; the seamstress names her price, I find it too high, R. does not, and he writes to her, placing the order! . . . All I can then do is laugh heartily and tell

R. that since I do not possess his genius, I cannot expect to have his rashness!

Wednesday, January 8 "Fourteen days ago there was humming going on downstairs, but you didn't notice," says R., after telling me that he slept well. We have a lot more fun about the dress he ordered yesterday, and he says, raising a clenched fist, that he is "horribly" annoyed with himself for not having ordered one which particularly pleased him last year! He works: "Exactly ten bars today," he tells me when he fetches me for lunch. He has received news of the death of the stout-hearted Herr Müller, and he recalls his friendly judgment on me back in 1857— "She is a real thoroughbred"—he (R.) had been so pleased by this, and also by his delight when he saw us come together. "That must have been a real weight off the minds of all my friends who knew about my disgraceful life. What they all had to put up with from me! Something like an avalanche lies between my former life and my present life." — He looks at the photograph of Semper which friend Lenbach has sent me, the exact image of an old lazzarone. "That's how I shall look one day," he says. I: "Oh!" He: "No, I believe I shall always look well, for I grow happier every day." I tell him I have been reading his "Stabat Mater" and enjoyed it very much, whereupon he: "Yes, after having spent two years in Paris! And after only one I was completely finished with it all. I wrote that article in my little room, when I had stopped going out, and saw and heard nothing—from that point of view these things are not uninteresting." We then return to the subject of Semper, whose genius had so astounded me at our first meeting in Zurich. R. asks whether I would have married him. I: "Before Hans, yes, after Hans, no." It would have been a bad match, R. observes. We then recall Semper's assertion that it did not matter at all to him for whom or for what he did his work, also his antipathy toward Christianity. R. says, "For the plastic artist things can only come from the outside world, and Christianity can't produce any buildings." — It is very cold, but R. goes out both morning and afternoon, and it does him good. When I return home, I find him walking up and down in the *salon,* so cheerful and content that my heart laughs to see him. "Things are going so well for me," he says! We celebrate the "*quinzaine*" of my birthday, I in *white,* as on every Wednesday now, and we remain alone together. Hans's birthday brings our thoughts back to the past, we recall J. 8, 1868, in Munich, R.'s moving speech at the little celebration; it is all so sad; in the morning R. had thought of my father's visit to him at Tribschen, during which my father was filled with deep pity for his loneliness but could do no more than point as consolation to the portrait of the King! — R. says: "Nobody believes in real love—even

Hans thought I was just amusing myself. The fact that I had often been prepared to accept money made them all contemptuous of me. I knew what my feelings were when I accepted it, but for them it was a matter of pride not to accept anything from anybody." A letter from E[lisabeth] Nietzsche brings back to us our experiences with her brother. The news that he, N., wants *Parsifal* to be staged makes R. smile bitterly— "Now they think I have no other wish but to stage another such performance"—whereas all that concerns him is how he can avoid it. I: "It is only necessary not to wish it." — R., with a sigh: "Oh, one would like it to happen, and yet one doesn't want to do it"—that is our sadly conflicting position. — But all these reflections melt into joy, today as on all other days, in the knowledge that we found each other in this terrible existence!

Thursday, January 9   R. slept well; while I was watching gratefully over his dear sleep, gloomy pictures passed through my mind—oh, Fate, be gracious toward me! R. works and tells me at lunch that he has completed 6 bars, but they are very significant ones. Before his work he reads Plutarch, which is just the right thing for him, since it does not overexcite him. He goes for a walk and enjoys the air. I have to stay indoors, and in the evening he drinks his grog in my room, after bringing me a belated Christmas gift! — He talks about his composition after we have spent some time, prompted by the parcel from London, talking about extract of roses, whose perfume (a particular favorite of his) he describes as "rapturous." He says: "During the morning I was thinking something I could not tell a soul—that in a scene like this the words and music are concentrated, more or less like this extract, to make a frivolous comparison; I could talk about all kinds of subjects, say things only I could say, there is so much concentrated inside me. Yet one walks the earth in silence and is then forgotten." I: "Forgotten!" He: "Oh, what is posthumous fame? I always think of Schopenhauer's likening it to oyster shells. What does the world know of Goethe and Schiller except the shells? Till someone comes along to whom they mean something." Draft announcing the cancellation of *Parsifal,* to be appended to the "Retrospect"; I observe that he can easily afford to let the year go by, make his announcement to the patrons, and return their money. While we are passing the evening in chat, he looks back on his life and says, "I do not know whether I am dreaming now or was dreaming then—it must have been then, for I was always creating illusions for myself and deliberately keeping them alive." He tells me of his sudden departure for Paris (1858), for which he borrowed money from Semper and Müller: "I was always wanting to go away and not return—if anything had turned up in Paris, I should not have returned, but nothing did.

That's why I cannot believe in those novels in which princesses in hooded cloaks come along—or a friend." We laugh heartily at this thought, and then he speaks very warmly of Blandine, whom he met on this journey. He is much enjoying the *Memorabilia*.

Friday, January 10   R. had a nasty dream about me; when I complain about this, he says I ought to be pleased that nothing else works, and that if he has to be frightened into waking up, I am the only effective means of achieving it. — He works, then goes for a walk, is looking well when he returns to my side, and we have such a cheerful and friendly lunch in the children's *salon* that, after he has left, I feel that in one's youth love could never shine and bestow its blessings so purely. Devout people wish to be good in order to secure their place in Heaven, I wish to be worthy of my Heaven, and so I close my heart to all wicked impulses. As R. sits down at the table beside me, he says: "Every day I become more and more conscious of the terrible facts of existence. Today, for instance, I thought of the earth's vapors, which come from its inner fires and return to us as rain; this means that the human being is nothing but a form of combustion, self-consuming— dreadful!" I tell him that I am almost continually aware of life's justice, punishment for bad deeds, reward for good ones. We quote several examples, small and great, and he cites Buddha and the stone thrown into the water which causes a widening circle of ripples. R. goes for a walk in the afternoon, and in the evening I read the *Memorabilia* to him, a very great pleasure for us both. "When one compares the people of the 18th century to those people, with their lovely costumes, their sandaled feet, their way of looking for the beautiful in everything, courage, virtue, justice, all such things—how pitiful they look!" And: "We moderns are like the Greeks, who replaced Asiatic pomp with a natural civic sense, something we also aspire to nowadays. But how do modern people look—Machiavelli, for instance, who was closest to the Greeks in spirit—in comparison to them? What a background of corruption!"

Saturday, January 11   R. slept well but once again dreamed that I wanted to go away with my father! . . . "And then, to my great good fortune, the cock began to crow," or, rather, Georg brought him his Ems water. After saying this, he tries to translate it into French and sings, "*Et là pour mon bonheur, le coq se mit à chanter,*" or, correcting himself, "*le coq se mit au chant!*" Much talk about the French, R. says he is ashamed that their instincts about the Germans in 1870 had proved correct (Schuré, for example). Of the approaching silver wedding anniversary of the Emperor and the Empress [of Austria] R. says, "They'll ask for the presents to be changed into gifts for charity and a few nice cannons." R. goes out twice today and is feeling well.

In the evening I read the *Memorabilia* to him with all our usual enjoyment. He writes down another theme for a symphony. In the evening, when he fetches me for supper, he comes back to "But I will," then says, "I will not, but I must." "A human being must acknowledge necessity," he says, "that's what makes him divine." — At our last parting in the evening, after countless other partings, he says to me, "When Parsifal falls in a faint—that is when it begins (the meadow will not be a separate thing in itself); it will be the loveliest moment—I already have much of it in sketches."

Sunday, January 12 R. slept well, woke up only once; in his first dream Marke sang an Italian chorus! The other dream was "creepy" again: "Minna was involved in it, she was supposed to return to me." — Discussions about his attitude toward the patrons. R. says, "If it were not for Wolzogen, I should cancel the whole thing." He works, but afterward does not feel well and decides not to go out—yesterday's walk in a biting east wind did him no good, he says. Naples at lunch! Plans for next winter. Then he tells the children his dream about Marke, saying his chattering teeth were probably responsible for this Italian choral accompaniment of the sort one hears in theaters—a builder's apprentice sang and Marke did the accompanying! — But I find it hard to be merry when he does not feel entirely well, when he is not, indeed, bursting with good spirits, and all day long I hear inside me Tristan's "Wherever Tristan goes, is Isolde resolved to follow?" I hear it as I am reading the *Odyssey* to the children and accompanying Lusch to an afternoon party, it forms the melodic swell on which the poor bark of my existence is borne today. But when I return, R. is feeling and looking well. I find him at the piano, going through *Médée,* from which he plays me some very beautiful things. In the evening he remembers that, having just read his article "On the Overture," I wished to hear some of the things mentioned in it. He starts with *The Water Carrier,* and at one point remarks how pretty it is, how it expresses something of the pleasure one takes in a good deed. Then *Les Abencérages,* whose second theme is particularly delightful, and afterward *Anacréon.* R. says: "Cher[ubini] was certainly the greatest of musical architects, a kind of Palladio, rather stiffly symmetrical, but so beautiful and so assured. All the rest—Auber, Berlioz—are unimaginable without him." He also points out to us details in which the influence on Beethoven can be seen. — We end with *La Vestale* by Spontini—"warmer in feeling," "more passionate," "less of a master"; he says the first finale in *Lohengrin,* with its continuous melody, could be traced back to Spontini "rather than to Weber." — Over coffee he gazes at the wall on which Beeth., Goethe, and Schiller are hanging and says, "There Makart ought to paint a fresco for us, illustrating the

Dionysian element in the introduction to the A Major Symphony." He literally divides up the wall for it and says, "Even if the painting should not please us particularly, or its connection with the present not be very apparent, we could still take pleasure in the idea." He thinks that Genelli would have been able to do it. Like a monarch of all the arts he could assign each of them his tasks! He sang something from *La Vestale,* Julia's lovely words following the departure of the High Priestess, and it did not tire him. — R. remarks that not a single one of the people he mentioned (in his "Retrospect") has had a word to say to him about it. — The publisher Schmeitzner has sent copies of Nietzsche's books to Bismarck, who used the occasion to admonish the publisher for using Latin lettering, recommending German lettering instead! R. says, "That's just like that uneducated Pomeranian *Junker,* who does not even know what the good German J. Grimm had to say on the subject."

Monday, January 13　R. slept well, and he leaves me in cheerful mood to go to his work, after talking about *La Vestale;* among other things, he says: "It is a dramatic mistake, which I myself should never have allowed to happen, to leave Julia alone in the street to sing her aria. I should have thought of something, my imagination would have come to my aid. But as it is, all plausibility is lost, we are back in the opera house." When the water in his bath becomes very hot, he is reminded of death, and he wonders what it would be like if one were treacherously to be scalded to death like that, how natural instinct would rise up in a scream of protest. I tell him I often ask myself whether one would not at once bow to the inevitable. He thinks not. He is well and does some work, which makes me feel as if I had wings! But how foolish is the assumption that possession robs love of its dreams—how much I think of him, how often I gaze upon his picture, how dominant the *"wahnloss hold bewusste Wunsch"* ["the undeceived sweetly conscious wish"] of his presence! — At lunch I tell him that I have finished the first volume [of his collected writings]. "Then I have at least one reader," he says, and adds, "I must admit to being glad that even in my youth, urged on by my inner feelings, I always expressed myself in a simple and natural way, never just striving for effect." About *Opera and Drama* he remarks, "It is a very curious work, and I was very excited when I wrote it, for it has no precedent in the history of art, and I was really pursuing a goal nobody had hitherto seen." He is glad that Herr Musiol has so much respect for it. In the afternoon he goes for a walk and returns looking well, the dear, splendid man! — Visit from Herr Levi, very pleasant. To start with, R. goes through Beeth.'s F Major Symphony with him, pointing out to him the passages he would like to see somewhat differently orchestrated; he repeats his view that "nobody has ever grouped strings and woodwind more ideally than Beeth., but just here and there he failed to judge the sound relationships quite correctly." He points out the *sf.* in the trio of the minuet, which Herr Rietz gave to the horns as well. — Then he reads to us the translation of the libretto of *Les Abencérages,* and, later still, he plays us his third act, up to the worship of the spear. . . . He declares that Gurnemanz (whom he wishes he had described as an armorer) is his favorite character—he and similar figures such as H[ans] Sachs, Kurwenal. Later he tells me it would have been better if we had done this when we were by ourselves—all the same, it was indescribable! . . . Friend Levi stays behind after our other friends have gone, and when he tells us that his father is a rabbi, our conversation comes back to the Israelites—the feeling that they intervened too early in our cultural condition, that the human qualities the German character might have developed from within itself and then passed on to the Jewish character have been stunted by their premature interference in our affairs, before we have become fully aware of ourselves. The conductor speaks of a great movement against the Jews in all spheres of life; in Munich there are attempts to remove them from the town council. He hopes that in 20 years they will be extirpated root and branch, and the audience for the *Ring* will be another kind of public—we "know differently"! — Alone together again, R. and I discuss the curious attachment individual Jews have for him; he says Wahnfried will soon turn into a synagogue! . . .

Tuesday, January 14 R. slept well, he leaves me in cheerful mood to go to his work, and around noon he fetches me and sings to me Gurnemanz's narration to Parsifal, up to the words *"er starb, ein Mensch wie alle,"* which is as far as he has got. When I attempt to explain to R. how moving I find this simple fervor, he says, "Yes, one could describe that as its essentially German quality, simplicity combined with immovable faith, and the urge to prove this faith through good deeds." Before we enter the dining room, R. says to me, "I feel well, and my only wish is that it may go on like this forever." Lunch with the children, much fun regarding our pet Israelites, R. thinks the only feeling they have in regard to his compositions is how well he does things. After lunch I beg R. to mark in the scores of Beeth.'s symphonies all the things he would like to see altered. He says, "After *Parsifal.*" In the evening, when I come down to supper, he shows me the alteration he has made to *"er starb, ein Mensch wie alle."* "It was too much like Cherubini," he said. — In the evening the *B. Blätter,* went through manuscripts: Herr Lipiner on Prof. Lagarde, unfortunately again quite impossible. Then, to our utter delight, the sextet from *Le Nozze di Figaro;* R. can never impress on me too much the artistic mastery of this work, its delicacy, wit, charm, and fluidity.

Wednesday, January 15 R. had a good night, but he complains of congestion in the chest and wishes me already to book the villa in Naples for next year. Yesterday afternoon he came to tell me that the royalties from Vienna have been good—all his works, even *Rienzi,* had earned something. I: "So they are good children, after all." R.: "Yes, they have to go begging for me." — He fetches me for lunch and says, "I have got Parsifal to the point of fainting—I'm always glad when I've got my people where they ought to be." Over coffee he says he can only bear his state of well-being when composing—otherwise it seems to him like a sin. He looks into the *salon* and says, "This is where I want to be carried when I die." I reproach him for using the singular. He: "It's better when one knows nothing about it, but all the same, when one is very old it must be nice to die in full awareness." I tell him my only wish is that we do not leave the children while they are still dependent on us. He: "What do you expect? In 10 years I shall be Kraussold's age, and Fidi will be 20; by then one knows who one is. We shall live to see Fidi's children." — R. does some more work in the afternoon, and in the evening we go through Berlioz's overtures to *King Lear* and *Benvenuto Cellini* with Herr Rubinstein. "Oh, Cherubini, Cherubini!" R. exclaims. Long discussion then about Berlioz, which he concludes with me upstairs by saying it would be better if such music had never been written. Barrenness, touches of vulgarity amid great eccentricity, overattention to detail, yet some true inspiration: "There are themes of his I remember," R. says. "One them in the Adagio of *Romeo* is wonderful." "But he belongs entirely to the French school." Taken on the whole, a very unpleasing impression.

Thursday, January 16 R. slept well, he laughingly tells me of his dream "while turning over in bed": "I was between Minna and Mme Wesendonck. She was making horrible advances to me, to annoy Minna, at whom she kept looking. 'All right, neither of them,' I thought, and tried to get away, went around looking for a purse, in which there were some gold coins. 'Is this devilry starting again?' I said to myself on waking, but I was not driven from my bed." He works and says at lunch that he has reached the point where Kundry arouses Parsifal again and he proposes marriage to her. Since the children were at a ball yesterday, R. again tells me how repulsive he, as a young man, found the balls to which his sisters went. In the afternoon R. goes for a walk in the palace gardens, and when he returns, I hand him the (Zurich) stories of G[ottfried] Keller, which Herr Levi has just sent me. I do not know why, after a cursory glance, I recommend to him the last story in the second volume; when I come downstairs, he says, "I have been spending one of the pleasantest hours of my life."

Everything in the story he has begun he finds gripping, he says. In the evening he reads it to us, and we are truly moved by both melancholy and merriment. Ursula's spiritual state quite shattering, utterly feminine and folklike.

Friday, January 17 R. slept well; our conversation in the morning is devoted almost exclusively to the story; he leaves me with the greeting "Schiller, before he was raised to the aristocracy" (this because friend Gl. wrote that he calls our busts the Riga Goethe and Schiller!). Around noon, as I am dressing, I hear the cherished voice calling from upstairs, "Cosi—I want to play something to you." I fly into his room, he sings to me Gurnemanz's words "*Nicht so*" and all the rest up to "*so weiche jeder Schuld Bekümmernis von dir.*" — After lunch we talk of Naples, whether to go at all—it is so lovely here, he says. Over coffee I tell him about the orthopedist who was here to see the children, and he remarks that I am doing too much; this makes me laugh, but he continues: "Things are going so well for me that I want to work, in order to earn my happiness." — But in the afternoon he feels pain in his chest and decides after all on Naples for next winter; he says how quickly the 10 years of our happy life together have flown. When he goes, I call out after him, "I think only of you!" He: "And I only of myself, for that means you." — In the evening we finish "Ursula," I doing the reading since he has slight chest congestion. We remain enchanted to the end; R. says: "Oh, if I could only find a contemporary like that in the musical field!" Fortunate Switzerland, where such a writer is still possible! Zwingli, because of his quarrelsomeness, feasible only within a narrow community, impossible to imagine Luther sword in hand in the general "mishmash" of the German empire.

Saturday, January 18 R. had a disturbed night. . . . I find it hard to bear all the love with which he nevertheless always overwhelms me! . . . However, he does some work, and at lunch he tells me he is satisfied with it, but he does not wish to go out of doors. We admire the lovely frost-covered landscape and talk about Italy—Naples next year. When I go to him in the afternoon he has just been looking through [Mendelssohn's] *Saint Paul* and is filled with utter disgust for it, calling it Jewish through and through, facile in form, shallow in content: "To serve us that," R. exclaims, "after we have known Mozart, Beethoven, and Weber! — And as if one could ever hope to imitate Bach!" He is sorry that my father writes oratorios. — We read the first half of another of the Zurich stories ("*Das Fähnlein der sieben Aufrechten*") with great enjoyment, except that I do not care for Frymann's speech, which seems to me too Periclean; R. says the Swiss get this sort of pathos from the pulpit, but he is inclined to agree with me. — After that three preludes and fugues from the second book of the *48,* and we are particularly affected by the 9th. (Dr. Eiser is asking for the Prelude; R. annoyed, for nobody is supposed to know that it was performed here.)

Sunday, January 19 R. again did not have a good night, and he has chest congestion. It is very cold. He works but does not go out. (At supper yesterday he talked about an article in the *Illustrirte Zeitung,* "The Elk Fighting the Wolves," and said it had taught him some very curious things—how in Nature even the most heroic must perish, men as well as animals, "and what remain are the rats and mice—the Jews." — I told him that I had seen friend Wolz.'s two sisters-in-law in the mental hospital, and he talks with horror of the maintenance of such poor creatures, "which uses up the energies of the healthy and the good.") —

I am kept very busy with the children, since the governess is away. R. has a short session with Herr Jäger, the scene between Siegfried and the Norns, which soon exhausts him! — In the evening he reads to our small company (Jäg. and the Wolz.'s) more of the "*Aufrechten,*" which causes very great merriment.

Monday, January 20 But R. had a very bad night, had to get up three times; a little dessert at lunch, then in the afternoon a glass of Ems water with milk, following the session with Jäger, gave him real indigestion. He does no work, but rests, and at lunch does not look too bad. He also ventures out on the ice today. In the evening we finish the nice story. Recently, talking of G. Keller's personality, R. said, "When he started talking and had something good to say, words poured from him like potatoes out of a sack." — Then he puts his hand on Mendelssohn's *Antigone* and we go through parts of it with amazement, noting that M. does not once pay heed to the Greek verse meter, and declaims it in the most nonsensical way. R. also draws my attention to the markings—"allegro," "tempo di marcia"—that, in this terrible tragedy! Then he takes up *Figaro,* plays the concluding finale and the two Cherubino arias so beautifully that—as always when he plays anything—I feel as if the secrets of art are being unveiled anew. I have a vision of a performance of this splendid and lovable work in our opera house here under his direction. "But with which singers?" R. asks. "Preferably Italians—Patti and Nicolini!" At once I have to admit the impossibility of achieving any sort of effect. —

Tuesday, January 21 It seems to me like a victory over life that R. had a good night! Toward one o'clock he says to me, "I have also done some composing, have done everything!" We drive out a little, paying calls, and are very cheerful; we discuss my present reading, *Die Wibelungen,* and enjoy the wintry yet bright sunshine. In the afternoon R. goes for a walk, and this does not appear to do him any good, for he is not feeling very well—at any rate he says the air felt unpleasant. But the evening passes in a very lively, cheerful way; first of all he goes through the choruses from *Antigone* with W[olzogen] and R[ubinstein], and we are once again astounded by their glee-club ordinariness; the allegro of the Overture also horrifies us with its triviality. Then several things from *Die Entführung [aus dem Serail]*, after which Herr R. recommends *Idomeneo,* but this does not please us and we go on to [Gluck's] *Alceste.* R. plays through the Overture with R[ubinstein] and sings the Herald; this is both touching and uplifting—even antique, R. observes. Before that he had sought out some fine metrical examples (by Bach), since he cannot get over his amazement that Mendelssohn could find no way of matching the rhythms of Greek verse—he, a philologist, and so well educated! — Speaking of his own work, R. says he now has only 9 more pages of his text to set to music, and all the epic scenes are finished.

Wednesday, January 22   R. got up once during the night but did not have to take refuge in reading. A nice letter to him from the King. He works, but at lunch he complains of a stiff neck—his walk yesterday did him no good. Even when he is well I am never quite free of worry, but now any occupation is a strain on me—oh, this mortal life! . . . Ought one to envy the less favored? . . . R. is reading G. Keller's "Hadlaub" (in the first volume); yesterday he looked up the minnesinger poem quoted in it, and greeted me with "*Augentrost,*" also telling me about the bitten hand. — When I tell him that I have written to Porges, as he asked me, instructing him in what he has to do—though I doubt whether it will do any good—R. says, "You are right; when Jews go along with us, they turn stupid; they're clever only when they are against us." — In the evening I read to him "*Der Narr auf Manegg*" and the beginning of "*Der Landvogt von Greifensee*"; the latter story gives us great pleasure, particularly "Hanswurstel" and the Tyrolean Marianne. — But R.'s indisposition weighs on my mind like a gray sky, and I find no salvation except in prayer, summoning up all my faith in my good star!

Thursday, January 23   R. did not have a good night, but he says he does not feel ill, and at lunch he tells me he has been "composing well." (The day before yesterday he told me he had used a reminiscence which would touch me.) I read "The Nibelung Myth" and *Siegfrieds Tod* and talk to R. about them. Later he tells me that he originally designed this more in the mode of antiquity; then, during his secluded life in Zurich, he became interested in Wotan's downfall; in this work he was more a kind of Flying Dutchman. I am surprised by the increased *inspiration* in the revised treatment of the subject and its ever-growing feeling and intensity. When I tell R. of my great pleasure in the Valkyries' scene (up to Brünnhilde), he says, "It gave me my Valkyries' theme." In the evening we finish the story of "*Der Landvogt von Greifensee*" with great enjoyment.

Friday, January 24 R.'s night was a good one, and he works. At two o'clock we receive Dr. Jenkins, who has come to examine R.'s teeth, and he starts work immediately after lunch; R. wonderfully patient and cheerful throughout. He takes a rest, and in the evening a curious conversation develops. The excellent American is certainly surprised by present conditions in Germany, but he has no doubt that the Germans will rise splendidly to the occasion. R. says, "Yes, because we have had men like Goethe and Beethoven—but ask *them* what they feel about it!" He then enlarges upon the shortsightedness which has prevented efforts to bring the neighboring countries which are related to us (Holland, Sweden, Denmark, Switzerland) into an alliance with us! No ideas even of colonization! "The German people," he exclaims, "that is the poor man here in our district of whom Schnappauf recently told me; he spent ten nights out in the open, and then came into a barn where there was a stove, by which he sat down. Suddenly the other people notice that his clothing is on fire; they go to put it out and discover that the man is dead." And if Bismarck were to come here, he continues, we would all creep around on our bellies before his arrogance. When I smile skeptically at this, R. goes on: "That is to say, he would remark with such superiority, 'Of course, my dear Herr Wagner, we have already considered all these ideas, but this wretched Empress Augusta and this What's-his-name—so now we are going to have protective tariffs.' And so on, till one says to him, 'Excuse me for being such an ass as to have ideas!' " — The speech he put in Bismarck's mouth is so witty and so like the renowned statesman that we all burst into laughter. — Dr. Jenkins tells us some very interesting things about the Negroes, whom R. can hardly visualize taking part in public affairs; he feels that what has made them significant is their touching submission to a cruel fate. Dr. Jenkins also talks about the admirable qualities of the Germans in America, and R. says, "Yes, the emigrants—those are the good ones, just as the earlier wanderers were the heroes; the ones who stayed at home were the Philistines." When Dr. J. mentions the misfortune of having no fatherland, R. says, "Yes, where would the mourning come from, if one didn't love it so much?"

Saturday, January 25 R. slept well, but he does no work, and after we have had a light lunch at twelve o'clock, he undergoes the operation proper, which is painful and exhausting; he takes a rest afterward, then goes for a little walk, and we eat at 5 o'clock, when, if not as cheerful as yesterday, he is nevertheless just as hospitable. (Alone with me in the morning, he came back to the King's letter and remarked what nice things he had said about the "Retrospect," they reminded him of my father's comparison with the golden bucket.) In the evening I have to take Lusch to a ball, but I return home at once, going again to fetch her later. When I come into the *salon,* R. is playing the American march with Herr Rubinstein; before that they had played something from the 2nd act of *Parsifal,* and R. had been pleased with it. Then R. talked about his experiences with the festival, saying, "I was quite right at the time, when I said we had entertained the public and now we should have to pay for it." To me he says in the evening, "The finest thing I have ever done is what Tristan says—'Let me die'—with what went on before." He is sleeping deeply when I return home at 3 o'clock.

Sunday, January 26 Up early, after having had to tell R. of yesterday's "experience." But an evening like that with all the people taking part forms a grotesque barrier between me and my inner self. All the same I am able to open my heart to the sacred tones when R. plays to me the passage from where Kundry brings the water up to Parsifal's words, *"dass heute noch als König er mich grüsse."* — R. says goodbye to Dr. Jenkins, after having yesterday given him the *Ring des Nibelungen* with a humorous dedication: Dr. J. had spoken about an art-loving Welshman, King Jen, and said his people were the "kin" of Jen, this in connection with R.'s joke that he learned his English in Wales and consequently spoke a bad dialect! — A sunny winter day tempts R. out of doors, but the air does not entirely agree with him. However, when I go downstairs to greet him, I find him reading Xenophon and very cheerful; after a little while he comes up to my room and says he must read to me a dialogue which he has just finished and which he finds heavenly; he then reads aloud the conversation between Socrates and Theodota, and it really is beautiful, charming, and witty beyond all words. — In the evening we read some more, but at ten o'clock I fall asleep! . . . And Burchtorff (the district president who held the ball) becomes a catchword in our home.

Monday, January 27 R. had a good night, and he works; as he tells me at lunch, he spent the whole time improving a passage. — He is delighted with Loldi, says she will grow up to be like me. After lunch we discuss his "Plan for a German National Theater," which I am now reading, and R. says he "made the mistake of counting on finding efficient people." I: "Like C. Frantz in relying on the princes to restore the German empire." He says he will put down all his thoughts on this subject in his final articles for the *B. Blätter.* When he returns from his walk, he is delighted to hear Fidi singing an English song, and says his voice echoed so prettily through the house. In the evening, when friend W. and R[ubinstein] have come, R. talks about the *Memorabilia* and reads to us the dialogue between Socrates and Theodota and the one with the young Pericles, also the report on the death of Socrates; and afterward R. goes through the first finale from *Le Nozze di Figaro* with Herr R., from the scene between the Count and Countess in which he opens the door. R. says, "This is Greek in spirit, with its wit and its grace." He says it could not make an impact against the grotesqueries of Rossini, and people could not discern the melody in its light and delicate themes, so accustomed had they become to big arias.

Tuesday, January 28 R. slept well, and he does some work; yesterday, he said, he had spent all his time working on a correction. At two o'clock a "banquet"—that is to say, our neighbors the Staffs and their family, and ourselves, a total of 18 people; it is all very cheerful and friendly, except that, when the ball is mentioned, R. betrays his disgust for this type of entertainment, saying that he knows very well how the men speak about the women. Apart from that, he is very benevolent and witty, and it makes us laugh a lot when he remarks about the new general that he seems to be less *gene*ral (pointing to his head) than *corpo*ral (pointing to his body)! — R. goes for a walk, then takes a little rest, and in the evening seems not at all fatigued by the children's party—on the contrary, he speaks of it with pleasure, saying how pretty they all looked. — Later a nice letter from E. Nietzsche brings the conversation around to her brother's dismal book, and R. remarks that, when respect vanishes, everything else vanishes, too: "That is the true definition of religion; unlike Jesus Christ, I cannot be without sin, but I can respect the sinless state, can beg pardon of my ideal when I am disloyal to it. But our times have no feeling for greatness, they cannot recognize a great character. There can be no bond with it." — Then we take up *Le Nozze di Figaro* again, from the beginning to the Countess's first aria, which R. says is so beautiful because it does not go further than it should—an aristocratic lady at her toilette, looking at herself in the mirror and asking herself what is happening— melancholy elegance. — When today he fetched me for supper, he came through my gray room and stood still on the staircase, while I waited for him downstairs in my "Marajah" dress. I: "You are standing there like Walther von Stolzing." He: "You have guessed my feelings exactly."

Wednesday, January 29 R. slept well, and he works; at lunch he tells me that he has sketched Kundry's baptism, and he hopes I shall be satisfied with it. We go for a walk together in the palace gardens but soon return home, since I feel the air is too keen. R. does some more work, and I get the impression that he has had a slight rush of blood to his head. When Herr R. comes, I go through *Parsifal* (Act II) with

him, while R. watches us and listens. Apart from a few deficiencies of
tempo and execution, we are astounded by the way Herr R. plays from
the sketches. But after he has played Parsifal's cry following the kiss,
R. springs to his feet and sings this passage, in a way the world will
never hear again! . . . Reports about *Rheingold* in Cologne (rehearsal),
it makes me think of the remark he made yesterday (at the "banquet"),
pointing to the statuettes: "Those are my sons, they look after me, I
do not concern myself with them." — Before we start on *Parsifal,*
R. glanced at Beethoven's C-sharp Minor Quartet and pointed to the
3rd bar in the second line; he says he finds it unpleasant, it does not
sound well, altogether he finds the whole movement distasteful;
when Bach does similar things, it is quite a different matter.

Thursday, January 30   R. had a tolerable night, he got up only once,
after dreaming that I was startled by a noise; he went to see what it
was, and as he went I called after him, "Don't leave me!"; whereupon
he: "I shall be back at once." — Waking up, he goes to his room, reads
Plutarch, and finds nothing but ghosts in it, then finally the cave of
Trophonios. He says, "Devil take it!," shuts the book, and returns to
bed. All this I find uncanny, for I am debating in my mind whether I
shall not, in order to keep up the surprise, have to go to Munich to
have my portrait painted for his birthday! — R. works and tells me a
canon is going around in his head, and he really does seem preoccupied.
Over coffee he tells me that his greatest happiness, "which you share
with me," lies in creating, in the way it sometimes comes to him in
various ecstatic moments. But one must take care then, he adds, not to
do too much. R. goes out—as always these days, just into the palace
gardens, which are now completely bound up with *Parsifal.* News of
Rienzi in London. In the evening continued with *Figaro* to the end;
great delight in almost all of it. R. points out to us how, in the Count's
aria, the nobleman's sinister contempt for the common people is
expressed; then the lovely instrumentation of various entrances—the
bassoon, for example, in Susanna's "*Deh vieni*" aria, and the flutes in
the introduction to the Count's aria; then the splendid basses at the end,
the incomparable dance, which is so characteristic, for that is what they
are really like, we heard such things in Naples. — In the morning he
thought of his sister Klara, how beautifully she had sung the Page
[Cherubino]. — When I betray symptoms of a severe cold, most unusual for me, R. recalls Socrates's daemon, which also announced its
presence through sneezes, and he reminds me of the story, which I was
recently told, of the wise man who turned back halfway!

Friday, January 31   R. had a good night, that is to say, he only had to
get up once. In bed he says: "How many dismal things I have lived
through! When I think of those visits to Minna in Brestenburg! And

how glad I then was to be by myself again and to have my work—what would I have done without that . . . ?" — After lunch I tell him how much I like his introduction to the 3rd and 4th volumes (of his collected writings), which I read again today; also how pleased I am that he has given the whole edition such simple accompaniments as the introduction to Volume 1. Then we talk about friend Wolzogen and his character—how nicely and how quietly he and his family arranged their move here, etc. — R. goes for a walk and returns with the news of MacMahon's resignation and the election of Grévy. — Curious France, now with a sober, entirely bourgeois government! He also shows me the development of American activity in the following account: [*not found*]. Art and religion, depart in peace! But perhaps somewhat more truthfulness in the world. In the evening R. reads to us Plutarch's splendid chapter about garrulity, also Socrates's turning back on the advice of his daemon. "I so much enjoy immersing myself in this world," he says. After that we take up Bach's *Preludes and Fugues* again, after a long break: numbers 4–8 in the second book. Of the seventh R. says, "One can see the Countess from *Figaro* in that." And of the 2nd of these four preludes he says, "He wanted to do something especially beautiful there." After one of the fugues he says, "Canonic devices—they are repeated, too, so people should be able to put up with the repetitions of my *Leitmotive*." — Before our reading Herr R. played to us the Overture to *Das Liebesverbot,* in which the banning theme seems to me very good—soulless, legal, harsh, dramatic; when I say I like the Overture to *Die Feen* better, R. observes that the other (*L.-Verb.*) shows more talent. He searches out a few passages, but apart from the "*Salve Regina*" (*Tannhäuser*) he finds it all "horrible," "execrable," "disgusting." — It is well orchestrated, he says—"That I could do in my mother's womb"—but the Overture is all thunder and lightning.

Saturday, February 1 R. has slept well; he goes downstairs to work in ink while I arrange the "meadow" in his room upstairs. It turns out looking very Klingsor-ish, but that amuses him; he says, "Things are going so well for me—but that is because my previous life was so abominable." Lunch with the W.'s and friend Rubinstein, discussion of the state of affairs in France and Germany (R. says Bismarck's name comes from "every bite [*Bissen*] a mark"!). After lunch R. reads the *Fl. Blätter* with great enjoyment, then he talks about *Das Liebesverbot* and says he is surprised how bad it is: "What phases one goes through! It is hard to believe it is the same person." He takes out [Rossini's] *Otello,* the music in the second act as Rodrigo goes off and the following, plaintive aria of Desdemona, and talks of the impression it made on him, whereas *Euryanthe* always seemed stiff and false in spite of its heavenly music. Frau Schröder[-Devrient] always had to content herself with these Italian things, since she could make nothing of such Marschner nonsenses as "Leave me the veil, I beg." "Above all," R. exclaims, "you need a good play, and the important thing is what one puts into a good play or takes from it; but that is the basis, and I always knew it—that's why I could never understand *Euryanthe*." — In the afternoon he reads the *B. Blätter* and is very pleased with W.'s article, "In the Coming Year." "He is truly my expert," he says, and wishes he had a musician like that, too. — Memories of concerts. Then R. says, "Nothing is so dear to me as the room in which I bide, for opposite, my fairest wife dwells there by my side." — In the evening R. and I are alone, and as usual we then get immersed in our memories— "but nothing compared with their contentment." We remember how we wept over *Minna von Barnhelm* at Tribschen and think with pleasure of all the many things we have achieved in these 14 years—*Meisters.*, *Nibel.*, the marches, the collected writings, *Parsifal,* the house, the theater, the biography. — R. reads to me two legends by Keller, the "Dance Legend" and "Virgin and Nun," very pretty; but above all we like the short preface the author wrote for the book.

Sunday, February 2   R. had a good night, and he works (from pencil to ink), he says his canon will surprise me. — At breakfast he suddenly calls Bismarck the great tax collector, since he is trying to put taxes on everything. After lunch we are amused by the sudden idea of calling R.'s previous life, in memory of G. Keller, the *Falätsche,* which consists in nothing but detritus. Before that R. said to me, "You are right, the King does belong to us; he has caused us a lot of trouble, but from the point of view of Fate, he does belong to us." The same thought I encountered again, in his *Braunes Buch,* which I glanced through during the decorating, and where it is written down! Yesterday, when many thoughts, both large and small, were going through my head, they found their expression as we parted after lunch in "Laughing death!" "Not at all," said R., "weeping life!," and today he asks me what I had in fact meant by it: did I wish to die?! In the evening some more of the *Preludes and Fugues,* five of them today; the 4th (no. 12 in the second book) R. calls a complete transition to more modern music. He says Bach must have played it to his wife. Previously he had emphasized the extent to which these works were written by their composers for themselves, and how superficial the works their successors wrote for other people seemed in comparison—the sonatas. "They have also given us some good things, of course, but this is like birth itself." He then goes on to point out the difference between Bach and the Italian composers of the same period, talks of a figured "*Kyrie eleison*" and tells us how as children he and his sisters imagined they were singing fugues when they sang these figurations to themselves. — Candlemas brought us glorious sunshine, and R. went out twice today.

Monday, February 3 R. complains that for him the latter part of the night, from 4 o'clock onward, is always bad. But he works and says to me, "Do not expect too much from the meadow—it must of course be short, and it cannot express delight in nonexistence, as in *Tristan*." Then he laughs and says, "Rubinstein will ask, 'How does it happen that Parsifal recognizes Kundry?'—if indeed he does recognize her." And he continues: "It is all unspoken ecstasy, as Parsifal returns home and gazes upon this poor woman." Oh, if I could only reproduce the expression on his face and the sound of his voice as he describes the state of Parsifal's soul! — Then he tells me once more something I forgot to note down on Saturday: when he was walking beside the pond he heard a curious horn sounding, very absurd, and it was probably blown by the watchman on the ice; everyone vanished from the pond and he continued his walk alone; suddenly he saw on the snow the very faint shadow of himself and the two dogs, and, glancing up at the sky, he saw the moon in its first quarter. It had been a very mysterious moment; probably as a child he would have laughed heartily at the horn, but nobody had laughed. When we part I say, "You divine man!" and he replies, "No, you," then adds, "Unspoken ecstasy!" Ah, yes, that exists between us! . . . A wonderful head of Hermes from the new excavations at Olympia (illustrated in the *I. Z.*) gives R. another opportunity to talk about the ancient world, and he says, "How pitiful we look in comparison—like barbarians!" — R. goes out, is pleased with his room, which I help to arrange, calls it his shaman, and then goes down to his work. But suddenly he is upstairs with me again: "I shouted to the children from the hall, asking them to call you, but nobody heard; I have come upstairs to tell you that the entry of the kettledrum in G is the finest thing I have ever done!" I accompany him downstairs and he plays to me the anointment of Parsifal by Gurnemanz, with its wonderful canon, and the baptism of Kundry with the annihilating sound of the kettledrum: "Obliteration of the whole being, of all earthly desire," says R. — In the evening we come back to a declaration by Herr R. which yesterday astonished us—that on his first encounter with them (when he was a student at the Vienna Conservatoire) *Tannhäuser* and *Lohengrin* made no impression on him at all! — It is intellect which has brought this poor man to his feeling for these works. . . . Later R. discusses with me the inner loneliness of such a piteous character, and says this makes Rubinstein interesting in his eyes, he has found his way back to him in spite of the gulf which divides one from such a person. At the end of the conversation R. says to him gently, "We are trying to explain a phenomenon to ourselves;

it is not dislike but liking that sets us on this path." And he concludes jokingly, "You'll probably take that again as an affront." We then go on to a Brahms symphony, which R. plays as a piano duet with Herr Rubins. and which again downright disgusts us. R. talks indignantly about its vulgarity, and we then seek salvation in the final pages of Plutarch's essay on garrulity.

Tuesday, February 4   "I have been awake since five o'clock," R. says, "and I feel as if I were made of glass: I am quite conscious of all the functions going on in my body, though they are supposed to be working involuntarily." — He dreamed that he was again engaged in Dresden as a conductor and had undertaken in his contract to sing as well; he was expected to sing Max in *Der Freischütz,* and was indignant about this absurd clause in his contract: "Get Herr von Lüttichau to do it, I can't sing a note." Then he woke up. (Recently he told me of frequently recurring dreams in which he travels through Asia, finding Turkestan very different from what he supposed; he has also gone wandering through Africa.) Then yesterday's pitiful impression leads us to Beethoven's symphonies, and R. remarks on Beethoven's splendid instinct in avoiding all plaintiveness or other forms of excess; he departed from his usual rule only in the Ninth and in the first move-ment of the C Minor (full of defiance), but this is something quite different; these works depict Nature before the emergence of human life, he says: everything was struggle and destruction at that time, too, but in a different way. "I hate pathos," he exclaims. "People will be amazed, when I publish my symphonies, to see how simple they are, though they have already had examples of that in the marches and the *Idyll.*" He tells me how Weinlig advised him against dissonances, saying they would either sound ugly or not be heard. "I shouldn't have minded the ugliness so much perhaps," says R., "but not being heard—that annoyed me." — After lunch I stroll around in the garden, R. comes to fetch me, and I go with him into the palace gardens, where Marke's curious way of chattering his teeth amuses him: "No doubt he thinks he's talking!" I: "He sees us moving our jaws like that and does the same!" (This is what gave R. his dream a little while ago of Marke as an Italian chorus singer.) R. walks on farther, he does not care for the thaw, preferring the cold. On his return home he talks of a pretty theme for a symphony which he has downstairs: "It will all be done, the symphonies as well." We part with thousandfold greetings and blessings. — In the evening the string quartet from Munich; at R.'s request they play Sgambati's quintet together with Herr R.; it still pleases us very much, but it seems somewhat long and is the kind of music which does not raise one's spirits.

Wednesday–Saturday, February 5–15   Have not written in my book. I felt unwell during the night of 5–6 and had to stay in bed for three days, till Sunday; R. kept a loyal watch beside me, full of divine love, read to me Plutarch's glorious discussion of Socrates's guardian spirit and also his own still more beautiful letter to the King about Fidi. In the meantime he fully completes the *meadow*. On Monday the 10th I again eat downstairs, in the evening we go through *Euryanthe* (Scene 1), which, R. says, does not give him as much pleasure as he expected, too much glee-club music in the choruses. "That is a master stroke," he says of the place where Lysiart enters treacherously, "but still so little awareness." Then R. thinks of the finale to the first act of *Il Barbiere* ("All this tumult and confusion") and we all delight in it. R. works on Tuesday (Monday, too); in the evening we go through the first act of *Parsifal,* but it gives R. no pleasure, since Herr R. does not get the accents or the tempi right. Arrival of "Scheherazade," the new dress which R. has given me and which I put on! — Wednesday the 12th, a wretched day; R. has a cold, and I accompany Lusch to a ball. Though I remain there only two hours, I still find it depressing! — Thursday the 13th, R. had a good night, is well, and goes to his work; in the evening he reads to me the strange, original, and profound conversation between Circe and Odysseus (Plutarch). Friday the 14th, R. not well, speaks angrily about Lusch's long stay at the ball (I had asked a friend to take care of her), feels indisposed and spends the day in bed; in the evening I read to him Gogol's *Hetman,* that is to say, a scene from it which he wanted to tell me about after reading it himself and finding it very remarkable: it is the scene in which the new hetman is elected and the maddest confusion leads to a declaration of war. Saturday the 15th, R. well, returns to his work, tells me at lunch that I must write some words for him—he already has the melody, which conveys the sense of the matter, but the words are lacking. — In the evening we read the discussion about the guardian spirit again, with genuine delight.

Sunday, February 16 R. had a bad night, disturbed by ugly dreams about money. I myself wander with him in a dream along a wooded walk and feel a painful start when he says to me that he is beginning to feel old. Waking up, I say to him, "Please don't leave me just now—I have had such a bad dream." He: "But I am just coming back!" He had also experienced some fear of ghosts downstairs. At lunch we laugh about it, and R. talks of his terrors as a child, which had never been of ghosts, but of lifeless objects suddenly coming to life: "I should have been frightened of this siphon—of a chair—of anything." In the evening we finish [Plutarch's] discussion for the benefit of our friends. Yesterday R. prefaced our reading by saying: "I have read Balzac—good—and Keller—good—and Gogol—good—and Turgenev

—good—but what barbarians we are! It was only the ancient world which brought forth truly great men; in comparison, all that is really effective is Christ and the Sermon on the Mount, the denial of the world; in the acceptance of the world only the Greeks are great." Astonishment at the long life span of the Greek spirit: 600 years later Plutarch still speaking as if he were living at the same time as Socrates —and how do we regard Wolfram von Eschenbach? — Delight in the comparison with the mirror, though otherwise "The Cave of Trophonios" proves somewhat wearisome. R. looks at his old edition of Plutarch, "transferred with incredible effort" into German—and speaks of the timid and petty character of the Germans at that time. — My spirits are overshadowed by learning that R., who went out this afternoon but gave it up on account of the violent wind, showed some blood in his saliva (*not from the lungs,* the doctor says).

Monday, February 17 R. had a good night—at any rate he had to get up only once. Eva's birthday; when we, R. and I, drink a toast, he says, "What we are drinking to is so touching that we cannot even mention it." And, as always, *"Things are better than they were!"* — Then R. joyfully informs me that he has words enough—he had overlooked one verse (*"der liess sie so gedeihen"*). He takes pride in not having had to alter his words: yesterday he recalled the melody of the "Prize Song," which came to him before the words, and was pleased with it; today he recalls Sachs's last speech and asks if any other composer could have done it better (as far as voice leading is concerned). — Referring to what he is doing now, he says he is taking care not to put in too many figurations—something he has sometimes done, as when Brünnhilde pleads to Wotan in Siegmund's behalf; I remark that this was just because Frau Materna did not have the personality to act it—she was overshadowed by the music, as it were. — Recently he spoke of his absent-mindedness, the way his head is always full of his work, and he mentioned the example of Archimedes, whom the servants had to remove bodily from his work in order to bathe and anoint him, and how he continued to draw figures on his leg with the ointment; in the same way, he himself was constantly making notes on scraps of paper. — When we were talking about the dialogue between Odysseus and Circe, R. said that the fine thing about the Greeks was the way all these sagas continued to live in their thoughts; with us nothing now remains alive, and to this extent Keller's experiment with legends is interesting and as it were folklike. — Delight in Fidi, whom R. always finds so beautiful when he compares him with other boys—as if from a different world. (Fidi brought me the first flowers of the year; on the very day of Eva's birth—she herself one of life's blossoms!) — R. goes out for a while and drops in at Angermann's, where he causes ringing laughter by telling the barmaid, who is leaving, that she ought to offer her services to the theater committee in behalf of the ballet! (A committee to promote the theater has been formed here.) In the evening the three younger children gather around a little table to play cards; they make a very amusing picture, and R. says, "*Tristan und Isolde, Meistersinger,* and *Siegfried*—I myself am *Götterdämmerung!*" Then: "The three lansquenets." It gives him the urge to play, too, and with Miss Murchison we make up a whist table with "bids"! . . .

Tuesday, February 18 R. had to get up once during the night, but he does not feel unwell in the morning and we chat merrily at breakfast. — Toward noon he comes to me and says, "I have found a transition which is worthy of you," leads me into his room and plays to me this divine transition from "*will ihr Gebet ihm weihen*" to "*ihn selbst am Kreuze.*" "The main thing," R. says, "is that it doesn't cause a shock— there must be no feeling of shock." — This morning he said he would like to compare his works with those of other composers and see whether his do not contain ten times as much music—that is something which has never been acknowledged. And for this reason he was willing to believe that his works would have a great future. He is so well and cheerful that today seems like a really sunny day: "I am so happy," he says, "I feel like a god." When we go upstairs together and I notice that he has ordered all sorts of things for himself, he admonishes me jokingly: "Always the attitude of Rome toward Venice—permitting nothing, but overlooking faults once committed!" I have to love him like a child or like a god! . . . Snow flurries, but he goes out for a while with Brange, who, having run after him, touches him by demanding to return to her newborn puppies. — In the evening we go through the first act of *Die Meistersinger* with much enjoyment; but R.'s delight turns to bitterness over the treatment this work has received.

Wednesday, February 19 R. was up during the night from 3 to 4 o'clock, but otherwise he is feeling well, he slept peacefully before and after, and our morning conversation covered all sorts of subjects— the aristocracy, who have lost everything except their vanity, the German language, and many other things. Yesterday, when the filling in of the spring in Teplitz was mentioned, R. said, "For Teplitz that is as much of a loss as if Schnappauf were to leave Bayreuth!" He works and is in cheerful spirits; he also goes for a short walk; in the evening whist with bids again, and after it champagne! . . . (News of the success of the *Ring* everywhere; R. says, "Who would have thought such a thing 20 years ago, or considered it possible?") When I tell R. that I happened to glance through the *Theologia Germanica* and am truly amazed that Schopenhauer discerned its deep metaphysical basis through its language of naïve faith, he says, "Yes, it was Schopenhauer who revealed Christianity to me." (Much enjoyment from the children who are developing a strange talent for mimicry.)

Thursday, February 20 "If from night's cares you seek your ease, drink champagne and eat some cheese," R. answers me when I ask him what sort of a night he had, the reason being that I have often asked him not to eat cheese in the evening. — He works and is satisfied with what he has done. In the afternoon he goes out for a while and then reads friend W.'s article on *Siegfried,* his object being to help him cultivate a simpler and more correct literary style. In the evening three Bach preludes and fugues from the second book, very well played by Herr R. Of the first and most beautiful (in F-sharp Minor, No. 14) R. says, "That is like Nature, uncomprehending and incomprehensible, and it is also unending melody!" He then continues: "That was his language. In life he could expect nothing but trouble and vexation, and probably he never spoke a witty word, but in his music he let himself go." Talking about himself, he says he is still very pedantic and thinks hard before writing fifths, etc., but when he needs to, he throws the rule book out of the window; Bach did the same, and that is why R.'s teacher Weinlig never really liked him. (Very nice letter to R. from the King.)

Friday, February 21 R. had a good night, and around noon I see him radiating happiness—he has found it, he says, and he sings me Gurnemanz's words. He is taking a long time over it, he adds, and that gives him pleasure. After lunch he talks about the bad times in Vienna and says, "Nothing of all that was really necessary." At lunch he recalled how he had always been forced to break off his work— *Tannhäuser,* for example, and others. — My wish to give him my picture for his birthday coincides with earache and toothache; I ask to be allowed to go to Munich. He wants to come, too; my anxiety about his health does not permit it. A sad evening—disconsolate mood—

Saturday, February 22 Journey! No diary until Tuesday the 25th, when my return takes R. by surprise; traveled in the night. Glad that he did not fetch me from the station or travel after me. (For all else, see his letters, telegrams.) [*Enclosed between the pages are ten telegrams addressed to Cosima, giving news (entirely domestic) of Wagner and the children during her absence and signed variously by Wagner, Wolzogen, Rubinstein, and the servant Georg.*] R. not entirely well, he had bad dreams about me, he did not come to join me because he also dreamed all the children were ill. Was I wrong to inflict all this on us just to bring him pleasure? A difficult question! May the heavens protect us! The children very affectionate! — I give R. the letters to read which he wrote to Schumann in earliest times; Herr Levi was kind enough to have them copied for me.

Wednesday, February 26 R. had a better night, though not entirely good. I feel as if the heavens have reopened when I hear his sounds, the only music in the world for me! R. laughs and says he does not know what to make of it: when I went away, music abandoned him entirely, but now he has his head full of themes again! In the evening we are unfortunately not alone; Frau Jäger brings us some news from Vienna, the Emperor has commanded a performance of the whole cycle for as early as next March; amusing, on the other hand, the episode between A[nton] Rubinstein and Herr v. Hülsen. We take refuge in whist. After that, however, R. and I alone together for a while. (The "swan"!)

Thursday, February 27 R. had a tolerable night, we breakfast "like an eagle with two heads," and he then goes to his work. His reading matter before starting work is Gogol's short stories. Yesterday evening he wrote to Herr Levi to thank him for his kindness to me. Arrival of a pamphlet by Herr Marr, *The Victory of Judaism,* containing views which are, alas, very close to R.'s. R., who went out today as well, in very melancholy mood: "This lack of relationships!" he exclaims. When I tell him about Prof. Zöllner and the spiritualist medium Slade, he says this is the modern, realistic way of approaching a subject, which Schopenhauer has already so beautifully explained.

Friday, February 28 Again R. did not have a good night, he got up twice, and I also woke him from a frightening dream. He jokes that for this my absence was to blame, and says laughingly, "Since the corn was beaten down, it rose no more: that was its death." When I reproach him for his cruelty, he replies, "You ought to be pleased to have my life and death in your hands—Richardism has been completely merged into Cosmaism." In spite of his wretched night he works and plays to me a transition (from the meadow to Kundry's flower theme). Over coffee he recalls that it will be a week tomorrow since I went away, and he says this two-day absence was like an unending Russian steppe in his life. — Returning home after going out, I ask the servant if his master is well and where he is; immediately a sound comes from his room, telling me he is there! — He comes to bid me good evening, and when I ask him what he has in his hand he says, "My paper from *Seville.*" He goes down again to the *salon,* where I hear him continuing with his work. In the evening reminiscences of friend Serov, whom Herr R. also knew. Herr Rub. tells us that 6 weeks before his death the Grand Duchess Helene got from him the admission that he was *"un homme d'esprit"* ["a wit"]. Then four of the *48 Preludes and Fugues,* from No. 17 of the second book on; R. often sings to himself the theme of the 17th fugue, and he likes it to be played lightheartedly, like a rondo; the following one, in G-flat minor, is, I believe, even more beautiful, a truly wonderful wonder! — R. says one only has to compare them with what others understood by fugues, for example, Handel in the Overture to *The Messiah;* since we do not have this work we look at *Samson,* and R. says the allegro theme denotes the Philistines.

Saturday, March 1 R. had a better night, got up only once, right at the beginning, but went to sleep again immediately. I dream for the second time that I have no flowers for his birthday—the first time the roses had not yet begun to bloom. — In the morning R. tells me that he considers it very important for everything to sound well, including the subsidiary voices, and that is why he likes to have a piano at hand, he is not satisfied until it all sounds right. In Beethoven there are frequently passages which sound "squeezed," making R. say to himself: "S——(!), if he had listened to it, he would never have written it down." — "Stay just as you are," he exclaims to me, "don't take anything away, and I want nothing added"—he is speaking about life. He works, and around lunchtime he fetches me and sings to me "*Du weinest, sieh! es lacht die Aue*" . . . Bright and sunny weather. — The children well, but at times my impressions seem to overwhelm me, after lunch I have to lie down; I come around only very gradually and write to E. Nietzsche about her brother's book. In the evening we read the pamphlet *The Victory of Judaism* (in which R. very much likes the comparison between Bismarck and Constantine)—it makes me feel very melancholy! After that, read with great enjoyment the two scenes between the student and Mephisto in Parts One and Two of *Faust.* We also go through some songs by R. Franz—"*Du bist elend*" and "*Ich grolle nicht,*" which Franz once asked R. to sing to him. R. enjoys the songs, and some by Schubert which we mention he finds "unutterably beautiful" ("*Sei mir gegrüsst,*" among others); he says that was Vienna as it used to be, the Vienna in which Beethoven lived, and an ardent, naïve fellow such as Schubert was living under its influence. And then there were Strauss and Raimund as well. Now all that is gone.

Sunday, March 2 R. again did not sleep well, and I very worn out— I almost think it is because of my letter; R. wants to know what I have said, I tell him and am pleased by his approval. At noon he again fetches me and plays to me the wonderful transition to the bells. Then lunch, at which my reappearance is celebrated! Afterward R. goes out for quite a long walk. In the evening conclusion of the *48 Preludes and Fugues;* the B-flat Major Fugue, which we call the "pleading" one; R. sings to it, "Please do not be angry, please will you forgive?," and makes an imploring gesture. R. has the last prelude played quickly

and with great passion, he finds it quite remarkable that Bach concludes in this way, says that the entire sonata of the future is contained
in it, and at a certain passage he observes, "*Tristan und Isolde* cannot do
that better." — Then the entrance of the Flying Dutchman, with which
even R. himself is pleased; I ask for the Overture as well, and with it
feel my youth sounding within me again, with everything that filled,
elevated, and powerfully influenced it. I am wearing the "Scheherazade," which gives R. pleasure, and in his usual flattering way he says,
"Let the whole world see that we love each other." Blessed in faith—
blessed in love!

  Monday, March 3   R. slept well. In the morning we talk a lot more
about *Der Fl[iegende] H[olländer]*, which he intends to revise slightly.
When I tell him how offended I feel if people prefer one of his works
to any of the others—for the same great spirit is in all of them, and
each is unique and incomparable in its own way—he observes that it
must be a human characteristic to be exclusive and condescending with
love. Most people, he goes on, judge things by the amount of work in
them: not the beauty of the picture, but the number of colors used in
painting it. "If there were still any Germans left in the world," he says,
"*Der Fl. Holländer* would have been bound to make an impression, for
it was something new in opera—but there are no Germans." A picture
in the *Illustrirte Zeitung* of an opera ball in Berlin vexes R. with its
princes and Jews, Prussian epaulets and moustaches; the only thing in
the picture which pleases him is a Chinese man. — We come to the
subject of Schiller's *Wallenstein,* and R. says that if one excepts Shak.,
as one of course always must, Schiller is the greatest dramatist; when
Herr Rub. expresses the view that the episode of Thekla and Max
stands outside the main action, R. explains to him in what way they
are a part of it, how the catastrophe comes about when Max, supported
by Thekla, abandons Wallenstein. R. says it has now become the
fashion to point out weaknesses in Schiller, though still professing
great respect for him. — He is very pleased with the lines about
Lessing in W. Marr's pamphlet, and he talks of Lessing's journey to
Italy, observing that there he must have felt as R. himself does—
melancholy, solitary, alien. — R. is amused by the continued success of
Das Rheingold in Cologne; he says it is probably due in the main to the
machinist Brandt. — Much conversation in the evening with Herr
Rub. about his origin and the position of the Jews.

  Tuesday, March 4   R. had a good night; he works in ink, in order, as
he says, "to give you an audition soon." At lunch, however, he feels
worn out, but he goes for a long walk; I go to meet him, and we watch
the most magnificent sunset. R. called out to me, "I arranged that for
you." "A while ago the orb was there, now the hero is shedding his

blood." — We play whist in the evening; R. seems to be looking rather tired, and consequently I suggest the game, which seems the right thing for him.

Wednesday, March 5 His foot caused him pain during the night; perhaps he walked too far? Yesterday his dear cherished face looked tired, and he complained of feeling languid—is his work proving a strain? . . . This morning we talked about the awfulness of a certain world in which women are not respected and the most horrible things are talked about. R. says, "Until I was quite old I used to feel like a callow boy, because I knew nothing of so many things I heard about from this person or that one." I feel that the existence of such a world turns ideal art into something ghostly, and I tell him that a sense of an unknown yet suspected perversity has always filled me with melancholy, and if I had been obliged to take note of such perversities, I think I should have been driven to suicide. Yesterday R. told Lulu very movingly about Hans's flight to him from St. Gallen when he was in Zurich. — Over our after-lunch coffee R. recalled his previous life and said to me, "In Zurich that time I should have gone away with you, but we were just like Tristan and Isolde, we didn't understand each other—'the dream of premonition.' " I go for a long walk with the children, R. comes to meet me, then goes to Angermann's with Fidi, greatly pleased with the boy; returning home, he works something out and plays it to me in the evening. —

Thursday, March 6 R. slept well, but he awoke very early and waited impatiently for daytime. He tells me, "When I have finished a part of my work, I ask myself, 'Will I succeed with the next?' " Talked a lot about the Villa d'Angri, for which we have received the plans. R. is very tired of the climate here. In the evening we chat together, R. reads me some things from his *Braunes Buch,* and we recall with delight our activities together. — He is now reading Plutarch again, since he found little satisfaction in Gogol, in spite of his talent. Sad feelings about French illustrations to R.'s works—appendix to the translation of *Parsifal!* A little volume by Daudet astonishes us with its talent—and silliness (the latter wherever the Germans are involved). R. says, "We are quite stupid and ridiculous enough, so why do they have to make themselves look ridiculous, too? They should study us closely."

Friday, March 7 R. had a good night, and he works. At lunch he suddenly exclaims, "That is a good idea! I must write it down at once." We bring him a pencil and some music paper, and he writes a harmonic passage to accompany the bells. Afterward he asks me if I know what the $\frac{6}{4}$ time means while the bells are sounding. It shows Gurnemanz and Parsifal in the act of listening; one hears the bells from a distance. He is completely absorbed in his creative work, and I am permitted to share it with him! . . . Otherwise we talk of hardly anything except Naples. — In the evening whist with Herr Rubinstein, as always with "bids." Watching R. as he plays, I have an indescribable feeling; I should like to take him in my arms, carry him up to Heaven, shield him from all suffering—I feel that this is my task. He often says that were it not for me, he would long ago have quit this life here below, and it is to make this *here below* pleasant for him, to shield him, look after him, sustain him, that is my dearest wish—indeed, I feel it as an imperative! Yet what can I do, what lies in my power? It is he who does everything! . . . His eyes, his cherished glance, how to bear the world without their radiance? . . .

Saturday, March 8 R. slept well, but he is still complaining of pressure on his chest; he feels unwell in the morning and goes out. A small lunch party in our house, cavalry and government, R. very hospitable. Then he and I go for a walk in the palace gardens and listen to the blackbirds, which, as R. says, are addressing "questions" to the air. — Yesterday he told me that he would not be able, as he had thought, to use the *Romeo and Juliet* theme for Titurel's funeral; he would find a use for it in a symphony. In the evening we play whist with the children, as the enclosed pieces of paper show. [*Enclosed between the pages are two pieces of paper with the scores of the games, on one of which is written:* "Everybody won! R. W."] Before that R. showed me the phrase in *Faust* which had utterly delighted him, when Mephisto says to Faust, "Let's think what to do." "It is things like that—so unimaginable!" He never stops admiring the way Goethe continually came back to this work and at last completed it. — Yesterday he talked about the Alps, their noble tranquillity above the growth line: "Where a blade of grass grows, there is still a place for Goethe and Schiller; but where there is nothing but stone, there we have tranquillity: it is a place for gods."

Sunday, March 9 R. had a disturbed night, at one point he laughs at me, for I slowly exclaim, "Now at last one knows what that is," and then say nothing more. He works, however, and I go out with the children in fine sunshine. At lunch the news that Semper is dying in Rome; solemn feelings. — In the evening we go through the "Good Friday Music," up to the bells, and celebrate in tears, tears of bliss, the salvation of mankind. R. is not satisfied with the piano downstairs and says merrily, "When I am upstairs, I close everything up, put on the soft pedal, and bang away at my stupid noise." (Before *Parsifal*, Bach's motet "*Singet dem Herrn.*")

Monday, March 10 R. had a tolerable night, and he works. "How utterly differently one works now!" he says, recalling that he completed the sketch for *Lohengrin* in only 6 weeks. Lovely spring weather; delight in the poultry yard; in the afternoon we have a splendid walk home through the palace gardens; the earth, still covered with white snow, nevertheless sends forth its fragrance, and through the brown branches one sees the rosy blue-and-golden sky; given new life, one's soul rejoices, feeling at one with the brightness and the fragrance. — In the evening another game; R. laughs over the fact that when I sit beside him, watching, he always has bad luck. But one thing he says grieves me: "People will say of us: They won't last long, they are too happy." And the fact that he takes a mourning card to write down the scores also bothers me. Such is happiness! And I feel more and more that love and a longing for death are one, as in *Tristan;* life can bring it only pain or worry.

Tuesday, March 11 R. slept well, and we chat about all sorts of things at breakfast; of Christianity he says, "We lack even the rudiments of the education needed to understand such a phenomenon—we are in a state of complete barbarism." It was the words of the requiem, which happened to fall into his hands, that evoked this remark; he pointed out to me how Jewish the words are. Our feelings of barbarism find an outlet in laughter when we contemplate *"Die Wacht am Rhein,"* a recently designed monument! — R. works and goes for a walk in the afternoon. In the evening Herr R. plays to us Bach's B Minor Organ Fugue, the Prelude to which delights R.; he says that after such things one can scarcely listen to Mozart, who still has so many *empty passages*— only to Beethoven, for he also shunned empty passages, and we go through the C Minor Sonata. "How divine was this urge of Beethoven's, R. exclaims, "to pursue the simplicity of melody!" — Then, regarding Bach, he says to me, "He was the culmination of the medieval world— Wolfram, the mystics, A. Dürer, Luther; after that a completely new world begins, the world of the sonata, the aria, which has also produced some fine things." — (Yesterday he praised Hans's *Nirwana* very highly and recommended it to Rubinstein's attention.)

Wednesday, March 12 R. slept well, and he works. Unfortunately the weather is so rough and stormy that one can feel it even inside the house. News of the wretchedness of the German people and reports of the tariff negotiations fill him with great bitterness, to which he gives vent in the evening in a description of the "frivolous manner" in which Bismarck is dealing with the matter; he wants money, R. says, and so he gives the Reichstag *carte blanche,* telling them, "Please choose whatever you want to put a tax on, we shall tax even bread and salt if you like, but only a small, a very small tax, so that people don't notice it." "And the whole nation is dying off, and we maintain a huge army to defend this dead body." — I suggest a game, because it hurts me to hear him talking thus: "What can one do but turn away with a shrug of the shoulders, not bother oneself with it any more?" Even the "swan," which I was wearing today, could not divert him from his sad thoughts, though he gazed at me with pleasure for a while.

Thursday, March 13   R. had a good night, and when I tell him about my reading with the children (Alex. the Great) he says, "Yes, there is something so clear, so pure, about such figures; our great men seem so unclean, so blurred—Heaven knows why." I feel the great German emperors should be excepted, and he agrees with me. He tells me what Plutarch says about the absent-mindedness of Archimedes, who would draw figures on his leg with the oil with which he was being anointed; this reminds R. of his own absent-mindedness and preoccupation. — A lunch party, the infantry in our house; R. says gaily at table that we ought now to hold a Piccolomini banquet and oblige the officers to pledge themselves to the art of the future! In the evening to the Wolzogen house, a game of whist. — But he was dissatisfied with his work today.

Friday, March 14   R. slept well, does some work, and is satisfied with it. Toward evening I hear him playing *Tristan,* and when I go down, he says, "I wanted to entice you down; if you only knew how I talk to myself and tell myself how happy I now am!" — As we sit down to supper he says, "You, children, are a part of our happiness"—with that radiant kindness so unique to him. Then he laughs. "So you can see how creative work and life belong together: in former days I wrote *Tristan,* now I am writing funeral music," he exclaims. "Poets alone he understands, who once has lived in poets' lands." When Herr R. comes in the evening, we go through *Tristan,* Act 3, from the curse on love to Isolde's death, to the end, and I feel as if I could never stop, were I to begin to say what this work reveals to me! . . . R. tells me that for him the loveliest moment is when the theme enters three times with muted horns and violins, as Isolde's only response to the sympathy of the others.

Saturday, March 15   R. had a good night, and he works. Today we celebrate the recovery of our friend Wolz., and after lunch Herr Rub. plays his arrangement of "Wotan's Farewell." At one point—I forget where—R. says, "That always pleases Lesimple so much," an interjection which utterly disturbed my mood for a while! . . . But then he plays to us the crowning of Parsifal and Kundry's tears, and it echoes inside me like an eternal blessing; I see Tristan full of yearning, stretched out on his bed, and hear sublime consolation, deepest peace. — In the evening games, ending, however, with a deep, deep sorrow which Lulu causes me.

Sunday, March 16   R. had a restless night, but he recovers in the morning and goes to his work. Toward noon he plays to me the passage in which Titurel is carried in. After lunch we go for a walk in lovely sunshine. R. tells me things from Plutarch about the painter Nicias and others. In the evening he reads to us the 19th canto from the *Odyssey,* the 1st conversation between Penelope and Odysseus, and does it in so sublimely moving a way that I shed tears, as if over a tragedy.

Monday, March 17   R. did not have an entirely good night, but better than the previous one, and he works; decides, however, not to complete *Parsifal* until a nice spring day. The weather is still raw, and he feels it severely. In the evening we go through Beethoven quartets, the Scherzo of the E flat and the *Grosse Fuge.* (Recently Herr Rub. played to us Weber's *Invitation to the Dance,* and R. was really astonished that the interpretation of even this simple piece went astray, a piece his sister Klara, for instance, could do quite well. He laughs at the ending, so typical, he says, of the cold manner in which a modern dancer takes leave of his partner after their passionate cavorting!)

Tuesday, March 18   Again not a good night; R. wandered about and took out Goethe's poems to look up a phrase in "*Stirbt der Fuchs, so gilt der Balg.*" "With us sought to play" delights him, and in the morning he reads the charming poem to me. In spite of his restless night, however, R. does some work. He goes for a walk in the afternoon, and in the evening we play whist—he, Lusch, Bonus, and I. And when the day is done, there flows between us the stream of love that never dries up.

Wednesday, March 19   R. had a good night, and he works. He goes for a walk in the morning, wants to meet us since we are also going out, but my steps lead me to a sickbed (Melanie Staff) which may become a deathbed. I have to tell R. about my sad impressions, and the children weep many tears over their little playmate. A gloomy day, lit by bright sunshine and greeted by the trilling of larks! R. sees the first shoots. He is worn out in the evening, and the thought that I may have caused him suffering is so unbearable that it turns into concern about his health, which then finds refuge in prayer: Oh, thou great force who created him, who wished him to be, let, oh, let him remain, desire his presence here below!

Thursday, March 20   The night was restless to start with, but later on it was all right. When I come from my bath, R. sings, "If a man will not let you sleep," and goes from there to the words of *Die Schweizerfamilie.* At lunch a toast to Boni, whom R. addresses and congratulates with all his deep sincerity, recalling my sister, my feelings for her, the meeting in Reichenhall at which R. was present. He says he was also yearning, seeking someone to whom he could yield utterly and say, "Come with me, to Hell with everything else!"

"But I always found everything—all the tables—already booked!" [*Added in margin:* "Yesterday, in connection with the scarlet fever, he thought of Friederike Meyer, who behaved toward him 'with very great nobility.' "] — Before that he recalls his visit to Berlin shortly after Boni's birth, when he proposed a drive, which I accepted: "You were always *smiling beneath your tears,*" he tells me in a touching voice, then adds gaily, "Very interesting!" R. goes for a long walk (as far as the Students' Wood) but returns home not entirely content, he has a great longing for the South. Impressions from the outside world are also not calculated to raise one's spirits, and in connection with the Szegedin catastrophe he says bitterly, "It does not go far enough for me—something terrible is needed to bring people to their senses, to make them think seriously." In the evening he reads to me passages from Plutarch about religion (in the conversation about Epicurus), and we have to admire this author's fine way of saying the right things, and with what noble reason, as R. points out, he steers a path between the utilitarianism the English employ to protect religion and the ferocity which destroys it. We are particularly pleased with the sentence "Few fear God, so that it would be better for them not to fear him," and what comes after that. — At lunch R. said that he would allow himself plenty of time to complete *Parsifal,* this final realization of a series of images which had arisen in his mind. He says he does not believe he will presume to create anything more that is new; the symphonies are different, but he wants to complete everything in peace and contentment. Before supper he comes up to my room, talks to me about the "elegy," and says he would like to play it to me; and he does so—this unique elegy, the process within Parsifal's soul when he becomes once again "an ordinary mortal" before he becomes a king. . . . "You have no idea of all the things in it," he says. I: "I believe I have." He: "Yes, of course." — Before that he said he could not understand how they did it, those composers who wrote one thing quickly after another, like Raff and Rubinstein "and others as well." "But their work shows it."

Friday, March 21 Not a very good night for R. The Battle of Torgau, which he dreamed I had put into a pastry, caused him trouble. But he soon recovers in the morning. When we separate, each to his daily task, he exclaims, "There is always separation," and this remark awakes in my soul the feeling, always slumbering there, that lovers can only, like Tristan and Isolde, long for death, since life means separation, not just the world! — When R. left me yesterday, I scrutinized his picture and recalled the look he gave me; when he came back to me, I told him how foolish people were to maintain that possession, union, deprives love of some of its ecstasy. He laughs and says: "*People* never applies to us!" — The bells are causing him difficulty, since he has too many alternatives and is still uncertain which to choose. In the evening he is content to play a little whist, but then we celebrate Bach's birthday with fugues from the *48 Preludes and Fugues* and with Parsifal's entrance into the Temple, up to the appearance of Titurel's body. — Once again R. stresses that this will be his last work; he says he will write the words of *Die Sieger* when he is very old, "and then Fidi can set it to music." Today, before having that feeling of separation in life, we talked about Gretchen in *Faust;* R. went into rhapsodies about the beauty of the ending to Part One, how she, full of her love for him, takes leave of him in order to assume for his sake a higher calling. Did Goethe plan his final ending? We are inclined to believe that he did.

Saturday, March 22   Still a raw wind, bringing R. a cough and tightness in the chest; ever-increasing yearning for the South. He works. Returning from a fairly long walk with the children, I tell R. what a curious impression the theater made on me in the bright sunshine—exhortation, consolation, reproach, hope—which of these, or all of them together? R. says, "Sad." — This leads us, goodness knows how, to the Sistine Chapel, I remember quite clearly R. saying to me as we entered it, "This is no place for lightheartedness—it is like my theater." R. says no, his first feeling had been one of great repugnance, though he had gradually tried, "for your sake," to be fair to the artist. I stick up for my memory and say that I had been so struck that he had at once seen through all the drawbacks—the disharmony of the building and its decorations, the ravages of time, the absurdity of the task—and felt warmly for the artist who had used even these poor conditions as a steppingstone for his flight; in the same way that here one had been able to grasp his ideas in spite of Unger, Niemann, Doepler, and many others, he himself grasped M[ichel]a[ngelo]'s genius. But he disputes this! . . . He goes out, attempts a walk in the palace gardens, but is scared off by the raw air and goes to Angermann's with Fidi, pleased by the boy's intelligence. On his return home he tells me that he fell flat on his face near the post office; he counters my alarm by saying that he always falls safely, he cannot forget how he once fell down on the Brühl in Vienna, Porges and the others thought, "The master is dead," but he had not even hurt himself. I leave him at about eleven in the evening to fetch Lusch from a party; on my return I find him awake; he was looking at the *Illustrirte Zeitung* and showed me the King of the Zulus, who pleased him very much with his finery and his melancholy face. Then he told me that he had written to the conductor Steinbach, having read that he had given *Die Msinger* in Mainz without cuts, but there had been no audience even for the first performance. Yesterday, before we began to play cards, the vision of Nietzsche's behavior rose once more in his mind. He said, "N. wrote his thoughts out of season, thus acknowledging that what he admires does not belong in our time but goes beyond it, and now he uses the fact that my enterprise is out of season to criticize it! Can one imagine anything worse than that?" . . . R. connects a remark by Herr Lindau the journalist with his description ("Retrospect"); this gentleman, it seems, has said, "Better to be bad than to be bored." R. finds this very typical—in Paris they had also said (about *Tannhäuser*)*: "Nous voulons nous amuser, nous ne voulons pas de récit"* ["We want to be entertained, we do not want recitals"].

Sunday, March 23 "For all guilt is avenged on earth." With these words R. comes to me from his bath; a curious experience is responsible for this quotation. Yesterday our friends Gross and Feustel held a *soirée,* and it seemed that an invitation to Lusch could not be refused without giving offense; since there was no mention of dancing, I arranged for her to drive there with Frau Feustel and to spend the night at her house. Since R. did not think this proper, he first declared that he himself would go, then in the end I. We sent Lusch off with Frau F. at 8, and I promised to be there at 10:30; but as the moment of separation approached, R. became more and more disgruntled, and his vexation fastened on the child: he said she did not belong here. I believe that in earlier days I should have been deeply offended and utterly cast down, but the god of love permitted me to discern only R.'s distress over the fact that on the heights on which we dwell we can still be reached now and again by the common herd. I was very sad, but before my departure I was able to embrace him with a pure heart, and when, at one o'clock, I find him waiting for me, reading, he has calmed down completely. But he did not have a good night, he does not do much work, and he complains of pressure on his chest; he says it is as if something were in constant possession of him. R. relates to me the biography of the Zulu King, the killing of the cows when his mother died, so that the animals might know what it means to lose a mother, and he ends with the words: "No animal is as cruel as a human being, it is only the human being who takes pleasure in tormenting; the cat playing with a mouse does not know what this means to the mouse, but a human being does know." He also talks about the military organization of the Zulus and says one can almost find in them the raw beginnings of the Lycurgian constitution. — Snow flurries, but R. goes out anyway (though only into the garden). In the evening a visit from our friend Feustel, questions concerning the tariffs and a good answer, to the effect that the extreme need of the German people demands such measures at this moment. After that a six-part fugue and the "Chromatic Fantasy" by Bach, kindly played by Herr Rub. at my request. Great delight in it; R. says Bach still belongs to the Reformation, to Luther, rounding that period off; then came something quite different, which could be equated with Goethe and Schiller, etc.

Monday, March 24   R. had a good night; letters about Naples, the Villa d'Angri becoming somewhat problematic. — R. works. He also attempts a walk, but the weather is so raw he is very upset and vexed by it. The Steinway grand piano returns to us equipped with a *"pulsator"* and delights us with its splendid tone. It is christened with the strains of *Parsifal;* a merry episode in the evening as we search for the name of the English composer Wallace and, after constantly renewed searchings, at last find it. R. showed us the picture of the Zulu King and thought of Wallace among the cannibals (Berlioz's *Soirées d'orchestre*). He says Wallace was a Wagnerian. — When I talked of Frau v. Hülsen, saying that in the 2nd act of *Tristan und Isolde* she was reminded of "the pretty evening star," R. says the trouble is that people can never call things by their proper names, and that is what matters. The princes, for example, such as the Grand Duke of Baden, who had held out hopes to him of grandiose schemes which never came to anything—he could not mention their names without employing the language of the gutter; but mere hints were not enough, one must name names— Lasker, for example, once reduced Roon to complete silence by mentioning names, though in that case Lasker was playing a treacherous game. — From *Parsifal* the consecration of the King and the meadow, then R. looks for his new sketches and plays to us the responses up to Amfortas's first outburst. He feels that his interpretations from the penciled sketches cannot have made things clear to us, but when I go to him upstairs, as he is putting the pages away, I tell him what a wonderful picture they had conjured up, how lifeless these singing and marching knights seemed, the whole thing working on one like a ghostly parade, until the tender and sorrowful laments of Amfortas enter suddenly like a living experience and move one profoundly. R. observes that I am the only person who could get such clear impressions from these "muddled pages"—ah, it is the inspiration of being per- mitted to follow him that gives me the power to do it! . . . [*Added below:* "R. tells Herr Rub. that the art lay in playing the seconds in the bass heavily, like the very footsteps of the knights bearing the casket."]

Tuesday, March 25   R. complains of tightness in the chest, and the weather is cold. He works, but nothing comes to him, he says, except a few bits and pieces, among them a scherzo theme for a symphony. He goes out in the afternoon, discovers that the *Bayreuther Blätter* has arrived, and when I come down to supper, he embraces me in great excitement; Glasenapp's article, the reports of the growth of the Society have moved him greatly and instilled in him a sense of obligation, since nothing like this has ever happened before. He remains in this state of excitement all evening and is also preoccupied with his composing. I do not know how he suddenly comes to the idea—though of course in a joking way—that Fidi may turn out to be a practical man of the world, who will find his papa and his mama terribly old-fashioned. If that were to be the case, all the papers would have to be left to one of the girls. But R. adds that it is a good thing Fidi has not yet betrayed any signs of knowing what sort of person his father really is.

Wednesday, March 26 The weather still cold. R. had a tolerable night in spite of a bad dream, brought about by a cat in the palace gardens which climbed swiftly onto a tree stump and from there triumphantly mocked the dogs; in it I was cold toward him (my father always behind it), and he had been the barking dog! All the same, he works. After lunch we talk a lot about Phocion, and R. remarks how decadent periods suddenly produce such men, whose greatness and strength become even greater and more noble precisely on account of the decline. — Yesterday he told Rubinstein that what he needed was a *Peabody* to leave him a large sum of money in his will. In the evening he writes a few lines to friend Wolzogen about the 3rd issue, and since the latter at once comes over to the house, he is rewarded with some music making: the first act of *Tristan*. R. says with a laugh that people will later think our era must have been a strange one, when one could offer the public works like that. In fact, he says, he has produced nothing new since *Tristan*, whereupon I observe that even from a technical point of view *Die Meistersinger, Siegfried,* and *Götterdämmerung* contain new ideas. But what he meant was that there had been no need for him to write a single note more; he could just have said, "Do it as I do." So he thinks!

Thursday, March 27 R. was somewhat restless during the night, and our home is not filled with music today. He writes to the King, and over coffee he says to me that there is something artificial about these letters, and he has feelings of shame and injustice toward me when he indulges in such dithyrambs toward another person; his situation and the King's own letters are to blame for it. I reply that in earlier times I had perhaps been hurt by the feeling that truthfulness was being made to yield to fiction, also hurt by the extravagance of expression, but now all I could do was to suffer and rejoice with him (I do not put it quite like this—much shorter!). I review in my heart all the things which have ever caused me pain, and the shadows melt in the sunshine of love, which is matched today by real sunshine outside. We all go out, but unfortunately the wind is still very keen, and we soon return home. R. completes his letter and tells me what he has said in it: that being engaged in completing a work is pleasant, but not its final completion—and people already have enough things to spoil! — The enclosed report [*not found*], from which I tell him only our good friend Lesimple's deed, gives him great pleasure. — The advertisement I read to him over our afternoon coffee rouses him to send the parson a telegram, asking the price of the cow. Answer: half its value would be sufficient! . . . Now R. is writing. — In the evening we begin Carlyle's essay on Cagliostro, which we find very gripping; R. was so pleased with the introduction that he decided to read it with me.

Friday, March 28 Last night it was my turn to dream a sad dream, and it was about R. I tell it to him, and at lunch he says he was so affected by the thought of having been nasty to me that he could write no music, but sought some literary activity instead. He took up his [*German*] *Art and* [*German*] *Politics,* but this, instead of restoring him, made him angry about all the things he had already said and must now keep on saying all over again! But the sad mood induced by my dream had finally led him back to Amfortas's sufferings. (He is not pleased with Dr. Schemann's article in the 3rd issue; he says he would have been able to write his drama just as well even if Wolfram's poem had never existed—from a book of folk tales, like *Tannhäuser.*) Something must arouse his anger before he can write literary pieces. R. goes out in the afternoon, and in the evening we finish Carlyle's sketch about Cagliostro, with much enjoyment, after R. has told me some very amusing things from Tappert's newspaper.

Saturday, March 29 "South wind, south wind!" I hope it is spring at last! . . . At breakfast R. and I discuss the positioning of Titurel's catafalque and decide that it should be placed high up in the arch from which Titurel's voice is heard in the 1st act, thus leaving the middle of the stage free for Amfortas's outburst, Parsifal's act of healing, and the blessing. — Yesterday R. played to me a theme he brought back from the palace gardens ("which now contain much of me")—for a symphony. Today he asked me jokingly how long I thought he would continue to be productive: "I still want to write symphonies," he says. In the evening read with much enjoyment about Cagliostro, or, rather, the story of the necklace; but for Carlyle's philosophy, the "Maker" which frequently peeps through, we do not much care.

Sunday, March 30 R. had a tolerable night and goes to his work, wants to see whether the rhetorical and dramatic part will suit the symphony. (Yesterday he was in Angermann's with Friedel and Jus Staff and was very pleased with our son!) In the afternoon he takes the girls and Friedel for a walk, goes a long way, but has trouble with the dogs and a cat. In the evening a whist party at Frau v. Schoeler's.

Monday, March 31 R. somewhat restless during the night, but he works and goes for a walk in the garden before lunch. I occupy myself with the Sistine Chapel, showing the children the lovely photographs of it. R. casts a glance over it and says I am right to admire it. In the evening we finish the necklace story, though R. does not permit me to finish reading C.'s speech at the end, finding it distasteful. We conclude the evening with Bach's "Chromatic Fantasy" and the Adagio from Haydn's C Major Symphony, which strikes us as quite divine.

Tuesday, April 1 A warm spring day, a long time in the garden, R. at work, but also out of doors a lot. In the evening, since I have a sore throat and R. must not overexert himself, whist with the children. During the day the Sistine Chapel. And so the days pass by! What it is that illumines them I cannot describe, only hold the "fair and calmly contemplated wish" tight within my breast.

Wednesday, April 2 An almost summery heat—I have completely lost my voice. R. works and strolls around the garden, in the evening silent whist and music, Haydn's E-flat Major Symphony, of which R. once wrote out the score from the parts. In the evening R. tells me he has some ideas for his next article, but they would have no influence on me, since they were in line with my own: to everyone his own individual manner—the Frenchman has his taste, the Englishman his public opinion, the German his tasteless private opinion. — We have to laugh heartily when our conversation at lunch leads us to *la dame blanche,* who appears as what R. calls "a girl sweeper," and he says: "I should like to have some white-robed fellow like that here in this house to sweep everything up. I could do with a ghost like that." R. is looking well, but the least exertion makes him cough.

Thursday, April 3 R. had a good night, but still this tightness in the chest; our breakfast is rather silent, since I still have no voice, but R. works. Herr Jäger calls at coffeetime and tells us about the great success of the final performances of *Götterdämmerung,* but says all other opera performances remained constantly empty. R. laughs and says: "So Herr von Hülsen is quite right when he says I am ruining the theater—where the *Ring* is being performed people will go to see nothing else! Now the question remains how long they can hold out before performing it. I could bring audiences back for the old works, too, by producing them myself as they ought to be done." R. contemplates the three younger children with delight, calls them love, loyalty, happiness, love, hope, faith! — At lunch he tells me about Carlyle's "Voltaire," which pleases him so much that he would like to send Carlyle something of his own. The fact that he is a theist hardly bothers him; he says this is what gives him his peculiar character. In the evening, on account of my throat, whist, and then, at my request, several pieces by Chopin, which R. enjoys, too. He counts him among the figures of the French Restoration. Then he points out several things in *La Muette* [*de Portici*] which especially please him, and he praises the work highly: "Such people I like; it is only our Germanic *Nuppler* whom I can't bear."

Friday, April 4   R. got up once during the night, and I also disturbed him with my coughing, but he works and is satisfied with it. He says to me: "You do not even notice how I keep all my melodies in a certain style, so that it all looks the same but is in fact different. Just to string one melody to another, splish-splash—there's no art in that." Over coffee he tells me about his plan for arranging some concerts here with the patrons' money, spread over two months, with the aim of showing conductors how to interpret the classics. Is my reaction due to concern for his health (though I hardly think so, since what he wishes is good for him), or to fear of once more having closer contacts with the world and having again to concern myself with so many things I have put behind me? In any case the news hardly pleases me, and I betray my apprehension, but when R. says to me, "You would surely like to hear these things again," my gratitude for his kindness makes up for the lack of pleasure I derive from undertakings of any sort. — R. returns from his walk and comes to sit with me: "The key to *my* music is the A-flat major from *Tristan:* Beethoven, Bach, and Mozart, well and good, but *that* is my music." I observe that everything he has written is his. — Spring was here, but then it disappeared again, the day before yesterday I was very touched to hear a blackbird singing, and it seemed particularly fluent since I was silent; if we hear more acutely when we are still, then death should make us all-perceptive; I have a profound longing for it, and I welcome any indisposition as a messenger telling me that I shall not have to tarry long once my mission is fulfilled. With these thoughts in my heart, my eyes met Loldi's, and her melancholy gaze seemed to tell me that I should long be exiled here, to help bear the sufferings reflected in it. — We play with the children, and then R. reads to me Carlyle's "Voltaire," excellent characterization, so just, so subtle. "For him, in all matters the first question is, not what is true, but what is false"—R. finds this particularly excellent. Between game and reading we went through Ännchen's aria from *Der Freischütz*. R. says nothing more charming and graceful has ever been written, and he points in particular to the notations for rests in the oboe part, just before the words *"Blicke hin und Blicke her"* ["Glances here and glances there"], as if each glance were being depicted musically: "It is unique," he exclaims, and he recalls his oboist Kummer—"a short, fat fellow he was, but what soul he had!" He also remembers Julie Zucker, "with whom I was so much in love when I was seven years old," and how at this point in the aria she would lift her apron, cover her face, and allow her eyes to wander. "The French and Italians have nothing like that," he says, "however much they pride themselves on their gracefulness." "Oh, we were also talented enough in that direction, we Germans." (R. wrote an autograph for the Spohr album.) [*Written on an enclosed loose sheet:* "He sends the *Fl. Holländer* motive and beneath it something like 'In Kassel, where Spohr lived for years, / *Der Holländer* found willing ears.' He says he can now only write jocular verses."]

Saturday, April 5 After a night plagued by coughing fits I feel so weak that I spend the whole morning in a state of lethargy. At lunch R. complains of feeling very torpid, says he is utterly dissatisfied with his work—what he did yesterday, which pleased him so much. "If we don't part in a mood of rejoicing," he says, "nothing is any good." He takes a long walk at a swift pace, "to shake off my torpor," and returns home contented. When I come downstairs in the evening, he says, "What is this—a portrait of my wife in a printed book?" — He holds up the memoirs of Charlotte v. Kalb and shows me the picture, and I feel such deep and heartfelt joy that he should see a resemblance between me and this rare being! — Ye heavens, make me worthy of his love, take from me the last remnants of self-will, cleanse me, grant me humility, through which courage is regained, as this noble-hearted lady so beautifully says! R. gives me the memoirs as a present, and I read them while R. glances through the *Aeneid* and says, "It is typical of the whole Renaissance and all the Latin races, the way they clung to Vergil." — Yesterday he quoted to me an amusing example of declamation in *Der Vampyr*. The words read "with soul*less* gaze," but the melody unmistakably points to "soul*ful*."

Sunday, April 6 Conversation in the morning about Charlotte v. K. and Schiller. "In the life of a young man," says R., "the value of a woman like that is incomparable." Then he speaks about a performance of *Nathan der Weise* by several Israelites in honor of Lessing, and he tells me the theme for his final article for this year's *B. Blätter,* which will be "*A human being needs necessity.*" He works and is satisfied with his work. But he has several things to vex him, as always when he comes into contact with the outside world; the dogs have killed a cat, Brange is accused of spoiling the local hunting of hares, and appeals are made to R., both in person and in writing; to one man he says in reply, among other things, "I did not wish to do harm to the Bayreuth population by settling here." On top of that, the gas is not burning well, and other such domestic troubles. All this irritates him, but he soon recovers, and after a short game of whist we read *The Winter's Tale,* the unique shepherd's scene! "What, art so near?"—the old shepherd's question which shows all of Shakespeare's immediacy, how he hears the raging of the storm, which prevents the old man's hearing his son's voice, and which accounts for his surprise—it is this immediacy which R. again singles out.

Monday, April 7   When I was unable to sleep during the night and was thinking about what we had discussed, I told myself that Shakespeare was certainly the most powerful and most naturally creative of all dramatists, but the others, Schiller in particular, should not be dismissed; to whom does one more readily go for guidance and indeed consolation than to Schiller? I tell R. this, also my impression of the book by Ch. K[alb]. — While we are talking about Schiller, we recall my brother, R. talks about him and says, "He was too good to live— that is how I consoled Blandine at his death." — In the afternoon I show the children and some acquaintances the pictures of the Sistine Chapel, with explanations; recently R. said to me, half in earnest and half in jest, that he could not bear all these people with their books: nothing but books—that had been the misfortune of the Reformation. — Unfortunately R. had more vexations today: Friedel came to complain of the improper behavior of the gardener, and R. got into an argument with the man, whose coarse and limited intelligence made me beg R. never again to waste his words in this way. R.'s magnificent sense of justice showed through even in this—and, in spite of his anger, his composure. However annoyed, he will accept an excuse when it appears to him justified and truthful. In the evening the Jägers and the Wolzogens, and R. explains his plan for the concerts. Then some music, from *Siegfried* ("Forest Murmurs") and from *Götterdämmerung* ("Departure"). "I like the Nibelungs," says R. "They are so heathen; not a spark of Christianity anywhere." — Unfortunately our little party does not prove very enlivening for R., and as always we find cause for regret in moving, even as an exception, beyond our most intimate circle. — I gave R. Renan's inauguration address to read and, like me, he found it pitiful. He says: "I would never pay compliments to Frenchmen in front of other Frenchmen, and what he has to say about Germany he should have left to the English. I would never tell Germans anything but the truth." When we are already in bed, he says to me, "My fate is the same as Shakespeare's: retirement to Stratford, and after my death I expect to be forgotten for a hundred years."

Tuesday, April 8   R. does not feel well, yesterday evening was a strain on him, he did some singing, too, and the tightness in his chest is worse. On top of that, raw weather! — But he does some work and is very pleased with it. In the evening we first of all play whist with the children, then we finish Carlyle's "Voltaire" with great enjoyment; R.

is very much taken with the remarks about Christianity and the summary of his whole personality in the words *"highly accomplished trivialist"*; I follow along, echoing his feelings. Ch. K.'s book put me in a melancholy mood today, on account of the preface—so this unfortunate creature was also mauled by the outside world, and the publication of these pages I find so moving brought her only mockery and shame! One could almost say of books, too, when one considers their fate, better if they had never been born. — When I tell R. that I believe my inclinations would have been toward Schiller rather than Goethe, since Schiller appears to have been one of those beings who could never be brought into harmony with the world, whereas Goethe strove to achieve such harmony, R. says, "Yes, and from this there arises in Schiller a great need, whereas Goethe is all seduction." He then recalls his own youth and the "pitiful social surroundings" in which he spent his whole life—"but I remember I was always very easygoing and dragged everyone along with me, like Apel, for instance." —

Wednesday, April 9 R. is looking better, but he still feels the tightness in his chest, severe enough to send for the doctor, who comes and prescribes Eger water, then two or three weeks in the South, which produces from R. the remark "Are you out of your senses?"! . . . During the afternoon strolled with R. in the garden; mild weather, but the barometer is showing "world's ending," as R. says. R. so preoccupied with his work that at lunch he suddenly gets up from the table to make an alteration. In the evening whist, and after that read Carlyle's "Diderot" with great interest. R. says he has a mind to send something of his own to Carlyle, and he adds, "The English are justified in expecting something from their literature, since a writer there is somewhat different from a writer here; he is a free man, has a cottage of his own, or, like Grote, he is a banker and does not live off his writings."

I ask R. whether he would approve my going to Communion this year with the two elder girls; he says yes, and with the feelings that this prospect arouses, we part.

Thursday, April 10 The possible arrival of my father, the need to inform the dean, Loldi's birthday lead me to the children early, after wishing R. a good morning, and delay me there a while; this greatly upsets R., and when I try to make my excuses, he says, "Why did you make our routine so pleasant for me?"—meaning that he now cannot bear even the slightest deviation. Vain wait for my father. For lunch Herr Levi, who stays all day. In the evening *Parsifal*—from the 1st act the entrance of the Knights, from the 2nd the Flower Maidens; from the 3rd the anointment, the "Good Friday Music," and (still in the penciled sketches) the "elegy." While Rubinstein is playing, even singing quietly, and Levi listening with great emotion, R. says softly to me, "What touching figures they are!" — Beatific high spirits following our ecstatic bliss.

Friday, April 11   To the sounds of R.'s music I go off to Communion with the children, my soul at peace. The raw winter wind blowing the blossoms about, the cold gray sky, these are indeed dismal, but in my heart the meadow blooms! . . . R. does a little work, yesterday he told me he now has only one printed page of manuscript left to complete. At lunch he tells us that Bismarck is dissatisfied with the slow progress of the tariffs and is threatening to dissolve Parliament and hold new elections in order to make the deputies give way—"questions," R. adds, "which cannot be considered carefully enough." Then he talks about the Egyptian problem and how "whole countries are now being bartered on the stock exchange." At three o'clock to church again with the smaller children, I wished my profound wish and prayed, read Tauler. In the evening read Carlyle's "Diderot" with R.; masterly description of the encyclopedist. — R. writes to Herr Steinway to say that in no art form—neither in painting nor in architecture, scarcely even in music—has there been such perceptible progress as in the construction of pianofortes. Of Beethoven it can be said that he never sat down to write unless he had an idea in mind, R. says; only the Fourth Symphony contains a lot of note spinning, it bears no relation to the 3rd and 5th symphonies; this can also be seen in some of the sonatas. — I tell R. how lovely today's service was in its great simplicity; I am now sustained by the blessings of his poem in everything, even in greeting acquaintances after the service, a task I previously found somewhat disturbing; now I think of the Knights of the Grail and their kiss of brotherhood at the end. — Yesterday R. wondered what the effect would be if after the service Pars. and Gurnemanz were to remain alone together, Pars. completely dazed by what he, fresh from the woods, has just experienced; Gurnemanz, accustomed to it, simply eager to find out what he knows. This had struck him in the poem, even though it was all quite different there. — I do not know what led him to the subject of the King and the buildings he is putting up (Versailles, etc.); he exclaims, "Oh, he is bad [*this obliterated in ink by an unknown hand*], and the falsehood of this life—to speak of the Trinity in connection with that!" — We then seek to find out for ourselves from what point of view life would not be a falsehood, and we find it! . . .

Saturday, April 12   R. is pleased with the return to normal routine; he says it had been a veritable flood of holiness. At breakfast he tells me how yesterday he imagined the Crucifixion to himself—"not possible in our climate, the wounds need the hot rays of the sun"; he pictured in his mind the languishing, then the cry, and he felt very moved. He explains that it was not Christ's death but his resurrection which gave rise to the religion; the death all but destroyed the poor disciples, but the women's not finding the body in the morning, and seeing Christ in their exaltation, created the community: "In the disappearance of the corpse a strange and subtle fate was at work." He quotes Renan, who sees the foundation of Christianity in a woman's love. R. works; after lunch he speaks to me about the strange compulsion exerted by a poetic conception, which restricts all one's freedom, and he says one cannot create many such dramatic works, or work on other things at the same time. He recalls the ending of *Tannhäuser*, saying, "It is good that Elisabeth dies just as the pilgrims are returning." "Children," he says at lunch, "you see what a man looks like who is writing his last opera." Goethe once said that it made a great difference whether one was born ten years earlier or ten years later, R. continues, and he can say of himself that he arrived either ten years too early or ten years too late—actually too late, for he should have stood in the same relationship to Beethoven as Schubert did, and then he would also have been in touch with people like Carlyle and Schopenhauer; in music he had known Weber, but no writers or poets. The weather is very bad, snow, rain, cold, and a constantly gray sky! — Just as I am writing this, R. comes in with the children, bearing whole masses of flowers which the King has sent, along with some beautiful and apt words. R. replies by telegram (for poem see red file). — In the evening finished "Diderot," much delight in it.

Sunday, April 13 White Easter, snow outside! But R. slept well, and he works. He goes out in the afternoon, and in the evening, after a game of whist with the children, he takes out Rossini's *Guillaume Tell* and shows the children the nice things in it, such as the arrival of the people from the various cantons, and the silly ones, such as the yodeling of Mathilde and Rudolf. — He has been reading the story about Struensee in the supplement to the *Oberfränkische Zeitung* and says it has once again revealed to him the nature of the aristocracy, and the existence of certain spheres into which the commoner should not venture; Struensee behaved wretchedly, the Queen and a count (?), on the other hand, with great courage and energy.

Monday, April 14 R. slept well and he works; he says he has so many possible ways of concluding his work. Wolzogen at lunch, chat about all kinds of topics, agreement on plans for the concerts. I then go for a walk with R., mild weather, pleasure in the town and its surroundings. Friend Heckel's telegram is answered, the reply ends,

"Oh, Albert!" This is because R. thinks our hotelkeeper is to blame for the laurel wreaths! (This is to take place tomorrow.) Herr Rubinstein in the evening, R. goes through Auber's *Lestocq* with him, then at my request he plays the Venusberg music, which gives R. much pleasure, too.

Tuesday, April 15 Presentation of gifts today—the Easter bunny and three birthdays; 42 candles are lit, and R. plays the *Tannhäuser* march to greet the three girls; his great delight in the children, Fidi's shining eyes, good news from Mannheim, R. not unwell, working, the blessings of existence, bliss of sharing in the joy of my beloved! — In the evening the *Idyll,* played as a piano duet by Herr R. and R.

Wednesday, April 16 R. slept well, and this brings me, as now almost every morning, a divine greeting. — Before work he reads Carlyle's "Novalis" with great enjoyment, and he reads several passages aloud to me. At lunch he says to me, "With my ending I am now like General Bonaparte and Venice; I can say, 'I know how to take you, it's all clear to me now.'" — In the afternoon vexation caused by Herr Feustel, who is of the opinion that the concerts would not be in accordance with the agreement! (An Englishman has sent 2,000 marks for the fund.) — And an overcast sky frowning down on the vexation! . . . R.'s head always full of construction plans, but he promises not to carry them out. In the evening cards and chat. Over coffee he told me some things about Novalis's life and quoted Carlyle's remark that renunciation is not the aim but the beginning of education; then he says that the thought of losing a child makes him shudder, he knows it would drive him mad. I tell him that, for all my constant worry, I have been granted unquestioning faith, and I do not believe he could ever lose anyone he loves. May Heaven not punish me for this seeming blasphemy!

Thursday, April 17 R. had a bad night, had to get up twice, and stayed up a long time. Whether it was the business vexations or the overcast sky, he goes so far as to talk of stomach cancer; I try to laugh, and am indeed confident in my heart, but what gloomy shadows oppress my mind! R. goes to his work. For lunch Wolz. and Feustel, over coffee discussion of the concert affair, R. finding it very difficult to retain his composure. Decision to place the application made to the Society of Patrons before the Cabinet secretariat, and to add a new clause to the contract. Friend Feustel seems to think that the King will either not live long or in any case not be sitting much longer on the throne. R. goes for a walk in the palace gardens, then reads some articles by Feustel about the tariff question and writes him some words of praise, disagreeing only with his fears of France. — When I come downstairs in the evening, he plays me a wonderful figuration and says,

"That is for Wilhelmj!" Afterward he says, "I have closed the book today," and when I reproach him for saying this in such an offhand way, he replies, "But I am by no means finished—the celebration will come when I give you the sketches." Rubinstein plays to us the fine B-flat Major Fugue, and after this R. asks for Beethoven's A Major Sonata, into which, as he says, he has dreamed many things. "That is like spring breezes," he says, and then, "Hymetto's yearning"; then: "Like heavy wings dipping." During the trio of the march (which he likes to be taken rather heavily) he says, "It moves like a brook that has overflowed its banks." He describes it as a work written by its author for himself, to be played by himself; for example, the syncopations in the first movement cannot be heard, he would have them repeated in the bass. When Herr R. has finished playing, R. says, "He dedicated that to Countess Erdödy—what a look she must have given him!" . . . Herr R. did not play it quite as he likes it: "But where could one even begin?" says R. — When we withdraw upstairs, he talks about his *Parsifal,* saying it has not been possible to avoid a certain restriction of feeling; this does not mean that it is churchlike in tone, he says, indeed there is even a divine wildness in it, but such affecting emotions as in *Tristan* or even the *Nibelungen* would be entirely out of place. "You will see—diminished sevenths were just not possible!" I remind him that all his divine works are gloriously unique and different from one another. He can be pleased with them! . . .

Friday, April 18 Snow, and yesterday I noticed the first hints of green in our garden! But R. slept well. At breakfast we discuss the articles on tariffs, and R. says: "One might ask why we fought a war with France if nothing has come of it but this fear. It is even worse than it was before, to have this specter of a French threat eternally before our eyes." — R. works, tells me he will probably be happy with his conception by the end of April, and then he will take some time off: "If it weren't for my love for you, no God would ever induce me to orchestrate *Parsifal.*" — Herr Rubinstein at lunch, R. very lively. He does not go out, and gaily calls out "Cuckoo" to me when I look out of my room, where I am sorting through some pretty things which have arrived for May 22, to see whether he might not perhaps be there! . . . In the evening he plays to Herr R. a part of his "*Fantasie*" (a youthful work), and then he reads aloud some things by and about Novalis from Carlyle's essay; much pleasure in Novalis's judgment on W[ilhelm] *Meister,* also on Klopstock; I can follow him, though only because of R.'s writings—R.'s words about Mignon, about the role of illusion in a nation's development, etc.

Saturday, April 19 R. dreamed about Mendelssohn, whom he addressed in the second person singular, then, secondly, that he had to steer a pontoon across the water, nobody could tell him how, and R. turned to General Moltke with a military salute; but he was a total simpleton, and R. said to himself, "What false ideas people have of him!" He works, but at lunch complains of tightness in his chest. It is still very cold, and he decides on a week's break, to the Rhine district, Baden-Baden, Mannheim. . . . I saw off our niece E. Ritter, who has been staying with us during the last 4 weeks; a nice child. — R. enjoys the *Fl. Blätter* and above all an article from the 15th century in the *Illustrirte,* which he reads with me; it is about a Saint George, and it does indeed conjure up a complete picture of the German character, with its imaginativeness, its earnestness, and its naïveté. — R. is not feeling well, says he could not bear to spend another winter here. And in the morning we parted with such tender good spirits! — In the evening our Wolzogen friends, but under no good star; R. reads aloud his sketch for a New Year farce, plays his *Romeo and Juliet* theme, but our friends' silence irritates him, and he comments on it, which does not improve their conversational powers! An attempt to read a preface to Shakespeare's sonnets also fell flat, though R. is very pleased by the interpretation; all the same, he stopped reading it, saying it was too philological. And so the minutes dragged by, until Herr R. suggested playing my father's *Tasso.*

Sunday, April 20 R. had a good night. As usual on Sunday, Fidi bathed with R.; R. talks of his pleasant, unemotional nature, wondering whether he will acquire some fire. . . . We hope so, and hope that hot temper is not an essential part of a fiery soul. — For me and the children, first rehearsal of the May Festival; coming home, we see R. in the garden beside the poultry yard. Delight in our first fine day! But in the afternoon the sky clouds over and the wind returns, so that we cut our walk short. In the evening R. reads aloud the first half of Diderot's *Rameau's Nephew.*

Monday, April 21 R. had a somewhat restless night, but he seems to be well. Confusion everywhere; Wahnfried is to be spring-cleaned, and we begin with the *salon.* R. works, now in ink, in my room; his reading matter in between still Carlyle, who is becoming a real friend; he likes the study of Jean Paul, and quotes me bits from it. (Difficulties are arising about the concerts.) In the evening conclusion of *Rameau's Nephew,* with increasing interest; admiration for Goethe's translation. Sat in the garden in the afternoon with friends Wolzogen and Jäger— only for a short while, but a beginning.

Tuesday, April 22 R. had to get up during the night and wander about, but not for long. He works while I and the children dust and clean up the main library. It pleases R. to see the children working in this way. It takes us almost the whole day, and R. walks in the garden;

toward evening he does some more work in my room, and in the evening he reads to me Carlyle (on W. Scott); he is particularly pleased by what the English author has to say about popularity and greatness. Otherwise our conversation today mainly concerns *Rameau's Nephew.* — (On Sunday we talked a lot about the ever-decreasing quality of indignation: moderation—a necessary invention of the Israelites, who cannot vent their anger in foreign lands—has been raised to an ethical and aesthetical maxim. When we change the subject, R. says I ought to write for the *B. Blätter;* yet it seems increasingly absurd to me that a wife should become a writer; I see her as a housekeeper, a weaver, a sibyl, taking part in all creative acts, raising the patience of a beast to the level of a holy offering; but philosophizing, writing, arguing—less and less do I care for it; and if I am permitted to live as an individual, I want it to be only secretly in the memories of my children's children.) R. today recalled the impression which inspired his "Good Friday Music"; he laughs, saying he had thought to himself, "In fact it is all as far-fetched as my love affairs, for it was not a Good Friday at all—just a pleasant mood in Nature which made me think, 'This is how a Good Friday ought to be.'"

Wednesday, April 23   R. wakes up cheerful after a good night—I do not know how he comes to talk about our death, but he does so in a cheerful and humorous way, saying one can never know what nonsense one might talk at the time—French, he fears—or we shall just sit ourselves down when we are very old, and we shall be gone. R. works, I tidy up with the children. (Around midday a visit from our neighbor Frau v. Staff, R. congratulates her in his sincere and cordial way for having come through the illness of the children (scarlet fever) untouched.) [*After the parenthesis Cosima has written* "Thursday"; *see the following entry.*] He goes for a walk, while I read *Wallenstein* with the children. In the evening, which we spend in my room, he reads to me from Carlyle's essay on W. Scott, and since he grows tired, I take over the reading, and we finish the essay; it seems to me that C. has not paid sufficient attention to Scott's *naïve* quality, which he just calls healthy; C. has also not quite understood or appreciated the artistic exaltation, which reveals itself in the many buildings and adornments, and the relationship with animals (both characteristics which remind me of R., even though with R. they take quite different forms); but most of his judgment is incomparably excellent. Much discussion about it with R. after studying the novelist's portrait.

Thursday, April 24   R. slept tolerably well and goes with pleasure to his work; yesterday he said he now knew exactly what to do. I have things to do in Wahnfried. (Visit erroneously entered for yesterday.) Having lost some time through our friend's visit, I tidy the *salon* after she has left, so that R. can use it again this evening, and once more I experience how a consideration like this can dispel tiredness and improve one's strength. We thoroughly enjoy our evening in the *salon;* R. reads me Carlyle's latest essay, on Dr. Francia; both subject and treatment highly interesting. Concern about Fidi, who is complaining of a headache.

Friday, April 25 R. tells me that at a quarter to six he went downstairs and altered a passage in his sketches: "I have got rid of those stupid syncopations." He shows me the passage and tells me that while he was doing it, a bird tapped on the window and demanded to be let in. Hardly has he said this when Georg announces the sudden death of Herr v. Staff during a hunt in the forest. I take leave of R., look in on Fidi, who is still unwell, and then go to the poor wife. When I return around noon, R. greets me with the news that *Parsifal* is finished, he has been working very strenuously! Though our conversation at lunch revolves around the sad blow in the neighboring house, it does not affect the mood arising from this event. And when, after lunch, R. sings to me Amfortas's last lament and Parsifal's words, and plays the ending, I once more feel that pain and mourning make the soul even more vulnerable to music—I breathe in this blessing deeply, and tears of joy follow on the tears of sympathy I shed in the morning like transfigured sisters. Bless you, dear heavens! — I spend the afternoon with my poor friend. Friend Wolzogen and Herr Rubinstein come to us in the evening. R. finishes reading the essay on Dr. Francia, to the enjoyment of all. — He says that never before has he been permitted to work so uninterruptedly. I: "Oh, that I have lived to see it!" —

Saturday, April 26 R. had a somewhat disturbed night—overwork, perhaps? And he feels the tightness in his chest, but it is decided to celebrate the completion of *Parsifal* today, since it is not until today that he can sort out and arrange the pages to present to me; I lay my very modest return gift at his feet, and the lamp holder is fixed to the table. At lunch we drink to the 26th. Meanwhile I go to the house of mourning and accompany my poor friend to the station, seeing her off on her very sad journey. Yet all deep things are akin to one another, today I can both weep and feel joy, in my heart a single harmony; it is only distraction which engenders discord, this is the destroyer, in both love and art. With *Parsifal,* spring has arrived, and R. seems happy! I am somewhat overcome by the wealth of my emotions, and over coffee I fall asleep without being aware of it; I am woken by a slight noise, and find R.'s blessing! [*Enclosed is a piece of paper containing, in Wagner's handwriting, the words:* "My dearest wife! Sleep well!"] All weariness is swept away, and I take the cherished sketches and arrange them, thinking of the children, who will one day find them. — Evening of chat, then something from *Rienzi;* delight in the nobility of the melodies, which no Italianate frills can obscure. For me it is a pleasant occupation to discern in this bud, still so tightly wrapped, the divine flower which was to unfold from it. —

Sunday, April 27 R. slept well. I tell him he will not know now what to do with his time! . . . I write in my diary and read Malwida's book, just arrived. Silence, no more sounds of music in Wahnfried—instead, a hideous military band! R. reads the *B. Bl.,* pleased with all three, Glase., Wolz., Schemann; he is vexed over the misprint in the old edition of *The Artwork of the Future*—"heavenly [*himmlisch*] beauty" instead of "sensual [*sinnlich*] beauty" (returning to this in the evening, he says the fact that Glasenapp has retained it could lead one astray about the whole thing). He says our confederation still lacks a musician to write a critique of modern music. R. is annoyed with M[alwida] for speaking out against religious acts; he agrees that the church has nothing to do with marriage, which is in fact alien to its spirit, and which it simply tolerates; but birth and death are both its concern. He says he cannot understand how one can hold out against baptism when one has been born into a Christian community, though he does admit that if one has been born outside it, there is no point in seeking admission to it, since the church is now in such a bad way. He can think of nothing more unbearable than a priest, but that has nothing to do with the act of baptism or the symbol of redemption. — After lunch we start to talk about the actor Jefferson, and R. recalls the ghostly scene on the mountains and the wonderful power of music—how the threadbare, indeed pitiful accompaniment elevated and transformed the over-all impression. — In the evening we ask Wol. to join us, so that we may congratulate him on the periodical. The very numerous performances in Cologne (mostly of *Holländer*) have brought in new members. We go through *Parsifal,* from the 2nd entrance into the Temple up to the end; R. said yesterday what he has said before: that the orchestration would be completely different from that of the *Ring,* no figurations of that kind; it would be like cloud layers, dispersing and then forming again. The naïveté which had kept sentimentality at bay in the "Forest Murmurs" would also keep it at bay in *Parsifal;* in the former it was the naïveté of Nature, here it would be the naïveté of holiness, "which is free of the dross of sentimentality." He plays certain intervals to us, saying, "That would be absolutely impossible in *Parsifal.*" "And so that you can see what a foolish fellow I am," he tells Wolzogen, "I'll show you what I intend to alter in the first act." He looks for the chord in the first act, but cannot find it: "Yes, of course, it is in the Prelude; when I heard it, I said to myself, 'Not bad on the whole, but this chord must go.'" He thinks it is too sentimental. Discussion of the final, wordless scene. R. says he will cut some of the music if the action on stage is insufficient, but it gave him pleasure to be able to show that he was not wearied. Talk of Amfortas, his weakness, his exhaustion, and just the one terrible moment when he tries to force them to kill him. Perhaps the most wonderful thing about the work is its divine simplicity, comparable to the Gospels—"the pure fool" who dominates everything. . . . As R. himself said, "It is all so *direct!*" . . .

Monday, April 28 R. had a good rest. He is using these quiet days for correspondence, today he writes to friend Heckel and congratulates him on keeping to the *spirit* of the work in the production. At lunch we talk about the incident he laughingly mentioned to me at breakfast: the King of Saxony is said to have been set upon and roughly handled by vagabonds during a hunt; an emperor (in Russia) who ran away, a king being thrashed—sore trials of respect! . . . For me and the children in the morning, simple devotions in the house of mourning. All that now remains of spring is the wind, and a cold one—it is not kind of Heaven to repay R. in this way! On the other hand, he takes the liveliest pleasure in the children. He told me that often, when he saw himself with me and the children like this, he asked himself whether he was still the same person. — "Eva in Paradise," I recently exclaimed to our little daughter. R. took me up: "Siegfried in Valhalla, Isolde in life and in sorrow!" The fact that you have brought him pleasure, my children, this blessing will be with you all your lives—let me thank you! — In the evening we play whist with the elder girls. Before that he looks through the window, sees the new moon coming through behind a cloud, and calls us to look. To me he says, "It stands there so shyly, so questioningly, this inverted Cosima—but God sees her from the right side." R. then reads some Carlyle to me, about the French Revolution, Mirabeau, Danton, Robespierre—it gives us much enjoyment. However, he does not wish to read Malwida's recently published book; he says at lunch, "I shall not read any book by a woman until you write one." He does glance through one chapter but soon puts the book down, finding all the philosophizing distasteful: "They are all materialists, after all," the ethics they derived from Schopenhauer, whose first book they did not understand, he says. —

Tuesday, April 29 He was up once, at 4 o'clock, but he is not unwell, it is just, as he says, a curious feeling when a work like this has been completed. He goes through it in the morning and tells me at lunch that he has already made several pencil marks in it; several things were too abrupt, leaving the listener too much to fill in as far as music was concerned, and that could be put right. — When I tell him that I cannot help thinking of the middle part in the *Faust* Overture, he says it is strange how in one's youth one does not dare let oneself go. Without this later middle part, he continues, the *Faust* Overture sounds so forbidding, and his symphony also lacks such sighs of relief. — In connection with this youthful propensity, I tell him I am always asking myself why the writings of women, whether in prose or in verse, are so curiously dry. R. replies, "Because there is something artificial about a woman who writes; it is her nature either to love or to hate, whereas for a man writing is a natural means of expression." He goes out (into the palace gardens), watches the military maneuvers, and says to Councilor Kraussold, with whom he is strolling up and down, "This is the way the Zulus now carry on, too." Over coffee he said to me that in fact Siegfried ought to have turned into Parsifal and redeemed Wotan, he should have come upon Wotan (instead of Amfortas) in the course of his wanderings—but there was no antecedent for it, and so it would have to remain as it was. — In the evening we read Carlyle's "Mirabeau" with undiminished enjoyment. (The "triviality run distracted"—R. much amused by this way of describing the Revolution.)

Wednesday, April 30 R. slept well. He spends the morning writing letters, but he feels something missing. However, he is looking well. Over coffee I read to him the description of the procession in Vienna, he expresses his great repugnance for such things, and the portrait of the Empress in the *I. Z.* downright disgusts him. — Yesterday evening friend W. sent us a copy of the periodical *Alma Mater,* Israelites poking fun at "Germanomaniacs" and also at our friend W.'s article about linguistic style in R.'s writings. R. looks through it, and the whole situation is brought back into his mind: "This is the true pit of Hell," he says regarding Jewish dominance, "and who is there to fight against it? C. Frantz in Blasewitz, I in Bayreuth. Oh, Lord!" — When we part after coffee, R., moved by the tenderness of our farewells, speaks of the harshness of such separations, however short they may be; a sacrifice one makes to life's labors! Yesterday, when he called for Georg, he said, "I wonder how many more times I shall shout, 'Georg, put out the lights'?" At coffeetime, as he is drinking his glass of cognac, he says, "I shall soon be 70, then I shall become very temperate," and he quotes what Dean Dittmar said to him about life between 60 and 70; I observe that the rules do not apply in the least to him. In the evening, when he makes some sad remarks about life, which brings one so much sorrow, nothing but unpleasantness, I tell him that things no longer affect me, but to see him out of humor makes me only too aware of my helplessness. "In a sense it is all your fault," he says with a laugh, "for if you had not come along, I should long ago have found a hole to bury myself in." And then it comes out that it is only the bad weather which is vexing him; he wanted to go out in the morning and had been forced back. In the evening reminiscences of Tribschen with the children, the *Christkind* and much besides. After that, Carlyle's "Mirabeau" to the end. — I received a not exactly encouraging letter from the King's secretary, telling me that the King does not seem to be in favor of the concerts. I keep silent about it for the time being. R. is looking well and is cheerful in spite of everything; I do not wish to be the cause of an unpleasant impression on him. — I close this book with a word of thanks and a fervent plea; never before was my end so constantly in my mind. May I be granted the much-desired boon which I am afraid to express! . . .

Thursday, May 1   R. slept well only till 4 o'clock, then he became restless, had to get up and apply compresses. The weather is cold and raw; three blackbirds have frozen to death! R.'s morning work the perusal of a Wolz. manuscript for America, which R. will have to sign and which seems to him very immature. Talked a lot about Fidi. R. tells me that at the age of ten he wrote sacred poems with a friend (Lauterbach) in a mood of religious ecstasy. The aim at 12 was to produce *Der Freischütz!* The sky clears, and R. and I go for a long walk with the two girls, Loldi and Eva (Boni and Fidi in bed), and the two dogs, to the Students' Wood and back on the road past the powder magazine. During it R. recalls Tribschen and says, "We should have tried to keep it for ourselves and make a pilgrimage there every year for a few weeks, for it was a good place—the storms were still raging, but they did not harm us." — In the evening R. plays my father's *Hamlet* with Lusch as a piano duet and says it aroused the impression of a disheveled tomcat lying there before him. Then we start on Carlyle's "Playwrights"; his judgment of Grillparzer very good. — Coming back to *Hamlet,* R. says: "Musicians should not concern themselves with things that have nothing to do with them. Hamlet offers nothing to musicians." We continue speaking about this subject until quite late, when an embrace and a blessing both part and unite us. [*End of the twelfth notebook of the Diaries. The thirteenth begins:* "The notebooks are piling up; the volumes which previously sufficed for years now hardly suffice for six months. And yet I feel as if I myself were less and less present. Will I succeed, my children, in conveying the picture I want to preserve for you? Will our love live on in you? . . . I do not know, but I shall continue."]

Friday, May 2   R. had a really good night, and we are pleased with the success of our long walk. But today it is even colder than yesterday; it is reported that the vegetable crop has been killed by frost, and at breakfast we make all kinds of speculations about the world's coming to an end through cold. R. says we should look ahead, rent a house on the equator in good time, and bring Fidi up to be an African explorer, so that he can discover the right place for his children. We part in gay tenderness, and at lunch R. tells me he has found a starting point and begun his work for the *Bayr. Bl.* At breakfast we talked about the biography. R. wonders whether he can continue to write truthfully in such detail, and he decides that he can, for truth and fiction, he observes, both suffer precisely because they are in fact neither the one nor the other. — I do not know what makes him think of *Der Freischütz,* but he points out to me how good it is that Caspar (in the Wolf's Glen) speaks below while Max is singing above; maybe Weber did not deliberately aim for this effect, he says, but the over-all impression is quite wonderful. In Paris, of course, Caspar sang, too. The raw weather permits only a short walk in the palace gardens. R. then writes to Herr Tappert, returning his article—a very nice letter, kind and truthful, as is always his way. — In the evening read Carlyle's essay on Burns, and some poems by Burns as well, with interest. — Georg calls us to watch the ratcatcher, in attendance at Wahnfried to protect our poor hens! We are amused by the lively owl, sniffing about everywhere. — R. said recently that our peacock was like one of those vain poets: nobody takes any notice of him, and so he puffs and blows himself up and rattles his feathers.

Saturday, May 3 R. did not have a good night, being burdened with congestions, and he complains of tightness in the chest. But despite this he is cheerful in the morning and calls out to me as I come from my bath, "Not every woman comes in like that"—and the day's blessing hovers between us. He works on his article: "I must do something that will please you." — Then he sends a telegram to the King in memory of their first meeting, 15 years ago. He goes for a short walk, though the weather is still raw. In the evening friend Wolzogen, with whom there is a long discussion regarding a much-desired critique of present-day music. R. explains his views on instrumental music and how it should be kept distinct from dramatic music.

Sunday, May 4 R. had a good night. I do not know what association of ideas brings him to doctoral titles and similar honors, but he says, "With me it is not resentment because such things never came my way—even as a conductor in Dresden I should have shied away from accepting one." — R. works on his article—slowly, because that is the beauty of it, he says: "Once one has expressed one's thoughts, as I did in my first writings, then—if one has to speak again—the pleasure lies in *how* one says it." — R. goes out, talks to some cavalry officers in Angermann's, and returns home in cheerful spirits. In the evening read Carlyle's "Burns." We intended reading a pamphlet on socialism by Father Felix, the Jesuit, but the table of contents put R. off right at the start, he found it far less significant than he had expected, having felt that the Catholic party people would have had the sense to master the problems, whereas this appeared to be nothing but an expression of loathing. — After that, conversing by ourselves, looking back on our 15 years together! A great joy, the world virtually nonexistent: "We do not have a single bitter feeling," says R. . . .

Monday, May 5   R. dreamed twice about my father, saw him in a brocade cloak, was annoyed by Lusch, who was being deliberately tiresome with her piano playing, woke up twice in agitation, had to get up, and then read Carlyle. "I know what it was—how childish one is!" And he reminds me that yesterday he wanted, against my advice, to eat some of the only dessert (whipped cream) he really enjoys. "That's what we're all like," he sighs. — He says of a book about Helene Dönniges and Lassalle, "The surprising thing about it is its nakedness, everyone mentioned by name, everything cynically open—another Frau v. Kalb," he jokes, thus making me really conscious of the difference between that time and this. In the evening a slight argument with friend Rubinstein, revealing once more the unbridgeable gulf between people of his kind and ourselves. R. uniquely kind and friendly, so touching in all the ways he tries to inspire trust in this poor distrustful man. — Whist and even lansquenet, both without money! — In the afternoon we went out with the children and the dogs; a lot of wind and dust.

Tuesday, May 6   R. dreamed that I came to show myself to him in a mauve dress. He is so tired that he falls asleep for half an hour in his bath. In the morning he works enjoyably on his article. I clear away letters and am touched by three from him to me, which I reread, one from the year '64 (Nov.), one from the year '67, and one from the year 1872 (from Bayreuth). All the struggles, all the sufferings and love rise up before me, recalled by these cherished lines. . . . This morning a letter arrived from the King—he does not mention with a single word the postponement of the performances or the concerts. The letter makes a pleasant impression on R., as does a letter from Heckel in Mannheim, enclosing one from Herr Schön; this gentleman from Worms wants to make an annual contribution to the school and inquires about the situation in a serious, understanding manner. R. reads the letters to us over lunch. He takes a long nap in the afternoon, and then we both go out into the garden and the palace gardens; the air is springlike—at last!—and though he has first to deal with all sorts of worldly nuisances (bricklayers, fitters, etc., dogs breaking in everywhere), lively spirits gain the upper hand. He takes from his waistcoat pocket the enclosed piece of paper, saying it cannot be understood out of context, but I ask him for it, and he explains to me something of its connection with his present work. [*Enclosed is a piece of paper bearing in Wagner's handwriting the words:* "2 lives. Undistinguished—deep—religion. | Celebrated—great—art." *The lines are bracketed together, and beside them is written:* "tragic."] Reverting to life's absurdities, I amuse him by saying that only too often do I find myself singing Figaro's "Of all else I say nothing" in connection with the many things I have not told him. — In the evening we remain by ourselves; R. plays the duet from *Médée* between the heroine and Creon, her pleading and his harshness; there are certainly some fine things in it, such as the appeal to the gods, but it leaves us quite cold. R. says, "I can't bear these raging women," and, "I find such arithmetical drama and such arithmetical music repulsive." I am reminded of the diatribes in *Rameau's Nephew* and feel how pale all this so-called dramatic art is in comparison with a single Weber melody. "And yet," says R., "there is something in it which completely eluded such donkeys as Marschner—a sense of form." — We finish the study of Burns and agree that, though some of the repetitions are wearisome and much of it looks like unnecessary preaching, it always gives evidence of a deep and remarkable mind; the parallels between Burns and Byron, for example, and the assertion that both of them, though true poets, were not poets enough to mold their lives to their poetic calling. Both these points are significant, and in connection with them we talk about the artist's relationship to life. We are in fine spirits as we take leave of this day, which bears the promise of spring.

Wednesday, May 7 R. had a good night, did not have to get up. In the past few days he has been greeting me with applause when I come up from my bath, but now he desists; he says he feels I do not like it, and I ask myself whether there is in fact anything coming from him which would not be welcome to me! He wants to finish his article today: "I wonder whether it will amuse you?" — After I have received from him the day's blessings he says gaily, "You can always say to me, '*If it were not for me, you would long ago have quit this earth'!*" — But spring has not come; a north wind is blowing, and it feels cold. He works without rushing himself, as he says, and enjoys his work. In cold wind and rain R. and I go to visit Frau v. Staff, the poor widow, and she thanks me and asks me to thank him for his divine kindness. R. then wanted to go to the palace gardens and to Angermann's, but he soon returns, saying that Marke ran after him and forced him to return home. When I come down to supper, he says, "I have been pursuing philology." He has looked to see how the passage in which Luther translates the word "*barbaros*" as "*undeutsch*" appears in Greek, Latin, English, and French—French the least felicitous with the abstract word "*barbare*," which is also so ambiguous, the English somewhat better; but Luther is splendid! R. cannot stress too strongly what this touch means to him; he returns to it once more late in the evening and says: "These young people! Do you remember how I once showed that passage to Rohde and Nietzsche, and they saw nothing in it? Such lack of understanding and imagination!" R. and I spend the evening alone together, and R. first of all looks through the 2nd act of *Parsifal* in the arrangement by Seidl and Rub.; he finds this act "completely strange" to him. Then we read Carlyle—"Midas," and also some passages at random, including a splendid digression on Cromwell. R. passes over only his writings in imitation of J[ean] Paul. Today was once again a "swan" day; this beautiful dress pleases R., and for me it brings back the fairest memories with its folds! R. makes fun of his absent-mindedness: inscribing the word *"barbaros,"* he wrote down the first beta quite correctly, but when he came to the second, he had to ask himself how to write it!

Thursday, May 8   R. dreamed that he and I wanted to drown ourselves in the bathtub; he says it had been a sort of legal affair, his sister had died, and he told himself, "Cosima always does as I do." — This re-emergence of my reflections in a dream arouses strange feelings in me—could I but prove worthy! — Much discussion in the morning about Carlyle, "who did not have sufficient regard for W. Scott's poetic talent." R.'s astonishment over characters such as Shelley, who leave him quite cold, however much they pile on the horrors; how different the Spaniards, whose manner seems like a natural phenomenon. — Then R. says how strange he feels when he regards his completed *Parsifal*—the time spent on it seems to have passed in a flash. He works on his article and says at lunch that he has written only one page. — Tariff disputes, R. observes that Bismarck is handling tariffs like the *"suffrage universel,"* to get them through he is now allying himself with Windthorst, "with all and sundry," at random. In the afternoon we follow in each other's footsteps, R. and I: first of all to see friend Gross, then to various shops! R. buys little rakes for the bank he has planned for this evening! All our neighbors come along, 6 in total, and the Jägers as well, and R. revives "youthful memories"; sets up the bank, taking great trouble in and getting much enjoyment from arranging things properly, then initiates all of us ignoramuses into the secrets of a "gambling hell"! Lusch and Boni are his *croupiers,* he calls them Hugin and Munin. Great amusement, and R. sets it up so that winnings shall be valid only for our guests. When they have gone, R. says it is both strange and touching to see this family which has settled here in order to follow his star. R. and I seem to me like departed spirits who have returned to this world and, once alone together, talk about their home! — A nice letter from Herr Schön, directly to R.

Friday, May 9 R. had a good night. He delights in the call of the peacock which he heard last night, says he feels as if he is in India; the character of the call seems to him to be that of a question, and its first note reminds him of a muted trumpet. At lunch R. praises his *"croupiers"* and gaily recalls last night. — After lunch news of the so-called Wagner Concerts in London, which are reported to have attracted no audience, and then of *Lohengrin* in Paris. The statement that the audience burst into applause after *"Einsam in trüben Tagen"* brings from R. the remark: "That is typical of the French—the nice side. But how difficult it is to find good things to say of the Germans!" — R. goes out, and I, too, but when I return home I find he is not well: the rough wind has upset him, and he eats no supper. He was in Angermann's, was pleased by the strong and handsome figures there. "Ours is no vanishing race," he says. — In the evening he reads to us all sorts of curiosities from the newspapers, about the nihilist movement and observations concerning the female skull! When Rubinstein remarks, "The female nihilists in Russia should be told about that," R. says, "But at least they are listening to their hearts; they think, 'If only we knew as much as men, we should soon change the state of things.'" This nonsense about the value of knowledge leads to a discussion on vivisection, which makes R. very angry. But he does not feel well, and we soon go off to bed.

Saturday, May 10 Raging storm; R. up all night. — His sleep disturbed; he dreamed that I went to Chemnitz for a christening, having promised it to Lulu; he, beside himself, exclaims about his sister, "What do they need to have children for?!" He also had another disturbing dream about Chemnitz. He asks me whether I shall go on being nice to him when he is always complaining! — But as usual he soon overcomes his disquiet, and our morning conversation covers all sorts of things, among them the fact that Cromwell had already embarked for America when Charles I, "the donkey," stopped it. R. works on his article. Our friends at one o'clock; friend Wolzogen believes he has found the music critic in a certain Herr Scheffer from Berlin, who in an article on singing draws a parallel between Schnorr and Niemann. In the evening R. asks me how he can possibly permit a critique of Niemann in the *Blätter* after all there has been between them. That is the curse of a situation in which obligations are involved, he says, it means one can no longer tell the truth. In his "Retrospect" he had been reserved about Niemann's achievements, but he had also not caused offense. — Regarding the concerts, R. suggests putting advertisements in the newspapers, inviting young players to come along, for he has no intention of attracting players here with heavy fees. If nobody responds, well and good—all he can say is, "Here I am." R. goes for a walk. At the end of the day the weather becomes very fine; R. said he was curious to see whether the sun would not come out at last on the "Sabbath," composed by Meyerbeer, and out it came! — In the evening we look through two little French books, about China and Brazil. The etchings interest R. very much; the slim girl from Lima reminds him of Calderón, and he says, "They could play Calderón at any time." The Chinese actors he also finds very pleasing. — Then we play something from *Parsifal;* I ask him whether he is not pleased with all his spiritual children; the best time is the process of creating, he says, the peculiar state of fervor in which one works. Of *Tristan* he says it will probably remain a sort of mystical pit, giving pleasure to individuals, but its performance presents too many difficulties, fascinating people are imperative for it. We finish the evening in chat, reminiscences of Frankfurt (*Lohengrin*), Vienna, etc. He shows me the photograph of the Crown Prince in the appendix to the report of the General Staff, and sighs: "That as our next emperor!" Of the present one he says, "No wine, no—" [*The foregoing sentence obliterated in ink by an unknown hand.*] His coming here was an act of courtesy, he says, a chivalrous gesture toward Frau v. Schleinitz (he makes a gesture, clicks his heels, and snorts: "A national festival," exactly like the Emperor). When I say laughingly that our King is completely different, he says, "Yes, the exact opposite—he does nothing out of chivalry." — Jokingly he recalls that two emperors have supported him out of courtesy (N[apoleon] III for Princess Metternich, Wilhelm I for Mimi).

Sunday, May 11 R. had a good night; he works on his article, and I do a lot of shopping. The weather is raw and gray, no sign of a change. Yesterday R. thought it would be fine on the Sabbath, and there really was a wonderful sunset. Today it clears up, and R. goes for a walk that is new to him, from the Birk via Konnersreuth. He is very vexed with the two dogs, whom he could not get away from Swallows' Pond! — In the evening we read a book, *Monodramen,* which has just arrived, astonished as usual by such productions.

Monday, May 12 R. had a good night; but he complains of a headache when we meet again at lunch. Overwork, perhaps? His article is keeping him very busy. He goes for a walk, I follow my little paths of preparation! Several visits have been announced for the 22nd, R. seems not unfavorably disposed, and so they are accepted. — In the evening R. talks about religion and says he has been thinking a lot today about Christ; he has come to see clearly that it is Christ's sinlessness which distinguishes him from all others and makes him so moving in his mercy. All the other founders of religions and saints, like Buddha, for example, started as sinners and became saints, but Christ could not

commit a sin. — After that, the third act: first from the funeral procession to the end, then from the introduction to the procession! —

Tuesday, May 13   Several nice letters following a good night for R.,
who says *Parsifal* drove away his headache. He finishes his article,
because his paper ran out, he says, which was fine, since otherwise one
thing would have led to another. — Visit of a Frenchman, Herr
Seignobos, a very singular person, he loves Munich, hates Paris, but
also the German universities, with which he has been given the task of
familiarizing himself, admires the *Nibelungen*—in short, an original
character! He lunches with us. Afterward I receive Herr Fricke the
ballet master, an unexpected meeting with R.! Embarrassed excuses,
but a very good atmosphere finally achieved. At 6:30 R. reads his
article "Shall We Hope?" to us (Seignobos, Wolz., me). In the evening
joined by the ballet master and Rubinst. Reminiscences of earlier
times with Herr Fricke, Rosalie as *La Muette,* for example. Then one
of Herr Rub.'s "Pictures" and Beckmesser's song with an ending.
When Wolz. inquires what to do about the circular, R. says it should
be abandoned this year, but he would very much like young musicians
to be invited along: in this way the school would in time become
established. Herr Schön has subscribed 10,000 marks and offers 500
marks annually. — [*Added later:* "A nice example of Lusch's presence
of mind: the Frenchman asks why R. did not compose a ballet for the
2nd act of *Tannhäuser,* for then everything would have been all right.
R. at first offended, then angry, the Frenchman becomes confused,
until Lusch whispers in her father's ear, 'Papa, he is speaking ironically'
—which turns the whole conversation into a jocular vein."]

Wednesday, May 14   R. had a restful night and is looking well; we
talk about our silver wedding anniversary, which we hope to celebrate!
In the afternoon we immerse ourselves in memories, Hans, the departure from Zurich, how for a long time there had to be silence
between us, a deep, subconscious silence based on fear! Departure of
our Frenchman, who after all appears not to be entirely free from the
limitations of his native land. R. takes him for a little walk in the
palace gardens, and I then find R. sitting in the summerhouse. A lovely
afternoon hour, the two dogs at our feet, and we feeling content! . . .
In the evening we read Carlyle's history of the Abbey of St. Edmundsbury; very gripping. R. very taken with King Henry II (in his judgment on the newly elected Abbot Samson). He is also highly amused
by the monks' Latin. A pleasant and lovely day, on which I was
permitted to occupy myself solely with the 22nd and be alone with him.

Thursday, May 15   R. got up once but was not dissatisfied with his
night; mine was a wild one, my head in a whirl, and sleep chased away
my fears of losing all my faculties. — At lunch R. says he spent a

"lazy" morning; I am glad about it, but he says he would like to be doing something, the hours of creative fervor are the best. Then we talk about some past experiences, our Tribschen guests, Nietzsche, Rohde, etc., how miserably they failed us. Then about the Jews; R. recalls a Herr Wiener in Prague in his youth, a Herr [*left blank*], how talented they had seemed to him in comparison with a Dr. Adler or a Herr Marsano—then Börne, then Heine. He feels their influence everywhere, and in his case they are just waiting for his death, for then, as they well know, all will be ended. I: "Siegfried will still be a stumbling block, for he will propagate your ideas; he will not have your genius, but I hope he'll have your character." R. thinks he will, too. Oh, my Siegfried, when you read these lines, may they give you strength and increase your courage! People say you resemble both your father and me—of what is mine, keep only my adoration of your father, for that was my salvation! Accept my blessings together with my hopes! — A nice afternoon, though still windy; a walk via Birk and Konnersreuth with R., children, and dogs, I thinking a lot about Siegfried, the ardent wish that we might be permitted to protect his youth to the end. R. in very good spirits, but a sad ending to our walk. We meet a basket maker and his son; they ask for alms; R. gives them a mark; when they have already gone on, I ask R. to buy a basket, which he does. In the man's face we see honesty and hunger, he has sold nothing, has been walking for 9 hours, still has to get to Wolfsbach! Dear God, thus it is everywhere now in Germany, our good people starving! The man is pleased, but my feeling is one of guilt for not having asked R. to let him sleep and eat in Bayreuth, and to buy all his goods. In my compassion my thinking powers froze, and anyway I am shy of making suggestions to R.; he always does what is right. But I suffer much from my failure to speak, and I can still see that pitiful face. — When I tell R. of some expected arrivals for the 22nd, he says the celebrations ought really to be for ourselves alone, but he has no objection to Mimi's coming. — Abbot Samson in the evening, with increasing enjoyment. R. laughs heartily over the idea of "a defect of telescopes." — Splendid ideas and feelings, such as: "He is not there to expect reason and nobleness of others; he is there to give them of his own reason and nobleness." (Bust of [Amalie] Materna set up; R. sends a telegram to "Brünnhilde.") Wagner Concerts in London empty!

Friday, May 16 R. had a good night. We chat about all sorts of things, he then goes to his "lazing about," as he calls it, though he would like to have good weather for it. Letter from Malwida with suggestions for Rome and Naples. "I want one element, not an assortment," says R. and sticks to Naples. He shows me an Englishman's remark about *Tristan*. The gray weather at first permits only a walk in the garden, but then he gathers all the children, including Lusch, and takes them to Angermann's after a short walk. To Lulu he says, "You can do anything together with your father," and tells her how I was once willing to seat myself in a wheelbarrow in Frankfurt a/M., when he asked me to. To me, of course, it had seemed more like the celestial Wain! . . . In the evening he is much vexed at seeing a manuscript of his being offered for sale. He sends a telegram to the publisher. A game of whist with the ballet master and Herr Rubinstein. (R. rather agitated.)

Saturday, May 17 R. did not have a good night. He tells me he dreamed about Weber, about encountering him in Stuttgart, speaking to him, and asking him whether he had really felt that he (R.) had musical talent, reminding him of his mother; when Weber gave no reply, R. said to himself, "Well, he is dead, he just doesn't want to say it, he's embarrassed." This makes us laugh heartily. — Then our conversation turns to Homer (after R. has called me Pan-elopeia), and he says that Homer was really the poet *par excellence,* the source of all poetic art, the true creator. We recall several things in the *Odyssey,* and then he talks about the *Iliad,* how interrelated it all is, like a drama, and he talks of the difference between the two epics. — So the minutes tick by, and R. laughs as he looks at his watch, saying how good we are at prolonging this morning hour together. Ah, it is a golden time— the day still far away! Then, when we meet again, I can see from R.'s face that something has vexed him—Herr Fürstenau has written to say that Frl. Uhlig does not wish to return the letters! — R. writes his feelings concerning this to Herr F. — Then an absurd article about *Götterdämmerung* in Kahnt's periodical. R. tells Lulu in his name to forbid the delivery of the periodical. — Over coffee he tells me his experiences in the early hours: he woke up before four o'clock, got up, went downstairs, took some magnesia, checked the weather, cold and misty, arousing a longing for the South, then listened to the cocks crowing—one after another. Then upstairs again, regarded me as I slept, returned downstairs, looked at the bust of Materna, went to the window, the chorus in the poultry yard reminding him of the laughing chorus in Offenbach's *Orpheus* (heard in Mainz some 20 years ago). Upstairs again, it was five o'clock—if it had been seven he would have taken his bath, but now he got back into bed and had at least 8 disturbing dreams. — Then in his bath he falls asleep again! — When we are discussing various things, Hans, my father, R. exclaims, "How rare to find a person who makes a religion of truthfulness and who cannot do other than he does!" In the afternoon R. corrects his article, then goes to the W.'s to fetch him back here. He returns home without being cheered up, but the children's chat soon overcomes his mood. In the evening whist with Rubinstein and a dummy. — Then something in passing from *Parsifal* ("*sah ihn und lachte*" and the page after that). Afterward I recall that some days ago R. told me that Kundry was his most original female character; when he had realized that the servant of the Grail was the same woman who seduced Amfortas, he said, everything fell into place, and after that, however many years might elapse, he knew how it would turn out.

Sunday, May 18 R. was restless in the morning, but he says the *conducteur* has not unhitched his horses. When he is in this restless state he compares himself with the driver in [Victor Hugo's] *Histoire d'un crime,* who exclaims, "*Bon, je sais ce que c'est*" ["I know what's going on"], and at once unhitches his omnibus for the barricades. R. says usually he would get out of bed, but this time he remained quietly where he was. (Yesterday he wrote to Herr Schön, telling him that when he started his undertaking he had counted on having 300 people such as Herr Schön—now there was only one, but he was *schön* [fine].) He comes to me around noon to tell me about what he has just been reading in Carlyle (about religion, the Pope, the London hatter) and has so much enjoyed. He is very annoyed by the Würzburg publisher's demands and intends to write a little article about it. — Yesterday, when we read something in Tappert's periodical about Beethoven's relationship with Giulia, R. said, "I never had any contacts like that— it is terrible, the company in which I always found myself." He then names some theatrical women and adds: "I can assure you that among all these Minna seemed downright aristocratic. In Dresden Frau Tichatschek was the prize exhibit—but no, I am forgetting I had Frau Schröder-Devrient there, too, but she had some impact on my life." — R. goes for a walk in the afternoon, and the evening brings us Herr Fischer, now a celebrated conductor in Mannheim, along with his Wotan. The latter sings for us, revealing, in spite of some hoarseness, an imposing presence and a powerful voice. But R. very vexed by the evening; the ill-humor of our friends, when they are of his circle, upsets him badly, and the many women annoy him as well! He falls asleep, grumbling.

Monday, May 19 R. had a good night, "not unhitched." — We talk gaily about our trials last night; as he recently said, "I should like to know who has anything to offer us." Then he talks of men who marry early, saying they are lost souls, Frau Schröder-Devrient despised him utterly on that account and accused him of being tied to his wife's apron strings. Fine weather, he goes for a walk with Eva and Boni, a new route to the Students' Wood, where they stop for a rest, and a butterfly settles on R.'s scarf and stays there a long time. In the evening we finish Carlyle's story of the abbey, which moves us greatly, particularly the exhumation scene. Before that I had the task of informing R. of Semper's death. Solemn mood, silence, then to Fidi (we are at supper)—yes, Fidi, we shall have to hold out a long time, you and I. Aspects of Semper's character, "What relates to antiquity in the qualities of such a person looks like distortion in our modern world." — R. recalled the supper given by Semper in honor of *Tannhäuser;* Herr v. Birk was invited, also Meyerbeer, who did not come; a very violent argument between R. and S. Semper: "I am not the only one who thinks like this, there is Birk, too—" They look at him, find him snoring, whereupon much laughter! . . . The end of the day is rendered particularly significant for me by Novalis's remark about the body, quoted by Carlyle. The poet expresses what the loving heart performs.

Tuesday, May 20 R. had a good night. At breakfast we talk about Parsifal, and he feels I am not entirely wrong when I tell him that each of us bears within his soul a fellow feeling for the tragedy of Tristan and Isolde as well as of Parsifal—the power of love; each of us feels at one time the death wish within it. And the power of sin, of sensuality, I think, too, and its longing for salvation. Wotan's experiences, on the other hand—his feelings toward Siegfried and Siegmund—people do not feel those inside themselves, the man of genius lays them bare, people look and are overwhelmed. I part from him covered in kisses: "You must take these off first." — At noon he comes to tell me about the delightful things (regarding overproduction) he has just been reading in Carlyle. He says, "When one thinks what excellent things have already been said, although the world goes on talking the same silly rubbish, one realizes that the only remedy is silence." The weather still overcast. In the evening Carlyle.

Wednesday, May 21 R. had a good night. A gay parting after joking about the *"tableaux vivants"* I am preparing for him. — Final rehearsal of pantomime and festival play, all in excellent shape, the good children dedicated heart and soul. — After the rehearsal I inquire at the Reichsadler about rooms for Mimi. Just then she arrives, along with Prince Liechtenstein and his wife. Greetings. A splendid thunderstorm, Donner cleaning things up thoroughly for tomorrow, it is now warm. R. stands at the door of Wahnfried, impatiently awaiting me, I tell him about the guests. In the afternoon R. corrects his article. After finishing my arrangements, I visit our friends. Unfortunately R. is vexed by a misunderstanding with W., but it is soon forgotten, and we spend a very pleasant evening with the L[iechtensteins], Mimi, and Frau v. Wöhrmann.

Thursday, May 22 The day of days! . . . It is also Ascension Day! Bells pealing and glorious weather. — Setting up the stands; everything

has arrived in time except the *Parsifal* sketches. At 10 o'clock I am able
to fetch R., and he is greeted by the Pilgrim! Everything comes off
well—Fidi indescribably moving as he sits before my picture in the
costume and hairstyle of Ludwig Geyer, painting it. We gaze at each
other as if in a dream—thank you, my children! — All the gifts have the
good fortune to please R., from my picture down to the glasses—after
he has gone, one of the Moorish bowls falls down and breaks; go thy
ways, Klingsor's glory! R. takes a rest, I receive the birthday guests,
and we then go for a walk in the palace gardens, where extracts from
R.'s works are being played. At 2 o'clock lunch, the guests from
outside, among whom is also friend Lenbach—Wolz. provides a dinner
for the Bayreuth colony. Fidi proposes the toast to his father. R. is
pleased with the song, "*An den Geliebten*" ["To My Beloved"], tells
me he has found the right ending for it, since he has not slept! After
lunch he leads the children in song, and slips into "*Wer ein holdes Weib
errungen*" (from *Fidelio*): "Oh, if I could die!" . . . Around 6 o'clock
R. goes to Angermann's with friends Levi, Lenbach, and Liechtenstein,
and when he returns home we are able to perform our pantomime,
which is so successful that R. thanks us with tears for our little bit of
nonsense. Oh, my splendid children! In the evening R. has the dance
repeated for our guests. When I appear to receive the guests, R. greets
me with the same song from *Fidelio,* but this time just played on the
piano. "Ah, there is happiness without remorse"!

Friday, May 23   R. had a somewhat restless night, but he is looking
well. He goes off for his morning rest, I do a bit of straightening up and
await the guests whom R. invited to listen to *Parsifal.* We play it
through in his absence—he comes in only at the finish. Lunch with
our friends (only Lenbach has left)—we come together again at 6
o'clock for the 2nd act. Most unfortunately, R. allows himself to be
stirred by it into singing; this puts a great strain on him, and in consequence there is a gloomy shadow over the evening for me.

Saturday, May 24   R. had a very restless night! . . . At 10:30 the
guests arrive for the 3rd act; R. there at the end, saying goodbye to
Mimi, amid all the emotion caused by *Parsifal!* — Lunch alone with R.
and the children, R. using the Rembrandt glasses for the first time
(Michel and the Pilgrim clinked them during the play). In the afternoon a drive to the Eremitage, to which our friends had gone on
ahead with the children. Nice evening. Then a merry party with our
friends in Wahnfried until a late hour. R. has the glasses brought, we
drink to our next meeting and then say goodbye with much affection.
Then at last alone, immersed in each other! . . .

Sunday, May 25   R. slept well. Our conversation is confined to the
birthday, my picture, the Pilgrim, Michel, the Gedon folio, the surprise

lists—all mentioned and discussed, with smiles and tears. Then R. reads the play and laughs at the way Wolz. has written in so many things of which he knows nothing; I have to laugh, too, but I recall gratefully how amiably the good man followed my instructions, accepting all suggestions and corrections. R. almost the whole day in the garden in spite of some thundery rain: summer really arrived with his birthday! . . . In the evening talk with friend Rubinstein. — Pleasure at supper in being by ourselves again. R. says we belong together and only we—all else is a masquerade.

Monday, May 26 R. slept tolerably well. — He sets about arranging his things; the clearing away has already been done, and now Webia's and Michel's gifts must be assigned their places—a nice final task, for now all the friendly cares are done with, the rehearsals, everything; the children and I are missing them! . . . Yesterday evening Marke began to bark loudly, R. ran to the window and rebuked him severely. Coming back to me, he says, "I remembered how, when I was a child and cried in the evenings, I was not content until my sister scolded me. That calmed me down, and that is what Marke wanted, too." R. spends most of the day in the garden, toward evening he goes with the children to the poultry show, and then comes straight up to my room. I notice something in his face, and he admits to me that he has spat some blood—the consequences of straining his throat. Oh, if we could only live for ourselves alone! Everything else, however well intentioned, is a disturbance. In the evening the doctor comes, he advises R. to put off the start of his cure a little while. His pleasure in my picture delights R. — Gay and peaceful game of whist with the two girls. The *Bayreuther Blätter* containing R.'s fine article has arrived, he is a little vexed about the misprints, and he also thinks much more attention should be paid to its appearance. — He recently told me that it irks him not to mention me by name—how can I tell him that all my happiness lies in becoming absorbed in his identity? —

Tuesday, May 27 R. had a good night. He also enjoys the summer-house in the morning, reads there while I am putting away the winter things and arranging the *salon* downstairs. R. comes to me and says: "In music, melody is everything—it is what line is in architecture. I think I have already expressed this idea somewhere." I think it was in *The Artwork of the Future,* he in *Beethoven.* [*Added four pages later but referred back to here:* "Toward evening he played something and said, 'Line—that is what distinguishes the human being from Nature.' "] — Many memories of the children's dance; he says that when Columbine (Lusch) appeared he thought to himself, "Ah, now things will start to happen!" Then delight in our furnishing arrangements—the carpets, the bathroom, the ceiling—everything pleases him. He writes to friend

Lenbach and to Gedon and then gives orders for a drive in spite of
the rather threatening skies; much driving hither and thither as we
chase the patches of blue, all very gay. In the evening a short game of
whist with the two girls, then a part of the section on Cromwell in
[*Heroes and*] *Hero-Worship*—and Napoleon to finish off with! The fact
that in St. Helena Nap. could not understand how the world could
continue without him amuses R. greatly. — In connection with our
studies of England R. said to me recently, "One day an industrialist
will have to come to the rescue, someone who has got rich through
work and now begins to think of his workers, looking to the future,
not just the present." —

Wednesday, May 28 A good night for R. Cheerful breakfast, "the
eagle with two heads," as he says when we both remain in bed. I
return some calls by birthday well-wishers while R. writes to the
King, and unfortunately I find him somewhat irritable when I get
home—he says I should not leave the house. Over coffee he tells me
that these letters are always a burden to him, he feels he is not being
truthful, and what does one not have to pretend to oneself in order to
prove that it is the truth after all? "I have not yet fought clear of it all,
magic still dogs my footsteps." . . . I am very tired, go to lie down, R.
goes into the summerhouse. Later he tells me how he came to my
room, saw me sleeping, gazed at me for a long time, and decided that I
was looking very worn out. Then, when he returned, he says, he
found me gone, and like a little child he cried out, *"Oué Mama?"* I find
his dear handwriting. A stroll with him in the garden, delight in everything! Inspection of the new hens—everything budding and blossoming all around us, we feel united. We think lightheartedly of the
Society of Patrons: "What will become of it?" asks R. with a laugh.
We then go up to his room, which delights him, and he thanks me for
recognizing his tastes and supporting him in them; he says for him
they mean abundance, and he owes them to a sort of instinct. — "And
I alone am permitted to follow you!" is my reply. The evening which
follows this blissful day is no less cheerful. Discussion about masks,
following on our "ballet"; R. once actually saw Columbine, Harlequin,
and the other figures, which have now disappeared, even in Italy. He
also remembers the "greeting" the children sang to him. (Recently he
said: "Who dares to suggest that I never had a heart? Always, whenever
the opportunity arose, I showed it and acted on it." He then describes
again the fine ceremony of the King's greeting and how well it succeeded.) As the evening comes to an end, R. asks me to drink some
champagne from the Rembrandt glasses, which he likes. And before
night a kiss upon his feet, to set the seal on this day spent lost to the
world in single-minded devotion!

Thursday, May 29 A restless night for R., wild dreams, raw weather, gray skies—are you envious, worldly daemon, or do you just wish to show us yesterday, compared with the day following, as the uniquely radiant treasure it was? R. mocks the specter and blesses our star! At lunchtime he comes to me to show me his letter to my father, which is celestial in its goodness. He would like to write to Doepler, whom he did not mention, and explain to him why. — He has been reading more Carlyle, with continuing pleasure; he says he is a dilettante and lacks depth, metaphysics, but his heart is in the right place. R. is also much struck by a coincidence: Carlyle pins his hopes on a proficient and goodhearted industrialist, and Turgenev shows us just such a person in Solomin in *Virgin Soil.* — The gray skies clear; we part, after we have once more thought of the room upstairs and R. has told me that he will still compose all he has in mind—symphonies, everything. He says the room seems to want him to tell it things, and I could say, "You see, I have looked after my husband so well that he just had to write *Parsifal* for me." To my "Oh" he replies, "And now you are trying to deprive me of the stimulus of knowing that I am giving you pleasure." He says the time of composing *Parsifal* went past like a dream, never before had he been able to produce a work in such a way, never had the outside world remained so silent. We stroll together through the town, buying birthday presents for Fidi. — In the evening a game of whist with friend Rubinstein.

Friday, May 30 R. had a very bad night, the disturbances and apprehensions began the instant he fell asleep and continued throughout the night. . . . Is some mistake in his diet to blame? God knows, but I am very, very worried, and in my preoccupation I have lost even my memory for his words. He reads more Carlyle (*History of the* [*French*] *Revolution*), with continued enjoyment. Toward evening a drive to the Riedelsberg, where our children have been spending the day; R. well enough to enjoy the journey home in the sunset. He is also pleased with our children. Previously Loldi reminded him of his ideal sister, and she also reminds me of family things, of mystical relationships, and we are moved to see ourselves reflected like this in our child. In the evening Herr Rubinstein plays to us my father's arrangement of the tarantella from *La Muette* [*de Portici*]; R. finds it rather too long, for it is definitely intended to create excitement; the repetitions and pauses in particular strike him as not being good, but the arrangement is excellent. A letter from my father which arrives today gives R. great pleasure; he praises the individuality of the expressions and says he never writes empty phrases, but speaks only when something has made a special impression on him, and then says something extraordinary. [*Added below:* "Recalling the past years, he told Herr Feustel how glad he was that the theater was there; every time he saw it he felt moved; nobody would ever be able to do anything like it again."]

Saturday, May 31   R. had a somewhat better night, but he did have to get out of bed, and I find him looking worn out. Not even his kindness and love can lighten my concern, my limbs feel as heavy as lead, everything seems wrapped in oppressiveness. But in the afternoon R. says a rest in the summerhouse has done him good. We stroll together through our beloved home, he reads to me some passages from *The French Revolution,* and then we go to see the sculptor Herr Geier, to order an aquarium for Friedel. Now, as I am writing this, the trees are gleaming gold in the sunshine, the blackbirds singing ceaselessly, and he wandering around below, and everything seems good again, instilling hope in my heart. . . . In the evening I read aloud to R. and the children one-half of Carlyle's first lecture (*Hero-Worship*). Among other things, R. finds what he has to say about allegory really outstanding. Then some research into the seasons, why summer in Brazil begins in December. Many lexicons—we laugh heartily at our ignorance.

Sunday, June 1   My hopes did not betray me: R. had a good night. . . . We parted last night with memories of Switzerland; R. recalled a Corpus Christi procession at the foot of the Matterhorn, at its head a clarinet and a drum playing a sort of French march—behind the monstrance a race of cretins, and before it this music! . . . He is reading Carlyle's *Fr. Revolution* with great enjoyment. Frl. Uhlig has sent a copy of part of his letters, and we read them in the summerhouse in the afternoon. Much delight in them; in a curious way they make one realize to what extent R. has always been the same person; no wonder that for most people he remains incomprehensible. We then go for a walk in the palace gardens, and in the evening I greet R. in "Scheherazade"; he sings, "*Sei standhaft,*" etc., and says with a laugh, "I am so contented that I am becoming stupid." — In the evening an attempt to finish reading Carlyle's first lecture, but R. interrupts, saying that Wotan was a man, a thinker, and the conclusions drawn from that fact are drivel. We proceed to "Mohammed," in which there are very good things, about the sincerity of heroes, for example (certainly applicable to R.), and that sincerity does not consist merely in speaking the truth in this case or that. R. mentions at lunch that the King is now having novels written for him about the times of Louis XIV and XV; this raises sad thoughts!

Monday, June 2   R. had a good night. Our conversation turns to the letters; R. is pleased with them, and I always come back to feeling how splendid it is that his character appears so consistent at all periods of his life. As then, he is still expecting socialism to take over, the only difference being that he does not foresee its happening at any particular time. We then indulge in speculating whether, just as our great men found a way of linking their outlook to the newly discovered ancient Greece, future generations, having devoured our present times, will find a link to our kind of art. I express my hope that every substantial community will have a theater like ours, thus replacing and renewing the Passion plays. In the morning R. reads C.'s *Revolution* with great enjoyment. After lunch we continue reading the letters in the summer-house, I truly entranced. We find it almost painful to be interrupted when we are in this mood, and have to listen to reports about Vienna from our friends, the Wolz.'s and the Jägers. Oh, God—how remote it all is! Just as remote as the prospect of R.'s having a success in Paris in '49! — The letters are the finest ones I have ever read. . . . In the evening we read in them his introduction to "Theater Reform," and then we finish "Mohammed"; we are very moved by the miracle which is a human being—"ye have compassion on one another"—that is where God begins, says R.

Tuesday, June 3   R. had a good night. The letters still dominate our conversation. In the morning he writes to friend Cyriax with a little verse for his small godchild: "that Richardis Cyriax may bloom and wax" was all he told me of it. He also writes to Herr Mosely. In the afternoon he continues reading the letters with me, immense enjoyment. — Oh, my Siegfried, what you are heir to! There never was such a being as your father. — R. is delighted with the way the hairs shed by Brange are carefully gathered by the birds to build their nests. . . . In the evening Dr. Schemann pays us a visit with friend Rubinstein; R. talks about Carlyle, saying that he has found exactly the right tone for the period which began with the founding of the Catholic church, and nothing but lies and deception since, a few great individuals who fell foul of these lies. It would be quite improper, he says, to treat the history of this time with solemn pathos, in the way Thucydides deals with the events he describes. Mention of Mommsen and his cult of J. Caesar annoys R. He says that M. is now championing Bismarck, too, though it is true that J. C. had a bit more genius than Bism. R. denies Caesar's magnanimity toward his opponents and maintains that Cromwell was 10,000 times the better man. I say that I always take the poets as law; Dante forbids me to regard Cato as a fool (as M. calls him, which R. finds so heartless), and Shakespeare shows me the theatrical element which seems to me to have entered the world with Caesar. After laughing at himself for becoming so heated about these things, R. then becomes heated about the Schumannians (Dr. Schemann belongs to Schumann's devotees), and he voices his utter contempt for this composer. He calms down at last. When we are alone again, we talk about the confusions in which even the best of our supporters are involved. "I am now back again in Putbus," R. says with a laugh, thinking of the letters which provide so much evidence of his isolation; things are not very different now, he feels. Except that his home has changed so completely.

Wednesday, June 4 R. had a dismal dream about Loldi; he sighed; "Lost!" he cried, and woke up—but after that he had a good night. — Over breakfast we talk of the trials we have been through: my secret visit to him in Munich with Eva, my journey to southern France with my father—almost the hardest experience I ever went through. R. says, "I believe that, if you had said to me, 'I love another,' I should have had the strength to remain silent; I should have suffered but said nothing." Dr. Schemann at lunch; when I come downstairs, I find R. again conversing about Schumann with the two gentlemen; R. had looked through the Symphony in C Major and was once again struck by its triviality and its *rosalia* devices. — Dull weather, Fidi somewhat unwell. In the evening R. reads to us from Carlyle, about the women's uprising led by Maillard. In this remarkable description R. once again points out that Carlyle never introduces his people with speeches or allows them to talk; he shows their acts, and in that way reveals their characters to us.

Thursday, June 5 "Frau Sigurdrifa," R. calls me today as he embraces me! He had a good night. Unfortunately a letter from our good musician Fürstenau leads us to the subject of the Uhlig letters, which are causing so much vexation. . . . Fidi still not entirely well, but out of bed. After lunch I read to R. a circular written by W. to the patrons, declaring that *Parsifal* will not be performed next year, describing the plan for the school, and inviting contributions. R. very much against it —he says he is here, and if people care to approach him, he will not be found lacking, but he cannot commit himself to anything or offer his services for anything. A drive to the Fantaisie, R. a little put out by certain happenings, in me just the feeling that I am to blame when everything is not exactly as he wants and needs it. Everything—worries, intentions, feelings of helplessness, the overwhelming burden of loving thoughts—I leave to my star, begging it to take charge and to exert its influence, to punish me when I am remiss, not to praise me when I succeed, but simply to shine on me. My star! How often does my spirit gaze upon it! It is my good wish, my good yearning, that I see in the invisible heavens in the form of a star, which shines on me and comforts me when the waves of my heart break darkly and stormily over the depths from which it came—at times in their ferocity they obscure its light, but only now and again and for short periods; my call sounds to it from the depths: Let me be good, as my fate has been good!

Friday, June 6 Fidi's day—when we recently recalled R.'s past life, R. exclaimed, "How different, how different!" Today R. writes to Vreneli, inquiring whether we might be able to spend a few days in Tribschen. Devout thoughts of that blessed day! Presentation of gifts at one o'clock; the main present, the aquarium, causes great delight, and R. says Fidi should always be given something which gives pleasure to all. At lunch R. proposes the toast—"Let Fidi be buried today— long live Siegfried, Siegfried the First!"—and it is decided that from now on he shall be given his full name. Spent part of the afternoon with R. in the summerhouse, R. then pleased when the 10 boys, Siegfried's guests, shoot toward him like arrows and bid him good day. In the evening we go with Herr R. through the three Mendelssohn overtures, of which the *Hebrides* impresses us as truly masterly, *Calm Sea and Prosperous Voyage* less so, because of certain weak sentimentalities, and *A Midsummer Night's Dream* perhaps least of all. R. says he is outstanding as a landscape painter—but, oh, when his heart starts to stagger! And: "It is a pity he saw elves as just like gnats, but musically it is very well done." — Before that R. dictated to me a note for the management committee of the *B. Blätter*. — When we are alone upstairs, R. tells me he wants to say something that sounds very much like self-praise: he has been thinking of *Lohengrin* and has come to the con-clusion that in it he has provided a complete portrait of the Middle Ages. Among other things he mentions the sentries sounding their trumpets, and also the preceding fight. I add that *Lohengrin* is the only monument that shows the *beauty* of the Middle Ages.

Saturday, June 7 R. had a good night, and we plan an outing to "Franconian Switzerland." After that he intends to begin his cure and then "do something." He wants to start on the orchestration of *Parsifal* with infinite leisure and enjoyment. — He is continuing to read *The Revolution* with great pleasure. He tells me that after reading a chapter he found particularly moving, he said to himself, "You must do everything with Cosima." But then he had the feeling that we should wear each other out, dissolve into tears, get immersed in each other, and so it would be better if each of us had his own circle, and that we then came together again; but he is always thinking of me and talking to me! — Somewhat later, after he has rearranged some things in his room and we are strolling in the garden, he returns to this subject and says, "Whenever I felt like telling you everything at once, I told myself, 'Better after I have thought about it; on first impact it is all too exclamatory, telling you later means it will be deeper.'" — A glorious

evening, which R. and I enjoy immensely in the garden, though R.
does say, when we are walking on the avenue, "One doesn't feel
strongly enough how green everything is—one should break out into
hymns of thanksgiving, praise Bacchus and all the other good spirits."
— In the evening R. reads to us Carlyle's magnificent description of the
festival of the Confederation. We then immerse ourselves in a discussion of history and nations; then of our form of art, and R. says,
"Whoever pins his faith on hope must be patient." I tell him that I can
understand love, faith, even bliss here on earth, but hope does not
seem to me easy to achieve. We pursue this subject, and R. agrees with
me that evil never fully triumphs, that good is never in vain, though
it is only for each great man individually, even in defeat. World
history as the universal seat of judgment—it is precisely this idea
which can bring us comfort and inspiration, but not hope. Thus more
or less the outcome of our discussion, which became linked with
"Pandora's box" when R. observed that such Goethe poems as
"Elpenor," "Pandora," and "Palaeophron and Neoterpe" had all been
forgotten; he describes *Hermann & Dorothea* as dispensable, and
concludes the conversation with the grotesque remark, "He dealt
with his genius like a blockhead." [*The last three words obliterated in ink
by an unknown hand.*]

Sunday, June 8   R. had a good night, though we were a little worried
at the beginning: the snake in the aquarium has disappeared, and we
feared it might crawl into Siegfried's bed; we both go there, one after
another, but all is quiet—just a silent gulping in the aquarium! —
Toward noon, when I see R. again, I find him a little unwell and in
low spirits; he thinks that a glass of his mineral water, which he had
had put on ice, may have disagreed with him. But by coffeetime he is
already somewhat better. I tell him about the church to which I had
gone with the children for the confirmation of the young Staff girl;
about *The Imitation of Christ,* which I have been reading and which
much affected me; and about a lovely, pale peasant girl dressed in the
ugly costume of the Hummelbauers, a strange kind of loveliness to
which one has literally to accustom oneself. He exclaims, "Oh, it is
terrible, this chasm that exists between us and the church—it is quite
evil!" Yet to how many people is it a comfort! In the afternoon he
reads in the summerhouse, and we then stroll together in the garden.
The sky was overcast in the morning, but now it is bright, and the
birds are tireless in their greetings. The weather is so fine in the
evening that we fix our long-projected drive to Franconian Switzerland
for tomorrow morning. Hasty packing and giving instructions—R.
calls me Napoleon! An evening of chat, nice telegram from the Knights
of the Grail. [*Added at a later date but referred back to this day:* "R. tells

me that he saw the two girls, I[solde] and E[va], sitting on our grave, and when he asked them what they were doing there: 'Looking for worms for the tortoise.' This answer amused him very much."]

Monday, June 9   Sky completely overcast, but we put our faith in the barometer and to the strains of "When my master starts his travels" we set off in the gayest of spirits, eight in all! . . . It is raining when we meet up with our carriage in Pegnitz, but by Pottenstein the weather has already cleared, and we have a merry meal in the little inn in Gössweinstein, walk through the park to the Stämpfer mill, sit for a little while in the pretty bower awaiting our carriage, and then drive on to Muggendorf, where a splendid evening greets our entrance. Great amusement to see the six heads looking out one after another from the windows and greeting us both on the balcony. Walk along the banks of the Wisent; meeting with a poor cripple who also has only one eye, the result of an accident. R. speaks to him, and we learn that he is walking to Streitberg to mend shoes, carrying his tools on his back. R. gives him alms and hopes he will find some others to help him as well. Coming upon such a sight when one is enjoying oneself, how impossible not to help a little! On the way from Pegnitz to Pottenstein we had already passed a young man with sore, bare feet; he was not begging, but R. called him over to our carriage and gave him something, and a grateful and cheerful look was our reward. To the cripple, who gazed at us like a character in a fairy tale, R. says, "See that you meet someone else who will help you further." — Returning to our hotel, we read Carlyle with the loggia door open, his account of the death of Mirabeau. We go to bed in cheerful spirits.

Tuesday, June 10   Although R. lacked many things—there were not enough pillows, no wide bed—he slept tolerably well, got up only once to fix his night light in the most ingenious way, whereupon I called him "Polymetis," which much amused him. Cheerful awakening; French rhymes to start with: *"Quelle bêtise, j'ai changé de chemise"* ["How stupid, I have changed my shirt"], then *"Quel plaisir d'être en voyage"* ["What a pleasure to be on a journey"], with endless rhymes on *"-age,"* and, to finish at last, "R. *Wagner ist gar schöne, der Liebling der Camöne"* ["R. Wagner is a fine man, the favorite of the Camenae"]'. — We leave at half past eight, delighting in the charming countryside, the lush meadows; the weather is kind to us, and—a happy moment—we meet our cripple again outside Streitberg; he greets us, and shortly afterward we see a peasant giving him a lift in his cart; so R.'s repeated good wish has come true. In Bayreuth at 3:30, joyful return—here is our home, R. says as we bid each other welcome! Renewed pleasure in everything here, after a meal at 4 o'clock each to his own room, great fatigue. In the evening friends Rub. and Wolz., R. a bit irritable, but he soon regains his spirits, gets Herr Rub. to play the wonderful Adagio from Haydn's D Major Quartet.

Wednesday, June 11   R. slept deeply and well, we talk over our little adventures, in particular the cripple, symbol of the people's destitution, while at the same time there are national celebrations, exactly as in the time of the great revolution—today the Emperor's golden wedding anniversary! . . . Bayreuth decked out in flags, and yet another starving basketmaker coming to our door! After having in this case, too, dispensed what we can, we enjoy the glorious weather; R. still reading Carlyle, for whom his admiration continues to grow. In the evening conversation with friend Rub., Isolde's apotheosis, remarks on tempo, that virtually unfathomable subject. Pleasure that we have been so successful with the education of the children, how numerous our blessings! Just to be alone together—we want nothing more. Nice letter from the King.

Thursday, June 12   R. had a good night's rest. But yesterday he again said he wanted to write symphonies for me, though not in many movements: "I must do something that pleaseth me well," he says, quoting from the poem *Alexander*. Over coffee we read the curious but, for us, heartening letter of a man from Charlottenburg, Herr Förster. A rainy day; I have many business matters to attend to, some to do with Naples, which is already starting to cause vexations! I hear R. playing parts of *Die Meistersinger,* and in the evening we continue with this divine work—the second act, Eva and Pogner, Eva and Sachs. Discussion on tariffs; R. says he feels this decision will spell the ruin of the German nation. His mind is full of all kinds of ideas about writing poetry and music, and he means to set them down, for he says he is having too good a time, he must do something! . . .

Friday, June 13   R. had a good night, except that toward the end he had *his* dream, as he calls it—about his wife Minna: "This time the mere sight of her was enough to wake me." Our morning is so sweetly cheerful that we can find no end to our words of love, R. follows me out yet again, and during our embrace we tell each other laughingly that it is now time to be serious! He starts on his article: "I must do something, even if it only makes you laugh." — At lunch, when the conversation is about performances, he says he does not wish to attend any apart from our house festivals! . . . Wet weather—"horrible," as R. says, but we are able to take a short walk in the palace gardens; in spite of the dismal sky, delight in Wahnfried, in our life together: "We are so happy," R. exclaims. — When Herr R. is with us in the evening, there is talk of war with France being inevitable; R. says this would be a great catastrophe, and he would not send Siegfried into it—we should have made it impossible on the last occasion for France

ever to cause trouble again. This morning R. was talking about the
facial features of the French, and he said they lacked something—they
were neither German nor Italian, and there was a smudged quality
about them. But how sad it is to have to tell ourselves that we would
take part in a war "coldly," as R. puts it, after having followed the
great deeds of 1870 with such feelings of sympathy!

Saturday, June 14 R. had a good night; he dreamed about [Auber's]
Fra Diavolo, which he was supposed to conduct in a hall in which he
could not even see the orchestra, and his vexation over this stupidity
woke him up. — Wet weather; he works on his article. In the late
afternoon we are able to stroll through the garden for a while, and R.
voices his great longing for fine weather. In the evening we play a
little whist, then R. reads to us the enclosed description of a session of
the French Parliament in Paris [*not found*]. This could be the funeral
dirge—or, rather, din—of the republic. R. observes that a man such
as Gambetta does not even have the courage to bring a session to an
end and call the dissidents to account but, being a Jew, just wants
everything to be smoothed over. — R. then reads to us the description
of August 10. "That is what is so awful about it," he says. "Things are
destroyed not by the strength of an aggressor, but always by the weakness of the degenerates on the other side." — We talked to Herr R.
about Schopenhauer's philosophy and urged him to get to know it, for
his own good.

Sunday, June 15 R. slept well; we breakfast again as an "eagle with
two heads," then each to his own affairs after the blessing has been
spoken. R. talks about his article and says it will make me laugh a lot.
We are able to have our coffee in the summerhouse, and R. remains
there all afternoon in the company of Carlyle, between times strolling
with me in the garden. In the evening a short game of whist, then some
movements from the Beethoven symphonies, the first movement of
the B-flat, which R. says ought to be played very quickly, it is a Mozart
allegro, as distinct from the so much more ordered Allegro of the
Eroica. Then the Andante from the C Minor, which Herr Rubinstein,
like everyone else, takes too slowly. R. observes that this reflects two
worlds side by side, two planets revolving around each other: "Here
they are united," he says at the end. — Return of Siegfried, who has
been to Himmelskron with his tutor and two other boys, joyful reunion
at 11:30. In the summerhouse today I told R. that, if I had to explain
the difference between happiness and unhappiness—though all must
suffer on this earth—I would say that the happy ones are those whom
necessity leads to a state of blessedness, and the unhappy those whom
necessity exposes to misfortune. My necessity led me to him, my
struggles against it, caused by good intentions, were my misfortune—

everything that prevented me from becoming wholly him, from ceasing to be myself, breathing only through him—these were my sufferings. But there are others for whom the accidents of life provide salvation— they are the unhappy ones! — When I ask R.'s pardon for my lack of clarity, he says, "No, no," and the look he gives me shows that he has been following benevolently the somewhat confused expression of my thoughts.

"Apostles of freedom I always found repellent"—this G[oethe] epigram, which Carlyle quotes as the motto for the 3rd vol. of his R[evolution], delights us as only a Goethe saying can—his "*dare* to serve the multitude" quite unique in its way.

Monday, June 16   R. had a good night. I do not know what led us, in the morning, to the play *Isidor und Olga,* but he says he can remember from his childhood the actors who appeared in it in Dresden (Schirmer, Julius, Paoli), though he did not see it, whereas he has forgotten so many actors in plays he did see. He works on his article, as he says, "*non multa sed multum*" ["not many, but much"], he has got to Homer today. Glorious weather, a cloudless sky, R. arranges an outing to the Waldhütte, and at five o'clock we all drive out there. With R. alone I walk to the "Wagner spot," the children go exploring, and suddenly Loldi is with us—she seemed to shoot out of the heather. Much laughter, walked the whole long way back with our child. Drive home around eight o'clock, the children begin of their own accord to sing the "Greeting to the Beloved," which touches us deeply! "You gave me all this," R. says, and adds jokingly, "Now I have wife and children enough!" With deep emotion I thank my children in my heart. [*Added two pages later but referred back to this day:* " 'You are a full thirty years old,' says R., thinking aloud about the song the children sang, among others, in the carriage. When I ask him what he is thinking of, he says, 'I was straying far—how good our nation is, after all. The Prussian heart—who invented this expression? The people! Loyalty toward greatness is sometimes more valuable than greatness itself.' "] — In the evening R. reads to me the death of L[ouis] XVI in Carlyle. — Lovely last farewell to this day in R.'s embrace.

Tuesday, June 17   R. had a good night, but he still cannot start on his cure, after which he intends to set about the *Parsifal* score, beginning with ruling the lines neatly and carefully: "I should like work on it to last until my 70th year, and then we would perform it." He continues, "On the other hand, it would be nice if I could rely on Fidi sufficiently to leave the performance to him." — R. works on his article, but with some misgivings today; he says one achieves nothing by writing. He is becoming more and more aware of the need for an end to the present era—it is only the worker, he feels, who now has a claim on life, as it were. Today he describes to the children (Lusch) the consequences of the emancipation of the Jews, how the middle classes have been pushed to the wall by it and the lower classes led into corruption. The Revolution destroyed feudalism, he says, but introduced Mammon in its place—oh, how comforting it is to turn one's back on all that and just gaze at the trees! A blackbird, hopping before us on the grass, brings from R. the remark "Like Materna—birds with good voices are never particularly beautiful." — Spent the evening with our two friends Wolzogen and Rubins., first of all reading Carlyle on Dumouriez and Danton. Our reading leads us to N. I, Nap. III, and others who, skillful strategists or statesmen though they might have been, nevertheless failed to face death squarely, and saw everything as a game of strategy. R. says: "These men lacked faith in themselves, and therefore greatness as well. Gustavus Adolphus was not afraid to die, and Frederick the Great always exposed his person to danger, but not these others." — We go once more through the *Fingal's Cave* Overture, which R. says is undoubtedly M[endelssohn]'s masterpiece. In the *Midsummer Night's Dream* Overture he remarks on the gnats, and mentions Faust's furs, from which the vermin fly when Mephisto beats them: "It's like that." — "That is tremendously beautiful, ghostly," he exclaims, pointing to a sustained progression of the oboes against the staccato of the other instruments (pages 25–26 in the score of the *Hebrides* Overture). — Then, to please me, he plays his *Liebesmahl der Apostel;* I asked him for it because I do not know the work, and he tells me I should not expect too much. By recalling to myself the occasion, and by visualizing the Frauenkirche, I come to the conclusion that the work, with all its theatrical, Catholic brilliance, must have given an appearance of pomp. R. laughs at the theatrical entrance of the Holy Ghost, and when I tell him my feelings he says, "Yes, it's a sort of Oberammergau play." — Putting the music aside, he says, "There one is fully aware of the composer of *Tristan und Isolde.*" He talks of the plagiarisms of his youth: only recently, when we played M.'s *Calm Sea,* he realized that this was his *Columbus* Overture! He also relates how he wrote his overture, in a room with Minna and Apel, and how—since he was jealous of Apel—he kept looking at them, to see whether they were not flirting too much! . . .

Wednesday, June 18 R. did not have a good night. A gray day; he cannot start on his cure yet. We went to bed last night with much merriment, thinking of Eva's inexplicable talent for mimicry: in Muggendorf she gave us a wonderful imitation of the wife of a confectioner here. Yet this morning I find R.'s face very drawn, he looks run down. Oh, life, oh, death! . . . However, as always, our tired spirits, once joined together, succeed in reviving; I tell him all the funny stories my life in Bayreuth brings to my ears, and he laughs, saying he hopes I shall soon be finished with the education of my children, so that I can write it all down. Heavens, if my poor little inspirations have taken his mind off things for an instant, they have more than served their purpose! At lunch he announces that he has finished his article; he says he has taken things very far. — Coming back to the swarm of insects from Faust's cloak (the *Midsummer Night's Dream* Overture), he says, "Weber depicted elves differently." — Over coffee talked about Charlotte Corday, of whom he has just been reading in Carlyle. "Through madness we express what is divine in ourselves; such deeds are akin to madness." — This morning, when I told him that through him the Germans could pull themselves together and come to despise the Jewish element which had kept him from them for so long, he said, "Yes, the fact that men like Hanslick in Vienna, for instance, have been left in peace by young people is not a good sign—it shows that they have lost their nerve." — It is wet all day, and R. can manage only a short walk in the palace gardens, which he does not enjoy. In the evening we are alone together, always a pleasure. — We chat for quite a while, and then R. reads Carlyle's *Rev.* to me. — The phrase "Barrack-room faith" greatly delighted him yesterday, and he observes that here in our country everything is now barrack-room faith. During the evening he told me he had had an idea which he still had to work out; he preferred not to tell me what it was, for then he would give away his "point." "Or shall I tell you?" "Whatever you feel is right." He: "*Homer blind, Beethoven deaf*—those are the two poles."

Thursday, June 19 R. had a good night, he goes to his work, and at 1 o'clock he comes to read me the first part of his article, "On Poetry and Composition"; glorious moments! And then the ensuing discussion about it. R. says, "If only we had written down all our conversations, for you know it all!" — He intends to make some insertions (about the Cottas, etc.). — When we are having coffee after lunch, our conversation turns to women; "The Tale of the Third Kalandar" from *The Arabian Nights,* which I am reading with Siegfried, led us to the subject. When I describe the charming scene of the 40 women and their love, R. says, "It is only the man who does not come out of it well." I: "He has always previously performed some heroic deed which has earned him the women's devotion." — Survey of the position today. I: "There is always at any rate one thing left for the woman to do—to keep silent." He: "And, should the occasion arise, to gain great influence over the man, however brutal he may be. If, for instance, there is a decision to be made which demands some sacrifice, a woman can exert untold influence, even in the humblest of circumstances. If

Minna had been like that when I wanted to give up my conducting job, what a great help she would have been! But as it was, she had to put up with hearing Frau Müller, a slave to drink, saying, 'That is your husband's greatness, that he is able to make such a sacrifice.' " — "Schiller shows us a woman like this in *W. Tell*, in the person of Stauffacher's wife. And it is a mystical quality, it occurs in Tschudi. Women think that, since men are good-for-nothing, they can arrange the world for themselves." A long walk with R. in the evening (along the road to Konnersreuth), more about his work—delight in the countryside. In the evening whist, then R. plays some things from his symphony for Herr Rub., who does not, however, quite know the right approach by which to listen to and judge such things. R. wanted at first to give it to him to look at, but then decided against it.

Friday, June 20 R. had a good night, and at lunch, when I ask him about his morning, he says he is content. News of the death of Nap. III's son gives rise to reflections on the righteousness of history. "Crime is never a good beginning," says R., and "There is no sure foundation made on blood" comes into my mind in this connection. — In the evening discussed with friend Wolzogen the latest debate on currency reform; R. feels Bismarck has now realized where the Jews have landed him! However, he does not tell the truth, but takes refuge in bragging. — Thinking of Dr. Schemann, R. says again how *young* and immature his friends are. The lengthy linking of R.'s work to W[olfram]'s *Parzival* he describes as pedantic, saying his text has in fact no connection with it; when he read the epic, he first said to himself that nothing could be done with it, "but a few things stuck in my mind—the Good Friday, the wild appearance of Condrie. That is all it was." — We search for the "inventor of wild tales," since R. is suddenly uncertain of his quotation, and are delighted to find it in Grimm and Behn (?).

Saturday, June 21 R. had a good night, and he works happily on his article. A close day, but it clears up, and we are able to have our coffee in the summerhouse and enjoy an afternoon rest, both reading the currency debate! . . . Would it not perhaps help if Bismarck were to call things by their right names? Around 6 o'clock a walk to Birken and beyond through the fields; a glorious evening. The meadows more gaily colored and lush than I think I have ever seen them, forget-me-nots, marigolds, daisies, wood pinks rising above the rosy blades of grass, which in the sunshine cast a reddish-gold veil over the flowers; a celebration of rebirth—how to express one's gratitude? A lark does it for us, trilling forth our thanks exultantly on high. R. leads us along a narrow path through the middle of a field of grain, and our figures vanish in a sea of grain; lost in it, we espy innumerable cornflowers, like greetings from Heaven—the blue ether transformed into stars, the blue star of the deep. Where Friedrichstrasse ends (and the meadow begins) R. shows me a farmhouse dovecote which has taken his fancy, and then we return home, along paths new to us, amid the scent of elder blossom. During the evening we think frequently of the meadow and the wheatfield. And we see our house, too, with redoubled pleasure. R. loves my picture, says it contains "a noble reproach." — Discussion about opera texts in the evening, R. says that one would be unjust to even the worst of opera composers if one did not read the text before listening to the opera. — R. asks Herr Rubinst. for something by Bach, and he plays to us the C Minor Organ Prelude and Fugue; R. finds it beautiful, though toward the end rather *un*fuguelike. We examine the portrait of Bach at the front of the French edition of the *48 Preludes and Fugues* (Czerny), and R. says, "A typical musician's face, like Mozart and Beethoven; they are men of feeling." And when it is mentioned that there is some doubt whether Bach really lost his eyesight through copying by moonlight, R. says: "Why? When I think of my two years in Paris, all that penury—people might feel like doubting that too, for I was not a mere peasant lad, and at that very time my relations were living in a big house in Leipzig." Talk of the fate of great men, Shakespeare, Cervantes, Beethoven. — R. somewhat tired.

Sunday, June 22 R. had a good night, but he has some pain in his foot. He works. Unfortunately we have an experience in our home which causes him much vexation; our gardener and his wife (four years in our house) turn out to have been unworthy of our trust. R. is much affected by this, and he demands the immediate dismissal of the gardener. I am grieved that, though I was aware for a long time of what was going on, I could only keep silent about it and was not able to deal with the trouble without his noticing. — In the evening we come to talk about the death of Prince Napoleon, and R. again refers to the righteousness of history, which in this case has been directed against his mother. R. observes that she started the war with Germany, encouraged it, only in order to relieve her son of the necessity of exacting "vengeance for Sadowa"; now, also for the sake of glory, she sends her son out on a sort of hunt against the Zulus! Fate takes a solemn view—Zulus are also human beings like ourselves, and he dies, not gloriously, but surprised, fleeing. We play a game of whist, and then R. asks Herr Rub. to play the G Minor Symphony with him as a piano duet. R. is vexed because his hands refuse to obey him, and he says he will never again play duets.

Monday, June 23 In spite of his vexation R. had a good night, and since, notwithstanding the confusions in the house, I read *Prometheus* to the elder girls yesterday, our conversation develops from that; I feel that, apart from R., Aeschylus is the only writer who makes his gods speak with such familiarity and nobility. R. finishes his article today and reads it to me; he says he hopes my father will not take the things he says in it about Brahms to apply to himself. I reply that, although I impress consideration both on other people and on myself, my sole thought as far as he, R., is concerned, is that he should feel completely free, come what may. In the afternoon he reads his splendid article to me in the summerhouse, and then we take Siegfried to the swimming school. — In the evening R. reads his article to our friend Wolz. but suffers somewhat from his lack of communicativeness, so that he tells me later that from now on he will read things only to me.

Tuesday, June 24 Midsummer Day! R. dreamed that he was at the Staff estate and wished to draw a curtain, and everything fell down. All kinds of domestic affairs for me, for him the revision of his article. Many gloomy reflections on his isolation; no one is really close to him, he has to show consideration on all sides. In the evening he reads to me Carlyle on Dante (in *Hero-Worship*); what he has to say in general about poets is rather amateurish, marred by the same weakness—the lack of a basic philosophical training—which is almost invariably discernible whenever he is talking in general terms; but his judgment of Dante as a person and of his poetry, and also a few things about poetic art, please us greatly. Today is Midsummer Day, but it is not the Midsummer Day melody which haunts me all day long but, rather, Sieglinde's words to Siegmund, her description of Wotan; these glorious scenes and sounds are like guardian spirits to whom my day is dedicated—I feel then that the common round cannot affect it.

Wednesday, June 25 R. had a good night, and he continues revising his article. We talked again about my father; R. tells me how he first saw him talking in front of a mirror, and his first impression was not a good one: "But now he is a complete original, and that suits him splendidly." — Our gardener is a very curious example of human folly, spurred on by wickedness: an unfathomable mystery. One is astonished by it—and has to laugh! — The weather still not bright; we go for a little walk in the palace gardens with the two dogs. In the evening R. gets Herr Rub. to play Beeth.'s E-flat Major Sonata, delight in its youthful bloom; the minuet is one of R.'s favorites, it brings to my mind Raphael's young Madonnas—the same grace, modesty, the same individuality within its dependence on great models.

Thursday, June 26 R. had a good night, and after we have once more set the world to rights (to use his expression), he goes to his work. The weather is still not good enough for him to begin his projected cure, but we spend some time in the summerhouse and enjoy an evening by ourselves. Despite much "blathering," Carlyle says some very fine things about Shakespeare; R. remarks in particular on the way Nature rewards the poet by allowing him to appear as a part of itself. He is excellent on Luther, and we are particularly pleased by his remark that the Catholic church will last as long as it retains the ability to satisfy noble spirits; as long as it offers mortals the possibility of being good and devout, just so long will it survive. In the evening, when I go to greet R. in his little room, he tells me he wants to hold a celebration for me in it. "When?" "When I get my first real inspiration." — I remind him that this month, 15 years ago, I came to join him in Starnberg. Memories of the external circumstances, and a sigh! R.: "I regret my whole life." I: "But we discovered each other." R.: "Yes, but fifteen years too late." —

Friday, June 27 R. dreamed of some danger to which Fidi was exposed (on the edge of a terrace), and it woke him up. Close, stormy weather; at about twelve o'clock I see R. strolling in the garden, fear that he is feeling unwell or vexed, go down, find him cheerful, already back at his desk, writing something down; he says he intends to give his article a different ending: "My one and only!" he calls out to me gaily; and, relieved, blissful, I return to my work, to life! — The promised heat does in fact arrive; coffee in the summerhouse, friend W. joins us, and, speaking of his article, R. says he is going to write once more about religion, and he develops his idea that the new religion will one day evolve from the workingman, from an industrialist who loves his workers. Around 6 o'clock we set off with the children for Angermann's cellars (or, rather, gardens); very merry stop there, return via the lovely village of Altstadt, across the meadow, great delight in places new to us, and in the gathering dusk the solemn palace gardens provide us with a lovely entrance to Wahnfried. A blissful day, in which all jarring notes are banished by the power of our love and our star. [*Added at bottom of page:* "I had to write to Mr. Cusinah (?), who had asked R. to compose a song, offering 630 marks for it; since R., as I believe, could do with the money, he gives me a smile and says, 'But the humiliation of it!' "]

Saturday, June 28 Was it the sounds of *Tristan*, which Herr R. played as we were getting ready for our meal and which I absorbed greedily, or dreams in the unconsciousness of sleep? Anyway, I awoke in so melancholy a mood that I felt life's tasks to be beyond all mastering. I believe that every blissful moment that life affords also demands that life should cease. — However, the day sees to it that my mood finds no outlet. The possibility of a fire in our bedroom causes us great merriment; R. then goes to his article, I to house and children. It is very hot; around seven o'clock we drive out to the Bürgerreuth, where we have supper by moonlight. Before that we stopped beside the theater, admired the growth in the surrounding plantations, and recalled the chaotic times when the place was teeming with people. The sight affects me unutterably, my thoughts are filled with sublime melancholy, R.'s greatness depicted here in all its isolation! He says, "It stands there like a folly, and once I had emperors and princes here." — My sense of his greatness is almost crushing, for at the same time I am aware of my unworthiness, and the dreamlike melancholy which possessed me this morning now turns into a real burden on my heart; he, the world, I—how could I ever make up for what the world has done to him? The thought that he loves me, that his love for me gives him happiness—this is my refuge from inexpressible emotions. And as if he knows what is going on in my soul, he watches the children, who are rollicking "in a Dionysian sort of way" in the meadow, and speaks of his contentment. Oh, my blessings on all things that give him joy, greetings to thee, thou noble, silent building, symbol of the highest might and the deepest misery! See though my repentance, my love, and my longing, all in one—Amfortas!

Sunday, June 29 R. slept well and at 7 o'clock this morning begins his cure, two glasses of Rakoczy water. — (In the Bürgerreuth yesterday he told me his dream: he had to conduct a Beethoven symphony; when he was ready to begin, the 1st bassoonist was talking to the 1st oboist; he tried to remonstrate, and the bassoonist gave him a blow on the ear which caused him to fall backward—into the position in which he was lying in his bed!) The pictures of the golden wedding anniversary sadden us—the old, bent Empress, who does not look benevolent, in a low-necked dress with an enormous train, beside her the Emperor in a tight uniform, around them the Court preachers and the Court officials. "It is nice to see the world in which we live," says R. In contrast, our theater in its simple grandeur! A very close day; R. must not excite himself, and so the afternoon sees us already at the whist table, and in the evening, too, with Herr Rubinstein. A very severe thunderstorm clears the air.

Monday, June 30 The night is spent in opening and shutting windows, two thunderstorms in succession, but at last R. falls peacefully asleep and gets up in lively spirits to continue his spa cure, of all the children only Boni in the palace gardens with him. A fine day, the air cooler, R. starts C. Frantz's latest book, which is about federalism, and he is so pleased with it that he wants me to read aloud the first chapter in the evening. R. says C. Frantz bears some resemblance to himself in the way he constantly refashions his basic idea. Before that R. read to me the new ending for his article. In the evening he says it would be a good thing if we could marry off our girls well; certainly it would be a good thing, but one our star will have to take care of, for it is not in our power to do anything about it. — This morning R. thought of Niemann and his strident manner and said, "Oh, never again to have anything to do with such people!" And yet during our recent evening near the theater, we were recalling the rehearsals and how everybody always arrived on time, we were full of sincere praise for all of them. Sad, this belonging together yet feeling separated at the same time— sad like so many other things in life.

Tuesday, July 1   R. had a very bad night, he was walking around until nearly 2:30! I wanted to put off the lunch to which we had invited the colony today, but he did not wish it, and in the course of it he is so lively and cheerful that there seems no question of his feeling unwell. Earlier, when I was in my bath, he called out, "Let's have the curtains," for he wanted to read something to me; I shut myself in like Beckmesser, and he comes in and reads to me Frantz's description of the attitude of the Jewish socialists toward the stock exchange, which they ignore entirely. Alarming evidence of yet another idea falsified. Some time ago R. pointed out how disastrous this law against the socialists was, he said that a prudent statesman would have seen the advantage to the nation of having representatives of socialism as members of the Reichstag, to learn from them or to reduce them ad absurdum. At lunch R. outlines C. F.'s views, and so vividly that, turning to old Frau von Schöler, he says, "So now I have explained it all to your son!" (He had spoken excellently to Wolz.) After lunch Herr R. plays us Schubert waltzes, and R. says, "Only in South Germany is there any talent," adding that by talent he means what Schub. possessed. Then Herr Jäger sings "Adelaïde" to us; R. reproaches him for his overemphatic accents, saying it ought to be like moonlight. — Around 6 o'clock R., the children, and I drive out to Ottmannsreuth; a fine evening. We walk across the meadows to Wolfsbach beneath a lovely sunset and very much enjoy this outing and the drive home; we also took a short rest in the woods. The less luxuriant wheatfield with its cornflowers, the somewhat overcast sky, gave us a completely different picture from the wheatfield through which we wandered some time ago; it was quieter, more resigned, a sense of yearning about it which matched the Beethoven songs we had listened to earlier. In the evening R. is very tired, and he falls asleep on the "Biklinium" by my side.

Wednesday, July 2   Unfortunately R. again had a very bad night, so bad that he comes to breakfast irritable. But his kindness triumphs over circumstances, and despite my concern and his fatigue, we part in laughter; "in laughter die"—I really believe we could do that! We thought of our walk yesterday, and, as always when R. thinks of fields of grain, the Lord Jesus comes into his mind. He says: "Considering his disciples' lack of understanding he could not have kept going for long; it was a good thing that he could now and again visit the centurion in Capernaum—but his great bitterness later, that was due to the company he kept. He had to express his idea, never mind to whom." The doctor visits R., and his call has a calming effect. R. talks of Frantz's book with ever-increasing admiration, says he would like to trumpet to all the world how good it is, and at lunch he tells me what he has to say about forestry; in this connection he remarks, "Fidi can become a political economist, then he might be of some use." — A letter from his friend Nuitter gives R. great pleasure, and he says he would like to introduce him to me, for in his attitude toward him (R.) he has never wavered. And indeed R. answers him at once, today. The dull weather does not permit an afternoon walk; I sort things and search in my books for a passage in *Euryanthe* which R. describes as a master stroke, and for which I must leave a blank, since I cannot find it. [*Added at bottom of page:* "Here is the passage which R. called a master stroke: it is Lysiart's very swift answer, '*Alles nach Gefallen, wie schön wirst du mit Kranz und Zither wallen.*'"] Instead, I read a great many things and am shocked by the pallor of words, their inadequacy in spite of all prolixity, above all, their lack of clarity. Oh, Siegfried, I am attempting the impossible! Shall I go on? . . . "For thee, beloved, let it be done!" — Much conversation with R.; after we have been enlarging upon Goethe, Schiller, Aeschylus, R. says with a laugh, "Eckert once said that one could talk so well with me about music; I say one can talk so well with you about poetry!" — "We shall never grow old," R. says to me over coffee, and we then discuss the fate and the character of many of our female friends (M. Muchanoff, Mimi). — In the evening we play whist with Boni and Miss Parry; during the day R. continued reading C. Frantz with great enjoyment; in this connection he said to me in the morning that C. F. was always spinning the same thread anew: "This is what everyone does who has an idea and lives for that idea; people who are fighting only for some abstract system can't do that." — At supper an additional remark about the composer of Weber's last idea occurs to him.

Thursday, July 3 A very terrible night for R.; hardly is he in bed when congestions begin to torment him, he walks about, and finally my concern gives me no rest, I go down to him in the *salon*. He has been reading Herr Glagau's *Des Reiches Not,* and he quotes to me Bismarck's statement "No decent person writes in my behalf," which produces peals of laughter from us in the dismal night. Still laughing, we return upstairs; R. goes to sleep but is visited by the wildest dreams (Jewesses mocking him, etc.); I remain awake, hear our cocks beginning to crow one after another, think of R.'s remark about the peacock spreading its tail: "Just like royalty—all pomp in front, fear behind." I at last fall asleep, while R. drinks his water and takes his walk. He returns home, he has spoken to the doctor, and during breakfast he is curiously lively. [*An addendum based on untranslatable word play omitted.*] Then, becoming serious, he says to me, "Make-believe starts with the human being; the ability to see truth, and not just the outward appearance, is what makes a god." But at lunch he is very worn out and can hardly eat anything, and he feels so unwell all day long that one is at a loss what to do. But despite all misery his genius still shines through; having left the room for a moment, he returns and says to me: "What a splendid stroke of Weber's, Rezia's reply to Fatima in *Oberon* when Fatima says he is found, 'Found? Where?' That is superb." And he plays the glorious passage to me. — Whist, then half an hour of chat; at 10 o'clock with dull fear to bed!

Friday, July 4 R. *had a good night!* All the miseries of life overcome in a flash; it matters not at all to me that the sky is overcast, we laugh at the "farmer's weather," as it is called here, and also at the cure, which R. is giving up for a while. — In the afternoon he plays passages from the 3rd act of *Parsifal*. He brings the dreary heavens back to life; the angels who came to Titurel, it is they in whom we believe. Then we stroll in the garden, delight in the roses, except for the yellow ones, which for R. are not roses at all. — R. is still reading C. Frantz with great enjoyment, his only objection being that he is not sufficiently aware of the damaging effect of the Catholic church on Germany's development, regarding the Reformation as the prime evil. In the evening whist with Rub.

Saturday, July 5 A good night! . . . Cheerful breakfast. At the end of it he wishes me God's blessing—the "true and good" god, whom he knows and can define—and he adds jokingly, "You are the goddess, so now ask yourself who the god is!" — Bad weather, cold and wet. R. reads C. Frantz, then goes through Cherubini's *Faniska* by himself, dismayed by its dryness and turgidity, despite some interesting features. In the evening some things by Glinka are played through (from *Russlan and Ludmilla*), and R. remarks how nothing is ever learned from the great German masters, and foreigners base themselves exclusively on French stereotypes. Then Berlioz's "Queen Mab" and parts of the love scene, with little enjoyment. To end with, R. explains to us C. Frantz's ideas on taxes. A sad reflection on the careless, heartless manner in which such things are written about nowadays! [*The following postscript in the lower margin was obliterated in ink by an unknown hand:* "R. says he feels downright disgusted with Frederick the Great for establishing the Prussian monarchy, which has brought us so much misery; and he himself is only interesting for a few individual features, otherwise a kind of caricature!"]

Sunday, July 6 R. had a good night. Our lighthearted breakfast conversation includes the emancipation of women, a question which is so well treated by C. Frantz. R. says the ladies are always thinking of Portia in *The Merchant of Venice,* but she got a lawyer to tell her what to do. "What a scene that is!" R. exclaims. Then we recall the courtship scene, and how badly it is acted as a rule—was it ever performed better? "Perhaps," says R., "perhaps there was a flourishing period once." — Speaking of the beauty of this scene, he says, "The poet saw what possibilities lay in drawing three separate characters, just as in *Siegfried's Tod* I visualized the Valkyrie and young Siegfried and did not want to let them escape me." At lunch our good mayor; his visit concerns the announcement that it will not be possible to perform *Parsifal* next year, which R. has phrased very succinctly; the management committee is unwilling to sign it, for fear of acting contrary to the agreement and getting into difficulties on that account. R. very much put out, and he says angrily that the declaration must be made, even if he has to go off to America to give concerts. He cannot eat a thing, and leaves the table! The old trouble, always the same kind of cooperation—sufficient to cause obligations, insufficient to be helpful! R. is also unable to take his afternoon rest, he tries a walk, whist in the evening—all under a cloud. Siegfried unwell.

Monday, July 7 As might have been expected, last night was much like the previous ones; R. got up, read C. Frantz, took a sip of cognac, returned to bed, and then went to sleep again. The weather is bad, cold and wet. A nice letter from Dr. Schrön relieves our fears of being taken to court over Naples, and from Bremen a cigar merchant named Wagner asks R. very naïvely to become his son's godfather, promising to bring him up in such a way that R.'s "all-round reputation" will not be affected. — In the afternoon I go to see Herr Gross with my letter to Herr Bürkel (in which I ask to have a new paragraph inserted in the contract), learn from him of the difficulties—that the King's end is felt to be nigh, and that Herr Feustel and Herr Gross have been assuring the skeptical bank in Coburg in particular that the contract would be observed without fail. I ask Herr Gross himself to edit the announcement, which everybody feels must be made. When I go to R. to report on the success of my mission, I find him stretched out on the *chaise longue* (the "Muchanoff") in the *salon,* much upset. The weather, his own position, which in a certain sense remains unaltered, the enormous expenditures revealed by his current account—all this is indeed enough to depress him. Already at lunch he had been talking of emigrating to America. But he rouses himself to write a letter to the

King in which he says that he wishes to produce *Parsifal* only when funds are such to ensure that performances can be given every three years, financed from the interest on the capital. After writing these 7 pages he looks refreshed, but he explains that, out of joy at having completed them at all, he has drunk too much beer. At supper he tells me that he personally has taken C. Frantz's book to the mayor. He is also presenting it to Prof. Fries and K. Kolb. — Around lunchtime he wrote a verse in the copy of *Parsifal* belonging to the 7th Infantry Regiment. Whist in the evening; R. very amused by the bad luck we both always have at cards. — Trials in the evening, again the question of emigrating! "Each seventh year he went a-wooing!" . . . R. recalls his hopes that a group of people, "select" if not large in number, would follow us here. What will become of our children? I stick to my view that whoever grows up under his protection can be called blessed.

Tuesday, July 8 R. had a good night, and once again in our conversation we set the whole world to rights, as he says laughingly when we part. I do not know what led us to purely human factors; R. said Goethe had also tried—in *Tasso,* for example—to dissociate his characters from historical costume, whereas a similar sort of Venetian play by Hugo is stuffed full of historical local color. R. is inclined to agree with me when I compare Goethe's Iphigenia with one of Canova's Greek goddesses. He says the Greeks were fortunate in that their costumes corresponded so well to Nature, whereas in Shakespeare one really believes that men were born the way they appear, with their lordships, etc. — As we part, he invokes upon me the blessings of the god of kindness and truth—oh, may this blessing destroy the last spark of *"will"* inside me! In the afternoon R. writes to Dr. Schrön in Naples, and to the cigar merchant in Bremen, telling him that his godson could learn patience and perseverance from him. — The acquittal of Cassagnac amuses R., he says he knows his Parisians and how they hate the liberals, the gentlemen like Gambetta all portly, etc. — Herr Gross sends us his draft of the announcement, in a form the management committee is willing to sign; R. rejects it, since on no account does he want to commit himself to the year 1881. In the fear that he will now start tormenting himself with new drafts, I quickly write down a few lines; these he accepts and improves, and thus this tiresome intermezzo is disposed of. — A new composition by my father in memory of Petöfi tempts R. to play it. "He wrote that for pianists like me," he laughs, "now I, too, am a Liszt pianist." We are also amused by the work's resemblance to Brünnhilde's question *"War es so niedrig?"* — Then the 2nd act of *Tristan,* from the beginning up to the dream of love, properly sung by R. himself. An indescribable impression—what performance could ever convey the same effect, what singer ever achieve these accents? And then the work itself! If the *Ring* rouses men's hearts to heroic deeds, *Tristan* gives us Nirvana, the non-existence of anything besides love. How gloriously does universal emotion resolve into personal dialogue—and, as R. says, in all the bitterness there are still sparks of wit! But the impression is almost overwhelming. We talk about it, as well as one can after having such an impression, and then R. says with a laugh, "The Emperor exclaimed, 'Wagner must have been very much in love at the time.'" From this quotation he goes on to describe an artist's vision, how completely dissociated it is from personal experience, which only clouds it. He thinks that no artist ever describes what he is experiencing at the moment, not even Dante with Beatrice—he sees all the possibilities contained in it. Our parting today is a silent embrace.

Wednesday, July 9   R. had a good night. He continues reading C. Frantz, still with great pleasure. When I say at lunch how glad I am that yesterday evening did not harm him, whereas *Parsifal* on May 23 had been bad for him, he says: "Oh, that is completely different, when there are other people there. But when I see your face, ennobled by pain, I find it all quite easy." Have I the temerity to write this down? For you, my Siegfried, for you alone, and not to vaunt myself before you, but just so that you may know how we were permitted to live our lives, we who feel so homeless. Over coffee R. once again told me that he is thinking of America, whether to take the children—if leaving them behind, then I to stay with them. I: "On no account. I go with you, I can make arrangements for the children." R.: "For me there isn't a glimmer of hope anywhere, nothing to which I could pin my hopes. What I am living on is due to the popularity of works of mine from which I now turn away in disgust. [*Added at bottom of page:* "Yesterday he received his royalties from Vienna, which still show that *Lohengrin* possesses the greatest drawing power."] This is terrible, and if I continue to put up with it, it is my personal happiness which is to blame, my life with you." The question whether to return or not. The children not with us, so that all would not be lost in case of a catastrophe. To earn enough to pay off the deficit and to be able to set something aside, so as not to have anything more to do with the outside world. Despite the gloom, we part in cheerful spirits! We take a walk, though the weather is unfortunately very windy; then R. goes to Angermann's with Siegfried. In the evening we are visited by Herr Huth, the clarinetist (he took part in our festival and also played under R. in Moscow!). After he has gone a game of whist with the two girls, and after their departure R. reads to me Frantz's excellent character studies of Bismarck and Fr[iedrich] W[ilhelm] IV.

Thursday, July 10   R. had a good night; he retains his good humor, in spite of the terrible weather! He is preparing a continuation of his article and in this connection he looks through the texts of Weber's operas. — In the afternoon, during a huge storm, to the church concert [*program enclosed; see notes*]. All kinds of mishaps: a carriage that does not arrive, then does not shut ("I wonder whether the cabs in St. Louis are better," says R.), then takes us to the wrong door! But the concert we find interesting, some things, such as the "Responsorium," moving and uplifting. But R. is put off by their not singing the published text. He points out how, in the Mendelssohn aria, he first ignores the Holy Ghost entirely and then pays it a compliment! In the evening much about Schumann, whom R. calls a mere village musician, devoid of soul, devoid of inspiration. Herr R. has told us that he is planning to write about him.

Friday, July 11   A restless night for R.; he caught cold yesterday; talked a lot about Naples—to console ourselves for the wild, blustery weather, which robs us of our pleasure in the roses. R. revises his announcement, and immediately afterward the reply comes from Herr Bürkel, the secretary, granting my request. Satisfaction! — R. shows me two portraits in the *Illustrirte:* General Manteuffel, now governor in Alsace, and Lionel Rothschild. These two pictures tell the whole story—Prussianism and Judaism! — In the evening we read Calderón's burlesque *Cefalo and Pocris,* but only the first act—I in particular find this kind of wit embarrassing.

Saturday, July 12   R. had a good night and looks so well that all my worry that he might have caught cold is removed. He is still very much occupied with C. Frantz, whose book he is literally studying. However, over coffee he listens to me telling him things from *The Arabian Nights,* which I am now reading with Siegfried. Yesterday I finished the story of Zobeida and began the story of Amina, which I today complete. Our conversation leads us to the Arabs' sense of form; R. says that in their nomadic life they found time to take pleasure in someone saying things well! — We attempt a walk, R. and I, but we soon return home. I feel very languid. In the evening chat about Bismarck; R. read his latest speech to us: still nothing but vulgar bragging. I wish one could forget all these things. This morning, as we parted, R. said, "I wonder whether God loved the world as much as we love each other?" . . .

Sunday, July 13   R. had a good night, and in the morning he reads C. Frantz and starts on the revision of his article, with which he is quite pleased. In the afternoon we go for a walk, the weather is not good, but at least it is warm. Then R. holds his own "Angermann's" in the summerhouse with friends W. and Rub.; much about C. Frantz;

R. would not feel able to write him an open letter, since there is a sort of crypto-Catholicism about him: "That's how it is with us," "What a wretched state we are in when a man like C. Frantz has to resort to such things." Then he reiterates his thought about "human make-believe, God as truth through compassion." He asks himself whether one should assume that Nature deliberately set out to produce this phenomenon, step by step. But even if one discounts time and space, he says, it has always been thus. The passages in the Bible which try to bring everything into harmony—this is bad, he remarks, but one must have something definite to hold on to! — In the evening R. talks admiringly about America and the American war, the only war whose aim was humane, and we jocularly discuss the founding of a new Bayreuth. He believes we are heading for a complete political breakdown, with social problems coming more and more to the fore, held back by wars. — An hour of whist.

Monday, July 14   R. slept well, and the difficulty with which we part in the morning, always seeking each other out again to obtain another glance, another embrace, reminds me of "Day" in *Tristan!* . . . Life is separation even in the midst of union, and every intense feeling, every impression contains within it a longing for death. — The weather is still bad, showers and cold as if it were April. R. finishes C. Fr.'s book, and in the afternoon, when I go to greet him on my return from some shopping, he tells me he has to write to Frantz, he must get rid of it, his head is so full of it. And after a while he comes up to my room, telling me it is done, he has written himself into a state of dizziness, must go out into the garden a little, then he will read it to me. I am soon summoned and acquainted with his splendid letter. . . . In the evening we read a little bit of Marr's pamphlet, recently sent to us. It is rather superficial. — (Yesterday R. played a theme; the first bar made me think it was an Italian melody, but with the second I knew it was something of his own and guessed *Rienzi*—but it was from his *Liebesmahl* [*der Apostel*]: "That's how I got by, poor fellow that I was," says R.)

Tuesday, July 15   R. had a good night and as he is embracing me exclaims, "The sun is inside us, let the weather outside be as it will!" — Much about church and state; he says, "For me Christianity has not yet arrived, and I am like the early Christians, awaiting Christ's return." — But in the search for ideality, he adds, things look different! — I get Lusch to make a copy of the letter to C. Fr. (see folder 1 in the corner bureau). [*Added two days later but referred back to this point:* "Toward evening R. watches the golden clouds and the sun sinking down like a hero (he quotes K. Moor), and he thinks in a mood of mild reconciliation of his own death."] In the evening we are visited by two American ladies, mother and daughter, devotees and patrons, etc. Some music from *Euryanthe* is played, R. singing Lysiart, Herr Jäger Adolar. Then the *Parsifal* Prelude, also one of the "Pictures" (Siegmund and Sieglinde). The fine and majestic simplicity of the Wagner themes, their nobility, uplifts me once again and brings me consolation. — The American march is also played in honor of our visitors.

Wednesday, July 16 R. slept well, and I had a very delightful dream of a walk with him and the children along the banks of a river, a young, pink-and-mauve-colored eagle alighting on my hand, being put back into a cage, and then reappearing on R.'s shoulder. R. works on his article, still hoping for the weather to turn fine at last, so that he can begin his cure. In the afternoon friend Levi, coming from Paris— he brings me news of my sister Claire and also has many tales to tell about the capital city *par excellence*. We do nothing else but chat, and in the evening the "upright men," Rub., Jäger, Wolzogen, are invited to join the conversation.

Thursday, July 17 R. slept well, though he was up at three o'clock, went downstairs, and saw the waning moon still gleaming as a very pale C on the distant horizon. The weather is fine; a cheerful meal with our friends Levi and Cyriax, who has just arrived from London. The latter tells us of Richter's "triumphs" as a conductor in London, and both speak with enthusiasm of the Comédie Fr[ançaise]. Herr Cyriax has brought me a picture of the house in which R. stayed in Boulogne! R. meets Herr Levi at Angermann's, I send Siegfried there with a note and receive in the lovely sunny evening the following sweet card. [*Enclosed are an empty envelope inscribed in Cosima's handwriting* "Herr Richard via Siegfried" *and a piece of paper on which Wagner has written:* "Oh, how wise! In these temporal problems—as in the eternal ones—I am utterly and completely in agreement with you. Fidi comes running to you to cancel the evening meal. A couple follows more slowly— but follows: God, the infinitely kind, etc."] The "couple" arrives, and R. exclaims that they have set the whole world to rights, Christianity, Judaism, Mohammedanism, everything. In the evening the "upright men" with wives; we make music, Beethoven's *Battle of Vittoria* and *King Stephen,* of which the first is R.'s particular favorite, on account of its popular tone. Then he tells us how he remembers having seen Weber playing with his son on the balcony of his house as the miners were passing by, and on the market place there was a man standing before a placard and singing, "A new murder story to tell you, my readers." Years later R. hears a Weber bassoon concerto being played in the Gewandhaus and recognizes this same melody he had heard sung so roughly on the market place, now appearing as a delicate theme on the oboe! "What does that signify?" R. then asks, referring to the tremendous popular flavor of Beethoven's themes.

Friday, July 18 R. slept well; in the morning, when he leaves me, he goes into his room and plays a rondo theme, which he then elaborates in the course of the morning. A fine day; the children to the Eremitage. I am beset by overwhelming melancholy, which gushes forth in torrents of tears. Can it be that all contact with the outside world is now too much of a strain on me? Or that the lessons today wore me out, and the revision of the domestic account books? That the news about Claire took me back to my youth, to a sort of home which has completely vanished from my memory? Or the coarseness of my external surroundings, of which I am at times only too clearly aware? I do not know, but anyway I was robbed of all strength, and my hand reached out for *De imitatione Christi;* I read several chapters, and life in a nunnery, which spoke temptingly to my youthful spirit, as to all others', once again seemed to me something desirable! — I struggled free of my confusions and in the evening was able to laugh with the family over my "swollen eyes"!

Saturday, July 19 R. had a good night and arranged a drive to Dommayer's. I spend the morning at the photographer's with the children. In the afternoon we drive via the Waldhütte to the Fantaisie, where we have supper in the best of spirits. Really I have never before seen the place looking so pretty as today, when we gazed upon it from the restaurant garden. R. enjoys sitting beside the highway, and with great delight he watches the haycarts passing by; we take a little walk through the Fantaisie itself, thinking of the times when we lived here and everything was full of hope—but then came the fulfillment! ... As we were walking at the Waldhütte, R. spoke about his work and about rhyme—how Beethoven quite rightly constructed his theme in accordance with the first lines of the poem, but subsequently he had been unable to sustain the principle of correct stresses.

Sunday, July 20 R. had a bad night; he thinks that, led into rashness by the happy mood at Dommayer's yesterday, he ate too much trout. I write letters, R. works on his article, also corrects his last one, with which he is pleased; writes to Sascha Ritter, starts legal proceedings against Herr Roeser, and writes to Herr Rühlmann about the MS. of *Iphigénie en Aulide.* The weather is bad again, but we have a cheerful evening with Gogol's *The Government Inspector.*

Monday, July 21 Again a bad night for R., Putz howling in quite a fantastic way; R. goes downstairs, is glad to see the two big dogs sleeping quietly, sees a light in Georg's room: "What spooks' meeting is going on in there?" Georg is fast asleep, having forgotten to put out his light! Then R. went back to sleep, and was awoken, as he tells me, by a pleasant dream: I had come to him in very high spirits with a blue ribbon and had wanted to do something with him, to bind something around him or cut it off. Bad weather! And the books R. is reading are not very enlivening—a new pamphlet about the Jews by Marr, Glagau's *Des Reiches Not*—what would we not give to hear nothing more about politics! An article on Schumann by Herr Rub. gives us pleasure, his ideas are good and his style concise, though he is just a little too spare. A short game of whist and finishing *The Government Inspector* in the evening.

Tuesday, July 22 Another restless night! . . . Letter from Dr. Schrön in Naples, the Villa Maraval no good either, too far from Naples. Five months of negotiations with nothing to show for it but a threatened lawsuit! — R. works on his article (telegrams back and forth with my father about the title of an opera by Hiller!). — In the afternoon Dr. Landgraf; R. is not to start his cure—because bad weather is on its way! Much laughter about this, as also about the suggestion that R. send his extra bottles of Rakoczy water to the town hall, to maintain the water supply! In the end he says to the doctor, "My dear doctor, if you are feeling ill, come to me—I now know all the tricks and dodges!" — Conversation in the evening with the upright men, Rub. and Wolz. Friend Wol. tells us about a miners' revolt in Silesia, due to attempts to reduce their pay; the lancers attacked them, four men dead. Miners! The most wretched of human beings—people shoot them—and we call ourselves Christians! — R. wrote to Dr. Schrön.

Wednesday, July 23 R. again had a restless night, but this does not stop him from going to his work—he says it is the last thing he will ever write. At noon, when I go downstairs, he is playing things from *Die Folkunger;* I do not know what to make of all these reminiscences mixed with glee-club choruses, but I am reminded of a friend who once saw a photograph of her cook in one of her own most elegant dresses! . . . After lunch the following news report [*not discovered*] leads us into the most dismal of conversations. "How can one continue practicing art after that?" he exclaims, and talks of a tour in behalf of the dismissed workers, but then he says with a sigh, "We are too tired." It makes us think again about the poor miners: never mind what madness drove them to their terrible deeds, is not our first duty to help these poor people? Instead they are shot at—oh, God, what a world it is! "And I," R. exclaims, "feel like an utter fool with all my plans." — As if to set the seal on all these sad thoughts, we receive news in the afternoon that the municipal gardener, a splendid man who resourcefully took over the care of our garden following our recent upsets in Wahnfried, has suddenly shot himself. [*A newspaper clipping enclosed; see notes.*] Young, cheerful, active, seemingly without a care, a friendly, helpful man—yet he, too, changed, a mystery, and the plants now blooming in the garden (which years ago he laid out, too) expound the mystery to me, and the trees shake their tops! — R. today read Carlyle on Rousseau, and he quotes to me the pretty remark, "The nobles did not know what to do with Rousseau, but he knew: he had them beheaded" (*French Revolution*). — Books about ghostly apparitions, written by *professors;* R. says, "Really, the Germans are imbeciles." — The day before yesterday, when we were talking at lunch about death, I said I always feared that with the loss of physical strength we should also lose our moral strength and set a dismal example of lack of courage, whereupon R. said: "All I fear is that I shall babble nonsense about the past; a lot of stupid stuff, as the brain becomes confused. And that's why it is right what people say—that a good death is the greatest of blessings." — Toward evening he tells me I am in for a surprise, but he will not say what; then I hear him working on *Parsifal.* "Familiar sounds," I say. He: "And some unfamiliar ones—" (entrance into the Temple, 3rd act). In the evening a very lively game of whist with the children—how children, with the obligation they impose on one, always help merriness to triumph! R. says of Lusch, "She is the cleverest person we know here." (R. is starting proceedings against Herr Roeser.)

Thursday, July 24   R. slept well and today reaches the eleventh page of his article. He is pleased with the quip he wrote at the end (all the operas from Italy, France, and—Judea!). At breakfast we talk about state aid for our cause. Herr Schön wants to approach the Federal Council; R. would claim an allowance of three million marks. In the evening, as we take leave of each other with an embrace, he says, "If our union leads to nothing, then I'm at a loss." We enlarge upon this theme, and I am constrained to tell him my belief: that the Will felt the need to manifest itself in the festival theater, and thus it came about; what people would then do with it was their affair. — In the evening more about Schumann; Herr Rub. plays the Andante from the Sonata in F-sharp Minor, and R. laughingly agrees with me when I compare it with the drink known to no other nation but the Germans, the *Maitrank,* with strawberries, giving a curiously fuddling effect. — Toward evening, before our meal, he read to me the beginning of his article. Much concern about Fidi; fears of his falling into bad company! . . . Melancholy delight in the garden, which the municipal gardener laid out so neatly for us.

Friday, July 25   A good night. R. is greeted by six little chicks, born during the night, which give him great delight (Georg brought them to him in a basket). — Conversation on all kinds of things in the morning: Dante's and Milton's Satan; Doré's illustrations (which R. much admires); and finally, on having thought as he got up of "the high-minded Tithonus," Schiller's *"Die Götter Griechenlands,"* and the fine feelings it aroused. R. works; in the afternoon, since all the children are away on an outing, we stroll in the garden, inspect the poultry yard, and then have the horses harnessed in order to drive to the Bodenmühle. A very lovely walk; a true idyll, so close to the town! . . . Siegfried meanwhile at the funeral of our poor municipal gardener. — In the evening a wide-ranging conversation: R. explains to Herr Rub. Schopenhauer's theory on the origin of the human race and the emigration and return home of the first Indians. We go on talking till late into the night.

Saturday, July 26 R. slept well and again settles down to his work, from which he tells me another very funny remark (about Brahman marriages). The weather is fine, the children are at the Eremitage, R. and I follow them there in the carriage, a lovely evening, intoxicating scent of linden blossoms, delight in the children ("Our only link with the outside world," says R., who feels he should be paying them much more attention, living with them much more, taking part in their education!). The photographs after this year's May Festival please him greatly; he thinks Fidi looks like the Goethe in the small edition (1834). In the evening he reads the final pages of his article to friend Wolzogen and me. He also gives him C. Frantz's reply to his letter, which is very distressing, in regard both to the circumstances which are now pushing this talented man in the direction of the Catholic party and to his own lack of clarity in philosophical matters, which makes him look like a complete fanatic.

Sunday, July 27 Heavy thunderstorm during the night which kept us awake, and today it is wet and cold. R. works, I have to lie down, for my fatigue literally forbids me to stay up. But I go downstairs in the evening. R. has been to Angermann's with Siegfried and laughed heartily to see Fidi being served in a glass of his own, marked "Herr Siegfried Wagner." In the evening whist and perusal of modern operas, *Armin, Folkunger, Königin von Saba;* it turns out that the Israelite's work is after all the best, musically more refined; but one cannot take any of these things seriously. The libretto of *Armin,* with its repulsive and superficial patriotism, aimed merely at effect, is truly horrifying. — (Prof. Rühlmann, son of the trombonist in R.'s orchestra, promises to send the manuscript of *Iphigénie en Aulide.*)

Monday, July 28 R. slept well, and I am again in control of myself! He works, I prepare the apartment for my father. Letters from poor Herr Tappert, wasting away in Berlin—how to help him? It is unutterably sad, looking at the outside world! R. has the satisfaction of securing an engagement for Herr Zumpe, the oldest member of the Nibelungen Kanzlei, in Frankfurt a/M. — R. works, but spoils his whole morning by reading the libretto of *Die Königin von Saba* and looking at the music. — I pay some calls, and when I come home I find friend W. and Herr Schloemp, the publisher from Leipzig, and R. in a kind of despair, which makes us laugh, however, when we are again united and face the hardship together! — In the evening whist and—chat.

Tuesday, July 29 R. slept well and finishes his article, telling me about it at the end; he is somewhat tired and says he does not intend to write anything more. Fine weather; outing to the Schlehenmühle via Wolfsbach, splendid walk through the woods as far as Bruckmühl, nice drive home; we were 16 in all; stop on the highway, a merry sight, R. in very good spirits, and his slight vexation over a detour and the coachman's heedlessness is soon forgotten. Delight in our pretty countryside. In the evening friend Feustel; much politics, he entirely for Bismarck, whereupon R. with splendid vivacity points out to him in what way B. is unequal to the task Fate has imposed on him. The evening not too unpleasant for R., and he goes to bed in good spirits.

Wednesday, July 30 Since the weather is nice, R. starts on his cure, drinks a glass of Rakoczy, and goes for a walk in the palace gardens with Boni. Perhaps it did not agree with him, or the outing yesterday put too much of a strain on him, for he is again complaining of tightness in the chest. "You are troubled in your soul," he says, "I in my chest, I feel very limp and have to push myself to do anything." R. had a letter to write to Breitkopf und H[ärtel], who have brought out a "popular" edition of *Tristan und Isolde!* He urges them to engrave the score of *Lohengrin,* which after all has caused them no losses. — Herr Rubinstein told us recently of a poem in *Kladderadatsch:* "It is decreed in Bismarck's plan that all he owns must every man pay tax on"; this leads us to Mendelssohn's song, and today R. plays to me the moving strains he himself discovered for the first line of the text: '*Es ist bestimmt in Gottes Rat.*' " — He wrote this down in his notebook in the winter of 1858. — When I tell him I have been dictating to the children how paper and ink are made, R. says, "Nobody ever taught me that, and yet I knew it; I once saw a poor scribe making ink for himself out of oak apples, since he had no money to buy any." Everything is like that with him—he knows, though nobody has in fact ever taught him. He copies his article and shows me the many alterations he has made. In the evening we are disturbed by some particularly harsh treatment of our Siegfried. R. so upset that I regret having told him about it; I did so in order to receive his advice, out of fear that I might be becoming too insensitive. But it would be better to spare R. such things. — Since we are alone together in the evening, our proximity soon dispels all lingering discords. We look through the notebook containing his very first sketches for *Tristan*. Then we become immersed in a discussion on art, remarking that the Germans have not discovered their own true form. I: "In your works." The cosmopolitan significance of these works: if the French, the Italians, the English were to learn German, they would recognize the fully developed form in them. Coming to his article, R. says, "If I now give everything up—my writing, the Society of Patrons—as I so often have a mind to—then that is the end of us, the theater will molder, and our idea will have departed forever." — I observe that we must be patient and just go on firmly reiterating our point of view, however difficult to keep persisting and however much we should prefer to lapse into complete silence—and this even when we expect nothing from our persistence. — Before that he read me something from Aristotle on perception, and he also began on Polybius; I, for my part, show him the passage on fear in Plutarch's life of Cleomenes; I ask him whether with this he does not mean "awe" in Goethe's sense of the word, and he agrees in part; in connection with this we discuss the great men whom the ancient worlds of Greece and Rome brought forth in such vast numbers; we, on the other hand, tremble at the thought that Bismarck might hand in his resignation! . . .

Thursday, July 31 R. did not sleep well; the consequence of some vexation he experienced yesterday—or the cure? He takes a bath, which refreshes him, and in our breakfast conversation we come via C. Frantz and his Schellingianism to Schopenhauer and his "Will." Yesterday R. said that everything manifests itself as *a hunger,* a splendid name Schopenhauer gave to "something hollow and ungraspable." Sad that so few are capable of accepting this doctrine; because it makes no concessions to politics, ignorant people believe that it inhibits activity. — The fact that human beings fashion laws in accordance with their understanding of things, that does not prove the validity of these laws, nor does it explain the things themselves; "Will" is an explanation. — R. has received a letter from a woman in Wiesbaden who sends him a book about vivisection and in well-turned phrases asks him to join in taking steps against such cruelty; she believes that its rapid growth is due to the great numbers of Jewish doctors. R. deeply moved and incensed by it; he says if he were a younger man he would not rest until he had brought about a demonstration against such barbarism. He says religion should be linked with compassion for animals; human beings' treatment of one another is already bad enough, for they are so vindictive they put up a resistance to one another, and the noble teachings of Christianity are scarcely applicable. One should begin with quiet and patient creatures, and people who felt compassion for animals would certainly not be harsh toward human beings.

"We must preach a new religion, you and I." This conversation, which he resumes in the evening, leads quite naturally to his deeply moving *"Es ist bestimmt."* — It resounds within me like a terrible exhortation—and how many partings have I already experienced! R. himself describes it as "sounds like those outside the portals of a monastery, and even more—complete renunciation, mortification." "You can imagine my dismay," he says to Rub., "when I saw Mendelss[ohn]'s song—ah, that is something quite different, quite different, I thought to myself." — In the morning he read Calderón's burlesque to the end, and he finds it horrible, a precursor of Offenbach; after the 1st act I did not wish to continue reading it, and now I am reminded of this cold, hairsplitting author, his humor, and the Catholic Renaissance rears up before me; against it the Protestantism of Luther, Goethe, Schiller, Dürer, Bach, *Parsifal*—and Catholicism itself, when hidden within it were the seeds of Protestantism, pre-Jesuitical! Dante, Palestrina, perhaps Shakespeare. R. also reads some pieces in a little book by Daudet which I recommended to him and which made a very good impression on him (*Contes choisis:* "*Le Décor,*" "*Les Deux Auberges,*" "*Les Douaniers*"). In the afternoon R. continues with the revision of his article. He is not well—is his cure perhaps doing him harm? — In the evening Herr Rub. plays Beethoven's *Waldstein* Sonata to us; for all its mastery it appeals to R. less than the sonatas of the first period; he calls the theme cold and stiff and exclaims, "I cannot bear cold music." Then he remarks how incomparably less significant B.'s first symphony is than the first compositions for piano: B. went through a period of relapse into pedantry, he says. In connection with the repulsive wit of the Calderón farce we were reminded of the two shepherds in *A Winter's Tale,* the carriers in *Henry IV,* and in addition the sturdily dignified language of the kings and nobles: "One sees a whole nation before one's eyes."

Friday, August 1   R. had a bad night, the subject of vivisection on his mind. He tells me in two parts about a curious dream: waking up the first time, he says Pohl told him his wife was earning him so much money, 17,000 marks annually; then R. goes to sleep, wakes up again, and tells me he has just dreamed that Pohl's wife is earning all this money with acrostics, which she composes for newspapers. — Is this sleeplessness due to moral impressions or to physical causes? Yesterday R. told me in great agitation what Herr v. Schlör had to say about the present policy of compromise—it drives one to despair! — But in the morning R. is tolerably well again, and when he looks at me on our first parting and feels that I am looking rather languid, he puts new strength into me, saying, "She shall never weep!" — A visit from Buonamici at midday, much pleasure in his gay and lively Italian character; in the evening he plays to us Beeth.'s Variations in F (Opus 33?), which R. calls a "lovable work" and which he plays quite splendidly, bringing out the motives so beautifully and shaping it with such refinement that we are truly entranced by it. Then R. gets Rub. to play some passages from *Parsifal,* the Flower Maidens and the entrance into the Temple (3rd act) with the altered bars; when he hears the chords on which Parsifal receives the robe of the Knights of the Grail, R. comments on the awful change which is now taking place inside him, now that everything has been decided; I tell R. that it arouses in me the feeling that "*Es ist bestimmt in Gottes Rat.*" R. agrees and tells me that this theme expresses the awful disgust with life he was feeling at the time he wrote it; I tell him that what I find so curiously magnificent about it is its lack of sentimentality, its almost Lutheran character.

Saturday, August 2   R. had a good night and decides to have breakfast in the summerhouse. Friend Heckel is announced. — When I am in my bath, I hear R. laughing loudly, and he calls out to me, "It is decreed in God's great plan that all that bores him most must every man go through again," which makes us both laugh a lot; but though the verse occurred to him during Heckel's visit, it does not apply to our friend, whom, in his capacity as theater director, R. sees as a Götz von Berlichingen, and who is a true German. After R. has gone, I listen with the greatest pleasure to his description of the *Ring* performances in Mannheim, in which he once again displayed all his efficiency. — I repeat it to R. at lunch, and he, too, is very pleased. *Faust* arrives; he has given me his old copy, which came from Minna and which contains his markings for the *Faust* Overture and the Ninth, and I lay an identical copy at his feet. — Over coffee, on the subject of Heckel, we talked about Germany, so difficult to understand. — My sister, so talented, never to be won over to it at all, I myself won over by *Tannhäuser,* the prayer in *Lohengrin.* Regret that it had to be Hans through whom I came to R.; R. asks whether we would otherwise have discovered each other; he thinks that, if I had been with the Oliviers in Paris, that time in '59, we should have got to know each other. But it all had to be won through blood! — In the evening a drive to the Eremitage with Heckel, supper there, return by moonlight, everything dream, dream, dream—Nibelung figures and melodies flit past in moonbeams and linden-blossom perfumes, in the distance the plain and noble building!

Sunday, August 3   Unfortunately R. did not have a good night— very hot; he remains downstairs in the *salon,* reads, and does some writing. We also, for once, have breakfast in the *salon.* The heat allows us to go outdoors only in the evening, we have supper in the open and then go for a moonlight walk in the palace gardens; delight in the glowworms in the shrubbery, "They're telling themselves, 'Dark's the time for sparks,' " says R. — It is ten o'clock before we return to the *salon,* and R. sings "Leave me the veil, I beg" as an example of absurd declamation and the desire for "melody at all costs"! We accompany Rub. to the gate and then stroll in the garden, R. and I.

Monday, August 4 R. slept well. . . . He works and is cheerful, reads Daudet, even things I did not recommend, such as *"Le Pape est mort,"* and despite various slight domestic vexations, our supper in the garden is merry, as also another walk in the palace gardens; after which we go through *La Dame Blanche* (the auction), which R. regards as a model of what the French spirit can produce. "In comparison with that we are a nation of drunken artisans," he says. — R. is pleased with my picture, the bold positioning of the hand, etc. Discussion about my father, his uncongenial life; R. says: "I am a bit odd myself, but I had quite different ideas. The domestic life I have achieved was, of course, dependent on you; I could not have stood it in Zurich—it would have been too stuffy for me; and Paris, where I again got Minna to come, was the last attempt; after that I was wiser: never again! I suppose I, too, tended toward the extraordinary." —

Tuesday, August 5 R. had a good night; our morning conversation is devoted to England, R. says he would like to read a witty writer's precise description of that curious country, of which Carlyle had given him some glimpses. — A volume of V. Hugo (dramas) with illustrations brings this gaudy and already so outmoded world very close to us, and the sight fills us with astonishment for its talents, and with repugnance. At lunch reminiscences of R.'s sisters; he describes them to our children, telling them they were much more efficient than his brothers; touching memories of Klara Wolfram, how beautifully she sang to him the Siegfried theme, which he had just written down to remind himself; poor, lost creature. — Over coffee he tells me the story of *Marie Tudor* and also of *Angelo,* in which Minna had been very touching. — He finishes his article today. Supper in the open. [*Added later:* "Very merry. R. said, 'I want nothing else but the children, have no desire to modulate, am content with C major.' "] Then fireworks—somewhat unsuccessful, but fun all the same. A long evening; R. reads his article aloud and then shows us some passages from *Templer und Jüdin,* the loveliest of all Bois-Guilbert's whisper to Rebecca in the final act and his reply to the Grand Master. — But as the evening ends he talks without joy about his article: "I feel I am being a fool—it won't do any good at all."

Wednesday, August 6 R. wakes up with a headache, the reading was a strain on him; he looks through his article again and corrects it, so as at last to be rid of it—very relieved about that, as he says. Yesterday he read—and in the morning tells me about—the story of the *Turco* in Daudet, which seems to him very well done—by comparison V. Hugo just looks like an ogre, he says (he reads some pages from *Hernani*). Herr Rubinstein brings along his article on Schumann, which R. finds excellent and which he sends straight to the printers. Wolz. is his philologist, he says, and Rub. would be his musician. Whist in the evening. In spite of his headache we have much fun during the day; R. describes his continual battles with the law of gravity—how he had wanted to draw the curtains up, had got entangled with them, and then it took him ages to sort it all out. — Glorious sunset, delight in the view from the dressing room, delight in his dressing room, "a convolution of pleasant things," as he says. But before these delights I hear him say, "How sad it is!" "What?" "That when one wants to say something one finds nothing to attack now beyond bogeys like Schumann—that is sad. Oh, what a world we live in!" Recently we told ourselves that, if we had not had the children, we should probably have been constantly traveling about, first India, then Brazil, etc. — From such reflections I prefer to direct his attention to our home, and it is my triumph to hear him exclaim once again, "I think things are going too well for me." Today over coffee in the summerhouse he proclaimed that between the ages of 70 and 80 he would "become a very quiet and pleasant gentleman," adding, "but not shrivel up mentally!"

Thursday, August 7 R. had a good night; in the morning reminiscences of earlier days; what would have become of him, he asks, if the King had not come into his life? "I had no friends in the sense that they took a truly genuine interest in my life. Just think of people like the Willes, who were really close to me yet meant nothing to me." — A young man asks permission to call and R. receives him: "A very handsome Jew," he tells me afterward, "or *métis* [half-caste]"—fairhaired and sweet. R. observes that we ought to give Fidi a crooked nose. — Around lunchtime I find R. engaged on a once familiar task— he is ruling a score! He has "pinched" my copy of the Prelude, since I would not give it up; he also knows what alterations he made in it. He says he is now going to write the score and keep it in a safe until the world becomes worthy of a performance. — In the evening the mail brings us an appeal to women to demonstrate against vivisection, announcing a meeting of the animal-protection society in Gotha; R. resolves first to go, then to get someone to represent him there and to write an article. — Many thoughts on religion; I tell him various things about the life of Cleomenes, which I have been reading to the children; among other things, his restoration of equality of possessions: "Something like that must come, and a man of genius, of great feeling, will take the lead." In the evening he says he feels so ashamed before people like Schuré and even Herwegh, having expected so much from men such as these German princes, this Emperor: "Just look at him!" — I observe that it was not by people but by the movement itself that one expected people to be drawn along. "Yes," he says, "but that can be misconstrued."

Friday, August 8 R. was up twice during the night, but he does not complain. "I am now already ten years older than Beethoven was." I observe that B. was left alone to die; he says that perhaps he was untamable, like my father, but people had nevertheless taken care of my father—though certainly not the Germans. R.: "Heaven preserve me from German women!" He laughs and says that when one talks of deep inside, things look so horrible in the human body, but he uses this as a starting point to enlarge upon ideality and the thing-in-itself. At lunchtime he plucks for me the rose whose scent and color have entranced him. But he says vivisection is worrying him, he has not yet made up his mind how to take part in the movement. — He reads some more things in Daudet which I did not recommend but which nevertheless interested him (such as *"Le Concert de la huitième"*), then says he has now had enough, adding that he started on the Bible today and cannot get over his astonishment that in England and elsewhere this story of the Creation is still the basis of religious instruction; all the same, the sense of sin through knowledge is a fine one. He asks me whether I have been reading *my* or *his* copy of *Faust,* and the mere mention of our *German book* leads us to savor its splendid images. The greatest thing in it, R. thinks, is the "Classical Walpurgis Night," all of it dramatic, conceived for the stage, but without recalling what stages were like in a country with no popular art such as that possessed by the Greeks, who created a popular art for educated people. — We have our coffee in the summerhouse; vexation with the *Fl[iegende] B[lätter]*, which pokes fun at the animal-protection society; in the *Illustrirte* a portrait of Prince Napoleon; R. says he resembles the conductor Abt and N. I. — Walk with R.: kept an eye on Fidi at his swimming class; on our return he espies us in the distance and calls, "Cockadoodledo"! — In the evening friends Wolz. and Rub., R. somewhat silent, his mind occupied with his problem. — [*Added at the foot of this and the following two pages: "Postscript to the previous days.* Yesterday: I found R. in the *salon,* looking up the word '*Friede*' ['peace'] in Grimm's dictionary and feeling pleased that the meaning bore out his motto for our house: *Schutz* [protection], *Tutela, Einfriedigung* [enclosure]! He called the present way of the world a 'mummery.' — When we had Frau Dr. Herz here yesterday for Loldi and she talked about all the cures for cripples, R. said, 'That's the way it is: one tends the cripples and suffocates the healthy ones.' — When he recently read his article to me, he said, 'Love, its complete unfolding and its power—that has never before been expressed in music as it is in Brünnhilde and Isolde.' I mention Elisabeth, whereupon he: 'Yes, but she is only a bud, and killed off in bud.' — Thoughts of having the *Idyll* pulped after paying back the costs of it—after all, it was yielded up only in order to release *Parsifal!* — His reading of Daudet leads R. to look at Doré's *Don Quixote* illustrations, which fill him with disgust: 'The French don't understand that kind of humor.' "]

Saturday, August 9 R. had a good night, but he is awakened by a dream in which he wept: I had been cold and strange toward him and had wanted to leave him! — Not vivisected but vivified is our feeling as we invoke blessings on the day. — R. writes to the animal-protection society in Dresden; yesterday he said that when one joined such a demonstration, one must become like Kohlhaas; that reminds us of the beauty of this story, pleasure in which is spoiled only by the fairy-tale ending; when I observe that in *Käthchen* [*von Heilbronn*] the arrival of Emperor Maximilian also has a disturbing effect, he says, "The power of blood is raised to magical levels—she could not be a child of the people." We go for a walk in the garden and are delighted with the children's description of the arrival of the 1,600 singers. In the evening R. recalls it and gets Herr Rub. to play the 3rd act of *Die Meistersinger;* blissful delight—what nation ever had its great men so ideally restored to it as with Sachs, Wolfram, Heinrich? — R. had a talk with Dr. Landgraf about vivisection; the latter denies that the animals feel any pain, saying that if they did, one would be unable to make any observations on them. R. is sent a protest against the Jews from Dresden.

Sunday, August 10 R. had a good night; the overcast skies and cold, wet weather do have an oppressive effect on him, but he is firmly resolved to start on his score. He reads a book about the Old Testament and then, for fun, V. Hugo's L[*ucrèce*] *Borgia,* which disgusts him. In the afternoon the singers' procession, with virgins clad in white and much noise; R., the children, and I cannot help laughing heartily, for there is much absurdity to be seen. In the evening a visit from Herr Löffler (Kundry) and a Dr. Kienzl from Graz, conversation about many things, which R. brings to an end by having a Bach prelude and fugue played.

Monday, August 11 As I went to bed last night, I remembered that it was the night of the Perseids, and I invoked all their blessings on R., begging fulfillment of my single wish. R. slept well and receives a nice letter from the King, which he reads to me; then I am suddenly summoned, and the doctor tells me that Eva, since yesterday slightly unwell, has scarlet fever. Many precautions to be taken, the other children to leave the house, R. goes with them to the Fantaisie and then, since there is no room there, to the Sonne, where they also sleep. Our sick child very quiet and resigned. In the evening R. and I alone in the *salon,* curious feelings. I am particularly concerned by R.'s complaining to the doctor of pains in his chest. Maybe his first shock about Eva did him harm?

Tuesday, August 12 Eva had a restless night, but the doctor is not worried; breakfast with R. in the children's *salon;* the children are not being sent to the Fantaisie but will be put up at the Riedelsberg through friend Feustel's kindness. In this matter one can see both the difference and the harmony between R.'s character and mine; the Riedelsberg occurred to me because I found it hard to think of the children in a hotel (the Fantaisie), but I should never have requested it; R. wrote at once and arranged it all. Very fine weather. R. visits Eva, who cries when she sees him. At lunch R. says his feelings of sympathy prevent him from working, but over coffee in the summer-house he is cheerful, enjoys the fine day, and thanks the heavens for our life, in which even a heavy blow turns out well. While I stay at home with the little invalid, he visits the children and the Feustels at the Riedelsberg and returns home very contented. A letter from Prof. Nohl gives him cause to believe that Jews have taken over the two musical periodicals (Kahnt's and Leuckert's), and that gives rise to the theory that Jews are after all better than cultural Philistines! Then he reads to me parts of the biography of Beethoven; much delight in the words "No more operas, I shall write in *my own* way!" — The description of B.'s return home, however, after the performance of the 9th, his going to sleep in his green jacket, cuts me to the heart—nobody to receive the great man, just Schindler with an account of the proceeds! . . . R. tells me he dreamed that he wanted to play the A Minor Quartet with me but could not, since he wanted to take it in $\frac{4}{4}$ time. Yesterday he told me that he had had a very unpleasant dream about a "Mme Claudius" from Magdeburg, and he feared that in death all sorts of "stupid stuff" would come back to him.

Wednesday, August 13 R. got up at 5 o'clock and wrote down something which he told me yesterday evening he had composed. This touches me strangely; the stillness at the bedside of the little invalid had conjured up pictures in my mind which I wished to present to R. on the 25th; the quietness and the unity of our life made me aware of what was in my feelings. The children come from the Riedelsberg to eat with us, R. goes there but returns home feeling low—the children's gloomy spirits have upset him. — In the evening read about vivisection in the newspaper.

Thursday, August 14 R. had a good night, and our little girl's illness is running its normal course. . . . We continue to share the children between us, he the healthy ones, I the sick one. Luckily the weather is glorious, and though I have a headache, my mood is wonderfully happy, as always when I am alone with R., overshadowed only by the knowledge of my unworthiness, my worry about his health. He writes to Herr v. Weber, sends 100 marks for the society, and expresses his idea of reviving religion through the love of animals, the love of human beings, particularly with regard to vivisectors, being by comparison somewhat difficult. — In the evening Herr Rub.'s article on Schumann in proof.

Friday, August 15   R. was up frequently during the night, and since my worry brings me close to the most extreme thoughts, I ask him if he really believes what he wrote at the conclusion of his program note on the Prelude to *T. und Isolde*—that one is never further away from the blessed region than when one attempts to enter it by force—should the loving woman outlive her lover. We decide to leave it all to Fate—and conclude the discussion with peals of laughter: a friend of mine writes about the remarriage of a Herr Harburger and adds that it is always the men who have loved their wives who remarry most quickly! So today R. is known as Herr Harburger! — Eva's condition causing no anxiety. We talk a lot about her, she always has a charming smile but at the same time is very deep and serious and full of wit; she is like R. — I am pleased to find in her eyes the depth and sharpness of R.'s eyes, in Loldi's gaze their ecstasy, and in Fidi's their humor. R. not well, undertakes the proofreading of Rubinstein's article with reluctance. We stick to our division of the children, he the healthy ones, I the sick one. In the evening we read Nohl's popular biography of Beethoven—curious ancestry! The journey to Berlin R. puts down to the restlessness of a genius, seeking something which he never finds, and the favors of the Viennese nobility to pangs of conscience over their neglect of Mozart.

Saturday, August 16   R. slept well. As usual, he visits Evchen in the early morning. A periodical, *Mode Illustrée,* causes us to remark that with the French Revolution the naïve imaginative interest in costume disappeared; people are no longer able to dress themselves. — Over our after-lunch coffee it is again Beethoven's ancestry which occupies us; R. says one cannot sufficiently disregard time and space—an electric spark can still strike after skipping several generations. B. got nothing from Frederick the Great, R. says with a laugh, but he did from Frederick's father! — R. walks to the Riedelsberg with the children and returns on a zigzag course after countless adventures (Marke does not wish to leave Loldi) and wrong turnings. He walked for two whole hours. — In the evening the two of us cozily alone together; R. says,

"I shall always keep a child with scarlet fever on hand, so people will stay away from our house." It is only the children he wants—he misses Loldi and Fidi in the poultry yard. I read aloud a little from Nohl's *Beethoven*, R. objecting to the bringing together of *Fidelio* and the real-life love episode: "I shall have to write something one day about the manner in which the life of the spirit goes its own way and has nothing to do with actual experiences—indeed it is, rather, the things one does not find which provide the images." — He reads to me two scenes from *Angelo,* which he finds well constructed, one between Katharina, Angelo, and Tisbe, the other between Kath. and Tisbe, the latter indeed touching. We laugh heartily about *"avec votre manie de tout dire"* ["with your craze for putting everything into words"]. — Afterward conversation, reflections on the present world, Catholic services and seneschals and other uniforms, costume, comparison with the Antonine empire. I: "They had no music." He: "And so were spared a Schumann or a Brahms." — Actually a picture of the destruction of all existing things, the ravages of power of the most brutal kind, at last the emergence of a new preacher of Christianity, from whom one could get the feeling that it is all in its very earliest stages! . . . It is precisely because the Gospels have come down to us from such a narrow circle, R. says, that they are so divine; just like the Chaldean shepherd in the wilderness, who saw and observed nothing except the stars above him, they cannot be compared to anything that was said before or after them. — A book by Claude Bernard about vivisection, sent to us by the society, gives us a deeper insight into this horrible practice, which has now become the usual thing.

Sunday, August 17   R. slept well, but he is tired and complains of tightness in his chest and an inflamed throat; the doctor, whom I question about this, feels it is not good for R. to take such long walks as the one he took yesterday; he talks of overtiring the heart. — Eva's condition good, weather still fine; R. has a bridge put up, so that the children have a direct route to us from the Riedelsberg. In the evening we drive out to the children, after they have had lunch with us as usual and then immediately left. Concern that R. should not speak; he looks worn out. However, he tells me the story of *Ruy Blas,* which he has just been reading; grotesque stuff, but good theater.

Monday, August 18   R. slept well and appears refreshed. Today I am borne along on the wings of *"selig, wie die Sonne meines Glückes lacht"* ["blissful, as the sunshine of my fortune laughs"], and in the afternoon, while I am with Eva, R. plays it for me downstairs! — At lunch he tells me about his present reading—*The Old Testament,* the story of Sarah—and he remarks that Israel has always been what it now is; the fact that Christ was born in its lands does it no credit, for, as

from extreme poverty, a god must also emerge from extreme wickedness. Still much vivisection! Real horrors are coming to light here; the
Latin nations utterly unsympathetic, the English on the other hand
indignantly active, successful. — We drive out to the children in the
rain, curious feelings grip me at the sight of the little estate, lying there
like an isolated island—how remote from the whole world we seem, we
and our children, battered by storms, rescued from ruin, completely
estranged from the world! — R. plays billiards with the children, and
then we go home. In the evening Plato, Socrates's speech in his own
defense. Glorious impression! R. finds it praiseworthy that in his
negation he touches on the nature of philosophy. What would be the
positive aspect, one might ask? That which cannot be spoken, the
soul's peace which unfolds from the annihilation of all deception and
inspires deeds. [*Added below:* "A feature of R.'s life: Herr Tappert asks
for 600 marks, after failing to pay the previous 500. First of all R. asks
friend Feustel what to do, but he grows daily more and more impatient
in his eagerness to help, and although he does not possess this sum, he
tells Herr Gross to send it! — His feelings could be described as
impetuous sympathy."]

Tuesday, August 19   R.'s night was not entirely good, though also
not bad; our breakfast conversation is again about Socrates's defense:
"That is the height of art," says R., "but that came naturally to the
Greeks." I continue to reflect inwardly on negation, and, though I find
it hard to put into words (perhaps because I have not yet thought it
out clearly), it seems to me that art should not concentrate entirely on
positive aspects, either; abstract beauty produces the Byzantine Christ,
and representations of heavenly bliss produce unfortunate pictures and
not very good music; by comparison, the transmutation of Isolde,
based on extinction, Brünnhilde's blissful happiness, based on downfall, are beautiful, as, too, is the Christ of the tribute money, with his
bitter, individual mildness; and it is not the Madonna Gloriosa who
speaks to us in Goethe, but Gretchen! R. starts his birthday letter to the
King. Merry lunch with the children—then at about 7 o'clock we
drive out to them in the rain. R. is delighted with their very diverse
personalities and when we arrive home repeats, "They are all we have,
and it is always interesting to watch their development." — In the
evening, when we are alone in the *salon,* we talk about the King, though
first about Marie Hohenlohe, whose "wickedness" he can explain; but
of the King he says that this one year which turned him away from
utter devotion into vagaries of taste and a complete denial of our cause
is incomprehensible; I try to explain it by saying that the King is no
normal being: "The Will wished to help you, and knew no other way
of doing it in the present circumstances; an anomaly, such as you are,

can be helped only by another anomaly, an additional cause of suffering for you." — Regarding Semper's funeral, R. tells me that the Protestant parson in Rome and Prof. Moleschott quarreled about who should deliver the address at the graveside; in the end they both spoke—a nondenominational burial! — Twenty-two years ago my wedding day, journey to Zurich, saw R. there!

Wednesday, August 20 R. had a good night; today he finishes his letter to the King and tells me that in it he has also touched on the subject of vivisection. Coffee in the garden, a fine day, we walk through the meadows to the Riedelsberg, across the bridge R. had erected so as to give the children a direct route to us. Always creative in the small as well as the large things; and it is a constant source of amazement to me how, in the unsettled conditions of his life, he has always had this urge to found, to build, to achieve permanence! There is a curious connection between the vitality of his inner contemplation and the acuteness of his vision, which allows nothing in the outward appearance to escape him, whereas he soon becomes blind to external circumstances in general. — Beer with the children at the Riedelsberg, after which R. and I drive home. Greeted the theater! For other theaters in the world, marble and costly decorations; for thee, dedicated to higher things, just wood and brick, reminding me of the crib of our Saviour! A lovely evening, both of us deeply involved in our conversation; still pursuing the subject of negation; in the world of morals, for example, it seems to me that it is enough to make no reply when one is offended, to keep silent when in the extremity of pain, in order to enable goodness to emerge from us; also never to tell a lie, so that we may live in truthfulness. We come to the subject of *affirmation,* Domenico in the *Dante* Symphony! At the end of it R. goes to the French window and calls me to come and look at the sky, which glitters down on us wonderfully. One star in particular shines powerfully down on us. I think it is Venus, R. thinks not. I am borne up by a wonderful feeling, as on waves of ecstasy, the world so far away! All is still, no suffering that does not melt into joy—is it the even greater solitariness which produced this effect?

At the beginning of the evening R. improvised for me "in the style of Chopin"; he did it as a joke, but it was lovely all the same.

Thursday–Sunday, August 21–31 My father's visit—R. and he splendid together; R. remarkably patient, even when listening to music which gives him no pleasure. Much talk about vivisection, much whist in the evening, a great deal of joking by R. about the "old priest" he wants made into a cardinal. — On the 23rd R. starts on the orchestration, but soon breaks off. . . . He is greatly stimulated by his reading of Haug's *Old Testament,* and he tells me his ideas on our religion, which he intends to put down in writing again. Pleasure in Eva's patience. On the 25th deep and tender communion with R., who plays the *Idyll* to me; he tells me he wants to live, not to think of dying. On one occasion we go to visit the children at the Riedelsberg with my father. — On Friday the 29th, 2nd act of *Parsifal,* R. tired. — In the evening we three alone, whist with a dummy, impossible for me to play against R. or to see him in a difficult situation without wanting to help him. Nice letter from the King, who is pleased with our little gift. On Sunday, August 31, at 1:10, my father departs with Lusch; they are spending a day in Munich, from there he goes on to Rome, she to our friends the Bassenheims. Rainy day. We walk from the station to the Riedelsberg with the 3 children and bring their stay there to an end. Quiet lunch, much that cannot be spoken, in the evening the children to the Sonne hotel. R. and I alone; deep silence, a star shines gloriously in between curtain and window frame, a greeting full of promise! I feel it in the depths of my soul. R. watches it as it runs like a glowworm through the clouds and is lost in the heavens; but with what grandeur and benevolence it peeked in on me as I sat on the sofa beside the piano! We stay silent or chat, R. and I, deeply at one in all we do.

Monday, September 1   R. had a good night. Cheerful breakfast, then all sorts of domestic work for me, the children installed in the annex, papers sorted. (Received some autographs yesterday.) Eva has her first bath. R. corrects his article and reads Haug's book with great excitement, learning more and more about the Jewish character. The enclosed newspaper report [*not found*] interests him, and he says, "I know why I held on so long, I knew that things would one day turn out well for me; now I hold on because things are going so well." — Fine weather; a lot of military music and drum beating, which makes R. irritable; he says this eternal sprightly jubilation hardly suits the present state of our country. (A pamphlet by Herr v. Weber about the colonization of Africa has depressed him, German interests neglected everywhere!) In the evening whist with Herr Rub., after a discussion about a business advertisement planned by friend W. has strengthened our resolve to remain silent. — We are now completely submerged in our Wahnfried world, we do not, by tacit consent, talk about the things that oppress us, but let our feelings be ruled by all the things which enliven and inspire us.

Tuesday, September 2   R. got up once, but he does not complain; our complete withdrawal into our tranquillity permits us to give rein to the humorous high spirits which are both his need and his most particular talent. At lunch he tells me that he has gone back to work on his score; with facetious irritation he complains about the trouble transfigurations cause: it is always the same, he says, and one could leave it to others to do, then suddenly, "There have been very few comforters in the world—Beethoven, Mozart, Bach, Weber, the ones I call the original melodists." — A French newspaper prints the article in full; it sounds quite absurd, and the picture of a woman dressed in the latest fashion brings home to us the utter wretchedness of "*la vie moderne.*" In the evening friend Wolzogen; R. tells both him and me about Herr Haug's "crazy" book, full of the most curious things. R. says he cannot read much of it, but he intends to continue. He wants to write down again his ideas on religion. — Very nice letter from Lusch about the busy world, also a very cheerful one from Judith, and we in our love-enchanted haven of peace! . . .

Wednesday, September 3 R. brings me *his "extrait centuple"* ["essence reduced a hundredfold"]—"*pour charmer les maris*" ["to charm your husbands"]! He did not sleep very well, had to get up once. At breakfast a letter from Herr Levi, which we open with some eagerness to hear about father and daughter, brings us the extraordinary news that during a discussion of his *Christus* my father flew into a rage with the poor man, who could think of no other way to extricate himself than to take his departure! — Long discussion, frequently resumed during the course of the day, of this curious incident, reflections on the character and life of my father. Dismal conversations! — Yesterday morning we were occupied with Shakespeare! R. recalled the murder scene in R[*ichard*] III, which had seemed to him so long in London, whereas in his memory it had been short. He continued by saying that every one of Shakespeare's characters contains material enough for a sustained role, though circumstances do not permit it, but each one is interesting, each person an individual. — Splendid weather; walked in the garden. In the evening whist with Boni. R. thinks Herr Haug must be crazy! — The prospects for the wine harvest seem favorable, but the grain harvest is said not to have turned out well, so that there will be a great need for products from abroad. "What taxes we shall have!" R. exclaims with a sigh. He complains of his left eye, which is watering, and his left ear, which is dull of hearing. He resolves to make no more complaints, but I thank him for doing so, for otherwise I should die of worry.

Thursday, September 4 R. again did not have a good night, though he dreamed of a very beautiful district full of flowers; the result perhaps of a letter from Mme Gautier, who invites us to Dinard. Our breakfast hour is again splendid. R. talks about Beethoven's conciseness and says, "One comes to admire it more and more." Mozart, he says, poured into an existing mold ideas which did not necessarily break the mold, but with Beethoven, the formal precision he preserves is something tremendous. He works in the morning after reading Haug's

Old Testament, which he is almost inclined to give up on, for it is too crazy. — Walked in the garden with R., in the evening Mozart's *Requiem,* which R. loves greatly, particularly the Benedictus and the Recordare; comparison between this melodic charm and the charm of Raphael's Madonnas; much about the *Sistine Madonna,* thoughts of R.'s next work about religion in relation to art; the beauty of Raphael free of desire; I compare Titian's *Assumption of the Virgin,* on the other hand, with Isolde's transfiguration. Completely immersed in these discussions, we seal them with an embrace.

Friday, September 5 R. had a better night; still more about Raphael and Mozart, and then some merry remarks about the house, the children, Princess Wittgenstein. As R. leaves me, he says, "I feel as if nothing ever happened to me before"—he means he never lived before. He is pleased with the way the children are developing, he calls Boni the beauty. — Yesterday he said to me, laughing, "If the Society of Patrons were now to raise the three million for me, I should run away—I must tell Wolzogen that." Fine weather, but somewhat close; R. groans about how slowly he is orchestrating: "When I was doing it for your birthday, how quickly it went!" In the late evening another walk in the garden, we are not venturing beyond Wahnfried and are content with that. In the evening a telegram from Hans to friend Rubinstein pleases us greatly. "Bravissimo! Bülow"—thus runs the brief and informative document. — Much drumming and piping all around us, one has the feeling that a "ballet militaria" is being performed, or that one has been set down in the middle of a Shakespeare play!

Saturday, September 6 R. slept well and is cheerful—we have been rewarded with lovely autumn days. Our conversation leads us from the military character in general to Cromwell, the Lord Protector. This naïve title, which R. also chose for his Lohengrin, leads R. to reflect on the character of this "gigantic" human being, his enormous understanding, his relatively less developed powers of reasoning, a man in whom everything taken to be hypocrisy and dissimulation was in fact naïveté; he could not express himself in any other way. R. also talks about Charles II, who with his black wig was particularly repulsive to him. R. does some orchestration, and again jokingly remarks how slowly this progresses now and how quickly it went last year. His eyes are somewhat strained, he works in my room, where the light is better. Over coffee a discussion with friend Wolzogen about his task for the next issue of the *Bayr. Blätter.* In the evening R. reads several scenes from *Romeo and Juliet*—there is nothing one can say about it, and time and time again one feels the need to express one's astonishment. Everything, the most delicate as well as the most vulgar, he saw and vividly portrayed—the latter, as R. says, apprehended but not repre-hended! R. also reads the scene in *Coriolanus* at the house of Aufidius and points out to us how the conversation among the servingmen, besides being witty and original, is dramatically important, telling us in the most economical way what we need to know. (Yesterday R. wrote to Herr Jauner, who has requested him to attend the per-formances, asking how he could possibly believe he would ever again set foot in Vienna.)

Sunday, September 7   Eva's reawakening! — She returns to us after an absence of four weeks! . . . R. not satisfied with the enthusiasm of the other children—they seem to him too casual about their reunion. But he was pleased in the morning to be able to take his bath with Fidi, who told him of a dream in which, while swimming, he rescued several people from the water! Nice letter from Lusch with all sorts of details regarding that curious incident in Munich. In the afternoon R. invites Rub., Wolz., Jäg. for beer (Angermann's at Wahnfried) and discusses with Herr Jäg. his latest engagement for a guest performance in Munich. In the evening R. feels tired and heavy, desires neither music nor reading, but calls for whist. Herr Rub. played parts of the 2nd act of *Tristan*. These sounds echo inside me like an irresistible call from and to my homeland: "Know'st thou where my homeland is?" — People talk about the magical attraction of the eyes, through which snakes draw birds to them; it is just such a fascination these sounds exert over my heart—I feel as if I were following some secret power without knowing whither it is leading me. When it suddenly falls silent, a desert opens, and life returns, for which I have again to summon up my strength. But this is something I cannot speak about.

Monday, September 8   R. did not have a very good night, he lacks exercise, and we decide on a drive, since the weather is glorious. R. orchestrates. Over coffee he talks of the lack of freedom now discernible everywhere, causing, for example, his farce, *Die Kapitulation,* not to be understood at all. Aristophanes would not be understood at all. He says he feels like writing a comedy for the *B. Blätter* in which people would appear under their own names, L. Bucher, Porges, Rubinst., Wolz., my father—all of it guileless, but full of nonsense. Drive to the Schlehenmühle, curious wrong turnings, a stop at the Bodenmühle, talk with the miller in which R. is struck by the word "*Wagschaft.*" Not far from the Bodenmühle we get back into the carriage, very tired. In the evening we are alone, R. and I, which is a great blessing; R. working in his head, and he at last finds the alteration in the Prelude which he has long been looking for! He plays it to me. Then he reads me the story of the ring from *Nathan*. A portrait and eulogy of Moses Mendelssohn, with the description of his shallow optimism, leads him to shape the scene in a nice and cozy way, but it all seems a very superficial conception of religion. And R. laughs at the celerity with which the other participants in the argument are always won over. I misunderstood the whole thing at first and thought that the three rings were not genuine, the genuine one having vanished. R. says, "That would be a completely different thing."

Tuesday, September 9   R. slept well, woke up when, while he was looking for me, more and more people got in the way. Concern about Fidi, rousing serious misgivings in me; we are disturbed by his equanimity—could it be that he lacks fire? — In the afternoon R. finds the ending to *Parsifal* and plays it to me as he has now finally written it. He says he went through the whole thing some 30 or 40 times in his head before giving it its present form. In the evening Rub. brings the conversation around to Nietzsche, and, reflecting on this whole experience, R. becomes very upset, he cannot get over the perversity of such a character. We pass on to whist, and to end the evening Herr Rub. plays the Overture to *Der Freischütz,* following it with the duet between Agathe and Ännchen, which truly uplifts our hearts in delight —what grace, what charm! (Immediately after supper R. read to me the summary of Haug's book; he is giving up reading it in spite of the pleasure he finds in some of its ideas. The Jews as "calculating beasts of prey," for example, pleases him greatly.) "He is another true German," R. says, "with very original and deep ideas, but crazy." —

Wednesday, September 10   R. had a good night. He brings me the news that the Emperor has commanded a world exposition in Berlin (1885)—our capital city girding its loins for a cultural idea! — R. receives two nice letters, from a lieutenant of the Guards, v. Einem, and from a petty official, the latter in connection with "The Work and Mission of My Life." — R. begins L[ouis] Lambert, which I recommended to him; he is gripped by the child's attitude toward the college and exclaims, "The best one could say to these people is, 'Your educational institutions are all right for small talents, but a child of fine feelings, imagination, and sensitivity would be lost among you.'" — I have to do some shopping in the afternoon, and when I return home, I find the nest empty! R. flown; he returns in a bad mood, saying that he had really wanted to work, Rub. had called, and so he went to Angermann's—we feel conscious that we have hardly seen each other all day! — In the evening Rub. brings along compositions by Herr Brahms and plays a concerto to us; very little pleasure in it, for to laugh at clumsiness, bombast, and falsity in art is no pleasure. Not a single melody, beginnings of themes from Beethoven and other masters, the composer's realization that it is not his own, hurried resorts to oblique harmonies and contrived curiosities. When Rub. says

Brahms has composed some nice songs, R. says that everybody has done that—"even I!" — Then R. shows me the two bars he has added to the Prelude, in order to bring out the one theme better. Wonderful internal spinning; to us the work appears finished, yet he feels the urge for still greater perfection. — When Siegfried saw the volumes of Brahms lying there, he asked his father to play the "Hungarian Dances" to him; R. tells me this in a tone of voice which leaves me in no doubt about his feelings; for me it is a stab—and there is nothing I can say, no way of preventing it—I also have not the courage in this case to plead for the strength of renunciation. — Taking leave of me in the evening, R. says to me, "If only you could hear the monologues I carry on regarding you!" —

Thursday, September 11 R. had a good night; he reads *L. Lambert* and works. At lunch he says, "It would do the French a lot of good to have a good translation of Schopenhauer," and he talks of the Swedenborgism of Balzac, whom he calls "a serious fellow." — He intends to write two more articles for the *Blätter,* one about the nature of symphonic music and "a long work" about the affinities between religion and art. He makes some more alterations in *Parsifal* and tells me, "If you only knew what torments I went through!" It is the *"nun such' ich ihn von Welt zu Welt"* passage—he was not happy with a sequence in it. — Departure of Herr Jäger, who is going to Vienna. I read friend W.'s manuscript and feel sorrow over Siegfried—he has been untruthful! At the conclusion of an evening during which we are visited by two French people (M. and Mme Lascoux), R. complains of a pain in his heart, and so going off to sleep is a very oppressive affair, appearing to my imagination as if it were a direct path to death. Ah, worry! . . . R. was amused by the imperturbable seriousness of the French gentleman, who did, however, respond very well when he told him his thoughts regarding Parsifal. R. speaks very fluently. — Oh, my star, remain merciful to me, do not force me to act alone! Go out, vanish, but do not brighten an existence without light—do not bind me here below when my sun no longer shines!

Friday, September 12 R. got up only once and is not dissatisfied with his night's rest. He works. At lunch the French people, whose detailed knowledge of all R.'s published works is truly amazing. In the evening Herr v. Weber, the antivivisectionist and African traveler, a very serious man. Herr and Frau Lascoux arrive, too, R. writes in French to friend W., bidding him come to us; to this curious gathering Rub. plays the Prelude to *Parsifal* and the second scene from *Die Walküre.* "Good people, do go away!" R. says to our German friends after the French people have left; and finally a bat flits around above our heads; on the evening before Eva got up she had a similar visitation, and a mirror broke in the children's room. — These portents, if such they are, do not alarm me, they just seem to me a reflection of my worrying thoughts, and it is curious how, when people come between R. and me, their liveliness only serves to augment my fears regarding him, instead of distracting me. I feel that there is nothing more I can do for him, it is as if he is surrounded by danger, and I, completely paralyzed, can offer him no aid.

Saturday, September 13   R. had a good night; he makes me laugh heartily with his comparison between the little French boy and Siegfried; and indeed the little stranger was remarkably lacking in manners. I do not know what led us from that to Bismarck, whom R. compares with Robespierre; just as the latter could think of nothing to do with his absolute power except keep on seeking out suspects and having them beheaded, so, too, Bismarck can only keep discovering new dangers, as an excuse for strengthening the army. — At lunch we come to the subject of the letter the Crown Princess sent to Herr v. W[eber], in which she ranges herself fairly clearly on the side of the vivisectionists. When I say to R. that this is a shame, for she has the reputation of being a good and sincere woman, R. replies, "It is easy to be sincere when one is vindictive and possesses power." He says he will never forget her "Oh, no, Fritz" when the Crown Prince was about to take up some certificates of patronage. — Nice weather, R. reads the pamphlets which Herr v. W. brought with him; I beg him not to do so, to participate as much as he can but not to concern himself with the horrors in detail, for then he would find it impossible to work. Herr v. W. has supper with us, shows us some diamonds which he dug up, also petrified animals in amber. The children greatly interested in these. Talked a lot about colonial life, so neglected by the Germans. Herr v. W. speaks highly of the Boers, the Dutch settlers, now being ousted by the British. Again a bat flutters around us toward the end of the evening. In the morning R. worked on his score, with some vexation over frequently writing things down incorrectly.

Sunday, September 14   R. had a good night; the meeting with the French people leads us to his time in Paris, the most wasted years of his life, then Vienna, and, finally and worst of all, the three weeks in Zurich: "The King came along when I was at my wits' end," says R. — Very fine weather, he corrects his article. In the afternoon we drive out to the Waldhütte, visit the caves; a very nice walk, but somewhat too long, worry about Eva and about R. During a rest at the inn, R. talks about his wild youth, also tells us how in his childhood, recovering from an illness, he had said, "Things are not quite right with me," which made people laugh. — Whist in the evening.

Monday, September 15   R. did not have a very good night, he also dreamed that I "offended" him—something to do with the earlier relationship with my father! But he recovers his spirits and tells me he has read an American story in Loldi's magazine and begun his article for the November issue. I occupy myself with friend Wolzogen's article, which is really unique. In the evening, when I come down to R., I find him busy reading a pamphlet by Dr. Hammer, which interests him to the highest degree. We read it together in the evening and take pleasure in the language and outlook of this doughty man. But the glance one is thereby forced to cast on human affairs is so horrifying that one feels with one's whole soul the wish to take leave of a world in which no crime is too terrible. —

Tuesday, September 16 A poor night! R. gets up frequently and catches cold in the process. His mind is occupied with his letter to Herr v. Weber. Is it autumn, is it the approach of old age, is it my preoccupation with the dismal subject of vivisection which so overwhelms me with melancholy? It is certainly because R. does not feel well, he goes to bed at 6 o'clock and at first feels better, but his mind is restless, all kinds of mishaps disturbing his sleep. During the evening, when I was in the *salon,* a bat once again fluttered around me with its heavy flight.

Wednesday, September 17 In spite of his bad night R. wants to go for a drive to see something more of the military exercises. He takes pleasure in the drive, in the countryside, in a glass of beer at Dommayer's; but after lunch he feels very languid, and he still cannot rest properly in the afternoon. By evening he is completely in the grip of his cold, coughing, too. Whist. To bed at 10 o'clock.

Thursday, September 18 R. had a good night's rest, but he is still coughing; a compress and a quinine capsule help a little. But good spirits, all the same. Yesterday we joked about "science"—"One should exclaim, 'God grant it may all be for nothing,' " R. observes, "when one sees all this equipment made in the name of vivisection as well as militarism." — The philosophy in *L. Lambert* does not appeal to him at all, but the novel itself he finds gripping. — If it were not for the children, he observes, everything would be easy to bear, for one could turn one's back on the world, but they form a link to it. I reply that he has already been of help to the children by pointing them in the right direction in almost every sphere of life and by awakening correct feelings in them—that is in itself a great deal. — When we were driving home yesterday and caught sight of the theater, R. called out to it, "Be silent!" M[ichel]a[ngelo] called out to his Moses, "Say something!" — On this same journey R. saw an old woman on the outskirts of Donndorf and the look she gave the artillerymen: "There was so much awareness of the seriousness of life and so much resignation in it."

In the evening whist with a dummy. [*Added later:* "At lunch I mention that I always found the laurels on Tasso's head a little disturbing, particularly in the 2nd act. R. says, 'Yes, it's easy to write it, but it is not *seen*.' He says that Emil Devrient's ideal appearance got him over the difficulty, but all the same, laurels are a symbol bestowed in public and by acclamation—in the play they are just a convention. — Over coffee he thinks of Prince Hal's 'hanging nether lip,' pointed out by Falstaff; this touch causes him great amusement."]

Friday, September 19   R. had some difficulties during the night, but on the whole he did not sleep badly; however, his head feels confused, and the article he has just begun seems almost to irritate him—"abstract stuff," and "how much scribbling have I already done!" — He also has to correct a passage, for he went too far in asserting that Mozart regarded the symphony with the eyes of a dramatist, and exaggerated the boldness of a certain passage. Over whist yesterday he suddenly exclaimed at the beauty of the first movement of [Beethoven's] A Major, particularly from the second part on—everything hovers in it, "pure as the air." On the other hand, Sgambati's quintet, which he has been looking at more closely, no longer appeals to him; he finds in it the same exaggerations as everywhere else. — Herr Schön's announcing his visit makes R. exclaim: "If they think I am going to set up a school—! My school is performances—which others do when I am not looking," he adds with a laugh. In the past few days I have been occupying myself with last wishes, a very painful task for me, since my will and fortune consist in having no will of my own. But for the sake of the children let it be done, in R.'s name! My head feels exhausted, weary; old sufferings, old wounds keep breaking open again, and in one's feelings of sorrow one sees the unreality of time; all that one gains from it is a stillness in the suffering, which, as if drugged, ceases to speak, no longer stirs—but it is still there in all its strength, seemingly immortal! "Calm my thoughts, give light to my needy heart"—in the morning, with this prayer in my head, I stroll with the children to the woods via the Bruckmühle, great peace and pleasure in everything; a glance at the theater, silent greeting; forget-me-nots on the banks of the Main; a blue, unknown bird—"king's fisher" in English, the "*roi pêcheur*"—arouses wonderful thoughts. Driving home, I realize that death can be a release to us only when we pass into it as from slumber to sleep; when there is peace inside us, when we have achieved ecstasy in suffering, serenity in renunciation. Mere ending does not by itself bring us rest. Not just forgetting, either—a vain endeavor, anyway— but recalling in love what is destroying us. — Why do we find help above all in Nature, in which desire and the will to live are expressed so strongly—why does it bring us peace more readily than all the poets? — In the evening I read aloud to R. the introduction to Gfrörer's *Philo of Alexandria;* in this excellent description R. discovers the starting point for his big work; if Protestantism had remained on a popular level, completely untheological, it would have been capable of survival; theology was its downfall. — In the evening much delight in the children's wit, and R. tells me that Fidi's gaze made a wonderful impression on him, there was something utterly familiar about it, an intensity of intellect, impossible to describe. "There am I," he had thought. Blessings on you, my child, threefold blessings for the joy you have given him!

Saturday, September 20 R. had a good night; in the morning the children were mentioned once again, their individuality, the joy and hope they bring to us. R. then settles down to his letter to Herr von Weber. In the evening we again take up the introduction to *Philo of Alexandria*. The comparison between the Protestant and Catholic churches in it seems to us very good. R. says, "I do not believe in God, but in godliness, which is revealed in a Jesus *without sin*." — Over coffee we talked of the possibility of my father's having come into contact with R. in his youth—whether he would have influenced him, or *vice versa;* R. says: "I was persuasive, I know. I turned people's heads and then I ran away from them—it has been like that all through my life." Memories of Friederike Meyer, the poor, good creature!

Sunday, September 21 R. had a rather restless night, and he seems to me to be run down. The problem of vivisection affects him, and his letter is keeping him occupied. We make an attempt to watch a Chinese man doing his tricks here in the Sonne, but the terrible music drives us out immediately, after R. has shouted, "Do stop it!" and begun to whistle himself. We have to laugh over this attempt to take a look at the world for once. — In the dusk we, R. and I, sit in the *salon,* and our conversation leads us to death. To die well, he says, is the greatest happiness; I observe that to die well one must already have died in spirit, so that death is then hardly an event, and I maintain to R. that there are many things of which he understands nothing, since genius has no part in original sin. He: "I live like a sort of animal." I: "Yes, in innocence." — Whist in the evening, R., Boni, and I, after R. has awakened from a short sleep with renewed signs of a cold. But the whist is very merry; contrary to his usual wont, R. has luck with the dummy, and a curious, harmonious gaiety settles over our quiet evening. —

Monday, September 22 R. did not sleep too well, and it almost grieves me that Herr Schön is arriving from Worms just at this time. When I am taking a bath downstairs, I hear a very delightful theme, then hear the cherished voice, "She probably thinks I don't know she is taking a bath, but it was just for her I was playing." Recently he told me that themes came into his mind all the time, but they then vanished, since he made no use of them. He says he sometimes wishes he were just a musician and did not have other thoughts. Herr Schön arrives; a pleasant man who also tells us very pleasant things about his relations with the workers in his factory. R. welcomes him very cordially, and he then goes off with friend Wolzogen to discuss the public campaign. In the evening R. asks for the *Idyll* from Herr Rubinstein; I feel as if I am wrapped around by magic threads, which soothe away all cares, my soul melts in the blissful sounds, and my dreamlike state prevents any activity. R. asks me why I never look at him—he had sought my gaze; I could feel his eyes resting on me, but I could not direct my own; the bliss of ceasing entirely, of complete extinction, possible only in the sound of music, his music. R. gave many examples of singing, breathing, this evening—how our singers do it and how, by contrast, Schröder[-Devrient] did it. — When the others have gone, R. complains about the way even someone like Rub., with all his understanding, plays the triplets, that is to say, unthinkingly, like a light figuration, whereas he takes them rather draggingly in this otherwise very smoothly flowing piece. "It's so intimate," R. exclaims, "absurd to play it in a concert hall!" — As R. is going off to sleep, he says to me, "Now the spasm is going away—do you believe one can die smiling?" — (Reached agreement with Naples.)

Tuesday, September 23   R. did not have a good night, and I find it hard to understand how he can nevertheless still manage to talk so tenderly with me in the morning, with all his usual love and kindness, and indeed cheerfulness. — He works on his letter. At lunch with Herr Schön friends Feustel and Gross, reminiscences of the beginnings of our venture. Unfortunately politics are also discussed, and R. has to make an effort to put up with the eulogy of the Berlin peace treaty. — In the afternoon I drive with friends Schön and Wolzogen to the theater; to the former I impart my views on bringing up a boy—not with a view toward a career, but to turn him into an independent, capable human being. R. comes to join us, delight in the building, in Faf, who guards it, memories of our poor municipal gardener. Had some beer at the new railroad station, which pleases R. very much; impressive entrance to the town, due to the view of the theater. In the evening Herr Schön works out almost all the details regarding a public campaign, a petition to the Reichstag! R. is glad that this excellent man is still young. And yesterday, when he was speaking of his workers, R. recommended to him Carlyle's essay on conditions in England. During the evening R. played to us the Prelude to *Parsifal,* which he called a preamble, like the preamble to a sermon, since the themes are merely laid out side by side. — Late in the evening we talked about the motives swarming around him, and I tell him I consider it my triumph that they fly around him like the seeds of flowers and flutter around him like butterflies. In Munich, he observed, he had not had any music at all inside him. —

Wednesday, September 24 Again R. did not have a restful night. But at lunch he tells me that after our breakfast together he fell into a very deep sleep and then, feeling completely refreshed, settled down to his work, the form of which interests him (letter to Herr v. W.). He is looking well! Keeps telling me that he intends to live for a long time, and today says that at the age of 82 he intends to ride along the *via triumphalis* in Metz! — I say goodbye to Herr Schön and believe I have discovered in him a friend for Siegfried. — In the afternoon R. calls to me, asking me to walk with him in the garden, splendid sunset, pleasure in Wahnfried! We go indoors as it grows dark; over beer on the "Muchanoff" we immerse ourselves in talk; first of all the capture of Cetewayo, then I show R. the little photograph of the oldest theater in Dresden; he recognizes it: "I played there, I saw Weber there—oh, it was all magic to me! I remember how in *Preciosa* the triangle began under the balustrade of the royal box. Oh, what fascination! I could not see the people, since the box projected outward. My father acted there." — Then as always back to vivisection; R. tells me various things from his letter. — Whist in the evening. — When I part from him after our conversation and call him "angel," he says, "That's nothing—such an ancient penwiper, tottering around, but when I say 'dear wife,' that means something, that is much more."

Thursday, September 25 R. got up once, but he is not too tired. Cloudy weather; one's thoughts turn gladly to Naples. All sorts of absurd things in the mail: a lady wishes to erect a conservatorium in Bayreuth, a gentleman in Kaufbeuren asks for a melody of his own to be turned into a march, and offers a telescope for it! — By rail a Spaniard who traveled to Munich to see the *Ring;* a lively, not unpleasant man. A very good English translation of *Parsifal* (so it seems to us), sent by Herr Schott. — R. continues writing his letter, and in the evening occupies himself by drawing lines for his score. Visit from the Spanish painter, much about Paris, about his native land. Thoughts of spending a winter in Seville as well. But R. gets tired of speaking French.

Friday, September 26 R. had a good night, and when he extravagantly demonstrates his love for me, there arises in me such a longing to make him happy that I feel the stars should fall at his feet. But nothing happens, the skies remain overcast and gray, since the blazing is within, and day claims its rights. Departure of the Spaniard, who declares he loves only the music of Beethoven and R. Wagner. — It is very cold—should we light the fires? — But we remain indoors; R. visits me up-

stairs just as I am engaged in writing down the lines for the 27th, but I
am able to conceal them from him. Then he calls me downstairs with
the "Sailors' Chorus" from *Holländer*. We discuss the distribution of
his letter and decide to give it out as a supplement to the *Bayreuther
Blätter*. In the evening R. reads to us the article which he started but
then broke off on account of the letter—what for Beeth. is a pre-
requisite is for Mozart a restriction—how fine! Then the first movement
of the Ninth Symphony; at the return to the tremolo and the opening
R. says, "That is the cauldron, the daemonic one which has been seething throughout, but one just didn't hear it." I admit to R. that in this
work I feel no need for a program, and I even put his, based on *Faust*,
right out of my mind. R. says everyone conjures up his own images
for it—but in my case not even that happens, and I can compare what
goes on inside me only with the springing up of mysterious seeds and
buds, the spirit being just a guide to the enchanted ground where this
magical act of creation is taking place, its role merely that of a myrmidon,
bereft of all power. R. plays the adagio, breaking off after the first
variation to exclaim: "That is an adagio—and what wealth of imaginative feeling in the variation! There is nothing like it." When I mention
Saint Cosmas, R. laughs and says there has never been a more typical
Catholic than I am, and it is a wonder he ever managed to convert me.

Saturday, September 27 Saint Cosmas celebrated after all, in the
morning, at lunch, and again toward evening, for a friendly fate
ordains that *Alexander and Darius,* ordered by me, also arrives during
the afternoon. R. shows me in it what made such an impression on
him 50 years ago that he has still not forgotten it; he says he can still
see Hephaistion's fury; the "Hurry, my dear one," the anecdote
regarding which he has often told me—this makes us laugh; and the
cover (Lyra and stars) transports us back to that time. — "Not a bad
time," R. exclaims. This was in the evening. In the morning there was
the news of at least not a bad night, and when, on parting, he gives
me his blessing, he is pleased that I am looking so well, remarks on a
"gleam" in my eye—probably the little pleasure I am hoping to prepare
for him shows in my face! Thinking how to arrange my little surprise,
I have the feeling that painters can only really paint the persons they
love, for what does a stranger see in us? And everything is strange
that one does not love, and love fervently! Much blissful chat throughout the day. When I am returning from some shopping, I hear R.'s
voice in Siegfriedstrasse and, wishing to catch him quickly, take the
path through W.'s courtyard; expecting me, he goes to the street
railings to meet me, and thus we spend some time seeking each other,
laughing in the end about the curious mischance which kept us apart!
At supper we talked about our first stay in Italy, at a time when "the

future held no prospects." "What a time!" R. exclaims; "how meaning-less everything else seemed then—the art of the future and all that!" — Then whist and Beethoven's first quartet, which R. enjoys, though he describes it as cold music, a good piece of music making, in which feeling also has its place. —

Sunday, September 28 R. had a good night. He works on his letter and tells me at lunch that he never does more than a single page (though a closely written one) each day, because he is taking a lot of trouble with the formulation; he says he is trying to express briefly in a sentence things which, if he were to deal with them one by one in separate paragraphs, would cause him to lose the main thread; but the clarity of the sentence must not be allowed to suffer, and this means hard work. — When I return home in the afternoon, I find R. in the garden, looking unwell and in a rather bad mood. He had been looking forward to hanging up the "Cosmos-Eos," but the servant had dis-appeared and been absent a long time. At last he returns, and we start our hanging work, during which R. displays his remarkable dexterity, his liveliness in overcoming all difficulties. Various things have to remain uncompleted. R. vexed, unwell, the dull weather oppresses him as much as his preoccupation with the subject of vivisection. He spits some blood and says at whist, "I have no wish to die yet." — Why is it that I write this down, something which grieves me so unutterably, yet a kind of shame prevents my setting down all the signs and sacred words of his love? I have the feeling that worry takes flight in the act of expressing it, I must confide it to this page at least, for the burden is too great for my strength. It is a weakness, an expedient, words lift the oppression; but silence shall shield all that inspires me, and prevent it from melting away!

Monday, September 29 R. did not have a good night; late rising in consequence, but he is cheerful, thinks of the work we did not complete yesterday and exclaims, "What is life without a lambrequin?" — News from Wiesbaden [*telegram enclosed; see notes*]; R. replies to Herr Niemann. Around midday he tells me he has finished his letter. Before work he read the first act of *A. and Darius*. In the afternoon I do some hanging for him, and he is satisfied! When I have finished, he takes me down to the *salon* and reads to me his moving letter, written with such manly restraint. — Over our afternoon coffee we talk about painting, the representation of the female body, which R. thinks an unsuitable subject, since it too clearly expresses its natural functions; he recalls Titian's Venus, saying that the relationship of the head to the body can be made to look graceful only through decoration, the serpent's head, holding out its cornucopia longingly: "But of course the Turk does not see that." Herr Jäger comes, bringing news of Vienna; R.

finds his visit, like all visits, disturbing, and I laughingly tell him that he took refuge in his silence, which is so stony that one feels one can never break through it. At times, incidentally, I feel his loquacity to be a complete shutting off of himself, a way of keeping everything at bay which might get inside his defenses; very few people understand those turbulent waves of wit, through which I see to the mysterious and fertile depths. — In the evening whist, R., Boni, and I. — Recently R. talked about the ruling of his score, which is now keeping him occupied during the afternoon and in which the various instruments are so precisely indicated that, as he maintains, another person could write the score by following it!

Tuesday, September 30 R. had a bad night. . . . All the same, he manages to be cheerful, something which always astonishes me. He sings the song "The Storm Breaks Out"—and laughs at its pedantic Germanity, something unknown in Goethe, for he never wrote empty phrases, even though he had a very good idea of what was German. He also sings the Queen of the Night's aria and, thinking once more of the high-minded Tithonos, says, "Probably because he allowed Eos to leave him every day to strew roses." Since we got up very late, we do little in the morning; R. reads the play and describes it as somewhat green—how, for example, Alexander seats himself on Xerxes's throne and—the curtain falls! Letter from Herr von Stein, announcing a visit; he wants to see whether he and Siegfried will get along together. Malwida the intermediary! — He plays bits from *Tannhäuser,* and we are pleased with the heroic character of the song to Venus. — I leave him to go shopping, and he intends to rest but does not succeed, and when I go to greet him around 6 o'clock, I have to disturb him while he is trying to sleep! . . . I leave him in a calm mood after a short chat over beer, and then have to endure the experience of Dr. Landgraf's coming in and making a joking reply to some remark about vivisection, which puts him into such a rage that he himself is shocked by it. It all ends with mutual soothing remarks, but R. comes upstairs to tell me about it, and in the mood aroused in me by his account I lack the courage to "make myself beautiful" as usual for the evening; I sit on my spiral staircase and reflect, reflect, until the mildness of my thoughts lulls and calms me; and then from downstairs I hear music: R. is also dreaming, he in music, strangely melancholy but, like all music, soothing. And so the evening, too, is introduced in a conciliatory spirit, and R. softly praises music; later he plays to me the theme which he does not wish to be called a theme. Friends W. and R. with us in the evening, further quartets from Op. 18; cold music, says R. [*Added later:* "I have noticed that the sonatas from the same opus are much freer and show much more feeling; is it that the artist, who played them, wrote them for himself, giving himself more than he gave the four people whom he liked to imagine as real musicians? Until it all melted together, and mastery gave him the ability to write down his most intimate thoughts for interpretation by others?"] — Discussion of Dingelstedt's impressions, which appear under royal patronage, decorated with a Minerva: "Palla*sch* Athena," R. exclaims! And then there is mention of our young neighbor's journey to Tunis, he says he is seeking there people of his own sort—*Tu nichts* [idlers]. — He is pleased with the gate, which he points out to me from the spiral staircase; everything that comes from inside us is joy—but the world! . . . "It is common," he says with Hamlet, and we recall to ourselves this expression of disgust with the world, finding in it the best definition of those feelings which force one to remain inactive.

Wednesday, October 1 Very bad night, which leads to a morning with disagreeable associations; I cut it as short as possible so that R. may get some rest, and when the hours have passed, I find these sweet lines on my table. [*Written in Wagner's handwriting:* "People behave quite wretchedly toward me in this house. All the same—I ask *Verseihen!* An enslaved *monsieur.*"] "*Verseihen*" [instead of "*Verzeihung,*" forgiveness] is what Fidi used to say when he had done something naughty and wanted to be forgiven. And at 12 R. comes up to me and cries, "*A genoux!*" When I go down on my knees, he immediately does the same, telling me that I misunderstood everything, he meant it for himself! The sunshine does him good, he goes out, hears Siegfried, as he is digging in the sand, singing the "greeting to his loyal subjects." Discussion about the visit of Herr v. Stein; will we really be granted the boon of educating our son according to our own ideas, bringing him to Communion as a devout Christian, in a non-Jewish way? R. says, "We must wait for a miracle." When I say that it is too much for me to be able to believe, he advises me not to think of it at all. — After lunch, when he is crushing out his cigarette and making sure it is extinguished, he thinks of Othello and Desdemona, and I remind him of the remark he once made to me—that O. killed Desdemona because he knew she must one day be unfaithful to him. He continues by saying that natural tendencies hold sway over acts of enthusiasm, and once the image had arisen in his mind, even if put there by such a despicable rogue, life became impossible, everything was finished, and the only saving grace that D. die with her purity unsullied. Beyond words—also as drama; *Hamlet,* through the nature of its material, weakly based in comparison, R. remarks, it tends to lose itself in length; not killing [Claudius] because he is at prayer, making the journey to England—these are dramatically almost embarrassing, though entirely necessary for displaying character. I do not know why R. mentions

Jaques in this connection; I tell him that what I find so remarkable about this character (among other things) is its pronounced French flavor, the curious, resigned melancholy which laughs even at profundity but is itself profound. R. agrees and wonders whether he remains in the forest. I believe one can assume that he does, and he says, "How superficial in comparison do all the princes seem, who return to their thrones!" "Except for Prospero," I say, and together we reflect on this most moving of characters. As we part, R. calls me "Prospera." I: "You are Prospero, you have his magic and his benevolence." — R. does not manage to sleep in the afternoon, and in the evening he looks very run down. He reads something from Herr v. Hagen's book, I note in it the quotation from Nietzsche and have to acknowledge in tears what we have lost in him. Visit from the doctor, he advises against a bath in the evening, which I had recommended to R., recommending camomile tea instead! Whist.

Thursday, October 2 Unfortunately the camomile tea does not work, and though R. calls it *"calmatif,"* I am too sad to laugh from the bottom of my heart. R. wakes from a very bad dream, gets up, goes off to sleep again, only to wake up once more, this time for a longer period, and to read Hagen's book. At last, toward morning, he falls asleep. Laughingly he remarks, "A doctor here would never order a bath and forbid beer—he doesn't know what effect the former has, and the latter he likes too much!" I am awake almost all night, tormented by ideas which, of no importance to me during the day, rise up alarmingly before me. I believe that his preoccupation with vivisection is much to blame for R.'s depression, and there is nothing coming to him from outside to refresh him; he says it is only when I go out that he hears enlivening news; I tell him what I hear in the shops about life in the town, all sorts of funny stories which amuse him. In the evening he gives me *Crito* to read out loud, but this glorification of the state does not much appeal to him, it is not one of Plato's best things. I feel moved by Plato's love for his country and the way in which, despite the execution of Socrates, he weaves, as it were, a halo around Athens by showing how Socrates loved the city. And then the dramatic wit and the consummate artistry in the speech about the laws. I always find myself thinking about what he says. When I tell R. this, he says I am right. Before whist a quotation from Nietzsche's book in Hagen again leads to astonishment over this fall from grace; I believe that here was committed the one sin which cannot be atoned for—the sin against the Holy Ghost. No words could be more moving than those contained in this quotation.

Friday, October 3 Last night R. did not sleep well, either, though somewhat better. He reads Herr v. Hagen and works on copying his article. At lunch we come to the subject of Marie Muchanoff and via her to women in general. R. says: "I cannot in fact talk to any woman. Now people might say that you have spoiled me; but previously I did not really know any of them." Even Marie M., with her great and noble spirit, remained a stranger to him, in spite of her sympathy for him; probably what people said about her was to blame for that. I tell him jokingly that he is too inventive and that this is why he does not see people in their true character, he makes them up for himself: if good, they disappoint him, if bad, they remain strangers to him! . . . Over coffee *Crito* discussed again and defended by me. — R. goes to take a rest, and I do some shopping, during which I consciously notice our beloved town; the irregularity of the houses gives, as a sign of life, a more pleasing impression than all the ornaments on the more uniform modern houses, which look to me like the grinning countenance of death. Through the Brautgasse past the church and the house with the bay windows, much enjoyment at the sight, then farther down the hill and home via Birken—peculiar feelings of belonging here, which I impart to R. when I see him in the house; he has had some rest. In the evening we play whist with Loldi for the first time, and at eleven o'clock we all go by omnibus to the station to fetch Lusch. The moonlight on the silent streets, the rattling omnibus, which forces us to keep silent, the unaccustomed journey, it is an absurd dream. Alarm caused by a man who suddenly appears at the door, then swings himself onto the carriage—all this puts us into the gayest of spirits, and we meet our child amid laughter and bear her home, where we drink champagne in welcome.

Saturday, October 4 A good night for R. Talked a lot about Lusch's excellent report; this little expedition was a complete success, and the child has experienced much of significance and observed it well. I spend the whole morning talking with her, and at lunch her very lively accounts continue. In the afternoon arrangements are made for the celebratory fireworks display; over coffee R. had told me that the fireworks man, a cobbler by trade, has a chest complaint arising from his exertions during the war, can no longer mend shoes, and is helping himself out with all kinds of foolish things; he looks wretched, R. says. Reflections on militarism, whether it does not sap the strength of a nation . . . At 7 o'clock the very fine fireworks display, celebrating Eva's recovery and Lulu's return home. Afterward Herr Rub. plays us Beeth.'s Quartet in F Major, Op. [*left blank; should be Opus 59, No. 1*], and R. says he almost prefers hearing it on the piano, where he can dictate the tempi, to having it played by fiddle scrapers, whom he cannot bear.

Sunday, October 5 After a good night R. gaily looks through my fashion journal in bed; he is always interested in costumes, but unfortunately we cannot help finding everything incomprehensibly ugly. Strange boys at lunch, Latin scholars, and we hear about the questions set for them in examinations, which greatly shock us: to know the ABC's so completely by heart that one can say with the greatest rapidity which letters come before and after this or that one! Then Schiller's poem *"Der Alpenjäger"* ["The Alpine Hunter"] to be written down in prose, thus depriving the child from the very start of the divine element within it, the "thus it must be"! — In the evening Herr Jäger sings something from *Die Walküre;* at the passage in which Sieglinde relates how Wotan appeared, R. turns to me and says he is pleased with it—it is like something from an old legend, something long since past, even for Sieglinde herself. — Earlier several things arrived from Straubing, where the animal-protection society has put up a very good show, and since Herr Mottl, who has just arrived here from Vienna, is composing a Romance in A Minor, R. gives him a pamphlet with a joking dedication. [*Added three pages later:* "On Sunday he wrote to Frau Lucca, saying she should seek out a respectable tenor, and he would then produce *Tristan* in Italian."]

Monday, October 6 R. gets up once and comes back after a while, saying he has found his Plutarch—he lost it a long time ago and now finds it at last in his room, acting as a support for his coverlet. At lunch he speaks of the first movement of the F Major Quartet, the theme of which he describes as "inspired shuffling," "divine pomade." He says Beeth. was not yet completely free in it, as in the F Major Symphony, for example, which he calls the most divine of all. He quotes a lot of things about animals which he has read with great delight in Plutarch's essay on terrestrial and marine animals. — In the morning he talked appreciatively of Hildebrandt the landscape painter and, reminded of him by the similarity of names, says: "What is a literary person like Hillebrand compared with the painter who gives us such pictures of distant lands? How pitiful he is in comparison!" In the evening Herr Rubin. plays the E-flat Major Quartet, to R.'s great delight; in the afternoon R. was shadowed by the "three little boys" and returned from his walk rather vexed over it.

Tuesday, October 7 R. had a good night, and he writes a new page in his article about animals; we talk a lot about the question with which he is wholly occupied. He says man's variety of motives makes him, if he is not fully mature, little superior to an animal in terms of truthfulness and simplicity. The artist is also assailed by too many motives, and the only genuine artist is the one who is able to tame them to form a whole. Much about the regard in which ancient civilizations held animals; he says the difficulty of his task lies in not going too far, not putting in too much, for there is no end to the material. In the evening we read half of Plutarch's essay on terrestrial and marine animals, with infinite enjoyment.

Wednesday, October 8 R. had a good night; still busy with the revision of his letter, and he also writes to the people in Straubing. Some newspaper reports about the scorn with which doctors are treating our movement upset him greatly, and he says he could bring himself to devote all his energies to it and become a socialist in addition. In the afternoon I read *Hamlet* to the elder girls, at their request! R. gets somewhat impatient that Lusch has not yet finished copying his letter, for he wants to make some additions to it. He is very taken up by it, indeed worn out. I suggest a game of whist. — As reading material he has E. v. Hagen on the 2nd scene of *Das Rheingold;* today he tells me that he has not grasped the difference between "eternal" and "infinite" —"eternal" simply means outside of time. Otherwise it would be nonsense to have spoken of "the end of the eternal gods." — Recently he observed that in the *Edda* and the ice-licking cow Andumpla one could see something like traces of Haug's theory (the poles). — At supper he said that on a recent walk he had had an amusing encounter; he had spoken to a stone breaker, and the man paid scarcely any attention to him, but when he saw Rubinstein with him, his face broke out in delighted smiles, and it turned out that the latter often gave him a few coins.

Thursday, October 9 The evening ended in melancholy mood, I believe vivisection is proving the most dismal of occupations! — All the same, once he has at last managed to get to sleep, R. sleeps well, and he goes off to his work, which today is devoted to additions to his article and, at last, its dispatch. I have to stay in bed, and the evening is spent in my little room. To start with, R. reads to us some extracts in the *Revue* from an American book about animals—some splendid features, which grip and please the children as much as they do us. Then we finish Plutarch on terrestrial and marine animals. — (Richter recommends an American tenor, R. writes to him.)

Friday, October 10 R. got up once but on the whole had a good night. I arrange some little things to celebrate the 10th. R. comes in, and all is spoiled. However, the cup with the façade of the old [Dresden] theater makes up for everything, and when R. laments my little misfortune, I really feel what a triumph it is that the delights of love have managed to overcome the vexations of chance! R. praises me for still taking such great care to preserve the joys of life—ah, it is my soul's gratitude which finds expression thus. Many memories of that time 26 years ago—also of Weber and L. Geyer on account of the cup. After lunch I return to bed, where these last pages are written. In the evening R. reads *Twelfth Night* to us, to the delight of us all. I always live again through these hours as they will appear in the future memories of our children, seen now so blissful before me. All kinds of droll incidents, the palm continues to be uncooperative, I could not set it up in the afternoon, and now, when I move it to protect it from the night frosts (the window had to be opened to create cross ventilation!), it pricks me, and I fall over with it in the dark. My celebration was spoiled, but that does not stop us from celebrating. (R. wrote to Herr Angelo recommending Herr Mottl, and to the conductor Herr Jahn about *Die Meistersinger* in Wiesbaden.) When I spoke to R. today about Dannreuther's description of musical life in England, he said, "Yes, one ought to start again every 30 years, that is to say, put the successes one has had in the past 30 years to some use."

Saturday, October 11 R. got up once, but he is not dissatisfied with his night's rest; in the morning he is much occupied with the eagles' chorus in *Agamemnon,* and he would like friend Wolzogen to write something about this profoundly mystical feature; the eagles, he says, are Zeus himself, they proclaim a victory, they pull to pieces a pregnant hare, and for that Artemis demands the King's daughter; she appears as protectress of animals and of peace against the god of war. R. then recalls the Princess of Rudolstadt: royal blood for oxen's blood. — Very cold, trouble with the servants, R. says, "Instead of friendly repentance, he shows concealed resentment." — He writes to the King and announces to me through "*Freude schöner Götterfunken*" on the piano that he has completed his 7 pages; later he tells me that he has talked a lot in it about the family, also a great deal about vivisection. He always finds writing these letters a chore. In the evening we wanted to finish the play, but a sore on his tongue, which he suddenly feels, prevents it, and I read a very good speech by the preacher Stoecker about the Jews. R. is in favor of expelling them entirely. We laugh to think that it really seems as if his article on the Jews marked the beginning of this struggle.

Sunday, October 12 Not a very good night, and the sore on his tongue still causing difficulties, but we think gaily of the 10th and the half-spoiled celebration. R. already said to me on Friday, "I am like some sort of beetle," and today he remarks with a laugh, "You used me to make things easy for yourself!" — He then tells me that, when he holds the cup in his hand, he is always reminded of something in his childhood (from about the age of 5); he had been on the Brühl terrace, going down the steps, when a sudden gust of wind from the river Elbe stirred up a swirling cloud of dust, and in the midst of this turmoil the church bells had begun to ring; he had seen right down the mouth of one of them, for the alcove in which they were swaying was open, and he had felt such terror that he had burst out crying—nothing on earth would have persuaded him to cross the square! . . . Lusch's birthday—our friends (the W.'s) with us; the Senta theme. Much affection and gaiety! Later, R. somewhat out of humor; but in the evening he appears in his new velvet jacket and long waistcoat as "Louis XIV," and again expresses his disgust with present-day fashions. — Whist in the evening, and at the same time some talk about vivisection, for Herr v. Weber has written to him; then the Jewish question is discussed once more. — While R. is playing the "Spinning Chorus" after lunch, he says, "Meudon and Bellevue inspired that, in somewhat the same way as the Quai Voltaire inspired *Die Meistersinger*—and our dear Emperor thought I must have been very much in love to write *Tr. und I.*" — He then tells us how Reissiger tried to find inspiration for composition by making a trip to Vienna. —

Monday, October 13 R. got up once and is somewhat run down; today he wrote letters—to Merz about a mistaken interpretation of Herr Jäger's attitude toward the school, and then to Messrs. V[oltz] and Batz. His tongue hurts, and he looks worn out at lunch—with him the slightest little thing immediately betrays itself in this way. The doctor comes and files the tooth which has been causing the inflammation, and everything is all right again, the wonted good humor and the gleaming eyes restored. In the evening the conclusion of *Twelfth Night* and a story about Minna and her family to the children. Their sympathy; R. says he really does not know how he stood it all: "It could not have continued, either." — Of the house in which he was born he says, "The white lion turned red with rage, and the red one white with alarm." — We talk of going on with the biography in Naples; I am delighted, but R. says only if he is not too much taken up by other things; the affinities of music and the other arts, all sorts of curious things are going through his head. — In the evening I see him suddenly come to a halt beside his bed: "A silly theme—I don't yet know whether it will be of any use or not." — He continues ruling his score in the afternoon and says he could now dictate the orchestration, so clear is it in his mind.

Tuesday, October 14 R. had a good night; recalling some childhood memories in the morning, he says he remembers how the Queen, angry with a baker's wife (Frau Hammer) for having bought a shawl which was too expensive for her, imposed an "iron cow" on the house: "You can imagine how this 'iron cow' exercised my imagination! Later I learned it was a form of tax." Over coffee we discuss *Twelfth Night,* and R. remarks how right Carlyle was to observe that the English might lose their colonies, but they would still have their Shakespeare. R. regrets that Sh. did not devote more words at the end to the transference of the Duke's love from Olivia to Viola; the comedy has a permanent flaw, he feels, and the happy end seems somewhat contrived. R. read this last scene so beautifully, put so much secret feeling into the Duke's words, addressed Viola with such a meaning look, that I could understand how, when he discovered that Viola was a woman, his whole soul overflowed with love for this being, and his feelings for the other were like a forgotten dream. — We then talk about the children's education, and he observes that he himself was never really educated at all—how often did he lie to his mother, and he went around with the wildest and roughest of boys. While using the cup, he is also reminded of the *yellow carriage* which he saw driving across this square and which took him to Leipzig for three days. We speak of dreams, and he says Frau Wesendonck has recently been appearing frequently in his, but unfortunately always in an odd and unpleasant way; once with her mouth so lax that it opened only to utter malicious things, which caused him to say to himself, "Well, that's the end of that." What he had subsequently said and done had been for the sake of propriety. "It is a pity," he concludes, "that memory takes such forms in one's dreams, for one would like to remember only the pleasant things; they were the first people to reward me with a certain amount of comfort and to feel a desire to take care of me." — On the other hand, he dreams only good and touching things about Hans, whom we shall probably never see again. . . . Over supper he tells me I can have no idea how lazy he is; today, for example, he looked through and read the complete supplement to the *Orbis Pictus:* the nebulae and the [*space left blank*] in the sun had raised many thoughts in his mind about the universe. "The whole thing is a fireworks display," he exclaims, "all so barbaric, so powerful, yet at the same time so undeniably subject to mathematical laws: and what is our earth by comparison? A mere speck." We play whist, the winnings to go to the stone breaker to whom the physician for the poor said, "What am I supposed to do with your old bones?" and who is now seeking his revenge by claiming admission to the hospital! . . . R. read aloud the poem of "Alexander's Feast," since Herr Rub. needs Handel's work for his essay on Brahms; afterward R. points out several ineffective and arbitrary harmonies in it and stresses how in Bach everything seems magnificent, necessary, and significant.

Wednesday, October 15 R. slept well; in the morning we continue talking about *Twelfth Night,* then R. says that when he first read Calderón, he was greatly moved by the delicate passion of the speeches; I observe that in them one is less conscious of the truthfulness of feeling than in Shakespeare. R. replies: "What is truth? It is a tremendous nervous excitation which can easily turn into the very opposite." — More discussion about the universe—and how splendid of the philosophers to have made ideality the basis of their outlook! — R. comes to lunch with Gfrörer's *Philo* and says he does not intend to finish it—all the theological subtleties stem from him. Herr Levi for lunch, and toward evening the 1st act of *Siegfried* with Herr Jäger! Great delight—indeed, enchantment! R. is also pleased. In the evening a gathering of all the stalwarts. Some talk about the King.

Thursday, October 16   R. slept well. — At 12 o'clock the 2nd act of *Siegfried;* when R. sings the words accompanying the burial of Fafner, the figure of Siegfried seems to become daemonic, overwhelmingly huge—superhuman! And when he sings of the doe and the human mother, I feel—through the music, as it were—that the connection between human beings and animals, with the human beings' superiority over them, is being movingly proclaimed. — At 5 o'clock the third act—and this is too much for us poor mortals! R. is worn out, our good conductor completely ill, Herr Jäger somewhat exhausted; so we have a family whist party, the two daughters, R., and I, after R. has sent for friend Wolz. and read to him and to us the remarkable passage in Carlyle's *Heroes and Hero-Worship* (Shakespeare) about infinity, music, melody.

Friday, October 17   R. is worn out, and so we have no music, neither morning nor afternoon. — Lenbach's pastel drawing arrives, it is good, and I am glad to have it to give to R. on the 19th. In the evening whist with the conductor and the two girls; R. somewhat tired, but gaily talkative.

Saturday, October 18   R. had a good night, but he prefers not to hold a rehearsal in the morning. Lunch with the conductor, conversation about the Jews, and the conductor also tells us of the horrifying infant mortality in Bavaria. Many sad accounts. — In the evening the first act of *Götterdämmerung!* — When after supper a Beethoven quartet is played (Op. 59), it gives us no pleasure at all; it seems to me that if one has been listening to dramatic music, the other kind makes no real impact—also this particular quartet strikes me as rather academic. R. calls such music note-spinning.

Sunday, October 19   Presentation of the picture in memory and celebration of the 19th twenty-three years ago, when I heard the *Tannhäuser* Overture and R.'s music for the first time. R. is pleased with it! — He says the curious thing about Lenbach is that at first sight his pictures strike one like an idea; afterward one might find this or that not very good, but the overall impression is always a convincing one. R. drapes and hangs the picture himself, and frequently during the day he shows it to me. He calls me his gift of a giver, and many other things also flow from his lips! . . . I spend the day reading the text of *Tannhäuser,* and my heart sings along with it. — Unpleasant episode with friend Rubinstein, though I hope it will eventually do some good. In the evening the first act of *Coriolanus* for the young people, and whist. R. writes to Prof. Overbeck for news of friend Nietzsche.

Monday, October 20 Bad night for R.; however, he takes pleasure in my picture and says it calls to him, "Richel, Richel, ideality." The event of the day is the arrival of Herr von Stein, a young, fair-haired, fine-looking man, a true German, very serious, but at the same time friendly. He is indeed willing to undertake Siegfried's education! We still cannot quite believe it; and in the evening friend Wolzogen as well—"a black one and a white one!" — The only thing that alarms us is the discovery that our new friend is a supporter of Dühring! Also an opponent of Christianity—but it all emerges from him in an unaffected and indeed noble manner.

Tuesday, October 21 R. slept well, and with astonishment and amusement we discuss the new element in our household; we owe it to Malwida, and when in great satisfaction I tell R. of my walk to the theater with our new friend, he at once sends her a telegram: "Devil take me, Münchhausen, you did that well—voice from the clouds." — But a little booklet of materialistic poems written by our young friend alarms us a little. R. tells him frankly all his ideas about universities, etc. The young mind is assailed from many sides, but holding its own staunchly and well. In the evening the second act of *Coriolanus;* for R. and me the object of unceasing, ever-recurring expressions of astonishment and admiration. — (Unfortunately a very sad letter to R. from friend Rub., to whom he replies very emphatically.)

Wednesday, October 22 R. slept well; much to-ing and fro-ing with Herr v. Weber about the open letter, which is to be published in the *B. Blätter* as well as in separate copies. The Conservative party appears to be supporting the antivivisection movement; also, R. read to us yesterday an advertisement for the new periodical *Die deutsche Wacht,* containing an attack against Israel; R. thinks it well done. First lesson today for Fidi; the elements of geometry, and planing with a cabinet-maker. R. and I feel as if we are dreaming, [*Wilhelm Meister's*] *Apprentice Years and Travels* now being translated into reality here—God grant that the noble spirit of our young teacher and friend will now gradually begin to feel at home with us and abandon all this modern rubbish! He is touchingly zealous in his approach to his task. — "There is a real devil in you," R. tells him with a laugh, encouraging him to be merry. In the evening the third act of *Coriolanus;* after the scene between C. and Volumnia we have to break off to exchange exclamations of admiration and to point out various details; and with cries of "Shame!" for Volumnia's disjointed ravings and utter lack of control, we acknowledge that one can never know these works too well; the poet's urge to reveal this character in all its shadings up to the point when even the highest breaks beneath the weight of wretchedness.

Thursday, October 23 R. had a good night, at any rate he got up only once, and he calms my worries about his cough, which disturbed him only in the morning, "when everything became active." — I cannot eat my breakfast, but he forbids any *Ottilie,* "after we have got past Ophelia." Around lunchtime he tells me that he has been reading Wolz.'s article with great pleasure; he really has something to say, and his way of dealing with the Jewish problem is new and very humane. It has given him the idea that the city of Leipzig, as the place of his birth, might perhaps be persuaded to make a substantial endowment for Bayreuth. Delight in Herr v. St.; discussion about the problems of socialism, our young friend hopes to see them solved in an amicable way, R. on the other hand feels there are bound to be convulsions. The enclosed quotations from the newspaper [*not found*] show where we are heading, and the nation will collapse under the strain. "We are not being ruled wisely," R. exclaims with a sigh! In the afternoon R. goes to Angermann's with W. and St., but on his return says very little came of it, and on such occasions he always has to make jokes and talk about himself. In the evening the last two acts of *Coriolanus.* — The mail brought us a very fine letter from Frau Helmholtz about Eckert's death, a touching one from Franziska Ritter, and one from the Catholic woman who asked me for *Parsifal* to give to a nun who teaches literature in a convent. I sent her Dr. Schemann's articles.

Friday, October 24 R. had a good night, he works on his article and tells me that in it he praises Hans's *Nirwana* very highly. — Good letter from Rub., who seems to be one of those people for whom harshness is more beneficial than kindness, but we are pleased that it has had this effect. At lunch we talk about *Coriolanus,* and R. says only the fifth act does not much appeal to him—indeed, all the fifth acts, including that of *Hamlet;* he says the tragic catastrophe has already taken place, and death adds nothing. From the way in which he depicts the common people it is easy to believe that Shakespeare was an aristocrat. Discussion with Herr v. St. about Siegfried; in response to R.'s ideas on surgery, he says he would consider it right to have models of the human form, including the internal organs, in the schoolroom we are going to build. R. thinks: Later; first of all, allow him to take pleasure in the outward appearance, the naked body as depicted by the Greeks, which will enchant him, and *only when the daemon begins to stir within him* show him the inner workings. At this stage he would perhaps feel revolted. He then talks of Fidi's willing nature: he is lighthearted but not unthinking, "the youngster enjoys life." — R. finds the *Illustrirte* interesting with its pictures from Alsace, the Emperor's visit, and once again he voices his utter scorn for the spiked helmet. The Supreme Court's ball also evokes many remarks from him: "How solemn and dignified we are—we open the Supreme Court with a ball! And all those bearded men—beards are all right in the wilderness, but with frock coats . . . !" — In the open letter, which is now ready for distribution, Herr v. Weber asks R. to alter "the inscrutabilities" of God into "the mysteries," since religious people are supporting the cause. R. tells of our meeting with Herr Windthorst and says that he came to us wearing large white kid gloves, which had almost certainly been sent to him by Pio Nono after the final blessing. In the evening whist with Herr v. Stein, after R. glanced with enjoyment through the *Fl. Blätter.*

Saturday, October 25　R. had a good night, and he goes to his work. In the morning he asked me if I felt Hans might be annoyed with him for praising *Nirwana;* I reply that I fear he might, since malicious people would perhaps make nasty remarks about it, and that would be bound to offend him. He decides to leave it out, and reads to me what he has written about the transition from program music to the music drama. All sorts of things keep us busy—the movement initiated by Herr Schön and Prof. Oncken, for me in particular the Wagner lexicon with friend Glasenapp, then the vivisection affair. R. has an idea that Leipzig, his home town, might perhaps be persuaded to make an endowment for Bayreuth. — A fine October day tempts us to take a walk to the Eremitage, the children, Herr von Stein, and I; R. joins us later in the summer carriage, a merry stroll through the park. R. tells us that the Chancellor is again trying to form an alliance with Herr von Bennigsen! . . . A visit to the inn, then the drive home, 9 people and so many rugs that we have to laugh out loud. At home our guest gets news of the sudden death of Dr. Dühring, his guiding star till now; this seems to us both cruel and significant. — R. says, "Life is so unseemly," and indeed, it does do things very drastically. When we are alone together, we discuss this strange occurrence—has this young man been sent to us by an inexorable fate? In the evening we begin *Don Quixote* and read up to the first homecoming; R. finds it so admirable that Cervantes does not reproduce the conversation with the peasant, but just tells about it; he says: "These people knew what to treat as epic and what as drama."

Sunday, October 26　R. had a fairly good night but feels heavy and run down, and, quite contrary to his usual practice, he takes a walk in the morning, telling us at lunch that he saw the exact place on which his statue would be erected—in the middle of the round border on

Cottenbacher Strasse—but he does not know how they will place him, facing the theater or the school; this calls forth many jokes. In the morning he told me that Siegfried had dreamed he was dead; why can I not bear any mention of old age or anything else to do with the laws of Nature in connection with him? — We talk about *Don Quixote,* and R. says, "What makes these few works eternal is simply that they are always new to us." — We take another walk like yesterday's, R. comes to meet us and, turning in the palace gardens in the direction of the Birk, shows us the architectural effect which pleases him so— when one enters from the nursery gardens and sees the gate, the single statue, the vase, and the trees grouped here in a grove. [*Added later:* "I have sent for patterns of furnishing materials, Pompadour style, to please R.; he finds all the modern things so stiff, so unpoetical. Twelve years ago he found in Paris some flower patterns of the kind he loves. — During the walk in the palace gardens R. talked about Swiss battles, which he calls the most heroic in modern history; he tells us about the Battle of Näfels."] Letter from Prof. Overbeck about the wretched state of our poor friend Nietzsche's health—and not to be *permitted* to do anything, let alone to be able to! — In the evening much talk about Schiller, arising from Tischbein's portrait; R. deplores Goethe's influence over him, which was responsible for the present form of *Wallenstein;* he talks about the excellent idea of wanting to present a picture of the 30 Years' War, and says that both Goethe and Schiller thought of Bernhard von Weimar as a subject, but then the first question had always been how, and in what meter—iambics or what? "Goethe at that time was a complete ass," he says in his characteristic way, adding that, if he had not finished *Faust* and written *Elective Affinities,* one would not know what to make of him. — Of [Schiller's] essay on the naïve and the sentimental, he says the beginning is splendid, but then it peters out. — More *Don Quixote,* up to the gallant Basque—we skip the list of books.

Monday, October 27 R. had a very bad night, I had to rouse him from wild dreams, try to calm him down! Blockages in circulation are supposed to be the cause, but what do names mean? . . . It can scarcely be a mistake in his diet—when we discuss what agrees with him, he says, "Joys, such as your picture, for instance, and every time I go upstairs and see the portière." He reads Herr v. W[eber]'s account of his African journey and says that it is certainly somewhat curious, and people might make fun of it for the way he is always talking about Offenbach quadrilles, but the subject interests him. A book sent by Herr Levi containing Busch's "*M[ax] und Moritz*" and other things by the same humorous writer amuses him greatly for a short while. But he eats almost nothing at lunch (Herr R. is with us), and he feels increasingly unwell. Dr. Landgraf prescribes vegetable pills—but at R.'s instigation, who recalls that Dr. Gide recommended them to him! — In the evening whist, we break up early, and I find R. upstairs in his room, pleased when I arrive.

Tuesday, October 28 R. had a much better night and is also looking much better; as we embrace in the morning, he says to me, "We shall become quite young again." — Before that we talked about the *B. Blätter,* and I told him what I had said to friend W.—that with every article a new category is introduced, and it is subsequently expanded by one or several other writers: with Semper's obituary it was sculpture, with Dr. Dühring (Herr v. St. wants to write this), education. R. feels I am right, and we agree that the important thing is not adding to our community, but strengthening its outlook in all directions, by always keeping our artistic ideals in the forefront and observing everything from that point of view. At lunch R. speaks of new members gained and tells Herr v. Stein about Kroppenstedt, Pössneck, etc., places in which we have members! "Yes," he says to the surprised young man, "we don't know ourselves, we Germans." — Telegram concerning the *Götterdämmerung* performance in Brunswick and its success; speaking of the Duke, R. says that in his experience it is precisely the frivolous, utterly uncultivated people on whom his works have the most powerful effect, as, for example, *Tannhäuser* on the Poles in Dresden at the beginning. — R. was able to do some work, he goes for a walk in the palace gardens and starts a new diet—at least he drinks no grog. — In the evening the quartet, Op. 74, which reminds R. of his uncle's remark: "One thinks one has got hold of Beethoven, but constantly he eludes one's grasp." "That is right," R. adds; "when one thinks a platitude is coming, something unexpected emerges, and one realizes he has been playing around with the platitude." —

Wednesday, October 29 R. had a somewhat restless night, but not too bad. He tells me merrily that in a speech in Essen Herr v. Puttkamer said with extraordinary naïveté that the Emperor had steeled himself to make the sacrifice and had concluded the alliance with Austria! Also that what was now leading us back to the Liberals was nervousness on the part of the Emperor, who had heard that the synod was discussing the abolition of the changing-of-the-guard parade on Sundays! — Then R. tells me that now, when he lights his *Lubin,* he finds himself thinking a lot about my mother, since I told him that she, too, used to fumigate her apartment with it; he talks of her relationship with my father and says he can understand why she was unable to tolerate his unfaithfulness. Much about this dismal relationship between two significant people, then jokingly to us: "You will also leave me!" Gay memories of that daemonic night in January nearly two years ago; the sudden flaring of the flame which told me, as I sought him in concern about his rest, that paper had been burned here, his return to the *salon* after it had been put out, his surprise over my question whether something had been burning—how pleasant that one can speak gaily of dreadful memories! When I leave him, I find a butterfly on my window, a large tortoise-shell; I go to ask R. whether it would be better for it to stay in my room or to be put outside in spite of the cold. R. goes to my room, the butterfly hops onto his finger, and now it is free! R. says it is like my portière (and indeed the colors are the same), which has small ones on it; for me it seemed like the free-flying messenger of our loving conversation. — Lovely sunshine tempts us to undertake an outing to the Fantaisie, I walking ahead with the children, R. following in the carriage; nice walk and drive home. In the evening a visit from a M. de Fourcaud, an editor of the *Gaulois,* who traveled in vain to Munich to see *Tristan und Isolde.* R. tries to explain to him (1) why he feels, and could feel, no *rancune* [resentment] against the French on account of *Tannhäuser;* and (2) why his works cannot be presented in France, and the French must come to Germany if they want to get to know them. R. plays the Prelude to *Parsifal.* And when the friendly stranger has departed, we admire his remarkable gifts of expression, the ability to put into words all one is feeling at the moment. His physical appearance, on the other hand, is peculiar—he comes from an old family and is small and inconspicuous in a way one rarely finds among the German nobility. When we were talking about Ollivier's position, R. said jokingly that Bismarck would send for him to become minister of culture, since he now had need of one!

Thursday, October 30 R. had a tolerable night; in the morning we discuss the visit of the *Gaul,* who is by no means handsome, but R. says his expression at first meeting had been nice, "a rapturous taking-in." We also comment on the fact that in France this class of person is becoming increasingly small and insignificant in appearance. The pact with Austria will, it is said, lead to an alliance of the three emperors, and thus to peace. "Against the English," says R., "all you need is to win over a lot of Jews." Our Gaul comes to say goodbye, but misses his train, stays for lunch, and surprises us with his questions, such as: "*Maître, aimez-vous Raphael?*" — R. goes for a walk, and in the evening, when he returns, writes to Herr Rudolphi. In the evening we are by ourselves and play whist. He gives Herr v. Stein Dr. Dühring's book about R. Mayer with a short inscription. Recalling his conversation with the Gaul, he says with a laugh, "I am not suited to the Socratic manner—I fall upon people and force my views on them." — When our guest called himself a Gaul, R. maintained energetically that the Gauls were Germans. A book on America with many illustrations has aroused his interest, and he wants to keep it.

Friday, October 31　During the night R. was rather restless at first, but the second part was better. When I come up from my bath and sit down beside him, he says I am so surrounded by brightness, whereas he by darkness—"thou in light, I in shadow"—this quotation brings us to Starnberg, all the suffering and all the high spirits, the jubilant surging of love. He recalls his poem and the feeling he expressed in it that he would never possess me: "It turned out all right in the end," he exclaims. — Yesterday the *inquiring Frenchman* wanted to know which of his works meant most to R. R. said he did not know, he soon forgot all about them, perhaps he could say *Parsifal,* since he wrote this in the most congenial circumstances. — R. joins with me in deploring Hans's foolishness in not seeing Lulu, saying that no other female person could be such a comfort to him. He works on his article and feels he has now said enough—he mentioned yesterday that he intended to cite Saint-Saëns's works as an example of how instrumental music has now gone astray, but he has decided not to do so, since it would be taken personally, as an act of harshness toward a friend. "When I get too carried away," R. says, "I make a swift change of direction"—and that is indeed very characteristic of him, his spontaneousness, even in his reflective moments, and his inability to "tell fibs," as he himself calls it. — At lunch our conversation touches on [Goethe's] theory of colors, and when Herr v. St. says it has long been superseded, R. says, "What interests me is the intelligent man who discerns something, not the number of learned discoveries." When mention is made of Eckert's sudden death, our young friend observes that it was a pleasant death; R. says no, a pleasant death means dying at a ripe old age, aware of it as the true aim of living. R. goes for a walk, taking the dogs with him, but complains about Brange, who looks at him "like a mother of God" but, once she picks up a scent, abandons him without mercy. At supper we come back to Goethe, reminded of him by a picture of Prof. Oken in the *I. Zeitung;* R. says Goethe did not like him: "He was a fine *monsieur.*" But he can understand his dislike of Fichte and says with regard to ideality: "It is exactly the same as with the valve trumpet—hardly was this facility discovered when all melodies were played with it. The same with ideality: hardly had Kant discovered it when everybody started making nonsense of it." R. is delighted with Luther's goblets in the *I. Z.,* and that leads our conversation to this great man. Another item about the Communards brings from R. the opinion that a plebiscite should have been held, for the people to decide whether they wanted the exiles back or not.

R. then tells about having experienced a vote of this kind in Switzerland (canton Glarus); from that subject to Sulzer, whom R. mentions with great warmth, finding the outcome of his austere life—the inevitability of his downfall—very moving. — Talking about large cities, R. tells our friend, who likes Berlin, that he himself cares only for Paris; this city had always interested him, and when the streets he knew so well were being demolished to make room for the new opera house, he had been too vexed to be able to watch it happening.

Saturday, November 1 R. had a good night, did not get up at all; he goes to work on his *"air varié,"* as he calls his article. Talk at lunch about Robert Mayer, and over coffee R. asks to be told about the new law this scholar has discovered! — He goes for a short walk, and in the evening we read G. Keller's "Dietegen" with infinite enjoyment. R. keeps exclaiming: "No, who would ever have thought of that? They are very first impressions, bubbling up as if out of a bottle." R. does not feel very well and takes some pills—my impulse, God knows, is always to advise him to take nothing at all. On the doctor's recommendation he goes to the Café Sammet instead of to Angermann's, and finds everything there, the beer as well as the people, very unattractive; the only thing that amuses him is a witticism in a paper—that in the morning recruits are bombarded with words of abuse and in the evening, as extras in *Lohengrin,* are addressed as "Ye nobles of Brabant!"

Sunday, November 2 R. had a very disturbed and bad night. A bath restores him somewhat; at breakfast we talk about the laws our friend described to us yesterday; R. says it all seems to him so childish, the most we could expect from it would be coffee machines in which the coffee would grind itself! — As he leaves, he tells me he has discovered that all virtues are negative except for fellow suffering, for the suffering is positive—whereupon I say that is exactly what I wrote to Lusch four weeks ago! After we have parted, we meet again, when he has found my All Souls' Day flowers. I am *Webia,* he tells me, I am the *"Urlögtrygia,"* spinning together all the strands of relationships. But at lunch he chides me for thinking so much of All Souls, saying he has only one soul. He goes out, I visit a widow, and when I return home, the skies are alive with indescribable colors. — I walk around in the *salon;* he, having seen me return, comes in: "You All Souls' woman!" Put on my white dress for the first time since May 22. R. is pleased. We have sent our friend Stein to Munich to see the *Ring,* we play whist with the two girls and then start to read Keller's *"Das verlorne Lachen";* the felling of the oak tree has a shattering effect on us both, and a little later R. says, "Yes, we Germans owe our downfall to the fact that we cannot be tradesmen." Shattered though we may have been by the episode of the oak tree—such things are rare, R. says, even in the greatest of poets, such as Schiller and Goethe—we are equally amused by the parson's sermon, which we can scarcely finish for laughing. (Yesterday, when I spoke of death by opening one's veins, R. said, "Arteries—the arteries are the hexameters, the veins the pentameters, in which the blood drips melodically.")

Monday, November 3   R. slept better, if still somewhat restlessly. He works on his article, says that he is now coming to the point for which he set out to write it in the first place. The weather is very cold. At lunch we talk about K.'s Protestant parson, and R. says, "He is unique—he abandons God, turns Christ into a good man, but the church—that remains." — Then R. talks of going to America, to return a rich man; doubt whether I, too, for ships can sink. I: "Without me you will get no farther than Nuremberg." Lusch: "No farther than Creussen." — Toward evening R. receives Herr Wölffel to talk about converting the annex into a schoolroom for Siegfried and Herr v. St. — In the evening conclusion of the lovely story, which remains gripping from all points of view. R. observes that such conditions could not be found in Germany.

Tuesday, November 4   R. did not get up at all during the night, which is always a triumph, and I also hear him laughing loudly as I go to my bath; he then tells me he has been thinking of that sentence in Falstaff's speech to the Prince, when he says he would not believe him to be his son if it were not for a certain feature of his nether lip. — He goes to work on his article, and when I ask him not to overstrain himself, he says, "Oh, no," adding that when he just sits and reads he gets melancholy in the evening. He has been much occupied in the past few days with Grétry's *Raoul Barbe-Bleue,* and tells me again about Raoul's white plume, which as a child he wanted so badly; then he shows me the score, the instrumentation, so empty—what a difference when one compares it with *La Dame Blanche,* he says! I tell him there is a difference also between his scores and Weber's. He: "If one were faced with doing what Weber did, one couldn't do it a single jot better." Alarming rumors regarding Frau Feustel's health induce us to address an inquiry to Dr. Landgraf; he sends us a short bulletin, so careful and precise that R. breaks out in praise of our good doctor, who has now, he says, replaced the parson. [*Enclosed here a note diagnosing Frau Feustel's complaint as:* "a typhoid type of illness with high temperature."] Whist with the children and a start on the story "*Kleider machen Leute.*" R. sings the finale of Beethoven's E-flat Major Sonata (one of the early works) and says, "This kind of melody has gone forever—innocent sweetness, it is a lost paradise." — Hans has resigned his conducting position in Hanover following a dispute with the tenor Herr Schott! — So once again homeless! . . .

Wednesday, November 5 R. wakes up with a slight sore throat, we send for the doctor, who confirms that the tonsils are swollen and advises gargling and rest. Bad news of Frau Feustel, which affects us very deeply, for we love this *good* woman. R. intends to eat with us, but he feels very run down, could do no work, either, he stretches out in bed. I stay downstairs, awaiting friend Gersdorff, and Richter comes in, with beaming face and spirits, the old Tribschen youth again. The children overjoyed, R. calls him up to his bedside and then has supper with us on his account, much about the present agitation against the Jews. After an hour R. goes off. (Friend Gersdorff has also arrived, to tell me of many things he has on his mind; R. says to me jokingly that I am Macaria, the All Souls' woman—everyone comes to me.)

Thursday, November 6 R. had a restless night, but he comes down to say goodbye to Richter, who, the complete Tribschen youth again, tells us many amusing things and is inexhaustible, particularly on the subject of the Israelites. Lunch with friend Gersdorff, during which R. remarks that he has regained his appetite and does not know why! Great concern about Frau Feustel, seriously ill with typhus. — R. does nothing all day except read the account of the African journey. New books sent to us arouse nothing but astonishment and disgust. In the evening conversation with our friend Gersdorff.

Friday, November 7 R. had a good night, the heavens are bright, his mood also, and he works on his article, which Lusch is copying. A constant stream of jokes with friend Gersdorff, whose amorous affairs enliven our lunch table, and the news that Dr. Dühring is not dead increases our gaiety still further. Herr v. Bürkel writes that the King was very willing to allow Herr v. Stein admittance to the special performances, which, it seems, have turned out very well. In the evening conversation with friend Gersdorff and Frau von Staff; we come to talk of friend Rubinstein, always a painful topic! — When I bring R. the copy of his article, he asks me whether I have read the "predigested tea"—he wrote it for me, and anyway he can only make jokes now, he says, serious things seem to him too absurd.

Saturday, November 8 R. had a restless night, he talked a lot in his sleep and afterward imparted to me how yesterday morning he had told himself that disharmony between us was an impossibility; now a cause of dissent had arisen through his "speeches," since, upset by the presence of other people, he sometimes did not know what he was saying. "I am so sad," he says with a pale face and tears in his eyes after we talked energetically together in the afternoon, I in particular about Héloïse, and he assured me that it suited me very well! But the gloom passes, and we spend the evening gaily in conversation, half of it in finishing *"Kleider machen Leute,"* which makes us remark that

Keller always rises to a sublime conclusion; we had almost feared that the story was becoming rather trivial, but then he suddenly changes direction, and the last sentence is excellent in its humor.

Sunday, November 9   R. had a good night, the sky shines brightly, we decide to eat late and to go for a walk before lunch. We stroll to Birken in various groups. R. stays behind to work on his article, then walks, not to Birken, but in the direction of Konnersreuth. At lunch he is so gay and exuberant that friend Gersdorff is swept up into joining in. Friend Stein appears at coffeetime, very happy with his visit to Munich; a little later the Jägers, his guest appearance was a complete success, which is very pleasant news. In the evening our neighbors and Rubinstein. R. maintains that this article is the last he is going to write.

Monday, November 10   R. had a good night, but when he wakes up, his nose is very red and swollen—we fear erysipelas! — He works on his article. Prof. Zöllner sends him his book on transcendental physics with a very nice letter, and in this connection R. remarks on how a misunderstanding of Kant and Schopenhauer can lead to such aberrations as the assumption of a fourth dimension; ideality, he says, is difficult to grasp, and particularly difficult to keep in mind, and people are constantly losing sight of it. "If Schopenhauer and Kant were really understood, how could new philosophical books possibly keep on emerging?" — After lunch our conversation touches on the connection between color and key; R. says he knows someone who suggested that he should turn it into a system, but in fact he has never seen colors. He then tells us about Baudelaire, who very wittily translated the Prelude to *Lohengrin* into colors, but he was not a musician. And how could this theory be reconciled with transposition, musical pitch? Everything lies in the relationship of one key to another, he says. Much then about Baud. and Champfleury, those two delightful oddities. "Just as the divine principle can be seen as a negation of the world, such people are a negation of Paris, but only possible in Paris itself." He goes for a short walk, revises his article, and, when I visit him at work, tells me delightedly about the children and the dance he has been watching: "My heart overflows when I think what happiness I have been given." — But his cold is getting worse; he does indeed joke about it, saying his nose is swelling up like a hippopotamus's, but both he and I are worried. The doctor prescribes inhalations of marshmallow tea—these clear his brain a little, and he is able to laugh heartily over the beginning of Keller's story "*Die missbrauchten Liebesbriefe.*"

Tuesday, November 11   R. did not have too bad a night, but his condition is worse, and the morning is filled with vexations; the revision of his article, the inhalations, the inopportune arrival of the barber—all these things, aggravated by pain, have made him resentful when he comes to lunch, but by the end his spirits are restored, through either his own efforts or the stillness which sympathy brings about; and at last he laughs heartily, telling us of all the little mishaps with which he has had to contend, getting his jacket caught up, losing his velvet cap, the tea boiling over, etc. Unaware of all this, my mind is taken up almost entirely with the death of Frau Feustel—our best, indeed our only female friend here. When R. asked me about her during the afternoon, I had to tell him of a turn for the worse; he wanted to visit her, and when I tell him that she is unconscious, he replies, "I shall soon restore her to consciousness." Now she is dead, and with her the soul of our identification with Bayreuth has gone, as well as a truly good and brave being. — R. finishes correcting his article, and in the evening we read the *"Liebesbriefe"* to the end; unfortunately we cannot really take to it, and have the feeling that it was written just to fill out a volume. — In conversation before our reading R. quotes the Bible saying: "For all have sinned, and come short of the glory of God." He says his first wife often quoted this saying; he admires the translation of the word *"Doxa"* by *"Ruhm"* ["glory"] and stresses the beauty of Luther's work and the wretchedness of modern learned "corrections."

Wednesday, November 12   R. did not have a bad night, but the condition of his nose is, if anything, worse, and he feels severe pains in his brain. Dr. Landgraf comes, and precautions are taken that the steam, passing through a funnel, does not rise too violently into R.'s face; the preparation of the paper cone amuses him, and he says to the doctor, "We shall have to send this to the next World Exposition." [*Added on a later page, but referred back to this point:* "R. calls the cone the nose of God, in contrast to the eye and the finger of God."] — In the morning he reads [Weber's] account of his African journey with interest, but is sorry that his new friend should have spent his time digging for diamonds. At lunch, probably recalling the effect Keller's story had on him, he praises the artistic economy of *Don Quixote,* how sparing he is in describing the adventures, so that they always have their effect. He had already said, after our reading last night: "We are no longer artists nowadays. The short stories of Lope and Cervantes may be insignificant, but what form they have! Whereas even Goethe and Schiller were always just searching, experimenting." — Today he has been reading *Othello,* in connection with something Herr v. St. said to him about the acting of Salvini; he says to me: "Women are better than men, that is something I realized today, and I thought of a lot of things which moved me very much. But the poetry I do not like at all, this realism tears one literally to shreds, it's terrible." I remained with friend Gersdorff in the *salon,* and R., coming from his afternoon rest, found us there, sat down, and asked us to stay; he talked in a splendid and very touching way of his happiness, which he is enjoying just as it is, wanting nothing changed. He says he posed a question, the answer was "Ba ba!," and now he has stopped searching and is happy, enjoying his life without any abstract nonsense. [*Added on a later page, but referred back to this point:* "He says, 'Let me be a child, and you be the same—I cannot say be a donkey, since I am asking someone else to be it with me.' "] When he hears Lusch playing the piano, he is pleased and says to me, "I have no idea how that came about, how you educated your children at all—it has happened without any fuss." [*Added on a later page, but referred back to this point:* "He calls the bedroom the 'well-tempered clavichord room,' since the sound of the children's practicing comes to us in a muted form. During a merry game of whist he says to Lulu, 'It's only for your sakes I look after myself; if you weren't all here, Mama and I would know what to do.' "] Our mood is a curious one, calm and pleasant, and it is blessed by our being entirely alone together, our friends having been invited to the W.'s. But I am beset by unutterable concern when I notice at the whist table how very run down R. looks. Whether it is due to pain, the fact that he is forbidden to take snuff, or the air in the room, only God knows, and God also knows how I manage to bear so much worry, however much in His abundant goodness He thinks of me—oh, who can measure, describe, or even guess at the feelings within my soul! R. talks to me again during the evening about Othello, who, he says, becomes downright repulsive. I: "That is perhaps what Shakespeare wanted." He: "Wanted—rubbish! He had no choice—that is how he saw it." "And Desdemona, the silly goose—not to guess what was tormenting him, always bringing up Cassio!" "That is how he had to show her naïveté and innocence." He finds Desdemona the purest and most complete female figure in Shakespeare, and mentions her exclamation "O, these men, these men!" The fact that we were alone together today brought home to me the utter bliss of his company—no discord, no irritation, just love, even in the midst of worry!

Thursday, November 13 R. did not have a bad night, and the doctor does not seem at all worried. At lunch R. is very cheerful, and at coffee bubbling over with good spirits. — In the afternoon he works on his score, that is to say, he continues ruling it, and when I go to him to ask whether he is sufficiently cheerful and well for me to wear my *Parsifal* dress, he says yes and he wishes me to. He comes back to Othello and Desdemona and says that in her and her fate he can discern the world's woes, but Othello is interesting only from a pathological point of view; he says he did not read the final scene—"it requires a brute like Shakespeare to write something like that!" — In the evening the presence of our friend Gersdorff leads us to the subject of war, and R. remembers how astonished Garibaldi was to see the Germans advancing in *"passo di scuola"* ["marching in step"] under shellfire: "He must have thought to himself, 'You can't wage war on such donkeys—they're not a bit nervous!' " — R. says it might well be asked whether this showed the privates' heroic courage or just fear of their sergeants. He says he has always supported the organization of the army, and he is also convinced that our officers have heroic courage, but the present state of affairs—an exhausted nation, constant new taxes, and the army's being constantly reinforced—that is barbaric. Conquering new territories and not waiting to inquire how they might be won over, never stopping to think how to make friends with Holland, Switzerland, etc., nothing at all but just army, army! Another speech by the preacher Stoecker provokes from R. the exclamation: "Oh, it is not the Jews—everybody tries to further his own interests— it is we ourselves who are to blame; we, the nation, for allowing such things to happen. The same with the stock exchange, a free and good institution to begin with, and what have we let it become?" And he talks of the present loan the state is making, which will just give further rein to this evil speculative urge. —

Friday, November 14 R. and I continue yesterday's conversation, and he remarks how disillusioned we are with the German character, since we so clearly see through it! . . . At lunch a recollection of Aeschylus's chorus (the female hare and the eagle) causes him to remark on the nobility of this outlook, and he feels it was things like this that might have led to accusations of blasphemy against Aeschylus, this connection between holiness and Nature was probably at the bottom of the Eleusinian mysteries. In our times, R. continues, religion should seek to influence ethics, and allow faith to be represented by art, which can transform illusion into truth. — During the evening he reflects on what might have been in history—if, for example, the Elector Friedrich had been king instead of Charles V, what would have become of Germany? How different from now!

[*End of the thirteenth notebook of the Diaries.*]

Likewise, too, his own project, if the Crown Prince had taken an interest in it, which would have been possible. One always builds on such possibilities, he remarks. — In the evening friend Rubinstein plays to us the *Idyll,* his "picture" of Siegfried and the Rhinemaidens, and the American march, which enchants me anew with its expansive, vigorous picture of a bold, peaceful nation. — Siegfried's run-down appearance gives us cause for reflection regarding his present studies; a difficult problem here, too—and a worry! . . .

Saturday, November 15   I asked R. last night to repeat to me the thoughts on religion which he had expressed at lunch; this leads him to say jokingly this morning that he will introduce a new religion for me alone. Siegfried's indisposition causes us to send for the doctor, and when he looks through the exercise book (geometry), he, too, has his doubts, though he does admit that mathematics is a very necessary subject nowadays, even in medicine, with optics, for example, being applied mathematics. "Applied mathematics and denied experience," says R. Over coffee he tells us the Goethe verse [*newspaper clipping enclosed; see notes*], though the way in which it is introduced throws an alarming light on the customs of our own day. In the evening *Don Quixote,* with a great deal of laughter and untold pleasure in following the all-knowing writer into the smallest of details. Before we go to lunch R. shows me the orchestral sketch of *Parsifal* and his ruled score; in the former all the instruments have been written in. These preparations provide his final pleasure in his work, he says, for once it is written down, pleasure vanishes—all that is left is piano arrangement, publication, and, worst of all, performance!

Sunday, November 16   R. is somewhat better, though he is still not allowed out of doors. However, he is having good nights, and today he continues ruling according to his method. The book by Herr v. W[eber] which he is reading gives him little pleasure, since the intellectual level seems very low—joy in discovering the *Kölner Zeitung* and the *Gartenlaube* in Africa, in playing Offenbach quadrilles, etc.! — The postcard from Leipzig [*enclosed; see notes*] gives R. pleasure, and he says, "If I were to go to Leipzig now, they would certainly harness four donkeys and drive me through the city," which makes us all laugh heartily. — Goethe's saying about uncongenial and insignificant people [*newspaper clipping enclosed; see notes*] also pleases us greatly. And we linger long in spirit in Italy, our friends describe Paestum and much else besides, whereupon R. turns to me: "God, how uneducated we are! They already know everything, we nothing at all." R. talks about Sismondi and stresses his pleasure in his book; talking about one of the many Italian adventurers, he says, "All these people needed was some great territory in order to become a Hannibal or an Alexander." The history of the various cities reflects Greece in a curious way, he says. — He always speaks of Pisa with particular feeling. After taking his afternoon rest, he collects his two friends for a glass of beer, and after a while he comes to tell me that he has been speaking very passionately, is feeling rather tired, and would like me to go down. I am met by silence and, I think, emotion. Yesterday friend G. remarked to me: if only he could write down all the things he had heard! — It had been so moving when R. questioned our young friend about his thoughts and his views on life and then gave a short account of his own life, how his disgust with existing conditions had so taken possession of him that he did not wish to accept the conductor's position. Later R. also tells me in brief what he said—I know how, too—the fire that is expended, enough to melt whole icebergs, but also to devour the straw and destroy the undergrowth! [*Added on a later page but referred back to this point:* "When I come down to supper, I see R. in the hall, Marke and Brange playing the organ."] — *Don Quixote* in the evening, somewhat trying since much of it is not designed for being read aloud to women. However, R. with divine calm continues equably to read, and we put a brave face on it. — (This morning R. received a letter from Herr Gützlaff, a head teacher in Elbing, along with a book containing quotations from Schopenhauer about animals. We are pleased with both.)

Monday, November 17 Just as Posa [in Schiller's *Don Carlos*] can exclaim, "All the same, life is sweet!" when he has sacrificed his own, so, too, do I, after experiencing all the awfulness of it and recognizing its tragedy, exclaim, "All the same, it is sweet!" At our morning separation I exclaim it. — "It must be: *go!*" R. says to me in English. Life is parting; at all such outpourings of our hearts I feel that death is, as it were, the unfolding of the yearning blossom of love, life the winter frost before which it must close in order to survive. When one lives, love dies, when one loves, life dies! — Frau Heim has sent me photographs of Zurich; R. goes through them with me and shows me his window in his various apartments; I gaze on them all with emotion and see the pear tree he climbed on the first morning of my stay at the Asyl. At lunch he talks about museums and says, "I have never visited the museum in a town—I never had time for it; I have never seen the Green Vault; I was only once in the Louvre, with a Mlle Leplet, from whom I hoped to get some money—Kietz had told me about her." As lunch ends, he voices his delight in a leaf: "Like a tiger skin." He expresses his delight at length, and since I cannot see the leaf, he plucks it for me. — He talks again about America, saying that he might still perhaps go there in order to make his fortune, but then he would not come back. He believes that if he had settled there permanently with his family, the Americans would probably have stood by him, but not now, when all he does is demand contributions for this place. — He also talks at lunch about the study of history in childhood and where one should begin, because I had asked him whether one should start with specialized history. He thinks, from the beginning of mankind, the first migrations and the return to the region of the Ganges, then the figures of Semiramis, Cyrus, in order to arrive at the Greeks; and this without questioning the legendary parts, for what human beings have themselves thought out and imagined is more important than what really happened. — In the evening we read *Don Quixote,* and the noble speech to the weeping old convict reminds us of Plato's state! . . .

Tuesday, November 18 R. had a good night's rest, which is indeed a miracle, to be gratefully accepted, considering that he is still not allowed out of doors. A pamphlet containing quotations from Schopenhauer on the subject of animals has been sent to him, and this gives him occasion to talk about the nature of Sch.'s philosophy and to remark that all the people who criticize it simply demonstrate that they have not understood it. And then people always want to do something with philosophy, he says, whereas its function is similar to that of a cold bath; to believe no more lies; every loss in that sphere a gain. Then he comes to socialism and says: "The main thing is not to imagine that the forces at work in it can be channeled through ideas and organizations; if that were so, there would be nothing to them. But one can influence ethics and prepare human hearts for the violence which lies ahead." — Arrival of Herr Schön's appeal! We approve it with a sigh. "A great honor for me if it does not succeed," R. exclaims, "and torture if it is successful, for it will be based on a misunderstanding." Very merry lunch, R. in a splendid, exuberant mood. He talks about the nobility, tells us the anecdote about the courtier who got into the carriage ahead of Louis XIV, regarding his gesture as a command. "With Louis II (*deux*) I have followed the same rule." He goes on to describe the role he has assigned to the nobles in our present time. In the evening *Don Quixote,* for whom he last night, after the scene with the convicts, played the Siegmund theme: "He was the German Don Quixote." And after we have taken leave of D. Q. in the mountains, R. asks Herr Rubinstein to play him a Bach fugue. Rub. chooses the B Minor (for organ), to our supreme joy. "These things are elemental forces, like planets, endowed with psychic life." "There is the musician *par excellence,*" he also exclaims. — At my request he plays the Prelude in E-flat Minor, and afterward voices what was in my mind—how much femininity there is in these most powerful of works, so much tenderness and touching lament! — When we are alone again in the evening, R. remarks that all the beauty and sublimity with which we concern ourselves is in fact just a way of embroidering our separation, and we are only truly ourselves when we are alone together! . . .

Wednesday, November 19 R. again had quite a good night. Winter is here with a vengeance. R. continues ruling and finishes the Gützlaff pamphlet, which he finds very satisfactory and recommends to me to read. After lunch, when we are talking of the upper classes and the little that is to be hoped for from them, R. says the people, the workers, are not a hope, but an obligation. On the previous evening he spoke of various encounters on the streets, the poor basketmaker, the crafts-man's apprentice, and the authorities' attitude toward them. Also one hears from all sides of deficits which are to be made good through new taxes, on top of that the news that trichinosis has now broken out in Bayreuth! — In the evening we play whist, and R. is bubbling over with such high spirits that it is bliss to see him; he says he wants to have luck in cards, for he already has luck in love. — Over coffee he said to Herr v. St., "Just you wait, I shall found a new religion, chuck all the patrons' money into it," and this evening he says, "Whist is only played in convents." — Searching for the origin of the word *"Eskadron"* ["squadron"], R. sings the praises of Littré, who produced a book such as his dictionary all by himself, whereas "we idle Germans, what have we done?" He again highly recommends the pamphlet of Schopenhauer quotations and at lunch reads us several passages from it, about the ugliness and inferiority of the human race in comparison with the superior nature of animals. — Our army also produces some smiling shakes of the head from R., he imitates the gesture of the lower ranks toward their commanding officer and says he used often to contrast it favorably with the sloppiness, the cigar smoking, the indolence of civilian life, but now it seems to him nothing more than barbarism and cretinism.

Thursday, November 20 R. had a good night, and in the morning he rules his score. Herr Schön's appeal leads us to read Nietzsche's "Appeal to the Germans" again; R. does not care for its all-too-Thucydides-like opening, but he shares my admiration for it as a whole, and we resolve to call on R[iedel]. — At lunch R. talks about his first father-in-law; he starts with a joke, saying both his fathers-in-law were musicians, one of them an army bugler, the other Liszt. He tells us how much he learned from the former and his family about life among the people. In the evening our conversation touches on the Commune, and R. remarks how petty they were in their actions; if they had ravaged churches and convents, hanged a few Rothschilds, that would have had some effect, but just to pick on the poor Archbishop, as if to say, "We know we're finished, but at least we'll settle *his* hash"—that was abominable.

Friday, November 21 R. was somewhat restless during the night; but since the sun is shining, he goes for a walk in the palace gardens. Over coffee he reads to us from the newspaper that France has quite a considerable surplus, which it intends to put to some significant artistic purpose. In the evening we play whist, but only briefly, then R. goes to the piano and, after playing a few bits from the finale of the *Eroica,* plays the whole second movement, so splendidly that I have the feeling that all sorrow has been borne to the grave in this austere and manly lament. R. laughs when I thank him! . . . Letter from the King.

Saturday, November 22   A heap of activities prevented my writing every day, and so I have forgotten various things. R. tells us that the vivisectionist Schiff has had to leave Florence. In the evening we have Rub. and friend Wolzogen with us, R. shows us König's book on literature, which he is keeping to give Lusch at Christmas on account of its nice pictures; we look through it with great interest, but unfortunately we are beset by gloom at the end, when we see what our modern poets look like—Freiligrath, Uhland, Rückert! R.'s walk does not seem to have agreed with him.

Sunday, November 23   Today is the day of the *Mode Illustrée!* Regarding the picture of Goethe, I remark that I do not like the laurels around his head. R. says, "No, it looks as if he is about to be served up." R. said recently, "I always examine them closely, so that I can say to myself, 'This is the world in which you live, for which you wrote *Tristan* and *Der Ring des Nibelungen.*'" R. constantly mentions the Gützlaff pamphlet in praise of Schopenhauer, and he again comments significantly on Aeschylus's 1st chorus. Whist in the evening.

Monday, November 24   R. is sleeping well, in spite of not going out of doors; in his reading he stays with Herr Weber, despite not liking the diamond digging. News from Naples that our house there is princely, paradisaical, comfortable. In the evening a letter from Herr Levi, nothing will come of *Tannhäuser* in Munich unless R. writes to Baron Perfall; swift decision: then let it rest. — At supper R. remarks how little his teachers meant to him, apart from a few whom he named, among them Magister Sillig, who once asked for the causes of the Thirty Years' War; differences in religious beliefs was the first answer, but then R. suddenly stood up and said, without really knowing why, "The jealousy of the princes." He had in fact never given it any thought, but the teacher was very pleased. — Herr v. Stein reads to us the translation he has made of Aeschylus's chorus, and it seems to us very good. "That is religion," R. exclaims. We then take up our noble *Don Quixote* again, with ever-growing admiration and delight. — R., who felt yesterday that I showed too much concern over an indisposition of Herr v. Stein's, tells me that I do not know what men are like; he himself has a low opinion of them all. That leads us to *Othello*—"I like that not" —which seems to us so much more powerful than "*Es gefällt mir nicht.*"

Tuesday, November 25   During the night I see R. turning over in bed and hear him exclaim, "Oh, what a relief!" He then tells me his dream: I had wished to leave him, he could not understand why, tried to recall my features, saying to himself, "She seemed so well disposed—is it all finished? But the children must stay with me." Then, imagining himself and the children without me, he started to weep, and that woke him up. — We then talk about D. Quixote's divine fury against the guard, and particularly his discovery that the people were convicts; R. compares himself to him, saying his fury is aroused in much the same way. He rules lines and tells me that he will not be able to allow himself a harp, since I find it a conventional way of expressing sanctity! — I do not know what brought up the subject over coffee, I merely know that R. suddenly quoted Egmont's words, "I set you an example," and said this was what made Egmont so significant, this was the German conception of freedom—not to want to go on living when all one could look forward to was fear and the need for circumspection. R. spoke these words with great vehemence, as if he were telling me the basic conviction of his life. He goes out for a while and in the afternoon writes to friend Levi, refusing his suggestion and consoling him. Levi has also written to me, asking me to use my influence on R. Reminded that he had once before extended a hand to Baron Perfall, R. says: "I would not think of it. That time when I was forced by the deficit to visit the man, he was so stiff with me—so now they can do what they like. The least little thing one tries to do only causes unpleasantness." — "I am an anomaly," R. replies when I point out to him the curious fact that, at the very time he is in effect doing away with the need for theaters, new and very elegant theaters are springing up everywhere. [*Twelve lines dealing with an untranslatable philological point omitted.*] In the evening Herr Jäger sings "*Durch die Wälder, durch die Auen,*" and R. accompanies him so powerfully that Weber's genius exerts its full effect on us. Then, at my request, Herr Rubinstein plays the Prelude to *Die Msinger* and, after that, as a piano duet with R., the "*Kaisermarsch.*" During the Prelude R. kept raising the piano lid for the forte passages and closing it for the piano ones. — Before the arrival of our guests he told us inhabitants that there was talk of a closer understanding between Holland and Germany. R. asks jokingly, "Is Bismarck perhaps having great thoughts?"

Wednesday, November 26 When I tell R. my impressions of the Prelude he says, "It must be very difficult to write about music, for no one has ever talked, for example, about the new form of that prelude; it is in fact a march with a trio, the theme of the trio appearing first of all in a whispered, fragmentary way before emerging in its full breadth." What I find so wonderful is the soul in this theme, which so majestically reflects the stiff old forms; the spirit which preceded these old forms and met its death in them now brought back to life within them! — When R. fetches me for lunch, he sings to a melody from *La Muette* that they are bringing him the keys of Naples; and it does us good to think of these being handed over, so sad and gray is it here. And R. is still having to use "the devil Nasias," as he calls the steam cones. — He has been ruling his score, and he says to me, "Do you know to what theme Kundry and Parsifal meet each other?" He sings to me the passage in which the Knights rush toward Parsifal, saying it is similar to that used in the exchange of words between Kundry and P. in the first act. Herr v. Stein has gone through his translation of Aeschylus's chorus with me, and since I find it very good and feel that our young friend has understood it properly, I talk about it to R., observing that it should turn out to be a fine piece of work. R. then speaks again about this wonderful poem, which contains everything that one can call religion. From there our conversation moves on to Dürer, and R. says in connection with the woodcuts (*The Great Passion*) that it is as if he had been literally playing with his subject—one of the soldiers in the crucifixion, for example, and the snoring people in the ascension, could certainly make one think so. He agrees with me when I compare *Maximilian's Prayer Book* with Bach's *48 Preludes and Fugues*. Moving on to Nuremberg, he says, "It is all well and good, but it does not mean very much when one has seen the Italian cities." In the evening we read Don Quixote's speech about the value of military service, and all that follows, up to his being put in the cage. — As R. closes the book, he says, "That was, so to speak, the last *artifice* that was ever made." — Before that he spoke regretfully of Goethe's life in Weimar—after *Werther, Götz,* and the first draft of *Faust,* to make verses out of sleigh outings, *Claudine von Villa Bella* and things of that sort, then to go in search of classical form! It was fortunate that he returned to *Faust*. He prefaced these reflections with the remark that one cannot take pleasure in the life of any great man: "Shakespeare is the only one for me—unable to put up with home, running away, writing plays, getting fed up with the theater, returning home, writing *Othello* and *Tempest,* and dying." — Putting the Cervantes book back in the library, he says, "I wonder when we will take that out again?" — In the afternoon R. played some themes from Beethoven's violin sonatas and found them not very significant; even in the Adagio of the *Kreutzer* S. he finds only the first part of the theme great and splendid, the second is *thought up* to fit.

Thursday, November 27 Shortly before falling asleep R. exclaims, "I know what it means to gaze upon Heaven; beside the pheasant house at Tribschen, where we had had some of our meals together, I remember how I gazed up at it in my loneliness, because for me the earth had become so dreary and empty!" — In the morning he laughs and says he has been dreaming of very fat hams, and now a very lean one turns up, not a trace of fat on it. — A lot more about Aeschylus's chorus, he says one could write a whole book about it. — Over coffee much about Austria and Bismarck, after much has been said about the Teutonic Order of Knights, its achievements, and, on R.'s part, the absurdity of the present Order of Saint John of Jerusalem. The sun shining on Beethoven's portrait leads us to talk about his facial features, and R. feels that when Schopenhauer was talking of the large eyes of the man of genius, he was thinking primarily of Goethe—certainly not of a musician, who is a monster *in excessum* and *in abcessum;* with Goethe, he says, everything was directed toward seeing; for the musician there is no seeing, no outside world, he is a wild creature. — At lunch he told me he was curious whether I should manage in Naples to get him back to the biography; it would get shorter and shorter, he said, for it was only youthful memories one felt the urge to re-create for oneself. With Munich, for example, he would deal very briefly; he could not tell the whole truth, one never knew what would come out of such things, Fidi could buy puff pastry with it. He said he would work on the affinities between religion and art: "They do exist, as long as the religion is not synthetic." — Regarding the treatment of Ae.'s chorus, R. says the Germans used to be so eminent in this field in monographs, fastening on a point and not letting go until it was thoroughly elucidated. R. has done a lot of work, and he remarks on how much music has lost through wind instruments ceasing to be natural instruments, but becoming equipped with valves. He reads a book by Karl Ritter on the theory of tragedy, says it is cleverly done, but so tortuous, so unseeing, never asking when great tragedies evolved, in what circumstances, never seeing Goethe and Schiller for what they always were—seekers. In the evening he shows us a sample of Schlagintweit's work on India, which interests us greatly. R. then tells us (from E. v. Weber's book) about the Hindu maidens who were beautiful and so faithful that their lovers could not get rid of them, they swam after them, and one (an Englishman) had to hack off the hand of a maiden who clung to his boat. "We live in a fine world!" R. exclaims. "And how do we look, we Europeans, beside these Asiatic peoples? Like crude barbarians." That leads to other things: starvation everywhere, a weaver discovered starved to death in his room, unable to bring himself to go begging, another frozen to death! Spessart, Silesia, Upper Franconia, misery everywhere, in Ireland and England, too; Carlyle's prophecy! Much about England, where all live side by side and where the socialist movement will probably start. France, as long as it could export pomade and chignons to everyone down to the Kaffirs, would probably be spared. R. mentions Bakunin, who wanted to burn everything down, sparing nothing, and he says B. told him, "Then you won't need so many instruments, and that will be a very good thing!" For the suffering caused by all these reflections I know only one remedy, and I ask R. to play the Prelude to *Parsifal,* which he does; tears gush forth, and earth's children we are no longer!

Friday, November 28 R. growls in my room, while I am taking my lessons, "What's this? These eternal celebrations!" He has found the *Rheingold* buttons and is now teasing me in his own peculiar way, only to go around all day with rolled-up sleeves and shower me extravagantly with thanks for the pleasure I gave myself! — Over coffee he says that in Cologne Hans had not wanted to continue playing, since he caught sight of the "musical Jew" sitting in the front row; our good Lesimple then hit on the idea of turning the piano around, so that Hans could no longer see Herr Hiller. "Good, now I can play again," he said when he came on again. — [*A sentence based on a German idiom omitted.*] . . . R. often comes up to see me, showing off his buttons! — In the evening he reads to us Cervantes's *La guarda cuidadosa,* exclaiming, "It is quite inconceivable how he manages to pin down something which looks like a momentary inspiration." We then go through my father's *Tasso,* in which R. deplores the long-drawn-out lament at the beginning, the chain rattling and the excessive jubilation at the end. — To conclude this day I must mention a strangely daemonic occurrence at lunch. Just as I was having the Rhine coins melted down to make the buttons, R. showed me his buttons (from the King), which, I feel, were not a very good match, and said, "You will now probably be giving me some buttons." — At lunch R. read to us an idea he had jotted down up-stairs—that a stranger to our civilization would perhaps feel content with it, but not someone who was rooted in it. — Over coffee search for Goethe's poem on brooms and boys, also the "*Pustkuchen,*" but without success—no proper index! [*Added below this entry: "Unspecified day.* Passing my bust, R. says, 'She looks as if she were saying, "And another thing . . .!"' We talked of Alcibiades, who for all his genius achieved nothing; I say that he ought to have led the campaign against Syracuse all by himself, he would perhaps have been just the man to fight boldly for an unjust cause and then carry a civilizing influence right into Africa; R. says, 'For that one needs to be a legitimate prince, like Cyrus or Alexander, so that people look upon one as a superior being.' — *Friday.* Friend W. tells us of a new play, *Die Hexe* [*The Witch*], which has made a great impact; in it a lady of enlightened views during the 30 Years' War is struck down by a shot as she tears up the Bible: 'Hence the *Hexenschuss* [*literally,* witches' shot; lumbago],' R. says and explains why all this hack playwriting is so absurd in our country, which lacks a social basis."]

Saturday, November 29 When I tell R. that I have been playing Mozart's Fantasy in C Minor to Boni and what a beautiful impression it has once more made on me, he says, "Yes, I discovered it in Uncle Adolph's house, and it dominated my dreams for a long time." — Disturbing rumors regarding the health of the Bayreuth factotum makes R. observe how sad it is that for a few marks this man has to cover long distances on foot in order to carry out his exhausting work, looking after the sick and also, indeed, the insane. What would appear splendidly uplifting if it were performed through love, in the service of a religious order, seems humiliating and wretched when done simply to earn a living. Coming to fetch me for lunch, R. talks about K. Ritter's book, which on the one hand is written with much understanding and in a good style, but on the other reveals so much absurd perversity —as, for instance, when he calls Nietzsche's theory of tragedy a joke— that one feels it would be better to stop reading it. "Just because they are unwilling to admit something, they become stupid!" he exclaims. — At lunch he talks about Roman law, which may very well have been the proper thing for establishing a clear rule over subjugated peoples but is not suitable for us Germans. He adds, "That will all be terribly simple once the great revolution takes place." After lunch he asks what word the Romans had for the Greek conception of "beauty," and he cannot get over the fact that all they seem to have had was the ugly word "*pulchrum*"; he then, by himself, comes upon "*formosa*," a word the Spaniards also have ("*hermosa*"). At lunch he speaks in praise of Lecky's book. He goes for a walk today, meets the children on the ice. In the evening we play cards, and when we think of what Schopenhauer thought about that, R. says, "There is a difference between resorting to cards out of inner emptiness and boredom, which Sch. was referring to, and playing in order to distract oneself from too much mental activity." [*Added later:* "He follows the whist with a game of lansquenet, then recalls how passionately he used to play cards in his youth."] He jokes a lot with Lusch about his death, and yesterday, when it was mentioned that Tasso's corpse was borne all through Rome, he said he would forbid any such thing, he had no wish to be carried up to the Bürgerreuth.

Many memories of our difficulties with some painters and costume designers—and always incredible that the theater is standing there: "If I were told it was just a phantom, I should believe it!"

Sunday, November 30 As I am dozing off, I hear R. softly blessing me as he goes to sleep. . . . In the morning he tells me about a pamphlet, *Anti-Stoecker,* in which it is asserted that the Jews are so far from being a state within a state that they have even given up their own language. "Fine fellows," R. exclaims, "losing their own language, when that is what a people preserves longest. It shows they are there mainly to live like parasites in the body of others." — Then, when I speak of the

Prelude yesterday, he says, "Yes, I often have the feeling that, no matter how much I might leave out, it would still be the main thing." — I say that with the second note of its first bar one is already securely aware of being in the mainstream, whereas with the others everything seems still undetermined. What is schooling, what is tradition? The *Bayreuther Blätter* has arrived, and R. expresses his full appreciation of Wolz. as editor. Over coffee we come to speak of the application of a new law discovered by R. Mayer; Herr von Stein expresses the view that the application of it is of secondary importance, and one's pleasure in the discovery of a law is quite independent of it; R. replies: "That shows you are still caught up in the struggle of the will. Incidentally," he continues, "the pleasure of which you speak is more or less the same as one has in art." R. goes for a walk and in the evening is looking very well, is extraordinarily cheerful. He soon overcomes his alarm over Eva, who has caught a cold and is very feverish, and at table tells us merrily of a journey from Leipzig to Halle which he made with his friend Apel and two girls, one the daughter of a ribbon maker, the other the daughter of a jeweler. Both had an eye on Apel, a rich young man who was a very good match, but they both found him, R., more entertaining; suddenly under the traveling rug his hand met Käthchen Westermann's (it took him a while to remember the name), and she pressed his. He felt very flattered and thought to himself, "So that's all right—Apel won't get her." — He says he was not vain, in fact he considered himself ugly, which he was. Just very exuberant, full of high spirits. "That must come from my always going around with Philistines." He turns with a laugh to Stein and Gersdorff: "I beg your pardon, I don't mean now." — After lunch he reads Herr v. Weber's letter to us. — Then various things about recruits and the military life, the sober attitude the people have toward martial deeds. Finally he goes to the piano, starts with a few excerpts from the C-sharp Minor Quartet, then plays the beginning of the final movement of the 9th, and ends with the andante. As he gets up, he exclaims, "What that means—after constructing a whole passionate symphony, to make the double basses softly announce this theme, like something wrapped in cotton wool." In the whole of art it is unique, he says: "He heaps one thing on top of another, to give us at the end something like a glimpse into Paradise." Regarding the figurations in the andante, he says it is curious how many such figurations Beeth. wrote for the violin, and how variegated they are—he must surely have done some violin playing himself. When I quote various things from Jean Paul, R. says there must be some reason why he is so famous, and he recalls a few things in *Siebenkäs* which made an impression on him—for example, when the hero suddenly notices and dislikes the way his bride walks. —

Regarding Siegfried's education he said to me yesterday, "He doesn't have to learn anything at all, just grow up to be a decent fellow." —

Monday, December 1   R. had a night troubled by wild dreams. He dreamed once more that I went away, and to Siegfried, who forced his way in to him, he said, "Go away! I don't like any of you now," whereupon Siegfried, leaving him, collapsed, he lifted him up, finding him light as a feather, then he felt a hot breath on his mouth and chin, which was Brange licking him, and to her he said, "You know Marke is dead!" — At breakfast we come back to yesterday's conversation about natural laws, and R. says he will once more tell Herr v. S. that they are of no benefit, no help at all for morals and ethics—"and if on top of that their application is despised, nothing remains of it all but idle sport." — Today for the first time R. talks about our dying together! —

At lunch he says that K. Ritter declares *Die Braut von Messina* to be Schiller's best play. When Herr v. Stein remarks that *Die Räuber* and *Die Braut* represent the two poles of Sch.'s nature, R. says this is a sensible view, but the play which contains the most life is in fact *Wallenstein.* Over coffee he talks of his youth and the "horrible company" he kept, then mentions Pfau and describes his visit to the 1867 World Exposition in Paris, the children as they filed past him, the sister of mercy who on one single occasion took her eyes off her children to cast an almost stolen glance at something, saw him weeping at the sight, and gave him another look. — In the children's faces he read precocious vice, and if now and then one of them looked good and sensible, this only made the impression even more lamentable. — This and the butterflies had comprised his visit to the w. ex.! — And that is why he will not send Siegfried to an elementary school, he says. — When we were talking about Naples and Malwida recently, he said her whole life was based in the final analysis on concessions and allowances; her character was not sinister enough to carry out what she had begun in a spirit of magnanimity. The monument in Geneva to the Duke of Brunswick, coupled with the King of Denmark's visit for the purpose of returning the Guelph fund, gives R. occasion to compare the wretchedness of a republic with the wretchedness of a monarchy. [*Enclosed a letter from Josephine Gallmeyer, presumably to Hans von Wolzogen, concerning her veneration of Wagner, and on it an addition in Cosima's hand:* "When I mention in her favor that the celebrated lady is poor, R. says, 'She is passionate, so she must be poor.' "] — Some music making in the evening, [Berlioz's] *Symphonie fantastique,* which R. follows in the score. Once again, in spite of all the interest in it, it arouses very disagreeable feelings. "I wouldn't allow him in my state," R. says and points out how monstrous he is, in spite of his talent, even in spite of a

certain sense of melodic simplicity and inner feeling. The last movement caused actual pains in his chest, as if he had been singing, and he
even looks worn out! — Pleasure at being left alone together at the end
of the evening. — Before the music R. read to us some of Goethe's
Zahme Xenien; his search in the afternoon for his favorite, "*Johannis-
feuer*," had led him to glance through these splendid pages. Goethe is
this and *Faust,* he says, a tremendous genius flashes through these
sayings, a Greek sense of freedom, and yet at the same time something
thoroughly German.

Tuesday, December 2 R. feels run down after yesterday, though he
had no bad dreams during the night and did not get up; talking is a
strain on him. — Sitting at my writing desk, I am suddenly startled out
of my wits by a very loud bang. The cold winter seems insupportable
to me! R. does not go out of doors. His spirits gradually improve,
and he talks humorously about our friends. In the evening, so that he
will not be overtired, we play whist.

Wednesday, December 3 R. did not have a good night, this time it was
Thénardier-type manifestations which disturbed him. Our conversation is now very often taken up with the presence and occupation of
our young friend, and when R. finds him with me, and we then discuss
what a young man of fire and intelligence should do in these times, R.
expatiates on the theme of science, the physical truths "against which
there is nothing to be said, but which also have nothing to say to us,"
and points in the direction of ideality. He says he does not deny that
these things are excellent as a method, but what really matters is the
soul. He speaks in a warm and lively manner and undoubtedly makes
an impression on our young friend. Memories over coffee of the
chorus master Fischer; very touching. In the evening finished the first
part of *Don Quixote,* the idyll with the grazing oxen, the strange
conversation between Don Quixote and the canon. Delight in it all,
admiration of all its various features, as, for example, the conversation
between Sancho and his wife, the power of D. Q.'s idealism over
Sancho—Sancho believes in all his fantasies, whereas he sees through
the deceptions of everybody else; he is aided in this by his covetousness.
Extraordinary interweaving of spiritual motives.

Thursday, December 4 R. had a curious, ghostly dream, in which
the stairs suddenly vanished and he woke up calling "Minna." —
Departure of friend Gersdorff. Very cold day, packing; letter from
Dr. Schrön asking whether we shall want stoves—so it is cold there,
too! In the evening conversation with friend Wolz. and Stein. Once
again much about socialism; R. recommends C. Frantz's interpretation;
then mathematics; the assertion that two parallel lines meet in infinity
annoys R. just as much as the claim for a fourth dimension in space.

He talks about K. Ritter's book on tragedy, and then tells the whole story of the curious relationship between them, drawing the conclusion that the young man turned away from him in order to preserve his independence. — News that a proposal has been made to the Duke of Cumberland to renounce his claims to H[anover] and Br[unswick], in return for which he will be given back his property! — R. points out indignantly that nobody has castigated the unworthiness of this proposal. (Wrote the last 3 days during R.'s illness, in consequence very inadequate.) [*Added later:* "Thursday the 4th, evening, R. plays to me a lovely theme from the period between *Tristan* and *Msinger,* containing both elements, yearning and happy."]

Friday, December 5   R. wakes up in great concern, his nose is again swollen; he uses the steam bath, it continues to swell, and it soon becomes evident that it is erysipelas! . . . The cold compresses do him good, he sleeps a lot, around midday he takes some soup and roasted meat, and sends word to me that he enjoyed it; in the afternoon he is cheerful, says he is putting up with the compresses in order to please the doctor. When I tell him that our lunch was gloomy, he says, "The funny man was missing; you are the poet and director, but I am the jester." Then he recalls the many ridiculous things he has done in his life: several years ago, for example, in Zurich, he read *"Der goldene Topf"* aloud in Karl Ritter's apartment, in the presence of the Wesendoncks; in the middle of it he felt his erysipelas coming on, but he continued reading. "That was vanity—I was like Councilor Carus." — Severe snowstorm. This illness of R.'s fills me with gloomy thoughts; it is becoming increasingly clear to me that he cannot stand excitement of any kind, and I feel that his preoccupation with Siegfried and the consequent discussions with Herr v. Stein in this connection were too much for him. I talk about this to our young friend.

Saturday, December 6   The night was not too bad, and the trouble has not spread, his temperature seems to have gone down. Yesterday he saw himself during the day as a Turkish lady being borne along in a litter, a half-waking, half-dreaming state. — Today he calls himself "Rhodonasilos Tithonos," and he tells the doctor he is thoroughly enjoying staying in bed and resting, he has always wanted to be just such a lazybones. — It is typical of R. that, when I heard him call out something yesterday morning, I went into his room and he said, "That was because Brange had a sore ear, and he, Marke, wanted to stop anyone from touching it!" This arose from Herr v. Stein's telling us that the previous evening Br. had been very affectionate toward him, and Marke had come between them, as if he were jealous. — Around eleven o'clock I hear R. singing! . . . He bears his suffering and his treatment with patience!

Sunday, December 7   R. had a good and tranquil night. His temperature has gone down, but he still has what seem like mild hallucinations, and the inflammation is spreading. But fortunately his appetite is good, and his divine sense of humor is not deserting him.

Monday, December 8   In consequence of a slight error in diet R. had a very bad night and woke up in great agitation, feeling very unwell. I experience the happiness of seeing that, by applying compresses, I soothe him to such an extent that we attain a mood of great cheerfulness! As I hum, " 'Tis there, 'tis there," he says, "An Italian cannot understand that at all, and I could imagine that a Laplander, if he were to see all our trees in bloom, might sing, 'Know'st thou the land where the pear tree blooms?' " — "I am both Nero and Naso," he says when he discovers a smudge on his nose. — Yesterday he told me that he had been thinking of the stretta in the 2nd act of *Don Giovanni,* and was astonished by all this clashing of sound without any sign of a musical motive, nothing but codas such as he might have intended for his overture. He says that Rossini was the first to try building a stretta like this on a melody. — We begin a conversation (yesterday), are interrupted, after a long while I continue with it, and R. says in English, "Have you seen Bosco?" This refers to one of his stories, about two Englishmen who walked twice around the city of Leipzig; on the first tour: "Have you seen Bosco?"; on the second: "You must see Bosco"—nothing else! — When I go up to him after lunch, he makes a joke about his funeral, how I must clothe him and accompany him with military salvos, etc. I reply in accordance with my way of thinking, and he says, "If you die first, then I shall start looking around me like Andolosia after losing his moneybag, and shall go on searching until I die." — He is thinking a lot about his projected articles.

Tuesday, December 9   The night was not bad, and the erysipelas seems to be subsiding, though it has now spread to one ear, which is very painful. A little reading and talking, interspersed with sleep. There is one merry moment when I ask R. whether he would not like to smoke a cigarette; at that very instant he had thought of it himself, and I am able straightaway to give him one, which he smokes very happily. This constant identity of thought between us delights us, and he tells me to make a note of it! — Concern over the distress in Silesia, on top of that corn taxes and—no minister present at the debate! [*The* Bayreuther Tagblatt *of December 9 enclosed; see notes.*] — Here a man who killed his sweetheart in a fit of justified jealousy has been sent to prison for 12 years, as if it had been a dishonorable act! . . . There is no pleasure in looking at the outside world, and my constant prayer is that I may succeed in keeping R. in his element by concealing the realities of life from him as much as possible. R. told me I was doing with him what, according to a picture in *Charivari,* was done with the Queen of England when she journeyed through starving Ireland: people stood close together spreading out their coat tails to conceal the starving inhabitants from her. — Interrupted my diary from the 9th to the 20th—I shall now attempt to catch up.

Wednesday, December 10 R. woke up cheerful, and when I greet him affectionately, he says we are just like Titania and Bottom, but I should on no account look at him. — Various thoughts I had garnered from him lead him to the subject of his future articles, and he says he would really prefer not to say a single word more. He also knows nobody, he says, to whom he can say these things. I read Herr v. Weber's book to him, and it occurs to him how impossible it is for us to civilize these peoples (Kaffirs, Zulus, etc.). What clothes would we give them? The Romans, he says, had some claim to regard themselves as civilizers. Then he says with a laugh that he would like Cetewayo for company. —

Thursday, December 11 His eyes have now become inflamed! R. loses patience, but with some effort and prolonged reading I bring him into a better frame of mind. All the children in bed, one after another! When I am with them, I hear piano playing; I rush to R.—he has been playing! Read a great deal about Zanzibar, horror over human cruelty!

Friday, December 12 R. did not have too bad a night, but the inflammation has got worse, he thinks because of the ice packs which have been prescribed for him, and he becomes very impatient. On top of this, various domestic troubles, the pipes freezing, the bath overflowing, the bells out of order. In spite of all attempts at concealment R. gets to know a little about them. Great care over his eyes. Reading aloud! The whole day spent with him, and as a result good spirits restored at last. Finished Herr v. Weber's book and started on a book about the Talmudic Jews . . . R. wishes all Jews would drop off of him, "like warts," for which there is no known remedy; one should not try to check them, just ignore them.

Saturday, December 13 A powder, which made R.'s eyes better and also gave him a restful night, torments him in the early morning [*added:* "on Sunday"], and he is very tired of the eternal compresses. But his eyes are still very bad, and we continue as before to read about the Talmudic Jews, with real amazement at their peculiar laws. R. remains in bed all day.

Sunday, December 14 In the evening a dose of chloral, which R. calls the Jewish caustic and which at the beginning of the night from Sunday to Monday gives him the most absurdly horrible dreams—his sister Klara sitting on his neck to make him sink in the water, Frau Wesendonck trying to poison him! . . . But in the morning he feels better and is able to "circulate" for the first time; over coffee in my gray room, where he and I had lunch, he receives our whole troop of children, all of them back on their feet! Much gaiety and sunshine, all of us together again in the little room! Also in the evening for tea. Talk about the permanent effect of making faces, ghosts; Kleist's story *"Die Macht der Musik"* is mentioned, and I read it aloud; it makes a powerful impression on all of us. R. praises the way it is made to sound like a report, there is only one description in it, that of the thunderstorm—Kleist must once have seen a church lit up like that, he says.

Monday, December 15   Much joking on R.'s part about the chloral; the two doctors (the ophthalmologist Dr. Reuter and Landgraf) have to laugh heartily. — Toward eleven o'clock departure of Herr von Stein, who is going home for Christmas, R.'s splendid words to him; yesterday we received a report of a lecture in which Dr. Dühring mentioned R. in a regrettable way. "People should not talk about what they don't understand," R. said. "In the Jewish question many ideas have come from *What Is German?* and C. Frantz's essay." — Today his intention is to pacify our young friend, who is a supporter of Dr. Dühring, and to set his mind at rest, and I believe he has succeeded. — Siegfried unwell, Eva, too! The winter very cold, but sunny—unbearable, all the same. — In the afternoon the "black sheep," friend W. — R. talks of his desire to have an orchestra and to conduct here in the summer, he has heard that the conductor Fischer gave a splendid performance of "Siegfried's Funeral March," but on the other hand a very bad one of a Beethoven symphony. — In the evening I read K. Ritter's book on the theory of tragedy to R., and we are astonished by the corruptness of this mixture of good ideas and absurdities; it is as if, whenever the ghost of R.'s art appears to them through all their affectations, they immediately lapse into stupidity. R. laughs at the idea of setting everything to rights through reason and going to live in Italy for nearly 30 years, in order to occupy oneself only with theatrical affairs in Germany! But as an experience he finds it interesting!

Tuesday, December 16   Siegfried and Eva really ill! — R. somewhat better, but still chained to his upstairs room. I read to him from K. Ritter's *Virginia,* but it is no use, I get a yawning fit, and R. is vexed.

Wednesday, December 17   Siegfried still feverish, Eva down with acute rheumatism. — R. is still confined to the upstairs rooms; our imprisonment and above all the illness of the children make us both feel a little melancholy (Eva sobs violently when she sees her father again; during the night she saw us both lying dead!). — But we have one cheerful hour with friend Wolzogen, though the evening is rather gloomy, for Eva's condition worries us.

Thursday, December 18   R. once more down in the *salon,* feels like

Mary Stuart in Fotheringhay, plays some things on the piano, and says: "What can compare with a melody? What would the world be without these sorrowing, pure, uplifting sounds?" He is very happy to be in the *salon*. Siegfried gets up, too, and at least Eva is no worse. Discussion with friend Gross about our funds, which are not flourishing at the moment. — Over coffee R. says that what he finds most oppressive is that one can take no pleasure in what is now happening in Germany; in one's youth one had at least had one's hopes. — In the evening we read *D. Quixote,* the beginning of the second part—utterly splendid, but the Baccalaureus annoys R.

Friday, December 19 R. had a tolerable night; I, on the other hand, tormented by many things, imagine what would happen if I became seriously ill and died, and make my arrangements. R. cannot yet work, much as he would like to; he feels "stupid." The news from Italy is shocking—God knows what will come of it! R. talks of America, his intention of going there after all to make his fortune. Friend W. comes over; much about the Jews: "They can starve Germany to death," says R. But he feels that Bismarck has something in mind; Puttkamer's speaking out against the nondenominational schools and several other things suggests regret for what has happened, though nothing will ever be said openly, and since he (R.) now knows that the peasants and their fields are in the hands of the speculators, he has lost all hope. And now, since the grain is being taxed, the army is said to be receiving extra pay! . . . When I came downstairs around lunchtime, R. was playing the second act of *Rienzi,* and when he comes to the part just before Rienzi sings and proclaims the freedom of Rome, he says, "These are just empty passages one puts in when one has no ideas—something one has learned how to do from the classics." In the evening whist with the two eldest girls.

Saturday, December 20 R. did not have a bad night, and since the sun is shining, we wonder whether we might not go out; but it is too cold, exactly the winter one always wishes for and now cannot bear. R. would have liked to write his words for the New Year, but he is still feeling "stupid" and run down. He spends much time with Beethoven's sonatas; in the evening he plays the first movement of the A Major (Op. 101) and says it is a consummate whole, a spring day, it is the model according to which he writes his *idylls*. Elsewhere he finds many empty bits—even, for example, in the F Minor Sonata, things (runs) which one need not play, but merely indicate—yet the themes themselves are always lovely. This first movement of the A Major Sonata, however, is quite incredible, he says, everything in it is gripping, every link in the chain, it is all melos. — Thought of [my sister] Blandine. R. says, "How much you have been through!" I observe that it is no credit to me that I survived it. R.: "Oh, you were one of the chosen." — For the benefit of the children he gives a dramatic imitation of his friend Flachs, and a merry game of whist ends a day which was particularly welcome to us since Eva had no temperature; in his joy R. gives her a thaler. — A letter from a physiology student in Göttingen pleases R., he answers it, drawing attention to his "Open Letter." — In bed R. remarks with a sigh how little our civilization has to offer which is truly consummate; even with Shakespeare one is occasionally conscious of time, and as for music, one must remind oneself in whose service it was created—that of dissolute princes of the church, and this makes it all the more touching when an individual shows evidence of independence. With Aeschylus, on the other hand, one feels one is confronted with a forest of oaks, and anyone who did not share the general belief in it would simply have been thrown out! — With this sigh he falls asleep.

Sunday, December 21 In the morning R. recalls with a laugh his "vanity" dream: he had wanted to sing Amfortas and trained his voice for that purpose, as a friend of ours does when he sings Schubert songs! — First walk, blue spectacles, blue veil, in the palace gardens; it is nice, but we revile the winter! — In the afternoon R. reads Horace (the story of his life, to start with), and he says our world began with the Romans, rather than the Greeks. — In the evening Herr Rub. comes and plays us Beeth.'s Sonata, Op. 110—not entirely to our satisfaction, but it is a heavenly moment when R., who is sitting opposite me (on the little sofa next to the piano), suddenly crawls along the floor to me and tries to kiss my foot, I seize his head, and he slips back into his seat, whispering, "He didn't notice anything." Afterward a discussion about the interpretation of these works, which R. says he numbers among the mysteries.

Monday, December 22 When we greet each other today in our usual way, R. says, "We lost 15 years, there's no denying it, and we can't bring them back." I: "You didn't want me at that time." He: "You wretch, you were so intent on getting a husband that you couldn't wait." Around noon, with our blue protection, we go for another walk in the palace gardens; R. still vexed by the winter. At lunch his expression is completely changed, the children completely silent, and he hands me Gedon's letter. [*Enclosed a letter from Gedon, giving his reasons for letting Wagner down, and an accompanying note from Levi begging forgiveness for the mishap caused by Gedon's delay.*] R. tells me he has been pursuing this matter since last June, and all his hopes were pinned on it; last year I had been celebrated in music, this year it was to have been the visual arts. My victory today is that, though this mishap is constantly mentioned, we manage in the end to treat it gaily—though with scornful laughter for visual art and its "lying" ways! "These people are all enthusiasm but no backbone, and it all gets squandered in beer and silly sensuality! And that's why the South will never amount to anything. The Prussians are made of sterner stuff." In the evening I dress myself as nicely as I can (Scheherazade) to celebrate my surprise, which I still have in spite of all the vexation, and our mood is bright and gay; R. reads aloud the unique—and Shakespearean—conversation between Sancho and his wife. He ends the evening by saying that we should have come together 15 years earlier—those were all pure loss! . . .

Tuesday, December 23 R. tells me his dreams: he saw Hans, curiously changed, pock-marked, but with a peculiarly serene expression, which made R. say to him, "You have now reached old age, Hans." Then he, R., had inquired about Berlioz's *"Kaisermarsch,"* in order to write a variation on it, but nobody knew it; then he tried to play his own. Also he had been taken to a large Jewish synodal meeting, at which two large Jews standing at the door had received him respectfully! — Lusch plays Beeth.'s D Minor Sonata, and at one point R. says, "Those are the things, those runs, which say nothing and remind me of Rossini's *Gazza Ladra.*" Recently he said, regarding these runs, "Like Homer, Beeth. sometimes nodded." — Fine weather, but we do not go out, since his nose is again hard and swollen—he puts on the sulfur amulet which old Frau v. Aufsess sent him and writes her a little verse of thanks. "The sun is sending down its counterfeit gold," he says over coffee, gazing at the books. Our conversation (my quotation: "Sing, heigh-ho, unto the green holly: Most friendship is feigning, most loving mere folly") leads us to Shakespeare's play, and R. says, "That is the sort they are, princes in the forest as well as in their palaces, and they return home as if nothing had happened; they are just aristocrats— like Bassenheim in Lucerne, who also continued to eat from his silver dishes, unmoved." — I observe that the great poet would not have concerned himself with such personalities if he had not at the same time brought in such figures as Jaques. Talked a lot at lunch about the scene in Cervantes we read yesterday; we mention Cervantes's fate, taken prisoner in the victorious battle, then usurped by Lope, whom he could, however, admire (not like R. and Meyerbeer). R. says, "And for me one scene from *D. Quixote* is worth more than the whole of Lope." The living Christian mythology in *D. Q.* leads us to the conclusion that among modern peoples only the Spaniards can speak of a genuine culture. — "The sight of Cervantes!" R. exclaims. "As a young man I was always looking for such a sight—I would dearly have loved to see Shakespeare." — *I* know the sight he is looking for! . . . Eva still unwell. R. jokes with Loldi: "E. has acute rheumatism, you have suit-ruin-matism!" — "Beeth. is the only true melody maker," he stresses again today. "What Rossini gave the world in a vulgar way is already entirely there in him, in a noble form; everything in him is melos." — Visit from our friend Feustel, the first since his wife's death . . . "He is a character," R. says after he has gone, "and can be regarded as a true man of the people." "Heavens alive, not to have our dear auntie with us any more!" R. says to him. — Recently, when I was talking to R. about Goethe's life and return from Italy and mentioned Frau v. Stein's 46 years (R. had previously maintained that I was not getting old), R. replied, "It was not because of the 46 years that G. did not cast yearning glances at her, but because Italy had intervened, and a relationship which had greatly enriched his youth revealed its stiffness—for it must have been a stiff one." — Summing up his impressions of Karl Ritter's book, he says, "It is the dignity of ethics which so completely eludes these people."

Wednesday, December 24 R. had a somewhat restless night, and Evchen is still ill. A somewhat subdued presentation of gifts. Nice letter from an American professor of music, who is lecturing on R. in New Haven; R. will reply to him publicly through Wolz. — Many reflections about America, "which will swallow us up as if we were nothing." R. says that if he had known what experiences were awaiting him in Germany, he would have gone with me to America and planted his flag there. He says bitterly that the Emperor would probably be the main hurdle to overcome if Bismarck were really thinking of disarmament, as people are trying to infer from one of his letters (to Italy). "There one sees what vices we drag around with us," R. exclaims. — The newspaper reports enclosed [*see notes*], one on the birth of a child due to the cold and the moving one about the executioner, were told me by R.: "He knew how to tame intractable fellows and then kill them with a sword, but he couldn't face a repentant man and a guillotine. He must be a very curious character—when I find things like that in novels about crime they always fascinate me." — *B. Blätter;* at first we are quite horrified by the retainment of the pseudonym "Armand Pensier," but then R. is so pleased with the article that he sends a telegram in approximately these words: "Why A. P., when you please me so much as Herr v. Stein? Merry Christmas." — Presentation of gifts at 7 o'clock, Eva there, but very run down. — In the afternoon, after arranging everything, I looked out at the golden sky from the gray room and thought of the "melody"—R. comes to me, jokes at first about my "melancholy," then sits down beside me, and we reflect together. After the gifts in the evening he sits down at the piano and plays pieces from *Tristan* (2nd act) to me—ah, how wonderful! At our final parting in the evening, when I thank him, he says, "At that time I felt an uncontrollable urge to luxuriate in music," and "When I went off to Venice that time, you should have said to me, 'I am coming, too!' I was like Tristan, didn't understand you, and—you would have left Hans more easily than I would have given him up. I could almost say that it was our good luck that Hans did not remain on the heights. If he had, we should have been ruined. — But if I had had you with me in Venice, we could have got by with your little property, and nobody would ever have seen me again!" — To the strains of *Tristan* we go to our rest—however great my happiness, that melody is always sounding in my heart.

Thursday, December 25 When I enter my room, I find the splendid garnet-red velvet costume which R., as I discover, has spent months having prepared! As I am gazing at it in emotion, there stands R. beside the portière, scolding me for looking sad! . . . Dear scolding, cherished sulking! . . . A banquet in the hall with our neighbors and the Jägers; R. toasts me just between ourselves, and silence accompanies our tears. Eva present, but very unwell. R. feels it bitterly in the evening that nobody proposed my health, but I think it was our mood of profundity which did not permit any such vulgar sound! — In the evening we are by ourselves, and very glad of it; R. reads the scene between D. Quixote and Sancho, to our enchantment—more, to our gay edification! —

Friday, December 26 R. had a good night in spite of his little excesses, he makes use of the face spray and Frau v. Aufsess's sulfur amulet. — He thinks Rubinstein's article not at all bad, and observes that he is a civilized man. — On the lunch table I find the verse with the lovely fan! Eva eats with us, then goes back to bed. Over coffee R. once again recalls the executioner and says, "He regarded himself as one of God's chosen with his sword, but then he had to oil his machine a few times and use it for the first time on a deeply repentant man, and he was not one of those elegant people like the gentlemen in North Germany, who go to the coffeehouse with axes in their cases!" — Of *D. Q.:* "That is the finest gift the Renaissance ever gave us, but it belongs entirely to the Middle Ages." — He quotes from *Hamlet:* "I see him still." "We see him": "Heavens alive, what great things they are, and how stiff Goethe must have been in his old age to cut the first scene, because it spoiled the significance of the reappearance! After that one has to recall *Faust* and the epigrams, and also the fact that one doesn't know so much about Dante, for example." I observe that D.'s lesser writings are more worthy of the *D[ivina] c[ommedia]*. "Yes, he always remained truer to himself."

Saturday, December 27 A day in bed, and in consequence nothing to report. I am plagued by a severe headache and remain thus in numbed weariness until

Sunday, December 28 toward midday, when we are once more all together, including two cripples! R. reads the story to us, the moving story of the smugglers [*newspaper clippings enclosed of a story by Friedrich Axmann entitled "A Mortal Enemy's Revenge"*], and says it shows the divine spark in human beings! Yesterday evening he read to me some passages from poor Nietzsche's new book, and E. Schuré's saying about "*nihilisme écoeurant*" ["nauseating nihilism"] came into his mind. "To feel nothing but scorn for such a noble and compelling figure as Jesus Christ!" R. exclaims indignantly. He continues with it today and reads several more things (about *Faust,* for instance) which are horrifying. In the evening R. reads to us his article for the New Year, so serene in its melancholy, providing consolation in a way only a genius can. — Then he finds a volume of Chopin's preludes on the piano; having played the 4th (in E Minor) he remarks disapprovingly that an ambiguous chord has been interpolated at the end, as if to create a shock. I seek to excuse it by saying that this sketch is an attempt to reproduce something like a strange natural sound, but only long afterward, when he is lying in bed, does he say, "A natural sound—that is very good, but it is precisely these which one must try to reconcile with our laws of harmony."

Monday, December 29 R. slept well, and now we set about locking things up and packing! Traveling the day after tomorrow in a saloon carriage on account of the invalids. — Last lunch with friends Wolz., Rub., Gross; R. indulgent toward Rub., praises his article, says he has written a preface for him in his words for the New Year. Through his kindness a new spirit is created here! R. proposes a farewell toast which I cannot reproduce here. Only a few words, but so gently summing up all the good things which unite us with our friends and all the bad things which living in close proximity inevitably produces, that I would give a lot to be able to reproduce its unique blend of truth and benevolence. His words were like a delicate veil, softening the bad and enhancing the good; just hints, yet so clear that everybody understood, and solemn glances were exchanged. Nothing but packing from the afternoon until Wednesday morning. But I find time on Tuesday to convey to friend Feustel the feelings which the memory of his wife arouses in me on our departure from Bayreuth.

Wednesday, December 31 At 1:10 P.M. departure in the saloon carriage. R. and the children in very high spirits; much to eat. The journey, however, gradually coming to seem rather long. In Munich at last. Remarkable New Year's Eve with friend Lenbach, Levi, Bürkel, greeted the New Year with punch in the Hotel Marienbad. For me a particular joy that when L., seeking to excuse his friend Gedon, is describing his character and the circumstances of his life, R. interrupts to tell him how splendidly he is speaking. Afterward he tells me that no practiced speaker could have framed and delivered his speech more beautifully than this man for whom words are not a natural medium. He embraced him with warm emotion, and I experienced the happiness of seeing a friend to whom I have for years been devoted being recognized by him in the way I myself see him.

1880

Thursday, January 1 We did not get to bed until 2 o'clock, in consequence of which R. very tired, decides against visiting the studio. I there at first by myself, then with the children. R. has an inflammation of the eyes, Dr. Bezold not worried by it. For me and the children a performance of *Tannhäuser*. Very good in many respects, and for me overwhelmingly impressive; the first scene blissfully relaxing. I do not miss R., inasmuch as a few things would have vexed him greatly, and he was glad to avoid the ovation which would certainly have been given him here in the Munich theater.

Friday, January 2 R. did not have a good night, and I stayed awake with him, talking about *Tannhäuser*. He gets up for lunch, which we have with Len[bach] and Levi. Much bother about the carriage he wished to order, dissatisfaction with the hotel. Friend Lenbach is kind enough to send us his Bismarck, a wonderful portrait. R. exclaims: "Terrible! Such a strong will and such narrow-mindedness! For a man like this, you, my dear Herr Lenbach, and I are mere nothings; we can understand him—but he does not understand us." The sinner Gedon is also received; today I was in his studio, experiencing once again how talent is ignored in Germany. It is disgraceful. — In the evening to the theater with the children; when we return home, he tells me that Dr. Bezold also examined his eardrums and considered a slight cleaning necessary. An uneasy procedure, but R. is very pleased with the results. Early to bed. R. relates his Munich experiences to friend L.! . . .

Saturday, January 3 Departure at 9 o'clock; R. not interested in the scenery, the Brenner bores him. Trouble in Ala, where one has to pay again, trouble in Bologna (4 in the morning), trouble in the carriage, where the lighted stove gives off so much heat that we have to open all the windows, thereby letting in the severe cold; all the same,

Sunday, January 4 a fine, sunny day. Whether it is the scenery or the fact that the greater part of the journey is now behind us, all of us are in good spirits anyway, and it seems no time at all before we are in Naples, where friend Gersdorff comes to meet us. First trouble, the trunks not there, second and greater, a whole floor spirited away and all kinds of sharp practice, but on

Monday, January 5 bright sunshine and an indescribable view make up for it all. R. insists on having all the furniture moved around at once, and he supervises the rearrangements with great energy. Much vexation unavoidable in the course of it, but our spirits continually restored by our surroundings.

Tuesday, January 6 A good night, but the erysipelas reappearing, and in Eva the acute rheumatism! . . . So once again confined to our rooms; in the evening I read aloud passages from Chancellor Müller's *Goethe,* which I started on the journey and which I recommended strongly to R.; he also takes pleasure in it, and we are particularly delighted by the remark about the worthlessness of other people's ideas.

Wednesday, January 7 R. had a good night, but the erysipelas is spreading, and Eva has severe pain in her knee. Nothing to do but be patient! — R. reads *The Conversations of Goethe and Chancellor Müller* and enjoys many things in it, he mentions the "consolidation of errors" and says that in *Egmont* Goethe went against his own nature, which was one of lofty forbearance; this could sometimes look like coldness, but great benevolence was in fact at the root of it. The remark about newspapers delights R.: "I shall even stop reading the *Tagblatt.*" — In the evening he gets me to read the book aloud right to the end, and all he regrets is that G. never managed to rid himself of the idea of God as a part of Nature concealed by Nature, whom one should not seek, although He is there; in consequence of this, one is obliged to look upon Christ, God's son, as a problematical being. "It would be well worth the trouble to define what we mean by God, but who can do that?" — R. is much amused by the idea of finding world history on the Seifengasse. Otherwise, however, he is vexed with the ill luck that prevents him from enjoying this magnificent spot in all its glorious light. He explains the mysterious figure of Dr. Schr[ön] by saying that the Germans are such *donkeys*—in foreign lands they set store by pretending to elegance: "They want to be like the others, but remain stuck in their shabby ways."

Thursday, January 8 .R. had a good night, and the erysipelas is disappearing; Eva is also somewhat better and much more lively. Sunshine in rain! In the afternoon I stroll for the first time in the garden, absorbed and oblivious, accompanied by the melody of the three graces from *Tannhäuser,* which R. described to me as "sensuousness transformed into beauty." — R. is reading a book (*Thalysia*) by a French vegetarian (Gleizès), which has been sent to him—he likes it very much. — He cites to me the story of the two Arabs; one of them ate dates and scattered the stones around, the other ate a lamb and threw the bones away; through the one a palm grove sprang into existence, through the other decay was spread! — "World history begins at the point where man became a beast of prey and killed the first animal." R. somewhat disgruntled by his illness, his cotton-wool mask: "I know exactly when the weather will turn bad—when I am allowed to go out of doors again."

Friday, January 9 A good night for both patients. At breakfast, when we mention Goethe's remark about the absolution which one should administer daily both to oneself and to others, R. says: "That is the only true religion, and I should like to know how anybody could ever do without it—without communing with himself and asking himself truthfully whether he has harmed another person. These days people go off to bed and pat their stomachs when they have ruined someone. But what I can well do without is the priest with his ruff and his bands. The Buddhists atone by making public confession." — R. continues reading the book on vegetarianism and is pleased with Gleizès's "charming and elegiac" appearance; he orders the book and says it fits in excellently with his present project. — I take a long walk with the children, since R. and Evchen are both well on the road to recovery. R. has a serious talk with our friend Gersdorff and tries to extricate him from his confused and unhappy position by pointing out to him the only two ways open to him—that "either-or" confrontation from which everybody flinches, apart from himself. — Cheerful meal and quiet, harmonious evening after I have told R. all the things we experienced and met (a camel, monkeys, donkeys) on the heavenly path to the Gulf of Baia.

Saturday, January 10 R. feels unwell; though the erysipelas is clearing up, his stomach seems to be upset. When will he be able to get out into the air? He is depressed, and I am beset by gloomy thoughts which I will not allow to come to the surface, and which I seek to disperse by forcing myself to be optimistic. I spend the whole day with him, the children go looking for shells on the beach and return home entranced with everything. — I talk with R. about *Thalysia,* and he agrees with me when I say there is something peculiarly French about this man Gleizès; there is a quality in him he shares with Saint Vincent de Paul which recalls Saint Francis of Assisi, he says: "It was finding something of that in Renan which attracted me to him." — Nice letter from a woman in Züllichau, thanking R. for having given her inspiration through his works. — In the evening much discussion about the Italians, the French, and the Germans. I tell R. that what attracted me to Germany was a sense that it was the only country in which people prepared to devote themselves to idealism could be found. R. says, "Yes, in their youth Italians live for pleasure, and in consequence they turn in their old age into completely withered, mean, and dried-up fellows." —

Sunday, January 11 R. got up once, he fears dysentery, but in the morning he is feeling somewhat better. We listen with pleasure to a cock crowing. — I sing *Tristan*, and he laughs and says, "We are a hardy lot." — Much about Germany and Italy: "That woman's letter yesterday did me a lot of good; we must hold on to this sense of the almost religious power of music. I have so few hopes of a German revival." Whereupon I: "Yes, but one must do one's work, and your mission in life is art." He: "Yes, and in Germany there is so little art; it is as if Schiller and Goethe were, or might have been, something other than artists—philosophers, scholars, and so on—and then one day they asked themselves: might one perhaps also write poetry in the German language?" — He praises the 18th century, Rousseau's and Voltaire's sympathy with animals, and he feels that our present age, with its vivisection, can only be described as barbarous in comparison. "But they knew nothing about Christianity—all they saw was the church, and they did not understand how that came about historically. Schopenhauer was the only one; and before him Kant, but in a foolish way." Then he observes that one cannot get into a gloomy state of mind in this place: "We should have built Wahnfried here. Though in time we should probably become sad at having no purpose in life, not even for the children." — Last night in bed he said, "I've just been thinking of the theme of the Andante in the C Minor Symphony— there is nothing else either composed or written to compare with it." — Around noon a visit from Dr. Schrön, who speaks quite interestingly about the talent of the Italian people. — R. agrees with him when he says that the Germans have never produced political martyrs like Poerio and others. Toward evening R. feels so unwell that the gloomiest of pictures is imprinted on my mind; should I keep silent about it, or should I talk about it? I do not know. — But I have nobody in whom I could confide—except for this page, and I have the feeling that soon I shall have nothing more to say even to this page. . . .

Monday, January 12 R. looks somewhat better, has slept well, and is at any rate in better spirits than yesterday evening. It is a consolation to me that a cold wind is blowing, for this would have prevented his going out even if he had been in good health. Arrival of our friend Herr von Stein, a happy reunion; he tells us about Vienna, Richter and the 9th Symphony, Salvini, we tell him our troubles; when Herr v. St. tells us that he heard the *Faust* Overture in a concert hall in Dresden, R. says: "Have they really turned that into a concert hall? I suggested it thirty years ago and was refused." — Prof. Schrön talks about the Camorra, with which he claims to be in touch. (R. is reading Düntzer's life of Goethe with great interest, and remarks how fine the Weimar period was, on account of all the practical activity; he says the Weimar state undoubtedly owed to him all the things which Carlyle praised so highly—and all done under conditions of great difficulty, hated by the Court, forced to throw out most of the administrators; he had persevered only for the sake of his relationship with Frau v. St[ein], which he would otherwise have had to give up: "It must have been quite a splendid relationship," R. says.

Tuesday, January 13   R. had a good night, but he is worried by a possible return of the erysipelas. All the same, he is cheerful and exclaims to Herr v. St., "I am only serious once a week." — When, toward midday, Herr v. St. talks about the performance of the *Euryanthe* Overture, R. takes up the subject of tempo and the need in Weber's overtures to play the allegros with great fire, holding back somewhat the middle theme, which is usually a cantilena; of course, if one overdoes it, he says, one is lost, and that is why he would have liked to have an orchestra, so that he could show how these classical pieces should be played. We have been sent some reminiscences of the first performance of *Tannhäuser* by Max Weber—all of it untrue. So much for the testimony of contemporaries! In the evening talk about socialism, arising from a remark by Lassalle about the press; R. remarks how absurd he was to believe that the state could encourage socialism by recognizing the common right to vote; the state implies a guarantee of property, he says. Then our conversation turns to the Moravian Brothers and their way of life, and when Herr v. Stein expresses the opinion that, having shed transcendental faith, philanthropy will one day become even more powerful, R. flies into a rage; it is always the same, he says, people think only of the church and confuse this with Christianity—the true task is to glorify the pure figure of Christ, so that his example provides an outward bond. Humanity runs in two parallel lines, he continues; the one is concerned with nothing but plunder and murder, the other can be regarded as a reaction against that; no figure is more sublimely moving than that of Christ, and all the rest who affect us have been his imitators. He speaks very agitatedly and without all his usual clarity, and when—as is his habit after speaking at length—he goes out and then returns, he looks very pale, his hands are cold and damp, and he is coughing. He tells me the thought he has written down: "The path from religion to art bad, from art to religion good." He feels that I will not understand it expressed with such brevity; I do understand it, but worry, and with it the swarm of superstitious ideas which at times slumber in one's heart like the Furies in the temple are disturbed, creating a condition which is indeed worthy of pity.

Wednesday, January 14 R. dreamed that Beethoven came to invite him to attend the performance of a symphony. "Good Lord, is he not dead after all? No, this was a dream that he was dead." He went toward him, each attempted to kneel before the other, and they stood there, arrested in the act of genuflection. Then I came in, dressed in a pink-and-red morning dress, and Beeth. said, somewhat in the manner of Goethe, whose stature he had, "Ah, a lovely woman!" R. went to prepare a seat for him, turning Herr v. St.'s bed into a divan by quickly concealing the bedclothes, and his vain exertions woke him up. — He tells us this at lunch, then reverts to our conversation of last night, saying that it was the word "transcendental" which had so upset him. "It always seems to descend on you!" he says cordially. Splendid weather, R.'s first outing as far as the palm tree (with me), which enchants him! Roses and carnations are in bloom, and Dr. Schrön, whom I had summoned, calms all my fears. In the afternoon R. walks to the pavilion and returns home enchanted, though the penetrating cry of a beggarwoman had pierced him with its piteousness: "One can call it play acting, but it is terrible that such play acting is necessary— need has turned this woman's cry into her second nature." — We talk about folk songs; R. feels they scarcely exist here, for years ago he discovered that opera arias had already usurped everything else; he remarks on the extent to which Italian opera alienated the French from themselves; Boieldieu, Auber—they all paled before Rossini.

Thursday, January 15 R. did not have a very good night, he got up and read in Goethe's life the episode of his departure. He often talks now about this life, and recently, referring to the mark of eternity in Goethe, he said, "He was like an outstanding pupil, and the conditions in Germany, which constitute complete anarchy, are to blame for that." — He also discussed the present rules of orthography, finding them absurd. "Who are the people responsible for that?" He feels one could very well take the Middle High German style of accentuation as a starting point—the new measures will lead to endless confusions. Sirocco all day, rain and storms—it is really very sad that R. should be prevented from going out, when he is so much longing for it. At breakfast he tells us about his childhood, how in the house beside the old Dresden gallery he was afraid to go upstairs alone, because in the corridor where Herr Mattei, the director of the gallery, lived, there was a huge picture: "Nobody on earth could ever have got me to pass by that naked old figure." So he used to ring the bell downstairs, and the maid, or in her absence one of his sisters, would come down with a light. "Wretched boy, did you ring the bell?" "Did it ring? I was just sort of playing with the bell." After that he was always asked teasingly, "I suppose you have just been playing again?" — The raucous shouts of the people remind him of the alpenhorn, which he heard in the market place in Lucerne and which sounds like the cry of a wild goose. "I listened very intently, that is to say, in an abstract way, but then I wanted to write it down. I wanted the man to come down to me, but he was too shy, and some years later, when I wanted to hear it again, he was dead. So I had to do as best I could in *Tristan*." — In G.'s life he has reached the friendship with Schiller, and he says it is the only heartening aspect, for despite the "distinguished" people with whom he had to do, one is conscious that Goethe always felt himself a stranger among them. "They shook their heads over *Egmont,* they scarcely understood *Tasso,* but then he is rewarded with complete understanding from a man who is his equal; indeed, Schiller, with his ideality, was much surer of himself, whereas Goethe remained an experimenter all his life—always curious, like a child with his testing and trying out, but with a tremendous love of Nature." When I express my amazement that Empress Eugénie, even though she has the corpse of her son, can still visit the land of the Zulus instead of entering a convent, R. says: "It just shows that there are no longer any whole-hearted and genuine people left. Someone like Cromwell would be unthinkable, they are all hollow—look at Bismarck." Then he tells me the anecdote about Cr., how he asked whether it was possible to fall from grace. — Regarding poets, he says a poet is a visionary, and he tells me how Herwegh always needed a framework for his thoughts: "He grew lazy and, like all idle people, sought refuge in science, dissecting frogs. I wanted to get him producing again and suggested the subject of reincarnation, 9 cantos, three figures with 3 cantos for each, the same type recurring at different times—what I mean by God, who runs parallel with Nature up to the point where the parallels meet. But he didn't do it. The same with Freytag, to whom I suggested Julian, a tragic and interesting figure in whom one sees the whole ancient world rising up in protest against the abominable church, and himself a restless man of action. But Fr. thought that the person who had such ideas should express them himself, and it is true we lack a form for treating such subjects." The newspaper prints an article about the kindergarten schools here, which do not seem to be flourishing, and R. says: "What can Neapolitan children learn there? They know without being told how to pick a pocket!" Then, more seriously: "The idea of teaching children through play is a splendid one, and Fröbel was undoubtedly an excellent man, but we lack the power, and let us not think we can carry our cause by such means, any more than by vegetarianism!" He relates humorously how he came upon Fidi in the kindergarten.

Friday, January 16 R. had a disturbed night, but the sun is shining again; I stroll into the town with our friend Gersdorff, from whom we take our leave sadly, for in his present position he cannot be helped. R. tries to overcome his feelings in his own way, by saying jokingly to Dr. Schr. that Gers. has "a divorced bride." I order a carriage and we go for a drive at about 1:30, R. bursting into ecstatic exclamations: "Naples is the city for me, the D—— take all ruins, here everything is alive! I know only two cities which reflect their countries, London and Naples—Paris belongs to the cosmopolitan rabble." First of all we visit a barber and have many amusing difficulties, then to Prof. Schrön's (Corso V[ittorio] E[mmanuele]). I fear the open carriage is too much for R. and notice his difficulty in climbing stairs, but he wants the carriage to be kept open and takes delight in everything; all of it interests him, the man adjusting his cap, the ugliest of people, all these tell him something, he says. He is also pleased with Prof. Schrön's accounts of the Camorra: "The way such people get by!" He buys cheese from a merchant he got to know 3 years ago; when he gives his name, the man exclaims, "*Mais vous êtes mort*" ["But you are dead"]! — Start on Sismondi in the evening, but R. does not care for its fluent French, he looks for the passage which gave him his conviction about the present decadence that is leading us into barbarism, after which the founder of a new religion may perhaps emerge. But this new outlook would not be confined to the Old World, though it would probably start from there; like the Jews, it would be scattered everywhere, and we should probably fight our battles somewhere in the South. Everything belonging to our civilization, down to the very names, would be wiped out, he says, for it is all too evil and mendacious. — Putting his finances in order, he says all this arranging and calculating arouses a sort of gambling urge in him. — In the evening he exclaims to me with tender passion that things between us have been different from Goethe and Frau v. Stein. — But he finds the choice of [Christiane] Vulpius horrible; he had imagined her to be a brunette, but no, she was fair with blue eyes—and he shows me her portrait. — He is particularly pleased with, and remarks on, Goethe's explosion over "humor is nothing different" (in Chancellor Müller), saying it is splendid and so apt—today the whole world expresses itself in that fashion. He comes to the subject of Nietzsche, who, out of sheer malice toward him, distorts the passage he wrote in his *Beethoven* about the way B. listened to folk melodies, and he did it just in order to denigrate R., "ignoring the fact that Beethoven was the greatest melodist who ever lived. The way he took a folk tune and gave it back to the people, transfigured—it was like the condescension of a god, like the unknown maiden appearing to the shepherd. And to rank him on that account somewhere below Schubert! What Schubert was, B. had long known all about. Disgraceful—and so stupid!"

Saturday, January 17 R. slept well, and when worry woke me up during the night, it was like balm to gaze upon his tranquil features. What we had been reading in Schop. about the physiognomy came into my mind—he had never looked as fine as he did then! — He read this chapter to us, and at first he was struck by the repetition of something already said; but afterward he says how right that was, for Schop. wanted to deduce something from it, and if he had simply written "the fore-mentioned," it would have conveyed nothing. He also reads us some of Sch.'s poems, to our delight; they remind one somewhat of Goethe's epigrams, which R. says he would like to have in a special edition. This morning he answers the enclosed postcard from W. [*concerning editorial difficulties, Dr. Bernhard Förster's views on the Gospels*]. Less and less can R. tolerate mocking references to Christianity. Yesterday he exclaimed, in connection with the idea of people's being made happy through education, "How can one speak of such things, with beggars stretching out their crippled hands?" — He quotes to us several things from Düntzer about the education of Goethe's son August; the sentence beginning with "Only," following from what has gone before, is incomprehensible and unsuitable for reading aloud; even in this good and simple book R. finds traces of those affectations which nowadays disfigure the German literary style. In the afternoon he takes the streetcar into the city for the first time and returns very content, except that an encounter with a German headmaster somewhat spoiled his mood; he remarks how improper it is for a person he does not know to address him just because he recognizes him; it would be much more proper for people who do not recognize him to speak to him simply as a fellow countryman. In the evening to see *La Juive,* pleasure in the San Carlo, a genuine opera house, pleasure in the many beauties of the work, pleasure in the orchestra, outstanding, and in the two English-horn players, but dismay over the singing and acting and the production; continual discrepancies between music and theatrical presentation, continual shouts from the prompter's box. Grand opera, it seems, is now dead, surviving only as an object of study by specialists. R. remarks how this work, originating in the school of Méhul and Cherubini, is full of life and refinement and is not at all Jewish, even in its treatment of its subject—it is just correctly observed. He says of the circuslike duet between the Cardinal and the Jew, "This had to be a bold sort of march theme—since the time of *La Muette* something of that sort had been obligatory in the third act." He says that *La Juive* belongs to the same period as *Notre Dame de Paris,* when so many significant things were produced. When I say that this work seems the most significant of them all, he replies, "Yes, that is because of the power of music." Halévy, he says, was the first musical genre-painter, and he had more feeling than Cherubini: "I liked him very much; he was a yearning, sensual character, but lazy." — When I tell him, in the morning, that I cannot get Brangäne's theme in the first act out of my mind (*"wo lebte der Mann"*), and sing it to him, he says, "This work has now been published, yet nobody really—no musician—has recognized what kind of music it is." I observe that musicians are too limited in outlook for that, but in their place *Tristan* has won many fanatic admirers.

Sunday, January 18 R. slept well. Since I am still tired after last night's events, to which I am not used, I do not attend the family breakfast. R. then comes to my bed and reports rain, which persists all day. He reads Düntzer and talks about Goethe's life with his mistress in Weimar, saying it was incredible in its nonchalance, and it reminds him of my father. R. describes Karl August and says, "A talented dolt, who really cared for nothing except French literature." R. goes into the city by streetcar with our friend Stein and Siegfried, the former is causing us some concern. — R. is looking for a barber, and he tells us very funny things about his experiences. A merry late lunch, I talk about what I have read in the newspaper, among other things that England now seems to be going through a great crisis. R. expresses his annoyance with the Queen, the silly old frump, for not abdicating, for she thereby condemns the Prince of Wales to an absurd life; in earlier times, he says, sons became their mothers' guardians when they came of age. — Prof. Schrön paid me a call, and while carrying on quite an interesting conversation with him, I thought of what R. had said recently: "I have put him in his place, and now I get on very well with him." — In the evening we are visited by Herr v. Joukowsky, and conversation flows in a pleasant and lively way, causing R. to observe later, "The Slavs are the people most closely related to us Germans." Telling us of a remark made by V. Hugo to Turgenev about Goethe ("My attitude toward G. is the same as Joan of Arc's toward Messalina"), R. says, "Such stupidities lurk in every Frenchman, with all of them one can expect a remark like that on some point or other." — R. unfolds his views on Russia, beginning, "I know how to help Russia, but nobody is willing to buy." The Emperor, he says, should set fire to St. Petersburg and, to start with, set up his residence in Odessa, moving on from there to Constantinople. That is the only way of showing what the Slavic race is capable of. But for this one would need a great man, and there are none left. It is just the same as in North America, where they will have to take over the central territories before they can show what they are. We Germans will never become a world power, having no sea, but our task is a different one—to spread culture by colonization; I was very pleased to hear that the workers most sought after and treasured in America are the Germans. — I am alarmed by R.'s appearance late in the evening.

Monday, January 19 R. had a good night but is very nervous at breakfast; afterward, however, he shows me the portrait of J[ohanna] Schopenhauer and says she is the most significant and sensitive person in the whole book. He continues to read it with great interest. After breakfast he suggests a walk into town; we set out, but my appointment with Princess Ouroussoff, who is going to call on me, induces me to turn back. R. walks on with the children, returns home worn out, which comes to my notice most dismally when he decides to read *Don Quixote* to us and his voice sounds quite thin. And so the scene which years ago so amused us—Sancho's fabrication of his meeting with Dulcinea and his monologue—leaves no impression. — But the town enchants him in all particulars, and what delights him most is a *trattoria* opposite our house. "Lord, to have had something like that in one's youth! I remember an inn in Magdeburg where we went to drink wine (Graves)— even that, in the wretched state of our lives then, raised our spirits. And now this one here!" . . .

Tuesday, January 20 Very cold, Vesuvius covered in snow, R. run down, and on top of that unpleasantly affected by a letter from the poor singer Jäger. He writes at once to Richter. A walk into town, R. visits a barber and returns very worn out; to distract him, I talk of various things I read in *Pungolo,* including news of unrest in Hungary. R. remarks that one should not imagine that the days of the *Junkers* are past—they are still powerful and very sure of themselves. — In the evening I ask him to read to us the "Cl. Walpurgis Night," which he does. When we are discussing it the following day, he mentions the cranes and the dead heron, and how the plutonic emergence of such a mountain means the beginning of covetousness and tearing to pieces, whereas in the action of water Goethe saw the elements of gentleness and beauty. — Today he said that one is not bound to assume that mankind was born evil—it became that only with the beginning of history, the killing of the first animal.

Wednesday, January 21 R. slept well and attributes his good nights to the climate here. It is now fine again, though very windy. A visit from the San Carlo theater directors, to whom R., in his expressive French, outlines the damage caused by present-day opera, telling them how Rossini always demanded the best from his singers and how his strictness was feared in Vienna, whereas Meyerbeer ruined it all. Afterward he laughs and tells me that he used the word *imbu* [imbued] for the first time in his life. In the evening he has once again to resort to this language for Princess Ouroussoff, and he does so quite amiably, although today, when I was glancing through a preface by A. Dumas the younger to a translation of *Faust*, I swore never again to read a French book. — R. tells us several things from Düntzer's book, and when we talk about the conversation between N[apoleon] and G[oethe] and wonder why we know so little about it, R. says, "Because it was nothing, and certainly not worth reporting." Regarding Nap., he goes on to say that one ought to regard him as a bandit to whom the French Revolution gave tremendous power; his task was to wage war, unlike Fr. the Great, for instance, who was a man of culture and resorted to war only under pressure in an emergency. We are alarmed by Siegfried's health (jokingly, but concerned, R. says to him, "You look like a cretin, goodhearted, but monstrous!") [*the sentence in parentheses obliterated in ink by an unknown hand*], and it turns out that he has boils again. Dr. Schr. prescribes a great many medicines. He also examines R. thoroughly and says he is like a young man.

Thursday, January 22 R. slept well, he returns to me in the morning and reads to me the account of Goethe's death, which has much moved him: "So beautiful, with the knowledge of a completed lifetime; what was wrong about it was the time, his country. And how beautiful this dying head! Thus does a great and noble man die." — Of his relationship with U[lrike von] Lev[etzow] R. says, "It was a terrible strain on him—it was a farewell to life." — We go for a walk together, R. and I, very, very slowly, up as far as the vineyards; everything delights him, the brooms of laurel leaves used for sweeping, a magnificent sheep, workers calling to one another ("Man as a bird," says R.), the view, the air—his slow pace worries me! — When I talk about the unrest in Ireland, R. says, "Yes, from there, from England, something may one day come—not from those in power, but perhaps from the indignant common people." In an economic discussion with friend Stein he says, "The mere abolition of property will do no good; the Jews will gladly give up estates and everything else, as long as banks and stocks remain." Going on to Bismarck, he says, "If he had had any ideas, something could have been done after France's defeat—an alliance with the smaller states aimed at disarmament, forcing France to disarm by threatening to prolong the occupation. But that would have called for a Periclean spirit." — Whist in the evening.

Friday, January 23 R. slept well, the weather is fine, and he begins a letter to the King which, he tells me, will contain many complaints. The complete work, *Thalysia*, has now arrived, and he is reading it with enjoyment. In the afternoon he rides into town and returns, as always, rather worn out. In the evening Herr Joukowsky introduces his servant to us, a Neapolitan folk singer, who delights us with his singing and his passion; among other things, R. admires his breath control, and the things he sings are unique in their wild tenderness, their ingratiating gaiety and their seductive sensuousness. But what feelings come over me when the singer tries to remember the Rhine-maidens' theme (he has seen the *Ring*)! R. plays it, and all the beauty of Nature rises before us; where before we had seen the lustful animal, now we have the innocent human being! . . . Pepino himself very remarkable, sturdy, thickset, simple, and proud—a lovely experience! R. observes that it is true that Italian opera is based on folk song, but it has been so terribly spoiled.

R. has ordered and received Renan's *Les Eglises,* but he does not wish to read it, saying he knows it all already—Lecky has instructed him very nicely. The only thing that interests him is the mention of Marcion (that he wished to separate the New from the Old Testament). Before bringing in his servant, Herr J. mentioned the French people who hissed R.'s work; this put R. into a great rage; it was not the French, R. said, but the German Jews: "And never mind the Jews— it is we ourselves, we weaklings who can only sigh over all the horrible things going on."

Saturday, January 24 R. slept well, but still feels run down; he continues writing his letter to the King. In the afternoon we go for a walk together in the garden, it is windy and we soon return indoors. At 6 in the evening dinner at Prince Ouroussoff's. — A great variety of new acquaintances; the Prince, the most significant of them, reveals that fact by not talking to R. about music. At table R. causes some surprise by observing that he has no idea why Russia does not grant him a pension, for he has always maintained that Russia should have Constantinople. Instead, the Sultan took out certificates of patronage. "That was to win you over," says the Prince. — The others ask him about Raff, etc., until he says at last that he is no musician. And when they praise the pleasant sound of Italian music, he plays the theme from *Norma,* with its accompaniment of thirds, to show that here, too, one can be quite happy with terrible ugliness. — But R. is unusually lively and friendly, till he tires of the many introductions and calls for our carriage.

Sunday, January 25 R. slept well, but cold, rain, no sunshine! — He finishes his letter to the King, while Lusch and I go with Princess Ouroussoff to an Italian lecture; discussion of its utterly un-German character fills our conversation at supper. We then play whist, R. constantly without luck, which puts him out of humor; he is also upset by the news that never within human memory has there been such a severe winter here; he says he feels everything is telling him to get out of the way, for he succeeds in nothing any more! — He thinks of Wahnfried, of the hall, and regarding his work he says he knows it has all been in vain. — Were I to point out what, beyond the general sufferings of existence, is particularly painful, it would be the necessity of keeping some sort of contact with the world. Oh, Tribschen, oh, childhood days of the children, oh, the time of complete withdrawal from the world! Then came fame, then the children grew up, while we two were armed for only one thing—the tranquillity of love and creative work.

Monday, January 26   A good night; at breakfast R. tells me of Helios's oxen, the roasted flesh of which still spoke to their companions, and he is more and more convinced that men began to be evil when they began to eat meat. A gray day, R. rides into town, returns in an open car! At lunch he has no appetite, and at about [*left blank*] o'clock he takes to his bed with a shivering fit. For me many letters putting off visits.

Tuesday, January 27   R. has erysipelas and remains in bed in a state of lethargy, broken only by expressions of ill humor. His condition deteriorates in the evening to the extent that he can eat nothing, but the doctor is not worried.

Wednesday, January 28   R. had a bad night, and his discomfort is very great. Dr. Schrön does not seem worried, but what help is that? — R. tells me something about the Roman Senate in connection with Regulus's widow; all I hear is what gives me pleasure, namely, that his thoughts are unaffected. He has a repugnance toward all medicines: "I see all these boxes, but what I lack is faith," he says. He gets up for a while in the evening but returns to bed again at once.

Thursday, January 29   A somewhat better night, but the trouble now spreading across his forehead. Great weariness. Yesterday was a glorious day, 23 degrees [Celsius], the children to S. Martin, in all this sunshine R. lying exhausted in bed, I in suspended animation! — This morning, at almost the moment he awoke, he asked me the name of the last conqueror of Asia, about whom Corneille wrote a play; I cannot think of it, in the end he: "Bajazet," whereupon I mention Racine and ask him what brought it into his mind. "Because at the moment I am so interested in the nomadic peoples." He goes back to the vegetarian book, then mentions Elohim, who actually demanded animal sacrifices, as can be seen from the story of Cain and Abel. R. remains in bed, I tell the children about his illness in Paris (typhus), and how in delirium he always spoke French; after that I spend a long time looking at the photograph from England. How strange I feel when he tells me late in the evening that he has had two dreams, in one of which he saw me with a photograph of him on the back of my hat beneath the veil! The other dream was in Paris, at the performance of *Tannhäuser*, where he saw me sitting with a pale face in a box and came to me, saying, *"Comment as-tu osé avoir le courage et le mérite de venir ici seule?"* ["How did you manage to find the courage and virtue to come here alone?"] — And he says this talking in French woke him up! . . . He tells me that when he is feeling unwell this, the most terrible time of his life, always comes back into his mind; and the perfumed smell of the ointment also reminded him of Royer's idea of suddenly flooding the opera house with the scent of roses, an idea which at the time he found as repulsive as the scent itself was otherwise attractive.

Friday, January 30　R. had a very restless night, but the rash seems to be subsiding, and he gets up and spends the whole day in the *salon*. In spite of his weariness he becomes lively and tells us of what he found interesting in Renan's *Eglises,* namely the preface, and he thanks God that the French still possess some men of intelligence. — When we were having our late breakfast, we heard him playing the chorus of the young pilgrims from *Tannhäuser,* and I was completely overcome. Was it the fact of his recovery, conveyed to me by these sounds, was it the exalted exhortation always to keep the Redemption in mind, or was it just the sounds themselves? How shall I decide? When, weeping, I thank R., he says, "Yes, people ought to respect me for having expressed the spirit of Christianity in this—and, what is more, freed of all sectarianism." — He is very cheerful with the doctor, but that does not cheer me.

Saturday, January 31　R. had a better night, and the rash is subsiding more and more, but he remarks sadly that, though it is going away, the catarrhal rheumatic troubles are returning with renewed force. He counts up the days since London and notes that we have been permitted not a single good one (as far as weather is concerned), apart from our stay in Heidelberg. Yesterday he spoke about our isolation, the fact that nobody belongs to us; it was not a complaint, or an expression of arrogance, but a quiet statement of fact. "We have behaved reasonably enough." — R. dictates to me his letter to Herr Jauner, since he is coming down with an inflammation of the eye. — After breakfast he talks about philosophy and says that Kant found something eternal in his quiet avenue in Königsberg, an ideality of time and space, like Jesus in Galilee: "My Kingdom is not of this world." I leave him in fairly tranquil mood to pay a call, but on my return find him very agitated. A conversation with Prof. Schrön over conditions in Germany (our army is being increased by between 60,000 and 100,000 men) made him so aware of the wretched state of things that all he can think of is emigration. I am made sadly aware of the depth of his depression through the way he chides me for wearing the dress he gave me at Christmas; he says it distorts my gait, which he loves. Though hurt, I say nothing, and soon see how far his thoughts have taken him. "Our rulers are not just stupid, they are bad; they know it all, the Jewish problem and the rest, but that is how they want it, for they know that if something genuine and good were to come along, it would be all over with them." — He whispers in my ear that he will tell me his plan, and he tells it to me in detail when we are alone, on

Sunday, February 1 after a tolerable night. He wants to move to America (Minnesota) and there, for a subscription of one million dollars, build a drama school and a house. He would dedicate *Parsifal* to them and stage it there, for he can no longer tolerate the situation here in Germany. It is years since I have seen him as he was yesterday. Today the eye inflammation is worse, and it is tormenting him. — Again and again he keeps coming back to America, says it is the only place on the whole map which he can gaze upon with any pleasure: "What the Greeks were among the peoples of this earth, this continent is among its countries." He works out his whole plan while we are sitting in the room darkened for the sake of his eyes. — I read to him some things in the *I. Z.,* including a description of the people of Chile and Peru which, because of his great sympathy for the Chileans, he finds very interesting.

Monday, February 2 He did not have too bad a night, and his spirits are sufficiently restored for him to ask me whether I think that art has ever achieved what is meant by beauty—that is to say, something that excludes all stirrings of pain or discontent. I think it has, in isolated Greek statues, but not in painting. He says it is possible that the Greeks possessed this quality, for otherwise the theory would be absurd, but even in Greek sculpture it is nobility rather than beauty that one discerns. — Much complaining about Germany, he intends to make a collection of the heads of German professors, to show exactly what he means. "Where are there any true Germans left? The heroic tribes all perished during the migration period, and only the Philistines remained. The Prussians are there just in order to beat the French from time to time, when they get too arrogant, but the French remain the world's gods and rulers." And: "We Germans are now like Bismarck's body, puffed up and in a constant state of agitation." — In the evening friend Stein recommends to us Dühring's description of the Commune. R. says the Commune undoubtedly contained some people of integrity, but what he holds against it is its childishness in believing that the power of property, which has existed since Cain and Abel, could be destroyed in this way. Before risking human life, people should consider what they are doing and ask themselves whether they can reach their goal by such means. (At early breakfast R. told me that a way of altering Licinius's "all too monotonous" entrance in *La Vestale* had occurred to him, and he plays it to me; I tell him that his alteration makes all the rest sound dead. He calls Spontini, with his monotony and poverty of invention, the father of Italian opera, saying that Cherubini was different.)

Tuesday, February 3 R. slept well, and his eye is somewhat better; indeed, he goes out on the terrace and delights in all the beauty. Still many thoughts about America, he asks friend Stein to bring him a map of North America, proclaims his intention of writing to Dr. Jenkins, and says, "Yes, they will outstrip us, and we professors will be left behind with our *polyphonic spectacles*." — "We are a sinking crew." — Visit from Princess Ouroussoff with Countess Schulenburg and Count Arnim; on account of the latter I call R. to join us, he finds this sorely tested man pleasant and touching in his sickness and melancholy. In the evening R. plays the Andante from the C Minor Symphony and the "Spring Song" from *Die Walküre,* both wonderfully beautiful. — And in the evening, when I talk to him about it, he says, "I always maintain that we, Beethoven and I, are the twin melodists, we both have the grand line."

Wednesday, February 4 R. had a good night, and his eye is showing a marked improvement. He reads Renan's *Eglises* and is pleased to find in it an interpretation of the Gospel According to Saint John which agrees with Gfrörer's. Fine weather, R. goes for a little walk on the terrace and delights in our splendid surroundings. In the evening much talk about Greek history; R. always maintains that in comparison with it the Romans do not impress him at all.

Thursday, February 5 Since I went with Lusch to a ball at 12 o'clock, returning home around 5 o'clock, we arranged things so that R. should not be disturbed, and at breakfast I give him my impressions of Neapolitan society, which can arouse nothing but laughter. At 1 o'clock we drive with the children in two carriages to the Toledo for the flower throwing. During our drive there great pleasure in the city, the people, the sun, and the sky: "The only big city for me!" R. repeatedly exclaims in his delight. But on the homeward journey the traffic becomes congested, long waits, the throwing becomes violent, R. very annoyed, for those of us with him indescribable anxiety on his account. But the children in the carriage behind see only the fun, and when they tell us about it in the Villa d'Angri, our feverish mood soon resolves into merriment; the children threw flowers, entered into all the fun, both good and bad, and while we were suffering (I feared all sorts of things—that his spectacles would be broken, his eye injured; that when he lost his hat, he would catch cold; above all that his mounting annoyance amid all these reveling people would make him feverish), they were enjoying themselves, and their joy became our reward and our consolation! Much talk about it in the evening, then about Renan's *Les Eglises*. R. decides to remain here a full year. (A fire put out in Lusch's room, R. not told.) — Regarding the drive, R. says it was not a spectacle, but an experience.

Friday, February 6   R. had a good night's rest; morning brings the *B. Blätter* with his article, and he is pleased with it. The weather is fine, and we drive together into town, where he buys a hat for Siegfried. He returns from the drive in a contented mood, but I notice that his skin always turns noticeably red when he has been in the open air. — I had parted from him in order to leave cards, among others at Count Arnim's. In connection with this acquaintanceship R. says: "What has outraged virtue got to do with avenging a crime? If Count Arnim comes to me, I can be of some avail, but not when I go to him." — In the evening I read to him an article by a new contributor to the *B. Bl.*, Dr. Kirchner; it reads quite well. — His eyes are badly strained.

Saturday, February 7   R. had a good night, but he dreamed that I was not well disposed toward him. The weather is not good enough for him to venture out on a walk, I go into town, he watches me from the terrace, and we wave to each other at every turning. Whist in the evening. At lunch R. tells us an anecdote about Wallenstein, how the soldier advised him to go to Vienna with the 100 "men in armor" and set everything to rights; W. felt the advice was not bad, but "Who puts his faith in devils . . ."; this made such an impression on him.

Sunday, February 8   R. had a somewhat restless night and is impatient with taking all this medicine. He wants to stay here for a year, then return to Bayreuth for a year to see whether there have been any developments; if not, move to America in his 70th year. "Escape from these 15-mark contributions! But what horrifies me above all is having to live on bad performances of my works, even urging theater directors to give them!" We take a walk as far as the Villa Postiglione, he delights in the splendid road, its cultivated wildness, we walk very slowly, but in the evening he is very worn out, his skin red, and he finds talking difficult.

Monday, February 9   A very restless night, much rambling, great weariness in the morning—yesterday's walk was too much for him. R. writes to Dr. Jenkins about his plans. I take the children to the Gala Corso. Fun for them. On my return I find R. much out of humor; a splendid day, but it has brought him no enjoyment. Spent the evening talking to Herr Joukowsky. Comparisons between Pepino and Rossini.

Tuesday, February 10   R. had a very restless night, walked up and down, read Renan; but in the morning he is cheerful, and we spend a nice domestic day together while the children go for a long walk. We stroll up through the garden, greeted by many things in bloom, and when I say to him at lunch that he seems to me much better, he replies, "Because you were there." — But his thoughts remain gloomy; though his manner is more cheerful, he exclaimed: "I find it impossible to believe that anything can still become of us Germans. And I should like to remove my children from such a world." The thought of giving up his son for a war, whether with Russia or France, appalls him. "Outrages have been committed against the people's feelings; while a poor dying soldier is telling his captain, 'I die for Germany,' they are drinking champagne in Versailles, delighted that Bavaria has been brought around; the Devil is leading, and God limping along behind." — He recalls the fruitless battle at Spichern, the waiting for the Crown Prince at Wörth, for Prince Friedrich Karl at Mars-la-Tour. . . . Renan's book provides him with another opportunity to talk about "the most horrible thing in history," the church, and the victory of Judaism over all else: "I can't read two lines of Goethe without recognizing the Jewish Jehovah; for him Jesus was a problematical figure, but God was as clear as crystal." He explains to us how Plato's Theos paved the way for the Jewish God.

Wednesday, February 11 R. had a good night, and if it were not for his thoughts, he would be well, but he is full of resentment. He says the last straw is the knowledge that another approach has been made to the Grand Duke of Weimar in our behalf, and he tells of his experiences with the various princes. Lusch goes to bed with a temperature.

Thursday, February 12 Typhoid fever, which is a worry and calls for careful nursing. Diary laid aside until Eva's birthday, on the 17th. Lusch still in bed, but all danger past. During these days R.'s main preoccupation has been Renan's book, from which it emerges that the church, even in the second century after its foundation, was already showing all the wretched characteristics of later times. "*Si jamais on m'y prend* [may I never be tempted] to found a religion!" he jokes. And, speaking of Marcus Aurelius's government and the fact that there was nothing he could do about emerging Christianity: "So I am not surprised that Emperor Wilhelm and Bismarck have no notion of my ideas; even if they had any feeling for them, they would have no time." "What bunglers we Germans are!" R. exclaimed as we were discussing plays. I ask whether we are not all bunglers in comparison with the Greeks; R. thinks no, the Italians, Spanish, French had certain distinct genres. But Schiller, for example, went looking for material, and one can understand why. In connection with his state of health, he is reminded at whist of old Tiefenbach, and he remarks what a splendid sense of humor Schiller had, and what a pity it was that he was led astray and did not give rein to it. Thinking of his life, and recalling the theater director Hübsch, he says, "If I had been afraid of blows, nothing could ever have come of me."

Tuesday, February 17 Eva's birthday, the "Prize Song" played to her by R. at early breakfast. Presentation of gifts at 12. "You came very modestly into the world," R. tells her. — With the children in the afternoon to Herr Joukowsky's studio, Pepino sings in honor of the birthday and delights us all once more. R. plays something from the *Ring* which he thinks Pepino may have remembered, then the bridal procession from *Lohengrin*—a lovely hour, wondering what will become of the passionate Pepino. Will he continue in this existence, out of love for his master, who rescued him from the gutter? — In the evening to the Teatro Bellini (with Boni and Eva) for the *Barbiere [di Siviglia]*. Beautiful theater, but wretched performance—all tradition lost, even here! . . . When R. talked at length yesterday about the wickedness and mendacity of the present world, I asked him, for the sake of the children, to broach this topic less frequently; he says I am right, for how else can the poor creatures find the courage to go on living? — "The entire Renaissance, including its paintings, I declare to be a period of barbarism, in spite of all the great geniuses who were a part of it and based their art on it. How could this compare with the performance of an Aeschylus tragedy, which was a religious service?" . . . Lusch's illness introduces to our household a *soeur d'espérance* as nurse, and even R. is pleasantly impressed by the cheerfulness, the serenity, the activity, and the refinement which are reflected in her reserved and uninquisitive character: "She seems to me like a princess who has joined the people," he says, and "How ashamed does this sister make one feel!" It gives him a lot to think about in connection with the church, which is still capable of producing such people!

Wednesday, February 18 R. is not too tired after yesterday's expedition. At breakfast we discuss the performance; when I say that, though *Die Zauberflöte* reveals a completely different kind of genius, the *Barbiere* as a whole is more impressive, R. blames the text: "The dear souls were really a bit too childish." However, this will probably be our last visit to the opera. R. goes out in the afternoon and as usual has several adventures, annoying encounters, including one with a sculptor; he rescues a poor boy from a difficult situation—the boy was carrying some small pictures on his head, and he dropped them, breaking the glass; utterly downcast, he hardly notices R. giving him a few francs until a man draws his attention to it, whereupon a whole swarm of beggars gathers around R., who has to fight his way out. When I return from "leaving cards and praising God," R. tells me about all this and, indeed, his impressions of our life here generally: "To live here admiring the beauties of Nature, knowing that down in the street below us there are beggars, ill-treated animals, and some [*adjective illegible*] Italian lady riding in a carriage, neither observing nor caring—that is one world, and not only the one here. To what does Chicago owe its riches and its rise to prosperity? To the mass transport of meat. So the whole city contains nothing but slaughter-houses. To paint and carve statues" (here he makes a gesture of chiseling!) "and have aesthetic thoughts in such a world!" — "A delightful fellow, this Gleizès!" he exclaims, citing to us his opinion that even tigers became fierce only after the emergence of the desert. In the evening we are visited by the American consul, who talks interestingly about his native country. He tells us of mass emigrations to America from Germany and Italy! Like Wotan to Alberich, the Old World can say to America, "Take my heritage!" R. displays a remarkable knowledge of conditions over there, and he once again expresses his great admiration for the war between the Northern and the Southern states.

Thursday, February 19   Glorious weather, R. slept well, Lusch gets up for an hour. R. in good spirits, rides into town to the baker's, who comes from Kempten. I stroll as far as the palm tree, gaze with indescribable feelings at the blossoming almond trees, R. occupies himself with his biography and tells us he cannot believe that after such a terrible life he now has me and the children! The soul's sunshine, the earth's flowery greetings, the colored veil of Heaven, the murmuring of the sea, all lending strength to my single prayer: to be worthy of my office, to remember always, in sorrow and in joy, salvation—the salvation that was vouchsafed me! — In the evening Herr Joukowsky; another attempt on the Emperor's life (an explosion in the palace) leads us to the subject of conditions in Russia, and when Herr J. says that Peter the Great was a man of great understanding, R. totally disagrees: "Of enormous will power, but not much sense, otherwise he would have set up his residence in Odessa and waged war with the Turks instead of the Swedes." — R. is much amused by the nihilists' message to Count Tolstoy, who through his edicts as minister of culture was directly responsible for these unsettled conditions, when he went out accompanied by an escort; they wrote saying that His Excellency would be quite safe going out alone, since he was working so effectively in their interests! R. says this shows that the party consists of educated men. [*Between this page and the next a French newspaper clipping about Wagner's open letter on the subject of vivisection, and a page of the* Allgemeine Deutsche Musikzeitung *containing an article by Wilhelm Tappert on Bach's* 48 Preludes and Fugues.]

When, talking about the biography, I tell him that for his sake I find his account of the Vienna period very difficult to bear, he replies, "At that time I was still living off my inner resources, but now I have to be helped." He is happy with the work we are bequeathing to our Siegfried.

Friday, February 20 Lovely weather still, sunshine and blossom, Lusch gets up again for an hour, but it does her no good, and she has to return to bed, very weak. Talking of the countryside here, R. mentions its wildness and thinks of German meadows, parks, German woods. Nothing like that here, just utter wilderness. — In the afternoon Herr Joukowsky comes and starts work on my portrait, in the evening R. tells us some things from his "delightful" Gleizès, and we conclude the evening with a game of whist.

Saturday, February 21 R. had a somewhat restless night, but he does not seem to be unwell, and he continues going through our biography. Friend Wolzogen sends us details concerning Hans's concert in Bayreuth!! . . . R. and I very affected by it on account of the children. — After the sitting for Herr J., R. says to him jokingly that his picture will be a "Stabat *mater colorosa*," for the amiable painter wishes to paint me in the Marajah! . . . R. goes to join the children on the sea front, and he improvises a boat ride around the Donna Anna, which gives him great pleasure. Before going off for his evening siesta he tells us what Gleizès has to say about the Last Supper, which he sees as the abandonment of meat-eating, the spiritual lamb replacing the real one. R. says the book makes him feel melancholy, but he intends to finish it. — After he has had his rest, he calls us all out on the terrace, wonderful moonlight, peculiar feeling of being at home here, because away from the world, and a dream! Stillness and life— We end the day with whist. (Yesterday R. spoke of the Empress's curious habit of persecuting people about whom she once raved, just like Nietzsche. He said, "One can give up mistaken allegiances, as, for example, mine with Feuerbach, but one should not then abuse them.")

Sunday, February 22 R. had a restless night; in connection with it he says, "Some wild dream is sent to fray me," and we go on to discuss the lines that follow—"The God that in my breast is owned"—and R. says, "It is not the profundity of this poem, but its felicity of expression, the true strength of the poet, which is so striking." This leads us to content and form and the absurdity of thinking that one can have anything to say without finding the right form for it, as is claimed for Schumann and Cornelius, for example. "It is different in philosophy, which, as Lichtenberg rightly says, deals with things which language was not made to express. That is why the Indians created a language for it." "Byron has power of expression, this poetic gift, but only to utter banalities." — R. thinks that the short story is now the best literary form. He would like to read *Cain* again, to see whether [Byron] touches on the bloodless sacrifice, not acceptable to Jehovah. In the evening R. gets very heated about the nihilists; our friend Joukowsky observed that a picture by Raphael is worth more than whole generations of human beings, to which R. replied that his art stems from a state of rottenness which these people feel an urge to terminate, and once blood has flowed, the desire to protect pictures is despicable and false. "I shall not burn them"—with these words he goes off, leaving our friend deeply affected. [*Added two pages later but referred back to this point:* "Departure of the sister, whom R. describes as a moral genius; I thank her, not only for her nursing, but also for the example she sets."]

Monday, February 23   R. slept somewhat better, though not entirely well. He occupies himself with his biography and is amazed how much there is to note in each period; he has the feeling that it all happened yesterday, and it all repeats itself, except for one thing. I tell him that in contrast my previous life slumbers in deep caverns, and I am aware of it only from the time when he became my guide. — At the breakfast table Herr J. tells us something nice about the Emperor of R[ussia], which adds to R.'s feeling that the Emperor is a very good man who has been turned quite *totten* by the unaccountable attacks on him. Regarding the attempts on the German Emperor's life ("These attempts were bestial acts"), R. thinks the perpetrators should be locked up in lunatic asylums in the English way. But the nihilists are people of a different kind, he says. When Herr J. remarks that it is deeply moving to find so creative a person building solely on destruction, he says he would be glad if everything in Russia were blown to pieces, and out of personal gratitude he would allow himself to be blown to pieces as well. R. laughs at the way everybody thinks of his own personal attitude toward things and is incapable of recognizing or judging anything without asking himself what his attitude toward it is. R. rides into town, makes some purchases, and returns in the carriage. He feels that my portrait is not uninteresting, he says it contains an idea. In the evening Herr v. St. reads to us his translations of several poems by G. Bruno, and R. recalls that his uncle spoke to him as a child about the philosophers.

Tuesday, February 24   R. had a bad night and feels worn out, just goes for a little walk in the garden, where a flowering cactus gives him pleasure. In the evening our friends the Joukowskys and a lady from Vienna; the German language allows us to converse congenially. R. talks about sainthood and withdrawal from life, in Schopenhauer's sense, and in connection with that he plays the Prelude to *Parsifal*. To conclude the evening he reads to us his favorite scenes between Falstaff, the page, and the Lord Chief Justice, and we remark that it is less the subject than the genius which creates so harmonious a mood; we found little difficulty in passing from the Saviour to Sir John!

Wednesday, February 25 R. had a better night; today we are rewarded with brilliant sunshine, crowned by a glorious moonlit night. In the evening the Ouroussoffs and the Joukowskys, and despite the necessity of speaking French R. is very friendly and cheerful; but on all days when I have seen a lot of people I have the feeling that there is nothing to report. His preoccupations today were the biography and Gleizès.

Thursday, February 26 R. had a good night, and we spend the day in good spirits; R. corrects the biography and reads Gleizès, and I sit for Herr Joukowsky in the morning. At breakfast we talk mainly about conditions in Russia, which are certainly worth discussing. [*Added on the next page but referred back to this page:* "R. says the world will soon contain nothing but prisoners—'Louis XVIII, the principle of no principles—' "] Then R. and I drive with Herr Joukowsky and Herr Stein to secondhand shops to look for old materials. We come to an Israelite dealer on the Strada di Constantinopoli, where we see very fine materials at a price we can afford. From there R. goes to the brewery, and I with Herr J. to even seedier dealers, who let down blankets in baskets from upper stories onto the square, a square which is indescribably Neapolitan and where I buy several rugs for R. I find it great fun when, on the larger square where the carriage has been obliged to wait, I meet Prince Our., show him my booty, spreading it out amid an ever-growing crowd of onlookers, then go to fetch R. from the brewery and tell him all about it. One of the joys of the experience, imparting it to him. Splendid journey home, and in the evening such curious moonlight and cloud formations that one has the feeling of being part of the ether itself; layers of cloud cover all the mountains, the countryside has suddenly become a completely different one, the sea is like a blue sky, and we, on our balcony, seem to be hovering in the clouds. I invoke all the blessings of Creation on the cherished head my hand is touching.

Friday, February 27 Early today R. complains of the discomfort he always feels in the morning, which makes it so difficult to work, but his divine humor always breaks through triumphantly, and at our late breakfast, at which Herr J. is now always present on account of the sittings, he delights us all with his wit; yesterday, when the subject of Madrid came up, he said, among other things, that he would tarry there to weep on the grave of Ph[ilip] II! And when Herr J. stands up to greet him during the sitting, he says, "Don't stand up, otherwise it

looks as if I am paying you!" — After lunch, since his quotations from
Gleizès have led us to India, he relates to us the story underlying his
Sieger, wonderful and moving. He says he will write it in his ripe old
age, it will be gentler than *Parsifal,* where everything is abrupt, the
Saviour on the cross, blood everywhere. — In the evening he tells us
episodes from the biography concerning his life in Biebrich. — Before
that Herr v. Stein read to us a dialogue about Pompey which put us in a
somewhat heavy mood. In contrast, R. reads to us Herr v. St.'s
translation of a sonnet by Giordano Bruno containing a comparison
with Actaeon, a poem which R. finds very beautiful, and which fits the
sonnet form so perfectly.

Saturday, February 28   No sitting for me today, but letters, R. still
occupied with his biography. First drive out with Lusch, on the
Posilipo, always a delight. R. quotes to me a statement by Cato which
he has found in Gleizès and which greatly enchants him: "I do not like
dealing with people whose palates are more sensitive than their hearts."
— When I tell R. that I find it hard to reconcile Schopenhauer's
philosophy with the idea that human beings are made better or worse
by what they eat, R. says, "One does not have to assume for a fact that
Nature made men evil, but as we see them, they are evil, and this is
due to their habit of eating meat." — In the evening laughing displeasure over attempts at smoking. The decorators he had to call in
again to set up the "tent" annoy him. "I regret it! I have spent my whole
life regretting." — In the evening *H. IV*.

Sunday, February 29   Still glorious sunny days, and R. very well.
Today I stay at home to receive some acquaintances. R. reads Gleizès
and is increasingly convinced of the truth of the idea expressed in this
book.

Monday–Friday, March 1-5   Prevented from writing every day, so I
will summarize. On the 29th we began, at my suggestion, to read
Faust, planning to read it all through. On Sunday we get as far as the
appearance of the poodle. If yesterday we were once again battered by
Shakespeare's elemental force, Goethe's mild genius today has a deeply
moving effect; it is like a call from one's homeland, and to hear it
conveyed by R.'s voice—the dedication, the proclamation of the
resurrection, the poet's words—this dissolves all constraining bonds,
and what a twin might tell of the brother from whom he is separated,
thus he speaks to us of Goethe. My gratitude knows no bounds, and
again and again, overwhelmed, I throw myself into his arms. During
the reading he is particularly captivated by the dramatic dexterity of
the introduction, Wagner's interruption, Mephisto's two entrances
(though one thing does seem to him to be missing—namely, a longing
for M.'s return, which would show Faust ready to conclude the pact).

[*Added three pages later:* "Note on the reading of Faust: R. feels that most of the passages from *after* the scene with Wagner up to Faust's seizing of the phial, interpolated by Goethe, hinder the dramatic development, and the suddenness of his agreement to Mephisto's proposal precludes any 'intimate experience.' "] — On Monday drive to the Palazzo Reale, R. enjoys the sightseeing, though he remarks on the utterly monotonous way in which such palaces are built, room after room, all the same, a senseless madness. (I like the portrait of an old woman by Ravesteijn, a painter unknown to me.) — Then we go to look at the triumphal arch; R. expresses his repugnance at inspecting such things through lorgnettes; thinking of a Roman triumphal arch and imagining to oneself the procession of the conqueror is quite a different matter, he says, from admiring singly the lines of some dead and useless object. Laughing, we go on with *Faust,* up to the scene with the witch. On Tuesday nothing of note; a visit from the Ouroussoffs in the evening. R. very friendly, he plays the Russian national anthem, the "*Kaisermarsch,*" and, linking onto that, the "*Marseillaise,*" which he sings. (When after the "*Kaisermarsch*" he plays the "*M.,*" it strikes me how unreligious, unsacred, the French song sounds in comparison with his song; it is certainly powerful and full of energy, but not great, not aristocratic, and, to our ears, almost absurd when one considers that the "*féroces soldats*" who are called upon to *mugir* [bellow] are the Prussians of Goethe's *Campaign in France.*) — On Wednesday morning, in glorious weather, R. drives into town in an open *carrozzella;* when I hear him returning (the bell rings), I go onto the terrace in my dress for the sitting, and R. is pleased by this rose-colored greeting: no other opera composer has ever had such a reception, he says! — Walk in the garden, ever-recurring delight in our house, which R. calls Posilipo II. — In the evening we dine at Prof. Schrön's house with Prof. Holtzendorff and the Countesses Arnim (with son) and Schulenburg; both R. and I are struck by the lack of dignity in the suffering of these persecuted people. Later in the evening Frau Schwab appears as well, giving rise to much exhilarating fun! But Naples is lovely in the evening, when the lights are lit. *Thursday:* R. tired after last night's "entertainment"—he can no longer stand up to such things. He writes to friend Feustel, saying that he wishes to stay here beyond the end of May. We drive out to Pozzuoli and the straight road through the grotto, to show it to Lusch. We bring our friend Joukowsky, whose presence R. finds very congenial, back home with us, and when J. talks of the need to economize, R. takes two sous from his pocket and presses them solicitously into his hand, saying he must help him out! — In the evening he feels very tired, and the sudden arrival of our friend Gersdorff depresses him, since the poor man has returned even more sorrowful than he departed; R. jokes at first about his life in the catacombs "beneath the baths of Caracalla," asking whether he read newspapers there, but then he has an outburst of annoyance at the unhappy situation in which our poor friend has landed himself. Then R. complains to me about our friends, saying how little joy they bring him. *Friday:* Since the dinner R. has not enjoyed a good night, and in consequence he is depressed, he does not look well, I should like to have him entirely to myself, and I reproach myself for not being able to arrange this. Yesterday he received a letter from friend Wolzogen regarding the concerts; R. replies today, the letter has upset him; he will not hear of concerts with charges for admittance and is annoyed at the idea of trying to make progress by such means—as if he has not already given concerts enough and shown what he can do, as if the performances had never been! We spend the afternoon on the terrace, and it does us good. But in the evening R.'s depression returns, and not even Pepino, who comes to the house with the Wöhrmann family, can rouse R. with his splendid singing. Contact with other people is always embarrassing for R.—he finds it difficult to overcome certain impressions, and this evening he received some from Gers. [?] which led to a remark about men's craving for pleasure. But when they have all left and we are alone with the two girls, he is glad to be with us, and I very much hope he will keep reducing the number of social occasions, which have an adverse effect on him. "I never find my equal at such gatherings," he says.

Saturday, March 6 R. had a better night; we breakfast together cheerfully, and he then settles down to read Gleizès. When I go in to him, he says to me, "I now have great plans in my head, but first I must have a serious talk with the doctor," and he tells me the story of the Greek painter who, to gain strength for a large project in his old age, became a vegetarian, then painted the picture for whose sake Demetrios abandoned his attack on the island of Rhodes. R. feels that, with his aversion to fruit, nothing would suit him so well as a diet of milk and vegetables, and he thinks many of his violent upsets come from eating meat. — He has been reading about our life in Munich in his *Annalen* and tells me he cannot understand how we managed to put up with it. [*Added at the bottom of the following page but referred back to here:* "Seeing Siegfried leaping about in the garden, he says, 'There is our protector, the Lord Protector.'"] — I drive into town to do some shopping, and when I return, R. and the children greet me from the terrace! In the evening R. reads some scenes from the conclusion of *Henry IV, Part I;* at lunch, talking of Goethe and Shakespeare, he had already said, "In the former one sees the great poet, how he arranges his material, how he shapes it; in the latter one sees none of that, he remains unfathomable; the only one like him is Homer, and that is why people have the idea that neither Homer nor Shakespeare ever existed."

Sunday, March 7 R. did not have a bad night, but he looks run down and feels indisposed and out of humor. — I receive some visitors, he joins us, the singer Frl. Hauk does not displease him, but he finds it all a burden. He talks to Dr. Schrön about adopting vegetarianism, and the latter is not entirely against it. In the evening we play whist, but even in this R. betrays his low spirits, and his humor shines only dimly through his sufferings. —

Monday, March 8 A bad, bad night, he hears almost every hour strike, and when he falls asleep for half an hour, he is awakened by the wildest of dreams—I was haughty toward him, and ordered him out of the house! In this life the poor mortal feels like a hunted animal; when will one find rest? Toward evening he is somewhat better, helped by a sip of melissa water which I recommended to him, and our whist evening (in which he insists on my being his partner, since he says he cannot bear for me to win against him) goes off well.

Tuesday, March 9 A better night! Despite a terrible gale. — R. has no objections to taking breakfast with our friend Jouk., and before Lusch departs for Rome he talks to her warmly and kindly and movingly, as is his way. — Today Vesuvius is not to be seen for dust storms, nor are Sorrento and Capri. At lunch R. told us about the palaces in Venice, how fantastically beautiful they seemed to him, much more beautiful than "that boring Palazzo Pitti" in Florence; the conversation moves on to Venice, and he says that after a time it made him feel melancholy, and on one occasion he decided to go to Vicenza, arrived in Treviso, saw nothing there except dust and maltreated animals, and said to himself, "At least you don't have that in Venice." However, he continues, it is behaving like an ostrich to hide one's head from the world's cruelties. His indisposition is in line with his reading material, and his thoughts are tending more and more toward vegetarianism. In the evening he tells us many things about lions and wolves, ingenious hypotheses and inspirations thought up by his delightful Frenchman, including hopes for a uniform climate throughout the world, and that the lion's young look like lambs and the wolf's like rats, and they are frequently consumed by their parents. — Our whist (I again with R.) is cheerful, R. calls Herr v. Stein "Virtue" and Gersdorff "Vice," and he arouses much merriment. — With great pleasure I took advantage of an old lady's departure (Frl. Pauschwitz) to allow Lusch to be shown Rome by M[alwida von] M[eysenbug]; for, as my good children know, there is little I can show them, apart from our love.

Wednesday, March 10 A better night for R., though he is still run down. The weather is glorious, but everything is thirsting for rain—when I returned home yesterday I saw flowering plants lying on the ground, uprooted by the storm, and it reminded me of the end of the second act in *Parsifal*. When I tell R. about it, he says that all the flowers here hang loose, in every heap of dust these charming living things grow between the stones: "That shows one that the air here is impregnated—where there is the slightest chance, things blossom." — After lunch (we have returned to our German mealtimes) we once more attempt to reconcile Gleizès's optimism with Schopenhauer's view of the world; R. thinks that degeneracy set in during a period of change on earth, but it is not absolutely necessary for the Will just to consume itself; Nature is injudicious, he says, but it has no wish to be sheerly destructive; how otherwise to explain the Will's delight in genius, in which it sees itself reflected? The possibility exists for a gentler kind of tolerance, for desire not utterly uncontrolled; in India, for example, human beings during a period of adversity could calmly starve along with their domestic animals, without ever thinking of consuming them. — In the afternoon a walk in the garden and a rest on the terrace with R., friend Gersdorff, and the children, gay moments of happiness, oblivious of all else. — R. talks to the children of buying a donkey and amuses them very much by saying, "If only all the people who came to see us were donkeys!" — In the evening a visit from our publisher Frau Lucca, memories of her visit in Tribschen, Fidi not yet born. Many outbreaks of exuberance, yet throughout that peculiar southern sureness of behavior, comparison with Betty Schott. — R. all but promises his assistance at the rehearsals in Rome! — A short game of whist after her departure, with some new and very delightful English playing cards, but R. already tired out, even by Frau L.'s visit!

Thursday, March 11 R. up once during the night, complains bitterly about his attacks, which so affect his nerves. As he sits upright in bed, waiting for the spasms to subside, I see strange faces, hear mysterious noises—somber pictures pass before my eyes, somber as long as one is still among the living. In the morning Fidi amuses R. greatly with his conversation with Lorenzo, he is now gardening in Naples, and R. is pleased with the childhood of our children. — Letters from Bayreuth, differences of opinion among the committee members, friend Wolz. wants the Emperor's patronage, others are afraid of offending the King. R. is of the opinion that everything should be laid before the King. What happens when one *wants* something can be seen from this example, when the only pillar of our enterprise can be almost forgotten! We, who want nothing, feel this very strongly; the Emperor, who has never done anything for our cause, is to be approached and the King ignored, for him we have already. He who acts, must suffer; he who wants, must deteriorate, become bad, be corrupted. — R. is arranging another little room for himself, the light is very dazzling, he says he could do with the Franconian woods on these rocks! Severe drought. Went for a walk in the garden with R.; Siegfried goes by himself to his friend Alexis in the Villa Postiglione; when I expressed concern about it, R. asked Fidi, "If somebody were to tempt you, offer to show you something nice, what would you do?" Fidi: "I would go with him." Whereupon a warning. Thus is one obliged to teach a good soul distrust, fear of other people—what a world it is! — In the evening R. reads to us Gleizès's opinion of N. I and the kings of France. — After that, whist.

Friday, March 12   R. up once during the night, still feels very tired in the morning, but he cheers up at breakfast, sings Auber's "Tarantella," and says, "I can't understand how such a bad composer as Auber was able to think up such a pretty thing, with its pretty modulations. How vulgar Rossini's ballet music is by comparison!" When I say to him that in my opinion the Italians have no gaiety of spirit, no humor, he agrees with me and says such a thing as the waltz in *Der Freischütz* is unknown to them. "The Count of Schlabrendorf begs to be excused," he says as he goes off, not wishing to chat so much. He gives the decorators instructions, has turned one room into two. I drive into town to do some shopping; on my return R. greets me from the terrace; he seems tired, but the children tell me—and he tells me himself—that the afternoon hours have been splendid. — His article on vivisection, which he is reading again, makes him exclaim, "What place has my art in a world like this?" — Talked a lot about the King of Bavaria, then about the "agitation"—R. thinks I am right to feel that our cause will be strengthened not by what we do, collecting, requesting money, etc., but by what we do not do.

Saturday, March 13   R., up during the night, reads "Shall We Hope?" — In the morning, after a short but deep sleep, he says gaily, "*Avant de mourir* [before dying] I should like to sleep well for once." — Cheerful breakfast—Heaven knows how this is still possible—"Now I must go to my fine fellows," he says as he leaves me. The fine fellows are the decorators, who, I hope, will finish today. Severe gale overnight and today, but no rain; R. says, "God is saying, 'I can do things the same as you; I created you and thought you would do things better, but I can be like that, too.'" — After lunch he talks about Joachim and Wilhelmj, how the latter can make no headway, and he exclaims, "There is no nation as shabby as Germany, everybody repeating what the newspapers say—in Berlin they all praise Joachim, down to the last idler." — Yesterday, when we were talking about Dürer's *Maximilian's Prayer Book,* he said, "It is a shame what has become of us Germans"—and he compares the book with Shakespeare. — Regarding his room decorations, he says all he cares for is the tent. — He tells with amusement the anecdote about N. III explaining the difference between *accident* and *malheur.* — Yesterday the teakettle sang some curious themes, and he observed that Schumann must have listened to such things; but when I say they remind me of Berlioz, he agrees— "Queen Mab" is that sort of theme, he says. When we are talking about the advantages the Jews have over other people, he says, "They pursue aims, we are pursued by our aims." — And as I sat reflecting, he asked me what I was thinking about. "Nothing," I said. He laughed and observed that thought comes in flashes, thinking can only be about practical things, and Dürer's *Melancholy* depicts complete emptiness. — Whist in the evening.

Sunday, March 14 R. slept well and immediately reveals this with a joke, exclaiming in a deep voice at the children's breakfast, "Where is Loris-Melikov?" I visit several churches with the children and then receive a number of callers. R. joins us for a moment, then, alone with friend Gersdorff, shows his great concern about him by very vehemently advising him to sever an unfortunate relationship. — Some talk about the King of Saxony, his good nature and lack of intelligence, qualities which make such people "pigheaded." Much about India, "the stupidest Hindu is more significant than the wisest of Europeans." Pictures in the *Illustrirte Zeitung* of the Gotthard tunnel and the artists' ball produce remarks from R. Nothing worth mentioning comes from such works, he observes, for, as Proudhon says, *"Le génie est sédentaire"* ["Genius is sedentary"]. And today an artists' ball is described—last week we were given starvation in Silesia. — The Universal Pulverizer —this name amuses him, and he says one can get on in the world only with the help of a universal pulverizer. The day and the evening are spent in good spirits, and R. says a humorous goodbye to our friend Joukowsky, whom at the beginning of the evening he called "my benefactor, since there is not another soul who wants to paint my wife."

Monday, March 15 Left home in the morning, R. had arranged with Prof. Holtzendorff for us to visit the law courts around 11 o'clock; a fascinating experience; remarkable building, unfamiliar behavior and deeply affecting proceedings in the courtroom. The accused looked angry, the first female witness unforgettable in her beauty, energy, loquacity, shamelessness! Then some touching female witnesses. — R. says the criminal sat there like a monarch on a high throne, surrounded by his bodyguard—the majesty of crime. But the journey home is a strain on R., it is cold, yet in spite of everything, delight in the city.

Many things have arrived, reports from the Wagner Society, a nice article by a vegetarian (except for the remarks about Schopenhauer), and the *B. Bl.* containing Rubinstein's article. (Yesterday R. dictated a letter to Frau Lucca, explaining why he cannot go to Rome.) Many French people in Munich for *Tristan,* declare that they have collected 40,000 francs to pay for a private performance. At the ball the German Emperor said he had started out believing in the cause, now it has taken possession of him. — The day is dominated by the morning's impressions, R. says criminal cases always fascinate him, it is these he looks for in novels. The legal proceedings impress him with their fine humaneness, he is quite touched by a mother with her newborn child. (Siegfried with us, taken through the courtroom by his father.)

Tuesday, March 16 A good night; for R. yet another letter to Frau L. He has read through his articles in the *B. Bl.*—also Rubinstein's, with some effort. His room is finished, and he plays pieces from *Parsifal* to us to celebrate his domestic comfort!

I walk into town and on my return am greeted by R. on the terrace. In the evening friend J. with sister, very pleasant people, but R. no longer enjoys talking to others, contacts tire him and he becomes nervous. (Yesterday good news from Lulu in Rome.) — R. dreamed that Fidi's double came through the mirror, dressed in blue, and advanced on Fidi, then disappearing through the door, an uncanny experience. I am struck by the blue, for at twilight I had a lengthy discussion with Herr Joukowsky about whether we should choose a blue material to frame the picture and, if so, which, for I had seen a great many.

Wednesday, March 17 R. had a good night and is pleased with the new arrangement of his room; he told the decorator that, if the Bourbons return, they could say he had learned something from him (R.). In the afternoon he takes the streetcar into town, tells me on his return, "I must not go out without you, I get too sad, I see everything too closely, awful impressions; today an old man who made one wonder what a life of misery and vice he had led, and then all those stupid faces in the car, the men with their moustaches, the women with their hair over their foreheads, which makes even the prettiest look so vulgar." While he was collecting these impressions, I was sitting alone in the *salon* and reflecting on happiness, thinking how one would like to die during love's embrace, the life that follows it seeming like a betrayal of this sublime death wish; that life is enduring—it could never be enjoying, for its highest yearning points to death. And when I turned from meditating to gazing, I saw a rainbow in a huge dark cloud, a sign to which I sent a greeting! Reconciliation with acceptance—silent blessings on R. In the evening R. plays the Prelude

to the 3rd act of *Tannhäuser* and the chorus of the young pilgrims. —
Oh, who can depict the emotions, who describe the inner melting,
sublime softening, transfiguration, which envelop our souls? After
that something from *Parsifal* (conclusion of the 1st act) and then, as he
puts it, breathing exercises, the *"durch des Mitleides"*—how that should
be sung. Singers have no idea how to do it, and when I tell him I
cannot understand how singers could so have lost touch with all the
old traditions, he says that Meyerbeer is largely to blame, because of
the demands he made on them. ("Next year on your birthday I shall
take you to Leipzig and perform the *Parsifal* choruses for you with
the Riedel choir.") Talking of priests' hats, R. says, "It is said that God
cannot make a round square, but he can make a round triangle—
priests' hats." He finds them extraordinarily ugly. Otherwise he likes
the costume, and he admires the way they wear their pleated gowns.
[*A sentence based on untranslatable word play omitted.*] — He comes upon
the quotations from Carlyle, is still delighted by them, and says:
"What he says about music is really extraordinary, quite unique; and
there is always something amateurish about it, like my good Gleizès,
even in Goethe when he talks about God, for the philosophical training
is lacking. Schiller was not amateurish in such matters." R. criticizes
the many underlined words in the *B. Bl.*, he says people do it to save
themselves the trouble of formulating a sentence properly [*a German
example omitted*]. A transgression by Boni gives R. occasion to remark
that one always does children an injustice by punishing them—I at
once give in to him and tell Boni that our relationship is the same now
as a few days ago, thanking him for all his kindnesses, his blessings.

Thursday, March 18 R. gets up with a headache, is already in an ill
humor when a letter from Dr. Jauner and the unavoidable reply
complete his misery. In the evening, when I refer again to the impression the sounds of *Tannhäuser* made on me, he says, "I cannot think
of any of my melodies without thinking of the theaters I now have to
push to perform my things." — And in the evening: "I have lost all
my illusions now. When we left Switzerland, I thought it a remarkable
coincidence, the victories and the culmination of my work, I asked
whether there were not 1,000 people in Germany who would be
prepared to give 300 marks for such an undertaking. How miserable
was the reply! I have coincided with the most miserable time Germany
has ever known, with this beastly agitator at its head. But all the same I
brought it off. No one else in the whole history of art has ever succeeded
as I did in building a big theater, bringing together through the
strength of my personality the best artists we have and staging such
performances. And what was my reward for it all? Baa baa! I thought
they would simply make up the deficit for me—oh, yes, they came

along, the women with their trains, the men with their moustaches, enjoyed themselves, and, since emperors and kings were also there, people ask: My God, what more does Wagner want? Does he want something else? — I believe that 25 years ago I could have done it better."

We talk about the museum, and R. says, "More and more I find myself turning away from the plastic arts, from painting—it is like a curtain one pulls to conceal the seriousness of things." In the evening he tells Herr Jouk. about the production of *Tannhäuser* in Paris, how magnificently the audience battled in its behalf, but they were no match for the "Jockeys," the very club to which our diplomats felt it an honor to belong. He talks of the beastliness of this social class which considered itself so refined.

Friday, March 19 Cold and gray weather; R. somewhat depressed, he says he intends to write the biography while he is here and to finish ruling his lines, so that in Wahnfried he can write his work on the affinities of art and religion and complete his score. "Wahnfried is the place to work in." — He thinks of the garden, which we shall now leave to bloom in solitary splendor. Today we arrange with Herr Lo Piccoli to remain here until the end of October. When he complains to Dr. Schrön about feeling so tired, the latter replies that this is unavoidable, but he will return home regenerated—only then will he really feel it. R. laughs and says, "Then I shall return home at once, so as to enjoy the benefits." — At lunch, talking of criminal cases, he recalls Balzac's Véronique and praises the book highly. Regarding our recent experience, he says that in such cases a jury seems to him to be entirely appropriate, but not in political matters, also not in cases of robbery, for, when property is involved, human beings are pitiless. He agrees with Prof. Holtzendorff's views on homicide. In the evening R. is very tired, and he looks worn out. We play whist after conversing for a while about England, where Parliament has been dissolved on account of the Irish question.

Saturday, March 20 R. slept well and is extraordinarily cheerful at breakfast. He talks about his barber Giamelli, a friendly man who always looks as though made of cosmetics, and about the decorator, "emotional and melancholy, with eyes which flash like an animal's when it fails to understand something." — Boni's birthday, R. extremely kind; I, elevated and sustained by him, embark with great fervor on this day, whose great event is—the resumption of the biography! Dressed in the Marajah I sit in his little room, to which he has added a skylight, as if in Heaven; R. feels everything is too lovely for such a life, but I am blissful at being his right hand again, and as I write, the feeling which has been growing in me for a long time comes to fruition: no achievement can bring us happiness, for what makes us happy demands that we abandon life; but then wise men deprived us of the happiness of death, saying that it is nothing, a constant journey along the same paths of suffering; happiness is inspiration, the inspiration of love or of creation, annihilation, yet at the same time affirmation of the individuality, creator of the universe with all its miseries and joys! — And today I am particularly happy to see Marie Muchanoff exonerated for all time; we laugh heartily over the situation in Bulwer's house—he, in love, distracted, she noticing it, quite willing to be left alone with him to achieve in person the aim which no reading could have effected. — At lunch R. is very gay, bubbling over with wit; a Herr Vitari is announced, and R. says, "That will be Herr Evitari." — To Jouk. he says, "One cannot make even an opportunity out of you, since you have no forelock to seize." (Herr J. is bald.) Thinking of our common work, he calls me his inciter to heroic deeds, and passing from this to Brünnhilde, he sings, "*Wunschmaid warst du mir.*" Recalling Eva and Loldi's age and approaching confirmation, he is also reminded of our friend Dittmar and our Communion. We drink to it, profoundly moved—whoever was recognized by him and held his own before him remains immortal! — After lunch a pleasant episode with flowers, Baroness Wöhrmann comes to wish Boni many happy returns. Since she talked about *Carmen,* R. improvises for me a conversation on this subject between her and her husband (who did not say a word). A walk in the garden, a cloudless sky, but it is cold; R. reads some of the Neapolitan stories but soon feels worn out and goes off to rest. Whist in the evening, R. and I together enjoy good luck! — Watching a glorious sunset above Vesuvius: "Beautiful," says R., "but where can I grasp you, Nature without end?" — "Grasp me," I say to him, and we put our arms around each other as we stroll. "You are the God that within my breast is owned," he replies to me, and utters a variation of the lines that follow—I cannot write it down exactly.

Sunday, March 21   R. had a bad night, he read the Neapolitan stories from 11 to 2 and then dreamed about Minna: "This time she was enough to upset me." But he dictates to me all the same, and I also have a half-hour sitting for the painter. He gradually begins to feel restored, and gaily tells me about the *condottiere* who threatened to make the Pope read 100 masses for one cent. — When somebody inquired about the King of Saxony's translation of Dante, R. says, "He called on the scholars of *Kladderadatsch* for help," and, when Herr v. S. tells us about Prof. Witte the *Wunderkind* [child prodigy], R. breaks in, "Hence the name Wittekind." — I receive several visitors, but R. does not put in an appearance, he walks a little in the garden, and in the evening we read the first scenes from *King John* and the first act of *K. Lear*.

Monday, March 22 R. slept well but is somewhat worn out from his "raging" in *K. Lear!* I do not have breakfast or lunch with him on account of pains in my knee which compel me to lie down. He talked about a melody from *I Puritani* which he was singing and about Bellini: "There is still a lot of naïveté among these people here, and so there is something touchingly simple in these themes by Bellini; one can understand what a great effect they had after Rossini, in whom everything was dissolved into runs." He quotes the dying Romeo's *canzona* from *I Capuleti ed i Montecchi,* which he once heard sung by [Wilhelmine] Schröder [-Devrient], a very simple *canzona* which made such an impression on him that he thought to himself, "To the D——with all classical music." "But Bellini was too poor a composer, he knew nothing of all the available musical resources." In the evening he plays the hunting chorus from *Euryanthe,* and when I express my delight in it, he says: "Yes, but one must watch what becomes of such a man, how he develops. His starting point was the Körner songs; then he wrote the hunting chorus in *Der Freischütz,* which had so much success that there had to be hunting choruses everywhere, but whereas in *Der Fr.* it is just hunters singing a song, in *Euryanthe* it is like something experienced, like a forest coming alive. God knows, the chorus in *Der Fr.* was well done and, in comparison to other hunting choruses of the time, unprecedented. Oh, it is impossible to say how much Weber has meant to us—and he is so little recognized!" — He plays the chorus from *Der Freischütz;* then a song by a young composer from Rome, sung by Loldi, its banal melody laced with modulations, leads the conversation to the modern manner of composing. As an example of a model song I mention "*Mignonne,*" which R. then sings to us. — The "Open Letter," translated by a Dutch woman into her own language, brings us to a very nice piece written by the translator herself. When I mention it to R., he says: "Such signs are very touching, and there are many things which might cheer me, but my concern about the general situation keeps me from enjoying the particular aspects. What I am now looking for is results, and they cannot come from Germany, spoiled by too many Jews and too many professors." "If I don't go to America, it is because I am too old, because I have again let 10 years go by." When, referring to Dr. Jenkins's letter, I remark how little the Americans overestimate their native land, however much they love it, and relate with what heavy feelings Miss Tilton, after 4 years in Italy, is returning to her home, R. says: "Yes, if you view everything from a historical standpoint and only want to stare at the past. But if you want to see what the German spirit is still capable of, and is indeed producing, then things look somewhat different. It is not the worst Germans who have gone over there, and Schurz's example shows what a proper German can do." He goes into the next room and plays something from the 3rd act of *Parsifal!* — When he sees how moved our friends are, he observes that this is not possible unless one sees the action and follows every word. "It is different when I am telling you everything at once—then we are working together." We think of the poor members of our Society, who have done so much—the cantor in Zittau, for example.

Tuesday, March 23 Cheerful rising, caused by a minor incident yesterday: I heard a moan and rushed to R., thinking he had called out; R. later discovered that it was some cats up to their tricks on the terrace! Early this morning he was still laughing about it, and, remembering how I rushed to his side though I am not supposed to walk, he says, "When you are alarmed, you could dance a ballet." — A vegetarian pamphlet leads R. to that subject over coffee, he describes what things would be like if we stopped murdering animals: "Perhaps we should have no more art, but if we were morally more secure, that would be no hardship." But he does not wish to have anything to do with the vegetarians, since they always have the utility principle in mind. When Herr v. St. says they are mostly lacking in compassion for the poor, R. replies, "It is very difficult to preserve one's compassion for other people, even for the poor, since the thought must always be in one's mind that, given the chance, they would be just as cruel as the more fortunate ones." "The only thing that still remains fascinating about the human race and is responsible for the poets' not withdrawing their attention entirely from it, is its occasional heroism, instances of which, though in a confused enough way, come to us like glimpses into a lost paradise—Alfonso's behavior in Gaeta, for example, when he spared his enemies simply because he felt sorry for the wretched people. — Otherwise history is a wilderness." — Dust and wind—I drive into town, and during this time R. plays pieces from *Tannhäuser* to the children, is very pleased with the way they listen, and says he will do this often, for it is good, after children have seen a performance, to revive their impressions. — In the evening he talks about Weissheimer, Cornelius; I am glad that these things are being preserved in the biography—a true book of justice! — How touched I was to devote to the memory of Serov the fine words which he dictated to me today! — Whist in the evening.

Wednesday, March 24 Yesterday evening Loldi sang "Like a Young Cockerel," a song by a composer from Rome which, with its trite theme, spiced with the oddest of modulations yet not made thereby to sound interesting, has a very distressing effect on us. At lunch R. sings

Beethoven's "*Herz, mein Herz*" and says no modern composer would write it this way, yet in this naïve form it is so typically Beethoven. In the evening the performance of a young pianist (Reisenauer) provides another opportunity for talking about the contemporary ways of making music. He plays the F Major Symphony, and the difference, when R. plays only the first theme, is like day and night. The talented young man can find neither the tempo nor the correct accents for the *Siegfried Idyll!* . . .

Thursday, March 25 Letters from Bayreuth; friend Wolz. wants after all to present concerts in Bayreuth under Hans's direction this summer. R. very saddened by his friends, even the best of them; says, "I am in fact just in the way, without me everything would be all right." I have the task of conveying his "no" to our friend. "Oh," says R., "if only I could find myself a pleasant wilderness!" — He almost decides to drop the school idea entirely and to consider presenting *Parsifal* with the Munich company, on condition that the King appoint another opera director, perhaps Herr v. Bürkel. — In the afternoon Frau Lucca appears with Cossa, the poet, to invite R. on behalf of the syndic of Rome to attend the performance of *Lohengrin* there. Frau Lucca imprudently noisy, but the poet listens intelligently to R.'s expatiations, which grow more and more heated with the urgings of this turbulent woman! — Great concern over R.'s allowing himself to be goaded by such nonsense. They leave at last, R. tries to sleep but cannot! He comes out onto the terrace and after some grumbling calms down. I want to cancel the carriage, but he says he wishes to go to the church to hear the *Miserere*. — Long drive to the Conservatoire—"The moon is flirting with Vesuvius." — Arrive in a splendid courtyard along a narrow alley, then enter a lovely vaulted chapel. Received by the charming Duchess of Bagnara; wailing of psalms, worshipers passing in and out, R. is led off by the Duke and the other gentlemen from the Conservatoire, since the service still has an hour to run. He returns, and in the darkness the choir begins to sing. — "What an awesomely noble impression the music makes!" says R.; then, "This is true music, which makes everything else look like child's play." The work (by Leo) rears up like a mighty cathedral, severe in outline, noble and essential; every modulation of tremendous effect, since dictated by the logic of the part writing. The performance suffers because of the pauses the conductor feels impelled to make in the interests of security. But the boys' voices sound touchingly naïve. — We think of *Parsifal!* Afterward R. accompanies the delightful Duchess, who, surrounded by her lovely children, pleases him immensely, while the friendly Duke escorts me to our carriage. We drive through a tumultuous crowd; driving is not permitted today, one must go to church on foot, and the people hiss at us; moonlight, the houses like palaces from *The Arabian Nights*. — We have supper at Dreher's, where the vulgar gaping makes us somewhat uncomfortable but does not spoil our good mood. Long after our return home, still talking with R. about this church music— art of the noblest, most impersonal kind.

Friday, March 26   R. unwell—I think more vexation than possibly catching cold in the church; he spends the day quietly, reads Marc Monnier's *Nouvelles Napolitaines* with great enjoyment, praises the French people, and says he is becoming exactly like Nietzsche! — I find it a great burden to have to receive calls in the afternoon (Cossa), but just as I am summoning all my strength to make a wish, R. comes to my room, and with a kiss I am permitted to tell both him and God what it is that fills my being! — When I tell R. that I should have found it painful to see people (the Liechtensteins, among others), he says: "To have certain days set aside for celebration denotes a cult, a common interest, something we can no longer have. No doubt it was the desire for it which led to the founding of sects." — In the evening Boni reads to us something from the *Nouvelles Napolitaines,* and we go to bed early.

Saturday, March 27   R. well again, does not know whether he owes it to the medicine or to the rest he had yesterday. As I am sitting for my portrait, he comes and reads to me Schopenhauer on the subject of language; he is much taken by it and tells me he can literally visualize how Schop., while writing, suddenly saw before his eyes the people he was addressing, and flew into a rage. In the evening R. reads to us more about language, and follows the reading with this remark: "Progress stretched from the birth of the human race up to the invention of a Sanskrit language. Progress is prehistoric, and when men lose the instincts which have brought forth languages, these then decline. Great men such as Pythagoras and Plato were not really progressive people—they went in search of a lost paradise, they looked back and yearned." — When, referring to the *Iliad* and the *Nibelungenlied,* I say to R. how sad it is that, since our old legends are not connected with our religion, we are constantly dependent on foreign influences, he replies, "That is why music is the only thing." — A visit from Herr Tachard, conversation about Bismarck. (Of the Italians, the educated ones, whom one comes across in the street, R. says, "They are like clowns who have lost their sense of fun.") — A game of whist in the evening. (I dictate to R. a letter to the syndic.)

Sunday, March 28   R. had a restless night, and in poor spirits summons me to dictation. How sad it sounds when he calls this a *corvée!* . . . We have come to Moscow, and the dreariness of that period is hard to bear even in retrospect—I ask R. to call me whenever he is in the mood.

He reads Schopenhauer, and his ideas for his article on the affinities between art and religion are growing ever clearer in his mind. — Visitors, some of whom R. receives himself. To the gentlemen of the Conservatoire, whom the Duke of Bagnara introduces to us, R. recommends the foundation of an opera school; he says that Italian opera still dominates the world and will continue to do so, whereas one can get to know his works only in Germany; consequently it would be a good thing if the Conservatoire were to set up an opera school here in which good ensemble and correct performances would be insisted on; in this way the extravagant demands of singers, both male and female, might be eliminated. — Afterward we joke, R. and I, that he always finds connecting links with education; but I mean it seriously when I remark that he, so bold in his desires, pays no regard to what exists already; and yet, whenever he sees signs of movement, whenever he comes into contact with an existing state of things, he always shows ways and means toward improvement. A lovely spring day. In the evening Herr Tachard, very noisy about Alsace and Bismarck. He would like Alsace to be neutral and Metz to become a federal garrison, whereupon R. replies with great passion: "I am not in favor of the present state of things, I find it as bad as it can possibly be, and I expect so little from the Germans that, if I were 10 years younger, I should emigrate to America. But when I hear talk of French susceptibilities, how they cannot tolerate our regaining a province which was snatched from us by an arrogant despot at a time when we were shedding our blood for our faith, then I say: the D—— take them all—and the French must be beaten once again." — A dismal state of affairs, Moltke is urging war, since everyone is expecting France, its strength restored, to attack us! . . .

Monday, March 29 R. run down, he had a restless night—but he calls me for dictation, first reading to me beforehand something from *Parerga* about the hopeful assumptions which the rare appearance of good, of genius, permits. "He is so truthful," says R., "that he has to allow that." — He is cheerful at lunch, relates to us several things from the *Fl. Blätter*. — But in the afternoon he feels very run down; last night had a bad effect on him—he himself invited Herr T., but everything now tires him out. — He goes to bed, but leaps up to play a merry game of whist with Loldi, Boni, and me. (I asked Herr v. St. to go out for a while.)

Tuesday, March 30 R. did not have a bad night, but still a somewhat restless one; a telegram from Wiesbaden, to which, he tells me, he feels like replying, "The D—— take you all." — He complains bitterly about his situation, about these 3 years since the festival, the continual projects occupying him, never any rest! . . . But at breakfast he rouses himself to formulate an idea which he says he cannot write down: "Nature is blind, possesses only the will to know; in its blindness it was unable to measure the convulsions which were so to change things that animals and human beings, designed to live on mild nourishment, became fierce, meat-eating creatures. Now it is the task of human beings to attempt through reason to recognize the urges and instincts of Nature and to live according to them; to do in all spheres what, as Sch. puts it, developed reason had to do with regard to language." "Human decadence stems from the fact that blind Nature was unable to foresee the effect of certain convulsions." — (Yesterday he spoke of the injustice meted out to Schiller, even by Sch[openhauer], who spoke of his Alba being painted black. The same injustice is done to Weber.) Before whist two evenings ago R. read to us the fine dissertation on language. In talking about Germany and the French, R. said, "But the dear Lord likes the French too much, and there's nothing one can do against Him." — He is still very run down, I hope it is the sirocco which is to blame, but above all it is his mood. He gives expression to it in a letter to the King—reply to a letter received today. In it he talks about his thoughts of America and desires Herr v. Perfall's removal if he is to produce *Parsifal*. He writes only a part of the letter today. To Lulu, on the other hand, he sends some nice, humorous lines. In the evening whist with Loldi.

Wednesday, March 31 R. did not have a bad night, but he is still not well and is in very gloomy spirits. In the afternoon he finishes his letter to the King. He tells me what else he has written in it. Otherwise, he finds pleasure in Schopenhauer, and he reads to me what he has to say about Augustine and "the poor fellow from nowhere." We play whist again, in order to avoid conversation and thoughts.

Thursday, April 1 Joyfully I greet April, which enters in bright sunshine, for R. had a good night, he jokes with the children and laughs at me when I tearfully beg him to be patient with life! He dictates to me our second meeting in Berlin! "We were like children." Then he deplores the unavoidable artificiality of his letters to the King, though "It was he who brought us together." — He is so well that he is able to talk with Jenkins about his thoughts of emigrating. The two of us go for a walk in the garden, he is delighted with the many flowers in bloom. In the evening a visit from the Liechtensteins, whom R. invites to spend the night with us. Much merry chat. (Of Frau Hedwig R. says, "She has eyes like caviar—much glistening, but no glancing.")

Friday, April 2 R. had a good night. I let him sleep as long as possible, so he writes no biography today. But after my sitting he plays part of the 3rd act of *Parsifal* for me! To my emotion he responds with quiet satisfaction, saying the work does have a color of its own; a melancholy yet mild one, I add. After lunch conversation comes to the superior beauty of the male over the female in the animal world, and R. says: "The females resist, the males have to dazzle them with their beauty. This shyness has led to the female virtue of modesty." — I ask him whether some connection might not be found between the resistance of the female and the idea of redemption. R.: "If one probes very deep, yes." — We accompany our friends the Liechtensteins back to Torre del Greco. R., however, unhappy with the long journey, and it is very windy. We are tired, too tired even for whist, and we chat about this and that. We are amused by our friend Joukowsky's accounts of old Liphart, who hides his bills of exchange in books, then forgets which book and searches through the whole library, cursing and raging.

Saturday, April 3 R. slept well, but he dreamed about Meyerbeer, whom he met again in a theater and who said to him, "Yes, I know—my long nose," as if R. had been poking fun at his nose, whereupon R. more or less apologized, and the audience applauded their reconciliation. — There is some dictation, although R. says at first that he is not enjoying it, but during work his spirits revive and he finds it pleasurable. A visit from the Liechtensteins in the afternoon vexes him, for he had just been sharply criticizing the character of the wife and the nature of the marriage, and insincere relationships are unbearable to him. A drive with the children to the Sejanus grotto; everything in bud, but it is still windy. In the evening a merry meal and whist, during which R. quotes Hafiz's line, "Sinning, to be a sinner," and says how intoxicating the Anacreontic style becomes when transposed to the Orient. Its meaning, he says, can be both understood and defended, but it is not exactly a precept for young people. — He spoke at length yesterday about Goethe's "The moment one starts to speak, one goes astray," and says, quite rightly, that when one is speaking one is no longer thinking.

Sunday, April 4 R. had a good night. At breakfast we mention a slight discord which Boni caused yesterday through inattention, and I have to admit to R. that I lose my composure when he is disturbed by the children. — Biography around noon; the Goethe-like flavor of certain descriptions (for example, of the relations with Mathilde [Maier] and Friederike Meyer) gives me great delight. — Gladstone's campaign against Disraeli, which will probably be successful, delights us. R. says: "If only they would keep pointing out that he is a Jew. — And he does not know his country, either, or he would not have dissolved Parliament and called for a general election." — Pleasure in the *Fliegende Blätter*, "the last remnants of the innocuous German character"—one anecdotal story in particular amuses R. very much. — A walk in the garden with R.; fine day; thoughts of home: "When we return, we shall lock ourselves in and get down to work." — Thoughts of staging *Parsifal,* following which the theater going up in flames, emigrating to America, and settling down there with our family. The shoemaker Forte, who comes to take measurements, pleases R. greatly with his amiable, artistic character. In the evening a discussion about *Alexander,* since Herr v. Stein has woven the Clitus episode into it. R. approves of this and says it is a good thing to select an occurrence like that in order to reveal a person's whole character. But he advises him strongly against the idea of bringing in the burning down of Persepolis and the figure of Thaïs, as he has done. He talks of Shakespeare, the urge he felt in the discussions between Glendower, Percy, etc., to reveal character, the whole person—how he expanded this scene, then dealt with other matters very briefly. "It is not political plots he is showing us, but people, as he also does in the farewell scene between Percy and his wife and Mortimer and his." This leads us to the court- ship scene in *H[enry] V,* as providing a similar example, and R. reads it to us, including the preceding dialogue in French. "He seems to have been a great favorite of Shakespeare's, and here he is shown in all his charm." — "Extraordinary that we know nothing about Shake- speare, nothing at all!" he exclaims. Then he reads to us the epitaph, "We are such stuff as dreams are made on," mentioned in *Heroes and Hero-Worship,* and, after reading the second line, "and our little life is rounded with a sleep," he reflects a while, then says: "What a magical effect that has on one! Life surrounded by sleep, and consequently a dream." — Very disagreeable pictures in the *Illustrirte* from Norse mythology provoke from him the exclamation: "Oh, were I but rid in my halls of *Kvasir* and *Odhrerir,* too!" — And the unveiling of the monument to Queen Luise reminds us once more of the drab uniforms, the scanty costumes for women, and the students in their "togs" (thus printed in all earnest!). (Last night R. dreamed in French.)

Monday, April 5 A good night; in the morning much from Rome about *Lohengrin.* — No dictation, R. thinks about his article, would like to begin it soon. The letter to the syndic of Rome amuses him: "You clever creature!" he says to me, and "Who can stand up against us?" In the evening whist, and a sudden visit from a Herr Cottran with telegrams about *Lohengrin. "Ah! quel bonheur, j'ai réussi"* ["What happiness, I have succeeded"]! R. exclaims merrily.

Tuesday, April 6 R. had a tolerable night, and we work nicely on the biography. I told R. about a visit I paid to a milliner and the ridiculously exaggerated prices now demanded for articles of clothing, and the impossibility of wearing them for long. R. is reminded in this connection of Nietzsche, who for him represents French fashions: "Just to liberate himself from me, he succumbs to all available platitudes!" In the evening a catalogue of an autograph collection, containing Hölderlin's letter to Schiller; remembering that Hölderlin was N.'s favorite poet, I read the letter and tell R. about it; he finds it so striking that he asks me to keep it. R. attempts to go out of doors, but the wind prevents it. In the evening the Liechtensteins and Pepino.

Wednesday, April 7 R. had a good night's rest, but he is run down, and since he still has pains in his chest, he does not dictate to me today. — In the afternoon he attempts to go out of doors but finds the wind disagreeable. Whist in the evening. He is depressed at feeling so weak and having no appetite for work. He tells Prof. Schrön about his idea of moving to America. The latter very rightly observes that what the Germans lack is instinct, which reminds R. of Pepino, who, when R. sang something to him, immediately accompanied him on the guitar. The Duke of Meiningen told Prof. Schrön that Germany would very shortly become a republic, since the present state could not continue much longer. — Following a remark by Prince Liechtenstein about the 3rd act of *Lohengrin,* R. tells me that the horn player Levy also once asked whether he had no human warmth whatsoever, for such a thing was unthinkable! — "That's what they call human warmth," says R., "sensual desire!"

Thursday, April 8 R. likes Prof. Schrön's remark that the Germans have lost all their instincts; he finds it correct, and compares these Germanic characters with the Italians (the common people), also with the French, observing that it is remarkable to what extent their second nature has profited from culture. He laughs when I tell him about Renan's book, how nicely dished up all the people in it are—Hadrian, John the Presbyter, etc.—though it is all very scholarly. — Letters about the success of *Lohengrin* in Rome arrive, and when we talk jokingly about them, he says: "Lord, how ungrateful we are! It reminds me of Gaspérini, who told me how impossible I am to satisfy: 'When Rossini is given a good beefsteak, he is delighted and gives thanks to God for it, but you despise such things.'" A young German businessman, whom R. had received, sends a large bunch of flowers; R. mentions the visit and that the man said, "After your battles it is understandable that you need rest." "I have had no battles," R. replied, "I have had no opponents, I have just had to wade through a lot of mud." — Regarding *Lohengrin,* he says that what interested him about this work was to ensure a completely correct performance of it, and now to have experienced that! Perhaps he could rehearse and stage *Tristan* very well here. He recalls *Euryanthe,* his sister Rosalie's adoration of it, and how he said to her, "It is not Euryanthe at all—it is Ariadne." He then goes on to Bacchus and says he can understand the festivals and processions and everything else, but the god's personality does not appeal to him, he can make nothing of it. (Unpleasant experience with Herr v. Stein, whose severity toward Siegfried is very embarrassing to us.) R. reads *Parerga* aloud to us.

Friday, April 9 R. slept well, but I am worried, because yesterday his voice sounded so tired. Today, however, he seems somewhat better, and he summons me for the most moving dictation (November 28!). — This mood dominates our day—impossible for me to think of anything else. We take the streetcar into town, very merry, and go for a walk in the Villa Nazionale, where everything pleases R. except individual faces in which one can read a horrible and sinister brutality and no good nature of any kind. The streetcar is full, we hire *carrozzelle,* R. is afraid of catching cold, jumps out of the moving *carrozzella,* and walks home on foot; I drive Boni home, then walk to meet him, and we return home together in peaceful harmony. In the evening much about Gladstone, who has won Midlothian. A great deal, too, about *Lohengrin* in Rome, photographs, enclosures, expressions of gratitude, etc.! [*Inserted in the Diaries a telegram in Italian from all the participants.*] . . . Then whist. R. wishes not to do any more dictating, but to settle down to some work. He wants to put off the dictation until after the production of *Parsifal,* when he wants also to take Siegfried's education in hand and revise *Der Fl. Holländer.*

Saturday, April 10 R. dreamed of some sachets which I prepared and sent to Prof. Rohde in Jena. Great amusement about it, and touching thoughts on Loldi's birthday. Memories of *Tristan!* [*Inserted in the Diaries a poem by Wagner on Isolde's birthday, copied in her handwriting; see notes.*] After lunch a drive with R.—visits to the Ouroussoffs and the Bagnaras. Before lunch a walk on the terrace in glorious sunshine— buying clothes for Siegfried. In the evening the Liechtensteins, light and pleasant chat.

Sunday, April 11 R. did not have a good night, then he dreamed that Minna had run away from him, he in pursuit, and then he sees a moon: "But it is early morning." It turns into a sun, then a second and still more, and finally a voice says, "There are 13 suns." — I tell R. they were the 13 letters of his name (Richard Wagner). — Dissatisfied with the tea at breakfast, he says he would ask for *chocolate,* and he speaks this word with such a comic Saxon accent that we all burst out laughing—the mail arrives and brings me news of the death of our dear Brange! [*Letter inserted in the Diaries; see notes.*] I am able with the aid of another death notice to conceal this from R. If only I could remember whether I received a sign on the day of her death! So that the dear faithful creature did not leave us unnoticed. Oh, how hard, how terribly hard this mortal life! I find it impossible to overcome my sorrow, and the day passes as in a gloomy dream, unheeded R.'s conversation with Liechtenstein, all other callers, Lusch's homecoming.

Monday, April 12   Woke up in a fever during the night, thought of Brange—oh, how to tell him, and how to bear it that I must tell him? — R. is delighted with Lusch's return, much merriment between them. Rainy day, but we celebrate Loldi gaily with gun salutes as we drink her health. In the afternoon we go to our friend Joukowsky's studio, where Prince Liechtenstein reads a short story to us. R. comes to fetch us, he planned it as a surprise; the surprise misfires and he is a trifle vexed, but we return home in great high spirits. In the evening he reads *The Merchant of Venice* to us, leaving out the scenes with Portia (except for the first), and we are amazed—and R. gives expression to our amazement—that a poet living 300 years ago should have defined the type of person who so flagrantly confronts us today, and how, in addition to this type of person, he describes the debased world around him, the thoughtless spendthrifts! But the hero remains the melancholy Antonio. "Is that anything now?" . . . With this question Shakespeare reveals to us both his hero and his hero's world! And the court scene, how it is done—the Jew exactly as today, so cold, alien, unapproachable! — These more or less R.'s words. And when we part and he tells me of his delight in Lusch's development, my overflowing feelings burst forth, and I have to tell him that all, all of it is his doing, that to each of us he is the salvation and the blessing (yesterday, at dictation, I was privileged to hear him giving expression to our feelings at a time of deep distress).

Tuesday, April 13   R. slept well, and the weather is so glorious that we go for a walk before lunch; as we go downstairs, R. engages in a whistling duet with Siegfried (in his room)! . . . R. takes advantage of the lovely weather in the afternoon to drive into town with Lusch and Siegfried (to buy straw hats). I go to meet them and come upon the small company in merry mood! In the evening our friends the Liechtensteins. Present-day social conditions form the topic of our conversation, above all the growing influence of the Jews—R. is vexed by a remark from the Prince, more or less to the effect that nothing can be done about it. — He says of Bismarck that one presumed him to represent the power of the German spirit, but now there is no sign of the German spirit! — Then R. expatiates at length on the treatment of children, and he says that one always does them an injustice when one punishes them, for what they do is very rarely malicious, and he relates the story of Fidi and the soap bubbles.

Wednesday, April 14   R. slept well, gets up early, and walks to the palm tree drinking Aqua di Leone. In the vineyards he meets Siegfried with the gardener, and they whistle to each other: "How nice it is, previously it was a parrot who answered me, now it is a son!" —

Today we work together on the biography; much Bissing nonsense, which makes us laugh a lot, in spite of its sad side, all this lying and deception! R. very gay at lunch and at coffeetime, pretends to be dissatisfied with me, and he relates how, when he complained of being ill, Dr. Schrön replied that was because he could not stand living with me! — Much laughter about this. R. on a walk with the children, I to meet them after paying a call on the Liechtensteins. R. enchanted by the hill above our garden. — In the evening friend Rubinstein, straight from Bayreuth. Somewhat perturbed by R.'s hopelessness! "He wants to become a saint, like the Strömkarl," says R.

Thursday, April 15 R. goes for a walk in the morning, notices the flowers which open during the day and then close up again, and tells me about everything he has seen. Regarding our friend Rubinstein, he says he cherishes a firm belief—the prospect of finding salvation through the German spirit—and that is why he is so perturbed when he sees R. casting doubt on the latter. We are silent for a moment, and suddenly he asks me, "What are you thinking?" I was thinking of [Cervantes's] *Numancia* and a return to Nature, and that in my youth an old professor told me that Cervantes was more objective than Calderón, who was frightened of the Inquisition. — When I talk at lunch about vegetarianism, he says, "You don't know how much this subject preoccupies me." — My wretched appearance, probably the result of the constant tension I have been in since Brange's death, torments R., and I am obliged to invent excuses to explain it! — Sirocco weather, the younger children to the races, return home very happy, and R. praises the naïve elegance of the women in Naples, who drive out during the day in the richest colors, conscious of both their clothes and their rank. This is what distinguishes Naples from Paris, he says, where only dismal women display their finery in the street. R. and I go for a walk in the garden after I have written in his name to Baron Hofmann in Vienna and to Herr v. Bürkel about the decline of the Munich theater. Regarding the *B. Blätter,* which has arrived, R. says of Dr. Förster's lecture, "I am like a ghost, I care nothing about what is said of me, whether good or bad." — In the evening he plays *Tristan,* the middle of the second act, the Prelude to the third (he sings the first scene) and the apotheosis. The piano score annoys him with its "fussiness," he says the arrangement is not bold enough, work of this kind should be a complete reincarnation, something like Schlegel's translations of Shakespeare.

Friday, April 16 Strong sirocco. "God has a grudge against me, although I hardly ever denounce him," says R. "Friedrich von Schiller," he exclaims, as he sees me leaning on my elbows, reflecting. He writes several letters, including one to Seidl in Leipzig, who has annoyed him by reporting that the letter to the director has been mislaid. The Liechtensteins to lunch and with us all day; the Prince tells vividly about how Baron Hirsch engaged his stepbrother, Count Schönfeld, in Vienna. R. tells him one could make use of such material (with the reward from the banker who, it seems, feels disgust for anything to do with money or business), even Balzac had nothing better. Walk; in the evening Prof. Schrön, friend Joukowsky, Rubinstein, etc. — A party, about which I never find much to report, since R. says little of note. (Recently R. remarked in connection with Beethoven's symphonies how manly they are, how utterly lacking in sentimentality, how strict in spite of all their imaginative ideas.)

Saturday, April 17 Bad weather still, but R. walks to the palm tree all the same, returns somewhat tired, and says, "Take cover, Richard, the world is cross with you." — Joke about the "venerable poet-philosopher" of Dr. Förster's lecture, whereas he would never give anybody the impression of being a venerable old man. Lunch with our friend Joukowsky. Very pleasant. — In the studio the singers Pepino and Alfonso and the violinist; R. launches into a veritable duet with Pepino, "*Ciceronella teneva,*" and the violinist also pleases us. R. exclaims, "If only these people could find a genius to make use of all their talents!" Whist in the evening, afterward R. reads to me Renan's *Life of Jesus,* Chapter XVII (?), "On the Final Establishment of the Doctrine of the Arrival of God's Kingdom," which makes a truly deep impression on both of us. R. says, "He loves Jesus, whereas Strauss does not."

Sunday, April 18 R. slept well, he goes for a walk and says to me, "It is enough for me to know, 'She is there at home waiting for me,' then I can also enjoy walking by myself." — We do some work on the biography—oh, how sad and wonderful, the stay in Munich! — As we talk about the school, R. tells us how shocked he was when Rubinstein played some of the *48 Preludes and Fugues,* to see how mannered he has become. — After dictation the Duke of Meiningen and his wife are announced. R. is pleased to see him again and welcomes him very warmly. Over our late breakfast he says the Duke gives the impression of being a direct descendant of Witikind. — Some visitors in the afternoon; R. receives Prince Ouroussoff and embarks with him on a long discussion about the church. The Prince maintained that it was unavoidable for the church to interfere in politics, etc.; R. maintains that, if religion had any influence at all on our lives, our customs would surely be less pretentious. — In the evening our Posilipine friends and, besides them, the Duke and his wife; Herr Rubinstein plays to us his "Picture" from *Die Walküre,* "Wotan's Farewell," and then R. plays the Prelude to *Parsifal* for the Duke, with explanations. When the

Duke says he is curious about the production, R. replies, "I have called my work a stage *dedication* play; it would be unthinkable in our ordinary theaters, and it is very bold; but, if our sweet secrets can be taken so lightly, I do not see why one should not also deal with them in the noblest way." — The Duke once more pleases R. with his personality: "He looks like Wotan, like Barbarossa, there is nothing in the least modern about him—he is the only German prince who makes one think of his origin, completely heathen." — The musicians strike up, and R. again does his duet with Pepino. (Before beginning dictation he said to me, "I come to it fresh from Lord Jesus." —)

Monday, April 19 R. somewhat tired, down in the dumps, as he says; on top of that, eternally gray skies. He reads Marc Monnier's description of the Camorra, which interests him. We stroll together in the flowering garden, R. and I, and enjoy this lovely world. In the evening whist with our friend Liechtenstein, and after that a reading of Chapter XVII, to which R. supplies an admiring commentary.

Tuesday, April 20 R. did not have a good night, wild dreams, perhaps the result of our social activities, not always agreeable. At lunch he talks about the Camorra and about his fondness for crime stories: "The Gospels are also a crime story." — We walk into town, take a *carrozzella* as far as Pincio's, get out there, and return home on foot, a walk such as R. has not had for years! And he enjoys it. In the evening the Liechtensteins, R. explains his views on vegetarianism, which he will set out in his next work.

Wednesday, April 21 R. slept well. Around noon we get ready and visit the Conservatoire, a nice room, nice friendly reception, nice choir, but the operetta . . . ! R. suffers but is very forbearing. [*Inserted in the Diaries an Italian newspaper clipping about the visit.*] It ends at 2 o'clock, and we take refreshments in Vermouth de Torino, where we meet Siegfried! We thought he was still in Cahadoli with the Liechtensteins—much merriment, and then drive home via the Corso V. E.— R. as always increasingly delighted with Naples. In the evening the first scenes of *Hamlet* (not the very first one) and some of Polonius. — (Yesterday we happened to talk about *Tasso,* and R. says it is downright horrible the way he makes Tasso *cling* to Antonio; one gets utterly confused, not knowing what the author means by it.)

Thursday, April 22 R. somewhat run down, the fact that our children have been invited by friends to an outing in Amalfi annoys him: "I feel it as an attack on my domestic pride, for all I have is you and the children, and nothing besides." I go to refuse the invitation, R. comes with the children to fetch me, and there we meet the Meiningen couple. He feels unwell and returns home immediately. In the evening friend Rubinstein and the Liechtensteins, to the former R. explains his views on the deterioration of human beings since they started eating meat.

Friday, April 23   R. still somewhat weary, but he goes for a walk in the morning. He tells me his ideas for a letter to be written to the Duke of Bagnara, and after I have drafted it, he dictates to me, up to the arrival in his life of the King of Bavaria, at which point he intends for the time being to conclude! — In the evening the most glorious moonlight. Then sketch of the life of Saint Francis of Assisi in the King of Saxony's translation.

Saturday, April 24   R. had a good night, we laugh over my letter after he has been for a walk and amused himself with lizards—he stops them from flitting away by whistling, and they then look at him with glittering eyes. Visit from the Duke of Meiningen and his wife. Shortly before that a nice letter from the Cabinet secretary, saying that the King is following R.'s suggestion of changing the theater director. [*Letter inserted in the Diaries; see notes.*] — Much consideration, no one to suggest for this position! . . . Thoughts of going back to the Vienna pamphlet and desiring no director at all. Somewhat to my surprise, R. discusses the matter with the Duke and asks him whether, together with the dukedom of Franconia, he would not take over the directorship. — After the visit, to town with R. and Lusch, visit the museum. The portrait of Paul III utterly shocks R.: "Beasts of prey!" he exclaims. Pleasure in the old masters, a Ghirlandajo attracts him, the saint to the left of the onlooker reminds him of Gleizès, "a head like the beginnings of a peach." — Above all a Lucas from Holland, *Adoration of the Magi,* and a nativity by Dürer. — In the former picture the king on the left with the wonderful hood enchants him: "As Nature clothes its creatures, so does the painter clothe his here." "And how beautifully it is painted!" — We feel quite carried away as we leave the little room in which we have been so refreshed by German spirit, German humor, diligence, and art. We go into Caflish's, where R. has a conversation with a young female street urchin, who pleases him with her liveliness and her understanding: "We ought to take her right away and train her as a parlormaid." — He laments the way in which this very gifted people has always been maltreated by conquerors, "because they were good and their country so beautiful!" Evening on the terrace; the children with us, Siegfried imitating the cries of the street vendors; wonderful moments: "With all these children's voices one feels as if one were surrounded by birds and grasshoppers!" The noonday hour was splendid, the evening is divine! — I take some notes for my letter to Herr v. Bürkel.

Sunday, April 25   A good night and an early walk for R.; he accuses himself of being lazy, doing nothing! I write the letter to Herr v.

Bürkel and R. thinks it good, just laughing at me for still making mistakes (datives and accusatives). — While talking yesterday about the 9th Symphony, which is to be performed in Meiningen in the fall, R. says it is curious that this work, not so well proportioned in its form, should have become so popular—and when I reply that people want sublimity rather than serene perfection, he replies, "Yes, they prefer 'Wotan's Farewell' to Beckmesser's serenade." — Visitors in the afternoon, among them the gentlemen from the Conservatoire, to whom R. describes the state of music in Germany. In the evening our friends Stein and Liechtenstein, returning from the outing in Amalfi, make all kinds of reports. When they have all gone, R. and I stroll on the terrace; Vesuvius is putting forth its rays, the flowers spreading their fragrance, the moon shining, and we can enjoy all of this together!

Monday, April 26   R. slept well and begins the day with his walk. Friend Joukowsky, back from Amalfi, comes to resume his painting. R. has difficulties with Leipzig and writes to the director. In the evening the Liechtensteins; R. embarks on a long discussion with him, at first about certain aspects of etymology and old religious practices and customs in Germany; he points out their sophistication. Then he goes on to global conformations, parallels between the Old World and America. Late in the evening, when a painful memory pierces me and, to rescue myself, I immerse myself in a prayer, R. asks me what I am reflecting about. "I am praying." — "Prayer is the cessation of desire," he says. — At lunch he amused our companions with his statement that we (he and I) are pure mercury! — Yesterday he spoke about the many dogs, faithful creatures, he had already lost. —

Tuesday, April 27   R. has a slight chill, Loldi and Fidi not well. News that *Siegfried* is not a success in Cologne! — Much talk about Dante in the past few days, R. is put off by his receding forehead, and the rigid dogmatism in his poems is disturbing. He says there are certain things human beings have been able to express only in symbols, and the church has committed the crime of consolidating these and forcing them on us as realities through persecution; it is permissible for art to use these symbols, but in a free spirit and not in the rigid forms imposed by the church; since art is a profound form of play, it frees these symbols of all the accretions the human craving for power has attached to them. But Dante did not follow this method. And even the appearance of Saint Francis has proved an embarrassment, he says, since it was wrongly used to gain support for the church at the very time the most genuine Christians, the Waldenses, were being persecuted. — R. does not feel very well all day, and he does not go out of doors. Visit from Herr Plüddemann, who makes quite a nice impression on us.

Wednesday, April 28   R. tells me the comical dream he had, which made him laugh very heartily in the morning; he wanted to greet the Khedive and his escort, these gentlemen were already solemnly engaged in exchanging greetings, and he could not take off his hat, a sort of straw cap which kept falling farther and farther over his eyes. — He then looks at me and says he cannot rightly remember what I looked like when I came with Hans to visit him, but he feels that what he calls my beauty came to me later, through suffering. I: "Probably through love." He: "I did not really know whom you loved!" . . . The enclosed leaflet on how to improve our agriculture [*not found*], the continuing mass emigrations, Rothschild's purchase of the Jamnitzer centerpiece (for 600,000 marks) produce bitter remarks from him. On the other hand, a letter from the conductor Levi evokes the remark: "I cannot allow him to conduct *Parsifal* unbaptized, but I shall baptize them both, and we shall all take Communion together." He says he will find a way around the difficulty. We go for a walk in the garden, and when I tell him that I was deeply upset by a passage in L.'s letter about Lenbach, who was painting a still life of a freshly slaughtered chicken: "Painters are like that, to them all things are there to be looked at, to feast their eyes on; poets, too, are cruel—Homer, for example; they depict heroism in all its cruelty and heartlessness, and then someone comes along like Jesus, who is all heart. He is at his greatest when he is bitter, when all his fury breaks out, he will separate the father from the son, everything will wither—then he shows his divinity. Of all the arts, music alone is entirely detached from all that, pure and redeeming." In the evening Herr Rubinstein plays to us the sonata [Opus] 111: several times during the piece R. came to me and said, "It is heavenly," and at the end he exclaims: "There lies my whole doctrine—the first movement is Will in its suffering and heroic desire, the other one is the gentler Will which human beings will possess once they become reasonable. Vegetarians!"

Thursday, April 29   R. goes for a walk and says, "The path up to the palm tree, that is Mathilde's garden—the last movement of yesterday's sonata, where there is no more suffering except fellow suffering, a sweet melancholy, spreading and leading ever upward to Beatrice." And as he describes this state of bliss, "which knows no boredom, and which only music can bring us," he embraces me and says, "We are in this garden, on the steps to final salvation." As we part, he exclaims, "All is well!" — At lunch he tells me he has been communing with me, reading *Measure for Measure*—I am Isabella, down to the last detail! Recently he reread the first act of *Othello* with very great interest, and he feels it is the most terrible of all, because so close to us. *Hamlet* is much remoter, he says, it seems by comparison a sort of farce (he speaks the word "farce" very calmly and deliberately). And always returning to Opus 111; so splendid of Beethoven to have written it for the piano, although certain things go far beyond it and clearly seem designed for the intensive sound of violins. In connection with the conclusion, he repeats his image of a paradise to which human beings might still aspire. He says, "It is literally as if, caught up in a gentle tumult, one feels oneself taking part, approaching it; tender yearning is not excluded, and there is no feeling of boredom." — Yesterday he spoke of his *final work,* the long one about religion and art. This he still wants to write, though he approaches the subject with a feeling of real trepidation, but otherwise he finds the thought of literary work utterly repulsive. Some strenuous climbing in the garden in an attempt to reach the children. R. tired in the evening.

Friday, April 30 R. had a good night's rest, and toward noon, while I am still sitting for the picture, he talks in a nobly impetuous way of the impression made on him by *Measure for Measure,* in which the nobility of convention finds expression as in no other of Shakespeare's plays. He finds the Duke's mildness unutterably moving. He promises to read it to me. When I return from town, I find our friend Liechtenstein with R., both talking happily, but when later his wife also joins us, and in the evening R. feels no desire either to read or to chat, the atmosphere becomes oppressive, and I begin to feel all too deeply how bad it is to become the slaves of circumstance.

Saturday, May 1 R. not very well, he explains to me the reason for his vexation yesterday: he had wanted to be alone with me, to read me the play, and we had been prevented. — On top of that, an invitation for a 2nd visit to the Conservatoire; R. instructs me to inform the old librarian of his feelings about the operetta, and to say that he would regret having written his letter if he were obliged to represent it in person. I do so. However, when I return, I find R. worried about a recurrence of his erysipelas. We spend the evening alone together, in silence and in quiet conversation, and I have the satisfaction of seeing the gradual return of a mild tranquillity. — How often these days does my soul cry out, "*Io ti vedo*" ["I see thee"]! The noble countenance of our crucified Lord rises suddenly before my eyes when my inner strength wavers. Dear God, do not abandon me!

Sunday, May 2 R. is well again in the morning after a good night, but later he unfortunately feels somewhat indisposed. Our friends the Liechtensteins to lunch; Prince Rudolf talks vividly about the former aristocratic world. R. says, "Now the Jews are the *grands seigneurs.*" Via Bulwer-Lytton, came to talk about the English and Germany's shame in connection with the Berlin Congress. Some visitors, including professors from the Conservatoire; R. comes back to his letter and says on the one hand they have the most rigid form of pedantry and on the other utter dissoluteness. — Then, beneath gray skies, R. and I stroll together through the villa; when we come upon a cactus of unusually rugged appearance, R. says, "That looks like an ox, which is really what it wanted to be." — In the evening farewell visit from the Liechtensteins, sad in many ways. As they depart, I hear from the street, hoarse and high-pitched, a prolonged sorrowful cry.

Monday, May 3 Fine weather, a good night for R. — I have some business to do with secondhand merchants in the morning. On my return I find him ruling lines and in good spirits. Final sitting for my picture. In the evening R. reads to us the three main scenes of *Measure for Measure;* an indescribable impression, the noblest and artistically most perfect of works. R. and I in tears, justice and mercy in their fairest forms; the Duke's transition to mildness, his unspoken love for Isabella (Isabella herself divine, as R. exclaims), the two scenes between Angelo and the virgin, the final scene, with its polyphonic construction —how to count up and point out all the many details which enchant and move one? — We can scarcely leave each other's side, and on

Tuesday, May 4 our very first words in the morning concern the advantages to a poet of solid religious forms—how lovely it sounds when Isabella speaks of the strict God who chose nevertheless to intercede! And how seriously Shakespeare took the idea of majesty! Again and again we come back to talking of this most glorious of works. — I have again some things to do in town, and I find R. completely absorbed in preparing his lines, so that he cannot at first eat any lunch, having overexerted himself. He says, "I could be like the young men of today, not bother my head about the outward appearance of my score, but it leaves me no peace—I must set it out so that it is nice to look at." Three dukes approach R., wanting to make him an honorary member of the Philharmonic Society; R. says, half joking, half vexed, "One thinks one is strolling in an orange grove here, but it turns out to be a grove of misunderstandings." More sittings (R. recently introduced our friend Joukowsky to someone with the words "A genius who paints with his emotions").

Wednesday, May 5 R. had some amusing dreams—that my father, in Indian costume, desired to have homage paid to him and said to R., "Kiss my hand." Then that Dr. Schrön fell off a chair and broke into pieces like a doll, the head divided from the trunk, and Frau Schrön treated it as something quite normal. He still takes his walk in the morning and enjoys the garden. Today what is now really the last sitting, after it lunch, which starts very gaily but ends on quite a serious note, when R. relates what he actually intended to keep to himself, that a decision has been made in Berlin on the question of vivisection: that it is a necessity. [*Newspaper clipping enclosed; see notes.*] R. wants to leave the Reich and take out American citizenship. He asks what his art has to do with these cruel and indifferent people. Deep distress. — Drove into town in the afternoon, separated from R., kept meeting him again, and drove home, merry on account of it. Whist in the evening.

Thursday, May 6 Not a good night, either for R. or for me, but he goes for a walk in the morning and returns for breakfast in good spirits. My journeys to town and the friendly encounters I always have there amuse R. when I tell him about them. He spent the morning on his score. In the afternoon he writes to friend Wolz. and sends the biography off to the printers. In the evening a curious visit from three English Wagnerites, whose imposing manner permits no conversation. The second act of *Tristan* played by Rubenstein; R. sleeps, Joukowsky and Stein, too, only the English people and the children and I awake: Lusch and I moved, the English people holding out nobly. Much amusement about it and discussion of the English character in all its steadfastness—enduring things in the assumption that they are special, but without in fact having the slightest idea.

Friday, May 7 Yesterday evening brings back to R. the idea of making some cuts in *Tristan;* he says it demands too much of the audience as well as the singers, and he would do this in both the second and third acts, reserving the full work for performances in Bayreuth, for he wishes *Tristan* to be staged there, too. — At lunch he announces that he intends to arrange the choruses from the first act of *Parsifal* for our children; he says he will not be able to prepare it as a surprise for me, for it would have to be practiced "mercilessly." — Otherwise, only dismal remarks about the present mass emigrations from Germany! However, delight in Siegfried, his cheerful temperament, which will make things easy for him. In the evening R. reads the scene from *The Merry Wives of Windsor* in which Slender is unwilling to come in for the meal, to our great amusement. "What I find so wonderful," says R., "is how he wrote it all down, stuff like this—what a tremendous mind!" — He quotes Falstaff's "No quips now, Pistol," with much laughing delectation. — From *Much Ado About Nothing* the constables' scene, with less enjoyment, on account of the verbal jokes. A violent thunderstorm, which does us good after the closeness which almost ruined our morning walk.

Saturday, May 8 Harking back to our conversation yesterday about Fidi, I tell R. I am convinced that in his own childhood he was equally cheerful and gay, and it was only his life which prevented this cheerfulness from finding expression, giving him this apparent frenetic quality which many people interpret as capriciousness. He admits it, but says that even in his childhood the poverty of his home did not permit his gaiety to unfold to its full extent, as with Siegfried. — We discuss what we read yesterday, and R. says it is remarkable how rich in characters and situations he made his *Merry Wives,* for which he had no previously existing story; he says it is all done with great artistry, but it is precisely this absence of an existing story which gives it a slight air of artificiality. — Then my portrait—R. praises its sublimely childlike quality. But his favorite picture of me is the photograph with the veil; what he adds in telling me this shall, however, remain my secret, which I can hardly admit even to myself! — Letter from a clergyman in Hesse about vivisection—R. pleased by it. We talk about the subject, and R. says: "We are too stupid, like the dodo, which was condemned to extinction! — If one disturbs an anthill with one's foot, the ants come together again and rebuild what was destroyed." Joukowsky: "But we have no instinct." — R.: "Knowledge should take its place and help the human race to restore what was brought into disorder by blind force, earthly convulsions. Moths fly into the lamp because Nature is imprudent, whereas for human beings the task is to extinguish this light—not the light of knowledge, but that of a false science, a science which the princes foster while at the same time they continue building up their armies." The socialist elections in Hamburg, Bismarck's idea of taxing *Pauli* provoke R. into violent expressions of indignation: "We are governed by bulls and oxen." [*The last seven words obliterated in ink by an unknown hand.*]

Sunday, May 9 A rainy day. Daniel's birthday, R. recalls the way in which he was abandoned and says that in a certain sense this is what has made him so cold and utterly unable to make allowances for individual qualities. Some callers. A Duchess Ravaschieri impresses me as a woman of sensibility. In the evening R. reads *Faust,* Part One, overwhelmingly beautiful and moving. But we feel that the poem lends itself as little to being read aloud as to dramatic presentation; R. says he needs to assume an almost artificial tone, and the scene with Mephisto after the meeting with Gretchen comes close to offending me. — In the morning we talked at length about religion and art. R. describes how art works in metaphors and allegories as such but at the same time conveys to the emotions the truth behind the dogmas. Aeschylus's *Oresteia,* he says, is undoubtedly more profound than all the Eleusinian mysteries. He also speaks of the godlike qualities manifest in Christ and says it is understandable that the birth of such a being should be presented as a miracle—the Immaculate Conception repulsive as dogma, but wonderful as legend and in art (painting). —

We were talking recently about the year 1857 in Switzerland, and he said, "I was truly like a good seed: if the earth in which I was planted was at least reasonably good, I would start to grow." — He talks of making money with *Parsifal,* giving concerts, in order to gain his independence.

Monday, May 10 Quite a nice morning. R. slept well. I have a sitting in the Villa Postiglione, return home in a rowboat, and my pleasant journey gives me something to relate. For a walk with R. in the afternoon. Whist in the evening, somewhat upsetting, for R. has no luck and I bring luck to Herr v. Stein! Glorious sunset.

Tuesday, May 11 R. announces at breakfast that we are to make an excursion to Vesuvius. Swift preparations, hasty lunch at Figlio de Pietro's. R. sends word that he is unwell, and he does not join us at lunch, but nevertheless wants the outing to continue, feeling it will do him good. Silent journey. Arriving at the observatory, we seek a room—none to be had. The children off to the crater with some guides; R. feeling worse, I suggest returning home. We do that, home at 9:30. R. to bed. The children, exhausted, do not return until close on 11. Strange, dreamlike day, saw nothing, just experienced the reality of worry!

Wednesday, May 12 Much indisposition, even I laid up; the children splendid, however, God is with them, and when I can do no more, He takes over! They are under His protection, so how can there be trouble? — Visit from Rubinstein, cheerful conversation. He tries out the pianino and plays the *Don Giovanni* Overture; R. interrupts him, saying the allegro is too fast, it should not be rattled off. He reads Sch.'s *Parerga.*

Thursday, May 13 R. appears to be completely recovered. I visit the foundlings' home here and receive a reassuring impression, of which I speak at lunch. In the afternoon a walk with R. in the garden, the sky looking whitish all day, and in the evening a violent thunderstorm. (He has written out the *Parsifal* voices.)

Friday, May 14 R. tells me of his dream: in it he saw his uncle Adolph, was surprised that he looked so young, then with him listened to a Mozart symphony, and his sister Luise stupidly exclaimed, "Ah, the name Mozart is hovering over us!"—but then he was weeping with me. R. somewhat depressed at lunch, but over coffee he becomes very cheerful again. He relates various things from Schopenhauer regarding time, the reflected image of which lies in ourselves; in the same way that one can discern a moving object only by reference to a stationary one, so within ourselves we carry the reflected image of time. — A walk in the garden with R. and the children, he takes great delight in the hills with their vineyards. Surprised by rain, we flee into the cave amid much laughter. In the evening R. reads to us a very tiresome speech by Bismarck and what seems to us an unsatisfactory reply by Windthorst.

Saturday, May 15   R. had a good night, goes for an early-morning walk with the children and is cheerful at our breakfast together. He likes the embroidery on his cloak, and he tells me once again how strong lines make work impossible for him, whereas the dreamier colors, and the refraction of light from the material, have a pleasantly distracting and concentrating effect. I drive to the *"Urbild,"* as R. calls my picture, to have my fingers painted. We talk about painting, about the gallery in Leipzig, Delaroche's picture, and R. says, "Napoleon on the Mount of Olives." — Then he tells us about his cousin Kühnlein. He makes some corrections to the biography. And in the afternoon he goes to town on foot; Loldi and I watch him for a long while, he frequently turns to wave, and all the blessings of love follow his rapid steps! He walks as far as the palm tree and returns home in somewhat less than an hour! He has written a cheerful letter to friend Wolzogen, greetings from *Haus* to *Maison,* and in spite of his tiredness is in a gentle and cheerful mood in the evening. Delight in the starry sky and the moonlight.

Sunday, May 16   R. had a somewhat restless night, and he works out a little poem to attach to the picture of himself which he is giving to friend Joukowsky. — He is in good spirits at breakfast and says to me, "Without you I am nothing; now make use of your comfortable position." — Some callers. In the evening starry skies and moonlight again.

Whitmonday, May 17   R. slept well, but he still does not feel quite at ease. Since his lack of caution with the soda water he is complaining of abdominal catarrh. He works on the biography. Arrival of Malwida, Corso del Monte Virgine, in the evening the Knights of the Grail; too much for him. He goes to bed in an ill-humor.

Tuesday, May 18   Not a good night, skies still white, he still retrospectively vexing himself over the obligations of partisanship, having to concern himself with people who can do nothing whatever for him. — Telegram from friend Feustel, he has lost his son; R. tells me about it and asks me to write something; all I can think of is, "Blessed are they that mourn, for they shall be comforted." R. incorporates it in the telegram he has already begun. Melancholy atmosphere. In the afternoon a walk with R. and Malwida as far as the belvedere. Since R. is still complaining of his sufferings, I send for Dr. Schrön, who comes late in the evening.

Wednesday, May 19   R. had a better night, though he was up once and wrote down an idea for his article. At lunch he is much more

cheerful, and he himself says, "Wit has returned: the Earth takes back
her child." — The whole company has to laugh heartily when he says,
"It would be my greatest triumph if I were to make you all laugh in
my final hour." — We reflect gladly that in the biography we now have
only 4 more years to write down, and R. earnestly resolves to write
these, so as to throw light on our personal destinies. In the evening he
reads to us the episode of the marionettes in *Don Quixote,* in which the
figure of the Showman particularly fascinates and pleases us. — Before
that he rehearsed the choruses from *Parsifal* with the children (already
begun yesterday)—so lovely, so touching, his dear hand strews
blessings over them with every movement indicating rhythm and
stress! Much rehearsal necessary, and intertwined with it the delight of
the children—every moment an outburst of laughter. R. says, "Now the
children are unhappy again!"

Thursday, May 20 Merry early breakfast; continued pleasure in the
thought of the children—R. remarks on Loldi's sense of humor and
how well she understands his witticisms. Yesterday, he says, he
greeted Herr. v. St. with the words, "Pardon me for not getting up,
but I just sat down," and Loldi, sitting in the corner, laughed. Then
he reads Schopenhauer to me on the subject of professors of philosophy,
and we laugh heartily over the words, "who cannot live without
theism, that is to say, eat and drink." — After lunch yesterday he
spoke about the festival, the fine spirit shown by his singers, and how
disappointed they must have felt when, after such an unheard-of
expenditure of all their powers, nothing happened. — At lunch he
addressed Siegfried as "obstinate innocence"! — Over coffee he told
us how curious childhood impressions are: when he was ten years
old, he and his sister Klara saw a play in which Mme Hartwig had
to speak the line, "You can do it *if* you will." She said "whatever you
will," the audience laughed, and R. asked Klara why, whereupon she
explained, "It should be 'if you will.'" This made an indelible impression on him. — Discussion about spiritualists, occasioned by an
exposure in Munich. R. says: "How foolish to object to a person for
that! It is like forbidding a poet to call his play *King Lear.*" Speaking
for himself, he would be delighted to see a person flying, whether in
the dark or by daylight. "But the stupid public wants to achieve
religion through hocus-pocus." To have a showman like that arrested,
he adds, is too absurd, for his powers, like those of an actor, lie in
some kind of deception. — R. wants to go into town, creeps off, I
catch up with him, and we drive in together; at Detken's we separate,
and he says with a laugh, "So the bookbinder is making the triumphal
arch?" Yesterday, when he saw the decorator taking away a carpet, he
crept in to find out what was going to happen on the 22nd, to catch a

glimpse of the triumphal arch! Toward evening a visit from Mme Stella Bonheur, the Ortrud in Rome; she tells us very pleasant things about the performances and our good, energetic Frau Lucca. R. says, when she has gone, "A complete lack of false modesty." — Always in this connection with a disapproving side glance at the Germans! — *Timon [of Athens]* in the evening, the scene with the painter, the poet, and the cynic. R. says the play seems to him "very personal": "The material allows no chance of a reconciliation, the characters are observed in all their wickedness." — Before *Timon* R. told the story of our journey through the floods in Ticino.

Friday, May 21 As we sit down to breakfast, R. says to me, "How different it will be tomorrow!" — Then he reads to me Schopenhauer on beards and also the introduction to the "Apparent Deliberateness" chapter, praising Sch.'s hypothetical skill. — The weather is gray and showery, and R. says the good Lord owes it to him to behave nicely, since he is taking so much trouble with him. — Friend Gross sends me news of a death, I interrupt my little preparations to express my sympathy for him. Yesterday, while I was shopping in town, I was vividly reminded of the stultifying effect of a big city at the café, where I was ordering champagne; beggars; in the carriage in which I returned home flowers, put there for me by R., while, as I get in, a funeral procession meets my eyes—and all of this accepted without reflection, my mind full of my shopping. And thus is life, day after day, for city dwellers. — At five o'clock rehearsal of the *Parsifal* choruses, separation at last at 10 o'clock, after a day containing five rehearsals!

Saturday, May 22 Wonderful night! The gardeners and decorators hammer and knock, contrary to all agreements. My concern for R.'s sleep expands into a conscious concern for his whole existence, into feelings of concern that I am unworthy of him and the task of caring for him, and my feeling, growing ever more intense with the outward noise, turns into a fervent prayer within me; with this it seems I might hope to overcome not only this night noise, but also all other disturbances, and I see the cherished reflections of this victory in his sleep, which lasts until the morning! A shining morning brings him my greeting! At about 8 o'clock the children bring him theirs, a greeting from the stars, and amid tears and sobs our souls intermingle, while the children hear from their father things they will never forget. He rests, we move the festivities from the hall to the *salon* and arrange roses, picture, and fabrics, so that R., entering the *salon* around 11 o'clock, is delighted; he spends an hour there, looks at Loldi's drawings, and when I go to greet him, I am permitted to see his happiness in his transfigured appearance and hear it in his very moving words. — Lunch at 1 o'clock. R. was not in favor of the number 13, to which I had linked the Last Supper and *Parsifal,* the suns and the letters of his name, also the year '13 of this century; we invite a 14th guest and change the form. All spoke well and with deep emotion, and R. replied, repeating what he had already told me in the morning—why he is now superstitious, whereas previously he had always liked to think of himself as the 13th! He does not wish to spite his good fortune, he says, and he mentions 7 as the number which means everything to him, the children and the two of us—all that is well disposed toward him derives from that; about this relationship he says many things which you, my children, have certainly noted, and which were accompanied by the tears of all present. Over coffee we hear "*Mignonne,*" sung by Pepino. Then a rest, a walk to the palm tree, and finally a trip on the sea. Five boats rock their way along the blessed shores, bathed in a moonlight which seems to wrap us in gentle warmth, Naples glittering in the distance, Vesuvius like a dream image behind it; yet more blissful than all outward appearances the harmony of souls binding us all together. — We return home to the illumined *salon,* and the day and the evening are brought to a close with the choruses from *Parsifal,* sung by our children, our friends Plüddemann, Rubinstein, Humperdinck, and R.

Sunday, May 23 R. had a good night, and he christens yesterday "the day of youth"! — Now cleaning up and restoring order, gray and cold weather to accompany it. — Friendly calls, which, however, tire R. because of the need to talk French. The sitting room is in order, and we spend a cozy evening together, R. remarking in connection with Mme Minghetti's visit how disturbing people are when they seem to respond to the boldest of ideas yet always remain in their wonted paths. With his very harsh remarks about the Italian theater—among other things, he said he could not understand how a lady of breeding could still go to the theater—Mme Minghetti was in full agreement, and took leave of him saying, "*Je suis amoureuse folle de vous*" ["I am madly in love with you"]—whereupon R. replied jokingly, "*Nous sommes au bord d'un abîme, mes devoirs compliqués à M. Minghetti*" ["We are on the edge of an abyss, my complex respects to M. Minghetti"]. —

Monday, May 24 Fine weather, which vexes R. inasmuch as, having reckoned on bad weather, he had canceled the outing to Amalfi. As a small consolation I suggest a drive to the Villa Floridiana, which gives us much pleasure—particularly when we go inside. In the evening a discussion of the outing, which ends in great laughter when—after the weather has been considered the deciding factor—R. declares, "Whatever the weather, we are going tomorrow!" —

Tuesday, May 25 Preparations, at noon departure from the Villa d'Angri in some agitation, since we are afraid of arriving too late. A saloon carriage awaits us, through the good offices of friend Joukowsky, to the delight of R., who sings, "When my master starts his travels, what things there are to see!" — Heavenly journey to Amalfi, visit to the cathedral, which vexes R. somewhat, but the evening, spent on the terrace of the Hôtel des Capucins, restores his good spirits, which had already begun to emerge during the meal, when he teased me for my curiosity about Saint Andrew, "viewed by daylight."

Wednesday, May 26 Merry breakfast and drive to Ravello, lovely beyond description. Discovered Klingsor's garden in Ravello. Late breakfast at the Villa . . . (?), then coffee with Mr. Reed's manager, whose wife, a Swiss, pleases us very much with her serious air—she reminds us of Vreneli. Drive via Santa Chiara to the little pavilion (the view from Santa Chiara the loveliest, in my opinion). Rest, with songs from Pepino. Meditative descent and lovely evening on the terrace, conversing about the stars, which glitter above us, and the moon, which looks down upon us—as it is claimed—"with swollen cheeks and foolish face." (In the book in Ravello R. wrote, "Have found the 2nd act of *Pars*.")

Thursday, May 27 Corpus Christi Day, much noise and banging, brutish affair which would shock anybody of a humanitarian or religious turn of mind. Siegfried full of it, six times to the cathedral, back and forth! Sea trip to the grotto in two boats, really splendid, as also the return journey to the beautiful Vietri and after that the journey by rail, during which R. becomes increasingly exuberant. As we arrive, Naples exercises all its powerful and imperious magic. R. remarks that compared with this everything else looks like an idyll, and one feels here as if one were in the main center (he said "main city") of the world. — In the evening, as if to celebrate our return, Vesuvius keeps sending up its flares, so regularly that one feels an eruption is nigh.

Friday, May 28 A good night and a cheerful day. R. writes today and tomorrow letters to Wolz., Lenbach, Schemann, and corrects the biography, which he sends to friend Wolz. for the printers. A curious mood overtook him yesterday and overtakes him again today as he contemplates our surroundings: sorrow at the prospect of having to take me home to the North. When I try to tell him what pain he causes me by saying this, he observes that, since I have no wishes of my own, it is all the more important for him to wish in my behalf! — And he adds that he himself is so completely finished with everything that this is now really all he cares about. We chose a spot up in the vineyards to settle down and spent a cheerful evening there, though cut short by our fatigue.

Saturday, May 29 R. resumes his early-morning walks. In the afternoon by boat to the Villa Postiglione, where our good friend Joukowsky, kept indoors by a fever, has nevertheless managed to work out a sketch for the 2nd act of *Parsifal*. Return by boat with R. and Malwida; the children also returning from the Villa Post., on the Posilipo road above, constantly waving to us! R. somewhat tired in the evening; he tells us of the interlude between Herr v. Rudhart, the Bavarian ambassador, and Prince Bismarck, continually remarking on the attitude of Bismarck, who had nothing to say except "I do not have to put up with that!"

Sunday, May 30 R. slept well and goes for a walk in the morning with the children; later in the morning he begins a letter to the King. Some callers in the afternoon. R. looks tired, the steps from the sea up to the Villa Postiglione were a strain on him. In the evening he asks friend Rubinstein to play the second movement of 111, after which he gives friend Joukowsky the plan for the 2nd act of *Parsifal*.

Monday, May 31 R. woke up very early, he goes for a walk with the children, tells me of his letter to the King, to whom he wishes a day such as the 22nd. He begins Flaubert's *La Tentation de Saint Antoine* and laughs over the curiously prosaic tone of the opening, in which the saint talks like a secluded epicure. He admits that the peculiar use to which the French language has been put in German detracts from the effect of French works—"*charmant*," for example. Over coffee he talks about Spohr and his last—so very childish—opera, sent to him for consideration; its rejection brought Spohr's anger down on his head, until he met him personally, and "I told all the lies I could." The bookbinder brings the folios, and R. excitedly enjoys himself setting them up—altogether he takes much pleasure in his "makeshift study." But in the evening he feels tired—ascending those steps really did strain him. But he gaily tells us a joke: "How to put a stop to the mass emigrations?" — "Make America Prussian, then not a soul will go there." —

Tuesday, June 1 R. is not entirely well, he had a somewhat restless night, but he settles down to his big work and says we will be amazed by what he is producing. I write letters of thanks on his behalf for the 22nd, and read with Herr v. Stein his piece on G. Bruno. Photographer and painter in the afternoon, and R. poses good-humoredly. Uncontrollable emotion as I see R. and Fidi sitting side by side and their picture is taken. In the evening friend Joukowsky brings his sketch for the 2nd act of *Parsifal*. Several things have to be altered, but occupation with it is in itself a pure delight, as is also the zeal of our friend. — Lovely views—R. observes that Vesuvius and Capri are like man and wife, sun and moon.

Wednesday, June 2   R. slept well, goes for a walk early in the morning, although it is already very hot, then goes to his work. I visit an institute for poor children, a former Augustinian monastery. Splendid Gothic hall looking out onto cloisters, the poor children there— probably less unhappy, one feels, than anywhere else! All the same, a disagreeable impression of the sisters of mercy. R. very content when I return, teasing me as he always does when he is well and cheerful. At 5 o'clock walk up to the palm tree, around 6 settle down on the big terrace, which is at its best at this hour, and a lovely, long, glorious evening beneath a haze of stars, flares from Vesuvius lighting up fishing boats and Posilipo. Few words, a tender inner awareness of the gentle omnipotence of Nature here, which I can compare only with his love.

Thursday, June 3   R. cheerful and playful, he says he talks nonsense to me in order not to become ecstatic. Drive into town with R. and Malwida in great heat, but R. is happy with the warmth, he gets out at the Municipium, I go on to the Conservatoire for a performance by the pupils. The children in Pompeii (Richard says it could just as well be named Cneius). Late return, the daily routine upset in consequence and R. not well.

Friday, June 4   R. did not have too bad a night, and he is able to work on his long article, the outline of which he described to me at breakfast; with such a subject, he says, one must be more circumspect— it is not like a review of an opera. — A gray day, sirocco, R. not entirely well and somewhat out of humor—but always kind to me; when I return from town with Malwida, I find a heap of popping pods on my dressing table, for me to burst! This is now his and the children's main amusement. In the evening Herr Rubinstein comes and plays pieces from *Parsifal*—R. not satisfied with his playing—and how little one can teach others. He allows himself now and again to be tempted into singing, but it is a strain on him, and after some expressions of disgust he ends by comparing himself with the bass singer Kneisel, who, losing his memory during Matteo's aria, stopped singing, went off into the wings, but kept returning to the stage and striking up again. He glances through the Schiller-Goethe correspondence, but says it is all very familiar to him, and it does not give him the impression of two masters talking together—rather, two pupils, two experimenters. — He has finally given up Flaubert's *Tentation* and puts the book down in disgust.

Saturday, June 5   R. works on his article, but the weather remains cool and gray. He misses the heat very much. All we do is walk in the garden together, but going uphill is something of a strain on him. In the evening he reads to us several of Schiller's letters about *W. Meister* and says that the first of them is the finest, so truthful and so full of veneration, and it contains his genuine feelings, which he then modified somewhat out of respect for Goethe.

Sunday, June 6 Siegfried's birthday! He comes to bring me good wishes in the name of his father, who, along with Boni, has already been jokingly serenading him with *"Jungfernkranz"!* Presentation of gifts around 1 o'clock. R. gives the boy a nice book about America. The weather not very good, but all the same a boat trip to Cape Posilipo; R. recalls the Norwegian cliffs, where one has the feeling of being protected. He told me yesterday about the orange sunrise and asked me whether I felt like fetching my blankets again! In the evening friend Rubinstein plays his "Picture" of the three Rhine-maidens, Siegfried's apotheosis, and the conclusion of *Götterdämmerung,* to the joy and entrancement of us all. Before that the singers arrived, having seen the illuminated terrace from below, and sang some songs for Siegfried. As our good boy says good night, one sees his inner gratitude and solemn emotion. Here a blessing, too, my child! (The children played Cinderella.)

Monday, June 7 R. had a somewhat restless night, and as we are having breakfast together, he tells me why it is that he sometimes jokingly drags me into the conversation in a way that might seem irritable; he says it torments him at table to be sitting not beside me, but opposite me; we surely owe this custom to those heartless French marriages, but he has no desire to talk to anyone except me—"not even if a goddess descended from Heaven"—and when he then sees me talking to other people, he feels impelled to comment on it. — He works. A letter arrives from Herr v. Bürkel, a petition to the King which occupies our entire afternoon conversation. R. writes down some points, which I am to set out for Herr v. B. [*Wagner's points enclosed in the Diaries; see notes.*] In the evening R. becomes increasingly merry, and he tells us all kinds of anecdotes—also about a letter from Schiller concerning Baggesen's remark on the *Musen-Almanach.* He takes much delight in Schiller's wit.

Tuesday, June 8 R. slept well, and he goes for an early-morning walk, but then complains that there is no shadow and no level path, it is all so hilly. Thoughts of the palace gardens! I wrote to Herr v. Bürkel and add to R.'s notes, at his request, the remark that what would be best of all would be a director of good will and under-standing. R. says: "Though the Court theaters are bad institutions, all it would need to have things put right would be a few well-disposed theater directors, as well as a princess on the throne with sympathy for my cause. But the princes all have other ideas in their heads!" At lunch he reports that he has been writing about Raphael. — R. and I sit on the terrace in the afternoon, then walk to the palm tree and to the vineyards, where we settle down. Contented mood, delight in Siegfried, who is so easy-tempered, so obedient. [*Enclosed a sheet of paper with drawings by Siegfried: villas and churches on hills, and a head. Also, on the back cover of the notebook is written:* "Note for Tuesday, June 8: The children tell me that R. said to them, 'I know that Brange is dead.' — We did not speak of it—he understands my inability to tell him sad news."] We take our leave of Malwida and Stein early, and R. tells me what he has so far written of his article, though without reading it to me. (It will be his last, he says.) In the afternoon, talking about the Indians and the dramas which convey such a fine idea of their refined culture, he remarks that it has now all been undermined by the Mohammedans, and that is the usual way of history.

Wednesday, June 9   R. slept well and comes to call me after his walk. Whether because of a dream or a chain of thoughts, I am looking "pensive," R. asks me why, and I tell him that my reflections were concerned with love and happiness, how life always demands acceptance (for instance, that others have been loved before us), and the moment this turns into forbearance, the happiness one expects from love is lessened. R.: "The only refuge is faith, limitless faith, at the risk of being deceived; but even so one will have known faith." — R. works and is satisfied with what he has done. I write to Herr Schrön and to the gentlemen of the Academic Wagner Society in Vienna, but R. is displeased that I have not told the latter that he will never again go to Vienna. And he adds that he will himself tell them one day that he expects them to beat up a few reviewers. Malwida's immediate departure provokes remarks from him about alienation and lack of affinity, due to people's always having something else important to them, which determines what they are. And it is true that one must yield oneself to him entirely. A lovely, idle afternoon spent beside the palm tree, where, however, it is somewhat cool. In the evening R. reads to us the letters of G. and Schiller concerning the distribution of *Die Horen,* since for him they so vividly illustrate German wretchedness. — When our friend Joukowsky remarks, over coffee in the afternoon, that he would campaign in Russia for our cause on the heir's accession to the throne, R. says, "It would be a humiliation for us," but he adds: "I must admit that it is precisely in Russia that there may be people, perhaps living on remote estates, who are concerned with the influence of the French and would therefore be the most likely ones to adopt my ideas. I expect nothing more from Germany."

Thursday, June 10   R. is very put out that there is no level walk here, and so we work out a plan for him to take the streetcar to the Villa Nazionale and have his walk there, riding up from the gates on a donkey. — He works and tells me that he has been writing about Michelangelo and Raphael. When I jokingly ask, "Is that perhaps due to my influence?," he replies, "No, I have taken care not to go into detail, and have come to the conclusion that a picture such as *The Last Judgment* is really an absurdity—something that cannot be painted." Malwida mentions the botanical gardens to us, and we decide to go there. At 5 o'clock all 9 of us take the streetcar, to R.'s great joy. He says one feels like part of some great element, and indeed one does have the pleasant sense that reputation, power, position [*end of the fourteenth book of the Diaries*] mean nothing here—one is "a man among the rest." A most delightful journey through lively working-class districts; R. jokes, "Just as in London, everything here takes place in the streets." All of it picturesque, and the botanical gardens truly enchanting. The streets become more and more lively, and, to crown it all, the gracious Queen of Italy drives past our streetcar. On R., who salutes her, she makes a very charming impression, and this gives our expedition its first happy conclusion, which is soon followed by another. R. presses my hand, cries, "See you again at the Torretta," and swiftly leaves the streetcar. He literally runs to Dreher's! We ride on, and at the Torretta there he is again. I send the children ahead and walk slowly after them with Malwida in almost total darkness, wave to a *carrozzella* which I first took to be empty, though in the very same moment I cry, "R. is in it!," and, quite true, he is in it, and amid much merriment all three of us squeeze ourselves into the little carriage! Quite an incomparable journey, from beginning to end a vista of palm trees against the evening sky, the Chiaia softly illuminated; after the previous teeming throngs, to which the gracious female figure gave an air of ideality, the meeting with R., and the final entrance into the silent, noble Villa d'Angri! R. thought with pleasure of the Queen and said, "What a moving impression people in this position can make, even when they are not conscious of the extent to which they are the symbols of human suffering and life!" — We talk with friend Joukowsky about painting, and R. observes how much talent is used, more or less unrecognized, in newspaper illustrations. He concludes the evening with a vehement apostrophe to Malwida, reproaching her for her pseudo-relationships and saying that she should come to us and let the others come to her, not she to them. He mentions my father with "his 3 flagpoles," Pest, Rome, Weimar, and all the important faces, and he says it is quite worthless and betrays an emptiness which has to be filled out with pseudo-obligations of this kind. "Cosima did it differently—you marry Liszt!" With this joking remark he concludes his very earnest and vehement address, in which the extent of his passionate truthfulness once again enchants and moves me.

Friday, June 11 R. slept well, and he tells me that in the morning he enjoys reading what he wrote the day before, and seeing whether it is of any value. Loldi unwell, giving us much to think and talk about. Untamable Nature! — At lunch R. says that he has finished the first part of his article and is glad now to have got to religion. "With art one is always obliged to think of Lübke," he adds jokingly. — We have coffee on the dining-room terrace and enjoy the glorious weather. While I am in town, looking at R.'s portrait, just begun, R. takes the streetcar to Dreher's to have a glass of beer, and returns by streetcar. We spend the evening on the big terrace, R. reminiscing about Poland. — Mimi Schl. has told me that Bismarck revealed to her his antipathy toward vivisection, and R. remarks how terrible it is in that case that he did not have the courage to fight for his convictions, but preferred to leave so far-reaching a problem to chance. Mimi has sent me the 1864 album leaf! . . .

Saturday, June 12 After a good night R. expresses to me his delight in Naples and the pleasure he felt at Dreher's, watching people and carriages passing by. Only one thing he noticed gives him a bitter feeling—that no beggar ever approaches a priest! We spend the evening on the terrace, and R. recalls Venice, the light he saw shining in his *palazzo* when he returned home of an evening in a gondola, its magical effect, "and yet my whole life was trouble and strife—not the sufferings and preoccupations of love, but the difficulty of being left in peace long enough to write my score." He then goes on to Paris and talks about *Tannhäuser,* also about Niemann and my father, who could have helped him then but did not, for which reason he, R., still harbors a certain bitterness. — After our friends have gone, Lulu brings me the domestic-accounts book; I exhort her to thriftiness, since her father has twice told me that the housekeeping is costing a lot of money. A violent outburst of anger from R. on this account, he completely misunderstands everything I say. The night begins for me in great sorrow. Was some god giving me warning? Was he punishing insufficient strength, or was it just a demon tormenting me? I believe that R. was upset by his memories. However, he goes off to sleep. While I am seeking and finding the reason for this trial, I hear a moaning sound; anxiety about Loldi, who is still occupying Lulu's room; I rush to her side; but she is asleep; then I hear the sound again, it is coming from the sea, a musical instrument or a human voice; the lament fills the silence, and what my heart does not utter I hear sounding from outside!

Sunday, June 13 R. looks quite indisposed. He heard the sound, too, and thought it was an unusually powerful female voice; we are told later that it is ships' sirens announcing their presence at sea during the night. Perhaps from the English ship the children visited and on which they today attend divine service—R. is pleased that they have inherited such a facility for languages. Toward noon I explain to R. that my exhortation to Lusch was not meant in an offensive way, and today he listens to me and my explanation. Fear of the demon who makes sport of us poor mortals! Some callers arrive, R. receives them with me and is cheerful, though he looks run down. When we show off the cabinet and one of the visitors says that portraits (medallions) should be affixed to it, R. says, "Yes, of the German consul general in Naples!" — Afterward we visit friend Joukowsky in his new apartment. Pleasure in the Sunday Posilipo. Quiet evening.

Monday, June 14   After a good night R. gets up feeling completely restored. When I greet him at breakfast, he says to me, "All I have is you, for you have spoiled everything else for me." — He works on his article, and in the afternoon we decide to go out by boat to the English ship. But as we are about to embark, R. feels some drops of rain, declares that everything he undertakes turns out badly, but gaily transforms the whole outing into a streetcar ride to Dreher's; all 9 of us sit down at a table out in the open, where we are gazed at in wonder by some ladies in a carriage who recognize R. Then a visit to S. Francesco Paolo, which pleases us greatly, except for the row of boxes. In the streetcar R. said to me, "One day I shall travel to Dresden with you in secret to look at the *Sistine Madonna*." — We ride home in two carriages and, turning in at the Villa d'Angri, witness a wonderful light effect. In the evening R. reads to us Schopenhauer's dialogue about death and life after death. Our starting point had been the sinners who fear Hell (Pascal), whereas a character like Goethe knows nothing of such things!

Tuesday, June 15   R. had a very bad night, tormented by indigestion, and we do not know exactly what can have disagreed with him. But in spite of feeling unwell R. went out of doors in the morning, saw Fidi with the gardener's boy, and was so delighted with the latter that he decided we should take him with us as Fidi's *Kurwenal*. He spends the day very quietly, does not have lunch with us, merely— when we are drinking coffee on the dining-room terrace—raising his fist to me as a joking sign that he is in good spirits. In the evening he feels sufficiently restored to join us for supper, and when I tell of my visit to the Fioretta and to Mme Mennikoffer, who presides there, and how she told me that to experience sorrow one must be living in luxury, he asks me whether she did not offer me something in her dining room, as if to say, "What are these titbits to me, now that I have lost my husband?"! — In the evening we look at a folio belonging to our friend J.; *The Temptation of Saint Anthony* by Teniers causes us the greatest amusement, the works of Rembrandt the greatest admiration; but about Rubens he protests at length, he finds his women with their "vulgar, indolent sensuality" repulsive, and considers Rubens a perfect pupil of the Jesuits.

Wednesday, June 16 Happy, cherished day! R. is well; at breakfast we continue talking about the pictures. And at 11 o'clock he calls me in to dictate to me, making jokes throughout about our work for posterity. At lunch conversation about Bismarck, who now wants to throw out the Catholic party, lock, stock, and barrel, since the Pope will not place it at his disposal, though he would have been willing to make all sorts of concessions to the Pope. The only condition would be that they support him in everything. But the Jesuits say they prefer to be martyrs. — The unveiling of the Goethe monument also provides us with entertainment, the Emperor was present at it, and the monument has been raised on borrowed money, for the full sum has not yet been collected. — R. is vexed by requests for conducting positions: "Always appointments! They have nothing in their heads except appointments! And my whole strength lies in having kept myself free. With such people I am supposed to found a school!" — Regarding Bismarck's rage against the Catholics, R. says, "The matter is one between Jesuits and Jews; they sit at the two ends like the hedgehogs in the fairy story, and the hare (ourselves) wears itself out." — He is invited to sign a petition to the Reich Chancellor demanding emergency laws against the Jews. He does not sign it: he says (1) he has already done what he can; (2) he dislikes appealing to Bismarck, whom he now sees as irresponsible, just following his own caprices; (3) nothing more can be done in the matter. — We walk to the vineyards with the children and settle down in the belvedere beside the pine trees. Telegrams from Genoa! In the evening R. offers to play *Tannhäuser* to the children, and they rush from the terrace, as if touched by a magic wand, to arrange the room. "They are a part of it all," R. exclaims to me in his gratification, then adds jokingly, "I have gripped them in the only way I can." He plays the 3rd act, up to Tannhäuser's narration, and indescribable emotion takes possession of me, bringing forth warm tears.

Thursday, June 17 R. had bad dreams—that I had gone away and that he called loudly after me, but could not hit on my proper name. But he goes for a walk, greets Malwida, and at 11:30 calls me in for dictation. Splendid things about the *Sistine Madonna*. At lunch he seems somewhat run down, but he is soon cheerful again, and the list of members of the Order of Maximilian makes merry reading, even if unpleasant memories are also attached to it. After his siesta we go by streetcar, "the ship of the desert," to Santa Lucia, and from there in two boats out to the English ships. Lovely view of the city, and the ships themselves interesting in their way, but it all arouses sad thoughts, and, as R. says, "All done just to give the Jews more opportunities for financial transactions." The crew makes a rather sorry impression: "Paltry people; but the world has always been ruled by people like that." — How different the wild, unruly crowds in Santa Lucia! — Home in a convoy of 4 *carrozzelle*. — (Before taking the streetcar we sat down in front of our door, and an old beggarwoman, well known to us, came to join us—"Mme Rembrandt," as R. calls her. The crazy creature becomes very bold, plays tricks on us, including one on Herr von Stein, "*bello bambino*" ["handsome boy"]; she purloins his stick and refuses to give it back unless he allows her to kiss his hand. The laughter grows, until Herr v. Stein goes off in vexation and the old rascal gives the stick to me.) — In the evening I read aloud Kleist's "*Das Erdbeben in Chile*," in which R.'s only regret is that the happy central episode is not executed in more detail. The descriptions of Donna Elisabeth he finds superb. When I go out onto the terrace, much moved by it, I find myself—I do not know why—thinking of *Tannhäuser* again, Elisabeth's sacrifice, giving herself up to death like a flower blooming, Wolfram heroic in his renunciation, his great compassion for Tannhäuser, all of it so sublime, so powerfully ennobling. When I mention this to R., he says, "Yes, I have never concerned myself with things of a gross nature." — Glorious moonlight, we stroll on the terrace like blissful spirits.

Friday, June 18 R. had a good night's rest, and he takes his walk in the morning. I go to him at 11 o'clock, and he dictates six pages to me, which include the splendid passage about *The Last Judgment*. In connection with a book by Daudet R. says: "The people in Paris all imagine that the entire world worries about them; they think, for example, that I have always borne an *aigreur* [resentment] against Paris because I have never had a success there! The best thing would be not to worry about them at all—except that the rest of the world is far too wretched to be able to provide clothes and perfumes for itself." — When I went to him for the dictation, he read to me part of a letter by Goethe about the vulgarity of people, with whom one must just put up patiently, since it is customary to wish to tease and vex others. Also the comparison with cretins at the end. Great delight in it. In the evening he sings Beethoven's Gellert songs for Lusch, who asked him for them, and, seeing us moved, he says, "That is Protestantism." Before that he played the end of the *Battle* Symphony and said, "Extraordinary, they had such noses for what was popular—nobody could think up such a thing nowadays." — Evening on the terrace by moonlight, all of us with indescribable feelings of well-being. Though I have to lie flat on account of a backache, I enjoy it, too, and above all the happy atmosphere around me! R. moves me indoors to hear the songs, turns me around so that I can see the loveliest view, and his joy in this blissful evening is the blessed outcome of all these rays. R. feels it is only here that one could always find so many new sources of delight—on one of the lakes in northern Italy, for example, everything would probably come in time to seem monotonous.

Saturday, June 19 R. had a good night's rest and was out walking by half past six. At breakfast he says to me, "When I came home, I felt tired and depressed until I drank a sip of coffee and used the nasal spray, and then I thought to myself, 'What a stupid substance it is, the brain, which can be so revived by external means, and the human being, everything in him constructed just to look outward and discover himself anew!' " When I tell R. that materialism seems to me to owe its origin to similar considerations, he says, "They leave out of account the Will inherent in every one, something which strives to avoid pain and to find well-being, until it perceives and becomes compassionate." Thus *approximately* and according to the sense, for unfortunately the actual words at times elude me, because I am too fascinated by his meaning, and I myself am usually engaged in thinking and talking at the same time. When I go to R. for dictation, he says, "It is after all a good thing that materialism has evolved from similar observations, for they show that feeling is everything." His work has been giving him a lot of trouble, but "I know now how to do it, as Napoleon said to Venice." — He dictates to me the conclusion of his splendid introduction. — Continuing his reflections on the world, he says to me, "How anyone can ever believe that during the short span of time through which one lives any radical changes can take place!" — We ride into town, R. and I, in the streetcar, "in which one feels as if one were hovering," to Dreher's. R. has a glass of beer and then, surrounded by *carrozzelle,* we seek and find the streetcar again, in which, undisturbed by other people, we talk about his introduction. In the evening friend Rubinstein plays to us several things from *Die Zauberflöte,* and then at my request the A-flat Major Sonata; he is not entirely successful with it, and when we are alone, R. talks to me about the work and says he does not feel it to be a masterpiece, like 111, for instance, he finds it abrupt, very personal; he considers it a weakness in Beethoven that in his final period he was so fond of writing fugues, for that was not his line. "Schools!" he exclaims. "How can one teach people to play such things? Though I think your father can." —

Sunday, June 20 R. slept well and went for an early-morning walk. I say goodbye to Malwida in great sorrow. R. says that he always feels in a state of suppressed rage with her for not staying with us permanently. After lunch we all go to friend Rubinstein's: Salita S. Antonio, to see the procession in honor of the saint. Again a unique and splendid picture of life here, the saint surrounded by fruit and flowers, boys singing the ancient Neapolitan call, which is taken up by the chorus, a ship is brought in, and goods of all kinds! — We gaze at the merry people and ask ourselves what one could take from them or give them. Luther! . . . In the evening, Sgambati with wife and child; yesterday R. had already reminded him of the subject in the history of Siena and encouraged him to do something for the stage. This evening he plays to us his new concerto, in a fine and masterly way. Then Rubinstein his Rhinemaidens' "Picture" and the conclusion of *Parsifal*. Talking of his working methods, R. said to Sgambati, *"Quand je me pose en compositeur, alors"* ["When I play the composer, then"]—an expression which caused great laughter.

Monday, June 21   At breakfast R. and I exchange impressions of the concerto yesterday. R. says, "Music has taken a bad turn; these young people have no idea how to write a melody, they just give us shavings, which they dress up to look like a lion's mane and shake at us!" "It's as if they avoid melodies, for fear of having perhaps stolen them from someone else." "It is always as if the world is having to be created anew, so forceful, so pompous, while I am always looking for melody." "In painting, one has the advantage of shape and form: when a painter paints a cock and does it badly, it still remains a cock, but here I do not even have the cock." — R. writes a page of his article today. The necessity the Swiss, too, now feel to reform their army brings the whole wretched situation before our eyes. — In the afternoon R., the children, and I to the belvedere, where we spread ourselves out; since Isolde has a volume of Shakespeare with her (*H. VIII*), R. reads to us the little scene between Katharine and Griffith about Cardinal Wolsey's death, which grips us all; when I remark that, after the Queen has first received the news compassionately as a good Christian, she then, through reflection and absorption, comes to a truthful judgment, R. says, "And what a great historian Shakespeare looks like at this moment! An unfathomable being." — Glorious moonlight in the evening, visit from Sgambati, but no music. At the conclusion of the evening R. reads to us Goethe's letter to Schiller about Darwin's poem, the description of its contents causing us much amusement. — Very early in the morning R. woke Herr v. Stein with *"Steh nur auf"* on the piano, a sign of his good mood; he says that the shrill tone of the pianino always tempts him to play popular, even vulgar things on it (including, at coffeetime, the "Egyptian March" from *Moses*). — Looking at the *Illustrirte Zeitung* we feel something like horror over the fish exhibition, and R. says, "We would not feel this disgust if human beings had not been designed for something besides gobbling one another up."

Tuesday, June 22   R. slept well and went for a walk in the morning with the children. At breakfast we talk about *W. Meister,* and R. says, "There is too much mawkish sentimentality in it." He tells me of the letters between Goethe and Schiller about *"Die Kraniche des Ibykus"* and says jokingly, "Goethe didn't want a rumpus, nothing excessive, and so he always wanted the cranes to be recognized more gradually." — R. vexed by the formality of the post office, which is unwilling to hand over a money order; however, he gradually recovers his spirits, and we come to the subject of *Don Giovanni,* R. once again voicing his opinion of the looseness, lack of cohesion, and disturbing elements in this work which contains such splendid things and in which the exposition, for instance, is so masterly—but unfortunately all so lacking in integration. Of *Fidelio* he says it is a big lie to admire it unconditionally, just for the purpose of withholding recognition from something else; he recalls the nonsense E. Devrient talked about the interesting character of Rocco. When the question is raised why Beethoven composed such a work, he says, "Rescue subjects were fashionable at that time, the central situation attracted him, and they were all like children, divine beings such as will never again be seen in our world." [*Added in margin:* "R. comes to *D. Quixote,* the scene with the old duenna: 'The temptation which he will doubtless resist, but to which he is brought as close as possible.' Comparison with *W. Meister,* a much greater poetic talent. In *W. Meister* mawkish sentimentality, which tells one nothing."] — He also ridicules the false cult of Gluck and Handel and says, "What was extraordinary about these personalities is quite unknown to the gentlemen, who indiscriminately admire what was really only prolificness." Of Mozart's *Requiem* he says, "It is beautiful, written by a naïve Catholic, a person of religious mind who enters a church and is moved by it; not at all churchly!" — In the afternoon we walk in the garden as far as the palm tree. [*Added in margin:* "In the afternoon, under the pepper tree in the front garden, looked at *Maximilian's Prayer Book,* with great delight in its divine humor; the text, '*Jesus fabricator mundi,*' amuses him, he says this was probably thought more refined, more elegant than 'factor.' "] There is still a fresh breeze and no heat at all. Moonlit evening, bringing us great delight.

Wednesday, June 23   R. had a good night and is looking well, but on his left nostril he has a small growth with a black center which worries me, although it has already been shown to Dr. Schrön. R. also seems to me to be preoccupied. With his work, perhaps? — During the morning I read a few of my recent diary entries, and I fear that I am wasting my time! Apart from his remarks, it all seems to me empty and dead—will the children be able to recover even a single memory from it? Is my "I" not always standing in the way, hindering full appreciation? Not to speak of the things that are beyond description! . . . R. and I drive into town to fetch the letter, miss the streetcar after a wait outside the door, during which the old witch again makes something of a nuisance of herself. In the *carrozzella* R. tells me about a dog which, sold to someone in England, escaped in Dover and swam and ran back to its former master in Aschaffenburg! . . . "And its master," says R., "will have seen that just as an extra burden, will have sent it away again! This is what is contemptuously called 'doglike devotion'!" [*In margin:* "The first time R. said, 'I wonder if its master sent it away again?' — On the second mention he was sure that he had."] — "Yes, one must not take dogs too lightly," he says gloomily. I: "Are you thinking of anything in particular?" — R.: "Yes, of home." Then at last I speak Brange's name and tell him how she died—not of pining. He remains gloomy, shut up within himself, and at last asks me not to keep watching him—it makes him uneasy. The letter is given him straightaway, and in a more cheerful mood we walk to Dreher's, where Herr v. Stein joins us. A man from Bologna, completely different in both speech and manner, is offering perfumes for one franc; we buy some and are pleased to have encountered him. Cheerful journey home. — The moonlight brings conversation in the evening around to Goethe's poem, which R. reads to me, but without enjoyment; we go on to the *"Urworte,"* and suddenly R. remembers a long unexpressed desire of ours and calls for Aeschylus's *Agamemnon.* He then reads it, and I feel as if I have never before seen him like this, transfigured, inspired, completely at one with what he is reading; no stage performance could have a more sublime effect than this recital— Cassandra's first cries of warning quite heart-rending! . . . After the first two choruses, R. says, taking a pinch of snuff, "Lovely moon, you rise so silent," in which even the finest of our lyric poetry is made to look so childish. —

Over our afternoon coffee R. quotes from Gleizès the following thought by Xenophon: Sheaves of grain give those who have planted them the courage to defend them; standing in the fields, they have the same significance as the victor's prize in a tournament—and this once more brings home to us exactly what the ancient world means to us! Various passages from Schiller and Goethe about the German public, which they call the least aesthetics-minded of all: "Perhaps there is something in that," says R. — Early in the morning R. played *"Der Schweizerbub"* again, Palumbello [the dog] howling along with it, Eva comes in, R. tires again, but Palumbello keeps silent: "He is shy," says Eva!

Thursday, June 24   Are impressions such as those of last night too powerful for poor mortals? Or at least for poor me? I wake up in melancholy mood, concerned about R., although he has slept well, with a feeling that my death is near and I wish nothing else. But perhaps it is just the sirocco which is to blame for this mood. When I see him looking well at breakfast, all is in order again, and we luxuriate in memories of yesterday. R. says, "I declare that to be the most perfect thing in every way, religious, philosophic, poetic, artistic." — "One can put Shakespeare's histories beside it, but he had no Athenian state, no Areopagus as final resort." — I say I would put only the *Ring* beside it. R. says, "But that stands outside time, it is something thought up by an individual, only to be made a mess of immediately, as happened with newly established religions." — We recall many single features, he mentions Clytemnestra's weariness, her contempt for the chorus, which has indeed condoned the murder of Iphigenia. "Those are these individual, unfathomable features; and all so bloody, drenched in blood. If Thyestes had been a vegetarian," he adds jokingly, "none of it would have happened." Then, becoming serious, "It fits in with my work." — Then he tells me that today in the garden he and the children saw a lizard seize a beetle, which struggled and resisted, and he exclaims with a sigh, "If human beings had evolved into gentle creatures, they would still have found enough to remind them of the tragedy of existence!" R. works on his article and seems satisfied with what he has done. I spend a large part of the day with the *Agamemnon* choruses. At lunch R. sings to us Mendelssohn's "*Vieles Gewaltige lebt*" chorus and mimes the chorus as it was done in Dresden, led by Mitterwurzer: two steps forward, one back. — I do not know what led him at coffeetime to Cromwell and his question whether one could fall from grace, followed by relief when he knew he had not. "Strange as this looks, it does, however, have a deep meaning: a person must know that he has acted according to his deepest impulses. Politics, the world's reactions, come later, and that is why he asked." — To my inquiry what Frederick the Great would have thought of Cromwell, R. replies: "Surely exactly the same as Voltaire—Fr.'s feelings were rooted in his legitimacy." He describes his answer to his father regarding his disinheritance—"and arising out of this feeling his resolve to sacrifice everything within his power to the people, who had sacrificed so much for him. Cromwell's roots were quite different, and two such men can never understand each other." R. drives with Fidi to Dreher's, returns home in good spirits. In the evening *The*

Suppliants, just as moving as *Agamemnon.* R. says, "In former times I was particularly impressed by the intoxicating musicality of the choral lament and the song—all this raving, forever starting anew." And to me, when we are alone late in the evening, "What I see here is the musical philosopher, the priest; and what a poet!" He quotes Clyt., where she says that Ag. would be welcomed by Iphigenia.

Friday, June 25 R. slept well, he walks in the garden with the children, again sees a lizard catching a glowworm, but the children rescue it. "If it were not for the assumption that the world was made by a good God, one would find it all easy to understand. But none of them, not even my good Gleizès, can free himself of the idea that once all was Paradise, and then they relapse into sophisms." Glorious days, still not too hot, the loveliest summer we have ever experienced. When I say this to R., he replies, "To know what our northern climate is like, all one needs is to glance through the correspondence between Goethe and Schiller, those eternal complaints about the cold, catarrhal conditions and so on." — Recently (yesterday) he spoke of the wretchedness of life in Jena for a person like Schiller, "all beer and cheese," and nothing as a model for the diver and the maelstrom except a mill wheel! — I say something (I forget what) about Schiller; R. agrees and says earnestly, "He was an ardent soul." The task of seeking and laying down rules for literary composition seems utterly childish to him. "We are plagued with a nice civilization," he said yesterday as he put down Aeschylus. — Over coffee he said, "What I find typical— and it says everything—is the story of the petition to the Reichstag on vivisection." [*In margin:* "On the terrace at coffeetime we hear a donkey braying. 'That is supposed to express joy,' R. exclaims. 'How terrible that the degenerate human being finds something ridiculous in this doleful sound!' "] — In the evening he relates with mock solemnity, "The Emperor wants the bishops back: 'Look here, Bismarck, you are quite right of course, but the bishops must return, I have Catholic subjects, and we must be methodical.' " — R. works and is still somewhat immersed in serious thought around lunchtime, but he then becomes more lively. Speaking of the first scene in [Aeschylus's] *Choephoroi* with its surgings and its constantly returning flow, he says, "I know something else like this: *Trist. and Isolde* in the 2nd act." — At lunch conversation about animals, Darwin's absent-minded ape, and the possibility of measuring the talents of a human being by his ability to concentrate his thoughts. — A curiously characteristic feature of R.: turning to Jouk. he says, "It is typical of the Russians that they have the knout kissed before they apply it." When our friend says he knows nothing of this, R. becomes very angry and says he is prepared to admit everything about the Germans, but he also intends to say all he knows about other nations. But then, noticing that he has hurt our friend, he mentions it in the friendliest and kindest of ways, as always utterly truthful and infinitely kind. — A new sketch of the forest has been made: "One must not see the wood for the trees," says R. Dr. Schlemm has sent some terrible opera librettos in doggerel verse: "And that is my school!" R. exclaims sadly. — After he has had a rest we go for a walk in splendid weather to the belvedere. In the evening the *Eumenides;* a glorious conclusion to the day, arousing wide-ranging thoughts and comparisons. I exclaim to R., "Do you know in which work I see a link between the ideal and the real world, reminding me of the institution of the Areopagus? In *Die Meistersinger*—Sachs's address at the end," "I was just about to say the same thing," R. replies—and, tired but exalted, we go off to bed.

Saturday, June 26   R. gets up early, goes for a walk, enjoys the air, which, he tells me, was like milk of roses. Much at breakfast about his work, he is pleased with the curious relevance of *Parsifal*—that his conception of sanctity, which makes seduction, conflicts, etc., impossible. In splendid spirits we greet this day, on which in my behalf R. invokes blessings and good fortune, and which for that very reason it brings. — "If in patience we bear, God will take care," he says jokingly in the midst of utterances of the most solemn kind. [*A sentence based on untranslatable word play omitted.*] — Over coffee after lunch he reads to us two fine letters by Goethe and Schiller, having previously remarked, "What they always brought out in each other!" Then he reads something quite splendid and profound by Schiller about language, and Goethe's equally fine reply with reference to the French, which reminds R. of Berlioz's *"digérer"* ["digest"]. In the evening, sitting on the terrace, we come back to these letters, and R. says: "One could write whole books about what is contained in this correspondence, and what have we done with it? As my brother-in-law used to say, 'What use is nutmeg to a cow?' " — He goes to Dreher's in the streetcar, and on the Piazza dei Martiri he feels a hand on his arm—Fidi had seen him from a house he happened to be in and ran swiftly to catch up with him: "What a feeling that gives me! I, who for two whole generations was like the Tannhäuser I wrote about, that is to say, a completely finished man! You, Joukowsky, were not even born then. Sometimes I feel like the Flying Dutchman—and then to see this boy before me!" He then tells me how, sitting in the streetcar with Siegfried, he saw Herr v. Stein boarding it and sitting down in front of them without seeing them, till, his attention caught by the conversation between father and son, he turned around and saw them! Lovely starry sky, later moonlight, curiously melancholy on account of the framework of little clouds, the air glorious! — R. talks a lot about the universe, the globe, also the South Pole. "What is the earth in comparison to this huge expanse of water? Like a few scraps rescued from the deluge." — He asks Herr Rubinstein to play something, I ask for the Venusberg music from *Tannhäuser*, and R. begins the 3rd act with him, starting at the point at which he recently interrupted him—from "*da sah ich ihn*" to the end. We then talk about the first scene, and R. says: "That would be a task for a king, to spend a long time preparing something like this, so that it would be done really beautifully, for it calls for choreography of a completely new kind, and there should be actors in it, too. If only in all the theaters I had directors who were sympathetic to me! Instead of that—well, just look around!" — Herr Rub. then plays us some fugues from the *48 Preludes and Fugues:* "They are like the roots of words," R. says, and later, "In relation to other music it is like Sanskrit to other languages." —

Sunday, June 27   Still thinking of that meeting with Fidi! And the difference between then and now: "I believe it is this that makes me appear so unchanged and still so full of good spirits." — R. works on his article. The news that a man went into the Chamber, threw stones at the deputies, and reproached them for being useless leads our conversation over afternoon coffee to the parliamentary system, brought into being in England through King John's demands for money—quite understandable there, but here so absurd. — Then: "Since among animals the fox came to dominate the bear, why should not the Jew (the fox) dominate everything here?" — "The fact that war has now become nothing but a mathematical exercise, that a soldier no longer sees the man he kills—that is what Hegel calls progress. What things people think up—it is extraordinary!" — R. takes a rest, and afterward we stroll to the palm tree. Watching Palumbello, he remarks, "Since human beings were responsible for breeding dogs out of wolves, why should they not produce the right sort of creatures from human beings?" — I: "But who is going to make humans out of humans?" R.: "Ah! The founder of a new religion." He says he feels his new work will not be unwelcome to a limited number of well-wishers. — In the evening we look through some folios; an engraving by Marcantonio [Raimondi] after Raphael (*Pietà*), which pleases me greatly, R. rejects entirely; classical beauty applied to this subject he considers reprehensible, and the reason for our decline. The head by Leonardo (sketch for the *Cena*) he finds too effeminate. On the other hand, he says what a different impression the Christ in the *Cena* made on him (he mentions the fine positioning of the hands), but he regrets the wealth of detail and the too great activity among the other figures in the picture. He then plays the first theme of *Parsifal* to himself and, returning, says that he gave the words to a chorus so that the effect would be neither masculine nor feminine, Christ must be entirely sexless, neither man nor woman; Leonardo, too, in the *Cena,* attempted that, depicting an almost feminine face adorned with a beard. He must appear neither young nor old, he says, the god within the human being. — The engravings by Nanteuil, which interest me, arouse no sympathy in him—he asks me whether I have not seen enough wigs by now! . . . On the other hand, he listens willingly to all I have to say to him following my becoming more closely acquainted with Aeschylus, and he speaks highly of Droysen and the influence he had on him when, self-taught, he set about building a library and was obliged to acquire these things in translation. He also recalls Otfried Müller, who showed him the Doric style in a different light from the familiar *Apollo Belvedere,* and Hermann (not the famous one).

Monday, June 28 R. did not have a good night; he reads Goethe and Schiller on "Pygmalion" and is pleased with Schiller's assured and independent judgment, which he imparts to me. The unveiling of Goethe's monument, raised for reasons of self-esteem "with other people's money," as R. adds, gives rise to many remarks, both merry and sad! "How ridiculous one feels when one thinks of anything in the German Reich with any sort of emotion!" In connection with this statue, still not paid for, we come to talk of the Schiller monument and the Gendarmen-Markt, and R. tells a very funny story about a *gendarme* who came upon an urchin behaving improperly outside the theater and directed his attention to the church with the words "What are our churches for?" — The monument of Goethe in his 40's leads him to himself at that age: "Where was I then?" "Recollection of the concerts in Zurich?" Then his 50's: "I was very much alone then." — In the afternoon he writes to Herr Schön and reads his letter to me: "There, now I've knocked off his head," he says in a voice like Punch. — He relates that the house of Rothschild has more or less given notice to quit Russia, if these measures against the Jews continue; the newspaper adds the comment that it is just as well that things are out in the open. R. says, "I am now on the side of the *Kreuz-Zeitung,* am becoming completely orthodox." We walk to the belvedere; passing the flowering aloe, R. says, "That is what I call a panaritium, a tumor!" As we are sitting on the wall of the belvedere, R. says, "I should imagine that in relation to Indian culture the Persians stand more or less as the Latin races do to the Greeks." He reflects, and is interrupted by the singing of a boy in the vineyards, a cry which dies away in the depths and keeps returning to surprise us. Palumbello also listens; recently he amused us greatly by joining in a fugue being played by Rub., and on the right note, too. In the evening R. reads to us the introduction to his article, but then regrets having done so, saying that one should read such things for oneself in print.

Tuesday, June 29   R. did not sleep very well, and during the night Palumbello singing in concert with someone! Today is Peter and Paul, a feast day, at breakfast we talk gaily of the heathen ways of these people, no sign of Christianity, and difficult to imagine English reformers; it must all end as with Miss Ouragan, who is herself becoming a Catholic. — I ask R. about Riga, of which he was speaking a few days ago, and he tells me of the river covered with rafts, of the people who came streaming in, perhaps as many as 70,000, of the balalaika, an instrument akin to the bagpipes, on which the peasants played for dancing: "I got to know all about folk life there." — He works, and at lunch we drink a toast to our friend Joukowsky: "Wake up, all, and let us toast Paul!" — Over coffee we talk about Moscow, the remarkable treasure in the Kremlin; R. says he saw nothing there, he was ill, and all he cared about was earning some money with which to furnish a little house in Biebrich, so that he could write *Die Meistersinger*. At lunch we recalled our meeting in Starnberg at the end of June 1864, I with my two "ladies," he forbidden by the doctor to go to meet me (on the previous day a storm had hurled his hat into the lake; caught cold, doctor sent for, put off, but came after all), he furious, took a long time to regain his composure. "You with your black hat and the poppy flower, always friendly, gay, and natural, 'milkmaid and marchioness'— marchioness when there was something to be gained by it!" — R. rests for a while, then he comes to me and suggests a ride in the street-car for "*gelati*" ["ice cream"]; the children jubilant. When I say that our friend Paul is staying at home to do some work, R. sings him a tune from *Jessonda:* "Joukowsky (for Nadori), you will come with us surely," and all of us set out for the Palazzo Reale café. R., full of high spirits, does not want to leave; he is so happy among the children that with every spoonful of ice cream he cries, "Lord, how nice it is here!" — Unfortunately no streetcar for our return, we are separated, and on arrival there is again an altercation with the coachman, and the screaming, the gaping of the crowd, the impossibility of understanding or making himself understood, upset R. so much that he feels utterly wretched, complains to me of the pain in his chest, and I have the greatest difficulty in calming him down. He comes to join us at supper but talks about the incident and becomes so vexed and angry that he has to leave the table; only some time later does he return to us. — Visit from the Schröns.

Wednesday, June 30   R. had a good night after all, and as usual our breakfast time is indescribably amicable, sweet, and fair—"Day" has not yet come between us! He tells me about the girls, who went for a walk with him, I tell him about Fidi, whom I heard gardening with Antonio and Lorenzo, speaking Neapolitan and giggling. We talk about art, and when I tell him that what I now find so interesting is the artist as seen in his works, leaving aside his circumstances and the subject of the work of art, a Mercury by Marcantonio [Raimondi] for instance, R. says, "Yes, but it is all just playing around, and it shows the decline, however great the artist may be." I then tell R. that I have taken Fra Bart[olommeo]'s Savonarola out of the folio for him, and I go on talking about him, whereupon R. says jokingly, "You have deprived me of the originality of my ideas—I wanted to bring up Savon[arola]." — I: "Oh!" R.: "With my things you can always say, 'That is *my brooch*' " (anecdote about Frau Beer with Frau Schröder-Devrient). — Before that he sang to me a delightful theme which had just come into his mind—"unless it has only too obviously been stolen from something else," he says. Around lunchtime he calls out to me that he has completed his 2nd article, and I should send a telegram to Sorrento, saying we will be going there tomorrow. He is cheerful and good-humored at lunch, and at coffee even exuberant, as we talk about Heaven and Hell; in connection with my weeping eyes, for which God would reproach me, I speak of Dante and say that he saw God through the eyes of Beatrice: "What, he used her as a pair of binoculars?" he asks. At lunch he recalled a line in *Der Freischütz,* "*Wie, was, Entsetzen!*" ["How, what, oh, horror!"], and he thinks the change of rhythm in the words when Ännchen joins in particularly good. — I show him Fra Bartolommeo's picture of Savonarola, and he talks at length about this face and the significance of this man. He says it cannot be imagined otherwise than that people were carried away by some tremendous emotional energy, a certain lucidity which has nothing to do with intelligence. "But I shan't mention him—that would lead me too far astray." — Of Christ he says one cannot imagine otherwise than that he was a person of great and gentle beauty. — He places the cigarette box in the center of the floor as a sacrificial altar, does a dance, and tells Joukowsky that he will also have to perform this dance if he wants a cigarette. Recalling the painters who burned their pictures for Sav., he says to me, "I wouldn't have burned you," and creeps out on all fours. — (This morning he again spoke of his desire to make a fortune in America.) — R. goes into town to buy himself a hat, returns home somewhat tired, and is rather worn out all evening, which we spend in chat.

Thursday, July 1 R. up very early, goes for a walk, but still suffers from the sun. I tell him about a letter from Wolz.; R. reflects on performances and says how reluctant he is to concern himself with all these things, for example, a performance of *Tannhäuser.* — He then asks what the stage decorations are like in Munich, and when I describe them to him, he says, "When menials build, monarchs have their hands full." — Our friend J's. *Pietà,* now on show, leads him to its subject, which he says one should not have paraded constantly before one's eyes—it should be kept in some secret place, in a crypt. — When I say that one of the advantages of our age has been to acquire a closer knowledge of Christ's personality, R. adds, "And without any loss of his divine qualities; all the trimmings, the endless talk in the 4th Gospel, all that is discarded; it would be a task for a great poet to write a pure gospel." R. is worn out at lunch, and he complains of our "stuffy conversations," which come from our not finding it easy to ignore his state of mind. — Our friend's picture, the *Pietà,* leads him to the subject of modern painting, which does nothing thoroughly, just daubs, whereas in Titian, for example, the coloring has a spiritual quality. — "Extraordinary," he says, his eyes still resting on the picture, "that the mother, who in real life disappears entirely, should be called upon to fill such a role." — We part; as we were sitting in silence, he suddenly let out such a sigh that I asked him if he was not feeling very well. He, calmly, "I am not feeling very well," then with a smile, "No, it is just my thoughts going to and fro and the restlessness of my brain which makes me sigh." After our first embrace he comes back to me and says, "We shall stick together!" — Yesterday, toward the end of supper, he said to Stein, "I am coming closer to your view: human beings do not have to be so evil, I know what needs to be done in order to regenerate them, and then we shall play them the *Pastoral* Symphony!" — "They will have long to wait, as Schleinitz says, before they get an emperor like that." — "Before they get a God as good as that," I say. We stroll to the belvedere in the afternoon; here R. often sings a theme from *La Sonnambula* (chorus gathering on stage), and when, as we stroll back, I sing the first theme of the F Major Quartet, he says, "That is a real *shuffling theme.*" In the evening he is feeling so unwell that he goes to sit by himself in the *salon* with Goethe and Schiller, while we, at his request, sit on the terrace chatting as best we can; we break up at 9:30, and R. goes through what he calls a crisis, after which he feels better. He told us of the death of Gräfe, the foreman bricklayer who built our house and with whom we had much to do; now he has fallen from a scaffold. Many good creatures have now left us:

Dittmar,	the foreman,
Luise Feustel,	Rus,
the municipal gardener,	Brange.

Good souls, both human and animal, who have been close to us in various ways.

Friday, July 2   R. dreamed of an intimate meeting with N[apoleon] III and his consort, Eugénie, the latter very modestly dressed, the former speaking German (in exile). At 7 o'clock we are all gathered in the breakfast room, and at 8 o'clock we drive to the steamship for Sorrento. R. in very exuberant spirits. The boys who retrieve coins in the water enchant him, the human animal, he says, and though he finds the game an ugly one, he throws many *sous,* in order to watch them diving. Lovely view of Naples; R. is attracted by a family which he takes to be North German but which is in fact Italian: "Those are the sort of people I should like to know, the older woman so motherly, the daughter serious but lively." — Delight on our arrival in Sorrento; greeted by [*name illegible*], R. is pleased for Lusch, who was not with us on the previous occasion. While the children go for a walk on the road to Massa, we sit on the main loggia and rest. Then Rub. light-heartedly plays to us some passages from Hummel's septet, some Strauss waltzes. Lunch is a success, R. drinks meaningfully to Lusch's health, recalling to himself why she was not with us before, and how well things have now turned out. — He is pleased with the fine trees in the garden, and he draws my attention to the beautiful hanging lemons, which remind him of udders, an association which leads him to pleasant and solemn reflections. We go down, R. plays with Ercole (another old friend!), he relates his dream and adds, "That is the way with princes—in spite of all their humanity and education they can only maintain their positions through murder and absurd behavior." Return journey at 4 o'clock on the upper deck, the children and our guests in very merry mood, Vesuvius looks much lovelier from the vicinity of Naples, and to R. the city itself again seems uniquely sturdy and significant: "There it is idyllic, *Hermann and Dorothea;* here it is heroic, could be the *Iliad.*" — [*Added later in the Diaries but referred back to this point:* "Speaking of Naples and the unique delight it gives us, R. says, 'And I am convinced that people despise us for our taste, since in Naples there is no art at all, nothing these people can understand!' — When we are on the ship, he notes how the sail is hoisted and even the unpleasant wind put to some use: 'The sailboat, that was a true discovery, it speaks to me, whereas all these machines tell me nothing.' "] And when we arrive back at the Villa d'Angri, we recall our previous visit to Sorrento and how much better things are now: "We are no longer deceiving ourselves." — Spent the evening on the terrace talking of various things, particularly the coming times; R. recalls the industrialist in *Virgin Soil* and feels such a man could burst the bubble of state as if it were nothing, but it must be done in a religious spirit. — In the morning he had already remarked that one can never get the better of things by delivering oneself over to them, and Gladstone, for example, would have been wiser to remain in opposition, and not to have become prime minister.

Saturday, July 3 R. slept well but finds the air somewhat tiring; in particular he feels the absence of shadow on his morning walk: "I had that in Bayreuth, but no sun." — At eleven o'clock he calls me in to dictate the beginning of the 2nd part of his work; recently I showed him the lines I had written about the chorus in *Oresteia,* and he noted something down, saying he would also like to mention it. He put down the [Goethe-Schiller] correspondence at once to read our friend Stein's work on G. Bruno. From the correspondence he mentions the "sect for good" and applies it to Bayreuth, saying that we should be the sect for good. We make music in the evening; the waltzes yesterday reminded us of [Weber's] *Invitation to the Dance;* talking of Berlioz's orchestration of this piece, R. says he considers it a complete failure; today he asks Rub. to play it to us, before that the conclusion of *Die Meistersinger,* beginning with the "*Wach' auf*" chorus (which the children sing). R. says there is so much good humor and merriment in it. In the evening he talked about Lenbach's manner, which he thinks bears some resemblance to that of the sculptor Hähnel, because both of them are witty and both regard their own things as clumsy; he does not really finish anything, daubs rather than paints. — (Recently he told friend J., as he was covering a canvas with charcoal, "Humans love blackening whatever shines.") —

Sunday, July 4 R. slept well, only he wishes he could take his morning walk in J.'s *Pietà,* since it is shadowy there. Dictation at 11 o'clock, after which he says, "It must seem rather odd to you, taking down things which are so familiar from our conversations." — The Schröns and Rubinstein to lunch; the latter refuses to eat fish, so as not to return to earth as a fish, and R. criticizes so personal and literal an interpretation of symbols. Everything, he says—birth and rebirth, life and death—is always present, and it is for the common people that one is obliged to set such symbols in the context of time; and he repeats what he recently said to us in Sorrento, when someone spoke of a person who would not travel on a Sunday so as not to make work for the people on the railroad: "Do not imagine that the individual can ever dissociate himself from the state of sinfulness." — Talk at lunch about the Germans, their addiction to beer, their beer halls and tobacco-smoke arguments: "In beer halls, that's where they discover their wit." — Also about our accursed climate, which he says makes us so materialistic, so immoderate. After lunch R. talks of the human being's finest achievement: the dog; this act occurred before recorded history, he says, but now they are being chained up, virtually turned back into wild animals. — Speaking of the Queen of Italy, R.

says, "This is how I like a queen to look nowadays, sad and amiable; the gay ones or maliciously peevish ones are repulsive." — The evening spent with our friends; R. says to Herr v. Stein that he is sorry to hear he is soon to leave us, and when I say that I hope the period of separation will pass as quickly as the time we have spent together, R. says, "There is no such thing as hope—only acceptance: all the good things in life are like a pleasant dream in a troubled sleep." — To end the evening he reads to us a passage in Goethe which particularly pleases him, his remarks about astrology and the way it is used in *Wallenstein*. — I still want to mention a little domestic incident, since it reveals an aspect of R.'s character: When I spoke of the invitation to the Schröns, friend Jouk. said to Herr v. Stein that in this case they had better go out to eat; I took them at their word and invited the Schrön boys instead; our friends would, however, have liked to remain with us, and in the evening they tell us of their difficulties. R. said, "I should just have come to the table, as if to say, 'Send me away if you dare!'" — [*Added in margin:* "Of Prof. Schrön's strange fleeting glances R. says, 'That comes from dissecting corpses.'"]

Monday, July 5 R. slept tolerably well and is cheerful at breakfast and also during dictation, less so at lunch, but his spirits revive over coffee, and when, among other things, I talk about the Princess of Meiningen and her great lack of kindness and amiability and wonder in what guise such a character would be reborn, R. says quickly, "As a spittoon." — In the morning, when we are talking of people who are not our kind, R. coins the phrase, "Your coming be borne, your going blessed!" — And when I talk of my diaries and the trouble Fidi will perhaps have with them, R. says, "Yes, perhaps it is not such a good thing to drag such a father around with one"—whereupon I explain to him my desire to allow my children as much freedom of outlook as possible. — Before dictating he tells me that wherever he turns he hears Nietzsche speaking; his judgment on Beethoven is a disgrace, he says, and also on the Jews. — In the evening R. reads Stein's piece on G. Bruno and says it is excellent, and indeed, because of its excellence, quite unsuitable for the *B. Blätter*. Later he reads the scene from *As You Like It* in which Jaques appears, and when we are alone, he points out to me how good it is that Jaques's attachment to deer is mentioned previously: "He cannot weep on stage, where too much is going on, but one knows his feelings, and that gives significance to each one of his words." —

Tuesday, July 6 Not a very good night for R., but at breakfast he is lively as always, except that the subject he brings up (the regulation of the Greek border, the loan, and the agio) is a very disagreeable one— in everything nowadays, he remarks, all one can say is "*Cherchez le banquier."* When I go to his room for dictation, he repeats to me Schiller's fine saying that the only approach toward the public which one need not regret is the warlike one; he also mentions Goethe's joking redress against conceited poetasters—to regard them from the point of view of natural history. — At lunch and also over coffee R. is out of humor and seems to me to be ill. A lampoon addressed to him—"To the pseudo-poet R. Wagner"—he does not read, but he is annoyed by a renewed request to sign a petition against the Jews addressed to Prince Bismarck. He reads aloud the ridiculously servile phrases and the dubiously expressed concern: "And I am supposed to sign that!" he exclaims. He writes to Dr. Förster, saying that in view of what happened to the petition regarding vivisection he has resolved never again to sign a petition. Arrival of the Swiss painter, M. de Pury, R. sits for him for a quarter of an hour; when he professes to find a resemblance in the chin between R. and Nap. I, R. says, *"Le menton, nous sommes tous deux des menteurs"* ["The chin, we are both of us liars"]. [*Wagner's remark obliterated in ink by an unknown hand.*] Walk to the palm tree, R. and I. In the evening much talk with Herr von Stein about the *B. Blätter;* the conciliatory tone which some of the members would now like to see adopted annoys R., who would like to have much more criticism in it, reviews of performances, plays, etc., instead of "a lot of drivel." — Then he talks about Goethe and Schiller, the miseries the latter had to endure in Jena and how long it took Goethe to summon him to Weimar: "Always just a matter of 200 to 300 thalers." — Then he laughs heartily about the Goethe-Meyer classification of painters: Correggio, Raphael, M[ichel]angelo, G. Romano: "What business is it of his, and what is the point of it?" —

Wednesday, July 7   R. rises early, goes for a walk, and tells me about a holly tree in glorious flower. He also tells me that the sea and the sky were both the same color, a deep blue. — He then talks with a certain amount of bitterness about Munich and Bayreuth and says, "Should one really sacrifice to these matters the few years one still has to live?" He takes a bath in the sea, and since his movements are too violent, it has a bad effect on him, and he spits up a little blood! . . . But he feels that on the whole the bath did him good. — Music in the evening; the Sieglinde "Picture"; only the passage of thirds should be played more lightly, he says, not too broadly—they depict Sieglinde's actions, of the kind made when one has been given something pleasing. Recently, regarding *Die Meistersinger,* he said that the themes he sometimes brings in again at the conclusion should not be played with the full expression belonging to them: "I have written them here in place of arabesques." — Then various pieces by Weber—*Euryanthe, Preciosa,* the *"Wilde Jagd."* — We go to sleep laughing, because R. told me of a

Philistine who sang, "*Das ist Lützows wilde verwegene Jagd—jewesen*," and one could hear the last word still reverberating. — In the Overture to *Euryanthe* he highly praises the beginning, up to the "*O Seligkeit*" theme, but then come the weaknesses, he says: "He wanted to show he could do things like the others, Spontini, etc., only better."

Thursday, July 8 R. dreamed of Lord Byron, that they had been together and R. had spoken about Schopenhauer. — In the morning we walk together in the garden, he shows me the splendid flowering holly tree, whose trunk hangs over and along the cliff, as if to greet someone—him—on the path below! — He is not feeling very well, and that overshadows our day; he frequently spits up blood, and he complains to the doctor that he always has some irritation, like a heat rash, etc. When I return from visiting a boarding school, I find him much occupied with thoughts of America; his earnings, reported on by friend Gross, have not been very good, and at the same time there arrive greetings from America and news from Dr. Jenkins which he finds very affecting. — His favorite simile now for the indestructibility of the mob is an anthill, which after rain always regains its old form. In the evening chat about all sorts of things, including Constantinople, of which Dr. Jenkins has given us a frightening description.

Friday, July 9 R. did not sleep very well, at 4 in the morning he is on the terrace, then back to bed, where he rests again. At breakfast we talk about the "Picture" of *Tr. und I.* which Herr Rub. played to us yesterday; R. finds little enjoyment in such extracts from his works. — After a silence he says to me, "Actually, one can only visualize the Will as negative, resisting things it does not desire. That is awful! And so it was a great stroke of genius on Goethe's part to depict Mephisto just as the spirit of negation. And after all, the insights he gave us in the first part are not repeated in the 2nd, when the poet takes over; he loses himself in fabrications, which make it impossible to appreciate the splendor of the conclusion." — He reverts to America: "So far it is the only country from which I have learned anything." — Throughout the day discussions about our friend Stein's departure; R. recommends looking on the bright side, saying that their friendship represents a gain: "You are young, I old, and yet we have come close to each other." — Over coffee he read to us what he has written in his article about Moltke. — Sea bath for R. and for me! Amusement over who is first in the water! In the evening R. reads to us the castle scene from *Götz von Berlichingen;* the toast to freedom and all the fine qualities of equanimity and justice which in the midst of Nature's turmoil dominate Götz's character remind me of R. and the German spirit, which to me seems to remain alive only in him. We drink to freedom with our friends!

Saturday, July 10   R. had ordered a farewell coffee, and though he did not have a good night, he had us all assembled around him at 8:30, and cheerfulness prevailed. But we do not know whether sea baths agree with him, for he is worn out; anyway, he does not take one today. I keep him company during his sitting for Herr Pury, but it wears him out, or, rather, upsets him. We then take a stroll and delight in the holly trees blooming all over the place; R. tells the story of the bishop in Belgium, which amuses him greatly. But he is worn out in the evening, he has received a pamphlet about vivisection and the German Reich which utterly depresses him; he is also complaining of pains in his chest and his heat rash, says he is in constant torment!

Sunday, July 11   R. slept well, and we enjoy a cheerful breakfast, though it soon gives way to bitter thoughts: "One cannot be blamed for feeling nothing but disgust for such a nation, for regretting that one has to speak the same language as these people." And he begins to talk of the petition concerning vivisection. "One's own thoughts, too—one could be disgusted with them, seeing how they are represented. Our crime of settling down in Bayreuth was a fond delusion; I am coming more and more to feel that the only thing for us now is a vagabond life, with no home at all for ourselves and our children. We should be like the old woman who sat down to rest: We are running *Botsch* (*Botschaft* [messages])!" In our amusement over this idea we talk about America, I am to write to Jenkins for next September. — At our last lunch he spoke words of encouragement to our friend Stein and said: "At your age, 23, I got married, and I had already written two operas and many overtures. You see how far one can get from the fact that at the age of 68 I have to think of traveling to America in order to gain my independence." (He also wants to keep *Parsifal* free.) Since he is not feeling entirely well, there is no sea bath today, for he has severe congestions. After a siesta he plays the *Pastoral* with Lusch as a piano duet. Herr Rub. surprises us in the middle of it and continues with it (storm and finale), to our great delight. R. feels enchanted anew by this wonderful work. But only too soon he reverts to his usual line of thought. Beginning with joking remarks, such as, "I should like to see field marshals turned into meadow marshals," he breaks out into expressions of indignation. "Oh, this nation of ours!" he exclaims at supper, "no other is quite so wretched—the English are at least dealing with this problem properly." — In the evening he discusses various musical matters with Herr Rub., and when the latter mentions, among other things, the witticisms the Papageno in Vienna is now making, R. says, "Oh, he can never be done with too little wit." — Later he reads some of Goethe's letters to us.

Monday, July 12   R. did not sleep very well, for which the great heat is probably to blame. But he takes his *"peau de chagrin"* ["shagreen"] walk. At breakfast he greets me with Goethe's letter of dedication to King Ludwig I of Bavaria, which he finds very moving and which touches me deeply when he reads it to me. He intends to mention it to the King of Bavaria, for he entered his life at just the right moment, he says. "The very last moment," say I. He: "Yes—and how much energy had already been frittered away!" — "When I have put my religion in order, I shall set about earning money," he says, "and then I shall write nothing but symphonies—I'm looking forward to that." To the telegram, he remarks jokingly, he will have to reply "Tantara!" A letter from Herr v. Stein gives us much to talk about concerning this unusual person and our remarkable relationship with him. Yesterday Lusch told us about a dialogue he had read to her, Bruno and Shakespeare in a London tavern. Jouk. observes that if he had discovered him he would have remained in London—"or moved to Bayreuth with him," R. interjects. Over afternoon coffee he talks about our friend and says, "He is like a tender and ethereal little cloud coming from a race which, though talented, possessed perhaps some streaks of brutality; the brutality and strength have gone, and all that remains is this little spark of intellectuality, and none of the robustness." —

(I am again beset by great worry and concern over the physical condition of the two elder girls. Last year Frau Herz allayed my fears, but now Dr. Schrön's examination has revealed a bad state of affairs! — Great inner efforts to keep this concern to myself and not to upset the girls or R. with it.)

America constantly in our conversations, R. would like most of all to go directly there in September in order to make his fortune. — We take a sea bath together, R., two of the children, and I, he is pleased with Eva's graceful swimming. Siegfried still in bed with a headache, but nothing to cause any anxiety. — Vesuvius very active for a while—until, as R. says, "the devil's coffee has been brewed." —

Tuesday, July 13 R. slept well and praises sea baths! Then America again: "I am already looking forward to our fortune!" he says with a laugh. He works on his article and tells me that he will soon be dictating to me again. But he is suffering from heat blisters and also complaining of a soreness in his nose, though he dismisses the latter with a joke, saying out loud to it, "One impulse art thou conscious of, at best—oh, never seek to know the other!" — We go to the beach, R. is delighted by Eva's swimming, but as for himself, it does not seem to do any good, he has congestions in the evening. — (Before the bath he dictated to me a letter to Dr. Jenkins about his journey next September.) — In the evening Herr Rub. plays the finale of the C Minor Symphony to us; R. is not very happy, either with the execution (the triplets never expressive enough) or with the arrangement—he feels that the figurations obscure the themes and that much in the manner of writing for the piano is contrary to symphonic style. I realize that this symphony in particular can only make its effect when played by R.; it is quite deliberately aimed at rousing the audience, there is something oratorical about it, and a person who does not himself command this noble art is certainly incapable of reproducing it. While with the other symphonies I can imagine that a sensitive musician need only get the tempo right to achieve the full effect, this one calls for a person of strength and power.

Wednesday, July 14 At breakfast R. talks about the C Minor Symphony, says he has been thinking a lot about it, and it seems to him as if Beethoven had suddenly felt the desire to set aside the musician in himself and appear in the guise of a popular speaker; here he spoke in broad outlines, painted *al fresco* as it were, left out all musical detail, which in the finale to the *Eroica,* for example, is present in such richness. — At lunch, after his work, R. is very cheerful; lavish praise for Heinrich von Stein. And again and again America. [*Added later but referred back to this point:* " 'This will fulfill my boyhood desires, for the constant thought in my mind was: What, die before I have seen this little earth for myself, and all there is in it? At least that, since one cannot get to know the stars! — Till I came to realize that the spirit is everything.' He utters the last turn of phrase with such a comical emphasis and such a drolly significant look at me that we all burst out laughing."] Visions of us all arriving in California in a royal carriage! When friend Joukowsky says he wants to come, too, and to paint, R. says, "In earlier times, when business was bad in the small towns, theater managers used to attract audiences by announcing that a pig would be raffled after the performance; so I will get you to paint me, and that will be raffled." — He tells us many things that he has read about the dispute between Russia and China and says, "We Western peoples, the conquerors and educators, could not do better than first of all to study the civilizations of the peoples we want to conquer, and then to reflect on them." — When our friend observes that the Russians would not wreak such terrible havoc as the English did with the aid of opium, R. says quickly: "Then with the aid of schnapps. Do not ever believe that from such methods, applied from outside, any good can emerge." — And when our friend observes that in San Francisco the Chinese fill the role of the Jews, sucking the land dry, R. says, "With the difference that they are industrious, and therefore entitled to gain these advantages." — The second half of the day is, however, very dismal: R. does not feel well; he spits up some blood, and though the doctor seems unconcerned, I am inconsolable when I see him worried and depressed and full of complaints. How to prevent it, how to help him? This feeling of helplessness produces probably more pain than anything else, and whoever is burdened with such feelings will certainly realize what it was that made the saints, casting a glance at the nature of life without having experienced it, turn their backs on it. Now there is nothing to do but bear it! And I truly believe that no penance and no castigation demand more resolution than retaining one's self-control under such circumstances. "Oh, that I can never feel free except in moments of ecstasy!" R. complains, "and that I always have to think of some enterprise, and always as if at the beginning of Creation!" — Moonlit night. Yesterday R. pointed with delight to the crescent above the mountain. When somebody remarks today that it is terrible to think that for the next 3 months the weather will remain constantly fine, R. says, "One must look on lovely Nature as a garment—something one must have, but not keep looking at; one must at the same time live one's life and carry out one's task." — He is pleased with the Swiss because of canton Basel's decision to provide free education up to the university level. "The Swiss could have been a good example to us." —

Thursday, July 15 R. feels somewhat better, he took a bran bath for his heat blisters and went to sleep in it, had some wild dreams, and now talks about the "unlimited possibilities" of dreams. — He also talks again about the Wittelsbach Foundation and about reprinting Goethe's letter in the *B. Blätter.* — Yesterday he read to us from the *Tagblatt* an absurd criticism of *Faust,* which reminded him of Nietzsche's "*Nähmamsell*" ["seamstress"]; after considering the absurdity and unworthiness of such criticisms, he goes on to say, "There is something in what is said about Faust's unloving attitude; just as one finds it upsetting that Egmont recommends Klärchen to Ferdinand, while she dies for her love; but it is not made to seem offensive, and through it the writer's truthfulness is particularly emphasized." — R. is cheerful at lunch; afterward he plays something from the Venusberg music, and when we talk of its beauty, he says: "I have never gone through any experience which could have given me that. Indeed, anyone who has, like your father—what remains for him except disgust and a rosary? And then he comes up with something like the *Via crucis.* That was sad." — Our conversation also comes to Frau Helbig and her intellectual gifts, he tells us of the circumstances in which he met her and Herr v. Keudell, and how her gifts yielded no results at all for him, he met with nothing but "dead ends." "From such people one never hears a sigh, a question, and so they can mean nothing to one." — He warns our younger friends against drinking cognac and says it is a bad habit which he himself took up only late in life. Before lunch he brought me some "Eau de Richard," his latest perfume concoction, and, when I smilingly reflect that, though previously I did not care at all for essence of roses, it has now, through him, become my favorite scent, I find myself wishing that my whole self might be changed in the same way and nothing remain except what he himself has created. — To R.'s great pleasure we go to town with Lusch by streetcar for ice cream; the way we are besieged by beggars irritates R., we ride home feeling tired, and in the evening he is not well. Conversation about comets, Copernicus, and Kepler.

Friday, July 16   A restless night for R.; we stroll on the terrace, he shows me a splendid star, Jupiter, and we enjoy the mild air and also the great noise, for the people are again setting off fireworks. He then reads the Goethe-Schiller correspondence and quotes various things from it to me, which causes him to remark that he, too, has many ideas which he has neither used nor fully worked out, and a whole book could be made of them all. Today he spoke of the Greeks and their tragic drama (I forget whether I have already noted that he recently said the Greeks were the only ones who treated the world's miseries in positive terms, whereas writers such as Cervantes and Goethe had also made use of irony). — As he leaves me after breakfast, he says, "We have lived for each other, and that has brought benefits for other people as well." — He works and is satisfied with what he has done. Over coffee he reads aloud Schiller's opinion of *Die Hermannsschlacht* and says he is right about its heartlessness, indeed he feels that he has even depicted this heartlessness in Wetter vom Strahl and brought it into conflict with the soul. — He is still not taking sea baths and is trying to overcome his chest congestions and his heat rash through rest. On the terrace in the evening I relate various things I have just been reading, for example, the behavior of the popes toward the Hohenstaufens. R. says: "Yes, but what was to blame for it, what made such things possible, if not the dreadful circumstances of the time? The excommunication of Friedrich II—the people allowed that to happen. This is something historians never pay sufficient attention to: how peoples, nations, meet their end, all of it quite frightful. They concentrate on the great individual personalities and do not see the whole, how it grows progressively worse." — I listen to but do not really hear what R. is saying, for something I find deeply painful has preceded it. The children draw his attention to a chirping sound nearby, and he cannot hear it. And only recently I was thinking with apprehensive pleasure of the bird he had not heard in Tribschen and believing that this anxiety was now past! Now once more I have to hear something he cannot hear—oh, life, oh, death, must the cup be drained? Ah, who has the strength? And who can honestly say: Thy will be done? When

Cosima Wagner, 1879
Portrait by Franz von Lenbach

Garden of the Palazzo Rufalo, Ravello

"Richard Wagner with wife and children.
Klingsor's Magic Garden has been found!"

Richard Wagner with Siegfried, Naples, June 1, 1880

Richard Wagner, Naples, July 1880
Painting by Edmond Jean de Pury

Richard Wagner, November 1880

The Holy Family, *tableau vivant,* posed Christmas 1880, painted 1881.
Front: Siegfried as Jesus, Daniela as Mary; back: Eva, Blandine,
and Isolde as angels, the painter as Joseph
Painting by Paul von Joukowsky

Richard Wagner,
Palermo,
January 15, 1882
Portrait by
Auguste Renoir,
replica, 1883,
by the painter

Count Joseph Arthur
de Gobineau

Reception at Wahnfried, 1882. Front, from left: Siegfried, Cosima,
Amalie Materna, Richard Wagner; back, from left: Franz von Lenbach,
Emil Scaria, Franz Fischer, Fritz Brandt, and Hermann Levi; at the piano:
Franz Liszt, Franz Betz, Hans Richter, Albert Niemann; right front:
Countess Schleinitz (sitting), Countess Usedom, Paul von Joukowsky
Painting by George Papperitz

Cosima and Richard Wagner, Franz Liszt, and Hans von Wolzogen.
Wahnfried, 1882
Painting by W. Beckmann

Family picture in Wahnfried, August 23, 1881. Richard and Cosima Wagner,
Heinrich von Stein, Paul von Joukowsky, Daniela, and Blandine

Orchestra pit of the Bayreuth festival theater during
rehearsals for *Parsifal*, 1882
Drawing in India ink by Josef Greif

Cap for the Knights of
the Grail, "designed by R.
in hasty fury (jumping up
in the midst of supper)"

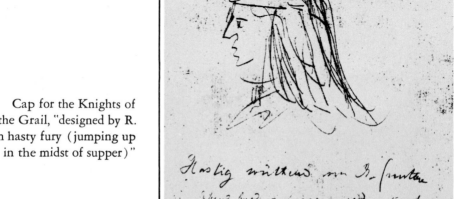

The Baptism, *Parsifal,*
Act III, 1882

Amalie Materna as Kundry, 1882

Heinrich Gudehus as Parsifal, 1882

Siena Cathedral. Its architecture was used as a model for the Temple of the Grail.

Temple of the Grail in *Parsifal*
Scene painting by Paul von Joukowsky

Parsifal, Act III, final scene, 1882
Woodcut after a drawing by Ludwig Bechstein

Palazzo Vendramin, Venice. The Wagners' quarters were in the rear wing.

Teatro La Fenice, Venice

Richard Wagner while
playing the piano,
Palazzo Vendramin,
February 12, 1883
Pencil drawing by
Paul von Joukowsky

Franz Liszt, 1884

Richard Wagner
Death mask

nothing else matters, there yet remains the capacity to suffer and grow weak with worry for the one who means everything, and to feel the sufferings of the whole universe in the emotion that is bliss! — Oh, life!

Saturday, July 17 In bed R. hears 11 o'clock strike, and he knows what that means, he says—that he will have a bad night. But a little later he goes off to sleep in spite of the heat rash, which is tormenting him greatly. And in the morning he talks gaily about his pleasure in colors, saying that life in fact begins with pink. Yellow, blue, etc., all the rest are props, cheerfulness or whatever, but pink is life itself. — He works and reads the Goethe-Schiller correspondence but unfortunately is still unable to take a sea bath, he consults the doctor but learns little. All the same, he enjoys the terrace in the evening ("No one in Naples should come to life until night, and the night watchman should be seen only during the day!"). —

Sunday, July 18 A very, very bad night for R.—indigestion and feeling hot; we stroll around, and he reads. In the morning he talks of *dispiritedness,* which Schiller mentions in his last letter! — But he becomes more cheerful at breakfast, tells me how much he envies the children, whom he has just heard laughing. His envy is pleasurable, however. He works, and the day passes quite bearably, and we even go to bed amid great laughter, for R. declares that he cannot tell whether our servant Georg is "hurling" furniture around as he tidies up or whether fireworks are being set off: "I thought just now it was a chair, but it was probably a rocket." — And yet—

Monday, July 19 —the wildest of nights, at 4 o'clock R. and I find ourselves out on the terrace watching the sunrise. [*Added in margin:* "I notice a bat circling almost directly above R.'s head."] R. points out to me the boats going out "to plunder," and we gaze upon all this beauty with tired feelings of indifference. All the same R. works, finishes his article, and is in consequence very cheerful at lunch, indeed boisterous. When I talk of the beauty of Schnorr's mother and call it a real and not an apparent beauty, he turns to Lusch and says, "Not like your mother's, which is already fading." He talks about the powerful geniuses in Dresden, Schnorr, etc., and when I ask how it is possible that falseness should so have gained the upper hand in Germany, he says, "You can depend upon it, the Jews are to blame." Over coffee we talk about *W. Meister;* R. finds all the women in it somewhat unbearable, apart from Marianne, Mignon, and Philine; he likes Philine, he says, and he knew her, "Malchen Lehmann from the Böhmes' house," whom as a boy he liked to be with, he enjoyed stroking her curls. "I always blushed red as a beet when she came into the room." And in the most expansive of moods he leaves us, after lunch, when I spoke of the unbearable age of L[ouis] XIV, having said gaily, "I don't know whether I shall get old, but unbearable certainly." [*A marginal note based on untranslatable word play omitted.*] — Recently he said that, if he is to be painted now, he must be made to look as he was about 12 years ago, for the signs of age have become too apparent. I believe that genius retains all its beauty in old age. In the afternoon he reads his work to me (conclusion), and I am enchanted by it. Before that he had read my words about the Wittelsbach celebration, and he praises them so highly that it would be coldness in me to describe myself merely as happy on this afternoon during which he confides to me the richness, profundity, and greatness of his thoughts and at the same time welcomes my few words as a melody! "Mine is a fugue, yours a melody." Thus in defiance of all that is bad or evil we pass as if in a trance into the evening; a flaming meteor, as it falls, takes with it the single wish (*"wahnlos hold bewusst"!*) I cherish—eternity will fulfill it for me. — Around 11 o'clock we go to bed, after R. has taken a coal-tar bath, but all too soon he leaves his bed, and since he does not return, I follow him; in silence we sit on the terrace, bathed in light, hear strange sounds, a woman whose call is reminiscent of Hungarian melodies; then we leave the terrace and stroll in the garden before the door, exchanging words and lost in contemplation. The loveliest night, perhaps, that we have ever experienced! My whole being immersed in his, in the richly consoling sea of his thoughts, and both of us silently lost in the still, mild glory. He laughs at the idea of wanting to sleep when one cannot! Memories of Sulzer. — Between 2 and 3 we go to bed, and at 9 o'clock on

Tuesday, July 20   we are having breakfast and thinking of the night, so rich and significant! At 11 o'clock he dictates to me, and when, while we are working, cannons roar to signal the arrival of the King, R. remarks that here people celebrate more than the whole of Nature, and, "It would be nice if one could assume that the entire population were really glad when the King arrived." — He had summoned me with sounds from *Parsifal,* the passage where the hero comes to the Temple for the second time, "having surmounted the death of his mother and much else besides"—and when at coffeetime he plays some of the Venusberg music (having told us that in spite of all the wrong notes he would in his own way provide the accents with all the necessary energy, something nobody except my father could do), I say that here is proof that everything in art is ideal, the fact that these sounds and P.'s sounds came from the same being. — R. says, "Everything *cries!*" and also: "It is the same in the Venusberg as in *Tristan*—in the one it is resolved in grace, in the other in death. Everywhere this cry, this lament, and these accents come from a rather different place from that of Berlioz's Sabbath affairs." (One evening recently he said that this work had been a vain effort: on the stage it cannot be done properly, and in the concert hall it sounds bad, just a wild noise.) — We speak of his trouble, the wretched heat rash: "One must pay for everything," he says. "When one has the kind of skin which enjoys touching soft things like my cigar case, then it easily gets overheated." — He continues talking about the time of the composition of the Venusberg music and says, "I was never restricted to a single element." — He receives a pleasant surprise from Leipzig, a larger payment than he was expecting, and the cashier, Herr Rosenheim, asks him for his photograph; R. sends one to him with the words, "*In der Kasse gern daheim, grüsse ich Herrn Rosenheim*" ["I send greetings to Herr Rosenheim, happily at home in his cash office"]. — In the evening much about Goethe and Schiller, the eternal complaints arising from the climate; then he enlarges upon the unbearable Lothario (even the name is horrible, he says), and repeats that if Goethe had not spurred himself on to *Elective Affinities* and finally *Faust,* no one would know what we possessed in him. — Before these evening conversations he enjoyed watching the children in the sea from the terrace, then he is pleased with the "Decameron," our little company sitting to the right of the terrace in the moonlight, listening to Pepino's songs. He is also pleased by what I tell him of Fidi's lessons with me. — Our conversation touches on December 2, and after a description of its horrors, R. says, "And that is how one becomes a humane ruler and one's nation's benefactor, which he undoubtedly was." And when I utter the words "*économie de sang*" ["saving of blood"], which some people use to describe December 2, "The French have a word for everything, which enables them to shrug things off." — "You need cynicism like that to remain cheerful and well disposed after such horrors." — He takes a coal-tar bath toward midnight and then gets into his "vexation machine," his bed. But he soon leaps out, and we are up the whole night, watch the sunrise, but this time without pleasure, with unfeeling indifference, for R.'s state is a pitiable one. — The only thing he tells me with a certain amount of enjoyment is that he has seen the singers, who during the nights have been irritating him so with their singing, taking their departure between 2 and 3 o'clock, and that it touches him to think of them now playing their instruments (guitar, violin, flute) by themselves.

Wednesday, July 21 In the evening he had remarked that they had copied their bad tremolo habits from the opera, for the street calls were entirely free of them. — He also reflected on the donkey's cry: "The tragic thing is that it seems ridiculous; I remember its heehaw, its whistling, high up in the mountains; now it tries them down here, but they make no sense and sound quite different." — No dictation today, on account of our fatigue. In the afternoon Prof. Schrön and a sea bath, which R. finds very agreeable, he is pleased with the children. When we are sitting on the terrace in the evening, he says sadly: "The German Emperor! When I think how pleasant this man was—I am not forgetting his friendliness in Bayreuth—and yet I cannot imagine meeting him again and maybe telling him my ideas." — Recently the sight of a very poor drawing of the Crown Princess (Roman boy) brought melancholy words from him about Germany's future; he frequently feels the urge to describe all his experiences with dukes, grand dukes, and crown princes in a letter addressed to an American; among other things he mentions the Grand Duke of Baden and his cordial, warm handshake. — In the evening the children ask Herr Rubinstein to play us something from *Das Rheingold*. We go back to the terrace, where R. has been waiting, to find the sky altered and clouds everywhere. All very lovely! The reflections in the water suggest to R. all kinds of pictures, such as the Persian troops crossing the Hellespont.

Thursday, July 22   R. had a good night. . . . He is cheerful at breakfast, to which he summons me with a chorus from *Euryanthe* and at which, as he says, he appears like Aurora on the snow-capped mountains. — We talk about *Das Rheingold,* and that soon leads him to the melancholy theme of the uselessness of great men. At around 12 noon he dictates to me, and when the possibility of a league for peace is mentioned, he says, "The French should show us how, the rascals!" He then gazes happily around his little room, in which he has the pink color which one can no longer find, and he says that is the reason he rails against our whole modern civilization—because it does not know how to produce this shade of pink [*a piece of pink material laid between these pages*]. At lunch we again talk about *W. Meister,* Therese's attitude toward Lothario (at first not to marry, since possibly his daughter, then to marry after all, since her mother, etc.). He says, "Those are chemical assumptions; they remind me of the Jew who thought it so nice that birds hatch their young—I should just say: Wife, hatch me a boy, or a girl, or a pancake." Then he suddenly exclaims, "It is quite scandalous, such a relationship!" — When friend Joukowsky says he now wants to paint his portrait, R. is glad that the full-face photograph is to be used for it, saying that this is a good one; the Lenbach portrait is striking, he feels, but exaggerated, one-sided, lacking in contrast. — After his afternoon siesta he corrects the manuscript, but says he is altering next to nothing in the style: "I am not a writer." — In the evening he brings up the subject of the uselessness of great men, asking of what avail Beethoven had been: "They have learned nothing from him—all they do is try to imitate him. And Aeschylus—could his wisdom stop his people from heading for downfall? And Shakespeare!" — He recalls the impression the Adagio of the E-flat Major Quartet made on him in Paris, how he wept and felt exalted. Glorious moonlit evening, mild and tranquil atmosphere; when we talk about wishing on shooting stars, R. says: "I have everything the world could not supply to the remotest degree! All I now wish for is good health, and then enough money to give us freedom of movement."

Friday, July 23 R. slept well, and in our gladness we continue with the dictation; when we come upon the word "pessimism," R. says, "If the optimists only knew what a bad time they would have had under their improved conditions!" — After the dictation he reads to me a page from a letter by Schiller about Christianity, very, very beautiful and profound. "Certainly," R. says in response to my remarks, "he was the profound one—Goethe was the wizard." We agree that he should use a part of this passage as a motto for his article; he cannot use the whole of it, for they had not yet become aware of the real and terrible problem. We go to the beach, and it has a pleasant effect on R. No *Rheingold* in the evening, owing to a broken piano hammer; conversation about all sorts of things on the terrace by moonlight; reminiscences of Bohemia, the romantic land of his youth; of Riga, which he knew when it was a completely German town, but to which was suddenly sent, as head of police, a Russian cavalry captain who could speak neither German nor French—"a fine state of affairs." — Thirst brings us to the subject of Christ on the cross, and he relates his death, as differently envisaged by Renan and Gfrörer.

Saturday, July 24 R. slept well, he does not wish to wake me, so we do not have breakfast together. All the more joyfully do we come together for dictation, and as I write, R. sings, "Nothing is so dear to me as the room in which I bide, for opposite—" He is very cheerful at lunch, tells of the bank note for £100,000 which Rothschild has hanging, framed, in his room, and, when we get a letter from our friend Stein describing his estate, he says: "Ah, how good it is, an inherited property like that! One knows then where one belongs, whatever happens. For myself, I should choose Rothschild's bank note as my basic property," he adds merrily, dispelling our serious mood. — He is continually saying that he wants to write symphonies, and our children bring him continual joy. Fidi recites Goethe's *"Der Sänger"* to him, and R. then reads it to him as a reward. In the evening a visit from the painter Böcklin, a peculiar, powerful character, turned bitter through experience; R. is soon tired.

Sunday, July 25 R. slept so soundly that he did not notice an earth tremor which I and others in the household felt very strongly. —

Böcklin's surprising view of Lenbach forms part of our breakfast conversation. Lengthy dictation, conclusion of the much-loved work. — In the afternoon to the beach; R. tries to swim, but he finds it a great strain, and we spend a tired and gloomy evening, which even the conclusion of *Rheingold* cannot enliven for me. Yesterday R. exclaimed to me, "Brahms is advertising in the newspapers for an opera libretto; I have described my views on composition in the *Blätter,* and now he thinks he has got a recipe." — A portrait of the Frenchman Daudet in the *I. Z.* does not please him on account of the wild hair, he observes that even in the most intelligent of Frenchmen there is something, some obtuseness, which cannot be overcome. — And when Lusch tells us that even the *I. Z.* is showing hostility to our cause, R. says: "Like everyone else; and then I am supposed to rejoice when somebody for some reason or other says something nice about me! This paper wants to stay on good terms with everybody, and so with us, too." — At lunch he talked about Wallenstein, he said jokingly to Lulu that she probably wished she could meet a young man like that, and then adds with a laugh: "Curious that the young German is an Italian." —

Monday, July 26   R. had a good night, he says he is longing for rain at last. "All you are fit for is day and night." Letters from Bayreuth cause him vexation because of printing delays, he writes to friend Wolzogen about it and also, jokingly, about his article; he says, too, that he can hold out no hope to friend Schön for 10,000 marks, indeed, not even for 100,000, for the hope he offers is an ideal one. — He is run down and is still spitting up a little blood. At lunch, when I tell him about what I am reading, Sismondi's history, he says, "Yes, it's frightful what historians tell you in cold blood—not one of them expresses horror at such a state of affairs." — Evening on the terrace, no bath for either of us. Sudden concern about Loldi. R. cheerful, however. Saint Anne is being celebrated with a great variety of fireworks.

Tuesday, July 27   [*Added in margin:* "He spoke during these days about the legend of Heracles, said it left him totally indifferent, meant nothing to him."] R. had a good night, but he is still much tormented by his heat rash. At breakfast he is pleased by a letter from Berlin: a Herr Oelten offers a large plot of ground in Berlin for the erection of a Wagner theater. In view of the attitude of the Court theater, this would be quite acceptable to R., and he instructs me to ask friend Feustel to look into both the offer and the man. He laughs and says, "The Emperor will surely come when I stage my *Ring* there, he will not consider it beneath his dignity." — He also talks of the curious character of the Jews, in connection with some anecdotes about Prof. Bernays: "A strikingly alien element has come among us." — He is still run down, but the doctor treats the matter lightly. R. goes into town to have a glass of beer at Dreher's, but he does not enjoy it; however, we have a nice merry moment when he drives up in the *carrozzella*, I go to meet him in a pink bathrobe and he gives me a lift. The thing that struck his notice in town today was: a very charming and elegant lady reclining in her carriage, languidly talking to her companion, while behind them a boy clung awkwardly to the carriage. R. observes that this is typical of the elegant world—not to know what is going on around and beneath one. "And yet for this elegance to be maintained, one has to imagine a husband making financial transactions, getting mixed up with unsavory people. And then the stupid look one would get from a woman like that if one were to try to interest her in anything at all." — Goethe's reflections on the Jesuits (at the start of his *Italian Journey*) produce from R. the remark, "He just happened to discover that, after all the other orders had disappeared, this one had managed to create some sort of life for itself, and that interested him." — When I tell R. of the Franciscans' struggles with Pope J[ohn] XXII, he says, "Yet the horrible thing about all these saints is their recognition of the Pope as Christ's representative." — Evening on the terrace: he yearns for the Villa *Angermann* and a glass of good Rhine wine; but when I suggest that we return home, he will not hear of it. His rash seems to be disappearing somewhat; recently he said, "The dear Lord must think that I have no nerves and no feelings and be asking Himself: What can I do to pinch and torment him?" — Our standing joke is now Palumbello, the dog, whose name has become an epithet, used for everything to which one is unable to give a name. Yesterday it was even "The relationship of Saint Catherine of Siena to Palumbello!" — Over coffee talked of clothes, how unnatural and unbecoming; R. would like to wear a shirtlike robe, and he speaks of the curvy lines of the female body, which are spoiled by the present fashions. We wonder how in such unnatural circumstances proper humans can be born! He says the Empire costumes were much better. He quotes Feuerbach's words concerning the abdomen: "In men a restaurant, in women a temple of love." [*Added in surrounding margins:* "Next summer he wants to go to Gräfenberg, and then to America, perhaps to stay there, if only to put Fidi out of reach of the 'horrible soldier business.' — In connection with our discussions of astronomical calculations, he says that previously their purpose was just to enable wars to be fought more safely; now, when the main thing is already known, it would at best be an idle pastime to occupy oneself with it."]

Wednesday, July 28 R. has erysipelas! Brought on yesterday by a drafty room (at Loldi's bedside) . . .

Friday, August 6 No complications, but the most dismal of spirits!

Since the heat rash gets no better, resolve to leave. The children are staying here, we pack our things. Curious feelings about Naples—though it is still nice, I, too, feel as if all this splendor were poisoned. — As for books, R. has been reading short stories by the American, Hawthorne, with much enjoyment. I read parts of Goethe's *Italian Journey* to him, but he soon became irritated by all its "wafflings about art." — During the six days of his illness, particularly at the beginning, R. had many wild dreams. — He finds all the medical treatments repulsive—"All doctors are vivisectors"—we decide on Gräfenberg. — Our complete isolation, our life together which was for me so utterly dear, yet at the same time so utterly sad, earns me the name of his "beloved saint." — His bed by day was in the *salon,* so this brightest of places also a sickroom. — On Wednesday the bed was removed. — Two things I remember about the day before his illness—that he said it had all happened 15 years too late, and that, when I was about to leave him talking to Lusch in the dining room, a bat flew in and circled around, causing me to exclaim, "It is bringing me misfortune."

Saturday, August 7 R. again took bromine. Apart from that, concerned only with packing. I go once again with the children to the vineyards—overcast sky, sudden violent thunderclap, and heavy rain, we rush home, there to find a most wonderful sight; R. calls me out to the terrace, Naples completely green, the Posilipo colored pink, Capri in a pale-blue light, the sea red, and before us golden clouds. Indescribable, and we so sad, the phantom of erysipelas constantly before our eyes! (R. sends picture and poem to Prof. Schrön.)

Sunday, August 8 R. slept, with the aid of bromine. Breakfast at 12 and then taking leave of the children. Under what circumstances shall we see one another again? Lusch, Boni, Eva in tears, Loldi and Fidi composed. — In the Rocca Secca region R. feels the benefit of the air, a mood of hopefulness. In Rome at 10 in the evening, Hôtel Quirinal, run by Herr Guggenbühl, a Swiss. Able to talk German even with the chambermaid.

Monday, August 9 R. froze the whole night! We visit S[anta] M[aria] d[egli] A[ngeli]; the Carthusian monk sweeping there is a German, and he welcomes us as such. R. very tired in the church, we drive around a little, the new Rome beside the ruins very unpleasant; curious round trip with a Swiss coach driver; at last, 10:52, in our compartment, where we are alone again. R. regains his spirits, we dine cheerfully, the Nierenstein wine from the Quirinal hotelkeeper has an agreeable effect. Tuscany, with all its flowers and cultivated fields, delights him. Nice memories of Naples, of which R. always says, "That is Africa, this is Italy, the southern tip of Europe." At the railroad station in Florence, old Beppa recognizes us and overwhelms us with friendly attentions. — Between 8 and 9 in the evening arrive in heavy rain in dark Pistoia. A nice apartment in the Hotel London and a pleasant Italian supper. R. very tired, however, his head feels hot.

Tuesday, August 10 R. had a tolerable night, at 10 o'clock we set out for San Marcello; uphill journey of 3½ hours, at first very hot, but then noticeably cooler. Curious accommodations in the village, where fleeing Ghibellines once settled. The road was reminiscent of French Switzerland, the village is something like Berneck or even Faido. — Gay mood to begin with, thoughts of Magdala, of flight, jokes about the Ghibellines, but R. becoming increasingly irritable, though a drive out toward Lucca gives him pleasure; in the evening, however, his skin is even redder, and he has fits of shivering, extreme anxiety; helpless and powerless as I am, I beseech the heavens, ecstatically accept a night of violent toothache, and pray, pray, pray that he be allowed rest, which on

Wednesday, August 11 he is, he looks better, and we laugh once more over the incredible place in which we are staying, without a garden, without a view. A cornet-à-pistons sounds, we think of R.'s method, and then I hear the Lucia fantasy! R. has been reading the *Causes célèbres* for several days now. — Earlier, in the Villa d'Angri, he had read Hawthorne's *The Scarlet Letter* with great interest, particularly in the young clergyman. I read it after him, the idea seems to me outstanding, the execution, however, rather amateurish. — Now we are here, and over there the familiar Wahnfried, the enchanted V. d'Angri. [*Added in margin:* " 'I put up with all this (such mountains) for 10 years in Zurich, now I have to land myself in such a h——!' "] — It could look as if there were a warrant out for us, says R., or as if we could not pay and were waiting here for money. Much laughter at first, but then increasing depression on R.'s part. We decide to go on to Abetone, to see whether there are rooms to be had there, and when. But during the journey R. is so irritated by the green mountains and the bare ones that, cursing them jokingly, he decides to turn around and go back to Pistoia, where we once again arrive in black night after a drive of nearly 6 hours. (In S[an] M[arcello], R. told me, he had immersed himself in thoughts of Isolde's apotheosis, but here it is the "Good Friday Music.") —

Thursday, August 12 Early in the night R. was much disturbed by his rash, but washing himself down helps considerably, and he sleeps well. Decision to go on to Perugia. He feels he has got thinner. We spend the day quietly in Pistoia, around 6 o'clock we drive through the town, which gives us great delight in spite of R.'s fatigue. He, too, finds pleasure in the reliefs of Luca della Robbia, and the cathedral, the Prefettura, the Baptisterio, individual elegant houses, leave behind an indelible impression. In Florence put up at the Hôtel de Rome, where friend Buonamici visits us and where very strange telegrams cause confusion and laughter; in one of them R. had put down *"wäre dieses schön"* ["this would be nice"], the official forgot *"wäre"* and wrote *"dieses Sohau,"* which then becomes a motto for everything causing embarrassment, all the more so since at first R. could not remember what he had originally written. He is very run down and early in the night is tormented by his rash, but at last he goes to sleep, and sleeps well.

Friday, August 13   Early departure; inflated bill, which gives R. the idea that he is a prelate, for he is being *geprellt* [cheated]. And the Germans, who otherwise left all business dealings to the Jews, would now probably come to be looked upon as cheating landlords—in which connection their servility would also come into its own. He describes Sgambati's concerto to B[uonamici] as "tears shed but nothing said." In the train he reads the *Causes célèbres,* including one about a killer of poor servant girls and his punishment. "How can one imagine," he exclaims, "that in the present state of things any sort of improvement can be expected, through either the death penalty or anything else?" — He is indignant about the Irish question and the brutal way in which the English are trying to solve it, and he calls England the most wicked of nations. — We like Perugia, also the Albergo Perugia, we decide to enjoy rest and fresh air here. At last! After six days. R. observes that in S. Marcello we were looking for the nut-brown maid! . . . He calls to me on my balcony, "Do you want to see something nice?" He empties a bottle; in reply to my question he says that it is his cognac—he feels that it is bad for his rash. — Around 6 o'clock I leave him to visit the Helbigs, who booked our apartment in the hotel. Strange impression of the place, darkly gleaming, powerful! I tell R. about it—also the comical fact that he is famous here as Morlacchi's successor! — We go to bed early, glad to be staying here. Read a little of the dismal history of lovely Pistoia!

Saturday, August 14   R. was restless early in the night, but it got better, and he woke up refreshed. After breakfast I visit the *cambio* [exchange], which I resolve to show him, and the gallery, to which I shall not take him. At lunch we talk about all sorts of things, including the cunning of the Greeks, and he says, "Their abilities were their gods." — Thoughts of settling in Italy: "I should feel safe from harm," he says, but it would be a means of dreaming away one's existence. "I still want to write *Parsifal,* then symphonies, then I will complete various bits of my work." He becomes absorbed in the thought that nobody understands anything about him, that nobody could represent him after his death. — We go for a drive through the city, which pleases R. greatly, then go via the Helbigs' house, S. Erminica, to the Tiber valley. R. enjoys it, but he is run down in the evening, and a slight error of diet again spoils the early part of the night for him. A letter from Lulu tells us that Antonio has been stealing in our house, and R. at once decides to abandon the adoption. My father is said to be in the vicinity, we invite him here; Frau Helbig wants him to stay in her house, which puts R. into a rage!

Sunday, August 15 Up late, R. slept well after all, and in the morning he reads *Faust,* Part Two; a few things in it annoy him, such as Helena's "significant group" after the words of Phorkyas, but much delights him anew, our "Let the phantom do what it will," the "inquisitive Proteus," etc. In the *giardino pubblico* [public gardens] with R., he is pleased with the clever use of the narrow terrain. We dine with the Helbigs. — At one point R. grows heated when the German Crown Princess is praised, and he describes the heartless triviality of this type of person, as shown in her behavior toward him. — Frau Helbig plays us a Beeth. sonata very well; R. begs her to play one passage with more meaning, saying it is good not just to let everything sing, but now and again to allow something to speak. — Since regret was expressed over the burning down of the library, R. said to me, "It would be very much better if Mommsen had been burned and his books and manuscripts saved, for everything worth while about such a person is contained in his books." In the evening he reads to me some fragments by Schop. about intellect (*Parerga*), and at such times I almost always have the feeling that it either comes from R. himself or refers to him.

Monday, August 16 R. did not have a good night, probably an error of diet to blame—he also regrets having left Naples, since his rash is not improving. In the morning I visit the cathedral, S. Severo, the Oratorio of S. Bernardino, return to the cathedral and there to my surprise meet R., whom I was just about to fetch in the carriage. We walk to the *cambio,* which disappoints him, since he expected it to be bigger. He is very tired, takes a bath when we arrive home. In the afternoon we drive to the Tiber valley and on the homeward journey visit the graves of the Volumni, which make an impact on R. as well. Thoughts of the Etruscans, their civilization, their absorption by the Romans. In the evening I read to R. Sch.'s chapter "On Apparent Deliberateness in the Fate of an Individual," with great enjoyment.

Tuesday, August 17 R. had to endure another spasm at first, but he finally slept well and is in cheerful spirits at breakfast. The proofs of the biography arrive, and both of us read them with enjoyment. In the morning he wrote to friend Wolzogen and ended with the words "Germania hurrah!" At my suggestion we have supper earlier and let it consist of tea and cold foods, and afterward we go for a walk in the last rays of the setting sun and in moonlight. — It is really lovely, or would be lovely—indeed, glorious—if R. were not feeling so tired! — Returning home, I write to Mimi Schl. about Gräfenberg, the idea of which already alarms R., since, as he says, he likes civilized places.

Wednesday, August 18 R. slept very well! — In the morning we decide on a meeting with the children, who are still managing splendidly. While I visit the lovely S. Pietro, S. Domenica, and a third church whose name I do not know—also the cattle market, full of splendid white oxen—R. corrects the biography and writes to the children. When I return home and during lunch he is very irritable, the flies, slight signs of negligence in the service, annoy him extremely; he is upset that the King does not reply to him in connection with the change of theater director, and says the King is probably awaiting his birthday telegram, so that he can ignore that subject entirely; he is upset also by his position in relation to the Society of Patrons. The pages of the biography are hardly encouraging, either! It is all very sad, and I myself cannot tell him my feelings about the works of art I am seeing, since I am so painfully aware that he cannot enjoy them, and that also leaves me with only the most melancholy of feelings. We part for our afternoon rest, and he comes to my room to ask me to forgive him—oh, dear God! In the evening the same arrangement and a visit to the Helbigs'. R. becomes angry twice, over the indifference revealed in a discussion on the subject of giving Rumania up to the Jews, and over a contemptuous opinion of Garibaldi. — Otherwise, however, the lively conversation of this woman who is so well versed in almost every subject is quite to his liking—only I must be there, too, he says.

Thursday, August 19 A bad night, R. feels we had supper yesterday too soon after our lunch, he had alarming dreams about the children! But in the morning we decide that, when I return home from the gallery, I am to show him S. Pietro. This visit succeeds beyond all expectations, he is thoroughly pleased, particularly by the choir. A very strict diet does him good, and around 4 o'clock we set off on a drive around and through Perugia, which at sunset and moonrise has a decided effect—on me a very heartening and inspiring one because of R.'s delight in everything, which delights me, and the fact that he is better. In the evening he declares in the most humorous way that he will not go to Gräfenberg—he laughs over pine trees, spa guests, spa music, in fact the complete prospectus, which has much alarmed him. He keeps exclaiming, "What an ass I should be to leave Italy during the loveliest months for—pine trees and rain and a thick winter paletot!" Much sending of telegrams canceling everything, with R. in high good humor.

Friday, August 20 I go straight to the Helbigs' in the morning to ask about Siena, where R. has resolved to live. Not very favorable information about villas. I myself should like to stay here, where there is a villa which is recommended, in order to save R. further upset, but he does not wish it. He wants first of all to wait for the children in Florence. Much joking about Gräfenberg, he recalls Vaillant and his difficulties: "He was like me, he liked the truth but wanted to be comfortable." — At 2 o'clock departure from Perugia. In the hot carriage great concern on my part over not having opposed him. I always regard his wish as inspiration and my own caution as the stupidest of "wisdom." Now, as always, all that remains for me is to place my hopes in Heaven, in the stars, that things may turn out well! — R. delights in the countryside and keeps exclaiming with a laugh, "Pine trees, indeed!" He says he will hang the prospectus on a wall. In Florence at 7 in the evening. Buonamici is to find a cook for us! R. and I stroll to the cathedral, splendid in the moonlight, then sit down on the stone steps of the Loggia [dei Lanzi]—a dream, our wandering together like this through Florence! — Comical to receive, on our departure from Perugia, a telegram from the conductor Herr Levi, advising us against Gräfenberg! When R. happens to say something about Garibaldi to Buonamici, the good man observes that G. lived too long and did some stupid things. R. says, "Don't tease me, now," and amid the laughter he adds seriously, as if to himself, "Bayreuth was utter folly."

Saturday, August 21   Hot, noisy night, R. sleeps for several hours. Decision to wait for the children not in Florence, but in Siena. Departure at 6:30, the air fresh, the scenery makes a good impression on R. Since I did not sleep during the night, I doze off, and awake in R.'s embrace. — He says he has been writing to my father in his thoughts—and now I hesitate to write down what he said—though I should like to show you his love for me, my children, I just cannot; such things one may scarcely even acknowledge as having been spoken! — Arrival in Siena around 10 o'clock, immediate inspection of villas, great heat, the position not very pleasant, for me at least Perugia still standing very much in the way of proper appreciation. But then a visit to the cathedral! R. moved to tears, the greatest impression he has ever received from a building. How I should love to hear the Prelude to *Parsifal* beneath this dome! In the midst of troubling thoughts, blissful to have shared this enchantment with R., gratitude toward my destiny. Comfortably installed in the Grand Hotel. Vexations caused by telegraphic muddles. Visit to villas, one of which—Torre di Fiametta—pleases R. — Negotiations with the landlord for me; apprehension on my part about settling down again in a completely strange place amid inhabitants of whom nobody speaks well, and who from the outside do not make a good impression. — In the evening a walk with R. in the dark gardens. In Schop. he has been reading many things about medicine and physicians which have given him strength in his present mood.

Sunday, August 22 R. slept well, the children are in Florence. Breakfast in good spirits—R. wishes to leave all the arrangements in the villa to me. For himself he has now adopted the motto "Let the phantom do what it will," to remind him to be patient! At 12 in the villa with the councilor. At 3:30 drove to the station to fetch the children. Waiting, arrival of the train, the children not on it. Vexation, worry, tomorrow he will send Georg to meet them; I want to go to the post office to see whether a telegram has arrived—nothing, provoking thoughts that they might have stayed in Florence to see the sights; return to the carriage, the coachman and Georg tell us that it was a different train. Cheerful and animated return to the station. At last the train, the children with us again, all of them good, healthy, affectionate, happy! Siegfried very tender. Meal at 5 o'clock! No end to the chatter! Then to the cathedral and the villa. Some concern for me in that the children traveled very expensively! . . .

Monday, August 23 Tolerable night and breakfast all together. I settle the rental terms and the preliminary arrangements to be made in the villa. In the afternoon R. visits me there with the children, who are astonished and delighted with their new world, so swiftly arisen. R. is satisfied with everything I have done.

Tuesday, August 24 R. did not have a bad night, and the children say he is looking very well and is very cheerful. He talks of the peculiarities of the Villa d'Angri, of its "ghostly insidiousness," that is to say, everything in it seemed to have evolved as if by magic, there were no benches there, an eternal changelessness of light and air. I arrange things in *Torre di Fiorentina,* go back to the hotel at one o'clock for lunch, drive to the villa at 4 in order to welcome the children there permanently. In the meantime R. and the children look over the cathedral and its *libreria,* and how can I help being touched when I am told that, every time he saw something which pleased him, R. exclaimed, "How glad my wife will be!" Between my two journeys I send off the telegram to the King [*copy enclosed; see notes*], carry off some fine fabric in triumph from an antique dealer as a gift for R. [*Enclosed an envelope inscribed by Wagner* "15 mètres for little Richard" *and containing a piece of the fabric and Cosima's sketch for a dedicatory poem.*] And so in the space of four days we have once again set up a household in this completely unknown town! Merry first supper (salami and risotto) in the tower! [*Enclosed a page torn from an account book, inscribed by Cosima:* " 'To see justice in every test of self-will—is this a consolation? I believe it is—it is like the transition from wounding to death—in acknowledging justice, self-will becomes no longer painfully, but mortally wounded, and its disappearance opens the way to a life of grace.' — His words on August 24 in Torre Fiorentina."]

Wednesday, August 25 Most unfortunately, R.'s night was not a good one—probably the food somewhat indigestible! But he is utterly delighted with my little present. For me the day passes in household arrangements, but he makes corrections—in the copy of his article. At lunch we drink to the King in a sparkling local wine—also to ourselves and to Bürkel—and are in merry mood. Several hours on the terrace; R. keeps saying, "This is Italy, in contrast to Africa." — When we are talking of the curiously passionate quality of our house moving, R. says, "In people of our sort excess is aimed solely at procuring a pleasant tranquillity, so that the spirit can roam free." — We go for a walk in the vineyards, but R. feels slightly unwell; in the evening it looks as if he has caught a cold, and I am as full of concern as he is of vexation.

Thursday, August 26 The early part of the night was very restless, but later R. slept soundly and well. He tells me of a dream: he had lent somebody his golden pencil, and a woman kept giving him another one instead, finally a tin one, though he kept on saying, "Give me back mine, it is a souvenir from my wife," and she admitted that, but continued to offer him other ones, until he woke up. To me the curious thing about this is that yesterday I was bothered by a golden pencil, preoccupied with it. — A little incident of which Lusch told us proves annoying to R.: when friend Rubinstein played in Frau v. Schleinitz's house—to begin with something by R.—Hans, who was present, cried, "Bravo," but when he then played the [Opus] 111 Sonata, Hans exclaimed, "I find that quite unrecognizable," and walked out. R. says he hopes Hans knows him well enough not to see his "school" in this. But the incident has once again made it clear to him how things stand with him and his cause, for not one of them, he says, remembers a tempo set by him. — He says of the Jews that in the long run they are a great burden; when they are any good, they have their souls to contend with! — The newspapers are reporting a bad harvest in Germany, and the *Illustrirte* is concerned only with festivities— shooting competitions, gymnastic displays, etc.—in connection with which, R. is much annoyed by the Emperor's clothing: "When our Emperor unveils his mother's monument, he comes in a short jacket like a silly little boy. Why not use judges' robes for such an occasion?" — Nice reply telegram from the King. — (I now remember how on the journey from Fl. to Siena the sight of this on a bottle filled R. with pained indignation; such things were not proper, he said, yet nowadays one saw such pictures even on matchboxes.) — Conversation in the evening, somewhat dejected, since R. does not feel well.

Friday, August 27 A fairly good night, and in the early morning a cold pack, which seems to lead to great exhaustion and irritability. He is extremely vexed by the very unfriendly manner of the German servants. I take the children to go look at several things, including the lovely *Three Graces* on their pedestal. — R. tells me his dream: a handsome greyhound followed him and spoke to him; getting more and more affectionate and troublesome, it placed its paws on his chest; R., believing the animal to be bewitched, pushed it away, whereupon it said to R., "Take me with you, I promise not to be troublesome any longer." — R. sends off his article and writes a few words to W., saying that this will probably be his last work, some points of which he might later elaborate a little further. As for his activities, he intends still to stage *Parsifal* for some very few of his friends. — He is very, very tired, but he orders an outing to Monte Caro, which turns out quite well and gives us a good impression of the charming Siena countryside. — In the evening great weariness on R.'s part, he goes to bed around 9 o'clock. In the middle of the night

Saturday, August 28 he wakes up and says he has had a terrible dream about me—I wanted to leave him. He calms down, however, goes to sleep again, and tells me that he has had a pleasant dream about us: we were playing a new Beethoven composition as a piano duet; the theme consisted of four notes, the entrance was difficult, he missed it, wondering whether I had noticed, for I continued playing without faltering. Then he tells me the nasty first dream in detail. We were in a public garden, and I declared loudly and at length that I no longer wished to live with him and could no longer put up with his grumbling, and others agreed with me, including Cornelius, who was sitting nearby and nodded his head. R. got up and went to one side, where someone said to him, "You are a fine *monsieur*— everybody knows what you said about Weber, too." — "Do not speak to me, my dear sir, about Weber," and in his pain and anger it occurred to him that he had not had any coffee, and he ordered some; it took a long time to come, and in the meantime his terrible situation went through his mind, in the fullest detail! . . . Very pleasant breakfast in the *salon,* with a view of "the theater," always hope. [*In margin:* "An article entitled 'Mozartiana' reminds us of the wretchedness of Mozart's final year—quite terrible and upsetting; R. says it could not be otherwise in this world of ours. I find it much more difficult to understand his friends than the outside world."] Through all our miseries I see in my mind the *Three Graces,* see their convolutions translated into movement and hear the music from *Tannhäuser,* and the lovely sounds and moving limbs bring solace to my heart! — R. plays *Parsifal* (the "Good Friday Music") before breakfast. He works, and at lunch says jokingly that he is not obliged to say on what. In the afternoon we go for a walk in the little wood opposite, but R. finds the steep paths all the more of a strain since he was not able to sleep in the afternoon. But the site pleases him, and in the evening we experience a few happy hours, made unforgettable by the fact that R. plays to us the beginning of the Adagio from the 9th, and [Schubert's] *"Sei mir gegrüsst"* is also played. We read about the cathedral in Burckhardt and discover in his supercilious, coldly dismissive tone traces of his influence on Nietzsche. R. says, "From where does he get these rules which enable him to criticize the builders of the cathedral, for instance?" — R. read the scene in *Numancia* where the boy throws himself from the tower. [*Enclosed a postcard from the president of an American theater society; see notes.*]

Sunday, August 29 Mosquitoes ruin the night for us! . . . R., severely affected by it, faces the day in a spirit of disgruntlement, for if he does not sleep at night, he is usually unable to rest during the afternoon. Gray skies dominate the day, but R. decrees a walk through the vineyards, and this turns out to be very delightful and beneficial. In the evening he reads to us the 4th act of *Faust*, Part Two. When at the end Lusch admits to me that she has been unable to follow it, R. says she is quite right, for the main points are dealt with so incidentally and fleetingly that one needs only to breathe heavily to lose the thread; and all the details are so painfully drawn out—the description of hills and valleys, then the Court ceremonies and the two appearances of the three mighty men. But the monologue and the following scene between Mephisto and Faust produce all their old effect, and the scene between Mephisto and the student, which R. read beforehand, enchants us anew.

Monday, August 30 With the help of ventilation, *sogni tranquille,* net curtains around the beds, etc., we procure ourselves a very good night, and, relieved, I set out in the morning with the children on a quest for art treasures. First of all we look at the fine altar and the *Sibyl* in Fontegiusta; the latter fresco brings home to me the impossibility of basing a school on a man of genius; in the main figure Peruzzi, under the influence of M[ichel]angelo, seems to me to have produced something which goes almost beyond his own abilities, but in the process the whole style of an epoch has eluded him; having once caught hold of sublimity, he—and then all others after him—lost forever the sense of beauty and fine proportion. I should describe this *Sibyl* as transcendental in a popular sense. — In the noble and simple spaces of S. Domenico, on the other hand, we discover in the *Saint Catherine* with the stigmata a full manifestation of inspiration. After this I find it difficult to look at anything else, and the three female figures remain in my mind as an eternal exhortation to nobility. — While we were gone, R. wrote to Prof. Schrön, and he is in good and cheerful spirits, even if he always tends to greet the return of the sightseers with a certain amount of irony! — At lunch an article by Tappert gives rise to many jokes. "People are fighting over the degree of my divinity," R. says laughingly. A Bohemian (Prokrok) declares that it would be a very good thing if all writings except the *Ring des Nibelungen* were destroyed by fire, for then one would be able to study this work unhindered; he also says that the reason he does not call Wagner a god is that all the gods are too puny. And E. von Hagen asks what the entire world of women signifies compared with these three notes (from Eva's motive). Fictitious realities. — In the evening he reads to us the 5th act of *Faust* up to [*left blank*], giving us unqualified pleasure.

Tuesday, August 31 Unfortunately, through the negligence of the servants, another mosquito-ruined night! On top of that wet weather— many reminders of the North! — At breakfast R. again comes to speak of his "school" and the absurdity of it, since nobody, nobody at all, has so far learned even a single tempo from him, and he says that people can only learn from what they discover for themselves—a person who for years has heard Beethoven played in the wrong tempo will not suddenly hit upon the right one by reflecting and under- standing and reasoning. Or at least not unless he has been given the example from the start; anyone, for instance, who heard Weber con- ducting his *Freischütz* would have the tempi stamped on his mind. — The fine arts provoke him into some bitter statements: For whom did these painters work? For the worst men of their time. Whereas music addresses itself, rather, to the hearts of the people. — He also takes no pleasure in the King's proclamation in connection with the Wittelsbach jubilee, for he says, "There is not a true word in all these things, either." — Friend Rubinstein comes to visit us, and we show him the cathedral, the *libreria*. I show R. the *Saint Catherine,* and it seems to me that it makes some impression on him, though he says it is not ascetic enough, too round, too colorful; it is precisely this unimpassioned mildness which I find so moving, her gentle resignation is uplifting. In the evening Rub. plays to us music from the 3rd act of *Parsifal;* before that (before supper) the minuet and allemande from *Don Giovanni* together with R., and R. says that Mozart undoubtedly visualized different rooms for the various dances to be played in: "But who would have provided the poor fellow with the necessary scenery?" Some Schopenhauer, then discussion on the nature of matter. — I have to listen to much joking from R. over the fact that I was so extraordinarily moved at seeing the *Saint Catherine* again! . . .

(R. was very worn out after his walk from the post office to the cathedral, but he found the sight of the great square entertaining.)

Wednesday, September 1 A good night for R. He wakes up after it and jokes about my stigmata. Friend Rub.'s departure brings him to the subject of his own situation. He says he is sick to death of the *Nibelungen;* now that he has released it to all the theaters, a manager in Königsberg is demanding it; instead of simply refusing, he has to negotiate with him, since he needs the money. This is why he wants to go to America, he says, to earn money and at least to keep *Parsifal* unencumbered. Departure of friend R. Recently, discussing his unevennesses, R. said, "One cannot just let him go, because he will not go!" R. writes to Richter, demanding an engagement for Jäger. In the morning he ruled lines, and he says how remote orchestration now seems to him. In the afternoon we go for a walk along the highway with the children, a refreshing, German walk. In the evening Pepino sings folk songs to us; R. then plays something from *La Muette,* pointing out the tremendous difference and what an artist adds to a folk melody.

Thursday, September 2 R. wakes up saying, "What rubbish! It is at Christmas," and he tells me we had been with friend Joukowsky in the morning, the bell rang, and I said, "Ah, that will be someone bringing me good wishes on my birthday," whereupon R. was beside himself for having forgotten it: "Is it on September 29?" "Yes." "I am going mad, I cannot remember dates any more." . . . Then awakening. This fills me once more with strange and pleasant feelings. On the previous evening, wanting a frame, I remembered that I did not have the wherewithal to buy it, wondered whether I should request it for my name day, then reflected that, since my name day (September 27) does not mean anything to R., it must in consequence pass unrecognized. — Talking of Christmas, he says he will be giving me only spiritual gifts, since he has no money. — In town with the children. R. rules lines. Over coffee he tells us a curious story: in Dresden, when, before the first performance of *Rienzi,* he was completely penniless, Herr Schletterer, founder of the Leipzig Gallery and an intimate friend of his sister Luise, sent him through her 6 pairs of yellow kid gloves which had been made for him in Paris and were too big! . . . No walk—R. remains in the garden with the children, while I write letters; Hans is said to be ill again in Munich! — Conversation in the evening, R. keeps coming back to the disgraceful decisions of the Berlin Congress, then he expresses his pleasure in the brave Chileans; talking about architecture in general, which follows from a sketch of the cathedral as a study for *Parsifal,* he puts forward the conjecture that the term "Gothic" originated in Spain, that the Gothic style in the Gothic realms of the

North arose through contact with the Arabs, it spread from there to France and then to Germany, and for that reason the term is quite correct. — He gives energetic expression to his aversion to turning the Last Supper into a theatrical performance in the Mass, and when we wonder how it was possible for the very evil power exerted by the church to be supported even by great rulers, he says, "There are very deep-seated reasons for that."

Friday, September 3 R. slept very well, and since the weather is splendid, he proposes a drive. He is looking well, and we anticipate our day gaily. In the morning he comes to my room to tell me that he finds my article good. He does so with such lavish words of praise that I should feel oppressed by them if his love for me did not shine through them all and bid me accept praise joyfully, even when it is extravagant and undeserved. — (Today Mass was said in our chapel; Fidi ran along to watch, a paletot over his shirt, but the sacristan caught sight of his bare legs through the balustrade, and he had to leave.) R. is very merry at lunch, and when I mention the roses Pepino brought me, R. declares that Joukowsky sent them in the vessel containing the flowers of the nun whose appearance at the window Ritter Toggenburg was always awaiting! — Glorious walk to the Osservanza monastery; return by a very lovely path which gives us an enchanting view of the town and its surroundings. The reward of this outing is Robbia's altar in the monastery, which also pleases R. — In the evening conversation about this splendid art, so soulful and naïve. Unfortunately in the monastery a veritable caterwauling from the monks, whose rough peasant voices are truly horrifying. — R. comes to talk about Renan's and Gfrörer's interpretations of the Resurrection, prefers that of the latter, whom he finds the most sensitive of writers in his handling of religious matters. He observes that one cannot overestimate the burning glow of ecstasy at times when a new religion is emerging. — Letter from friend Feustel with a note from Hans, who is giving 12,000 marks to the fund, on the assumption that he will no longer be able to play the piano. . . . [*Letters from Feustel and Hans von Bülow enclosed; von Bülow, writing on August 31 from Bad Lieben-stein, states that he is suffering from neuralgia.*]

Saturday, September 4 R. gets up feeling very unwell, and since he thinks it is an attack of dysentery, I send for the doctor; he says it is not dysentery, but he finds that R. has a temperature and prescribes bismuth, laudanum, and rest. The last of these does R. so much good that he gets up in the evening and talks in a lively way (about the Franco-Prussian War).

Sunday, September 5 Not a good night, R. got up 5 times and was running a temperature! — In such ways have the joys of Friday had to be paid for! When we spoke about that yesterday, he said, "Life is a task." — Today, too, the doctor is not at all disquieted, but what help is that? I see him looking tired, his dear features pale and drawn! . . . He spends the whole day quietly lying down, I with him, finally reading to him a story by Tieck (*"Der Geheimnisvolle"*) which the children begged from the clergyman who says Mass in our house and talks to them and welcomes them in a very friendly manner. A former tutor with the Strozzis, he has been without occupation since the dissolution of the monasteries, has built himself a house with a chapel in the vicinity of our house, lives there with a weak-minded abbot, and now travels around (Spain, England, Egypt); he knows Bavaria well, possesses, among other things, the collected *Fl[iegende] Blätter,* knows all of R.'s works, and would have come to Bayreuth if he had had sufficient means. We laugh over this acquaintanceship of the children's and make use of his richly variegated and, it seems, rather unusual library. The story is unfortunately very flat; although its subject should have interested us, we do not finish it. In the evening R. seems to me to be running a temperature.

Monday, September 6 R. slept well and is feeling better. We rest together side by side in the papal bed until eleven o'clock; in the course of our conversation, when I call him "my angel" in my usual way, he says, "There are fallen angels and good angels, but no sick ones." I: "Somebody has to take care of the normal courtesies." He: "You can always find words for your feelings, but I find none for my pleasure in you," and to this he links so much, so many things that cannot be repeated in words, that even now I do not dare think of them myself. — At my request to take good care of himself, he settles down on the day bed (the striped one) and reads the clergyman's collected *Fl. Blätter:* "This is my favorite way of communing with the age in which I live, it gives me the best picture of it, and the drawings are excellent." — Yesterday a poem by E. Geibel in celebration of Sedan aroused utter disgust, and today a "Germania" in the *Illustrirte* the same feeling; R. says, "I have only to see a fellow in a winged helmet and I feel sick." — And the description of the battle itself produces from him an outburst of indignation: "The dead horses alone are enough! And it all shows the barbaric times in which we live." — The Emperor's latest speech to the army, which ends with the words that his final thoughts will always be for the army, evokes from R. the exclamation, "I should have thought for the ballet—a person like that is nothing more than a dim-witted soldier, and that's about all they know!" [*Wagner's words obliterated in ink by an unknown hand.*] He wonders how to save Fidi from having to do military service—through naturalization elsewhere? Continual thoughts of America, above all in order to gain independence for himself and particularly for *Parsifal,* from which he cannot expect much anyway, since he does not wish it to be performed. And since one has so little protection in foreign lands, he says, it would be best if only the piano score were to appear during his lifetime. And perhaps the King would understand that *P.* is to be performed only in Bayreuth, not on a stage where *Flick und Flock* would be done the following day. And in that way Bayreuth's position would be safeguarded. But for all this America will be necessary, for he is already in debt to Feustel and has to sign his current account "to your credit." — In the morning we intended to finish the Tieck story, but it was impossible. And yet the subject should not have been uninteresting. R. tells me that he has many times heard people expressing views such as that we owe everything to France; he agrees with me when I say that I can feel nothing but profound pity for Germany's fate, for all its good and great qualities have been exposed to exploitation, and we sorrowfully realize that it would above all have needed good princes, since its outlook has always been loyally monarchical, even up to the present day. "They" (the Germans) "were the only originals in Europe (since the ancient world)." — R. is amused by Rothschild's request for an audience with the Emperor in order to explain to him to what extent the Jews in Germany are endangered, and he says with a certain satisfaction, "I have played some part in that." However, he does not see much significance in the movement. The news that Bismarck has now become minister of commerce is greeted only with a shrug of the shoulders—it is just to push through the tariffs, on grain actually imported to avert the threat of starvation! And on top of that, all these factions in the Reichstag! R. counts them all up—no other country has anything like it. . . . R. is not yet taking his meals with us, but in the afternoon he feels well enough to sit in the garden, and in the evening he has supper with us, and once again we are all together in gay spirits. The children show us their drawings of the cathedral— Fidi will become an architect and Loldi a painter! R. says he will present Bayreuth with a fountain designed by Fidi, but first he will have to earn some money. Delight in our stay here. Much talk about items in the *Fl. Blätter;* we announce our intention of bringing out a Wahnfried magazine every month, and when in speaking I make a slip of the tongue—instead of *"Peitschen-Knall"* ["crack of a whip"] I say *"Kneitschen-Pall"*—it is laughingly decided to call the magazine that. — Jokes about my preoccupation with Saint Catherine bring the conversation around to a serious consideration on R.'s part of the nature of a saint; the question was raised (by Jouk.) whether cleanliness was not reconcilable with it. R.: "In fact it is not, for the saint sees himself as a

dead person, kept here on earth a little longer through the will of God."
He tells the story of Saint Francis and the pigs: "The Pope realized
then that he could not be lightly dismissed." — I append to that the
story of his running after a robber to whom the porter had refused
entry, kneeling before him and begging him to enter. And when Jouk.
declares that other people, not saints, might also do the same, admit a
robber into their house, R. says, "Yes, but not run after him, kneel
before him, admit to being worse than he is." He touches on the
difference between the saints and Christ, whose life in Galilee he
described to me in the morning as "a noble idyll," and he goes on to
talk of the impressions which moved Buddha to renunciation, and of
the sickness which made Saint Francis see the whole world as if
through a veil. The saints were certainly not people of unusually great
intelligence, he says, but they had enormously warm hearts. He talks
about this with great warmth, interspersing now and again various
items from the *Fl. Blätter.* Thus, after I have finished telling the story of
the saint and the robber, he says: "A sentry challenges a passing
captain: 'Who goes there?' The captain, deep in thought, gives no
reply; the sentry fires and misses: 'Three days' detention for missing
me,' cries the captain." We also discuss the utter confusion saints
cause when they interfere in worldly matters; and how—according to
R.—the world has always been getting worse and worse, for in earlier
times the brutality had been open and honest, whereas now hypocrisy
prevails, particularly in the church (he recalls the principle that it
must not shed blood, so it burned people instead), and this is now so
great that people are not aware any longer of the true state of things,
but believe we are still making progress. — R.'s delight in the country
here.

Tuesday, September 7 With the words "This is scandalous!" R.
wakes up, and since I hear him laughing repeatedly, I ask him what is
the matter. He tells me that he was dreaming of a performance of
Tannhäuser under Richter; the bass clarinet was missing, and in consequence the singers felt obliged to speak, rather than sing; he had still
hoped that at least the *"Abendstern"* would be sung, but no, and
Richter did not seem at all disturbed. — At breakfast we come back to
our conversation about the saints, and R. says, "We artists can only
scratch the surface, particularly the painter, who has to express martyrdom with folds—the musician perhaps delves a little deeper!" — R. is
not dissatisfied with his state of health; on the contrary. For lunch we
invite our friendly "spirit," whose combined house and church are
exactly what is now happening almost everywhere in Italy, that is to
say, the monks set themselves up privately and gather together again.
In the afternoon R. and I go for a walk in the vineyards adjoining our

Benedictine monks' church. Delight in the countryside, which has the characteristics, R. says, that so enchanted him in Lombardy when he visited it from Switzerland. — He is in good and cheerful spirits, and many memories from his childhood and youth come back to him, among them his brother Albert's debut and how a Dr. Marcus, who was courting his sister Cäcilie, confided to him weepingly during a walk that he could not marry her, since he was a Jew and his practice depended on Jews. In the evening our conversation turns to the army and its world; we tell the story of Schrenck, and R. observes, "In the army one might perhaps still find uniquely sturdy and proud characters, but they would peter out in such isolated cases." — When Jouk. mentions the Court, R. says he cannot think of a single one among all the princes who would be worth depicting. Altogether there is nobody in that sphere who could calmly consider the questions which occupy us. — He tells about his evening with Bismarck, which never went beyond the confines of parliamentary gossip. "There are only two people who seriously discuss serious questions—C. Frantz and I," he adds, half in fun and half in earnest. — At my request we take up *The Sorrows of Werther,* and everything in it charms and moves us. Just the exclamation "Klopstock" tempts us to laugh heartily, but even the tears on the grave of the unknown man, which our friend Joukowsky finds somewhat superfluous, we are able to interpret to ourselves as an expression of a great and mildly melancholy awareness of the ways of the world.

Wednesday, September 8 R. had a good night and is not dissatisfied with his condition, declares that a beneficial crisis has taken place. At breakfast he comes back to *Werther,* says: "It is Goethe's work *par excellence*—all the rest is a sort of covering up of the main point. This is how a poet must present himself to the world, and really he should never have written anything else, for even *Götz* is a kind of diversion. Shakespeare and I, we could do many things, for we always held to the main point. And his" (Werther's) "feelings are entirely without bitterness, for instance, his objection to bad moods, whereupon Lotte complains that he always takes everything so much to heart—with such a character Werther was bound to come to grief." — R. rules lines in his score during the morning. At lunch, when we are talking about Fidi's and Jouk.'s journey to Perugia, we come to the subject of N[adine] Helbig: "Such people lack concentration," R. says, "they know too many things." — I showed him the ideas about Christ and the saints which I had written down, he says: "I understand you all right, but the others won't. For one can only visualize redemption as a negation." — After lunch he continues ruling lines, then we go for a walk together through the vineyards, taking great delight in our splendid surroundings. In the evening we continue reading *Werther,* still moved by the beauty of the book. But R. is annoyed by Lotte: "I suppose she has to be like that, but it is incredible; she would have been quite content to see Werther pining away for fifty years, would have become a mother every year and enjoyed having him at her side as a sort of lovesick swain!" — In the evening he grumbles a little about his condition, saying the crisis is wearing him out.

Thursday, September 9 R. is not very satisfied with his condition, but he is cheerful, and when he notices Fidi's frequently open mouth, he says to him, "Beethoven would have composed much more if he had kept his mouth shut." [*The foregoing words, from* "and when he notices" *on, obliterated in ink by an unknown hand.*] I speak to friend J. about the portrait of R. which I so much want to have, R. says, "It should have been done ten years ago, now there are too many signs of old age." — R. rules lines in the morning. An attack of dizziness prevents me from going to lunch, in the afternoon R. comes to me, we read the poem "*An Werther,*" and R. laughs heartily over the line "A fearful death has brought thee fame." But when I read to him the "Elegy," he stops listening, saying it is conceivable that one might feel the need to define a serious relationship poetically, but such things one should then keep to oneself. He settles me down on the balcony after a thunderstorm has cleared and refreshed the air splendidly. In the evening we read *Werther* to the end, I as far as Ossian and R. from there on (cutting short the embarrassing quotation) to the conclusion, all of us still greatly affected.

Friday, September 10 R. slept well, gets up in good spirits and returns to the bedroom, saying it is nice here, particularly when one knows there is someone there who "means something" to one—this happy expression is followed by the remark, "You are Werther and Lotte in one, passionate like him and sensible like her!" — He finds the narration in *Werther* excellent, Werther's outpourings in the middle section, on the other hand, rather long-drawn-out. — He thinks it incomprehensible of Lotte not to say to Albert when he arrives that something has happened, and to tell him of her first meeting with W. — R. asks plaintively whether Fidi is devoid of wit—he seems not to like it when one makes witticisms. I visit the picture gallery and have to put up with much joking about my preference for gilded backgrounds! Another thunderstorm, and between times the *Fl. Blätter,* which R. finds extremely entertaining; he tells us a series of anecdotes from it and is much amused, among other things, by the statement that someone has the writer's itch. Another thunderstorm, no going outdoors, his work still ruling lines. Toward evening R. plays the various national anthems (also his "Nikolai" hymn); as he is playing the

"*Marseillaise*" I am once again struck by its unreligious, popular flavor. R. says, "With that they have brought many thousands of people to their feet, and we Germans have no folk song like it—just think of '*Die Wacht am Rhein*,' which they sang *in Versailles!*" I mention the "*Kaisermarsch*": "A very good thing," says R., "that so little notice is taken of it." — In the evening I ask for *Tasso*, and R. reads the first scene; but he finds its chatter, as he calls it, repulsive, and he puts it down. "All in falsetto—not a single genuine tone," he exclaims. He goes on to *Egmont* and is utterly delighted by it; in particular the scene with [William of] Orange is quite shattering.

Saturday, September 11 No mosquitoes. [*Sentence based on untranslatable word play omitted.*] — Much merriment over his description of the scene between the two women in *Tasso*, both so wise, so good, all just vapor and hot air, "in which there is no place for a donkey like Tasso"—and all the time one knows how things really were! — He praises *Egmont*, though he feels that such crowd scenes would have been unthinkable without Shakespeare. Shakespeare or the *Nibelungen*, Hans Sachs—those are the two directions. He takes *Tancred* with him to read, in order at long last to acquaint himself with the subject, but the *Fl. Blätter* prevents him from getting down to it. He rules 12 pages. I go with the children to look at various things in town and have to put up with jokes from him about it. In the afternoon we take a splendid walk, R., I, and the children, through the vineyards, and he is not tired by it, or by reading aloud; he finished *Egmont* in the presence of the deeply affected children. Nobody could possibly describe his facial expression, the tone of his voice, the movement of his hands, as he speaks the final words. And everything in it delights us, he thinks it is almost the most perfect thing Goethe ever did. But he does say that on the stage Klärchen's scene amid the people makes little effect—it is very tragic, but almost too vivid. He emphasizes its fine humanity, its complete lack of empty phrases. This time it all seems to me lovely, I am moved, even by Brackenburg. Only Ferdinand seems somewhat spun out, but R. feels Egmont had to have someone to talk to in prison.

Sunday, September 12 He got up once during the night and is somewhat agitated; he also speaks of a soreness in his ear, he fears it might be a small abscess! — Talked a lot at breakfast about *Egmont;* he finds it curious the way the scenes suddenly break off; for example, the scene between the regent [Margaret of Parma] and Machiavell, they could have gone on talking together for a long time; also the way in which [William of] Orange comes to Egmont, Egmont to Alba, and they start talking right away without any introductory greeting: "Schiller was much more at home with the dramatic form." He laughs over the manner in which *Egmont* was received in Weimar and says: "They must have asked themselves whether the relationship was a platonic one. But seriously," he adds, "there is no way of telling whether it was not just a need in Egmont for an intimate love relationship. It is not openly expressed as with Faust and Gretchen, where all the power of sensuality is depicted." He rules lines and is in good spirits. Toward evening, following the thunderstorm, we all set out on a walk which gives us much pleasure. R. is delighted with the countryside, its richness, its beautiful lines. In the evening Schopenhauer's chapter "A Man's Place in the Estimation of Others," read aloud by R. — When we are talking about the attachment of certain Jews to R., he says, "Yes, they are like flies—the more one drives them away, the more they come."

Monday, September 13 R. had a somewhat restless night, but he rises in cheerful spirits, goes to bang on the children's door and imitate the thunderstorm, hears Eva and Loldi crowing in competition with each other, is pleased with them all (yesterday very much with Fidi and the stability of his character), and settles down to some ruling even before breakfast. When I greet him, he says, "I have the strength to work on it only because I have made up my mind to go to America and thus achieve what I want—to free the work, to stage it only in Bayreuth, and to become completely independent." He intends to take all the children. — He is hurt by the King's failure to reply to him about replacing the theater director, hopes nevertheless to get from him the promise that, if *Parsifal* is performed in the Munich Court theater, it will be for himself alone. — Lovely walk with R. through the vineyards, we drink milk still warm from the cow, and I have the pleasure of seeing him looking well. [*In margin:* "He reads *Tancred* to the end! — Then he is pleased with the words of a Frenchman about *Tristan*. Then he is also pleased with Fidi's drawings inside the cathedral."] — In the evening he reads [Goethe's] *Die Geschwister* to us. And all day long he is in good spirits. The picture of Saint Catherine which he finds in my room brings from him the exclamation, "Heavens alive, to be surrounded by such women!," and when, in the evening, we come to talk about Brackenburg, whom nobody cares for except me, and I wonder what trade he might have pursued, I receive from R., who usually agrees with me, a reply which brings forth peals of laughter: "A bandage maker." —

Tuesday, September 14 R. slept well, and he works before breakfast; during this he tells me that he was just about to send me a message saying that the Pope was summoning me, to Avignon! — Earlier he had played the spinning song from *La Dame Blanche,* and also the ballade, and he says that such things are peculiar to the French, something in which no other nation can compare with them, also such figures as Gleizès. Then he brings up Shakespeare and says people ought to perform one of his plays and then, having thus been brought into very close contact with the horrors of life, go to Holy Communion. And especially the historical plays—they ought to be seen every year. One might almost say that a play like *Egmont* owes its origin to a mood, a philosophical mood with which one can wholeheartedly agree; but in Shakespeare there is neither mood nor purpose, a veil is torn aside, and we see things as they are. Particularly in the histories. In *Hamlet* we find a situation similar to our own: we recognize the wretched limitations of our animal existence and, not having the power to change it, leave it as it is and take refuge in irony. — I then told him that this was why I did not like to talk about perceived truths which I was not permitted to obey. "One only does so in order to impart one's perception to others." — And, in between all this, constant jokes from the *Fl. Blätter*. I feel rather unwell at lunch and finally have to be borne off in a faint. Perhaps the thundery atmosphere. — I recover so quickly that I am able to go for a drive with R., which gives him much delight, since he is growing more and more attached to this locality. In the evening conversations about the Russo-Turkish War and the Franco-Russian War; R. remarkably well informed on both. — He tells of a mass emigration of Englishmen from two provinces to America. —

Wednesday, September 15 R. slept well, at breakfast a great deal about the children and rules of education. Then R. talks about the socialists, who have just been holding a meeting in Switzerland, and he says, "I am amazed by the stupidity of their program, always just state and no religion, no faith at all." An article in *Italie* reproducing a conversation between Bismarck and the French ambassador, in which peace was offered with a view to restricting Russia's and England's advance toward world dominion, astonishes R. greatly, he laughs and says: "Incidentally, that is C. Frantz's idea, of which he wrote in the *B. Blätter*. We are still ruling the world!" —

Thursday, September 16 At 4 o'clock arrival of my father from Rome. We all go to fetch him, in splendid weather. R. very sweet: "They can't get rid of the gay old sparks," he says.

Friday, September 17 We drive (without R., who is ruling lines) with my father to view the cathedral, and here I become aware how different R. is, how youthfully energetic he has remained. My father is all but unmoved. But our life together is happy and gay, R.'s wit helps overcome all difficulties, he calls himself Werther, Jouk., Brackenburg, and says my father is Albert and Egmont combined. But he is somewhat vexed that our conversation never seems to go beyond personalities.

Saturday, September 18 R. slept well, but the very cool weather makes him wish increasingly for Venice. — A letter from Malwida, in which she speaks of the extent to which the Reformation is to blame for the dullness of the German people, provokes him into an indignant denial: as it looks to us now, he says, the Reformation was deplorable, but it is not the idea which was at fault. Luther wanted to win the Pope over to the Reformation. — R. here shows all his greatness and the deep roots he shares with his people—to my utmost delight. — He is reading Mérimée's *Le Faux Démétrius* with much enjoyment and says he, more than anyone else, was on Russia's side, but it behaved so stupidly during the war. (Whist with my father.)

Sunday, September 19 I had to disturb R.'s night's rest somewhat because of my toothache, but he soon fell asleep again. He continues ruling lines. — But cool, almost cold weather! Amicable conversations about this and that with my father, who today and yesterday played piano duets with Lulu. — In the evening a slight misunderstanding; my father observes that R. thinks nothing of his piano playing; R. at first very vexed, but then he puts things right in his own way, and it all ends gaily and peacefully. (The day before yesterday R. aired his views about professors in the most delightfully amusing way and ended with the words, "If I were emperor, the first thing I should do would be to close all the universities.") — (On Wednesday, when R. was looking at a picture of the adoration of the infant Christ, he said: "In childhood all these signs of veneration, the shepherds and the kings and the angels—where were they all later on? That's what happened to Mozart.") (On this same Wednesday R. talked about the butterfly, "this consummate image of the movement which in fact never dies.")

Monday, September 20 A good night for R. — But a wet, cold day. This adds very much to our resolve to leave here. Discussion about my father, R. says, "He has been taught to distrust me, no one has ever been allowed to say even a single word against him." He rules lines industriously and ruminates on his American plan. At lunch he calls my father to account in his cordial way, and the result of his truthfulness is a merry mood. My father has acquainted me with three Petrarch sonnets he set to music: "*Pace non trovo,*" "Benedetto," and [*left blank; see notes*]. "Benedetto" in particular pleases me greatly, I tell R. about it, and he gets my father to play it to him; then he says to him with much warmth, "I am glad to see something of your worldly side once again." — In the evening R. and my father play so the children can dance; R. is delighted with the skill with which Siegfried dances (particularly the mazurka). After that whist, with many remarks on R.'s part, he keeps teasing me about Saint Catherine of Siena. At the end of the day he observes that such rainy days have their good side, providing an opportunity for more social pastimes.

Tuesday, September 21 R. slept well, tells me it is a lovely day, and he is pleased, not only by the sun, but by an inspiration for the 3rd act of *Parsifal,* the prolonging of the clarinet after the violin, he writes it down and is very cheerful. Before lunch he sees the *Smaller Catechism* among Eva's books and is so affected by the foreword that after lunch he reads it to my father and me and exclaims, "Luther was the greatest patriot of all!" In the afternoon we go for a walk through the vineyards; unfortunately his inclinations entice him away from the wide paths, and that results in fatigue in spite of the most splendid sunset. In the evening my father delights us with his playing of two Beethoven sonatas (*quasi Fantasia* and D Major), which leads R. back to the crazy idea of a "school"—who could ever learn to play these works that way?

Wednesday, September 22 R. had a cold and restless night, Italian beds annoy him; and he is vexed that today we cannot have our cozy breakfast room to ourselves. "With me it is always paroxysms," he says, "indifference is unknown to me, and everything is a paroxysm, either of joy or of pain." — In the afternoon R. and I take a very lovely walk to a country house, and we are often overwhelmed by the beauties of the heavens and the earth! In the evening my father plays his "Dante" to us, R. has serious reservations with regard to the material. — We then play whist. — Talking of the Prelude to *Parsifal,* R. says, "Nothing here and nothing there—it was from nothing that God made the world." What he means is that he has simply placed his themes side by side, like a preacher his Bible passages. — When my father goes off to bed, he asks for Luther's *Smaller Catechism* again.

Thursday, September 23 R. had a good night, and today he is quite content that we are three at breakfast. To my father he says, "I shall still make a Lutheran out of you." — To me he says he would like to see a catechism drawn up for Schopenhauer; he has seen the need for it in the work of a Prof. Volkelt, who wrote him a very nice letter but at the same time sent along such a confused paper on Hölderlin that one cannot help feeling strongly that a correct and disciplined knowledge of Schopenhauer is urgently required—for example, of the chapter "On Apparent Deliberateness in the Fate of an Individual." Went for a drive with the children, R., and my father, first of all to the Palazzo Pubblico; it gives me very great delight that R. admires Sodoma's Christ (*Resurrection*); otherwise he is interested much more in the architectural aspects than in anything else. He is enchanted with the view from the new churchyard and delights in the pleasing architecture;

we finish our drive with a visit to the cathedral, which as ever exerts its magic on us. And on our return home, the departing sun and the sky set the crown on these impressions, and R. speaks in praise of our stay here. — In the evening my father plays several pieces by Chopin to us, and a game of whist is appended to calm us down, though R. and I hardly participate in it. Unfortunately a glass of ale he drank in the afternoon at the hotel did not agree with him.

Friday, September 24 R. did not have a good night, twice he woke up pursued by the evil dream which always plagues him when he is not well: that I am about to leave him. This time the children also joined in, looking at him with spiteful expressions and telling him they would probably be seeing him once a month. At breakfast with my father we talk about his departure, the country to be traveled through, dreary around Rome; R. tells the story of the marshes, and via this oppression of the spirit of courageous peoples we come to poor Germany; R. describes the Thirty Years' War and exclaims, "We were treated disgracefully!" Today I finish R.'s article (revising the proofs) and find it so utterly splendid that I cannot help telling him so repeatedly. R. says he likes hearing what I have to say about it, for he always has doubts about the possible effect of his literary writings. He finishes ruling his lines today, thus has completed what is actually the most important preliminary work in his score, and what remains, he says, is just the pleasant part—and the final joy. We walk a little in the vineyards. R. enjoys the countryside, but also the prospect of going to Venice, particularly since there he will not see the leaves falling. — But on the whole he is not in the best of moods, and he does not come to supper—nevertheless, my father, through what he says about *Parsifal*, gives him the urge to play something from it, and after supper almost the whole of the third act is played by my father and divinely sung by R. — "Scarcely have I discovered a sensible wife when she must turn out to be your daughter and for that reason placed beyond my reach—" R. says jokingly to my father.

Saturday, September 25 R. again had a bad night; having to rise early for my father's departure, then the hasty final corrections to his article—all this puts him out of humor. All the same, he gaily brings me—"Tasso to the Princess"—the ruled score, 334 pages. He also reads Schopenhauer to me, on the artist's imitation of Nature, and when I start to talk about his article, he expresses the wish that the *B. Blätter* might gradually take a different path, and that the contributors, modeling themselves on this article, might proclaim their intention of doing battle on all fronts—not merely for the Society of P.'s, but as a public periodical. — Regarding the passage in Schop. on Gothic art, I tell him that it seems to me unjust to judge this only from its outward aspect; it emerged out of the jumble of houses in medieval times, and the Gothic builders erected their churches outward from the inside. He agrees with me and in the evening says that I really should write something for the *B. Bl.* on Gothic art! — My father's character gives rise to many observations between us, and indeed not cheerful ones, since we are feeling a little tired. However, we go for a walk in the afternoon and again stray onto the stubble fields, which is hard going for us, but it does not prevent our taking pleasure in many things; for example, R. suddenly points to a peasant pushing his barrow across the sun-drenched horizon: "A picture of antiquity," he exclaims. And all the time talking about Schopenhauer, then about the Etruscans, who, R. declares, must have resembled the Indians, a gentle, cultured people, honored in fabled stories by the Greeks. Talking of architecture, he says palaces make no impression on him, since they consist of two stories of openwork, and two rows of windows, one above the other, rob space of its ideality; he would wish to see a fine window once and once only; but he has nothing against Gothic, castlelike palaces, he says, which allow one to imagine defending warriors—it is the Renaissance palaces which leave him unmoved. Thought of Fidi (who is now in Orvieto) and his talent for architecture; R. feels one should not allow this too much nourishment, as happened with my father's virtuosity, otherwise the other aspects would be too much neglected. — He talks of electricity and hopes to see it used on the railroads, to reduce the number of coal workers. — A vegetarian menu earns his disapproval: "There is no point in all this playing about, ignoring religion." — I forget what in a recent conversation led me to make the remark, "There is no such thing as a depraved artist." Whereupon R.: "No, he might perhaps look that way and be misunderstood by many people, but depravity begins with artificiality, hypocrisy, and an artist is genuine." He then quotes the Indian proverb, "It is not badness which is bad, but mediocrity," etc.

Sunday, September 26 R. slept well, immediately on waking he begins to talk about the Indians, their culture and their meekness. — A gray day, but a happy breakfast. Thoughts of America; decision to save *Parsifal* at all costs, to allow Schott to publish only the piano score, for a payment of 50,000 marks. At lunch a temporary clouding of our bright sky through a joke of R.'s for which I am unable at first to find the correct response, and which the children also find surprisingly humorless; but the sky soon clears, and we gaily welcome Fidchen and Joukowsky, who have much to relate concerning Orvieto. I am much impressed with the photographs of Signorelli's frescoes, but R. is constantly put off by the subjects, though he remains fair to the artist. The façade of the O. cathedral strikes him as being more in the nature of theatrical scenery, bearing no relation to the rest of the building. Conversation in the evening, R. again gives vent to his antipathy toward the Romans in both ancient and more modern times— as oppressors of the civilized Italian peoples in the ancient world, as the embodiment of papacy in the modern one. (I fear I may have forgotten to note that R. gets much pleasure from the heads of the popes in the cathedral; he finds such ornamentation much better than "a Greek knot, which means nothing to us, though it certainly meant a lot to the ancient Greeks themselves.")

Monday, September 27 It is my delight to celebrate Saint Cosmas with a little gift to R.; he is much surprised by the work with Loldi (the letter C), and when Fidi now also comes out with a huge dome, R. laughs and observes that the children must be goblins. He does not realize that it is my name day, thinks it is his own, and this leads to much hilarity at the end of the day, when it comes to light. He starts on a letter to the King, while I look at a few more things in town and say farewell to lovely Siena. The French situation interests R. very much, he is glad that the good Ferry has managed to get a government together, and convinced that Gambetta will hatch out as many intrigues as he can; he says he has a good mind to write to Ferry, "*Après les Jésuites faites attention aux Juifs*" ["After the Jesuits, look out for the Jews"]. — In this connection many memories of Ferry, of Blandine, he finds a resemblance between her and me, which pleases me very much. "Just flashes," he says, "such things are in the spirit." — In the evening R. reads some passages from his biography to us, and he laughs over the fact that because of its light and flowing style, everything gives the appearance of having been nothing.

Tuesday, September 28 R. wakes up cheerfully with the remark, "In this bed there could have slept not only a pope, but the whole schism as well" (Pius VI once occupied our bedroom). But then the sight of the leaves turning yellow fills him with melancholy, and he wishes he were already in Venice, so as to miss the fall. In connection with his letter to the King, he thinks with a shudder of having to concern himself with singers, with the scene painters Döll and Quaglio, and he is vexed by the lack of resolution there. — Many thoughts of Venice, he recalls his favorite hero, Morosini, also Schulenburg. — Much at lunch about my father, impossible to describe him, I think. R. says, "Yes, one side of him would always be exaggerated, he eludes all the rules." He thinks I would be able to do it. — R. says he himself is not an original, which gives us cause for laughter and reflection. — In the afternoon he plays the *Midsummer Night's Dream* Overture and the *Egmont* Overture with Lusch; he still has some reservations about the beginning of the former, and about the trio in the march he says, "There he ran out of ideas!" — When I say that the *E[gmont]* O. will remain eternally young and popular, he says: "Yes—it is Klärchen, Egmont seen through Klärchen's eyes. The scene invoking the citizens —that is what inspired Beethoven, and this is as it should be; whoever tries to convey the many aspects of a drama one by one will come to grief; it must be tackled from a single viewpoint." — We stroll to the little cypress wood in a sharp north wind, carts in antique style please R. In the evening he is somewhat tired, but well, and he looks cheerful and full of health. He reads his biography to us, which leads to a discussion of Friederike Meyer; he agrees with me when I call her the most interesting of his female acquaintances. — (Yesterday at lunch he talked again about *Tasso* and said, "Goethe makes one doubt Tasso's character when, after showing Tasso's deep and genuine bitterness and having him put everything into this one feeling, he allows the Princess to feel nothing but the impropriety of such behavior, so that he then clings to Antonio." Previously I had also wished that, instead of hurrying off, she had cried "Tasso!" and collapsed—now, however, it seems to me to show the poet's inexorable veracity, which is stronger than himself. But R. says one can assume that he would have asked Schiller: How shall I end it, Schiller?) — A few more remarks about my father's diffuse character with its constantly recurring flashes of significance. — Pleasure in Ferry and the fact that a minister of education was made minister for foreign affairs: "I should like to see matters dealt with here as they are in France, and I should gladly give them Metz. They are going about things in the right way."

Wednesday, September 29 R. slept well. — A book by the younger A. Dumas, sent by my father, brings back to mind a description by the same author of the curious present society within a society. I ask R. if he does not feel that the seeds of a new religion could be planted in such a society (with the prospect of fervent reception), exactly as previously in Corinth. R. says, "But then money would have to be abolished, certain things would have to cease to be obtainable with money, and to that it seems to me the social economists are not paying sufficient attention." — Our landlord visits us and reveals so much hardness and miserliness with regard to his servants that R. is vexed over it all day long. — R. writes to friend W[olzogen] and invites him to Venice. He is cheerful at lunch, but soon afterward he feels tired, indeed in an ill humor, and since I am unable to go out with him on account of a toothache, he says, "Nobody wants anything to do with me." — It is cold, and he finds the whistling wind disagreeable. But in the evening he reads his biography to us. (A letter from Lenbach to Jouk. reveals that the former was in Paris; we wonder what he has been doing there; R. observes that, compared with Italy, Paris is what the bowl of punch was to the Englishman who wished to make himself drunk and tried one bottle of wine after another in vain.)

Thursday, September 30 R. had a good rest but is in poor spirits, and a suggestion I make to him—to allow Siegfried to see Ravenna with Jouk.—unfortunately irritates him greatly. He then observes that everything is making him melancholy, all his thoughts, the fact that he is not feeling well, the view from our rooms, and the remoteness of the town, indeed even the town itself, which has little to offer him— all this depresses him. He longs for Venice, and we pack and settle the inventory in haste. — (Yesterday he talked a lot about the false Demetrius, saying the Russians did not consider him genuine because he sprang agilely onto his horse, whereas "genuine" people always allowed themselves to be led!)

Friday, October 1 Up early; R. lively, plays the finale of the C Minor Symphony as a farewell! Glorious sunny day; six oxen pull our luggage, at ten o'clock in Florence. Very nicely accommodated in the Hôtel New York. In the afternoon a drive with R. and the children to S. Miniato, after R. tried to surprise us in the Loggia—unfortunately in vain, for we were in S. Marco and the Medici tombs. R. much delighted with the glorious church and particularly the wonderfully beautiful view. The cathedral gives me the impression of being the mother church. — The drive home is also very lovely (R. says he cannot understand what M[ichel]angelo's *David* is doing there in the square). In the evening our friend Buonamici, who makes us laugh with his very humorous description of his vain 12-hour wait for us in the railroad station at Pistoia.

Saturday, October 2 R. slept well, and if it had not been for the failure of another surprise he had prepared for us in the Pitti Gallery, this day would also have been a wonderful one. Toward evening he goes out with me, searches for a dress which caught his attention, finds it, and orders it for me; he then invites me to go to the Ciompi (beerhouse) with him, is pleased that I do so, and we then return home beneath a blazing sunset, to receive in the evening the news that we can now be accommodated tomorrow evening in ·Venice after all, which had at first seemed unlikely. Since R. insists on having a saloon carriage, he sets out with Lusch and is told at the station that we cannot have it until Monday, so we stay on in Florence.

Sunday, October 3 Early to the galleries with the children, met R. in the Boboli Gardens, which please R. enormously. In the afternoon we drive to Cascino, and in the evening R. begins *"Der Geisterseher"* in preparation for Venice.

Monday, October 4 Off early, unfortunately vexation at once, and a very great one for R., since the saloon carriage does not arrive—it takes him a long time to calm down; but gradually the journey restores his spirits, and the town of Padua, among other things, makes a very pleasant impression on him. At 4 o'clock in Venice. — Immediately went to look at the Palazzo Contarini, which pleases us, then got off at the Danieli and in the evening showed Lusch Saint Mark's Square.

Tuesday, October 5 A good night for R., who is glad to be in Venice. Very busy arranging the house while R. and the children are sightseeing. He is not entirely well toward evening and gives up an intended visit to the theater. (Two dreams of R.'s fall within these days, though I no longer know exactly when. In one of them he was supposed to marry his first wife, and he found it all the more embarrassing in that he had a relationship with me at the time. — In the other he was playing something he had just composed while I was sleeping, and in my sleep I made signs of disapproval—"Ah! Ah!"—and he himself thought his composition affected.)

Wednesday, October 6 Much to do in connection with the move; we have to spend another night in the hotel. Arrival of our friend Wolzogen, R. quickly explains the situation to him. — In the evening we move into Contarini, and all are satisfied with my little activities. Tesarini.

Thursday, October 7 R. slept well, but he is annoyed by the bad weather which greets W. We visit the Scuola di San Rocco; for him there is too much going on in the picture—Tintoretto's *Crucifixion*. — In the evening Pepino sings to us, then comes the first "Picture" from *Tristan* and the Prelude to *Parsifal*—to Tristan's yearning question Parsifal seems to me to be the answer! — This morning, when I quoted "She who kept silent pledges me to silence," R. said, "That is the realm of poetry, where everything has to be wrapped in cotton wool; the other, where it all bursts out, is music."

Friday, October 8 A day of pouring rain, Wolz. the bringer of bad luck! R. says to him gaily that he wishes him and Schemann to the Devil, for they are forcing him to keep on bothering himself with the Society of Patrons! — In the afternoon there is a ray of light on Saint Mark's Square; R. talks to W. about turning the *Blätter* into a public periodical, but this tires him and he decides to walk home in silence. In the evening he bids our friend a very warm farewell.

Saturday, October 9 Glorious weather, which R. enjoys with all his heart; his delight in the city is unbounded, whether going by boat or on foot. Reunion with Mimi, still the same friendly person. In the evening the 2nd piece from *Tristan*, by J. Rubinstein, after which R. sings some passages from it.

Sunday, October 10 I hand over my salute to the 10th, and R. is pleased with the missal-like Flower Maidens. I go by myself to the

Belle Arti, in spite of the rain, and afterward, beneath the arcades, with R. to a photographer's shop, where I show him a head of the Virgin Mary; it moves us both to tears. I say "Isolde." He says no, this shows much of the rapture of suffering, which Isolde was spared. Recently he said that ecstasies of this kind were based on sensuality, that is to say, sensuality was one grade, saintliness another, of a sort which gratified sensuality could never provide. I visit SS. Giovanni e Paolo with the younger children; the older ones are causing me concern, which I am able to bear only with the help of R.'s deep sympathy. In the evening he reads "*Der Geisterseher*," but he finds it tiring and we give it up.

Monday, October 11 As usual, out of doors twice with R., once at midday, once in the afternoon; in the afternoon we wander through the Merceria, and when I go into a shop to buy a muff for Lusch, R. bids me make haste; I start explaining to him that I shall need a little time, but he interrupts me and stops the whole thing in the most charming way by exclaiming, "How beautiful you are!" — In the evening he is so merry that he plays a joke on our friend Joukowsky, removing the lamps in his absence and allowing him to think we have all suddenly gone off to bed.

Tuesday, October 12 Lusch's birthday, I go with her to the Belle Arti to pay our respects to [Titian's] *Assumption*. At lunch R. greets her with the name Husch [flash] instead of Lusch. The Schleinitzes in the evening; R. takes Mimi aside and begs her to give some thought to Lulu's fate, because in our seclusion we can do nothing for her. Though I was of the opinion that his star would take care of everything, nevertheless it must be given every opportunity. Before the party we went to Dreher's.

Wednesday, October 13 R. as always rather worn out when our very close circle is widened. He arranges to meet the children, who have gone for a last swim in the Lido, on the Piazzetta; the fact that the gondola does not arrive there puts him into a great rage; when I beg his pardon and tell him what happened, he says I should always just let him rage, it is a need in him and he can listen to no reason, he is like Othello, whose fury was only made worse by Desdemona's innocence. And in his explanations of his state of mind he is unutterably kind and divine. In the afternoon we go on an outing in fine weather, and in the evening to the theater, to see Paesiello's *Barbiere di Siviglia;* the children enjoy it and we are amused by some drastic things in it.

Thursday, October 14 R. dreamed that I had had many objections to make concerning the *Nibelungen* and that I described my doubts in a twelve-page letter to him. Much amused by this absurdity, we embark on a splendid day. In the afternoon a trip to Murano, which brings many jokes from R., since he finds it ridiculous to leave Venice to see Murano; the cathedral makes him downright indignant, but Bellini's picture, particularly the Doge in it, attracts his earnest attention. In the evening Rub. plays the *Eroica* under R.'s very lively instruction, and afterward I read "The Children Next Door" from *Elective Affinities*. Certain words used by Goethe (such as "*Societät*") strike R. again and again as signs of his curious dependence.

Friday, October 15 R. reads to us the beginning of a letter from Wilhelm Meister to the Abbot, to draw our attention to the whimsicality of its style. We go to see S. Sebastiano, and it is R. who shows us the pictures in it, which he remembers from the year '58. In the evening a pleasant hour at Princess Hatzfeldt's with all the children; while Rub. plays the *Msinger* Prelude, R. acts out the scene between Walther and Eva with Mimi. When we return home, he tells me he cannot bear listening to his own music.

Saturday, October 16 R. dreamed that I went away, he following behind; running after the train, he cried frantically, "To Ansbach!" — I call for him with the punctuality which always puts us in good spirits, on the stroke of twelve, and we go to the Doge's Palace. Great impression of decadence. After lunch our conversation touched on women who smoke, and R., after energetically voicing his repugnance for it, says that it comes, however, from men who smoke in the presence of women, and altogether from their incorrect attitude toward women. — Today he has on his mind the allegretto theme of the C-sharp Minor Quartet (2nd tempo): "What a serene lament!" he exclaims, and, "A man who invents something like that I could worship as a god." — Excellent letter from Herr von Bürkel, saying that our matter is now settled, *Parsifal* assured for 1882, orchestra and chorus from Munich at our disposal. — We are still tired from yesterday, so unused are we to social occasions.

Sunday, October 17 R. slept well; I am somewhat worried on account of Lusch, R. tremendously kind and consoling. — He goes to the Belle Arti and returns with reservations about the *Assumption,* since he is so disturbed by God the Father in it; the encounter in the temple seems to him more perfect if she, striving toward and arousing sublimity, does not spoil it "with a blot." I read Schiller's poem "*Das Glück*" ["Fortune"] aloud, and R. finds it so beautifully directed at Goethe. Walk with R. and the children on the Riva, very, very lovely, but in the evening a visit to the theater is a complete disaster. —

[*End of the fifteenth book of the Diaries. The sixteenth book begins:* "Venice, October 1880, written in Bayreuth, November 20. As always for Siegfried." *Opposite the first page:* "On October 4 I received from Herr

v. Stein the news that he will not be returning to us; his father wishes to keep him at home. R. writes to him very nicely and makes the decision easier to bear. —"]

Monday, October 18   R. had a good night. But the weather is rough. R. works on his article "What Boots This Knowledge?"—then goes for a walk, takes delight in everything, including the Manin monument with the cannonballs. In the afternoon we go for a long stroll with him through the lanes. In the evening we read Schiller poems; Rub. plays to us his *Tristan* "Picture," and R. then sings the first scene with Kurwenal from the 3rd act.

Tuesday, October 19   R. had a good night. He works while I look at apartments, and when I return, on the stroke of 12, I find him still at it. Schiller and Goethe—the latter a poet who based himself on physics, the former on metaphysics. — In the morning I had attempted to defend Titian's kind old God, which brought jokes down on my head. Over coffee R. came back to the Indians and maintained that all other civilizations were like planetoids in comparison with this one great sun. — Short walk with R. on the Riva dei Schiavoni. — *Tristan* in the evening, R. sings Marke and everything else up to the end, his voice is wonderfully clear and on "*wohin Tristan geht*" I feel as if my heart will burst.

Wednesday, October 20   The impression too much for me, I have a wild and agitated night, R. divinely kind and patient—I get up but soon have to lie down again, and I sleep all day. R. works—the evening spent chatting.

Thursday, October 21   R. had a good night, and at breakfast we have to laugh heartily when he says to me, "I am very . . . run down; for a moment I did not know what I was." — He works and wants to know from me what the cardinal virtues are, is annoyed about them. — We take a trip together to the Palazzo Loredano, which he likes very much, and then to the Modena, he believing me to be very fond of it, but he has no desire to have it. In the evening we chat, and our conversation touches on the Cologne Cathedral festivities, in which Herr Oppenheim played a major role.

Friday, October 22   A good night. In the morning he expresses to me his utter antipathy toward Bismarck. He goes to his work, reads through the Ten Commandments, and tells me that he has invited the doctors who came out against vivisection to contribute to the *Blätter*. We drink my father's health and then take a gondola to Saint Mark's Square, where the children are given ice cream. — As we glide along, R. remarks that here in Venice the gracefulness of the architecture takes the place of flowers. In the evening Count Gobineau comes to visit us, undoubtedly an interesting and significant man; but the French language is causing R. increasing difficulties—not only speaking it, but also listening to it; he finds it "horribly hard." —

Saturday, October 23 R. dreamed that he was to conduct *Der Fl. Holländer* in Munich, he had already seen the children to their seats, was going to his place, was held up; to his great annoyance, the work began without him. — I feel my neuralgia again, the dark, cold room bad for it, we move downstairs, and again I have to stay in bed. (R. introduces Joukowsky to the doctor as Count Mattei.)

Sunday, October 24 I feel somewhat better again, receive some visitors, including my dear Mimi—R. receives a letter from a Dane asking for advice, he wants to give up everything and devote himself to music. R. talks ill-humoredly about the disastrous effects of music, saying it is a way of doing nothing. — Return to the green room.

Monday, October 25 A good night. R. finishes his work. He surprises me around 12 o'clock at Princess Hatzfeldt's, where I am having a late breakfast with Mimi and Count Gobineau. He goes out around 4 o'clock and decides to do this every day, in order to enjoy golden Venice in the sunshine. — While I am seated at my writing desk, he comes to my room, very melancholy; he has been reading a letter from my father and shedding bitter tears at the lack of harmony in it: "On the one side the impulse which led him to write the letter—that is splendid—but then so much conventionality, nothing complete, nothing." — We mourn together, and in mourning regain our peace. In the evening Rub. plays to us very nicely [Beethoven's] *Adieu, absence et retour* and the *Pathétique,* in connection with which R. says, "Goethe and Frau v. Stein." — Between Beeth.'s first and last works he finds similarities, as in the melodic line, but the works of the middle period seem to him to be in the nature of masterly playing around.

Tuesday, October 26 R. is somewhat restless today, and also it is cold. He goes to the Belle Arti and finds pleasure in the older pictures, which seem to him more accomplished. We take a communal walk to the Giardino Popolare, then he leaves us, near Lavena, to have a glass of beer at Dreher's; he returns to us in a very agitated state, having been kept waiting too long for 2 lire. I pay a farewell visit to Frau v. W[öhrmann]; on my return I find him looking sad, he says he had been bored without me. — In the evening R. plays Beeth. sonatas to us; in the first movement of the F Minor R. says it is a dialogue between decent kindness and noisy mischief. He comes to the subject of Saint Mark's Cathedral and says it is a stroke of magic; every time he sets eyes on it, he feels it might just as easily vanish overnight. He talked about Brahmanism and Buddhism, saying that the former petered out in a sort of conceited intellectuality, like all philosophy apart from Schopenhauer, whereas Buddhism placed all its emphasis on morality.

Wednesday, October 27 A letter from our friend Feustel pleases R. very much; he says people of this efficient, practical sort are the kind he likes best. A letter from the King, requesting us to come to Munich in the second part of Nov., causes dejection. Is it that he does not wish to see R., or that he does not want him to know about his private performances (*Aida,* Louis XIV plays)? R. sends Herr v. Bürkel a telegram, saying he has to be in Munich during the first half of the month. I go to the Belle Arti—to look at [Longhi's] *Concert,* which caught R.'s attention; he says he likes pictures of this sort. We go to an antiquarian's, there R. discovers some nice Renaissance fabric, which we buy at once. — In the evening he revises his work. — He recalls the Mozart symphony (D Major) whose allegro movement he prefers to that of the C Major Symphony. In the evening he gets Rub. to play it, and he shows us how everything in it can be seen as a dance.

Thursday, October 28 R. is suffering from rheumatism and pain in his right leg. He revises his article, and in the afternoon we go to the bank, whose director, a Jewish enthusiast, R. finds very unpleasant. We have seen how our old friend Tesarini's stay here in Venice has been made downright impossible, all because of Israel. He has been deprived of all his lessons, and slanders of the most virulent sort have created a kind of wall of destruction, looming ever closer over the poor rogue. We are alone in the evening (the children at Princess Hatzfeldt's), R. reads his article aloud.

Friday, October 29 R. feels tired, although he had a good night. We meet around noon in the Belle Arti, after I have visited Tesarini's daughter in the convent, a very charming girl of 15. In the B. Arti the Carpaccios and the Callots capture his attention, and he says how much he likes such pictures; the Laurentius, on the other hand, which I find enchanting, does not appeal to him at all. — He then goes to the station with friend Jouk. to reserve the saloon carriage. His unwillingness to meet women is becoming more and more marked, and he does not pay a farewell visit to the so friendly Hatzfeldt house. In the evening we go for a walk in Saint Mark's Square with the 3 younger children (the two elder ones are with Mimi). — For the last time we delight in the lovely square, which looks, he says, as if the Doge received the whole of Venice there.

Saturday, October 30 "Then goes he, led by a friendly hand, depressed and sad to a colder land," sings R., who feels great agitation and uneasiness, rising to fury, after having inspected the saloon carriage, which he dislikes exceedingly, in rough weather. He is sad at having left Naples. — Departure at 6 o'clock, after bidding a warm farewell to Mimi, so touching in her friendliness. The singers who had so often upset R. arrive, and this time they really please us and rouse our spirits as, singing all the while, they precede our gondola and accompany us as far as the station. Farewell, Venice! Departure at 6 o'clock. The saloon carriage much better than expected.

Sunday, October 31 We all more or less slept and are merry, glorious sunshine greets us in Germany. — Much drinking, the bottles are called Odysseus's companions, R. recalls his brother-in-law Brockhaus, who once told him that debts were nothing to be ashamed of. Also his sister Rosalie, who, when he did silly things, told him that, having done them, he should not suffer so terribly on their account, should be more carefree. He also tells us of his delight at being transferred from Magdeburg to Königsberg, a larger town. The air is good in Germany. We arrive in Munich at 6 o'clock in very good spirits; met by Lenbach and Bürkel, Levi comes along later. Lodging at Jungfer Schmidt's house, Briennerstrasse 8c—strange, but full of feeling!

Monday, November 1 A good night, though arrangements to be made once more; thoughts of moving to the hotel, but the friendly Frl. Schmidt proves the decisive factor in our staying where we are. R. is pleased that I make all the arrangements with good humor—the King sends some flowers. At last, in the evening, Beethoven's *Mass*. Fine, if somewhat mixed impression: "You will write a Mass," Beethoven must have said to himself, "and it will be something quite different." When I express my feeling that Italian church music has a different effect, R. agrees, and when the conductor takes the opposite view, R. says, "There speaks the musician, but my pleasure begins only at the point where I cease to be a musician." —

Tuesday, November 2 Bad, restless night; all the same R. goes out in the morning, but soon returns on account of the wicked wind; however, on his short walk he sees a photograph of the *Sistine Madonna,* and that fills his thoughts. — He writes a few lines of verse to the King for the flowers, and in the evening we see quite a good performance of [Méhul's] *Joseph,* a work which both moves and delights us. That is style.

Wednesday, November 3 R. slept well. In Berlin Herr v. Hülsen is inquiring about the *Nibelungen,* having heard that Herr Neumann is to stage it at the Viktoria Theater. R. sends a telegram to Tappert, saying he does not intend to release any of his works to the Berlin theater. Around noon we visit Lenbach, R. sits for him but says in the course of it that he is tired and would like best to close his eyes. — Herr v. Bürkel visits R. Reports concerning the King arouse melancholy— among other things, the K. does not travel around, because he fears for his life (assassinations). A very nice evening at Levi's with [Wilhelm] Busch, Lenbach, and Gedon. Much joking with the latter. Laughing admiration for Levi's arrangements and conducting fortunes; Lenbach laughs heartily when R. says in connection with the singers in Venice that his miserliness was always in conflict with the pleasure they gave him. — But his remarks about the Renaissance and about the fine arts in general offend L. However, R. abandons the subject and goes on to the Indians, citing Manin, who said that at death a human being is deserted by everything except justice. (R. continues reading Jacolliot's book.)

Thursday, November 4 R. had a good night but wishes for more heating and says gaily that the Heating of Mary would make a better feast day than the Annunciation (our maid's name is Mary). — Sitting with the photographer and then a visit to Herr v. Ziegler. Continued negotiations with the Leipzig director [Neumann] about the *Nibelungen* in Berlin. In the evening a performance of *Der Fl. Holländer,* R. affected in spite of the shortcomings of the performance, he frequently bursts into tears.

Friday, November 5 R. asks me which I would prefer—correct singers without any great talent or the other way around; he says he prefers the former; I observe that there can be no artistic correctness—that is to say, no living performance—without great talent. Bad weather, R. does not go out; for me and the children *The Merchant of Venice;* R. goes to bed.

Saturday, November 6 Morning discussion about *The Merchant,* which completely fills my being, in spite of the dismal performance. — Then much vacillation about spending the evening at Lenbach's, R. wants not to go, then to go, in the end we do go and have a nice party, which does not tire R. But at the conclusion there is so much agitation and fury on his part, and as a result such a terrible night, that the miseries of life and original sin trouble my soul almost more than ever before!

Sunday, November 7 Only in the early hours does R. fall asleep, and he has a wild dream about Fidi falling in the water. We rouse ourselves to a sort of conversation about the previous evening: Bernays's absurdity (always as if bidden to lecture on everything noble) and a happy accident which resulted in young Muncker's hearing R. speak of his father in a very friendly way. But the saddest of days, on which even what R. likes to call my beauty becomes a source of sorrow, for he tells me that I stand in the way of my children. *Tristan* in the evening, probably never before heard in such sorrow; R. very affected, tells us that he feels with every character, with Marke, with Kurwenal, he feels he is each one of them. — The orchestra very good. The second act the crowning glory.

Monday, November 8 R. dreams of a white point which turns into a white horse, this white horse brings the Emperor of Austria into his dream fantasy, the Emperor affably offers R. his hand, which, of enormous size, turns out to be Gedon's. — A kind God lends me words which satisfy R., he tells me that I can see from his madness that I mean everything to him, excluding all others. I: "But you are my salvation." — Our lunch is then a very cheerful one, and when there is mention of Lenbach's remark that in life we are like the donkey, always following the bundle of hay retreating in front of its nose, then of his loyal and not exactly requited love for Marie D[önhoff], R. says, "Now I know how I should address the Countess: 'Honored bundle of hay,' whether she understands it or not." Whereupon someone adds, "At any rate she would understand that the donkey is L." We part amid great laughter. The evening was spent at home with friends (Heckel, Pohl, Levi), joined later by Prof. Bernays with fiancée, which gave rise to a part-joking, part-irritable mood. R. gets rid of them all, suggesting to our friends that they come back, and this ruse succeeds. But when R. advises Heckel and Pohl of the altered situation of the Society of Patrons, refers to the deficit, and says that no one has yet thought of returning to the children the sum of money that belongs to them, Heckel says, "That is the difficulty." Then R. explodes: "The difficulty! While I abandon my whole idea, charge admission for the performances! — What are you there for, you Societies of Patrons?" He gradually calms down, excuses Heckel in particular, who has done all he can and performed real miracles.

Tuesday, November 9   R. slept well but is nevertheless still very tired. First of all we have a sitting for him with Gedon, who with boundless excitement is starting on a bust, then with Lenbach, who seems to be on the best way to painting a magnificent picture. R. is pleased, when Jouk. joins us and draws Lenbach's attention to various things, that L. simply gets him to sit down in his place and paint, and this gives rise to all kinds of friendly jokes. Feustel with us for lunch, warmly welcomed. — In the evening an old comedy and afterward *Coppélia,* a French ballet which, pretty though one might call it, nevertheless puts us out of humor. — It is only in the dance of the mechanical figures that the true ideal of ballet emerges. — In our evening conversation we come to Schiller and Weber and constantly have to count the young people lucky for having such poets.

Wednesday, November 10   Our morning conversation leads us to *Coppélia,* a vulgarity of melody that is peculiarly Parisian, which reminds us of pictures in newspapers (such as *La Vie Moderne,* which L. has sent us). We have a sitting at Gedon's with Lenbach. A magnificent bouquet from the King inaugurates the *Lohengrin* performance, R. watches it from the royal box, we from below. Otherwise a completely empty theater. On me it is the tragedy in particular which makes an impact—R. dissatisfied with the tempi, tells Levi that conductor and producer deserve to be sent God knows where. But he got much pleasure from his meeting with the King, whom he found completely unchanged.

Thursday, November 11   R. and I up very late, for the performance lasted until midnight, and R. wanted to chat a little afterward. He works out the program for *Parsifal,* and we talk a lot about the tragic element in *Lohengrin,* which offers no reconciliation. — Love produces faith, life produces doubt, which is punished unatoned. The lovingly faithful Elsa has to die, since the living Elsa must put the question to him. And all the scenic splendor, all the glory of the music, seem to be built up to throw light on the unique value of this one heart. — Drove with R. to the town hall, in Lenbach's portrait of the King he does not see the King as he knows him. Sitting for Lenbach. We dine at 5 o'clock and then go to see *Die Zauberflöte.* — R. describes this work as the genesis of the German character, and he draws our attention especially to Pamina's aria (G minor). Back home, much about Mozart's amiable genius. When Herr Levi is talking about concert programs, I tell him my view, which is that it is now too late for the works of Berlioz or my father, and that these should have been played in public immediately on their appearance as interesting novelties, not 20 years later as classical works; I say that the head of an artistic institution should possess the gift of recognizing original works which are worthy of the attention of their time and should support them, as happens in both painting and literature. R. agrees with me, which is why I note it down.

Friday, November 12   R. had a good night—I visit the painter and costumier, R. Seitz, in order to discuss with him the costumes for *Parsifal.* In the meantime R. finishes Jacolliot's book and is irritated by his arrogant dilettantism. At 3 o'clock rehearsal and [*Parsifal*] Prelude in the Court theater. The orchestra's pleasure in seeing R. once more in their midst; a flourish, he very cheerful, friendly, pleased among other things by the expression on the face of the violist Toms. The Prelude is played twice, then the King demands the Prelude to *Lohengrin.* R. very put out by this. He summons me to his dressing room, where he is cheerful in spite of it all. But at home he is tired, and when Lenbach makes some unfortunate remarks about Bismarck, R. loses his temper about this bulldog face which is always being painted. — Lenbach takes his leave after R. has sought to explain to him the reasons for his anger. He reads the death of Falstaff in *H. V,* is much struck by the passage about kings having curious humors, and repeats it. Late in the evening he goes for a walk on the Dultplatz with Jouk.; on his return he says merely that he has an antipathy toward Lenbach, who irritates him. — Altogether very agitated, he says in a conversation with Levi that he—as a Jew—has merely to learn to die, but Levi shows understanding.

Saturday, November 13 R. had a wild and restless night, he cries out "Joukowsky" and "My son," but he soon recovers from his fatigue, and in the evening he greatly enjoys *Staberl's Abenteuer,* he laughs a great deal, and after the performance goes to thank the actor Lang, who pleases him very much. He is greatly delighted with what he calls "the animal bourgeois quality" of his interpretation. He is now reading Count Gobineau's *La Renaissance* with much interest.

Sunday, November 14 R. slept well, and a fine sunny day puts him in good spirits. He writes to the King, then goes for a walk with Jouk., meets Frau Vogl, and says teasingly to me that he embraced her. — Members of the orchestra, singers, Knights of the Grail in the Orlando Lasso, where it was very cheerful and companionable, he says. We meet again in the theater; *As You Like It* is being performed, and the first scene grips us at once with all Shakespeare's usual power; unfortunately the performance then gets so bad that we leave after the 2nd act. R. is above all indignant with Possart's Touchstone, in which he sees all the usual Jewish qualities. He says Touchstone must be in the nature of a sharp and spirited old courtier, "something like Schleinitz," but instead of that we saw him lazy, expansive, speaking not one natural word. Twelve years ago I saw a charming performance of the play, and now this! — We return home in lovely moonlight, stop to look at the Kleine Residenz garden, then, back at home, forget the performance, thank goodness, and think only of the play. I was particularly struck by the lifelike scene between the women and the young man, Rosalind's return ("Did you call, sir?"), but above all the description of Jaques's words to the wounded stag; this description, entirely lacking in sentimentality and in its irony revealing more emotion than is actually expressed, fills me with admiration for the masterly use of language and the faithfulness of the characterization. I tell R. my feelings, he is glad that my enthusiasm has the power to overcome my disgust, and the evening passes in good spirits.

Monday, November 15 R. has a cold, has to keep to his room and miss today's performance of *Die Meistersinger.* The book, *La Renaissance,* interests him. He receives Herr v. Bürkel, who makes a very good impression on him and who, among other things, tells him that he must not imagine that "beneath this fleshy bulk" there does not dwell a warm sympathy and understanding for his ideas. — But R. remains in poor spirits, and my reports on the very good *Msinger* performance do little to cheer him up.

Tuesday, November 16 R. did not sleep well but has made a good recovery. From *La Renaissance* he tells me M[ichel]a[ngelo]'s remark about Leo X, that the Pope did not love art, only luxury. He drives to the photographer's with me. We see Lenbach for the first time since the explosion; I had also been avoiding him, but Lusch told us that he had been downright ill on account of it. R. explains his feelings to him, and we then drive with him to his studio, where quite an agreeable conversation develops. At lunch R. is completely cheerful, and he says we do not admire him enough for having sacrificed *Die Msinger,* to which he had been particularly looking forward. And today I am able to tell him all my feelings about this divine work, and what a triumph of ideality I see in his ability, amid all the dreary realities of his situation at the time, to conjure up such a vision of a lovely reality and a noble fatherland. That he fled from disagreeableness into the worldlessness and night of *Tristan* seems to me less wonderful than this creation of a "daytime," and this affirmation amid the very worst of experiences. He goes out, meets the whole world in the street, and is much fatigued. However, he is pleased by Herr v. Ziegler's visit; this influential man, whose task is to keep the King informed on all political matters, professes to be a grateful devotee of R.'s, intends to recommend everything (in the matter of the rail connection to Bayreuth, for instance), and, on leaving, kisses R.'s hand. In this place in which we previously experienced nothing but hostility, we now have two loyal and enthusiastic men. — Before supper R. goes through *Lohengrin* with the conductor, and at table he talks about the dismal influence of the Jews on our present conditions, and warns Levi against the implications for him, which Levi accepts good-humoredly but nevertheless with some melancholy. [*Added in margin:* "A few days ago he told him that he fusses too much about his soul!"] We also talk about Gedon and the lack of recognition for his talents, and finally Lenbach enlarges interestingly upon the state of technique in painting. R. had said to him that painters were lucky in comparison with composers—all they had to do was to create their works, then they were dependent on nobody. L. says that, on the contrary, technique in painting has got into such an appalling state and been passed down to them by such bad predecessors that there is still everything to search for. — Very friendly parting from this peculiar man, of great stature, certainly, but nervous and high-strung.

Wednesday, November 17 Cheerful rising with much talk from R. in Saxon dialect. "If you do not go to *Die Msinger,*" he says, "you will not get typhus." Friend Levi at the station to see us off. Cheerful spirits in the saloon carriage, though somewhat impaired by the bad rail journey. Otherwise much joking about the dreary scenery. First greetings from our beflagged theater, Moritz and Fuchs wave to us. In

Bayreuth we are met by our doughty friends Feustel, Gross, and the mayor's wife, the mayor being ill. — Marke at Wahnfried. — Everything in good order, a curious feeling: Have we been away? Are we back? — Neither seems real. — In the evening the Wolzogens—R. run down, because of either the heat or the unsympathetic elements, very irritable, and when there is talk about decorating the walls of the *salon,* perhaps with Gobelins, he almost loses his temper. But he calms down before going to bed.

Thursday, November 18 R. had a good night and is in good spirits. We have a cheerful breakfast, friendly sunshine lighting up the *salon.* Are we here? — The new cook, sent from Munich, is acquitting herself well. R. goes for a walk in the palace gardens with Marke. Toward evening friend Wolzogen; all kinds of Society of Patrons affairs, which rather tire R.; but he is touched by such evidence of good will as renewed gifts from Herr Irwine (a Scot in Leipzig) and from Herr Rosenlehner, who still does not wish to be named—last month brought in about 8,000 marks. — The need to adapt to conditions here, the heat, the wind, all of this seems to oppress R., he is again very irritable, but an evening spent by ourselves restores calm, and the *Illustrirte Zeitung,* reporting a gathering of astronomers, provides, if not exactly pleasure, at least some amusement.

Friday, November 19 R. slept well; in the mornings he is now reading *La Renaissance* with ever-increasing interest. Talking of Italy, he says, "Naples is an intoxication, Venice a dream." Here, beneath these gray skies, he says, the sad tune is sounding. — He invites our friend Jouk. to stay with us until his studio is built. — The many utterly useless letters annoy him. — A biography of my father by a lady called Ramann has arrived here. Two pages about my father's life with my mother in Como before my birth catch my attention; I show them to R., and he is pleased. "There must have been something like that," he exclaims, and now everything friendly in relation to me is called "Bellagio"—even the expression on Loldi's face.

Saturday, November 20 R. slept well. Much arranging for me. He tries to go out but gets a pain in his chest. — The heavens press down on us, heavy and leaden-gray; R., all but exasperated, talks of Venice. — Count G.'s book continues to give him pleasure, however. — (He reads to us the scene of Propertia's death and the scene between Titian and Aretino.)

Sunday, November 21 R. did not have a good night, and I, probably through overtiredness, a very agitated one. R. dreamed again about my being cold toward him, and departure! At breakfast R. says: "Worst of all is probably the indifference one feels toward everything. When I hear people talking about a work like 'Religion and Art,' it all seems to me utter nonsense. You and the children are my only link with the world—in fact only the children, for you are 'moving with me, considering well, from Heaven through the world to Hell.' " — He finishes *La Renaissance* and comes to me around noon, the book in his hand, much affected by the final scene between M[ichel]angelo and V[ittoria] Colonna. He gives it to me to read, and it makes a quite wonderful impression on me. How many of his characteristics can be seen in M., too, and he says he was reminded of himself when M. talks of the inordinate violence of his temperament, combined with great energy. We discuss M.'s attitude toward the Renaissance, very perceptively described by Gobineau. R. says of himself that he is the plenipotentiary of downfall (this he sees increasingly): "If my ideas were to strike root, all these great men would be listened to as teachers and would not, as it were, have lived in vain." — He goes out with Jouk. but is annoyed both with the weather and with Marke, who runs into all the houses; he takes refuge in Angermann's. — In the evening Jouk. tells us that Pepino is feeling homesick, which is only too understandable. We conclude the evening with a game of whist.

Monday, November 22 R. slept well. He discusses several of his acquaintances with considerable equanimity: "There must be some such queer fishes about, I know," he exclaims, "but it is bad if they are all there is." At midday I find him truly indignant over the biography of my father and the way all his relationships can be discussed like this during his lifetime. I continue arranging things, and he is pleased: the banner of love, or Isolde's seal, is now spread out above the door. R. says it is as if the whole of Naples were sailing toward him. We dine merrily and seek the sun, lacking out of doors, in wine. R. then goes to Wolz.'s with Jouk., intended to go farther, but returns home on account of the bad weather. In the evening Wolz. and Rub., the latter bringing good news of Boni. At table he spoke of our first journey to Italy, how he had wished to remain there with me, "for when a step is to be taken, better at once, without much talk. However, V. Colonna wanted to suffer in the correct manner," he says jokingly, "though Nature was on my side—the gods did not want us to return home, and the heavens were emptied upon us."

Tuesday, November 23 A good night. — At breakfast R. again expresses his delight in Gobineau, says he has no desire to read any more modern German books. Skies still gray. R. settles down to his score but is dissatisfied. He goes out for a while, then returns to his work. He is not happy with the brass music on stage, he seeks and, he believes, finds what he wants. In the evening he reads to the children the 1st act of *Der Bauer als Millionär,* which makes us feel very much at home. Our conversation then leads us to Frederick the Great, and R.

observes that he belonged much more to the Renaissance than to modern times—Machiavelli would have admired him. He also talks about the debate in the Reichstag on the Jewish petition and finds it despicable on both sides, particularly a remark by Windthorst. — In the evening, when we go up to bed, he has forgotten his watch, goes down to fetch it, alters something in his score, picks up the case, forgets the watch, goes downstairs again, but all very gaily. He cries out to me that I must always remain pretty, gay, jolly.

Wednesday, November 24   R. slept well. — I walk to the theater with the children, he comes to meet us in the carriage. Pleasant weather, we show friend Jouk. the old opera house. A new volume by C. Frantz about Schelling annoys R. very much, he says, "As long as he (Sch.) believes he has got hold of God Almighty, then everything is all right." He says he once thought Schopenhauer was too harsh in treating these people as charlatans, but he had been quite right—it is sheer windbaggery. — After lunch he talks of his indifference toward the performance of his works, and says what he finds most painful about it is that he has to pretend it is important to him. — He is disturbed about *Parsifal,* says he would like to compose the whole thing anew. — He goes out for a short walk. In the evening our friends Wolz., Jäger, Porges, Rubinstein. R. expresses his indignation with Schelling and reads to us a truly incredible passage, proving the existence of God by its impossibility! Then he indicates some cuts for *Tristan* (2nd act).

Thursday, November 25   R. had a good night, but he is in no mood for work, makes writing mistakes, is absent-minded, has great feelings of anxiety, and when the Voltz and Batz affair crops up (they want to sell back to him their rights in his works for 60,000 marks), he is quite beside himself with rage. In the evening, before supper, he goes back to his work, glances through the conclusion of *Götterdämmerung,* and says that never again will he write anything as complicated as that. — Frl. Uhlig has sent the final copies of R.'s letters to her father; R. reads many things from them to us, and we are astonished at how unchanged his feelings about his art and the public have remained. — Delight in our children, who are cheerful, amiable, and good-looking. —

Friday, November 26   R. had a good night, he does some work and then goes for a little walk, but it takes hold of him again—what he calls the *crab* in his chest. — Our friends the Grosses, whose warm friendliness does us good. Feustel's idea of publishing the piano score of *Parsifal* on subscription, which would perhaps make America unnecessary. [*Added in margin:* " 'My *bel âge,* Belgiojoso'—thus R. addresses me in the morning."] — Wolz. comes in the evening, R.

talks about Schelling, how sad it is to see such good minds as C. Frantz's going astray—with us genius must always be original genius, all on its own. Then he explains his thoughts on the way to look at history—from the standpoint that all history shows decline. He also talks about emigration for religious reasons, in order to establish new communities and a new humanity, since our climates are unsuitable. After supper he reads an act of *Der Bauer als Millionär* to the children, and to me, after the children have gone to bed, some more of his letters to Uhlig. He is pleased with his words about my father, and that he never failed to recognize him. Also his opinion of the Wagner family. —

Saturday, November 27 R. slept well; he goes to his work and is satisfied with what he has done, but much less so with the weather; he feels so run down that he does not go out. In the evening he reads me the letters to Uhlig.

Sunday, November 28 Business day [*added in margin:* "but first, festive day, R. accepts my little gift in a very kind and friendly way"]. First of all, friend Gross's report that Voltz & Batz want 100,000 marks for selling back their rights, R. rejects all suggestions, wants to wait and see what happens. Then Herr Neumann comes and reports that Herr v. Hülsen has offered him the opera house in Berlin, together with the orchestra and chorus and whatever singers he wants, for the *Ring*. R. much against it, wants to see it all done in the Viktoria Theater, though he leaves the decision up to the promoter; however, he promises to make a visit to the Viktoria Theater, but not to the opera house. The theater director asks for a certificate, which makes us laugh! — Very good report on Seidl's activities, which pleases us greatly. In the evening a visit from Rub., discussion of the Jewish question and again of *La Renaissance,* with great praise from R. Our good theater director could not understand at all that R. should think nothing at all of the Emperor and royal family's attending the performance of the *Ring!* — We compare Neumann's energy and resourcefulness with Hülsen's narrow-mindedness and vindictiveness and have to laugh over Israel's predominance. —

Monday, November 29 R. has an eye inflammation! But it is slight, and when I exhort him to be patient, the only medicine I know, he goes downstairs, comes up again after a while, and says my advice has been a great success, he has been sleeping and now feels better. After lunch we drive to the mayor's, and in the Reichsadler see the preparations for Jouk.'s rooms there. — Friend Stein writes to R., telling him of the publication of a book R. had suggested to him, *From Naples for Bayreuth,* and R., very pleased, replies to him at once. — Fidi starts woodwork again, Voltz & Batz seem to have calmed down. In the evening there are discussions with Wolzogen about the extended *Blätter,* the basis of which R. wishes to be his own view of the decline of the human race and the need for the establishment of a system of ethics: intellectually, he says, people will always remain unequal, but one could aim for a greater moral equality. We might not achieve anything, but we could prepare the ground. In the morning he spoke to me of human aberrations and how far they can extend when people cling to basic errors: the gentle Melanchthon approved the burning of Michael Servetus at the stake, and Protestant theologians have supported slavery, because nothing is said against it in the Bible. Wolz. tells us many other things about a man in Vienna who has been completely captivated by "Religion and Art" and wants to devote his life to the spreading of its ideas. Someone in Schweinfurt has written to him, "Fortunate we, to have experienced 'Religion and Art.' "

Tuesday, November 30   R. did not have a very good night. — In the morning he talks to me about the present debate on the Jewish question, saying that the government has been pushed into a curious corner, for if it were to come out in support of the Jews, it would be identifying itself entirely with the Progressive party, with which, however, it wants nothing to do. He then goes on to discuss the present state of the stock exchange, saying that the power of the Jews could be dealt with only if all that ceased to be. He thinks it a great stroke of genius on Goethe's part to have set the ball rolling in the Emperor's Court with paper money. — Now nothing can be done, R. says, but he himself would ban Jewish holidays, on which they will not sell merchandise to Christians, and also the boastful synagogues. "What then will be the significance of our feast days?" R. works, then goes out for a little while, but without any pleasure; indeed, the dampness makes him feel as if he were at the mercy of those hostile beings who are sometimes revealed to him in dreams. However, since I wish to do some shopping in the afternoon, he goes out again with me, I abandon my shopping, and we stroll in the palace gardens, very merry, though it is a rather macabre kind of humor. "Yes," he exclaims, gazing at the parade ground, "arm yourselves with cannons, so that this lovely land shall not be occupied, so that the French shall on no account take Bayreuth!" — In a climate like this, he observes, the only possible life is in taverns by lamplight, though, to be sure, it spells ruin for everybody. The Philistine figures passing by, the old maids, annoy him, but when we speak of them we remain merry—impossible for him, he says, if he sees them when he is alone. He works in the evening, but says he had to do a lot of erasing. His best-written score, he adds, was *Lohengrin.* In the evening read the letters to Uhlig, still with great interest. Even at that time he was finished with everything, all things vain and worldly. We talk of Fidi's publishing these letters after our death, also those to his wife Minna, to A[lwine] Fromann, to my father. But our own, those between R. and me, must never on any account be presented to the public. I solemnly pronounce this here as their sacred duty. — Shortly before going to bed R. and I discuss the future of the *Blätter,* with some misgivings. It is only the views of people of genius which can prove absorbing! —

Wednesday, December 1 R. did not have a good night, he got up, went into the children's *salon,* and read the article on New Zealand in *Orbis Pictus.* Thoughts of emigration still occupy him very much, and he feels that, if one were young, it would be the only thing to do. In this ability to colonize he sees the main quality of the Anglo-Saxon race and a sign of the productivity of the Reformation, whereas Catholicism has been completely sterile in this direction since the Reformation. In the morning he tells me that Bismarck and Bucher sat down together and considered the problem of the socialists; help is now to come from a compulsory savings bank. — He works out an advertisement for the *Blätter.* At lunch he talks about the past, says, thinking of former times, that the eternal feminine drags one downward. "It took a rather long time for things to change," he adds. — We go for a walk in the palace gardens: "Brooms, oh, brooms, be as you were," he says, looking at the trees reflected in the water, and talks with the same humor as yesterday about the earth and sky, which are wet, cold, and gray. Friends in the evening. — R. talks once more about Schelling and C. Frantz, and when somebody mentions the former's philosophy of mythology and recalls Creuzer, R. says: "All these people like Creuzer saw something, they made mistakes but they saw something. Their successors see nothing, just think they ought to say something, too." — Letters from Herr Neumann to R. and me, very friendly in tone. R. is insisting on the Viktoria Theater. — When our friends depart, I remain chatting with R. in the *salon,* and the subject of outward appearances, an outward image of some kind, crops up between us. (Over coffee R. had made me responsible for our having settled in Germany; he said he had wanted to stay in Genoa in 1868; once a decision had been made, it should be put into effect at once, but I had had too rigid a sense of duty, and all the gods had been against my decision; we probably would have come to Bayreuth, but only for a short time, for the festival, to the Fantaisie.) I tell him that Lenbach said to me that, since I had not become an empress, I had dedicated myself to a great cause; whereas he as a person has always meant everything to me, and the cause is something entirely for him. R. says nobody can understand this, and that is why nobody has been able to paint my portrait, the assurance of my manner leads them astray. "They are too stupid," he says with laughing earnestness.

Thursday, December 2 R. did not have a good night. He dreamed of a hare which was running as if on air, rushed close to his side, and hid itself there; he looked for me to show it to me, but I had gone! — I had to ask him in the morning whether I might go to fetch Blandine; since he tells me that even a single day's separation from me makes him gloomy, I give up the idea. — Telegram from Hans, whom I had asked on Lulu's behalf whether she might see him and at the same time hear the 9th. [*Bülow's telegram from Meiningen, in French, states that he finds it impossible to answer at once; he was laid up for several days and is still indisposed.*] — This reply brings R. back to the idea of adopting all the children, which is his wish. — Before this conversation, still in bed, he suddenly laughed and said, "Since someone like Shakespeare sees figures nobody has ever seen before—Polonius, Hamlet—the way people think they will now be able to do likewise!" — He writes to the King. A dense fog makes a walk impossible, but we go for a drive, "drop cards," and are in high spirits throughout. Once again considered the question of Neumann-Hülsen. R. is still very much against the opera house, and he advises me not to send off a letter which I have already written to the director. In the evening we finish the letters to Uhlig. Then R. reads to me part of his letter, his reply to the King, who asked him what had been going through his mind in the royal box when he suddenly got up and clutched his brow. — I should find it hard to say why I find myself wrapped in melancholy as the evening comes to an end: the correspondence with Uhlig, also his lines to the King, everything, both the good and the bad, deception as well as truth, reveals life to me in all its melancholy, and I feel that nothing can any longer alleviate this melancholy, not even one's own personal good spirits. — We talk about *La Renaissance*, R. says I ought to write about it; what good does it do, he observes, that I talk a lot with others, since nothing but nonsense seems to come of it? We part in deep feelings of harmony. — R. went through parts of *Joseph* with Lusch and is very pleased with her, her intelligence and her integrity, no less with Fidi, whose way of saying Mass continues to amuse R. — My Parsifal dress gives him pleasure; he says I have never looked so well; in Munich, he says, I suffered too much, and in consequence became shy.

Friday, December 3 R. dreamed so vividly of a large black wart that he got up in the morning and looked at himself in the mirror. We laughed. Shortly afterward, however, he says, "You were sad yesterday evening, and I am sad now." But our conversation soon becomes lively again, and he says that in the Middle Ages the idea of honor took the place held by beauty among the Greeks, for the Greeks had no morality—everything seemly and everything heroic was for them a part of beauty. With the Romans it was *honestas*. In more modern times this absurd conception of honor had been worked out to take its place. We discuss Goethe's [*Wilhelm Meister's*] *Wanderjahre*, and R. says I should write about this as well as about *La Renaissance* for the *Blätter*; I reiterate my inability to address myself to the outside world, however glad I may be to tell him everything that comes into my mind. The weather is very fine, R. invites me to go for a walk with him in the palace gardens at 1 o'clock; when the military band strikes up, the mere sound of it coming from the distance has a tremendous and startling effect on us. "What a divine thing music is— how a brass instrument like that stirs one's blood!" Then he laughs and says, "It must throw a poor soldier into ecstasies." — I mention a passage in Joukowsky's letter and observe that, because the *Sistine Madonna* and the *Tribute Money* have become so much a part of him, he can no longer really appreciate them when he sees them. — This cannot happen with music, I feel: however much one thinks of it, a melody, when one hears it, always has the power to surprise. R. agrees with me. In the afternoon we go for another walk and are very grateful for a lovely sunset. — R. then makes a cozy nest for himself in his little study and says that even in his younger years he had spoken to Uhlig of his longing for comfort. "At that time, though, because you had no love." "So much the better if it is combined with love." — Over coffee he recalled his remark to Uhlig about the *Ring:* "Things like that I used to say just in fun, but I always had a high opinion of what I was doing and felt that nobody else could do it." — In the evening he reads the paragraph on "song" in J. Grimm, and we are pleased by the words, "It is always Nature one comes to recognize, the spiritual nature of the human being." — We discuss the reorganization of the *Blätter,* whether viable—it would depend on finding people with much wit and intelligence. Taking its lead from Schopenhauer's *Parerga,* it must devote itself entirely to criticism—of history, literature, education. R. remarks again and again how splendidly Schopenhauer, while showing the fullest and freest awareness of things, stresses the moral aspects, always showing compassion, the need to recognize oneself in one's neighbor, and to sacrifice oneself instead of him. — We were alone, R. and I, and glad to be so—oh, if only there were no outside world, were it but possible to live like this, exchanging thoughts, peacefully watching the children growing up! But—this is asking too much, even if R. says that he would stage the festivals for the children! — Such ideal happiness brings to R.'s mind the quotation "But nothing compared with their contentment," and we conclude the day with memories of this second part of the lovely work. "In *Wilhelm Meister* they are just phantoms." An illustration for *Hermann und Dorothea* with some of Goethe's lines beneath provokes him to exclaim, "How badly they are done!" —

Saturday, December 4 During the night I could not sleep, and R. was restless. In the morning he says to me: "Yesterday one instance gave me a real insight into the tragedy of life; it is nothing new, but I saw it very clearly—the fact that those who mock the idealists and the heroes are seen to be right—Mephisto, for example, Sancho Panza. The hero is inspired by something which they can never understand, but which also goes beyond the reach of life." I: "That is also the tragic thing about love: it requires happiness, which is not possible in life." — R.: "Yes, but for the very reason that it does not stem from life, it alone makes life bearable." — Coming to his correspondence with Uhlig, he says, "Oh, that time of lethargy, of not being able to do anything, when my whole being was possessed by the urge to create!" — The weather is bad, and his eyes are troubling him. A quotation from Herr Ehlert in Fr[itzsch]'s music periodical—to the effect that this formerly so significant man (R.) is dissolving into his atoms— causes me to remark to R. that the only thing wrong about "Religion and Art" is that it has been printed; this does not displease him. — He tells me that the countertheme in the Andante of the A Major Symphony came into his mind with particular vividness when he was in his bath, and it affected him like a revelation! "How divine it is that something like that can suddenly sound in our world, something so beautiful!" — Beethoven melodies and Shakespeare scenes, these are everything to him, he says. — In the evening he discusses the expansion of the *Blätter* and comes back to the idea expressed in "Religion and Art," also to emigration and the single inspired being who must work religiously to bring it about: "Unfortunately he would have to be a rich man." — Then friend Rub. plays Beeth.'s E-flat Major Quartet to us, and very well, to R.'s very great delight. At the end he embraces me, and after each movement he utters expressions of joy. — I hear it only as if it were coming to me from a great distance and indirectly, as it were, for my head is very tired and I am overcome by feelings of inadequacy. — He works on his score.

Sunday, December 5 Again my night was entirely sleepless and R.'s restless. — In the morning he receives a telegram from Herr v. Hülsen [*enclosed in Diaries; see notes*] which, as R. surmised, requests *Die Walküre* as a result of the "joint performances" with Herr Neumann. R. decides not to reply at all. Wolz. has sent his plan for the enlarged *Blätter,* I read it with some misgivings; I find it hard to envisage the possibility of R.'s far-reaching ideas being propounded by his pupils. I show R. the MS. over coffee, R. makes a few deletions, we experience the same feelings of embarrassment, without, however, going more deeply into the matter. He takes a walk, returns to me after a while, and says, "I believe I shall be complying with a growing thought in you if I decide to leave the whole thing as it is." I am very much in favor, our spirits revive, and the word is spoken between us: "subscription for the decline of the human race" (Wolz. had appealed for subscriptions); I do not remember who said it first, but it turns a mood of depression into one of tremendous gaiety. — But his eyes are troubling him, he cannot read, in the evening I read *Preciosa* to him and the children. — He then shows me a page of his score.

Monday, December 6 For me a sleepless night meant the loss of our breakfast conversation. R. waited for me till 11, then had breakfast alone. He came up to me around 12, when I was still alternating between sleeping and waking. He reads to me—partly to our horror, partly to our great amusement—passages from Schelling's transcendental philosophy, in which God is treated more or less as a tumbler doll. At 1 o'clock friend Stein, great joy at seeing him again, particularly because of Fidi; hopes that it will after all be possible to maintain the connection, that Stein will come to us for a few months each year and later Fidi go to him in Halle. — He intends to lecture on Schopenhauer at Halle, this at R.'s urging, for he considers it essential that the doctrine be used as a basis for education. Friend Joukowsky has also returned home from Dresden. Stories of all kinds. In the evening R. comes back to his cosmogonical ideas and says, among other things, that in Africa one can actually see from the natives how they came into existence as awkward afterthoughts (other expressions, too, which I have unfortunately forgotten). In the shape of America he sees a repetition of the shape of the other world, but slimmer, more complete. He is in very gay spirits, and when our sudden departure from Naples is mentioned, he says, "It was when I got corns on my face." Then he says that he is in the youth of his 3rd period of life.

Tuesday, December 7 We had a better night, and the light shines upon us. Our conversation leads us to life, I say that to me it seems to be just. R. says, "Certainly, and when we look at the difficulties in a life such as that of Cervantes, we can tell ourselves that the world's will had quite other things in mind than just providing him with honors and riches." I feel that if that had been what he wanted, he could also have achieved it, and I see a streak of nobility in his gaiety, his contempt for despair. One has what one *wills* (not what one desires). — He says that Will had required him to persevere, and that is why it had given him a good little wife and a king (recently he pointed out how unusual their relationship was, since the King demanded nothing at all from him). Around lunchtime R. comes up to my room and tells me with merry exasperation what happened to him when he wanted to go out: first of all, too warmly clothed, changed again, then fastened his cuff buttons in the wrong holes, at last the sun, which hid the very moment he went out. But in the afternoon we go out together, through the palace gardens with Stein to visit Joukowsky, deep in house-moving troubles. There R. is provoked by a luxury edition of Frederick the Great into venting his opinion of such "nonsense." "One reads about barley and hops in magnificent lettering, while the most valuable things are cheaply printed." — Then he takes us to Angermann's, and we return home by moonlight through the palace gardens. — In the evening R. again explains to us his thoughts on cosmogony, and then we go on to *Die Meistersinger,* the 2nd act, the greater part of which he plays to us, sharing our incomparable delight in it. — After our friends have departed, R. and I chat together, and we are joined by Boni, just returned from Munich. Various things worry us concerning the children, but my sense of being blessed does not waver. (At lunch today R. made a significant remark—that a human being must never feel *obliged,* but always *impelled.*)

Wednesday, December 8 R. had an agitated night; an eccentric whim of Lusch's had caused us concern. But our morning conversation is as usual very good-humored. It was today that we talked about the justice of life, and R. keeps coming back to his belief that this world has a moral significance and that the important thing is resignation, that is to say, a recognition of the tragedy of existence. He goes out, and in the evening we pass our time in reminiscences of Italy, above all, Siena and Venice. (The *Assumption* was mentioned again at lunch, and R. said that in the facial expression the pain of a woman in childbirth is mixed with the ecstasy of love, and this is why the closeness of the apostles and disciples and all these false relationships are so disturbing. But when I tell him that Joukowsky agrees with him, he is sorry, and he says I am right to follow the artist so unconditionally in his work and to defend him.) Jungfer Schmidt in Munich is also mentioned, and when we part after this amiable chat, he tells me I am the good principle which unites everything. — And it is only his sun which warms us and bestows its rays.

Thursday, December 9 R. had a good night and is cheerful in spite of some business matters (among other things, Voltz and Batz, though Feustel writes that this affair is taking a favorable turn). At lunch we discuss Fischer's appointment as conductor in Munich, which has just taken place, and R. says, "All a person has to do is come within 20 paces of me and he wants me to make him a conductor." He has received a newspaper containing a report on Robert Springer's lecture on "Religion and Art"—it seems to have been a very nice lecture.

Regarding another report, which says that Wagnerians proclaim him (R.) to be Christ, he says gaily, "Thank you very much indeed." — We go for a walk in the palace gardens in order, as R. says, to obey the 11th commandment. Boni's paleness causes him concern—"The girls are going crazy one after another"—and he breaks the ice in his own peculiar way by saying to the child at lunch, "Tell me, are you in love?" — "Too much chatter and too much food—that's what is wrong with me," he says. In the morning we went through former times of separation: "We would not have stayed alive much longer," he says, "and that is why I seized on Röckel's misdeed as if it were a salvation." — Chatting about all kinds of things with our friends in the evening—Africa yet again ("Mother Earth's delayed birth"), then coal mines, hopes that electricity will make coal superfluous. Also about salt being less necessary with vegetables than with meat: "Yes," he exclaims, "we wander over the face of this earth like the gods in Valhalla and never think of all this night and this horror beneath us." — He now has a new volume of the General Staff's report, and he tells us of the heroic deeds at Belfort: "It is impossible not to admire such things, but what was the point of putting all these forces in danger?" He talks of his intention of staging a mourning ceremony and says he still wants to write some funeral music, for which he would take as motto the reply of a dying sergeant to his officer: "Sir, I die for Germany." — " 'I die for Germany,' " he exclaims, "what a state of ecstasy!" I observe that this was our mood in Tribschen, and he says, "True—and what came of it?" — When our friends have departed, we sit for a while longer in the *salon* with the two elder girls and enjoy their chat and their prettiness. "*Gnautis auton,*" he says to me. "Know thyself—it is we ourselves in whom we take delight." — [*Added in margin:* "R. plays the Benedictus from Mozart's Requiem."]

[*The following postscripts have been added at the bottom of this and the next three pages:* "Yesterday he said, 'At every word I ask myself what it is and whether one is not talking nonsense.' At supper he tells us that he had conceived all his works by the time he was 36, from then on he just carried them out. — After reading the newspaper report, he says, 'With the Germans everything is mixed up in confusion like Marke's supper—a carrot here, a bit of cabbage there, all good things in themselves, but no specific identity, and covering it all a lukewarm broth, neither hot nor cold.' Recently R. jokingly quoted Antonio to Lusch, who had become a little overexcited: 'Were I now like, etc.' — We talk about *Tasso,* and when I say that I admire the poet's truthfulness, which forced him to that 'Begone' of the Princess's, however embarrassing we might find it, he says, 'But in that case the poet should not select such motives.' — About Kundry's kiss R. said recently,

'What he cannot learn from any doctor or armorer, a woman teaches him.' Recently, too, when it was suggested that R. had carried on the Beethoven type of melody, he denied it emphatically, saying that had been something complete in itself: 'I could not have composed in the way I have done if Beethoven had never existed, but what I have used and developed are isolated strokes of genius in my dramatic predecessors, including even Auber, allowing myself to be led by something other than opera.' — 'Bismarck is now regaling Germany with scraps from France, with the tobacco monopoly, which had already been introduced in Alsace.' "]

Friday, December 10   Gale and gray skies. And with them for R. as reading matter, Schelling's transcendental philosophy! But around lunchtime R. comes in with the *Fl. Blätter* and shows us the final page: performance of an opera in the presence of "the master." — We go for a walk in spite of the weather, R. at first puts up with the raging wind and the lack of light, but gradually he becomes impatient. We talked about Hans's silence; when we return to Wahnfried to leave Marke, the groom hands me a letter from him; we continue our walk to see friend Joukowsky, who has installed himself very comfortably in the Reichsadler. (R. is designing a studio for J.) I read the letter and show it to R.—solemn feelings! At home R. brings up the question of his adopting all the children. Solemn feelings, fears of erysipelas; to cheer him up a little, I put on the Scheherazade dress, and that does restore his spirits. Cervantes does the rest, I read the story aloud, and we take a friendly leave of this dreary day on which the forces of the soul had literally to fight a duel with the external powers. When, as in our case, they conquer, then it can be counted a blessing. — R. tells us about Ireland, where once again a policeman has been murdered, and he says England may be in danger of war, since the Irish in America are supporting their compatriots. — (A Jew, R. said, can only be demanding, greedy, cunning—if he were not those things, he would have to look very touching and worthy of pity. —)

Saturday, December 11   R. slept well—at breakfast he says to me, "Perhaps I shall read Freytag's *Die Ahnen* after all," but then he adds, "No, to have to attend to inventions by people like that!" And when I remark that there is little talent in Germany, he says, "Yes, a sense of form is enough to attract attention." — The wind blows unceasingly but does not dispel the fog; R. maintains that it is a *monsoon,* the most extreme form of south wind. He gaily reproaches me for having on that earlier occasion, by returning to Germany, merely obeyed the inner voice of duty in quite a useless manner—"All these *monsieurs* are not really worth it"; we should otherwise now be settled in Italy, probably in Como. — In the morning he continues with Schelling, and toward noon he works on his score, leads Amfortas to his bath. At lunch he indicates the atmosphere of gray and brown and says, "There is your Gobelin." All the same we go for a walk in the palace gardens, and he decides to go to the Villa Loredano next winter, via Seville and Palermo. "To regard Germany just as a concert hall and then to derive enjoyment from what grew up in adversity." — Yesterday, watching Marke happily sniffing around in the palace gardens, he said: "What a poet he is—Ossian in the mists of the past! He is utterly immersed in the ecstasy of scenting things out." — In the *salon* he is pleased by the frames of the two pictures (him and me by Lenbach), since they make the pictures invisible. He says he likes this beveled gold, and then he talks of pretty varieties of marble, but "The pleasures of furnishing begin only with folds." — In the evening he does some work, and when I come down in the Swan dress, he wants to "form a group with me" and sits down at my feet. But before that we talk of the melancholy of Amfortas's theme, then of his second "*Sterbe, höchste Gnade,*" which I find gentler. R. says it denotes collapse in his agony. — In the evening he plays the Overture to *Jessonda* with Rub., remembers having heard it under Weber's direction. Then the C-sharp Minor Quartet, and since friend Jouk. tells me frankly that he did not understand the first movement, I ask R. to read us the words he wrote about it in his *Beethoven,* which move me to tears. Then the "*Kaisermarsch*" as a piano duet, and, scattered in between all this, Jn. Pérès. — When we are alone, R. says more about the quartet to me: "Everything lies in the first 4 notes at the beginning, then he busies himself with some fugal writing, which is not very interesting—even for musicians. As I said, it was a point of honor with a musician to write a fugue. But through the roughnesses and awkwardnesses there emerges a mood such as I can well imagine him to have had. And it is splendid that he felt the urge, after the E-flat Major Quartet, to write this. And all the passion lies in the last theme." — But Rub. could not get the tempo of the theme in the second movement, R.'s favorite theme.

Sunday, December 12 A wretched night followed these lovely stimulations, and I feel as if my poor head is going on strike! In the morning R. observes that we are now in the mood of the first movement. — He goes to his work but complains that he requires instruments he does not have, and he would need to invent some—not in order to make more noise, but to express what he has in mind. Later he tells me he has decided on trombones and trumpets (it concerns the exit to the lake): strange as it might seem, it should prove as successful as previously the trumpets and flutes in the *Faust* Overture. — At lunch our friend Stein's views on the right to sacrifice lives for the sake of an idea (Marat) results in R.'s adopting Carlyle's opinion that revolution is a triviality run mad; and he says if the idea is such that it must be sealed by human blood, one must in that case sacrifice oneself. Over coffee memories of the festival performances come into his mind, particularly the first scene of *Rheingold,* and he feels that its achievements were not properly appreciated. — We attempt to go out of doors, but the weather makes it impossible. I go to his study to greet him, and tell him that he was wrong to say that the day would not fulfill any wish—for me at least all wishes are fulfilled when he is content. Where-upon he: "It was also wrongly formulated; we have no wish—it is only that what comes to us from outside gives us no pleasure, we just have to bear it." — In the evening with Stein the question of how to educate a boy; R. would like to see the gradual emergence of embryonic states and their development explained to a child in a religious sense, in the way the Brahmans taught the creation of the world to their people. We then continue reading Cervantes's story with unalloyed pleasure.

Monday, December 13   The night is bad and long; the gray light of dawn persists a full twelve hours! R. declares that he has all the rivers of Hell in his eyes and nose, Styx, Acheron, etc. Quite clearly, he says, the gods are telling him to get on with it, if he still wants to stay alive and do something. The children tell us it is Lenbach's birthday, and R. edits a telegram to him (see folder 1). He works, and in the evening cheerfulness breaks through, and we have to laugh when, speaking of Spain, of the town Xeres, he says: "How Xeres lost an X, an unknown quantity." — (Yesterday he got Stein to explain to him how to calculate with unknown quantities.) We finish Cervantes's story; in the morning R. had already remarked on Cervantes's preference for gypsies; he says: "Everyone has felt the longing to create for himself some refuge outside this world, as it were. In the case of the mule, the gypsy stands up for the animal, which the nobleman sacrifices in order to save him-self. It is all observed and shown, but none of it is stated directly." — In the evening he says to me what a significant step it would be if Stein really worked out a plan for educating our boy. — Our evening conversation led us to N. III, and R. said, "People who bring about such things as December 2 subsequently become wise rulers, their country's benefactors." — Regarding the German Emperor, he says he cannot join in the enthusiasm for his well-being, if only because he knows him to have been among the most relentless opponents of the revolutionaries.

Tuesday, December 14   R. did not have an utterly bad night, but he got out of bed. — In the morning he tells me that the water dripping in the cistern made such a pleasant noise that it was just like listening to a piece by Chopin. — At lunchtime he comes up to my room and tells me with great liveliness of an altered comma in his article, and at lunch he enlarges upon the difference between German and French punctuation. — Regarding Cervantes's story, he says, "It is all there, but I have the feeling that these people were of a very special kind, and they appear in a particularly charming light." At lunch he exclaims to the "Gobelin" weather, "Just carry on, don't be shy," which makes us all very merry about the inclemency of the weather. A book about him by Marsillach, translated into Italian, amuses him, and when, over coffee, we talk of his friends, he recalls Schuré and the fact that he has now lost touch with him. He tells of his passion for a Greek lady, and when I rectify his account by remarking that the attraction was mutual, he says, "Well, then, no wonder I got it so badly"—which makes us all laugh heartily. We stroll around, he and I, in the *salon* and in the hall, he also does some work in the evening, and says he did something good today and is in exuberant mood, as always when satisfied with his work. — From a "violently tender" embrace he goes over to the wildest of joking, which he explains to me thus: "Otherwise one would go mad." Whereupon: "I'm gradually beginning to understand you." — He gets the idea of reading *Parsifal* and does so, as a parting gift for Stein. Afterward, as usual, he regrets it, but it proved quite easy for him, and though some somber remarks about his relations with his friends and with the world escape him, he is nevertheless in good spirits. — Giving me the newspaper report [*not found*], he says: "What one desires in one's youth, one gets in plenty in old age; if this performance had come to my notice when I was a conductor in Dresden, for instance, how excited I should have been! But how cold it leaves one now!" — In the evening the moon shines brightly and illuminates the glass in our skylight. — It pleases R., and it really does make Wahnfried look enchanted, since all day long not a glimmer of the sky was to be seen.

Wednesday, December 15 R. had a good night. At breakfast he tells me that he has been thinking a lot about R[ichard] III and his soliloquy, and how strange it is that he should hold in contempt all those people who amused themselves "to the lascivious pleasing of a lute" after the bloody battles. — Before lunch we go for a walk in good weather on the road to Konnersreuth; but by the end of lunch it has already clouded over; we are amused by encounters in the palace gardens—a solid citizen whom R. points out to me, who presses his nose with a finger clad in black cotton to add more weight to his words. Of an old man in cap and overcoat he says, "There is the Green Knave of the old German playing cards." The most amusing sight of all is always Marke with what R. describes as his "undulating gait," still containing traces of the serpent. — At midday we took leave of our friend Stein, looking forward to seeing him again. Talking of his still-imperfect manner of reading aloud, R. says he throws the verses out like rogues from some tavern: Here, you—I know you, and you, too—etc. . . . In the evening a visit from our friend Feustel, who tells us in the most comical way of the quarrel between Voltz and Batz, which has led to their books' now being deposited on neutral ground. The two wives (sisters) could not get along together, neither was willing for her husband to visit the other! And Batz, cut off from his father, is now reconciled with him again, having quarreled with his mother, who is separated from her husband, leaseholder of a *prison*. Balzac! — Then he talks about the currency changes and says that Germany must avoid taking any further false steps, for it is too poor.

Thursday, December 16 We get up very late after a restless night. Since the weather is bright, we go, R. and I, for a walk before lunch. He talks with ever-mounting indignation about Schelling's revelation, and says it is now impossible to communicate with C. Frantz, either. The Germans are like that, he says, disposed to reverie and each of them cultivating a bee in his bonnet, which turns him into an imbecile and then makes him spiteful. — R. is somewhat run down, but all the same we go for another walk after lunch and allow ourselves to be rained on in the best of spirits. In the distance R. points out to me a perambulating umbrella—there is no other way of describing the figure; we then watch Marke, and R. explains our delight in his beauty by saying that everything about it is pure Nature; when one touches his coat, it is as if one were plunging directly into Nature. — He works before supper. During the meal the humiliation of von Hülsen, who for 30 years has not behaved well toward R., gives rise to observations on the subject of justice, and R. says: "Every act, good or bad, has its consequences; it is of no account whether the individual lives to see it or not. If he holds out, he will see it" (as R. now with von Hülsen). "There is something sublime about the justice of Fate—for one cannot ascribe it to human beings." — The other subject of conversation is the adoption of vegetarianism by our friends the Wolzogens; with this R. sees his ideas reflected back to him as in a distorting mirror, a great perception mistakenly converted into a petty practical act. — Perceivers and followers, perhaps the most deeply divided of natures! In the one, everything is great, free, tranquil; in the other, narrow, agitated, restricted; the one exerting its powers for the world, the other just for a sect. — Rub. plays the C-sharp Minor Quartet to us.

Friday, December 17 R. had a better night, got up only once, but he is taking medicine, and this puts a strain on him. At breakfast he recalls his orchestrations and says he has never misjudged his effects— he may previously have overloaded the accompaniment for the singers, but he made no mistakes with the instruments. In the afternoon we again go for a walk in the palace gardens, and R. tells me of his desire to know once and for all what is genuine in the Gospels and what has been inserted, "shown literally in color, red for the one, black for the other." — He says he recently glanced through the Bhavagad-Gita and was dismayed by the chaos of additions; if only one could be shown what the original was! — He works on his score but complains of lack of concentration. In the evening he talks to friend Wolz. in an earnest and fatherly way about vegetarianism, and the latter listens—but will it be of any use? Friend Rub. plays the American March very nicely and to the delight of us all, including R. — We remember Beethoven's birthday, and I read reminiscences of him by a Herr Louis Schlösser, which remind us of R.'s short story and interest us very much, in spite of some curious features. — When we express our admiration of Beeth. for going to see the young man, R. says: "He was utterly delighted with him for bringing the Duke's subscription; usually people bring something useless—this really was something. It is like *us*." — When we embrace at our first parting, R. sings the joyful theme of Tristan's reunion with Isolde, then says, "That is not the joy of holding out and winning victories, but it's joy, all the same." — "Rather, joy in defeat," I observe.

Saturday, December 18 R. woke up suddenly and with such violence that he upset the table beside his bed; half grumbling, half joking, he picks up the objects and settles down again to sleep, which soon comes. We get up early, and each of us goes to his day's work. He begins it by reading *Amadis* (by Count G[obineau]), which particularly pleases him, he believes, because it followed Schelling—he would sooner have spent his time reading the dreariest tract of a Protestant theologian than that nonsense. — We go for a walk at one o'clock in pleasant air and visit friend Jouk., who is suffering from rheumatism, but whose nice furnishings please R. — At lunch we have the mayor, friend Feustel, and Wolz. — Many reminiscences of Italy, then discussion of the present state of the Society of Patrons and plans for a meeting. — R. and I then go for a walk, are caught in the rain; we are glad to have such friends as Feustel and the mayor; R. says, "It gives me so much confidence when businessmen like that show faith in a cause which seems so nebulous even to me." — The evening brings news from Italy about *Tristan und Isolde* and "Ride of the Valkyries" which makes us smile [*enclosed a letter from Tesarini and an Italian concert program dated December 15, 1880*]. But R. looks run down—was he not pleased with his work? He is also easily irritated, as by the subject of Siegfried's education; I hoped to have arranged things satisfactorily with Herr Vogler, the head teacher, but R. wants a house tutor and is annoyed at always being surrounded by incompetent people who are unable to help him. — I suggest a reading, and we choose Cervantes's "Rimorete and Contado," which gives us tremendous enjoyment. — The evening passes, we go upstairs, and when we are alone in R.'s little room, he begins to talk about Hans, with indignation on account of his behavior toward Lusch. He recapitulates the whole relationship and wants to write to him. I advise him that it would be better to state his feelings to Hans's cousin Frege, along with a repayment of the Bülow fund. A sad conversation; R. tells me this was the reason for his irritation—to hear about the performance of the 9th from friends who went to hear it (Gross, etc.), this cut him to the heart. — His decision calms him somewhat, we go to bed—but soon he starts again, asks me many things about the past, and thus the night is a very restless one. R. gets up and reads; at last he falls asleep! — Frau D[egele] has sent a photograph with a request for an inscription for her husband. R. complies: "All honor to women, for here is a wife who weaves photographs into Herr Degele's life." — Yesterday we were speaking of my age, and Lusch gave me one year less than is due to me, whereupon R.: "Whatever you do, take nothing away, for this is our pride, like the tines for a stag—with every year our antlers grow prouder."

Sunday, December 19 Our night ended with quite a good early-morning sleep—but R.'s countenance is grave as he wishes me good morning. He has already done some reading—Count Gob.'s *Amadis*—and is little edified by French poetry; he finds the syllable counting, which excludes rhythm, repellent. — At midday he reads to me the draft of his letter to Herr Frege for Hans. Solemn feelings. In the afternoon we go for a walk in the palace gardens, in the evening R. copies out his letter, and after supper we finish Cervantes's story with ever-increasing enjoyment. "I see the eye which saw all this"—I am often interrupted by loud laughter from my audience; every feature of it grips us, and all imitations seem to us prosaic and clumsy in comparison with the original. This charming masterpiece strikes him as so "light-footed"! At lunch R. came back to *Amadis,* he dislikes the light tone, taken from Ariosto. (Last night, before supper, he came to tell me that he had just seen a large spider in his study, and when he went downstairs, he found an advertisement for the Brunswick lottery lying there. He would like Fidi to buy a ticket.) He was vexed with the Grimm dictionary and its untidy editing. But Bismarck's pompousness toward the Greek envoys amused him. — A letter from Busch in a philosophic vein, which Herr Levi sent me, displeases him; he says he once knew a brewer's son who wrote just like that. But we women, he adds, we form a good opinion of somebody for one reason or another, and then we never drop him—and that is very good of us.

Monday, December 20 This night was also none too good, though not entirely bad. In the morning R. recalls the chorus at the end of *Die Zauberflöte,* how Levi had not understood it and took it too fast, clumsily allowing the men's voices to drown the delicate singing of the women. It just shows, he says, how conductors do not bother themselves about what is happening on stage. He copies out his letter to Frege and shows me that he has written it without mistakes, whereas he always makes mistakes when writing to the King. But for him this has been a happy and an important task, which came to him quite naturally. — At lunch a statement of his makes us laugh heartily; Vogl is said to have observed that the conductor Levi was going mad; R. says I was to blame for that, for I had turned a *Juif errant* [wandering Jew] into a *Juif concentré* [reserved Jew], a statement which produces loud laughter. We go for a walk in pouring rain, but are nevertheless in good spirits, always able to put many things out of our minds. In the evening he works on his score and shows me how carefully he has erased one passage. I receive friend Feustel, who tells me that his son-in-law was received in Meiningen by Hans with a flood of complaints about Bayreuth, and particularly about Wolz., who had misled him into signing the Jewish petition, whereas he sees that R. abstained and now stands well with the Jews. He, Hans, made the sacrifice and was hissed, etc. — This has a dismal effect. I suggest reading, and we begin Cervantes's "The Generous Lover," but such Turkish tales interest us very little. Our mood remains what it was, and we start reminiscing! It behooves us now to stand by each other, to recognize the justice of all hardships. . . .

Tuesday, December 21 The night was bearable; but some things said about Lusch upset us. We wonder whether Hans's attitude might not have an oppressive effect on the girls and disturb the even course of their development. If so, the blame is primarily mine. Ailinos, the good, may it triumph! In the morning the weather is so bad that we cannot even think of a walk, and R. feels thoroughly depressed. But in the afternoon we stroll around the palace gardens, and since I notice that he is much affected by the recent embarrassing occurrences, I tell him I should like to go somewhere far away with him, so that he would not hear of them. "But you don't want to go to Madeira," is his reply. He describes the Society of Patrons as the hypothetical *x,* with which Feustel is not reckoning but he himself is. Conference at 5—on friend Feustel's advice R. decides not to send his letter to W. Frege, lest it appear that the letter was the consequence of the altercation between Bülow and Gross. The problems concerning the production of *Parsifal* are also settled. Our friends stay to supper, and afterward their wives arrive. Pepino sings very nicely in the hall, and R. plays together with him as he sings, to the great delight of us all. Herr Jäger sings "*Am stillen Herd"* to us, not exactly to the satisfaction of R., who says afterward, "Germans have no idea of mildness or charm." In the palace gardens he said to me, "If I had an orchestra at my disposal, I should take great delight in rehearsing something like the last movement of Mozart's E-flat Major Symphony, bringing out all its subtleties, and in the fastest tempo."

Wednesday, December 22 Good weather, R. does some work, but he is still weighed down by recent impressions, and when at lunch Lusch talks about the performance of the 9th Symphony, he says to her earnestly, "If anybody had had an ounce of tact, not a word would have been said to you about it." After lunch he reads to us the debate on the Jewish question and then remarks that all talk and all measures are useless as long as property exists. World peace might certainly have helped in this matter, but as long as nations are arming against one another, the Jews will retain their power. They are the only free people, "for it is only through money that I can keep my son from becoming a slave to the state." When I ask him whether he could not express these thoughts in the *Blätter,* he replies that he would be very unwilling to do so, he has made many notes elaborating his major ideas, and these he would carry out. We go for a walk in the palace gardens, the elder girls occupy our thoughts and give rise to dismal conversations, which might have led to angry outbursts if we had not taken refuge in a sad silence. On our return home I cannot rest until I have begged R. to forgive me for not having sufficient strength to dispel certain moods in him. He says he would feel like weeping tears of blood if he had caused me sorrow, and our souls intermingle, freed of their burden. — Frau Niemann has sent a photograph of R. for her husband, which R. inscribes, "Wehwalt is my name indeed, since Niemann does not sing me." — In the evening we continue reading Cervantes's story, but not to the end, since we find this Turkish tale repellent. — When we are alone together, R. tells me that he slept a little before supper, and it did him so much good to stretch his muscles; he was feeling what a bore everything always was—the photograph for Niemann, receiving one friend or another, the talk—all of it such a bore. — And to end with: "One should be glad when wearisomeness turns into weariness." —

Thursday, December 23 R. slept well, and we both rise fairly early. R. tells me that during the shower Fidi reported that the weather was "horrible." And so indeed it is. Constant thoughts of Venice, and sad considerations whether our center of gravity should not be moved outside Wahnfried. Other difficulties on top of that; when I go downstairs at midday, I find R. engaged in writing to Herr Batz, a task which puts him in an ill humor. We do not go out, I make little preparations for tomorrow, a *tableau vivant* with the children, the Holy Family; we have finished but are still deep in discussions when R. softly opens the door. Some embarrassment is glossed over with much talk. In the *salon* he shows me the passage he has just been orchestrating ("*schon nah' dem Schlosse, wird uns der Held entrückt*") and asks whether I can appreciate how beautiful it is. Joy returns, and when friend Wolzogen visits us in the evening, a very fluent and pleasant conversation develops on all sorts of things, on the Boers in Transvaal, whom R. would like to see the Germans supporting against the English, on the Jewish agitation, on the etymology of German words; R. also frankly tells friend Wolzogen his true opinion of Jäger. [*Added in margin:* "Also on Gambetta, whom he wishes the French would get rid of, whereas he enjoys watching what Ferry and his colleagues are doing."] — Over coffee I tell R. a nice episode about a nun in a Balzac novel, R. says, "The French ought to do with Balzac what I wish the Germans would do with Schopenhauer."

Friday, December 24 R. tells me he wishes that Wolz. would ask Herr v. Weber to write a sort of appeal in favor of the Boers for the *Blätter,* so that future emigrations might be channeled in that direction. — The sun shines during the morning, and R. invites me to walk with him in the palace gardens, but it is soon obscured, and we return home. During our walk R. tells me that Jacolliot's journey is not giving him as much enjoyment as he expected, the constant abuse of the Germans is offensive, they are regarded as dogs and barbarians let loose by the English. How can people so lower themselves, he asks, as to disparage the opponents who beat them? We Germans had at least regarded the French as gods (1804, etc.). In the afternoon we go out again, and I tell R. how much I enjoy these walks with him, which make me feel as if, leaving all of life's ballast behind, we are marching toward a nameless goal. "The goal," he says, "is to keep the little candle alight, so that it will go on burning a while longer." — Then he talks to me of his childhood, how at the age of 5, since he could not sing, he imitated Kaspar's piccolo and flute trills [in *Der Freischütz*] with "*Perrbip,*" climbed on a chair to represent Samiel looking over an imaginary bush, and said, "Perrbip, perrbip." [*Added in margin:* "Over coffee R. tells us something funny which he heard from Schnappauf: the knacker here said to him that since R. was in such good standing with the King, he might procure him the executioner's post, which has just fallen vacant."] At 7 o'clock I give him the "golden robe" and tell him he is being expected as the *Christkind* (in order to explain why the children are not coming with us to see the lighted tree). — The *tableau vivant,* splendidly posed and held by the children, delights and moves him, and he wants Joukowsky to paint it. Marke's Christmas present also pleases him, and the evening, lit right up to the end by the tree, passes merrily. The portrait of Fidi, presented by Jouk. to R., also delights him. But above all the dear children, who looked splendid in the *tableau* (three angels playing musical instruments: *Boni, Loldi, Eva;* Fidi, planing, as the young Jesus; Lulu as Madonna, praying; off to one side Pepino as Saint Joseph). — During the *tableau* Rubinstein plays the first chorale from *Die Msinger.* — R.'s last word: "Now I can feel sympathy with your mother." —

Saturday, December 25 "*Geschreibsel, Gebleibsel!*" . . . How to describe, how indeed to write? . . . The children strike up their song after the first embraces and sing it splendidly—then they bring me "the locker," and what things there are in it! . . . The 9th Symphony, copied out by R. 50 years ago—he coaxed it out of Frl. Uhlig for me! Splendidly written, pleasing him, too, with its painstaking thoroughness, which, when I think of all the things that must have been going on in that 17-year-old head, seems incredible to me. Then a lovely old necklace, which R. calls "Frau Vogl's kiss," because, when he was choosing it in the antiquarian's shop, Frau Vogl rushed in and embraced him passionately. "You will never see anything like that again," R. said to the dealer. "You should let me have it 100 marks cheaper." "That's true," the man said, and R. remarks that much more and he would have given it to him for nothing. Then a gold heart, an old saltcellar, and many little things from the children, which I took one by one out of the drawers, with comments from R. and the children. In my room I discover a table carpentered for me by Fidi, and lovely sketches by Joukowsky, full of associations. The morning passes in friendly felicitations, and R. says he would like to go on drinking without a break, he can do or write nothing. — Since the King kindly remembers me in a telegram, R. thanks him, sending birthday bliss to the sun! At lunch R. proposes my health, I have difficulty in replying, for what exists between us cannot be expressed in words before others, not even those nearest to us. After lunch he says to me, "Forgive me for speaking like that." — Ah, he is well and in good spirits—how can I have any other feeling than overwhelming gratitude? — It snows in the afternoon, Frau Holle is congratulating me, says R. — I go for a rest, R., too, but then he gets involved downstairs in a philosophical discussion with Rub., who wants to do away with the world! — Our mealtime conversations are devoted to the difficulties connected with my surprise gifts: the nonarrival of the locker, the discovery that Frl. Uhlig had gone away, and much else. In the evening the *tableau vivant* is repeated, and it moves R. to tears; the splendid "*Geschreibsel, Gebleibsel*" is also repeated. Then R. plays the *Euryanthe* Overture with Rub., and after playing it he embraces me, exclaiming, "Oh, Weber! I love

him as much as I do you!" and then adds, "No, not quite as much."
He then becomes immersed in memories of W., whom the Dresdeners
called "Humpelmarie" ["Hobbling Mary"], he recalls his walk, his
expression, somewhat weary, and attributes his earnest application to
so neglected a genre as opera to forebodings of his early death. R.
is moved as he expresses this thought, and it is very affecting. Then
he says to the children, "Now I am going to sing something for
Mama," and he sings the passage in the first act where Lysiart comes
to fetch Eur[yanthe], turning to me on the words "When thou
appearest." — Then we start discussing *Fidelio,* which R. describes as
unworthy of the composer of the symphonies in spite of splendid
individual passages, and the finale of *Fidelio* is played. (Before supper
R. had played through the C Major Overture and given it preference
over the great *Leonore* Overture, which has more of an *al fresco* quality;
but this C Major was not designed for the masses, he says.) When
Jouk. remarks that Beeth. and R. are the composers of joy, R. observes
that he must be thinking of the finale to *Lohengrin,* but he has found
little scope for it, for drama always introduces passion. — My health
is repeatedly drunk, in both gay and solemn ways. Among jokes which
since yesterday R. has frequently been telling is this one from the
Fl. Bl.: One lieutenant to another: "How many cows are there here,
do you think?" — "77." — "How do you know?" — "Quite easy—I
just counted their legs and divided by 4." R. observes that all knowledge
nowadays is something like that! — The evening ends, I kneel in
prayer before Him whose blessing can alone make me worthy of him.
And as we lie quietly in bed, I hear his voice softly saying, "I am
happy, I am happy, now I could die, for it has all been fulfilled—what
is still to come is a bonus." —

Sunday, December 26 R. has a slight headache, calls himself an old
toper, but is in good spirits and writes a detailed "dog letter" to
Bremen, since the good news is being brought to Faf on the hill, and
now something must be done for Marke. At one o'clock, in very
mild weather, R. and I go for a walk in the palace gardens, then we
welcome Seidl, our old member of the "Nibelungen Kanzlei," from
Leipzig. Our conversation at lunch is concerned with the Berlin
project, and R. expresses his annoyance over the fact that it is now
being said that von Hülsen has withdrawn, and nobody is aware that
he, R., did not wish the *Ring* to be performed at the Court opera.
In the afternoon R. and I go for a walk in the palace gardens with
Seidl and Joukowsky. Yesterday morning R. spoke to me of the
beauty of the *tableau vivant* and wondered whether the painting could
reflect all its beauty, for it had been a living thing, whereas a painting
conveys only the memory of a vision. In the evening R. complains

about how boring our friends are. In the afternoon he worked on his score.

Monday, December 27   R. slept well. I occupy myself arranging the nice, dear things I was given, and delight in my little room, whose every corner arouses pleasant feelings. R. receives a nice letter from the King, who is sending him a Renaissance cabinet and a bronze model of his new castle near Hohenschwangau. — But we have very bad weather for our afternoon walk, R. once again feels his chest pains, lunch, for which he also retained friend Wolz., puts him in a bad mood, but his afternoon rest restores him, and in the evening a magician delights him and us and a multitude of children in the hall. His skill is really remarkable, and R. gives him his picture, under which he writes, "Herr Mennier can do more than I." — Some Batz affairs disturb him, but he is pleasantly stimulated by a telegram from Herr Neumann, announcing further ventures with the *Ring* in America, London, St. Petersburg [*enclosed a telegram from Angelo Neumann in Leipzig, requesting exclusive rights to stage the* Ring *for three years against a royalty of ten percent of gross receipts*]. Since the director asks for an immediate answer, R. replies something like this: "Somewhat tempestuous; confident that your intentions are upright, I give my consent." — It would certainly be a good thing if the *Ring* itself were to bring R.'s finances back in order.

Tuesday, December 28   Not a good night for R. But in the morning R. takes a short rest. At 1 o'clock we go for a walk in the palace gardens with Loldchen and Evi, the weather too mild. In the afternoon R. and I again, but in the rain, which now descends on us almost every day and gives more urgency to R.'s thoughts of Italy. In the afternoon Seidl plays passages from *Parsifal*. R. comes to listen and is pleased, for he says it has all become so strange to him. In the evening we again go through parts of the 2nd act and the Prelude. — R.'s reading material is now *A Voyage to the Land of Elephants,* he shows me the engravings, and while we are looking at them, I am reminded of the sect R. once told me about, which regards the spirit and not the flesh as being responsible for evil; I say that, seeing animals, the elephants in the rice fields, one gets the feeling that it is only human beings with their "spirit" who have brought cruelty and malice into the world. R. replies, "Yes, certainly, and in every sect there lies some truth, a genuine perception—but developed one-sidedly and thus leading to mistakes." — When we retire in the evening, he tells me about a scientific encyclopedia by Hederich owned by his father; he says he would like to have it for the sake of the article on opera; he recalls that in it opera was described as the worst form of art, and he says to me, "Strange to think that people like Semper and even Goethe looked on such isolated pieces—the cavatinas, the dances—designed for entertainment as the proper artistic form." — Yesterday he spoke of the private performance of *Lohengrin* and observed that it was not really the right way—for drama one needs people.

Wednesday, December 29   R. sleeps well, and since he is expecting a rehearsal with Jäger and Seidl, he settles down to read—now Gobineau's *Nouvelles asiatiques*. The rehearsal falls through, and at 1 o'clock we go strolling in the palace gardens in springlike weather. Seidl with us, which leads our conversation primarily to the Berlin venture. At lunch some more Batzish affairs. We discuss what we intend to do on January 1, so that we may continue doing it throughout the year. "Work," says somebody. "Pray," say I, and R.: "Take steps to ensure earning the maximum amount of money with the minimum of effort." — Much about Russia, arising from the *Nouvelles asiatiques*. The wretched state of Ireland is also discussed, and the American desire to come to its aid. R. expresses his great antipathy for the English rule there. We go for a walk in the palace gardens, and R. has the idea of surprising Seidl at a rehearsal he is good-naturedly holding for the amateur concert. After the concert in the evening, R. reproaches him for having done it, saying: "When one is under an obligation, as you are to Gross, one should discharge it in a homophonous way, but not with one's soul. Mount guard in front of Gross's bank, but do not conduct a concert. If Rothschild offered me a million to set a poem to music for him, do you think I would do it?" — He tells him that he went to the rehearsal in order to surprise him, take the baton from him, and beat time in such a way that they came to grief—but unfortunately, he says, the rehearsal was already over. — While the children are at the concert, R. and I talk about his new article in the *B. Bl.* — Then a glance at the pictures leads to a discussion about Lenbach. R. once again says that he really cannot bear him, in his type of person there is something ungenuine, like those fabricated cones on mountain slopes. — He tells me that 105,000 marks have been subscribed in Germany for Mommsen to replace his burned-out library. R. thinks it is the Jews, which is why Mommsen is now intervening on their behalf, but the Crown Prince heads the list. Krupp, however, has refused to sign, on account of the Israelites. — The children return, and there is talk of Meiningen, which on every occasion leads R. to express his great vexation and deep disgust.

Thursday, December 30   Our friend Seidl has departed with instructions for Neumann, also equipped with cuts for *Tristan*. Today R. writes to the King, tells him all kinds of things, everything, in fact; he continues his letter in the morning and concludes it in the evening. Over coffee he says that a dream last night ended with the words,

"Rise, all you tailors, you brave Bayreuthers." This was probably due, he thinks, to the following line of thought he had had: "In 10 years the French will celebrate the centennial of the great revolution; by that time the Emperor, Moltke, Bismarck will all be dead; the French are quietly setting aside a billion a year for army and navy, we are piling up, too, but will not be able to keep it up; I believe they will beat us and then do what Bismarck did not do with France—could not do because it is too unified—divide Germany into provinces, some going to Belgium. I can already see *la haute Franconie* [Upper Franconia] and all of us put to work as tailors when the Jewish genius, the Jewish Napoleon, makes his appearance there. The whole European mainland will be drowned in pomade. We getting poorer and poorer—though the German empire will not be much of a loss." — "Then," I observe, "will come emigration." "I should like it to come even sooner," says R. — We go for a walk in the palace gardens—Marke has a fight: "He is an enemy of the spirit—he finds all flesh blameless." — We go walking in the palace gardens with Joukowsky, R. very merry, he draws our attention to the faces, among them one he describes as "a perennial bellyache." He delights in the sunset, laughs, however, when we hear the drums rolling, and remarks how well they combine, how the shades of color are reflected in the drum rolls! In the quiet palace gardens there is scarcely anything to be heard except for the angry commands of a sergeant in the nearby barracks. — Yesterday, in connection with the bugle calls, which are not nearly so nice as the previous ones, R. remarked, "With these calls the Bavarians conquered, with the nice ones they were defeated." In the evening our friends the mayor, Feustel, Gross, Rubinstein, Wolz., Jouk. — I was rather weary today, had to go to bed during the day, which gave R. an opportunity of showing all his solicitous kindness toward me.

Friday, December 31 The night was a good one, also for me better than for weeks past, which is greeted as a sort of triumph. R. reads Gobineau and writes what he calls "an artificial letter" to Herr Batz. We go for a walk in the palace gardens at 1 o'clock and again later in the afternoon, when, however, our walk was "washed clean," as R. puts it, for it was raining. Over coffee we discuss Siegfried's development, and since R. talks about the importance of having a companion for his studies and his games, I have to laugh when he irritably exclaims, "These boys are all so precious!" — He feels that the parents, such as the Giessels, etc., will not let us have one; his instinctively felt right to demand whatever he wants is here expressed so clearly, and is so different from anyone else, that I find it a joy to observe. — An act of our friend Seidl's also gives him the opportunity of showing his whole nature: Seidl told us the day before yesterday that he would no longer go to the Sonne when meetings were going on, then we hear that he did go after all and stayed up until 2 in the morning. R. is annoyed about it, I observe that he probably made the decision impulsively, sitting lonely and melancholy in his room; R. disputes this and is indignant at the lie, also at "this stupid addiction to beer, which is driving the Germans to ruin." — "It is all right to lie out of shame," he observes, "when one finds oneself in a false situation, but this hypocrisy is despicable"—and his face is severe, and his voice rings out and his eyes flash! He also says, "Just don't try to make yourself look good—I see people as they are, then all right, then I accept them." — In the evening the candles on the tree lit again, and fortunes told with lead. — But before that R. plays to us the 1st movement of the A Major Symphony and tells us his ideas about it (Dionysian celebrations), as he has often done before, but this evening so eloquently, so absorbed is he by the picture and animated by the subject, that once again—but in a different way from at midday—his countenance gleams; it is now pale and rapt, and he does not even notice that Fidi has handed him his lead. — We do not stay up for midnight. — We experienced it yesterday in the *salon,* when we were hungrily seeking some rusks, and R. was pleased by my picture by Lenbach (the white one), both figure and pose. After reading us something from an article by Helm about the Beeth. quartets, which he finds very good, he ends by reading the invocation to the Graces by Aristophanes, whom he describes as the greatest of Greek geniuses; he recalls with pleasure the sense of lucidity with which he read it years ago in Dresden. — In the morning he tells us about Herr Förster, the theater director in Leipzig who demanded some music for *The Merchant of Venice*; when Herr Neumann made difficulties, he exclaimed, "I cannot present the *Merchant* without music—sooner *Götterdämmerung.*" —

1881

Saturday, January 1   R. did not have a good night, he feels that the tea he drank yesterday, against his usual rule, did not agree with him. But he forces himself to stay quietly in his bed, out of fear of meeting his double; I myself was frightened last night by a noise (probably a mouse). But in the morning he is cheerful, and he continues our discussion about the introduction to the A Major Symphony, which, he maintains, musicians do not know what to do with, and which he would like to reorchestrate. "Everything is either a march or a dance, there is hardly any absolute music," he says. "Beeth. did not have the idea I connect with this introduction—the procession I see so clearly and in such detail that I could stage it—but the thematic figures imposed themselves on him, and then he had to work them into a symphonic form." [*Added in margin:* "F, C, D sharp in the 1st movement of the A Major—'what a cry of sensual delight that is!' R. exclaims. 'What sighing and squirming! What is a musician to do with it when it suddenly chimes in? And how one has to rehearse with orchestras in order to bring such things out!' I tell him that in Mannheim it had perhaps not been so much heard as felt. He laughs and says: 'Yes, when they play with me, they do not know what is happening to them. "What was that?" they ask themselves. Tausig once said to me about the *Freischütz* Overture, "I don't know what you did to the ending, but it was incredible." ' "] — He feels vexed about the "stupidity" of most of the people he talks to—the way, for example, J. Rub. listened to him yesterday and then wanted to have a full mathematical exposition of his idea. And he observes that intelligence is everything, and in living together differences of character are far less an obstacle than differences of intellect. We walk to the mayor's house and bring New Year's greetings to our excellent friends. At lunch our friend Feustel, a person R. always enjoys talking to. R. looks back on the past and says that in his letter he told the King of Dr. Schanzenbach's remark about what a pleasure it was for those who had been there during the bad times to see us all again in the same Munich theater, and to see R. being given a cordial welcome by the public: "One must be able to persevere," says R. — When, after coffee, we bless our meal with an embrace, R. says, "Two stars encountered each other"—our eyes met and exchanged our spirits! — We go for a walk in the palace gardens and again there is some agitation because of Marke, but less severe. In the evening R. tells us feelingly about a blind starling, which a flock of starlings are looking after, feeding, taking with them on their migrations. Rub. brings along Mozart's concertos, we talk about this man of genius, and R. plays and sings the quartet from *Don Giovanni,* which he considers a consummate masterpiece. "One cannot see from his symphonies and piano works what an artist M. was—there are some splendid themes scattered among them, but the construction is loose. But here—what a host of things are gathered together in one single piece of music! A repulsive situation, if it were spoken, but turned by music into Elvira's lament. Oh, music! In it all the world's sufferings are transformed into a gentle lament, and all sin appears as suffering. How does one respond to this?" He plays the piece once again. Then he reads an article to us, "Fashion and Industry," written in connection with an incident in Vienna (the wedding of the Crown Prince and costumes ordered from Paris, demonstrations against this). R. is in agreement with the argument expressed in it—that fashion must of necessity be dominated by Paris—and says: "One might have expected something from the last war, but now we see that it was just a soldiers' affair, nothing in it, and thus Paris must continue to dominate, and it is utterly ridiculous to talk of a German fashion. The best thing would be for women to wear military costumes." His final word in bed is an exclamation over the stupidity of Gladstone, who is practicing the policies of the former government, though he himself previously stood up for the Boers. — (But for the boors one is doing things, he adds.) Before that he expressed a wish to see Carlyle. — Delight in each other, in our children. — Once more harking back to Zurich. — If only I had said to him then, "Come!" But Hans was there—Tristan! I: "We had to prove ourselves to each other." — He urges me to take my medicine and says that with every sip of my iron salts I should toast him! —

Sunday, January 2   R. slept well, the weather is cold and fine, in the morning we go for a walk in the palace gardens; as we go out, he says he always tends to the left, and he dislikes it if someone he loves sits to the right of him. — In the evening he orchestrates, but he looks worn out and fears that he might have caught cold. We start [Cervantes's] *"La Española inglessa"* and are astonished over its conventional charm; it reminds one of the pictures of Veronese, dating from the same time, of the later ones by Tiepolo, of the treatment of subjects from the ancient world in opera, in which everything ends in a dance. R. points out to me how trivial all the aristocrats are, always the same, no figures of note. R. sums all this up with a single word, "Renaissance."

Monday, January 3   R. did not have a very good night, but he is in cheerful spirits. "In seven years we shall celebrate our silver wedding anniversary. Since then I have belonged to no other woman. Before that I did not know whether Frau von Bissing or Frau Wesendonck was the one meant for me." — We laugh, and he recalls the three girls in blue (Boni, Loldi, Eva), how pretty they looked in the theater. Lulu as well, in a different color, in the box. — We walk in the palace gardens both morning and afternoon and delight in the "springlike winter's day"—all the trees white, it is cold, but mild and sunny. — In the morning R. looked through his articles in the *Bayreuther Bl.* and was pleased with them. He still intends to add to them. — In the evening the Feustels and Wolz. and Rub., general conversation. R. reports that Phidias's *Athene* is said to have been discovered. Also, on learning that Bismarck is trying to dismiss Parson Stoecker and that the Emperor is still vacillating, R. says that the same thing will happen to the Jews as happened to the "Jockeys" in Paris at the performance of *Tannhäuser:* the police will be brought in, not against them, but to protect them. — Departure of Lusch, who is going to Mimi in Berlin. When we are alone, R. and I, we immerse ourselves in the picture—we think of Malwida and some other resigned souls. — When he sees the children gathered around him, R. says, "To think, after 30 sterile years, of now having five children all at once around me!" He decides to send the letter off to Hans, 4 weeks after the date on it.

Tuesday, January 4   A good night for R. and for me—lovely weather. R. reads Gobineau's stories and finds them interesting. — We go for a walk in the palace gardens around 1 o'clock. [*Added in margin:* "When I asked him at 1 o'clock what he had been doing, he said, 'Putting on a shirt,' and he complains about all the difficulties it caused him. Recently he said, 'My hands are more absent-minded than my head.' "] A sketch of Kundry, brought along by Jouk., pleases us a lot. "Actually," says R., "she ought to be lying there naked, like a Titian Venus." — Now this has to be replaced by finery. A nice letter from Standhartner pleases him and starts him reminiscing about Vienna; St. is proof, he says, that one can get through to the Viennese with music—how much had he done for him when he settled in Vienna! He describes the bone structure of Standhartner's skull as frighteningly Slavonic, yet at the same time pleasing. In the afternoon we go for a walk in the palace gardens, delight in the fine winter weather (the sun gladdened us in the *salon,* "and it is always the setting sun," says R., "which gives us this light—like the smile of a god"; the transfigured picture of Beeth. delights him), the ice, the evening glow, the crescent moon appearing; now and again poor women, to whom he gives something and who bless him. We also stroll in the garden, and there it is begging children who besiege us, and the evening star which delights us. — When I tell R. that, bad as my sight is, at table I clearly see his countenance as something impregnable, reserved, as it were, protecting and shutting off his inner being from outside attack, and his gaze as that which gives, bestows, reveals his inner thoughts, he tells me, "It is your [*deleted:* "splendid"] will which allows you to see all that." (I have deleted the adjective, since I am not sure what the word was.) — And in deep, harmonious peace we part; the glow of the setting sun, the moon's chaste gold, the gleaming purity of the evening star have left their blessings deep in my heart, all, all that is, speaks of the land of nowhere, the never-never land for which one's heart is always yearning! — In the evening we intend to finish Cervantes's story, but we find it quite impossible. Instead R. reads us Councilor Tusmann from *Die Serapionsbrüder;* we enjoy it, and R. says, "He is an original talent—I am glad we Germans have someone like that to show, and everything by Hoffmann always contains an idea."

Wednesday, January 5 R. did not have a good night, and he feels oppressed. In the morning he reads Gobineau's stories with enjoyment, much enjoyment, he particularly likes "The Persian Magician," and he feels that of all modern languages French is the best suited for conveying an impression of Oriental courtesy. — At 12, when he comes downstairs to begin work, he finds some business letters; these delay him and vex him. Believing him to be working, I pay some calls with Boni; as we return, I see him in the avenue, coming toward us. He had been watching the other children skating; but he is not well. And a walk we take in the palace gardens does nothing to restore him, for it is very windy ("Devil take ozone!" he exclaims in the middle of it). — At lunch our conversation turned to violent emotions, and whether there can be love without jealousy. R. says, "It is a terrible thought, and one is deprived of the basis of everything, of one's whole roots, if one assumes that somebody else can be the sharer of one's joy—that just shows what a risky thing the love bond is." — Yesterday R. said that he still intended to write about his ideas on property for the *Blätter;* how sacred this idea has always been can be seen in the fact that every robber, every conqueror, starts with the assumption of its sacredness. How would it be if nobody possessed anything? — In the evening he works a little on the orchestration of *Parsifal* and says how curious it was that, while orchestrating "*in heilig ernster Nacht nahten sich des Heilands holde Boten,*" he happened to open the book at that passage and saw that in his sketch he had left out the word *dereinst;* this he immediately put back in, for rhythmically it was very welcome to him; words like *Heiland* should never be extended, he says. In the evening

R. reads "*Die Brautschau*" to us, up to the end—that is to say, not right to the end, for R. feels it is amateurish and loses itself in insipidities. — R. considers the form of the Mozart concertos extraordinarily clumsy, with some nice ideas scattered throughout.

Thursday, January 6   R. procured a better night for himself by taking medicine. He jokingly calls me the Napoleon of sleepers. Napoleon is now his main word for everything. — While still in bed, he says, "If you look after me well, clothe me well, feed me well, then I shall still compose *Die Sieger*." — "My difficulty there is the locality and the speech. Christianity is all noble simplicity, but in Buddhism there is so much education, and education is very inartistic." We talk of the fact that in both, *Parsifal* and *Sieger,* more or less the same theme (the redemption of a woman) is treated. "It is impossible to judge what an effect the 3rd act of *P.* will have if it is well done." — This is why for Kundry he wants some other singer than [Amalie] Materna, whose face does not appeal to him, for she should be capable of deep and noble expressions. — "I wonder if some formula could be found," he continues after a while, "for baptizing some such poor creature as Levi—I believe I could discover it." — And he expands on his idea concerning faith, love, and hope, as described in his most recent article. "One cannot speak too harshly against all the things that make up our modern culture. When I think that Bismarck has applied for the dismissal of Parson Stoecker, and when I think of our future with the Crown Prince—and particularly *her*—! When I recall that women like her simply refuse to discuss certain subjects (such as vivisection)—!" — I say that the women cannot be held responsible for everything, but he exclaims: "Oh, yes, they can. The men are just wretched soldiers, the women are the only ones to whom one can turn in idealistic matters; and if all one finds there is leather, it really is appalling." — When, referring to religious statements, I say, "I hope for eternal peace after our death," he replies, "Those are all secrets—we should not run around as we do with our five senses if we knew the answers." He orchestrates, asks me whether I like flageolets and says I cannot know what it is like when a passage has to be reorchestrated three times. We go for a walk in the palace gardens, where Fidi is skating. — At lunch he comes back to Hoffmann's story and says it is utterly unworthy of being read aloud to us, he is downright ashamed of having suggested it. Whereas he highly praises Gobineau's stories. — Countess La Tour's action in sending us the Count's picture starts a discussion over coffee about relationships of this kind. When I say that the Countess would be very shocked if one were to assume anything beyond friendship, R. says: "But what is that—spending their evenings in intellectual conversations together? In such cases it always turns out that she is a goose and he a silly fool, for if one assumes that such contacts are not at the same time—how shall I put it?—physically beneficial, then all this homage to Plato is ridiculous." — He works in the afternoon, three bars cause him trouble, and he cites to me Helm's 2nd article about the quartets—the freedom of the voice leading in the [Opus] 133 Fugue. He says that with him it was more or less the same, he felt this urge, and he promises to show me a subsidiary voice in Gurnemanz's narration. — The question of costumes and decorations is discussed in the evening. [*Added on a later page but referred back to this point:* "R. shows us the article on the philosopher Hartmann in Spamer's encyclopedia, and we are much amused by the expression 'his cowardly personal renunciation.' — R. thinks these pieces are now all written by Jews."]

Friday, January 7   R. had quite a tolerable night and works on his score in the morning. In the afternoon we go for a walk in the palace gardens, where R. finds the windless, mild cold very pleasant. At lunch we had friend Heckel, who has come here for a conference. *Nibelung* reminiscences in plenty. R. works, it is still the three bars (*es neigten in heilig ernster Nacht*) which occupy him. He feels tired. In the evening much about Count Gobineau, whose *Ottar Jarl* I find very gripping, and it leads to a discussion of old Nordic customs. — A letter from Lusch delights us with its naturalness and its discretion. (R. expressed his antipathy for the English again today.)

Saturday, January 8   R. had a tolerable night. In the morning we talk once more about Lusch's letter. "Yes," he says, "if she imagines she will ever again find someone like you—!" And he observes that in the social world there is in fact a great deal of vulgarity to be found, even among the women, while the men can talk only about horses. — "A man like Schleinitz is extraordinarily rare, heartless though he may be." — R. is not entirely pleased by our friends' coming here for a conference, he says he feels no great eagerness to stage the work, though it gave him much joy to write it. — At 12 R. calls me and shows me how he has placed his nice slippers beneath his big chair; things like that give him pleasure, he says, when he enters the room. When I tell him I can understand that, he says, "Yes, but your way of making your room pleasant is just to put up nasty pictures of me." — Then he tells me that he feels like writing his article about the present Jewish problem; I had suggested it to him, and he would like to do it now, to ask, "What does a Jew find when he comes to us?" — R. works after we have been for a stroll in the palace gardens. — In the evening Herr Schön, Pohl, and Heckel; R. annoyed, first because, not wishing to retain his informal clothes, he feels uncomfortable, and second because he has no desire to talk about these things. He finds the good people all too unsatisfactory and insignificant, and the first moment of meeting is tart on his side and rather off-putting. But he soon recovers, makes jokes with and about Pohl, and when Rub. plays my father's arrangement of the Hummel septet, R. is in high spirits and finds much amusement in this old-fashioned, worthy piece, with all its padding. Afterward he plays with Rub. the Overture to *Rienzi*. When our friends have left, R. and I remain alone together—it is as if we discover each other anew, and how beautiful, how splendid the discovery then turns out to be! (R. wanted to drink Hans's health, I asked him not to.)

Sunday, January 9 R. did not have a good night, but he cheers up during our breakfast together, and we start a long discussion about *patience;* I have often spoken in praise of it, R. says I am right and praises it as the true form of courage; he quotes as examples Frederick the Great, Marius, and Morosini, and the Christians who refused military service and submitted to torture. — "Spring is here," he cries when he hears me opening my egg, and declares that it sounded like a woodpecker tapping on a tree. He also appears to be cheerful around lunchtime, when he shows me his dress suit and says he wants to look formal for our guests. — But when the meal arrives he looks ill, is out of humor and so unwell that he leaves the table. He soon returns and gradually regains his spirits. The conclusions of the conference are discussed, as well as the present relationship of the Society of Patrons to the performances, seats for which are now after all to be put on sale. — We then go for a walk in the palace gardens, since R. is feeling better. In the evening, before our friends arrive, he comes to sit beside me with a serious face: "My reverence for you grows and grows," he says, "but everything else leaves me increasingly indifferent." Evening comes, and with it our guests, and R. is told what was decided at the conference. He is satisfied, and he tells me that a social gathering of this kind, at which matters of common interest are discussed, is by no means the worst. He is cheerful, exceedingly friendly and kind toward everybody. When we are alone together, he reads me several things from Count Gobineau's stories, after I have told him what I have written to Stein about patience and about happiness, which I regard as a treasure to be unearthed—hence the verb "to treasure"; such happiness is perhaps all the harder to snatch for oneself when an apparent fulfillment (our festivals) has already been achieved. R. observes that feelings of this kind would not be easily understood.

Monday, January 10 Our morning conversation concerns that disinherited part of humanity to which no ray of religion, let alone of art, can penetrate. We feel the irony of talking about Christian renunciation, when all around us are hunger, need, oppression, apathy. — Molle arrives from Bremen, a good and handsome creature. Also a letter from Herr Neumann enclosing very large announcements. R. tells the children he would become so rich that he would have his trousers made with holes in them, so that money would spill out in all directions! — We go to Jouk.'s studio to look at the Magic Garden, which is still not quite right. R. feels rather run down; but over coffee we get immersed in a long discussion following what I have to say about *Ottar Jarl*. When I declare that Gob[ineau] has vindicated medieval poetry's claim to be regarded as original, R. disputes this view and says that it drew very largely on the Orient, and only the confused ancient heathen traditions were genuine; Wolfram [von Eschenbach]'s *Parzival* is not genuine, and that is why it does not make much impression on one in spite of some very lovely features. "The first original work is my *Ring des Nibelungen*. The second part of the *Nibelungenlied* is original, too—the first part is a compilation." — But he remarks on the Count's sympathy for the heroes of the 11th century, who because of the vigor and independence of their characters were able, following their deeds of plunder and conquest, to bow down before holiness and become saints themselves. He continues, "It would be nice if we could also recognize some special qualities in the German character, some peculiar enlightenment, capable of absorbing quietly all that is foreign to it and reproducing it!" — We go for a walk in the palace gardens, watch the children skating—Fidi the Quaker (on account of his round hat). In the evening R. writes to Herr Neumann, complaining about all the business matters he now has to attend to. Afterward our friends Schön, Heckel, Feustel. R. shows considerable composure, though he loses it when friend Feustel talks rather airily about the present prosperity and says that the farmers are pleased when they see some Jew who has come to buy their cattle. R. grows angry, regrets it, and says to me afterward that nothing upsets him more than having to listen to a string of platitudes and being provoked into making a reply which in any case will not be understood. There is an amusing moment when Feustel, after observing that it is not only the Jews who are to blame for swindling the people, asks earnestly, "Who has the control over my purse?" "I," says R. — Developments in France still continue to interest R. It is said that anti-Semitic demonstrations are assuming ever-increasing proportions!

Tuesday, January 11 "Well, what does that have to do with me?" I hear R. say during the night. I: "What?" "Corfu's neutrality, of which I have just been dreaming." He slept quite well, and at 12 o'clock settles down to his work, after writing to inquire what he owes for Molle. At breakfast and also at lunch we talked about friend Feustel's optimistic sophisms and also about Empress Augusta, who appears to have

directed some malicious remarks at Lusch. R. says, "These creatures
are such utter nobodies, they cannot even make people happy, for
when they bring someone into their entourage, they then find it a
bother, and all that's left to them is to make malicious remarks." —
Over coffee we again talk about Gobineau's stories, which R. finds
very absorbing. In the palace gardens he tells me about the Chileans,
who are now outside Lima. In the evening R. jokes about a present I
have given to Fidel, saying he wants to see the gold pencil, too, he is
hoping to become Fidi's heir. He expresses his happy feelings of
certitude that nothing can happen to our children, and so foolish am I
that, instead of being pleased, I am gripped by a kind of fear; I betray
this only through a movement and an exclamation, but how unjust of
me, how lacking in self-discipline, not simply to be pleased when he
expresses pleasure! I read *"L'Illustre Magicien"* aloud, and R. is much
delighted by it even on hearing it a second time, particularly the scene
in which the magician teaches Kassem wisdom and in which only the
effect on Kassem is shown, then the first scene between Kassem and his
wife and the return of the sister. — R. has taken a little notebook up to
his dressing room, since, as he tells me, musical ideas always come to
him while he is dressing. — Letters from Lusch to her sisters entertain
and delight us.

Wednesday, January 12   R. had a rather restless night, but he works,
and his face wears its merry and sparkling expression at lunch, when he
drinks Wilhelmj's new wine, "Rauenthaler Richard Wagner," with
enjoyment. We drink our health. R. says, "I drank silently to the
children's health," and I feel as if, for my sake, he has been making
up for yesterday's rashness. Still delight in Gobineau. A walk in the
palace gardens at 4 o'clock, the air very pleasant. Then R. settles down
to the joyful exertions of work, and comes to fetch me in the evening
as at midday. — At lunch he was even more inwardly absorbed by his
work. In the evening friends Jouk., Rub., Humperdinck. — R. talks
about Mozart—"How lonely such a man is!"—and how after him there
followed such commonplace works as *Dorfbarbier, Donau-Weibchen,*
etc. "Schools, alas!" he cries ironically. "Now, after 30 years, they are
looking at *Lohengrin,* to see more or less how it was done!" — Recently,
when somebody said that Jesus was a Jew, he replied that this was more
or less like saying Mozart was a credit to the people of Salzburg. — But
today was a really nice monastic day, tranquil and industrious, and with
those words of his to me which I often do not dare to write down, like
starshine in the evening, like dew in the morning. And the constant
feeling of communion! Today I wrote to Herr Marsillach about his
book, and almost everything I said in my letter R. brings up today as
table conversation! — In the evening he says, "I am glad that I shall

not need to go to America, *Ich-Neumann* will be going." "Your alter ego," I cry, and we laugh heartily over R.'s notion. A pamphlet against the Jews by Prof. Dühring is truly dreadful on account of its style.

Thursday, January 13 A good night, and all day the same nice monastic atmosphere. Our friend Jouk.'s birthday gives R. an opportunity to display all his usual kindness. At 4 o'clock our old comrade-in-arms Karl Brandt! Against Feustel's advice R. has turned to him and invited him here to discuss the staging of *Parsifal*. Many memories, but above all much good sense, all conceivable technical questions; the music for the walk to the Temple listened to in order to assess the time needed for the transformation scene. — At the end of it R., turning to Joukowsky, quotes humorously from the *Fl. Blätter:* "An officer cries out to a volunteer, 'Listen, you are not at college now.' " — We are not in the studio now, he says, the time for dilettantism is past. On the one hand R. regrets, but on the other he is glad, that things are now beginning in earnest. And that means Brandt. It is truly curious to hear the spear now being discussed—how it is to be held up with wires—whereas up till now it was only his soul that mattered. — R. is still taking great pleasure in Gobineau; he exclaims, "What a shame that I find the only original writer so late in life!"

Friday, January 14 A good night, good work, and much Brandt: "This cold brand," R. exclaims. Our old friend has been to the theater and pleases us with his delight at the way everything has been preserved. Maquettes are brought down so that he can show friend Jouk. what he wants. — In the afternoon, while the expert and the amateur are deliberating, R. and I go for a walk, watch Fidi tracing curves for the first time, delight in the two dogs, who look very funny in all the snow and come bounding toward us over the bridge. The cold is severe. R. takes delight in the full moon, standing very proudly in the sky "as if Gottlieb had put it there." (He tells us that during a theatrical performance a voice was suddenly heard saying, "Gottlieb, pull out the moon.") — I, with a shawl over my head, am Dürer's Saint Hubert. At lunch he toasted me as "our dear lady of Wahnfried"! . . . In the evening he has to write a letter to Herr Batz, who is again behaving in a most presumptuous way in connection with the *Tristan* production in Leipzig. Feustel admires the precision of his letter, but R. complains about having to cope with all these Neumann and Batz escapades. — In the evening many, many memories with friend Brandt of *Nibelungen* tribulations; R. also discusses various things with him, such as the lighting for the dove at the end, and laughingly says over and over again that it is noses to the grindstone when Brandt appears. And when we are then alone together again, it is as if nothing remains on this earth but our love. And my whole day is a prayer that I may be worthy of it. [*Added in margin:* "In the evening R. talks in grateful praise of the King."] — When I talk to R. about [Thomas à Kempis's] *Imitatio Christi* and say I should be interested to know if it would appeal to him, he replies, "I am in the clutches of the Devil of art!" — In the morning a letter from Lusch, received the previous evening and containing comments on the nature of worldly society, produced the remark that she will certainly never find a husband there. It makes us laugh heartily when, after I mention a friend of Stein's (Delbrück) in a completely different connection, R. exclaims, "Delbrück—wouldn't he do?" —

Saturday, January 15 R. had a good night and does some work; but at lunch he is feeling some discomfort. It is very cold, but all the same we go for a walk in the palace gardens, talking a lot about Brandt, whose visit has pleased him very much. — In the evening I read Gobineau's story *"Gamber-Ali"* aloud. Friend Feustel has sent me the minutes of the committee meeting, and I am pleased to see an alteration in the final paragraph which will enable R.'s wish to be fulfilled, namely, that the Bülow fund should go to his children. (Lengthy examination of the map of Asia with R. after the story reading.)

Sunday, January 16 Reflections on history and the development of mankind's predatory activities lead me to ask in the morning whether these have not brought about art. "Certainly," says R., "and that is why it is an evasion and a dismal substitute; it becomes something worthwhile only when it is religion, but not when robber chiefs set themselves up as judges over the art of their dagger thrusts. Keep that in mind," he adds jokingly as he embraces me on our morning's parting. He works and is pleased that the 30 pages of his score already look imposing. But before he goes to work, immediately after our parting, he comes to me wearing my old fox fur, which he has had covered in black velvet in a single day as a surprise for me. He is happy to have brought it off and reproaches me for denying everything, the cold and all the rest—as exuberant again now as ever before!

He is still enjoying Gobineau's stories. We go for a walk in the palace gardens, I in my new furs—this time just with Molly, since Marke has a glass splinter in his paw; she is very obedient. Before that, a letter from "an enchanted prince," as he calls himself, containing much talk about the purely human factor, produces from R. the remark: "At the time I was corresponding with Uhlig I should have been in the right frame of mind for it and should have taken a look at this man. In those days I wanted at all costs to discover the purely human factor in everything, in Karl R[itter], Uhlig, everyone." —

He works in the evening as well and summons me to his side to drink some bock beer which he has had sent along and which he likes very much. I found him conversing with friend Jouk. about the minne-singers, in particular the poem by Emperor Heinrich, which I am asked to read aloud. Its delicate phrases please R. greatly, and he goes into raptures about that period, saying how cultivated it was, and how diversified. — We spend the evening in conversation. Among other things, R. says, "If the Russians took Constantinople, they would still stay up in St. Petersburg and rule the new territory from there." — When R. and I are alone, he goes to the piano and plays a passionately imploring melody from [Bellini's] *La Straniera,* then another, in character not dissimilar, from *I Capuleti ed i Montecchi,* remarking on its long-drawn-out character, something one also finds in Spontini, whereas in Mozart almost everything is unfortunately shortly phrased. He then goes on to *Rienzi* and says he can understand my father's and my delight in the work, since there is this streak of aris-tocracy in it. — As we part to change our clothes, we have the most blissful feeling of inseparability, he asks me to look after his health, "for I wish to live disgracefully long, fifteen years more than the allotted span, in order to make up for the time we have lost." — [*Added at bottom of page:* "An engineer in Helsingfors writes very nicely to Wolz. about his Wagnerianism and the *Blätter.* He regrets J. R[ubinstein]'s article about Schumann, and R. is inclined to agree with me when I observe that this article, while remaining just as sharp, should have been more comprehensive and more detailed—Schu. as composer of oratorios, as symphonist, as opera composer, etc. —"]

Monday, January 17 R. dreamed thoughts which had been much occupying my mind! And did not have a very good night. But he works. At lunch he tells us about the war against the Turkomans, another of the Count's stories. My report of a visit to the Berrs' and the growing insanity of the husband produces from R. the remark that everyone in the grip of passion is close to insanity, that is to say, clinging to one fixed idea and ignoring everything else. We talk about *Othello* and he recalls what "was not very long ago." — In one's memory, he says, names disappear first of all, since they are a con-vention which has nothing to do with the person, whom one can still see quite clearly. We read the Crown Prince's words to Councilor Magnus, and when the question is raised what he can do now, R. says, "Keep his mouth shut." — When I observe that this aggressive attitude probably stems from fear, R. says, "Yes, and from the idea of being liberal, moving with the times—ideas which the Crown Princess brought with her." He would never forget her "Oh, no, Fritz," in connection with Bayreuth, he said recently. In the morning a remark

by an acquaintance brought into my mind the question of the confirmation of the two girls; I talk to R. about it, and as a result he
decides to send the letter off to Herr Frege. When I come down to
supper, after we parted very amicably on returning from our walk, I
find him in a very agitated state of mind; bills, the eternal trouble with
the new water supply, perhaps the dispatch of the letter as well—in
short, he is in a very bad humor, and when some of our friends arrive,
their presence does not help to dispel his gloom. He tries Mozart's
E-flat Major Symphony with Humperdinck and talks of the difficulty
of doing the Adagio properly, showing us how it is usually played at
concerts. But then Rub. plays us the first part of the [Opus] 106 Sonata,
and our delight is boundless! In fact, we cannot get over the impression it makes on us, and when we are alone, R. and I, so many
words of liberation and happiness escape our lips that I shall have
difficulty in remembering them. R: "It is like being taken into the
workshop of the Will, one sees everything moving and stirring as if in
the bowels of the earth." — "Anyone who could translate this into
words would have the key to the enigma of the world." — "Cries of
passion to which the workshop opens its doors." — "Not even
Shakespeare can be compared to it, for what he has created is too
closely connected with the world's misery." — "In the symphony
Beeth. lets others play, here he himself is playing." "And all that in
the form of a sonata—what a sonata!" — We end this enchanted
evening by recalling that we have now been living together for 17
years.

Tuesday, January 18   R. is rather unwell, has a buzzing in his ears.
When we part after breakfast, he embraces me: "Blessings on you,
pardon everything as I beg your pardon for still being here, for by
rights I should long ago have joined the hammerklavier." — He comes
downstairs later, supplies a dedication to Mimi in the biography, looks
at clothing fabrics, since he wants new paletots for his children; I feel
that the old ones are still all right, but he wishes it. Over coffee we
talk a lot about Semper; only recently he recalled with pleasure that
he bought a copy of the text of *Tannhäuser* for himself. He remembers
that Semper worked out his book on style during late sessions in the
tavern with Herwegh, and that Herwegh was a good listener. When
mention is made of his great admiration for the French, R. says, "They
possess the ideality of our reality." — At lunch he complained of his
catarrh and said he would like to be given two slaps on the face at
once, so that the cold would fall out through his nose! [*Added in margin:*
"At lunch R. again proclaims his intention of living to be 94."] A
walk in the palace gardens, delight in the *Quaker* (Fidi), who, R. thinks,
looks exactly like my father in his hat and long paletot. "All of the

children must turn out like your father, I shall just keep Eva!" — He works before supper, and after it Fidi does some magic tricks for us. Then we read Gobineau's story, and R. is pleased with this new acquaintance, so rare a mind; he praises the Cervantes-like flavor of his stories. In the evening, stretched out in his big chair in his dressing room, he says, "And now I am supposed to be looking forward to *Parsifal,* to coaching Jäger." — But when, to distract him from all solemn thoughts, I admire his robe, which is pink, he says, "Yes, this is what makes me feel good, something Feustel would find it completely impossible to understand." — Yesterday, when we were passing through his workroom, he caught sight of my picture over the piano, but he talks about the other pastel drawing by Lenbach: "It looks at me in a ghostlike way, reminding me of all that is solemn and good." —

Wednesday, January 19 R. did not have an entirely good night, and he does not feel well. He begs my pardon for complaining, and I say that it is the great drawback of love that it cannot overcome all the trials of life. "No, but it makes us forget them," R. replies, and, truly, in the course of our conversation together they are soon forgotten. — But then, as always, comes day! — Many thoughts of Andalusia in the past few days, and it is constantly being declared that we shall spend next winter in Seville. R. speaks glowingly of the good Italy did him, particularly Siena. — I tell R. about old Frau von Aufsess's 14-year-old dog, which the police have taken away from her on account of the present precautionary measures. R. says: "It's like everything else, they do not bother their heads about food being adulterated, animals being tortured, but someone suddenly hatches the abstract idea that at a certain age animals turn into corpses. I don't know what I should do if somebody came into my house and took away a dog." — Today R. goes for a walk in the palace gardens by himself, since I am not quite well. Friend Levi arrives toward evening, and music is played—that is to say, R. sings some ballades by Loewe, in order to show, as he puts it, "what has been lost in us Germans." — We always take great delight in these productions, in which, as R. says, the poetry makes more impact than the music. Then he announces to Herr Levi, to his astonishment, that he is to conduct *Parsifal:* "Beforehand, we shall go through a ceremonial act with you. I hope I shall succeed in finding a formula which will make you feel completely one of us." — The veiled expression on our friend's face induces R. to change the subject, but when we are alone, we discuss this question further. I tell R. that what seems to me to be the difficulty here is that the community into which the Israelite would be accepted has itself abandoned Christ, though it might write about him, whereas previously blood was shed and everything sacrificed in his behalf. R. says he himself has certainly remained true to him, and in his last essay he more or less outlined what the formula would be. "The trouble is," he exclaims, "that all great personalities reveal themselves to us in time and space, and are thus subject to change." When we have our first parting, he exclaims jokingly, "What an accursed subject you have brought up here!" and when we come together again, he raises it once more, and we agree that this alien race can never be wholly absorbed into our own. R. tells me (and I write it down here, for he has repeatedly said it to me, with very great earnestness and not a trace of mockery) that when our friend modestly approached him and kissed his hand, R. embraced him with great inner warmth, and from what emanated between them, he came to feel with extraordinary precision what a difference of race and separateness really mean. And thus the good Jew always suffers a melancholy lot in our midst.

Thursday, January 20 R. slept well. He spoke softly as he was falling asleep, and I heard, among other things, the words "the best woman in the world." When I tell him this, he says, "That is how it is—when one's sleep is peaceful, one knows nothing about it." — But at lunch he does not feel well, agitated, and his digestion out of order. — We talk about Saint Augustine, whom friend Levi carries around with him, into whom I glanced and who does not please me on account of the God Creator he is always praising. R. criticizes the conductor's gloominess and says: "I should think that being taken up in such a friendly way by people like us would be enough to make anyone cheerful. Or are you superstitious, having trouble with your souls?" He then speaks of Rub., how he is always preoccupied with himself, and in spite of his good qualities can never throw this off. He compares him with Levi, who is much more fortunate, since he has his own field of activity. He advises "a carefree expansiveness." — R. calls me Flower Mother, since at present I am frequently wearing asters, but he chides me for dressing *à la vieille,* is unwilling to admit that I am old! He goes for a walk with Jouk. and Levi, then he works, after complaining humorously that the story *"Les Amants de Kandahar"* keeps him so absorbed that he always comes to his score too late. Despite the corrupt state of the Orient as described in it, he says, Europe nevertheless seems to him a land of barbarians, with all its epaulets, etc. — France, where the new elections have turned out in Ferry's favor, pleases him, as also Gladstone's reply in connection with the Boers. He is still hoping that, with the collapse of external power, the right man will emerge in England's interior. — In the evening we ask Rub. to play us the 1st movement of 106 again, and it gives us the same ravishing delight. — Whether at a certain point it should be a sharp or a natural, R. says, he finds it impossible to decide, whereas with the famous passage in the *Eroica* he simply tells himself that to him it doesn't sound right, and if anybody wished to do him a favor, he would play it differently. [*Added in margin:* " 'Marry my wife, then you'll be cheerful,' says R. to the gloomy-looking conductor."] — He talks of the new version he made of the ballade in *Der Fl. Holländer,* which he has unfortunately lost. The same thing happened with the "*ich sank in süssen Schlaf*" passage in *Lohengrin,* he says: he had it quite wonderfully but never found it again; as it now stands, it is an approximation. — When we are alone and I meet him again after our first parting, I find him much irritated by his two fingers (thumbs), which are painful and which he keeps stubbing. But I succeed in coaxing him out of these feelings of annoyance, and I have the joy of being able to tell him that, since for me he so completely is and represents the divine principle, I am constantly becoming more and more religious and able to follow the mystics with ever-increasing understanding, learning thereby to despise the world and accept the blessings of peace. — Perhaps this is why my greatest sacrifice is keeping in touch, for his sake, with a world in which there is no choice but to suffer! . . . And, turning to his nature and the way in which it finds expression, I tell him that he is the only person I know whose speech and language are what color is to the leaf and scent to the flower—something involuntary, devoid of ulterior motive and in consequence very often made to look inconsiderate; when he then notices that he has offended someone with an involuntary remark, he tries with every means to put it right, even to the point of denying his own feelings. — Many people without understanding have taken him to be insincere because of this! Nothing any longer disturbs me, I see it all. — I follow each and every utterance like a river whose pure source and outflow in the infinite deep are known to me.

Friday, January 21   R. slept well, and he goes to his work. But when I go down to lunch I find him in poor spirits. His finger is hurting him, and a letter from Herr Batz annoys him and makes him regret having spoken even a single word, he says that by doing so one places oneself on the same level as these people. Our conversation at lunch leads us to various women, and R. sums up his repugnance for them thus: "Very gifted, but they have no souls—but the same can be said of some men. — No person can mean anything to me, and that is why I have created a family for myself. Only those who fit in with the family mean anything to me." — Over coffee he reads to us with much amusement two anecdotes from an anti-Jewish newspaper, one about Rossi, the other about the parson Delitzsch, whom he once knew. — "The fact that D. was a Jew explains many things to me as well; he was an unpleasant character," he says. — Somewhat boldly, I tell him that when I join him, however poor in spirits, after we spend a little while together he is again in a good and cheerful mood. "We should come together to die," he replies earnestly! — We go out, the dogs almost knock R. over in their joy, and in this devotion of animals to him I see one of the signs of R.'s wonderful connection with Nature. Animals like me very much, too, but it seems to me that they greet him as if no division had ever taken place. When we return home, R. feels Marke's ear and finds that it is still stiff: "Things like this don't just go away," he says. "It is like my finger, but he puts up with it better." — I: "He has no *Parsifal* to compose." "That's true," says R., "and every page calls for some new invention." — A letter from Frau Pusinelli pleases him, she announces her daughter's engagement. He works, is looking forward to leaving the epic part behind him and starting on the drama with Parsifal's entrance. In the evening we read the very charming story "*La Guerre des Turcomans*" to the end. — R. then looks at the map again, and as he is doing so, I recall what he said today at lunch— that among the peoples of the earth it is always the stupidest tribes which are destined to rule over the others, the strongest arrogantly placing their paws on everything: the Macedonians in Greece, the Moors among the Arabs, the Prussians among the Germans, the Turks in Asia. — He praises Count Gobineau highly and takes great delight in the story "*Les Amants de Kandahar.*" (While looking at the map, I also recall that he recently described the Gulf Stream as the brutal element which ordains everything: "Then everything depends on whether one goes along with or resists it." — As always with him, physics and metaphysics merge, rather like the memory of Max and Jupiter in Schiller's *Wallenstein*.) — This morning he told me how musically Fidi said, "Adieu, Papa," as he left him after their shower. — He complains about the tar ointment and the fact that he can now detect only bad smells.

Saturday, January 22 R. slept well. — At breakfast we come to the subject of the dispatch of R.'s letter to Frege and the possible consequences. I remember the time when this action, and what it will mean for the children, would have caused me boundless anxiety, but now I am ready to accept in complete confidence everything that R. does, and determined to bear it all joyfully. — R.'s finger is tormenting him, and I find him in very poor spirits when I come down to lunch, it turns out that tar was not the proper treatment. — All kinds of things have arrived, including a pamphlet by Paul de Lagarde. R. glances through it and finds it written in such a way that one does not know whether he is for a certain matter or against it. — Dr. Förster has sent an appeal for the founding of an anti-Semitic newspaper. R.

relates that he wrote to him from Naples, "Find out whether you fit into Prince Bismarck's plans." — And it seems that they fit in with them, for they are adopting his whole program. "We Bayreuthers will remain very isolated with our ideas." — At lunch, in connection with Ollivier and Ferry, R. thought of Blandine, saying that Ferry, whom Blandine idolized, is carrying out Ollivier's program, which is, as he once told R., to effect all reforms by political means. During lunch R. gradually regains his spirits, and he even exclaims, "Good food chases off a bad mood." — The walk, with its prelude of joyfully barking dogs, delights him in spite of the cold and what he calls an "ironic" sunset. He works in the evening and reaches Parsifal's arrow shot. — In the evening we turn to Gobineau. (Yesterday, when I informed him that Gobin. had a malicious wife, R. exclaims how terrible it is that a youthful urge to find fulfillment must then be dragged in misery through one's whole life. He mentions the naïve method of divorce among Orientals, and says how wrong the woman's place is in our society—on the one hand making a show of chivalrous devotion, yet on the other, holding her in contempt.) — Friend Wolz. pays us a visit, we abandon our reading, and many things are discussed —the response to reproaches for throwing the performances open to the public, then the guarantee certificates and also the subscription for *Parsifal,* to which R. is looking forward: "I look forward to having a little capital—always supposing that I have paid off my debts with the rest of my earnings." It is Mimi's birthday, we drink her health and sing her praises. We have sent her the biography; now five of our friends possess it: the King, my father, Wolz., Glasenapp, and Mimi. — When our friends have gone, I say, "How sad that there is nothing more in our glasses." — At once R. calls Wolz. and Jouk. back, and another half-bottle of champagne is sent for! In very merry mood—"No one else has half our talents," R. exclaims—we conclude the evening for the second time. — R. has written to Lilli Lehmann about engaging the Flower Maidens. — R. tells Wolz. that he has been thinking about the meaning of the word "free" and has gladly adopted the Swiss sense as he once heard it used: in the canton of Appenzell a guide was recommended to him with the words "He is a free man." "Free" means "true," someone who has no need to lie—otherwise "free" would always have something negative about it; "freedom," free of this or that person—but in this case, he says, it is the lie which is negative. The root of the Greek word *"eleutheros"*—*"lud"*—says Wolz., has a connection with our word *"lauter"* ["pure"], so that it is not very far removed from the meaning favored by R.

Sunday, January 23 R. had a good night. In our morning conversation he talks profoundly and at length about the mother's womb, the life within it, the sacredness of it, and he ends with praise of Goethe, who recognized the divinity in these manifestations of Nature. But how could one ever have visualized a personal God who created all these things! He also says he can well understand why Goethe, out of his sense of the sacredness of Nature, felt the urge to examine things individually, for one can never pay too much attention to the individual element—to pursue Nature as a whole, to see it as a cosmos, is foolishness. — While we are immersed in these reflections, Isolde and Eva come in to thank us for their new paletots. R. is pleased with the girls; things are no longer going on *en cachette* [by stealth], here they are, grown up. — He comes to me before lunch, announcing himself as "the old clog-maker"—he has just noticed the great likeness between them. I tell him of my feelings of boundless emotion when I recently glanced through *Lohengrin* again and read the "Bridal Song," then the finale of the 2nd act; I say I cannot understand why everybody in Germany did not burst out cheering over its "chaste fire." "The German brain can only be reached through a sort of stuffy head cold," he says. — His royalties from Vienna seem very good; now that *Die Msinger* is beginning to make an impact, he says, he hopes things will get better and better. Some friends at lunch, we drink retrospectively to friend Feustel's birthday. Then we go for a walk in the palace gardens, a lot of people, our children not among them. Memories of Tribschen, its solitariness! — In the evening a great deal about the anti-Semitic agitation, then the Count's story "*Les Amants de Kandahar,*" read with great and genuine delight. R. is still much taken with it on second reading, he finds the first love scene wonderful.

Monday, January 24 Not an entirely good night for R., or for me. The morning somewhat affected by this, and also R. has business troubles with Leipzig, which, it seems, has not shown the number of performances correctly; I admire R.'s astonishing memory, even for things of this sort. Severe cold—I do not go for a walk with R., since today everything is causing me excessive difficulty. In the evening we read in Herr Glagau's newspaper, *Der Kulturkämpfer,* a good article criticizing natural science today. — R. says he is carrying all kinds of (literary) ideas around with him. His finger is now cured! — Yesterday, when we were talking about Lenbach and various immature things were said about him, R. stated his own opinion with his usual prudence, saying: "Very well, he does not reproduce the Moltke you all know, in a wig and an assumed pose: it is not this he sees; what he sees and depicts is the idea of Moltke, at times exaggerated. What people call his prattling comes from the false position which this man of the people, not highly educated but now famous, occupies in society. And if the reproach can be made that he speaks slightingly of all other painters, that is softened by the fact that he does not value his own painting a whit higher." —

Tuesday, January 25 R. dreamed of quarrels with Minna, of the salary which, almost always in his dreams, he draws from the Grand Opera (sometimes 12,000, sometimes 6,000 marks), and then of the children—whether he would part from them, but this unresolved. He says, "I only hope I do not blather about such things in my dying hour." — He works, and we go for a walk in the palace gardens, content with the hard, clear winter. — Fidi had to undergo a little examination with the head teacher at the primary school today; he passes it successfully and is gaily praised by us. We also enjoy watching his curves on the ice, and we bless them all. — W. Frege's telegram is answered to the effect that R. will be perfectly satisfied if only the letter is transmitted! — In the evening R. tells us of two letters, one from Herr v. Weber giving his reasons for abstaining from the anti-Jewish movement in spite of the most comical bad experiences, the other from Lilli Lehmann. R. answers the latter right away, in order to clarify for her benefit the position with Hülsen regarding the *Ring*. L. L.'s "Germanic deed" makes us laugh, and R. says, probably with some justice, that Hülsen would certainly have got the better of them if he had not intervened with his "No." — The conversation then moves on to Heine, and R. tells how he showed him his French text of *Der Fl. Holländer,* in which, among other things, he had written *"amateur"* instead of *"amant"* (Erik to Senta). R. also gives a friendly personal reminiscence of Halévy. — The evening passes in congenial conversation, though R. says to me afterward that when several people are present, he feels as if he must never stop talking. On other occasions, when he is explaining something, I compare him to Frederick the Great giving instructions to Ziethen before the Battle of Torgau. He speaks of the superfluity of the *B. Blätter* since the new turn of events. (Weber's and Lilli L.'s letters in one of the green cardboard boxes in the *salon:* correspondence with friends—the reply to the telegram in the corner bureau, red folder 1.)

Wednesday, January 26 "Dear wife, we shan't be returning to Bayreuth—Cicero has invited me to stay here." Thus I hear R. speaking! But in the morning he has entirely forgotten it. This leads us to talk of the Romans, and though R. does not care for the cold and wise ones, he says, "With the ancients there is always the possibility of linking onto something, but the further one progresses in time, the more this diminishes, and that is why I regard decadence as a wholly incontrovertible fact." — Fidi has told us how badly an apprentice is treated in the workshop, and that gives rise to reflections on human brutality, the pleasure a person finds in torturing someone weaker than

himself. If it is not a human being, it is an animal. Around lunchtime
R. calls me and shows me the landscape gardener's letter and his
reply to it (see corner bureau). — In the evening he relates in a humorous way his experiences with the Order of Maximilian and the final
confusion between owl and lyre! Then we read Cervantes's "*Vidriera*"
with great delight. In this we once more see him whole, the writer
with his melancholy smile, his knowledge of the world, his sense of
absurdity and the part it plays in all significant things; the cruelty of
human beings, the goodness of convents, etc. R. is frequently struck
by the popular use of the word "will" in its Schopenhauerian sense. —
And all so personal, always pulsing with life, speaking to us with a
smile. — Before the reading R. once more touched on the first movement of the *Eroica,* expressing his unbounded admiration for it.
Beethoven must have felt downright alarmed, he says, when he wrote
that. And everything in music so direct, whereas in literature everything must always be explained. — I tell R. about the French history I
have been reading with the children (episode of Duplessis-Mornay
and H[enri] IV), and R. comments, "Acceptance of monarchy is an
expression of pessimism." —

Thursday, January 27   R. had a good night, and when I am in my
bath, he comes to the door and, standing outside, imitates Siegfried's
voice bidding me good morning. Our conversation at breakfast
revolves around yesterday's reading, which brought Cervantes so
close to us again. A letter from Jouk.'s sister, which R. saw on my
desk and read, also provides material for a serious discussion. — When,
around lunchtime, I go through the *salon,* R. is sitting at his writing
desk, and he calls out to me: "Do you know why I am so absent-
minded? Because I think too much about you." And to this he adds
such words that, back in my room, I beseech the God who has allotted
all this to me to grant me humility! — The mail brings all sorts of
things, including a letter from Lusch, after reading which R. exclaims,
"She is a genius!" — We go for a walk, R. and I, in spite of the windy
weather, watch Fidi, who, almost alone on the ice, is tracing his
curves, and who amuses R. by telling him that he trod on a pair of
spectacles at Herr Popp's, but they had cost only 80 pfennigs. — He
has given young Giessel—also to R.'s great amusement—20 pfennigs
for magic tricks, and he tells us the boys have advised the magician
to buy herrings with it. — Before our walk Jouk. showed us his sketch
of the Grail, which won R.'s approbation. In the afternoon, as a result
of my request to Herr v. B[ürkel], sketches of the same subject arrive
from Munich and turn out to be completely unusable. In the evening
we read Gobineau's story "*La Danseuse,*" and afterward R. discusses
with Jouk. the fate of his sister. When we are alone in his dressing

room, R. asks me whether family affairs upset me. I: "No." Then he tells me he has received a telegram from Prof. Frege, saying he is returning the letters without passing them on. — After we remark with a fleeting smile on such courageousness, long discussion about what to do. I end by saying to R. that everything he wishes or does is acceptable to me, even if I expect blessings only from what goes on between ourselves, sheltered from the world—and none at all from what we attempt outside. — After lengthy and sustained discussions we go off to bed.

Friday, January 28 R. slept well, and though our morning conversation returns anxiously to the subject which is foremost in our thoughts, it does so in such a way that at lunch R. can refer to it jokingly through the story of a man who spoke of obstacles in a horse race. "What was the obstacle?" "I didn't have a horse." — R. observes that he also has no horse—that is to say, Hans will not read the letters. But he does some work, and even though he says, "*Parsifal* bores me, I should like to do something else," his spirits are raised by some good work. In conversation he recalls my arrival at Tribschen and how I said to him, "Now get down to *Siegfried*," and how he eventually completed the whole thing after long interruptions, and with pleasure, despite his momentary mood of disgruntlement. Yesterday he talked about the puppet theater in Heidelberg, our delight in it. Blessed memories return, how cut off from the world we were, and how alone in the world, the children still small! — Our friends in the evening, Rub. plays us the Adagio from Sonata [Opus] 106, in which R. sees the beginnings of all modern music (Schumann, Brahms), and I realize, with something like dismay, that a piece of music held to be the highest degree of art no longer makes very much impression on me—it seems to me more like an improvisation, left to a great artist to interpret, than a work of art in itself. "How different is 111!" says R., who can discern little genuine Beethoven in the piece. — After that the conversation turns to my father, St. Gallen (1856), where he played the 106, life at that time, "such a subsoil of manure and snuff for such a thing to flourish in." — And again and again, in the evening and during the day, Hans and what we should now do. — (An absurd photograph has been sent to him for signature, beneath it he writes, "I am not so handsome as this.")

Saturday, January 29 As a result of all sorts of things, particularly the one matter, I am so tired and heavy in the morning that I oversleep through breakfast and have no conversation to note down. But soon everything is back in hand again, confirmation arrangements and also a visit to a poor neighbor whose husband has become insane; she told me all her troubles, and I advised her to consult a doctor. — But R.

thought at once of Dr. Falko's institute, and I passed this good advice on to her. R. works, but has first to write to Herr N[eumann] on business matters, performance rights, Paris, etc. — Over coffee he explains to our friend Jouk. what universal guilt means: he says it has now come up for reckoning, just like a son inheriting the sins of his father, and renunciation wipes them out. R. goes for a walk with Jouk., I wait for Councilor Kraussold; since he does not come, I go to him, then again to the dean. The question of certificates of baptism brings R. back to his main desire for legal adoption. After supper we read the story "*La Danseuse de Samakha*" to the end, much moved, particularly by the climax. — R. then enlarges upon how vanishing races like these Lezghians still bring forth heroic women: "The Renaissance was brought about by women," he says—adding that it is remarkable how closely this corresponds to the Sch[openhauer] theory that one inherits character from one's father, intelligence from one's mother. Returning to the subject of guilt, he says: "Perception and idea, however, are free of sin, except when they are guided by the will. But it is terrible how this will exists in a constant state of desire; from the moment a child leaves the womb, it desires, with all the violence of Genghis Khan laying claim to the world." — Reverting to the question of interrelationships, he says, "Nobody dies before he must, and this produces the interrelationship, the link to everything else—also the incurred guilt." — A report of my conversation with Coun. Kraussold arouses in R. a desire to read Rothschild's letter to Parson Stoecker, in which he makes fun of the parson. "Of course," says R., "this question is connected with the continued existence of property, and, as long as things remain as they are, they will be our masters." — The movement interests him, however, and he laughs when I say to him that it seems to be peculiarly German, for in any other country it would simply not be understood. — "Good night, my poor Djéhâne," says R., who earlier had recalled how in past sad times I could fly into such a rage that I would smash things and even hit people. This makes us laugh heartily, for it is not at all like me. He jests at scars, that never saw a wound!

Sunday, January 30 R. slept well. Our morning conversation turns to perception and its freedom from sin; yesterday R. told Jouk. that the best thing one could do was to occupy oneself with art, but not in the service of any great power; he comes back to this and says that art is the transfiguration of perception, just as religion is the transfiguration of the Will. At lunch, too, in connection with the fish, he says how terrible it is that the human being, the only creature to whom Nature has given feelings of sympathy, should then stifle them. R. works, but he is somewhat depressed, our conversations are serious, and my preoccupation with the fate of my neighbor is not exactly conducive of gaiety. — In the evening Rub. plays to us Beeth.'s A Minor Quartet, to our very great delight. "Nobody knows all there is in it," R. exclaims; he recalls his impression in Paris and says how curious it was that it should have happened in Paris of all places: "When I returned to Germany it was all just plop-plop, like putting things in a sack." — Rub. says that he owes his understanding of the 9th to R.'s program note, and when I express to R. my astonishment that a musician should need such a thing, R. says, "Particularly a musician, for the first movement, for example—which in fact has no melody and begins with those fifths—this tells the true musician nothing, but makes an impression—a ghostly one—on an imaginative layman to a far greater extent." — He is of the opinion that he and my father have done much toward disseminating Beeth.'s last works, and he tells us how they were regarded "in olden times." — Loldi's shy nature reminded him at supper of Joan of Arc, and he talked about her mission (in connection with the King of F.) and her terrible fate. He then expresses his pleasure that it was a German who revived the memory of this being. — His reflections on the dreadfulness of history and of existence lead me to remark that it is a curious trial to have to work for a world one sees in this way, and that for him it is the creative urge which has made it a source of pleasure. — Regarding the Catholic church, which R. mentioned today in connection with the experiences Joan of Arc had to undergo, pointing out its horrifying realistic outlook, he recently remarked what an active role it has played in attitudes toward Blandine, Daniel, and myself. Princess W[ittgenstein] described us to my father as having been born under a curse, and the preservation of our lives thus of no special account. —

Monday, January 31 R. tells me his dream: we were at home, but not in this house, in a *salon,* he was standing by the fireplace, and I, very melancholy, began to play the piano; he asked himself what it was—perhaps something by Chopin—but he almost dozed off; I gazed at him with an expression of mournful ecstasy, a look with which he is familiar, and went on playing, more and more sadly, like an improvisation; he approached me, touched me with his hand, saying: "Please stop," and at the same time noticing that I was kneeling. "My father is leaving today, I must go with him." "Oh, then I must also get ready." He goes into his dressing room, wants to light the fire, but the matches will not ignite; trying hard, he notices one of the big dogs: "How did he get in here?" — Then he wakes up. After this R. does not have a very good day; he does in fact work, but complains of restlessness and nervousness, his fingers are hurting. Herr Levi returns from his journey, tells us all sorts of things about the theater world, not particularly edifying. — R. talks with great satisfaction about Stein's article, and he is also content with the other contributions in this issue. — We go, R. and I, for a walk in the palace gardens; the air is springlike, very mild and pleasant, and we stroll around for a long time with the two dogs. — But in the evening R. does not feel well, he is very nervous, and it can be regarded as a stroke of good fortune that our discussion of the game of hand-me-the-slate, and whether, with the words "Here stands your uncle," one should really take the slate, leads us to *Hamlet*. R. decides against the slate, and says that everything in this is agitation, dawning madness, Hamlet the modern man, disintegrated and incapable of action, seeing the world for what it is. — We are glad to be alone together for a little while after our friends have gone, and R. complains of the state of nerves to which he is subject and also about his uneasy relationship with the Israelites, with whom one must always be so "exalted." —

Tuesday, February 1 R. had a restless night and is feeling very strained; in the morning we have another discussion about *Hamlet* and also talk again about the Jews; I say in connection with Rub. that it is precisely because of them that one would feel bound to become a Christian, which makes R. laugh. Around noon R. comes to me and shows me a passage in Prof. Dühring's essay to the effect that "a German can be meaner than any Jew"—and it is true that the two pages about R. are deplorable. On the other hand, R. reads to us over coffee two statements by a Moslem in Count Gobineau's story "*Vie en voyage*," one about life, the other about Europe, both remarkably pregnant, and when we then go for a walk in the palace gardens, we talk about the superiority of the Moslems, to whom the idea of submission to an unfathomable god is so familiar, a feeling unknown to the Jews. R. works. In the evening friend Feustel, whom R. instructs to reimburse the 40,000 marks to Hans, telling him that he can discover the reasons for this reimbursement in letters to Prof. Frege. Friend Feustel very understanding. — A. Rothschild's letter to Parson Stoecker is discussed; it is taken to be a hoax, even though one feels certain that Israelites do speak in this way. At the conclusion of the evening memories of Tribschen, of Richter with the children—in the morning I glanced through my first diary. Of our journey across the Brünig (1866) R. says, "That was our best time." I say Tribschen was our good time. R. promises to complete his biography after *Parsifal*. — When we return from our walk, I tell R. that I call an expression in his face—a complete change of both manner and look—a *Schwendi Fluh*, and I feel very flattered at being permitted to live on this rugged and forbidding crag! He says yes, now and again he suddenly becomes aware of the nonsense he is talking, and he then withdraws into himself. — He sees a blackbird in the palace gardens, yesterday we heard what sounded like siskins, and they seemed to be following us from tree to tree: "Gentlemen, you are too early." — When friend Jouk. says that Levi is always stripped of so many illusions when he is here, R. says with a laugh, "Yes, they are removed from him by the cartload, like piles of snow."

Wednesday, February 2 R. slept well and settles down in the morning to some literary work. At lunch he tells us that he once again fell into a deep, deep sleep, after which he got down to his article, though first he read his *Braunes Buch* with enjoyment. A letter from Lusch gives us pleasure, but also slightly alarms us with its sharpness of observation and hastiness of judgment. After lunch a walk with R. in the palace gardens, we hear a woodpecker tapping quite loudly, and R. also sees it. He then talks to me about his article. Dr. Landgraf visits us toward evening; a serious court case against young Staff is preoccupying everybody here, also to a certain extent R., who after the visit comes up to my room and says, "I like gloating, in some ways I get a malicious pleasure from seeing people behave badly," and he shows me an anecdote told in Vienna about the young man, which is really very sad. — In the evening we read Gobineau's story "*La Vie de voyage*" with great interest. R. feels that the Count must be unhappy; his companion, Countess La Tour, seems to him to be insufficiently equipped to make a man happy, for, "A woman who paints—!" he exclaims. — He also says one cannot love the human race as such, one must begin with the family. And that we are solitary and the festivals mean a sacrifice for us—R. laughs and says, "But after all a doctor's certificate can always save one from such rubbish." —

Thursday, February 3 R. looks worn out; but he goes to his work, and around lunchtime, when he fetches me from my room, he is satisfied with the result. After lunch much talk about monasteries, the Trappists, and R. jokes that one is obliged to choose between *l'attrape* (meaning the world) and La Trappe. We go for a walk and have to laugh heartily over the nature observations in the newspapers, which report, on the one hand, that the hares have acquired a second fur, and a week later that the starlings have arrived. We attend a drill parade—"Epaminondas on horseback," as R. says—and think of Fidi. R. reports that Bismarck is said to have his pockets full of proposals for new laws, including one against drunkenness: "What is the cause of the evil no one inquires about." — In the evening we read a short story by Cervantes, "*La fuerça de la sangre*," and find it not at all edifying; indeed, we are much repelled by its coarseness of feeling. "That is the Renaissance," says R., "all this fine talk even in the most terrible of situations." — "Even Shakespeare is not totally free of it, though only in the comedies." — "Cervantes never got beyond the antechambers of the great, he learned nothing from them; the common people he knew, and that is why I enjoy only the stories set among the people." — As the evening ends, he looks at the globe and is amused by the thought that, if the Gulf Stream were not forced back by Panama, our Europe would be a mass of ice. — In the palace gardens, when he sees a soldier (green with red facings), he is reminded of a dream, and he tells me that in this dream the red facings were turned into bleeding wounds as a punishment.

Friday, February 4 R. slept well—he works with pleasure on his article. He no longer intends to reply to letters from Herr N[eumann] about rights in Paris. — At lunch conversation with the two candidates for confirmation about the prophets, both major and minor, memories of Michelangelo's figures, whom R. sees as figures grieving over decadence. Jokingly R. adds, "About M[ichel]angelo I feel like Spontini about tubas: '*Je ne veux pas bannir cet instrument de l'orchestre*' ['I do not wish to banish this instrument from the orchestra']." Boni at her first ball yesterday, the two girls preparing themselves for confirmation, Lusch out in the wide world, sending us melancholy reports! Fidi the only one still displaying childhood in all its innocence. Fine weather—"The starlings win"—we go for a walk, R. and I, meet Dean C[aselmann]. "You in place of Dittmar!" R. exclaims, astounding me with his memory; he recalls what I told him about the dean's first visit, how he had asked to be accepted as a substitute for Dittmar, even in our game of whist. This last request stuck in his mind as typical. Returning home, we hear the soft chirping of a little bird: "He is saying, 'I want to be brought into the world like the Homunculus,'" R. observes. — At supper joking with Loldi about the major and minor prophets and with Boni about her experiences at the ball. After that our friends; an attempt with *La Vestale* miscarries somewhat, but then Beeth.'s last quartet—ours! R. summarizes our feelings during the playing thus: "It seems something like an act of grace that one is allowed in one's stupidity to listen to such a being." [*The word* "stupidity" *subsequently written over and changed to* "isolation" *in an unknown handwriting.*] — When all have gone, we "wash down the evening" with champagne, R. and I, and talk of Beeth.: "If only one had known, had seen a being like that! He would not have put up with us, but what tremendous outbursts there would have been—cries of bliss and ecstasy! He would then have gone his own way, rather like your father. It is quite unimaginable. I have seen both him and Shakespeare in my dreams—toward me always gently consoling." — Today in the palace gardens we wondered whether any more great men might still be expected. . . . Italy, Spain, France as good as dead, and Germany?

Saturday, February 5 The children's voices delight R., and he says about Fidi, "He is a pure nightingale." Then he reverts merrily to the "silly theme," saying: "That a person like Beeth. wrote such a silly melody! And what we clearly see in it is some animal pretending to be stupid." [*This last sentence obliterated in ink by an unknown hand.*] Since my toothache is still troubling me, and I am keeping silent about it, R. inquires, "The Napoleon of toothache?" — He writes, and since that is happening upstairs—"in the fresh air," as he says—he comes to fetch me for lunch. He talks about Gob.'s *Les Pléiades,* which he says is somewhat immature but contains some nice passages. Delight in Fidi over coffee: because of his carpentry work his hands are full of blisters and calluses, but he does not complain and allows a callus to be cut off without any flinching. — Then a book arrives which I ordered for yesterday (R.'s day), Hederich's *Real-Lexikon.* The article on opera which R. thought was in it is not there, but there are other articles which he also remembers, and which are really indescribable, such as Lais and Thais. — Our reading leads to a discussion about German literature and how the great intellects fashioned everything for themselves. We go for a walk, the cold is again severe, the hares are proved right, and R. seizes the occasion to remark on the unity of Nature, which takes precautions of this kind. In the morning we also talked about the superiority of animals, if only on account of their fur, whereas poor humans have their posture and gait impeded by heavy clothing. — Over coffee R. also talked about Count Tyskiewicz, who once accompanied R. to *Die Zauberflöte* and found it all so poor and childish; in contrast he mentioned the friendship duet in the 1st act of *La Vestale*—that really was something, he said! This declamatory French manner of haranguing reminded R. yesterday of the election meeting he attended in Paris in '49, where he heard the 7 Montagnards, all of whom spoke excellently. — In the evening Hederich again, the articles on Aspasia, tragedy, and drama, also Pericles, to our great amusement. Then R. asks me what Shakespeare we should read, and I beg for the scene between H[enry] IV and his son at the King's death. — We do not regret our choice, and are lost in emotion and admiration over practically everything: the language, which R. describes as official and heavy at times, but always natural; the initial behavior of the Prince, no grief at the death of his father, exactly as in the previous scene, but then his emotional response to his father's words; and the King, too, just mouthing words of wisdom, after having been so moving: all of it the simple truth, like Nature itself. We also look for the passage in which the King sighs, wishing that one might read the book of fate, because we had been reminded of it in the palace gardens. — "Everything is terrible, and if one never achieves an enlightened glimpse of freedom, the whole of life is not worth very much."

Sunday, February 6   R. somewhat restless, but not until the early hours. — At breakfast he says, "Lessing and I, we got our first impressions in the theater—with Goethe it was more through amateur acting." Then he talks again about Shakespeare's language, its dignity, in both wit and irony, and its majesty—he calls it pedigree. (Yesterday we compared the English with the German, and the German strikes us as much nobler.) R. works. At lunch we have friend Feustel, an always welcome guest. Walk in the palace gardens; talk about the way one has to expend so much energy in this climate. "And now I am about to do it all over again," R. says reflectively. "And then I suppose the Grail will shine on you of its own accord," I add jokingly. This amuses R. very much: "I can already see Levi unveiling it," he says. And then, "I have always been fated to carry out in prose (in life) what I have put into my poetry—that scene with the swan, people will think it came from my views on vivisection!" — I add that there is something daemonic about the hunt in *Tristan,* it is like a deliberate sin, in contrast to the tragedy of the lovers' original sin. He works on his score; comes to fetch me for supper and tells me that all his writing and creating is an endeavor to prove worthy of the kind of life I have given him! — And various other things which I do not dare to think about! — In the evening we read the first act of [Calderón's] *El mayor monstruo los zelos* and are completely swept up by the surge of passion in it, the familiar tragic outlook. As a prime example of this style R. also reads the sonnet to the pale star at the end of the battle in his *Muger, llora, y vencerás.* — Of the scene in *H. IV* he says on our return from our walk, "It is exactly like overhearing a scene between a king and his son— something one would not otherwise experience." — I remind him of green Naples following the thunderstorm, saying that Shakespeare always arouses in me a similar feeling of astonishment. — "In Calderón one can see the artist," R. observes.

Monday, February 7   I ask R. for the "silly theme," so that you, my Siegfried, will know exactly what he means. Much about the first act of [Hebbel's] *Herodes und Mariamne.* R. works. Some friends at lunch, and in consequence less to report about R., for though he is in very good spirits, he seems to me to be not quite his usual self. He goes for a walk with Loldi and our friends, because toothache and concern for our little neighbors keep me at home—he says he treated Loldi just as if she were me. — In the evening he writes his score, though he keeps saying how much he would rather be writing symphonies: "All the time I am putting aside themes for the sake of the drama—I cannot do things as, for example, even Weber did, when he introduced his hermit with a dance tune because it happened to occur to him just at that moment." "Not so much brooding," he exclaims to Rub. "In your place I would be playing the piano all day long." — In the evening R. reads to us the extract from the Reichskanzler's speech, and after that we read the last two acts of *Herodes und Mariamne*—gripped by it throughout, if also often disturbed by its curious mixture of passion and dryness, poetic flight and prose, profound perceptions and operatic quality. — Impossible to compare him with Shakespeare, yet there is truth in it, for example the reappearance of Octavian, the resurgence of passion when he learns that M. is being maltreated; those are motives from life, says R.

Tuesday, February 8 R. slept well, and he works with pleasure on his article. At lunch he is worried by Isolde's obstinacy; Fidi the only one who seems normal, if frequently absent-minded; R. says of the children's obtuseness that they have always got something in their heads, as he had, for example, when he decided to build himself a ship and imagined to himself his family's surprise when he arrived with the boat on the Elbe. And then he had decided to start breeding rabbits—his mother had discovered that when she heard the animals thumping around in the cupboard. In spite of strong storm winds we go for a walk, and are cheered by our resoluteness. On the difficult little path from the fence to the avenue, R. says, "Just like the German character, no energy left, everything just muddy and messy." — In the evening R. sings the ballades "*Herr Oluf*" and "*Der Wirtin Töchterlein,*" and in the latter he corrects Loewe in the run at the end, giving eternity its proper solemn character. When our friends have gone, he talks about us, at least 15 years too late, and, referring to another relationship and all the useless disturbance it caused, he says jokingly, " '*J'ai si peu dîné*' ['I have had so little to eat'], as I could say," quoting Chopin's remark when he begged his hostess's pardon for not playing the piano. — He describes Bismarck as a caricature of the *homme fort* [strong man] of whom George Sand speaks. — He also tells me that today he found a place in his article for an idea written down in his *Braunes Buch* in '73. — Today, while singing at the piano, he looked so beautiful, so noble, with a childlike radiance, that I had to tell him of it.

Wednesday, February 9 The gale tears open our window during the night, we awake, both of us spring out of bed, I fear for R., but he returns gaily to his bed, saying, "The storm was so violent that it pulled off my compresses"—and, laughing, we go to sleep again. — When he gets up after breakfast, he says orchestrating is no fun, he prefers writing, orchestrating is just arranging. When we come together again at lunch, he complains about his fingers; I tell him how sorry I am to see a person with his temperament exposed to such petty torments, and he says, "It is the temperament which produces them."

— We talk of Wolz.'s manner, of his eyebrows, which give one the feeling that he could turn the world upside down. "And I, who am energy personified, have none at all," R. adds, in such a humorous tone of voice that we all burst out laughing. [*The words from* "We talk of Wolz.'s manner" *to this point obliterated in ink by an unknown hand.*] Over coffee there is talk of starvation in Russia; R. says he feels like writing to the Grand Duke, the heir to the throne, suggesting that they transfer the capital to Odessa, but princes who would do such a thing no longer exist, he says; whatever happens will come about through suffering, through the people, and piecemeal. At the same time there is praise for France, which, since it has done away with religion, has now banished its ghosts as well. We go for a walk in the palace gardens: "The worst weather thou find'st will show thee"—"that you, Richard, are with Cosima," I finish. "That would be nice," I suddenly hear him say. "What?" "I can't say just now," and then: "If one melody were to accompany another, the first one were to disappear, and its accompaniment be turned by the cellos into the main melody, and so on alternately. I have got something of that sort in the '*Kaisermarsch*.' " He adds, "The '*Kaisermarsch*' is probably the nicest of my instrumental compositions; it shows what one can still place beside Beeth." — Of Carlyle he says how right he was to describe the French Revolution as "an urge to face up to truths." — Boni's ball gown delights him. — In the evening we chat together about all sorts of things, my father, the Israelites—and finally [Wilhelmine] Schröder-Devrient. Jouk. asked whether she was beautiful. R.: "How shall I reply to that? Everything about her was life, soul, warmth, and an expression of delight such as I have otherwise seen only in Cosima. — A face easily expresses suffering, but true delight—I once saw such an expression in Grisi, when she uttered the word '*gioia*' ['joy'], and there was something of it in Judith." Of the latter he said, "At that time, in 1876, I found her natural warmth very pleasant in contrast to all the prevailing stiffness." He says once again that he is longing to do some instrumental compositions, adding that it was a similar mood which gave rise to *Tristan*. He enjoys writing, but feels it will be some time before he writes another text: "I have posed enough riddles," he adds.

Thursday, February 10 R. reflects on the German language, and how everything is to be found in it, for example, the word *Recht* [right], from which has been derived so abstract an idea as *die Richte*—putting a thing "to rights." — Toward lunchtime he calls me and reads to me his new article, "Know Thyself." — Whether the Jews can ever be redeemed is the question which, in connection with it, occupies our thoughts—their nature condemns them to the world's reality. They have profaned Christianity, that is to say, adapted it to this world, and from our art, which can only be a refuge from prevailing conditions, they also expect world conquest. — Letter from Lusch, very characteristic and original—R. feels that Hans's temperament shows a strong influence, but, helped by a better education, she would surely never be tempted into such injudicious statements as "a Christian converted to Judaism," etc. R. also says that he has the feeling that seeing Lulu again would be bound to have a very beneficial effect on Hans. — Today, in spite of the weather, R. goes for a walk with Jouk., as far as Senfft's—while I drive out to the mental institution with our neighbor's poor wife. In the evening we read in *Deutsche Reform* an article which as good as implies the complete dependence of the anti-Semites on the Conservatives. Then the second installment of W[olzogen]'s article "The Wagnerite as Writer," which so touches us that R. sends for him and drinks a toast to this Wagnerite in particular. Much about the Jewish problem, R. keeps coming back to the question: Who are we? Of a photograph of Carlyle he says, "We should look like this, righteous and sad." — He maintains that I do not like his article, which sounds very funny. — At supper we turn to the subject of Frederick the Great, and R. says, "One forgives him everything, one accepts him as he is, just because one sees before one's eyes a true character."

Friday, February 11 I reproach R. for not realizing that I consider his article to be of the greatest value. R. replies unbelievingly, "You are quite correct: everything one writes, all articles, are silly nonsense." And when I protest, he says I should learn to recognize a joke: it is just like the president saying, "My wife finds me boring." "That's what I am saying—you know it all, all the ideas have been discussed between us, and so it can be no pleasure to you to hear an article like that read out loud. At least, to my way of thinking." — We laugh about the president and part in cheerful spirits. Around lunchtime I find R. altering the ending of his article, to my regret. — At lunch he is a little irritable to start with, his fingers are hurting him, but he gradually regains his spirits, and over coffee he is in a very good mood, even if the bad weather makes him talk at length about his Venetian projects. I do not remember why Mozart is mentioned; R. says: "In him one can really see what the world is. How easy it would have been to make things easy for him, to say to him, 'Come here, Mozartl, you'll be treated well'—and a person like that was obliged to struggle with the most abject poverty." — Some days ago R. said, "How touching it is when he, this Salzburger, this Austrian, describes himself, in the horrifying state of our empire, as a German musician." We go for a walk in the palace gardens in spite of the bad weather (heavy showers) and speak in praise of Italy, where such things would be possible. [*Two newspaper clippings enclosed here between the pages.* "Music in Hospitals" *begins with the sentence,* "Our great master Richard Wagner's fine idea, to make use of music in the treatment of illness, has become a reality in England." *Marginal comment by Cosima:* " 'Thus,' R. observes, 'does one become a fable in one's own lifetime.' " *The second clipping, from the* Deutsches Familienblatt, *is a reproduction of a picture by A. H. Bakker Korff, depicting three women in a* salon. *Beside this Cosima has written:* "R. is touched by this picture—he looks at it for a long time—is pleased that someone has seen things in this way—in particular he finds the 'old maid' singing extraordinarily full of feeling —the women listening also full of surprises, whether old maids, widows, or wives. The prosperous bourgeois life depicted there, it all interests him, also the costumes—with our restricting clothes, he observes, such a thing would not be possible."] In the evening *cercle:* Zumpe from Frankfurt, W.'s, etc. — Rub. plays first of all the Flower Maidens and then [Beethoven's] *33 Variations,* to our admiring delight. R. remarks on the richness of these "extraordinary" compositions: "With any three of these variations he could have written a symphony." — When our friends have gone, he reads to me the revised ending of his article, which seems to me more fitting than the first, and R. himself says that he always meant to write about us, not about the Jews. And yet I have to tell him what strange feelings it arouses in me when he alters anything at my instigation; I say that for me every idea he has is sacred. — "You foolish girl," he says. "As if we were not always in harmony!" — And indeed it happens quite regularly with us, in both the deepest and the most trivial things. Today, for example, he said he was now reconciled to the Freemasons' new building, and a few moments earlier I had wanted to make the same remark. And so I believe that what I said in connection with the first ending merely expressed his own feelings. When we finished reading, he thought of the sad music which the shahs of Persia ordered played to them before going to sleep. — "You could do that better than anyone—it would be something like 'O *sink hernieder, Nacht der Liebe.*' " — "Oh, no, that is happy, not sad, a luxuriating after their wild discussion of their predicament." — "I still find it incomprehensible that an audience can follow all that with interest, as in Munich." I: "And yet it is the favorite work of the *barbarians* in particular—Lenbach, for example." R.: "I gladly admit that there is something intoxicating about its big musical complexes." — In the palace gardens he was pleased by the sight of a little girl with a red scarf around her head and some school folders and books: "That is something I like to see," he says, "there is something so respectable, so dutiful about it." And he mentions Br[uno] Bauer's remark about the Germans' being placid, a remark which has always pleased him greatly. I say it seems to me that in their contacts with Israelites the Germans come to grief on account of not only their bad qualities, but also their good ones: for example, their undemandingness, which makes them so capable of idealism; now, under the pressure of these rapacious people, this is turning into indolent insensitivity. —

Saturday, February 12 R. had a very restless night, and all morning he feels uncomfortable, but he does some work, and after lunch we go for a walk in the palace gardens, pleased that it is again dry and cold. In the evening we read Stein's article and find it very good; his character gladdens us, and by contrast we think of Nietzsche's! . . . R. observes that Stein's and Wolz.'s more distinguished birth had been an advantage to them. R. is on edge, but not unwell. At lunch he read to us an article in the little *Oberfränkische Zeitung* about longevity. — After the reading of Stein's article R. said it made him feel very peculiar to hear himself mentioned in such terms, compared with Shakespeare, and he again laughingly quotes his favorite story: *"J'aime votre rude franchise"* ["I like your brutal frankness"]. —

Sunday, February 13 R. slept well, copies out his article, and is very good-humored with Colonel Schäffer and his wife, whom we have to lunch to thank them about Boni. When we are walking in the palace gardens afterward, R. tells me it made him feel very strange to see how much the couple had aged—no doubt they had thought the same about him. In the evening read [Cervantes's] *"El zeloso estremeño,"* which makes a great impression on us. — For reading material R. has landed on Pott and is pleased to encounter Gobineau in its pages right at the start. — It was cold today, and we crept, rather than walked, through the palace gardens, which are "saturated with *Parsifal,*" as R. remarks.

Monday, February 14 I had a difficult night, and in consequence sleep the whole morning. Around lunchtime R. comes to me in his new hat, sent to him by the "Order of the Holy Grail." It suits him splendidly. R. finishes copying out his article. At lunch he talks of a book by a Prof. Pott, in which he suddenly found Gobineau's book on the inequality of the human races thoroughly discussed and criticized. He describes to us Gobineau's main idea of the downfall of humanity after an existence of 14,000 years, which interests both him and us. Over coffee he brings up his Italian plans again—on my account, he says; when I assure him that the climate here is doing me no harm at all, he says, "Then let your good health be the excuse." — The *Parsifal* meadow reminds us of Switzerland in spring, the magic of it, and of Tribschen altogether. "That was a refuge," R. says, and relates how he was able to keep me hidden from view. — We go for a walk, watch our abbé on the ice, return home; the operation is performed, that is to say, R. allows me to cut off one of his eyebrow hairs which has grown too long and to place it in my locket. In the evening I read his article out loud; R. listens, standing, interrupts me now and again with signs of approval, and then embraces me. The loving intensity with which he listened and watched did, I believe, increase my powers of interpretation, and if he was satisfied with the way I imparted his ideas, to me it was bliss to express them. Our conversation starts with the article and touches on all subjects, including Gobineau's theory, to which R. links the remark that it is by no means impossible that humanity should cease to exist, but if one looks at things without regard to time and space, one knows that what really matters is something different from racial strength—see the Gospels. And he adds jokingly: "If our civilization comes to an end, what does it matter? But if it comes to an end through the Jews, that is a disgrace." He talks of starting a new article, "Herodom and Christianity." — He once again speaks in praise of the *Nouvelles asiatiques* and says that beneath the majestic foolishness of Mohammedanism the peoples of the Orient have retained a certain childlike quality; and they also have dignity, as can be seen, for instance, in the two silent people in the first story. — He feels that the Russians are more capable of civilizing the Orient than the English, who have imposed themselves on it in the manner of a countinghouse. — When we are alone, we yield completely to the mood which the reading has induced in us—oh, could one but die at such moments!

Tuesday, February 15 R. tells me the comical dream he had—that the stuttering Count Du Moulin read his article out loud and stuttered so much over the word "Bitz*barkeit*" (I had drawn his attention yesterday to this mistake) that we all had to laugh. — He tells me some things from C. Fr[antz]'s article, which criticizes Moltke's remark that war comes from God, and he concludes: "But it would have to be a king— he would have to be concerned for his people and make the decision to abandon this militarism. But just look at them all!" — He writes a little verse for the Knights of the Holy Grail, which I then send off. At lunch he tells me that he gets more pleasure from working on his score after breaking off to do some other work. Over coffee Dr. Landgraf performs a little operation on his finger, which is still painful. — He talks of Prof. Pott's quarrelsome tone and his absurd fury with Gobineau, since the latter believes in decay and is not impressed by the fact that we now have railways! — We go for a walk in the palace gardens in glorious weather; R. suddenly says, "I can understand why Beeth. liked the variation form so much; he could be much more creative in it than in any other, for after all, what matters most is melodies, shaping things, and the conventional symphonic form restricted his creative powers much more than variations." — At supper I find R. rather irritable: was it his work, or the book? "I'm reading German flour again, and it's like getting badly ground flour between one's teeth." — On the other hand, he is increasingly attracted to Gobineau's idea, and when I say, "If we disregard time and space, there is surely no such thing as decay," R. replies, "The thought I am occupied with is whether morality should not be preserved as being that to which everything tends—survival is then a matter of complete indifference." — He remains more or less in this mood until Bach's B Minor Fugue is played. "What a world that is!" he exclaims. "Planets circling around each other, no feeling, yet all of it is passion, will—no intellect; Beeth.'s art, by contrast, is a dancing couple." — We then ask for *Die Msinger;* after Rub. has played the Prelude to the 3rd act and the first scene, R. says to me, "H. Sachs has married Eva," gets up, declares, "The entire condition of German art is contained in this first scene," a remark the others do not understand; he has it played again, singing it up to the "Prize Song." "Never before has the master given us such a friendly greeting." — R. then enlarges upon Germany, which, he had been convinced, would acclaim this work, though of course it has been so badly performed—and he becomes agitated in a way which is not good for him. — I send our friends away, we remain alone. "What does it matter whether it is performed, whether Germany behaves in this way or that way? We still have it." He: "It's only to the others that I say such things," and we immerse ourselves in happiness and memories! "None of it fits," he says, "I have married Eva." — I: "But according to Herwegh you are Sachs and Walther in one, and according to me you are all of them, Tristan and Marke, Lohengrin and Parsifal." And to this we link congenial memories of Herwegh and all who congratulated us sincerely on our marriage, Sulzer, Marschall, and several others. And we keep coming back to *Die Msinger;* of the Prelude to the 3rd act he says, "That is the loveliest thing I ever wrote." He then speaks about the specks of dust playing around Sachs in the morning sunbeams, and keeps exclaiming gaily, "But it doesn't fit, none of it fits." — He becomes reflective, I ask him why: "A bassoon passage." "Orchestration is your way of cobbling," I say. "You are probably right," he replies. Then he expresses his annoyance over always having to deal with apprentices, like the musicians around him. But we soon go back to the topics that concern us and to Schopenhauer, who, in R.'s estimation, would probably have gone along with him as far as *Loh.* and *T.,* but certainly not from then on. Regarding his errors in the application of his theories, so right in themselves, R. says, "It makes one feel that an artist can be a philosopher, but not a philosopher an artist." — (Previously, in reply to a question from Rub., he had described Mendelssohn's "daemonic" and impish manner, all the more sinister because of its taciturnity, and suggested that possibly *Tannhäuser* might have had a strangulating effect on him, for he died not long afterward.) — And we part happily, after our souls' spirits have become immersed in each other! — Before lunch R. chose watches with me for Eva and Loldi.

Recently R. expressed his pleasure at having provided in *Der Ring des Nibelungen* a complete picture of the curse of greed for money, and the disaster it brings about.

Wednesday, February 16   R. recalls his childhood days; how, returning from a visit to his godfather, Träger, who had presented him with a worn-out gray dress suit and a Turkish waistcoat which R.'s mother laughed at, he had been welcomed very affectionately by his family in Dresden. He goes to his work, but his fingers are irritating him. He fetches me for lunch, and I show him the letter I have begun to Lusch, which, without my having intended it, is devoted entirely to Hans Sachs, and that in French. At lunch conversation about Gob., who prefers Brahmanism to Buddhism. I observe that, if one looks at the reality of things, he is probably not wrong, for Buddhism dissolves everything. R. goes for a walk with Jouk., returns home disgusted with the military music he has just been hearing: "And to these sounds my son is expected to march!" This arouses in him thoughts of emigration. Meanwhile he was amused by Marke, who because of his stiff leg fell down like a human being and then, when R. and Jouk. laughed, would not jump over the ditch before them, but waited until they turned their backs. — The lawyer Hofmann reports the loss of our lawsuit regarding the autograph in Würzburg; R. sees in that a typical example of German justice and wants Wolz. to write about it. — Read Cervantes in the evening, "*La illustre fregona,*" with tremendous enjoyment. "Oh, the south!" R. exclaims, and frequently, "Shakespeare." He hopes to see these places, which are not yet as well trodden as Italy, and where people play guitars and sing for their own pleasure, not for the benefit of foreigners, as in Naples. — And in the evening, when we are once more by ourselves, he says that we came together 15 years too late: "We would have founded a town of Wahnfried in America." He recalls previous relationships which he kept going and idealized because he did not wish to admit to himself how pitiful they were; I tell him that this is his tendency in all relationships: he must present the person with whom he has to do in an ideal light to himself, and in that way he makes him for a while look better than he is; if that is not possible, he, R., will have nothing to do with the person.

[*End of the sixteenth book of the Diaries. The seventeenth book begins:* "To my Siegfried—begun on Eva's birthday. May family love be preserved among you, my children!"]

Thursday, February 17 "Eva was born today," I say to R. after we have talked about all kinds of things; after leaving the room, he comes back, embraces me, and says that I surely did not believe that he had forgotten the day! At 1 o'clock we give Eva our good wishes, first of all in my gray room, while R. plays the "Prize Song" in his. — At lunch he reminds me that I once called her the child of loyalty. We talk a lot about the *Odyssey,* since Jouk. has given Eva a fine edition of it, and we go through many of the splendid features of this divine work. — Talked over coffee of Eva's birth, my inner happiness in spite of everything. Then R. recalls a childhood experience in Possendorf, how he went for a walk with his comrades, and one of them, Bernhard Lingg, son of the owner of the Lingg baths, threw stones at a bird, a yellow bunting, and R. can still see the bird after it was hit, fluttering and at last sinking down. We go for a walk, R. and I, actually —since it is muddy on the paths—on the ice, which is still firm, but no longer good for skating. Much about Cervantes and Shakespeare. — The two girls in their confirmation-candidate mood R. calls the two Vidrieras—he says they look as if they were made of glass! When we return home, we part tenderly, and after a while, as I am changing my clothes in the bedroom, he comes up and takes leave of me again. — We end the story with great delight, and the anecdote about the tail reminds R. of his gambling night when he was a child; he tells Jouk. about it and says: "How must I have looked then, poor boy? And what an expression on my face when I won again!" I observe that in this single incident one could have foretold his entire fate. — When we are alone, he plays the piano and says the sustained tone with the pedal down always pleases him—it is like calling into a valley. — Previously he talked about the Germans and their lack of talent, the wretchedness of the anti-Jewish agitation which is relying on Bismarck (he still feels his misunderstood remark to Dr. Förster might be at the bottom of that), the impending mass emigration. In the morning, talking about Schiller, he said that he was the most serious and profound of them all; in the evening he says that Schiller really did manage to write good plays, whereas Goethe had only dabbled in it, though he was undoubtedly the greater poet. Regarding Grillparzer, he says he saw a play of his in the Königstädter Theater in Berlin which pleased him: at that time Sch.'s influence was still predominant; then came, under Schlegel's influence, the trochees and the tragedies of fate, and all was lost. [*Added in margin:* "Jouk. told me that R. said that Heyse had made the drama impossible. 'I said that they should just write a good comedy—that would certainly please people, beside R.'s works,' but R. had felt they were incapable of doing it. Of Kleist he said that in relation to Schiller he was like Schubert to Beethoven."] When we go upstairs, renewed memories of former times; he observes that Hans has never got beyond the age of 15–17, never become a man, whereas Fidi would reach fulfillment only as an adult man — I observe that for R. himself this age of fulfillment would be old age, since only then would all that he is become apparent. "We shall remain very much alone," he says, and, jokingly, "Isolani"—a play on words, such as he enjoys making—he calls Marke Lomellino, from *Lümmel* [lout], and when I tell him that Dr. Strecker is demanding *Parsifal,* he says, "I suppose because he has *vorgestreckt* [advanced money]." — Yesterday he said to me jokingly, "You must have a very bad conscience toward me, since you always give in and adapt yourself to me"—and this makes me feel very solemn, as if I have no right even to the happiness of being permitted to obey him! And for me the main burden of my life is that, though I should like to surrender myself utterly all the time, I still hold firm, desist even from expressing many things, in order not to disturb the tranquillity which is better for him than ecstasy. . . . But yesterday I had to tell him that on the night of Eva's birth he spoke a word to me which transported me beyond all the sufferings of mind and body; he wanted to know what it was, I could not say it—for you, my Eva, let it be written down here, as a blessing on you: "I have never loved before." — This is what he said, showing me the full extent of his love. . . . "Good night, you big and pretty girls," he said tonight to these two beings who have so flourished beneath his star.

Friday, February 18   A good night, but his fingers still painful. — At lunch (and also yesterday) he tells me how revolting he finds the German scholar in this book of Pott's; there is no need for him to have a single idea, it is all nothing but quotations; W. v. Humboldt seems to R. very shallow. — Then R., with much enjoyment, quotes several things from today's *Fliegende Blätter*. After lunch a portrait of George Eliot gives us quite a shock on account of its ugliness. — We go for a walk, the weather is not particularly good, we watch a blackbird busily bathing in a little puddle beside the fence and then flying into our garden. — In the evening we receive a visit from Herr Irwine, the donor who wishes to remain anonymous, a quiet and serious Scotsman. Rub. plays Bach organ fugues. R. says to me, "This is something rather like Cervantes's stories, but nobody would understand what I mean." I think I do—he means all the life, the apparent confusion, which in fact represent the variegated and ordered life of Nature, in which one can discern accents of supreme passion, of a deeply sorrowing sensibility. Then R. gets Rub. to play [Mendelssohn's] *Hebrides* Overture and delights in this beautiful work, though he feels it requires a program, for when he heard it for the first time, in Leipzig, under the title of *Hebrides* Overture—which meant nothing to him—he did not understand it at all. — My feeling is that in this work the heroic saga has been turned into a fairy tale, Brünnhilde into the Sleeping Beauty. — When our friends have gone, we remain together for a while. The Scotsman made a good impression on him, but he remarks that Nature is now no longer producing beautiful mouths! — And then he exclaims: "How nice to be alone! We must keep inviting people to our house, so that we can always enjoy this happiness again" — and he sends for a half-bottle of champagne, so that we can drink to that. And memories return, and tender reproaches are made to me, and when I take them to heart, we laugh together! — (Yesterday, when I spoke of the doubts I previously had whether my way of doing things was right for my children, R. said, "Well, your eldest daughter is now a real enchantress.")

Saturday, February 19 "I am the Napoleon of the breakfast table." With these words R. turns to me after finishing his tea and eggs. He tells me about Fidi in the shower. And then, after rising, he recalls the *Hebrides* Overture and Mendelssohn, that uncanny man, silently lying in wait, then suddenly breaking into violent speech. — After lunch he tells us how handsome he was, and how at the age of 30 he became so Jewish. Taking off from an article about Vienna and its Israelites, he enlarges upon the subject of how terrible it is to have this foreign Jewish element in our midst, and how we have lost everything. We go for a walk, R. and I, the starlings are now here, as well as other little birds, tweet-tweet, and R. speaks of the nightingales promised him 6 years ago, which gives me quite a shock, for I am at present engaged in negotiations for birds of this kind. Marke's barking at a cat keeps us waiting at the gate for a while; when he sees R. lingering there, he does not do the same, but jumps over the ditch, sniffs at the trees, and in the end follows us in a *nonchalant* way, which amuses us very much. In the evening a glance at the staircase of the Paris Opera and revulsion at such splendor! — A picture of some gypsy women, on the other hand, reveals true pedigree. [*Added in margin:* "And, in contrast to the gypsies, a transport of slaves in Africa. 'This is us!' R. exclaims, then says it would do as a performance in the Paris Opera!"] — The reading of Cervantes's "*El casamiento engañoso*," since it is difficult to do, taken over by R. Splendid conversation between the two dogs! — R. showed me his wind instruments, the trouble they have caused him, and he says his work has been "not at all Rossini-ish." Boni caused us concern through her lack of understanding (she was unable to withdraw gracefully when we found the story embarrassing on her account). R. lost his temper, but he immediately followed her upstairs, finding it unbearable to be in conflict with the children. And I feel compelled to tell him that all the emotions I had previously laid before the Godhead I now offer up to him, and it is in him that I find, not my happiness, but my salvation. — Much then about Cervantes and Shakespeare, and Goethe added to their company, as the author of *Faust,* as a perceiver and portrayer of characters. — The Spaniard's gracefulness of form R. ascribes to Arab influence, as in Italy, too, where in the Sicily of the Hohenstaufens, which the Saracens had previously dominated, Italian poetry began.

Sunday, February 20 Thoughts of decay and downfall do not abandon one; when the subject comes up first thing in the morning, R. says, "What is eternity?" And he recalls [Cervantes's] *Numancia,* the child who wants to be rescued but then prefers after all to die, a living proof of Rome's triumph. "Tremendously important, however," R. adds mockingly, "that such a town should be taken," and we recall Moltke's speech attacking the peace, and the opportunity France had at that time to give the world peace, to raze fortresses, Alsace-Lorraine to become independent like Belgium, and the small states relieved of the need to maintain large armies. — Yesterday, in our conversation about Mendelssohn, R. recalled Disraeli's *Tancred,* in which it is asserted that all significant people are Jews. R. says, "Most of them are German Jews, and Disraeli overlooks the fact that it is German talent which is being used in this way." — When I hear R. going downstairs toward lunchtime, I wish to greet him, but he is much irritated by his fingers, which make any kind of manipulating difficult for him. But when I come down for lunch, he has regained his cheerfulness. He talks a lot about the German scholar's book, which is once again demonstrating to him that German science knows nothing: "If I had my way, not a single cent would be spent on them." "On the one hand this army, on the other these professors," he exclaims. Over coffee I read out loud a letter from Lusch. Then Dr. Hess arrives and tells him about rubber fingers; that consoles R., and our walk turns out to be cheerful, with some twitterings from starlings and woodpeckers. Over coffee R. relates that he gave our handyman Krug a little lecture because the heating was late, and the good rascal made a peculiar impression on him. "A character of that sort is like some strange embryo. Heavens, when I compare him with Molly—what assurance, what completeness in her—!" I say it is difficult to imagine what such a person would be thinking if, say, caught up in a revolution. "He would be like the Turco in Daudet," says R.—a thought which had already occurred to me as I asked my question. The marriage of Count Hatzfeldt's daughter to Herr Bleichröder, who is turning Catholic along with his family on account of it, gives rise to gloomy reflections. Presumably it has come about through the Count's debts. When we return home from our walk, R. recalls the passage in *Parsifal* which he is just orchestrating, "*Waren die Menschen, die mir wehrten, bös'?*" He is pleased with Gurnemanz's laughter in reply, and he says it was necessary in order to show the childlike qualities which make Gurnemanz believe that this is the creature for whom they have been waiting. — In the palace gardens R. recalled the portrait of Louise Michel in the *I. Z.:* "Such are women: when men fall, heroism finds refuge in them. But in a horrible way; from a wit one might expect pity, but not from such a humourless woman." — In the evening we had a different seating arrangement at table; R. did not wish to sit in the middle opposite me, but beside me at one end; we do it according to his wish, but it displeases him, and he wants to be put in the middle again, as our king. — We read some of the conversation between the two dogs again, then R. does some improvising, something approaching the style of *Tristan,* and he also begins the Prelude, I having reminded him that I have heard it played so beautifully by him. He says he used to play frequently, among other things the Prelude to *Lohengrin*—in the Willes' house in Mariafeld, for example, for Frau Wille had been a very good listener, artistic impressions sent her soul into a shiver. — I recall that I first heard *Tristan* when my brother was lying mortally ill in my house, and he breathed in the sounds of it with me—love and death entwined! After our conversation R. told me that the wind instruments are causing him trouble, and he shows me what he has erased and altered in the "*wer ist gut*" passage. —

Monday, February 21 In the morning our conversation comes back to Moltke's assertions; previously one had thought that a Christian was in conflict only with himself—"No, with the French," R. interrupts me merrily. We talk of Amfortas's wound, which for me has something unutterably moving about it because of its symbolic character, and we enlarge upon it at length. When I come downstairs for lunch, I find R. very cheerful; the rubber fingers recommended by Dr. Hess have arrived, and they do him good, take away the irritation, and that is enough to restore him to the most splendid of spirits. We go for a walk in fine weather, enjoy each other, which makes R. say, "Our relationship is coming along." In the evening we read with real pleasure the episode of the witch in the conversation between the two dogs. Impossible to define wherein the power of this story lies, impossible to think of anything else. One is reminded of Kundry, of Diotima, the prophecy is unfathomable in its depth. "Good God, what things these are, what a human being he is!" R. keeps exclaiming.

— Unfortunately this reading was preceded by another, assertions by Herr v. Hülsen which come back to R. at the conclusion of the evening, and he wants me to reply to them.

Tuesday, February 22 I occupy myself during the night with the reply, but in the morning I am able to talk sensibly about Cervantes with R. An inexhaustible subject, but at the same time unapproachable! R. is now inclined to leave Hülsen be, but when he sees what I have written down, he is in favor of immediate publication in the *A. A. Z.* — At lunch I tell him that I cannot get the conclusion of the C Minor Symphony out of my mind, and he says this is very remarkable, for during the morning he had been analyzing this song of victory—this happy rejoicing about nothing, he adds gaily. Jouk. presents his sketches; the Magic Garden is still not right. We go for a walk—on the ice, since the surrounding paths are all muddy. Fidi skating on it all by himself! We part in contentment, but when I come downstairs, R. is not feeling well. He goes to bed, and we spend a musical evening with *Tristan* in his absence!

Wednesday, February 23 When, reunited with R., I asked him last night how he felt, he said, "Don't talk—I feel like a plant." — And in the morning he is feeling better. Herr Neumann writes to me to say that there is a growing danger of the Jews' staying away from the *Ring* in Berlin; R. is advising him to abandon Berlin and go straight to London; the ordinary citizens have no money, the aristocracy and the Court will stay away on account of Hülsen, and the Jews on account of the agitation. But all of this is unpleasant to a high degree, like everything else outside! Although R. is feeling run down, we go for a walk in the palace gardens; he tells me about Pott's book and Gobineau's very bold, very aristocratic assertions. His article "Herodom and Christianity" is ripening inside him. But in the evening he feels run down, and it requires Cervantes's genius to restore us to our usual path. We finish the splendid conversation; try then to read Hoffmann's continuation of it, but find it impossible. "It is like *Kladderadatsch*," he says.

Thursday, February 24 R. had a bad night, his fingers are tormenting him, and today he cannot even write. He does have a moment of gaiety before lunch, but it soon passes, everything pains and upsets him. Dr. Landgraf, who joins us for coffee, thinks that the rubber fingers have overheated him, he takes them off. He finds the conversation with Dr. Landgraf entertaining; the latter talks about the school—that the children who have received bad marks just think they were born to be graded 3 and 4. And he relates that once, when he wrote a German essay for his son, the boy was given the same bad marks. — (Today Siegfried has his first Latin lesson.) We go for a walk with R. as far as

the Birk, delight in the pretty little place, but at the same time remember Siena! — At supper R. talks of his father Geyer, his kindness,
his consideration, and his at that time predominating interest in the
theater. Yesterday R. recalled an anecdote, told him by his mother,
about a woman who sat in a stall outside the theater selling meat pies,
and how in the intermissions the students, knowing that she had no
more pies to sell but wanting to annoy her, would demand these from
her, ignoring her nuts and other merchandise, and that brought curses
from her. — In the evening friend Wolz. visits us; R. tells him that we
cannot champion special causes such as vegetarianism in our *Blätter,*
but must always confine ourselves to defining and demonstrating the
ideal, leaving those outside to fight for their special cause; for the same
reason we cannot join in the anti-Jewish agitation. — All sorts of
things are discussed, and my reply to Herr v. Hülsen also receives an
amicable mention. — When our friends have gone, R. and I remain
cozily together. R. drafts a telegram to Herr Neumann about abandoning Berlin. — "Intellectual equality cannot be achieved," R. says, as if
replying to Count Gob., "but moral equality, attaining that—this
one could urge." — In the evening, before going off to sleep, he says,
" 'Stay a while, you are so fair'—this one can say of the moment when
the day is cast aside, and, in a larger sense, of death."

Friday, February 25 R. did not have a good night, and he is also
feeling unwell at lunch. — A telegram from Herr Neumann says that
Berlin cannot be abandoned. After lunch Jouk.'s relationship with
Pepino discussed in much detail, brought up by a sad amorous incident. I allow myself to be provoked into describing it as *silly,* and I
regret that. We talk about it with R. as we go for a walk together amid
snowflakes to the Birk, and for R.'s sake I almost prefer this subject
to the anti-Jewish agitation, Berlin, etc. From the *Tagblatt* R. reads
to me the debates in which Prince Bismarck declares that all he cares
about is the greatness and unity of the German nation, in other respects
he will rule with all parties. It sounds a little arrogant and somewhat
hollow. Whist in the evening. R. is irritated and exasperated by his
fingers. — About the relationship with P., R. said: "It is something
for which I have understanding, but no inclination. In any case, with
all relationships what matters most is what we ourselves put into
them. It is all illusion." — (Today R. sent for a map of Germany, to
show me *das eichelne Taus,* with which he compares Marke on account
of his tongue. —) Late in the evening a letter from Herr Neumann, he
is not relinquishing Berlin.

Saturday, February 26 R. had a very wretched night, and his fingers
irritate him more and more; he dreamed, among other things, that I
did not return home until midnight and announced quite calmly that I

had been trying out costumes at Lenbach's: "Are you trying to drive me to suicide?" he had asked, beside himself. — The doctor comes, looks at the trouble, prescribes compresses! — We go for a walk and to friend Jouk.'s with both dogs; Marke literally examines the pictures! — Our friend is ill and probably sad as well. — We then stroll in the palace gardens, hear a blackbird in the distance, a sad sound amid mud and snow! In the evening great abstinence, and completely alone. R. talks of alterations which Hans has made in Weber's *Invitation to the Dance,* he finds them patronizing and utterly unjustified. We glance through Jacolliot's books on India and are each time revolted by the way Europeans behave among the Asians. —

Sunday, February 27 The night was really wretched, hardly any sleep at all. All the same, to my surprise, R. is cheerful at breakfast. He also works on his score, and when I come downstairs around lunchtime, he shows me a letter from the Société des Amis du Divorce [Society of the Friends of Divorce], appointing him an honorary member. At lunch a telegram arrives, reporting the success of *Lohengrin* in Naples. Our guest is Prof. Toussaint, who is giving Siegfried Latin lessons and who seems quite bright. R. and I then go for a walk, and on our return he recalls Hans's birthday in Munich (1868), how, after the dinner he had given us at Queroy's, he wandered alone through the streets of Munich. In that moment he had a curious feeling of relief, he says, as though everything were in a complete state of suspension, it was like a pause. — "It was people's malice which restored us to life," I say, and R.: "Yes—we should otherwise have gone under in silence." — R. works in the evening. Then we have friends and music, the C Minor Symphony, played by Rub., and scenes from the 1st and 2nd acts of *Siegfried,* Siegfried and Mime, R. as Mime, Herr Jäger as Siegfried. — During our walk R. was vexed about the mud, and he swears never again to spend a winter here! —

Monday, February 28 The night was quite tolerable, and R. says he now knows what he must do in order to sleep well: just eat and drink a lot. We talk a lot about the C Minor Symph. R. says that with the march the curtain is suddenly torn aside, for the previous flickering is like the soft fluttering of larks, and it does not actually lead into it. — R. works and with a smile signs the letter of thanks to the Friends of Divorce. He is still not content with his fingers. A letter from the King pleases R., and another from Lusch diverts us, though as always it gives rise to some earnest reflections. — We go for a walk in fine weather along the Konnersreuth highway. The dryness delights R., also the fact that a farmer looks at the two dogs and loudly praises them. Then we talk about the Jews; finally, however—know thyself!— about German professors, and R. calls them truffle-snufflers. Since this makes me laugh heartily, he says that in fact the expression comes from his uncle—literary t.-snufflers, he had said. In the evening we read with friend Wolz. J. Rub.'s article, much of which R. finds good, for example, what he says about tonality and its significance in Mozart's symphonies. — Dr. Landgraf visited us at coffeetime, and our conversation turned to the prison and a woman shut up there for killing her child. The doctor found her completely lacking in conscience, which would suggest that she was not really responsible for her actions, but for practical reasons she has to be punished. Our conversation ranges very wide and deep; the inequality of moral tendencies, whence that derives, and whether it cannot be overcome, whether it should not be humanity's goal to achieve equality in this field. The doctor speaks with much appreciation of the prison governor and his influence on the people under his care; R. cites an instance from N. America, mentioned by Gleizès, in which prisoners have become quite docile as the result of a vegetarian diet.

Tuesday, March 1 R. slept well, and our day begins very gaily. He looks with enjoyment through a Spanish illustrated periodical. At lunchtime, too, although his fingers are not yet cured, he is in good spirits. He dwells upon the mouth, and praises Nature's mastery in having made this feature, which had only to be a slit for eating, into the noble instrument of speech. — New tidings confirm the success of *Lohengrin,* and there is news from Spain that the production of *Lohengrin* in Madrid will coincide with the centennial celebrations for Calderón. When I tell R. that this would provide an opportunity for saying some nice things, he observes that everything there is dead. — He sees the proofs of the letter from "more Wagnerites"; he was against the use of the plural, but I begged to be allowed to retain it for the mode of address, "we," which seems to me more dignified. We go for a walk, the Konnersreuth highway again, but gray skies and bad underfoot, and on top of that a very strong wind on the homeward journey. R. feels a chest spasm, and this causes me concern, but he recovers and calls out, as he goes downstairs from his siesta to work, "A son has arrived." — Since I was downstairs myself, he tells me about it and says how much he regrets that, owing to all kinds of pressures, he is not constantly alive to the "glories of happiness" he enjoys. — The boys, Fidi's friends, skylark in the gallery, celebrating Shrovetide. R. then corrects the proofs of "Know Thyself," and in the evening, besides the happy author Rub., we receive Herr Köhler, a schoolteacher who was here three days before he made himself known to us and, after being very bashful at the start, seems to be developing into a lively character, if still rather confused. — Since he has fallen out entirely with the authorities, R. recommends him to Lesimple and, on a hint from me, holds out hope that he might come to us at Easter as Fidi's tutor. He has a liveliness of manner peculiar to the Rhineland. When he has gone, we take up *Parsifal,* Gurnemanz's first narration. It seems to us good to celebrate Shrovetide in this way. When I talk of the impression made on me in former days by being marked with ashes in the form of a cross, R. observes that there have been some fine customs, and the only sad thing about them is that they have become so meaningless. In the evening, when I go to him in his room, he tells me that, looking at himself in the mirror, he spoke his name, "Richard," and immediately felt that this had nothing at all to do with him: "What is that—Richard? So stupid!" I tell him he once told me how much he liked hearing me call him that. "Oh, that is different," he says, "then it is like the union of two beings." —

Wednesday, March 2   R. slept well, though he talked a lot in his sleep. It is a bright day, the sun already bringing us warmth. R. works on his score; but his fingers are still tormenting him, and the doctor, who comes today, seems unable to help at all. Lusch's letter, in which she describes her presentation at Court in connection with the wedding celebrations, amuses R. and me, too. We speak of it during our walk in the palace gardens, which is more wading than walking. Before supper R. comes upstairs to my room singing the C Minor Symphony, but unfortunately he is vexed by a lady visitor who happens to be with me, and he again feels pains in his chest. In the evening we read the first act of [Calderón's] *La dama duende.* Afterward looking at Schlagintweit's book on India.

Thursday, March 3   R. had a good night; the telegram from Frau Lucca amuses him and he has it answered in Italian. He puts Pott's book aside and is vexed at having now to write music for the scene painters (transformation scene in the 1st act). At lunch he jokes about the Bible lessons, makes the other children laugh, but Loldi weeps. I mention yesterday's *La dama duende,* observing that the characters give the impression of a shadow play; R. says yes, and one in which the confusions into which they fall are turned by one of them to good, to the breaking of the will. Since, to look up something for R., I spend much time in the morning searching through Indian literature, our conversation is much concerned with India. But over coffee R. talks about the Boers and says he has joined the committee set up to support them—at present looking after the wounded. And he talks of a recent perfidious act on the part of the English, though it has been of no help to them, for they were beaten by the Boers in spite of their superior numbers. — R. says the Boers come from the same stock which gave the Spaniards so much trouble. In fine sunshine we set out on the

highway to the Eremitage: "On Kunigunde the heat comes from under
—guess who said that," R. says to me. — "Schnappauf," he continues,
"and he added, 'I didn't notice it.'" — I remember Saint Kunigunde
and her walk over the red-hot grill—and we are pleased with this
folk saying, which combines Nature with religion. Pleasure, too, in
the theater: it looks like Valhalla, says R. — I enjoy a little triumph
when R. tells me I was right about Perugia; the view and the colors and
lines of the hills are finer than in Siena—he had just not wanted to
admit it to himself. We separate on the homeward journey, R. returns
home with Marke, I go to Frau Berr's with Molly; when I reach home,
Marke is unusually affectionate toward me; R. tells me that he kept on
giving him long, long looks as he went indoors, as if asking him
where I was, since I always return with him! — In the evening friend
Wolz. — Much about Indian wisdom, R. reads aloud the final conversation from the Upanishads; then we talk about races and the
formation of the earth with reference to Gleizès's theory, which gives
him hope, and to various things in Jacolliot. [*Added in margin:* "In the
course of his diatribe against history, R. mentions the Assyrians, whose
carvings in the Louvre and the British Museum had filled him with
amazement and admiration."] Then indignation from R. about the
way our scholars treat Indian matters, and against the whole school of
history. — When we are alone and continue talking about the un-
fathomably deep wisdom of the Indians, I ask R. whether he does not
feel that they are nevertheless at a disadvantage compared with
Christians, appear indeed even petty: they sought to arrange and
regulate the world, whereas Christianity leads us away from it. He
agrees with me; and during our walk he had already told me to what
reprehensible lengths the Brahmans went in order to hoodwink the
poor, despised common people. — Yesterday R. talked about the
symbolism in his works, saying that there is nothing of that kind in
Shakespeare, for it lies in the nature of music; the fact that Calderón
made use of symbols is a bad thing, for it brings him nearer to *opera.*

Friday, March 4 First thing in the morning R. is somewhat irritable,
his fingers are tormenting him, and the plumbing, again out of order,
deprives him of his bath. — But he soon recovers, tells me how
disturbing these little things are, for his head is still full of his score,
and he also wants to start on his new work. Our after-lunch conversation brings us back to Brahmanism, to the religion of intelligent
people: "We belong among these," R. says. "We perform hocus-pocus
with our art." — Though the weather is not good, we go for a walk
in the palace gardens; among other things R. says, "Every state is in
fact a collection of denunciators; fear of being denounced governs all
communications." — As we are happily watching Fidi, alone on the

ice, and the dogs chase after him, he is suddenly shouted at by the keeper to take the dogs off the ice; R. very angry—he cannot bear such admonishments—and his anger at once gives him chest spasms. — He writes to the palace gardener, and by supper has overcome his vexation. When, arising from my reading with the children, I talk about Cardinal Richelieu, he says he cannot bear these fellows in their red robes, lace collars, and four-cornered hats! — In the evening we read with unalloyed pleasure the last two acts of *La dama duende.* — [*Added in margin:* "Yesterday, when a pamphlet by a Prof. Ihering about the law arrived, with a very courteous letter, R. said, 'It must be pleasant for you to have such a renowned husband.' " —]

Saturday, March 5 R. says to me in the morning, "At times I become very much aware of the problem of existence, the problem on which everything depends, and which is the very essence of Christianity." That leads us to Brahmanism, in which, R. says, hardly any traces of benevolence can be found. We read Count G.'s work together—that is to say, he early in the morning and I around midday. After I have made him compresses and he is going off to his work, we linger at the top of the stairs, talking about the Count's views on civilization and Christianity. R. laughs at us over coffee and says we are mad! The palace gardener has sent him a polite reply; R. is pleased and says, "So you see these people do not regard one merely as trash." — Bismarck's appearance in the Reichstag annoys R. — We go for a walk in the palace gardens in spite of the rain. In the evening he sings a folk song which he finds unutterably moving, then much from the 3rd act of *Die Msinger,* the rich variety of which completely astonishes him. — When we are alone together, we lose ourselves in the remotest regions of religion and philosophy. He still holds out hope of man's regeneration, believes in the establishment of a community, but will hear nothing of it when, speaking of Loldi, I say that I believe she has a leaning toward a withdrawal from the world. — Fidi brought home good marks from the Latin teacher.

Sunday, March 6 A good night, but terrible weather; R. says the cocks began to crow before midnight—that was a sign. — R. writes some additional music for *Parsifal—4 minutes of music.* — We dine at the Grosses', R. sees the Kolbs for the first time in years. He talks with passionate feeling about the Boers, indignant that nothing is being done by us in their support. When we leave our friends, R. says, "I find a dinner like that much more agreeable here than at the Ouroussoffs'." — We spend the evening in chat.

Monday, March 7 Since my voice has deserted me, I stay upstairs on my chaise longue. R. comes up to my room for coffee, is annoyed with the photographic transparency on my window, particularly with the way the lower part of the face juts out, jokes about how pleasant it is downstairs without a "quarrelsome woman," without me. I spend the day worrying about Lusch—that is, her character. I send off three letters to her, and after I have confided to R. what Mimi has to say, he also writes, seriously and nicely. — In the evening a brief chat in my room, various things about Bismarck, who has publicly castigated the town councilors. Then R. and Jouk. go downstairs to look at the new installments dealing with India.

Tuesday, March 8 Our first conversation concerns Gobineau, whom R. praises as a "crazy, excitable fellow." [*Added in the margin two pages later, presumably for insertion here:* "He says Pott gives him the impression of being a stiff German student in heavy armor, whereas Gobineau comes in lightly, flourishing a foil."] Turning to me, he says gaily, "I have parted company with the German Reich, I am very willing to part company with the world order." Over coffee discussed with Dr. Landgraf the question of the Boers, the German Reich's attitude toward them when they asked for protection: "Then I will join in, and at the same time put my signature to your anti-Jewish campaign." — Another letter from Moltke gives us little pleasure; what this great genius and expert has to say about the need for and benefits of war is in fact nothing but words. — Jouk. shows me a new sketch of the Magic Garden; it is still not right! R. rather vexed about it. On the other hand, he is entranced by the installments of *India,* asks what our cathedrals express in comparison with these splendid works. It is looking like spring; R. goes for a walk, the hurricane drives him home after he has heard some blackbirds singing: "Nature in its life instinct is so good." From there we pass on to Aeschylus, Calderón, Goethe, Shakespeare: "Since in your presence one must always discuss such nonsense." — "Goethe, Cervantes, Dante saw and created characters, D. Q., Sancho, Faust, Mephisto; Dante, Vergil were wanderers who looked around them, whereas Aeschylus spoke like a priest in the midst of a community. Shakespeare neither the one nor the other, the most enigmatic of them all." Thus he speaks on parting, as he goes to change his clothes after his walk and return to his composing. It is causing him trouble: "Yesterday I was dissatisfied with what I did the day before, today with what I did yesterday—so you see how it is." — In the evening he shows me Captain Darmer's letter and his reply, tells us also of Boer successes, finally reads aloud a modern Indian play which charms and indeed deeply moves us. We have no hesitation in placing it higher than the *Intermeses,* and all things European sink deeper and deeper in our estimation next to the Asiatic. Continued for a long time to talk about and go over it in detail.

Wednesday, March 9 India again in the morning, and in particular the little play. After lunch I have an anecdote about the teacher Gutmann with which to amuse R.: the former did not wish to continue going with Fidi to the Latin lesson, because the Latin teacher recently gave out the following sentence to be translated: "Among the Romans the boys were taught by slaves"—otherwise he is polite and friendly toward him. At lunch R. speaks gaily about jealousy, and says he makes a solemn oath never to have anything to do with another woman! — Much about the Boers, the English are giving in here and there. — Bad weather, R. does not go out; when he wants to join me, he finds me giving a lesson to the girls (French history) and laughingly calls me Aspasia! In the evening we go through the 3rd act of *Tann-häuser,* which moves me like something from the Scriptures. R. is particularly pleased with the "Prayer" and its utter simplicity, and that, so young and poorly equipped technically as he had been at that time, he had nevertheless had the self-assurance to keep this long piece so free of ornament. — We talk about his present work; the fact that he found the swelling trombones in his book is helping him to compose his additional music: "But if you imagine I write a single bar without thinking of you, of your Catholic look, may the curse of ultimate Hell fall on you!" he says as we go upstairs. — And as he is undressing, he thinks with pleasure of the *Ring:* all the other works are to a certain extent conventional, but this one dwells in the forest, and he ends with a reflection on the German peoples, who never again succeeded in evoking anything from that source.

Thursday, March 10 All kinds of things, but nothing unpleasant, from Lusch. — R. had a good night, I a bad one, in consequence of which I sleep through breakfast and R.'s rising. He comes in later and teases me, saying I sleep only when he is present, but after that I get up. He leaves me, and shortly afterward calls out, "Now I can see it all," and he plays to me his new incidental music. (Yesterday, while he was sketching it out, I again lay down and went to sleep, and in my dream I heard him playing the scene from *Tristan* in which Isolde arrives, with so much passion that I cried out, "He is calling me"—and then I woke up. — Friend Feustel dines with us. R. again does not go out of doors, on account of the weather. He works in the evening, is somewhat out of humor, but speaks affectingly of his reading (Jacolliot's *India*). He is vexed that people are thinking of theater boxes in Berlin, when the whole of Berlin revolts him, but he is pleased about the Chileans, whom he has always liked.

Friday, March 11 R. had a good night and goes cheerfully to his work, but when I come downstairs around lunchtime, I find him vexed by the abdominal troubles from which he continually suffers. He talks about India, that consoling aspect of the Brahman teaching which permitted a pariah to tell himself that, if he bore his earthly lot without complaining, he could look forward to a noble rebirth; the teaching that the whole genesis was constantly present in its entirety. — R. is having trouble with the Magic Garden, which friend Jouk. still cannot get right. He drives off with the latter and with Fidi and takes a walk on the station platform, since the weather does not permit anything else. — R. then works before supper, and afterward we read the Englishman's curious letter and look with great enjoyment at H. Burgkmair's splendid work, *Der Weisskunig,* lent me by the royal library in Munich. "The power in these robes!" R. exclaims. Then R. plays the *Oberon* Overture and several things from *Oberon:* he feels he is coming home, he says, when he takes up Weber. The *Hebrides* Overture is a much greater artistic masterpiece, he observes, than the *Oberon* Overture, yet how much soul, how much fire it has! — A sad conversation about Hans between R. and me, I resolve to keep silent on the subject from now on. At ten o'clock, when we were still all assembled in the *salon,* I heard a distant sound, we open the door into the hall and hear Isolde and Eva singing his *"Gruss seiner Treuen"* in bed to themselves. It touches us greatly and leads R. to tell us about this nice episode in his life. And it is then the dear children who bring us to Hans!

Saturday, March 12   Not a good night for R., he has severe abdominal troubles. But he works on his 3-minute music, literally with his watch in hand. — At lunch he complains about his state of health. — But he goes out and brings me the first snowdrops from the garden—touching, cherished greeting! [*Some dried snowdrops pressed between the pages.*] In the evening friend Wolzogen, with whom everything is discussed— cosmogony, Indian and Christian wisdom, everything! —

Sunday, March 13   Very bad night, R. tortured by his old abdominal trouble, and in consequence he is much out of humor in the morning, also looks very run down. But he talks at lunch about his reading (Jacolliot). At coffee visit from Herr Löher, a privy councilor and archivist, who tells R. that in the years around 1852 the *Tannhäuser* Overture gave him the courage to see himself as a German. — R. goes for a walk, still without me on account of my cough; he then works on his score and brings me a page, which we send to Herr Bovet in Paris; at supper friend Feustel, who tells R. that he called on Hans in Meiningen, did not see him, and asked to be told within a week where he might talk with him. — In the evening Rub. plays us the music from the Paris *Tannhäuser,* and I see R., actually for the first time, taking great pleasure in it: "If someone were to tell me to do such a thing, I should find it impossible." He is pleased with its fullness, for he says it is no easy matter to write such an extended allegro. He also asks himself, when we are alone, what it is that makes the old *Tannhäuser* Overture so significant, for from a musical point of view it is in many ways much inferior to Weber's, and Mendelssohn would certainly have looked down on it in scorn. It is the vividness of the motives, he thinks: "I have never been grudging." — It consists entirely of motives, he continues, and his theme for Tannhäuser, for instance, broke with the usual custom of making the second subject a graceful one; he believes that, placed beside preceding works of greater musical accomplishment, it nevertheless looks new. — And in conclusion he says he enjoys watching me while his music is being played; he will stage performances and seat himself with his glasses so that he can watch me, for that is something worth seeing—and he blesses me, and blissfully we go off to bed!

Monday, March 14 "So they have got him at last," says R. in the morning, and he reads me the dispatch reporting the assassination of the Tsar. [*Newspaper clipping enclosed; see notes.*] I am very shocked; but R. ponders with great calm on the forces which have been unleashed here, and he is particularly struck by the fact that a second bomb was thrown. Our poor friend Jouk. utterly downcast; at lunch we talk a lot about Tsar Alexander, whose limited outlook, combined with good intentions, led to this tragic conclusion. — R. then goes out, he is pleased that the snowdrops have so stoutly defied the cold, and for that reason he does not pick them for me. In the evening we read Cervantes's "*El retable de las maravillas,*" taking pleasure in its happy inspiration. Otherwise R. continues with the book on India. At lunch he tells us about the Arab horses. — He replies on a postcard to an appeal from an anti-Jewish newspaper—does not wish to have anything to do with this affair, or indeed with the German Reich at all, after its behavior in the vivisection matter. (Page of the *Parsifal* score sent to Herr Bovet.)

Tuesday, March 15 R. slept well; a remedy from Dr. Landgraf has had a good effect. He writes to the King and in the evening reads a part of his splendid letter to me. In the morning we come to our main topic, the world's morality: "We philosophize too much," he says with a laugh. Count Gobineau has sent us a piece about India for the *Blätter.* New details concerning the assassination still coming in. R. arranges a drive to the Eremitage, bright sunshine, but the wind still very strong. R. says to me, "It was nicer last year!" In the evening friends Wolz., Herr Rub. Concerning the assassination, R. says it is an example of stupidity; as a dramatist he is interested in the assassins— if he were to treat the subject, he could not make them entirely uninteresting. There was madness on both sides, he says—two bombs of stupidity which burst against each other. The Tsar, who did not wish to have any contacts with the Liberals, leaving such matters to his son but not abdicating—as if events would wait! "Oh, the madness of rulers!" R. exclaims. And now his successor, who out of filial piety must hang, banish, and imprison, and cannot be humane. "You would need a genius in this post," he says. — We ask Rub. to play the Venusberg music again. — R. tells me that during the rehearsals in Paris Wesendonck said to him, "What utterly voluptuous sounds these are!" "I suppose he was afraid I had been dancing something like that in front of his wife," R. says! And then he calls the passage with the Three Graces "the bit Wesendonck likes." When our friends have gone and we are talking about various things, he tells me he once heard the following statement from an actor called Stein: "It is stupidity which ought to be punished—only stupidity." At the time he had thought it very strange, but now it has come back to his mind. — A remark about Humperdinck and Rub. reminds us of Rosencrantz and Guildenstern, and R. recalls the passage in which the King and Queen send them away, and we read the scene again. And, as always, with renewed amazement! . . . Then we come back to Hans. R. feels offended when Lusch writes "my father." It is being said that he cannot receive his children since he is not living alone. [*These sentences concerning Hans von Bülow obliterated in ink by an unknown hand.*]

Wednesday, March 16 R. slept well, and bright sunshine persuades him to arrange a drive to the theater. In the morning he finishes his letter to the King. At lunch he waxes very merry about it, and our drive is also inordinately successful. The dog Faf, offspring of Marke, enchants us with his beauty. And letters to me from Count Gobineau, expressing a half-spoken wish to settle here, and from Herr Levi, affected by "Know Thyself," have on the whole a pleasant effect on R. In the evening he wants to play whist, after joking gaily about Balzac and other things: "*La femme de trente ans commence à 40 ans*" ["The woman of thirty begins at 40"]. — He remarks that no Frenchwoman has ever interested him, and he asks where all these interesting Balzac women are. — Among the women of other nations, whom he enumerates, he also finds few to remind him of these interesting figures. Over whist he recalls a certain party in Magdeburg who in a state of complete drunkenness took him to see his mistress! Today he bubbles over with humor as seldom before! He maintains that it is because he does not wish to make me speak, on account of my cough. His good spirits and his wit also extend to Hans, of whom, over coffee, he says quite simply that he is unbearable! Which, in my depressed state of mind on this subject, causes me great amusement. [*These sentences concerning von Bülow obliterated in ink by an unknown hand.*] But again and again it is Faf's beauty which gladdens R. to think about. The fact that he did not recognize us reminds R. of Siegfried and Wotan!

Thursday, March 17 R. had a good night; he woke up with the intention of singing to the children a students' drinking song, which he sings to me while still in bed. — Around midday he comes up to my room, thinking that I would also have read the *B. Bl.;* the fact that I have not yet received a copy is a disappointment which finds expression in a kind of vexation. He praises the "Open Letter" so highly that I feel quite ashamed. We go for a walk as far as the little wood, larks fluttering in the air! R. is amused by a hare, and on our homeward journey the little town looks cheerful in the sunshine. In the evening some whist and *Don Giovanni;* of the mask trio R. says, "That is what I always strove to emulate in my youth." He laments all the mixing up of beautiful music and mere strumming, and finally sings to us the final scene, the Stone Guest, to the admiring astonishment of us all. He then shows us how it is the poet who is responsible for bringing forth such music!

Friday, March 18 Not a completely restful, but all the same a tolerable night for R. He reads the newspapers in the morning, and is made uncomfortable by Herr S[ain]t-Saëns's remarks, since it always offends him when people assume, or pretend to assume, that he is looking for success in Paris. He works. Evchen, who has a cold, is missing from our lunch table! A supplement to the *B. Bl.* (a paper on vivisection) leads R. to talk of life's dreadfulness, and he concludes with melancholy humour, "One keeps on top of it only through a hotchpotch of ensemble." — Gobineau's book, which he is now reading, is giving him less pleasure than Jacolliot's, which he describes as "green pastures." — Springer's article, with its fine quotations—particularly the idea of Buddha, to which R. especially draws my attention—gives us pleasure. We go for a walk in the direction of the Konnersreuth highway, the skies are gray, but our mood is cheerful. In the evening our friends; with Feustel R. always starts talking politics; once again he puts forward his views on Russia and says Tsar A. was the "victim of his own stupidity." Then we have some music, from *Tannhäuser* (2nd act). — When all have gone, we again experience the pleasure of having each other!

Saturday, March 19 R. had a good night, came back in the morning to St.-Saëns's remarks against him, asking himself what might be the cause. Does he really believe that he, R., desires success in France, or does he pretend to believe it, or does he want to prevent R.'s works from being performed? — R. works on his score, is pleased with a passage which explains the reason for a *piano* marking Rub. had not understood, and he says how quickly his works become strangers to him. Letter from Lusch to R., who insists on believing that it was I who suggested it. We go for a walk, R. and I, in the palace gardens, since one is more sheltered from the wind there. In the evening R. reads aloud [Calderón's] *El medico de su honra,* and its impact is so marked that R. exclaims, "What fools we are not just to keep on rereading these tremendously rare great poets!" — Much then on the subject of jealousy, one can understand Don Gutierre. (Riddle at lunch: What is silver in front, gold behind? Mama! — On account of my hair.)

Sunday, March 20 Boni's birthday—Evi unfortunately in bed. Our night was rather restless, since the reading lasted until past midnight. However, R. is not unwell, just a little run down. Much about Donna Mencia—why she does not admit to her husband that the Infante is there, the reason being that she loves the Infante. Then we have the feeling that it is because the Catholic church does not permit suicide that the most terrible things are turned into a spectacle—often, indeed, treated in a spirit of comedy. After the lines in the first act in which Mencia admits to her maid her love for Enrique, R. exclaims, "There is a poet, an artist!" — At the presentation of gifts Boni is greeted by R. with an improvisation on Elisabeth's theme, from which he then goes over to the march as she is receiving her gifts. At lunch Jouk. and Rub.—the latter, always somewhat singular, asserts that R. has been advising him to marry an Italian woman. R. recalls early times, when he visited me 18 years ago. The gray carriage and many other things. — We then go for a walk in the palace gardens, pleasure in the blackbirds, whose song R. finds the loveliest of all except for nightingales. At supper he recalls Minna, says that he married her out of jealousy, remembers with horror that Minna was not shocked by certain intimacies in front of her superiors. In the evening he plays pieces from *Die Zauberflöte* and *Oberon.* Regarding the latter, he relates how melancholy it made him as a boy of ten not to be able to find it as beautiful as *Der Freischütz,* and how later he then found pleasure in its various individual beauties. The C, E, A, G, F, C, D, C of the fine aria had vexed him. "Oh, we are poor creatures, we Germans," he exclaims, discussing Weber's being forced to go to London, his longing to do things somewhat in the Rossini style. Today he again declares how much he would like to write symphonies, how much he enjoys working with orchestras, how little with theater singers. He says he would call them "From My Diary"; but then he finds the title too pretentious. — And he pictures to himself the birth of the universe, some central sun which begins to revolve, out of desire, no, out of fear, and how this agitation born of fear was everywhere, and everything a matter of indifference until one gave things a moral significance.

Speaking of our society, he tells me that personalities such as Voltaire seemed to him so individual and so detached from it, and consequently without any real power.

Monday, March 21 R. had a good night. At lunch he tells us Count Gobineau's opinion of France, which he finds very convincing. We go for a walk in spite of the weather, he points out to me the tiny buds showing on the bushes and says, "They are like Eva's sneezes" (so unnoticeable!). — The form of oath of allegiance now being imposed in Russia makes us indignant—and this petty precaution also seems to us so useless. — Toward evening I wish to greet R. before he goes downstairs to work; I go into his little room, he is already in his dressing room; I wait on the spiral staircase and hear him say, "I should prefer cures to newspaper reports—well, all right, he knows the child has relations in Brazil—" and, after a pause, "It's as if it were predestined, they occupy all the southern countries." I ask him what all this means, tell him what I heard, he reflects, laughs, and says: "When I looked at my finger, I was reminded of the doctor; he has gone into the country on account of the murder of a child, the girl has disappeared, and within me arose a romance about Schnappauf having concealed the girl in his home (knowing of rich relations in Brazil) in order to marry her off to his son! And, as regards Brazil, it occurred to me that all immigrations there are in the hands of the Catholics, and all that remains for the Protestants is the North." — We laugh heartily over this spoken monologue. — In the evening he says he heard Fidi singing all kinds of things from *Tristan, Lohengrin;* and his mother's words to him, R., came into his mind: "Oh, my son, with whom I am well pleased." He says he expects a lot of Fidi, but will probably not live to see it. At supper he complains humorously of our having so many girls—there are no men around, and they will become old maids. — In the evening friend Wolz. — Memories of the *Nib.* performances; R.'s sorrow over Betz. Then many general topics, the birth of the universe, our civilization less imposing than its forerunners, the Assyrians, for example, the aims were different. He also mentions the Russians and observes that they could do with a brutal barbarian like Bismarck to lead them ruthlessly into Constantinople. — He regrets that his texts have not been discussed from a somewhat wider point of view—the *Ring,* for example, in relation to the significance of gold and the downfall of a race caused by it; *Die Msinger* for the German type as depicted in Sachs, rather crude, if you like, but something distinct from the Latin type. — When we take leave of each other in the evening, we think of our simultaneous death, and we feel that this is the way I would greet him in Nirvana—and that we have rediscovered each other, not just met here for the first time. — (As evidence of his hard work he shows me page 80 of his score, which he completed today, and particularly the bassoon passage in it.)

Tuesday, March 22 Hohenzollern weather, that is to say, snow at the beginning of spring! — When R. wishes me good morning, I tell him how beautiful he is; he replies gaily, in the tone of Bottom, "Not so, neither," which leads us to talk about this scene in Shakespeare. — Then he goes off, first to his reading (Gobineau), later to his score. Lunch and coffee pass without any particular conversations, except that R. advises Jouk. against giving Russia anything more than an expression of his submission. — Toward 4 o'clock Brandt and the Brückner brothers; much of a technical nature; Brandt excellent as always. When they have all gone, R. and I wax very merry over our curious contacts with such peculiar creatures as the worthy painters. But when R. offers me his pity for having had to spend most of the time with them, I declare how easy and pleasant such an obligation is, which produces something useful, as compared with the usual social obligations; and at the same time I can tell myself proudly that I am taking something off his shoulders! — (When Rub. and Humperd. sang the Flower Maidens yesterday, R. said, if not Fl. Maidens, then at any rate Radish Boys!)

Wednesday, March 23 R. dreams in audible French about thieves and calls for the police. We are both somewhat tired, but at lunch, for which our guests are again present, he is bubbling over with good spirits and wit. Brandt says he has not seen him like this since Tribschen. Both his confidence in Br. and the curious appearance of the two painters rouse him to utter exuberance. We then go for a walk in the palace gardens. "Smiling through tears, a mood of snow in spring-time." (Thus R. describes our mood at rehearsals at that time. Many memories are exchanged with Brandt—the serpent without a neck, the blackbird which turned into a magpie—and then, again and again, the assassination, the Tsar's fate all the more tragic in that he, a good man but no genius, could in no way understand it—advantage of the nihilists over the rulers, the former are unafraid, the latter afraid.) — Marke throttles a chicken. Whist in the evening, R. has good luck, which pleases him. To end with, he reads *Hamlet* with such moving penetration that one feels nobody in the whole world could match the warm, refined, bitter, ironic, reserved, and expansive tone of the hero better than he can. He describes him as the embodiment of the Renaissance, a being in whom the naïve actions of the Middle Ages cease to exist. His reproaches of Ophelia (the painting, lisping, etc.) R. accompanies with the exclamation, "What else do people like ourselves have to put up with when they deal with people at Court?" And after the conversation between Polonius and Hamlet he says, "God, if one could only hear such a conversation!" — R. is much intrigued by the news that Emperor Wilhelm is said to have remarked, on hearing of the assassination, "So escorts are of no use after all." — (At lunch he said he intended to become a vegetarian, all he would now eat would be lambs' tails.) When we are alone, R. talks about "To be or not to be," and remarks how free these reflections are of any churchly ideas. Hamlet stands there like the first man ever to confront death and feels the fear of awakening from the dream of life, awakening to the sleep which will perhaps contain dreams—reincarnations.

Thursday, March 24 R. had a good night, but at midday, after his work, he does not feel well and frequently gets up during lunch. And unfortunately my statement that the nihilists are more remote from the people than the Tsar arouses his violent displeasure. When I observe that these conspirators have no right to act in the name of the peasants, R. exclaims: "Right? And what right has the Tsar? This is a matter of strength, of right as *jus,* power as the Romans defined it; there is no strength in the rulers, but there is in these conspirators." — In the evening he relates that his brother-in-law General Meck used to have his Cossacks flogged and then made them kiss the knout! These people could not have changed so swiftly, he says. — He goes with Jouk. for a walk in the palace gardens, I, tired after an errand in the morning, stay at home and read about Brahmanism, which permits me at supper to bring the conversation around to this, and that in turn leads to the reading of the first *Oupnekhat* (Colebrooke), on death. — (I came in for such merry teasing about my "golden-mean" views in the matter of the nihilists.)

Friday, March 25 R. slept well. Our conversation concerns Brahmanism, which R. praises as the religion of intelligence, but then he places Christianity above it as the religion of suffering. When he comes to me around lunchtime, I tell him that Count Gobineau's account of the Hunnish invasion has provided me with a clue to the nihilist movement, since it seems as though all that now matters is destruction. At lunch our conversation comes back to India. But R. is still feeling oppressed. We go for a walk after he has inspected Jouk.'s costume sketches. The gale drives us home. R. works and rejoicingly shows me a page on which he has filled in only a few instructions (as Gurnemanz and Pars. are conversing). In the evening he has the new incidental music for *Parsifal* played to him, and then he goes through *Die Entführung aus dem Serail* (Osmin, Osmin and Blondchen, the Turkish music), to the very great delight of us all. When we are alone, and R. has ordered a half-bottle of champagne, he talks about the birth of this inspired work, about Mozart's relationship with his future wife: "It was like my relationship with Minna Planer, except that in my case it produced no blossoms." —

Saturday, March 26 R. had a good night. (Around lunchtime he comes to me to express his pleasure in Gobineau's chapter on civilization. [*Inserted:* ("That was yesterday.")] — The costume design for Kundry is discussed and settled. We then go for a walk in the palace gardens, start talking, R. and I, about *Hamlet*—an inexhaustible topic between us! In the evening we read the preface and introduction to [Schopenhauer's] *Will in Nature*. Today R. again complained of pains in his big toe. ("Kings nowadays are the pensioners of civilization," R. says, adding that it is the Jews who are keeping them.)

Sunday, March 27 R. slept well, but we have two children, Boni and Loldi, down with throat infections. Reduced lunch table. R. annoyed by Feustel's accounts to me of the impossibility of getting hold of Hans. But he gradually recovers his spirits, and over coffee he cites an idea which has now become his favorite: "I can make mistakes only in things I understand; in things I do not understand I proceed according to the authorities, I shall make no mistakes in my strategy." — Recently he said that he would trust himself to know when to deliver the final blow in a battle, and I can well believe it. — Walk to the Birk after Jouk.'s costume designs have been accepted. A strong wind is blowing, proving very troublesome, constant thoughts of Italy. — Whether to give up here entirely—but in that case R. would want to burn everything down, for he would find it too painful to see alien, common furnishings here, as in Tribschen. In the evening continued with *Will in Nature* after R. related several things from Gobineau and read aloud the song of a pariah from Jacolliot. — Before today's reading R. improvised beautifully, and he says he always enjoys doing it.

Monday, March 28 R. had a good night. — The most perfect spring weather tempts him out into the garden before lunch, and after lunch we walk as far as the Students' Wood, accompanied by the whirring of larks! R.'s delight in them, and sad thoughts about human beings, who can think of nothing better to do with birds such as these than to "stuff them in their mouths." — It would be a good thing for human beings of perception to reflect on these expressions of Will. As we are walking home, R. catches sight of smoke rising, as straight as the lark itself, from a factory: "The one singing, the other stinking." — He works on his score. The evening brings friend Wolz. R. says he would like to set the *B. Bl.* free, like a baby severed from the umbilical cord. Then: "Gobineau says the Germans were the last card Nature had to play—*Parsifal* is my last card." — When we are alone, he enlarges upon music: "Oh, what a triad like that means to me! Everything else vanishes before it. When it comes in again, after all the raving and raging and straying, it is like Brahma returning to himself." "You can keep all your pictorial arts." He then comes back to the glories of music and says that when he thinks of the sounds of Palestrina and Bach—for this is what he means by glories—he is also reminded of Herwegh's poem to me, and to this he appends fair and cherished sayings! — "How cold were I to call myself just happy!" R. cries out to me as we part after our walk.

Tuesday, March 29 R. had a good night, and he is still happy at his work. Glorious spring weather. We drive to the Fantaisie and go for a walk there. In the evening we play through [Beethoven's] *Battle of Vittoria;* R. points out the childlike quality of the opening, praises the glories of the victory hymn, and is pleased by the way in which B. then "gets tired of the dry tone and plays the Devil." Its naïve, folklike manner reminds him of *Egmont,* and we go through some of the music from that. R. himself plays the music for Klärchen's death wonderfully. "She really dies," R. exclaims, "and he recommends her to Ferdinand! But that's the way it is, and it is this truthfulness which makes the work so appealing. Beautiful, the way she appears to him." — We talk of the fact that this music, written solely for the play, in fact gets lost at performances of it. R. thinks it should be performed here in our *salon,* just for a few people. He went to a lot of trouble with it in Zurich, he says. At the famous oboe passage, which he compares to the whirring of the larks, he recalls Kummer in Dresden, saying he would never hear it played like that again. Between the 1st and 2nd parts of the *Battle of Vittoria* he reads to us the account of this concert in his biography. When we are alone, he speaks of the chords which sound as if they are part of the liturgy, and he says how moving they are. At the conclusion of this music he exclaims, "We musicians are prussic acid—when the music starts, nothing else matters!" —

Wednesday, March 30 R. slept well, and he teases me about "the old Saxe." This is because I noticed that a bowl from this china service had been brought into use, and I am said to have cried out piteously, "But the old Saxe!"—a remark which amuses R. enormously. Unfortunately R. is not well, and the change in the weather gives him chest spasms. We go for a walk in the palace gardens but are not refreshed by it. — At lunch, talking of Count Gobineau's book, R. remarks that distinguished Frenchmen seem able to understand all the peoples of the earth with the exception of the Germans. "We may not present ourselves well, but when the right man appears among us, we produce what are probably the only completely universal and unprejudiced minds." He feels that even Carlyle is prejudiced in many ways. "But," he says, "we do not present ourselves well, we are thoroughly unpleasant." — In the evening he feels oppressed—a letter from the theater director in Cologne has brought him much vexation. — This evening's page of the score (88) caused him a lot of trouble, he says. At lunch he told me that I would be pleased with the trumpet.

Thursday, March 31 R. had a somewhat restless night; he read a lot of Gobineau, who annoys him with his Celts and various other things, but he retains his satisfaction with this intelligent man. He works. Our Friedel is hoarse, and it looks as if it may be something serious. Rough weather. All the same, we go for a walk in the palace gardens, and the wind gradually dies down. Delight in a blackbird which is singing splendidly. Before supper R. goes to Fidi, but he admits to me that he does not really know how to speak to him, he felt he was being so affected when he tried to play the piano to him. In the evening we look through some pictures of costumes (Racinet); R. finds Renaissance rooms (gallery in Fontainebleau) stiff and uninviting. Then we play whist with a dummy, and at the conclusion of the evening R. dictates to me the distribution of singers in his chorus for Herr Levi. — At lunch he was somewhat vexed about the food, etc., he jumps up with his coffee and goes to his score to erase something, saying to me as he works, "Now you can understand what it means when I babble like this—what is going on in my head." — (I have just thought of the joke he made to Humperdinck on Tuesday evening, when he advised him to compose *Egmont* as an opera, taking the words from Goethe and the music from Beethoven.)

Friday, April 1 R. slept well. At breakfast he says he will write another opera, in which the hero would bear the name of Lenardo. This leads us to the choice of names, and R. describes it as incredibly thoughtless of Goethe to have sought out Italian names (Lothario, Lenardo) for his German novel. Friedel is hoarse, and it sounds very sad when he answers the Siegfried theme, whistled by his father in the hall, with a soft, hardly audible whistle of his own! R. is also somewhat irritable at lunch. We go for a walk in the palace gardens, and the first day of April brings us no merriment! But we are quite gay in the evening, listen in a cheerful mood to an organ fugue by Bach and the *Eroica* Variations; of the former R. says there is much conventional stuff in the fugue (not the prelude), in the latter he is surprised that B. does not modulate at all. When everyone has gone, R. dances and orders a half-bottle of champagne, and we chat contentedly, though tears are streaming continuously from my eyes. Weariness of the eyes or of the heart? I do not know. At the start of the evening R. talked about his dread of the journey to Berlin, and for me there is the added heartache (on Lulu's account) concerning our probable meeting with Hans.

Saturday, April 2 R. slept well. Our morning conversation touches on how ill-natured musicians are (Brahms, Berlioz); R. says they are perhaps more irritable than other people. I realize ever more deeply that when he (R.) sometimes says things which are offensive and deeply wounding, he does it with complete innocence, and he has a daemonic instinct for being right. The fact that one is so defenseless against it is what makes one feel so uncomfortable. Today he writes three pages of his score and shows me that he has arrived at the "*mein Sohn Amfortas*" passage. — Over coffee we go through newspapers of all kinds. — We then take a walk in the palace gardens; but the raw wind does not agree with R., he is attacked by chest spasms, and when we reach home, he sits down on the biklinium, unable for a time to go upstairs. In the evening whist, and afterward Count Gobineau's article. — When we hear that Herr Förster has been maltreated by some Israelites, R. says, "The Germans have never thrashed reviewers, but the Jews thrash Germans!"

Sunday, April 3 R. had a restless night, read much Gob., and has to take medicine in the morning. We do not go out, I spend most of my time with Fidi, pleased by his patience and amiability. Letters from Lusch and Countess La Tour enliven our coffeetime. Speaking of Count G.'s book, R. observed that one becomes conscious of his immaturity, and really people should not write long books; he would find it difficult to make up his mind to read Grote's history, but he would reread O. Müller's work on the Dorians at once. In the evening we read E. v. Weber's lecture on the Boers. The book about races is discussed at the same time, and it is very stimulating. At the conclusion, when we are quite alone, R. and I, discussion about the staging of *Parsifal*. In the morning R. had counted up how many English governments he had already lived through, and he talked of Canning's head, which as a child he had seen on pipes with the inscription "*Liberté civile et religieuse pour tous*" ["Civic and religious liberty for all"]. — When I take leave of him in the morning after coffee, he says, "Oh, grant that with rapture I may thy breath inhale!" . . . We then discuss Lohengrin, Elsa's dismay when she hears that his origin is splendor and bliss! — "Quite a nice subject," he says jokingly. And the nation has also recognized it.

Monday, April 4 R. slept well; he dreamed, probably because of our final conversation about *Parsifal*, of Holy Communion; receiving it and snatching the wine woke him up. — Our topic is still Count Gobineau's racial theory and R.'s ideas arising from it. — A keen north wind prevents our going out today as well. Sad reflections on the climate, our nice house, which it will always be difficult to leave. One pleasant piece of news today: Herr Neumann writes that we need not be in Berlin until the 30th. When there is talk of great riches and what to do with them, R. says, "Nothing good can be done with money, one cannot change the human race with it; it must be abolished." — A Herr Wanner suggests readings of the *Ring* in towns in which it will not be performed. — Another man sends some dramas "conceived in W.'s spirit." — R. does not look at them and says, "I can provide an example, but no encouragement." — In the evening Rub. plays to us [Bach's] "Chromatic Fantasy," to R.'s infinite delight. "How can one talk of progress?" he exclaims, and explains to us how since that time forms have become trivial rather than otherwise. — When friend W. stays behind and is alone with us, R. explains to him our attitude toward Hans in the clearest possible way.

Tuesday, April 5 R. slept well, I woke up suddenly as if I had heard some inner cry from my heart—who might be in danger? — But Richard was all right, and this stab was probably a stray memory of old times. The newspaper reports a speech by Bismarck about prestige; R. says, "The French speak a language with no knowledge of its roots, just according to convention, and then we use it without understanding the convention." I pay a call on our poor neighbor and report that she has been to see her husband in the mental home and that he was quite mild and resigned, which R. finds very touching. Much about the costumes and stage properties in *Parsifal;* Jouk. shows us the Knights' mourning garb. We do not go out of doors, on account of the north wind. In the evening I go downstairs to see how he is getting along; he is working busily on a viola passage, does not wish me to go away, but reproaches me for being the cause of his writing something wrongly. In the evening Herr Rub. plays to us one of Beeth.'s first sonatas. R. does not enjoy it. Before that he read to us the women's scene in [Calderón's] *Hombre pobre todo es trazas,* quite intoxicating in the wealth and depth of its emotion. But following that, the first act of *Macbeth*—terribly beautiful! — When everyone has gone, we stay together talking, and after we have separated to undress, then come together again in the lower green room, we continue talking, and R. looks forward to the better times in which such men as Shakespeare, now prophets in the wilderness, will be brought in to form, as it were, part of a divine service. Thus the world once *was*— first a ceremonial act spoken, then to Holy Communion.

Wednesday, April 6 R. slept quite well and goes off gladly to work. Friend Gross, who has lunch with us, thinks that he is looking very well. When we embrace following the after-coffee grace, R. tells our friends that we are still on our honeymoon, for we still have at least 15 years to make up. I pay various calls on our neighbors (diphtheria there now on top of everything else), also visit the Jägers, since the poor man is ill. When I tell R. all this, at first he chides me, and when I ask him not to be angry, he quotes Schopenhauer's remark about a kind heart, "What is Francis Bacon in comparison?" He finds this splendid of Schopenhauer, and from there he goes on to talk of emigration and the future community, saying that it must be held together by a vow—for instance, only to eat food of one kind or another. At supper he tells me that his mind is full of the music for Klärchen's death, the change into A minor. He says he could write a whole book about it—about music as an emanation of religion—and he comes back to it in the evening: "What this C natural means in A minor!" — We have a cozy game of whist, Boni, he, and I. [*Added in margin:* "During whist he sings *Tristan,* which I have been singing all day, and he says that at the time he wrote it his life had been '*une tempête dans un verre d'eau*' ['a storm in a teacup'], then he thinks with a shudder of the present-day public—in *Tristan,* for instance, nothing but hooked noses, and on top of that, those accents!"] Afterward the two of us chat together downstairs and then once again upstairs (in the green room!), this time about the Gobineau article I am translating, about the industrious and securely instinctive Chinese. — (We were out of doors, much sweet twittering of birds, but a north wind.)

Thursday, April 7 The outing was bad for R., and his intensive reflections on the Klärchen music get mixed up in a dream with Fidi's indisposition, so that he hears it as if in relation to Fidi and wakes up filled with melancholy. He tells me this from the neighboring room as I go off to my bath, but he does it in French, which at once reduces it to a laughing matter. He works, reaches page 103, begins the 2nd volume of Count G. with enjoyment. Friend Humperdinck has lunch with us; he inquires about the tempi of the *Pastoral* and feels that the mood flags somewhat in the final movement. R., after speaking in defense of the finale, says: "That is the question—how to end! The best thing is probably to let it all fade away like a dream! In the C Minor, one can say, the finale is the main thing, all the rest a sort of preface to it. With the F Major he succeeded completely. In the *Eroica* he was at the height of his imagination and produced one inspiration after another, but most people haven't the slightest idea what to do with them." — We do not go out. Toward evening Herr Francke from London comes to see R., about *Tristan* and *Meistersinger:* the project, it seems, is assured. — When the conversation touches on the people in Meiningen and what they are doing, also on the Duke himself, R. says: "He looks like an old Saxon duke, and one can easily imagine him leaning on his sword and talking familiarly to Charlemagne. And now all that has been blunted into artistic dilettant-ism!" — When Herr Francke tells us at supper that his father was the town musical director in Königstein, R. says to him, "Say, rather, 'town musician,' for that does us honor; my grandfather was gate collector in Leipzig." — But all these excursions into the outside world worry me, for they tire R.; he can flourish only in an atmosphere of creative tranquillity; what comes from outside just produces fatigue. A few mornings ago he was talking about Pest and had completely forgotten that I was there with him, so disembodied do we feel when we are "outside"! — Yesterday we were greatly amused when, at the conclusion of the evening, we discovered a silver laurel wreath and two bronze candlesticks by the stove in the *salon*—no idea where they came from or how long they had been lying there! . . . R. praises the English in comparison with the Germans; when they think there is something they do not know, they become all attention, and on this it is then possible to build. "But we—we know it all, we are horrible! I can say that, because: *J'en suis* [I am one of them]!" . . . When Herr Francke remarked that Hanslick was just a gnat, R. became very vexed and demonstrated to him what such a man can do in the way of creating obstacles for existing talents and destroying means.

Friday, April 8   R. slept well, and he works. At lunch we have Herr Francke, and the final details of the London enterprise are discussed. R. then goes out, unknown to me, and returns home with a chest spasm and great indignation over the climate here. By evening he has gradually recovered; the first two movements of Beeth.'s E-flat Major Quartet are very nicely played by Rub., to R.'s great delight, then we go on to *Fl. Holländer,* and the tempi are wrong—R. sings the Dutchman's first monologue movingly. — When we are alone again, chatting together, I confess to him that, in order to enjoy the quartet, I have to be free of all preoccupations, whereas his works affect me even in a whirlpool of worries. Now, for instance, with thoughts of Berlin and many other difficulties, I can only feel in a dreamlike way how beautiful this is. He agrees with me and repeats that sublime things such as these are for future times of bliss, should they ever come.

Saturday, April 9   R. had a somewhat restless night, but not a bad one, and at the farewell lunch we hold for the Staff family he is bubbling over with gaiety and such wit that I can only regret not being able to repeat it all here. The wind is still very piercing, and we do not go for a walk, R. just for a short while in the garden. The *Fl. Blätter,* with its rules for soldiers, gave us a lot of amusement yesterday, and again this evening. The *I. Z.* publishes a picture of the murdered Tsar, and in connection with it R. makes the sublime remark that he can imagine what a great feeling of peace must descend on such a frightened person at the moment of death: "The pacification of the Will—certainly no awareness of it, but in the words 'to die in the palace' there lies submission, and I can imagine a great feeling of release: 'No more worries now!' — Whereas in our Emperor I see something trivial following the assassination; immediately after the attempt listening again to reports about this regiment and that regiment." — At the conclusion of the evening R. reads aloud the first scenes from Aristophanes's *The Frogs,* to our great amusement. R. sees it all before him, the people, the poet, the actors, and he delights in its freedom and its genius. Afterward he points out to me how much more genuine this kind of comedy is, however difficult for women's ears in its bluntness, than our own kind, which shows human beings only as they seem, their positions and other things of that sort. Whereas this turns its attention to the generic animality of the human being, shows it in conflict with his qualities as a god, and this, in the middle of a ceremony in honor of this very god, with all the invocations of his priests who are sitting there, must have produced inimitable comic effects. Cervantes had sought to do the same with D. Q. and Sancho Panza. — When we are in bed and I think of Isolde's birth, I ask R. to bless me, so that I may become good—"What am I supposed to say?" he replies. I: "Goodness does not need to be good." —

Sunday, April 10 R. had a restless night, dreamed of wounded people and cries of fear. He does not work in the morning and feels run down at lunch. However, he celebrates Loldi at the presentation of gifts and in the evening with the sounds of *Parsifal.* We continue to talk a lot about Russia and about Count G.'s theories. We go for a walk in a still very raw wind. In the evening we are visited by a conductor from Frankfurt named Kniese who offers his services as an assistant at the performances. Our conversation turns to tenors, etc., and telegrams from Herr Neumann, alarmed on account of the Francke project, also provide things from the outside world—and thoroughly unpleasant ones—to talk about! R. laments that among musicians he has only the most primitive handymen to represent him! Now we are returning to the old miseries, and both of us are apprehensive, in our own ways. — An enthusiastic letter to Kotzebue from Beeth. made us laugh in the morning. —

Monday, April 11 In the morning, after a better night, R. reads the nihilists' manifesto to me! Then, around lunchtime, he brings me the manuscript from Count Gobineau, whose urgent need for the *B. Blätter,* as he gaily says, he will now prove. But the article interests him and provides material for conversation almost throughout the day. "If the farmer is greater than the hunter," R. quotes, and continues, "If the musician is greater than the statesman—but they are too unwise," he exclaims. Again we do not go out of doors; R. works on his score, and in the evening we discuss once more with friend

Wolz., half in fun and half in earnest, the invasion from the east, the Chinese flooding everything with their work.

Tuesday, April 12 R. tells me in the morning that he dreamed of his "old sweethearts"—all mixed up into a single person—who pressed around him, urging him to go to the theater, so that he would have been glad if a policeman had misunderstood and arrested him. — He works, and is pleased with the effect the chorus will have in the first act. We go for a walk, a short while in the garden, then in the palace gardens. In the evening our friend Levi is here—it all goes quite well, but when the *cercle* assembles, there is much suffering for R., on account of the great dullness of our good friends. He reads some scenes from *Hamlet* (beginning of the 2nd act), and Levi quotes to us from *Cymbeline* a passage which could serve as a motto against vivisection. "Shakespeare has everything," R. exclaims in delight. After the company has departed, R. and I stay up, R. at first commenting gaily on the absurdity of such reunions, while I have the curious experience of not feeling at all bored—immersed in my own thoughts, overwhelmed by the scenes from *Macbeth,* I was not conscious of the leaden quality of the evening. — The evening ends with a discussion of the nihilists; when the conductor says that the manifesto, as indeed all the behavior of these poor people, fills him with admiration, I say that, though I may feel boundless pity for these people, I cannot admire them. R. disputes my view and observes that one should not talk in this case of murder: these people act as one emperor against another in a war, placing mines. He cites Thrasybulus and a few others, I mention the fanatical Jesuit assassins, who also believed they were serving a cause. R. says no—these were treacherous, wicked people, whereas among the others he could very well visualize a loyal and good peasant countenance. When I say that murder is un-German, he laughs at me, saying that certainly the pensioners in the palace gardens are not murderers. Gladly will I remain silent and resign myself to it all, though it seems to me that since the advent of Christianity we should no longer be taking our example from the ancient world. — Over coffee R. thought of Saint Paul and observed that he might have said, with W [*remainder of name illegible*], "If only I had put my trust in blows"; he visualizes him on the Areopagus and says the Roman world still managed to produce such naïve figures—unthinkable nowadays.

Wednesday, April 13 Great merriment in the morning between R. and me about yesterday evening; R. declares that people always expect from him a sort of "Bring on the clowns"—he should entertain them! — Then we come to Shakespeare, the absorption of a whole race by an individual; we discuss this first scene of Banquo's departure, the meeting with Macbeth, and feel distinctly that a whole potentiality of Nature was embodied in such a man and then vanished forever. But music remains! This our ever-recurring theme! — But at lunch I find R. unwell, very run down; Herr Seitz's costume sketches reveal to us in their "masterliness" all the wretchedness which divides us from all others—Flower Maidens like cabaret Valkyries—yet all of it lovely. — Deep gloom hangs over R. in consequence—at times he looks just like Siegfried! — He calls Levi the Assyrian, and jokes about the "*assürana*" with which he plays whist. — At lunch he talks about the bells to be obtained for *Parsifal* and about the glass bells in the Munich theater. R. laughs and says such Cyclopean cheese-covers would be just the thing.

Thursday, April 14 R. had a restless night, fetched and read in Gobineau's *Essai*. However, he is not out of humor in the morning and is able to work. At meals our talk revolves mainly about casting. In the evening R. tells our friends about his disappointment with the costume designs—"shopworn women" where all should be innocence: "Everything in my art is chaste," he can say with pride! *Parsifal* is played, Amfortas in the 1st and last acts and conclusion. . . . We stay up late, in a blissful mood.

Good Friday, April 15 I dreamed of falling stars and the wish I then made; it was on the Posilipo, and the children showed me that what had fallen were fragments of glass, breaking apart. I am touched that the dream relieves me of the fervor of wishing, which the daily toil may not allow me to do, and that it brings to my mind all that fills my inner being. In the morning I hear the *Parsifal* Prelude, quite nicely played by the conductor. At midday we fast, R., the children, and I, and afterward I go to church with Loldi and Eva; the children and I all have Tintoretto's *Crucifixion* in mind, and also the hour of three, when one is allowed to make a wish! — R. works, and in the evening Dr. Schemann visits us with friend Wolz. But R. declares himself to be worn out by these evenings on which he is always obliged to talk about what is currently occupying him. He says he expects nothing more from societies; he had once done so, but now it is individuals from whom he expects everything.

Saturday, April 16 R. does not feel well; he is tired and wants to see no more people in the evening. At lunch we have the Wolz.'s and Dr. Schemann, and it proves quite bearable. After lunch R. and I go for a walk—spring is here. All kinds of things for me, including the newly arrived Herr Köhler—a wild sort of creature—can he be tamed? In the evening whist. (Siegfried still hoarse.)

Sunday, April 17 R. did not have a very good night, but he recovers sufficiently to come to my portière, after we have separated, and to say to me, "I shall set the Christian religious holidays to music—those will be my symphonies." — Happy about this, I stroll with Dr. Schemann up to the theater and the Bürgerreuth, on a splendid Easter morning. But on my return, I find R. indisposed; he comes to lunch but soon gets up and goes off to bed. The doctor finds he has a fast pulse, prescribes something soothing for him. — He reads in bed, I write to Lulu in the next room. In the evening, however, he gets up, only to return with me to bed at about 9 o'clock. (Telegram about the unveiling of the bust in Leipzig.)

Monday, April 18 R. did not sleep, but he lay still and is lovely enough to call out to me in my bath that I should look on my writing desk, and I find the enclosed note. [*Enclosed in the Diaries a sheet of paper bearing in Cosima's handwriting the words:* "I shall be out today, my friend, and should I not come, then . . ." *and in Wagner's handwriting:* "Prepare for death! You still have 2 hours! Don Gutierre di Wanfredo."] He also works on his score. Count Gobineau's book tires him, and he once again declares that one must beware of thick books. We go for a drive in lovely weather and delight in the pretty countryside. I then go with Loldchen and Evi to their examination and confession, and we return home much affected. R. has meanwhile been reading the Saint Matthew Gospel and is put off by the many references in it to the Old Testament. — A whist party. — The doctor is not sure whether R. will be permitted to attend the ceremony tomorrow.

Tuesday, April 19 R. slept well. Our first conversation leads us— I do not know how—to the ancient world; I say to him that clothing seems to give life a particular flavor, because, as it were, it leads one to expect the movement which these copious folds would encourage; nakedness, rather, arouses feelings of stillness. — R. agrees with me and says that painting in particular is on the wrong path when it depicts the nude female figure, which, from an aesthetic point of view, is not really beautiful. Then we part and are reunited in the church, to which R. comes after the sermon for the holy act. He, too, is moved, deeply moved, and he tells me he was again inspired by great hopes; the clergyman had nothing to do with it, he says, it was the black robes which gave him the feeling of something distinct from ordinary life, and he was delighted to see how moved we all were by the ceremony. He wishes to baptize Levi and to admit no Jews to Holy Communion. In the evening he plays for me parts of *Parsifal*. Our conversation comes back to statues. — I wrote to Lusch of our feelings and answered Herr Seitz, who wrote to me very cordially but has withdrawn his work.

Wednesday, April 20 R. slept well, I dreamed of some danger threatening him, he woke me up because I was groaning. He works, and we go for a walk; he observed in the morning that his idea of the Christian festivals would not perhaps be possible, since he has too many gay themes, and that would not be Christian. Herr Köhler at lunch, rather heavy going. No double windows since yesterday, the transfiguration of spring. We go for a walk. In the evening Feustel, bringing important news about Batz & Voltz, and much joking as well. Asked by the *auteurs* about royalties, R. has written to friend Nuitter inquiring whether he is still alive. — The evening ends with great agitation on R.'s part, since friend Feustel starts, in his usual wordy style, to sing the praises of the German Reich. R. tries to point out to him how little wisdom there is to be found in it, and to what completely different uses the situation and potentialities could have been put.

Thursday, April 21 It took R. a long time to recover from his agitation, he praises my good sense when I also have feelings on the subject. Many letters, Herr Seitz has definitely withdrawn, Herr Francke sends the contract, Count Gobineau writes in very friendly fashion, the lawyer in Würzburg makes demands! R. writes his score. In the evening we have a merry game of whist.

Friday, April 22 R. dreams that a pope looking like the composer Bruckner visits him, brought along by my father (somewhat like the Emperor of Brazil), and when R. goes to kiss his hand, His Holiness kisses his and then takes with him a bottle of cognac. Lunch with friend Feustel, who in the Voltz-Batz affair is extraordinarily [*sentence uncompleted*]. R. has begun his introduction to Count Gobineau's work. We go for a walk in the palace gardens, still brooms. Departure of our neighbors the Staffs. Conversation about them. In the evening friend Wolzogen, still much conversation on the subject of race.

Saturday, April 23 R. slept well, and his work gives him pleasure; many jokes arising from the fact that his bust has been placed beside Benedix's. Less innocent are the remaining events, and in the evening he has several business letters to write (to Voltz and Batz, to Dr. Strecker regarding London). Merry lunch beforehand with the Wolzogens; conversation about the climate (it is still very cold). We go for a walk, but only for a short while. A letter from Loulou tells us that my father is leaving on the very day of our arrival! That ferments inside R., and he writes to my father with utter frankness! I tell him I myself would not write this letter, he keeps it back, then demands it again from me and sends it off! He is so indignant over my father's passing us by. He keeps talking about it all evening, but without anger, because there is nobody to contradict him, and he goes to bed pacified. (Over coffee he thought of the Giorgione in Brunswick; he says the Adam looks melancholy, as if Maya were holding a veil in front of him.) Also some words about Ch[arlotte] Kalb, to my delight R. finds what I show him beautiful.

Sunday, April 24 R. slept well; but he is immediately vexed in the morning by the presumptuous announcement of the performances in London. He gets me to write in his name to Herr Neumann and Herr Francke. In spite of all annoyances we have a cheerful lunch, during which R. laughs at the children for being so touchy, and a nice letter from the King produces a very good mood. R. observed yesterday that, if we had not had the King backing us, my father would have ignored us. [*This last sentence obliterated in ink by an unknown hand.*] We go for a short walk. Then he settles down to his score, but he is tired at supper and says he is in a bad mood. I ask Herr Rub. to play us some Bach, which he does (organ fugues), first the famous A Minor and then the shorter one—No. 6, I think. At the start of the latter R. says he is pleased by its imaginative anarchy. He describes the theme as a human voice which turns into a bird's voice—it is the bird species speaking. Bach was a true musician, he says; the others, Mozart, Beethoven, were closer to being poets. He advises Rub. to be careful with rubato and repeats that it is impossible to indicate where it should occur, and no tempo marking can show it. Bach leads us to hymns, which nourished him, and to the ceremony of Holy Communion; R. says that the fine thing about our form is that it leads one entirely away from life, whereas the roses and the gaudiness of Catholicism are repugnant to him. Then he reads to us his "Introduction," which keeps us in the same mood. — When I ask friend Wolz. about Dr. Schemann's work, R. exclaims, "When a German is fiery, he is almost invariably lazy as well," which amuses me very much.

Monday, April 25 R. had a tolerable night but is nevertheless indisposed and later out of humor. [*Added after the entry for the following day but referred back to this point:* "In the morning he thought of Mistress Quickly's words on Falstaff's death and laughed loudly over them."] The matter of the contract with London, the journey to Berlin, Hans's behavior, it all weighs on him, and he complains that all he is conscious of nowadays is a state of either exaltation or deep depression. The weather is also vexing him—that probably most of all. To distract him a little, I tell him about the picture (a surprise) and the sittings. The Jägers at lunch, he arousing confidence in me. No walk, I arranging the little house for Herr Köhler; while I am there, R. comes in search of me to give me back the sketch of the first act—his first act is now completely orchestrated! — In the evening slight vexation for him, caused by a letter from Darwin in favor of vivisection, or, rather, physiology. We then play whist with Loldi, since Boni has rheumatic pains.

Tuesday, April 26   R. had a very bad night and is in a state of great depression all day. The news Lusch sends us of the presence of her grandfather is also not calculated to raise his spirits. He adds something to his "Introduction," having noticed that the same thing has happened to him in connection with the Gobineau article as with many other things (the Scherzo in the Beethoven quartet, etc.)—that is, that he first took it to be more significant than it is. The doctor calms my worries. — When R. says he wishes his whole character could be changed, the doctor says jokingly, "If I could do that, I still wouldn't—or at any rate, I should think carefully about it beforehand." — But he regrets that R. takes so much medicine. Whist, but no cheerful spirits. — Herr Neumann's telegram yesterday asking about the horse (Grane) has greatly annoyed R.

Wednesday, April 27   A better night for R., and a better mood, as always when he sees nobody. Feustel's telegram causes concern, Lusch's a sort of satisfaction. [*Enclosed Daniela's telegram from Berlin:* "Indescribably moved by today's reunion, I beg for your thoughts. Would it be possible to put off your arrival for one day on account of hotel and other considerations, await answer—Lulu."] — We postpone our journey. We try taking a walk in the garden, but rain and snow drive us back indoors. R. reads from Count Gobineau's book and agrees with his harsh judgment on the Greeks. In the evening we play whist, R. with the dummy. Then he reads aloud part of the Count's article, the passage on Russia, and very kindly goes on to the article about Jouk.'s father, which he describes as benevolently imaginative. He drinks a little champagne, and in good spirits we go off to bed.

Thursday, April 28   R. had a good night, dreamed about Frau von Kalb—that she made "advances" to him—laughs heartily when, with my thoughts on *Parsifal,* I let out a loud sound—calls me Chanteclair. All morning he is agog to hear details. Letters from Lusch and from Feustel provide little information, except that Lusch was much moved by the reunion. R. thinks it natural that she should now find it difficult to approach him—Nature is powerful, he says. My feeling, however, is that she might, rather, turn against me. At lunch some aggressive remarks of Loldi's cause him to comment on the peculiarity of the female character. After lunch we go to convey our good wishes to Frau v. Schoeler, and he is very gay, although he went out greatly vexed about the weather. He tells the old lady that we will transport her to Transvaal in a sedan chair. Our friends in the evening; R. proposes playing the final movement of the 9th, singing where we can.

He cannot sufficiently express his astonishment about the at times childlike and always sublimely naïve quality of this work, and he does not believe it can attain popularity unless given performances of a kind for which he claims to have the secret.

Friday, April 29 R. had a good night. He looks forward to events with some apprehension, to my father's letter, etc.: "With us everything always has to be smothered with pepper and salt." — He wants no farewells at the railroad station, because there one is not master of one's fate, and when I recall earlier times, he says, "There were no railroads for us, just places of execution." — At noon I receive a letter from Hans—four explosive lines of thanks! — At 1 o'clock departure with M[arie] Gross. R. soon in good spirits, keeps wishing for Jouk., to admire the scenery of Saxony. As we are approaching Leipzig, near *Luppa,* he talks of an impression from his earliest youth—a man who wanted to pay court to a woman in the mail coach and laid his hand on her knee; the woman repulsed him coyly—that was one of R.'s first impressions of female coyness. — Of whistling, he says that dramatists ought to travel often on the railroad, so as to accustom themselves to failure.

Sad arrival after a cheerful journey. Feustel all alone on the platform! — Lusch not even at the hotel! [*Added at the bottom of this page and the following one:* "When it gets late and I have written to the children (2 postcards) I fall asleep, and when I awake, I find R. deeply moved —and about me. — Once, when I opened my eyes and moved my hands, he placed them together again and then said to me, 'Go on sleeping, you are so beautiful!' And thus I feel his blessing on me and feel that it was he who brought about the reunion which has made me so happy. Gentle tears fall from our eyes—how blissful we are in this unblissful life!"]

Saturday, April 30 A good night. — At 10 o'clock Lusch! Many reports of the emotional reunion with her father—that he spoke constantly of me; R. somewhat dejected. Feustel's initial mediation very clumsily done. Visits to Mimi, then to the singers, L[illi] Lehmann —meal at the Schleinitzes', who cannot praise Lusch too highly. The Count very original, friendly, and interesting. In the evening Lusch with us again. The poor child wildly excited; R. in his truthfulness speaks his thoughts concerning her father—it pains me, for she is in such a state of turbulence, both physically and morally!

Sunday, May 1 In the morning Herr Neumann does not wish R. to attend the rehearsals, discussion concerning London, no result. A letter to me from Hans! I reply to him and ask him to allow his daughter a share in his life. — I ask R. to show a little consideration toward Lusch, he says I am right. — We pay calls, distinguished ones today,

R. waiting in the carriage, but he takes us to the Passage to see the waxwork figure of Beaconsfield (Rausch). He gets a very dismal impression of the people here (mongrels) and is despondent at not being able to start work. In the evening dinner at the Schleinitzes' again, after which the Helmholtzes arrive, and the famous professor goes to the most obvious lengths to demonstrate that R. is his friend. Afterward we drive around a little—we are both tired, R. and I, also sad, I deeply, oh, so deeply! —

Monday, May 2 R. slept well. A letter from Leipzig offers to sell him the house of his birth, whereupon R. says, "I can't be born a second time." — When Georg asks whether he should take along a change of underclothing, R. says, "No, I'm not conducting—today I'll only be grousing." We arrive on stage, R. is greeted with a flourish, replies jokingly, "If you make so much noise, I can't say a sensible word." The rehearsal begins (1st and 2nd acts *Walküre*), R. not with me at first, but then he comes; it goes reasonably well—the orchestra amazing—and when Frau Vogl, in fetching the utensils, does not match the action with the music, R. is still sufficiently good-humored to interrupt and call out, "We must do that again, or Herr v. Hülsen will run away." — And during another passage, "That will please even Herr v. Hülsen." The orchestra fills us with astonishment, and in our friend Seidl we are able to take genuine delight. Scaria confronts us with certain Viennese cuts. R. points out how absurd they are—for example, the entrance of the Wanderer—whereas it would be easier to make slight cuts in the course of the scene. [*Added in margin:* "This happened on the following day."] The tone in which Herr Scaria speaks is reminiscent of earlier, painful experiences. We eat alone together, R. and I, then drive to the rehearsal (3rd act *Walküre*)—much trouble with machinery and lighting, a Herr Scheibe (from Saxony) causes much vexation, he also at times causes laughter. We drive home, not too late, and are alone together. Lusch rushes in from a *soirée* at the Crown Prince's—her accounts of it are not enlivening!

Tuesday, May 3 R. had a good night. Lilli Lehmann visited in the morning; discussion about the Flower Maidens; joking mention of Herr v. Hülsen's preparing *Tannhäuser* here for the evening of *Rheingold* and the director in Hamburg, Pollini, preparing a cycle. Letters from the children! At 11 o'clock we drive to the rehearsals, R. with Mimi, I with Lusch. First act *Siegfried*. Mime "a Jewish dwarf," R. says, but excellent, Vogl also very good, clear and assured. But Seidl is greeted by R. as a pearl. He dines with us, at 6 o'clock Herr Niemann in a mood of enthusiastic excitement, we drive with him to the rehearsals (2nd and 3rd acts *Siegfried*), Scaria overwhelming in the scene with the Wala—Materna unfortunately gesticulating very strongly, making a cut ("*dort sehe ich Grane*") which throws Vogl off, R. indignant and provoked into a very loud exclamation. Vexation during the rehearsal, at the end much weeping and lamenting in the corridor. Herr Niemann thinks it was all because of Vogl's gratified expression! . . . Seidl quite composed.

Wednesday, May 4 R. had a good night. I write letters. He goes to see Materna, who starts to cry again, R. cuts her short by saying he has not come to hear all yesterday's twaddle over again. I also visit the singers. We come together again at 3 o'clock and eat cozily alone. Then to the *Rheingold* rehearsal, which is held with piano; the first scene just about all right, but everything else, lighting, scenery, etc., is very poor. R., depressed, says that he experienced such things in Magdeburg 50 years ago and never thought to see them repeated! We drive home in almost complete silence and eat our supper around midnight, what little conversation we have being continually steered by R. toward the sad experience we have just been through.

Thursday, May 5 The night was somewhat restless; I beg R. to allow me to accompany him wherever he has to go, because his mood is despondent; first of all we make some purchases for him, then we drive to the Viktoria, where he intends to surprise a rehearsal. The janitor receives him with "Your Excellency," and, arriving on the stage, which is still lit, we are told by a curtsying woman that it is all over. We drive to the director's in order to make some additional arrangements about the lighting, but before that R. was in such good spirits that he suggested going with me to the museum. Solemn and sublime impression made by the Pergamon group in the rotunda. Then upstairs to the pictures. We come upon a sign, "Entry Prohibited," stop, a man says to us, "For you no entry is prohibited," leads us through boldly, whispers something in the astonished custodian's ear, and returns: "I believe I have the honor of talking to R. Wagner?" "My name is Wagner." "May I shake your hand?" And he disappears. We look once again at the Greek discoveries and then drive to the director's. — The meal at the Schleinitzes' begins with R.'s being somewhat subdued, but he gradually livens up. His main theme of conversation is Gobineau's work. The minister, telling us about life in Berlin, is always highly interesting and original. We drive to the theater with Lusch. R. is received with a flourish and applauded enthusiastically. The performance is on the whole so excellent that R. has the desire to acknowledge the applause from the stage with the singers. He makes a little speech and indicates the artists—the merit is theirs and they deserve the applause. R. is much exhausted by his speech, and particularly by the urgings of the singers, who do not wish to go before the curtain with him. — We remain in our box for a while, and as the audience disperses, we witness, to our amazement, a machinery rehearsal in the darkened theater! — We drive home in a somewhat weary mood, gradually cheer up, and spend a while together, drinking champagne. Scaria excellent as Wotan and the whole performance extraordinarily lively. R. thought it not bad that an intermission was inserted. Unfortunately it was necessary to use steam between the Rhine scene and Valhalla in order to drown out the sounds of the scene changing—an embarrassing absurdity. A letter from Count Gobineau, he is at Wahnfried and seems to be quite happy with the children.

Friday, May 6 R. slept well, but he has caught a cold. Friend Stein is here, always welcome. We drive to the theater, R. stages the fight in *Walküre* with incredible agility. (Twice during a rehearsal he frightened me by climbing from one first-floor proscenium box to the other.) He is tired, goes straight to bed when we arrive home, and at our meal around 4 o'clock he is again in good spirits, declares it is due to Stein. But he wonders whether or not to attend the performance, decides he will. Reception, flourish; for us the first act something of a failure, he goes on stage, talks with the singers. Between the 1st and 2nd acts many visitors, who tire him. The acting better in the second act, the fight very successful. At the conclusion R. is all but exhausted and very irritable; he acknowledges the applause from the box; he had already said of the audience after the first act: " 'Today is Simon and Judah, the lake is wild and wants its sacrifice.' " — We go straight to bed. On the way to the theater we were pleased with a friendly and handsome blond policeman; R. did not wish to join the end of the row of carriages: "Herr Wagner, we won't hold you back." — And on stage he is addressed by a liquor manufacturer who, from his factory close to the theater, has provided the steam; he says, "It is the greatest moment of my life to shake your hand." (R. was satisfied with my appearance, found my hair properly arranged.)

Saturday, May 7 A bad night, R. sends for the doctor, he has a slight sore throat. Dr. Zwingenberg prescribes something for him, bows deferentially low, and says: "Now, having seen you, I feel a few inches taller. I first read *Opera and Drama* in 1851." — R. and I remain by ourselves, have a cozy breakfast together, but he soon becomes tired. — A letter from Frau v. Heldburg reports Hans's emotion over his reunion with his daughter. — R. recalls the look in the eyes of our dog Schnauz, whom we nevertheless got rid of! He reads to me the passage in Gobineau's book about the Roman Empire. — We spend the evening alone, R. goes to bed early.

Sunday, May 8 He had a very bad night, dreamed that Siegfried fell into an abyss, that we found him without a face (probably memories of the Pergamon discoveries) but nevertheless revived him; he wanting to walk right away, but we warned by a woman not to let him walk too soon—that had already caused the death of one child. We remain at home, R. reading Gobineau. Herr Neumann full of misgivings about the rehearsal. And in the evening the dream comes true: Jäger as Siegfried utterly unsuccessful, he actually provokes the audience to demonstrations. R. does not appear at the end. Impression of a failure and a Sunday audience. — R. compares Jäger and Vogl—the two singers —and says of the latter, "On the stage one wants brilliance; if there is no gold available, one takes silver, and if one hasn't got that, either, tin; but what one does not want is wood and leather."

Monday, May 9 My grandmother's and my brother's birthday. R. did not have a very good night. — We drive to the scenery rehearsal and from there to Herr Niemann, whom R. wants to take over Siegmund, since Vogl is to keep Siegfried. Since he is not at home, R. writes on a scrap of paper, "Siegmund I am, since Niemann is singing me after all." — We then drive home, and R. reads to me the beginning of Ch. 3 in Volume 4 of Gobineau, which pleases him very much—it revives thoughts in him of his "Herodom and Christianity." — *Götterdämmerung* in the evening; despite all the deficiencies in the acting, R. and I are very moved by it; with Brünnhilde's last words we are leaning against each other, my head on his arm, and he exclaims to me, "What we go through together!" — He goes on stage and makes a speech. We stay up together for a long time. (The Crown Prince wished to see R. in his box, R. begs to be excused.)

Tuesday, May 10 R. writes to friend Wolz. about Jäger and tells Neumann that in this case an amputation will be necessary. — A small young man whom he saw taking care of things in the Hôtel de Rome pleased him so much that he wants to engage him as a "groom," and this morning he speaks to his father. — Lusch's and Boni's first nursemaid visits me, many memories—very touching that she joined the crowd lining the street to see us drive up for *Rheingold*. Then for me Dr. Herrig and poor, oblivious Herr Jäger! — We breakfast with Seidl at the Schleinitzes', after which R. goes to an artists' dinner in the Hôtel de Rome, which to his annoyance turns out to be a Jewish family-hotel dinner. In the evening we receive old Prof. Werder, whom R. holds in most cordial memory, Helmholtz, the Niemanns (he will not sing, for reasons we do not quite understand), etc. — At last, at 11 o'clock, we are at the station with Lusch and take our departure.

Wednesday, May 11 Toward night R. is amused by the voice of a boy, loudly and melodically offering "Sausage . . . rolls"—and this cry remains with us. In the morning coffee at the station in Leipzig, and in Saxony again the "fuss and bother." Arrival at one thirty—all the dear children, Count Gobineau and friend Paul [Joukowsky] as well, Siegfried gazing fixedly at his father with radiant eyes. — In the evening R. very tired, we break up early. —

Thursday, May 12   R. slept very well and is very cheerful. Great delight in the children. — To work at once, that is to say, a sitting with Joukowsky, the Count reading aloud his *Amadis,* and endless discussions with the Count about everything. The weather is raw—R. thinks of his score. — In the evening R. reads to the Count the pages in his book (Volume 4, Ch. 3) which he so loves, and afterward he plays the Prelude to *Parsifal.* After which a discussion ensues between R. and Gobineau about the word "Gothic"; Count Gobineau does not share R.'s view of this expression, but explains it as coming from the Renaissance.

Friday, May 13   R. had a good night; the day begins nicely. A good telegram about *Rheingold* gives us pleasure, and R. again voices his astonishment that such a success was possible in Berlin. — When I return from the studio with Lusch, the lunch bell sounds; I, not realizing that he is ringing it, complete a conversation with the Count; he is vexed that I did not guess who it was—and a humorous, grumbling conversation ensues at lunch. In excuse I explain that the Count was in the middle of telling me a Chinese proverb, and suddenly it is "All my wife cares for is listening to Chinese proverbs—they mean more to her than anything else!" In the evening R. and I are both very tired.

Saturday, May 14   R. dreams of my leaving him. He is unwell all day. In the afternoon he comes to Jouk.'s to look at the picture (the "surprise"). He is at first amazed by the technique, but the portraits please him. He is not with us in the evening, goes to bed early. — A good telegram about *Walküre.*

Sunday, May 15   In the morning R. thinks of the *Ring* and is pleased with it, including *Das Rheingold.* He looks run down, and I fear the quinine he is taking does not agree with him. He reads Gobineau, and in the afternoon spends a long time with me in the garden. He takes pleasure in the fresh greenery, the animals, and, when Count Gobineau comes to join us, a lot of stories are related, including anecdotes about falcons. We sit in the garden until nearly 7 o'clock. In the evening R. reads from his biography the passages relating to Bakunin. He shares my pleasure at having written what he has about this personality.

Monday, May 16   R. had a good night after getting up once. In the morning he reads to me a report on *Die Walküre* which shows much understanding. At midday R. takes to Wolz. the corrected proof of his "Introduction" and surprises us, Lusch and me, in Jouk.'s studio, wearing cap and jacket (the weather is very warm). In the evening Rub. plays the 3rd act of *Götterdämmerung* to us. — R. vacillates between pleasure in the work and an embarrassed feeling that the Count cannot be getting a proper impression of it from such a performance.

Tuesday, May 17 R. dreams that on account of unhappy love I wished to die, was already clothed for it with a wreath of flowers over my hair; he, furious, cries out to me, "But only a few days ago you were calling me Puschel!" — He starts his letter to the King, and that puts him slightly out of humor; he says, "Oh, finding a form of address to match those of the King!" — Also, in spite of all assurances, he insists that the Count could not have received any impressions from *Götter-dämmerung,* since it is not a symphony. — In the afternoon the Brückners and Herr Brandt show us the maquettes of the temple and the Magic Garden, which are thoroughly satisfactory. In the evening our conversation touches on the French, and when I say that they have produced no poets, R. supports me.

Wednesday, May 18 R. was up once during the night. In the morning he is amused by the peacock's call, he says it sounds like the cry of a greatly astonished woman—*"Herr Jeses!"* — He finishes a letter to the King in which he defends the scene painters, whom the King has criticized harshly; R. laughs and says, "You can't do that with me— I'm all for being just." — We drive up to the theater with the Count, R. looks at it with cheerful pride; and in the evening, when he reads that many people in Berlin find the *Nibelungen* tiring, he is extremely glad to see this mentioned, because he thinks it is correct. — On coming down to supper, I find him in melancholy reflections watching the last rays of the sunset; he is somewhat absent-minded toward me, and then he tells me that he has been writing a few words about Herr Heim, the musical director in Zurich, at the request of some friends. — Undoubtedly he was thinking about his death as he looked out of the window. In the evening a quarrel develops between the Count and him about the Irish, whom Gob. declares to be incapable of working. R. becomes very angry, says he would not work under such conditions, either, and he castigates the English aristocracy. The Count goes so far in his ideas as to reproach the Gospels for interceding in behalf of the poor. But it all ends very amicably, R. admits that he does not know the problem in detail, and the Count says to him, *"Vous voyez la chose en philosophe et moi en homme d'affaires"* ["You view the matter like a philosopher and I like a businessman"].

Thursday, May 19 [*Written at the top of the page:* "The diary resumed on June 7."] R. had a good night; yesterday, before the discussion about the English, the topic of conversation was the Franco-Prussian War; the Count relates the most curious anecdotes about the stupidity of the French, including a general who, asking for the third time the name of a river and receiving the answer, "It is the Marne," exclaims, *"Ah, mais c'est une mauvaise plaisanterie"* ["that is a bad joke"]. R. comes back to that today and again laughs heartily. At lunch the Count tells us some things about Persia which show us how philosophically inclined this nation is. R. jokes, saying he is going to his score *de race mélanésienne.* In the evening the Count's descriptions of Athens arouse in us such an urge to go there that the Count has to promise to write to friends there about accommodation for the winter.

Friday, May 20 R. had a good night, and he is sitting at his work when I come in from the neighbor's house around 1 o'clock; he opens the door of the *salon* for me, in doing so stubs his finger, and is in consequence of this and various other mishaps (no ink, his pen bent) very ill-humored at lunch; he says he feels as if he will never be able to start his work! — The Ritter children arrive, most welcome at the rehearsals, which we begin immediately. The weather is unfortunately very unfavorable, and when R., to take his mind off things, goes across to Jouk.'s, he is annoyed to see that he has altered Fidi's portrait; I find him in this mood and do not quite know how to ask him to allow the Eyssers to work in the *salon* tomorrow; but I do it, and when I see him later, I find him in tears—moved by thoughts of me, he says. The evening passes peacefully. — Over coffee R. quoted Thomas à Kempis's saying, "To suffer this, one must be God," and he thought it right to see godlike qualities in the sufferings of humiliation.

Saturday, May 21 R. dreams that I go away and that I tell Jouk., who tries to intercede, that he is a sheep, which makes us all laugh. There is nowhere for him to go—the Eyssers are working on the surprise, and in the hall we are holding rehearsals! At lunch he says merrily that he wishes he could be given his presents right away! At coffeetime the Standhartners appear, father and daughter; introductions and memories of Vienna. For us "juvenile rehearsals." In the evening R. talks about the Count's essay, and the Count explains his ideas to our friends. Cheerful atmosphere.

Sunday, May 22 R. slept well; the Flower Greeting takes place at 8 o'clock and is very successful, the clock presented by Fidi-Parsifal delights R., and he is pleased with the flower costumes. The coats of arms of the Wagner Society towns genuinely surprise him, and he is pleased with the ceiling. In a mood of divine happiness he strolls to the summerhouse with me in the blue robe, and we exchange gold pens and little poems! Our lunch table consists of: Standhartners 3 (with Gustav!), Ritters (the parents), the Count, Jouk., Boni, Lusch, and Fidi; in the hall Eva, Loldi, Ferdi Jäger, Julchen and Elsa; the latter two have to slip away unnoticed, so that the singing of the verse will float down from the gallery. Siegfried speaks Stein's poem very well, splendidly proposing the health of eternal youth, and then in a full voice Elsa movingly sings *"Nicht Gut noch Pracht,"* etc., from above. — Over coffee Faf from the Festival Theater appears with the program for this evening on his back. The dear good children act out the little farces by Lope and Sachs magnificently, and Lusch speaks Wolz.'s linking epilogue particularly well. To the conclusion of the Sachs play J. Rub. linked the Prelude to *Die Msinger,* and when R. went into the *salon,* the children, in different costumes, sang his *"Gruss der Getreuen"*; at the conclusion of the evening, after the meal, came the *"Kaisermarsch,"* with altered text. All splendidly done by the children, though we are not entirely successful in sustaining the mood. Before lunch R. was upset by the military band, which he—somewhat to my concern—had allowed to take part, and it required Siegfried's toast to raise his spirits again. In the evening he was irked by the dullness of our friends, he asked Standhartner to remain behind, without considering that the stepson would also then remain, and the presence of this man whom he cannot bear kept him from expressing all that was in his heart, and that made him almost painfully unhappy! The successful parts are what delighted me—the fact that unbidden things intervene no longer bothers me, however much it once used to pain me: I keep remembering that "all transient things are but an image."

Monday, May 23   The children's giggling draws me into their room. "Yesterday Papa had 12 surprises: (1) the Flower Greeting, (2) the coats of arms, (3) the military band (!), (4) the toast, (5) the song, (6) Faf, (7) Lope, (8) the epilogue, (9) the Prelude, (10) the *"Gruss,"* (11) the *"Kaisermarsch,"* (12) U-August (Gustav Schönaich). I report this merry notion to R., and it makes us laugh heartily. But he again flies into a rage when he is obliged to say goodbye to this man whom he detests. Lunch at 4 (the children eat with the Ritters in the Sonne), R. is rather tired. But in the evening he calls for the plays, and the children act them out for us in the *salon,* very gaily and well. Departure of the good Ritters.

Tuesday, May 24   R. had a good night. A telegram from Herr Neumann inquiring whether we are coming to the 4th cycle. I think it is in order to express his thanks to the children that R. decides to do so, and when I am a bit startled, he exclaims, "Let us not be Philistines." Great turmoil, hither and thither with friend Gross, saloon carriage reserved, I timidly ask whether I might not be allowed to stay here with the Count, who is very tired, but it is no use, a special train to Neuenmarkt is ordered, and to friend Gross he says humorously, "When it comes to throwing away money, you can always rely on me!" — At midnight we are all sitting ready in the dining room, at one o'clock we leave, and on

Wednesday, May 25 at one o'clock in the afternoon, after a merry and exuberant journey, we are in Berlin, installed with our two friends in the Hôtel du Nord. (In the morning our sausages-and-rolls boy turns out to be stupid!) At 7:30 P.M. we are all sitting in *Das Rheingold!* During which a few things unfortunately cause R. vexation. But the row of children's heads cheers him up.

Thursday, May 26 A good night for R. — A nice speech to him from the vegetarians. A pleasant letter from the King. Then a talk with Herr Neumann in which R. learns that 10,000 marks have been deducted from the receipts for seats for the press. R. drives with the children to the zoological gardens and then visits the Countess *par excellence* with them. Lusch visits a Frau Overbeck and there hears strange things about her father, which upset her. In the evening to *Die Walküre,* the Count in a hat borrowed from Jouk., which amuses us greatly. The performance both good and bad, Frau Hofmeister effective as Sieglinde, Frau Vogl less so as Brünnhilde, many crass errors of production which upset R., and when, afterward, he has to stand in the middle of a gaping crowd awaiting our carriages, he loses patience entirely. Concern for Lusch, the great and sublime effect of the work on me, and R.'s mood of vexation form a complicated whole to which my humor cannot measure up, and I wake up on

Friday, May 27 with my head in a whirl, preventing me from adapting myself to R.'s unconstrained mood as completely as I should like. I take the children to the museum (yesterday to the palace); returning home, I find R. unwilling to go to the breakfast arranged with the Countess for all the children together. The misery of finding myself in the "outside world" comes over me in full force, and I burst into tears! R. promises to come, and he does so; if to begin with he is much out of humor in the home of the friendliest of our friends, he soon recovers, and in the best of spirits he listens to a tenor's voice. We spend the evening peacefully in the hotel. To a Dr. Herrig R. explains how helpless the Wagnerite journalists are, because lacking in courage—they did not dare print his letter to Hülsen.

Saturday, May 28 A good night. I walk with Daniela to the photographer's, since her father has complained of having received no picture of her! From there to the Museum of Applied Arts and the New Museum, where we suddenly meet Siegfried, who is out seeing all the sights of Berlin. Lunch in the hotel with our good Seidl. Then to *Siegfried,* some of it good, much not, the enthusiasm still as great as ever. R. sad, says he is gradually being made to lose confidence in his work. His pleasure today lies in finishing the Count's book. (Yesterday he said of the Berlin population that it contains much *race grise* [mixed race] with red noses.)

Sunday, May 29 A good night. The children drive out to Charlottenburg, I in the morning to the museum, then with R. to see our friend Kathi Eckert, whom I found the day before yesterday very ill. The poor woman is almost paralyzed, but she stammers out the words "Dear master." — We soon leave her and drive through the Tiergarten —lovely spring breezes and the most painful impression! My poor child again so unsettled here that I have to reproach myself for not having brought her up in a more Christian spirit of resignation. R. tells me sharply not to worry, I withdraw into myself and feel something like bliss in the midst of my pain. — Was it the unconscious proximity of death which I felt? At lunch in the hotel the Count relates that his sister, the Benedictine nun, had inquired about *The Artwork of the Future* and what it means. R. replies, explaining that the less recognizable the races, the lower humanity has sunk: all the more strongly and clearly must art assert itself. Lusch, whom I ask for some wine, thinks her father has finished speaking and asks him on my behalf; R. becomes violently annoyed, and violent, too, are my little one's tears, overtired as she is by all the things happening to her. Not exactly well prepared, but with our spirits restored, we go off to *Götterdämmerung*. Various things again upset R., and when Herr Neumann starts an ovation for him according to his own taste, he rushes away. I notice that he is very agitated, follow him, and prevail upon him to acknowledge the audience for the last time from the box. — Luckily we manage to laugh merrily about it on the homeward journey, for truly there is something disconcerting about this Israelite affair. In laughter and melancholy we go off to bed!

Monday, May 30 R. frequently wakes up crying, "The illustrious house—Devil take it!" — I set out for Potsdam at 10 o'clock, to show it to the 5 children, R. stays at home and receives Herr Neumann's letter, which he answers. At 4 o'clock he is at the station to meet us, unfortunately he misses us and is annoyed by the mishap. We all drive once again to our friendly Countess's, dine there, and spend the evening very pleasantly up to 10 o'clock. Back at home, we receive Herr Schön, who tells us about his reception by the Crown Prince, whereupon R. very forcibly states his opinion of his behavior toward him over the years. (At lunch R. expressed his delight in the Count's book, *Dogme et philosophie*.) At eleven o'clock we depart, after Herr Neumann, in a 2nd letter, has asked R. to make public amends, that is to say, attendance at *Die Walküre* with some kind of "theatrical participation." At the station Seidl declares he knows nothing about it all and that he has broken with Herr N. A nice saloon carriage, the night quite bearable, the Count kindly considerate of the children. Arrival on

Tuesday, May 31 at 2 o'clock. Delight in being back at home. The garden very beautiful, R. pleased with his armorial *salon*. Fatigue soon drives us up to bed.

Wednesday, June 1   All slept well, and the weather is glorious. In the morning R. reads *Dogme et philosophie* in the summerhouse and feels content; we spend a long time in the garden. Molly presents us with some puppies and abandons them to follow R. We have our coffee in the summerhouse and talk about lyric poetry, on which subject the Count agrees entirely with R., declaring incidentally that the Italian language is thoroughly unpoetic. While I am enjoying the lovely air with R., I tell him one really ought to spend the whole day in the woods and in the evening listen to one of his works; he says I am right, and that watching a drama together is a desirable occupation, for then one feels part of the human family. In the evening we have a philosophical conversation with the Count.

Thursday, June 2   Yet in spite of the fine and harmonious day, R. did not have a good night. He wants to get back to his score. We rest together in the summerhouse during the afternoon. Then we drive to the Feustels', who visited us yesterday. He shows us R.'s letter, and we are quite agreeable to its being printed. A glass of beer with the Count in the garden produces much talk about animals, particularly dogs; then R. shows his snuffboxes and I my green stone, and I relate how I lost it on New Year's Eve and then found it again! — A report in the *Tagblatt* about the King's relationships with actors distresses R. Then we talk about Shelley, whom R. does not see as a true poet, and in the evening the Count tells us a lot about Persia, compared with which Europe always makes a sorry appearance.

Friday, June 3   R. had a bad night, and he is not well. At lunch he is downright explosive in favor of Christian theories in contrast to racial ones. The doctor advises a drive, and we undertake one to the Eremitage. — Cheerful mood, but in the evening he feels worn out and goes off to be by himself.

Saturday, June 4   R. had a good night and spends the morning reading *Dogme et philosophie* in the summerhouse. He quotes from it a saying by Thomas Aquinas about justice, and observes that we have now gone beyond that. We all drive to the Fantaisie and take enormous delight in the lovely blossom time. Friend Wolzogen in the evening. R. plays the Prelude to *Lohengrin*. He presents his collected writings to the Count, with a dedication extolling the bond between Normans and Saxons. (Blandine brought us the news of K. Eckert's death!) [*Enclosed in the Diaries a letter to Cosima from Ernst Dohm, written from Berlin on June 3 and conveying the same news.*]

Sunday, June 5   R. had a restful night and wanted to have breakfast in the summerhouse, but I am hoarse. He tells me of a ghost which

Siegfried and Georg saw at 10 o'clock last night—we connect it with Rausch, who is very ill in the hospital. And I use the conversation to inform R. of the death of our poor good friend K. Eckert. At 12 o'clock Rausch comes to the house in a high fever, half dressed and looking terrible, and asks for his room! The topic of our conversation is ghost stories! R. is upset by all these experiences; first thundery heat and then thunder. We have our coffee in the summerhouse, then R. walks into town with Jouk., to see whether, in spite of its being Whitsuntide, he cannot buy a chain for S.'s watch. He is successful. In the evening he plays the *Idyll* with Rubinstein—much emotion and much reminiscing, he talks of the birth, and we are moved, though constantly disturbed by uninvited guests.

Monday, June 6 Siegfried, child of joy, child of peace! Presentation of gifts at 2 o'clock. Afterward 14 at lunch; R. asks who is to propose the toast, friend Feustel gets up, says a few words, which Siegfried interrupts with an alarmed cry: "I haven't got any champagne yet!" — Great amusement over this. In the afternoon the first act is gone through in an arrangement by Herr Rub., only up to Amfortas's outburst. Unfortunately rather restless. In the evening much about Siegfried, who, when his father tells him that it is rather absurd for him to have a gold chain, replies, "Perhaps you can take it back." — R. thinks he looks like Byron.

Tuesday, June 7 R. has a wild dream about Herr v. Staff killing his dog Peps with a shotgun! — I manage to tell him what I wrote yesterday to Mimi about my feelings of consolation on the death of our good Kathi. He agrees with me, saying that in her vain battle against adversity she suddenly lost the will to continue. We remember with emotion her telegrams during the 2nd cycle, then my visit, when she said to me, "I shall not see you again"; then the visit together with R. and her paralysis ("Oh, death is very solemn," R. remarks here, "it no longer smiles"), then the doctors' encouraging reports, the comforting letter from her daughter; and now her death—she was cured, but did not wish to go on! — Farewell to the Count very cordial; over coffee R. reads to us an anecdote from *Dogme et philosophie;* he had meant to read it to the Count on parting, but had been prevented from doing so by the farewell fuss (visit of Wolz.), about which he is sorry. At 5, conference on the production. Then R. visits Wolz. and Schemann. At supper he tells us that he has been sent Herr Lindau's article about his behavior during Neumann's speech, and he says that against such shameless creatures one is utterly defenseless. — Discussion of the fact that Herr Nmann is quite incapable of understanding R.'s indignation, since he meant it as an act of homage! — In the evening much talk about our good and excellent guest. When we are in bed, R. says,

"Vanish, you arches," and remarks how ridiculous it is to sing this, whereas an instrumental piece would convey the idea; Goethe made use of words, he says, precisely because he had no music.

Wednesday, June 8 R. had a good night, and he works. But the cold gray weather puts him in a bad mood. He declares his intention of covering over the whole lower part of the windows during the winter. Still much about the Count, who in every particular has become so valuable an enrichment of our lives. At coffee an anonymous letter. — Apparently a great deal of dust has once more been raised. R. goes for a short walk with Marke in the palace gardens. In the evening Herr Köhler vexes him with a description of his difficulties in Berlin. He sends for friend Wolz. and Dr. Schemann. Then he dismisses all what he calls refractory elements, and we have to laugh heartily over his merry and sparkling, childlike expression as he regards the serpent among the leave-takers. [*The last eight words of this sentence—referring to Wolzogen—obliterated in ink by an unknown hand.*] —

Thursday, June 9 A good night, but the weather is raw. R. works, however. At lunch he tells us how much he loves the peacock's call, the wildness of it, and how much he enjoys being surrounded by living things. Again no walk; R. writes to Herr Levi, saying he hopes the Vogl couple will be received with the proper signs of respect. Letters like this (containing friendly words) are what he best likes to write, he tells me. In the evening our friends Wolz., Schemann, Rubinstein; R. expounds the idea of honor to Rub., talks to Schemann about Byron and in particular *Don Juan,* the final cantos of which he found very boring. To end with, our favorite, the E-flat Major Quartet, is played; the Scherzo R. calls the "Nutcracker." — He praises the perfection of these works. — When we are alone, we become more lighthearted, we think of Molly's young ones, then of mine; I say I cannot really believe that I brought these five into the world, and R. says: [*blank left here; see following day*] and he quotes the passage from the *Iliad,* between Diomedes and Glaucus. — (Letters from the Count, from Frau Helmholtz, who is making a collection for the Eckert children, accounts from Neumann's cashier, the debt to friend Feustel repaid.) —

Friday, June 10 R. had a good night and goes to work in the morning, after reading Count Gobineau's book (*Dogme & phil.*). The weather is raw, overcast, and cold—a planet is said to have come too near. This leads to far-reaching reflections, we discuss the Count's ideas and finally come to Schopenhauer. That he would like to be "sonfi," and once mentioned it to R. in a—for the Count—humorous way. We snatch a breath of air in the garden together, then he works, and I ask him to write down the Greek sentence for me. [*Enclosed in the*

Diaries a sheet of paper bearing the words, "dien aristeuein kai hypertaton emmenai allon" [always to be brave and of all beings the best]," *referring to the blank left on June 9.*] In the evening we chat together, and as I go off to sleep, I hear R.'s final words, "My dear wife's love keeps me alive, nothing else." — (R. has demanded a precise explanation following Seidl's telegram.)

Saturday, June 11   R. had a chest spasm in the morning, and the cold, raw weather puts him in utter despair. An article in the newspaper about the dire state of the farmers in Bavaria (most of the farms are said to be mortgaged) forms the dismal theme of our lunchtime conversation. In Russia a conspiracy against the Tsar has been discovered, and in Paris believers and atheists are quarreling over Littré's body! — One stays indoors and thinks of heating. In the evening *Don Quixote* (the episode with the lion and the puppet show) produces a friendly and more cheerful mood, and R. and I cannot tell each other often enough how singular this work is. —

Sunday, June 12   R. slept well. A letter from Seidl brings news of Herr Neumann, unfortunately in a rather brutal way, and in consequence R. writes to Herr Förster. At lunch he says how embarrassing he finds such relationships, when he is obliged to write to untruthful, narrow-minded, phrase-making people who are nevertheless devotees. Over coffee he reads aloud his letter, in which he complains in particular about Herr Neumann's stage directing and demands changes in it; he laughs about it, saying he knows of no single person whom he could recommend. The weather clears up, we go out on the summerhouse turret, and before our evening meal R. sits in the garden with the children and Jouk. After the meal we chat together, discussing our relations with the neighboring house, which was with us today *in pleno* for lunch. R. recalls how this whole family, through the enthusiasm of the son—literally following his star—settled here, without making any difficulties, and how one is under a genuine obligation to them, which makes it easy to overlook their lack of charm. [*The last ten words obliterated in ink by an unknown hand.*]

Monday, June 13   R. had a good night and works diligently. A ridiculous story read aloud by R. over coffee, in which Jews make a frequent appearance, brings from R. the remark, "Certainly much has been won in the last six months, since one mentions the Jews by name." In the afternoon R. and I visit the mayor and are overtaken by a storm; we seek refuge under the portals of the church, and R. complains about the wind, which reminds him of an officious policeman setting upon and grabbing him, a fear which used to haunt him during the revolutionary years. After the visit to the mayor the wind has died down, and R. suggests going with me to Angermann's. We carry out his suggestion and then stroll home, where we walk a little while longer in the garden. The wind has died down, but R.'s thoughts are full of the bad climate, and he speaks definitely of spending next winter away from here. In the evening memories of Switzerland, the lovely days, but also the floods. R. compares me with Sieglinde: "Further, further!" When we are alone, we talk about our relationship. "Tristan and Isolde," says R. I ask him whether I should not destroy our correspondence, since we may perhaps die before Siegfried is sufficiently mature. R. says, "Not yet, but later perhaps; there is no trace of the Goethe-Stein relationship in it—there was blood everywhere." Previously, when we were speaking about our journey, he said he was glad it had been so agonizing for us, since things must have been agonizing for others, too. — Hans's letter to Daniela also provides us with a melancholy topic; he is bitter about his stay in London; and this renewed relationship, though desired, also produces quivers and qualms! . . .

Tuesday, June 14 R. slept well, and after his reading he goes to his work. The weather is improving, and after coffee we walk up to the tower, where we have a long rest. Before that we strolled in the garden, inspecting our animal stock. Comparing the white peacocks to the colored ones, which represent life, R. says, "They are more sublime beings, like the ghost of Hamlet's father." — We are amused by the little puppies, the children have already given them names. When R. is about to return to his score (after having received and answered a long and tiresome business letter from Herr Batz), I beg him to take advantage of the comparatively fine day and stay in the garden. He does so, and we spend quite a long time chatting with friend Wolz. In the evening, too, when R., talking of his childhood, relates how at the age of 5 he was thrown out of the carriage against a steep bank on a journey from Dresden to Meissen, but was uninjured. — Still much about the Count and his works, a telegram from him gives us pleasant news of his arrival in Auvergne.

Wednesday, June 15 Each morning now I have a sitting at friend Jouk.'s with Lusch, since she dearly wishes to take a picture of herself to Weimar for her father. R. works on his score. When Alexanderbad is mentioned, he says he would prefer Hyderabad, if that by any chance were also a *Bad* [spa]. In the afternoon we are in the pavilion, delighting in our life among the treetops. A very curious letter from Dr. Schemann gives me food for thought about the relationship between master and disciples! A newspaper from Berlin has published a nice article about our friend K. Eckert, also a letter by Mozart which R. declares to be not genuine, or, rather, a compilation. We talk about

Lusch and Hans, and I tell R. that in her excitement, which takes forms I am not always happy about, there lies perhaps a providential aid, as it were, against the impressions she will now be exposed to.

Thursday, June 16 Today I allow Lusch to attend the sitting without me, so that I can reply to Dr. Schemann's singular letter. R. works on his score and tells me that the aversion he feels for magicians and evil beings will perhaps induce him to write *Die Sieger,* since in that everything remains gentle. Sultry weather and thunderstorm, but all the same we undertake a projected outing and the skies are kind to us; we drive via the Eremitage to the Riedelberg, where the sight of the gardener makes a bad impression on us as evidence of the harshness of rich people; we then drive to Bürgerreuth, stop there a moment to enjoy ourselves, visit Faf at the theater and our good doctor on his little estate, and return home in very high spirits. In the evening conversation with Rub. and Humperdinck; the album for the shipwrecked gives us something to talk about! . . . Then R. says he is actually rather glad when we have an evening without music, since for him music means ecstasy, and he does not care for that to be regarded lightly. — When we are alone, we keep coming back to Hans—who writes to his daughter, declaring among other things that he has continually been betrayed, in both small and large matters.

Friday, June 17 Though R. had quite a good night, he does not feel well. He begins his letter to the King. We drive to the Waldhütte with the three younger children, but the lovely journey seems long to R., and he has feelings of anxiety. Once we are seated at a table in the Waldhütte, he feels better and becomes more cheerful. The homeward journey begins with a little scene; Loldi tells me the coachman has caught a bird, which he intends to take home in a box; I demand that the bird be set free, R. joins in, argues, and orders its release, whereupon the coachman gives in. We are silent on the homeward journey, all R. says to me, after the children have got out, is: "Even Gobineau's book I now find distasteful, like everything else to do with history. And I am always on the side of the rebels—now, for instance, the persecuted Bahais." — We reach home at 9 o'clock, a letter from a man in Duisburg, wanting to link a study of *Parsifal* to a review of Wolfram's *Parzival,* irritates R. He says, "I could just as well have been influenced by my nurse's bedtime story." — He turns to the subject of women's fashion today, and when Lusch replies that at least it obliges women to take short steps when they enter a *salon,* he becomes very indignant; talking alone with him afterward, I acknowledge my feelings of melancholy that the children, having been educated for the world outside, cannot adapt themselves entirely to our world. R.

regrets having insisted on her seeing their father again. I—leave it all in God's hands and wish, wish from the bottom of my soul, that good may triumph.

Saturday, June 18 R. tells me that in a dream I spoke aloud and demanded admittance to "the place where nobody speaks." R. says to me, "You are right—one says useless things and hears stupid ones." — In the morning and afternoon he continues his letter to the King. Over coffee our conversation brings us to the saints, and R. gets heated about the idea, so common nowadays, that they are virtuous in the hope, as it were, of future profit. We spend the afternoon with our friend Jouk., R. comes along after finishing his letter and brings a new picture of himself, painted by the Spanish artist Egusquiza. It does not give much satisfaction, there is a feeling that nobody ever finds the right colors for him, but all portraits of him please me. — R. and I return home alone and sit down in the garden, delighting in the acacias; and it does us good to know the children are enjoying themselves, and we all alone. In the evening conversation with friend Wolz.—about the Bahais in Persia. We go off peacefully to bed.

Sunday, June 19 Talking about climate, R. says there is one way of having done with all that: dying. I agree with him, telling him how often this thought occurs to me when I am feeling too weak for life's battles! And the most consoling thought of all is that death is inevitable. Then we pass on to the things that one does, and how absurd it is to talk of compassion, since here below, active participation is everything. R. says that one can, however, achieve it with the aid of thought and by taking steps to avert terrible situations, for which Nature surely has no desire. At lunch the conductor Mottl from Karlsruhe, at one point we talk of Brahms, and R. admits his utter antipathy for him. When R. goes off to rest, we ask the conductor to play us the 3rd act of *Tristan;* this he does, so well indeed that we are all utterly transported. Friend Jouk. leaves for a short excursion to Baden without saying goodbye. — We tell R. of our experience. We spend some time in the summerhouse amid the treetops, where we are caught in a heavy shower of rain. In the evening R. wants *Coriolanus,* and he delights in it, saying, "Here is race, this is something for Gobineau." I: "*Tristan* is the music which removes all barriers, and that means all racial ones as well." — A letter arrives from Herr Förster in Leipzig, very carefully phrased.

Monday, June 20 R. had a good night, we have breakfast in the garden, and I read to R. a nice letter from Count Gob., after which R., reflecting on him, says, "He is my only *contemporary*." At lunch we are still talking about the impression the 3rd act of *Tristan* made on us. R. says, "Oh, none of that is true," but then to me, "Of course you know it *is* true." — A letter from Herr Neumann indicates that the conflict is as good as over. R. replies to him, and he will probably visit us in mid-July. Herr Brandt is here, and we spend an hour with him "in the treetops." Unfortunately R. again feels a chest spasm, and I cannot think of the preparations for next year without misgivings. In connection with these preparations he himself recently quoted Brünnhilde's words, "Heavy weigh my weapons." — At lunch he talked about the Bahais and observed that this would be the future religion of Asia. In the evening our conversation deals with the relationship of the artist to the public, appearances on stage, speeches, etc. — R. felt that the element of enthusiasm brought about these obligations.

Tuesday, June 21 R. starts on his cure, drinks two glasses of Rakoczy water, and we have breakfast in the summerhouse. He then works on his score, and we spend virtually the whole afternoon in the garden. Herr Köhler, Siegfried's tutor, comes; R. counters his singular, abstruse manner with a calm, attentive earnestness, and then exhorts him in the most splendid words to be cheerful, to look around himself and stop brooding. — In the evening more about Gobineau and Bahai. — In the afternoon, as we were strolling together beneath the pergola, R. and I, he told me his plans for his next article ("Herodom and Christianity") and said that even in such things he proceeds like a dramatist, dividing up his work as if into acts. — R. does not like looking at the death masks of Beeth. & Weber; I remove them. He compares it to playing games with the crucifix.

Wednesday, June 22 R. had a good night, he continues with his spa cure. At lunch our friends the Wolz.'s; Hans finds beneath his plate instructions (in verse) to go to Stockholm with his wife. — Great heat, we stay at home, but around 7 we go to the summerhouse, R. and I, and eat our supper alone. The children are again out on a very long ramble. A thunderstorm approaches, they return home, very cheerful. We, R. and I, contemplative. — Before we went upstairs, R. amused himself greatly with the little puppies, who are now crawling out of their box. — (R. did not work.)

Thursday, June 23 Heavy thunderstorm during the night, then off to sleep again. — Letter from Hans Wolz., to whom last night R. sent another note, for fear of not having said enough. [*Wolzogen's letter of thanks enclosed in the Diaries.*] Yesterday he told me that, hardly had he made the arrangement we long ago discussed, when a request for the *Ring* came from Frankfurt; today Herr N. also requests rights for Frankfurt and Prague. Around 5 R. comes to my room and reads to me what he has just been reading in Gobineau's book about the theater. My idea of spending the last evening with Lusch and friend

Brandt on the Bürgerreuth is accepted by R. We surprise the doughty man working on the stage and join forces for a simple meal on the Bürgerreuth. The theater seems like a miracle!

Friday, June 24 Midsummer's Day! Up very early, listened to the birds, great melancholy. Departure of Daniela, who is going to see her father in Weimar. Then to the hospital on account of our good Rausch, who died last night. Home again—many tears (R. told Lusch above all to remain cheerful!), interrupted by Count and Countess Nako; I show them the "sights"; R. admires my ability to do such things, but I scarcely hear what the strangers around me are saying! Thunderstorm. — A short evening, since my sleepless night left me very tired. R. came across Mozart's "Lacrimosa" and played it to me; our "flowers and ribbons" for this year! — R. reads to me several things from the Count's book. We go to bed early.

Saturday, June 25 R. had a somewhat restless night, but he takes his waters. I have a discussion with poor Herr Köhler, who is very difficult! . . . In the afternoon our good Rausch's funeral, moving in its simplicity; the superiority of Protestantism over the Catholic church in terms of its detachment and lack of power symbols. — Visit from Herr Brandt and Herr Staudt—to everybody's astonishment the gas pipes are still in good condition! . . . In the evening a Persian play from the Count's book, *Kassem's Wedding*—extremely moving!

Sunday, June 26 R. and I are up early, he takes his waters, and we have breakfast in the summerhouse, from which the rain soon drives us. Our conversation revolves around yesterday's reading, and it is an inexhaustible subject. In the afternoon a visit from our friend Herr Levi; discussions about the performances. In the evening chat—still much about Gobineau, whose book (*Religion, etc.*) R. has finished.

Monday, June 27 Letter from Lusch—dismal reflections, R. mentions how difficult his position has become through the attitude taken by Hans, who talks about me but avoids mentioning him. At lunch discussion on finding a cast for the chorus. Then various things from R. about his life, with this remark: "I was never in love. When the great demon gets going," he says, turning to me, "that is a different matter—that is not being in love, and it doesn't stop, either." Herr Köhler comes to us in the evening, but in spite of all my efforts we cannot establish any sort of contact with him. The conductor plays us some Bach, including the final chorus from the *Passion*. R. then speaks of how much he likes the one chorus in [Mendelssohn's] *Saint Paul* following the stoning of Saint Stephen. He remarks on what a period of decadence we live in; Mendelssohn still had some ideas, then Schumann, a foolish brooder, and now Brahms with nothing at all! (No waters.)

Tuesday, June 28 Not a very good night for R.; all the same a walk, with Rakoczy water and breakfast in the garden. Lulu again and again, and complaints about the climate, and concern over people's incompetence, which has obliged us today to have poor, beautiful Molly clipped. R. dictates to me a letter to the veterinary surgeon. It is cold in the evening, and R. feels it severely. But we go through the first scene of *Parsifal* with great delight.

Yesterday R. praised Siegfried's gentle will: "He is a good boy," he said, "he has a gentle will, but at the same time he is lively, and so good-natured and sensible." Also the way he is musical and whistles everything, but has no desire to learn the piano; R. says it reminds him of himself in his youth. — Of the girls he says they are now no longer children: what we have is the flower, no longer the bud. — A theory about the stars amuses him: if the light we see from stars is now several thousand years old, he says, then they must be seeing us as we were at the time of Abraham! . . . Over our after-lunch coffee the talk was of Bismarck and the jovial spirit in which all our interests are being pursued; R. says he no longer has the slightest interest in any of it. —

Wednesday, June 29 R. had a good night, but the bad weather keeps us from having breakfast in the garden. Around lunchtime he comes to me in a state of some excitement: "Here's a nice letter." I: "Something bad?" "Oh, you'll see." I read it, am at first astonished, but then join in R.'s lively merriment. But when the letter is shown to the poor conductor, he cannot master his feelings, it seems that such instances of baseness are something new to him! . . . Marianne Brandt comes, R. offers her the role of Kundry. Then R. and I take Siegfried to the headmaster of the technical college, for gymnastic lessons. In the evening some things from *Tristan* and *Götterdämmerung,* R. not very pleased with them, in a mood of melancholy with regard to everything concerning his works.

Thursday, June 30 Toothache for me, the doctor diagnoses an abscess on the gum; I would like to stay in bed, but there is Hans Richter with all his sunny good humor to receive, and poor friend Levi—who cannot recover his composure—to take leave of! — Lunch much enlivened by Richter's countless anecdotes. He also talks about the unparalleled success of the new Venusberg music in London. He is confident about the theatrical venture. Memories of Tribschen the happiest of all! For me poor Frau Jäger in the evening! R. sends a telegram to friend Levi. — Life, and people who expect something from it!

Friday, July 1 R. had quite a good night, and he takes his morning walk with the children, but, out of consideration for my toothache, has breakfast with me in my room. Around lunchtime he brings me a letter from our poor conductor, who asks to be released from his obligations. R. writes to him, asking him to take courage and not to make things so difficult for him. Lunch with the Richters and M. Brandt. — Letter from Lusch, saying that Hans wants to see me! R. upset about it; I feel that for my children it will be better if I comply. We drive together to the Eremitage, where the children already are with the Richters. R. says he regrets having brought about Daniela's reunion with her father. In the evening Kundry's second act gone through with Marianne Brandt. R. despondent about the discrepancy between the tasks he sets and the people who carry them out.

Saturday, July 2   A good night for R., fine morning, he goes for a walk in the palace gardens with the children, we go with the Richters to meet him, and all of us have breakfast in the upper pavilion in cheerful spirits. Richter's departure. At 1 o'clock return of our poor friend Levi as a result of R.'s splendid reply to his letter. Very relaxed, indeed even very cheerful mood at lunch. R. calls for *Hebrew* wine! He tells us a lot about the elephants in Jacolliot's book, and Richter contributes much to the conversation. In the afternoon I write to Lusch, telling her my reasons for agreeing to a meeting, and I inform R. of it. In the evening R. relates many things from his life, the rehearsals for *Rienzi,* something, he says, which never happened to him before or since. When friend Levi tells us that he visited the cathedral in Bamberg, and shows evidence of a leaning toward Catholicism, R. talks about the ceremonies in our church and praises their simplicity and feeling. He indicates to Levi that he has been thinking of having him baptized and of accompanying him to Holy Communion.

Sunday, July 3   R. had a wild and restless night and, as a result of a shower in the morning, a chest spasm which keeps him from taking his waters. At lunch he is still sad about it, and a foolish letter from our friend Heckel, who requests a reply in his own hand, does nothing to help raise his spirits. He also has to write to Herr Batz. I am happy when his thoughts revert to his reading (Jacolliot) and the elephants! A fairly long letter from Jouk., written in various places, also annoys him; he does not like people whom he considers as belonging to him to go away, and when he sees the roses in bloom, he wants to show them to Jouk. — A review of other friends leads us to declare that many of these relationships were dependent on time and place, were indeed of merely local significance—a remark that horrifies our poor friend Levi. But, after considering many instances, we have to stick to our view. — The children bring reports of glowworms, we hasten to the palace gardens and are rewarded with a wonderful display of *Midsummer Night's Dream* magic. Great delight in it! Unfortunately the memory of

Heckel's letter brings back all the wretchedness, and mention of the musicians who have persecuted my father in the past produces a veritable explosion from me. But we nevertheless bring the evening to a pleasant conclusion by reading the chapter about the Persian theater (Gobineau).

Monday, July 4   R. had a good night, he takes his waters, and we have breakfast in the pavilion. He says goodbye to the conductor, telling him jokingly to stick to his telegram and remain "ruefully resolute." I receive a letter from Lusch: her father insists on a meeting. I discuss it with R., who is vexed when I tell him that I should like to spare Hans a discussion after a long hot journey, and I myself would therefore travel as far as possible in his direction. I am overcome by an overwhelming sadness; R. bemoans the fact that in this matter he can only be silent; and that, consciously or unconsciously, Hans is using the situation maliciously. [*The last eleven words obliterated in ink by an unknown hand.*] We are alone at supper, my strength deserts me, and when R. reads to me some nice things about the elephants in India, I am unable to hold back my tears. However, the glowworms help, as well as lovely moonlight and a balmy night and, above all, the dear, dear children: "You mustn't be sad," says Loldi, and she is right. Oh, how right! How could I dare to complain?

Tuesday, July 5   A good night for R., although he got up once to adjust something at the windows; two stars shine down on him, he thinks they belong to the Wain and goes into Siegfried's room. But they are two single stars which he does not recognize. In the morning we listen gaily to the cock, then the peacocks and other birds. We have breakfast in the garden pavilion. R. curses his score, but he does some work on it. In the afternoon, following lunch with the entire family next door, our friend Jouk. returns and is given a jokingly hostile reception by R. Accounts of all kinds from both sides; walk in the palace gardens, illumined by moonbeams and glowworms. — A telegram from Lusch puts my mind at rest about my father, but saddens me at the same time; she says his weakness is persisting. R. suggests that I travel to Weimar, since he notices my mood. — In the morning, when I say to him, "Think well of me," he replies, "Only too well— otherwise I should be less perturbed." — (Today R. looked as radiant as a god.)

Wednesday, July 6   I tell R. in the palace pavilion that I dreamed Jouk. took his departure, Loldi ill at the same time, whereupon R.: "He seems to me like a living departure," an expression I find curious. — R. works. I go to meet our friend Countess Schl[einitz], who is charming and amiable and spends the day with us. We go for a walk in the palace gardens, and to end with, R., at my request, reads to us the first act of *El medico de su honra,* since Mimi told me that up till now she has been unable to take an interest in Calderón.

Thursday, July 7 The hot weather has cooled down somewhat. R. takes his promenade in cheerful spirits, though he has much to preoccupy him—for instance, expenditure greater than income, which means we have a debt of 5,000 marks. Lunch with our dear friend and her departure, after R. has made jokes about the way women can chat together. Letter from Lusch, who tells me that Weimar would suit her father for our meeting; however, I decide on Nuremberg, since I can travel there and back in a single day, and R. is content with that! In the evening conversation on India, brought about by Jacolliot's book.

Friday, July 8 R. had a good night, and we have breakfast in the summer pavilion in fresh and pleasant weather. Then I walk to friend Feustel's to discuss all kinds of business matters, particularly the publication of *Pars.;* the contract with Schott is bad, but I believe I have found a way of persuading Dr. Strecker to cancel it. The Emperor has refused to take up a guarantee certificate, but I do not tell that to R. He is working out the performance dates with the help of next year's calendar. He is somewhat worn out from his cure, but he organizes an outing to the Fantaisie and a trout supper at Dommayer's; this turns out very well, and we receive the liveliest proof on the highway of what it means to be traveling. R. sends Siegfried in pursuit of two journeymen whom he sees passing by, to give them alms unbidden. — We return home at 9 o'clock, very content, and then start talking about the *Ring;* R. remarks, "Wotan's rage is very fine, since it leads to the breaking of his will." — It is also decided that Jouk. will now paint R.'s portrait for me. — When, referring to the maliciousness of various people, I say to R., "Forgive them, for they know not what they do," he replies, half in jest and half in earnest, "Don't say that too often—I am using it in my next article."

(Nuremberg, 2 o'clock in the afternoon
Goldner Adler!)

Saturday, July 9 R. slept well, but during this night, too, he greeted his star (we think Mars). My night was taken up by toothache, and so we do not have breakfast together. He is run down all day, and I fear that the waters do not suit him. Visit from our friend Glasenapp from Riga; in the evening R. gets me to read aloud a fable from Jacolliot's book. Over coffee he mentioned that it was probably the beauty of India which had made all visual arts superfluous, and he adds that these probably arise simply as an expression of longing.

Sunday, July 10 R. calls me at 8 o'clock, I make haste, he and Siegfried take me to the station. Parting! Oh, how strong the feeling that we should die together! Journey as in a dream, and dreamy delight in lark song and villages. At 1 o'clock Lusch at the station, very, very good, the poor, dear child! [*Telegram to Wahnfried enclosed, announcing C. W.'s safe arrival in Nuremberg.*] Sad accounts of her father's state of health. She leaves me at 2 o'clock. The sad tune! Who could, who would wish to be happy? Hans with me from 4 to 6:30. Attempt to quell the violent outbursts on his part and overcome his unfairness toward Daniela. Unsolvable task! He begs me to stay here through tomorrow morning, since he has not, as he intended, explained to me what he wants. I consent. [*Enclosed C. W.'s telegram to R. W., sent at 7:25 P.M.:* "Good spirits, if little yet achieved, another interview arranged for tomorrow morning subject to your approval. Would then catch 1 o'clock train. Also perhaps dentist. My whole being comes to you in greeting."] Evening all 3 together! Melancholy animation!

Monday, July 11 Strange night, toward midnight I hear a loud explosion. R.'s telegram sounds more than sad: "What couldst thou do else, unhappy wife?" [*Enclosed R. W.'s telegram, sent from Bayreuth at 7:40 A.M. on July 11:* "What is now to be approved that has not already been approved, since domination of situation conceded to the other? Your telegram reached me yesterday at 9:30. May good triumph!" *Also enclosed, C. W.'s reply to this, sent at 9:10 A.M.:* "Sadly recognizing that greeting had to be thus, report with thanks and greetings that departure is 1:32 P.M. Hope to clear up misunderstandings in evening. All else when we meet."] — Second interview, Hans tells me he does not know when white is white or black is black, he no longer has a guiding star. He is overcome by a nervous twitch, we take leave of each other. I go to fetch Daniela, would like to speak to him again, but he does not wish it. Journey home in tears with Daniela. Arrival in port; R. happy to have us back again. He says that last night he organized a whist party but was in a disgracefully bad mood. What I have to report is all sad, but still the feeling of being at home together comes over us, and we can discuss it all without embarrassment. However, one thing is clear to me—that I should and can only be with him and the children, that all other contacts, with strangers and also with friends, are a trial and an injustice! . . . I enter this house after this meeting as if a new life were beginning for me, unconsoled and yet in peace, made happy entirely through his happiness, and deep in my heart the knowledge of my unatonable guilt. To enjoy the one, never to forget the other—may God help me to achieve this! — For Lusch R. plays Kurwenal's theme, "*auf eigner Weid und Wonne,*" for me he recalls —joking, yet all the same moved—the finale from *Die Schweizerfamilie:* "He's mine again!" — Kurwenal's melody is for me a reflection of my feelings in Wahnfried, pain and misery everywhere; sorrow deep within my heart, and yet the possibility of recovery. But only here, and by confining myself to those I love. [*Added in margin:* "As R. goes to bed: "You are my Heaven on earth—"]

Tuesday, July 12   A good night, also for R., and cozy breakfast in the pavilion with Lusch. R. asks her if she thinks her father would come to *Parsifal* and whether he would see him. R. feels a meeting would not be possible in the house, for what would be their words on parting? — But perhaps in the theater. — Around lunchtime R. summons us with folk songs and we go off to the Feustels' for a family meal. Strange feelings as we think of his first wife, and the completely different tone now prevailing there. R. gives drastic expression to these feelings as we drive home. In the evening friends Glasenapp, Porges, Wolz., Jouk.; with the last of these R. gets into a kind of dispute: someone says that Turgenev has immortalized our poor friend Pohl in one of his stories; R. says how ignorant the French and all the foreigners who follow them are about Germany; all they can ever bring up is sausages and pipes: "I am the first to complain about the Germans, but when I see such superficialities, then I feel like saying to them that Bismarck is quite right. And it is bad, because the French dominate the world with their *article de Paris*." When Jouk. replies that the Germans are no less prejudiced against the Russians, R. replies: "But that is something quite different; in Russia everything can be seen easily, there is a certain barbaric grace of openness, whereas we are very difficult to understand. And what we know of the Russians we know from their writers, such as Turgenev and Gogol; whereas no writer now shows us as we are, and one can't get to know us even through our best writers." — We come to the subject of "The Pied Piper of Hamelin," and R. says he has recommended the poem, yet it has happened here as with so many others: "First of all, in the urgency of youth, under the sign of Sirius, a person produces something, and then it gets worse and worse, nothing else succeeds." — He cites Halévy, above all Marschner, even Spontini, and also to a certain extent Weber, who, however, was hindered by illness: "Whereas with all the genuine fellows like Beethoven, things become more and more astonishing; it is quite impossible to say what Mozart, for instance, might not have produced." — He even cited Goethe with his *Werther:* "Except that *Faust* stands in relation to *Werther* exactly as Goethe does to Goethe." — The sketches for the stage properties spoil the mood, and finally R. tells our friends that they are boring—they expect him to entertain them. He gives each of us 5 thalers from the royalties he has received. — Letters from G. Sand to my mother, which Daniela brought me, give me the impression that French society at that time was completely different from now. As regards German society, R. says one can only ask oneself whether there were more Jews then or now, or what they were like then compared with now. He asked whether I would ever expect to find similar letters from a German woman; I mention Frau v. Kalb: "Yes, she belongs to the previous century." R. has orchestrated half a page. —

Wednesday, July 13 [*Enclosed a newspaper clipping about a cup in the theater restaurant in Berlin, bearing an inscription to the effect that R. W. drank broth from it during the dress rehearsal of* Die Walküre.] R. and I have breakfast in the summerhouse; it is somewhat sultry, and R. is feeling the effects of yesterday's lunch. We again come to the subject of Hans, and R. says, "I could be helped—he could not be helped." — I tell R. that this case makes me so clearly aware of the tragedy of life and the unatonable guilt of existence—that is to say, *my* guilt; for nobody had been better equipped than Hans to follow R., nobody more in need of guidance than he, and then I came between them— how can one ever close one's eyes to my sin? And when R. tells me, "Your crime was a beneficial folly," I may be enabled thereby to give him a look of serene contentment, but never to deceive myself about the misery of having ever been born! — All day long R. complains of his "poisoning," and he is not looking at all well. Over coffee he talks about Indian customs, which look terrible because of the misuse to which they are put by the priestly caste in dealing with the people. In the evening we spend a long time sitting in the garden. R. gets up, strolls around a little, and I see him emerging, like a shining Wotan, from one of the paths; in his hands he is carrying a glowworm, which he brings to me. (In the morning, when I spoke of Hans's curious attitude toward living with D., R. said: "Yes, people would prefer to hear you complaining, but in our house there reigns such horribly monotonous peace. The way we live together is something completely unknown to them. Think of your father, for instance, and his relationships with women.") — In the afternoon he reads the interminable program of the Magdeburg Festival, including the description of the "*Kaisermarsch.*" "Nothing but misunderstandings!" he cries, and in our thoughts we see ourselves wandering like ghosts through the *school*— the things that will be done there in the name of Wagnerianism! [*Written on a later page and referred back to this point:* "In the garden in the evening I said to R. that I was reading a manuscript about Schop. in which his theory of music is criticized. R. mentions the image of three-part writing, according to which the melody may lie only in the soprano part; this, viewed as a law, is a mistake, but one not worth mentioning, since the image is at the same time clever."]

Thursday, July 14 Still fine weather and spa cure. From America a request to supply an unpublished opera for next year's festival, from Italy a commission to compose a Mass. I tell R. that, when I see this heap of fame steadily mounting, I regret that my place is not occupied by some other woman, who would be pleased by it. R. does not at first understand my absurd remark; when I beg his pardon for it, he says, "No, idle things do not have to remain unspoken." — He is longing to return to his score and be finished with the cure. The fact that L. Lehmann has not replied disquiets both him and me. He goes off to his reading (Jacolliot's *India*) after I have related some things from the French *Revue Nouvelle* to him and we have both come to the conclusion that Germans have entirely lost the capacity to observe and to describe their observations. R. feels that what is observed by us would always look very trivial. He has business letters to write, among others to Herr Vogl, since Königsberg wants to do *Tristan*. At lunch he tells us all kinds of stories from Jacolliot. We have supper in the pavilion as Family Rest ("in all treetops is rest"). The conversation turns to my father and his relationships, and R. says it speaks badly for a man when he cannot live happily with a beautiful and noble woman, yet on the other hand remains faithful to ugly ones out of complaisance. He adds that it does tell one something about a man to see the kind of woman he can live with; he finds an ugly woman terrible, unless her face radiates kindness. In the evening the Jägers, Wolz., Porges. Once again R. exclaims, "My God, what bores you are!" An edition of Grillparzer, sent to Lusch at Hans's request, brings us to *Sappho*. R. reads the first scenes and is astonished by their flatness. "Oh, Germania!" cries R., who had read much of it in a very comic way—among other things always speaking the name "Phaon" as if it were a peacock's call.

Friday, July 15　　I meet R. in the palace gardens, where he is walking with the children and dogs. We then have breakfast in the summerhouse. The *Tagblatt* prints a description of the storming of the Bastille: "Not a heroic deed, but an event," says R. When we then talk of the meeting with Jäger, and I express my regret that he turned down engagements which were offered him, including some not very long ago, R. says: "He views himself as the Sibylline books—the more he shrinks, the more valuable he becomes." — He asks me how many Sibyls there were, and, reflecting on M[ichel]angelo's work, he says the Christian idea of this prophecy seems to him very fine, particularly in comparison with the products of Brahmanism. Everyone is yearning for the Last Judgment. We talk about yesterday's *Sappho,* the images, such as the full breast and the empty breast, and we wish we could find for the *Blätter* a critic who could denounce all this idol worship. There is probably no prospect of that—"and yet," R. observes, "I am now sometimes being quoted in political papers, and I like to think that something might yet come of our little periodical. I shall be glad when *Pars.* is finished and I can write symphonies and articles." — He works and reads. At lunch still more about *Sappho* and his father Geyer's parody. In the evening we have supper in the summerhouse and stay out in the garden till 10 o'clock. R. is somewhat despondent and irritable, he finds the abstentions imposed on him by his cure hard to bear. However, he again thinks of the Sistine Chapel and tells me he wants to be present when I next describe it to the children. He says that Brahmanism is heartless, even in its doctrine of compassion, just understanding without feeling. — When we talk of Count G.'s companion and her painting, R. says: "There is something awful about a woman who owns a studio. A woman who writes is bad enough, but people do talk, people do write letters, and the rest follows from that, even if a woman with her own study, library, and reference books is awful, too. But painting—so specific a profession—I find that dreadful." —

Saturday, July 16 I come upon R. in the garden turret with Dr. Landgraf. The cure is finished, and for his convulsive cough R. will need sea air. — Our conversation at breakfast reverts to Hans! As always, his state of wretchedness. — I tell R. that Hans has also quarreled with Herr Hillebrand in Florence over the Jews. R. observes, "All these Renaissance people are friends of the Jews." The young trees surrounding us attract our attention—they are like olive trees; we talk about caring for them, about botany, then about animals, oysters, and the wonderful way in which pearls are formed, snails and their shell-houses; we come to human beings, and I ask R. whether I am wrong in my feeling that the beautiful decorations of the ancient Germans were, so to speak, innate, rather than the result of a lengthy period of civilization. He thinks I may well be right, and then talks of the Greeks, saying that the human body meant everything to them, to the Spartans in their own persons, to the Athenians in representations, and this was also a factor in making them free. R. does not work today, but is all the same in good spirits, says one of the good things about the Jacolliot is that one can skip much of it. — Thunderstorm. In the *salon* conversation about Schott and the publication of *Parsifal*. R. decides to write to him himself. Frl. Uhlig has written. R. feels no inclination to buy the originals of his letters. Some talk about Levi, who has become distasteful to R. — After coffee R. played the *Freischütz* Overture, utterly splendid. [*Added in margin:* "Today R. talked a lot about his dogs."] In the evening Rub. plays us some things from the same work; at the duet between Agathe and Ännchen, which enchants us, R. exclaims, "*La brute germanique*—this brought that about!" The *Don Giovanni* and the *Egmont* Overtures are played by Rub., and the latter is at the same time played on me by R., causing great amusement: he gave only the *Bullrich*—as he calls it—to the sofa, the repeated high

C's on my head! — But he has many criticisms to make of the performance! — He takes leave of Lusch, with jokes on both sides, and when I, going off with R. to bed, pass through the bathroom, he says: "Do you know what I have just been telling myself? This girl will be able to say in her epitaph, 'He was fond of [me] as well, and that is a great deal, for he loved only my mother.' " [*The word "me" inserted in pencil in a different handwriting.*] — (Dannreuther reports the purchase of a tom-tom for the bells.)

Sunday, July 17   After a good night for R. we have breakfast in our bedroom—butter for the first time, but also cold! — He comes back to the subject of Schott, the letter he intends to write, and says how hard it is to attain life's flowering, contemplative thinking! As he leaves me, he feels his chest and heart, then says, "As long as that is still warm and beating, everything is all right," and he tells me how he recently enjoyed watching his watch charms moving to and fro in time with his heartbeats. It occurs to me then that his speech seems to bear a direct relationship to his heartbeat, whereas in other people the slow pulse is not strong enough to inspire the words, which are then supplied from outside, emerging either in a parrotlike fashion or as the result of laborious thought. All in him is compulsion. — We also talk about Hans in the morning, and he agrees with me when I say that for such a person death does not seem like salvation. "It is a cry," he says. He writes his letter to Feustel about Schott and Dr. Strecker in the morning, then we eat alone, since the children are on an outing in the country with the Grosses. Yesterday, when he mentioned that he had no need of friends, he added, "On the contrary, the children stand between us—an intrusion I could not do without." — Lunch passes in a welter of chat about all sorts of things, including the present-day extravagance of Paris, which R. says would still look petty in comparison with that of ancient Rome. Over coffee I relate various things, among them the rabbi's curious statement. He then reads to me his letter concerning his relationship with the firm of Schott, and it is really excellent. What he finds most disagreeable in his contacts with such people, he says, is their silence when he has explained to them how things stand. — He revises the letter in the afternoon. Then we settle down in the turret, where he drinks a glass of beer; after that we set out to view the public baths; we feel as if we are in the country, walking from our estate onto common land. The baths please us, we stroll in the finest weather across the railroad track, through the palace gardens, and home—to our own amazement, for R. these days hardly keeps the cobbler busy! Supper outside the house, conversation about Hans, R. severe—I beg him not to say that Hans must either die soon or go mad, for such statements frighten me. Wolz. and Porges arrive. R. goes through *Templer und Jüdin,* the court scene, and relates what an impression it made on him in his youth, when he saw it done by the very talented singer Hammerstein, this scene between Bois-Guilbert and Rebecca. He says he has often asked himself where it was that he gained the impressions which enabled him to set to work with such a will, and then he would recall the many good singers he has seen, both male and female. — (In the palace gardens during our walk home he told me about his stepfather, how he arranged a shooting party and sketched Frau Hartwig as she aimed at a bird; then how he, father Geyer, invited some boys to a party on R.'s birthday, and was very sad when they turned out to be rough—something prepared in such a friendly spirit proving a failure!) — Around 10:30 we say tender goodbyes, both to each other and to this so harmonious day. We gaze at the moon from R.'s room, and I remember how he recently mentioned the stars he had seen in Naples, hanging like a net let down from the arch of Heaven; I gazed upon them with my naked eye and saw them large and magical, whereas through glasses they appeared small and insignificant, and I attached much importance to this discovery. — When R. is in bed, he says, "This century has performed one good deed: it brought you into the world," which makes me laugh, yet at the same time serves as a solemn warning and an invitation to prayer. — (I am writing this on Monday to the noise of a military parade—R., when he heard it recently in the palace gardens, said, "This crude speech—as if everything always has to be uttered in rage and fury!") — Over coffee, when I say, in connection with the letter to Dr. Str., "With the interest on the sum you have demanded we can travel to Palermo or wherever we wish," R. laughs and says that is like the story of the boy and the foal. [*Two lines, incomplete and in consequence untranslatable, omitted.*] He says his mother often quoted this—she and his first wife introduced him to popular sayings. — The puppies are already coming to the supper table to beg; R. is very amused that they already know what *souper* means! — At lunch we also talked about Platen's article, begun yesterday, then about Goethe and his dramatic skill in *Faust*—"when he does not get lost"—"true, when he does get lost, the detail is still interesting." —

Monday, July 18 The children arrived home at 11:30 last night, I welcomed them from the window of my dressing room. At 5 in the morning I hear R.'s voice raised in great alarm. From the bathroom he saw Krug allowing one of the puppies to fall unnoticed into the pit! He calls the gardener's assistant, who drags the little creature out with a rake! — I read some things in the newspaper to R., including a quotation from Schopenhauer criticizing the Jews, and R. makes a joke about *"one Jew too many."* He completes his letter to

Feustel about the firm of Schott. Lunch with the Wolz.'s, the last before their departure, chatted about all sorts of things; R. talks about fjords and sailing into them, he praises Helsingør, saying he saw it from the sea and felt Shakespeare must have known it. — We talk about visiting Tribschen again some time, but R. feels it would make us melancholy. About a week ago he was singing the praises of this cherished spot and recalling all the things he wrote there; the children noted it and thought we wished to go back. He is very pleased with a turn of phrase in his letter about the stupid legacies of Schott of blessed memory, which occurred to him today! — But he is unwell, the beer did not agree with him, and we retire early.

Tuesday, July 19 R. had quite a tolerable night. We have breakfast in the turret; he is amused that the signorina calls Fidi "Sigfredo" and laughs over this "idealization which makes nonsense of everything." Recently he criticized women's names which are modeled on men's; he says the ancient Germans bore women's names. From the newspaper he reads to me a translation of a fine sonnet by Camões. The announcement of the Reich Chancellor's speeches provokes him to exclaim, "If that is the only statesman worthy of the Germans, *tant pis* [all the worse]!" — Departure of the Wolz.'s—R. goes to them around 1:30. At 1 o'clock Herr Neumann, whom R. does not dislike. Talk of a theater to be built in Berlin for the *Ring,* which the director would use as a base for the foreign tours he is starting. We drive up to the theater, great pleasure in the work going on there, a splendid sight, this stage teeming with good workmen! The whole thing a source of pride. How it rears up, huge and simple, dedicated wholly to the sublime! — Herr Neumann inspects the machinery with a view toward purchasing it. Supper in the garden, the scent of linden trees. Departure of Herr N., who asks R. whether he has forgiven him, whereupon R.: "You did nothing to me, you just didn't appreciate who I was. I could not have remained, not at any price, though I admit that it was a horrible situation for you." —

Wednesday, July 20 R. had a somewhat restless night, he dreamed first of all that I did not love him, then that he was surrounded by Jews who turned into worms. We have breakfast in the turret. R. thinks of our visit to the theater, which gave him great pleasure. "It was a very nice day yesterday," he says in referring to it. His opinion of Herr Neumann is also a favorable one, he says he has personality; and he adds that he no longer knows any Germans at all, everything has become so blurred. He recalls having maintained in the year '52 that no Jew would ever become an actor—and now! R. works on his score morning and afternoon. In between, lunch with our friends the Grosses; Adolf [Gross] photographs us in the *salon.* During his siesta

R. reads an Indian story in Jacolliot, and it fascinates him so much that he recounts it to me in the evening. We eat out of doors. Yesterday R. said to Joukowsky, referring to their mutual liking for soft things, "The Indescribable, here it is done: the pleasant and soft things one likes to put on." — He changes that today into, "The gently strokable, and we are done: the pleasant and soft things one likes to put on!"

Thursday, July 21 A toothache night robs me of the pleasure of having breakfast with R.; Lusch takes my place. At lunch all sorts of reminiscences of Schiller and, among other things, of *Fiesco;* when the ending is mentioned, Verrina plucking F. by the coat, R. says, "And sings, 'You're a full 30 years old.'" Over coffee the *Egmont* and also the *Leonore* Overtures come into his mind, and he says: "It is true that a completely different spirit has come over music—certain bits of padding in the accompaniment are no longer possible—had already disappeared in Weber, and appeared in Beethoven only when he wrote for the theater. His symphonies are entirely thematic, and one could also study his quartets of the middle period in order to learn how to avoid them." — He works. The weather is raw; we do not go out. In the evening we are visited by a singer, Frl. Wülfinghoff, which reduces R. to a veritable paroxysm of despair! He finds it horrible to have to concern himself with such beings.

[*End of the seventeenth book of the Diaries. The eighteenth book starts:* "Dedicated to my Siegfried / July 1881 / Our Father which art in Heaven!"]

Friday, July 22 The weather is cool, we have breakfast in bed. R. had a good night, and he works diligently. In the afternoon friend Brandt visits us, reporting all kinds of things about the theater. R. makes all kinds of jokes about Frl. Wülfinghoff. — He reads to us, translating as he goes, a pariah fable (about a jackal thanking the gods aloud for guiding it to some hams, thereby betraying itself, and being choked to death). He tells us many things about this pariah existence. — After breakfast, as I was going to my daily work, R. came to me and showed me Dürer's portrait of himself as a young man in the *I. Z.;* very, very charming. Then at lunchtime a dialogue in the *Fl. Blätter* between a forester and a prince which R. says is the best thing the *Blätter* has ever published. — But in the evening he is very tired.

Saturday, July 23 R. had a restless night. "You are a Devil's brood," he says to me, referring to the little drive the children and I take this morning. At one o'clock we find him well and cheerful again. He has been working. He continues to recount many things from J.'s book to us, and he says to me in the afternoon, as we are strolling together in the garden, that he will have something more to say about the elephant, a creature which has remained unchanged for all time, whereas the favored human being, with his culture, has been reduced to decrepitude. In the evening reminiscences of various operas, *Robert le D., Norma, Straniera.* — Then, however, *Die Ruinen von Athen,* the Muses' chorus, which R. particularly loves. — He has orchestrated three pages today, and we have a merry meal in the garden and spend most of the evening there.

Sunday, July 24 R. very dissatisfied with his night's rest; complains bitterly of a chest spasm; he fears that showers no longer agree with him, is ill-disposed toward the air here, which "huffs and puffs" and always makes him feel as if a policeman were grabbing hold of him. But when he talks of climates elsewhere, I succeed in diverting him to India, and our conversation soon takes a cheerful turn. He works and reaches the middle of his score (less 3 pages). Jouk.'s new Flower Maiden makes him joke about these bean blossoms being Klingsor's kitchenmaids. The weather is fine, we go for a walk together in the palace gardens and plan all sorts of outings. In the evening we are visited by friends Porges and Gross. — The group picture phantom-like, and R. says, "This is how the modern world has learned to live with art (as far as the visual arts are concerned)—through photography, which is to art what glee clubs are to music." —

Monday, July 25 R. resumes his cure and goes for a walk in the early morning, then has breakfast at my bedside. He had a tolerable night. I spend a fair part of the morning in bed. R. works on his score. Dull, wet weather. After lunch 4 of us go to old Frau Sänger's antique shop, R. soon loses patience and returns home, where he reads and works. Toward evening he comes to my room to talk to me about a mistake Wolz. has made in his article: Wolz. confuses Titurel with Amfortas and connects "his line fell to me" with the Knights of the Grail! In the evening we read Jacolliot's chapter on elephants, to the great enjoyment of the children as well.

Tuesday, July 26 We are greeted in the morning by military music; at first it gives us some pleasure, but then its vulgarity puts us off: "And only yesterday," says R., recalling the chorus from *Die Ruinen von Athen,* "I was thinking lovingly of music as something far removed from the visual world which rises up to say friendly things!" At lunchtime Herr Brandt reports that we can now inspect the Magic Garden scenery. In tones both grave and gay we discuss Germany and its constitution, particularly its princes: "I can't see myself bowing down before such people," R. says, "with the exception of the King of Bavaria; this is a good relationship, he is my friend." — The fact that our worthy gardener's assistant is being taken from his work to serve three years in the army, and will thus lose his eagerness to work and pleasure in working, arouses R.'s ire. The climate also disgusts him; we set off for the theater, and a storm greets us before we have even got beyond the foot of the hill. Inside everything in darkness; also rain is falling on the stage. Much vexation, but we decide to wait. After-noon snack in the artists' room, beer, rye bread, and butter offered us by the friendly foreman, Kranich; R. very mild and cheerful, he recalls our moods in the year 1876, we feel a similar kind of enthusiasm, the children play tag with Marie Gross and Jouk. The sun shines, Kranich calls, the Magic Garden is set up, and the tom-toms are tried out; fine bell-like sound. R. goes on stage, he speaks the words "Thou know'st where thou again willst see me" and points to the spot, feelings of unreality, life a dream, happiness! We return home with the good mayor in very high spirits. In the evening we try to read Calderón's *El mayor encanto amor* but are downright repelled by its false, trivial spirit. R. observes that one must draw a sharp line between the mythological and the Spanish subjects in C. This play reminds me of certain compositions by Tiepolo—pyramids in the air, etc.

Wednesday, July 27 R. had a restless night; and his vexation with the climate is great. But he thinks with pleasure of yesterday afternoon. — A letter from poor Nathalie gives rise to reflections on his past life. I tell him I am utterly convinced that few men (if any at all) would have seen and accepted this relationship as understandingly as he. We resolve to help the poor woman as far as lies in our power, but we do not yet see exactly how. In the evening our friends Rub. and Hump. R. somewhat vexed by the latter's lack of energy. I remind R. of the idea he expressed earlier in the day to read to us the scenes with the fairies and the artisans in *A Midsummer Night's Dream,* and to our delight he does so. The fairies so touching, as if making their appearance for the last time; the quarrel between Titania and Oberon: "One ought to show that to those French gentlemen," says R. "Has anything more delicate and refined ever been seen?" — Less and less, even in one's thoughts, can one think kindly of the Mendelssohn music in con-nection with it. — When I tell R. that I still recite the Lord's Prayer, he says, "It is an appeasement of the Will." —

Thursday, July 28 Our morning conversation revolves around *A Midsummer Night's Dream,* and we find ourselves still laughing heartily at Bottom's "Not a word of me," which shows him to be a complete original, a being such as only Nature and Shakespeare can bring forth. And how individual all his comedies are, whereas in Calderón the characters are always the same! We surrender entirely to the magic of Oberon and Titania in our memories. R. works. At lunch he looks somewhat run down. The weather is fine, we walk in the garden. Jouk. brings a Flower Maiden; the costume problem worries me a little. — The score of *Der Freischütz* is lying on the piano, and R. says, "I have just brought it out to show you who my master was," and he shows me the two orchestral bars preceding Agathe's "*Wie nahte mir der Schlummer*" aria—the wide spread of the wind instruments—"He was the first to write like that; it occurs in others in flashes, but with him it was deliberate." — Toward 5 o'clock, conference with the management committee; after the men have been together for a while, R. comes to fetch me, telling me that he does not know what to say to them. We discuss the building of the King's box, copyists, and also the subject of N[athalie] Planer (which makes R. smile incredulously at his first wife for finding it in her heart to conceal from her daughter that she was her mother!). Afterward we joke about how he dislikes being with other people in my absence. I tell him it is because he does not like talking nonsense, which I can do so well. We recall the times in Munich when he was always sending for me, and I often could not come. "Altogether the idea of me without you—that would be a nice thing!" — In the evening, thinking of the Calderón play, he reads the canto in the *Odyssey* about Aeolus and Circe. — Glorious impression; when the sacred valleys are described in which Hermes appears to the hero, R. remarks: "How sublime it is! And however great the sorrowing and suffering, Nature itself always objective, always sacred." With a final laugh about Bottom from R. in bed, we bid the day farewell.

Friday, July 29　R. had a wretched night, then a prolonged chest spasm in the morning. He stays in bed, the doctor diagnoses it as indigestion combined with a chill. We lunch without him! But after I have been with him all day, he gets up in the evening, is, however, quite exhausted. Recently R. described one of our acquaintances as being covered with "an icing of triviality."

Saturday, July 30　R. slept well, and he receives the doctor very gaily, praising the splendid summer, in which we have had 6 good days! He gets up as usual and works on his score. After lunch we drive via the Rollwenzel to Aichig, he delighting in the charming countryside. — In the evening prolonged discussion about the relationship of animals to human beings; about Nature's cruelty, which does, however, allow for the possibility of good. It is our task to conform to this possibility, and from all else arises the sorrow which afflicts us and the significance of religion. — At lunch, and again in the evening, he mentions how painful it is to see the French being always so childish, not to say silly, in their remarks about the Germans, even when, as in Jacolliot, for instance, their judgments on everything else can be so pleasing and so independent. — During our drive we talked of the possibility of our all being descended from animals, because Evchen suddenly looked to

R. like a tortoise, with her long neck, small head, and glittering eyes. R. joked of having been a flea, Loldi thought I was an elephant, R. said, "A pelican, or an ostrich with me the Moor sitting on its back." —

Sunday, July 31 We resume our conversation from yesterday, and R. says he has been thinking a lot about the subject, "to save taking refuge in words." — I express my doubts whether anything could ever be done for the world in general; one sees from politics what becomes of the efforts of great men; what they do remains, but only rarely is it carried on and the goal reached. R. returns after having already left me and says, "But the masses have a certain feeling for justice," and he cites a factual example from French history and the occupation of India. He works, and tells me that he has reached the point where he no longer enjoys his work. Our neighbors to lunch, Rub. and Porges as well, the latter reading to me and the children his piece on *Tristan*. R. rather ill at ease, as always when strangers are present, but friendly. He recalls Alwine Frommann with expressions of warmth. Dr. Landgraf comes around 6 o'clock and finds R. well. We talk of the present way of treating children, using the headmaster here as an example: without any kindness or understanding, thus making the boys insensitive and indifferent. A stroll in the garden, a mood of tenderness. — In the evening R. speaks of Rossini's *Guillaume Tell* and plays parts of it, highly praising certain things, such as the meeting of the cantons (the 3rd in particular), and laughing at others for their superficiality and vulgarity. The yodeling of Arnold and Mathilde in the love duet particularly amuses us, and I remark that they could just as well be milking cows or making butter. — "What has outraged virtue got in common with the vengeance of vice?" R. exclaims, thinking of the curious fate which has put his art on the same level as products such as these. "They don't belong together; better throw out the new entirely—except that the old is now somewhat sterile." — We talked in the afternoon about *H[ermann] und Dorothea,* and he pointed out Goethe's leanings toward efficient and genuinely strong women such as Dorothea and Elisabeth (*Götz*): "And that is how a German woman should be—for she will never be like an Indian one."

Monday, August 1 With "Now Get Up" and yodeling I am called downstairs. We have our breakfast in the summer turret. A letter from Count Gobineau about the French gives R. pleasure, he says it is so genuine. I play excerpts from *Götterdämmerung,* arranged for piano duet, with Loldi. R. says he is pleased with the work. Unfortunately in this edition there are a lot of markings such as "wanderlust motive," "disaster motive," etc. R. says, "And perhaps people will think all this nonsense is done at my request!" Sultry day, R. works—at 6 o'clock we set out on the path which goes past the mental institution, in spite of an overcast sky. We enjoy the nice scenery, rest in the woods, and return home toward 8 o'clock. During the evening R. reads to us his article "Art and Climate"; while we are discussing it, he says, "It was supposed to say something like 'Stop talking about art,' but in fact I myself did not believe in a future, all I wanted was to have nothing to do with this world and its art institutes; I planned the *Ring,* and in it I have remained true to myself: there may have been some deviations, but no concessions." R. shows us the night sky, Wain and *Coffee* Way, that is to say, long, striped, thin black clouds! [*Added three pages later but referred back to this point:* "In the evening we talked about Cherubini's Masses, and R. observed that the design of the Mass is not artistic—the need, for example, to set the whole of the Credo to music, and then the isolated pieces."]

Tuesday, August 2   Resuming our discussion from yesterday, R. says, "Need is the spur to activity; if the spur is of an ideal kind, it soon yields to insight, and activity continues, as it were, just as a means of sustaining existence, since we lack a community of noble beings." When I tell him that a statement by an eminent personality, however bold it may be, fascinates me, since it shows how a great man helps himself through life, he says to me, "You have got much further with all these questions than I have," and all day long he teases me about it, saying I get gooseflesh whenever he has a constructive thought, and that I do not believe in the art of the future. — I make an awful error: when giving the pages of the score to Herr Humperdinck, I wrap them in one of the prepared sheets. R. quite beside himself with rage; we do in fact get the page back immediately, but he has lost half an hour and is very angry. However, afterward he is infinitely kind, regrets having been so vehement toward me, while I am disconsolate about my carelessness. At lunch friend Porges irritates him, though without actually having said much, but R. assumes him to be a supporter of Schelling. When a man like Kant expresses a great thought, he declares heatedly, it falls into the hands of charlatans; and to pay attention to these is to show oneself incapable of understanding the original thought. He leaves the room during coffee but soon returns, and the conversation proceeds more calmly. Toward evening, when we return to it, we discuss the subject of supporters; one can share in sanctity, but can one in genius? Very questionable. Schopenhauer's true supporter is R., who went his own way, was himself productive, and could have given Sch. at least as much as he took from him. — In the garden R. recalled the Suleika songs and the fine manner in which Tichatschek sang them, and he goes through some of the songs. In *"Wer nie sein Brot"* he points out to us how impossible it is for music to illumine a word like *Brot* [bread], and he declares that the whole of lyric poetry is an absurdity, and no poem can be set to music; it is the task of music to enter at the point where words at their most expansive become action. — When *"Die Forelle"* ["The Trout"] is mentioned, he says, "Schumann no doubt composed the herring!" — In Schubert he is often disturbed by the prosody. We go on to *Tristan,* R. plays to us the Prelude and part of the first act, up to the second conversation with Brangäne. He says he gets more pleasure out of accompanying himself in this way, and these are divine moments for us. . . . The furnishing of Stein's room at Jouk.'s brings us to the subject of the visual arts in the 15th century and the miraculous emergence of whole generations who saw and reproduced things in this way. R. feels there is something similar in the dramatic literature of Spain, but probably Italian painting was more significant. — About the climate in Bayreuth R. improvises the following verse [*written in the Diaries in Wagner's own handwriting*]:

> *Upper Franconia, children, may have a*
>> *horrible winter;*
> *However, the summer there is*
>> *much more terrible.*
>>>> *RW.*

Wednesday, August 3   Again we do not have breakfast in the garden; R. complains about the wind and is vexed with the meteorological observations: changeable winds, showers. "Herodom" is being worked out in his mind, and once again he humorously reproaches me for not believing in the art of the future! He works, and since we are expecting our friend Stein, he writes a poem about him. Cordial general delight at this dear friend's arrival in our home. Recollections of his first visit, now almost two years ago; in between, Italy. R. in a very cheerful mood; among other things we talk about Berlin and mention that, when we were speaking yesterday about the present year, '81, and Jouk. observed that he had not achieved much, I remonstrated; R.: "And I, if I had not run away from Neumann, I should have done nothing at all!" R. pursues his joke further: "Oh, heroism! . . . Reason calls for putting up with things, but necessity compels." — Over coffee R. chides me teasingly for listening to Porges's readings on *Tristan,* and when I tell him I find it somewhat difficult to explain the concatenations to him, he interrupts me good-humoredly: "You know cuckoos? They have a habit of laying their eggs in strange nests, which elephants never do," etc. — Then exuberantly he goes on to my appearance, connects it with Porges's reading, and comes out with one comic notion after another. In the afternoon we drive to the Eremitage; he talks about Gobineau, India, the Orient in general—"It lives—is older than we are, but is still alive"—and he adds, "There is no triumph

of priesthood comparable to the unshakable faith of the pariahs." —
Supper in the garden by moonlight. "I am a happy man," R. exclaims.
— In the *salon* we take up *Tristan und I.* again, he speaks and sings it
up to the end of the 1st act; he feels he has been too drawn out in the
confrontation between Tr. and I., except when it is in the hands of
really great actors; and to convince himself of it, he reads the scene
between hero and heroine: "Neither will speak it or admit it until the
moment of the embrace, when the whole moral world seems to collapse
into ruins." — When Molly comes into the *salon,* R. says that during
the afternoon, as he was reflecting on and singing the allegro theme in
the 1st movement of the A Major Symphony, the two dogs had leapt
around him, licking him, as if saying, "What's the matter with him?"
— He says many thoughts had come to him about this divine portrait
of the world (the symphony).

Thursday, August 4   Breakfast in bed; R. finds it cold outside. But
he works, and our lunch with Stein, Köhler, and Jouk. is very merry.
Siegfried very happy to have Stein again. Talk about the German
tribal names, Vandals, Suevi, etc. Coffee in the turret. Friend Brandt
comes to invite us to say farewell to his workers. In the evening supper
in the garden and then music from *Götterdämmerung* (conclusion), to
our unutterable delight.

Friday, August 5   Still unable to have breakfast in the garden, R.
finds the air unpleasant. He works and happily shows me the inserted
half page. We are in the theater from 12 to 1 and see not only the Magic
Garden scenery, but also its transformation into a desert. All of it
magnificent—I find this technical work in the service of the imagination very affecting. For me much discussion with Stein regarding
Siegfried. In the evening a singer—Carrie Pringle—who sings Agathe's
aria very tolerably (R. observed recently that some people one could
only refer to approvingly as "tolerable," "bearable"). When he takes
up the new piano score and sees the arrangement of the first chord, R.
says, "I cannot play from this—look how Weber composed it." —
Then the duet with Ännchen is sung, the trio, and (by Jäger) the
"Durch die Wälder" aria. Afterward R. draws my attention to an
absurdity in the duet, when Max, as accompanying voice, repeats the
words *"Die Sonne verfinstert,"* etc. He says, "If I were conducting it, I
should simply say to the singer, 'Leave it out.' " —

Saturday, August 6   Breakfast in the turret. — Yesterday R. worked
out a plan to complete his score by January and then to take us via
Venice and Corfu to Athens, and from there to Palermo! — He works
diligently today to do his two pages. We say farewell to Brandt, who
eats with us and drinks to Richard's health. In the evening a sudden
thunderstorm chases us from the garden; discussions of all kinds with

our friends Rub., Jouk., Stein—about Schopenhauer, about the old form of opera, which still produced real singers. "Now all we have is music drama," says R., and he brings out the term "music drama" in such an indescribably comical Saxon accent that we all burst out laughing. "If she is called Caroline," he quotes from W. Scott's *The Heart of Midlothian,* "if it is called music drama . . ." Opera led us to *Guillaume Tell,* this to the opera's so comical notion of the Swiss; and R. speaks very much in their favor in connection with their resort to arms in '52. Over coffee, on the other hand, he spoke of Bismarck's wrongheadedness and all the legislation he has now had to repeal. At lunch about Kundry—how she should look in the desert; he thinks I may be right when I suggest that she should not fade like the flowers, but during the dramatic action should appear to be tearing her clothes, casting off her jewelry. — The fact that our friend Humperdinck has won the Meyerbeer Prize (4,500 marks) gives rise to many jokes. — Regarding Rubinstein, whom R. apostrophizes on account of some peculiar behavior, R. says afterward, "If he knew how difficult we find him, he would make things easier for us."

Sunday, August 7 Breakfast in bed, thought about August 25, in connection with which R. says, "He was a great benefit to me; as far as we are concerned, it was not necessary, but it was a good thing." He works on his score, he is now doing 2 pages every day. — The newspaper contains an article, "Kant and Darwin," and R. points out how much superior Schopenhauer's interpretation of instinct is to that of Darwin. The day brings us Herr Francke with requests for London; R. little pleased by it, the participation of Herr Pollini is particularly distasteful to him, and he says humorously how right Gobineau is to talk about "Semitized" art. In the evening the gathering of our acquaintances is a downright torture to him, and a piece of tactlessness on the part of the prize-winner puts him into a real rage. Concertmaster Francke offers to play Beeth.'s Sonata Opus 96, and does so; R. comically finds fault with the squeaking of the violin, which cannot play a melody and sounds like a Nuremberg toy. However, he asks to have the trio of the Scherzo repeated. Of the final movement he says: "Curious! One can hardly call that civilized music." — When our friends have all departed, R. complains most bitterly about all this company, and since speaking about it does not calm him down, I leave the room. A few moments later I hear him singing "O Mathilde" beneath my window, along with Jouk. He had fetched him and Stein, and he invites me to go for a walk. The four of us stroll through the deserted palace gardens by moonlight, and a lovely mood of gaiety takes hold of us.

Monday, August 8 R. is still laughing over his serenade and Stein's excuse for not singing—that Jouk. has such a good voice. Nice weather; R. works; at lunch Humperdinck's case is much pondered; R. declares that all these prize-winnings are very mysterious, the Westphalians altogether curious people, and when he talks of "veallike malice," we all laugh heartily. In the afternoon R. signs the contract with Herr Francke and in so doing again shows his great grasp of business. In the evening Ernst von Weber, much about the antivivisection movement—that the Crown Princess attended an experiment carried out by Herr Du Bois-Reymond and declared herself to be thoroughly satisfied. Then much about colonization and travel; he whets R.'s appetite for Madeira and for Zante. — Steingräber called in the afternoon to receive R.'s commission for the construction of the "bell piano."

Tuesday, August 9 R. had a good night and works both morning and afternoon. Herr von Weber's accounts of Zante are occupying his mind, and he finds it a curious coincidence that, when he opens the newspaper, he sees Zante described as "the flower of the Levant." Herr v. Stein gives me and the children an introductory talk on Schopenhauer's theory of art, and we tell R. about it at lunch. Stormy weather keeps us indoors. Dr. Strecker writes to R.—regret at not being able to oblige him as they would like. R. starts a reply which is so humorous that he laughs as he tells me about it, and in the evening we read the whole correspondence to our friends. Then R. sings the scene between Evchen and Sachs, and afterward complains good-humoredly to me that it has not been sufficiently recognized. When I tease him about that, he says—completely in earnest—that he is really glad, when he looks at something of his own after a period of time, to find it good; for during his work on it—even now, on *Parsifal*—he gets the feeling that it is all bad.

Wednesday, August 10 Weather still dull, and R. has a chest spasm! I read to him a letter from Malwida and discourage him from talking. Then I set out for the Eremitage with poor friend Rubinstein, who has once again lost his composure, and listen to his laments. R., to whom I relate this on our return, is astonished and jokes about it, properly pulling my leg about it in fact, but he agrees with me that at times there is nothing else one can do, though he says that to an onlooker it seems curious and extravagant. When I compare myself with Jungfer Züss, he says, "Today it was more like Catherine of Siena!" He thinks I am looking well, and when Dr. Landgraf says the same thing, he remarks that it is because of my good deeds. Alas, if only it were possible to help by showing a willingness to do so! Much with Stein yesterday and today about Siegfried's education. In the evening merry chat with our friends, he advises Rub. to get married; at lunch he said to us: "The Italians—they eat the Jews for breakfast!" — Then he talks about the second theme in the *Euryanthe* Overture and plays another one by Marschner, so similar that we have to laugh heartily, saying it is probably the result of "training." We talk of opera: "All the same," says R., "one feels a sort of pitying respect for it when one sees what has been achieved in this absurd genre." — While we are teasing Stein over the fact that he is about to be made a professor, R. says it is perhaps not a bad thing to have to go through this in a place like Halle. "In the same way," he says, "I had to go through the complete career of an opera conductor. And when one looks back on it later, one tells oneself that nothing could have been different from the way in which one experienced it." — Talking of the war and the peace treaty of 1871, R. said, "It is impossible to be too cynical about how heads of state play around with the destiny of whole nations." — When Jouk. told us that Herr v. Weber had not once looked at him, R. joked, "I should have introduced you as 'Jouk., who did not educate Tsar Alexander III.'" — Recently, when R. mentioned the pipes of the Prussian military band, he observed that there was something utterly wild about them: "But to these gentlemen it is all the same whether they look like grand moguls or whatever." —

Thursday, August 11 In the morning the newspaper brings us Tappert's article on 8 letters from R. to Herbeck, which have just been published in the *Neue Freie Presse*. He is so disgusted that he throws the newspaper away. At lunch we discuss the aspect of our law which makes a letter the property of the receiver. Coming back after breakfast to my walk with Rub. yesterday, he says jokingly that he is going to have a diver's outfit made for me and Malwida, for the rescue of people of all sorts. Then he jokes about having been given eternal youth and when I say, *"Brüderlein fein,"* we laugh heartily, for with him one can always talk playfully about old age. After lunch he goes on from the bold joke that Stein should get his father to marry to the question of emigration, alliance with the Boers: "Even if one doesn't live to see the idea put into effect, at least one has got a goal, which can be left to another generation to achieve." — He is much occupied by his work on his score, he shows me how he has had to turn something he intended as a quartet into a sextet. — An article about anti-Jewish demonstrations makes him remark, "That is the only way it can be done—by throwing these fellows out and giving them a thrashing." Regarding emigration, he observes that in view of the bad times which would be bound to come, a fund of a billion marks should be raised and used to cover all the costs of establishing the new community there. The people to be selected and the religious basis of the community laid down beforehand. — In the evening R. spends some time in the garden and then invites us to go for a walk in the palace gardens. After that we play a merry game of whist. (He has written to Dr. Strecker, a cheerful and friendly letter.)

Friday, August 12 In the *Illustrirte Z.* there is a horrifying picture of the Algerian rebel leader Abu Hema, which raises in us all kinds of reflections about mixed races, and a very moving article about Körner with Friesen, Lützow, and some others on the evening before his death. This magazine shows us a completely different epoch and different—joyfully inspired—human beings. In Körner R. sees our friend Stein over again—"on the evening before his emigration," I add. Toward noon Jouk. brings along a picture which gives us pleasure; yesterday evening, when R. withdrew for a brief rest, Lusch had surrounded me in my chair with Oriental rugs, Jouk. brought out the globe, and, getting the children to work it, I asked Stein to name the places to which one might emigrate, pointing to them with a finger. Our friend has now charmingly recaptured this moment. R. is delighted with it. "That is how it should be," he says, "always seeing and doing things." Our climate (the weather is again raw) keeps bringing R. back to the question of emigration, he says Siegfried should be brought up with this in view, and then Stein would have two generations before him. Stein gives his second talk in the afternoon, in R.'s presence—about Sch.'s views on architecture; it is very good, and R. is very pleased with it, saying that Stein is our pride. — In the late afternoon I practice my part in the *Götterd.* piano duet with Lusch. R. comes in, listens to me, praises me! Then I to him: "The girls are gone now!" And he shows me the page of his score and again explains to me the problem of sextet or quartet. At supper he relates a nice children's legend about Krishna from Jacolliot, and then talks about the divinity of the Gospels, due to their artlessness: "And then, suddenly, all the suffering!" he exclaims. The Greeks have also been in his mind, the connection between their history and their epics; the Battle of Marathon, the 1,000 Plataeans, the retreat of the 10,000 bring him to the *Iliad,* whose subject is little to his taste; he is repelled by the quarreling over Briseïs, and "instead of Agamemnon's being put to death, Hector is killed, for whom one has more sympathy than for Hector." [*The second "Hector" altered in pencil in another handwriting into "Achilles."*] When he goes off for a short rest after supper, we look through Dürer's *Life of the Virgin Mary,* which contains among other things one of R.'s favorites, a picture of Saint Joseph planing with the help of angels. I do not know why the verse *"Es waren hochbedürftige Meister, von Lebensmüh bedrängte Geister"* ["They were masters in great need, oppressed by life's labors"] comes to my mind with such force that tears spring to my eyes. I recall my overwhelming feelings when I heard for the first time of these sorely tried beings, and what it meant to me suddenly to see these masters, whom one likes to regard as joyfully triumphant conquerors, revealed in their *Ecce homo*. And it is Dürer who brings this back to me! — R. comes to join us, he supports Jouk. against me in the feeling that the Pergamon reliefs are the work of a school, whereas the early Renaissance works in the same Berlin museum are the expression of a single idea. He talks about *Actors and Singers,* which he wants to read again in connection with "Herodom and Christianity"; he feels he did justice to singers and actors there. Later we play whist.

Saturday, August 13 The weather ("in winter it is hardly possible to skate, in summer hardly possible to swim," is R.'s summary) as well as observations of external happenings—among them the Berlin Congress and its treatment of the Oriental problem—arouse in us thoughts of a complete withdrawal from everything after the production of *Parsifal*. "To depart like Lycurgus," says R., "and then see what they make of my ideas." In the afternoon he stands at the glass door of the *salon* and considers whether it would be right to tear the children away from their roots. At lunch much about the climate, but he is busy with his work, with which he is thoroughly pleased. In the evening our friend Cyriax; in his cheerful, frank way R. asks him about his income from his business, and thinks it rather small. Then we talk about large cities, and R. disputes that poverty is easier to bear in Paris than in London. In the evening the *Pastoral* played by Rub.; R. says one must take care not to fall into emotional accents with it. Here and there in the first movement he exclaims, "That is done with a cadence." He deplores the repeats, which make it all sound insignificant, and finds the whole thing has something of the spirit of 18th-century *bergerie*. At one point he quotes Polonius: "Pastoral, pastoral-comical, tragical-comical-pastoral." — When I tell him afterward that the piano often sounds very painfully thin to me, he says: "Oh, how we think the same in everything, it is terrible!" — He is becoming more and more averse to associations. (He has rejected the contract with Frankfurt.) A letter from Herr Vogl about the role of Kundry for his wife reminds R. all too clearly of the whole dreary theatrical scene, and he bemoans having to work with such vain people. He says that after *Parsifal* he will write nothing but symphonies.

Sunday, August 14 R. slept tolerably well, but the irksome weather—constantly cold and gray—annoys him. He works, and today completes page 201. In the newspaper there are again reports of Jew-baiting in Russia, and R. observes that this is all that is left, expression of a people's strength. He says, "Gobineau is right, they—the Russians—still see themselves as Christians." We spend an afternoon at Jouk.'s. R. comes over, looks at the photographs of the Sistine Chapel, recalls

Nietzsche's childish and malicious remarks about it: "How bad a person can be, just in order to make an impression!" — The evening passes in chat; among other things, the relationship of the earth to the sun, and that the latter is cooling off and gets its heat from bodies falling into it. R. reads the conclusion of G.'s work. I feel he is right, but it all seems to me rather insignificant in comparison with the death of a great person; if such have to perish, what do masses and celestial bodies matter?

Monday, August 15 [*Enclosed in the Diaries a poem of thanks and greeting sent by Wolzogen from Krokan, Norway.*] Bad day, which for R. begins with chest constrictions. He takes his mind off it with work, but in the afternoon his eyesight starts flickering. We set out for a walk, he and I, but soon turn back; first of all he is pained by the faces he sees, and then he finds the air unpleasant. In the evening he reads to us from Jacolliot a somewhat overdetailed account of the funeral of a Brahman, a repellent picture of exploited superstition; after that, "to restore your spirits," the dialogue in Thucydides between the Athenian and the Melian, and we are brought to life again by its simple, plain, so highly civilized language. This reminds R. of Pfaffe Lamprecht, and he reads aloud his favorite passage between Candacis & Alexander. — "I find it insulting," R. says to himself as he is changing his clothes; he is thinking of our walk and the faces which on top of everything else gape at him.

Tuesday, August 16 R. was up part of the night, he feels very unwell and is deeply depressed by the horrible weather. But he works, eats with us, and even attends Stein's talk. The last, however, with some effort—he then takes to his bed, very exhausted and at the same time agitated. We spend a while together, I tell him I should also like to go to bed, and as we lie there, we think of Egill and his daughter, who wanted to die yet did not. We get up, laughing; R. has his tea alone in the *salon* and sends to our table a word of praise for Stein on his talk. We then gather around him, and from Gobineau he reads aloud the parts of the chapter he intends to quote (in the 4th volume, where "*l'homme est l'animal méchant par excellence*" ["the most vicious animal of all is Man"] occurs). The doctor comes, prescribes pills, at 10 o'clock we go off to bed. — Wandering around my room, R. finds a volume of G[oethe]'s poems and reads "The Metamorphosis of the Animals," which he finds rather bad, in both form and content.

Wednesday, August 17 The night was not as bad as the previous one for R., but all the same disturbed, and he spends most of the day in bed. The weather is very bad, and R. exclaims, "Oh, if the wind were to carry off the d—— theater, I should certainly not build it again." And when I say something flattering to him, he says, "We have nothing to do on this earth except love each other." When I talk to him about the electrical experiments in Paris, he says, "Yes, we are well on the way to becoming cretins." — He reads Stein's article about *Wilhelm Meister's Wanderjahre*. In the evening he attempts to play whist, but it soon tires him. — Today he gaily compares Lohengrin with the mandrake being pulled out of the bottle (the Grail the bottle).

Thursday, August 18 R. had a better night, and we are cheerful at breakfast; he thinks, among other things, about Goethe's hexameters and observes: "People should write such things only if they are able to. One must be out of one's mind to write hexameters." Dr. Helferich visits us for the purpose of examining the children's figures. The costume designer from Frankfurt-am-Main also visits us and pleases us with his liveliness and understanding; we feel we might do very well with him. Jouk. gives him the sketches. Dr. Helferich tells us some interesting things about his profession. But the evening brings us a rather unsuccessful rendering of the "Entrance into the Temple of the Grail" by Porges and Humperdinck and a performance by Rub. of the *Msinger* Prelude which also does not appeal to R., producing a discordant atmosphere which finally dissolves into jokes. "Oh, were I but rid in my halls of Isis and Osiris!" exclaims R. And before going off to sleep, he says he feels as if he is living amid "rotten lettuces." [*This last sentence obliterated in ink by an unknown hand.*] — (In the evening he recalled his visit to Eisleben and complained with great bitterness about the neglect of this venerable town, also of the cathedral in Magdeburg; from there he goes on to a condemnation of the Prussian character, which had no feeling for or pride in preserving such monuments.)

Friday, August 19 R. had a somewhat restless night, with wild dreams. — Another gray day; we take leave of our friend Rub. as from an unsolvable but affecting enigma. Dr. Helferich also leaves us. At lunch Stein and Jouk.'s socialistic talk leads us to Socrates, from him to Plato and Xenophon. Over coffee a glance through the *Illustrirte Z.* produces from R. the remark that in all German celebrations (Kyffhäuser here) a beer glass is the main thing. The Munich shooting match and the procession displease him greatly—like all masquerades. — Toward 5 o'clock, after he has written his page, we drive to Bürgerreuth, to which the children have gone ahead; he is worried about the preparations for *Pars.*—the singers, etc.—he feels there is a lack of true enthusiasm. The sky is overcast, but our stay on the hill is pleasant —except that R. is downright horrified by the people there, mainly women and, to look at them, old maids. On our return we take delight in the playing puppies, which R. recently compared to his heap of cupids (*Tannhäuser*), telling me that he had wanted a heap like that resting on the ground and then suddenly shooting up to fly in the air and dispatch their arrows from there. — In the evening he plays and sings "*An die entfernte Geliebte*" to us, greatly moving us with it. "The whole of Schubert can be found in this," he says, and that brings him on to Nietzsche's maliciousness (about Schubert and Beeth.) and the whole dismal experience! The eternally denying, head-shaking trees give us a sad picture of life—resign yourself, resign yourself.

Saturday, August 20 R. has a chest spasm and feels run down, but he works and begins a poem to the King for the 25th. — The sky clears toward evening, and we take a walk through the meadows. In the evening friend Feustel, discussion of the relationship with Dr. Strecker; friend Feustel thinks that R. might get his way. A newspaper article about socialist movements in China in the 12th century produces from R. the remark that we are behind the Orientals in everything, starting with our imagining that the world began with us.

Sunday, August 21 R. had a restful night, and he sketches the 4 verses of his poem. "I am lavish," he says gaily, after joking about the fact that, when one is lost for a rhyme and nothing comes to mind, "I write 5 verses." — At lunch he recalls the splendor of the Gulf of Naples and says that after seeing that, one cannot really be satisfied with anything else, on account of its magnificent lines; he compares Vesuvius to Marke—something belonging to us, familiar, yet exotic! The newspaper prints a nice letter written by my father about R. (1849): "Oh, what Liszt is—that he is a being *hors de concours*—this I know; I have only to tap my brain case to see him complete before me. But I deplore the fact that through bad influences we have become strangers to each other—or, rather, we are not really that, but we mean so little to each other." — In the afternoon, after we have been watching the dogs together, he comes upstairs and shows me the 4 verses! . . . Oh, silence, silence! . . . In the evening the tenor Herr Winkelmann, who had already presented himself during the afternoon. He sings a few things from *Rienzi;* our conversation turns to the difficulty of doing justice to works like *Die Zauberflöte* or *Die Entführung* in our gigantic modern theaters. R. also observes that the introduction of Shakespeare onto our stages sends us into the theater with different expectations. And singers have now lost the naïveté needed for Osmin, etc. R. says that he and other serious-minded people had even enjoyed *Der Dorfbarbier*—that would be impossible today. — R. has advised me to study orchestral scores in order to appreciate fully the joys of musical lines.

Monday, August 22 R. completes his poem and sends Siegfried to me with it around midday, in return I send him the box! As we go in to lunch, he says, "The last verse should have been quite different, but one can never know," and later on, "Oh, nonsense, we shall not write poems to each other!" He has also written to Herr v. Bürkel about the construction of the royal box. At lunch a dispute flares up about Latin beauty and German beauty; I come out too strongly in favor of the latter and somewhat offend Jouk., so that R. says I am wrong. However, peace is then restored in the summerhouse, when we concern ourselves with the costumes. — Some old pieces of jewelry have been sent to us to look at, and from them R. chooses some necklaces for me, saying I have none! — Since Herr Winkelmann is too run down to sing, R. takes out Loewe's ballades and sings them in his usual splendid fashion, pointing out that it is precisely these thoroughly amateurish works which reveal such German talents. — As we part in the evening, he says, "We shall live as long as we love each other—that is bad, we shall never die!" — [*Added at bottom of page:* "Someone inquires whether Loewe did not write a '*Braut von Corinth*'; this leads us to Goethe's poem, which seems to us almost childish—at any rate not in the best of taste. — On the other hand, a short conversation with Eckermann gives us much pleasure. (The book was lying on the table, R. picked it up.)"]

Tuesday, August 23 A newspaper article about medieval peasants contains a poem in which the knight calls himself an *Edelkunne;* the expression pleases R. greatly, also that the peasant is called "*Baumann*" (instead of "*Bauer*"). Then he begins his article and says gaily that he went through his old ones and is scribbling a new one from them! Friend Gross is with us at lunch, which brings some business talk, and afterward photographs are taken in the *salon* and in the garden. J. brings along the Grail's chalice, and it is accepted by R. Telegram after telegram on account of Seidl, who, enchained by Frau [Reicher-] Kindermann, is reluctant to come, which seems to me to mean that we must dispense with him. Drive to the Fantaisie, very nice, the children going with their friends to the Schweizerei and then through the village, R. and I by a short path to Dommayer's to await the rest of the company. Gay spirits. In the evening Rienzi's recitative and Rienzi and the Cardinal, followed by "*Fanget an*" and "*Am stillen Herd*"! As we are going into the garden in the afternoon, R. recalls the beginning of *Henry V* and exclaims: "How utterly and incomparably inexplicable Shakespeare is! The way he allows the death of Falstaff to be related by a boy, who then dies a heroic death! — And how the ground is prepared, as it were, for the subsequent shallowness of the King, as revealed in the French wooing—all of it unspoken, but it is all there. Nowhere else can one get to know the world as one can through him."

Wednesday, August 24 R. writes his article and is satisfied with its beginning. Then he coaches Herr Winkelmann, who proves teachable; but R., as he tells me, is very tired of always having to begin again from the beginning and having to work with bricks instead of marble blocks. Our lunch is somewhat subdued because of his weariness; over coffee the subject of race comes up again, and R. says he is writing his article with Gob. in mind. — He takes a rest and then calls me into the garden, where we again get much amusement from the family life of the dogs. In the evening he plays the *Parsifal* Prelude in an indescribable way—almost too much rapture! As we go to bed, he calls out to me, like Othello, "And when I love thee not, chaos is come again!" That leads him back to Shakespeare, and he says others always seem to skirt a subject, whereas he is always so direct.

Thursday, August 25 Ludwig Day! To church, but beforehand set out roses and boxes for R. He is delighted, and when I return home, it is to a heavenly atmosphere. He takes the cover downstairs to show our friends, telling them that it is the children's work. Seidl has now joined them, and R. makes the merriest jokes about his relationship with Frau H. [Reicher-]Kindermann. The children also in very cheerful spirits. R. works on his article, then, after spending some time with me in the garden [*added later but referred back to this point:* "with delight in Marke, whom he calls 'one of Nature's original themes, completely undecorated' "], he arranges for a drive. In the evening Herr Winkelmann sings the "Forging Songs," and Seidl plays the "Entrance into the Temple of the Grail" to the delight of us all and to R.'s complete satisfaction. — Today R. sings the melody from *Die Msinger* and says, "When a melody leaves no place to draw a breath, then it is beautiful." — He talks of cuts he intends to make in *Tristan,* including the third act, since it goes beyond the permissible—and all through the day he keeps saying tenderly to me, "All that now remains for us is to die with each other—we shall die together!" — The photographs have turned out very well. (At breakfast, I do not remember in what connection, I found myself repeating the line "Hurrying clouds, you aerial sailors." R. says, "Those were the things which made Schiller so popular—one felt there was no poetry but that.")

Friday, August 26 R. has a slight headache, but he quickly recovers; he is pleased to see in the *Ill. Z.* a picture of Schloss Püchau, to which our little puppies have now been sent. He works on his article. The presence of the Sachse-Hofmeister couple at lunch threatens at first to disturb him a little, but we slide past the difficulties. And since the weather is quite summery, we first sit in the pavilion and then take a drive with M[arianne] Brandt, who has just arrived. After that there is work to be done until suppertime, and the evening is spent in chat. A lovely starry sky shines down upon us, but R. and I are still feeling strange in this changed existence. "Oh, were I in my halls," etc., he whispers to me.

Saturday, August 27   First rehearsal between Kundry and Parsifal! R. divine in all his instructions, in his identification with, his clear understanding of his characters, down to their slightest movement. But unfortunately little hope that he will be followed. Lunch with the entire small company, the weather overcast, but R. is in good spirits. In the evening he brings out on the spur of the moment the piano score of *Otello,* and with Seidl and M. Brandt he sings the trio from the first act with unbelievably comic effect. Because of this the evening takes on a very gay color, but our feelings with regard to the production of *Parsifal* are subdued. He sends off his letters to the other artists. [*Entered on the following page but referred back to this point:* "At supper Herr Wink. tells us that he spoke to the Duke of Brunswick, and that he affects a broken German, somewhat like the Hungarians; also all his servants are French!"]

Sunday, August 28   The weather still dull. R. concentrates all the objections he has against the appearance and the singing of M. Brandt on the fact that she cannot pronounce the letter *s.* He said very emphatically at lunch yesterday that she would have to consult a "mouth doctor." But he admits with a sigh that not a single member of the public would hear an *s!* — Again today at 1 o'clock rehearsal of half of the scene between P. and K.; in the evening, from Herr Wink., bits of the conclusion and the 3rd act. Weariness amounting almost to despair. But his rendering of the 3rd act of *Siegfried,* that is to say, Siegfried's entrance and awakening of Brünnhilde, brings us out of our ill-humor. The evening concludes with Neapolitan songs, sung by Pepino. R. praises P. highly and tells me he felt as if a Greek sky were opening above him. — ("I play wrong, but correctly," R. said to Herr Humperdinck as he took over the accompaniment from him.)

Monday, August 29   R. slept well, but complaints about the weather are now part of our daily bread. He works on his article and tells me that he has had a sudden inspiration, but he does not want to tell it to me just like that, since it would look like a joke, and it is meant seriously. Working on the rose portière. Since M. Brandt has a cold, there are no rehearsals, and we are by ourselves. Seidl's personality is discussed, and R. points out how he makes up for his lack of education with a silent manner. Fine weather, though very autumnal. R. orders coffee in the turret, I read passages from a pamphlet, *Germany and Its Professors,* by the spiritualistic Prof. Zöllner. Among other things, a note to Empress Eugénie from the Jesuits, very confused and farfetched stuff. R. arranges a drive via the Fantaisie as far as the redoubt, and fine weather permits a glorious view; the short stop at Dommayer's does not fail to have its usual beneficial effect on R., and he talks gaily to the host, says he enjoys speaking to such people, and continues, "One notices how isolated from the people one feels when, going through the fields and arriving in remote villages, one talks to the countryfolk." As we set off on the drive home, he exclaims, "Oh, this blissful day—not to have to wrestle with impossibilities!" [*Added later:* "During the walk he thought of the line 'Let the phantom do what it will,' in connection with the freedom we allow friends and children, and this leads him to a panegyric on *Faust* and inspirations of this kind: 'This is Goethe. If someone vaunts *Iphigenie* or *Hermann & Dorothea* to me, I should say, "Well and good, those were experiments, but *Faust* and also *Wilhelm Meister's Wanderjahre*—those are the man himself!"' "] — In the evening much chat in the gayest of spirits; the air was invigorating and certainly did R. good. He looks at the family picture and asks Jouk. to do it in oils, never mind the "mistaken attempts at deception," as he merrily expresses it.

Tuesday, August 30 R. had a good night and, after the rug has been hung up, he goes to his work, which he then reads to me. Friend [Marianne] Brandt enlivens the house with solfeggios and the sounds of Kundry, which at times get on R.'s nerves. But he goes to his score after writing a friendly but determined letter to Dr. Strecker on the question of publication. He was somewhat out of spirits in the evening, but he soon recovers and gives us dramatic accounts of theater experiences from his youth, including *Fortunatus' Abenteuer* in Vienna, splendidly imitating the Viennese accent. — To me he is extravagantly kind; when I come downstairs in the afternoon, he says he is quite beside himself at the thought that he has been unfriendly toward me. And in the evening, "The fact that I have put up with all the vexations and the difficulties shows what a good life I have—but if I am not in harmony with you, then it all comes to a halt." — "In music lies hopeful resignation," R. says today. [*A sentence based on untranslatable word play omitted.*]

Wednesday, August 31 A good night for R.; he calls out to me in bed, "Anyone who finds you comparable will have to reckon with me!" The rugs give him pleasure, and he works. Early in the morning an idyllic scene pleased him greatly: two ducks, which the cook bought, bathing while the whole poultry yard looked on; R. gives orders that the happy birds are not to be used in the kitchen. A letter from a vegetarian in Slavonia amuses us, and otherwise the day passes harmoniously, with a drive to the Grosses' and solfeggios and exercises from friend [Marianne] Brandt. Only a piece of inconsiderate behavior on the part of Herr Köhler, which strengthens the decision to dismiss him, causes me serious concern—a dismal experience! — Loldchen unwell; R. says she looks like the Medusas we saw among the Etruscan graves near Perugia; talking of these, he goes on to say, "Curious, no sign of emotion, and that round shape, like a full moon—a completely Greek culture." — At lunch we discuss the possible use of the palace of the Office of the Royal Household as a residence for a prince, which produces a comment on Bismarck's manner of dealing with people he does not like! — In the evening R. goes through "Hagen's Watch"— to see, as he says, what he has stolen—and he then links Waltraute's scene onto it; our good [Marianne] Brandt sings it—beautifully, in spite of her hoarseness, making an indescribable impression. (Yesterday, before going to bed, R. sang something from *Tristan* and, delighted with its rapturous melodic beauty, wondered where it came from: "Oh, of course, it is from *Tristan!*") — A quotation which suddenly came into his mind—"That is a seignorial right in Arras"—leads him to the incredibly high moral tone which pervades Schiller, and we then pass on—I do not know how—to the dialogue between Odysseus and Circe in Plutarch, finding all our old delight in it. R. calls our good [Marianne] Brandt, whom I like very much, pure animal, but in a positive sense: there is nothing in any way false about her. And when someone says that everybody looks like some animal, R. says, "I look like a flea—hence the King's favor." — All kinds of memories of Königsberg, of the first days of his first marriage, are brought back to him by Frl. Brandt's mentioning the theater in Königsberg. R. tells how the students hissed him, because they thought he wanted to oust the conductor!

Thursday, September 1 R. had a good night's rest and faces the day, apart from the bad weather, cheerfully. He works on his article and also on the score. In the latter he makes a small harmonic change in *"holde süsse Mutter"* and says, "One could spend a lifetime working on a thing like this." Our good [Marianne] Brandt does some studying in our house; R. turns to Handel, takes out the "Ode for Saint Cecilia's Day" and asks M. Br. to sing his favorite piece from it, "The soft complaining flute"; she does not know how to sing it and R. demonstrates it to her. He also plays the march from *Judas Maccabaeus,* which he likes enormously, and at supper he maintains that Handel must surely have composed "God Save the King": "The fellow was a scoundrel, but a genius as well." — His appearance reminds me somewhat of Rubens, and when I recognize elements of Beethoven in the march, it occurs to me that in his *Battle of Vittoria* Beeth. had no better model for the English character than Handel's style, and the two then became identical. — Before lunch I was led to my room, and I laugh heartily on seeing that R. has had Egusquiza's portrait painted over by Jouk.! Some days ago he reproached me for keeping all these bad portraits of him; he also dislikes the Lenbach sketch; he says he does not know what to think of me! All in the gayest manner—and now the Spaniard has turned quite pink! — Today was R.'s Saxon day; he says, among other things, "When I sit here *cackling* at the piano . . ." And he talks of *Fitji*. And he teaches Siegfried to whistle with him and to answer him! — In the afternoon, as we are strolling in the garden, he talks to me about his article, and in the evening he comes back to it, saying that he hopes to have developed Gobineau's views to the extent that there may now be something even consoling about them, although he has accepted these views in their entirety. — In the evening he exclaims: "How little it speaks for human intelligence that they settle down in places with such climates and—have beggars among them. What can one make of such a species?" — Mentioning the luxury he saw in Herr Fould's house in Paris, he says, "Marble statues stand and gaze at me, yawning—why have you been brought here?" —

Friday, September 2 R. had a good night, and the day brings the very pleasant assurance that Marianne Brandt will be able to sing Kundry well. R. summons me downstairs, since he is so pleased with her, and she touches us very deeply with her first words to Parsifal. Her outward appearance, we feel, can be overcome, since, as R. tells us, "Everything about Kundry is costume—her ugliness, her beauty—all of it a mask." — The affair of the newly installed Bishop of Trier, Dr. Korum, who has in the end been exempted from taking the oath, brings R. back to the manner in which Bismarck deals with things, even the struggle with Rome! I read a reporter's account of a visit to Dr. Korum, in which the Bishop's amiable reserve reveals all the superiority of the Catholics: "They are the only ones among us who still follow in the footsteps of the Brahmans," R. says. — R. is much taken up with his work, and he tells me in the evening that its significance depends on the detail and the settings. We play whist, I always with R., since he is quite happy to lose with me, but cannot bear me to win against him. Still dull and damp weather, we do not go out of doors—R. says the air *barks* at him. — President Garfield's condition seems to have improved slightly, and R. tells me that, when he said farewell to his wife and asked her to return to their home, telling her that, unless a miracle occurred, their final separation was nigh, his wife is reported to have replied with great energy, "The miracle will occur!" And now his condition is indeed said to have taken a turn for the better! — We talk of separations, and how irremediable they are—that is to say, the impressions they leave behind. And R. recalls old times and all our many torments! "Things have become much nicer, much nicer," he repeats. — There was a discussion about the desire for money, one that does not affect me. R. says, "Certainly if it weren't for you and the children I don't know what I should need money for, but as it is, in a saloon carriage on the railroad, for instance, with all the children's heads at the windows, or in the theater watching them sideways leaning forward in excitement—that is joy." —

Saturday, September 3 Dull day, rain, gray skies, R. has a backache. He works on his article and also on his score. All day long, he tells me, the sounds of the mourning music—Herzeleide—which accompanies Parsifal on his second entrance into the Temple have been going through his mind. We play whist in the evening. R. went for a walk in the palace gardens by himself and then visits our neighbor Frau v. Schöler, in whose house we meet. In the evening the conversation turns to costumes, and R. says, "What makes the Greeks so noble is their simplicity—suddenly, amid all this Assyrian and Persian luxury, the divine simplicity of their costumes and their buildings!"

Sunday, September 4 The children and I finish reading *Beethoven* with Stein, then Lusch and I play the Prelude to *Götterdämmerung,* after which R. reads his article to me, and I float in the sublime. At lunch we had Herr Humperdinck, whom R. is able to praise for the way he accompanied Marianne Brandt. R. and I go for a walk, it is a fine day, the life of the dogs here a complete idyll; R. turns the fountain on, is pleased with it, appears as Wotan in a blue robe, and in the evening reads to us many poems by Hafiz. Beforehand he insisted on having the whole household, along with our friends, admire the fountain! While I am changing upstairs, he enlarges upon music and melody, and at the conclusion of the evening he wonders whether he will perhaps be entirely forgotten, ousted by someone who will make things easier for the audience. However, he concluded, "it won't be easy to make it easy." —

Monday, September 5 Farewells, departure, saw Loldi off in Hof at 4 o'clock; R. reads [Gobineau's] *Trois ans en Asie,* he is pleased with the countryside in the Erzgebirge, but most of all with Tharandt. (He, I, Eva, and Siegfried!) — The 2 elder girls in Kaibitz, Isolde in Bug.

Tuesday, September 6 A good night at the Hôtel Bellevue [in Dresden]; the children's first walk is to the dentist's; I leave them there and visit the gallery alone, afterward going with R. to Dr. Jenkins and then back with all of them to the gallery. R. is pleased by some of the things I show him, including Bol's picture of the Holy Family at rest. "A lovely picture!" he exclaims, and as we are talking about it, he says, "Perhaps going somewhat beyond art, since the subject in itself has a sentimental appeal." — We had breakfast beforehand at the Belvedere, and R. was pleased by its lovely surroundings. While I was in the gallery by myself, R. heard the chorus rehearsing the *Holländer* in the theater as he was shaving, and he was as pleased by the good voices as he was annoyed by the tempi. He sends word to the chorus master, asking to have it taken a bit slower. We have lunch on the Bellevue terrace at 2 o'clock and then drive through the beautiful park to the zoological gardens, where the elephant and other animals give us pleasure, but the people and their absurd behavior with the animals very little. In the evening *Holländer.* — For me much emotion, for R. a good impression of the singer [Therese] Malten, and he tells her so immediately afterward in her dressing room. He shows me and the children many things from his childhood years, including the old Kreuzschule. — The theater, quite imposing from the outside, satisfies us very little inside.

Wednesday, September 7 R. had a good night; in the morning he stays indoors reading *Trois ans en Asie* with much enjoyment, but he is interrupted by a visit from the conductor Schuch, who, however, as he tells us, was very modest, and he was able to put him right on the tempi without difficulty, particularly in the ballad (beginning too slow, continuation too fast). I stroll through the gallery with Evchen, then we go to the dentist's, where the main joke between us is the additions R. makes to a letter I am writing to Jouk.! We have a late breakfast at the Belvedere, and since I have been telling R. much about the Canalettos, he says of a man who keeps looking at him, "He takes me for a Canaletto!" We drive out to the Waldschlösschen, where R. has a glass of beer and also gives one to the coachman; since the latter drinks very slowly, R. is greatly amused when the waiter remarks, "The coachman can't lift his elbow." — R. shows us the Albrechtsburg (previously Finleder); his nurse's house, not far from the statue of Augustus the Strong, which he often visited as a child; the Stille Musik; the path to the Weisser Hirsch, where as a boy of 12 he shed so many tears, having gone in vain with his sister Ottilie to meet their brother Albert and having to return home late on foot. Then in Kietz's studio, and finally a very pleasant dinner at Jenkins's. The various climates are discussed, and R. declares that where we live summer and winter are the same, and the trees turn green out of boredom. — The pictures from Athens give the impression of a desert.

Thursday, September 8 Yesterday R. invited several people to a late breakfast, these now arrive and disturb him greatly. He speaks frankly to Elsa Uhlig about the sale of the letters. Dr. Strecker, who had sought him in vain in Bayreuth, also turns up, but when the conductor Wüllner finally arrives, he sends him off to find me in the gallery. I drive with R. to Jenkins's, where he always makes all kinds of jokes. At 2 o'clock we have lunch on the terrace with Dr. Strecker, to whom R. says, "My dentist has advised me to demand a lot of money from the house of Schott for *Parsifal.*" After arranging with Dr. S. to have another conference with him in the evening, we drive out to Pillnitz. R. shows me the courtyard in which he performed the music for the returning King, he also shows me where Baron v. Lüttichau sat. A gentleman unknown to us (Councilor Braun), who saw us waiting for the guide, took us in, but since a swarm of other people followed us, we soon took our leave. We then drive to Gross-Graupen, where *Lohengrin* was first sketched. From such a cramped and indigent place did this world of brilliance and beauty shine forth! R. shows us the paths he often walked, and we come to the romantic Lochner mill, where we stop for refreshments. In darkness, late in the evening, we return home. Dr. Str. arrives; to begin with, R. speaks to him very severely for having imagined that he had him in his power, having published the text; then, when Dr. Str. apologizes, R. accepts his explanation that, in spite of their great success, his works are still not a good business proposition, and the terms of the contract are agreed upon. R. trusts this man, who behaves with great propriety, and he reduces some of his demands. — A curious and frequently recurring characteristic of R.'s is the way in which at the end he asks after Dr. Strecker's fiancée, and the latter, surprised, indeed almost disconcerted, announces that he became engaged about a week ago. And so great is R.'s sense of justice that, when we are alone, he regrets having made an additional demand for 15,000 marks. [*Added fifteen pages later but referred back to this point:* "At tea in the evening, R. talks about *Der Fl. Holländer* and says how sad he was to note so much in it that is just noise or repetition, that is to say, so many things that spoil the work."]

Friday, September 9 R. had a good night, is satisfied with the business arrangements, and says goodbye to Dr. St. in a very friendly way. — At 12 o'clock he comes to Dr. Jenkins's, and from there we go to the Pusinellis', where we are expected. R. is greatly affected, embraces our good Frau Pusinelli very heartily, and talks feelingly about our loyal departed friend. On returning home, he has a chest spasm; the visit of the critic Dr. Hartmann wears him out, and we go, feeling somewhat worn out, to see *Preciosa*. The performance of this charming work is disappointing, the tempi wrong, though, curiously enough, the march which the conductor had dragged is played correctly by the musicians on stage. The declamation absurd throughout, much Israel, and in consequence everything a masquerade.

Saturday, September 10 R. had a restless night, he cancels his visit to the dentist. We eat in our rooms and then drive to the churchyard to visit Weber's grave, then go on to the Marcolini; R. shows us all his familiar places, including the beautiful Neptune fountain; he tells about my father's visit there—and I am pleased that *Lohengrin* was completed in this lovely room. Before that he showed me the route

Weber's funeral procession had taken. And thus Dresden has become virtually a second home to me! In the theater we see *Figaro*. Much suffering over the subject and the conclusions, both all but unbearable to me, thus making it completely impossible to enjoy its beauties. (R. visited Tichatschek.)

Sunday, September 11   R. did not have a good night, he rests in the morning, Fidi goes to church, and then we all drive together via the pastry shop to Jenkins's. From there to a late breakfast with our friends of London memory, the Schlesingers. A gay meeting, for R. finds the pretty wife very pleasant. In the evening *Der Freischütz*, a joy, a solace, fragrant as a forest. But one thing greatly astonishes R.—that the traditional manner of performing these works has been forgotten to such an extent that the Ännchen did not even know the characteristic movements (with her apron, to the accompaniment of the clarinet). R. draws my attention to the use of the bass register of the oboe, also of the flute—all Weber's own inventions. At the conclusion of the opera he is approached shyly, but enthusiastically, by a Frl. von Zettwitz, who says she could not miss the opportunity of thanking him.

Monday, September 12   R. has another appointment with Dr. Jenkins, which proves a great strain on him. Our missing each other at the china collection, where we had arranged to meet, makes him angry. Dismal meal. After that a walk to Loschwitz and Blasewitz. He is pleased to see that Weber's house has been preserved, and he shows us the Ziegenbach, the stream on which he attempted to build himself a boat to sail to Dresden in, imagining the surprise of his family. We are pleased by the countryside, R. praising the way the river curves. How painful to hear that the Queen does not care for Pillnitz and is seldom there—R. observes that none of them cares for the people! When we arrive home we find two pretty girls waiting with flowers; in reply to R.'s inquiry, they say they are the daughters of the deceased headmaster of the Kreuzschule, and they admire R. so much! — In the evening we go to see our friend Frau Pusinelli and say goodbye to her very affectionately.

Tuesday, September 13   Many bills to pay! . . . And a final appointment with Dr. Jenkins for R., after which he goes for a glass of beer with Fidi and shows him the Klepperbein house, in which he spent so much time as a child. (He also showed me the apothecary's shop from which his mother received a bill for "mixed teas for little Richard.") Departure at 2 o'clock, the Hartmanns at the station. When R. jokes with Frau H. about her showing so much feeling for a conductor, she replies that she does not bother herself with such insignificant people, but with Wagner, Shakespeare, Beethoven. He says, "Oh, we two are not fit to tie Shakespeare's or Beethoven's shoelaces." And when she expresses delight over his "we," R. says, "Enthusiasm makes equals of us all." We arrive in Leipzig at 6 o'clock, Herr Neumann with the conductor Seidl at the station. R. calls the former "a rose exuding earnestness." He goes for a drive with the children, and then we go to the theater, where Israel again predominates. Curious voices, above all. Benedix's play *Der Vetter* seems rather clumsy.

Wednesday, September 14 Departure at 6 in the morning; Herr Neumann, whom R. later calls an Assyrian inscription restored to life, pays—curiously—for our tickets, and he has to listen to many jokes about it from R. We are welcomed at Neuenmarkt with a hailstorm. In Bayreuth, however, the children and our friends. Unfortunately R. immediately has a chest spasm! But at lunch he is cheerful. When someone mentions the Saxon royal family, he says, "They are all worse than just ghosts—they are the descendants of ghosts." But a letter from Herr Batz vexes him greatly; he has to reply to it, and thus our evening has a subdued beginning; but spirits are gradually raised and news exchanged.

Thursday, September 15 R. slept well, but it is so cold that he is put out of humor by it; he busies himself with his article, and after lunch reads to us the very nice letters from singers accepting his invitation. In the evening he has to put on his blue robe, and in consequence he does not wish to receive the French people who send in their cards. The Wolz.'s visit us and tell us a few things about their journey.

Friday, September 16 He feels indisposed, talks of Constantinople— then of the *B. Bl.* and the establishment of a committee which will continue his work here when he goes off and leaves this place permanently. At lunch we have M. and Mme Lascoux, very formal Wagnerites, who tell us a lot about Munich and also the prospects in Paris. In the evening he works on his article, and when I suggest that he dictate it, he says jokingly, "That's no good with something that is superfluous." — Yesterday he said to Wolz., "We are both overhasty in our writing." — The Lascoux couple spend the evening with us. R. plays the Prelude to *Pars.* But he finds the French conversation afterward very onerous, he disappears, does not wish to say goodbye, then, however, follows the guests out, takes leave of them, calling them Isis and Osiris, which they will hardly have understood!

Saturday, September 17 The *Blätter* and its demise and rebirth are still keeping us occupied; R. comes to the subject of Jews as actors— the fact that in '53 he could write that there were none, whereas now...! And the way they treated our language! — Today he completes his article. Friend Gross, who has lunch with us, tells us about Herr v.

Bürkel and says the latter now thinks that the King will after all finance the orchestra. — R. talks to me about his work, describes it as "*very bold.*" In the evening we play whist.

Sunday, September 18 Today R. calls me the fair miller's wife, because I grind everything down into something good, restore equilibrium! God grant that I live up to that! — R. writes to the King and reads some passages to me about the sketches, the orchestra, and its conductor. Toward midday I find him indisposed, he drinks some tea immediately before lunch; however, his mood improves during the meal. Afterward he reads to us the wine merchant's letter, which he finds amusing. He arranges a drive to the pretty spot beyond the Fantaisie, but a wind is blowing as he is walking through the meadow, and he has a chest spasm. He thinks longingly of Corfu. In the evening he plays some pieces from *Der Freischütz* which bring him great inner contentment, then parts of the Venusberg music, pleased that "it, too, is melody."

Monday, September 19 R. tells me for the second time that he believes *Parsifal* will please people, saying it is the most remarkable thing he has ever done. He works on the score, reads reports about Thomas More's *Utopia* in the newspaper, thinks the book insipid: "Those ancient Greek fellows were much more advanced in their ideas," he observes. — In the morning he sends Fidi to me to announce that the weather is fine, we go for a walk together in the palace gardens, sitting down twice for a rest. In the evening Stein reads to us his letter for the *B. Blätter,* which R. thinks very good. When we are talking in the palace gardens about ways of changing the *Blätter,* R. says, "Let the ghost do what it likes."

Tuesday, September 20 R. had a restful night, and he works. Over coffee, when our conversation turns to Eros and Anteros, scorned love, R. says that Anteros is Parsifal. He says the Greeks did not know love in our sense. The news of the death of good President Garfield, after a long struggle, makes a solemn impression on us; the fact is mentioned that he was of humble origin. — At 5 o'clock R. has a conference; just before it he feels greatly indisposed, goes to sit in the garden. But the discussion goes smoothly, agreement is reached on advertisements, prices of seats, etc. We then drive to the Riedelsberg with our friends to fetch our children. R. expresses his wish to have a "*strapontin,*" as he calls a coupé, amused by the name of the little seat inside it. In the evening the contracts with London cause him vexation, he makes certain stipulations to Herr Francke and sends the contracts back. A bat flutters around us, which I find very ominous; R. drives it away.

Wednesday, September 21 R. busy on his score. Our expecting my father leads the conversation to his relationships and his life, in which we feel we are no more than an item. [*The preceding sentence obliterated in ink by an unknown hand.*] We again discuss the fact that in their later years men by themselves are much more helpless than women, citing M[ore] as an example. R. says, "Yes, if only because women like to show they are something in themselves—men do not need to." — We drive to the theater, inspect the construction of the royal box, on which the brother of our good foreman Gräfe is now working. — Then the workshop, in which the rollers for the transformation scenery are being planed. R. is much pleased by all this activity, all this effort in the service of an ideal aim, and he thinks of Brandt with gratitude and appreciation. Very foolish behavior on the part of the children, following the mildest of scoldings from him, makes me angry; but he is filled with feelings of having been unjust to them. And in the evening he sends to the Wolz.'s for [Scott's] *Woodstock* and reads aloud the scene following the search in the castle. — Over coffee we talked a lot about Minna, acknowledging both her beauty and the fact that a correct instinct led R. to her: "In that way I was cut off from all acts of foolishness and thought only of my work." — He pities her for having married him.

Thursday, September 22 R. receives 40,000 marks from Dr. Strecker today and offers us all money! At 3 o'clock my father arrives; R., I, and everyone else at the station; he looks much better than we had anticipated; R. tries very cordially to persuade him to remain with us permanently, and concludes, "But you are exactly like Köhler—you must have your freedom." — (His describing the snuffbox I gave him on August 25 as the work of an amateur is for me another sign of that perspicacity I always find so astonishing in him.)

Friday, September 23 R. had a good night, but he feels indisposed, and the cold is severe. In the morning he has to swear an affidavit for Herr Fürstner, much to his displeasure, and we discuss the dismal necessity over lunch. — Then we come to the subject of vegetarianism, and my father amuses us greatly by singing to us in English the words the Temperance Society sings to the melody from *Norma*: "We belong, we belong, we belong to the Temperance, the Temperance Society, to the Temperance Society!" [*Added four pages later but referred back to this point:* "Over coffee R. talks about the American war. 'Very well,' he says, 'one says all these things about America' (he himself, observing the arrogant young Jenkins, had said, 'Possible that such people enjoy this world, but now I know why I do not enjoy it') 'and that we have nothing in common with it; but all the same this war is the only one to have been waged for the sake of humanity and an idea.' My father listens attentively to his ensuing description, something he notices with pleasure."] A letter from Batz brings vexation; R. and I drive to see friend Gross. He replies to Batz. In the evening we play whist, but he soon goes off to read *Woodstock,* in which he is struck by many weaknesses in description. He said recently that W. Sc[ott] was like Gobineau; the legitimate rulers—in this case the Stuarts—could do whatever they wished and still remain divine, whereas someone like Cromwell, however fairly treated, was nevertheless presented as a unique curiosity. At midday, as Wolz. is going off to see my father, he throws him a 50-pfennig piece through the window! — Letters about *Tristan* wring from him angry exclamations that his thoughts are now elsewhere—do these people imagine that one never moves on from such things?

Saturday, September 24 The weather has taken a turn for the better, the barometer has risen. R. works on the proofs of his article, and he tries to surprise my father and me in Jouk.'s studio, but he misses us. The Wolz.'s lunch with us; that always provides some good etymological conversation between him and R., but at table he is already somewhat out of humor. Then in the evening all sorts of things arise— our manservant drunk, for R. bad luck at cards, which he then abandons, but above all, I fear, the *Mephisto-Walzer,* played by my father, along with a conversation with Porges while the rest of us are playing whist— quite an appalling atmosphere. He flares up, and everybody goes away in some alarm. I stand at the top of his spiral staircase listening to him in order to decide what to do, and to my joy I hear him say: "Still so-and-so many pages to do! I shall be glad when I have finished my score." — I then go to him, and together we pour out our hearts over, oh, so many things, among which the *tête-à-tête* with Porges and the tipsy Georg with the guitar (Pepino had been singing) provide the moments of light relief. (Before supper I inspected a *strapontin.*)

Sunday, September 25 But R. did not have a good night. In the newspaper is a description of the Jouk. costumes, containing many mistakes; it is by F. Muncker, and for R. this is yet another proof of the hasty way in which things are always done nowadays. He works, complaining of lack of concentration. At lunch we have the mayor's family, it all goes quite well, and at half past four the *strapontin* arrives! . . . R. and I ride in it together, everything amuses him, even the way the people stare, the coachman, the horses—and the weather is fine, too. I had been offered the carriage just for inspection, but he wants to keep it, if only for the reason that a man here built it at his own risk, and who will otherwise support him? In the evening we have a merry whist party (I unfortunately never with him!); but he withdraws and just looks on, constantly exclaiming, "Porges is missing—something is missing!" To my father he exclaims, "If you had such a nice house, we should visit you much more often—or such a wife!"

Monday, September 26 "All I care for now is tranquillity. *Tristan* came storming along and gave rise to *Siegfried,* too, but now I find emotional scenes repugnant, and it is something which disturbs me in *Parsifal* as well; all I want to do now are things like the scene in *Die Walküre* where she goes to fetch the water, or the scene in the 3rd act of *Parsifal* (anointing and baptism)." At lunch our friend Judith Gautier; I do not yet know whether this is pleasing to R., or just embarrassing, as he says. He goes for a drive with me in the direction of Heinrichsreuth, talking of when coal was first discovered, and whether one could hope a day would come when people no longer went down mines—an American jungle would surely suffice to keep the world supplied with fuel. But, above all, the climate—he keeps coming back to that. Then, seeing some geese, he laughs loudly: "They are the victims of civilization, so clearly designed for swimming and flying, and now forced by human beings to waddle." — Strange evening with Mme Gautier—when the others sit down to a game of whist, R. says, "This is Porges all over again!" — My feelings are strange, I leave the room; when I return, R. is reading aloud his material for *Die Sieger* from Burnouf. — For me Loldi, now returned, is everything today—indeed, all the children, who show me the point of living. What do children ever owe to their parents, compared with what they give to their parents?

Tuesday, September 27 Saint Cosmas! . . . Yesterday I desisted from responding to R.'s remarks about Judith's character, which he finds embarrassing; instead, I kept bringing the conversation back to the children. He is sad today about that, weeps, and says that, if anything were to come between us, it would be all over with him; I seek to explain to him in all mildness the feeling which makes me so intensely aware of this strange woman in our house that yesterday I had to leave the room for a moment. We part in good spirits, I blissful that I have been able to account for something that could so easily have been presented in the wrong way. Even before I went to my bath, he appeared in my room: "What shall we make our coffin of? Which do you want—lead or wood? For until death comes this nonsense will never cease—death is all that remains to us." — I arrange my little gifts and lay them in his room while he is dressing. He then comes to me: "Again I have forgotten your name day! — Oh, yes, you live for me more than I do for you, and that explains why I get so little joy from my work." Then he comes in with the atlas and shows me the journey Gobineau made in two months. — When I go to greet him as he is working on his score, he observes, "Art and love don't go together," but he is using the new snuffbox with much pleasure. At lunch he praises my father for having given me Cosmas, the healer, as my guardian angel. But then he comes to *Faust* and the thousand antics which disfigure life—how well Goethe expressed that!—and he tells Stein about the coffin, whereupon Stein reminds him that in Naples he wished to be lying on his deathbed. Mention is made of cuttlefish and the way they save their lives by disappearing, and R. says, "That's what God did after creating the world—He disappeared." — Previously he said to my father, "You invented me, and then you were obliged to push your wares." — We drive with Loldi along the avenue from the Eremitage to the theater and then home, much contented. Then he works and pastes over two bars in Parsifal's reply to Kundry which he felt to be Meyerbeerish—one works toward something like *grace* and then does not know how to handle it. At supper he comes to the subject of vivisection and says, "Our attitude toward animals is so simple, we find it so easy to be kind to them, whereas toward other human beings it is so complicated and difficult; that would be a way of finding it." — When I come downstairs, I discover R. at the piano and our friend Judith in rich, rather revealing finery: "I was taken by surprise," he tells me; he plays the *Prelude* and later some other things. Much amazement among the children and demonstrations verging on the comical from our friends!

Wednesday, September 28 R. complains loudly that everything, everything is a lie! He feels, for instance, that since my father played the waltz, the innocence of our relationships has vanished. "The Prussian state also consists of lies, of which they are unaware." He works both morning and afternoon and tells us that he has inserted a solo violin in place of a clarinet at the words "*so schüttelte sie die Locken.*" At lunch we have, besides our friend Judith, the poor Jägers. R. and I drive out to Mistelbach, and he feels that all is well when we are together. — In the evening he plays whist, the beautiful Judith sits down beside him and then declares that she wishes to play with him, and the group (Lusch with my father) makes a charming and merry picture. — Eva causes much amusement with her talent for mimicry. — But an explosion against Porges on account of the Jägers.

Thursday, September 29 R. reads in the newspaper that the discovery of a diamond mine in America has led to the building of a complete town in the shortest possible time: "That shows what people are—when metal, which was intended only as a symbol, a means of facilitating barter, becomes *eo ipso* a means of creating life." R. works, goes through the 2nd proof of his article, and takes it to Wolz. He returns from his little walk with a chest spasm. At lunch Judith and her friend Herr Benediktus—Israel, R.'s remark about the smooth, somewhat oily voice of the Israelite. Fine weather—for R. and me a drive along the pretty highway to Konnersreuth. Much pleasure in the countryside; R. somewhat beside himself over the growing numbers of Israel. In the evening he feels pains in his side and sends for the doctor. At supper he is still cheerful, he tells the story of M. Jadin, in whose house in Meudon was nothing but *"crapauds* and *araignées"* ["toads and spiders"]. But he is vexed at having to speak French and he soon withdraws, after the doctor has seen him, diagnosed his trouble as rheumatism, and prescribed a compress. *"Ma chère enthousiaste, prenez pitié de moi"* ["My dear devotee, have pity on me"], he says to Judith, as he takes leave of her and makes his excuses. During our walk we discussed that curious and daemonic habit of his of wounding people without the slightest evil intent; today, for example, in the disquiet of his restless mood, he said that if he were king, he would distribute ministries for this and that, and, turning to Joukowsky, he says, *"A vous celui de la chétiveté* [to you that of puniness]." Since Jouk. is very puny—and that is also the reason why his talent can never amount to much—he was very hurt, until I explained to him that it is always a sign of R.'s inner disquiet when he sticks out his claws in this way, though he has a daemonic talent for hitting unerringly on one's weak point. — Today he wrote, along with my father, to the wine merchant Feldheim.

Friday, September 30 R. had a restless night, the doctor's treatment has only made things worse. Three leeches are applied—R. calls them the Three Graces—and he has to stay in bed. He complains that his score is shagreen in reverse—the more he works on it, the longer it becomes. I remain upstairs, and since the doctor shows no anxiety, I return to my wonted mood. "This is what I love—to be by myself with you." He: "And I by myself for you." — I read his article over and over again and tell him of my heavenly delight in it. He reads *Trois ans en Asie* with much enjoyment, only deploring the remarks in favor of the Catholic church. Thus do we spend the day; only in the evening he sends me to my father, and I play whist with him and our friends. The doctor came in the course of the day, and he remains unperturbed, although the rheumatic pains are severe.

Saturday, October 1 R. slept well. But a misunderstanding about his bath upsets him greatly. However, he soon calms down, and we have a merry breakfast in spite of his pain. He gets up but cannot work on his "shagreen," contenting himself with reading. At lunch much about our friends: the things about them that seem alien to us the consequence of their race, which has allowed no established practice to emerge, the good in them their own individual possession—we agree on that. All sorts of business matters, Neumanniades, London, etc., also Levi-orchestra. I settle everything with friend Gross. Supper without my father, who is in much pain from an inflamed gland. [*Two sentences of purely etymological interest omitted.*] — In the evening he asks me to read aloud from *Trois ans en Asie,* but before that, before supper, he plays "*O sink hernieder*" from *Tristan* to me. — And continual discussions about his heavenly article. — An anecdote told by Jouk., about a general who pocketed 10,000 francs, leads him at supper to the French conception of honor; they will do anything, he says, but always observe the convention of keeping silent about it; anyone who is foolhardy enough to say what he has done will be put to the knife.

Sunday, October 2 R. had a comparatively quiet night, he takes his bath and tells me gaily that my pronouncements concerning his article have given him complete confidence in it. He reads *Trois ans en Asie* and works; writes a few lines to Marianne Brandt—a variant on "*fühlst du im Herzen nur andrer Schmerzen*" to facilitate the breathing. Our lunch is harmonious, R. talks a lot about the massage he intends to have. My father is also somewhat better, but we do not venture on a walk. In the evening R. studies the atlas, the route to Corfu! He then goes to work, but complains of having a cold. The evening part whist, part conversation with Wolz., to whom he demonstrates his error with regard to Parsifal. When he talks jokingly to and about me and I tell him he is being naughty, he says, "If I were to try to do you justice, I should go mad!" And this morning, when we greet each other, he keeps on gulping, telling me it is to make sure that no kiss escapes into the air! At lunch he told the children about the comical dream he had because of falling asleep with a finger in his nose; he says it showed him a cave with stalactites, then a milk pond, and finally the pulpy brain substance! — When my father expresses his dislike of present-day Goethe literature, R. says humorously, "Goethe has altogether gone down in my estimation for having so little money; I thought he had 100,000 thalers, but now I see that he, too, wrote for money!"

Monday, October 3 R. had a good night, and he works. At lunch we have a medal maker, H[ermann] Wittig, who would like to do R.'s portrait, and whom R. teases on account of the blue spectacles behind which he withdraws. Then he says to him, "Do me in the act of creation, with an eraser in my hand." Cold weather, no outing. R. thinks of Venice but is put off by thoughts of all his acquaintances there. Since the medal maker has also done a portrait of the Pope, R. remarks on the latter's mouth, "an imposing eating instrument fashioned for eloquence"; he says he is certainly incapable of mercy— and nowadays most mouths are like that. Whist in the evening; between games he goes to his desk and asks my father whether he has ever used the kettledrum below F. My father says no, since it does not sound right, but R. says he will use it all the same, and he whispers in my ear the passage for which he needs it: "*ich sah ihn—ihn.*" — Then he plays the Overture to *Lumpazivagabundus* and is altogether very cheerful, if sometimes immersed in thought. "If only God lets me off unscathed!" he exclaims jokingly. "But he is torturing me dreadfully with the law of gravity." —

Tuesday, October 4   A letter from a friend who says that if the world were to collapse she would save only *Tristan* brings from R. the remark that he can understand this, for in *Tristan* he gave himself up entirely to music; in the other works the drama had imposed a tighter check on the musical flow. He has another massage. When that is over, we have breakfast in cheerful spirits, and he cites a suckling infant as the most drastic expression of the will to live: all that raging when it is hungry, and the calm once it is satisfied, followed in some by laziness and in others by a desire to play. He says he observed this among the puppies. He works and then sits for the medal man, after which, despite snow and cold, we go out for a drive and, during it, talk a lot about philosophizers such as Schelling, etc. In reply to my question whether he thinks C. Frantz will understand his article and be drawn by it away from Schelling and on to Schop., R. says no. But in the evening he does not feel well; he plays a little whist, then withdraws with W. Scott (he has finished *Trois ans en Asie*). "I do my work amid spasms and stupid people," he exclaims plaintively! We had some acquaintances here. He has to point out to friend Wolz. yet another mistake in his piece about *Parsifal*—that he makes Parsifal take part in the Communion.

Wednesday, October 5   R. dreams about me during the night, that I leave him, but he calls out, "Minna." He gets up, talks about it, and then dreams again; this time he says, "It was you, after all." In the morning he is not feeling well, he complains about the doctor, then says jokingly that one should just let him grumble, then it would all be over with. We think of distant lands, of Palermo, he reads about it in Baedeker and then goes to his work with a semblance of good cheer. But the fog is not conducive to a drive. In a letter Princess Marie Hohenlohe urges me to give Daniela to my father as a companion! . . . In the evening, to our very great delight, my father plays two Beethoven sonatas (E Major, A-flat Major). Afterward we play whist, and R. is glad that "nobody" is there.

Thursday, October 6   R. had a good night, and since the sun is shining on us again, I have hopes of a good mood, but the wind is blowing, which R. finds unbearable. To make up for it, however, Brandt arrives, with him the Brückners; when we return from our drive to the theater, where we inspect the box, the maquettes are displayed, to R.'s very great satisfaction; the transformation scenery in particular pleases us all very much. Some guests in the evening; my father plays Beethoven's Variations, and in such a way that R. asks whether one can believe that Beeth. himself ever played them thus. He thinks not, and he praises the simplicity which enables each melody to come to our ears as an individual figure. Both day and evening pass peaceably.

Friday, October 7 R. has another massage and goes to his work in good spirits, but when he takes a walk in the garden and sees Marke catching a little fish in the fountain, he gets very upset and tries in vain to rescue the creature. At lunch afterward he is very unwell and very depressed. All the same he talks in a friendly way with Stein about the latter's dramatic scene, "Cornelia." We drive along the Konnersreuth highway; he is displeased at being unable to persuade my father to stay here. And everything, every conversation, is a burden to him; he leaves the supper table, with my father's permission I follow him, calm him down, and the day ends with an amicable game of whist. At the request of the Princesses Hohenlohe and Wittgenstein it is decided that Daniela will accompany her grandfather. R. consents, though he is annoyed that commands should be given from outside, as he puts it.

Saturday, October 8 R. had a good night and is also in a good mood for work. At lunch there is talk of the Sedan celebrations, and we wonder whether other nations also celebrate their victories—the English Waterloo, for example. R. says, "Not they—for them it is just a job—*business*." — Today the sun shines on us, we go for a drive, R. and I, and delight in the splendid sunset and the moon. And when I am with my father talking about Lusch's journey, we hear someone outside singing, "We belong, we belong"—R. is standing there in the moonlight! We go to fetch him, he shows my father *"ein andres ist,"* which he has just done, and my father praises him for avoiding a feeling of precipitancy. Then R. and I walk through the garden in the moonlight. At supper he is very cheerful, yet, so it seems to me, on edge. Friend Wolz. comes along, conversation with him; the others play whist, and R. is vexed by the seriousness with which it is played. The evening ends, we remain in the *salon,* R. and I, I very downcast, since Daniela did not take well the news that she should go with her grandfather, and it also means much work for me to prepare for her sudden departure. The coats of arms in the *salon* are mentioned, the *salons* of Mme Minghetti and Mimi, misunderstandings occur, melancholy discord prevails, R. leaves his bed, but I follow him at once and calm him down and beg him, if I have said something unkind to him, to put it down to my overtiredness!

Sunday, October 9 He feels unwell and is sick; but he comes to Lusch's present opening, which we are holding three days in advance, I with very dismal feelings! After lunch our conversation turns to forms of burial; R. is not much in favor of cremation, he observes that in such cases the ceremony should consist of saying farewell to the corpse, which should then be borne off. But it is quite a different thing, he says, to rest side by side. — We go for a drive again today, and when we sit down to supper, R. tells me I should send a telegram to Princess W.—"My father is staying, my husband coming, Krug prevented"— which makes us laugh heartily (that was yesterday, Saturday). My father plays the [Opus] 111 Sonata and before that the A Major, which R. calls the coming of spring; R. wishes the final movement to be taken somewhat slower, since he feels passionate accents are out of place in this sonata. My father humors him, and R. takes delight in this "blossoming and rustling of spring." — While the others are playing whist, we speak with R. about Stein, and he says, "He is a big baby in swaddling clothes, who has still to be unwrapped." When we say good night, he calls me "you lamb of God!" and continues, "Agnus Dei—it really should be *'agnus mundi qui tollis peccavi Deus.'* " —

Monday, October 10 [*Added three pages later but referred back to this point:* "When R. came down to breakfast, we talked about voice leading, and he was very pleased when my father recalled the choruses in the 2nd act of *Lohengrin;* nobody but he has ever noticed that, R. observes."] Departure! Dismal weather—very dismal feelings. R. takes leave of father and child here, the other children and I accompany them. At lunch talk about my father's fate, also Carolyne W.'s, and since I recall only her good features and say that, when she became angry with us and goaded my father, it was only because R. had once offended her by forbidding a visit from her, R. replies, "All right, but if she had any nobility, she would have forgiven, sought an explanation, instead of just making trouble." We drive together to the theater along the avenue from the Eremitage, greet our handsome Faf, climb the boards of the future royal box, and return home. At 7 o'clock it is exactly 28 years since I saw R. for the first time; I bring him the little compass, and he gives me the ring he had meant for Christmas, a wonderfully beautiful opal! We immerse ourselves in memories, he also recalls his wife Minna and how she left him in Dresden! But at supper we think of Tribschen, of the *Christkind* there and the *Knecht Ruprecht,* all the blissful times. Then he reads to me part of [E. T. A. Hoffmann's] "Ignaz Denner." (R. plays a lot with his compass.)

Tuesday, October 11 R. had a good night, and not until the morning does he find the greeting I wrote to go with the compass. — His chest constrictions start again, and our table conversation consists in imagining a journey up the Nile. The news of the sudden death of the Austrian minister Haymerle, who, R. relates, suffered a chest spasm and then heart failure, has made an impression on him! — But his high spirits as always gain the upper hand, and when, at lunch, Fidi tells us that someone has given him an ostrich's egg, R. says, "If you open it, you'll find the life of Jesus inside." — We drive out in the *strapontin* almost as far as Drossenfeld, taking great delight in the countryside—a field in which cows are grazing R. finds "quite blissful." On our return home he receives Dr. Landgraf, who suggests he should send for Dr. Leube, an authority on abdominal complaints. R. then writes to Herr Neumann about Dresden—without, however, mentioning the Berlin project, to which he is unwilling to give his approval. Then he works as far as *"Mein ganzes Liebes-Umfangen"* (238), and in the evening we chat about all sorts of things. The children go to a lecture by Dr. Brehm. — R. goes through *Euryanthe,* as ever regretting its many banalities, revenge aria, finales, etc. Among other things, he points to the device of introducing the rustic lover, Rudolf, in order to provide a quartet! . . . News of Lulu—not exactly encouraging! Hans writes, agreeing to our daughter's journey, but ill! . . .

Wednesday, October 12 Lusch's birthday—R. toasts her at lunch. Otherwise our talk is about the journey up the Nile and Palermo, which Rub. describes to us in blissful terms. Some work is done, another alteration sent to M. Brandt, and Baer's *Urmensch* read, though with much displeasure at German books nowadays. We drive to the theater via the Eremitage, see our handsome Faf, and return home to work. In the evening friend Wolz. visits us with his guest, Dr. Hering, whose talkativeness somewhat irritates R. to begin with, but he is then pleased to be able to talk about previous acquaintances such as the philosopher Professor Weisse—"the young people know nothing." — (He wrote to Herr Neumann today.)

Thursday, October 13 Letters from and about Lusch. R. talks about the stars: why did they separate? It is as though God loved to individualize. The weather is very bad. Memories of the Villa d'Angri, the night on the terrace, watching everyone come and go: "One felt like God Almighty," says R. — R. works, and when the sun appears at about one o'clock, I hear him calling in the garden and see him walking with the dogs. After lunch we go for a drive along the Konnersreuth highway, he tells me various things from *Der Urmensch,* including the author's statement that there is nothing further to be said about the origin of man, since Prof. Müller has made no further researches! Which amuses us vastly. Then he rhapsodizes over the beauty of a Nubian pictured in the book and expresses his opinion that the white races do after all stem from the black ones. He works, and in the evening we read in Uhland the story of Starkardr, following that of Egill which R. had read to us on the previous evening, and which delighted us all. — In connection with them, R. plays the first bars of the C Minor Symphony! — We spoke of the sonatas; what R. praises in these final works of Beethoven, especially in the quartets, is that all extraneous matter has now vanished, and only thematic work remains. — Of Bach he said recently, "Like the world before the advent of man." —

Friday, October 14 R. had a good night; he receives a letter from the King, in which only one passage, in favor of tolerance toward the Jews, somewhat displeases him, though it seems to me that princes can hardly feel otherwise. He continues reading *Der Urmensch* and says jokingly that there is nothing in it but quotations from professors. But the pictures of the various human types interest him; he shows them to us and says of the Papuans that they could very well be in the Jockey Club, also that the Jews could be persuaded to dress their hair like that if one were to allow them "a few more locks and another little flag in it." — He is also interested in the hypothesis concerning the origins of human language. — He then comes back to his favorite idea, that our little community might lead to the formation of a core to promote emigration. "To set an example"—and he comes back to *Egmont,* that true German greatness which Goethe characterizes by contrasting [Egmont's] courageous refusal to put life first with Alba and his cautious clinging to this and that. In this connection I mention Schiller, whose correspondence with Humboldt is at the moment keeping me completely absorbed. (When we recently spoke of Alexander Humboldt and the apparently inexplicable world reputation of his *Kosmos,* R. said, "He traveled with a Herr von Hum—bug.") — R. and I drive to the Fantaisie, the air feels like foehn, and at the same time the colors are completely autumnal. In the evening we are visited by Herr Marsillach from Barcelona, with whom we discuss a possible stay in Seville! R. is very friendly toward the foreigner, but in the middle of it he says to us, "Oh dear, what a bore this is!" — The Spaniard takes his leave of R. with the words, "*Les gens du Nord sont faits pour créer, ceux du Midi pour admirer*" ["The Northern peoples are born to create, those of the South to admire"] — The *Bayreuther Tagblatt* reports that we are staying here; R. says I had that inserted, in order to exert moral pressure on him—as with Starkardr (he tells me) I was trying to trump his Egill. We talk a lot about the Normans, their wild pride, yet feel that the Goths and the Vandals were more civilized people, and one can understand Charlemagne's melancholy when he caught sight of the ships. But their pride, their intractability— that is what is interesting about these people, R. says, for all their heartlessness. — He comes back to Gobineau's book and says that so lofty an idea, so expert a hypothesis—that is what interests him, whereas all this cautious dependence on quotations he finds repellent.

— Regarding the German expression "It is all Spanish to me," R. has the idea that it must have come from the Netherlanders, who did not understand their rulers.

Saturday, October 15 Dreadful stormy night, and R. again had his chest spasms in the morning. But he works, and figures that he now has 90 pages of the score still to do. At lunch I ask him about Humboldt and Schiller; he observes that it was not until Schopenhauer that a certain precision in philosophical matters was achieved, before his time there had always been a tendency to drivel. When, in agreeing with him, I say that both he and Schopenhauer turned this whole world upside down, yet this did not seem to me to be what the preface is implying, R. does not allow me to continue, and this reveals a characteristic feature of him—namely, that when he has said something, he likes to regard the matter as settled, and he does not like people to take up an idea of his in order to raise another aspect of the subject. When we discuss this, he tells me it looked as if I were trying to say that this was not the standpoint from which to regard the book, and my remark did not at the moment interest him. — We also talk about history, in which he can no longer take much interest, since he has come to the conclusion that there is no hope of any improvement; I ask him whether it is not always interesting as a natural phenomenon. At lunch he again tells the nice story of Alfonso of Aragon, who was advised to choose 12 men who were just, brave, gentle, etc. "Give me one such, and I shall give him my kingdom," the truthful man replied. We drive out in a gale: to friend Gross, then home via the Eremitage, and once again to our friend, since 20,000 marks have arrived from Herr Neumann. When the postman delivers them, R. says to him, "I expect you wouldn't mind having these." "Oh, if I only had a quarter of them!" the good man exclaims merrily! — In the evening R. reads "Ignaz Denner," to the enjoyment of us all. Before that there was much talk about the first human beings, their descent from one couple; R. had already observed yesterday that present-day theologians base themselves on Darwin: "He can still be made to look completely silly." —

Sunday, October 16 The newspaper, which is now publishing the portraits of the election candidates—just like those of people being sought by the police—annoys R. extremely, and in particular because it is now also proposing a completely different Catholic-party candidate —this is what has now become of anti-Semitism! R. feels that the Catholics are not true Germans in any case, and he says one should stand by Luther, who would have been indignant for this reason. And thus, he says, the Southerners are no true Germans. I observe that they nevertheless have the greatest artistic tendencies. "Maybe so," he says, "and that is the black influence—as Gobineau sees it." — We get up laughing at this. He continues reading Humboldt's preface and is pleased with his assumption that human beings, when they invented language, must have been gentle and enlightened creatures, playing like children. — The young apprentice-copyist Hausburg has lunch with us. R. asks him whether he has any means of his own and, as if apologizing for such directness, adds, "Oh, at your age I had nothing at all, I was the great musical director of Lauchstädt." — We drive out to Drossenfeld and delight in the yellow buntings fluttering above a plowed field. Since it is R.'s wish, I promise him a game of billiards tomorrow, but observe that it will not be good for the girls, it might give them round shoulders, whereupon he: "And if I get round-shouldered, we shall all be able to carry our sacks of ashes around on bent backs!" — However, in the evening he feels so indisposed that we spend a very dejected evening and talk of nothing but plans for going away at once. R. very downcast. The air is so raw that he has no wish to move another step!

Monday, October 17 R. had a better night than I dared hope for. I was awakened by the cock, and quite distinctly after waking up I heard it call "Richard Wagner" three times. The billiard table arrives, R. finds it already set up when he comes downstairs, and he is much taken with it—after every page he goes back to practice with the cues. He also comes upstairs to me, commiserating with me for having such a restless husband! Then he sends the children to tell me that he is in the garden. He says that Neumann seems to him thoroughly eudaemonic, to him he now owes his highest income from the theater. He said that Berlin would bring in about 900 marks, and true enough, that is how it happened. The family gathers around the billiard table before and after lunch. Over coffee R. says very gaily, "All I want is to know the target which has been set me, so that I don't do too much—it is dreadful to think of doing too much." — Fidi's museum, to which he gains access through the window—since I keep the room locked—amuses R. greatly. — The inspector from Leipzig is also a pleasing arrival, since he has found all the scenery in the best of condition. So we can give thanks for this day. R. ends it by reading *"Frauentreue"* from the *Gesammtabenteuer,* or, rather, from its very good table of contents; we are greatly touched by its great respectability, indeed almost petit-bourgeois quality, for all its boldness. In the husband R. sees his King Marke. — Late in the evening, just before we part, R. says, "How can one even speak of human beings, when there are still slaves among us?"—and he enlarges upon this theme.

Tuesday, October 18 He continues with his theme in the morning, to the extent that he again thinks of human beings at the time they invented language, and he pictures to himself their gentleness, goodness, kindness, and skill. When we come together again at lunch, he plays the little melody to which the tightrope walkers in Eisleben performed their acrobatics, and which he later reconstructed. He speaks of the correspondence between Schiller and Humboldt, and the almost playful impression it conveys when they are investigating whether Schiller resembled the Greeks or not; he also deplores all the musing about verse forms. In the evening he plays billiards and is pleased at the way he hit the red ball.

Wednesday, October 19 He comes back to something I told him yesterday about my father—how, when he saw the doctor coming to see R., he remarked, "The author of *Lohengrin* and *Tristan* will be difficult to cure." As far as *Lohengrin* is concerned, R. says he is completely satisfied with it, but in *Tannhäuser* he would criticize some still-remaining traces of operatic tradition (which mean that in the duet between Elisabeth and T., for example, the singers have almost to change places). He also still seems to feel a certain discrepancy between the new scene and the work as a whole. A letter from Herr Schlesinger touching on all aspects of the Nile journey makes R. feel cheerful and eager. At lunch he is in very high spirits. [*A sentence based on untranslatable word play omitted.*] After lunch I receive a very lively letter from my good Lusch in Rome, which greatly entertains R. as well. We drive to the theater via the Eremitage avenue. On returning home, R. completes the 2nd act of *Parsifal!* — Friend Wolz. comes, and we spend the evening alternately chatting and, for R., playing billiards. — I mention that 26 years have passed since I heard the *Tannhäuser* Overture for the first time and—became engaged.

Thursday, October 20 R. had a good night, and since it is a very fine day, I suggest a drive to the Fantaisie around one o'clock. This we do, but unfortunately he finds the short walk from the restaurant to the Schweizerei onerous, the autumn air cold; he laughs at the "beauty" of the sky and repeats how boring it is. He had already said to me in the carriage that he was curious to see which of the children would be the first to climb a pyramid! . . . Home again, he is overtaken by a chest spasm, and it is some time before he appears at table. However, he soon recovers his spirits, and the Nile journey usurps everything, encyclopedias and maps are consulted, to Fidi he says, "You'll see nothing there but mummies, and cousins both male and female," and to us that he must get as far as the 5th cataract at least; he sees himself and us in turbans, will have himself fanned all day long—in short, the plan serves at least to distract him thoroughly from other thoughts. — In the morning he read Stein's new dialogue. When he first saw the manuscript, he said he felt like the French general who heard the Marne mentioned for the third time: *"C'est une mauvaise plaisanterie."* — "Still on Plutarch," he said. — But he reads it and finds one speech in particular—Solon on the Egyptians and their attitude toward life and toward Atlantis—quite distinguished; he praises Stein and in the evening reads to us the passage he means. Mention of Gobineau's book brings our conversation back to the Greeks and the mixture from which art emerged. What I find most remarkable in this connection is the way R. gets inside the ideas of others and reshapes them so that one comes to know the authors, and yet at the same time feels less satisfied by them, since, through his supplementary remarks, one has come to understand them so much more clearly. — At supper R. tells us that Herr Neumann has sent a telegram saying that he regards the contract as having been broken by the management committee, and he does not intend to buy the scenery. R. very little affected by this. A letter from Countess La Tour telling of the pleasure R.'s article has given Gobineau. — The evening, which was spent in such quiet harmony, ends with diatribes against the portrait by Lenbach in my *salon* and against what R. imagines to be my good opinion of L. Since I say nothing, he says, "And thus do the bats fly up, thus do we torture each other—that is to say, not we, it is I who do the torturing." — We laugh, but in his room, talking to himself, he comes back to it. He cannot understand why I have put the sketch on display! — I shall certainly remove it tomorrow.

Friday, October 21 We get up late, since R. had a somewhat restless night. In the course of the day he confesses to me that when he awoke, he wondered where he was, and the thought of the Nile journey suddenly seemed like madness, let alone writing his 3rd act there. He reads W. v. Humboldt and writes several letters, also discusses the Neumann affair with friend Gross and remains unconcerned. The *Fl. Blätter* and the *I. Zeitung* help to distract R., and he shows us an old portrait of Luther done on leather, and, most important, an illustration of dogs, in which he is quite charmed by the pinscher. — We go for a drive to Drossenfeld and then go to see Steingräber about the instruments which are to accompany the bells. We also go to the tailor's for Fidi. Back home, R. drafts the telegram to my father and asks me what I think of it. I tell him I would not alter a word. "In such a frame of mind, though, things can easily be misunderstood." — "That does not matter, since it comes from you!" — He then plays two games of billiards with Stein, in very cheerful spirits, but they prove a strain on him, and he listens to the news from Rome, Rub.'s letter about Palermo, with some disquiet. After lunch he plays another game of billiards, but somewhat later, after he has had a rest. — We read Feustel's speech to his voters and are astonished by its heartlessness, which comes from his talking so much sanctimonious rhetoric. The observations on the Irish question in particular make R. very angry. When a people has been brought to this state, he says, to reproach it then with a lack of diligence . . . ! — In the evening R. looks in *La Vestale* for the passage to which my father drew his attention: the *smiths* in *Il Barbiere;* he finds it, and we have occasion to admire Rossini's much greater skill in handling it, using it in a comic situation. — And, proceeding from the dogs, he comments on the professors' faces, saying they look like "*oxidized bulls*"! —

Saturday, October 22 R. had a restless night, he seems run down; at lunch he says he has been rereading his article "Shall We Hope?" Then he requests that the toast to my father be drunk soon, since he is not feeling well. Friend Wolzogen proposes it, but the atmosphere remains subdued, and when R. learns of the death of Councilor Kraussold, he says, "He was my forerunner—now I shall live another 10 years." We recall the prophecy of 94—he shakes his head and in the course of the conversation frequently regrets not having seen his old friend again. He recalls his speech at the concert on my birthday and says he feels that a cordial word of encouragement could keep such a person alive, whereas when he was left in a state of both moral and physical debility, life was bound to end. And he relates the story of a soldier dying after an amputation, whom his lieutenant restored to life through friendly questioning. — He leaves us early, goes to bed, the children celebrate the birthday with charades at friend Jouk.'s, and I remain close by until R. no longer feels content in bed and we both go downstairs to the *salon,* where he shows me the picture of Japanese officials being received by the Mikado—and in European dress! — In the evening farewell chat with Stein; R. agitated by the unsettling effects of our plans, feels we should take him along, not leave it to him to decide. He expresses sorrow at having to leave the house.

Sunday, October 23 Wretched night for R., but he gets up and reads his "Public in Time and Space," is pleased with it, and tells me, when he comes to my room around lunchtime, that he is now writing about male and female in art and religion: "And you are in it, too." — I consult Dr. Landgraf, who advises that R. should leave here as soon as possible. I book the rooms in Palermo, and R. seems content with the arrangement. He jokes with Jouk. about the latter's impending departure and says of him, "Until he frees his sister from her husband." — He expresses sorrow at having to leave our nice, comfortable house. We drive in the rain along the Konnersreuth highway, passing the "Krummstab," the countryside still pretty but the skies dismal. R. wishes that Count Gobineau could accompany us to Palermo. —

Feustel's speech once again fills all the columns of the newspaper and annoys him by interrupting the serialized novel, *In the Grip of the Nihilists!* — Yesterday he was interested in the news of gold coffins containing richly ornamented corpses, discovered in the Balearic Islands. — We go for a short drive, and on our return R. reads a ghost story by Apel which he finds so entertaining that he tells it to us at supper; at the same time he observes that the tone prevailing in the society of that time seems to have vanished completely now. — After supper he plays a game of billiards, while I play little games with the children; then he plays some excerpts from *Euryanthe* very beautifully, from the 1st, 2nd, and 3rd acts, with the usual mixture of delight and regret. But at any rate he cannot be accused of making the same mistake: he has given room on the stage to the melody, and not suddenly interrupted the general rejoicing with glee-club music. As an example he cites the finale of Act I of *Lohengrin*. When we are upstairs in the dressing room, he tells me that he feels exactly as he did in the years of his youth, so that at times it seems to him utterly ridiculous that his hair is gray.

Monday, October 24 R. had a good night and walks a little in the garden. After lunch Lulu's letter arouses concern, indeed even anger, because of what she tells us about Princess C. W[ittgenstein]. — Goethe's "eternal feminine" is mentioned, but R. feels that women would not thrust themselves forward in this way if the men were not so pitiful. Our maid Marie sobs as she brings in the lamp, since she has heard we are going away. I am very touched, R. as well—memories of Vreneli and leaving Tribschen. Earlier, R. came up to me again: "But you are going with me." — In the evening friend Wolz., R. talks about *Faust* and remarks how unique it is—there is nothing else to compare with these two parts; this meeting in the first part, whereas in the second, Goethe, like Beeth., felt the desire at the end of his life to write once more "in his own way." In the years between—*Iphigenie, Tasso*—well, yes, he showed with these what becomes of a man when he is not himself. The children perform a charade outstandingly well, then R. plays *T. und Isolde,* and all, all that is sorrowful dissolves, and the fair bliss of melancholy flows through our veins! — Then, after expressing his regret that we cannot take Wolz. with us, R. relates how [Wilhelmine] Schröder-Devrient once said to him in great passion, "Oh, what do you know about it, tied to your wife's apron strings?," and how strange that made him feel. He was 32 at the time.

Tuesday, October 25 R. had a restless night, he says goodbye to our friend Jouk., whose servant Pepino has preferred to remain here, out of fear of being left behind in Italy. We talk a lot about this singular case. After lunch a new installment of *India* keeps us occupied, and when I remark that India also possesses the legend of the virgin mother, R. says, "Yes, that suggests that woman was here first—that is to say, outside of time." Today he attempts to go out alone, but he returns home in great distress. He says people in the palace gardens must have thought he was drunk, he leaned for support on every tree; he will not take one further step here. In the evening I read aloud one of Apel's ghost stories, "Paulinzell," though it does not please R. as much as the first. However, he likes the way it makes use of the events of that time—the Battle of Möckern, etc. He feels such vivid descriptions would no longer be possible.

Wednesday, October 26 R. had a good night, but he has given up his article. My father thanks us for the telegram. He shows me an article in the newspaper about "Herodom and Christianity"; we regret that it is such an insignificant one and would have preferred it to be ignored entirely. R. regards me while I am reading: "I suppose I am still allowed to look at you? A noble human countenance, it transforms all creation—and how rare that is!" — When I speak of Lusch, he says, "Oh, all we can do is die, for the worries will not cease, the children keep bringing us back to them—the girls most of all, since they have to mingle with alien lives." — At 3:30 Prof. Leube from Erlangen. Long consultation, the best of results—R.'s organs completely healthy; only strict diet and much fresh air necessary. Abundant—indeed, super-abundant—joy following silent fears! A few moments of chat with the excellent doctor. In the evening the Grosses and Wolz. Much about our impending journey and friendly chat, also billiards. We talk about short stories, and R. tells us of something which occurred to him during his walks in the Sihl valley near Zurich; the rescuer—a man living quite alone and dispensing justice—turning into a mischief-maker. — He also talks about his work and regrets that one can no longer very well use the word *"Weiber"* for "women"—*"Frauen"* has an entirely different meaning. — Recently he praised Goethe for his great knowledge of the German language; he says he is constantly being astonished by it.

Thursday, October 27 R. had a good night, except that in the morning Dr. Leube's medicine had somewhat too strong an effect. — Yesterday he discussed the future of the *B. Blätter* with Wolz. and hoped that a community would be formed which, by criticizing existing institutions —the universities, for example—would prepare for the times following a complete breakdown. — A request to me from Frau von Marenholtz to promote the centennial celebrations for Fröbel makes him ask with a slight shrug of the shoulders whether people really thought they could avert the evil by educating the children. — A letter from Lusch provides us with another insight into the female character (P[rincess] C[arolyne]). — R. writes all kinds of business letters, and I read to him

Parson Stoecker's election speech in Dresden. It pleases us with its straightforwardness and truthfulness, but we regret the necessity to go along with the Reich Chancellor, hence this subdued acknowledgment of the military, etc. — Then R. plays a lot of things from *Oberon* and again from *Euryanthe,* and we delight in their beauty and delicacy.

Friday, October 28 R. feels a little unwell. He reads Lubbock on primitive man but soon loses interest in it. At lunch all kinds of trouble with the children, Loldi somewhat willful and rude toward me, R. feeling she has some cause, I sad. We drive to the theater, inspect the royal box, and then visit friend Feustel, who talks with great confidence about the performances next year. In the evening we discuss Parson Stoecker's speech with friend Wolz., and R. says what is bad about it is the appeal, "If you are against progress, vote for us." R. feels foreigners would be quite unable to understand that. Then R. plays pieces from Marschner's *Der Vampyr,* and we are astonished by the vulgarity of the text (for instance, in the vampire's aria) and the naïve plagiarisms of Weber and Mozart, though there are signs of talent, such as the seduction scene. "But it is a good thing to go through a work like this, so that one doesn't make too much of it." How it makes one cherish Weber's delicacy! — R. finds the beginning of the Overture superb, and he plays it—leaving aside the wrong notes— with a rousing sense of its character. — Late in the evening R. comes back to the subject of male and female and says the essence of the female is sympathy with the male in his struggles against the outside world; if the man perishes, the sympathy ceases, and the woman becomes hard. — R. spends a long time looking at the illustration of the socialists' trial in the *I. Z.* and says that the accused look like madmen, the judges very evil; and the watching audience—a dismal sight. By contrast, the *Fl. Blätter* provides much amusement and gives rise to many plays on words, such as "As Othello I visit many hotellos," etc. [*One untranslatable example omitted.*] But during our drive we are in a serious mood, and as the carriage turns away from the theater, R. asks me, "What would you have replied to Pilate when he asked, 'What is truth?'—something which cannot be said to a liar?" I: "I think I should also have kept silent, etc." He: "Quite right, truth lies not in words, but in deeds; its center of gravity lies wholly in morality." — Following this conversation, we drive down the Bürgerreuth highway in silence, in a glorious sunset. This part of our countryside is particularly dear to R., and today—because of our departure?—it seems to me more than usually transfigured. — Before the music in the evening R. read to us a passage from the preface to Kant's *Theory of the Heavens* dealing with the purpose of the Creation; the way it is described pleases him. — A picture of two Mongolians in a new installment of *India* brings from him—on account of their strange faces—the exclamation "This is what our conquerors will look like." —

Saturday, October 29 A good night, but a mood of seriousness, until an embrace solves everything and Schnappauf's errand evokes the best of high spirits. The latter comes to me and asks in the name of "the master" whether I have a message for him; I say no; the messenger: "I think the master meant, for him"—whereupon I laughingly send greetings, which he at once, laughing himself, receives. He has again been reading Kant, with pleasure on the one hand, but also with regret over some obscurities. At lunch (our neighbor with us) Gambetta's visit to B[ismarck] is discussed, G.'s curious, Israelite secretiveness and B.'s simple remark that he should leave his card, "and I will visit him later." Yet R. believes that both Bismarck and Europe want G., in order to satisfy Rome, which undoubtedly desires to see Ferry removed and hopes at least for unrest and all kinds of concessions from this International. Over coffee Dr. Hering speaks in favor of nondenominational schools, and with such pedantic obtuseness that R. grows extremely angry, after having several times explained to him that, caught between the Jesuits and the Jews, German Protestantism would be bound to perish. When Dr. H. says he is unable to understand how R. can talk of the decadence of these times, for he himself is a sign of their improvement and elevation, R. says, "The peaks which rise up are there just to emphasize the decay." — He withdraws and, during our drive, says he cannot understand why he flew into such a rage, but for him an individual like that is typical of the whole species, and he, R., then asks himself why he ever has anything to do with such creatures. We drive past the "Krummstab," which R. notices, and upon which he sees a raven sitting! When we return home, we see Fidi playing billiards with Ferdi, and when Fidi misses a ball, he whistles, "And though a cloud may now obscure it," which amuses R. greatly, and he continues, "The ball still stands upon the green." — In the evening some of Apel's ghost stories, including "*Der Totentanz*," which we enjoy very much, though it is somewhat farfetched. Then R. plays something for me from [Boieldieu's] *Jean de Paris* which he says is the troubadour's song—it seems a little monotonous, for all its French charm—something which, it seems, no longer exists in France, either.

Sunday, October 30 R. had a good night and spends the morning with Kant, also with letters. Brandt writes very nicely and takes on the management of the whole thing. A cold wind, R. attempts to go out, but soon returns home for fear of erysipelas. At lunch "Werbel and Swemel," our two musicians. Herr Humperdinck shows us his neat copy of the score; R. looks at the "*die Klage, die furchtbare Klage*" passage and fears he may have orchestrated it too heavily, particularly in the wind instruments. When I venture to remark that, since the actors would certainly not be able to convey the whole situation, it is a good thing for it to be carried by the orchestra, and that a powerful orchestra never disturbs, but enhances (as in the awakening of the Wala), he agrees with me and says, "The cothurnus is a necessity." He also says he was thinking of his theater. — We do not go for a drive, but stroll up and down in the *salon,* discussing domestic affairs. Then R. sits down at the piano and plays the 3rd act of *Pars.*—wonderfully! In the evening we have our friends from the management committee and the Jägers. R. has something from *Euryanthe* performed, from "*Unter blühenden Mandelbäumen*" on, he himself singing Lysiart. When the guests have left, he sends for Wolz., orders champagne, tries once more to persuade our friend to come to Palermo with us, then, turning to me with "I did not tell you," goes on: "I recently saw quite clearly in my mind's eye Prince Hal's face, a blotchy, ravished face with bushy eyebrows, and eyes which can at times flash with anger. His humor comes from indulgence, and his indulgence is drink. The scene with Pointz is repulsive, and the one with the King in which he puts on the crown, just affectation." I remark that it is a natural affectation; R. agrees with me, but not when I observe that awareness of his calling must also have been apparent in his face. However, he agrees again when I observe that all attempts at interpretation seem impossible, since, just as one is telling oneself that it must have been like that, it always turns into something different. "An unfathomable being, this Shakespeare— he wants to glorify the national hero, but he cannot help himself, he must show him like this. In *Hamlet*—there he really expressed himself. *Hamlet* provides us with a commentary on this world. But one could spend a whole lifetime reflecting on this scene between father and son. He, H. V, is the setting star, the end of a heroic line. In H. VI the weakness is already apparent." When our friend leaves us, R. exclaims to himself, "H. V—it looks like something, but is nothing," in his bitterness at being unable to persuade our friend to go with us. Then, upstairs, he tells me something from his childhood which I have now forgotten (the sentence completed in Palermo).

Monday, October 31 Packing and clearing up. Soon, R. observes, I shall be able to sing, "All flies delight," whereas here it is "All delight flies." I am very tired from all the things which have to be considered and arranged, and when we are talking together, and R. replies to a tender word from me—"without each other we are no longer conceivable"—with absent-minded indifference, my great weariness breaks out in ill-humor, and I sink into a deep sleep. When I awake, R. says nothing, but he is weeping; I see the sheet of paper, which he goes to tear up after we have embraced, but I rescue it and, having rescued it, tell him what happened; then back to work. [*Sheet of paper not found in the Diaries.*] Friend Wolz. in the evening; talk about the comparison between Wallenstein and Bismarck printed in the *Tagblatt,* and R. expresses his admiration for Gustavus Adolphus, admitting that there is some truth in the way the German princes, out of a kind of patriotism, behaved so badly toward the great King. Today R. was struck by how pretty Eva is.

Tuesday, November 1 R. had a good night, and we are busy with packing and farewells. At lunch our good friends the Grosses. Departure at 7 o'clock in the evening. Siegfried weeping! Before our departure R. drove to the station to look for our carriage; at the very moment of our arrival it had been shunted onto another rail for half an hour. When we are in our saloon carriage, R. says he can now see Georg spending all day playing billiards with his wife; I quote the line from [Winter's] *Das unterbrochene Opferfest,* "For husbands it is right and proper with their wives to dwell." "Except that here what is right and proper is not allowed," R. replies. — This line, which he considers the most stupid imaginable, causes me to remind R. that in Frankfurt (1862), when Antonio's remarks struck me as somewhat curious, he had aroused in me an admiration for *Tasso* which still persists, whereas he no longer cares for it. "I admit," says R., "that it is a truthful portrayal, but of a world which means nothing to one."

Wednesday, November 2 In Munich around 8 o'clock. Herr Levi awaits us with breakfast. Severe cold, the enormous station means a long walk for R., during which his chest spasms recur. Departure around 9 o'clock. R. reads with interest an article about Schiller and Sicily ("Diver," "Hostage," *Braut von Messina*) and gives it to me to read. We are soon in the mountains, snow scenes, R. tells me it always reminds him here of Parricida. He also thinks of *Tannhäuser* and, when it grows lighter, tells me of his first impression in Boulogne, when he saw in a French newspaper a quotation in German, "*Es föngt an*" [*instead of "fängt an," begins*]. — We look at patterns for the *Pars.* costumes. — When Fidi whistles the waltz from *Der Freischütz,* R. says it sounds like "And though a cloud may now obscure it." I observe that it was Weber's large hands which gave him his love for the ninth. "Yes," says R., "he played octaves wrong." — R. reads Kant's *Theory of the Heavens* and finds it curious, alien, its expressions intricate. In Bolzano friend Jouk., who accompanies us as far as Verona; discussed costumes and many other things.

Thursday, November 3 R. slept quite well in his little room, and the public welcome is performed in Pesaro in front of Rossini. From then on various happy impressions, much greenery, golden autumn colors, Ancona splendid, Osimo pretty. R. is unfortunately vexed by the children's untidiness; he scolds them severely. Slow arrival—R. says it is curious how long things take when one is almost there. At last, around eleven o'clock, in Naples. Moonlight and silence. Arrival at the Hôtel Bristol, all tired. R. worried about having scolded the children, he feels it is always unjust.

Friday, November 4 Not a very good night for R. because of the unfamiliar beds, but soon forgotten. Naples in blazing light stretched out before us! — I am oppressed by feelings of melancholy, for which I reproach myself, and when R.'s watch falls to the ground and stops, it seems to me like a punishment for my apprehension. Prof. Schrön comes to greet us, and then we drive, R., I, and Fidi (the others having gone ahead), to the Villa d'Angri. Reunion with our good gardeners, then drove as far as the Villa Postiglione around 3 o'clock. At 5, drive via Pizzi Falcone—unbelievable for us poor Northerners—to the ship. [*Added on the following page but referred back to here:* "R. much taken by fine maps of Italy, he talks about the earlier style of cartography and compares the methods of description to Kant's *Theory of the Heavens.* — And while we were on our happy drive to Pizzi Falcone, R. gazed at all the people and said, 'What we see here is unconscious suffering!'"] On the ship, vexation for R. over the cabins. Departure in moonlight at 6 o'clock. R. soon goes down to the cabin, I settle the children on the deck and sit beside them. R., who comes up at the crack of dawn, says I looked like Hecuba with the corpses! He tells me that the chloral pills Jouk. gave him against seasickness had worked as *agents provocateurs!* Gradually we discover all the things we have on our ship: horses, oxen, chickens, convicts, soldiers, and other Italians; it has been the first fine day for weeks, and now everyone is traveling. R. was pleased by a lively conversation between Fidi and a soldier.

Saturday, November 5 Arrival in sunshine at eleven o'clock. Much waving from boats, and the waiting people storming on board, which, since it hinders our leaving the ship, makes R. very indignant. But then he joins in our laughter. Arrival at the Hôtel des Palmes, rooms 24, 25, 26, with a conservatory terrace overlooking the garden, the children on the ground floor opposite; everything nice and homely and green. Rub. welcomes us, we have breakfast, unpack, and drive through the town, which makes little appeal after Naples. I observe to R. that this is hardly likely to become our permanent winter abode for the future.

Sunday, November 6 Quite a good night in spite of some deficiencies in the beds. The sun smiles upon us, and we smile back. Our first deed is to rescue birds, which are hunted with lures and cages smeared with birdlime. Drive to the Flora, which pleases R. greatly. Spent a long time in the evening sitting on the terrace (conservatory) in moonlight. The idyllic aspect of Palermo is beginning to captivate us. And R. in his contentment is infinitely kind toward me. — Melancholy news about Lusch and Father. R. intends to persuade my father to join us permanently.

Monday, November 7 R. had a restless night, since he had taken medicine, but he is looking well. He arranges his worktable in the *salon,* and the situation pleases him. In the afternoon we drive to Monreale. [*Added on next page, under Tuesday:* "Yesterday, on the journey to Monreale, R. notices a small and very independent poodle, a favorite breed of his, and in the evening he is still thinking of the little creature, having been struck by its intelligence."] Sublime impression: "What people they must have been to build such a thing!" R. exclaims. We are enchanted by the cloisters. The valley of oranges is like a fairy tale, and when we return home we feel that nothing less than Shakespeare will do. — We begin H[enry] VI, Act I, the children showing great interest. As he reads, R. looks so wonderfully young that I have to tell him so. And when we are discussing this first act, he says, "He is the greatest of them all." — "What images!" he exclaimed as he read Exeter's "Like captives bound to a triumphant car." — And at the conclusion of the evening he sat down at the piano to show me how homogeneous is the recitative of Agathe's aria in *Der Freischütz,* how its sole purpose is to lead in.

Tuesday, November 8 A good night, and sunshine until breakfast, then, however, an overcast sky. R. settles down to his score, page 1 of the third act, and he calls out to me, "I have made no mistakes." We have lunch with the children in a cheerful and harmonious mood and then go for a walk in the Via Maqueda, looking at the shops. The air is very mild. — Yesterday, when we sat down at table, R. brought up the subject of compassion for animals, and remarked how long it took mankind to come to its senses; I observe that it is wonderful enough that it happened at all; R. feels it did so through mankind's own suffering. — And, talking of the many stars and suns he finds mentioned in Kant, R. says he feels the same way about it all as the French general about the Marne: "*C'est une mauvaise plaisanterie.*" — In the evening R. reads to us the 2nd act of *H. VI Part I,* again making an indescribable impact, especially the scene involving the brawl with the roses. It is impossible to speak of anything else. When I say to R. that the play with the symbolic roses reminds one of *Tr. und Isolde* (the torch), he says, "Yes, it is musical," and, "When one person speaks in Shakespeare, one must always pay attention to what the other replies"—foolishness to try to compare him with anyone else. And: "If a community were to be created, one would have to erect a pulpit, in order to learn from Shakespeare what history is." He also feels that, because the Sh. histories include features from real life, they make a completely different impact from those in which he had only stories to work on—in these some traces of conventionality are still interspersed. And even where there is that Renaissance flavor he finds so repulsive, Nestor, Hector, it is full of life.

Wednesday, November 9 Battle with mosquitoes for R., I suggest changing beds, and that enables him to get some sleep; but in the morning and all day long he is in a wretched state because of great errors of diet yesterday (beer, tea, grog, champagne, one after another). It is stormy in the morning, but at noon the sun comes out. R. relates to me some statements by Lassalle about the press, which are very significant. We go for a drive, R. and I, and visit the Cappella Palatina, which makes a splendid impression on us. Details of the trial in Pizzo cast a gloomy shadow over the evening; and I have feelings of anxiety when I hear that Siegfried has been climbing Monte Pellegrino with Herr Türk. In the evening chat with friend Rubinstein, somewhat depressing, and reminiscences of *Robert le Diable* do nothing to enliven it.

Thursday, November 10 R. slept peacefully. A stormy morning prevents our having breakfast in the conservatory, instead we eat in the *salon,* his workroom. He is pleased with its furnishings, even the worn rugs and cushions: "I like friendly things," he exclaims, and when I remark that, even if they are old, they still look pretty, he says, "Yes, when the color fades, the ideality of the feeling still remains—when Makart vanishes, Lenbach remains." — We come back to Lassalle and his assertion that with such a press even the Greeks would have become stupid. "Except that they would never have produced it," R. remarks. "That is what I always say—what sort of people are we, to let such things happen?" When I remark that it seems to me that the Germans were never made to form a state, which always contains an element of sterility, he says, "Yes, it is an Assyrian-Semitic idea; we Germans were made to form small, industrious communities like the Boers; the French, on the other hand, for monarchy." — The fact that Bismarck is speaking against the anti-Semitic movement and the rumor that Parson Stoecker is to be removed from office make R. think that, having realized that it failed to get recognized in the elections, the Reich Chancellor is now abandoning the movement and making a pact with the Jews! . . . R. observes that one ought to leave the Reich, so as to keep it from causing one too much grief. R. works and shows me the completed page of his score. We do not go out but are able to stroll on the terrace, where, among other things, R. is much amused by the monkeys; he goes to give one of them a tap, but it anticipates him and hits R. In the evening delight in Siegfried, who is again drawing ceaselessly here. And the 3rd act of *H. VI,* in which we are moved above all by Exeter's soliloquy. Otherwise R. does not much care for the scenes in France. — And continually Weber.

Friday, November 11 Lovely sunshine, cheerful breakfast. Work for R., he is pleased to have overcome a bad passage at the end of the third act. In the evening, as he is writing his second page, he recalls the irrational way in which Berlioz at times introduced his instruments, and he is glad to have smoothed out this passage successfully. After lessons we—the children and I—go for a walk, as does R. for half an hour or so. After lunch we, he and I, take a lovely drive to the Villa Giulia, delighting in all the blooming vegetation; R. is pleased by a palm tree, its hanging leaves laden with fruit, also by large red blossoms which look to him like butterflies; sea and mountains give delight. There were no errors of diet today, and in the morning he talked about the wretchedness of strong desire. In the evening the 4th act of *Henry VI* and then, brought about by a chance quotation of "Believe me," etc., the first scene between Faust and Mephisto, to our renewed admiration. "Only a German could have written that!" R. exclaims, and at Faust's words "So to the actively eternal," etc., he stops, to allow us properly to appreciate their greatness and splendor. Whereas in the later conversation the "Then let thyself be taught, say I! Go, league thyself with a poet" seems to him artificial, constructed, and it displeases him. The fine freedom of the verses especially pleases him, such as "In names like Beelzebub, Destroyer, Father of Lies," which should be read quickly, he feels.

Saturday, November 12 Lovely morning, the curious and unpleasant scenes with Joan La Pucelle in *H. VI* are discussed; R. says: "One sees they caused him real trouble." On the other hand, we think with delight of the heroic idyll of Talbot and his son. At 12 Dr. Berlin arrives, making some changes in R.'s diet. At lunch R. again remarks how strange it makes him feel that he is 68; he says it always comes as a surprise to see that his hair is gray, he always feels as if he has Fidi's hair. Recently he made the remark, "I am not a ghost, after all—with my *Parsifal* I am again coming along with something new." — We take a 2-hour walk which enchants R., in the English Gardens [*Giardino Inglese*], heavenly air and indescribable colors. Returning home, R. writes his score, and in the evening we finish *Part I.* What patriotism does to a person, he says, we can see in the wretched scenes with La Pucelle, whereas a German, unaffected by any such barriers, Schiller, saw the truth. — When Schopenhauer's remarks are discussed, R. says, "He was a philospher, but no sage." — At the conclusion of the evening R. calls me out onto the terrace to show me the glorious summer night.

Sunday, November 13   A good night for R., and the morning air quite glorious; we enjoy it by having breakfast on the staircase landing. Some roses the landlord brings me seem to R. to have a quite special fragrance; he observes that at home they would no longer give off scent. We then go for a walk and visit friend Rub., and R. writes half a page. In the afternoon we drive to Punto Gallo and are enchanted by the homeward journey through the Favorita. R. completes his page, and in the evening he reads aloud the first act of *Part II,* during which we ask ourselves in amazement how it is possible to be so entranced by such alien relationships, which leave us cold, and such unsympathetic characters; yet every word grips us, even the children.

Monday, November 14   R. cried out in the night and told me in the morning that I had once again left him with some accursed painter, not a well-known one, after a picture had been taken from his room and a hole made in the wallpaper, about which he had had nothing to say. All the time he had had a feeling of great lack of breeding on his part, and he had indeed succeeded in making me return to have it out with him! He says he knows what was intended: that he should wake up—and, to ensure this, the dream produced the worst horror of which it was capable. [*Added two pages later:* "He then reproaches himself for his lack of breeding and talks of his 'vulgar habit of guzzling' —he says he cannot help eating huge amounts of bread and butter with his coffee; nothing else tastes half as good, though it is always bad for him."] — However, he is very cheerful at breakfast, and he says to me, "You will be amazed what I shall make in my next article of the fact that the sun is feminine." Then he comes to the subject of the firmament, how curious our understanding of its nature. "Though indeed," he adds, "even when the law is discovered, it still has to be applied," and suddenly, "What a stiff beggar a human being is, when he can think of nothing better than straight lines to get at the secrets of Nature, whereas Nature itself has none, until the artist comes along and takes his wavy lines from Nature." — Late last night he thought of Marie Hohenlohe and said that just how bad a creature like her is inside is shown by her spiteful behavior toward M. Dönhoff in connection with the certificates of patronage—that condemns her. — At lunch R. tells the children about his dream; Boni asks, "What happens to us?" "Exactly," says R. "I thought to myself, 'The children will stay with me, and then she will surely come back.'" — The children laugh. Then he talks to them about Italian history, the significance of Venice. Finally about *H. VI,* and he points out that Warwick simply represents the Norman character of the conquerors and the urge to set up a different economy. — Before lunch R. and I went out [*added in margin:* "along the Via Maqueda, which R. calls V. Macbetha, as he calls our Stabile Via Staberl"] to buy him a hat, and after lunch we go for a walk in the English Gardens; in the evening the 2nd act of *Part II,* deeply moved by it. Before that R. spoke of the 2 pages he has written and mentions how much he dislikes harsh effects, how he always tries to anticipate them, to make them understandable, prevent their sounding abrupt; and he points to the Gurnemanz passage, *"kalt und starr,"* pleased that today he has given it an accompaniment of muted horns. He says this is what pleased him when he heard the *Nibelungen*—that even the very boldest of the sounds to which he had had to resort did not come in unanticipated. With subjects such as his, he says, it is necessary to make use of eccentric colors, *"notte e giorno faticar"* would not be enough, but the art lies in not allowing them to sound like eccentricities. He points out how effective in *H. VI* mild and resigned words are in their wild environment—the two lines about the miracle I had found quite particularly striking. — At lunch we heard a shot, and I asked whether birds were being hunted. "Yes," said the waiter from Ancona, and he observed that the people here are so backward that only gradually can they be brought to behave with more propriety; otherwise there would be immediate revolutions. We reflect on this statement and wonder what examples have been set these wretched people by the nobility and the church. — Before supper, just after R. has completed the 2nd page of his score, our reading of Sismondi, which I am now studying with the girls, leads our conversation to heretics and their views, so deep and so similar to ours. "I believe," says R., "that it is conscious suffering which has brought us so close to the heart of things." — A letter from Count Gobineau gives him the idea of summoning him here with a telegram: *"Nous comprenons que vous ne comprenez rien"* ["We understand that you understand nothing"]. I prefer to write, urgently inviting our friend to join us here.

Tuesday, November 15 R. goes for a walk before breakfast. Then he writes his score, and at midday we go out in very bright sunshine, and in a garden square are enchanted by the sight of a bush of passion flowers. In the afternoon we stroll along R.'s favorite street—Strada di libertà; he works again on his score, and in the evening he reads to us the 3rd act of *Part II.* After such things nothing remains to one except silence, wonder, and the uplifting feeling of becoming a better person. —Before that R. showed me the *I. Zeitung* with two pictures from the world of royalty; he is particularly repelled by the uniform of the Austrian Emperor, shown proposing a toast to the Italian royal couple; he is offended by the shortness of the uniform, which does not even allow for cuffs and, when the sleeve is pushed back by the movement of raising a glass, reveals so much of the bare arm.

Wednesday, November 16 At midnight I was startled by a dream, I felt as if Fidi had called me; we make our way, R. and I, along the lengthy corridors and see him sleeping very peacefully; then we return, I very distressed at having disturbed R. by crying out. At breakfast he talks about music and how strange it is, how impossible, to set something like *Faust,* for instance, to music; in my father's *Faust* Symphony, when the chorus starts with "All things transitory," etc., one feels, "Why didn't he say that earlier?," whereas the Magnificat at the end of the *Dante* Symphony is quite different. Then we talk about *H. VI,* and R. remarks that in it the populace appears (at Gloster's death, demanding justice) for the first time in the manner it has since been so frequently used—by V. Hugo, for instance. Then he speaks of how short the speeches are, so that one could in a certain sense set them to music. Much walking again today, delight in the roses in our gardens. In the afternoon a walk to the marina, where we take much delight in the sea, the mountains, and the sunshine. Before supper our time is taken up in discussion of a letter from Herr Neumann and various things derived from it in connection with Paris and London. Difficulties appear to be arising. — In the evening the 4th act of *H. VI* makes us forget all these troubles! Before that R. gaily recalled the saying, "The hand that wields the broom on Saturdays will best, on Sundays, fondle and caress," and he read this nice scene from *Faust* to us.

Thursday, November 17 R. did not have the best of nights, and he is put in a bad mood by being deprived of his bath this morning, but he is soon able to talk merrily to me about it. [*Added on the following page but referred back to here:* "Fidi relates a melancholy dream: We were on a steamship, and R. as Flying Dutchman was saying farewell to me and all the children; I had said goodbye to R. down in the cabin and was tranquil—Fidi thinks in order not to make them sad; Loulou and Eva in particular were weeping."] Then Shakespeare ad infinitum. R. is glad that we have the sonnets here, for they bring him closer as a person; R. imagines him to have been a cheerful man, "somewhat like me." — He goes to work, and around noon we set out to inquire about the condition of friend Rub. We soon return, and R. and I walk in the garden, where he talks to me about music, and in particular the last movements of symphonies, pointing out that in the F Major Symphony, for instance, Beeth. kept everything short, as if preparing to throw the whole weight onto the finale—the same in the C Minor. "In the *Pastoral* he meanders, and the finale of the A Major, however fond one is of it, allows one to say, in a certain sense, 'This is no longer

music'—but only he could do it. The last movements are the preci-
pices; I shall take good care to write only single-movement
symphonies." — In the afternoon vexation for R. on account of
visitors, interrupted walk. In the evening the 5th act of *Part II*.

Friday, November 18   R. had a good night and takes his bath; some
irregularities cause him great anger, but it soon turns to gaiety. I look
at some apartments, and R. speaks to the landlord about alterations;
I do not know whether it is just this that makes him so agitated, but
during our walk he is bothered by all his old complaints, we have to
rest frequently on benches, and he arrives home very tired. — At
lunch he talks about *Parsifal,* saying it will amaze us all; he particularly
mentions the prayer, which reveals all, things impossible to put into
words, for they are concepts and must be seen as such. He tells me that
I cannot imagine what this prayer is like. I observe that I already know
it: "Oh, yes, on the piano, but that is nothing, it is the instrumentation
that matters." — No reading in the evening; I tell him about my
reading with the children, Sismondi, Manfred's fate, and this brings
us to *Die Sarazenin*.

Saturday, November 19   R. had a good night in spite of a huge,
raging storm. We finally agree on terms with the landlord and now
arrange things as we wish them to be; it costs much effort, but at the
same time—because of the result—gives us pleasure. The prefect calls
on R. and turns out to be a clever and well-informed man with a clear
idea of whom he is talking to. We do not go out today, on account of
the storm and the rearranging. In the evening R. reads to us the 1st
act and half of the 2nd of *H. VI, Part III*. — R. tells us about a monkey
which amused him during his time as music director in Magdeburg;
it was called Marianne and was to be seen in the "Damenkrug"; it
once threw an apple back at Minna, finding it too sour.

Sunday, November 20   Our first conversation concerns Shakespeare,
R. observes that his heroes, "whom one can in fact hardly describe
as heroes," are a lot like the ancient Vikings, and they remind one of
Egill; we go through the remarkable passage of Warwick's flight and
are astonished by the poetic richness with which Shakespeare has
invested a subject so lacking in appeal. R. intends to write a letter to
the King but does not find time for it. At lunch R. interpellates Bonus
and adds, "I know I can no longer fall from grace; and one can say
that whoever falls from it was never in it." He laughs at the idea of
falling headlong from grace! — We talk of the Semites and the way
they have always made common cause with the press. R. says not
Rubinstein; when mention is made of the fact that he is always remarkably well informed, R. says: "Yes, it keeps dragging him back; he
is like Ignaz Denner, who, after discovering the saint, was always

being bothered again by Trabacchio. It is things like this which have always attracted me to Hoffmann; he certainly didn't invent them, but he described them." — We visit the Palatina, which enchants R. After lunch R. has a long sleep; it is 5 o'clock when he awakes, so we do not go out again. We stroll on the terrace. One of the monkeys has died through the carelessness of a boy who gave it a cactus to eat; the other one is grieving for its companion! "What else can one expect from these creatures who go about on their two legs?" R. exclaims in disgust, and we leave the terrace, which has now been spoiled for us. — In the evening chat and enjoyment from the *Fl. Blätter.*

Monday, November 21 [*Enclosed in the Diaries a piece of paper on which is written in Greek letters, in Wagner's handwriting:* "Fidi is a donkey." *Beneath this Cosima has noted:* "Written in Fidi's room by R."] Our first conversation is now almost invariably about Shakespeare, and today, when I remark on the mild reproaches H. VI makes to Salisbury, R. says, "That is because Shakespeare *sees* everyone he makes speak; he sees everything." From Rome we receive an extract from Renan's *Marc Aurèle;* I find this figure moving, but R. finds in him a certain lack of self-control unseemly in an emperor. In the morning R. begins a letter to the King, in the afternoon we drive to the Villa Tasca, which is charming and pleases R. greatly. He is also pleased by the sight of the sea, quite rosy in color, and, when we arrive home, he calls me to show me the view he has from his couch—the splendid palm tree in the garden opposite—and I am happy to see him taking cheerful note of it! He continues writing his letter, and in the evening we read the 2nd act and the beginning of the 3rd act of *H. VI.* In the face of that, silence! When I jokingly remarked at lunch that things had been easier for Aeschylus with his few characters, R. says, "That is the difference between myth and history," and, after a moment of silence, "One thing Shakespeare always shows us—the terrible state of the world. In that sense one could regard him as the greatest pessimist of all."

Tuesday, November 22 Shakespeare still! Yesterday, after we had finished the battle scene, R. exclaimed, "It is beyond belief," and at the conclusion of the evening he says to me, "I feel it is only I and Schiller who understand this play." He remarks how great they all are at the moment of death. — This morning he ends his letter to the King and tells me that he has dealt particularly with the subject of the Jews, told him that they have preserved a feeling for genuineness which the Germans have entirely lost, and that is why many of them cling to him. — Then, that as a German he feels at home here, since he finds living traces of great ancestors; he remarks to me that this is one of the few countries in which the Germans are preferred to the French. We go for a drive to the Villa Belmonte, which we much enjoy, and the walk does R. a lot of good. We then receive Count Tasca, who invites us and the children to breakfast tomorrow. In the evening the 3rd and 4th acts of *Henry VI*. — R. tired, but with the feeling that the air here agrees with him. —

Wednesday, November 23 A beggar who, seeking shelter from the north wind against a doorpost opposite us, starts his day's work at 6 in the morning, attracts R.'s attention. But the local inhabitants seldom give him anything. At half past twelve we drive with the children to the Villa Camastra, Count Tasca's home; a very nice, lavish *déjeuner* in charming rooms of ancient style. Our hosts extremely friendly and natural, the elderly wife knows Germany, and she shows R. his photograph. The weather is splendid, and the garden enchants us again. All the same, R. is rather tired on our return, and since he cannot rest as he would like to, he invites me for another walk around 6 o'clock; we stroll in the lovely, tranquil air, gaze at the crescent moon, discerning the shape of the full moon behind it, and return home for our supper and reading. We finish *H. VI*, horrified by the picture of the world Sh. gives us. R. remarks how this world becomes increasingly harsh; at the beginning it is found difficult to get rid of Gloster, but now people are simply stabbed, and then—Edw. IV—they start amusing themselves. When I point out how indifferent one feels to the relationship between Lady Grey and Edw., whereas, despite the cruelty, one is gripped by Marg[aret] and Suffolk, R. says, "Yes, that is tragic." He draws our attention to the remarkable nature of the scene in which H. VI is murdered—how Gloster is able, as it were, to make himself out as having been provoked to a deed already planned! We consider the different death scenes and the affection among kin, the only kind in evidence here, and have again and again to talk about the play. This morning at breakfast, which we had in the *salon,* R. said: "Do you want to see Herr Tocqueville? . . . Look in the mirror." He regarded himself wearing his new cap, made for him by the children.

Thursday, November 24 *H. VI* is still our breakfast topic. R. goes to his work and today writes two and a half pages of his score, although the somewhat lavish meal yesterday, which he much enjoyed, did not entirely agree with him. We go for a walk in the English Gardens in the afternoon and spend the evening in chat. — R. tells of his constantly recurring dreams: among others, one in which he has left or forgotten Friederike Meyer in Paris; also experiences with orchestras. — The fact that Dr. Strecker now wants to publish the Prelude to *P.* annoys him, like almost all notifications from the outside world (Herr Neumann again announces his intention of taking legal action against the management committee!). He says how pleasant it will be next year on the Nile—he will hear nothing for 3 months. — Discussion about the Emperor's speech, in which everything hinges on taxes! And R. is much amused at a joke by J. Gallmeyer; he recalls this famous actress, her enthusiasm for him and the modesty with which she forbore from visiting him: "Such characters ought to be studied," he says. — I talk about Talleyrand's correspondence with L[ouis] XVIII, the sparing of Saxony; R. feels it would have been better to give it to Prussia and do away with the dynasty which is disloyal to Protestantism. — Today R. said he was convinced that modern scientific studies were making people completely heartless. — A glance at a newly discovered picture of N[apoleon] I in his youth brings from him the remark how much more racial beauty, and expression, too, there is in this head than, for instance, in Bismarck's—"I can't bear bald pates," R. exclaims drolly, "Caesar has spoiled them for me." — When I tell R. about the Congress of Vienna, he says, "It was Beethoven's best period—the concert brought him 4,000 florins!" — He relates that he made a mistake in writing and wrote a stage direction for Kundry next to the violas.

Friday, November 25 R. does not feel well, the result of indigestion. He does manage to complete his page, but he eats little at lunch, omits his walk, and goes off to bed at 6 o'clock, after being vexed by a letter to me from Herr Francke about *Tristan* in London; they want to do it in Hamburg first as a preliminary study. "One can't keep anything spotless," says R.

Saturday, November 26 Before breakfast R. writes to Frl. Malten in Dresden to tell her that he would like to have her for Isolde as well as for Kundry. He comes to tea, somewhat tired, but recovered, and we laugh a lot when he tells me he has already had coffee. — He talks about the brother-sister relationship and says it is a remarkable metaphysical and physical law that such alliances do not flourish. In the morning, as I am writing to Herr Francke, he comes to me and recommends that I should read his "Retrospect of the Stage Festivals," as he has just been doing; I find a similar pleasure in it, the fact that it has all been stated openly. We drive to the Flora and delight in the fantastic avenue of palms. On this walk it again happens that R. gives expression to what was in my mind. I will cite just one example. Gazing up at the clear sky, I asked myself whether even in Spain the coloring could have a more southern flavor; "You will have to see the Guadalquivir someday," R. says to me shortly afterward. After our return home he is soon with me again; he has recovered his health and is cheerful! In the evening the 1st act of R[ichard] III . . . Before that he spoke of how anxious he is to complete his score; he says he is afraid of dying before it is done, and that he has felt this anxiety with every work of his. Then he shows Rub. a subtlety in the orchestration with which he is very pleased (the 1st violins cease to play, replaced by other instruments). He talked of wanting now to write nothing but symphonies, adding, "But they are not wanted, the concert societies won't perform them." We talk of the fate of the *Siegfried Idyll* and recall with pleasure my father's recognition. "Oh, ho-ho!" R. exclaims. "However much he exasperates one, he is still quite beyond compare—the only one with a feeling for certain things."

Sunday, November 27   R. had such a pleasant dream about my father that it almost worries him. My father sang something from *Die Msinger* more beautifully than anything R. had ever heard, and afterward they embraced and gazed deeply into each other's eyes, as in the most intense outpouring of friendship. Sulzer was also present, and he had with him an album containing illustrations from *Die Msinger:* "I should never have expected that from you," R. told him. — At breakfast I see a woman having breakfast on the terrace, and I tell R. I can imagine such a solitary, meditative woman being happy, but not a man. R. says: "What do you mean? The times of solitariness were my best—Lucerne, Venice." That leads us to Minna and her sufferings, since she could find no sort of pleasure and enjoyment in R.'s company, but only anxiety and fears of complete estrangement, after poverty had brought them close to each other—for instance, when a little money had been earned, a kind of gaiety was achieved. — I take my first stroll through the town and talk at lunch about our impressions. Etna leads R. to Hekla and Iceland and the life of the Vikings there. — A letter from friend Wolz. about the *B. Blätter* arouses R.'s displeasure, and he bemoans all he has encountered in the way of assistance and understanding. [*This last sentence obliterated in ink by an unknown hand; see notes.*] He says he will sell Wahnfried, hand over the performances of *Pars.* to Neumann, settle down here. "Oh, Solon, Solon, Niemann!" he exclaims (since Niemann prophesied that our gravestone would one day be inscribed "Here lies Meyer Cohn.") — [*Added in margin:* "He also thinks of the King, having read that the King has commissioned some plays about L[ouis] XV and is paying 2,000 marks each for them, since they will not be done publicly."] — He is very tired and run down. In the evening he talks to Herr Türk about the modern pronunciation of *ai* in Greek: he himself says *ā,* but now it is *ī*—since when? And for him the cry *á* corresponds to the word "*Weh*" ["woe"], and there is something terrible about "*AiAia,*" which he has now lost through the new pronunciation.

Monday, November 28   He had a restless night, and my little anniversary gift [*enclosed in the Diaries a heavily corrected verse by Cosima entitled* "November 28"] finds him in a disgruntled mood, but it gives him pleasure, and he comes to breakfast with the cap on his head. — He tells me he is working on a difficult passage, and altogether he is longing passionately for the day when this score will be finished. At lunch I tell him about our morning walk with the children, hoping that his disgruntlement is caused by the sirocco. We drive to the Favorita but do not get out. I tell him about the B. *Blätter* and Kant's remarks, among them the one about life (quoted by Bruno Bauer), and I tell him I always feel like making an addition of my own to it when I think about us. R. repeats to me what he meant to say in the morning with his joke about "Monsieur Fate": "What mattered to the universal spirit was our preservation, and so it was ordained that in life we should persevere; none of the other things involved has anything to do with life." At lunch he once again said how much he always regrets that we did not discover each other ten or fifteen years earlier. — We spend the evening in chat; R. reads to us Porges's article about my father, to our amusement as well as our concern, since its lack of clarity in expression makes its good intentions and occasional judiciousness even more terrible! I then read aloud Bruno Bauer's article on Luther, which gratifies us all. R. thinks Stein's style somewhat overornate (letter to W.). — A telegram from Niemann—"*Tristan* today, remember us"—arouses smiling astonishment. I am glad that it is happening today. —

Tuesday, November 29 A very restless night for R., a sort of crisis which he himself regards as not unsalutary, but which wears him out— and on top of that a battle with mosquitoes. At the first light of dawn he sees a young girl in the street, a baby on one arm and a basket on the other, picking over the garbage and having at the same time to reprimand a naughty little brother. R. says he wishes he had had some money to give to this very lovely girl, and at the same time that he could have punished the little boy. He reads B. Bauer's article again and is vexed by the passage on Christianity, which, coming from this author, did not surprise me, whereas I was pleased that he had understood Luther. — R. is also annoyed that he criticizes Kant's judgment, as if considering himself superior to him—that shows he had not understood or paid any attention either to Kant or to R.'s preceding quotation from Schiller. When we tell R. of our morning walk through the streets, his curiosity is aroused, and we look at all sorts of things again, La Gancia, S. Francesco d'Assisi, which pleases him. We also show him how, by passing through a narrow door and a wretched kitchen, one can reach a charming courtyard and a chapel. R. is amused by Siegfried's confident opinions, and he observes that what the theater world was to him, with its bearded ghosts and other things to which one made music, Italy would be to Siegfried, who saw it for the first time at the age of seven. In the evening R. talks about Helm's analyses of the Beeth. quartets; he is pleased with them and only hopes that something similar will be done for his works. I observe that popularity must always precede analysis. R. says no, things like the last quartets could never be popular; if one does not study them, one cannot even get the tempi right; B.'s notations are frequently misleading, and the quartet in Paris, however well and melodically it often played, made great mistakes. He does not believe me when I tell him I have the feeling that these things live for the Germans, despite bad performances. — He is much amused to see my father being cited as a Jew-baiter: a very drastic extract from *Des Bohémiens* is now being prominently featured in the newspapers. During our walk R. says he cannot understand all this eternal philosophizing, he finds it absurd: "Good heavens," he exclaims, "I have also concerned myself with these things, but besides that I also live, I read my novel" (he is indeed reading *Princess Narischkin's Wig* and telling us about it) "whereas this idea that one must get close to a subject by brooding over it is utterly stupid."

Wednesday, November 30 R. had a good night, but he feels tired after his bath. At breakfast he comes back gaily to the quotation about the Jews: "Really—your father a Jew-baiter!" But the word "popularity" seems to him inappropriate for Meyerbeer—one might have said "celebrity," but not "p."; Weber was popular, he says. — We search around for popular figures; he names Garibaldi, Nap. I with his little hat, which he copied from Frederick the Great. The question whether it is possible for a true genius to grow fat is also discussed: "Not if he is well born, from the aristocracy," R. feels. We go on to the unpopular Caesar, recall Shakespeare's Caesar, agitated, angry, and bombastic at the same time, thoroughly unsympathetic, whereas Mark Antony's torrent of sentiment makes him seem like a god. Shak. reminds us that we thought yesterday of his "deliver them like a man of this world"; R. fetches the book and reads aloud the report of H. IV's death. Then he goes to his work, while I drive with the children to the Grotta della Regina. Before lunch R. tells me he is now writing "I am shorter, thou art longer" in the meadow, between horn and oboe in the orchestra (here he is recalling the poem by Walther v. der Vogelw[eide] which Lusch recited to him in Tribschen). But at table he complains about the "horrible tales of violence" which demand "an utter concentration of ecstasy"—he had already forsworn it in *Tristan.* — We come to the subject of anger, and when I remark that, confronted with an angry person, I always feel almost ashamed of my coolness, he says jokingly: "Nothing breeds gentleness more than living with an angry person. Minna, for example—her eternal state of agitation made me completely calm, and she once told me that nothing had ever so enraged her as my calmness during a scene in Zurich. There was no passion involved, deep inside me I was quite unmoved, so that I could say coolly to myself, 'This is something you have simply to put up with.' " Then he says, "With you it happens ever more rarely, but when it comes, then it is the end of everything, even of life itself." — Typical of his outlook is what he says to me: "The people who stay away from me vanish from my mind, they have their own destiny independent of mine, like Joukowsky" (he stayed behind in Germany on account of the costumes) "and also Lusch." — News from London about the Neumann affair is more unpleasant than otherwise. At three o'clock R. and I visit a villa close to the Favorita; the air, the countryside continue to delight us, R. feels decidedly well here. He is also working regularly. In the evening he reads to us the 2nd act and half of the 3rd act of *R. III,* and that is already too much for our way of reading it and the impression every detail makes on us. The introduction of the news of Clarence's death after the meaningless reconciliation, made touching by the King's condition, the Queen's shattering exclamation, and the portrayal of the pleading Stanley which brings Edward to pour out his suffering: "That is a tragedy in itself," says R. Then Hastings dying: "Wise art thou again in dying," one can say of all Shakespeare's characters. — When supper was finished, R. got up and played Italian melodies, mainly by Bellini (*Pirata, Lucia, Sonnambula*), saying that this music, in freeing itself from Rossini's ornate style, enabled the heart to speak, and it was all suffering and lament. Then he comes to talk of Schröder-D., how fine she had been as Romeo; she did not appear in helmet and armor, as she had been seen up till then, but in a coat of mail, and her blond hair had looked so beautiful; it also made a fine impression when she was Lucrezia and D. Anna. — He recently talked about ninths and their significance, saying how trivial the ensemble theme in the finale of *Der Freischütz* would be without them. — Boni told us that, when she was looking for gloves for me in a shop and chose a pair on the spot, she was told to take them all away without paying, since our name is so well known! —

Thursday, December 1 R. slept well. At breakfast he entertains us with his account of how the wig is snatched from Princess N.'s head, and he seizes the opportunity to enlarge upon the dreadfulness of wigs, all the things that are needed to produce this white mass of hair, and what an uncanny effect they always had on him. Then we come on to *R. III;* R. remarks on the sudden violence at the council meeting: "The people cannot really believe that in that moment in the garden his arm withered, but the terror has been spread, and one can picture the two of them, Buck[ingham] and Gloster, laughing uproariously." — We also discuss the scene with the two princes, and R. says how well drawn Clarence's children are, too. — Then R. is amused by the cries in the street. Little as he cares for Italian chatter, all the more is he amused by the cries, and by Schn[appauf]'s remark that for the sake of 10 olives a man would make a noise as if he were offering the whole world for sale. Fidi tells us at lunch that yesterday the whole street gathered around him while he was drawing a church (S. Domenico); this amuses R. — We then come back to R. *III;* what particularly impressed me is the way the poet, in the midst of all the dreadful reality, shows his characters transfigured by suffering: Margaret becomes a sybil; Elizabeth, with her "Welcome," a heroine; Anne a penitent through her acknowledgment of guilt. — R. says, "That is ideality." — Over coffee I read that a further 20 million marks are to be spent on the army; R. says jokingly: "Germany is a beggar armed to the teeth. It is as well not to meet us in the street." — He is constantly being annoyed by the newspaper reports on *Parsifal,* more or less suggesting that he said the same things about the *Nibelungen* as well. He talks of publishing something about it; I advise him against it. — It is raining; he goes out after his siesta, to the bookshop, and he tells me that when he got there, he could no longer remember what he was looking for: "Renan? Cosima is ordering that." Finally Jacolliot, of whom they had never heard. But he was attracted by some relief maps, which he much likes: "Everywhere one feels as if one were there and settling in." — He is repelled by the rococo Church of San Domenico and the pillar of the saint: "That's what the Renaissance led to." I observe that there is no more cause to reproach it for that than to blame Palestrina's music for the emergence of the operatic aria, but he holds to his opinion, saying that Greek art influenced the world long after its own downfall, but this eagerness to make things beautiful, to avoid harshness, resulted in rococo; in the core of things there was something corrupt. "Ideas such as Nietzsche's have found their voice in Burckhardt, the Renaissance man: Erasmus, Petrarch, I hate them." — At supper he talks about his page, saying he made a lot of writing mistakes. — He arouses the children to merry laughter by describing the picture he keeps before his eyes to characterize the present-day world: "Fine horses, noble, eager, fiery, with them a good, hard-working, capable, earnest coachman, and inside the carriage, master of all these creatures, a bloated Jewish banker!" — We continue to speak of this world, and he says that never again can he bring himself to write another word about politics or even mention such a name as Bismarck [*the last eight words obliterated in ink by an unknown hand*]. On the other hand, he would enjoy dealing with a subject such as male and female—"like driving clouds in front of one." In the evening he reads to us up to the end of the 4th act; amid all the horrors and moving scenes we frequently have to laugh at all the wit and humor; the people who only hear when the recorder speaks! The scene with Buckingham's *"Give me some breath,"* the exclamation about Richmond on the seas. — When Fidi says good night before the reading, R. says, "You are right, my boy, to go off to bed! And yet," he adds afterward, "when I was his age, wild horses could not have dragged me away. God, how these things gripped me!" — Later, when Fidi's teacher praises his diligence, R. says, referring to his passion for architecture, "That is just how I want it—I should have no use for a composer son."

Friday, December 2 R. had a good night, but after his bath he again suffered a spasm. However, he is recovered and cheerful by breakfast time, and he relates that in his bath he had been thinking of Buckingham's account of the attitude of the people, and the superb humor contained in this account. This leads to much else about Shake. One thing he finds particularly horrible, he says, is that Anne cannot sleep because of her terrible dreams about her husband. Then he bids the heavens with folded hands to grant him easy pages! Things such as *"durch sie ging all mein Glück verloren"* in *Die Zauberflöte.* He has had enough of ecstatic miracles, he says. — And he has also had enough of wallowing in sorrow with the bass clarinet. I sing the theme from the last movement of the F Major Symphony: "Yes, that—that brings delight." — He then talks about the transition from "Hagen's Watch" to Brünnhilde's monologue. "Always *Tristan,*" he exclaims humorously, "they never talk of anything but *Tristan;* all the tender, overflowing love that lies in Brünnhilde's reflections—nobody has noticed that." — He works, goes into the garden before lunch. At lunch I tell him about my visit to the museum. It is raining gently, but it is still clear, and R. shows me how transfigured Monte Pellegrino looks. We go for a walk through narrow lanes, R. shows me a palace which he discovered on his solitary walk yesterday and which is quite magnificent. Everything entertains him, the life in the streets, various views such as the one above the splendid towers of the cathedral, unusual peacocks; we go into a church (S. Oliva) and pay a short visit to friend Rub. — Fidi relates his drawing adventures, telling us that a man got rid of the crowd around him at S. Francesco by throwing heads of lettuce. In the evening we finish *R. III;* with him, R. feels, the interest ceases— now come the "flat" ones, as he himself calls Richmond. Buckingham's death again seems like a transfiguration. — Over coffee a letter from Herr Levi raised some questions concerning *Parsifal;* R. says he no longer has the necessary keenness, somebody else should do it for him.

Saturday, December 3 R. was up for an hour during the night and read the Berlin *Tage-Blatt;* after that he slept well, and before breakfast he went for a walk in the English Gardens. He did not see our doorpost beggar; but yesterday he talked about this deplorable state of affairs and observed that one should do nothing but keep repeating to the people who praise Italian progress, "Your beggars." Then he comes to the subject of gaiety and seriousness and says: "Do you know why most people have no sense of humor? Because they are always pretending. A truthful person can let himself go and play around with things, the liar must always be thinking of himself. Gobineau, for instance, who cannot tell us his true reasons for not coming—he has to be very serious, whereas you, who see through it, can joke with him." I tell him how much I am struck by this, since it is the theme of the letter I have just begun to Jouk., who has admitted to us his difficulties—on account of his sister. [*A sentence of purely etymological interest omitted.*] He works. Around lunchtime we go for a walk in the garden, he shows me the orange tree beneath which, and the lawn on which, he wants to "roll" with Fidi. He is content here and is thinking of always spending 6 months of the year here, and to live in Germany for the sake of music, which is undoubtedly at home there; when darkness falls, the lamps are lit: "Now for the theater." He recalls what lovely experiences we had last year in Munich. But this is where he wants to live. He says sadly how much he would like to share it with friends, but he has none. He has asked Count Tasca, who called on us yesterday, to recommend a villa to him. Over coffee I read aloud a letter from Stein, who writes about the callousness of the socialists when one of their number was abducted. "Yes," says R., "when there is no idea to inspire them." He says they should be shown a great example and brought to see what selfless sacrifice means. With regard to that he keeps coming back to relationships with animals. He goes for a walk with the girls, by the sea and through the streets. We chat in the evening; Siegfried tells us that he was stopped in the street, asked whether he were the son of R. W. When he said yes, the man (a photographer) said to the other one, "*Tutto il tipo Wagneriano*" ["completely the Wagnerian type"]. — R. shows me the newspaper report about the King [*not found*], observing how strangely it coincides with their correspondence; he scents trouble, he says. Then he gets annoyed with the language in which the weather conditions are described. I read aloud the historical survey in Baedeker, and at the conclusion of the evening R. calls me onto the steps of the conservatory, shows me the moon, and delights in the splendid air. I feel how dreary all this beauty would seem if we were separated. "We have experienced that," R. says, "and, if we did not have the children with us, we could not take pleasure in it, either, even though we knew them to be happy and content at home." — In the afternoon, when he sees that I am coming to the end of Talleyrand's correspondence, he tells me he does not intend to read it. All the same, he adds,

"Everything is interesting—it just depends on who is reading it."

Sunday, December 4 R. had a good night and rises early to have a cold sponge bath. He tells me that he has prescribed this for himself, knows very well what he is doing, is vexed when he is treated as a delicate person to be cosseted by artificial means. Exactly the opposite of what he said in Bayr. when he was feeling ill! — Over coffee he talks, half in jest and half in earnest, about the downfall of the human race, which one is always seeking to counter by erecting telegraph poles and building railroads. Then he said he would like to live in a district which has no beggars. — He is looking well, and he tells me over afternoon coffee that here it gives him tremendous pleasure to sit down at his writing desk. He is glad not to need a fire—and then the lovely plants. "How lovely it is," he thinks to himself, "that you are able to write such a score, without sweat or anxiety, completely at ease!" He says everything here seems homely—quite different from Naples, where there is so much excitement. Today he goes out by himself, I being prevented by a bad foot, and he returns after two hours, somewhat tired, it seems to me. — At lunch he tells me that he has given up *The Theory of the Heavens,* since he knows too little about the subject, and he is now starting on Kant's book about the human races. And at the end of the meal he says he would like to make the acquaintance of a gifted young man, but not a woman—they always cause a disturbance. After his walk he goes to work, and he tells me he has been asking himself whether he should use a bass clarinet. I: "In which passage?" He: "In the baptism." He adds that he has not yet got that far, but he is considering it: "The fellows must practice." — At supper he recalls Switzerland, which gave him shelter twice: "Twice I have crossed Lake Constance with the feeling of leaving all that nonsense behind me." Then he recalls the performances of the Beeth. symphonies in Zurich and feels that, as far as correctness is concerned, he has never achieved better ones, because he had sufficient time there. We recall the other splendid performances and old times in Tribschen. He gives Boni Bismarck's speeches in the Reichstag to read. We are amazed by their tone, this constant "I." — At the conclusion of the evening we open the doors of the conservatory; mild air bathes us, R. feels well here! . . . Today he speaks to me of the beauty of S.'s eyes: "The lad is all eyes." He also played something from *Parsifal,* expressing humorous vexation that nowadays it is always *Tristan* which is singled out. He then observes that, if our performance plans fall through, he will hand the task over to Herr Neumann, so that the latter can earn some money for him and he can travel through Spain, up the Nile, etc. Today he was sent a R. W. calendar from Vienna, some mistakes in it.

Monday, December 5   R. slept well, has a cold sponge bath, and comes
to breakfast in good spirits after having greeted the children through
closed doors, as he frequently does here, with Mendelssohn's music to
"Pyramus and Thisbe." When I tell him I do not really care for it, he
says: "Oh, it's wretched stuff! The trumpets for Peas-blossom are
witty, but none of this *Midsummer Night's Dream* music has ever appealed to me. Still, all the theater managers vied with one another to
present this masterpiece; Eduard Dev[rient]—he was exactly that sort
of cold, perfidious M. admirer." — (These not his exact words, but
what he meant.) We talk merrily about the celebrations of the 100th
concert in Bayreuth, and the speech in connection with it which we
read yesterday in the *B. Tagblatt*. That is so typical of these people, R.
says, their self-satisfaction—and the final chorus always proclaims that
nothing more need be said to the world! We think of Schop. and of
what a respectable life he led; R. says his concern over the dissemination
of his works was due to their nearly having been pulped. "Just think of
Tristan," he says, "if printing had not been invented, how soon it
would have vanished forever!" — He recalls that Hans told him of his
visit to Schop. and the question the philosopher put to him: "Did
you notice how the dog looked at you?" "And it is true," says R.
"Nothing else is quite like the intensive look with which a dog examines a newcomer." — The morning is nice, and at lunch R. relates
that he has been working. "Oh, music!" he exclaims. "Here one will
be able to see for the first time what potentialities it contains for
conveying sorrow in bliss! That is something in the Adagio of the 9th
Symphony which I do not like, that rousing of oneself for a sort of
triumphal song, a self-mastery which is quite unnecessary, since it is
already there *eo ipso* in the music." — Lunch is somewhat overshadowed
by Loldi's melancholy, arising from a reproof I was obliged to give her
during the history lesson, and R. cannot bear to see the children sad.
The skies are gray, too. We go for a short walk by the sea, in spite of
the rain, and then home via the Politeama; R. chides a boy who is
maltreating his dog, and since he can make little impression on him in
Italian, he resolves to learn the language. — In the evening I read to
myself the speeches and replies in the Reichstag; the parties are now
all split up. "Socialism," says R., "is the only thing left with any
strength, for at least everyone is still talking about it." In the evening
I read aloud the passages in [Goethe's] *Italian Journey;* R. is bored by
the description of the sea crossing, I skip a lot and come to the capers
of Prince Pallagonia; R. remarks that Goethe used to enjoy staying
with such old fogeys. Regarding the Reichstag, he says: "Why doesn't
somebody get up and speak a sensible word, say to Bismarck, 'It was
you who introduced these laws—it was you who brought us to the

point about which you are now complaining'? Instead of that, everyone just worries that he might resign." (Letter from Lusch, R. thinks the life she is leading is a trivial one.) The girls tell us they saw a crowd outside the cathedral (at the side), they go to see what it is and discover their brother drawing, surrounded by inquisitive people who have come from all corners to watch him. [*Added in margin:* "He completes a letter to Wolz. for the January *Blätter*."]

Tuesday, December 6   A mosquito disturbs our sleep. However, R. goes to his work early, even before our family breakfast. He would have liked me to surprise him, but I, unaware of that, call him. At lunch I tell him about my reading with the children (Sism., the Sicilian Vespers period), and he enlarges upon the power the church possessed, all the monasteries, buildings, canonizations—it all came from the church. The continual acts of destruction, the conspiracies show him that the universal spirit has little concern for the beauty of paintings or buildings. — At lunch he repeats his strictures on beards, those emblems of the animal in men which he cannot bear. After lunch we both are led to the 1st movement of the C Minor Symphony; R. plays part of it and says, "Nothing like this outburst of enthusiasm and joy existed before Beethoven; Mozart knew nothing at all about it, though Weber has an inkling of it; this is one of those passages which, if one could decipher them, would explain the world to us." He promises to perform symphonies between the performances. — "Oh," he suddenly exclaims over coffee, "why do I need to have the bassoon blowing low notes?" — I: "Where?" He: "In the baptism. Anyway, I can't bear the bassoon." Then he says he ruled his score lines wrongly in Siena: "It's terrible when one has been given pedantry and inspiration inside the same skin—a real torment." I observe that this is what produces genius. — "Oh, this world of ours," he exclaims, "it is terrible!" And a little later, thinking of a time and place in which he would like to have lived, he says it would be with Plutarch in Chaeroneia: he had been very close to the greatest and had experienced so much, then came under the wing of the Antonines, but always in Chaeroneia. "With Shakespeare in Stratford, no, one could not have borne that—he had to live among people who had no idea of what he was." — We go for a walk, the cathedral—exterior—enchants him, reminds him of Indian buildings, and he observes that it looks like a king's castle. He says he enjoys living in a town with a building like that, but the rainy weather conjures up within him a picture of a journey up the Nile. Today, when R. mentioned the girls' situation, it stabbed my heart, so much melancholy does it cause me to think of the children in our state of isolation and estrangement. Then I call upon God, the Silent One, and plead for the strength to dispel all these gloomy thoughts which weigh me down, and I do believe, my children, that by quietly accepting things as they come I shall bring down upon your heads more blessings than if I were to attempt, at the cost of peace, to win for you some other lot. Let the blessings which are certainly yours persist undisturbed by my worries, and everything be entrusted to God—and, dear Lord, give me, preserve in me the strength of serenity! — At lunch R. related things from Kant's book on the human races, which pleases him on account of the naïveté of its descriptions. In the evening I start reading to our little circle Bismarck's speeches, but R. interrupts me. We conclude the evening with a discussion of the *B. Blätter;* R. feels that it should be allowed to die, though he is concerned about Wolz.'s fate. He was somewhat irritable, and I frequently call upon the God within me to give me strength against evil spirits. When we are alone together, then everything is always all right! But that is not always possible. Today he wrote in his *Braunes Buch* that the reason he cannot get along with other people is the foolish questions he is asked, which drive him to despair ("What do you think of Gounod?," etc.) — This morning he compared the drenched palm trees with a Spaniard returning from a masquerade.

Wednesday, December 7 R. again rose early and had breakfast by himself, but he does keep me company for a while. I visit the museum with Loldi in very wet weather, which is also responsible for our going for a drive with R., instead of a walk. At lunch he tells us about his reading (Kant), which he finds absorbing. The great success of *Tristan und Isolde* in Berlin, of which our friend Mimi has told us, both pleases and surprises him, and he speaks appreciatively of Niemann's ambition, which keeps him alert. Musical reviews cause him to exclaim, "Nobody takes *Tristan* as seriously as I do, neither poets nor musicians," and he feels he is really unclassifiable. Yesterday, as we were talking about the *B. Blätter,* he described the kind of criticism it should have published, e.g., a condemnation of the whole piano mentality, etc. — In the evening Rubinstein brings along the first proofs of his piano arrangement and plays it, to R.'s satisfaction. — Today he was annoyed by a letter I read to him from friend Gross, then at lunch said he was ashamed of himself, but two things in life upset him—on the one hand, the sluggishness with which things are done, on the other, the wild rush. Such punctuality when there is something to pay, but when one is expecting something, such procrastination! — A letter from Princess Wittg. about the significance of visiting cards amuses us greatly.

Thursday, December 8 Immaculata! The children accompany their governess to this curious feast and tell us the oddest things about it. R. works, and at lunch, when I tell him about an episode in Pisan history (the Battle of Meloria and its consequences), he says what happened there is just as in Nature, the same naïve cruelty, and so it was everywhere up to the moment which he calls *Jesus;* for a sensitive person, he says, the impulses of Nature are horrible! — We go for a walk on the terrace overlooking the sea and enjoy the view in spite of the cloudy skies. R. then works diligently and with much exertion till 7:30, and even then supper comes too early for him! In the evening he reads "The Diver" to us; it moves us greatly, though R. misses in the description the sufferings the boy must have undergone when holding his breath under water. R. says he would not have forgotten such a thing, since his approach is always a practical one. When I recall that the episode is said to have occurred under Fr[iedrich] II, R. starts talking passionately about princes and great men and their cruelty. He comes to the present-day ones and says, "This ability to see 1,000 men go to their death before one's eyes, and yet to stay in some sort of good humor, to go to the ballet afterward, all in the name of epaulets, military duty, retreat, *à la suite*—! Above all, uniforms—they are the reason everyone thinks alike." He gets very heated, and I have the feeling that the presence of some alien elements is partly to blame for that, though he continues to express his opinions. — Today we called Mozart the musician of the Renaissance. — And as he was watching the raging of the sea, he said, "And to build a dam against that helps Faust to get over all his sufferings about Gretchen—what frivolity!" . . .

Friday, December 9 This morning R. had another chest spasm; but he is able to work, and at lunch he is entirely well again. The naïvely shameless beggar at the doorpost, "our pillar saint," causes R. to remark that we are doing him harm with our long stay, since he would get more from travelers coming and going. We walk to the English Gardens and there meet Count Tasca, who takes us in his carriage to La Zisa, a remarkable Arab house. In the evening R. reads to me several pages from Kant's book on human races, which we find very absorbing; R. said at lunch that Schop. was right to call him the most original of thinkers. [*Added three pages later but referred back to this point:* "At supper we talked with the children about the history of the ancient world. R. relates that Prof. Weisse once said with an eloquent gesture that the Peloponnesian War had wiped out the flower of Greece, and this had spoiled everything for R.—he had had no feeling at all for the Romans. 'And, God forgive me for my sins, I was always on the side of genius, of Hannibal against the Romans, even though one must admire the energy with which, for instance, they swiftly built a fleet and with it beat the Carthaginians. Regulus, too, amused me.' A leading article about Gladst[one] and the situation in Ireland, which I read aloud, annoys R. with its lack of fairness toward the Prime Minister, of whom he says merely that he should never have become prime minister.]

Saturday, December 10 R. had a good night, and at breakfast we continue our conversation about Kant and his theme of seeds dying out. He works, I go with the children to look for photographs for friends in Bayr. At lunch he is pleased that the Rhine wine has at last arrived. Afterward we drive to La Cuba, then to La Zisa, and finally we alight in the Florio Gardens, which are very beautiful and in which a magnificent owl arouses admiration in R. and all the rest of us. "That is Nature," R. exclaims in the evening, "without disguise, terrible but truthful; and that fellow looked like a lion—more beautiful than a lion." We spent a long time looking at it, and returned to it after the charming gardens had greatly refreshed our spirits. The town pleases him more and more; its dissection by the two great arteries as a means of controlling the confusion of the narrow streets seems to him completely right, and it gives great delight to see the sea through the Porta Nuova across the roofs of the town. In the evening he loses his temper again, this time in connection with the theater fire in Vienna, about which he was asked. He replies that the most useless people frequented such an opera house; if poor workers are buried in a coal mine, that both moves and angers him, but a case like this scarcely affects him at all. Then he comes back to the subject of the army, saying he would like to have Siegfried spared from military service; when someone says that soldiers die for glory, he exclaims: "Because they are more afraid of their sergeants than of bullets—a bullet is something merciful. Ask yourself whether the soldiers at Spichern died for glory." (When he exclaims at the end of the evening yesterday how terrifying the world is, I tell him that I dearly wish to preserve some happiness for my children, and for that reason frequently keep silent about my feelings; he says I am right.) He reads "The Hostage" to us (vexed to find Möros called Damon); he finds it not as good as "The Diver" and remarks that Schiller did not properly understand crucifixion, confusing it with the gallows; the significant point of crucifixion was the slowness of the agony. Then "The Journey to the Forge"; he thinks the dialogue between Robert and the Count too dramatic, Othello-like, but everything else pleases and moves both him and us, especially the description of the Mass going on in all its ceremony while the horrible deed is being done—"A glorious spirit is speaking here"—and he finds delight in the beautiful expression on S.'s face as he listens. — In the morning he was pleased by Kant's word constructions—"*das Anarten*" ["assimilation"], for example— whereas nowadays new constructions amount to a depreciation, are simply nonsense.

Sunday, December 11 A stormy night, R. restless, too. In the morning the sun comes out, but it soon has to give way, and the day remains overcast most of the time, though two rainbows are to be seen. Before lunch, when I go to greet him, he is still erasing the lines he ruled wrongly in Siena. At lunch our landlord visits us; he is a butterfly collector, and he really shocks us with the news that whole species of butterflies have been wiped out by widespread collecting. No outing beyond a short turn in the garden for R. — In the evening he works again, but he is so tired that he has to take a short nap after supper. The concentration and exertion of his work are proving a strain on him. I suggest reading Goethe again, and this gives him pleasure, except for a description of temples! He finds this very boring: "It's life we want." The expression "*Schrittstein*" for "*Trottoir*" ["pavement, sidewalk"] pleases him. When we are alone together—after he has encouraged young Türk, Siegfried's tutor, to regard our stay here with a bit more enjoyment—I tell him that I can well understand what he said yesterday, that in *Pars.* he will have none of the "polyphonic playing about" which he used in the *Nibel.*—the "Forest Murmurs," for instance. It is all too solemn, he says, too concentrated, there is none of the luxuriating in suffering that there is in *Tristan.* He continues: "God, when one thinks how I started, a Magdeburg conductor with 4 first violins, what a joy it is to write for 12 and to do oneself justice! I went furthest in the *Ring,* in order to reproduce effects of Nature." The news of the success also of the 2nd *Tristan* performance astonishes him: "Things must really have changed a lot there if that pleases them." But he would like to make some cuts in it, and recently he said he felt his orchestration was too heavy (2nd act). — He still complains a lot about his work: "If only I could write something like the A Major Symph.! I should not have Beeth.'s lovely ideas, but the work involved would be nowhere near as much as I am now doing."

Monday, December 12 Another restless night, but he is cheerful at breakfast. The name Mozart keeps us occupied (Muothart), R. thinks it sounds good, and he feels one should have formed Guiscard in the same way (Witzhart). "Mendelssohn should have called himself Händel'ssohn!" — Goodness knows how we come to talk about Princess Wittg., but I say jokingly that I should like to have seen how two such characters as his and hers would get along together: "Not for four weeks could I have stood it," he says, and drolly adds, "Ox and donkey fought one day to find out which of them was wisest; neither wavered nor gave way!" — At 12 o'clock we drive to Count Tasca's palace; R. finds a potpourri from *Die Meistersinger* on the piano and plays some of it, then we view the rooms, richly ornamented with a childlike variation in taste. — During our afternoon walk (English Gardens) R. complains about how his work absorbs him, and says he accepts to some extent what I said to him earlier, that he is growing more patient, for I cannot imagine how preoccupied he sometimes is, how an oboe can keep going through his head, etc. The walk gives us pleasure, as always, and we also recall the owl; R. laughs over the clarity of its call, as if it were learning to speak. Its ears remind us of Hermes, and we talk about the way in which the Greeks drew their motives directly from Nature. He works; in the evening he seems to me somewhat agitated. He talks of his childhood, of Weber, of "Humpel-Marie" [Weber], of an oboist called Wusstlich who had a ladylove from whom R. heard that he had played under Weber and was reported to have died of consumption, news which had associated the oboe with tragedy in his mind forever afterward; of concerts in the Grosser Garten. The difference now—serious concerts! . . . Then he talks about the Bach fugue, how, in connection with Mendel.'s performance of the Bach Passion, he had heard a musician in Leipzig say that Bach was a great mathematician but Handel had been more imaginative. He speaks of the Bach fugue as if it were a vanished species, compared with which the fugue in Sonata [Opus] 106, for example, is child's play. — I am concerned at not being able to have him to myself, when I feel I could bring him peace. — At supper he again became absorbed in reflections as to whether the sum of existence, which has already developed so nobly in some heads and even in some hearts, might not in fact have an ethical purpose, as has indeed been finely surmised. "Or are we really just here to eat grass? It's possible." — And then he says a good person is to be prized above all else, but how rare they are! — At breakfast yesterday we reflected on immortality, that is to say, living on in the memory of others, and how questionable this is, since even a being like Goethe was so vague and indeed almost conventional in his judgments of the deceased.

Tuesday, December 13 R. had a restless night and chest spasms both morning and afternoon. He forces himself to do his page. I wander through the town; then he talks to me about the letters which have arrived, and when I tell him that Malw[ida] writes in connection with the canonization that people are saying Moltke would now offer to restore temporal power to them, R. observes, "He'll do it immediately if the Emperor wishes it, he is like Schott" (who once said it made no difference to him what he printed), "it makes no difference to him whom he shoots." We go out; Count Tasca takes us to a villa almost directly opposite the English Gardens, quite splendid with its view and its trees. But on our return home he feels extremely indisposed. We succeed in spending a very quiet and peaceful evening. He says how bad the two novels he is reading in the newspapers have become— what was interesting in them was probably taken from memoirs, and all the rest added, but very poorly. No sun today! The Nile rising high in our thoughts.

Wednesday, December 14 R. had a good night, and he works diligently. In the afternoon we drive to the Villa Florio and visit the owl, after having received some callers. He gives his article on vivisection to a priest. In the evening our conversation begins with comments on Bach's organ fugue, which R. cannot imagine sounding good—clear—on the organ. Then we descend to *La Muette de Portici* and even *Fra Diavolo;* indeed, he played some things from *Le Serment* and *La Fiancée,* with emphasis on Auber's merits, ideas, and vitality. He complains about his task—but emphasizes that *Parsifal* is his most propitiatory work.

Thursday, December 15 During the night I heard R. groan and cry out, "My good Cosima!" He wakes in melancholy mood and tells me his dream: "We seemed to be in your father's house, Hans and Lulu, too, and I, as if to show that we had brought her up strictly, went to punish Lulu with a box on the ears; she tried to give me one in return. Then we wanted to leave, but Hans tried to appease and conciliate us; he kissed my hand, I his brow, we continued to kiss each other, and he said, 'I knew very well that you would not have fulfilled your love for me without giving me the highest prize.' Then he goes to leave the room; as he opens the door, his double enters, he and we burst into tears and sobs, realizing that it means his death." — I tell R. that I had mentioned death in one of my last letters to Lusch, in order to set her on the right path in her behavior toward her father. At breakfast R. says that in his case dreams of this sort have never been prophetic, and the afternoon brings a letter from Lusch with an enclosure—on the whole a reassuring one—from Hans! But our mood is melancholy. — Before lunch R. writes to Herr Niemann, saying, among other things, "Anyone who does not believe in you will not get very far." He also does some work; he still has 30 pages of score to finish, and thinks of them with a sigh! We drive to the sea, which is wild and raging, a sight which keeps us entertained. We return home along the Via Maqueda, and R. again goes to his work. Among other topics of conversation, we imagined what would happen if we married off all our daughters and then went traveling together through the world! Madeira, Ceylon—"I want blue skies." — In the evening we play whist, ending with vexation over his lack of luck, after first reading in detail about the terrible incident in Vienna. . . . Thinking today about human wretchedness, R. was also reminded that Schopenhauer saw it as a just desert for our behavior toward animals. — He reads aloud the advertisements in the *Musikzeitung,* laughing heartily over them. — Today he again complains that nobody understands his aims, that there is nobody to whom he can entrust the realization of his works after his death. He says he does not wish to bring up Siegfried for that purpose. — When we saw him beside the wild sea today, R. exclaimed. "What a happy childhood the boy has—what impressions!"

Friday, December 16   A good night for R., but at breakfast he is rather resentful, because I am coughing and cannot take the matter seriously. He works, goes into the garden around lunchtime, takes delight in the camellias, and at table chats with the children. Then he goes out with them and takes them to the Casa Rossa, which I liked so much; but on his return he complains that he had another chest spasm, had to sit down, is feeling very run down! . . . All the same, he works. In the evening we go through the newspapers. An article by an actor, containing many impossible and boastful things, arouses R.'s anger, and also his amazement that such stuff can be accepted and put into print. After all these various reports, and after an article on Ireland has provided an opportunity to discuss the insolubility of this problem— for the people there have now become like animals looking only for a chance to bite—and the awkwardness of Gladstone's situation, with nobody showing any understanding of it, R. talks about his lack of sympathy in connection with the catastrophe in Vienna. "It sounds hard and is almost unnatural, but people are too wicked for one to be much affected when they perish in masses. As I have already said, when people are buried in coal mines, I feel indignation at a community which obtains its heating by such means; but when such-and-such a number of members of this community die while watching an Offenbach operetta, an activity which contains no trace of moral superiority, that leaves me quite indifferent." I mention the war: "There people were at least inspired by great acts of sacrifice and a sense of living for an idea." — Earlier, in connection with the Irish problem, he exclaimed, "We shall all become slaves like them, for property has been canonized, and now the gentlemen from the stock exchange are in charge." A moment of amusement is occasioned by a postcard from Cyriax, from whom I had ordered a new kind of umbrella which had been recommended by the *I. Z.* and which R. thought good; Cyriax tells us it was a joke in a humorous journal, which the *Ill. Z.* took seriously! *Trist. und Is.* has now come to Königsberg, too. — When, in connection with the Vienna catastrophe, the lack of conscientiousness among the inspectors, etc., is mentioned, and someone says there would certainly have been more in Prussia, R. says: "Where is it to come from in Austria? A Slovak here, a Bohemian there, no one committed to community life, and as police chief a *Baron Marx.*" He again talks about the island of Ceylon and Orientals in general, who have gone furthest in recognizing the necessity of evil, who have accepted absolutism as the best form of government and bear with a series of bad rulers for the immeasurable happiness of occasionally getting a good one. — (When I first awoke this morning I heard him say, "Night is still glowing." Then he turned over and went back to sleep.)

Saturday, December 17 People arriving late from Catania make a noise, R. gets out of bed and calls for quiet. He took a bath in the morning and afterward suffered another chest spasm! He lies down in bed, we have breakfast, and he is soon so much recovered that he can embark on a detailed discussion of the passage in Kant concerning "seeds." "I can very easily imagine how a Laplander, for instance, evolves out of a Norman, however farfetched it sounds, and this idea opens many doors. The seeds of the widest variety are in Nature itself—for example, man's carnivorous tendencies are indicated by his canine teeth, and it all depends on the way things evolve. In Germany everything is in the process of dying out—for me a dismal realization, since I am addressing myself to the still-existent seeds. But one thing is certain: races are done for, and all that can now make an impact is—as I have ventured to express it—the blood of Christ." He then talks of the revolution which could be brought about by a manufacturer in Carlyle's sense, and of emigration to the Boers—he says he would like to know something about what Herr v. Weber said to Stein on that subject. "But," he says in connection with the first topic, "it is unthinkable that such a character should emerge, all the sources have dried up," and, on the second, "But the moment one tries to deal with the practical aspects, it all becomes foolish and petty." — When I say that this theory of seeds which need to be cultivated is a comforting one, and that I can see from a character such as Boni's what successes can be achieved by cultivating the good in it, he says, "Oh, yes, indeed!" — He works, before that read Kant, and again speaks of it at lunch: "One never regrets communing with a significant mind, and one should in fact occupy oneself only with such original beings." He then comes back to the theory, and says that the Germans are finished! Then I tell him of the pleasure it gave me today to do justice to Ariosto, hitherto so alien to us; in this I was helped by a quotation in Sismondi and his clever use of it—about the giant who forgot that he was dead and continued to wage a battle. This amuses R. greatly, and he says one should not allow oneself to be deterred by this and that, but should seek—"in the original language, I willingly concede"—to come closer to so great a name. — Letters at coffeetime, a very nice one from Herr Vogl about *Tristan* [*enclosed in Diaries:* "Königsberg did not shame your miraculous work!"], then another calendar "with good wishes"—we joke about the recognition now coming to R. from all sides. — R. goes for a drive with the children but returns dissatisfied; it rained, Favorita was closed, and at the Villa Ranghibile, where he wanted to show them the splendid fig tree, his vexation over the guide brought on another chest spasm. Very sweetly he tells me it was all because I was not with them that they had no luck. (My cough kept me at home, I played the piano score.) R. works, and we spend the evening as quietly as possible. Bonus reads to us an article by Dr. Herrig about theaters, which makes very sensible mention of the building in Bayreuth. R. says he does not know what is meant by the "people" for whom drama is supposed to exist; he knows nothing about "people"—what seems to be in everyone's mind are the 30,000 Athenians, and Greek drama had its chorus, but few individuals. One cannot say that a Shakespeare play is for "the people" —it was just created for the kind of stage on which one viewed the actors from all sides. He feels his remarks about a performance of *Faust* probably led Herrig to imagine something like this. The Albert Hall, with its audience of 10,000, he continues, does not entitle one to say that "the English people" was there. "I know no 'people,'" he exclaims, "they must have created one of their own in Berlin." — "In such a large space as the A[lbert] H[all] the orchestra ought to be in the middle, and only things like the last movement of the C Minor Symphony played there." — Rub. reminds us that today is Beeth.'s birthday, and that leads me to recall that R. recently sang the theme of the *Leonore* Overtures and said to me, "Only once does he introduce it in this passionate way, and then—quite correctly for the overture style—with an accompaniment in which there is something downright pedantic, and for us vexing." — We hear from Lusch that my father's condition alternates between apathy and irritability. "It must be particularly painful to him," R. says, "that he is completely ignored even in Paris, whereas my things, which are not at all suitable for concerts, are being played—and above all in Paris. Both time and place have let him down." — At lunch I talk about *The Arabian Nights,* which I am reading with Fidi, and R. spoke with particular warmth of Harun al-Raschid, "that good, humorous, greathearted ruler"; on the other hand, he says, the stories of Sindbad have never interested him. The fact that 416 Israelites died in the fire does not increase R.'s concern over the disaster.

Sunday, December 18 R. again has a chest spasm; we discuss the possible cause of these, and agree that it is his work which puts such a strain on him and disturbs all his functions. I implore him not to strain himself by hastening its completion. At breakfast he is cheerful again, compares me with some pope or other, then with Friedrich III (on account of my long hair). — Then he tells me about a recent performance of *Nathan* [*der Weise*] at which, when the line asserting that Christ was also a Jew was spoken, an Israelite in the audience cried "Bravo." He reproaches Lessing for this piece of insipidity, and when I reply that the play seems to me to contain a peculiarly German kind of humanity, he says, "But not a trace of profundity." He recalls Bernays, who accused Holtzmann of having no regard for Lessing. "One adds fuel to these fellows' arrogance by having anything at all to do with them, and we, for example, do not talk of our feelings about those Jews in the theater in front of Rub., 400 unbaptized and probably 500 baptized ones." He makes a drastic joke to the effect that all Jews should be burned at a performance of *Nathan*. — At lunch he talks about the story of the blessing Jacob won by trickery, saying that this is just how things are. I: "More or less: '*le ciel souffre la violence*' ['the heavens tolerate violence']." He: "And *La devoción de la cruz*—Calderón's —the magnificent result of it." — Sunshine. We drive down to the sea and through the Porta Nuova, still deep in conversation. But after his evening work he is worn out. The *Fliegende Bl.* takes his mind off it, but the *Bayr. Bl.*—an article on Kleist by Wolz., which I suggest we read—arouses his anger. He says one knows all Kleist's mental struggles by heart, they were those of an adolescent schoolboy; what is this striving for truth supposed to mean? One is truthful, and that's that. The bombastic style—"Corsican Imperator"—he also finds unpleasant, and he calls the whole thing *green*. The statement concerning the performance of *Pars.* also seems to him lacking in dignity: "I should have put that slightly differently." — Rub. asks him various questions in connection with his piano score, and this leads him to show us his last page and its orchestration (trumpet [*space left blank*]); of the worshipping of the spear he says, "Here I have done something which will earn me praise even from my wife," and, further, "For Parsifal's entrance I have horns and trumpets; horns alone would have been too soft, not ceremonious enough, trumpets alone too clattery, brassy— such things one must go in search of, and then I expect people to play them well." He persists in maintaining that he orchestrated too heavily in *Tristan*. When I say that we had certainly not noticed that with Schnorr: "At that time my mind was on other things." — When we are alone, I say to him, "Tristan and Parsifal, one dies because of his will to live, the other lives because of his dying will." R: "You must always have a *mot*," then, after a pause, "Parsifal sees Tristan" (in Amfortas), and, after another pause, "Something has come between them—the blood of Christ." —

Monday, December 19 A bad, restless night. He finishes reading Wolz.'s article, returns to bed, but in the morning has a chest spasm. Yet in spite of this, after we are together a few moments, he is gaily talkative. He takes up *Faust* and finds the things in which Faust finds satisfaction pitiful—ditch digging, he says, the loading and unloading of goods, and one cannot imagine what the angels and Gretchen are doing in this roadside digging affair, without any mention of brotherly love or of the idea of renunciation. "They are all magnificently contrived things poetically—from a poetic point of view the 'Walpurgis Night' is unique—but the concept is pitiful, and it is only in the conversations with Mephisto that Faust comes alive somewhat." Then he tells me he thought of Homer, who was an Ionian, and thus represents the feminine principle; now Gobineau will only allow the Dorians, who had to borrow from Athens a singer to inspire them— that is a bad thing. [*Added in margin:* "Writing is a wretched business, he says, and Schiller chose the right course when he decided to write plays, well-constructed plays."] And with a joke about how quickly he can become merry again, he goes off to his reading (Kant) and his work. — Unfortunately a misunderstanding by a servant vexes him. However, he recovers his spirits at lunch and tells the children about the custom in England—only recently abolished—of leading a wife to market on a rope in order to sell her. Certainly not a Germanic custom— it probably came from the original inhabitants; R. observes that the number of Anglo-Saxons had in any case been small. We drive to the Piazza Croce dei Vespri to visit the banker, R. enjoys the handsome palaces. In the evening he works, we have a merry game of whist, and after that he once more tells us about Kant's theories of races and seeds. — The extinguishing of the gas during the frightful event in Vienna brings him to the lamp at the approach to the bridge, which went out during the floods (1868).

Tuesday, December 20 A wretched night for R., he gets up, spends a long time in his room, does some reading, and in the morning is very tired. He works all the same. In the afternoon we drive with Count Tasca to see Princess Butera, whose *palazzo* shows great splendor and opulence. The Princess herself a curious, cheerfully abrupt person who keeps us much amused. But R. soon tires, and we return home. He works again in the evening. The second part of the first act in the piano score—Rub. plays it, it seems satisfactory to R. (except for the triplets, at which he exclaims, "Only Liszt and I know how to play triplets!"), but the whole thing bores and vexes him, he says it seems to him so stale. A game of whist concludes our social evening. When we are alone, R. says again that the problem of orchestrating the ending of his work is exercising him greatly—he would have to use a lot more instruments; he had the English horn made, he says, and now it is necessary to enrich all the wind categories in the same way, since he needs various groups. I cannot imagine how much this torments him, he adds. — A bit of nonsense, Gambetta's *coup d'état,* described in the newspaper *Figaro* in the fullest detail, down to a poem by Hugo attacking it, amuses him greatly.

Wednesday, December 21   Again a very, very restless night for R., and it is as if his digestion were completely blocked. He does not work. To distract him, I suggest to him Mme Rémusat's portrait of Nap., and that keeps him entertained, he particularly mentions the anecdotes about Talleyrand. He attempts to go out but has a chest spasm in the street and returns home in a state of violent agitation. He continues reading Mme Rém., and in the evening we play whist, after I have tried to keep the conversation as light as possible. Gobineau's denial to Ollivier of being the author of *La Renaissance,* about which Lusch has told us, pleases R. immensely as evidence of his great originality, and he tells us all sorts of anecdotes about the Count. — He still has 22 pages to write; he believes he now knows how to deal with the problem of orchestrating the ending—he will give everything to the wind instruments first, then bring in the string instruments. But he says he needs three sections (wind instruments) and has only one. He complains of the strain this work is putting on him, and as he looks back over the past years, he says what a strain they were, setting up the production of the *Ring,* then the rehearsals, finally the sorrowful times following the performances, and how, to help and to rescue himself, he wrote *Parsifal.* — In the morning he once more confided to me how unreal the whole world, all relationships, are to him, how everything had gone from his mind, become strange to him—"and I mean everything." — Nevertheless his cheerfulness still continues to break through.

Thursday, December 22   R. had a good night! He returns to me with a joke: *Salba venice* (he wanted to rub ointment on his foot, but there is not enough). Had been listening in the morning with enjoyment to the boy and his lively singing in the street. He finds his new reading entertaining, and he tells me many bits about Nap. and Talleyrand. He works. At lunch he makes a journey with us to Spain, which, a passing courier told Schnapp[auf], is much lovelier than Italy. Unfortunately his anger is aroused over coffee by Lusch's fate and the arrangements being made by my father, whose rules of life are repugnant to him. Nor does one know, he says, in which direction Lusch is moving. But after going off for his siesta, he returns to tell me the new idea he has had: after the glowing of the blood he will bring down the curtain, darken the auditorium, and allow the music to play thus to the end. — We drive to the Villa Camastra. [*A few words dealing with a false rhyme in Goethe omitted.*] We meet Count T., and he conducts us around his enchanting estate. — But R. makes an error of diet (lobster at lunch), and there are many complaints in the evening; only gradually do we manage to get a conversation going; a sonata by Beeth., played by Rub., brings us back to yesterday's topic: how inferior this type of music is to painting, how conventional, and R. cannot understand how one can compare Mozart, for example, with Raphael, though he is well aware that in his music there are things which cannot be compared to other things, either. — A picture of Iph[igenia] at Tauris in the *Illustrirte,* with temple, Italy, carved lions in the background, shows all the wretchedness of mankind! It is true, says R., that Goethe depicted even these Scythians as very civilized people. — Late in the evening he talks about his absorption in his work—he says he literally sees ghosts, fifths, sixths. — Rub. tells me of difficulties with his father and feels that a letter to his father from R. would improve matters; R., to whom I impart this, starts to write it right away, but the idea soon begins to worry him, and he even jumps out of bed in order to forget this task, which makes him feel rather uneasy.

Friday, December 23 "I shall write to Rub.'s father at once." With this joke R. rises. He is much enchanted with Frau von Rém.'s memoirs, and concerning an outburst of Nap.'s against *convenances* [propriety] and *bon goût* [good taste] he says, "That could be me." The weather is gray, we go out for a drive but soon turn back, and R. settles down again to his reading, which is giving him much enjoyment. Very drolly he applies to himself the joke Nap. I made about Berthier, of whom he said he really had no idea what he was supposed to do with him! In the evening he is unwell, and he goes to bed early.

Saturday, December 24 A good night, and R. gets up in good spirits. Schnappauf is sent several times to the post office, but nothing seems to have arrived. At breakfast we talk about the characters of Bonaparte and Talleyrand, the one very fiery and full of imagination, like someone from antiquity with his wild openheartedness and his naïveté even in mendacity, the other superior on account of his coldness. — R. says he is reading it as if it were natural history. — At eleven o'clock, as I am at my writing desk, R. comes in, followed by somebody I take to be Schnappauf, and he says, "Nothing has arrived." I: "An excellent thing that my birthday should turn into a calamity for you!" He continues to approach with his companion, and at last I recognize Joukowsky! . . . When the astonished laughter has subsided, I manage to learn that he has come bringing some things for R., in order to ensure they are here in time! The day passes in talk about our surprise; that is how people should be, R. observes. — Vexation at coffeetime—a sick lady, Princess Lieven, wants one of our rooms, which upsets R. greatly. But at 6 o'clock the tree in the conservatory succeeds in taking me completely by surprise; I had been told that there would be no tree this year, and now I find a little fir standing there—so for the first time a Christmas tree shines on us quite unexpectedly! What R. said to me on this occasion I cannot write down—not even for you, my Siegfried! . . . The evening passes very merrily. R. reads aloud various passages from Mme de Rémusat, anecdotes about Talleyrand, and he says the clever woman has observed things superbly, and a work like this is worth more than anything written by Mommsen, Pommsen, or whatever else they may be called. When I say it seems to me that a woman is better suited than a man to observe things in this way, he says, "Yes, women have a greater sense of truthfulness."

Sunday, December 25 "*Gratel, gratel,*" I hear in the morning beside me, and his mighty head appears to me like the head of a child as he merrily wishes me many happy returns. But soon things get serious, he calls me in, and with the children hands to me all my fair gifts—*Polonia,* the *Parsifal* sketches, the talisman ring, and—*pia fraus* [pious deception]!—the completed score! . . . The weather keeps us from going out but does not spoil our high spirits. At lunch R. proposes a toast to me, but he breaks off and afterward tells me that mists gather around his soul whenever he tries to talk about me. — We bemoan the gray weather for the sake of our dear friend. In the evening *Polonia* is played and all kinds of things from his life linked to it, just as yesterday, in talking about his indisposition, he touched on the episode of *La Favorita.* — Today he recalls the *Klepperbein* family, how every Sunday he was given roast goose in the house with fortune's wheel, and his father Geyer joked: "Klepperbein, my boy, that means death!" — When I say that *Polonia* seems to me to be exactly what it was meant to be, R. says, "Oh, with a military band for the people, as I thought of everything at that time, it would have sounded splendid and produced a great effect." — Mme de Rém. less pleasing—not she, but Nap., when he is made emperor and everything becomes theatrical.

Monday, December 26 Gray skies still, which upsets R. for our friend's sake. Today's joke is the news that *Lohengrin* has been banned in Paris, which in fact delights us. R. says with a laugh that it makes him look very important. R. works, I send the sheets from *my* score to Rub. and, besides that, write letters. We visit the Palazzo Gangi, and in the evening the children go there for the distribution of presents, which, after our very merry game of whist, causes a kind of upset in R., since he would have liked to see the children before going to bed, and they arrive home just at a moment when he cannot talk to them.

Tuesday, December 27 A good night for R. Pleasure in the *Fl. Blätter,* also in the gifts for me which arrived belatedly. Less in Mme Rémusat, since he has reached the point where Nap. sets up his court. The weather, however, is still not good, and it keeps bringing R. back to the Orient; as we are on the way to the Villa Camastra he talks of this ancient civilization, which we in the West have copied "like thieves." In the evening Blandine persuades Rubinstein to play the final movement of [Beethoven's] C-sharp Minor Sonata; when I remark to R. that this kind of music is not intimate, but demands a concert hall, he says, "Yes, of course," and goes on to deplore the many things in art which are dying out. Then, to our enjoyment, Rub. plays some mazurkas and also a Chopin waltz. The day before yesterday, in connection with *Polonia,* R. had spoken enthusiastically about the mazurka, a creation of the Polish people. — We play whist, and R. is in very high spirits, making jokes which are impossible to transcribe (one of them, for example, as he leaves the room: "I now withdraw like a hippopotamus"), and I go off to bed glad about this.

Wednesday, December 28   The sun smiles down upon us again. But we have our breakfast in bed, with all kinds of remarks about Nap. I, or, rather, about R. III and the heroes in *Henry VI,* who, R. says, are much more personal than N., much more personally involved in matters of life and death. He works and goes for a walk in the garden before lunch, but at table I can already see that he is in an ill humor, and the champagne he orders does not cheer him up. I can think of no reason for it, except that his work is absorbing him. However, we drive to Monreale and delight in the splendid cathedral, feeling ourselves transported back into the spirit of that distant time as we gaze on this ideal representation of it. The return journey is also splendid, even though the sun soon goes down. Unfortunately R. is not feeling very well, today's menu was not made out correctly, and—God knows through what combination of events—when we are sitting together in the evening and he starts talking about Munich and among other things about the coach the King had built at that time, he flies into a rage over the visual arts and artists. He describes how childishly they— Gedon, Lenbach—expressed their delight in this golden coach, whereas he and his plans were abandoned. They are only a little worse than courtesans, these painters, he says, and adds, "But my mama, too—she is not far off from taking delight in such things as that coach, either." — So well do I know, when he gets so angry and violent and tries to hurt someone or other, that his malaise takes complete possession of him and any reply, however conciliatory, only pours more oil on the flames, that I leave the room for a while. He follows me out, is soon pacified, and explains his all-too-justified grounds for bitterness, and we play whist, after I have made excuses for my attitude toward people by saying that I lack the ability to keep bad experiences constantly in mind; with Nietzsche, for instance, I can think only of his friendly aspects, and the same with Lenbach, Gedon, etc. R. says this is the result of my education, the influence of my father confessor, subsequently a bishop, to whom I owe what he calls my "pious serenity." — When we are alone, we discuss a few matters; yesterday, over coffee, Jouk. related a comical remark a previous acquaintance of his had made about me; R. feels he is thoroughly compromised by having once been intimate with such people. When I tell him that nothing can compromise him—on the contrary, he is to be admired for having extracted from such trivial personalities something which was at least a comfort to him—we come to the King and his taste for L[ouis] XIV, etc. It is a harsh review of all our acquaintances, and even my father is tacitly considered. (By mistake I have put this down for today, but it happened yesterday, while we were waiting for the children— today we only discussed his outburst. His old resentment against Lenbach came back to him, and his odd idea—which increasingly makes us smile—that I should have married a painter!)

Thursday, December 29 A good night for R., but all the same a chest spasm on rising. He soon recovers, however, and we have a merry breakfast in the conservatory. We cheerfully discuss his outburst against visual artists, recall the angry scenes which so offended Nietzsche, and R., recalling Jouk., goes out onto the terrace in his dressing gown to call him up to our room. Since he is unsuccessful, he sends a servant to summon him, and then says merrily, "My wife believes you are offended," which leads to an amiable conversation. He goes off to his work, and at lunch he talks about Nap.'s introduction of the *Schleppcour* and his impatient fury because it took so long! At lunch Herr Ragusa brings Jouk. a telegram, remarking that it must contain good news, or he would not have brought it. Jouk. reads it, does not understand it, and hands it to me, and I have to impart what is in it [*news of the death of Karl Brandt; see notes*]. — After the first somber surprise there follow reflections on this stroke of fate. "He has fallen into practically the same grave as Offenbach," R. remarks bitterly, and in the course of further observations he says, "I know that his son will be able to take over, indeed I was even advised to entrust things to him in the first place, but he was the only reliable man I had." And we go through all our experiences with Brandt. "It is all so stupid!" he exclaims. Before that, despondently, "It was not necessary." It reminds me of Schnorr's death, and R. says to me, "I, too, was thinking of that." We go for a drive after he has had a short rest; before that, over coffee, his thoughts turned to the uncertainties of life: "I shall consider carefully how things can be brought to a swift close." — He thinks of Fidi in this connection, and that there could be a sudden disaster. — "It is all so depressing!" We drive to the Villa Florio to see the owl, then the Strada della libertà, and R. returns in somewhat better spirits, even receives two calls with me. And in the evening we play whist, and when we are alone and think of his dying in harness but not in pursuit of his vocation in Bayreuth, R. says, "Oh, one can look at it in whatever way one likes, it is still terrible."

Friday, December 30 R. slept well, but after his bath he has a chest spasm. However, since the sun is shining, he is agreeable to having breakfast in the conservatory. But work costs him some effort, and he longs for it to be completed, saying it is a torment to him, he is afraid of orchestrating too heavily. In fine weather we visit the prefect and then drive to the Villa Belmonte; in the evening, to our surprise, we receive calls from Prince and Princess Gangi, Countess Mazzarino, her son, and his religious tutor. R. at first disappears, but when he sees that the guests are staying, he soon makes his presence known again with *Norma* and remains very hospitable throughout the evening; he gets Rub. to play all sorts of things from the *Ring*, does indeed leave the room, but is pleased, when he returns, with the impression made, particularly on the ladies; he then himself plays the "Bridal Song" from *Lohengrin*. — When the guests have departed, he speaks in praise of them, particularly the ladies, and tells me I should fix a definite evening for us to be at home to callers. — (This morning R. recalled the legend of Saint Geneviève and its unique beauty.)

Saturday, December 31 The sun is not quite loyal to us, it fights through only now and then, and R. again has a chest spasm. All too many things vex him—struggles with an ink which will not flow and a thousand other petty things of which he tells us vexedly at lunch, for which he arrives late; but his mood then changes to one of great merriment when I agree with him that life is terrible, in the little as well as the big things. After lunch we drive to the Orto Botanico and delight in the splendid trees there. He works in the evening, and when I ask him at table how much he still has to do, he says mournfully, "Fifteen pages," and then with quiet satisfaction, "Fourteen" (with a slight Saxon accent). — In the evening we begin G[ottfried] Keller's novella *"Sinngedicht"*; the opening pleases us, R. says he has seen women of this kind in Switzerland, and the form of expression seems felicitous; but when we come to Lucie, the educated lady, we break off, and R. says all that has been taken from books. He exclaims, "God knows, there are times when nothing seems real to me but music!" — Our Bonus goes to a ball, taken to Princess Butera's by Princess Filangieri; we enter the New Year sleeping.

1882

Sunday, January 1 R. dreamed that he was thrashing a boy, using a tallow candle, which proved to be unsuitable—too soft—for the task, whereupon he woke up! — We both look cheerfully toward the approaching year, and evidence of his good mood is seen in his telegram to my father [*in English*]: "We belong, we belong to the temperance society!" . . . He works but is still having trouble with the ink, feels like interrupting his work, which is tiring him, and comes to lunch looking tired. However, he soon recovers his spirits, and we are soon in lively conversation, mainly about what he is reading. — We then drive with the children to the Tascas' for a kind of New Year court, of which R. quickly becomes weary. We soon make our way home, where we are then obliged to receive the prefect and his wife, and are glad when we can sit down to a game of whist, after a lengthy talk about the world situation! . . . After whist, memories of Munich and its former intrigues come into our minds!

Monday, January 2 After a good night R. wakes up feeling well, and in our first conversation he talks of [Schiller's] ballad "The Glove"; he laughingly calls it a curious subject for poetry, says he much prefers the episode of D. Quixote and the lion, and gaily recalls it. He works; at half past twelve we go for a walk in the garden and take delight in the plants, with their blossoms and fruits. He says he has written only a quarter of a page, and altogether he has now decided to work only when everything else bores him. At lunch he is very cheerful and full of fun, and quotes at random lines from various Schiller ballads; afterward talks of *Maria Stuart,* the scene between the two queens, and remarks how fine it is that the wide-ranging and apparently entirely political play builds up to this one scene which expresses its whole meaning. He says that this play, which he now finds so good, made little impression on him in his youth; he was not able to follow its emotional subtleties, and it seemed that the mourning at the beginning belonged more to the end of the play. His talk alternates between jest and earnest; he suddenly stops; we ask him what is the matter: "Well, when all I see after my jokes is puzzled faces . . ." (Apparently some joke he made had not been understood.) I: "But who is making puzzled faces?" Whereupon from the far end of the table, quite calmly, Fidi: "I am," which amuses us indescribably. — Among other things, R. also mentions the Englishman who, out of boredom with having to put on his clothes, etc., every day, hanged himself, and he goes off into the most comical descriptions of the vexation every routine task—cleaning his teeth, for instance—causes him. And when Jouk. agrees with him, and I remark how disgraceful it is when a person can find nothing in life to absorb him and raise him above such petty annoyances, R. says, "Yes, there is a world of ethics and a world of morals, but when one belongs to neither, yet all the same keeps going, one is trivial compared to that Englishman." — A well-phrased letter to me from Richter pleases us greatly. We go for a drive, R. recalls Fidi's reply, expresses delight in the boy and his character, so harmonious in his development, quiet, but in no way afraid of adversity, not at all soft. From the English Gardens we go on to the sea, which, bathed in a wonderful light, always has such a liberating effect on me! — In the evening R. reads the first two acts of H[enry] IV Part I. "It is terrible," he exclaims in the middle of it, "for after this nothing else seems worth bothering about; even ironic dialogues, as in *Faust*—what are they in comparison with these authentic characters, of whom, but for Shak., we should know nothing, yet who now come before our eyes like living beings?" — Before this he enlarged upon what he means by the Renaissance, and how the influence of Latinity spelled the death of everything. — He talks of his great admiration for the popular element in Cervantes, and after the scene with the two carriers, he says, "Anyone who does not know people in this way is no poet." The life of the common people here always gives him pleasure; today he addresses a beggar as "Paganini," and recently, when we were returning from the Martorana in dull weather and in somewhat downcast spirits, he was cheered by the sight of a bagpiper, standing alone in the rain, playing in front of the lighted altar of the Madonna; and not long ago, when we were returning from the Villa Belmonte, two children riding on a donkey which bore the exuberant youngsters off at a gallop. — At supper he suddenly jumps up, leaves the room, comes back after a while, and says, "How trivial are your lives compared with mine!" He wants to be asked but at the same time not to tell, and he interpellates the girls. I say I know he went to his score. "Yes, but what for?"—and he will not say. But at last, "I have found the bass clarinet!," and is teasingly brusque with us. —

Tuesday, January 3 R. had a good night, though his sleep was interrupted once. We have breakfast in bed, talking about *H. IV.* At lunch R. raises the subject again and observes that Jouk. cannot get the same pleasure that we do from the comic scenes, since Russian education, which is cosmopolitan, encourages other tastes: "We Germans have no taste at all, but that means we are at any rate now and again more susceptible to works of genius." When Jouk. protests against the assertion that he is closer in spirit to French literature than to German, R. replies, "When I say German, I am thinking only of *Faust* and possibly *Götz*, for with *Iphigenie*, with *Tasso*, etc., Goethe came nearer to what I call Renaissance culture." Late in the evening he returns to this idea that a painter cannot possibly appreciate popular things. One could not imagine Raphael, M[ichel]angelo, taking pleasure in such folk scenes, he says, but certainly Dürer, and also Leonardo, a man of breeding who could play around with things. In the course of this conversation he calls Shakespeare "a nonexistent mirage of reality." — But it torments him to see Jouk. disconcerted by his remark. He deplores the fact that, when he feels ill at ease, he has this urge to be abrasive, indeed to hurt others. And all through lunch he is on edge, also with Rub., whom he makes fun of for not having appreciated *Lohengrin* at first hearing. In connection with this we come to talk about Schopenhauer, whom I jestingly call a bad man, since he saw *Tannhäuser* and, "never mind how bad the performance was," could see nothing in it, even in the text. — A telegram from Leipzig reports the success there of *Tristan;* R. says he hears the message but still lacks belief, unless many cuts have been made. — We stroll down to the sea, R. and I, he is not feeling completely well, and when, in the evening, he and Jouk. complain about life, I say my contentment makes me feel quite vulgar, whereupon R. praises me for having retained this great strength. After that his mood changes completely, he is gay, accepts the newspaper description of Linderhof with good grace, and returns happily to the reading of *H. IV*. Unfortunately Count Tasca interrupts us, and that provokes R., after his departure, to an outburst against society. He then reads *H. IV* to the end, regretting the farce played by Falstaff with the body of Percy, though he admits that here, too, Shakesp. was being truthful.

Wednesday, January 4 R. dreamed of a performance of *Lohengrin* in which the singers, and particularly Scaria, had forgotten their roles. He again complains bitterly of his chest spasms and suffers from the cold in the morning. At lunch he complains of the exertions of his work. Also, the weather is dull, R. feels it and orders a fire. At supper we manage to amuse him with all kinds of accounts of the "evil eye" here. After supper we attempt to read a dialogue by Stein, "Saint Catherine of Siena," but R. soon interrupts the inadequate reading (mine); he also finds the subject distasteful—a saint involved with political interests does not grip his attention: "The most one can say is that a woman like that is stupid." — We then play whist.

Thursday, January 5 R. had a good night, and the familiar gay singing of the child—boy or girl—at 6 o'clock in the morning again delights him. We have a cheerful breakfast in the conservatory, unfortunately amid the stares of strangers, but that does not embarrass us. The street calls keep us amused, and the day starts in good spirits. R. works, goes for a walk in the garden before lunch, and when he returns and sees me waiting to go to table with him, he exclaims, "Mamsell Glorious!" At lunch he talks about the changes of fortune brought about by Nap.'s divorce, as described in Mme de Rémusat's memoirs, and says he cannot understand why this interesting subject has not been turned into a play. He takes quite a long rest after lunch, and then we drive, he and I, via the English Gardens to the Favorita. When I tell him I have just been thinking of *Parsifal* and am pleased that this last work of his is also his masterpiece, he replies, or, rather, interrupts me very excitedly, "No, no, I was telling myself today that it is quite remarkable that I held this work back for my fullest maturity; I know what I know and what is in it; and the new school, Wolz. and the others, can take their lead from it." He then hints at, rather than expresses, the content of this work, "salvation to the savior"—and we are silent after he has added, "Good that we are alone." — Then he suddenly mentions Brandt, saying very earnestly, "Oh, that this profoundly loyal person—for that he was to me—had to die!" And he recalls all his remarkable talents. I tell him that I have written to Frau Brandt, promising that he would write to her son. We drive farther on, and a kind God permits me to take such delight in the countryside that my gloomy thoughts disperse like clouds. He is pleased with the drive and orders the coachman to take us to the sea; we get out and walk on the quay near the railroad station. The view is quite wonderful, and R., after asking me what I find so beautiful about it, begins to enjoy it, too. And in gentle, indeed uplifted spirits, we return home. He goes to his work, completes two pages today, and joins us at table, somewhat excited but in cheerful mood. Lenbach's wonderful sketch of my father leads to reflections; when we mention that L. has never done such a picture of R., he says, "On the one hand I am too much of a Philistine, on the other, perhaps too intellectual," and he goes on to observe that this sketch, splendid and a good likeness though it is, nevertheless reflects only a single instant, an action, not complete repose; in his opinion a portrait should show this, and he is glad that the photograph of him—on which the engraving is based—exists. This is how he would like to look. He then talks about the visual arts and expresses his hope to Jouk. that he will understand what he means by this—not painting, which, as he very well knows, comes closest to his own art (the Greeks, for example, knew nothing about it), but architecturally decorative trivialities such as the saltcellar of Benvenuto Cellini, etc. "In my perception of the world, etc., such things seem utterly despicable." — He then talks about his instrumentation, compares it with painting techniques, then relates atrocities committed by the Russian government and declares that what is best in the nation can certainly be found among the nihilists, in the higher spheres everything is rotten and decayed. We then begin *H. IV Part II;* when he has to skip several passages, he complains about having to read it aloud in front of "womenfolk." Later I jokingly point this out, but he cannot remember having said it—as so often, his remarks are the involuntary expression of his thoughts, a mere indication of his feelings of unease. — Rub. plays Weber's A-flat Major Sonata and his "Polonaise" which again make R. feel that he is "no musician"; despite some lovely passages, the sonata reminds him of Kalkbrenner, and he finds its stiffness of form and applause-seeking brilliance distasteful; he says this piano literature shows not the slightest trace of Beethoven's influence. He does not listen to the "Polonaise," but enjoys the glorious moonlight and the mild air; we go into the conservatory and enjoy the delights of Nature. When the *Tristan* night and the *Walküre* night are mentioned, he says that in neither case was he thinking of moonlight, but just of warm summer nights, if only for the reason that on stage the moon looks ridiculous. Many thoughts of travel! From here we should go on to make the acquaintance of Athens and the Ionian islands; but he says Constantinople does not interest him at all, neither its founding nor its predominance means a thing to him.

Friday, January 6 R. had a good night, and we have a cheerful breakfast in the conservatory, talking about all kinds of things, including Cherubini, whom Schemann is trying to bring closer to our hearts: "Man should not visit the gods," says R. — R. describes this outmoded master as interesting and boring at one and the same time. Then he passes on to the French, saying that the way they have turned *pater* and *mater* into *père* and *mère* says everything. — R. then goes to his work, which, however, puts a great strain on him today. Page 331, with the harps (Parsifal mounting the steps to the altar), causes him much exertion, the weather is dull, and the news that Lusch is about to return produces from him only the remark that she is now just a guest in our home. We take a drive to the Favorita, but he does not feel well. At supper he discusses the news that it will be L. Bucher's task to arrange the Pope's new position in Rome as a free city. He already mentioned this during our walk: "Who possesses the rights, then?" he said, talking of the Piedmontese rulers. At lunch he defended Frederick Barbarossa against the accusation of cruelty: "They believed in themselves, those rulers, were caught up in a magnificent error. At that time the Pope represented the people. But one cannot call them simply cruel." I continue reading G. Keller to distract him, and the story of Salome offers us quite a lot to enjoy.

Saturday, January 7 Today we have breakfast in bed, after a night during which R. got up once and read in Mme de Rémusat a scene in which Talleyrand, after an altercation with Nap., exclaimed, *"Quel dommage qu'un si grand homme soit si mal élevé"* ["What a pity that such a great man should be so badly brought up"]—a remark R. jokingly applies to himself. He comes back to the news of the restoration of secular power [in the papal states] and says there is no longer any good faith anywhere. He works and is much worn out by it; we make an outing to the pier and then to the courtyard discovered by Jouk.— Villa Philippina. Women are not allowed in, but R. admires the curious courtyard with its terraces. Returning home, he goes through the Stein pieces of which I had spoken—"Saint Catherine," "Luther," "Homeless"—and is thoroughly delighted with them; he says he feels in some way implicated, seeing his ideas bearing such fruit, and he considers Stein to have a definite vocation. In the evening, when Rub. plays us one of his "Pictures," R. does not at first recognize the awakening of Brünnhilde, but then he is pleased with it, even though he does not at the moment enjoy hearing music. We finish [Keller's] story "Regine," which impresses us, and then discuss the curious habit among ordinary people of preserving silence. We are reminded of Minna's behavior toward Nath[alie].

Sunday, January 8 After a good night R. and I have breakfast in the conservatory, and he says, "It has occurred to me that we now seem to concern ourselves only with dead things; everything around us is lifeless, whereas previously our existence was concerned with living things, with plants, animals; Wotan carved his spear from the growing ash tree." When I say that it is perhaps this life within life that has given later generations a feeling for divinity, and that Siegfried and Brünnhilde give the appearance of sacred, living Nature, whereas the Gibichungs are already among the dead, he agrees with me. From this we go on to Keller's story, and I say how regrettable it is that our modern world has led him to subjects such as commercial secretaries, people one is almost ashamed to mention, remembering how the people of the Middle Ages brought forth such figures as Geneviève and Elisabeth. He then wants to rest, is disturbed by the children's reading, calls for me to help him, but there is no more question of work, and he decides to go to the museum with us. Memling's charming and masterly picture pleases him as a very delightful piece of trifling, but what most enchants him is the Greek ram. Unfortunately the happy outing ends for him in vexation and feelings of indisposition; he was too lightly dressed, he begins to feel cold, and the Rosario chapel, which we also intended to visit, has such a disagreeable effect on him that I send the children in alone and drive home with him. January 8 awakens memories of Hans, the dinner in Munich in 1868; he talks about Bülow in his youth, how, along with Karl Ritter, he had scoffed loudly at Reissiger, walking along the street behind R. — Toward evening R. feels he really has caught cold, he tries to work but then asks to be read to, and in the evening we play whist. R. extremely vexed by music coming from the room above his. [*Added on the next page but referred back to this point:* "At lunch he recalls the Norns' scene and is pleased to have written such a thing; he declares, half in jest and half in earnest, that nobody has ever mentioned all the things there are in it."]

Monday, January 9 The night passed fairly well, with a gentle perspiration, but vexation over unavailable precautions is unavoidable. A warmed jacket cannot be procured, but in the midst of his vexation R. asks Schnappauf how he puts jackets on madmen, and when Schnappauf shows him, R. begins to laugh heartily again. The day is spent taking care of a slight sore throat; we eat alone together, and I then go with Count Tasca to look at a villa (Airodi); this, at the same time too grandiose and too dilapidated, makes us think again of Venice, which R. prefers to all other Italian towns. In the evening I read aloud the touching story of *"Die arme Baronin,"* which R. had previously read and highly recommended—the metaphor of the little kitten particularly pleases him. — After the reading he returns to his idea of the dead world in which we are now living, and puts it into words. He also comes back to animals and their way of devouring one another, and he firmly pushes the thought from his mind. Talking of German fiction in general, he says he can think of nothing arising from our society except criminal cases, for example, situations caused by clashes of character, etc.

Tuesday, January 10 In the morning, before getting up, R. declares that he by no means shares Keller's opinion of the shortness of life, how swiftly one is overtaken by old age; he says that in his case everything has happened so slowly. How long was he obliged to wait for everything! During the day we talk a lot about this fine story, and R. speaks with pleasure of more to come. A letter from Princess W[ittgenstein] about Lulu's stay irritates R.; he cannot understand why my father does not put an end to this tedious relationship. [*A sentence based on untranslatable word play omitted.*] — In the evening we begin "Correa," and R. says he is downright glad to go from Mme

Rémusat to Keller, from history to fiction; and on hearing the sentence "She believed in herself, in prosperity, in the church," he exclaims, "There we have Sicily exactly!" The story holds our interest and pleases us greatly. Before this, R. played the second subject from the C Minor and pointed out how short it was, yet how eloquent! He continues to praise the wonderful concision of this work and mentions in contrast the *Eroica,* with all its "luxuriance." When I ask him whether he considers this concision to be evidence of greater perfection, he says, "It would be foolish to try to put the C Minor in some sort of higher category than the *Eroica,* but in it the human being has climbed a few steps higher."

Wednesday, January 11   When he hears a church bell in the morning, R. says, "The good Lord is sounding his repeater watch," and he gaily asks me if I know the female name for a rhinoceros, "Rhinoce-Rosine, or Rosine Rhinoc." — He works, and in the afternoon we drive to the Favorita; R. is vexed by the disappearance of the sun, feels the dear Lord has it in for him: in the morning he is unable to escape the sun, and in the afternoon it uses the clouds as a handkerchief. In the evening more about C. W[ittgenstein], then about theatrical people, the difficulty of getting along with them. In the evening "*Die Berlocken*" and the ghost story cause us much amusement; then R. tells a very drastic anecdote, for men's ears only, and it is very characteristic of R. that he is not pleased by our friends' first seeing its funny side. (Fidi is unwell.)

Thursday, January 12   R. had a good night's rest, and Dr. Berlin allays my fears; but we are alarmed to hear that an operation on his tonsils might one day be necessary. R. works. At lunch news about the Russian Emperor brings our conversation to the Russo-Turkish War, and R. says that he had been on Russia's side, but when he saw how talented Osman Pasha was, and how utterly untalented the Russians, his sympathy for them diminished, for it was vital to a sympathetic attitude whether or not great abilities were in evidence. — A letter from Herr Marsillach in Luxor raises the subject of the Nile again. R. dearly wishes to forget Europe for a while. We visit the cathedral, La Zisa, and on our return R. works. He comes to supper in an animated mood and assures us that he would not hesitate for a moment to sacrifice his works for the sake of the children, not for a single moment—*Tristan* for Isolde, *Meistersinger* for Eva, the *Ring* for Siegfried. "That is life," he says. Then he jokes about having chosen a bad country in which to get them married off, for here they would have to become Catholics, and that would seem to him a very great shame. In the evening he talks a lot with Rub. about the harp parts, then we read the story about Lucie, a converted Catholic, and we find it so delightful that R. resolves to renew his acquaintance with Keller. Yesterday he amused himself by telling me that "*Die Berlocken*" ends touchingly, so that, as the reader, I started off apprehensive of having to become emotional in my delivery.

Friday, January 13 [*Enclosed in the Diaries a sketch by Cosima for a poem, "Sangue reale,* true blood."] In the morning R. observes that I would have behaved like Lucie, run off to the convent during the night! — We think of these stories with pleasure, also understand the things which put us off them at the beginning. — Today is Jouk.'s birthday, and since we would like to give him something, I go to the antique dealer's with him and the children, but to no avail. Returning home, I find R. very run down, and at lunch he even leaves the table for a while, but he soon returns and proposes the toast very cordially. After lunch we visit a house which has been offered us. He then works, and in the evening, in honor of Jouk., the chorus from *Die Feen* is played, then the witch's ballad (sung by R.) and the Overture to *Die Feen*. During the last of these R. goes out, I go to see what he is doing —he is putting the finishing touches on his score: "It gave me no rest," he says. The splendid sounds of the *Tannhäuser* march ring out, he comes in, and—all is completed! With this, as with all his other works, he had feared being interrupted by death—that is what he told us at lunch today! As he is talking, I place the Monreale bowl on his desk, and when he goes to fetch something from his room, he discovers it, stays out for a while, then comes in with the heavy box. He likes it! He recognized Eva first, also Fidi. Then everything is told—how the theme of Monreale was adapted in this way by Jouk. at my request. We drink to *Parsifal*. Our friends depart later than usual, we stay up, R. and I, and talk of the various completions (*Tristan, Msinger*—), and of life in general, and go off to bed in a mood of exaltation and peace. — A few more things I have to tell about this evening: first, that R. told us the story behind his first ballad (boy and swan). Then, that he spoke about the orchestration of *Parsifal;* the wind instruments would complain, he said, but when he recalled how, in *Martha,* for instance, the four horns are used time and again in the stupidest way, then he felt comforted. — He tells me that the A-minor chord (as Kundry falls to the ground) will make an impression on me; the terror of sanctity flows from it, and it will have to be very beautifully played, he says.

Saturday, January 14 R. is rather tired; he reads Renan's *Marc Aurèle* (feeling that this emperor is overrated), and writes to Fritz Brandt, entrusting the supervision of the machinery to him. He then goes for a walk with the girls, and at 1 o'clock we have our meal in celebration of *Parsifal,* though R. insists that the work was finished on December 25, and this was the afterbirth. He tells with amusement an anecdote from Renan's book in which someone boasts that as an academician he could speak with Plato, and as a stoic with Zeno, but Pythagoras would remain silent with him; whereupon somebody at the meeting called out, "Then imagine that Pyth. is now with you, and keep silent." There is talk of portraits, and he says merrily that somebody should depict him with me offering him the apple of vegetarianism. I tell him that, since I heard him get so angry with Nietzsche over this subject, I have no longer had the courage to turn vegetarian. R. relates: "Yes, when he came to our house, ate nothing, said, 'I am a vegetarian,' I said to him, 'You are an ass!' " — Recently, though I do not remember in what connection, we agreed that it is only people with a limited outlook who, by not knowing or by ignoring many things, can set up a system. We go for a short walk, R. pays two calls, and as we are returning, we hear some long, sustained, solemn tones; the sounds come closer, arousing feelings of earnestness and exaltation in us; we listen; a funeral procession passes by, the music simple but not vulgar, extremely beautiful, expressively played; R. is completely entranced: "Oh, what a divine thing music is—how it transforms everything!" he exclaims. Unfortunately he is annoyed by the garments and faces of the prelates. We tell our friends about it. In the evening, after Rub. has played part of my father's arrangement of the *Tannh.* Overture, he says he was influenced by a passage in the first part of Berlioz's *Harold* Symphony; in youth one borrows from others, he says; he likes this symphony, the first movement in particular, also the serenade and the pilgrims' march. When I remark that it seems to me soulless, he says, "Yes, a landscape painter like Mendelssohn." I: "I think even more soulless than Mendelssohn." — "Yes, it is like the clattering of bones, a skeleton, but there *is* a skeleton." — And I cannot remember by what transition we come to stories about saints, and he recounts the tale of the Rhineland saint who sucked out a pestilence sore, and it seemed to her the sweetest thing she had ever tasted. He says that for him this contains everything, and he would come back to it again. "We artists," he says, turning to Jouk., "are sugar in comparison." — He also tells the story about Saint Francis rolling among the pigs on the Pope's command. We finish the evening with a game of whist.

Sunday, January 15 In the morning R. talks about Bismarck's statements on the responsibilities of a king, and he then continues to enlarge upon what he calls "this constitutional rubbish." At 12 o'clock a sitting for the French painter Renoir, whom R. jokingly claims to have mistaken for Victor Noir. This artist, belonging to the Impressionists, who paint everything bright and in full sunlight, amuses R. with his excitement and his many grimaces as he works, so much so that R. tells him he is the painter from the *Fl. Blätter*. Of the very curious blue-and-pink result R. says that it makes him look like the embryo of an angel, an oyster swallowed by an epicure. This sitting brings us to landscape painting, and from there to a discussion which becomes so heated that, when R. says, "I have been hearing the same thing for twenty years," I leave the room. That produces a turn in the conversation which gradually restores us to the best of moods. Regarding portraits, R. declared, among other things: "What does that convey to me? The best thing a portrait artist can paint nowadays is a bloodhound!" The weather was dull, no one went out, and in the evening whist was played.

Monday, January 16 R. takes medicine today and reads *M. Aurèle,* but without pleasure. After lunch we deal with various letters which have just arrived, one, for example, from Herr Neumann about his various enterprises. An interruption by a visitor vexes R. greatly. He replies to Herr N. and advises him to drop Paris, which arouses in him nothing but disgust. Then he looks at the book of etchings which Siegfr. has received as a present (a few days ago I found him at breakfast enchanted by the page devoted to Lucas v. Leyden: Joseph interpreting the dreams). Music in the evening: the two last movements of the C Minor Symphony, not entirely to R.'s satisfaction, and the "Picture" of Siegmund and Sieglinde, the construction of which pleases him. Reports of the von Bülow concerts in Berlin sound very favorable.

Tuesday, January 17 The air feels fresh, R. thinks of Spain, and I write to Marsillach in order to be prepared for possible travel plans. R. has a joint sitting with Jouk. and with Rub.; he asks the former how he wants to do him, profile or full face—Lucretia or Lucia. At lunch he tells us that the *Tagblatt* contains a report that a tree frog has been found at Wahnfried. He drives to the club with Count Tasca and Jouk., but when there is talk of venturing farther, he wants me with him, which brings from Count Tasca a joke about the "turtle-doves." We drive to the sea, which is rough but still lovely, even when the sky is overcast. He then writes to Feustel, and in the evening we play whist.

Wednesday, January 18 He had a good night, and he is very cheerful at lunch, when, among other things, he talks of his definite resolve to travel up the Nile, in order to see "where Barthel gets his cider." — His current account shows good revenues, and that as always delights him. [*Added seven pages later but referred back to this point:* "In the morning, when he went out with the children, R. met the Abbé Jecker, tutor to Count Mazzarino; at their first meeting he had made a good impression, but this time he seems fulsome and at the same time reserved. R. feels he has received a *mot d'ordre* [instruction], and he resolves to make clear to the mother and other relatives that he considers it a great shame to deliver this fine boy up to such slavery. — With regard to Lusch's nonarrival, R. takes out *Hamlet* and reads the final speech, adding, ' "The rest is silence"—that is my motto.' "] In splendid weather we take a very lovely drive to S. Maria Gesù, both the journey there and the view utterly enchant us. In the evening he reads to us a page in Renan about faith and certainty which pleases him very much. We talk about marriages, and how seldom one can be described as happy. [*The previous sentence was originally begun:* "A letter from Lusch talking of the prospect of a marriage, which caused great excitement among the children, brings our conversation to marriage." *This is crossed out, obviously because it was entered on the wrong date; see January 20, last sentence.*] Then we come to the subject of age, and when we tell R. he is becoming increasingly handsome, and the same amiable remark is made about me, he says, "You have acquired a beautiful serenity." — He then claims always to be hearing me "warbling" with the children! — In the evening, when we are assembled in my *salon,* our neighbors, a married couple from America, start singing hymns in two-part harmony; this at first makes us laugh, particularly since the husband sings the bass very inaccurately, but gradually it becomes almost moving, and at any rate arouses in us reflection and contemplation. Then at R.'s request Rub. plays a Chopin polonaise. (Bismarck's efforts, aimed apparently at revising the constitution, cause R. to recall his conversation with Herr von Lutz in 1865; the latter told him that they would rather go along with Prussia than with Austria, because Prussia would greatly restrict constitutionalism. According to this, R. observes, everything that has happened since has been a parenthesis.)

Thursday, January 19   R. had a good night, but he is much annoyed by the exorbitant demands of our landlord, and I notice it in the irritable way he talks about M. Aurelius at lunch, in the assumption that I harbor an unjustified admiration for this emperor. He talks with much emotion of the martyrdom of Saint Blandine. When mention is made of someone who wishes to see him, he tells me that the thought of any new acquaintances upsets him. At 12 o'clock he goes for a walk with the children in the Engl. Gardens, and in the afternoon we visit the Aumale gardens, which are quite splendid and which please R., too, even if his mood is still irritable. Seeing oranges growing beside a rose, he says, "How vulgar they seem beside that blossom!" — In the evening Count Tasca calls on us to arrange for tomorrow the outing to Bagheria which R. wanted to make today. We discuss everything, then R. plays the *"Kaisermarsch"* with Rub. as a piano duet, but finds it very exhausting. As the evening ends, he tells me of the alliance between the Liberals and the Center party against Bismarck! — A letter from the publishers [Breitkopf &] Härtel announces that *Lohengrin* is at last to be engraved, also a new edition of *Tristan*. R. considers whether he should make some simplifications in this, but then abandons the idea.

Friday, January 20 Glorious sunshine; R. had a good night, and in the morning he jokes about the success of *Tristan*—he says he feels like the long-legged grasshopper, "singing its wonted song in the grass." He likens Härtel to earthworms, which emerge the moment anything moves. And at 11:30 we drive off to Bagheria with Prince Gangri, Count Tasca, and the children in four carriages. The outing is a complete success; the view from Val Guarnero enchants R., it seems the loveliest thing ever seen. Lunch at Soluntum with the Prince is very pleasant. A lawyer toasts R. in both German and Italian, and R. proposes the health of the Princess; despite a slight adventure on the homeward journey (the axle of a carriage breaks), it was all a great success, and R. embraces our friendly hosts with great warmth. — At home we unfortunately find a report on the B[ülow] concerts in Berlin, the fêting of Brahms makes a dismal impression. A letter from Gobineau also brings some vexation, since R. is unable to understand why he does not join us here. "I need nobody but you," he says. "I moved Heaven and earth to get you, and nobody else; but I am glad when I can be of help to anyone." (Today Lusch's letter about marriage prospects arrived.)

Saturday, January 21 R. had a good night's rest. In the morning we again go through Lusch's letter, which has an enclosure from her father confessor; great vexation over the latter, a witticism about great men who have no heart makes R. indignant. We discuss Lusch's fate. — At 12 the fine weather tempts R. to a walk in the English Gardens with the children, I go to meet them. Our lunch is cheerfnl, the letter from the wine merchant *Kroté* makes us laugh, but the fatigue arising from yesterday's outing shows, and vexation with hotel life is growing fast. (Since, in response to R.'s request to take out this and that, Herr Ragusa was prepared to deduct only a minimum, R. has the whole bill paid, but he is no longer speaking to him.) We leave some cards, to provide an excuse for a drive. As I am talking to Jouk. about his departure, R. bursts out—why is he not told anything? it is a false kind of consideration—and he then goes on to talk very bitterly about Lusch, my father, the Princess, and soon asks to go home. I advise Jouk. to explain to him calmly why it is necessary for him to return; he does this as soon as we arrive home, and a telegram to Plett[ung] and Schwab, "Werbel and Schwemel," is drafted, asking whether they really have anything to show. (Jouk. had already wished to leave on Wednesday night, saying nothing to R. but just leaving a letter behind; however, R. instinctively guessed it, talked of evil omens, and, when we told him about the curious twittering of a bird—which we could not find—in the chimney before supper, interpreted this as a warning against departure, so that Jouk. remained silent, impressed by these daemonic utterances. He was then obliged to go to Bagheria with us, but now it has been decided that we shall give up Sicily and visit Lusch, and it is that which I touched on today.) — In the evening I read aloud parts of a lecture on Palermo by A. Springer; R. is fairly interested in the historical aspect, but when it gets to a description of the buildings, he grows restless, goes out, comes back again, sits down in the adjoining room, withdraws into himself, says to himself, "I shall not have the heart to do it," asks me, when I enter the room, to take no notice of him, and at last, when I return, shows me his letters to Lusch and to Gross. I am silent at first, but then I tell him that I find this letter easier to understand than the one which was sent last year. I tell him that my trust in the girl is now so great that I hoped from all this to achieve what was best for her. And gradually he calms down, and we return to the children in almost cheerful spirits and talk for a long time with Jouk. R. jokingly calls me Saint Catherine—so calm about everything that one can scarcely follow me. Then we talk about the children, who were today strangely muddle-headed—like a flock of sheep, R. says—and, joking, we release our friend and go off to bed.

Sunday, January 22   R. had a good night, and we discuss yesterday's reading, the significance of the Arab people, and Gobineau's over-estimation of the Normans, who in fact simply took over the beautiful things they found in order to enjoy them—they created nothing themselves. He writes a letter to Rub.'s father, praising his son, and around midday goes for a walk in the garden opposite, where Prof. Salinas, who came to fetch Siegfried for an outing, finds him. In this otherwise cultured man he detects the same limited outlook common to all people who occupy themselves with art, and he is glad when I arrive, since he "chatters too much." We accompany Jouk. to the ship and take leave of him there with much waving. At supper Fidi pleases us with his efforts to take over from our friend in our conversations; he talks about a conspiracy in Constantinople, mining disasters, etc. R. says, "He is saying, 'Please put me in his place.' " — We play whist and Chopin! The latter pleases even R. with his melodic refinement, which is indeed downright astonishing in one who, as a virtuoso, as R. says, had to provide scope for rhetorical brilliance. When we are alone, we come to the subject of Hans, his remarks against Lulu, his attitude toward me; we comment on the ability to say the most terrible things lightly, and we talk of Minna, too. When R. mentions that it was not until the year 1864 that he told me about her infidelity, I can reply to him that, when he told me about it in the garden at Starnberg, I had the feeling that only to me could he have said it; and the fact that he did say it left me with indescribable feelings. (The letter to Rub.'s father has put something of a strain on him, he complains about having things of this sort demanded of him, but—according to his account—he spoke very warmly of our friend.)

Monday, January 23   R. had a good night, but the topic which most occupies us is our living accommodations; we talk to a paper hanger, decide to drive to Bagheria to look at the Casa Ferdinande there. When I remark that I believe in good, R. says, "A yearning for good is part of Nature, though it is true that evil is also there in full." — M. *Aurèle* bores him greatly, and Renan's sugary portrayal makes him sarcastic. At 12 o'clock Prince Gangi appears with Count Tasca and offers us the former's villa in the country, which we then visit; it pleases us very much, and we accept it with much gratitude. R. replies as follows to a telegram from Jouk. [*not discovered*]. — He is tired from the journey, all the new arrangements upset him. He immediately gives notice to the hotel. In the evening Rub. plays us the symphonic poem *Dante* and arouses interest with it, as well as regret [*the last four words obliterated in ink by an unknown hand*]. —

Tuesday, January 24   R. had a very disturbed night; he reads a lot! — In the morning I hear him playing the enclosed melody [*four bars of music, inscribed by Wagner* "melody comp. by Shakespeare"]: "This is by the descendant of Dürer and Shakespeare," he says; yesterday he observed that he could not understand how someone in proper health could choose Hell as a subject. [*Added in margin:* "Otherwise our morning conversation is about the Fantaisie, which is being sold!"] — He answers Herr Ragusa's letter in person, and all is settled peacefully, R. as usual prepared to make payment in full. Now all our thoughts are directed toward the new house. Unfortunately R. does not feel well, we drive to the Favorita, get out in the Via [della] libertà, and frequently have to sit down for a rest. He notices an old and ragged man dragging himself along laboriously with a rake and a spade: "Always the aged who have the hard work!" R. exclaims. I: "Let's give him something." R. approaches him with our gift, the old man at first regards him with solemn surprise, then understands him, smiles, and continues laboriously on his way. "The earnestness of that look!" R. exclaims. I had felt it, too—the withdrawal from everything, from the whole world, which was expressed in this look. — We return home slowly, and R. has much vexation with the proofs of the piano score. We have supper later than usual and spend the rest of the evening in cheerful chat. (Fritz Brandt writes very reassuringly.)

Wednesday, January 25 But R. had another restless night. However, when I return from the new house around lunchtime with Boni and Count Tasca, I see him on the Corso, going in search of cigarettes and looking so well that it is hard to believe he had a bad night. Lunch is spent on reports and proposals regarding the move, also reports about Venice. Since I am somewhat tired in the evening, I let R. go for a walk by himself, he tells me that he saw the street laborer again and that the latter greeted him with a smile. He would like to make a donation to the man. He sits down beside me when he returns from his walk and complains of the constant unrest; to calm him down, I tell him that everything between us is so nicely arranged; he: "Yes, for leaving the world, but not for gaining a foothold in it." — In the evening Prof. Moleschott visits us, he recalls having spoken French with me in Zurich more than 20 years ago and asks me whether I have turned into a German. After that a singer, an Englishwoman, from whom R. takes flight, and in the evening friend Rub., who plays us his "Picture," to our great satisfaction. Then whist, and finally some words between R. and me about Renan, who R. declares must be a Jew, since the whole thing is a glorification of Judaism. "Nobody has ever written such popular songs as Beeth.!" he exclaims merrily today! — The length of the evenings and nights makes him feel melancholy and arouses in him reflections on the misery of human existence and the many things it depends on. He says that every time the sun disappears behind Monte Graio his heart feels heavy. Herr Neumann requests permission to call his enterprise the Wagner Theater. R. grants it. [*Added two pages later but referred back to this point:* "R. tells Rub. two jokes he made yesterday. To a shell collector: '*Dans la mer on trouve à une certaine profondeur des coquillages, plus loin des coquilles, et enfin des coquins*' ['In the sea one finds at a certain depth mussels, farther out, other shells, and finally rogues']. And about the *B. Blätter:* 'Strange that its circulation is not increasing, when Porges writes for it so rarely!' "]

Thursday, January 26 In the morning, after a somewhat restless night, R. plays the melody of Chopin's "*Marche funèbre,*" and that brings us at breakfast to a discussion of the Poles and their endearing qualities. Before lunch R. reads me Renan's passage on usury, in which he says that Christianity's ban on usury held up civilization for a number of centuries. This makes us laugh a lot. In the afternoon R. goes to the new villa with Siegfried, meets Count Tasca there, and brings him back; Fidi tells me that Papa was satisfied, but soon after-

ward I notice that R. is much out of humor, and then it comes out—
to our dismay—that he dislikes the villa and would sooner remain in
the hotel. Prof. Salinas's visit provides a pleasant distraction, and he
tells us a lot about the Sicilians, among other things, the frugal living
habits of the *Borghese,* opulent country people who eat practically
nothing. (Concern about Loldi!) [*Added three pages later but referred
back to this point:* "R. makes the children laugh heartily with his sudden
joke: 'Children, I won't go back to Bayreuth—Jäger is refusing to
sing Parsifal.' " —]

   Friday, January 27 R. slept well; our breakfast is cheerful, he is
reconciled to the move. He finishes *M. Aurèle* and gives me his final
summary; "*Une tendance vers le bien*" ["A tendency toward good"],
says R., "that I can allow, but on top of that *une grande bonté* [great
benevolence], which R[enan] finds in everything—such optimism is
worthy of [David] Strauss. Elegance and a narrow outlook, that is the
Frenchman of today." — At R.'s request I write to Venice about the
palazzo there recommended to us by Princess Hatzfeldt, and before
lunch we visit some carpet and wallpaper dealers, again in connection
with our move. Over coffee a letter from Lusch (she is not coming
until Tuesday) arouses his anger, and since he expresses this with
some violence, it makes me weep and complain, for I am worried about
Loldi, and the move is making me melancholy. However, it is very
soon over; he observes that when the words Jouk. enclosed with
Lusch's letter were read out, he was inwardly pleased that he had
yielded to my persuasions not to send his letter to her; the trivialities
in Lusch's present letter annoyed him above all because they prevented
him from giving free rein to his overwhelming feelings toward me. —
Count T. comes, I settle kitchen and carriage with him. R. takes a
walk along the Libertà but does not encounter his old man, for whom
he wants to set aside a sum of money, and that worries him. In the
evening, after telling us that the antivivisection petition has again
been rejected (Reichstag), he says that he recognizes no religion except
compassion, and it is precisely this which it is not only impossible to
arouse, but which is now being killed off entirely. Pity no longer
exists! — During the evening he indignantly relates what the *B.
Tagblatt* is printing about friend Schnappauf and his decorations [*newspaper clipping enclosed; see notes*]. He says he is writing to friend Gross
about it, telling him what it makes him feel like to live in a place
where such things are possible, and indeed tolerated. We play whist, and
in the evening, when we are alone, I go along with his melancholy
about the new house, just to avoid provoking him by contradiction
into being prejudiced too strongly against it. [*Added two pages later*

but referred back to this point: "R. asks me whether I believe Count Gobineau will be able to write his preface retracting various things which might give offense."]

Saturday, January 28　R. had a good night, but after his morning bath he has a prolonged spasm and joins me at breakfast looking run down. He gradually calms down and takes delight in the sky and the sun and the country. I drive out to Porrazzi, and since the sky is wonderful and the mountains make a glorious impression on me, I am able to give him a cheerful report and get him to regard our move favorably. Unfortunately the mail brings him an unjustified demand from the agent in Frankfurt, he immediately sends a telegram to friend Gross, telling him to withdraw the rights from the director there, Dr. Claar; then—out of humor—he tries to take a stroll in the garden, where he is "goggled at" by some ladies, which irritates him, and he comes to lunch dissatisfied. "What a world it is!" he exclaims in connection with the agent. But he calms down, and though he first of all feels my equanimity regarding Lulu's visit ("When the witch interferes," he says, meaning Princess W., "everywhere is Hell") to be stiff and cold, he gradually comes around to my way of seeing things, after I have assured him that, difficult as I may sometimes find certain things, I can never forget how much happier I am than others. A look from Siegfried, the sweet faces of the girls, even my ability to feel the greatness and sublimity of Nature as I did today—all this fills me with gratitude. And even some disquiet concerning how differently the elder girls have turned out—this, too, tells me in the mighty language of Nature that it was right to dissolve my first marriage, and teaches me patience and timid, though joyful, resignation. — R. agrees with me that this is the way to look at life, but he says, "Our union started 15 years too late!" In the afternoon I drive out to Porrazzi, R. follows with Eva, but he is in poor spirits because of indisposition, and he cannot bring himself to like the new house. In the evening friend Rub. plays the *Tannhäuser* Overture to us, but R. does not enjoy it, and we are filled with regret that a person so excellent in his own way should seem so alien to us; R. even goes so far as to say that he would prefer it if he were no longer with us, though he has the highest opinion of him. — Reading the final chapter of Renan's *M. Aurèle* together, we have to smile over the remark that Jesus resembled nobody as little as his followers! . . . The chapter itself is interesting on account of its subtle analysis, but it annoys one with what R. calls its "trivial mixing up of everything," its Jewish optimism.

(At lunch R. tells us that Schnappauf was today erroneously arrested as a thief, but was soon released.) — R. is still much upset by the

Tagblatt episode, he talks of writing himself, then of canceling his subscription, but then he decides to do nothing.

Sunday, January 29   R. was up once during the night, and for quite a long time, but then he fell into a good and gentle sleep. In the morning he tells me that he had been thinking of writing a piece for the *B. Blätter* criticizing Renan's final chapter. He points out how shallow his idea of a miracle is, and contrasts it with Schopenhauer's profound theory. He finds this all the more regrettable in that Renan has said excellent things about monasteries, the cult of the saints, and the way the masses have modified Christianity. How splendid R.'s eloquence as he describes miracles to me in Sch[openhauer]'s sense! — He has returned with enjoyment to Kant. — Around midday he calls on Countess Mazzarino, whom he fails to see, but Abbé Jecker shows him around the lovely palazzo, which pleases him. He talks jokingly of snatching this lady, "their prey," from the priests, but says this would probably lead to his being poisoned. He is thinking of writing friend Wolz. a letter he would not know what to do with, that is to say, whether to publish it or not. Among other things, he would like to forestall Schemann with Cherubini. — He has now given up the idea of a journey on the Nile, having read yesterday in the guidebook that it is bad for people with abdominal complaints. — Rub. dines with us today, since he is accompanying Boni and me to a concert; R. talks at table about present-day Italians and how they justify Gob.'s concluding chapter. He is annoyed that Gobineau cannot find a publisher for his 2nd edition and that he intends to publish it at his own expense. He comes back to his idea of dramatizing Nap., and says it should be done in the style of Abelard. News I have received from Princess W. about Lusch's abusive remarks on Rome upset me greatly, for I so dearly wish my children to be well behaved and dignified. R. defends Lusch, saying that he is pleased she should experience feelings of disgust there and also give expression to them. He says I am wrong to demand anything else. I observe that an experience such as Lusch has just been through should be given a more refined and elegiac form! But how fine and how kind it is of him to speak in her defense, and how willing I am to listen, alas! When I cite Marie Wittg., and how nobly she bore all the miseries of her youth without complaint, he says, "That is why she became such a passive person—everything in her was struck dead." We play whist in the evening.

Monday, January 30   R. had a good night, we have breakfast in bed in cheerful spirits, and I go off soon afterward to Porrazzi, return home in good spirits, although some things there seem to me somewhat primitive when I consider R.'s tastes, tell him of the fine carriage we shall have—Prince Gangi had just shown it to me—and the lovely location. At lunch R. talks about what he read today, Kant on earthquakes, which he enjoyed. But after lunch R. drives out to Porrazzi and is so struck by the simplicity of the house that he wants to make as many alterations and additions as possible; when I ask him to stop worrying on my account, since I should soon get things to my liking and do not like offending people who have been so friendly toward us, however alien they may seem, R. is at first angry, but then he jokes about what he calls my pride on the one hand and my aspirations toward sainthood on the other. We then talk about Lusch's arrival tomorrow and the celebrations in connection with it, and very sweetly Fidi says to us in Sicilian dialect as he goes off to bed, "*Allora domani non si parlano di questa casa, ma di Roma, di altre cose*" ["Tomorrow there will be no talking about this house, but about Rome and other things"] . . . Even yesterday, at the start of the disputes about Lusch, he said softly to me when I spoke my wish with regard to the children, "*Io capisco*" ["I understand"], and his gentle nature is a boundless delight to us. When we are alone, we read Stein's article on Rousseau in the *B. Bl.* and find it quite outstanding. R. then talks of the possibilities: "If one were to win over a person of as good a disposition as young Mazzarino for great ideas, where, to whom could he look for support?" And he mentions little Cavaliere Guccia and smiles. —

Tuesday, January 31 We come back to our theme in the morning, that is to say, the differences in our characters as seen from outside, and when he says to me in a friendly way that I am both pride and weakness, and I reply that this does not seem to me a very special mixture, he replies emphatically, "The best for sainthood!," which makes us laugh. Earlier than expected, as we are still chatting in bed, Lusch is announced. "With Lusch there must always be some excitement," R. says gaily. The girl arrives around 9 o'clock, and Fidi says, "*Tutt'un altra vita*" ["A completely different life"]! How much, how much is there to say, with never a pause! Once again the dear child has been looking into life's ugly countenance. R. immediately drives with her to the Via [della] libertà and the Villa Trabia and returns thoroughly satisfied with her—"a splendid child." The evening also passes in merry chat; a smiling sun greeted her arrival, and now we are together!

Wednesday, February 1 Weather somewhat dull; we are told that February here is stormy and cold. Bonichen doing much shopping in connection with the move, and Lusch telling us a lot about my poor father! We spend the evening at Countess Tasca's, where quite a large reception is being held; R. bears it all very well; he even gives some advice to the young lady who sings "*Dors, mon enfant*" and "*Mignonne*," and she heeds it well on singing them again.

Thursday, February 2 Candlemas, moving today, packing, amid many difficulties; it is reported that some English people in San Martino have been set upon and robbed, and we are advised to notify the prefect of our moving. Our final lunch goes off merrily, though what Lusch has told me about my father's condition, and the torments he is having to undergo, leaves me in melancholy mood; he is being told that R. and I are complaining about his visits to us and that with R. he is exposed to ridicule! When I am alone with R. after lunch, I have to shed some bitter tears. A man of such talents and a life so miserably squandered, as if in the clutches of an evil witch! While we are talking with R. about it, we suddenly realize to what an extent his gift of virtuosity has condemned him to worldliness, and this is the dismal explanation for the whole thing. We resolve, when the moment seems right, to make a final onslaught on him, in an attempt to persuade him to make a complete break and remain with us. . . . I ask Lusch not to relate anything more of what she has heard about the people close to us, in order to spare the other children and allow them to keep their youthful bloom. — We leave the room, remembering that here *Parsifal* was completed. R. says, "We are a large and very good family," and in a rough wind we enter the carriage. "What will you pay me for leaving?" R. asks Herr Ragusa, who replies, "I'll pay you something to stay on." Arrival at 3 o'clock, much confusion! But in the end a merry supper and a merry evening, for which Rub. joins us. A *Fra Diavolo* mood, since we are advised to keep our shutters in good order, but splendid moonlight. R. sends a copy of the Italian piano score to Prince Gangi with a little dedication. Downstairs in the *salon,* we recall the songs sung yesterday, and R. describes his move to the Rue de la Tonnellerie. The minuet from Mozart's E-flat Major Symph. was played yesterday on two pianos.

Friday, February 3 A restful night for R.; for all of us somewhat wild and frosty; mine was split up into various acts. Luckily the sun is shining, but it is very cold! . . . R. drives into town to pick out carpets while we arrange the furniture. The children go off at once on a walk. Our lunch is a cozy one, we drink to Lusch's health; R. does it first in German, solemnly welcoming her return, then Fidi in Sicilian dialect! After lunch R. takes a long rest, but on waking he feels very hot, and the simultaneous arrival of paper hangers, piano tuner, and Count Tasca upsets him greatly. The Count himself is anxious when he learns that the girls have gone off to the left for a walk without being accompanied, and, after sending the *facchino* [carrier] away, he sets out on foot to meet them. Once R. has calmed down, we also drive toward them, meeting the Count first and then the children, accompanied by Antonio with a powerful shotgun on his

back! Much amusement. We divide ourselves between the two carriages
and then drive through the enchanting countryside via Madonna della
Grazia, returning home through the town. The evening passes very
harmoniously; R. enlarges upon the German language, regretting the
loss of so many of its forms. Then he goes on to Herr Türk about the
foolishness of philologists, who devote all their energies to establishing
the purity of the text and do not bother at all about its spirit. —
Despite the unfamiliar surroundings our mood is a very good one; I
feel as if I have just arrived in Transvaal or been born here! And R.
shares my feelings; he also talked about Kant's theory of earthquakes
and described it to us, and, after drawing our attention before supper
to the magnificent rising moon, he takes me onto his terrace in the
evening to admire the splendid moonlight.

Saturday, February 4   A good night for R., but the cold is severe.
However, we are cheerful in the morning, and our conversation soon
takes off on a wide-ranging flight; the French Revolution, the terrible
fact that now property is all that matters, Rousseau, and many other
things enliven us as a brilliant sun shines down. At 12 o'clock we stroll
with R. to the Villa Camastra and return home very pleased with
Nature, but amused by our escort of two security guards, lent to us
by an anxious Count Tasca! In the afternoon I pay some calls with
Lusch, and when I return home, I see R. returning from Camastra,
still flanked by his two guards, and now very annoyed by it all. To
conclude our outing I had decided to visit our owl with Lusch, we
looked for it, could not find it, and were told that the fine bird is now
dead. "He must have been pining for us," R. says at first on hearing
about it; then we tell ourselves how miserable the beautiful creature
must have been in captivity. Fidi has a slight chill, I put him to bed
right away. The evening passes harmoniously, with the children we
look at etchings of German history, and I even read aloud [Friedrich
Wilhelm III's] "Call to My People"; but we are beset by uneasy
feelings of having been rash in moving here, and I go to bed in a
state of indescribable anxiety about R. — At my recommendation R.
has begun to read [George Sand's] *Le Piccinino,* after Count Tasca has
told us the most curious stories about Valvo the bandit, and the visit
paid him in the country by 7 bandits—things which make the way in
which we are guarded here understandable!

Sunday, February 5   Worry! I send to Dr. Berlin to ask whether it is
advisable to stay on here. The sun is shining, and we wait for Count
Tasca, an outing having been arranged; he does not arrive, R. and I
drive to his house, it was a misunderstanding. Above all R. wants the
bodyguard removed! After lunch the children go with the Count to
the flower throwing, R. rests but feels oppressed. Dr. Berlin advises

stoves. The children return home with the Count and Rub. — R. asks the latter to play Chopin's "Polonaise" to warm us up and is delighted with it, calling it a masterpiece. He is again delighted by the "flashing of countless spurs," and explains this to Tasca. In the evening we read "Correa" again in honor of Lusch, with renewed enjoyment. In addition R. is reading *Le Piccinino,* which he finds pleasing. — R. praises my cheerfulness under such conditions, thinks it must be the South; "I know otherwise!" — I must add that R.'s first dream in this house concerned Fidi: R. was with somebody like Math. Maier, and through a kind of embarrassment tried on his hat; whereupon Fidi presented him with a small one: "Here, Papa."

Monday, February 6 R. is unwell! Probably a cold; a stove is brought in, and it helps a little. He remains all day in his room reading *Le Piccinino,* which interests him in spite of its "sloppiness"; he remarks that the French cannot make anyone except modern characters speak convincingly. I purchase carpets in town, eat with the children, and in the evening put my Siegfried to bed with a temperature! . . . I read Keller's "*Die arme Baronin*" to the girls, then go at half past nine to R., whose condition is at any rate no worse. He is very kind to me, calls me goodness and beauty personified, and if that delights me even more unutterably than usual, it is because I see it as a sign of recovery.

The (for us) unfamiliar Italian style of furniture causes us to reflect that, in places where people are easily accessible, there is much less comfort; comfort is the invention of the English, with their "I am no slave" attitude. — We also come to realize why intellectual work is impossible in such circumstances; it makes me laugh heartily when R. says everything ends in noise, for our hospitable prince always gives his orders with extraordinary loudness and breadth.

Tuesday, February 7 But R. has a restless night, he wakes up, continually pursued by dreams of my turning away from him in contempt! . . . In the morning he blames it on his temperament, saying that anyone who puts his trust in it is exposed to continual wild-goose chases; he recalls our flight from Naples and now our leaving the hotel. — I start the day hopefully, since at any rate things seem no worse, either with him or with Fidi; and, since it is Saint Richard's Day I present him with Humboldt's *Kawi-Sprache,* which he finds amusing. He eats alone upstairs, while downstairs we celebrate Rub.'s birthday in spite of the inhospitable circumstances. The doctor visits Fidi, who still has a temperature. The doctor seems unperturbed but wants to wait until tomorrow to make up his mind. I had not told R. that the boy was in bed, but he unexpectedly comes downstairs to look for me and finds the doctor and me with Siegfried. Yesterday I was again struck by his uncanny powers of divination: I had scarcely put Siegfried to bed when R. went to see him, and his first words were "I hope nothing will happen to Siegfried—he always has his mouth open"! It costs an effort to keep the worst thoughts away from R. He has supper with us; Fidi, on a strict diet, falls asleep! — Downstairs we attempt to read Alexis's *Ruhe ist die erste B[ürger]pflicht,* but the vulgarity of the first scene puts us off. R. goes up to his room and continues with *Le Piccinino,* remarking jokingly that in women's books it is always women who play the dominant role. The novel interests him, even though he recognizes its weaknesses—trivial subsidiary characters described in detail, impossible conversations. — When I go into R.'s room in the evening and find it comfortably warm and nicely furnished, I tell him that every time I come to him I feel as if I am entering harbor; it is a reflection in miniature of my fate, although outsiders probably imagine life with him is all misery and unrest, as it indeed might appear from the outside. — He regrets that I have not furnished my own rooms like his, so that he could come to me in the same way, but he understands when I explain to him that I have no life of my own, and the children and everyone else in the house must be allowed to keep their share of me.

Wednesday, February 8   R. had a good night, but his cough is very persistent. He is in quite good spirits; lying in bed, he is overcome by the thought of how beautiful it is in music when one instrument joins in with another; one frequently has to deny oneself something, he says, in order to achieve a climax or to ensure that a new theme makes a maximum effect; these are things of which people like Marschner and Schumann have no notion. I observe that this is because they probably never saw a melody as a living form, and consequently never felt the need to give it special clothing. He spends the morning quietly, reading *Le Piccinino.* But Fidi's temperature is rising, and when, after a somewhat generous meal (during which R. says he needs only to eat and then he stops coughing), R. meets the doctor and the latter shakes his head dubiously, R. gets into such a state that his spasms return; a short walk with me does nothing to help him, and an anxious evening leads to a wild night for him. (Siegfried's temperature has risen to 40 degrees!) However, amid all this uneasiness and worry we achieve, thanks to the girls, some contentment in the evening; Lusch tells her father about her impressions in Rome, her lunch and dinner with the Cardinal, speculations on the stock exchange in which eminent people in Rome participated, producing a "crash" in France, with losses for the small people. R. says: "With my pessimistic outlook I actually enjoy hearing things like that! Before long not a single honest person will possess a cent. And let us hope there will be no inequality in other things besides property. States will no longer be able to exist—

Austria, for instance, which must now go to war, can find no money for it!" When we are talking about the Jesuits, R. asks himself whether this powerful, expert organization could be put to the service of a higher calling; he thinks not, since they would never desist from keeping the people in a state of superstition. — The absence of any kind of morality, of God-fearingness—this is what strikes him as typical of the superstition imposed by them. "Excellent fellows here and there who love their master, but not a trace of religion." — Since there is a parade ground in front of the house, we are constantly hearing the blaring of trumpets: "Nobody here but the sons of Nimrod!" jokes R., who finds these childish toy-trumpet sounds quite absurd—he would prefer drums. We draw out the evening, because R. is fearful of going to bed, and talk again about my father, his bewitchment and the possibility of winning him over to us entirely; R. observes that he can easily give up his fortune and everything else, since it is all in the hands of the Princess, and live with us. Our conversation turns into a discussion of women's power over men: "They take hold of them by their vanity," R. says. — And he observes that a better relationship was discovered in the East.

Thursday, February 9 R. had a wild, agitated night in consequence of an error of diet; Fidi was awake until two o'clock, his fever has abated a little, and he is quiet. R. soon cheers up, too, he talks to me about Lusch's friendly and cheerful character; then an article by Herr Hiller about my father's remarks on the Jews brings us to this subject, and R. says it is becoming more and more clear to him what damage they represent, rather than cause: "In a wound on a poor horse or some other animal one at once sees a swarm of flies." While I am with Fidi, he reads *Le Piccinino* and quotes to me with a smile a description of a fountain in the *"nuit parfumée"* ["fragrant night"]—there really is a great division between us and the French, he said before reading it to me. But he adds that even such reading is useful, it all helps to sharpen one's basic perceptions: G. Sand did not get beyond the hope that a worker, for example, would one day be ennobled, etc. He is looking forward to the book on the Kawi language, he says this period of mankind interests him—history and civilization are concerned only with killing. He intends to study the book when he writes his preface to Stein. "The character of our present society," he says, "is easily discernible in the fact that it assumes there is no life after death," and, in connection with the painter in *Le P.*, he recalls the portraits in Henri II costume, the tight jacket, long legs, cap with a feather, and he says, "I find them repulsive." He comes down to lunch and says I must now always put the food on his plate—this would also provide a good excuse in the company of strangers for him always to be sitting next to me. Before lunch he calls me to the window to see the lovely light on the Pellegrino, and yesterday, when we went for a walk despite his spasms, he pointed out Monreale to me, so curiously bathed in rays of light softened by the clouds that it looked "like a mirage." — In the evening Prince Gangi visits us, bringing jelly for Fidi in his own hands, and since the doctor did not seem dissatisfied with his condition when he spoke to R., we remain downstairs, and a conversation develops about all sorts of things; the popular movement in Sicily in which the Prince, like almost all the aristocracy, took part. Then about the stock exchange, and R. demonstrates with great clarity that a profit on the stock exchange can rest only on losses suffered by others. Before that he very splendidly explained Gobineau's system to us, saying that it deals not with *l'homme* [mankind], but with *les hommes* [people], and he says he has every reason to be harsh.

Friday, February 10 Fidi had a restless night, and R. has a slight sore throat, having yesterday, after a walk in the garden, sat down in the *salon* beside Princess Gangi with a bare head. Our dear son is ill, and the nature of his illness cannot be denied—it is typhoid fever! . . . I stay beside him and go now and again to R. In the afternoon, when the boy has quieted down and I go across to R., I find him reading the dialogue which Stein has sent us, dissatisfied with it and with the whole house, complaining about boredom, about bad country houses; very annoyed at having come to live here. Sorrowfully I leave him, after begging him to be a little patient. Whether this irritability is the cause of his illness or the result of it I do not know. When, in the evening, the doctor prescribes a cold compress to counter the fever, R. flies into a rage about the way the doctor wants this compress applied, and he becomes so violent that the doctor afterward asks me to see that he is no longer present during his visits, since he gets so excited about everything. Since Schnap. has spent two nights beside the sickbed, I take over for tonight the continual moistening of the linen; and our boy has a good night, he quiets down, his breathing becomes more regular, and when he opened his eyes once as I was pouring out the tepid water, he looked at me and softly cried, "How nice!" — But at half past two R. appears and is beside himself that I have not asked Schnappauf to relieve me; I have to speak to him vigorously and at length try to convince him that it is better for our child and for everyone else that I stay with him. R. goes off to bed, and at about a quarter to seven, after Siegfried has slept soundly and well, I lie down beside him.

(R. wrote very frankly today to Count Gobineau, among other

things exclaiming with Eteocles, "Oh, Zeus, why did you ever create women?")

Saturday, February 11   The doctor says he cannot yet speak definitely of an improvement, we shall have to let the requisite number of days go by. — R. has a slight sore throat and keeps to his room, complaining greatly about our stay here. He also does not care for his reading— Stein's dialogues on the Revolution—and he decides not to write a preface, since these pieces seem to him very juvenile. He transfers his attention to Shakespeare and in the evening reads to me the great scene between Beatrice and Benedict, pleased that in it the hollow wit and the cruel cynicism of the princes and counts are emphasized, thus allowing one to feel that Shakespeare took no pleasure in depicting these trivialities, but brought these Renaissance figures back to life only out of his sense of truthfulness. He is extremely delighted with Beatrice's reply to Benedict's desire for no tears, and this "peasant simplicity" enchants him as much as the jesting about eating the sword repels him. — He also finds the scene between Leonato and Antonio particularly pleasing. Telegram from Leipzig about the [*Ring*] cycle; R. is pleased with Herr Neumann. Then he talks to me about the Society of Patrons and what he might do to ensure that after our death the cause does not fall into the hands of petty people, hindering Siegfried in all he undertakes. He asks himself whether he will retain enough strength and desire to stage his other works, besides *Parsifal,* there; he says he ought to take them all up again, with close attention to detail—*Tannhäuser,* for instance. — In the afternoon, after having lunch alone upstairs (I had mine with the girls), he came down and, finding Loldi alone in the *salon,* he played to her "her themes" from *Tristan,* as he told me when I thanked him for the kind greeting I heard as I sat in the sickroom! — Today R. complained about no longer having a home anywhere, since Wahnfried has been spoiled for him by so many things. I reply that this is the outward sign of our detachment, and this leads to the subject of "no when or where," R. full of admiration for the fine way in which Schopenhauer expressed this condition. Regarding our present civilization he exclaims, "It cannot even invent any names"—the name "Emile" put this into his mind. I shall bring the day to an end with the blessing he uttered to me: "Whoever is tended by you cannot die."

Sunday, February 12   Friedel had a good night, and the doctor is very satisfied with his condition! R. has a cough, against which he is advised to take opium drops; however great his disgruntlement, his native humor keeps returning, and today, when the doctor was tapping Fidi to sound his swollen spleen, R. asks, "Fidi, do you think the Archbishop would put up with that?" — Yesterday he told the doctor, "Physicians live on our foolish acts." — Around 12 o'clock I go for a walk with him; the lovely air once again revives his desire to make a second home in Sicily. At lunch we are struck by coincidence; D[aniela] says Rub. was asking whether R. had received a letter from his father; she says he is disturbed at hearing no news. At this very moment Giovanni comes in with the book containing registered letters, gives it—curiously enough—to Daniela, who signs it for her father and then hands him the letter from Kharkov. — Rub.'s father writes in a very decent manner, and R., sending the letter on to Rub., advises him to do as his father wishes. — He comes to Fidi's bedside with all kinds of news about the imminent flight of the Pope, the losses in the recent crisis on the stock exchange, which have hit the Jesuits hardest of all; he suddenly finds it cold in the sickroom and says jokingly to S.: "It's all right for you, you have a temperature, but the rest of us are cold!" — In the evening our excellent friends Gangi and Tasca visit us; unfortunately R. is increasingly annoyed by the necessity of talking French, and by the end of the evening he is feeling very run down.

Monday, February 13　Fidi quiet during the night, but very listless during the day . . . R. had a tolerable night, but he does not feel well; our conversation takes us in many different directions, including Tunis. A (for him) very unwelcome interlude is the visit of our friend Rub., who is quite unwilling to obey his father and yet wants him to go on supporting him financially. At 12 o'clock a drive with R. through the glorious countryside; but R. is displeased by the bareness of the mountains. — Lunch is spent discussing Rub.'s fate. R. is very depressed and out of humor in the afternoon, his revision of the 3rd act gives him no pleasure, and the material difficulties of our life, such as the unsatisfactory furniture, arouse his anger. But in between, much laughter (before lunch). I had made inquiries about the owl, in order to have it stuffed as a memento for R. if possible. Then I receive the news that it was not the owl, but Herr Florio's mother-in-law who had died! *"Mi dispiace molto"* ["I am very sorry"], the servant said in conveying this correction! — But the merriment does not last long. Since R. did not feel the worry about F[idi] to the same extent, his joy over his improving condition is not sufficiently intense to prevent his disregarding the natural weakness of our child and loudly complaining that the conclusion of our stay here has been spoiled, since we shall be unable to make any excursions. In the evening, as we are going to bed, he breaks out into complaints about life, the world, and above all the state of his health. But he soon goes to sleep, while I lie awake enduring an inner raging of the most bitter melancholy! But the storm abates, and with the cry "My God, why hast Thou forsaken me?" I once again discover the paths my weakness had barred to me, and, sadly still, yet peacefully, I embark on

Tuesday, February 14 after hearing that Fidi had a good night and seeing R. sleep through it with only a few short interruptions. But he is still coughing a lot, though more loosely. At 12 o'clock we drive to Madonna della Grazia and return home via the town; the weather is glorious, though the sun burns somewhat. We make the trip in silence, R. enjoys the entrance into the town, its remarkable contours. Our lunch is a very happy one, and R. is again thinking of building a house here. — The doctor, who found Fidi with a temperature of 39 degrees in the evening, is not dissatisfied, however, and, after examining R., he can find nothing to cause alarm, though he admits that his condition must cause him great discomfort. And that is indeed present to a high degree; when friend Rub. visits us in the evening, R. surrenders entirely to his feelings of irritation, and when our normally dear friends Tasca and Gangi appear, he withdraws entirely. The piano score is also annoying him, and the pleasant things which also exist here amid all our sorrows have only a weak effect on him.

Wednesday, February 15 R. had a tolerable night, but is not yet free of his cough. To take his mind off things he reads travel books, and describes Constantinople to me on a drive to Bocca di Falco which he and I take around midday. At lunch, however, the sudden entrance of Count Tasca embarrasses him so much that he leaves the room with congestions. In the afternoon he takes a little walk to Camastra while I am with Siegfried. In the evening the doctor tells us it will be a month before S. will be able to move around quite freely. Rub. visits us in the evening, and R. treats him more gently than he did yesterday, when he told him that friends are people like the Grosses and the mayor, who never think of themselves. — (At lunch yesterday R. said, in connection with Lusch's journey to Rome, "I am jealous, I cannot bear seeing a person I love being ordered around by other people." —) Today for the first time he again praises the lovely air here. But the ever-increasing expenditure vexes him greatly!

Thursday, February 16 R. finishes the revision of the piano score and sends it off, complete with title page. Newspaper reports of the way Herr Ragusa took advantage of us cause us some amusement, though he himself is very angry about them. The air is lovely, R. feels its beneficial effect as we stroll in the garden. In the afternoon he walks to Camastra by himself, returning home rather tired. In the evening he tells us about the soldier who shot some children dead; he is furious about his acquittal and the state of war here. "Orders!" he exclaims. — Then he loses his temper over the way women dress nowadays and their luxury, and, when Count Tasca and the Prince visit us, he feels so worn out that he withdraws.

Friday, February 17 R. had a restless night, and he feels ill in the morning. I wonder whether my small birthday greetings will please him a little [*two much-corrected poems by Cosima in honor of Eva's fifteenth birthday enclosed*]. At lunch, before he finds them, he is in a friendly mood, and afterward he is kind toward my efforts to celebrate the day. He drives to town in the afternoon and buys a silver necklace for Eva. He is now reading German history; yesterday he spoke at length about fashion during the 30 Years' War, saying how absurd it was—people who dressed like that were not to his mind human beings. Today he talked about the bad behavior of the German princes at the time of Napoleon, how poorly Prussia was treated; he says that, if one considers that, one can understand and respect Bismarck. To ensure a good night's rest he takes a bath, while the girls go off to a ball under Count Tasca's protection.

Saturday, February 18 R. had the good night he hoped for, the girls enjoyed themselves, things are going in the right direction for Fidi, and so there would be reason enough for satisfaction. But R.'s mood does not improve, and lunch, along with a discussion with a paper hanger, upsets him extremely. I sink into sleep—very tired after many sleepless nights — Count Tasca's visit awakens me, R. comes in, very irritable, saying that strangers always make me wake up. We go for a drive to Parco, through glorious scenery, R. is somber, shut up inside himself, an almond tree offers him its blossom, which Eva, whom we have taken with us, plucks for me. On the homeward journey he reproaches himself, saying he can feel what a burden he must be on those around him. We succeed in bringing him into a better frame of mind, and since the children go out again, we spend the evening alone in intimate conversation, mostly about Germany and its history.

Sunday, February 19 R. slept well; in the morning he talks about the German princes with a mixture of gaiety and bitterness, observing that one could say of them what the Saxon mail-coach driver with the Prussian jacket said to the people who mocked him: "These . . . also deserve to be Prussians." The departure of Herr Türk, whom we are sending home, gives rise to much merriment, since Siegf., in his concern for economy, looks through Baedeker for all the cheaper hotels. In the morning we stroll in the garden, in the afternoon at Camastra; as we are leaving, we are greeted by a boy who, R. says, might just have been spat out by Mount Etna, and a few steps farther on we meet a beggar who is a complete "Carthaginian," black and wild; at Camastra the Count introduces his theater manager, who is reputed to have murdered *something,* but whose open, cheerful, and

energetic face pleases R. greatly. In the evening I am obliged to go to a ball at Prince Gangi's, R. insists that I go and looks on as I dress.
However, on

Monday, February 20 I find him still awake at 4 A.M.! On my departure he had gone straight to bed but was unable to sleep, and so he waited up for me! But he then goes off to sleep, and at around 11 o'clock I describe to him all the little happenings, which appear to amuse him. When, in the evening, I ask whether the girls might go to Princess Butera's for the final and most glittering ball, since I had been pressed to send them there with the Tascas, and Blandine in particular was very anxious to go, he flies into a great rage and says that he feels nothing but contempt for a girl who wishes to gad about 4 nights in a row, and if he were head of the family, he would forbid it. This final remark decides us, but also causes great dismay among the children. Many tears are shed; Lusch behaves splendidly, understanding her father's and my feelings completely, and that we are of the same opinion, but Loldi is beside herself, while Boni sheds a few silent tears for her lost enjoyment (she has both given and received much pleasure here). For R. and me also the night is much disturbed, but after shedding hot tears myself, I hear him getting into bed. After a few quiet words he gets up again, goes off to read, comes back, and says, "The Duke of Augustenburg is still laying claim to the throne." — Gladly would I have laughed at the change of subject, but my strength deserted me; some time later he falls into a half-drowsing state: "Here, take my foot," I hear him say; I lay mine on his. "Oh, you are good!" he says, and after a tender and silent embrace, I take his hand, and he sinks into a deep sleep.

Tuesday, February 21 In the morning he tells me that, half asleep, he had really wished to sacrifice his foot as a penance, like the fakir, and when I touched him, he had felt comforted—that was what he meant by "you are good." We merrily welcome Lusch, the "angel of death," and then, with a joyful shock, Siegfried, who, allowed up for an hour, comes to greet us! — As we are having breakfast in bed, we decide merrily that, as far as peace and quiet are concerned, the children might just as well have danced the whole night through. The problem of the Society of Patrons is discussed, the *Blätter,* the legacy of the festivals as a whole—whether we should let it all die, or retain certain things and try to introduce others. R. regrets feeling so little inclination for anything. It is cold, with snow and hailstorms. R. does not go out. In the evening we are visited by Count T., Rub., and C[hevalier] Guccia; Rub. plays the King's march to R.'s satisfaction, he is pleased with the way the work "flows." At lunch we talked about Berlioz, his restless rhythms, his embarrassing and inartistic realism (such as the oft-repeated murmuring of the pilgrims in the "Pilgrims' March"), his fragmentary themes; R. cites my father's melody for *"Die Lorelei"* as being legendary and folklike, then jokes about Schumann's *Weltschmerz,* this continual taking up and hurling of Jove's arrows. — The *B. Blätter* arrives, and R. finds Wolz.'s article good; but he objects to the announcement of a vegetarian menu. (In the evening Rub. also played the Prelude to *Die Msinger* and the conclusion of *Tristan und Isolde,* but R. is not satisfied with this—he says the whole secret of it is that the tempo should be literally suspended in the interest of spiritual freedom.) When he wonders what it is about these things which pleases our Sicilians, I suggest the pulsing life within them, and he thinks I am right.

Wednesday, February 22 R. had a tolerable night, he has a sponge bath in the morning and feels very run down after it. An article on Cherubini by Dr. Schemann which he reads (in the *Bayr. Blätter*) vexes him, and he writes ironically to Wolz. about the various tragedies: of Schumann, to have possessed no melodies, of Rossini, to have had no school, of Brahms, to be a bore, etc. That relieves him. He is much amused by a reply made by Frederick the Great to a clergyman. — The weather is fine but fresh, and he just walks to and fro in the little garden. We spend a peaceful evening chatting. I hardly dare to say it, but things seem to me to be taking a turn for the better. The distribution of roles among the singers is keeping R. much occupied, he fears there will be disputes about precedence, and that they will all want to take part in the first performance. I, on the other hand, believe that they will all behave well.

Thursday, February 23 R. slept well, and in the morning his conversation in bed takes the form of meditations on the world, on Gobineau's theories; he believes in a catastrophe which will open the door to migrations and the establishment of communities in Southern countries. Yesterday he talked about the English, saying that the expression "a nation of shopkeepers," however curious it may sound when one considers all the elegant lords, is nevertheless quite correct, since they rule other peoples only in order to safeguard their property in England. — The air is splendid, R. enjoys it. We go to Camastra for a walk, the purity of the air, the sharp outlines of the mountains, the blue sea in the distance enchant us. — His reading is now to be Turgenev's *Fathers and Sons* (since he is saving *Die Kawi-Sprache* for serious study, along with the Gobineau book, for when he starts to work out his "Male and Female"). But he is approaching it with trepidation, having seen Schopenhauer described in Mérimée's preface as the father of the nihilistic movement; R. observes that no other nation is as stupid as the French, he finds them more and more repellent. All the same, quotations in the *B. Blätter* from [Diderot's] *Le Neveu de Rameau* please him greatly, and the statement of Herder with which this article ends he also finds very striking. In connection with the *Blätter* we talk about partisanship, and agree that it is not a good thing when insignificant people attempt to meditate about something a man of genius has said. We drive to S. Maria di Gesù, R. pleasantly affected by the beauty of the day and the "magical forms" of the mountains. However, we do not get out, but doze in the carriage outside the churchyard while the children are strolling about. On the drive home R. remarks on the gnarled appearance of the olive tree, how curious it is, as if the tree begrudged growing! — In the evening, talking about our presence here, R. says quite openly, and in contrast to my own feelings, that he has no sense of obligation or gratitude; there are some people he likes, he finds them endearing, and then he takes pleasure in being agreeable to them; but not out of a sense of obligation. Yet only recently he said to me one morning that, by accepting favors from people who did not belong to him, such as Wesendonck, he had laid himself open to embarrassing familiarities. — Much jesting about Schemann's cypress branches for Cherubini, in whom R. recognizes tremendous talent combined with much dryness. He talks about the beginning of the *Fidelio* Overture (the first work by Beeth. he ever heard, and it made an overwhelming impression on him!), its courageous honesty, something which nobody could imitate without making it sound at once like an imitation; whereas Rossini could quite easily have used the theme from the *Water Carrier* Overture in slow tempo in his *Tell*. For all its guileless prettiness it is just an arabesque, he says. The most striking example of the Beethoven manner, he continues, is the opening of the C Minor Symphony: who could ever imitate that? — He then talks about Jommelli, Durante, and opera arias by these composers which he had heard and which gave him the impression of a grand style.

Friday, February 24 R. had a good night, but all the same he has a very severe chest spasm. He thinks of Schiller's sufferings and feels extremely dejected. The day passes in anxiety, we spend the evening upstairs in Fidi's vicinity. The children chat, I relate to R. various things from the correspondence between Goethe and Marianne Willemer.

Saturday, February 25 R. had a good night and is feeling very much better. Telegrams from Herr Neumann about Paris take up his time, but his mind is free enough for him to talk with me about *W. Meister*, which I have suggested for evening family reading. He regrets that its noble and humane community emerges with so little clarity, and that one never knows where one is or in which period it all takes place. —

He is persistently reading *Fathers and Sons,* in which he is slightly conscious of routine, but he finds some things in it to praise. At lunch, when in connection with reading we talk about the relationship of young girls to the world, he says in a low, agitated voice, "God, when one sees what society made out of people's natural urge to approach one another, and with one another to create something beautiful, there is not much one can say about anything else." — Then he mentions Gobineau's profound remarks about language and how the various races have handled it, and he regrets not being able to be of any use to this outstanding man. Gob.'s reply to his letter shows him that he has stepped right into a puddle. — A visit from Count Basewitz's family raises the question whether R. should not introduce himself to the Grand Duke's heir, but R. utterly rejects the idea. — We drive out in the direction of Parco and come in splendid weather to the loveliest of localities. When Goethe's line "When for six stallions I can pay" comes into our minds, R. says, "One always overlooks how terrible that is—when I can *pay,* then the 24 legs are my own—always property." — In the evening we chat again; Lusch tells us several things about Rome, but R. feels ill at ease, as usual when the world is being spoken of; Sgambati, whom Lusch praises, is repulsive to him on account of his coldness, and so it is with everything. When he is in bed, he says, "I have you, and otherwise nobody in the whole world; if it were not for you, I should have nothing at all, nothing belongs to me except you." —

Sunday, February 26 R. was somewhat restless during the night, but in the morning he gaily tells me two dreams he had. The one: "I came home to Minna, who asked whether I had been with Frau Tichatschek; I told her yes, but it had been a party, whereupon she flew into a rage, saying to me as I left, 'I am going to a hotel to sleep and tomorrow I shall go to a lawyer'; whereupon I said to myself, 'This must stop,' and she threw billiard balls after me." The second: "From the street outside I looked up at your father's room; there was a piano in the window; nimble as I was, I climbed up and played the Gretchen theme to your father as he returned; he looked up from the street in astonishment; so that he should not know who it was, I tried to go back through the window, but I stumbled, and then woke up." The mood today is very good, at 12 o'clock we stroll in the garden with Fidi, and in the afternoon I walk with R. to Camastra, where the red aloes are in flower. Though we often have to sit down, R. is not too worn out. Before that the appearance of Dr. Berlin with some bottles of beer cheered R. greatly. The great event of the day is the completion of the tent on the terrace, and beneath it we enjoy our coffee and also the beer. The air is wonderful. R. humorously scolds the children, the many "useless girls" who constantly want to be entertained, and in the evening he hospitably receives our good landlords Tasca and Gangi and rails amusingly, if energetically, against Chevalier Guccia's *monocle,* recommending that he wear an "honest" pair of spectacles. To the children he says, "Mama and I should by rights no longer be among you, but hovering on clouds up above." — At the conclusion of the evening he gets Rub. to play the Andante from Beeth.'s E-flat Major Quartet and the Scherzo (butterfly!) from another. And I thank the dear God who made me a present of this day!

Monday, February 27 R. slept well, but the weather is wretched, storm and rain; it makes us laugh to think that the tent was erected outside only yesterday! But this morning R. has no chest spasm, he is very careful with his sponge bath and manages thus to stave off an attack. R. begins a letter to the King and writes three pages about Fidi. He, still tired from yesterday, stays in bed and draws; his continued education gives us much to think about, where to find playmates as well as a tutor for him? This occupies R. and me during a drive into town. R. would like to take over Fidi's history lessons himself, but he complains about always leading such a restless life—now fully taken up, for instance, with his Paris affairs. — In the carriage in town he suddenly calls out, "Very well, you gentlemen overflowing with ideas, try to write a melody like the Prelude to the 2nd act of *Tristan und Isolde!*" — Then some goats claim his attention, and he says, "They have proper Philistine faces, like tailors—a sheep expresses much more suffering." — In the evening we begin the novel *Fathers and Sons* with the children; I do the reading; at half past nine we break up, and R. and I spend a long time in his room in intimate conversation, in effusions of love! R. pays tribute to what he calls my courage and my sufferings, and when I tell him that it is only because of him that I was able to do it, he denies that and says no, he is not even permitted to advise me, for in matters of love the woman must take precedence; when I still maintain that it was him inside me and not myself, he exclaims: "Oh, no! To have any sense of himself, a man must be loved—the life-giving power is female. — And things began to work again when you were with me—people had been saying that I would never do anything more, and then it all started again. One can live for a while on one's inner resources, but then one must be shown a picture of oneself in a mirror to know what one really is." And he recalls the terrible circumstances in which I showed my belief in him, and also the good King, who stood by us loyally, "and for that reason one can say a few flattering things to him." And his final words before going off to sleep: "It is now as it was on the first day, only better!" . . . [*Added in margin:* "On the drive home he tells me about Carlyle, whose biography he is reading, and he is pleased with the remark that he, Carlyle, vacillated between prophecy and comedy. Then R. expresses his surprise over his taking sides against the Negroes, saying how rarely a person is completely free; he feels that deism, the Jewish kind which inhibited even Goethe, also oppressed Carlyle's spirit. — R. is much amused by C.'s criticism of democratic government, in which he says that most of England's 30 million inhabitants are blockheads. He describes as an 'ironic ovation' the fact that figures from his dramas were used in a masked procession in Leipzig, and that from the pilgrims a 'Pulcinella and P. Carnival' arose!"]

Tuesday, February 28 R. had a good night and is looking very well. But his mood is soon clouded by the vexations which never fail to arrive—the fact, for instance, that the glazier from the town comes in the morning and keeps him from finishing his letter to the King: "It's always like that," he declares. Various things in the Carlyle biography occupy his mind, and he tells me what he says about the nobility and about Friedrich Schlegel's conversion. We visit—with an eye toward perhaps renting it later—a deserted Palazzo S. Elia, where we are confronted with a most curious set of people! All races seem to be represented in these deserted accommodations—bawling Negroid creatures, as well as genteel, quiet, handsome ones, everywhere children, life, and idleness, an extensive view, terraces and neglect—so remote from all civilization that it makes us laugh. From there we go to Camastra, where every day there is something new in bloom. We recently talked about the way in which nature poetry seems to be a peculiarly German phenomenon—the Italians, for instance, usually bring it in only in a realistic sense, and then mainly in the form of animals; trees budding, blossoming, and fading, deep shadows, dew— all this seems to affect them hardly at all. — R. tells me with some annoyance that the first sight of the *Parsifal* music the general public has had is in the correspondence columns of a newspaper (concluding bars of the first act). The impatience with which the piano score is being awaited reminds him of his own impatience for the piano score of *Oberon* following Weber's death. — General Skobeleff's statements amuse R., who has no sympathy with the Austrian monarchy, and Turgenev's story gives us a further lively insight into the Russian character. — But unfortunately the day ends in a regrettable outburst, since the supplement to the *B. Blätter*—an advertisement for books on vegetarianism, the description of the *Blätter* itself ("monthly periodical for the propagation of a German culture")—upsets him extremely. He reflects on how he might put an end to this relationship but cannot make up his mind, since, as he says, it is connected to some extent with the problem of Wolz's living. I hope I have managed to ensure that he will not write harshly to W. but will effect the dissolution in a friendly spirit, and with his consent. [*Added in margin:* "At supper R. expresses his delight in Kietz's bust of me and says it is the best portrait ever done of me, an excellent likeness, and he is glad it exists."]

Wednesday, March 1   R. had a restless night, and the sirocco, which is blowing strongly today, is a severe strain on him. — There are only the three of us for lunch, since the children have gone on a big outing to S. Martino. All sorts of things from the outside world, picture of the carnival, a speech by friend Feustel (which makes R. remark jokingly, "He knew nothing about me and has been gradually won over; he bases his relationship with me on my relationship with the world"), then news from Paris that nothing but R.'s things is being performed there. — We do not go out, and R. feels increasingly unwell, so that I send for the doctor, who again finds nothing to cause concern. (I read to Fidi the 1st act of *Götz*.)

Thursday, March 2   R. had a restless night, and he keeps returning to his dislike of our present house. — In our early-morning conversation we come to Feustel's speech, to the general question of growing fame: "It's quite true," R. says, "what one longs for in one's youth one has more than enough of in one's old age, but I can't say that I ever longed for fame—rather, for something that was different, a genuine melody of my own, something that was not Beethoven or Weber. From the beginning I composed for effect, never got myself immersed in meditation or brooding like Schumann." He is reading a second Turgenev novel, *A House of Gentlefolk,* with interest. He strolls up and down for a while on the terrace and in the little garden, then I hear him improvising downstairs, he writes down a melody, then shows it to me, saying that he has at last found the line he was looking for. He plays it to me and calls it an antidote—he had been reading my father's 2nd "*Mephisto-Walzer,*" and we agree that silence is our only proper response to so dismal a production. But I feel this apparition as a sort of renewed blessing on my existence—perhaps I might call it a reward for never having allowed my hopes to diminish—these sounds blossom before me like a water lily rooted in the depths of our being—how, dear God, shall I thank Thee? — After having read the 2nd act of *Götz* to Fidchen, I continue in the evening reading *Fathers and Sons* to R. and the girls.

Friday, March 3   R. gets up in a cheerful mood, we talk at breakfast about what we read yesterday; all R. and I find lacking is the "hidden fire," and he remarks that Russian women completely lack dignity. When I point out that Balzac possessed a daemon which this writer seems to me to lack, R. says, "Yes, one doesn't really know why these things get written." — All the same, he started the conversation

by saying that he would like to get to know T. personally. Memories of Baza[rov]'s falling in love lead to a joking conversation at lunch about R.'s affairs; he says, "No, I never danced attendance on any woman." — We drive into town, and R., after becoming vexed with the narrow streets through which we are driving, gets out and goes into humorous ecstasies about all things urban in comparison with Porrazzi! . . . The Garibaldi gardens, the terrace by the sea, various large buildings, he enjoys it all, and we return home in lively spirits. On the journey he quotes to me F[riedrich] W[ilhelm] I's final conversation with his valet, who told him his death was "unfortunately" approaching: "Do not say 'unfortunately'—how can you know that?" — In the evening we continue with *Fathers and Sons* (before that R. read some of [Goethe's] "*Reineke Fuchs*" to Fidi); at 9:30 we break up, so that Fidi can get some rest—his excited drawing and reading of Baedeker make R. very apprehensive—"With music I was not like that—I fear the boy will turn out quite cold" (he means without interest in other things). I try to calm him down; I succeed, and gradually—probably via Mme Odintzov—we come to talk about Marie Much[anoff], her first appearance in R.'s life after *Tannhäuser:* "But I was jealous of your father, for he had sent her from Constantinople—but no, I wasn't, for I was extremely modest and never thought that things could have gone differently for me from the way they had gone before!" — Quietly we go through all our experiences with this extraordinary, elusive friend of ours, and R. speaks in praise of her magnanimity and a certain naïve quality; we attempt to unravel the mystery of her life, but it will probably remain a mystery, though not one to spoil our loving memories. — We part in peaceful harmony. Yesterday he told me that he could not get along with anyone except me, I had spoiled him; when I can save him from becoming overexcited, as before with regard to Siegfried, then I feel exalted by my sacred task and bless life for it!
[*End of the eighteenth book of the Diaries.*]

Saturday, March 4 R. did not have a very good night, and a few slight vexations in the morning lead to a chest spasm. I observe complete stillness and read a little in his vicinity, and soon our conversation takes a quiet, cheerful course. Our subject is the Russian novels, and R. remarks on the complete absence of dignity in Russian women. — He chides Fidi severely for not noticing him at once when he goes to greet him. At lunch he talks about Kant's physical geography, which he is reading with interest, and he says he is learning more from it than from all the specialized books. His preoccupation with it inspires him, however, with his idea concerning poets and scholars (in his *Braunes Buch*), and he says that Goethe compromised himself, as it were, as a poet because of his "childish preoccupation with natural science." It makes people heartless, he says. Over coffee he tells me he read in the newspaper that the Jews in Palestine speak German. He says they seem to look upon Germany as the promised land—the defeat of Varus, the downfall of the Roman Empire, must have created the impression on the Jews that there was something to be done with Germany! — It is a windy day, and R. humorously expresses his vexation over our stay here. In the evening we continue *Fathers and Sons* with great interest, and are moved by the words of the nihilist's mother to her husband on the sudden departure of their son. The news of the assassination attempt on the Queen of England produces the following remark from R.: "He was a completely destitute man, before throwing himself into the water he wanted to shoot down at least one of these fortunate people." — And we recall the case told us by Count Tasca, in which miners killed an estate owner (father of the Count's daughter-in-law) before the eyes of his daughters. He said, "The people are taking revenge."

Sunday, March 5 In the morning R. talks at length about the Treaty of Passarowitz! The name Bazarov brought it to mind. Much gaiety, and I thank God for it. — We discuss the affair of the *Ring* translation (the English one)—Forman's is being very severely criticized; we have to admit that all these things seem to us of very little account. And even our great hopes with regard to a furnished palazzo in Venice, now dashed by a letter from Dr. Keppler, are taken by R. more calmly than he himself expected. However, he is tired from our stay here; the weather is wet, his spasms return. But in the middle of one I hear him laughing loudly, for a herd of sheep comes along, led by a donkey, seeking shelter from the rain. We drive into town with Siegfried, but he looks very pale and is weak and run down, which worries R. After supper R. plays the new melody, which he has altered a little, and can I permit myself to say that in it I see the present state of my soul fully reflected? I should not dare, were I not to feel that the yearning gaze of a worm seems to bear some relationship to the shining blessings of a star. — In the evening, in the presence of some acquaintances, R. gets Rub. to play the first movement of 106, and he takes tremendous delight in it, kissing me as it is being played and then telling me he was pleased by the way I was listening. After that the *Fl. Holländer* Overture is played; R. at first makes jokes about it, saying it depicts Garibaldi's entrance into Sicily, the King's prayer, the retreat of the Neapolitan fleet, but then he gives advice on the tempi and himself plays the ballad very beautifully. But later he complains how little has been learned about the execution of his works. When we are alone together, he remarks how right Schopenhauer was to say that anyone who could reproduce music in words would solve the secret of the world; and he cites the Butterfly Scherzo (E Minor Quartet) with its "Peasants' Dance"—who could explain that? Previously he had gone into actual rhapsodies about the wonderful concision of the first movement of 106, at the same time complaining that the Andante is too long. He regrets the unchanged repeat, when Beeth. was capable of so much in the variation form. He sees something of this error of length even in the "Funeral March" of the *Eroica,* whereas elsewhere in his works it is the brevity which is always so wonderful. At supper he told us very emphatically that he would have to make cuts in the third act of *Tristan,* since no one will ever again do it in the way Schnorr did, and even then it was so shattering that it went beyond what one should be allowed to experience on stage. Also in the 2nd act, where the "artificial metaphysical wit," though always full of emotion, cannot be followed by a large audience. "I permitted myself that in Lucerne, at a time when I had nothing." — "I love you very much—that is what I wanted to tell you," he says to me, raising himself up again in bed, and we drift off into the night.

Monday, March 6 Since, contrary to R.'s expectations, the weather does not improve, but the reverse, and since he is feeling the after-effects of last night, he is almost in despair, and an invitation to us both from the Grand Duke's heir and his wife to call on them today finds him if possible even less inclined than usual for such things. He feels that the good people could have come to visit him, observes that it has never done him any good to take such a step, and declares that he is glad to be free of such acquaintanceships. — At lunch he remarks that intercourse with other people, even the most amiable of them, is a torture to him, from which he extricates himself by becoming excited. When we are drinking our coffee alone, I tell him how completely I understand his feelings and how well I realize that with the children there is a need for meeting other people, whereas with us there is only one course: withdrawal. I go on to say that this does not make me bitter, all I am attempting to do each day is to procure tranquillity for him and a little activity for the children. I do not know what brings us from this to Christianity and the great Christian buildings, and how they express something which was completely alien to the ancient world—we call this the musical element. In the evening we finish Turgenev's novel with great interest, R. says of Mme Odintzov that her trouble is that there is nothing in her. — R. asked me the name of Parmenion's son, the King of Macedonia who appears in [Spontini's] *Olimpie*—he was thinking of Cassander, but we were led astray by naming Parmenion as his father. Yesterday he showed me in Fidi's copy of Grube's historical studies the pictures of A[lexander] the Great and Charlemagne, both as beautifully polished as Bruck-mann's picture of him. "That is today's Jewish art—no longer any truthfulness, everything touched up." When he learns that the trans-lator of *Parsifal* is a Jew, he says, "In ten years we shall have no one left to deal with but Jews."

Tuesday, March 7   R. tells me jokingly that "Frau Minna" appeared on his horizon in the form of congestions: "*Bon, je sais ce que c'est*" ["Good, I know what it is"], he told himself as he awoke, and he took some valerian. He says that in his dream the question of claiming a forgotten fee in Paris kept recurring. At breakfast he comes back to the problem of race and says that it has been changed by women—for example, when an Aryan marries a Semite woman, the Creole race appears. "And art," I add with a smile. From here our conversation turns to the Sistine Chapel; R. deplores the painting of all the walls and ceiling, saying that he finds it confusing, in a certain sense tasteless. "As in a certain sense Shakespeare's *H. VI* could also be called taste-less," I observe, and I attempt to explain my feelings about this work. From this to painting in general, its unfortunate position today: intended as a still and sublime vision, it is now placed on exhibition. — Since I am reading the 1st act of *Egmont* to Fidi, I ask R. to play the song "*Die Trommel gerühret*," and this virtually dominates our whole day with its awesome bravado. When I tell R. that I much prefer it to "*Freudvoll und leidvoll*," R. says: "Yes, because poems like that cannot be set to music, music cannot convey concepts. Lyric poetry!" he exclaims; "only drama exists." "And absolute music," I say. "Which is a kind of drama—I really believe that—a theme and a countertheme, which combine in a dance. Joyful, sorrowful, thoughtful—there is no music to be found for those words: at the most a repetition." — Our friend Levi's remark that only bad poems can be set to music is in this sense correct, he feels. At lunch there are only the three of us, since the girls are on an outing, and all three of us then drive to Terra Rossa, which pleases R. greatly. In the evening R. relates to us some things from his present reading, Dumas's *Les Garibaldiens,* and later in the evening he tells me of Garibaldi's greeting to his star before the entry into Palermo. "This is what matters," R. continues, "whether one is capable of such impulses, or whether they are completely foreign to one." — When the lines "Who can know the pangs of woe," etc., came into his mind today, he added, "A bit artificial." — In the evening he recalls the performance of *Egmont* in Zurich under his direction, for which he himself wrote the linking text. On our journey home, during which he tells us all sorts of things about Garibaldi, he exclaims: "The French and their generosity! Under the republic they had Rome shelled, whereas the English freed Sicily from Bourbon dependence.

They have an effective public opinion, a Parliament to represent it." He tells me of Gladstone's resignation.

Wednesday, March 8 (Written at Camastra.) [*A sentence based on untranslatable word play omitted.*] At breakfast we have serious thoughts about whether we should not after all send Siegfried to school, since he has no contact with other boys. Yesterday, for a joke, Fidi arranged his elder sisters' hair, and that alarmed R. greatly. At lunch and over coffee R. complains of his condition, his ailments, but he and I go on a lovely drive to Parco Monreale, thinking of Garibaldi's expedition, for this is the road the 1,000 took, except that it has now been nicely leveled. We delight in the fresh green which the rain has brought, the blossoming blackthorn, even, indeed, the monastic cells which in the distance look like vultures' nests and increase in numbers as we come closer to Monreale. The village itself amuses R. greatly, among other things he points out to me a gander on a balcony, surveying the scene like a grumpy paterfamilias. Also darned laundry—touching that such things are still mended—"The mama no doubt spends her winter evenings on improvements." These and the view into the distance, in short, things both great and small, distract him. In the evening we have visitors. For a while R. has quite a good conversation in German with Prof. Salinas on archaeology (the excavations at Olympia) and the archaeologists Springer, Brunn, etc. The Prof. confesses to me that he finds R. very difficult to understand on account of his rapid transitions from seriousness to humor. He ends the evening by singing Italian melodies, for the "Picture" from *Pars.* does not please him this time, particularly since Rub. is still unable to grasp the variations in the tempo. But R. is very tired, in fact agitated, at the end of it. We remain alone together for a while until he calms down a little. He sang Moses's phrase in the crossing of the Red Sea quite wonderfully.

Thursday, March 9 To have lunch today at Camastra or not, that is our little question in the morning; we decide that we will. A telegram from Herr Neumann, asking for the curtain, embarrasses him, but he gives it to him on loan. Today the tent is once more put up on the terrace, and we enjoy breakfast there in cheerful spirits. But around lunchtime R. breaks out in a fury over the shooting practice on the parade ground, he fears it will go on and on. Yesterday he gave our host to understand in almost unmistakable words that he does not like the house and its situation, and he even said that the bedroom was responsible for S.'s illness. Since we are here dealing with a very well meant act of kindness, it pains me to think that our departure might take place in a spirit of vexation. When R. goes downstairs to recall a theme, he meets Rub., and that disturbs and vexes him even further. We get in the carriage and drive off; R. notices my sorrowful expression,

I tell him what has made me sad. At first that arouses his anger, in Camastra he goes off alone to the left, I with the children to the right, but when we meet, we unite, and have a good and merry meal! Afterward R. takes a long rest in the sitting room, and the outing to Piana dei Greci, which R. arranged with the Count yesterday, is fixed, much to my concern. — A letter to R. from Jouk. contains a favorable report on the costumes. But Camastra gave R. genuine pleasure, he wants to come here often, indeed he asked the Count to build something for him at the entrance to the villa, saying he would pay the rent on it. He tells me that, if anyone were to offer him the choice between 3 years of complete rest in a comfortable home in a good climate, with no obligations to see or hear anything, or 12 years as now, he would certainly choose the 3 years. He adds with a laugh that one would then be glad to die out of boredom! — He tells me much about A. Dumas's bragging—he seems in his own estimation to have done everything for Sicily. After I paid some calls, I went to fetch R., who had again gone to Camastra. (Here I have made a mistake: the dinner at Camastra was on Friday, today we just went for a walk there and enjoyed ourselves so much that in the afternoon R. took himself off there again.) In the evening he reads a scene from [Goethe's] *Clavigo* and is pleased with the vividness of its description.

Friday, March 10 During the night I hear R. cry out very loudly: "You say to me 'your' Ottilie! Fellow, are you mad?" — It appears that he was dreaming of Georg, who had taken an improper liberty. R. takes a bath, gets his usual chest attack, and comes upstairs extremely agitated and annoyed. But after a while on the terrace he recovers his cheerful spirits; when I greet his improvised word *"Güllverständnis"* with a laugh, understanding it as *"Mis-t-verständnis,"* he says I am now like my sister, Blandine, who always completed his witticisms for him; I admit to him that I often understand him without revealing it, and our conversation then goes on to the source of the comical, when dignity and convention are suddenly upset by a natural law—for instance, a pompous statesman carrying out his office who suddenly has to let out a terrible sneeze, and other such examples. I tell him that this in itself might be considered a sort of convention—one could go one step further, to the point where the natural functions would not be regarded as ridiculous. He says, "Yes, for Nature is always serious." — It is then that he unfortunately goes downstairs and encounters Rub. (The vexation about the shooting practice was yesterday.) Sitting on the bench after our lunch at Camastra, we hear no birds as at home. "The world of sound has fled to Germany," he says. A letter from Herr Neumann brings no pleasure, since it contains a somewhat impertinent, headstrong invitation to attend the performances. Then he takes a long rest in the house at Camastra, until I wake him. Then our friends arrive, and the outing he suggested is discussed for tomorrow, and it is decided that, since it cannot be canceled, I shall accompany the children without him! In the evening we read Turgenev's *A House of Gentlefolk* with much enjoyment.

Saturday, March 11　And so at 8 o'clock I abandon father and son! My little package from Parco arrives in good time for my dear ones' lunch. R. had had a restless night, and I returned home in some anxiety, to find R. very well and cheerful. He says he spent an idyllic day with Fidi, they went for a walk together, and the little diversion my package caused seems also to have had a not unbeneficial effect. He has completed his outline for the open letter to Wolzogen. In the evening he tells us a moving story he read in the *Tagblatt* about the elephant in London (which we saw); this has demonstrated to him in the most striking way the nobility of animals and the stupidity of human beings. We chat all evening, telling him about our "Greek" experiences in Piana dei Greci.

Sunday, March 12　R. had a good night. We have breakfast on the terrace, and since the sun is quite dazzling, we hang up Schnapp.'s traveling rug as a "black sail." Our conversation turns to the French, and once more we are reminded of the old image of apes and tigers, that is to say, the feeling that nothing could ever come close to the pitiless cruelty of this nation, were it ever to conquer Germany. The children have accepted an invitation today to a late breakfast at Camastra, and I go there as chaperone. Since R. makes a remark about the family's wasteful abundance, I cannot help being most painfully conscious of the difference between the ways of youth and the inclinations of old age, and feeling how conflicting is my own role. I have to weep, but not violently, just such tears as a God will take heed of. Since the Grand Duke of Mecklenburg's heir paid us a first call yesterday, R. instructed me to make an appointment with the good people for today; we are received, very graciously, at 4:30; R. is very pleased with the friendly gentleman's free and open character, but he finds Her Imperial Highness thoroughly disagreeable: in her features he discerns a Phryne-like cruelty, and he feels that only extreme measures would be of any avail against such a character. In the evening we have some friends with us, among them the abbé, tutor of young Count Mazzarino, and a Dr. Cervello; R. teases the latter by remarking that the physicians always recommend caution because they well know that they can be of no help to someone who becomes ill! To the abbé he says that there are too many priests, and it is such a good thing that one ought not to subject it to abuse. He sits down at the piano and sings something from *Le Postillon,* then Rub. plays his

"Picture" of the Wood-bird, after R. has explained what it is about, to the enchantment of all. And somehow or other it comes about that the children sing his *"Gruss der Getreuen," "Wisst ihr, Kinder,"* and create a splendid effect with them. I feel overwhelming bliss at being permitted once again to enjoy all these moments of happiness, and I end this day with blessings in my heart.

Monday, March 13 We talk of Hans's character, and R. admits to me that from the beginning there was always something alien about it for him, amounting almost to repulsion. [*The last four words obliterated in ink by an unknown hand, the word* "almost" *still uncertain.*] He remarks how Lusch, for all her great resemblance to her father, nevertheless presents a completely transfigured image of his character. After he has broken out in humorous complaint about the need to get dressed, we continue our serious discussions over breakfast. About the Italians, for instance; I told him that in the village of Piana dei Greci it struck me how well the craftsmen played their instruments, with fire and rhythm, although the music was dreadfully bad; they therefore still possess the aptitude, but their taste is horribly coarse. Then we recalled a certain moment from last night: R. played (shortly before the children began to sing) the "Porrazzi Melody," which he had molded in the way he wished it to be. All of us stood around him, and when Count T. and Prince Gangi spoke of his fame and said they would give up all their lands to possess it, R. replied, "What is fame?" and quoted Schopenhauer's likening it to an oyster shell after the oyster has been consumed. I tell him today that I dearly like this idea but do not care for the image; R. agrees with me, saying it sounds as if it came from an 18th-century rake. Then we speak of North and South, their productive abilities; in the end R. says, "The longing to escape what is bad is the only really productive factor." — We are much amused by a droll remark from Siegfried; when Lusch tells us about the canonization and that the Pope fasted through it, Fidi asks, "Does the Archbishop fast as well?" — R. completes his letter to Wolz. Over supper he tells the children much about his family, his brother Julius, after talking to me a lot during the day about Ottilie—whether to invite her to the festival performances; he fears unhappiness may not have softened her. . . . In the evening I read aloud the Turgenev novel. A few evenings ago R. read to us some things from Kant's book on physics, and we were astonished by the great naïveté of the descriptions—of the lion, for example. — At the conclusion of the evening R. is still very vexed to think of Jouk.'s having shown his sketches to the King in Munich, since R. feels they are by no means sufficiently advanced for that. He is always complaining of being surrounded by "bunglers," and he takes this relatively trivial matter terribly to heart.

Tuesday, March 14 [*Enclosed in the Diaries a peacock feather wrapped in a sheet of paper bearing the inscription:* "A feather found a few days ago by R. on the steps from the *salon* to the garden and presented to me!"] But R. gets up in cheerful spirits, and our breakfast on the terrace passes off very harmoniously. Only the three of us at lunch, since the girls have gone on an outing to Pellegrino with Count T. He reads the text of *Die Msinger* in his collected writings, is pleased with it, and says this is really his masterpiece. Yesterday he expressed pleasure over his prefaces, but his criticisms of the state in *Opera and Drama* he now finds immature and erroneous as a concept, an idea. A letter from Levi brings all the difficulty with singers before his eyes; he replies in humorous vein, but he is not satisfied with our conductor's methods, he thinks of Richter's practical ways. Wolz.'s clinging to Jäger also arouses his displeasure. And I fear the whole thing is becoming a burden to him. (Packing for Acireale.)

Wednesday, March 15 R. had a good night. He reads the forewords in his collected writings, also *Die Kapitulation,* and expresses his astonishment over the lack of humor in Germany, people there have shown no understanding at all for his joke. "Genius demands the right audience," he says, recalling the Attic people. Today I am much preoccupied with the news, conveyed to me by Count Tasca, that Count Gravina is asking for Boni's hand. I tell R. first, then together we tell Boni, who appears very surprised. R. and I then dine with the Grand Duke's heir and family, the young Grand Duke Konstantin also being present. With all his usual splendid frankness R. talks of the Russian need to capture Constantinople. The Grand Duke's heir continues to please R. greatly, but the Russian aristocrats are distasteful to him, he finds them horribly trivial, with a certain sort of "robber mentality," he also feels that the noble lady should have given her arm to him and not to her cousin, with whom she also should not have spoken Russian now and again. He talks to the Grand Duke's heir about Fidi's education, and he tells me afterward how it felt to be talking in this way about a son! — In the evening some friends come over, and Rub. plays [Opus] 111, R. not satisfied with it, I unfortunately quite distracted.

Thursday, March 16 R. slept well. Our talk is devoted to Boni, and with some concern. At 12 o'clock I drive to see Countess Tasca, who has taken over from Countess Mazzarino the office of go-between! During our discussion R. goes for a walk with Fidi in the Flora. The condition I make, in view of the Count's unsettled financial situation, is that he take up some occupation. In the afternoon, since we have decided to round off our stay in Porrazzi with a musical reception for our friends, there is a rehearsal of the *Idyll.* A horrible orchestra, and yet great delight in the work. Memories of blissful times, also of my father, whose joyful approval of the *Idyll,* R. says, showed him what a rare being he is and how utterly different from anyone else.

Friday, March 17 R. slept well, although yesterday he was very languid. News of the Count's financial condition causes us increasing concern, but their feelings for each other appear to be mutual! — In the afternoon rehearsal with the military band; the marches for King and Emperor, both of them splendid, go very well, R. wonderfully cheerful and kind with the players, he tells them that Garibaldi is coming and makes one joke after another, so that they say, "If only we had a conductor like that!" The works make a tremendous impression, and indeed a downright ecstatic one on me, since I have not heard them for quite a long time. The battle-arrayed, God-fearing peace of the *"Kaisermarsch"* brings back to me all the things for which our hearts once beat so warmly, and in the King's March I can feel the "fair protector"! We return home in very cheerful and exalted spirits, R. not too tired. In the evening we chat and consider!

Saturday, March 18 R. had a somewhat restless night. I have many preparations to make for the afternoon. Our guests appear at 2 o'clock, and the concert begins. Unfortunately the people do not play the *Idyll* well, even when it is repeated, and even the *"Kaisermarsch"* gives R. no pleasure. When it is all over, we laugh at our rashness in letting ourselves in for such a venture. We remember Tribschen and decide it was desecration to perform the work in this way; we also regret the necessity for publishing it. R. is very tired; between the *"Huldigungsm."* and the *Idyll* he had a chest spasm.

Sunday, March 19 R. had a restless night and is very tired. For me a day of packing and shopping, also a conversation with Count Gr[avina], about whom R. says he should come to Acireale, so that we can get to know him better. The reports of him are good, and his behavior was excellent. Around 7 in the evening we go to bed, at 1 o'clock we are up again, and toward 3 o'clock, amid much turmoil, we leave Porrazzi, which R. could no longer stand. At the station the prefect, Count Tasca, Gravina, Guccia, Rubinstein. Friendly farewells and then sleep till sunrise.

Monday, March 20 During my slumbers I hear my dear ones talking, and even join in myself in the middle of the somewhat dreary country-side which leads us toward Catania, and which R. finds very disappointing. [*Added in margin:* "At one station R. gets out and is pleased to come upon a Wallachian woman, who talks to him with great distinctness and says to him significantly, in a voice filled with natural pride, 'I come from Wallachia.' "] However, our apartment in the hotel at Acireale pleases him greatly, the landlord seems a very decent man, and R. breathes again. Exchange of telegrams with our friends in Palermo.

Tuesday, March 21   R. slept well, and we have an enjoyable breakfast in the large *salon* while Schnapp. is arranging his bits and pieces. Since all other books are still packed, he reads Molière's *Les Femmes savantes,* which the children brought with them. He finds the play actually vulgar, and he considers Molière to be much overrated, but a few things in it amuse him. He then talks about its subject, that is to say, courtship, the eternal theme of the mating instinct, to which social conditions have given such peculiar forms; he says jokingly that we, too, are now caught up in them. We drive to Belvedere and delight in the view from there. R. ascribes the curiously ugly, broad faces to the original population, and he remarks on how the civilized tribes, thinking in fact entirely of trade, settled only on the coasts and ruled as robbers, then, as the least numerous, died out and left the inland folk behind. In the evening we finish the Turgenev novel, much affected by it; R. enlarges upon this kind of tragedy's arising out of social laws; if Lavrezki had divorced his wife, everything would have been all right; I observe that with Lise's tendency toward sainthood, her sense of the need to atone, this possibility would not be of much account. R. says I am right: in which case it all goes very deep.

Wednesday, March 22   R. had a good night, and he is extremely pleased that we have come here. Our morning conversation leads us to the development of mankind, and R., with Gob.'s theory in mind, says: "We shall perish, that is certain; the question now is whether we shall end with Holy Communion or croak in the gutter. It's not a question of quantity, greatness has always been rare." The weather is very hot, and R. feels it severely when he walks in the garden around midday. Our good Boni is causing us some trouble with her engagement. But throughout it all I have the feeling that every event brings us, R. and me, closer together, that everything leaves us more and more immersed in each other! . . .

In the afternoon we go for a walk in the garden opposite, visit the monkeys, which give us much enjoyment, and soon return home. In the evening we read *What Is German?;* I am pleased by the peculiar vitality of its observations—none of it can sound hollow when it is all so bound up with such terribly eloquent experiences.

Thursday, March 23   R. had a good night; we discuss Blandine's character and fate and agree that for her marriage is a good thing. Then R. expresses his delight in the refined tranquillity of this place and says he will find the desire to work—to write his preface for Stein, for instance. This brings us to [Stein's] piece about Bruno and Shakespeare; R. feels that in it Sh. is not significant enough, though he admits it is extraordinarily difficult, if not impossible, to put words into Sh.'s mouth—how, for example, can one imagine what he felt with regard to Catholicism and Protestantism? And what impression the fate of the Dominican monk made on him? — During the morning an inquiry from Herr Batz puts him in very gay spirits, but particularly his own reply, in the form of marginal comments to the letter, which he returns. Among other things Herr B. had spoken of Richard's "advanced age." R. replies with his death, which at an advanced age is only to be expected. — At 1 o'clock the arrival of Count Gravina, who will now of course have to be regarded as our son-in-law, and whose natural talents speak highly for him. — In the afternoon R. tells me of a very forceful letter written by Garibaldi about France; we then visit the good monkeys, who entertain us greatly, and in the evening we look through some English illustrated periodicals, R. as always very interested in the human types, while all the children play. The *Idyll* accompanies us, its fair tones our guardian angels.

Friday, March 24 R. slept well, and he rises in cheerful spirits. This reminds me that he told me his mother once called him the "children's friend" (saying he looked like the "children's friend"). Around noon he tells me that he has been looking again through C. Frantz's "Open Letter" to him, and he reads some of it to me, including the excellent passage on *Faust,* and we once again come to the conclusion that he is outstanding as a critic, but questionable when it comes to creative work. Then he goes to the piano, plays the Valhalla theme, which he thinks well described by Wolz. as "architectural"; he thinks of *Das Rheingold* with pleasure, also the performance of it in Berlin, and agrees with me when I say that music can make an impression in the memory as great as when one is actually hearing it. He also tells me that today he composed a true popular song, but he has forgotten it. We are nine at table for lunch, our conversation half in German, half in Italian, half in French. R. decides on an outing. When we part and he goes off for a rest, I hear him exclaim loudly, "Alas!" I go in to ask him about it, and he tells me, "I was wondering when we—you and I—would be in that other world to which we belong; there is nothing for us in this one—it was there just to produce us both." — Ah, how blissful is my feeling that life can give us nothing! Nor can it harm us. . . . After our little concert in Porrazzi I went upstairs to speak to Blandine about her future; after a while Daniela came in and told me that they, the children, had had such a fine conversation with their father downstairs. And I learned that he had spoken about me, even about my appearance, in fact; and he himself hints jokingly about it to me. I, however, feel the ecstasies of eternity; to have the image of myself planted in the children's hearts by him! It will live in their hearts as the image of our love. — A peaceful evening; the six children play and chat, R. plays some Beeth. themes to start with, among others from the Adagio of the 9th Symph., and he says, "To discover these two themes and to combine them, the one like a dream of Nature, the other like a fair memory, to produce something so divine—only a madman could do that, a person of sound mind could never find such things." Then he reads *The Tempest* and talks to me about the wonderful things in it, also about the peculiar vitality of Prospero's character, the fullness of his first scene with Ariel. R. also remarks on the way Prosp. makes the young prince chop wood, and we immerse ourselves in this wonderful creation.

Saturday, March 25   Yesterday we talked about the sonata form, agreeing that even in 111, for example, Beethoven still shows a certain stiffness in the first movement which does not quite match the freedom of the concluding movement. In this connection, R. says, he acknowledges only the A Major Sonata, which is utterly free, and the first movement of 106, which is certainly highly organized, but in which the richness demands this kind of organization; otherwise no sonata gives him what individual works by Bach can give him. — He slept well. At breakfast I tell him what Stein has written to me about the coal industry being replaced by electricity; he argues strongly against it. "It is still a machine," he exclaims, and tells me what crippling conditions have been brought about by machines. No, no improvements of this sort, but moving to fine climates in which one can live naturally. He then reads, first of all *The Tempest,* then Stein's essay on Rousseau, with which he is so impressed that he writes to Stein, bringing up again his old ideas for an educational institution; he wants to print an appeal in the *Blätter* and see whether he might not be entrusted with about six boys, who would enjoy a free education under Stein's direction. — A very great storm brings up the subject of the sea's erosions—every year estates worth 8 billion are being lost. Otherwise it is *The Tempest* which claims precedence in R.'s thoughts, he says he is only now beginning entirely to understand certain beauties in its composition. In the evening he goes to the piano again and to begin with plays the opening of the *Freischütz* Overture; this always opens our hearts, and I say to him how much vitality the art of music must possess if, so soon after Beethoven, something as novel as this could still be discovered. "Oh," he says, "Beet. was in the ninth Heaven, and this was a return to Nature." He remarked today on our (the German) aptitude for ideality, our return from beautiful Italy to Munich—so ugly, cold, and raw; but then one enters a hall—sometimes itself very ugly—and the music begins! He says that for this reason, as far as we are concerned, all is lost if music is put to the wrong use. In the afternoon, over a glass of beer, he looks at an English illustrated periodical and shows me a picture of starvation in India, served up as entertainment for the readers! — In the evening some whist, during which R. jokes a lot with Count Gr., telling him he will surely take him for a *fou* [madman] and find it difficult to believe that he ever wrote *Lohengrin*. Then he says that if he had to talk French for the next ten years, he would be dead in five. — Today I again find occasion to call him the "children's friend"; he then jokingly recalls the children's book of that name, which showed a boy with his hair brushed upright bringing in a cake— it was this boy with whom his mother compared him.

Sunday, March 26   A disturbed night, and I myself feel so run down that I believe I shall have to remain in bed, until, knowing him to be alone for breakfast, I feel there is nothing wrong with me and leap out of bed, to the great amusement of us both. We come to the subject of etymology, led to it, I think, by an investigation of the word "bold," the mythological origin of which R. discovers in Balder; when I tell R. that I feel greatly drawn to etymology, he says: "Yes, it provides everyone with his family tree, as it were, when one can explain to oneself where one comes from by understanding what one is saying. And in a certain sense it raises the lower orders above the aristocracy, to whom, as conquerors, the native language is foreign." That brings us to the theme of original inhabitants; though I share the opinion that the various civilizations were founded by predatory people, I still am not quite convinced that the original inhabitants were necessarily good. R. says, "Yes, they were, because they cultivated the land, and Humb[oldt] is right in maintaining that the human being who invented language must have been of a gentle disposition." — R. plans the outing to Taormina but then abandons it, since he has taken medicine; in the evening he humorously confesses all the things he took in the morning, and says it was discomfort which led him to plan an outing. R. very kindly writes to Prince Scalea in Gravina's behalf. Then he reads a little of *The Tempest,* but the clown scenes with Trinculo bore him. He plays the great march sequence from the *Eroica* and takes delight in it. At lunch we talk about the Russian character, and R. says drolly that they sent Jouk. to Europe to find favor, to make people think they are all like that. Of the wife of the Grand Duke's heir and the Grand Duke [Konstantin] he says, "Paltry and arrogant." We drive out to Belvedere, having heard that Gar[ibaldi] is expected today, but he does not arrive. In the evening, as he is having his cigarette lit, he tells Semper's English anecdote, "I am a gentleman, but not your slave," and also the anecdote of the courtier who at L[ouis] XIV's behest entered the carriage ahead of the King, taking the view that every word of a monarch is a command; R. says this made a great impression on him. While the children are playing, R. talks to me about *The Tempest;* during the afternoon he had already expressed his astonishment and admiration for Prospero's words as he breaks his magic staff. "He gives up everything, the miracle of knowledge—I have the feeling that I can understand that to mean the achievements of our modern world—for music!" — Then he reads to me what Gonzalo has to say about the natural condition when he sees the island, views which lead to his being scoffed at by the shallow nobleman—but what he says is exactly what R. himself also believes.

Monday, March 27 R. had a good night, and in the morning we immediately become absorbed in our subject, and R. remarks how platitudinously Rousseau tackled the problem. R. then says that he cannot understand how materialists can be optimistic, which they are— it is really only deists who can be that. He wonders whether one can hope that a community might be formed after the collapse of the existing order which, inwardly committed to a Christian outlook and veneration of animals, would emigrate to better regions. He says he would like to believe it! At my request he begins work on the subject of male and female. Fidi and Gravina go to Catania, return home for lunch, and tell us what they have seen. Over coffee R. talks about *H[enry] VIII,* which he has been reading today; he is astounded by this courtly world, so utterly different (from the histories), these cardinals and their feasts, etc. The cruelty is still there, but with more cunning, and mixed with hypocrisy. We go for a drive to a coastal village, whose prettiness pleases R. Returning, we wait for Garibaldi, who does in fact pass through around 8 o'clock. A wonderful sight, almost the entire population at the station, the train approaches slowly, first a ripple of movement as it is announced, then silence; at last, when the hero's carriage is recognized, hearty cries of welcome, lovely to hear, ceremonious procession of the sick man, whom no one can see, since he has to lie still; the white kerchiefs and the flowers give the children the impression of a funeral, Gravina bursts into tears, it makes a profound impression on R. and me as we stand on the balcony; when the locomotive, quietly moving off, lets out a long whistle, it sounds to me like Earth's lament for its finest sons. Bengal lights and moonlight illumine the scene, the people buzz like a gigantic bird's nest, making harmonious sounds, which pleases R. — Our conversation, when the children return, is devoted to the aged hero; R. praises him from the bottom of his heart and mentions the tragic fate which gave him, without his knowledge, a part to play in the comedy of Nap. III and Palmerston, but this time it was in a good cause; he became a nuisance in the politics he began by serving—"all these frightful politics which lead to the abyss." R. says that what he most admired was Garibaldi at Capua—there he appeared to have supplied the greatest proofs of his indefatigability and his persistence. But he lays stress on all his deeds, the retreat from Rome, etc., and it does one good to listen to him. While we were on the balcony, he considered how it would be if they were to meet: they would have nothing to say to each other; he, G., would ask R. whether he was a democrat, a Liberal. It is the deeds of such a person which one must recognize, in all else there was a gulf between. I observe that G. would surely admire the greatness and independence of his character. "Yes," says R., "but in what way would that come through to him?" We wonder whether the cheers of the crowd do not disturb the sick man. "Oh," says R., "he remembers how he was torn to pieces, how he had to send most of them away, it can't bring him much joy." — In the evening R. talks to me about Shakesp. "He is unbearable," he says, "because he is completely unfathomable! Aeschylus, Sophocles were the products of their culture, but he! And he knew everything." He again quotes Gonzalo and says he could in fact be made to look shallow and insignificant, and yet in his heart, which had produced a good deed, he held a true knowledge of what was desirable in life, and Prospero also calls him a good man. — Regarding Shakespeare's life, R. feels he must certainly have known penury, and he thinks the 16th century was no better than ours—one would need only to ask Cervantes and Sh. Before going off to bed, R. improvises on the Porrazzi melody, which once more reveals to me the most secret aspects of my soul, and I go to rest in a mood of bliss. (One incident I must note, since it is typical of R.; he was annoyed to see Gravina smoking during a conversation with me, and he feels it is wrong for us women to allow such things.)

Tuesday, March 28   R. gets up early after a good night, and we have breakfast in cheerful silence, since I fear the effect of stimulating conversation on him. When he asks me why I am silent, I tell him the things which are occupying my mind—the letter to Hans about Boni, and Siegfried's education. (R. has already abandoned his idea of advertising; he says he can imagine the sort of children who would be sent to him and what difficulties one would be piling on oneself.) [*A sentence based on untranslatable word play omitted.*] — As I am writing my letter to Hans, the maid tells me that R. is having a severe attack, I hasten to him and am confronted with a sight which so affects me that I faint. I soon pull myself together again and return to R. from the bed on which I have been laid; his condition gradually becomes calmer, he is given electric treatment, starts joking again: "If only Baron Pennisi were to come today!" and: "My intestines are tying themselves in knots, so as to remind themselves of something." But he is very run down. — Only yesterday we were talking about our end, I wished to do everything I could to be worthy of dying with him. He said that we must live, and this is much more difficult. My fainting today has now given me hope. Oh, my Siegfried, should I leave you before I have set you firmly on your path, remember me, be good and brave, flee from all that is contemptible, avoid all the usual distractions, honor noble women, shun all others! — The doctors say attacks like this are not dangerous, but when I see him in such a condition, see him suffering, groaning, and there is nothing anyone can do, then, dear God, my strength deserts me!

We pass the day quietly together. At about three o'clock R. has some food, and afterward he talks to me about *Henry VIII,* which he has been reading, admiring how freely Shakespeare has drawn this character; he says Kleist would never have permitted himself anything like it, even in the figure of the Elector Prince, so enslaved are we by court restrictions: "It is all Assyrian," R. says. He shows me the remarkable passage in which the Queen forbids Griffith to answer the summons. We spend the evening quietly alone. I read the *Lohengrin* text, and R. recalls that when he read it to Laube in his sister Luise's house, Laube said that the development of the second act was good throughout, but one ought to see Ortrud performing acts of magic in the background—the psychological processes meant nothing to him.

Wednesday, March 29   A good night for R.; he has a bath, which does him good. We talk about the strange conditions in Sicily, in which only 7% of the population can read and write, about Catholicism; and R. says a monastery such as Einsiedeln (where Abbé Jecker's brother is musical conductor) is a most curious phenomenon in our present age, having nothing to do with the modern Jewish framework, but for him it is the most alien of all. — He reads the conclusion of *Henry VIII* and the exposition of *A Midsummer Night's Dream* and says: "With Shakespeare one has only to think that something is unimportant, like the lovers here, to find oneself in trouble at once. I find there all my thoughts about love—indeed, I now find all my thoughts about everything in him." At lunch he explains Schopenhauer's interpretation of ghostly apparitions to our friend Gravina, jokes about the bridal couple—"Two sheep, one black and one white"—relates to Loulou over coffee some episodes from his biography—life in Zurich—and in between jokes frequently about my silent fainting fit yesterday. — He also says he would like to play H. VIII and Prospero. — The newspaper sent to us with the excerpt from Frau Dietz brings back old memories! "Use your head," etc. Then he reads to me the splendid scene between the lovers: "That is what I always say: the main thing is to remain faithful." Apart from this, he regrets all the academizing in *A Midsummer Night's Dream*—Cynthia, etc. In the evening we play whist, and after that he plays the beginning of the *Album-Sonate,* which the children have brought with them.

Thursday, March 30 A restless night, but a bath does him good. At breakfast he talks about the half-light in the *salon,* which he finds productive—the penetration of light from outside is not beneficial to his inner world. Around lunchtime I tell him about Garibaldi's arrival in Palermo, cries of rejoicing at first, then, when the people saw him, complete silence. This moves R., as it does me. — The weather is bad, but in the evening we are able to take a little walk; we visit the monkeys and spend quite a time enjoying the sight. The violent movements which, without any reason, suddenly stop, give one the impression of a lack of purpose in Nature, and when I remark on this to R. in the evening, he replies: "Yes, storms, earthquakes—all these stirrings of the Will. A spirit such as Goethe's rebels against them and tries to discern and introduce a gentle kind of order!" — When we arrived home, he was vexed that his advertisement has not yet appeared, and he writes to Wolz. In the evening whist, and in between, "*Lützow's wilde Jagd.*"

Friday, March 31 R. did not sleep very well. We give up Catania, which we meant to visit today, since the weather is not very favorable. Discussion about the engagement; letters yesterday from the Tascas raise some doubts in us. R. laughs over our amateurishness in such matters! It will be a hard task to find the right occupation for our future son-in-law, his education has not equipped him for anything! — R. writes to [Amalie] Materna about the role of Kundry and tells her not to worry about the low notes, what is needed is less a voice than a good heart, and that she has shown in the 2nd act of *Die Walküre.* For Klingsor, he feels, he requires more viciousness than voice. Around 4 o'clock (in the morning R. and I went for a walk in the garden, the sea looks exactly like the sky, he told me yesterday) we visit Baron Pennisi, who possesses a splendid collection of coins, which R. and I examine with interest. But in the evening R. is very tired, and he goes to bed around 9 o'clock.

Saturday, April 1 After a good night we take the early train to Catania and are utterly entranced by the journey. The handsome town, through which we are conducted by Marquis S. Giuliano, pleases us greatly; at lunch the Marquis quotes "The Landgraf's Address" in *Tannhäuser.* The little excursion does R. good; he is impressed by the sight of the Gravina tomb beside the royal ones. — In the evening the children sing, R. accompanies them, and we play whist.

Sunday, April 2 R. had a good night. Our breakfast conversation revolves around the children, mainly Blandine, with some apprehension! The laconic tone of Hans's telegram says a very great deal! In the

Bund, which a Swiss maid here receives, it is reported, to R.'s delight, that on the left bank of the Vierwaldstätter lake a parkland is to be leveled as far as Tribschen, "for some time the residence of R. Wagner." — The weather is uncertain, we abandon a coach excursion and take the 5 o'clock train to Giarre and Riposto, returning with the 7 o'clock train. When we get off at Giarre, R. calls out, "Herr Schnappauf!" The urchins surrounding him repeat "Schnappauf" like an echo, amid much laughter; we go down to the sea in very gay spirits, sit on the terrace of the little tollhouse and watch the moon rising. A splendid journey, which we greet with cries of delight. On our return we see Etna free of clouds for the first time, shining in the moonlight. A game of whist, made very merry by R.'s humorous vexation with his bad cards, ends a day on which R. has felt very well. He decides on a journey to Taormina tomorrow. [*A sentence based on untranslatable word play omitted.*]

Monday, April 3 A good night for R. He gets up early, and we feel pleased to be so favored by the weather. He writes to Feustel on account of the Batz affair (yesterday Herr Neumann wrote that the theaters were allowing him to give his guest performances on condition that they retain 10% of the performance rights)—now the question is whether Batz also has rights in *T. und Isolde.* The beauty here could drive one out of one's mind; we visit Taormina and are rewarded with a unique view! Before leaving, R. took Fidi for a walk in the garden opposite and told him how lucky he was compared with other children, and this obliged him to be particularly good! — In Taormina R. is particularly delighted by the columns. On the homeward journey he says how dreamlike is the sight of such things, one is not in fact moved by them at all. I understand this feeling only too well: when one's gaze is directed toward the depths, the surface no longer has much effect. Yet even in this lack of effect there is a peculiar feeling of well-being. — We met S.'s Latin teacher, Herr Toussaint, in the Hôtel Timeo, concerning which R. says we should have fled there in 1858 and spared ourselves many, many torments. The children could have lived on prickly pears! — But the meeting with Herr T. and also a letter from Stein bring up the education problem again. R. is against high school and says that what might have been all right for the Grand Duke's heir is not suitable for Siegfried. He believes that at school he would lose his innocence; he feels that everything will turn out all right for him; having in our home become sensible while still remaining childlike, he requires no further education. — We play whist and go to bed early. Saying good night to me, R. remarks, "How little pleasure the Will takes in itself we can see when we remember how silly loving couples always look in real life, how little sympathy is aroused by the exchange of yearning glances, whereas on the stage we find these things so interesting." — On arrival in Taormina R. catches sight of a little island; he says that in earlier days he always longed for something like that, in order to cut himself off from the world. "If only Wesendonck were to give me such an island," he had thought to himself, "and Minna had no great desire to go there with me!" And he adds, "It was the thought that there was much I could still do." — As the children are singing the "Shepherd's Song" from *Tannhäuser,* he tells me that he heard it sung by a shepherd in Schreckenstein, near Teplitz—though of course in a completely different form. — The feeling of strangeness, even when contemplating something as sublimely expressive of a national culture as this theater, the sight of the many citadels piled one above the other, arousing our laughter at such a display of caution—all this causes R. to repeat his remark that all these civilizations were robber civilizations. We review other possibilities. "Oh," he says, "I am becoming more and more Gobinistic," and this is why he is annoyed by Malwida's criticism of the book on race. He calls her views optimistic and justifies the grim veracity of his own by virtue of the serenity they induce in him.

Tuesday, April 4 R. feels worn out from our outing yesterday. Our conversation turns to Hans, whom R. criticizes severely; against this I set the blame attached to me for marrying him and thus perhaps exacerbating his tendencies. — Then we talk about emigration, which is assuming extravagant proportions in Württemberg and Baden in consequence of the tariff policies. "And it is the best part of the population which is emigrating," what remains is fodder for the Jews. I also tell R. my idea of a Wagner dictionary, touched on by Stein in his letter, and we talk about it. At lunch he seems somewhat run down, but he has a good rest in the afternoon, and the two of us set out for the Cyclopean Islands, with the idea of catching up with the children. However, they are not there. We go in the dirtiest of boats, rowed by three constantly chattering boatmen, in order to see the curious lava formations, and we resolve to return in the evening. The boatmen demand payment during the journey and then demand it again from our coachman, who—*un génie d'insolence,* as R. remarks while telling Grav. about it—gives them what they ask, luaghing cheekily at us, and on top of that cadges a pinch of snuff from R. [*Added in margin:* "On our return from Taormina he asks Fidi how much smaller than the earth the moon is, and he adds, 'A dreadfully big thing, this earth, much too big!' "] We return home in laughing vexation, visit the splendid garden opposite, admire Etna, and give up our evening drive. In the evening whist, during which R. explains to Gr. why he always likes to play with me: because then he can bear both good and bad luck, but he cannot tolerate my having the one or the other against him. — He praises the splendid air. He reads letters to D[aniela] about [?] Hans, declaring himself completely indifferent to this correspondence. He tells me about the minister Gerber's edict, which so delights him that he has half a mind to write to the minister. He is pleased with Fidi and feels he will be a better person than we are, since the things we achieved only through difficulties and torments he is receiving without suffering.

Wednesday, April 5 R. had a good night, even though he woke up once with the words "I am dying—oh, how beautiful!" There is a heavy thunderstorm, and he sees a flash of lightning which, he says in describing it to us, drew "passionate" signs in the air, and he then dreams he saw the name "Nadar" in the sky (the well-known Parisian who wrote his name in zigzag letters on all the walls). — At breakfast he mentions that he is expecting royalties for this quarterly period, but they will be small; *Carmen* is providing him with competition. Yesterday he expressed surprise that his old works were still bringing him in so much money, and he wonders whether the new ones will follow the same path. Before lunch he goes for a walk in the garden opposite and is amused by a "scuffle" among the monkeys. Then at lunch the question of upbringing is discussed; R. feels that punishment is quite unnecessary—either the child has a bad heart, in which case nothing helps, or it has a good one; what matters is whether one is born good, a child of love, and then everything rights itself of its own accord. Then he comes to his theme of male and female; since he calls it "boy and girl," I ask jokingly whether I fare well in it: "Yes, in the second part of your life, but not in the first, for in a woman's love for a man I see the first breaking of the Will, in the longing—as Schopenhauer so magnificently puts it—to produce the Saviour." — I recall Diotima, to be born again in beauty. "Certainly Plato knew it," R. says, "but he made the mistake of wanting to be constructive." — Over coffee we plan our homeward journey, then R. tells us things from the world of politics, that Bismarck is making concessions to the Clerical party in order to win their support for the tobacco monopoly, and that in France *gros bon sens* [plain common sense], *bonnets de coton* [cotton bonnets], and *les sabots* [clogs] now prevail, which heartens him; for example, they did not wish to dissolve the concordat. — We go for a little walk, first in town, but we find it unpleasant on account of the ugly, crippled people, so we go into the garden, which always delights us. In the evening whist, and then between R. and me a long conversation about love and, from there, the realization of ideas. It begins with R.'s pointing out to me the moonlight on the sea and adding how little such a sight now means to him; he mentions Schop.'s similar remark and stresses how wise he was to confine himself to criticism; invention leads to foolishness. We then go on to Christianity, which in its pure form was too fragile to gain ground and, in accommodating itself to the world, could only give rise to inconsequentiality. We come to see how this realization—that an idea cannot give rise to a corresponding deed, that such a deed can only be released by an urge—which appears to be such a bitter one, can nevertheless lead to serenity: it draws one away from the outside world and bids one dig deeper within oneself. We see that the Saviour had no community in the true sense of the word, and that he allowed himself to be crucified for the few who committed themselves to him. "That is sublime," R. exclaims. But the need to inform, to show others the truth one has perceived, that exists, he says—but it means monasteries! Feelings and thoughts pass to and fro between us, until it is just glances we are exchanging, and we go off to bed. — "I did the right thing, another the wrong," he says in our bedroom, thinking of Hans and his marriage. He mentions often during the day that, on account of the wrong done to him, Hans now expects to be absolved from responsibility. — Stein's enthusiastic response to the school idea, which R. has already more or less abandoned, leads him to ask: "Why does our son need other boys to play with? Isn't he getting to know the world best in this way? Let's leave it to Fate. Schools are for creatures who ought never to have been born!" he exclaims, and says that he must expect only an absurd response to his high-minded appeal, if he ever makes it. — Support for his works comes only from Jews and young people, he said recently. — An exclamation from Cervantes which he frequently uses—"Oh, you persecutor of God and all his saints!"—again makes him laugh today and leads him to say that he can clearly see the facial resemblance between those two, Shakespeare and Cervantes. — R. concluded our evening conversation with the remark that *Parsifal* ought certainly to be his final work, since in these Knights of the Grail he has given expression to his idea of a community. *Die Sieger* could only repeat this in a weak and insignificant way.

Thursday, April 6 R. had a good night, but he tells me he is still feeling down in the dumps. All the same I can be pleased with the way he is looking, yesterday he seemed so youthful—younger than everybody else! — The children go to church, Siegfried wishes to stay for the whole 4-hour service and comes home with strange reports! The lawyer Gilio comes from Palermo to give me a report on the property situation. It is complicated, not very encouraging, and my fears increase! — A drive with R. and Fidi; before that, visit from Marquis Giuliano. Since, talking of the Semitic problem, he pointed out Italy's advantage in having absorbed them, R. becomes greatly agitated, and he then, through Herr Gilio, sends the Marquis a copy of "Know Thyself." He jokes with me about it and says that the only way to treat such people is to make them mad, as Röckel once said about his brother Albert, to whom he had described the extreme consequences of the revolution as unavoidable necessities. — In the evening we play whist in earnest; the toss separated him from me, but after a while I ask to be allowed to play with him.

Good Friday, April 7 A good night, but bad weather; R. complains humorously of having nothing but the B. *Blätter* to read, and he reads Wolz.'s article "Present and Future." He says he understands Jouk.'s remark that it looks as if it had been written under the influence of hashish. When I told him recently I objected to this remark, he said, "Women always prefer hypocrisy," but he then added that one is in fact always a bit to blame for such things oneself. We go to church, the children and I, in very bad weather; it is quiet and empty, I am able to read the Gospel, and through its veil the cross speaks to me. And today I was in need of it. After an hour we return home; in the meantime R. had been reading the "Classical Walpurgis Night" with great delight, he then plays parts of *Parsifal* and finally the new melody. But when I go to take a rest, Lusch shows me a letter from her father which in offensiveness transcends everything so far experienced. However, under the influence of my hour of prayer and R.'s playing, I am able to accept it calmly and to dictate to Lusch a good letter to her father; I then try to forget it. R. visits me, opens the Shakespeare, and reads me various bits from Polonius in Lulu's presence. P.'s "Farewell" reminds R. of the "*Fahr wohl*" in the scene of the griffins and sphinxes. I am able to respond to this, but when we are alone I give him a summary of the scornful attitude Hans is adopting in the matter of Blandine. Supper is announced, R. jokes about our fasting, a curious story is told about the Bishop, and then we play whist. After a few games we leave the table to the children and talk about *Hamlet,* which on stage has an enervating effect, so awesome and magnificently truthful is it. And the same with all Shakespeare's tragedies—one leaves them exhausted and overwhelmed. The spirit of theater yearns for music, I observe, for the consummate ideality of sound. R. says in the modern theater that is certainly so, but things were different on the Shakespearean stage. The children say good night, we are left alone, and Hans's behavior is our topic, and what to do about it; R. wishes me, in the name of the children, to repudiate everything he has set aside for them and to forbid any further interference, and he wants to dictate it to me right away. I hesitate and promise to do it tomorrow, and we continue to reflect on it—for a long, a very long time! R. is violent in his expressions of repugnance and contempt, I tell both him and myself that, if I am to blame for such a deterioration, then may God protect me! — We go off to bed. (R. thought today of Good Friday in the North, which is often very beautiful and touching with its emerging buds and little flowers—in the Asyl in Zurich, for instance, where the first thoughts of *Parsifal* came to him.) — Along with this most serious of matters, the mail also brought the news that L. Lehmann has declined to take part, something I do not tell R., but which affects me greatly, for she is all but indispensable.

Saturday, April 8 R. had a somewhat restless night, I compose in my mind a letter to Lusch, a copy of which I would send to Hans; but today R. is for "letting it go," and so let it be forgotten and—to the extent that I have the right to say it—forgiven! — Then I write to the Tascas, before that to L. Lehmann, with all the warmth I am capable of expressing. Weather still gray and overcast. We receive Marquis San Giuliano and Prince Ramacca, Blandine's future father-in-law. R. very, very charming and kind. In the afternoon he reads to me an anecdote, which he finds touching, about a shepherd who, after getting tickets for himself and his dog, leaves his seat and goes to join his animal. Then he reads parts of the "Classical Walpurgis Night" to me, he much admires Erichtho's speech, but almost above all else the scene of Mephisto with the griffins and sphinxes, then Chiron— everything, in fact, in this most wonderful of conceptions. Talking about Goethe and whether he can be regarded as the sum total of the German spirit, R. says, "I think he can, if one considers how he absorbed all the revivals and discoveries of the 18th century in this free manner; and in the ultimate things he was always full of prescience." Speaking of Helen in *Faust,* whom he does not much care for, R. says he can see Goethe standing in Rome in front of the antiquities. In the evening whist, and Italian arias sung by R. — Then some more talk between us about H.

Sunday, April 9 Christ is risen! But here in Sicily in bad weather! Talk of leaving; R. enjoys moving about. Pleasant lunch with 10 at table; at one point R. loses his temper in earnest over the Catholic clergy. Then a joke from him about his interest in education brings from me my solemn assurance to Gravina that he did in truth educate the children. He tells me that he can well believe it, since they would have seen R. expressing only noble and great feelings. — Since this answer pleases me, I repeat it to R., and he, asking in protest how I could possibly justify my claim, says, "It was you who preserved my life, and it was this act of preservation which gave dignity to my life." — In dull weather we go for a walk in the garden; since many of the citizens are there, R. quotes Wagner's words about ten-pin rolling, fiddling, etc., and Faust's fine answer, "One impulse art thou conscious of, at best." — "That," he says, "is the Faust who grips us"; later we return to Mephisto. He intends to complete his work in June, and he says it will be more significant than he himself first thought or others expected; he says he will connect it with Gobineau, start with him. — The rest of the day R. finds thoroughly unpleasant. Dr. Strecker inquires whether the specifications for *Parsifal* are all right as they are, after R. returned the corrected proofs weeks ago! Then he finds the weather a trial, and he comes to supper in an irritable mood. But as soon as Pasquino's performance, which Gravina and I arranged, begins, he cheers up, and he is completely won over by the talents of these good people. Gr. had arranged a fee of 30 francs, R. raises this to 100 and then goes up to 200 lire, and is touched by the solemn expression of gratitude on Pasquino's face. The rest of us are pleased as well, I in particular by his delight in it all.

Monday, April 10 R. had a good night, but he is vexed by the gray weather. Our morning conversation concerns yesterday's show, R. says he was fascinated by the first entrance of the two women, since they took no notice of us, the audience, at all, but just spoke very earnestly with each other! — Excitement at lunch over Isolde's birthday, R. sings two themes from *Tristan,* then proposes her health with warm delight; but then he is embarrassed by the presence of the Prince, and our departure for Messina takes place in unfavorable circumstances. But he gradually recovers his good spirits, and in Messina, while the children are enjoying themselves on the sea, we two go for a splendid drive to the top of Mount Cappuccini, then to the cathedral. The sky is bright, and who could hope to describe all the rest? When I tell him how much I enjoy not seeing beautiful things before he does, that is to say, never without him, but always with him, he replies, "And I am glad to see nothing after you!" — We return home, confine ourselves just to swapping reports with the children, have a short game of whist, and go off to bed.

Tuesday, April 11 R. had a good night, but he is not well, and his indisposition gets so bad that he avoids going out and wishes to be left alone. I go with the children to look at the Antonellos, then accompany Fidi into some churches; R. takes a walk to the cathedral square, which pleases him very much. Our lunch is uncomfortable, and after it R. feels very indisposed and cannot make up his mind whether to go out or not; after a few changes of mind we decide to remain at home. R. reads some Turgenev stories and is particularly affected by one about a lame woman, since he is reading it at a time when he himself must avoid movement as much as possible. We spend the evening alone together; I have begun reading Sophocles's

Philoctetes with the children, and I talk about it to R. But *Faust* remains our principal topic. At lunch the day before yesterday R. said he could not really understand why, after depicting Faust's shattering experience with Gretchen and intending to have Faust redeemed by Gretchen, [Goethe] then leads him through all these inappropriate happenings, leaving him at the end with such a paltry field of activity. With considerable clumsiness I indicate that this seems rather fine; for a moment he is annoyed, but his view of the nature of *Faust* does not prevent his showing the utmost admiration for the way the plan is carried out. He reads the scenes with the Emperor, I likewise, and we admire the original and popular style in which it is all expressed. The character of the Emperor so striking in its combination of weakness and integrity. He observes that it is still a little-known book, but *the book!* Recalling [Schiller's] *Die Braut von Messina,* R. says: "One shouldn't hide dignity behind a mask; if it does not arise naturally out of the prevailing culture, as among the Greeks, where every appeal to the gods has so awesome an effect, one should leave it alone."

Wednesday, April 12 R. had a restless night, and we learn that the ship we were counting on has no room for us, since the ex-Khedive, turned away from Alexandria with his wives, has taken it over. R. says he wishes to see the ship! — I finish *Philoctetes* with the children, while R. reads the book of short stories, maintaining his interest in it to the end, and saying in its praise that the Russian people still provide a writer with naïve subjects, whereas French books have only repulsive things to offer. In the afternoon R. and I set out on a drive to the temple of Neptune, the sea is showing the most remarkable colors, mauve and green, and the shores are beautiful. But rain forces us to turn back. Issues of the *Fliegende Blätter,* discovered in the hotel, keep R. amused, and I tell him of a report in the *K[ölnische] Zeitung* about a German in Strassburg who has suggested the monopolization of electricity, since a nation can only assume control of an industry with advantage when it is in its initial stages, not once it is already flourishing. R. remarks that this is a peculiar idea and asks why we must always imitate what other nations have done a long time before us. — In the evening we play whist, and since I feel certain that R. prefers to be alone with me when he is feeling somewhat run down, and also that he does not care for all the Italian and French, even though we two always speak German, I soon send the children away, and we chat together, about *Philoctetes,* about *Faust.*

Thursday, April 13 After a somewhat restless night the sun shines on us again, and we start our day with a conversation about *Faust.* After I have quoted to him a few things, such as "We made him rich, and now we must amuse him," in which Schop.'s saying about neediness or boredom is summarized, he points out how much superior this poem is, on account of its freedom, to that of Dante, who was free only in his personal judgment, but otherwise completely bound by church doctrine. I ask whether it was not the time he lived in that worked to G.'s advantage, and R. replies, "Of course, as I remarked in 'The Public in Time and Space' "—there has never been a greater poet than Dante. He also said, before this, "G. could die in peace after having given us this portrait of the world's triviality and this glorification of love and the Christian idea." "He worked on it long enough," he replies jokingly when I say that without apparently ever having thought much about it, he had absorbed everything down to the smallest detail of Christian symbolism. "And one does not need to search for long—what one needs comes into one's mind of its own accord, one doesn't quite know how. I know something of that from experience." — Departure at 5 o'clock after a few difficulties and worries, of which R. tells us at lunch, saying humorously that he had wanted to inquire about the ship but in the end had gone to beer halls with Gravina. The weather is bright, but very windy, and after a few glances at the coast R. withdraws to his cabin. (He told me before this that he has been reading Sophocles's *Ajax,* and he criticizes the bad habit of bandying maxims about, calling it a mannerism. But he does say, "If only a few MSS. of Aeschylus and Soph. were dug up, instead of all the many statues!") — I remain on the upper deck, first with the children, then at last alone, gazing upon a starry night beyond compare, softly glittering, and a phosphorescent sea, till my gazing turns into a prayer. Sailing past Stromboli, Loldi even sees flames. It is after 10 o'clock when I join R. in the cabin; he is not actually sick, but feeling the strain, and he sleeps with interruptions.

Friday, April 14 We arrive in Naples at 8 o'clock, in somewhat gray weather; it is to Pellegrino that R. gives the honor of a salute, since he can raise no great interest in the cliffs of Capri. Naples itself, however, as unique as ever! Dr. Schrön to greet us; parting from our friend and son [Gravina], made very moving by R.'s words. "*Soyez homme et vous nous avez pour amis*" ["Be a man and you will have us as your friends"], he says, and expresses his appreciation of his good and honorable character—and what lies in its power to achieve—in such a wonderful way that all pain is dissolved in blissful melancholy. — We leave the city, which R. declares to be the loveliest of all (we had once more enjoyed the drive down the Posilipo), and now hasten away. The countryside beyond the Naples coast does not interest R. very much (I am fascinated by the sunset over Monte Cassino), but Tuscany on

Saturday, April 15 enchants us with its cultivation; when we come to Lombardy, R. explains to me the origin of alluvial ground. "That took quite a time," he says jokingly, whereupon I: "It must surely have happened before the calendar was invented"; he looks at me with a twinkle in his eye, then earnestly, and says, "I have you, and you are all I could or should have, everything else is a masquerade." Yesterday, as I was going to sleep, I heard soft words of blessing being spoken over me and felt his dear hand, grasped it as he said quietly, "Now we can say that we are happy." And when all is silent, all that exists is a prayer from me to him, a blessing from him to me—yet how many things come between us! In Naples an unpleasant business letter (Batz), during the journey inquisitive people, and how much else! In Mestre he is vexed by a completely inexplicable delay, also by the fact that it is raining when we arrive in Venice, whereas in Naples we had the brightest weather, as always. R. very tired, can scarcely eat a thing, goes straight off to bed, and, as I am writing these lines, sends me a message to say that he is feeling all right again, whereupon I go upstairs to greet him. — Soon afterward he comes to join me, and we chat for a while. (In the train he thought of Beeth.'s quartets and told me that they are the equivalent of *Faust,* playing with the theme in a completely free way, but in music this is more transfigured, a playing with sound!) — Then he considered the masculine and feminine names of the various rivers, believing first of all that the German rivers were masculine, *Donau* [Danube], etc., being Slavonic, but he satisfied himself that this view is untenable.

Sunday, April 16 Following a good night, delight in Venice, our curious apartments please us, and a walk he takes to San Marco around midday utterly enchants him; we are in no doubt that this is the loveliest place of all. Just one incident annoys him: the son of the American impresario Strakosch asks him how much he earns from the performance of his works, whereupon R. rebukes him severely for his impertinence. "If only I could say such things with biting coldness, but I always get emotionally upset, and I felt my spasm again." — In the afternoon we return to the square and go into the church, which R. was unwilling to enter in the morning, since a service was being held, then as far as S. Zaccaria, delighting in everything. The hotel, too, with its long anteroom on each floor, pleases R. — In the evening he reads to us three acts of Gozzi's *The Raven* with enjoyment. When we are alone, we talk again about Sophocles; R. tells me various things from *Ajax,* regretting only the way maxims are bandied about, but full of admiration for its other qualities, and particularly for the vividness of Odysseus's character; he agrees with me in my praise for *Philoctetes* and the aftertaste of racial feeling in it.

Monday, April 17 R. had a restless night—we believe as a result of his second glass of grog! He began to read an article by Hans in the

Musikzeitung, then set it aside, disliking its witty tone; however, when he takes leave of me, he picks the paper up again, saying, "Now that we have laughed over it together, I can continue reading it." Yesterday R. took the news of L. Lehmann's desertion very calmly, but something from Batz has annoyed him. I go out in search of palazzos, but without success today. On my return I find a letter to Lusch from Hans, from which I see that my mood of resignation has been rewarded, for he writes in a very proper manner, to Gravina as well. R. went out, but returned exhausted, and a ride in a gondola, which he takes with us, cheers him up, without, however, removing his feelings of discomfort. He is also vexed that the piano score of *Parsifal* has still not been published. In the evening I write at his request to Herr Neumann, saying he will not be coming to London, and to a Herr Schulz-Curtius, who has inquired whether R. would accept an honorary doctorate from Oxford, saying that he considers the time for his accepting such honors is now past. — His "Gondolier's Song" of '63, which I have now got hold of, amuses him. The children are with Princess H[atzfeldt]; we spend the evening chatting quietly in between the letters, which I am writing on his behalf, since he now feels very disinclined to write!

Tuesday, April 18 R. did not have a good night, and since the weather is wet, he does not go out; he passes his time with Homer, talks to me about it, and says that in spite of all its great qualities it seems to him, with so much talk and the sham battles, frivolous in comparison with certain succinct German sagas, particularly the conclusion of the N[ibelungen]*lied.* Delayed by my house hunting, I keep him waiting for half an hour and find his remarks on "Hunger" and also the melody [*see notes*] on my desk. The latter touches me all the more in that I had just been thinking of using it for his birthday! — After lunch we visit the P[alazzo] Desdemona—with Hebrew occupants! Perhaps! Then S[anta] M[aria della] Salute, whose cold interior utterly disgusts R. — He cannot understand how the warm style of Byzantine churches could ever have been abandoned in favor of this imitation classical whiteness. We return home, and I write to M. Meysenbug, giving her my reasons for accepting Gravina as a son-in-law. R. feels that my confiding in her goes too far; he says she is not so loyal to us as she should be, has other interests besides, is not permeated with our ideas! He thinks she is somewhat like Bakunin, whose biography he has just been reading in a newspaper, astonished by all the things he did as a conspirator and the people with whom he had dealings. R. also talks about the dominance of Jews in this country as well, and he is astonished that nobody is apprehensive about it— but of course all the rest are already Israelized. — Recalling these two curious people, he said: "No real life of their own—ghosts!

Nothing there but profit seeking and a pinch of voluptuousness!" —

Wednesday, April 19 R. had a good night, and it is a glorious day! I set out on my searches, and R. goes on his own to the Belle Arti, says he discovered me there in the first room: others might not recognize me in it, but this is how I look when I have been weeping. He is still enchanted with Venice. — When I return home, I find on my desk his reply to Herr Förster, who has deployed all of what R. calls his "play actor's" eloquence in an effort to persuade R. to go to London, holding out the prospect of an invitation from the Duke of Edinburgh—showing, in short, his complete ignorance of R.'s character. R. replies that it is very unfortunate that there is so much lying in the world, for no truthful man will be believed when he says that his health does not permit him to go. R. and I visit the Palazzo Morosini, look at Loredano, go inside S. Marco, stop at a jeweler's, where R. buys a necklace for Boni, having given fans to Loldi and Eva. — Our supper is overshadowed by the news that Prince Scalea's young son, whom Gravina discovered lying mortally ill and neglected in an institution in Naples, is being left there abandoned by his parents, in spite of Grav.'s urgent entreaties to be allowed to bring him home! ... R. wants to adopt the boy, at all costs to rescue him from the hated institution, but then, realizing his powerlessness, he relapses into melancholy and inveighs indignantly against these families. — With the children we go to the Goldoni Theater and see Scribe's *Bataille des dames.* The weak and wordy exposition annoys R., he wants action, but he is interested in the way the story is developed.

Thursday, April 20 R. had a good night. — In the course of the day we return to a reply Fidi made to me yesterday; I had observed that I would like to die in Venice; Fidi: "I in Bayreuth, for, lovely as it all is, one likes best to go home." — R. praises this home-loving spirit and says, "Woe upon those who do not possess it!" — I thank Fidi in my heart for understanding so well how to please me. — R. talks at breakfast about the *Iliad,* and he says the garrulous prolongation of the narrative is out of proportion to the cruelty of the legend, and from this he deduces that the latter is much older than the former. The narrative has a real Oriental breadth. The famous description of Olympus shaking as Zeus bows his head finds no favor in his eyes, as a dramatist he sees the foolishness of it, the lack of proportion. — Then our thoughts turn to that poor boy, abandoned in Naples. In connection with him R. said yesterday that night was not dark enough to hide in, and today he quotes M[ephisto]'s terrible words, "She is not the first"—that, he says, is the consolation the world offers! He enlarges upon the chapter on marriage with which he is now much occupied, this urge of Nature: "At any rate," he concludes, "it is always wrong to do anything against it." He goes out and brings Boni a necklace, with which the girl is very pleased. Before that he informed Herr L[evi] that he would be passing through—he feels there is now much to be done at home. After lunch we pay another visit to the P. Desdemona, then we go on a lovely drive to S. Giovanni e Paolo. Delighting in the blue sky, we think of the North; he feels the weather will get worse and worse, since everything is moving toward the end of the world. — At lunch we mentioned those friends who often reproached us for finding all other people dispensable; R. says, "What they are demanding is a sort of being in love, for we have shown them that we can be friends." Turning to the children: "There is only one person who has ever been indispensable to me, without whom I should find it impossible to live, and that is your mother. I was mad about her," he adds jokingly. — At supper, in connection with the appalling pictures of the Madonna which one sees here, too, our conversation turns to Cath. and Prot., and R. solemnly and penetratingly explains the difference to Siegfried. Then he reads to us the conclusion of *The Raven,* without much enjoyment.

Friday, April 21 In the morning R. recalls yesterday's play and remarks how curious it is that after G[oethe]'s and Schiller's works had already appeared, such rough and vulgar language could still be printed as that used in the translation of this play. — At lunch he says to me that all one can do in our time is to practice criticism, confine oneself to exposing the lie; and apart from that promote the work of art! I observe that criticism serves to prepare the ground for this art. — In connection with a mulatto (custodian at the Palazzo Loredano) he tells me, half in jest but all the same very much in earnest, that he no longer finds human beings at all pleasing, even to look at, and he shares Schopenhauer's feelings in finding no pleasure in the skin's whiteness. We visit this Palazzo Loredano, and R. feels attracted by it anew. From there we go to St. Mark's Square; R. asks the military band for [Rossini's] *Gazza Ladra* Overture, which is then played, and very prettily. In the evening he has some unpleasantnesses (Batz-Neumann, performance rights of *T. und I.*); at about 9 o'clock we go to Princess Hatzfeldt's; the singers are awaiting us below, and they lead us there amid singing, moonlight, and Bengal lights, and also take us home. With the friendly Princess, R. is in very lively spirits, though, it seems to me, somewhat on edge.

Saturday, April 22 Sirocco and a certain amount of confusion today, various letters and requests; but it is a great delight, when I return with the children from the photographer's (Boni for Gr.), to be met by R. (under the arcades). After lunch I negotiate with the agent for the P. L[oredano], which belongs to Don Carlos. Then we all go for a walk, R. wishes to make some purchases for the children, and finally we accompany Lusch home (to the Princess). During our stop at the confectioner's, R. tells me how desirous of rest he is. "Actually," he says, "we should now have all the children married off, and the two of us should be sitting for hours on end in a bower on the sunny banks of a river—that is the picture I have in my mind! We found each other too late—we should have been united much sooner." He also tells me the news of Hans's engagement. Is this perhaps the resolution of the discords Hans hinted at in his most recent letter? . . . I feel very apprehensive on the children's account. Since I am rather worn out, the evening is spent looking through the *Bayreuther Blätter*. R. is satisfied with his writing.

Sunday, April 23   R. has remembered a Verdi theme which he heard sung yesterday on the Grand Canal as a duet; he sings it to me, laughing at the way this outburst of rage was bellowed out yesterday; he made a note of its broken rhythm—"And *that* one is asked to call a natural line!"—there is nothing like it in Rossini. He reads the *Blätter* in the morning and feels that Stein's "Luther and the Peasants" is rather sketchy and bombastic. — Then he goes out, once again intent on finding presents for the children. — He tells me humorously that in Giarre, the village we gave up in favor of Riposto, a lawyer from Palermo was taken prisoner and released only against a payment of 75,000 lire—now they are about to clean up Etna. R. asks what priests are for; they are supposed to represent Christianity. Judas has triumphed, he says sorrowfully, and he speaks of Christianity, the relation of man to man—this will be his last work, he says. He reproaches Gob. for leaving out of account one thing which was given to mankind—a Saviour, who suffered for them and allowed himself to be crucified. — Over coffee we come to G[oethe]'s last letter to Frau von Stein, with Chr[istiane] Vulpius in it, and R. observes that Christiane's amiable disposition was a blessing for G. after all the "lovesicknesses," and as he was becoming increasingly serious, he surely wished to get rid of these excitements "with nothing behind them"; we talk about the moral courage required for the curious relationship with Christiane in that little town; R. asks how Schiller described her and then, going on to talk of Schiller's wife, he says earnestly and exaltedly, "I have fared better." My heart overflows at the thought that I have been permitted to share his life! — At 4 o'clock we go for a drive, wish to visit the Giardino Pubblico and hear something from *Lohengrin,* lose our way, however, and go on to the arsenal, a photograph of which attracted R. One of the ancient lions enchants him: "An ideal creature such as I have never seen before; that's how my Fafner and Fasolt should look." — And back at home, reading Baedeker, he exclaims,

"That lion is my Wotan!" He is staunchly and firmly convinced that it once stood in Marathon as a triumphal monument; it is symbolic, he says and is pleased that he felt so drawn to it, even in the photograph. — As we are returning home, a glorious sunset illumines the buildings opposite. Fidi asks regretfully why the monasteries were dissolved. R. replies to him earnestly, telling him what a pitiless power these magnificent buildings served, what symbols of arrogance they had become, though built for a completely different purpose. It is true, he continues, that the power which is attempting to take their place is not promoting the cause of sublimity, either, and so the situation is serious, and we are probably experiencing the last days of a pleasant illusion. "But we should strive to preserve, to see history as a great teacher, and not to begin again from the beginning, tearing everything down," he says, having been much moved in S. Marco by the thought of how much work had been done on this noble building over many centuries. — As he speaks, the lovely bells of Venice toll solemnly, the shadows lengthen, and the sun sinks down, gilding the other side. "You have one advantage over others—you keep me company," R. said to me before this; I scold him for expressing what I only tell myself. "But what I think about it—that you don't know," he replies. Once again I am struck by the way he expresses what I so fervently feel inside me, as also at times much more trivial matters. For instance, I had been thinking for a moment of *Der Dorfbarbier* [*The Village Barber*] for his birthday, and he says, "I must find some village barber for Fidi." (Fidi had been unwilling to let Schnappauf cut his hair.) In the evening R. reads "Signor Formica" aloud, to the enjoyment of us all.

Monday, April 24 Today at breakfast R. says jokingly, but seriously, "Truly, if there were no pope, there would be no Christianity left at all, not even sects"—to such an extent its spirit fled from the world. I visit some churches with S. while R. is reading Homer. (The report in the *B. Bl.* about vivisection in the Reichstag has once more aroused his greatest indignation.) The weather is not very favorable, we decided to stay at home, just going out in the evening to the Teatro Rossini, where once more there is a great deal of garrulity, but very good and natural acting, and a farce at the end amuses R. greatly. — R. tells us of Darwin's death.

Tuesday, April 25 R. had a good night. In our morning conversation we decide that one should only concern oneself with the very great or with "gifted eccentrics" such as Hoffmann, Carlyle, etc. Then we discuss Italian melody, and I tell R. that here it seems at times to be curiously effective, in spite of all its banalities—in some way in harmony with the air and the sky. R. agrees with me and says, "In our country everything must be locked in, and that produces a sound which has nothing to do with the visual world; it must all be locked in." — While the children are in church at S. Marco I go to the Belle Arti, spend an hour there in great delight, and am discovered by R. standing in front of M. Marziale's *Supper at Emmaus,* in which the man with the big hat makes a great impression on him, too—indeed, the whole picture, though Christ is handled rather conventionally. The small Bellini *Madonna* hanging next to it also gives him great delight, and then we rest in front of [Titian's] *Assunta,* and it makes a glorious impression. When I say that it is a totality, rather like the 9th Symphony, R. says, "Oh, we have nothing so perfect in music—that is all experimentation." — The glowing head of the Virgin Mary recalls to him his idea of the sexual urge: this unique and mighty force, now freed of all desire, the Will enraptured and redeemed. He is unable to do justice to God, the "bat," though he feels he is finely painted. However, he is captivated by the apostles. What blissful moments do we spend there! Every time he regards the head he gives an exclamation of delight. Then we stroll through the other rooms; a picture I find very attractive, *Thomas Touching Christ's Wounds,* has little appeal for him, but [Bonifacio's] *History of the Rich Man* and the one Bellini *Madonna* please him greatly. We end as we began, contemplating the old altarpiece (Annunciation) in which, R. thinks, the Madonna looks like me when I have been weeping; he says she has the expression which only he knows in me. And in contented and exalted spirits we return home. Over coffee R. talks about his future work, his greatest, in which he will loudly state what will become of a race which uses the most important, most powerful force of all, the sexual urge, merely as a basis for marriages of rank! — I have some house affairs to attend to; R. goes to the Church of S. Marco with the children, and then once again with me. [*Added two pages later but referred back to this point:* "When we left S. Marco, R. went with Eva and Fidi to the beer hall, saw there the man who once before delighted him with his imitations of animal sounds, asks him to do them, gives him a lira, but with instructions to thank him in his own way—whereupon the man bursts into the most grotesque *ringraziamenti* [expressions of thanks]."] A strange and inspiring impression, watching the surge of people making their way to the Lord's shrine; the crypt, brightly illumined, presents a similar view, but in the midst of the crush, not leaning against a picture of Christ but as if merged, kneeling, into it, a woman praying! Amid all this unheeding, yet all the same pious bustle, such fervor! Was it despair, like Gretchen before the *Mater Dolorosa,* or passionate adoration? We could not see her face. But the image gripped our hearts: this was love, this was holiness. Much did R. say about the need to preserve churches as houses for the poor, places in which love feasts would be celebrated, but without the false pomp of the clerics. — In the evening he finishes reading "S[ignor] Formica" to us, which unfortunately suffers somewhat from being too long. (A telegram from Neumann produces vexatious thoughts.)

Wednesday, April 26 A restless night for R., caused by the telegram. When I greet him at breakfast, he is reading a conversation in *Die Serapionsbrüder,* and he says, "The worst German book means more to me than the best French one—in German some mystical chord is touched of which others show no trace." But then he observes I should not take this too literally. All the same, we read with interest the remarks on quietism and the awesome quotation from Father Molinos. — Yesterday R. remarked that in his opinion the only consummate masterpiece is the *Oresteia,* though it is true that the Athenian people are in part responsible for that. He dictates to Boni his reply to Herr Batz, whose dropping out makes him very glad. But unfortunately he suffers another chest spasm on going out. Lusch tells me of a letter from her father which fills me with mournful alarm; the manner in which he announces his engagement seems to me worrisome; I tell Lulu what to reply. The weather is bad, we stay indoors and play whist, and R. reads another story by E. T. A. Hoffmann. In the conversation in *Die Serapionsbrüder* he found something which interests him greatly in relation to "Male and Female."

Thursday, April 27 R. slept well; he continues reading Hoffmann. He no longer feels like reading Turgenev, a passage in Prosper Mérimée's preface to his novel *Smoke* shows that the famous Rachel possessed all the Jewish bad habits of declamation in her French. In the morning we come to the subject of Marie Hoh[enlohe]; R. says he can understand her utter hatred of her mother, but not her sudden hostile silence toward him. We talk of the King's entrance into his life; before that his (R.'s) life had been an utterly rootless existence, he says. The weather today is stormy. R. returns from the Belle Arti with photographs of the drawings there, and these truly delight us, many by Leonardo and a splendid one by Caracci (R. calls the latter "a drama"). Later we give it to Jouk.

Friday, April 28 Today we are once more led to the subject of the "Classical Walpurgis Night," and R. calls it a veritable cathedral, so beautifully is it constructed. A fine article by Dr. Schem. in the *Blätter* brings us to it, but R. deplores the lack of humor in all these pieces. Singer news and difficulties, R. calls Vogl a bit of raw gristle! In the evening a farewell *soirée* at Princess H[atzfeldt]'s, at which R. feels ill at ease. He is embarrassed by Lusch's having gone somewhere else, and he tells me of his tendency to be jealous of his loved ones.

Saturday, April 29 A good night, nice weather, packing. R. goes out around noon and tells me he went to visit K[arl] Ritter, whose address he came upon by chance in the bookshop; given at first a wrong direction on the Riva, he sees a gray-haired gentleman at the window, asks himself, "Has Karl really altered so much?" Then, led into a room in which a lot of pictures are standing, he again asks himself, "Does he paint, too?" At last he sees his mistake, makes further inquiries, and comes to the right door, where a woman with a baby in her arms tells him that Herr Ritter is not at home; whereupon R.: "I think he is at home." The woman, embarrassed, asks if he is indeed Herr Wagner. "Yes, I am," R. says, writes on a scrap of paper, "What sort of a person are you?" and goes away. All the same, he is greatly upset by this experience; even before it, the feeling that he would have to take K. R. more or less by surprise in order to see him had brought on a prolonged chest spasm. — We also learn that our old friend Gersdorff is here and has not visited us! We leave the hotel at one o'clock, accompanied by the singers, a sight which draws people onto all the bridges, and we leave Venice, after having once again inspected the *entresol* of the P. Vendramin. We greet Verona and much else, and arrive unnoticed on

Sunday, April 30 in Tirol. At one of the stations R. is greeted joyfully by a Herr Gehring, a violist in the Dresden orchestra whom he appointed! — Concern over Boni's reserved manner. Looking at the clean houses—this is our way of doing things, he says. The country around Munich disheartening, as always! Arrival at 2; the conductor comes to meet us; Herr v. Bürkel calls on us; it is uncertain whether the King will attend the performances. To the theater with the children, *Around the World in 80 Days,* bad play, badly acted. Lenbach is with us, and R. finds him pleasant company, while to me he remains as invaluable as ever. Springlike air.

Monday, May 1 Left the Bayerischer Hof early; R. very irritated by the huge Munich railroad station, as almost always when there. In Nuremberg breakfast in the restaurant, and then great joy in the two churches, Sebaldus and Lorenz, warm satisfaction that our country, too, can offer such architectural delight. Nice impression of the countryside between Nuremberg and Bayreuth, woods and meadows. Constant waving as we approach, at the station a large crowd, our friends, Gross! Wahnfried at last, Jouk., Wolz. there. Reunion with the dogs, entrance into the *salon,* R. thanks me for our home, birds twittering— for me it is like coming into a haven of rest!

Tuesday, May 2 R. had a good night, and while I am in my bath, I hear him playing the Porrazzi melody! — There is a lot of chat with friend Jouk., then a walk in the palace gardens, where the swans from the Fantaisie both please and sadden us, since their water is not very nice. We stop at the poultry yard, the turkey amuses R.: "A butcher's shop in front, a fashion magazine behind," he says. In the evening our neighbors and the mayor, which makes R. irritable, and he flies into a great rage—I think about the newspaper here.

Wednesday, May 3 R. is still very upset from yesterday and has a great desire for peace and quiet. At lunch we talk about Saint Paul, whom R. describes as the first Christian. In the afternoon we drive up to the theater, we believe the new façade will look well. In the evening he feels very run down.

Thursday, May 4 R. slept well and wakes from a comical dream in which he was kicking the children! The Grosses and Feustel have lunch with us. Afterward we go for a walk in the palace gardens; the birds— not heard for so long—enchant us. After R. has taken me to call on the mayor's wife, I meet him again at Angermann's, where a comical incident has just taken place: he loudly criticized the beer from an outside brewery, saying it was adulterated; the director of the brewery was there, and he made a violent protest. In the evening he spent an hour by himself before supper, he is overcome by emotion, which expresses itself in a melody! — Wolzogen comes in the evening, and there is much talk about Kant. Then about vegetarians, and R. speaks warningly of deluding oneself that one is better than others. The piano score of *Parsifal* has arrived!

Friday–Saturday, May 5–6 Nothing written down, because busy with the start of rehearsals and other little preparations. Herr Levi and Herr Heckel are here for discussions about the performances.

Sunday, May 7 A warm day, and I go to the school to listen to the boys' choir, which I wish to have sing on his birthday. It moves me greatly! — Lunch with our friends the Grosses, R. in very good spirits. While he is resting, I hear Herr Jäger singing something from *Parsifal* —very well, it seems to me. In the evening, further decisions made with Levi and Heckel.

Monday, May 8 Siegfried is ill—muscular rheumatism, it seems. I hold a rehearsal with the girls, R. comes in. "I suppose you are reading a Greek tragedy," he says jokingly. He writes to the King. (In my little notebook I have written "then sang," but now, 6 weeks later, I do not know what this means.) In the afternoon he has a conference with the mayor and friend Gross which turns out very encouragingly for him. In the evening we see Fritz Brandt, the son! . . . Herr Merz is also here, there is much talk, also music (the Flower Meadow, as R. says, presented like a horseradish), and Italian melodies. When we are alone we ask ourselves when we shall be alone at last, by ourselves? The thought of our dear sweet children is our whole delight!

Tuesday, May 9 R. complains of a headache, and the weather is inhospitable. We receive a nice telegram about *Siegfried* [in London]. In the afternoon we drive up to the theater, the bells are effective, but R. is beset by great misgivings about it all as we drive home. In the evening various technical problems are discussed with Fritz Brandt.

Wednesday, May 10 Nice telegram from England. R. continues his letter to the King. Then he tells me the barometer is falling—he thought it too good to be true; he says he should sing, "Vanish, you dark arches above!" — R. says of the weather that it is like having drunk bad beer! — In the evening he plays pieces from *Die Msinger*. At lunch he talked about *T. und Isolde* in connection with his idea that Nature has a craving to produce something great and redeeming. *Tristan* is the greatest of tragedies, R. says, for here Nature is thwarted in its finest work. In the evening he talks about Beethoven, particularly the first movement of the 9th Symphony, which Beeth. marked *maestoso*—in R.'s opinion very significant for this wild, sorrow-laden piece; what this movement is cannot be expressed in words, he adds, though he had tried to do it. Then he comes to racial questions, to *Ottar Jarl*, which he is reading with interest, and the day finally ends with his longing to be alone with me. He said much more about *Tristan*—how absurd to perform a work like this for money!

Thursday, May 11 R. is not well, and we have a gloomy lunch with our friends the Grosses. A drive in the *"strapontin,"* suggested by me, does not cheer him up, either. However, he makes an effort to pull himself together when our friend Count Gobineau arrives unexpectedly. We chat about all his travel adventures, and the ill-humored mood is overcome to some extent.

Friday, May 12 R. had a good night's rest, he finishes his letter to the King. The subjects of our conversation with the Count are Catholicism, Christianity, also Asia. Alone again, we are overtaken by a mood of melancholy.

Saturday, May 13 Frau Materna writes that she would like to sing Kundry a few times at the beginning, then alternate with others. R. writes to the King (it is only today that he finishes his letter). In the evening he reads in Carlyle (*Frederick the Great*) the passage about Protestantism and Catholicism. We do not go for a drive today, spending much time in the garden; as I come down the steps from the *salon* to join him and our friends he says, "Circe approaching Odysseus and his companions!"

Sunday, May 14 R. had a good night, and he reads to me his letter to the King, in which he has mentioned Biagino [Gravina] at length. Over coffee a dispute about Italian and Flemish painters arises between the Count and Jouk. R. understood and added to what the Count said in favor of the latter, particularly Rembrandt—that he was the most significant of all by virtue of his intelligence and humor. We stroll in the garden, R. and the Count touching on a great variety of countries; in the evening he reads something from *Faust* (the "C. Walpurgis Night," I think), then he talks a lot about *Ottar Jarl,* which he finds interesting. But R. is in somewhat low spirits, though whether it is the French language or life in general which wearies him I do not know!

Monday, May 15 R. had a good night's rest, but again he has letters from Batz to vex him. I am very busy with rehearsals for the three plays. R. is still carrying on lively conversations with the Count, and when the latter praises the Persians so highly, R. raises the question whether it would be possible for us Europeans to become intimate with them. The Count thinks not.

Tuesday, May 16 R. had a good night's rest, but his first movements in the morning are always a strain on him. At lunch he talks about *Ottar Jarl,* which he finds very interesting in its details, if somewhat laborious to read. He also talks about a journey to Asia. At 12 o'clock he enjoys a walk in the garden, is pleased with our lovely dog Molly. He then visits Jouk., and is pleased with his nice portrait of his sister. Then the piano scores are sent off (Father, Mimi, Schön, Wolz.). There is much joking about the continual rehearsals, and in the evening he is extraordinarily cheerful. Among other things, he talks about Herr Schön's contribution, saying that, as with most other things, it is not enough to be of help, yet it puts him under an obligation.

Wednesday, May 17 R. slept well. He writes to Seidl about the London venture. We go for a drive, make a *"giro"* ["round trip"], as R. jokingly calls it. A letter from Herr Schön about the school idea greatly upsets R. But he calms down, and we embark on our usual conversations about "everything"; among other things, he says that popular melody was to Beethoven what doggerel verse was to Goethe. We drive out to the mental institution, where I have to order some straw mats for the comedy. Music in the evening, Boni takes part, quite well, in a duet of the *"Kaisermarsch,"* and R. plays the Andante from the 9th Symph., better, I think, than even he has ever played it before!

Thursday, May 18 The details of Ascension Day I have forgotten, remember only a very moving performance by R. of the 3rd act of *Tannhäuser,* then his decision to use the Society of Patrons for the purpose of collecting funds for the poor. Then some more Batz trouble. Also news of London from Cyriax, very positive, very favorable to Richter. Finally, the arrival of the "parson" (Else Ritter), greeted by R.

with much joking. We are still without our Eduard, since Herr Jäger has been delayed in Stuttgart.

Friday, May 19 R. had a restless night. We have our friends the Grosses at lunch. — In the evening there is much talk about the Orient; R. wonders whether Oriental people have a sense of humor. But conversation is always a little restricted when we are obliged to talk French. R. is still very much occupied with the 9th Symphony, the first movement with the marking *maestoso;* he says it is a wonderful piece, though to the shrewd professional musicians of its own time it must have looked like the work of a bungler. All sorts of tasks for me today, negotiations with Venice, selecting dresses for Boni, and rehearsals!

Saturday, May 20 In my notebook I find written down for today "Similar thoughts, symphony"—now, 6 weeks later, I can no longer explain this, remember only that R. and I so often had the same thoughts. When we talked about spas like Wiesbaden at lunch, he defined these as offering "cheap luxury and expensive vulgarity." — The skies are gray, and our evening guests, among them our two musicians, provide more vexation than relaxation.

Sunday, May 21 At lunch R. declares that he will now read only Gobineau, Schopenhauer, and himself. The first of these, he tells me, possesses much acuteness, but no real profundity. R. and I drive up to the theater. The sun is shining. The new façade of the royal box pleases us quite a lot. On the homeward journey I show R. the butterflies which I planned to release on the 22nd; he saw one of them, the first, lying dead on the steps, since the cold has been so intense the past few days, but he takes two of them from the boxes, and a swallowtail flies sturdily away. In the evening R. says with such amiable kindness that he is looking forward to what tomorrow will bring. He plays the march from the *Eroica,* describing it as truly heroic, since in its mourning it never abandons its solemn dignity.

(I remember now what the "similar thoughts" were: I decide to make use of R.'s symphony in the birthday congratulations, and I give it to Humperdinck; R., who has not mentioned it for a very long time, now asks me for it!)

Monday, May 22 Happy awakening; then, unfortunately, a chest spasm, so that the children have to wait before bringing their greetings. During this delay, sudden arrival of Gravina, joy and shock, I hide him with our Count, make signs to the children, who have all seen him, except for Blandine! At last the "Thespis Cart" can be held. R. comes downstairs, receives his congratulations. After embracing the children in tears, he goes away; Boni, still in her costume, is sobbing in the knowledge that this will be her last festival, we call her, she keeps her hands over her face, at last she hears Gravina's voice, and we withdraw! — Now our task is to surprise R. with this new arrival. The hangings are arranged in the *salon,* and after I have shown R. the little gifts in the garden—fish, golden pheasant, and roses—we enter the newly decorated room, the bell for lunch is sounded, Biagino is the first to enter. R.'s joy is very great, and he tells us the arrival has put new spirit into him, for he had been feeling very run down. A look from Else tells me that the boys have arrived. Blandine rises and speaks her toast very beauti-fully (R. tells me she looked completely transfigured) [*toast enclosed in the Diaries; see notes*], Else succeeds in disappearing without R.'s noticing, and, supported by her, the choir starts to sing quite wonder-fully, greatly affecting us all. R. hopes that his performances will go off as well as these little festival offerings! At coffee Fidi, dressed as a page, brings in the telegrams and the program for the evening, and while R. is resting and the children having a musical session at Jouk.'s, I decorate the hall for the performance. Then R. and I go off to see the black swans, which give him very great delight, and, returning home, we find the 50 boys, who, looked after by Siegfried, fill Wahnfried with the sounds of *Parsifal* and other merry noises. At 8 o'clock the company of players is ready! The first play, by Cervantes, is done in a very lively manner, but there is some nervousness with *Liebes-Not* (between the two plays Herr Humperdinck and Herr Hausberg play the Scherzo from the symphony). But it all goes as it should, and Daniela really distinguishes herself! The scenery arrangements also function without a hitch, and we have every reason to be satisfied with our success. R. remains in the best of spirits; nothing happened to spoil the day, and everything was allowed to succeed and to give R. a little pleasure. We were favored with lovely weather, and for me our success seems like a divine greeting!

Tuesday, May 23 R. slept well, and when I tell him merrily that I am not at all tired, he calls me a "splendid fellow"! But we are not allowed to remain in this gay mood; he is vexed by the hotelkeeper Herr Albert, whose arrival prevents his looking at the hangings from the King, just received, which I have put up. Lusch's slight irritation about Ferdi Jäger's success as Roldan brings us down a little from the heights, the weather is thundery, also the fact that all the young people have accepted an invitation to the Riedelsberg (R. wanted to visit the theater). But above all he is vexed by a letter from Seidl reporting on London. However, he cheers up in the evening, and Herr Albert's gift, a lantern attached to a pole, gives him the idea of marching through the garden "like glowworms," surrounded by the children, and surprising our neighbors. — (Over coffee he spoke in high praise of the "Mephisto" movement in my father's symphony and compared its style to Gobineau, who also, like Mephisto, is prepared to bow down before only one being.)

Wednesday, May 24 I am up very early in order to perform my various tasks. Els'chen works with me, pleasing me with her quiet industry. R. is content with my *West-Eastern Divan*. In the afternoon we drive up to the theater, where the scenery for the Temple of the Grail and the singing of the boys give us great delight. Unfortunately, however, the tom-toms (bells) have not been tuned, and since there is a misunderstanding with the coachman on the return journey (the Count and I are driven home, the others to the Eremitage), R. is put into an ill humor, which Pepino, requested to sing in the evening, aggravates rather than diverts. But the principal reason is probably Lulu's departure; R. says goodbye to her.

Thursday, May 25 I wake up early, accompany my daughter to the station, return through the meadows in the splendid morning air and am home in time to have breakfast with R. We have it for the first time in the turret. We take delight in the birds, and before that R. expressed his pleasure in the variegated colors of the pansies, which he compared to the equally variegated twitterings of the birds. In his reading R. is trying to establish friendly relations with *Die Kawi-Sprache,* but all the talk about spirit and matters of that sort vexes him, and he says jokingly at lunch that from now on he will read only Gobineau, Schopenhauer, and himself. In the afternoon we are again in the summerhouse with our friends, listening to the birds and taking pleasure in our good dogs. (In the morning R. wrote to Herr v. Bürkel and read his own *Beeth.*) With the Grosses, who ate with us today, R. discussed all sorts of things in connection with our performances.

Friday, May 26 Horses and coachmen come to Wahnfried, which is unfortunately covered by a gray sky. I use the former to drive to friend Gross's and report on many business matters. When I return home, R. receives me in a very cheerful way and says he has been helping Jouk., who is decorating my room; he says that some of the cloth was left over—enough for cravats for them both—but now, since an empty space remained, they are sacrificing their cravats. He is pleased that I should use what remained from the hangings in the *salon* in this way! He has been sent a printed leaflet about the significance of the Jews: they comprise our civilization, he says—that is obvious, and that is why it is worth nothing. When I come down to the *salon* around 6 o'clock, I find R. in earnest conversation with the Count; he has been asking him how he came to study such things as the Persian language, and he is pleased that I join them. He praises the Count's writings, saying that such work is the finest product of a lifetime. But they both tear lyric poetry to pieces, and R.'s motto, "I am like a flower," is seized upon joyfully by the Count and continually quoted. — In the evening R. reads to us the beginning of [Shakespeare's] R[*ichard*] *II,* to our enchantment; impossible to describe all there is in it, yet impossible not to talk about it after such a reading. — R. has read a new article by Hans which again, it seems, contains jabs at him! He uses this occasion to express his utter hatred for the musical establishment, and says, "That has been our ultimate ruin, to humiliate the only thing that could have ennobled us, in the way these concert managements, music festivals, etc., do it."

Saturday, May 27 Our main topic of conversation today is R. *II;* R. has been reading to himself the return from Ireland, and he cannot speak too highly in its praise. "He is my only spiritual friend," he says of Sh. — We drive out to the Eremitage, where R. has the fountains turned on, and this gives us tremendous pleasure. From there to the theater, where R. discusses various things with Brandt. On our return home we find a very nice letter from a Frenchman, which touches R. tremendously; he asks me to dictate a reply to him, and when this is done, he remains in a very animated mood, extolling his happiness but continually saying that it arrived 15 years too late. Wolz. comes over in the evening, and R. speaks to him quite openly, saying how much it weighs on him to have persuaded him to settle here, since he cannot bring himself now and again to share our travels. To Gobineau he also talks very animatedly, trying to persuade him to share our life completely.

Whitsunday, May 28 A lovely morning, we have breakfast in the turret; before that R. admired with Siegfried the many different colors of the pansies, and he tells me that, when he pointed out to the boy that they have completely human faces, the latter replied, "Yes, there is Prince Ramacca." I write a letter to Herr Schön according to R.'s instructions, and he signs it. In the afternoon we visit the black swans, R. and I feed them and are delighted by their tameness and their beauty, also their pleasure in one another, which they demonstrate to us literally by intertwining their necks. — In the evening R. plays to us the first two movements of the C Minor Symphony and the love scene from *Lohengrin;* he plays them wonderfully, though he himself is not satisfied; but Beethoven's genius is brought very close to us.

Monday, May 29 R. had a good night. In the morning I receive a letter from Lusch which is on the whole encouraging, but R. does not wish to know anything about it, since her departure has offended him. He reads *Die Kawi-Sprache,* would like to start on his large work, but cannot, because of the unrest the impending performances arouse in him, against which there is nothing he can do. At lunch he says that, if one wishes to describe our times, all one needs to say is, "Whereas all others respected their ancestors above all, we consider ourselves superior to everyone else." Then he talks about love and what can happen to a generation in which civilization thwarts Nature's most serious purpose. For example, he says, Romeo loves Juliet, she him, but civilization makes him marry Rosaline and Juliet marry Paris— what stock can come out of that? It is for this reason, he adds, that *Tristan* is his most tragic subject, since in it Nature is hindered in its highest work. — At coffee we receive news about London, a letter from Cyriax is read aloud, R. is upset by Grav.'s inability to understand it, and he scolds Boni for chatting with him alone, which she does to keep him from feeling left out. — In the afternoon we drive out to the Fantaisie, but unfortunately encounter many beggars on the way. However, the garden makes a charming impression, lilac and laburnum in bloom, and we are in very cheerful spirits, which rise even higher in R. when he enters our house again and from the hall catches sight of the garden through the *salon,* then the *salon* itself. He comes to me and tells me he has been looking for the children in order to say to them, "It is divine here, and my wife is divine"—now he will tell me so directly! . . . He sits in the garden with the Count while I change my clothes; soon I hear him calling me, and learn from the Count what R. has been saying about me! . . . That no man has ever had such good fortune. A charming hour ensues, surrounded by animals—doves drinking, dogs tussling with one another, blackbirds hopping unafraid on the lawn. At supper R. speaks of the Goths and how difficult it is to visualize men like Alaric and Theodoric, "beings daemonically full of themselves, yet regarded by the entire Roman world as rabble." — I observe that they were probably not unlike Alexander; R. says, "Much more daemonic." The evening is somewhat difficult; friend Wolz. comes over, but somehow it is impossible to get a conversation going, though R. is not tired.

Tuesday, May 30 The children have gone on an outing to the Waldhütte in spite of a thunderstorm. It is still very sultry, I remark on it and, after spending the morning with the Count, receive my greeting in music. [*Enclosed in the Diaries a note from Wagner:* "It is truly sultry—but I am violet—" *and a line of music, see notes.*] I go to R. and find him sitting on the *chaise longue.* "I am enjoying myself," he says and repeats that he never foresaw his present happiness, even in his dreams! We gaze with delight at the family picture and come to lunch happy and content. Over coffee R. tells Gravina that he is making it easier for Blandine to develop in her own way, since up till now she has been overshadowed by her elder sister. — In the afternoon we go to Jouk.'s to see the cover for the Grail, which has turned out too opulent-looking. R. expresses his dislike for all Israelite pomp and says that, if people even begin to observe details such as the shrine, etc., then his aim as a dramatist is lost. We return to our garden and delight in our lovely surroundings. We also delight in Isolde and Eva, who are looking particularly pretty today. R. had a dark moment this morning when he read the address on a letter from Lusch, "Frl. I. von Bülow," but the black fit passed, and he never ceases to delight in the children and to praise the womb which put its stamp on them! . . . The evening is enlivened by all sorts of things: first of all, a scene in the poultry yard in which we intervene; R., talking about it, bursts into rhapsodies about the brooding turkey hen, her self-sacrificing devotion to her young. A thunderstorm breaks, bringing hail, and the rain comes pouring into the dining room, causing a lot of commotion, but by the end of the evening all is outweighed by R.'s pleasure in the children, who really are a lovely sight. — Dr. Schemann drops in for a few minutes; R. reproaches him for his Cherubini and its mistaken approach; he says he was neither a tragic figure nor a forerunner, but an excellent musician, often indeed just a craftsman. On the other hand, he praises his piece on Goethe. (Telegram from Herr N[eumann] about the success of *Götterdämmerung*. R. replies, "The risk was great, yet Wagner says, 'Let's not spare our thanks and praise.' " —) At the end of the evening, after our neighbor's wife and Count Gobineau have left, he lets out a sigh about life, I reply soothingly, he: "I want to go away to some place with what belongs to me." . . . Yesterday, when I went to him, he quoted to me from *Othello*—"Perdition catch my soul, but I do love thee"—and says one has to have felt this in order to understand. —

Wednesday, May 31 The remarkable feature of our life recurs today: I notice that Loldi has many fair hairs on her cheeks, and this occupies my thoughts in the evening; in the morning R. tells me he dreamed that Fidi had whiskers on his cheeks! — The weather is sultry and overcast in spite of the thunderstorm, R. is much vexed by a rude answer from our manservant, he comes to tell me about it, but when he arrives, the chambermaid is doing my hair, and this prevents him; then, when I go to look for him, I cannot find him. At last I discover he is in the middle of a chest spasm, and he asks me to have lunch with our guests without him. But by the end of the meal he seems to have recovered. In the afternoon we go for a walk in the palace gardens, but the gray skies, the sudden timidity of the swans, and above all some very stupid military music do nothing to raise our spirits. A visit from Dr. Schemann and Wolz. tends to upset R. somewhat, he comes back to Cherubini and says that there should be much more criticism: "You bury your noses so much in books, while everywhere there are things waiting to be attacked. Military music, for example—am I to put up with my son or someone like Stein having to march to this— —music? Conservatoires, concert promoters—all these should be dealt with; instead of this we churn out God knows what." — In the evening, however, he is very tired, and when our Count leaves early, feeling worn out, R. also goes off to bed. (He told me recently that the government is issuing a law against vivisection.)

Thursday, June 1 R. had a good night, the latest news about the [*Ring*] cycle in London is good. Our friends the Grosses have lunch with us, and that gives rise to information of all kinds, also to many complaints about the local workers, who were to blame for the trouble in our dining room. For me today trousseau troubles, but above all concern about the Count, who really is not at all well. — A letter from Daniela about the music festival has a far from pleasant effect on R.; the fact that there is comment about the 44 violins of *T. und I.* which have to be fought against displeases him all the more since it is said in connection with the Brahms concerto, which Rub. had severely criticized in the *Blätter!* But our pleasure in our home outweighs all else, and even though R. says we returned two months too early, since there is nothing for him to do here, we much enjoy a drive to the Fantaisie today. At supper he talks about the Count's views on languages, their connection with the various races, and the worthlessness of mixed languages; and he warmly ascribes the clarity of his ideas on this subject to Gobineau. "Long life to you!" he exclaims to our tired friend. . . . In the evening he plays for Biagino the *Parsifal* Prelude, much annoyed by the piano score, and also the end of the second act of *Tannhäuser.* — Biagino tells me today, joking yet touched, how R. had commented on his own character, how he allowed such trifles to upset him, and how he had added, "I should have discovered Cosima fifteen years earlier."

Friday, June 2 R. had a restless night, but he is not aware of it in the morning. Around lunchtime he receives a letter from Herr Vogl, who declares himself unwilling to sing without his wife. R. sends the letter via Levi to Herr v. Bürkel. Meanwhile I have a consultation with the doctor about our friend—it is not at all encouraging! I resolve to do all I can to keep our friend here with us. Still having lunch in the hall; today is Saint Blandine's Day, R. gives Boni a lovely fan—the first Catholic feast day we have ever celebrated! — Over coffee there is talk about the part that life plays in fiction; the Count says he has invented nothing, and the motives which lead to a book's being written are more interesting than the book itself. R. says, half in German, half in French, "That reminds me of the King of Prussia, who once, in connection with *Tr. und Is.,* said Wagner must have been very much in love when he wrote it. Yet anyone familiar with my life well knows how insipid and trivial it was, and it is quite impossible to write a work like that in a state of infatuation. Yet probably it was due to my longing to escape from my wretched existence into a sea of love. It is this kind of unfulfilled longing which inspires a work, not experience!" — We drive up to the theater, the Temple of the Grail, Flower Garden, wilderness, highly delight us. [*Enclosed in the Diaries a telegram from the Brückner brothers in Coburg:* "Greatly pleased to have worked to your satisfaction, and many thanks for your telegram."] R., too, is still feeling much joy over our return home, and he calls out to me from the garden how happy he is: "You and I, just think what we are, and so we want others to share in our happiness!" — I go to him, the Count then joins us, we talk about our friend Gross, his absolute loyalty. Also about the attitude of the superior to the inferior races, the Negroes, for instance. R. says the greatest triumph for the intellectually superior person is to win the love and devotion of those beneath him, whereupon the Count says such love can be found among Negroes, but not mulattoes. — At lunch R. said that W. v. Humboldt was driving him to despair with all his drivel about his ideas, excellent as these may be in themselves. He also expresses his antipathy toward the English language; the fact that in it a Shakesp. has emerged does not disturb him—that is an anomaly; but imaginative writing is possible only in a language in which one feels every word to be alive. The German language is still half alive. He cites the verb *"sprechen"* ["to speak"] as a living word, whereas *"reden"* ["to talk"] is a constructed, dead word. I think I understand correctly what he then added: that English was a created language (under H. VII), since before that time French was spoken, and that Shakespeare was able to work creatively with a language in the process of creation, rather like Dante; however, by the time the *mixtum compositum* was finally established, poetry was already dead. — In the evening R. plays to us the lovely Andante from Mozart's D Minor Symphony, then something from the E-flat Major, later from *Euryanthe* and *"Lützow's wilde Jagd."* He speaks pityingly of the way Weber was forced to throw all his splendid inspirations into the operatic form. I had the feeling that the evening had been spent very harmoniously, but afterward I hear R. complaining of being "obliged to entertain all these donkeys." I beg him to do only what gives him pleasure.

Saturday, June 3 R. is somewhat indisposed, the Vogl affair is upsetting him, and the expected arrival of Herr Batz is a burden on him. He had hoped to see this gentleman only in friend Gross's office, but then he comes along with his wife and throws R. into a fury with his way of behaving. Nothing is accomplished today, and a conference is arranged for tomorrow with friend Gross at the mayor's. A nice

letter from Richter reports the great success of *Die Msinger* in London
and tells us, just at the right moment, how excellent the tenor Winkelmann was. At the same time we receive a French newspaper which
describes the encoring of *Tr. und Isolde* in Aachen as a sign of the times.
After all these somewhat varied news items, R. tells us of Garibaldi's
death, adding that he was a classical figure and belonged to the time
of Timoleon. — In the evening R. is very tired.

Sunday, June 4 He had a good night, but his disgust at having
anything to do with a person like Herr Batz, his having (as he puts it) to
keep starting over from the beginning, and also the unpleasantness of
his relations with the Vogls—all this upsets him greatly! And *Die
Kawi-Sprache* is providing insufficient enjoyment. He compares this
work to his *Opera and Drama* and says, "Such things are studies,
explorations which one makes for one's own benefit, but which ought
not to be published." However, he feels his *Opera and Drama* was more
clearly defined. — Friend Gross comes around with the mayor and
tells us they have just been having a discussion, the outcome of which
is nil. It is very revealing of this individual that Herr Batz thought
R. was in debt to these gentlemen, and that was the reason for their
taking his part in such a lively fashion! . . . However, R. soon recovers
his spirits and is firmly resolved not to have anything more to do with
this man whom he finds so repulsive. — He writes to Seidl today, I
to Richter. In the afternoon we are visited by a Dr. Druffel, army
physician from Minden and representative of the W[agner] Society
there. We spend a while in the turret, where the talk is much less about
the Society than about brigands; our Count openly expresses his
loathing of them, yet at the same time tells us things about their
behavior—such as their respect for women—which reveal such
generosity that R. feels they must stem from different and very ancient
times. — Garibaldi's death has caused a great stir in Rome; R. compares
him to Timoleon, though in our times the example looks less estimable!
For R. there is something great and epic about his final journey to
Sicily, and the fact that politics were behind the hero's great deeds in
no way reduces his greatness. — A thunderstorm is hanging threaten-
ingly over us as we have supper in the hall. R. thinks of *Lear* and,
recalling both this play and Othello, ruined by "a corporal's cunning,"
exclaims, "He was the greatest of them all." Then he reflects on Sh.'s
12 years of activity, his retirement to Stratford, drinking his glass of
wine with the rest after having shown us the world as it is, yet never
revealing himself. Then he opens *Lear* at the 3rd act, and Kent's question "Who's there, besides foul weather?" arouses his mirth. — And
again and again, in good times and bad, we are today as much aware
as ever of what we mean to each other, more fervently perhaps after

18 years than at the beginning! — And birds are building their nests in our *salon!* Yesterday we thought a little bird had got lost, and we tried to free it, but today we discover that three nests have been started, and there is a constant fluttering to and fro. This afternoon, R. tells me, when he came downstairs a little bird was trying to get in, but when it became aware of him it flitted away like Siegfried's bird before Wotan. — Over coffee the martyrdom of Saint Blandine was mentioned; the Count spoke of the misunderstandings behind canonizations: she had certainly been a heretic, but the church represented her to the people as a pure Catholic; R. argues heatedly that it is the example which makes so great an impression—what the church does with it, 10 years or so after death, is of no account; what is inspiring is the martyrdom. And such beings as Saint Francis—they ultimately unwittingly served the church's ends, even if they had nothing in common with it. Like, for example, the Count's lame sister, who from her 14th year had no thoughts but to become a nun; it is examples like these, R. says, which the Jesuits promote, and it is these which give them their strength. Before this we had been talking about mercy, about Calderón's play *La devoción de la cruz;* in it R. sees a very profound truth, which, however, was bound to lead to abuses of the worst kind.

Monday, June 5   R. slept well and is cheerful in spite of all unpleasant embarrassments. From his room in the morning he sings to me "We belong to the temperance society!" in connection with *Die Kawi-Sprache,* which he finds very boring. I go in, and we look at the portraits of me. "You can believe me," he says, "it is impossible to paint either of us." A letter from Lulu saddens us, and R. reproaches himself for having exposed the girl to such conflicts through his interference. What he finds worst of all, he says, is that even here there is nothing he can do. Since our Count is now feeling somewhat better, our conversations are also cheerful. In the afternoon R. and I go for a walk in the palace gardens. We chat in the evening, and R. amuses us with his remark that educated, intelligent people write boring books, but are very pleasant in conversation. At supper he expressed his dislike of Ariosto and the whole of what he calls Renaissance poetry, which is based on Vergil, another poet he cannot bear. Cervantes, on the other hand, comes immediately after Shakespeare, in his opinion. — Gob. talks about French audiences and tells us, among other things, of a man who, after seeing a Racine play, told him that such things make him feel like a better person! R. declares that German audiences, furthermore, are merely a copy of the French, and he utterly rejects my claim that they are better than French ones. — In the end he accepts my "neglected talents," but he says they will put up with anything, and their music-making, glee-club activities are a kind of hypocrisy. How would it be possible otherwise, he asks, for them to cheer all sorts of other things besides Beethov.? And articles by Hans, etc., can still be published, and a composer as wretched as Saint-Saëns is said to have written the best German opera after his, R.'s.

Tuesday, June 6 R. had a good night, and with untroubled hearts we wish our Siegfried many happy returns. R. proposes the toast at lunch, but says he cannot make a speech. The celebrations are continued at Jouk.'s in the afternoon, R. comes along, but he soon has enough of all the dancing, smoking, and shouting, and we return home with the Count, spending some time in the turret talking about great modern politicians, Thiers, Guizot, etc. R. says one glimpse from afar of this political world is enough to make him vow never again to take part in world affairs. In the evening he plays us the Prelude to *T. und I.* and moves us all deeply, with the exception of our good Count, who, the minute it ends, gets up to tell R. the Swedish verb we were searching for when R. asked where the English "*I am*" could have come from. — Much amusement over this!

Wednesday, June 7 We all wake up feeling well; R. reads through his *State and Religion* and is pleased with its good sense. At lunch we talk about the Greeks and the Persians, and the Count goes to the length of declaring that the Persians would always have beaten the Greeks! But R. intends to pursue his theory about Alexander and to read his history of the Persians. — R. and I drive up to the theater, summoned by Herr Brandt, and inspect the tower, meadow, and transformation scenery with satisfaction; R. is very pleased with it all. We have some beer in Herr Moritz's little garden, amid caresses from Faf and Freia, and R. exclaims that life among artists is the only pleasant life, only artists understand. He then talks about the use of painting on the stage, saying it is like the use of music in drama; people may hold it in contempt, but in fact it provides the living element; and he puts machinists above architects, who nowadays can only imitate. — Returning home, we say goodbye to Biagino. Then a letter from Daniela claims our sorrowful attention—oh, Lord! . . . R. reproaches himself for having restored the link between the child and her father. — A diversion is provided by Herr Seitz's publication of the costumes, an act which rather surprises us. In the evening R. reads the first pages of *State and Religion* to us, then his poem to the King, written almost 18 years ago. He finds the sentiments expressed in it embarrassing and deplores the things one does in order to escape the specter of boredom.

Thursday, June 8 Our conversations nowadays are absorbed by poor Lusch, R. now looks upon her as if she were "buried alive," and my heart is heavy on that account. After lunch R. and I drive to the mayor's, where we hear all kinds of things: first, Herr Vogl's final decision; second, a malicious report of smallpox in Bayreuth, which has led to numerous inquiries! [*A few words based on untranslatable word play omitted.*] In the evening R. reads to us from *Faust,* Part Two, the soliloquy and the scene between Faust and Mephisto; he was led to it by the quotation "Stench and activity," and our joy in this unique work is beyond expressing. (He writes to Plett[ung] & Schwab.)

Friday, June 9 R. does not feel very well, and he takes medicine. But at lunch, for which our friends Gross and the mayor are present, he is very cheerful; he is very glad that there are no difficulties in Munich regarding Vogl. He prefers not to read a letter from Lusch, and a letter from M. Dönh[off] produces an exclamation about "trivial" women—"penwipers," as he calls them, in whom there is nothing genuine, whom one cannot pin down. Before that he told me that I would not believe how dead, dead, everything seemed to him, lying around his feet like faded rose petals. Toward evening we again touch on the subject of Normans and Saxons with the Count; R. agrees with our friend that the Normans were the last heroic race, but he disputes the assertion that they brought culture to all the countries they conquered; what they did, he says, was to utilize the energies already at hand, particularly in England; and he quotes the line in *Faust* about the companion who "must goad and tease and as a devil toil to serve creation," saying that such were the Normans! The quotation leads us to the prologue, which he then reads to us. — Before the reading I mentioned what R. told me this morning at breakfast about Richard II's boldly spirited behavior during Tyler's Rebellion, and how he offered himself to the people as their leader. In the Normans R. recognizes these qualities of humor and courage, but he finds it reprehensible that they—alone among the German tribes—lost their language.

Saturday, June 10 R. slept well, we have a peaceful breakfast, after which I set out to make some calls and encounter difficulties with Dean Caselmann on the subject of duplicate weddings. My report on this at lunch leads to a conversation about the two confessions; R. tells the Count that, in defending the incarnation of Assyrian Semitism, he is contradicting himself; Protestantism is the final expression of the Germanic consciousness, and even the Protestants had been too few in number. Over coffee R. shows us some things in the *India* volume and says how pitiful Europeans look in comparison. I mention Greek temples as an example to the contrary; he says I am right and enters into a very lively description of the Greek character, which, he says, was unique in the world in terms of talent and vitality, since in this very small entity every part was alive. Later we set out on a walk, R. and I, but are caught in the rain; it is also cold, and R. shows me some wilting buds, the summerhouse is very damp; we return home, much depressed. But I soon recover, and the sun also emerges for a while. R. comes up to me and complains of our bad luck; I tell him about a letter from Herr Francke, but R. does not wish to renew his contract, on account of Herr Neumann. — Many times today R. complains of finding the world so unpleasant, he says he feels like giving everything up and moving permanently to Italy; he told me yesterday that he was in such despair about everything that it would not worry him at all if Fidi were to go his own way entirely. Reproductions in the *I. Zeit.* of portraits of Mart[in] Luth[er] and his wife by Cranach do not please him, either. He leaves me, telling me, however, that I should come soon to see what he is doing. When I go down to the *salon,* he is reading Hume's *History of England.* (At lunch he told us that he was occupying himself as, according to the Talmud, the Almighty occupied Himself: He read the Bible; R. was reading his own writings. And he humorously compared himself to the Almighty in the *Faust* prologue, in which, according to him, Gob. was Mephisto.) He does not much enjoy the evening; the Count talks a lot about Sweden and Norway, and R. finds the French language, with its lack of accentuation, disagreeable. — But he reads to us two sagas from Lachmann's collection, the ones about the skald in America who, without revealing his identity, gave the Icelanders a ring and a sword for Thurida; both he and the rest of us are completely gripped by the magnificent character of these things.

Sunday, June 11   R. is in poor spirits in the morning—the cold, raw weather is inimical to him. He starts an article for the *B. Blätter* about his school idea, and he says to me he is curious whether I shall allow it to pass, since he "grumbles" so much in it. "When the Bashkirs are on the march," he exclaims, "I no longer bother my head about music." Over coffee the conversation comes back to racial questions; friend Joukowsky argues in behalf of the bourgeoisie, the Count attacks it, until, through R., it is made clear that the Count is not defending a social structure, but the purity of the blood. The weather forbids a walk; R. strolls around the garden with the dogs, mainly Marke, always the most faithful of his companions. In the afternoon he continues reading Hume (on R. II), and he remarks how superior the poet is to the historian; in history everything looks just cruel and crude, but the poet reveals the suffering individual behind it all and thus arouses our sympathy. At supper he quotes Humboldt's statement on the difference between ancient and modern poetry—that modern poets fashion their characters from the inside, the ancients, on the other hand, from the outside, and this is what gives them the appearance of types, monotonous types even, but excellent with buskins and masks for an audience of 30,000. When Jouk. tells us that he is now reading Schiller's dramas, we start to discuss them; in *Kabale und Liebe* R. sees a true picture of the times, and he speaks with some emotion of the German spirit which raised itself from a state of submission and devotion to take its place among the most liberated of spirits. "One could really be excused for ascribing a special mission to the German spirit." "And it is not easy to renounce that." When, in the course of further conversation about poets—who, as R. says, must envisage characters such as Faust and Mephisto, D. Quixote and Sancho, some in Dante and Vergil, and all in Shakespeare—Goethe is mentioned, Jouk. remarks that he can recognize no characters in *Elective Affinities.* "In an idealized experience," says R., "that is a problem." — In the evening he reads aloud his favorite scene between Falstaff and the Lord Chief Justice, and then he plays us parts of the last movement of [Opus] 111 and the whole first movement of 101 (A Major), to our enchantment; we all agree with him when he passionately declares that with these works Beethoven opened up a whole new world, all of it melody, conjuring up figures no eye could see. "But music is finished," he exclaims sorrowfully, "and I don't know whether my dramatic explosions can postpone the end. It has lasted only a very short time. Yet these things have nothing to do with time and space." He recalls how in times of deepest trouble the German people discovered this refuge, this other world. Then he adds gaily how nice it is that one's precursors always mean the most to one—it is always the works of others which come into his mind, never his own. At our request he then plays something of his own, the conclusion of Act I of *Die Walküre.* He expresses the hope that my father will play something to us, saying that he is the only person with whom he can make music. — On coming in from the garden, he wrote down a symphonic theme: "All I need is quiet, then it swarms all around me." — In the evening he also looked at the score of [Gluck's] *Armide,* and amid great merriment showed us the *"ici l'on danse"* ["here there is dancing"]. — But over coffee he recalls the celebrations for his 50th birthday, which he spent entirely alone with Pfistermeister, a man whom he found repulsive, yet who was so important to him! I tell him how I imagined his life to be at that time, saying I could not but assume that his life was something of a gilded one. He says that, to judge by my father's, it is no wonder I assumed that.

Monday, June 12 R. works on his letter to Schön, I have the same difficulties with the Catholic parson as with the Protestant one! A letter from Lusch in Nuremberg deeply affects me, but the girl is conducting herself well. We drive up to the theater, where R. unfortunately gets very annoyed, since work on the King's box is making hardly any progress. In the evening we are faced with the problem of how to receive the Grand Duke of Schwerin, and it is indeed a difficult problem, since it seems the King will this time be offering no hospitality, and indeed the King is making the need to receive foreign princes his excuse for not coming at all.

Tuesday, June 13 The gray and windy weather makes R. downright indignant, and when he sends for more champagne at lunch, he says all that is left to do is either to drink or to grumble. In the morning he works on his letter to Schön and tells us jokingly that he is complaining about everything. In the afternoon we drive up to the theater and see things which do not please us—the first woodland scenery and the final transformation scene; the cupola of the Temple of the Grail also does not satisfy us completely. — The *B. Blätter* makes a good impression on R. with its account of the *Parsifal* reading by actors in Brunswick. Then R. talks with the Count about the religious reality of the Persian and also the Greek theater; he says the various actions shown in it suggest the priest taking the holy wafer himself; this no longer happens, and what he, R., is showing is the dream vision. In the evening R. reads to us *Faust,* Part One, the scenes from the walk up to the entrance of the "traveling student"—the first scene with Mephisto strikes R. as particularly masterly. Late in the evening, when we are already in bed and about to fall asleep, I hear R. say: "What makes a person beautiful? A direct communication between the heart and the brain." He was thinking of our girls. [*A sentence based on untranslatable word play omitted.*]

Wednesday, June 14 R. had a restless night and complains about the wild dreams which frightened him in the early morning. But he is in good spirits, and he talks to me of the absurdities arising from the music's need to repeat itself—thus, for example, in Klärchen's appearance to Egmont, when what she has already told him about his impending execution is repeated, it is as if she were saying to him: "Did you hear what I said? You are to be executed." The same thing in the second act of *Fidelio.* — We have many Batz problems, he extricates himself by sending a telegram to Voltz, saying he wishes to deal only with him, and surrenders a fourth share of the royalties. He summons us to lunch with the tom-tom which has just arrived from London, but he himself comes in later, since his vexation over these Batz affairs has quite spoiled his appetite. He welcomes Herr Levi, just arrived; many things discussed, but quite pleasant ones. After lunch he goes for a walk in the garden despite the bad weather, then he comes up to my room and reads to me things from his letter, about my father, then about Brahms's symphonies! — Later he joins the Count, with whom I am talking, and plays the "Meadow," but breaks

off, distracted by a blackbird, to which he listens in enchantment'
And it is quite true, the bird's call is beyond description in its variety
and "wit," as R. calls it—also R.'s own calls to the little fellow sitting
all by himself on the roof of the summerhouse in the rain and making
such efforts to attract a mate: "You poor little creature," "You good
boy," and many more! "The creatures are better than their Creator,"
he says finally. A telegram from Voltz, announcing his arrival "very
shortly," amuses R. with its formulation. The *B. Blätter* contains an
article against eating meat which impresses R. greatly; he says he
wishes only to drink milk, he finds the idea of meat repulsive. — In the
evening he plays his Bach prelude, then Levi plays an organ fantasy
as well as a fugue from the *48 Preludes and Fugues,* and finally a cantata is
played, "*Gleichwie der Regen und Schnee,*" which, however, seems rather
mastersingerish, clumsy. R. says that makes it all the more wonderful
that the pieces we heard earlier had emerged from this same world!
With regard to the Overture to *Die Feen,* R. spoke very strongly
against publishing these juvenile or occasional compositions, "which
in any case owe their origin to by no means the most auspicious of
occasions." —

Thursday, June 15   R. slept well, but it worries me that he will not
keep to his prescribed diet and is, for instance, now having milk,
coffee, and butter in the morning. — A great source of worry for me
today was Siegfried, whom I came upon very early in the morning,
already frittering his time away! This disturbs me so much that, after
the business talks with friend Gross are over, I tell R. of my concern
and the measures I feel it would be desirable to take. R. has also been
keeping Fidi under observation, his running wild, and he also fears
signs of effeminacy. We close the "chapel," Fidi's main pastime—R.
inspects it and thinks it no longer suitable for his age. — Over coffee
R. reads aloud parts of his article. — This is followed by many complaints about the weather, which is indeed very bad. A volume the
Count has given him brings R. to the subject of French poetry, which
he says is not poetry as far as he is concerned, since it makes use of such
prosaic expressions (for instance, "*avoir sous la main*" ["to have ready
to hand"]). He also says he is against the Normans, since they gave
up their own language—and for such an alien one. At lunch we came
to Hoffmann, and he says he cannot understand why a ballet has not
been made out of "*Prinzessin Brambilla,*" he has often suggested it. —
Then his rage over the bad weather gives him the idea of having a
saloon carriage built. We have no music in the evening, but the subject
of repeats is discussed; R. mentions an example in Cherubini's *Médée,*
and when I say that Gluck surely never made such errors, he says,
"Oh, yes, he did," and shows us a passage in *Iphigénie* which is simply

marked *da capo*. He repeatedly expresses his disgust with present-day music making.

Friday, June 16 R. slept well, but with a lot of dreams: twice about the German Emperor, who paid him a very friendly visit, and R. kissed his hand; the Empress was also very gracious, but when they left, they stepped not onto the staircase, but onto a sort of chicken ladder; while he was wondering at their choosing that way, R. woke up! For me much searching among papers, still in connection with Herr Batz. In contrast, R. praises Herr Neumann, who, before giving up his directorship in Leipzig, is staging all of R.'s works there. R. recently wrote to him, "I admire you." [*A sentence based on untranslatable word play omitted.*] Talking about some married couple and caresses, R. says, "Caresses should always be accompanied by tears." But today's great joy was you, my Siegfried! You were very good in the way you answered me today, and your father, to whom I sent you, was also pleased with you! . . . Yesterday evening your father said one felt like despairing when one thought of the offspring of great men, Goethe, Schiller, Weber (him in particular, says R., having bad memories of Max v. Weber); he said he realizes more and more how important it is to keep character and the need to strengthen it well in mind. Well, today we are hopeful, my son, and if one day you should discover these lines—perhaps when you are already straying onto wrong paths— may your mother's blessing, your mother's joy point the way! . . . Mocking at the weather, R. says how very necessary it is to keep 1,200,000 men on their toes in order to stop the French from taking over this country, but if he had his way, he would sell it to the French and go off to Taormina with the money! [*From* "but if he had" *to the end obliterated in ink by an unknown hand.*]

However, we snatch a favorable moment and go for a walk in the palace gardens, R. and I. The blackbirds delight us, and the swans are a poem in themselves. In the evening R. reads Stein's "Solon" to us, and we are astonished at the profundity of its thought and its intelligent construction; also by the characterization—R. finds Croesus, for example, a mixture of decency and excitability. (Yesterday R. was emphatically in agreement with Jean Paul's statement that the artistic temperament is rooted in intelligence; he says it is true that intelligence does not provide inspiration—"all our present-day gentlemen compose intelligently"—but it is necessary in recapturing the inspiration. —) — Over coffee he particularly singled out Hans's *Nirwana* for mention, and regretted that it would be impossible for him to say that he finds it much more significant than any other modern composition: "Hans would take that as mockery."

Saturday, June 17 A somewhat restless night. Severe cold, and departure of the Count, which fills us with gloomy thoughts. R. finishes copying out his fine letter to Herr Schön and brings it to me in the afternoon. At lunch our talk is mainly about the Count and his fate; but over coffee we talk about the state of the German Reich (Bism. is reported to have declared that he is uncertain whether F. Wilm. III had not been very wise to refuse the imperial crown). R. stresses the difference between the motives of Baron von Stein, who wished to see the German clans united in order to rescue something in the German spirit, and those of Bismarck, which reflected the arrogance of the Prussian *Junker*. — In the afternoon we go for a walk, and if the sky, the trees, the strolling people make us feel melancholy, the effect of the military band, playing the most vulgar of dances and marches, plunges us into utter gloom! — At supper R. tells us that he has written to Dannreuther, enclosing in an envelope bearing the most detailed address just one single word, "Excellent!" — After supper the distribution of the roles is discussed, and R. is firmly resolved to reject all the singers' pretensions (about "creating" the roles). I read aloud his letter, which makes the impression it is bound to do. He already told us at supper that he has cut out the joke about Niemann and his beard: "I remembered you; when I made it, I was not thinking of you, and so I was rude." — He says he no longer has any desire to be witty in public. He resolves to write something about military music and send it to Fritzsch's periodical, since he is still very well disposed toward Herr Fritzsch. He reads to us parts of Dr. Grysanowski's article (*Bayr. Blätter*), which he finds admirable (on the war), but he adds that it is quite impossible to exert an influence on anything, it is all the same whatever one writes.

Sunday, June 18   R. has a slight chest attack, but he decides not to pay much more attention to the diet, but to treat this complaint as a form of hiccups. Fortunately he is looking very well! . . . He corrects his article, takes it to the neighboring house himself (a letter has arrived from Herr Schön, but he does not wish to read it, preferring his letter to be published without prejudice). Before lunch he sits in the garden, Siegfried and Eva join him there, and he tells me he has been enjoying a wonderful ten minutes; a bit of sunshine makes one unutterably grateful, he says, and one would be content with the tiniest scrap of earth. Over coffee he delights in the blue wallpaper in the *salon,* the coats of arms, and he thanks Jouk. for the former. The costumier from Frankfurt, Herr Schwab, is here, also Fritz Brandt, and so we set out on a drive to the theater via the Eremitage with the entire "art of the future." R. is very merry. On stage he climbs right up to the rigging loft and tries out the tom-tom (which he calls the "*Adam-Dam*"). But already the sky is clouding over! . . . In the evening

I put on the Kundry costume, which does not entirely come up to our expectations. Our conversation turns to music, and R. points out how much finer and nobler—never mind that the whole idea came from Rossini—the prayer in *Moses* is than the *unisono* conspiracy chorus in *Les Huguenots*. When everybody has gone, I read to R. my draft of the letter to the mayor which R. asked me to write; he thinks it good. — Talking about his work yesterday, he said he now leaves so much out; to hear the peacock calling is enough to distract him (the peacock's call gives him great delight—he said recently that he felt as if he had been transported to India).

Monday, June 19   R. slept well, even if he now wakes up between 4 and 5 every morning. The weather is gray, and thoughts of his relations with Herr Batz not calculated to cheer him up. At times he comes very close to the idea of fleeing from all this senseless muddle. At lunch he jokingly described to Loldi how he could see himself with her on a desert island, with dogs instead of people; a cow would plead with her to milk it, which she would do; now and again one would see a sinking ship, bringing a letter from Eva, for Eva would give her letters only to sinking ships, these being the only ones which ever saw the island. — In the morning he strained himself trying to move his big dressing chair by himself, and he has to miss his preparations with the conductor. He reads Hume and is very taken with H[enry] V, intends to look at Shakespeare again to find out why we find him so unsympathetic there. He thinks it may be because of our feelings for the "genius" Falstaff. — At lunch he talks about *Die Zauberflöte* and remarks how seldom—except perhaps in the choruses—the music is superior to the text, and that is what is so nice about it. Then the case of Herr Vogl is discussed, along with his various achievements; in the course of the conversation R. calls him an "ironical court clerk" and talks of his policeman's sarcasm. Over coffee he reads a nice letter from Herr Scaria, whose participation pleased him; but when Herr Neumann is ironically referred to in the letter as "Herr Ehrenmann" ["man of honor"], R. says he stands outside all these things like [*not completed*], and he relates Richter's anecdote of the conductor Proch, who was always anxious to get things over with, and who, after the last word of the dialogue ("Rogue!") and the shot, immediately launched the orchestra on the elegiac melody about the clouds which cover the sun. R. also talks about the orchestration of *T. und Isolde,* which he thinks decidedly too rich in the 2nd act, particularly for the very insignificant singers of today. — Around 4 o'clock R. and I drive up to the theater in the *strapontin,* which always pleases him; costume session, which can be divided into three stages: (1) horror; (2) absurd comicality of the figures demonstrating the things to us; (3) earnest and worried efforts to alter them! However, in the end I feel we shall be able to save the day. But, oh, our feelings of having been let down! On our return home, when R. and I are alone, he has much to say on this subject! — In the evening R. is very tired; we have some music, and Herr Humperdinck plays a pretty song of his own, the only thing to criticize being the tremendous amount of modulation underlying a fairly unremarkable theme. R. and I agree that, just as Rossini foretold riches for the man who 50 years hence would invent the stagecoach, so it would be for the man who one day would revive *"Lützow's wilde Jagd"* or even *Der Dorfbarbier!* The American March is played, R. remarks that it was badly done, but once again it pleases me with its breadth and its fine popular flavor. — "If I did it right, I should not be Tell," R. says after trying to play a Beethoven quartet in an arrangement for piano duet and breaking off. We then recall our duets together in Tribschen and those lovely years of solitude. — (In a copy of Cramer's music encyclopedia dated 1783 R. read with interest the testimony regarding the 13-year-old Beethoven, of whom it was prophesied that he would become another Mozart; he remarks how greatly those times differed from our own in acuteness of judgment.)

Tuesday, June 20 R. had a good night's rest, and our first conversation concerns the Flower Maidens' costumes. Loldi makes us a drawing, and we decide on naturally wavy hair with no headdress. Around noon R. has a rehearsal with Herr Humperdinck and Herr Levi, and he seems satisfied, but he is worn out. At lunch we have the two army doctors who took part in the performance; R. read the script of the play and, with happy memories of my little jest, reproached me for not yet having shown the two gentlemen any courtesy. So they share our meal, and happy memories of the 22nd are exchanged. Over coffee our conversation turns to Schiller, and R. reads from Streicher's little book about [Schiller's] flight an anecdote that delights him— how transported Schiller was at a performance of [Benda's] *Ariadne auf Naxos,* while the others were just inclined to laugh. — R. takes a rest, and afterward we go for a drive together in the direction of Drossenfeld, which pleases him. Enormous delight at being by ourselves! We are silent, we talk—even our worries (about the singers, etc.) bring us close together! How I should like to "go abroad," as is inscribed on Dürer's grave, together like this, "unseparated, eternally united"! — The evening produces some vexation for R.: he dislikes the "authentic" helmets of the Knights, would prefer a cap with a cloth veil, and since Jouk. does not understand him properly, he loses his temper and leaves the table, then does a drawing himself and returns. He gradually calms down, and the evening passes in friendly conversation (for example, he relates some of his recurring dreams—

that he has not sent money to his wife Minna; that he is on intimate terms with King Fr. W. IV; that he is performing old operas of his which are unsuccessful; that in Paris he has to fetch some money of which he is ashamed, since it is a settlement; then what he calls his "coward's dreams"), and we crown the evening with the "Classical Walpurgis Night" from *Faust*. — (During our drive R. delightedly recalled its popular style, reminded of it by the Biblical expression "to kick against the pricks," which he believes occurs in Saint Paul's vision and which he finds splendid. "Hans," he adds, "kicks against the pricks and gets covered in blood as a result!" . . . This quotation brings to mind the noble simplicity of the Gospels, and R. remarks sadly that there can be no help for a world to which these "good tidings" mean nothing.)

Wednesday, June 21 R. had a restless night, and he confesses to me that this Voltz-Batz affair is always at the back of his mind, and that it is causing him constant inner anxiety. Today he rehearses part of the 2nd act. Before that Jouk. discovered in a book of costumes an illustration of the knight's cap he wants. At lunch R. remembers Gravina with high praise. We drive up to the theater. The discrepancy between the transformation scenes and the music provided for them becomes clearly apparent; R. at first jokes about it, saying that usually conductors make cuts, now they have to compose additional music for him. But it saddens him to see that even here his ideas are not realized in practice. The forest scenery in the first transformation is not at all the way he wanted it, and it is also bad that at the end the rocks sink into the ground. . . . But the weather is kind, and on his return R. is able to take a little stroll in the garden; that makes many things easier. — From the outside world we hear good news about *Tristan* in London and about a performance in Holland. Domestically, Fidi's difficulties in learning Latin cause R. to reflect on the whole system of study, and he says how sorry he is that one cannot be protected against "scholastic nonsense"—he says it was certainly not ancient languages which aroused in him his feelings for antiquity—that happened later. Return of our good Lusch—great excitement everywhere! . . .

Thursday, June 22 R. had a very restless night, he frequently awakes with a cry; he jokes about it, saying that I seemed to him like Lady Anne beside R[ichard] III. We go for a walk in the garden and then have breakfast in the turret. He then goes through the second act. Our friends the Grosses come along, always dear and precious to us. Fidi brings me good reports; I tell R., and he says he will turn them into an opera. We drive up to the theater (there are scenery troubles, the transformation scene too long for the music and the first forest not arranged as R. wants it). R. has to resign himself. In the evening the cap for the Knights of the Grail is decided on—a cap with a veil, to be made as much unlike a fez as possible. — Our friend Stein arrives, having walked all the way from Nuremberg—great, unmitigated delight.

Friday, June 23 We again have breakfast in the summerhouse, and our conversation leads us to Hans; yesterday I received news that he wishes the 40,000 marks to be used to pay back my 40,000 francs, which Boni will then receive. I find this a good solution, but R. is not satisfied, he does not wish any of the 40,000 marks to be put to use. The impossibility of obtaining permission to adopt Isolde and Eva is also a matter of great concern to him! — As regards practical problems, R. has decided that the Flower Maidens should appear in their costumes from the start, leaving only the headdress to be attended to. Around noon I drive up to the theater and select flowers, with which I adorn the children at home, and R. is satisfied. In the afternoon we drive to the theater, and this flower problem is settled; the throwing of the spear is rehearsed. On our return home we find a letter from Richter, reporting the success of *Tristan* in London. In the evening Nietzsche returns to memory, after we have been thinking joyfully of Richter! Then Batz, too, unfortunately! . . . R. regrets that there is always something distressing in whatever we discuss.

Saturday, June 24 Midsummer Day! We begin it in the turret. A pamphlet on the Pope, sent to me by Ollivier, leads us to the unfortunate French habit of haranguing in print, and from there to Mark Antony's speech over Caesar's corpse; we are astounded that Shakespeare, having just shown us this emotionally compelling man in all his grief, also has the power to show him as a politician, at this same funeral adopting exactly the tone which is bound to have the greatest impact on the people. We reflect how few people really read Shakespeare, and in this connection think of Nietzsche, whose strange character we sum up by saying that he possessed no real intelligence, but could be magnetized. R. goes through the end of the third act; a telegram from Voltz puts his mind at rest. In the afternoon we drive up to the theater, the transformation scenery for the 3rd act is rehearsed again, and it is decided to repeat the sentimental part of the music. [*Enclosed a piece of paper inscribed in Wagner's handwriting:* "Electric telegraph for the beat."] We are very pleased with the Temple of the Grail and its new cupola. Then, over a glass of beer beneath the arbor in Herr Moritz's garden, it is decided that Amfortas shall be given no special mark as king, that his cloak will be his blanket and his head left bare (only, in the forest, a light silk scarf). R. is very pleasantly affected by the way things are gradually emerging and by the decision. After returning home we sit in the garden, where we also have supper. Unfortunately R. learns that a Herr Strauss, who is connected with some of the most distressing memories of our life in Munich, is to take part in the performances. This throws him into a fury, which dies down, however, when he hears how zealous Strauss has been in the interests of *Parsifal*. Wolz. [*this name obliterated by an unknown hand and replaced by* "Something else"] also causes him pained feelings, but the evening passes in good, indeed even gay spirits, and at the end R. and I, kneeling on a stool at the window, see the head of Froh close by in the moonlight, leaning against an oleander. — We bid farewell to this Midsummer Day, R. and I, with tender impetuosity —may God grant us more such days!

Sunday, June 25 On the next day that wish was not granted! Whether it was the Strauss matter which affected him, or perhaps Wolz. [*this name altered in an unknown handwriting to* "Batz"], or even indeed the discussion in the morning about Jouk.'s disordered circumstances, who could say? He is overcome by a very severe spasm and remains in a tortured mood all day long. Since the children are away on an outing with Gross, the presence of our 3 friends is a torture to him, and, in spite of a few cheerful moments, he is deeply upset. — An interview I had this morning with the mayor has given me the assurance that for the time being R. will not be bothered with Batz-Voltz matters.

Monday, June 26 When I went to bed last night and thought sorrowfully of his day, I put all the strength of my being into a prayer; may I be permitted to say that I felt God quite close to me, as if a mighty protective spirit were enveloping my heart and its apprehensions? . . . In the morning I saw R.—who had been slumbering beside me— sitting on my chair opposite me, and his face did not alarm me; I simply knew that, just as I had fallen asleep with his image before me, so, too, did I now awake. R. had a good night, but he takes medicine in the hope of avoiding a repetition of yesterday's state. He reads *The Destiny of Opera* and is very pleased with it, says he has nothing more to say on this subject, which he has treated exhaustively. He is sorry that the article made no impression at all, for he is well aware that what he wrote in it about music was completely new and probably as worthy of being considered a landmark for a new way of seeing things as [Lessing's] *Laokoon* in another territory. He had previously told me, half in jest but half in earnest, that Goethe and Schiller had never done anything as good. Over coffee he comes to talk about Schiller and singles out as the main feature of his character his composure, in spite of his otherwise pronounced straightforwardness. This term, taken over by R. from Bruno Bauer, defines the true nobility of the German character, he says, and, as an example, he relates how, after his break with the Duke, Schiller calmly consumed bread and cheese and played skittles, saying at last in reply to inquiries that, yes, he knew he must make his escape. Not taking fright—this is what saved Germany from the Catholics, who were out to sow fear. — Unfortunately, however, R. is still in somewhat low spirits. We drive with the children to Wolfsbach, where they get out, leaving R. and me alone; we talk about Siegfried's education; R. does not agree with my plan of sending him to Stein in Halle for a year, and he suggests we look among the young people to whom free seats are to be given, to see whether a good house tutor cannot be found among them. As we were strolling in the garden before our drive, thinking of all the unpleasant things connected with the performances, R. swore this would be the last thing he would ever stage. We also talked about the Hannibal dialogue which Stein had just read to me; R. is surprised that he has not chosen for his theme Hannibal with Antiochus and his encounter with Scipio, the daemoniacally awesome and witty man and the old man dying a legendary death. But we are of one mind in recognizing the poetic talent of our friend, who reminds R. of Kleist. In the carriage R. reflects on his facial features, which he cannot reconcile with his talents. — Home again, there is more vexation: the dog Freia has run away from the theater, come back to us, and had to be removed, and our poor Molly seems to be really ill—the veterinary surgeon not to be found immediately! We eat in the garden, R. very agitated, but the evening finishes more peacefully than it begins; Rubinstein's obstinate insistence on having seen "*bar jeder Gefahr*" in the score and having to compose a note to match it leads to some head-shaking over the poor man. — R. sits down at the piano, turns the pages of *Parsifal,* then plays some Auber; this leads him to remark on the genius with which Auber wrote for the trumpet, and in contrast he shows how vulgarly Meyerbeer imitated him in the 5th act of *Les Huguenots.* — What music is in and of itself he demonstrates with an example from [Rossini's] *Otello* (finale); he says old Bierey had once pointed out to him how bad it was, but when he heard Schröder-Devrient singing Desdemona, the whole anguish of the situation had been conveyed to him. "Such is the power of music," he exclaims; "what are maxims and opinions in comparison with that?" — When mention is made at supper of the courage needed to compose music nowadays, R. says, "Music is the youngest of the arts, and it is a question of how it is applied, and whether one will just go on eternally reproducing for concert use that form of it which originated in dance!" — The G Minor Symphony, played by the children, yesterday brought him almost to the point of despair on account of all the padding between its "divine inspirations." "Nobody would be more surprised than Mozart to see things he wrote just for an 'academy' or a concert evening proclaimed as eternal masterpieces. Mozart had yet to show us what he was—had he reached the point of being able to work without worrying about earning his living." — R. then recalls Schnorr, saying that he ought to have sung Parsifal, how long he has been dead, and how many people he, R., has survived. "You have invented the strangest macrobiotics for me," he then says to me!

Tuesday, June 27 R. had a restless night, he got up 4 times, dreamed that he was on trial and having a difficult time in court! In the morning he is pleased by the peacocks, the white and the colored ones sitting together on the roof timbers of the poultry shed. He jokes about the "mousetrap for house tutors" he is setting in friend Gross's "den." Then we talk about a preface for Stein's dialogues. At lunch he remarks on the beauties of *La Juive,* the Passover celebrations, the final choruses, also the lively first act, and says it contains the best expression of the Jewish character; before that he had jokingly told Levi that frivolity did not suit him, yet when he was melancholy it was difficult for us to bear it sympathetically. (As far as orchestral work is concerned, he thinks *La Juive* more significant than *La Muette.*) He enlarges upon the difference between a Mozart allegro, which can never be taken too fast and which owes its effect to this liveliness, and a Beethoven one, in which every note has some significance. — In the afternoon we drive up to the theater, the forest is dressed with foliage, and I am overcome by strange feelings of contentment in the midst of this industrious quiet, with people devoting all their will and energies to an illusion. In this artificial forest thoughts flutter around me like friendly birds, and the work of art itself seems scarcely more enchanting than watching it emerge tirelessly into being! — At supper we at first discuss the positioning of the orchestra, and R. again argues heatedly against the practice of placing strings and wind instruments side by side; he says the orchestra must form a complete whole, the wind instruments giving the effect of lights; he had managed to reproduce the magnificent sound of the orchestra in Paris by adopting the positions he had learned from Spontini. The strings must also be divided up, in order to provide more *"points de départ"* ["starting points"], as Berlioz expressed it. Then we talk about Bismarck's speeches and come to the conclusion that he has described the state of things very clearly and will probably succeed in gaining people's sympathy, even if one cannot exonerate him from having caused the dismal situation. After that he reads to us the beginning of *"Prinzessin Brambilla."*

Wednesday, June 28 R. had a good night, although he had some very vivid dreams. He reads Bismarck's speeches and, as we are driving to the theater, tells me how wretched and unworthy he feels the left-wing hissing of these speeches to be. In the theater the transformation scenery for the third act is rehearsed again, there seems not to be enough music, but finally it all fits, and R. willingly accepts a suggestion made by Humperdinck. Then the positioning of Titurel is tried out, the placing of the benches, the arrangement of the orchestra—all kinds of things, in fact! "What a fantastic place to be, a theater like this!" says R., who is enjoying all the activity, in spite of the difficulties. I feel as if I am in a dream, and cannot understand how I came to be granted the good fortune of being permitted to stand beside him and share it with him! On our return home we find Herr Winkelmann's assurance that he will be here in time, and Herr Gudehus also announces his arrival; Frau Materna, on the other hand, wants to visit her mother first, which inspires R. to send her a telegram saying that those who are not present at the first rehearsals cannot in all fairness expect to sing in the first performances. He is pleased that, despite Vogl's withdrawal, he has three tenors, "each one better than the last—or at any rate two better than the one!" In the evening he continues reading "*Prinzessin Br.*" to us, and the conversation between Ciarlatano and the German, which he finds very pleasing, reminds him, in connection with masks, of a letter (Nov. 6, 1795) in which W. v. Humboldt enlarges upon Greek literature. R. agrees with him about its "sketchiness," also the difference between character and individuality, but he does not agree with me when I tell him that this way of apprehending the Greeks as writers (Humboldt does not mention Aeschylus) ought surely to have been superseded now, following his own writings on the subject.

Thursday, June 29 R. had a good night, but a letter from the theater director in Vienna first thing in the morning vexes him: Herr Fürstner is again claiming royalties on *Tannhäuser*. I then have to search through boxes for the papers, and I write to the lawyer Simson, who handled the case. At 12 o'clock R. has another worry: he goes through the role of Parsifal with poor Jäger and finds him completely unsuitable! . . . The first festival visitor—Miss Tilton from America—has arrived and is our guest at lunch today. She finds R. looking aged somewhat and, oblivious of the effect she is having on me, tells me so! . . . At 4 o'clock we drive up to the theater, lighting rehearsal. The need to repeat the mournful music is a real grief to R.! We stay in the restaurant with the children and eat there for the first time; in spite of the wet weather, all the bad and distressing things, R. is nevertheless cheerful. But we soon return home and finish up the evening with conversation on subjects of all sorts. An orchestra player (contra bassoon), who played under R. at Weber's funeral and was also here for the laying of the foundation stone, starts off by giving us pleasure but then feels obliged to tell R. that the orchestral parts have been ruined by the bookbinder. We do not quite understand why people tell him such things when there is nothing he can do about it, and R. says, "The violent urge of foolishness to make its presence known." There is also much friendly and considerate talk about Jouk.'s character, but above all about the difficulties with the transformation scenery!

Friday, June 30 Despite various vexations, despite errors in diet, R. has a good night, which leads him to make many merry jokes. We drive up to the theater, where the transformation scenery for the first act is tried out and things take a turn for the better. Returning home, I go to Jouk.'s to see the portrait of Blandine which he has begun, and there I find Callot's illustrations for *"Prinzessin Brambilla,"* which I take to R.; they give him much pleasure, at the same time bringing the conversation to this subject. From fantasy we move on to magnetism, and this so absorbs us that in the evening we seek to define the nature of daemonism. News of the death of a child provokes from R. the remark, "No, not that—for that I would throw my club at the good Lord's feet, like Luther." We recall his prayer over Melanchthon when he was dangerously ill—"What must that prayer have been like?"—and then he enlarges upon the Schop. theory of magnetism. — In the afternoon we walk in the garden, also in the palace gardens, delight in the swans, the roses, too, gaze in concern at our silver pheasant, now grown weak with age, though we still hope to save it, look after the dogs, and enjoy a few peaceful hours! — In the evening R. continues reading *"Pr. Bramb."* to me, with much enjoyment in the lively scenes with the actor and Abbate, the tailor, Ciarlatano, though we find the fairy-tale episode wearisome. R. wonders where this ironical treatment of magic derives from: does it stem from Ariosto, and how? But it is repulsive, he says—in *The Arabian Nights* everything is always full of passion and earnestness. The conversation is a long-drawn-out one, we search everywhere for parallels. At supper R. spoke in high praise of Lucian's story about the ass, and he says in connection with both this author and Plutarch: "We might as well give up. After 500 years people still spoke and thought like Plato: that is civilization. With us it is all a matter of individuals, we have no civilization."

Saturday, July 1 We continue talking about this subject, and R., who finishes *"Prinzessin Brambilla"* in the course of the day, speaks regretfully of its amateurishness. — The execution of the President's assassin brought him back yesterday to his idea of monasteries and the efforts of their inmates to bring the sinner to the point of wishing to atone by death. — A letter from Countess La Tour brings the fate of our friend Gob. very close to us! Today there was to have been a gathering of orchestra and chorus in the little restaurant, but the weather prevents it. . . . We drive up to the theater to arrange it all for tomorrow.

Reunion with Hill (Klingsor) at the moment of driving off, later Gudehus (Parsifal), in between Heckel at Gross's. In the theater the conductor arranging the desks, otherwise empty. In the evening Hill and Gudehus. In between (for me) poor Frau Jäger, on the verge of despair! Over coffee R. speaks in high praise of Jouk.'s sketches, and he is in favor of displaying them in the hall. "You are a remarkable man," he tells him, "but I cannot stand injustice" (a reference to the Brückner brothers).

Sunday, July 2 Start! Orchestral sounds heard again, R. says some friendly words to the orchestra, but dealing with masses of people wears him out. Materna and many others as well. The orchestra entirely lacks style, the players are unschooled, R. feels that very strongly, but there is no embarrassing hitch, the first act is played through satisfactorily. At home I find the news that the King is not coming! ... I tell this to R. after lunch, and he thinks the exhibition in Nuremberg is to blame. At 5 o'clock rehearsal of the first act with piano, the entire company on stage! (In the morning, after the orchestra rehearsal, we saw all the Flower Maidens assembled in one room—they made a charming sight.) A glorious impression! ... Celestial, in fact—blessed-ness brought to life! Herr Scaria wonderful as Gurnemanz, Herr Reichmann very moving as Amfortas, and everyone without exception so earnest, so absorbed in it, a unique occasion. Afterward a gathering in the "Blue Moor"—that is what R. has now christened the tavern, on account of the doorman from the West Indies, who has been given a gleaming royal Bavarian livery. We return home around 10 o'clock in pouring rain, R. satisfied, I deeply, deeply moved! I believe it was the divine will that he should refine his art to this expression of it.

Monday, July 3 In the morning R. discusses with me the King's decision not to come, and he says he intends to write to Herr v. Bürkel. However, he does not find time; first of all a visit from Herr Winkelmann, and then a conference with the poor little ballet master (Fricke), greatly aged! Lunch with the two Kundrys and Klingsor goes so well that R. exclaims to Jouk. and Stein: "They are real people! You"—to Jouk.—"have been spending all your time with elegant donkeys, and you"—to Stein—"with educated ones!" — Rehearsal at 5 o'clock (voice and piano); R. asks the people to pay attention to his rhythms: "I think I have got them right; I may have composed badly, but my rhythm is good." — He is extraordinarily merry and keeps putting new heart into his singers with his high spirits. At supper we are all merry together, he talks about his previous life, the revolution in Dresden, the happiness for him of no longer being a conductor—"no wine is as intoxicating as this feeling of freedom." While we are cozily chatting together after the meal, Herr

Winkelmann's letter arrives. We cannot help remarking how little this accords with the letter to Herr Schön, published today! After having written a few lines to Herr Wink., R. sets out, and surprises the good and simple man, whom R. soon brings around by telling him that all he wanted was to return his call, and was obliged to come so late since he would be leaving in the morning!

Tuesday, July 4 R. shows me a touching letter from one of the ladies in our chorus. He soon goes off to the scenery rehearsal of the 1st act, which lasts from 9:30 to 2:30 and causes R. great, great vexation and much exertion. The props are missing, the chorus leaders know nothing, the poor lady choristers have to stand in the rigging loft in the most terrible heat. We put off the little dinner we had arranged. R. takes a short rest, and at 5 o'clock there is an orchestra rehearsal (1st act) with the singers; this does not tire R., since he has had a slot inserted in the hood over the orchestra and is thus able to converse with the conductor in comfort; he is satisfied with the sound of the invisible orchestra. We spend the evening with Jouk., Stein, and Levi, and R. tries to show the latter how to wield the baton, since he finds that he conducts much too much with his arm, whereas it should all be done with the wrist! The evening passes harmoniously; in the morning, after the vexatious rehearsal, I told him what an overwhelming impression everything made, every movement, every sound, the smallest detail in the acting, and thus I succeeded in making him forget the vexations and recall the period of creation; in the evening I cannot help making a similar exclamation, and he says to me, "We have done a lot together." He then recapitulates it all and goes on to ask, "Why didn't you say to me at that time (1858), 'I wish to live with nobody but you'? Then I should have known what to do. But throughout my life love has never been offered to me directly; I was lacking in self-confidence, exactly like Tristan—but how was it with you?" He gradually drifts off to sleep, and we find it very comical when, after sleeping for about 2 minutes, he suddenly calls out "Tante Schinkel," having seen her in the Flower Garden.

Wednesday, July 5 He had a good night's rest, but he feels he has caught cold. We go to an orchestra rehearsal with singers, still the 1st act. The need to raise his voice tires him, but it all goes well. At lunch we recapitulate all our impressions, Herr Scaria quite outstanding as Gurnemanz. R. is pleased that his first act is not boring! In the afternoon another scenery rehearsal with piano accompaniment, the orchestra is permitted to look on, and breaks into hearty applause after the transformation scene, which does R. good, though he has many difficulties to contend with: the bells are not right, and our good ballet master is not much help! Much agitation in the evening, but no real indisposition, thank goodness! . . . (M. Brandt very expressive as Kundry today.)

Thursday, July 6   R. had a good night, he spends the morning quietly, and at 12 o'clock we drive together to the theater to try the bells, which are much improved this time. At 1 o'clock we give a dinner for the tenors, and the fine Amfortas (Reichmann) is also present. At 5 o'clock rehearsal of the first act. Trouble with the choral singers, the ladies do not wish to go aloft, and R. finds they do not sound right if they stay below. R. and I climb up and find that it is indeed very hot, but the trouble can be cured with lighter clothing. Everything else goes splendidly, and the impact grows steadily stronger. In the evening R. is very tired.

Friday, July 7   R. had a very restless night, and the morning brings me various burdens (Jäger, Countess Mazzarino, Ritter, Betty Braun). At around 12 o'clock we go to the theater to rehearse the choruses, everything runs smoothly, and they climb to positions halfway up. On our way there R. told me that he is giving up the idea of allowing the boys to come down and take part in the Communion ceremony, since they have not yet been confirmed and he does not wish to give any offense. Amfortas's litter is adjusted. We lunch by ourselves. In the afternoon rehearsal Herr Siehr sings Gurnemanz, and the choruses stand up above; Fischer takes over the conducting. The effect increases as it all gains in depth. In the evening we are visited by our friends Heckel, Brandt, Levi. R. is tired, but we stay up a little longer by ourselves, chatting about "everything."

Saturday, July 8   R. had a restless night; in the morning he writes to the King about his decision not to attend the performances, and he tells me he has done what Luther did to the Lord in connection with Melanchthon's illness—thrown his club at his feet! — I paid some calls. At lunch R. answers a warning not to eat cucumber salad by saying to me humorously, "Shut your trap!" and he then recalls his mother, who used to put a swift end to every discussion by saying this very loudly and emphatically. Costume fittings. The swords are missing and various things have to be modified, but the overall impression is lovely, and the effect as powerful as any theater can produce. R. is disappointed that the Knights' accolade does not fill the time required by the music written for it; this music is still being played as they start marching, but there is nothing that can be done about it, and for me this moment of brotherly love is one of the most moving of all. In the evening R. is tired, but on the whole pleased. (Yesterday he was upset by a member of the chorus who was making jokes about the bread, and he rebuked him severely.)

Sunday, July 9   R. had a good night, though enlivened by wild dreams. Around 12:30 he goes to the rehearsal and makes the conductor jump by calling to him through the slot, "Don't shout so!" — At lunch we have the three bass singers, and there is much gaiety. R. feels decidedly more at ease with his artists than with people from society. At 4:30 we drive through pouring rain to the first piano and voice rehearsal of the 2nd act. The Flowers (R. wishes them to be called that and not Fl. Maidens, since this reminds one of flower sellers) are enchanting. The big scene between Kundry and Pars. will almost certainly never be done in the way he created it. R. complains about how insensitive the singers are to all there is in it, and he thinks of Schröder-Devr., how she would have uttered the words "*So war es mein Kuss, der hellsichtig dich machte.*" Now the music has to do it all. — As we were driving to the theater, he told me that, when he thought of his times in Zurich and Paris and then looked at all the life going on around him now, he felt literally like a magician. At supper he tells us that he is reading Hoffm.'s "*Die Marquise de la Pivardière*" with great interest, also a novel in the *Tagblatt* which likewise seems to be a genuine crime story. In the evening he speaks in praise of the present Khedive of Egypt, Arabi Pasha, who is vigorously standing up to England and France, and gradually the evening moves on—strangely enough—to Strauss waltzes, during which R. recalls Penzing (Dommayer) and remarks how much more original the waltzes of the elder Strauss were, whereas the artistically more elaborate ones of his sons either are contrived or were greatly influenced by Chopin. — We find it very touching when, at the end of the evening, Blandine complains of hardly ever seeing me.

Monday, July 10 In the morning R. writes a correction to the erroneous news about the alleged text for *Die Sieger,* which a Herr Lessmann has again published in his periodical. We go to the orchestra rehearsal of the 2nd act, which turns out very well. Afterward we entertain Herr Hill and his wife, Frl. Dompierre, Herr Fuchs (Knight) at lunch. At 5 o'clock reading rehearsal with piano, Frl. Brandt sings Kundry. Gudehus pleases us with his magnificent voice; but R. is very tired. He wishes to be alone, we put off our friends. The conductor and Joukowsky call late in the evening.

Tuesday, July 11 After a good night R. and I go to a rehearsal of the 2nd act, orchestra and singers. R. willingly gives an explanation of Kundry's character to Herr Scaria, who requested it. We eat by ourselves with Stein, R. reads the two drafts, Wolz.'s and Stein's, about the new Society of Patrons and accepts Stein's draft. He also receives a copy of Herr Oesterlein's R. Wagner catalogue and remarks jokingly, "I am now enjoying myself 15 years after my death, how things will look then." A German translation of the *Oupnekhat* pleases him greatly. Yesterday he received an honorary diploma from St. Petersburg. He also tells us that Alexandria is being blockaded and that General Skobeleff is implicated with the nihilists. At 5 o'clock we have a scenery rehearsal of the 2nd act with piano. In the morning R. said he was not staging an old work of his youth, but a youthful work of his old age. However, he is very tired in the evening, and a visit from the Feustels, whom he does not receive, keeps us shut up in the dining room, which greatly annoys him. They do not leave until quite late, but we then spend a little time in the *salon,* where R. discusses with Stein Bismarck's politics, which are precisely that: just politics.

Wednesday, July 12 In the morning I express to R. my misgivings about Parsifal and Kundry's having to play out their tragic scene amid all the luxuriant flowers, and observe that, at any rate next year, a large expanse of foliage might screen them off during Kundry's approach. As we are about to drive off to the morning rehearsal, we meet Fräulein Malten, who has just arrived; she is very nice to look at, and she reminds R. of Wilh. Schr.-Devr., even in the way she looks at one. During rehearsal R. was vexed by the orchestra's having been invited to the Frohsinn, leaving the restaurant he has provided deserted. He talks to the orchestra about it, but this upsets him, and he does not feel well, though he jokes with the Knights. [*A few words based on untranslatable word play omitted.*] The rehearsal causes M. Brandt much trouble; the Flower Maidens are excellent. Frl. Malten has lunch with us and makes a good impression. In the afternoon scenery rehearsal with piano (M. Brandt, Gudehus), the orchestra looks on and again breaks out in applause at the transformation. But the exertion for R. is endless! . . . In the evening, after we return home, the weather clears up, and I sit at the *salon* door, listening to the birds; R. discovers me there and comes to listen with me—a moment (the only one) of recuperation. In the evening we are visited by Wolz. and Levi, our friend Jouk. brings R.'s anger down on his head with a somewhat ambiguous statement, and the evening comes to an awkward end! — Stein gave me great pleasure by responding to my request to begin a Wagner lexicon; he reads to me his articles on German and on culture, which are excellently done, and I find them truly uplifting.

Thursday, July 13 R. slept well but is very agitated. A letter from Herr Batz (statement of accounts) vexes him greatly. At lunch we have three of the Flowers (soloists). At 5 o'clock orchestra rehearsal with Herr Winkelmann and Frau Materna, the latter very good. But R. very, very tired, since he has constantly to show them everything. Because the weather is fine, we drive home via the Eremitage road. We are alone at supper, the children tell us that our dear good dog Molly is ill, the veterinary surgeon is sent for and says it is just a slight chill.

Some time ago, since her face was looking much changed, I asked Dr. Landgraf, and he told me that she was quite well but was eating too much and must get a lot of exercise.

Friday, July 14 R. feels weak and takes medicine. At around 10 o'clock Georg brings me the news that our lovely dear dog has died—and you know, my children, what she meant to us! ... After paying my final respects to the good creature, who suffered in such silence, I drive up to the theater to inspect the Flower costumes; then back home, to the Jägers', to do what I can to raise the poor offended man's spirits. At lunch we have 3 Flowers and 2 concertmasters. There is a rehearsal in the afternoon, I tell R. that the children have caught cold; they stay at home (the younger ones), and after the dissection they bury our dear Molly. — The rehearsal goes on with Herr Gud. and Frl. Br.! — Oh, how clear it is becoming to R. with what inadequate means he has to work—he feels it so painfully! He exclaims that he is dealing with bunglers. — Stein and Jouk. are with us in the evening: "For the one I feel sorrow, for the other pity," says R.

Saturday, July 15 R. asks after Molle, Georg tells him that we must be prepared for the worst, he goes into the garden around lunchtime, sits down in the arbor, notices Marke sniffing at the grave! At table, where we are alone, he utters the name, and we burst into tears, realizing that he knows all. He thanks us for not having told him. ... Toward two o'clock my father arrives, met by the children and looking well—we are overjoyed to see him! While the children and I are keeping him company during his meal, R. joins us, stands for a while unnoticed behind my father's chair, and whispers to me, *"Die Mutter!"* — Our dog came into my mind, too, yesterday when I heard those words! — When I return to my room as my father is resting, I hear R. calling out "Molle!" in the garden and sobbing. I rush to him, and we weep together in the arbor. ... Then we go to the costume session for the first and second acts. R. is so delighted by my father's presence that he hurries to me from the stage and says this is his only genuine relationship! We eat in the restaurant, between the first and second acts. The late evening, following the rehearsal, we spend with my father, Stein, and Jouk. (Reminded by the terrible example of Molle, R. comes back to the need for Fidi to study animal surgery.)

Sunday, July 16 R. fell asleep last night on his big dressing chair, I watched over him and prayed. Alas, we are both so tired, and our wish is to live for the children, only for the children! ... He then goes cheerfully to bed and has a good night. Toward 11 o'clock we drive up to the orchestra rehearsal of the 3rd act, in which R. particularly notices how the orchestra just bangs away, no longer playing with feeling, but just ignoring the sensitive, the passing notes. We return home feeling sad; R. accuses himself of having scored too heavily at times! In one passage he cuts out the woodwinds. Apart from that he talks about the killing of the Europeans in Alexandria, saying it was all happening "in order to protect government bonds." — A letter from Herr Schön in reply to his open one pleases him greatly. — At 5 in the afternoon we both go to the vocal rehearsal of the 3rd act. Unfortunately Herr Winkelm. arouses great anger in R. by not knowing his part. The evening passes in whist for my father; for R. and me a conversation between R. and the conductor about interpretation.

Monday, July 17 R. talks almost without interruption throughout the night. I hear, among other things, "Adieu, children"—to whom could I speak my thoughts? Not thoughts, alas, but cries of fear heavy as lead: he, the children, the children, he! I see Siegfried's pleading look! . . . At 12 o'clock the oboist arrives, along with the conductor; very humorously R. says it sounded like a young cockerel who "suddenly feels the urge to say something." Then he suddenly exclaims: "What is aristocracy? How does it reveal itself in a sound like that? By not saying anything stupid, and so I have advised the oboist to louden his tone at once, so that the trivial shall not last an eternity." We have a bearer of the Grail, a squire, and Dr. Strecker and wife at lunch. At 5 o'clock a rehearsal (of the 3rd act, reading, with piano). R. very thorough on the various points of significance, among them Parsifal's blissful smile, Gurnemanz's rapture, and his folklike simplicity. The impossibility of his being understood causes great depression. In silence we drive home by a roundabout route; the drive does R. good; now and again we exchange a word about the work. Arriving home, R. goes off to bed, and I receive Herr Neumann, whom R. sent for because of a letter from Herr Voltz received this morning, telling him that in spite of all R.'s concessions the court case in Leipzig is still proceeding. R. takes a bath and then some food, which is always connected with a certain amount of vexation. But I go to keep him company, leaving our circle to whist and conversation, and soon we are in lively, indeed almost heated conversation with each other over a glass of champagne. I only wish I could take him in my arms and carry him far, far away from it all!

Tuesday, July 18 R. had a good night's sleep, and he tells me in the morning that the Grail processions in the 3rd act are now in order (in his head). At 10:30 we go to the rehearsal, the violoncellos, which so annoyed him the day before yesterday, play better today, but there is still much which is not as he wants it, and when one of the musical directors draws his attention to something, he relates the story of the tailor in Heaven whom God rebuked for throwing down his stool. But his main trial now is not knowing what he should let pass, what comment on. He adds a drum roll to the crowning of Parsifal, but he is very tired. All the same, the presence of our friend Malwida at lunch pleases him. He jokes with her about their writings: "The whole world reads yours, I read only my own, because in all others I find embarrassing contradictions. But not in mine—I do what the Talmud says about God, who reads the Bible." During our conversation over coffee R. remarks that many people have broken with him, become angry with him, because he expected them to behave worthily, to be worth while. At 5 o'clock a rehearsal with piano to fix stage positions, much trouble for R.! No one to help him. Concern about the transformation scenery. We return home in silence. But he has supper with us, and when I pass on to him Herr Scaria's suggestion of cutting the second transformation entirely, he is pleased with it, sends for our young friend Brandt late in the evening, and arranges it with him. In the meantime he talked to my father about the curious "agitation" into which he (my father) had been drawn, and he remarks that the things one said 20 years ago about the Israelites (as in the first edition of *Des Bohémiens*) one must take good care not to say nowadays, since for some time Herr v. Bismarck has been using them against the Conservative party. "The corn must either sprout or go rotten," I said yesterday to R. in connection with characters. I write it down, since he was pleased with it.

Wednesday, July 19 R. is feeling unwell and cancels the rehearsal. We have breakfast in the turret, he then has lunch on his own, or, rather, he has no lunch and spends the whole afternoon in the summerhouse. After coffee I go to join him, he reads Hoffmann, I the *Oupnekhat,* now and again we exchange a few words and are happy. The doctor has given him something to calm him down, he looks in during the evening and finds him well, reassures me by finding all his organs completely sound. Herr Scaria comes and gives a good report of the rehearsal. — We have supper with my father and R., later Malwida arrives with Stein and Jouk. Among other things R. is preoccupied with the thought that there is no appeal against science, against medicine; vaccination, for example, which is now regarded as harmful, was made compulsory by the state for 20 years! — He complains about military music, the vulgarity of which does indeed annoy us. — When Stein tells us that Dr. Schemann is quoting his saying, "I am no musician," R. jokes about this misunderstanding and sings, "He is no musician, he says it himself," to the tune from *Figaro,* "He is my father," etc. After I have already said good night to him, he comes into my dressing room and says, "The nicest thing of all is when we are sitting side by side in silence, as in the turret today." While we were sitting there, he looked at me and said: "There has never before been anything like us. Absurd, eccentric relationships maybe, but never us two . . ."

Thursday, July 20 R. had a good night's rest. Over breakfast in the turret we read the King's letter, which arrived yesterday and which R. put aside. The news of the wretched state of his health is all too easy to believe. R. wanted to have lunch with us (me and 4 children, my father and Lusch invited out), but he got upset about something, and instead of broth he enjoyed Humperdinck, he says, then the ballet master, who did in fact put him in a good humor, but he is tired. He sleeps in the *salon,* and on awaking discovers me asleep in the hall; my watching over him amuses him greatly, he says I am turning him into the Emperor of Siam, who has a female bodyguard. At 5 o'clock rehearsal of the 3rd act (orchestra, Winkelmann, Materna), R. is satisfied with the orchestra. We again drive home together. In the evening my father plays whist, and we chat with the conductor. At the rehearsal R. merely asked that people not start talking when he has something to say. We are pleased that the curtain now falls and no transformation scenery disturbs the music. [*This last sentence obliterated in ink by an unknown hand.*]

Friday, July 21 R. slept well, but we are both very tired; he goes so far as to suggest in fun that at such times I might come to detest art! We have a very cheerful family lunch; R. talks a lot about Gobineau. Previously he spoke about the carnage in Alexandria. After lunch I visit our friends the Glasenapps, return home, and in my weariness fall asleep in the *salon;* when I awake, R. is sitting beside me (around midday he came up to my room to ask whether I was still alive), there are tears in his eyes, and he says very gently, "What sacrifices we are making!" — We drive to the rehearsal (orchestra, Gudehus, Siehr). In the evening whist is played in the hall, while R. refreshes his memories of Bakunin with Malwida.

Saturday, July 22 R. slept but talked a lot in his sleep. — He frequently cites to me a joke of Hoffmann's about the madman who rose very gently as the moon but, when he wished to rise as the sun, became wild and frenzied. We have rehearsals, Scaria appears as the aged Gurnemanz and is quite superb. R. had said 80 in the first act, 90 in the last. During the entr'acte we all eat in the restaurant. We spend some time by ourselves on our return home, with Stein and Levi. R. gives a detailed description of Kundry's character, but during it I have the feeling that he is overtired.

Sunday, July 23 R. very, very tired, sleeps restlessly, finding pleasure in the morning only in the crowing of the cocks. We have breakfast together in the turret in nice weather. He then stays in the summerhouse and lunches there alone, keeping himself amused with E. T. A.

Hoffmann. At 5 o'clock we go to the rehearsal, Mar. Brandt (whom I had to console yesterday after an imagined slight by R.), Herr Gudehus. But we spend only a very little time there. The foliage to screen off Pars. and Kundr. is tried out, but it does not entirely meet R.'s wishes. The tempi also dissatisfy him. We soon return home. The evening begins in a very cozy and humorous way, R. tells Fidi the story of *Pars.* after asking him how much of it he had understood; while he is doing this, my father explains the *Almanach de Gotha* to Boni. But toward the end R. becomes irritable with Malw. and taunts her about her many friendships with vivisectors.

Monday, July 24 R. had a good night's rest. I have all sorts of purchases to make in town; in the meantime R. strolls in the garden and, catching sight on Jouk.'s balcony of someone he takes to be Malwida, makes all kinds of gestures of humility and apology. On inquiry, it turns out that the woman was Judith Gautier. In the *Tagblatt* there are reminiscences of 1872, the 9th Symphony, the laying of the foundation stone, and R. is very touched. At 4 o'clock we have the dress rehearsal. R. finds the tempi in the first act drawn out rather too long; he is also not satisfied with the lighting. The 2nd act goes better. Between the 2nd and 3rd acts we have our supper. In the 3rd act he is very touched; since my father and Daniela leave in order to meet our friends the Schleinitzes, R. exclaims bitterly, "More of this obsequiousness—D—— take you all!" There are many strangers present; since there is applause at the end, he acknowledges it ironically from our gallery. — To me he makes the remark that as a member of the orchestra he would not like to be conducted by a Jew!

Tuesday, July 25 R. slept well, and since the weather is fine, we have breakfast in the turret. Suddenly we hear a noise, and like a voice from the grave R. hears Frau Heim from Zurich, whom I am greeting down below. We have lunch with my father and Herr Levi, with whom R. once more goes through the tempi. Before lunch R. called on our patron Count Schleinitz, whose appearance I had remarked on when I returned from my early visit. Judith visits us after lunch, I receive her in my room, since R. is rather tired. He reads *Die Serapionsbrüder* in the garden, and at 5 o'clock he holds another rehearsal with Herr Reich-mann and Herr Winkelmann, reading to them the salient features of their roles. At 7 o'clock we drive up to the restaurant, where, among other things, R. greets his artists; then the mayor proposes a toast to my father, whereupon R. gets to his feet and makes a wonderful speech about my father's value and significance to him. (R. greets M[athilde] Maier with much delight in the restaurant.) —

Wednesday, July 26 R. had a restless night, I hear him saying softly in a dream, "Children, I am going, suffering." — He is also not satisfied with the turn the toasts took yesterday, on top of that has forgotten everything he himself said, does not recognize it in the newspaper reports. We leave home at half past three, the weather unfortunately not good. The first act goes more or less according to his wishes [*the entries broken off here, the resumption, on September 18 in Venice, being indicated in a footnote*], it is just the large amount of "play acting" he finds displeasing. When, after the second act, there is much noise and calling, R. comes to the balustrade, says that though the applause is very welcome to his artists and to himself, they had agreed, in order not to impinge on the impression, not to take a bow, so that there would be no "curtain calls." After our meal R. and I are together in our box! Great emotion overwhelms us. But at the end R. is vexed by the silent audience, which has misunderstood him; he once again addresses it from the gallery, and when the applause then breaks out and there are continual calls, R. appears in front of the curtain and says that he tried to assemble his artists, but they were by now half undressed. The journey home, taken up with this subject, is a vexed one. Once we are home, it takes a very long time to calm R. down, since a host of different impressions are mixed up inside him. Even the fact that Schnapp. talks to him of Dr. *von* Liszt annoys him. At last I am able to hand over my little gift (a cushion), and gradually his thoughts are diverted; at twenty to one we go off to bed.

Thursday, July 27 The subject of our first conversation is once again the audience, and how to deal with it in such a way that the artists are not put out of humor by the absence of applause. We have a very merry lunch with the children, who amuse R. greatly with all they have seen. In the evening a reception at Wahnfried—Herr Schnappauf thinks 300 people, I think 200. (R. reads Hume's *History of England* in the French translation.)

Friday, July 28 R. slept well. At lunch he is amused by the children's accounts of all kinds of experiences with our guests. We drive up to the theater early. The Prelude is dragged out. After the first act there is a reverent silence, which has a pleasant effect. But when, after the second, the applauders are again hissed, it becomes embarrassing. At the end, believing himself to be in the presence of his patrons only, R. makes a short speech, presenting his artists and asking the audience to express its gratitude to them, after having himself first expressed to them—and particularly to the conductor—his own appreciation and emotion. (Between the 2nd and 3rd acts Herr v. Bürkel visited us.) In connection with his singers, he said to me that they moved and vexed him at one and the same time. However, the impression is a much more harmonious one than on the first occasion. We enjoy a quiet and amiable time with my father. A sonnet in the *Tagblatt* makes a pleasing impression, as also various newspaper reports.

Saturday, July 29 R. slept profoundly, if restlessly. At lunch we have the singers (Materna, Winkelmann, Scaria), to whom R. imparts some rules of enunciation—for example, not to say "*sein FLUCH*" (when the "*sein*" is hardly heard), but "*SEIN FLUCH*," and much else besides. At 3 o'clock we have a rehearsal in the theater with Frl. Malten and Herr Jäger; the former makes a surprisingly good impression on R. He is very tired in the evening. Today I had to deal consolingly with the complaints of our restaurant manager, who wants to give up on account of the lack of customers, and also to receive some gentlemen from the Wagner Societies, who appear to be not entirely in agreement with R.'s latest regulations.

Sunday, July 30 R. talks a great deal in his sleep. He is languid at lunch, which we have with our friends Mihalovich and Apponyi. But when the latter touches on the question of Christianity, R. takes him on in a very lively manner and says its sublimity is too delicate for it ever to become common property, and the old gods had been taken over to serve the church. At 4 o'clock we drive to the theater in bad weather. The performance is good, Frau Materna indeed very good, and R. asks me to congratulate her in her dressing room. Again silence after the first act, great applause after the 2nd act; calls after the 3rd act, and the curtain rises on the final tableau. R. expresses thanks on behalf of his artists from our box. "This is how I want it," he says. — Business is said not to be good, on account of the bad weather; we also hear all sorts of bad things about the way the visitors are being looked after. Very disturbed about this, R. writes—at nearly midnight—to our excellent mayor.

Monday, July 31 [*A newspaper clipping enclosed; see notes.*] R. wakes up with the same vexed thoughts with which he went to bed. He feels he will have to abandon the festivals because of the unsuitability of the place. The Dannreuthers have lunch with us, the Irish question and its insolubility are discussed, then R. talks about the *Oupnekhat* and reads a passage from it, incomprehensible when torn from its context. — R. then goes into the garden, a girl comes to him, asks for alms; R. chides her, saying she is doing it for her father: "Well, what about your father?" "He is in prison." . . . I, for my part, receive sad news about friend Gobineau. And a reception in the evening! A small, crippled Prince of Hesse, Mme Lucca, too, for R. very tormenting.

Tuesday, August 1 Memories of the beggar girl dominate R.'s thoughts today, he talks about her at lunch with Malwida and Stein and exclaims, "It is immoral of us to give thought to beauty in a world in which such things confront us." At 4 o'clock we go to the performance. It turns out only moderately well, the transformation scenery goes wrong because of a draft, the chorus wavers at the end, and several other things of that sort. Before the performance R. wept, and at the conclusion he cries out, "I am tired." — Rain.

Wednesday, August 2 Constant rain; R. sees it as a judgment on him for settling here at all. Yesterday he was still joking about the barometer, saying it is human, it lies when it is showing good weather. At lunch we have the former directors of the Leipzig theater, Countess Voss, and Frau v. Meyendorff. It is lively and gay, and in the afternoon R. can stroll in the garden, delighting in it as a paradise in which all the animals live in friendship together. R. and I are in the theater from 5 to 9 on account of a rehearsal with Frl. Malten and Herr Jäger. The rehearsal wears R. out but also satisfies him; it is truly moving how indefatigable and how unshakably earnest all our participants are, down to the least of them! Returning home, we find the children hungrily awaiting us, they misunderstand our instruction to eat right away, thinking we have already eaten, and have themselves served before we come in; this leads to vexation on our part, resentment from the children, and a whole scene, which dissolves into cheerful peace, however, after the children at first go secretly off to bed, then get up again! — The weather bad again.

Thursday, August 3 R. had a somewhat restless night and is not feeling well. Lunch with the Schöns and Frl. Malten takes place without him, though he comes to join us. After having spent several hours in the garden, he feels somewhat better in the evening, and at the reception he comes down and sits by the stove (to the right), among the Flower Maidens, with whom he jokes. In the morning he received a very nice letter from Wilhelmj. For me the day brought an examination of a tutor for Siegfr., recommended by friend Standhartner; unfortunately he will be impossible to combine with friend Stein, since his character is so utterly different from the North German one.

Friday, August 4 The wretched weather continues! For late breakfast at 12 we have the Dannreuthers, both of whom R. likes. At 4 o'clock the performance with Herr Jäger and Frl. Malten, the latter with very lovely, lively accents, but still somewhat immature. R.'s mood is one of great excitability, but he is always pleased with the diligence of his singers. He proclaims his thesis: "Here on my stage anarchy reigns: everyone does as he wishes, but each wishes well."

Saturday, August 5 R. is very tired and is troubled by a chest spasm. Between 3 and 4 in the morning he wrote to friend Gross, having read a report in Herr Lessmann's music periodical about the poor distribution of tickets, which upsets him greatly. My father's departure also arouses very great anger in him, and I am obliged to have both breakfast and lunch today without him. Friend Gross comes in great agitation to defend himself, R. has already half forgotten what he wrote during the night. In the afternoon he receives Frl. Malten to tell her a few things; and in the evening, since we are entirely alone, I tell him some of the stories now circulating in Bayreuth about spirit rapping, and these amuse him. He has sent repeated telegrams to his friend Sulzer, inviting him to the performances!

Sunday, August 6 The curious subject of spirit rapping continues to occupy us, since our poor friend Liechtenstein, who is interested in it, seems to have been the victim of an evil deception. — The persistence of the bad weather makes him curse ever having settled here. I cannot in all sincerity do other than stand up for our little town—and Germany —and I consider the drawbacks of our life here to be far less significant than the advantages. We are alone for lunch, and then we drive to the theater, where today Frau Materna and Herr Gudehus (Herr Winkelmann being ill) are singing. R. criticizes some things he finds not at all good—for example, Kundry's advances to Parsifal after the great outburst—but the eagerness of the singers as always touches him anew. However, the day is dominated by ill-humor. In the gallery he misses Siegfried, whom I have left at home for his own good, also Daniela, whom I have surrendered to the Schleinitzes, because I no longer dare ask them to our house, since recently he felt uneasy in their presence. But these concessions of mine do not meet with his approval, and I resolve to revert to my former ways. When he is in such an excitable state he makes errors in his diet, and late this evening he was still wandering excitedly in the garden.

Monday, August 7 First thing in the morning R. begs my pardon in his touchingly humble way for yesterday's irritable mood. He begins by asking me very gently how I am, whether I am still alive! Wilhelmj comes for lunch, very refreshing, with all sorts of stories and accounts, Malwida and Stein are also our guests. The conductor appears for coffee, and the casts for the next performances are determined. A letter from Herr Reichmann, whom the conductor has offended, is answered in a conciliatory way. At 5 o'clock Herr Neum[ann] is with R. for negotiations regarding his forthcoming tour (*Ring des N.*). Then the sun shines, and it is possible to stroll a little in the garden, where I show R. a telegram from Biagino giving favorable news about the P[alazzo] Vendramin—I had sent him to Venice with some anxiety, because of a misunderstanding which suddenly arose. Also a word of praise for my humble self in the *Indépendance,* which has been sent to me, amuses R. And the reception goes off very well.

Tuesday, August 8   But R. is very run down again today, on account of an error in his diet. In the morning I receive Herr Feustel and Herr Voltz, who, in order to extricate himself from the tangled situation, proposes ceding his interest in the business to R. For the time being I say nothing to R. about this visit, since he is very run down and has his second meal by himself; he does not follow the children and me to the theater until the middle of the 1st act and by the middle of the 2nd act has already left. Late in the evening, when I tell him about the performance, he is still very irritable.

Wednesday, August 9   R. had a wretched night and spends the morning in the garden, where he eats alone, without greeting Biagino, who has just arrived. I receive some friends, Passini, Liechtenst., etc., for lunch and, when we are having coffee in the hall and in my room, he summons Biagino to the *salon* with *Norma*. Unfortunately his device does not succeed, someone else hears him, and R., annoyed, exclaims, "The indiscretion of my friends spoils all my enjoyment!" Later he wants to go out, to visit Am. Materna in the Sonne, but someone immediately stops him in the street, and this sends him home in annoyance. In the evening he is in a somewhat irritable mood, and the necessity of talking French with Biag. is a torture to him. He sends for Malwid.—who never disturbs him—and Stein.

Thursday, August 10   R. had a wretched night, and our poor bride spends it with a toothache. After lunch, which he has with us, R. goes to bed and reads Hoffmann's "Mademoiselle de Scudéry" with much enjoyment. I receive guests in the evening somewhat reluctantly, the company leaves early.

Friday, August 11   R. had a restless night. He feels so languid that he does not attend the performance, just appears during the intermissions, and the only thing he hears all through is the flower scene, since the excellence of the performance always refreshes him. From our box he calls out, "Bravo!," whereupon he is hissed. Countess Tasca attends this performance, and we have her and our dear friends the Schl.'s in our home. — R.'s mood is changeable, but on the whole biased against Bayreuth—indeed, he even talks of handing over *Parsifal* and the festival theater to Herr Neumann!

Saturday, August 12   Another restless night, but fine weather. Countess Tasca, Frl. Malten, and Herr Gudehus lunch with us; R. is pleased to be able to show the Countess our house. He spent the morning in the summerhouse and avoided seeing even his family (Fritz Brockhaus along with his sister). At 4 o'clock the Liechtensteins paid their farewell call; he had been offended by R., R. learned about it and, in an attempt to reconcile him, exerted all the power he has over other people, making it seem ridiculous for anyone to take offense at anything he does. But the Princess-medium gazes wildly and fixedly at R., as if uneasily aware of his ability to see through things. Toward 5 o'clock we drive out to the Riedelsberg, to which the Grosses have invited several of the artists, we pick up the Glasenapps in the Rennweg and spend some time there very enjoyably. In the evening Malwida and Stein, while Biagino amuses himself with the children, since R. finds French very trying.

Sunday, August 13 Fine weather! But R. has a cold and spends the morning in bed. The children go on ahead to the theater, and R. and I arrive in the middle of the first act and leave a little before the end. The Liechtensteins, whom R. has persuaded to stay on, have supper at our house (R. does not join in). Scaria and Materna pleased R. today, particularly the latter, by paying attention to his hints.

Monday, August 14 R. feels somewhat better; for me a number of farewell visits, E[milie] Sierz[putowska], Alex[andra] Schl[einitz], whose excellent piece on *Pars.* pleased me greatly. Unfortunately tuna is served at lunch, R. eats some and suffers all day from indigestion! He had made an appointment with the chorus master, the conductor, and Herr Reichmann at 5 o'clock to discuss tempi; it is quite a while before he is able to talk with them, but at last he does so, then commits an error of diet by drinking beer, after which he has to go to bed. He reads Cervantes's story "Rintonate & Contadilla" while I receive people downstairs in a subdued frame of mind. During the night his pains increase, I make hot compresses for him, and in the joy of seeing him gradually recover and of being permitted to perform this humble little service for him, my soul sinks down in grateful prayer. Who never saw his dearest suffer, who never sat helping at a bedside through night's heavy hours, he knows you not, ye heavenly "powers"! I know you and your consolations!

Tuesday, August 15 He is still not feeling well, and he has some soup in the *salon* while I lunch with the children. He and I then drive to the theater with Loldi, and R. is so pleased with the success of his exhortations to Herr Reichmann (1st scene, "*Habt Dank,*" etc.) that he goes to him and gives him a 10-mark piece. At supper R. sits down with the children, but he is very agitated. My mood becomes more fervent as a result, and in my helplessness I call on the God who reveals Himself to the humble. And not in vain! The evening hours after the performance are spent in peaceful chat over a glass of beer.

Wednesday, August 16 And R. had a good night. When our friend Mimi is visiting me and we are strolling in the garden, R. calls to Mime (the dachshund): "Mime, find Mimi!" and is led to us. When the Countess says to him that he must be pleased to see what an uplifting effect his work has on everybody, he declares that he has no feelings at all with regard to it. We have lunch with the children. At 5 o'clock Herr Hill comes and sings Amfortas, some of it (1st scene in the Temple) with great power; R. points out to him his errors of enunciation. Then he goes to see the swans, is surprised by vulgar military music, which he can no longer bear, calls out some nonsense to the Wolzogens through the hedge of the palace gardens, and in the evening sits companionably with Levi, Stein, Malwida, Jouk., telling stories of earlier times (Unzelmann, Gerlach, who was always blamed for everything, now Levi). — A few mornings ago he told me of his first patriotic feelings, when his mother took him to the town council.

Thursday, August 17 R. had a good night, but there is never a day free from vexation: today it is a letter from Dr. Strecker making protests about the—indeed very surprising—Italian edition of *Parsifal* planned by Mme Lucca. We have a family lunch, and at 5 o'clock a rehearsal with Frau Materna and Herr Winkelmann, during which R. lays down the main points to be observed in the scene in the 2nd act. He divides up the character of Kundry: first the temptress, who has no recollection of what has gone before; then, after "*so flatterten die Locken*," remembering in wild horror, and desiring loving pity from her redeemer; and, finally, blazing with fury. He also arranges the stage positions of Kundry and Pars. in this scene. In the evening we hold our reception, and R. is unusually hospitable despite his exhausting work in the afternoon.

Friday, August 18 In the morning, since I am now reading the *Oupnekhat*, R. enlarges upon the difference between Christianity and Indian wisdom, stressing his preference for the former on account of its simplicity, and above all its ability to inspire art. After a late breakfast with the children we drive to the theater, and R. is pleased with the success of yesterday's rehearsal. Herr Levi sits with us throughout the performance, during which R. has much to say to him about incorrect tempi, and in particular the insensitive playing of the orchestra.

Saturday, August 19 R. had a good night's rest. With us we have young Fritz Brandt, who has turned out excellently, also Malw. and Stein. In the morning I had an interview with friend Glasenapp about the review of the performances, since our good friends have strayed far from R.'s intentions in their somewhat overhasty judgments. In the afternoon we experience all sorts of difficulties with regard to the wedding. I propose to R. an outing to the Fantaisie; but when he learns something of these difficulties, he insists on turning back halfway to visit the mayor. The Catholic parish priest happens to be standing in front of the town hall, R. promises to restrain himself (we have heard that the priest—angry that Blandine is not being converted—has written to Palermo saying that she will be no asset to the Catholic church; he also added that she is a baptized Protestant, and the parish priest cannot publish the banns of a mixed marriage without a dispensation, which in Italy can be given only by the Pope, not the archbishop). When we declare that we intend to wait quietly until all this has been cleared up, the priest says the Archbishop of Bamberg can give the dispensation! And we discover and experience many other things of a similar sort in connection with this affair! In the evening R. is extremely vexed by a report in the *Köln. Zeitung* about the meeting of the Wagner Societies here; it is true that there was some by no means gentle speaking. (We have signed the contract with Venice.)

Sunday, August 20 Rain! At breakfast Rub. with his father, who looks entirely un-Semitic, and this makes R. suspect that his family, like so many heathen ones in Russia, assumed Judaism, and the men then married Jewesses. At 4 o'clock to the theater, where unfortunately R. is faced with vexations, Herr Scaria curtly insisting that the casting problem should be decided in his favor, and Herr Siehr not prepared to give way. But he is pleased with Frl. Brandt's truly enraptured look in the 2nd act, and during the 3rd act he is in the orchestra and also on stage, where he is pleased to see everyone, even those who at the moment have nothing to do, following it all with keen attention. At home Biag. has received a telegram from his brother, saying that the marriage will be null and void if no public notice is given in Palermo, something which has not yet been done—deliberately, it seems.

Monday, August 21 R. had a good night. Otherwise we are living in a whirl of telegrams in both directions, since great misunderstandings still prevail. At lunch we have our dear Glasenapps. R. is also corresponding with Frl. Malten and Gudehus about appearing again; he sends her his photograph with an inscription, "So, too, thy tear became a dew of blessing"; to Frau Materna, "Kundry here, Brünnhilde there, the work's bright jewel everywhere." — He strolls in the garden and is gratified by Marke's affection toward him. Around 7 o'clock he comes to my room; he has just been reading the riddles in Calderón's *La sibila del oriente* and feels great aversion toward it; he is disgusted by the hairsplitting, artificial playing with the cross. His mood is melancholy, the sky overcast, I feel that all that is left for us is to die together. And in the evening there is a reception, following which R. is feeling unwell!

Tuesday, August 22 R. had a very wretched night, and he gives expression to his annoyance regarding the evening receptions. In the morning I have the contract to read through and sign. But the wedding difficulties still continue! At 4 o'clock we drive to the theater, where R. again finds things to vex him in the rivalry of the two Gurnemanzes, and also an appeal from Frau Materna, from whom, it seems, Vienna is trying to withdraw the role of Isolde. But she pleases R. with her correct grasp of the turning point for Kundry (2nd act). He gets the same good impression behind the scenes altogether. He has supper very late.

Wednesday, August 23   After which he has a very wretched night. On top of that the vexation over Scaria and Siehr continues, the latter intends to leave if he is not permitted to alternate on a regular basis. Herr Gudehus also writes from Dresden that it would be incompatible with his honor as an artist not to take part in the final performance! — We have a family lunch. At 5 o'clock Richter arrives, and he absolutely denies having been put in an awkward position in London by Francke's bankruptcy. Friend Gross came with him to see me; the general has suddenly withdrawn the military band for *Pars.*, which was promised for the whole period—impossible to find out why. We send a telegram to Herr von Bürkel—without telling R. about it—and he immediately sets things right. From Palermo comes the news that the wedding may proceed; we spend the evening in chat with Mimi, Malwida, Levi, Stein.

Thursday, August 24   R. had a good night. At last I am able to make my arrangements for Boni's wedding; he writes a telegram to the King and also a little verse for Boni (to be spoken by Fidi). My father arrives, we hold a reception in the evening. R. has vexations over the Lucca-Strecker affair. In the afternoon I utter my final words to Boni!

Friday, August 25   Preparations! At 11:30 the civil marriage ceremony at Wahnfried; around 11 o'clock the town councilors bring Blandine a pretty table centerpiece. The mayor's speech very dignified; at 12:30 lunch, 27 people at table. R. makes the first speech, turns to Blandine, recalling the poem she recited to him on May 22; he speaks of the crises of his life and describes that which led him to me as the crisis of salvation, remarks how lovely it is for him in this life of crises to see something so natural and so simple as the relationship between her and Biagino; then he comes to the King and calls him the good guardian angel of our lives! — Then Count Schleinitz toasts the Gravina family in a charming speech in which he recalls a saying of Prince Castelcicala. Whereupon the mayor proposes the health of Count and Countess Schleinitz, and the minister rises once more to toast the geniuses of the family in the most graceful and at the same time moving way. At 4 o'clock we drive to the theater, where Mar. Brandt plays Kundry. In the intermissions there is a fireworks display in honor of the day, and on our return home electrical illuminations.

Saturday, August 26   Much turmoil. The young bride very moved and touching. At 11 o'clock the church wedding, the priest, it seems, not very favorably disposed and keeping just within the bounds of personal propriety; his address, with all its sacristan trimmings and impertinent indiscretions, has an embarrassing effect. Biagio conducts himself splendidly, and when, gazing earnestly at Blandine, he places the ring on her finger, we feel that this was the truly sacred act! — The music literally acts on us like balm, an *a cappella* Mass conducted by Herr Levi and sung by our chorus. Then we see them off at the station. It so happens that R. and my father, who remained at home at my request, suddenly appear, to the surprise and joy of all on the platform! The children get in the saloon carriage provided by the railroad management and are borne away. Their departure for me a more than usually serious occasion! — R. writes to Dr. Strecker. He feels upset by the singers who are causing him such difficulties in the matter of casting. He is also upset by the King's failure to attend the performances. In the evening we had invited all our friends who had come for the wedding, and also the singers, who had all so kindly taken part in it. R. comes in, encounters Prof. Bernays first of all, and becomes so annoyed with everybody and everything that, long after all the guests have departed, he is unable to control his ill-humor. In the afternoon, as he was sitting at his writing desk, I went to him to ask how he felt, and he told me then that he wished he might die. Now, late in the evening, while he has some food served to him in the dining room, I sit alone in the deserted rooms and reflect and reflect, until my excited thoughts take refuge in slumber, and I know what it will one day be like! (Yesterday, to our great joy, friend Sulzer arrived, he also attended the wedding.)

Sunday, August 27 R. had a restless night, and his ill-humor persists. He sends a telegram to Herr v. Bürkel, expressing his concern at having received no word from the King. In the evening we have a performance in the presence of the German Crown Prince. For me it is greatly overshadowed by the illness of Count Schleinitz, who has to suffer a severe attack of his illness in the box! — In the course of the day we heard that the singer M. Brandt was in a high state of emotional agitation about some imagined disparagement! (R. invites orchestra and singers for tomorrow.)

Monday, August 28 R. had a tolerable night. A letter from Boni brings us good news and a nice picture of a well-formed character. At lunch we have friend Sulzer and his son (yesterday, too), and we take much delight in this unique man, though R. forbids me to ask him so many questions about political economy. At 5 o'clock the reception in the garden. All the artists, also the Grand Duke of Weimar and the Princess of Meiningen. R. is there at the beginning and is quite vexed by the arrival of the nonartistic guests. He disappears, then returns, makes the rounds of the garden with me, finally converses for a while with the Grand Duke, and even recovers his spirits with the Princess, when he sees that his unreserved and positive character is breaking down her stiffness. She told him that her father could not come because of his wife's illness. "Very wrong of him," says R. "He should have let her be ill and come all the same!" — But in the evening he is still depressed. The whist table is set up for my father with Jouk. and Stein. (Herr v. Bürkel has sent a reassuring reply.)

Tuesday, August 29 R. had a very agitated night. Returning home from farewell walks, I find him unwell. But he is very pleased that Frl. Malten has arrived, responding to his invitation to attend the performance. — We have a final lunch with my father, which leads to much expansiveness between R. and my father! At 4 o'clock I drive with my father to the theater. Frl. Malten and Herr Siehr watch the performance from my box, "heaping coals of fire on the heads of the others," as R. says when he appears during the intermission between Acts I and II. — Unfortunately he is put into a very bad mood when the Grand Duke passes through his *salon* and one of the princely ladies enters it! Everything on stage satisfies him, however, and in the third act, after the transformation music, he takes the baton himself and conducts to the end! Then from the orchestra he says farewell to his artists, after a storm of applause which threatens never to end. Not many of his words could be heard in the auditorium, and he himself tells me that he never knows what he has said. Once, he says, he succeeded in writing down what he had said for the King, and he believes fairly accurately—that was after the dress rehearsal of *T. und I.* But for several years now he has no longer been able to recollect his words. — Our drive home is quiet and solemn, I observe that we can be grateful, even if the achievement was bought at great cost and meant the sacrifice of almost our entire domestic tranquillity. But without a doubt such activity is a necessity for R., and the right thing for him in spite of all difficulties. — Late in the evening we talk with the children about what we have just been experiencing, and it is remarked how differently the orchestra played under his direction, how incomparably different Herr Reichmann as he sang his *"Sterben, einz'ge Gnade."* — I tell how I discovered Papa drinking grog in his dressing room with the conductor, while some of the Flower Maidens were waiting outside to see him once more. — Unfortunately the news of my father's departure tomorrow produces a great outburst of anger.

Wednesday, August 30 Rain! Leave-takings on all sides. For me from my father. For R., who gets up late, from Reichmann, Hill, Frl. Galfy. Herr Neumann annoys him by asking for *Parsifal!* The King's complete silence and failure to come he also finds disturbing. A visit from our friends the Schöns cheers him up at coffeetime, in the evening he also enjoys seeing our friends Mimi, Malwida, and with them Count Wolkenstein and Stein; he talks at length about the performances and remarks how much the singers have learned. He says that Materna completely astonished him, and she had told him that it was all quite different when he was standing with them in the wings! He also talks jokingly of Levi's concern that he might upset the performance. We, on the other hand, maintain that almost all of us heard what was happening in the orchestra, even if we could not exactly explain it at the time. He tells us that when he indicated the fifth quarter note for Herr Reichmann's benefit, he received a "Bravo" from the conductor for this recognition of the singer's weakness. And so these sixteen performances have come to an end, and never once did the spirit of eagerness and dedication desert the artists! And the audience, too, had the feeling of something out of the ordinary, indeed, in the highest sense of the word. I think we can be satisfied.

Thursday, August 31 R. had a good night's rest. Unfortunately he receives another court summons in the Neumann-Batz-*Tristan* affair! — For me there are still a few leave-takings. At lunch we have Heckel, Schön, the Glasenapps; R. speaks of the amazing achievements of the artists. "True," he says, "what impels them is the anxiety to please; but apply this anxiety to noble purposes, and you will still find them ready to serve it with the same eagerness." In the afternoon a discussion with friend Feustel about our business affairs. Then the Brückner brothers come, and the necessary alterations for next year are discussed. At supper R. remembers what he calls his sins, that is to say, his cruel treatment of animals in his youth, also of another boy. — With Herr Schön he discusses the question of the Society, which he wishes to see simplified as much as possible, and particularly to see the word "Patrons" dropped. As yesterday, we have our friends gathered around us; R. plays *Tristan,* the Prelude and conclusion, also the introduction to the 3rd act. Then he takes a very tender leave of the two Glasenapps. Afterward he talks to me about *Parsifal* and *Tristan;* in the introduction to the 3rd act of *Tristan* there is the melancholy of longing, it is "like a fish out of water"; but in the introduction to the 3rd act of *P.* the depression is complete, no longing at all.

Friday, September 1 R. had a good night's rest. I have a discussion with Herr Schön on Society affairs, R. feels uneasy about the King, particularly the fact that Herr v. Bürkel, present at the last performance, did not visit us. The *Fl. Blätter* cheers him up, and a very nice letter from Blandine gives us great delight. At lunch we have our excellent machinist Fritz Brandt, who cannot be praised too highly. The weather is nice in the afternoon, and Dr. Landgraf, whom R. meets in the garden, promises a continuation of the good weather, since it is Saint

Giles's Day. The tame magpie, which has been giving us pleasure for some time now, appears again, attracted by the brilliance of Wahnfried. In the evening we see our friends again, R. plays Bach's C-sharp Minor Prelude and the Prelude to *Parsifal*. These evenings with the last remaining guests are friendly and intimate, and, like me, R. does not find them unpleasant.

Saturday, September 2 R. had a good night, and the day is really fine. Unfortunately R. has a chest spasm after having committed an error of diet. He is worried about the King, whose lack of participation in the performances is very painful to him. We take a drive with the children in the direction of the theater, via the road to the Eremitage. The packing of the restaurant equipment and Herr Albert's complaints leave a sad impression. But it is always a joy to see the dogs again. In the evening R. bursts out in bitter complaint about Bayreuth, saying that nobody has followed him and settled down here, and that the town itself has shown him not the slightest understanding. With the exception of a few friends, everyone has remained aloof; we had made an effort with all classes of society, he had joined the historic Thursday gathering, but nowhere had he gained an influence, and at his performances it stabbed him to the heart to see the army officers lounging around, the Bayr. citizens looking on as if it were all just a spectacle—to none of them did it ever occur to buy a seat. (Departures: Malw., Mimi.)

Sunday, September 3 R. is very tired. A letter from Herr von Bürkel sets our minds completely at rest. Another, from Dr. Dorda (tutor for Fidi), leads to a discussion, but R. decides against him on account of his bloated, Bohemian nature. We drive to the Fantaisie after having had lunch with our three friends Levi, Jouk., and Stein. There we experience a wonderful golden light, due no doubt to the dampness impregnating the air. At supper we are much reduced, Daniela being on a visit and our good Siegfried having left today for Dresden to see the dentist; for my admonitions to the latter I have been compared with Polonius! Before our drive I spent a happy time in the summerhouse with R. We were pleased by the house, the garden, the stillness, and the walk afterward also gave him great pleasure. In the evening our conversation turned to Bach, the *Passion;* when I observed that it is out of place in a church, R. agrees with me. A musical journal ascribes the Amen of the Dresden Mass, used in *Parsifal,* to the conductor Naumann, but R. and I feel it is much older.

Monday, September 4 R. slept well. Our Siegfried leaves at 1 o'clock. At lunch we have our friends the Grosses; Adolf crowned indeed with fame, since his activities during the festival were quite beyond compare. Herr von Ziegler (secretary) writes to me on behalf of the King, or whom R.'s telegram seems to have had some effect. — R.'s word of thanks is in the newspapers. We drive to Bürgerreuth via Eremitage; R. talks about his reading of Hume, is pleased that the writer has so many positive things to say about the "Maid of Orleans," whereas Shakespeare only showed the witch in her. Again and again one is astonished by the French character, desecrating their national heroine through Voltaire! — We receive the thoroughly satisfactory accounts of the festival performances. [*Enclosed in the Diaries; see notes.*]

Tuesday, September 5 Return of our "Hanswurst," as R. calls Lusch on account of her jests, and from Schnappauf we receive news of Siegfried, who is now comfortably installed at the Jenkinses'. R. starts a letter to the King; I drive to the Fantaisie in the morning with the children. Poems by G. Keller, sent to us by Sulzer, do not entirely please us, but some of them, such as the "Goethe-Philistines," we do enjoy. Friend Gross visits us, and R. talks about the hotel plan which has been sent to him; unfortunately its very modern character is little to his liking. In the afternoon we visit the swans in the palace gardens, the damp air soon drives us home. In the evening R. recalls early memories, particularly of Weber, on whose sharpness he remarks—how he once called out to the man singing Kaspar (at the appearance of Samiel), "Here we sing this in the correct tempo." R. says that as a boy he happened to be in the theater on that occasion. — He then plays Siegfried's awakening of Brünnhilde, is pleased with the character of this work, its trueness to Nature: "Like two animals," he says of Br. and Sieg. "Here there is no doubt, no sin," he continues, and in his Wotan he recognizes the true god of the Aryans. He then takes a very friendly leave of our conductor.

Wednesday, September 6 R. had a good night's rest. Pouring rain in the morning. He continues his letter to the King. Around lunchtime I hear him in the garden laughing out loud, it was about the noise the hens were making after they had laid their eggs. — Over coffee the subject of genius is discussed, the word itself, the difference in the way it is used in German and in French, the curious fact that the Germans use a foreign word [*Genie*] for an idea so very much their own. In the afternoon we receive our friend Sulzer's warm and significant article about *Parsifal;* I immediately read it to R., then we drive together to friend Feustel's to settle some business matters. In the evening I read the article to Stein. Before this a telegram from Herr Voltz thoroughly annoyed R., as does everything connected with this affair. We play whist. During it R. says he misses the Flower Maidens, he had been unable to show them adequately how pleased he was with them, though at every performance he had loudly called "Bravo" above the heads of the whole audience.

Thursday, September 7 R. had a good night, but he suffers all day from catarrh, and the summons to the law court in October angers him. However, he continues writing his letter to the King and particularly mentions the Flower Maidens. In the afternoon he feels so indisposed that he sends for the doctor. In the evening we play whist, but he is not in good spirits.

Friday, September 8 R. had a restless night; he dreamed of Wahnfried, which had been completely altered; everywhere arrangements for a reception, and he being asked who he was, whereupon he loudly and angrily gave his name, and at the same time heard me laugh in a neighboring room, then he woke up. — In the morning he continues to write to the King. Earlier I drove to Laineck with the children. At 5 o'clock we have a discussion with friend Feustel and the lawyer Dr. Meyer about the Batz relationship. R. writes to Herr Voltz and concludes, "I should be ashamed to be in a certain person's place." Feustel attests to the fact that, though R. had not retained the papers, his memory is thoroughly sound and can be confidently relied on. — In the evening the conversation turns to Shylock, and R. reads the scenes in which he appears, after expressing his admiration for a representation of this racial character such as will never be achieved again. In the face of his ever-increasing admiration for Shakesp. his earlier predilection for Calderón is tending to diminish; in much of him R. discerns artificiality, a Jesuit outlook, and he takes very good care to read no more of it.

Saturday, September 9 R. slept well. Lacking something light to read, he takes up a book Lusch is now reading, Cooper's *The Bravo*. At lunch we have our neighbors the Schölers. I then suggest to R. the pretty drive to Laineck and the walk through the meadows as far as St. Johannis. The weather is very lovely, but R. finds the final stretch through the village onerous and calls for the carriage; Isolde, fearing that it will be in the place where we first ordered it to wait, rushes ahead; meanwhile the carriage, which had just been driving up and down, makes its appearance before R. and I arrive at that spot, and in indescribable concern we then set out to look for Isolde, whom we at last find in Laineck! — R. very angry, I just glad to have my child back! In the evening we play whist. Herr v. St.'s impending departure brings my worries about Siegfried's education so close that it is all I can do to keep them at bay.

Sunday, September 10 R. had a good night's rest. Since the children have gone on an outing to Berneck with our neighbors, R. and I are quite alone, as in the earliest years, or perhaps one day in later years, happy and lively and at peace. R. receives a letter from Fidi, I tell R. my worries, and since he can never bear to see suffering without doing something about it, he writes to friend Glasenapp, asking him to move here with his whole family in order to take over Siegfried's education. — The question of the W. Society, brought up again by Wolz. and Schön, is distasteful to him, he wants the utmost simplicity. In the evening, after the children have returned home, we go through the various relationships we have had with people. "Alas," R. exclaims, "we are as full of experiences as a dog is of fleas!" (We had spent the afternoon together in the garden, taking much delight in the animals.)

Monday, September 11 R. slept well, but too strong a dose of Karlsbad salts disturbs the tranquillity of his day. He writes to Herr Neumann, whose telegram has pleased him. Otherwise he is kept busy signing the many photographs he is sending to his artists. His delight in his artists grows ever greater in recollection, and thoughts of the consistency of the performances have a very beneficial effect on him. — In the afternoon he recalled his relationship with the Wesendoncks and remarked on Herr W.'s constant readiness to help him. In the evening, at my request, he reads to us [Lope de Vega's] *Fuente ovejuna,* which enchants us.

Tuesday, September 12 R. slept well, and he continues signing his photographs. Siegfried returns today, delights us with his lively eyes, and Dr. Jenkins's report on him is extremely encouraging. But we are soon concerned about his pale face. Over coffee R. speaks agreeably about the picture of my mother. In the afternoon Herr Feustel visits us in order to discuss the Voltz-Batz affair once again. In the evening R. plays the introduction to the 3rd act of *Parsifal* and tells us that Herr Zeisel the barber had singled it out as particularly impressive: "You see, it is not so!" He writes to Herr Levi, acceding to his wish to delete a pause as Kundry brings the bowl ("*Nicht so*"). He is in a merry mood and speaks in humorous phrases, most of them in a Saxon accent, about his attitude toward the world. Then he reads to us two intermezzi by Lope in Schack's edition, which give us much enjoyment. At lunch he said to Stein, who had replied reassuringly to my question about his father's attitude, "No father is eaten as hot as he is cooked," and to Jouk., "So you want to go to Weimar, where Goethe went to the bad!" — And to me he is unutterably kind and loving. — To friend Wolz. he sends his ultimatum (revised by Stein) concerning the Society.

Wednesday, September 13 R. had a good night and continues with his signatures. A lawyer, Herr Josephsthal, has been sent here by Herr Batz, and because of this there is once more in the afternoon a conference for R. with Dr. Meyer and Feustel. In the evening, as so often before, he plays something from *Der Freischütz,* including the part of Max's aria with the words "*Wenn sich rauschend Blätter regen*" ["When the rustling leaves are stirring"]. When he praises its peculiarly graceful lyricism, I tell him that in style it reminds me a little of Beethoven's songs, and he agrees with me, plays and sings "*An die entfernte Geliebte*" to our very great delight. The only thing he deplores in it is the brilliant concert ending. (All kinds of curious letters, including one from Frl. Uhlig, who offers R. his original letters for 3,000 marks. Then one from a Herr Langhans, who feels that *Lohengrin* contains a transgression of German hereditary law: Elsa would not have the right to offer him her country! Along with these are letters arriving daily from grateful schoolteachers to whom R. gave seats for *Parsifal.*)

Thursday, September 14 R. had a restless night. And he now gets down to clearing things up, a task we began a few days ago. Several business matters have to be settled. Hardest of all R. finds the parting from the dogs, Marke in particular, whom he feels he will not see again! — Siegfried's appearance is also worrying us, and me the unsettled nature of his young existence, also the sorrow he experienced in finding on his return that the large theater he had laboriously built for himself in the little garden had been destroyed on his father's instructions. We depart at 7 in the evening. Seeing the bookbinder Senfft, our manager, Moritz, and Schnappauf at the station, R. says, "For me they are Bayreuth." The journey to Nuremberg takes a long time, R. dozes off and says to me, "You are talking of roses, I can smell them here." In Nuremberg we say goodbye to our friend Joukowsky. R. sleeps but is restless, frequently talking aloud. When there is mention on the train of the Wagnerites' preference for *T. und I.* even over *Parsifal,* R. says: "Oh, what do they know? One might say that Kundry already experienced Isolde's *Liebestod* a hundred times in her various reincarnations."

Friday, September 15 At 8 in the morning we are in Munich; the station inspector, who traveled to Bayreuth 4 times to see *Parsifal,* offers us breakfast. Siegfried is worrying us, he is very pale, and since he complains of a headache, I make some cold compresses for him. In Bolzano we are greeted in pouring rain by our dear and honored friends the Schleinitzes. At 11 in the evening we are in Verona, where we encounter some difficulties. Since I am much afraid that Siegfried has a chill, I wrap him up in a long black fur, and he mounts the steps ahead of us, slow, pale, with a large round hat. R. exclaims, "Abellino, the great bandit!"

Saturday, September 16 Much noise during the night, and in the morning the din of a market; R. exclaims, "*Les doux accents de l'Italie!*" ["The soft accents of Italy!"] — But we soon learn that Verona is flooded, and to reach the station we have to make detours and drive through water. But the town looks magnificent. When we again enter our saloon carriage, R. cries, "*Dich, teure Halle, grüss ich wieder!*" ["To thee, dearest hall, once more my greeting!"] There is a real threat of danger, and the noise during the night was made by soldiers leaving their barracks. I express my surprise at these soldiers, and R. says they look like Slovaks. I amused him yesterday when, in connection with a very effusive newspaper article, I told him that we now accompanied our great deeds with Turkish music. In this same newspaper I read that the naturalist Wallace has become a spiritualist, "That is what is now happening to everybody who lacks patience, who cannot set his sights wide enough," says R. "Those of us, however, who can afford to be patient, since it is only from the downfall of this world of property that we expect anything, we live in a mood of hopeful resignation." — The countryside is lovely in spite of the rain. Since, recalling the forsaken people at home, I write at the various stations to Marie Schöler, R., very much against it, says to me jokingly, "With all your devotion you will make sure that when we die, only your coffin will be followed!" At half past two we are in Venice; the town pleases us in spite of the gray weather, and the P[alazzo] Vendramin, which we inspect immediately, greatly appeals to us. Our lunch around 4 o'clock is very cheerful, and over coffee he reflects on Nature's production of great individualities at a time when it is worried over the collapse of a generic idea. He compares this to the birth of twins following periods of war. — The children look at pictures in *Über Land und Meer*. And, commenting on the modern world, R. tells us of the silliness of student songs and sings to us "*Vif la Vif la la.*"

Sunday, September 17 A terrible storm in the night! In the morning we go to the Vendramin and arrange things there. When we return home at one o'clock, there is such a huge thunderstorm that we feel it will not be possible to ride in a gondola, but the gondoliers reassure us and perform a real masterpiece. R. feels depressed, goes to bed, but soon gets up again, goes out in spite of the rain, and returns in good spirits. A book belonging to the Hôtel de l'Europe, *Balzac chez lui*, gives him pleasure, like everything else that is lively and has to do with significant personalities. The mention of Montfaucon, Balzac's interest in crime stories interests him tremendously; he thinks of postmen, locomotive stokers, and exclaims: "What moral powers and capacities of self-sacrifice can be seen there! They encourage one to be hopeful." — In the evening all that finds its way through the floods to us is a telegram from the theater director Staegemann, instead of news from the children and our friends the Schleinitzes!

Monday, September 18 R. slept well, but Siegfried is still very pale. Our breakfast is cheerful, however, and R. tells us about the book on Buddha which he is now reading and which constantly states that one can know nothing for certain; he says this critical approach to history is fine, but it should not be applied to subjects like this. The news of the floods is dreadful, and R. asks me what I think of God's intelligence now! — In spite of the rain R. and I go out around midday to look at furniture, and in the afternoon we move into the Vendramin, worried about S.'s pallor! In the evening the singers appear; R. gives them a substantial gift, along with a request never to come again.

Tuesday–Wednesday, September 19–20 R. had a wretched night with wild dreams; first about Lusch's engagement, then about two cavaliers who were with me and who behaved scornfully toward R.; when R. turned to them and gave them to understand that he knew the sort of lives they were leading, I angry about it, they asking R. whether he had been speaking with this man or that; R.: "Yes," then, threatened, calling out, "Police!," and I to his relief also loudly crying, "Police!" along with him. — He has now decided either to find contentment here or, failing that, to return to Wahnfried forever. Over our breakfast together he talks about the book on Buddha and says that by giving much attention to B. one learns to understand Christianity, and people were surely now beginning to realize that the greatest heroic power lies in resignation. At lunch, after having taken some opium, he turns to that curious book about Judaism he once read and says that such clairvoyant, pessimistic people achieve some kind of progress, the present-day historians and scientists none at all. A telegram from Glasenapp consenting to R.'s proposal touches us greatly [*telegram enclosed; see notes*]. On the other hand, news of Frau Lucca's behavior and the King's plans with regard to *Parsifal* cause R. great alarm. In the evening Herr v. St. reads us his article about Renan's *M. Aurèle*. R. remarks that it is characteristic of Renan to maintain that the Christians, by forbidding usury, held up civilization for several centuries.

Thursday, September 21 Despite a bad night I hear R. singing to me in the morning, "Long may the King live, my Christel, and I: the King for all people, but Christel for me!" Our night was disturbed by thunderstorms and mosquitoes. In the house a little 70-year-old paper hanger is working with quiet, but frantic, zeal. The weather is fine, a telegram from Herr Neumann reports further successes. R. drinks some champagne, feels unwell in consequence. We ride to the Riva, where we take a leisurely walk, he recalling his visit to K. Ritter! Back home he is annoyed by reports in Herr Lessmann's journal. I write to Frau Lucca on his behalf. In the evening letters arrive from friend Glasenapp and Herr von Bürkel, both very good, but R. finds something to worry about in everything!

Friday, September 22 R. had a bad night, and he is weighed down by all sorts of cares! Even the Glasenapp family's move to Bayreuth, pleasing in itself, causes him concern. But he is very gentle toward me, and since I seek to reduce his turmoil just by maintaining silence, he feels this to be kind and loving! — But the town gives him much pleasure, he goes out before lunch and tells us of his delight. Unfortunately his room is not yet furnished, so that he still has to live amid much turmoil. All the same, his amiable manner does not desert him, and after coffee, when I ask Herr von Stein to read me his article about Luther and the peasants since I wish to comment on it to him, R. creeps in unobserved and then makes many jokes about us! After that we go to see the lion at the Arsenal, which makes the same magnificent impression on R. as before, then to the Giardino Pubblico, since R. wishes to inquire whether Siegfried can take riding lessons there. — We ride as far as the Piazzetta and from there walk to the Rialto, but R. finds walking difficult, his chest spasms always threatening. In the evening we talk much about Calderón, Rub. having returned the plays he borrowed. We recall our previous enthusiasm for him and decide that one probably needs to be in a special mood to appreciate these works of art.

Saturday, September 23 R. had a good night, but he has a spasm in the morning. His pleasure in our lovely dwelling he expresses in this melancholy way: "Lovely is it everywhere, till Richard comes with all his care!" Herr Hausburg's announcement that he will be able to come to us is agreeable in that it gives us a bit more time for the Glas.'s, but even this disturbs R. — He reads *Faust* and quotes what the Arch-Chamberlain says to the Emperor, "If thou but read my heart, I'm honoured as is meet," saying it is quite extraordinary, and he is pleased with all the subtle strokes in the battle, etc. R. and I go out around 5 o'clock, walk to the confectioner's (Lavena), and ride home in a splendid sunset, which is followed by bright moonlight. R. spends the evening quietly by himself, since he is feeling very run down (he made two errors of diet, beer and champagne, in the past few days).

Sunday, September 24 R. was up once in the night for a fairly long time, but after that he slept well. In the morning he tells me several things from Buddha, including sayings about women, taken from the book he is now enjoying. Around midday he goes for a shave and returns home by gondola. After lunch we have a thunderstorm, which upsets us, because we think of our dear Schleinitzes held captive in Bolzano. We go to the H. de l'Europe, R. and I, then to Lavena's; R. is feeling well and tells me he is always cheerful when he goes for a ride with me (the children at the time in the public baths). In the evening he reads to us and then gets me to read some very fine things from Buddha, in which he is pleased to note that B. never wished to talk about the beginning or the end.

Monday, September 25 R. had a very bad night. "Why," he says as he gets up, "hold on to a life in which I show nothing but grimaces to the people I love?" — At breakfast he tells me of an article in the *I. Z.* for the 16th, in which we and the children are talked about; he finds it on the whole quite pleasing. In another issue he is amused by the heroes of the 30 Years' War, though he speaks admiringly of Bernhard von W[eimar] as a true German, and powerful. His delight in Venice and our dwelling grows daily. The palazzo opposite, single-storied, as he likes it, pleases him immensely, and to watch the gondolas across the garden, "flitting past like elves," is for him the ultimate charm. In the afternoon he goes out with Lusch and Fidchen; the smoking men at the confectioner's, the familiar way in which a Prince Biron greets Daniela, these things make him indignant. Over supper he talks about the nature of Venice's history. Then he goes off for a rest and afterward comes back to us, saying that he will live for another 24 years. He talks about Buddha, the portrayal of whom he is now reading with great attention. Then we come to the common people in Shakespeare, who do not emerge very creditably, even in *Coriolanus,* and he reads to us Warwick's speech in *H. VI,* following the battle that was lost. [*The nineteenth book of the Diaries ends with the words* "reads to us from"; *the twentieth book begins:* "Sept. 25, 1882, continued: written on Saint Cosmas's Day—i.e., September 27."] — We are glad to be quite alone at the end of it. (News of the flooding sounds terrible.) (Good-natured letter from Frau Lucca.)

Tuesday, September 26 R. slept well, and I hope that he will stick properly to his diet. He writes to friend Glasenapp and jokingly praises himself for this deed. Over coffee, when friend Rub. asks him for his opinion about the orchestration of the "Pictures," he mildly but very definitely gives him to understand that he does not care to occupy himself with such things, which are a concession to publishers. Then all of us together view the Palazzo Vendramin, which pleases him greatly, and after that he goes with the children to Lavena's. For the evening a ride in the moonlight had been planned, but he does not feel like it, and the children go alone. At around 5:30 I went for a little walk by myself, and on my return R. reads to me wonderful things by Buddha about beginning and end. Yesterday, talking of Weber, R. said, "When I first heard his melodies, Mozart's ceased to mean anything to me." — And in connection with Rub.'s piano playing (I asked him, when R. was out, to play his "Pictures" to us), R. told me that he found all piano playing absurd!

Wednesday, September 27 Last night R. had his other regularly recurring dream, that is to say, that he had stolen, and behaved in a cowardly way, passing two men and trying to put the purse down so that they would not see it, but they noticed it, whereupon he woke up.

He got up once during the night and read the book on Buddha. In the morning he notices some photographs on my desk, among them those of Palma Vecchio; he finds the women lovely, but the Christ operatic, with his curls and too-great beauty. In the middle of breakfast he gets up and discovers the Saint Cosmas, which I think pleases him. We now talk almost constantly about Buddha; recently R. remarked how impossible it would have been for him to set him to music if he had had to concern himself with mango trees, lotus blossoms, etc.

In the afternoon R. and I go to the Piazzetta, where R. has the idea of taking the steamer to the Lido to fetch the children. On the steamer R. was delighted by a dog, and he said, "What a joy it is suddenly to see such a naïve creature before one's eyes!" We do find Siegf. and Stein, but the girls are unpunctual; we decide to say nothing to them and to play a joke on them, but at supper we discover that they were delayed by a horrible accident: a young lady was drowned, they saw it and also witnessed the despair of the father, husband, and brothers! . . . The evening passes in horrifying accounts of it. — After the children have left, I bring the conversation around to the Society, about which Wolz. has asked me. (At lunch R. told us that he had written "some flattering words" to Frau Materna, then to Niemann about Wilhelmj, since he could not bear such cases of injustice, then he went walking in the direction of the Cannaregio.)

Thursday, September 28 R. was restless during the night, and he feels the final topic of our conversation upset him. He writes to Wolz. in the morning and shows me the letter he has begun. But he is in cheerful spirits, and when I show him the pattern I have selected for the sashes, he says, in approving it, "They will be the gondoliers of the sad countenance." Around lunchtime, having finished his letter, he goes out, and at table tells us of the pleasure this always gives him. Over coffee we come to speak of how quickly the observation of certain rules leads people into strange conceits; I tell Fénelon's reply to an inquiry by the Duke of Burgundy: "Eat a whole calf on Fridays, Monseigneur, but remain a Christian." R. says that Fén., in his elegant priest's robes, did not get to the heart of the matter here, even if he had been right about the observation of Friday, and then he exclaims, "It seems that we (humanity) have not been put here to provide a picture of eternity." — And he goes on to talk about property, which he regards as the root of all evil. Of the world he says jokingly, "When the Lord felt like playing a silly trick in order to amuse himself, he created the world!" — Then he cites the theater devotee in [Tieck's] *Phantasus,* for whom even the worst theater was a symbol of eccentricity. — We then go to the Hôtel de l'Europe, where the unhappy family of the drowned woman is staying— and learn there that she had been married only a week! — Also that the accident was the result of negligence and cowardice. — R. then buys a hat for Siegfried and goes with him to look for a shower. We stay up late in the evening. While R. is resting I read the 3rd act of [Calderón's] *Amor, honor y poder* to the children, then we chat. R. tells us his dream: I had smilingly shown him a letter signed "Leopold" in which a prince had asked for Lusch's hand, and he says he awoke feeling in a certain sense flattered! Then we discuss his letter to Wolz., which he is glad to have written. — He recalls his sister Ottilie, then talks about his brother Albert, whom he describes as foolish and talented at one and the same time— the sort of man, Röckel had declared, whom one must try to drive utterly wild. — Then we read parts of the Anti-Semitic Society's manifesto, which seems to us both sad and comical, and R. makes jokes about the German passion for "committees" in particular! Then, more seriously, he remarks that nobody has paid any attention at all to what he wrote in "Know Thyself" about our own blame for our situation. When we go off to bed, he shows me the Cosmas portières which our little 75-year-old paper hanger put up for him with tremendous dexterity! . . . Yesterday he told me merrily that he was thinking of having his "extravagances" in Wahnfried gradually removed, so that after our death certain Wagnerites—R. mentions Dr. Schemann— cannot laugh at them. And very gaily we talk of the instructions, recalling F. W. I. At lunch he told us a legend about Buddha, how he was reborn as a rabbit and, unable to sacrifice anything but lowly grass to the Brahman who brought the animals their food, leaped into the fire and found it wonderfully cool. This day, too, we conclude by comparing the merits of Christianity and Buddhism.

Friday, September 29   R. slept well, and we have breakfast in cheerful spirits; I admonish him to place his eggcup farther in on the table, since frequently he has a very vexing mishap with it, but he does not do so, and when I say that this obstinacy, which is a weakness in others, is a divine power as far as he is concerned, he laughs loudly and seizes every occasion to say, "My divine power!" It also always raises his spirits to gaze at the little garden and see beyond it the gondolas flitting past "like silent ghosts." He thinks of Goethe and Schiller, who persisted in staying in Weimar and Jena; he finds that incredible, though certainly these places were better than Dresden, Vienna, or Berlin, for instance. When I observe that we would certainly have stayed in Bayreuth if it had not been for the climate, he says, "All the same, I prefer the sight of the town here to the road to the Eremitage!" At lunch, after we have talked about our morning walks, he tells us that he started his in the neighborhood of the M. dell'Orto and had two encounters with the common people, first of all with a man who, talking to someone behind him, did not notice him and collided with him, and was profuse in his apologies; but then a rogue who begged from him and could not tear his eyes away from the pendants on his watch chain. Over coffee—since Dan. replies to him in a very dignified way—he discusses my rebuke yesterday and says that I was wrong, that I had misunderstood the children's curiosity. As I am explaining myself, he gets up and leaves the room, but he soon returns and is quite gay and unconcerned. He says of the Italians that they deserve to be beaten, since they did away with the drum and introduced the "contemptible" high trumpet in its stead. He compared the flutes in present-day orchestras with steamship whistles. Yesterday evening he began to sing the *Leonore* Overture and said nobody before Beeth. had any notion of a theme like that. — R. goes out with the children while I copy his letter to Herr Neumann. They tell me at supper about their visit to Bauer's, where they enjoyed beer and chocolate, then about the rude waiters, all very lighthearted. In the evening Herr Wolkoff visits us and entertains R. with his lively conversation about the present problems of science, among them experiments with hypnosis. Then he amuses us with stories about the present-day painters called Impressionists, who paint "nocturne symphonies" in ten minutes! (At table recently R. said that for him portraiture was the main feature of painting, its true discovery. He said large historical compositions meant little to him. But tonight, expressing his preference for clean, not daubed, painting, he adds jokingly, "I am for Titian's *Tribute Money*.") At lunch there was talk of the natural age of a human being (200 years), and I recalled that R. recently said he would live to be 94, and we would have to put up with him for another 24 years! — At supper he thought of Marke on our last day, how he seemed to know that R. was going away. [*Enclosed in the Diaries a visiting card bearing the name Joseph Schroeder and inscribed by Wagner:* "Founder of idealism."]

Saturday, September 30 R. realizes that he has again made an error of diet with his beer! — At breakfast we discuss the appearance of the Russian painter and naturalist (Wolkoff), who certainly has no inkling of our world but made a pleasant impression because of the liveliness with which he looks at things. R. feels that Riemer and Falk must surely have been lively people, too, also the art expert Meyer, otherwise Goethe would not have put up with them; he says of our two North German friends, "One brings out everything with a crack, the other with a snap." — He does not go out this morning, but he is cheerful at lunch. Since Rub. has seen [Schiller's] *Die Räuber* here, and yesterday witnessed the audience's utter lack of sympathy for it, R. recalls having seen the same play in the Strand in London, followed by *Les Deux Frères Corses,* in which the duel made everyone hold their breath

—R. was also as fascinated by it as if it had been a real experience. — R. was reading *Faust* in the morning, and he tells us about it over coffee; he even jumps up to fetch the book, and he reads to us Faust's conversation with Meph. before the battle. The stage direction "Martial music behind the audience" R. singles out as proof of how right he was concerning the stage he had thought out for *Faust*. He says *Faust* is the finest book ever written in the German language. And at the conclusion of the scene, closing the book, he says, "Uniquely divine." — Through the doggerel verse it gains something undefinable. Wit, of quite a different kind from Shakespeare's, and the times in which he lived, "nearer in spirit to certain aims," offered completely new motives. "And how he did enjoy it!"—such features delight him. — A basilica designed by Siegf. astonishes R. We go out together, Stein, Siegf., R., and I, and R. leads us to S. Zaccaria; the church itself, the exterior, which he finds too effeminate, as well as the interior, which does not appeal to him, leave him indifferent, but Bellini's painting fascinates him. After looking at it for a while, he remarks how good work immediately stands out amid all the daubing (by this he means the other pictures in the church). And a little later: "It stands there like a dream image!" He is sorry to see a saint holding the Book in it— he finds that too Jewish. "When the saint is present, what need for the Book?" — But "It is good to live close to something like this," he says. — We sit down between the pillars of the portal on Saint Mark's Square, R.'s favorite place. We return home in a glorious sunset. In the evening he tells us, from the book he is now reading, that Buddha did not accept the sick and the crippled: "It sounds very harsh at first, and yet there is deep meaning, great wisdom in it; since the stifling of desire is all that matters, there can be no acceptance for people whose illness makes desire impossible." — He advises Stein to write a novel about the new life in emigration, and he praises Heinse for writing at the end of his *Ardinghello,* when the blessed isles are founded, that the colonists decided not to allow property to intervene between them. He reads to us further passages in *Faust* describing the battle; the Emperor's hollow pathos, the images Faust employs to help him over all the horrors, the essence of battle, the brutal might of blood lust, and the craze for booty—all this, with much more besides, arouses our delighted admiration anew. The verse in which the Emperor desires to meet the daemonic powers to whom he is indebted, in order to decorate them, arouses in R. a laugh of appreciative understanding.

Sunday, October 1   "For all guilt finds vengeance here below, and if you drink beer, it's bound to cause you woe": with these words R. greets me and at the same time tells me of his bad night, in which he had for company the croaking of the frogs and *Faust,* Act V. Of the latter he goes on to say that it is a sketch, that is to say, there is no continuity of action and the most significant moment could be dealt with in three-quarters of a page, whereas a very long time is spent on all the rest. He also discovered some completely incomprehensible passages in it, left in on account of the rhyme, and he also feels the pastoral description of the covetous bishop is rather out of place. It has enormous objectivity, he says, but also a great coldness, which makes it difficult to take an interest in Faust himself. — Around 11 o'clock we are surprised by the young bridal couple, very happy, it seems. R. writes to Herr v. Bürkel, referring very seriously to the possibility, mentioned in this gentleman's last letter, of an impending visit; he says how difficult it is for him to request from the King such favors as chorus and orchestra, knowing that the King himself will get no pleasure from them. At lunch much chatter in all languages; we go out for a ride around 4 o'clock; because of my bad foot I remain in the gondola. R. lets the children go into S. Marco and climb the tower, while he sits down again between the pillars. "I was Hagen on the Wasgenstein," he says, adding that it is so lovely that he will one day be found lying dead there. It is impossible to describe all the things one sees there, he says, and, apart from a few foreigners, nobody takes any notice of one. — In the evening the children go for another walk in Saint Mark's Square; R. then talks to Stein and me about the book on Buddha, which he praises highly, saying it is much more significant than Köppen's. Buddhism itself he declares to be a flowering of the human spirit, against which everything that followed was decadence, but also against which Christianity arose by a process of compression. Buddhism shows evidence of an extraordinarily youthful power in the human spirit, he says, not unlike the time when language was first invented. It exerts no compulsion of any sort, in consequence it has no church; the monk could return to the world if he no longer cared for the monastic life; no divine service, just atonement and good works. But it was this happy lack of organization which made it so easy for such a highly organized power as Brahmanism to oust it. — For him, R. says, the whole of Christianity is contained in Holy Communion. But it is the fact that it was possible to found a church, and that so gloriously gentle a character as Saint Francis had humbly to bow before its leader, that makes Christianity so questionable. — At lunch the English travelers had been referred to as "shopkeepers"; in this connection R. reflects that in England the most useful segment of society is regarded with contempt, and he remarks how far one has to go in order to say anything about it! And he frequently invokes Buddha and Rousseau; the first, who never said what he knew about the beginning and end of things, the second, who could not say what

had been his inner vision. — Then he talks about an article he intends
to write on Italian church music and German military music, finding it
utterly wrong that our army organization should be presented as
something positively good. He says this constant linkage with prevailing conditions—as, for example, in C. Frantz, who even considers
it a good thing that a part of Germany has remained Catholic—may
appear all right at first, but soon one begins to feel that all depth is
lacking; a person who expresses this opinion has never heaved a sigh
of horror concerning the world.

Monday, October 2 R. slept well; he dreamed that a (40th) jubilee
performance of *Rienzi* was being given in Dresden; he was to conduct
it, but he was held up with me on a bridge; when we arrived, he heard
church music from the 1st act and said, "The Court is bound to put my
coming late down to conceit." In the morning he reads *Buddha*. At
breakfast we talked about Siegfried, who is looking very pale, and we
feel he is finding Stein's company too much of a burden. In the afternoon a letter from Dr. Strecker, enclosing a copy of R.'s contract with
Frau Lucca (according to which she seems to have the right to publish),
causes R. great vexation. We go out with Siegfried, get out at the
colonnades, and, after visiting a decorator's shop in which the modern
things which attracted R. from outside displease him greatly inside,
come via the Piazzetta to the courtyard of the Doge's Palace; look at
many things in it. The high wall with just the 3 windows pleases R.,
too; he says, "What promise of ceremony that holds out!" We gaze at
the fountains. But the Roman statues make R. indignant: "What are
such things doing here?" At the exit the lovely single window delights
him, then the griffins, and we gaze at the Knights Templar, who gave
him the idea for the headdress of his Knights. Yesterday, when I
asked him to turn around and look at the gateway to the courtyard of S.
Zaccaria, he told me he knew it by heart; on his earlier visits people had
always brought him that far and no farther; I tell him jokingly that it is
I who have taught him a feeling for art! In the Giardino Reale he recalls
that it was there that he first received the news of *Lohengrin*'s success in
Vienna. On the homeward journey he is amused by the man in the
gondola who, accompanied by a barrel organ, imitates opera singers
and conducts. R. says he is without doubt a destitute orchestra player,
and he could write his whole life. [*Added at the bottom of the next two
pages but referred back to here:* "But afterward he relapses into thought,
then says, half to himself, 'All these experiences before getting ready
for *Parsifal!*' — 'A terrible world!'—again half aloud, shaking his
head—'small wonder that it should respond to the question of *Parsifal*
with Strecker, Lucca, Batz!' — And further: 'About church and military
music—a person like Wolkoff will laugh at the idea, find it facetious,

but nobody else ever thinks of such things!' "] In the evening R. plays and sings to us Tristan's appearance in answer to Isolde's summons. Then friend Rub. arrives and at our request plays us the conclusion of *Götterdämmerung,* R. joins in and sings Brünnhilde's last words, is pleased with it all, so heathen and Germanic! "It is so free," he says, "yet at the same time so tender." — "I am glad that I had the ability to paint in variegated colors." — He recalls Gobineau and the Germanic world which came to an end with this work, and says he wishes for strength to stage the *Ring* once more and do it well.

Tuesday, October 3 R. had a wretched night. His first words in the morning concern Dr. Strecker, and I know that his ensuing and prolonged spasm is directly connected with this vexation. I succeed in taking his mind off these wretched subjects at breakfast and gradually restore his good humor by talking about the pretty things in his room. When I tell him that the color of his jacket is the pinkish mauve the French kings used to wear, he replies, "With golden lilies, I shall have the golden mean embroidered on it." — He reads *Buddha* but feels unwell all day. He does not go out, wanders through the rooms and now and again writes down a joke to tell me, but he is indisposed. In the afternoon, after the children have gone out, I sit with him for a while; things are all right then, as always, but I cannot hold back life, which invariably introduces unrest! . . . Friend Levi visits us, by no means unwelcome to R., who, sitting in the smoking niche, is content looking back on the *Parsifal* days, and his only regret is not having spent enough time with his artists. In the evening he withdraws early, I follow him and lie down beside him. He cannot get to sleep and complains about the boring company he is keeping; indeed, he is even disturbed by all the bustle of the children, which he usually enjoys: "Oh, if only I were dead!" So he gets up, lights the light, and reads the *B. Blätt.,* Gob.'s article with his preface. Toward me he is always the same: "I wanted to see what the Atman was doing," he said when he came looking for me in the afternoon! — "Siegfr. is causing me so much worry that I woke up during the night with a start on his account!"

Wednesday, October 4 R. has finished the book on Buddha, and he reads to me the passage in it about deeds—that these, too, are finite and that the Atman is superior to them. This reminds us of the doctrine of grace in Saint Paul and Luther. At breakfast we come back to our vision of future times, and I ask him whether the lower classes of people we see here around us would not be better suited to the peaceful future state he envisages than the very different, proud race which produced history and art. R. reflects on this, but feels that among the emigrants there would be knowledgeable people familiar with and able to interpret the great poets such as Shakespeare and Aeschylus. With Herr Levi, who visits us, he discusses the pause ("*Nicht doch*") and decides that it has to stay on account of the structure, the melody; but he wishes the pause to be treated as a *fermata*. At lunch he is again full of high spirits; when his beefsteak is put in front of him, he tells a story about a bottle of medicine which worked on a man the moment his wife shook it! He writes to Frl. Malten. A photograph of the lovely Russian lady Frau v. Uexküll produces from R. a sigh of aversion: "Oh, these creatures, so alien to me! You can keep all such beauty." Then, turning to the children, he says, half in jest, half in earnest, "We have sympathetic faces." Herr Neumann's telegram gives him pleasure. Since the weather is very bad, he does not go out. The Calderón play I recommended to him, *Amor, honor y poder,* arouses his disgust; nothing but chess figures, repugnant trivialities—he attacks it vehemently over supper, and I defend my own view as best I can. In the evening we have some music, Herr Rubinstein plays us Beeth.'s F-sharp Major Sonata, Opus 78, R. gives him some tips and remarks what a very personal work this is: "If one were to suggest it in the Vienna Conservatoire as a model of sonata style—that would be the silliest thing imaginable!" — He goes on to speak of the second part of the first movement of the E-flat Major Symphony and says: "I know of nothing so perfect with regard to structure, the architecture of music. The way the themes intermingle, they are like garlands linked to each other!" He remarks that this movement never arouses storms of applause. "I suppose it is too spiritual?" I ask. He: "Yes, too spiritual." The conductor thinks the reason lies in the instrumentation, and R. remarks how regrettable it was that in Beeth.'s time the wind instruments were so restricted in scope—he was using the orchestra of Haydn and Mozart, with ideas transcending all other worlds! — When I observe that he should make the various corrections he feels to be necessary (he was speaking of the Andante in the E-flat Major Symph., among other things), R. replies that it would not be feasible—how to know where to leave off? Every conductor who feels something is lacking should find a way out without saying much about it. — We go off to bed in very good spirits, though there was some vexation when he came to fetch me from among the children.

Thursday, October 5 R. slept well. At breakfast I tell him stories about the children, which he enjoys hearing; I learned about them yesterday evening. In the morning he reads Calderón, but still without enjoyment. Then he writes to Herr Winkelmann. After lunch he goes out with Siegfried and me, first of all to Lavena's and then to Müntzer's bookshop, where he orders W. Scott. In the evening he plays whist, after the Strecker-Lucca affair has coaxed him into still-further explanations. —

During the whist various operas are discussed—*La Juive,* for example, always having an edge—and at the end he sings several things from *Rienzi* in that splendid way of his which no singer can imitate.

Friday, October 6   R. had a good night's rest, and at breakfast he thinks about the festivals; says he would like to stage *Tannhäuser,* which he regards as a consummate drama, but then again not, since he feels that musically some things are insufficiently expressed. He observes that *Tannhäuser, Tristan,* and *Parsifal* belong together. — He looks for something in W. Scott, takes up a novel he does not know, but does not read it, saying he would prefer to read something he already knows, for that gives him an artistic pleasure. In the afternoon the two of us ride (with Stein) to Saint Mark's Square in spite of the rain, meet the children there at Lavena's, and ride home in two gondolas. The news I have just received that Jouk. has sent Pepino home stimulates R. into writing him a congratulatory message. Biag. buys a sheet of illuminated paper, R. writes, "We congratulate you from the bottom of our hearts," and we all sign it. With the conductor R. goes on to the subject of what constitutes melody, and he cites as an example, in its long-drawn-out perfection, the theme of the Andante in Mozart's C Minor Symph. R. does not care for brevity. Several things are mentioned from *La Juive* and even from Rossini, the conductor cites the final aria in Gluck's *Iph[igénie] en Tauride.* Then R. has a splendid idea and reads to us the first two scenes of the 2nd act of *J. Caesar.* Portia's speech, as he reads it, brings tears to my eyes. After the reading he recalls Calderón, just to remark how incomparable Shakesp. is—not literature, which Calderón is, but just drama. This was written before the invention of music, he says, and at times it seems quite sober. Then he reads his favorite scene, between Squire Toby, Aguecheek, and Maria. He remarks what a living character even Maria is, first treating the squire as she does and then joining with him against Malvolio! Everyone in Shakesp. has character, he says; Brutus's boy servant—he would surely turn out to be someone very special if one could follow him up. — In spite of the wretched weather, which is affecting him, R. is cheerful. At supper he plays at spirit rapping and suddenly, to the astonishment of us all, knocks, while still seated, with his right foot on the table, a piece of agility which surely nobody else would be able to copy. He laughs about all the many daughters he has; he tells me that instinct connects Loldi with him—however far away she is sitting, she laughs at jokes of his which nobody else notices. And we, too, have to laugh a lot over his high spirits; when I tell him about a certain Frau v. B., saying that her financial position does not allow her to take a gondola, and hence she goes out with nobody: "That's a great stroke of luck for nobody!" And "Such friendships I approve of for you—keep that one up!" — Today he wrote to Herr Gudehus, but reproached him, as he tells me, for not coming back.

Saturday, October 7   R. slept well, but the weather is still gray. At breakfast we talk about the children. [*Six lines, with words missing and inadequate punctuation, omitted as untranslatable.*] After lunch he tells me that he now always tries to avoid emotion; he says I might have noticed yesterday how close he was to tears during Portia's scene. Yesterday and today he looked out of the window, regretting that *he* could not enjoy the sight of his mauve jacket! — The *B. Blätter* has arrived, he reads Wolz.'s article, notes the error of the 9 volumes of Gob.'s works, but is satisfied with the article. The name Anti-Progress Movement, which he sees in the newspaper, causes him to remark on its absurdity! And recently, when the phonograph was mentioned, he spoke of the foolishness of expecting anything from such inventions—people were turning themselves into machines. Over coffee he recalls Lassalle—I do not know in what connection—and his visit to Starnberg, saying what a *poseur* he had been, describing him, R., as Siegfried, Frl. v. D[önniges] as Brünnhilde, in order to win him over and, through him, the King. It had all been play acting, and through his vanity in passing himself off as a cavalier and fighting a duel with a cavalier, the demagogue brought about his own ruin. I observe that in such cases the manner of death says nothing, and indeed in general says little; it just says what life has already said. R. agrees with me. — R. goes off to rest and arranges to join us in Saint Mark's Square; we meet there at half past four after R. has bought some tins of tobacco; in this task he was helped by Biag., who happened to come along, an encounter which reminded him of Palermo and Eva's birthday. We again return home in two gondolas, and during the ride R. thinks repeatedly of the hook men, as he always does since being told that these were old *gondolieri* whom the state refused to employ any longer. — In the evening he reads to us the quarrel and reconciliation between Brutus and Cassius and remarks how incredible it is, the way Brutus acts out in front of Messala a sort of comedy of stoicism regarding Portia's death. "One cannot say it is either good or not good—it just is!" — "They are all improvisations!" he exclaims, laying the book down. — He mentions the question of the reason why—in which he always likes to quote Luther with his rods of Almighty God—as one of the most foolish of questions, and says he has taken good care not to deal with it in his article. The ringing of the church bells opposite brings from him the remark that it must be a lovesick sacristan who is tolling them so haphazardly; we gaily recall Cervantes and his "sacristan of my soul." —

Sunday, October 8   R. had a restful night, and in the morning he visits the children. Later in the morning he starts a letter to Frl. Galfy but then addresses it to Frl. Belce, since he no longer has any clear memory of Frl. G. He also reads friend Wolz.'s article on Gobineau's book and is pleased with it, regretting only the bringing in of Dr. Wahrmund and particularly the quotation from Dr. Ebers, both signs of that lack of judgment he recently noticed among his friends; he intends to write to W., fearing his letter may have hurt him. Around midday we visit our friends the Schl[einitzes], who have at last arrived here safe and sound. When we leave the Schl.'s R. suggests we view something; we decide on the Frari, but it makes no impression on him; he already has his three churches, he says at lunch: the cathedrals of Siena and Pisa and Saint Mark's. The apparatus of Catholicism he finds very repugnant, but he likes Bellini's *Madonna,* the perfection of its painting pleases him. — "And now we have seen Lari Fari," he says, sitting down beside me in the gondola. Yesterday, when he heard about the popularity in Munich of Schumann's *Manfred,* he said, "They feel about it exactly what they felt about *Tristan,* a sort of emotional tipsiness, but there is not a trace of artistic appreciation." In the afternoon R. goes out with the children, meets our friends in Saint Mark's Square, and stands treat to them all. We begin the evening with chat; Mme Beecher Stowe's simple reply to a question about *Uncle Tom* has led to a spiteful remark in the newspaper report against stirring up the slaves, and R. is so indignant that he no longer wishes to read this newspaper; he instructs Stein to write to Dr. Herrig. A letter from our friend Schön enclosing a draft of the statutes for the scholarship foundation makes R. realize with increasing clarity that he must decide everything for himself. The gray weather is greatly depressing him; he feels that he has been living in a constant gray mist ever since our return from Sicily.

Monday, October 9 R. had a good night's rest, and the sun is shining, but his morning is unrestful; he decides to write to Herr Schön and does so, but is interrupted, first by the barber, then by our friends the Schleinitzes; he is beset by a spasm, requires a long time after lunch to recover (during which time he is somewhat vexed by the absence of Lusch, who is with our friends). At 4 o'clock R. and I go out, and, gliding along in the gondola with contented feelings of being together, R. says, "One ought to be able to shut one's mind to everything, to hear nothing more; to put up with living one has to be dead!" On the Riva we meet the Gravinas, and R. takes us to see his lion, which he calls "the most antique antiquity" he knows; the lion of Saint Mark's also pleases him, he says it is so human and was certainly made by somebody who never saw a lion. Then we meet the other children, whom he takes to Lavena's. We ride home, and it makes him sad to see the sun setting in a threatening way; in the evening he complains that he has seen virtually nothing but gray skies since Sicily! — We spend some time in the niche leading to the vestibule, talking about the children, R. about Lusch's fate in particular, with fatherly concern. Later Voltz and Batz come into his mind; yesterday it was the thought of Mme Lucca which plagued him! . . . In the evening he talks to Biagino, whom he holds in great affection, about his experiences with *Rienzi* in Dresden.

Tuesday, October 10 Today is the 10th, and I lay my little memento at R.'s feet, but without an inscription, indeed without even mentioning it. I cannot really explain it even to myself, but for me silence is becoming a necessity in joy as in sorrow! R. goes out around midday, returns home with a gift for Lusch, and gives me his cardcase; then I tell him that it is the 10th, and he remembers. Before going out he read the proof of Glasenapp's chronicle, but decided not to publish it in the *B. Bl.,* since he intends to write about it himself. At lunch we come to the subject of youth and old age; he quotes *"Qui de son âge n'a pas l'esprit, de son âge a tous les malheurs"* ["He who has no feeling for his age has all the misfortunes of his age"], and when I add that an old woman should not behave like a young one, he replies emphatically, "And a young woman should not behave as an old one may not." Over coffee he mentions a remark in the *B. Tagblatt* to the effect that present conditions are untenable and all that matters is to draw the right conclusions from the collapse; he is struck by the similarity to his own idea. In the afternoon R. and I take a gondola to Saint Mark's Square; since he has been cheated by the jeweler, he tells him so in very drastic words; the man refunds the money he paid for the trinket and we go to another, who, when he sees R.'s card, is beside himself with joy. R. then leaves me at the Palazzo Malipiero, where Siegfried and Eva come to fetch me at the very moment I am about to leave. The journey home with these two dear, good, sensible children is like a blessing on me—we three are Wahnfried, wandering abroad in foreign lands! At home I find R. reading, and I embrace him at the very hour I first set eyes on him! "That was an encounter which has proved its worth," he says. — Herr Hausburg arrives to replace Stein with S. temporarily, until Glasenapp takes over. In the evening R. gets Rubinstein to play some fantasies by my father; one rhapsody he finds particularly pleasing, he says it is original, something newly minted which reflects my father's individuality. He then tells us about a Herr von Glümer, whom he knew in 1849 in Dresden, and who has now married a rich heiress, after having gone through much and spent years in prison. He is reminded by this that, when we left the Frari, a Herr Hampel introduced himself to us, saying he had been adjutant of the provisional government during those times, and R. had been particularly friendly toward him then; R. was completely silent, then said, "What right does that give you to address me now?" Later he told me, "He has lied about it so often to others that he now believes it himself." —

Wednesday, October 11   R. slept well. Around noon he sets out with the girls (Loldi and Eva) and visits the church of S. Giorgio dei Greci, which strikes him as pompous, with its black Madonna and Saviour! He talks about it at lunch, inquires about the *Maria Aegyptiaca,* and then, stimulated by the presence of Herr Hausburg, goes on to talk about the three gods of Lithuania. We then go out, after 4 o'clock, the view of the canal from beneath the Rialto Bridge also gives him very great pleasure; the bridge itself with its broad steps, indeed the marble steps everywhere here, give him a sense of security, and he holds to his opinion that no other town can compare with Venice. — At supper, looking back over our year, he says, "We are living just like Jews"—he cannot remember where he was a year ago! — He takes delight in Fidi's rowing, then in the walk on the Piazzetta. He advises the new tutor to be serious, since the good young man invariably shows his embarrassment by grinning. In the evening he tells us (saying in connection with Tribschen, "Those were happy days") that he has been rereading the final scene of *Faust,* Part One. He says Goethe took very good care never to wander along these paths again; Shakespeare never did anything of this sort; R. says he would describe his works as political-historical tragedies, whereas this was a social-historical tragedy. He recalls having seen Ch[arlotte von] Hagn play Gretchen in Riga, and she made a very great impression on him. Later he talks about W. Scott's novel *The Pirate* and says he makes the inhabitants of the Shetland Isles talk in the Ossianic bardic style of the previous century, though the Icelandic sagas have shown us completely different customs.

Thursday, October 12   Lusch's birthday—celebrated in Venice for the 2nd time. — In the morning R. talks to me again about the Greci church, saying that it does not give any warm feelings of Christianity but, rather, an impression of stiffness and pomp, like a relic of ancient Assyria! — Around 10 o'clock the presentation of gifts, at 11:30 R., Lusch, Siegfried, and I ride to Saint Mark's Square, go into the church, visit the vestry, which pleases R. very much—particularly the inlaid work. As we leave the church he says, "The Crusaders certainly trod this floor before us." At lunch he asks Siegfried to propose the toast; when he shyly refuses, R. says very humorously that Lusch has not married because the family loves her so much that she does not wish to leave it; Field Marshal Moltke is completely in despair, and so on. Around 5 o'clock we go out, in the worst weather! R. is very cross about it; and when we are told in the evening that this persistent rain is bound to lead to an outbreak of fever, I am also filled with concern. This is dispelled by *Götterdämmerung*, from which Herr Rubinstein plays us "Siegfr.'s Journey" (following which R. sings "Hagen's Watch") and the conclusion. "How perceive it, how to leave it, all this rapture" . . . R. jokes about the way people never want anything but Isolde's apotheosis—and *Die Walküre* (with the false stress)—that is to say, "*Du bist der Lenz.*" It is the women who want these, he says, the men do not count. — "I wish for Katharina von Bora," says R. in connection with the weather—in other words, a north wind. We laugh at his joke, but the weather really is desperately bad. Today R. says about S., "He is a penetrating boy—when one looks long at him, he looks back at one in the same way." — When he was riding with me in the gondola today, he told me he was still toying with the idea of asking the King of Bavaria to show him no more favors; the news that the King is also having a deer park laid out in the style of L[ouis] XV at his newly built castle has truly appalled R.! The news about the plays the King is having performed for his own amusement also has a painful effect. — At breakfast R. thought with mild regret of that time in Zurich when Minna had her heart ailment and people were forbidden to excite her. "It was difficult for me," he says, "since she took advantage of my consideration for her condition to become malicious." — We are informed that these floods bring a virulent fever in their wake, which adds unutterably to my anxieties.

Friday, October 13 R. dreams that he was about to leave for a journey with Sulzer, then they both realized they had no money or belongings with them but, laughing heartily, decided to have these sent on after them; however, R. turned back to Vreneli, who had in the meantime become a bluestocking and was deep in conversation with a literary historian! . . . He got up once during the night, but he comes to breakfast in cheerful spirits, and when he says, "I am Torquemada, cruel like T.," I have an opportunity to tell him about Hugo's curious play. He then tells me about a women's theater, in which all the roles and the orchestra were filled by women—the exact opposite of Shakespeare's times. We then talk again about Gretchen and about Shakespeare's female characters; when I somewhat obscurely observe that the latter stand in the normal relationship of woman to man, whereas Gretchen absorbs our complete sympathy, R. says, "The motive of Nature's naïveté in conflict with bourgeois society did not exist then." — Telegrams arrive from Barmen! At noon R. and I go to the canal on which S. Michele lies, Fidi rows us nicely, takes us past Zanipolo, where the Colleoni monument always impresses us deeply, then to S. Maria dei Miracoli. In the afternoon we go out again, this time R. and I alone, we stroll through Saint Mark's Square and see the church in a most curious golden light. Our conversation concerns the *Ring;* R. says he cannot blame Gobineau for clinging to this depiction of the downfall of a species and caring nothing for *Parsifal;* he has no need for Christianity in the pride of annihilation through love. We then eat ices together in the Café Florian and feel at ease and gently calm in each other's company. "There is always too much humanity between us," he said yesterday, but he has asked the Gravinas to stay on, so as to have another nice day for an outing to Torcello. — As we are returning home, he says it is indeed curious that though one claims that men are intelligent, in legends they are always foolish, Tristan, Siegfried—"it is just that women take the one thing with terrible seriousness." At supper he reads to us that a group of bandits has been organized to plunder the flooded districts! He also tells us of excesses against the Jews in Pressburg. We play whist, though R. is then much vexed by the children's departure (in a gondola) to fetch Lulu (from the Schl.'s). But in the end he suggests a game of lansquenet, which goes very merrily, and in the middle of which the children arrive home.

Saturday, October 14 R. did not have a good night, the sirocco and perhaps also the ices yesterday did not agree with him. But at breakfast he is cheerful, and he sings, to the tune of the duet between Valentine and Marcel, the words *"Qui n'a pas l'esprit de son âge, de son âge a tous les malheurs."* But around noon, when I go to fetch him, he is having a spasm. However, he soon recovers and goes out with me. After he has told me that he finds W. Scott's *The Pirate* boring, we start to talk about the book on Buddha, and R. says that the credit for having discovered and clearly expressed the truth that the world as we see it is a figment of our imagination, for having defined its complete ideality, belongs in fact to Kant, "the most original of minds," as Schop. put it. We make several purchases, from the baker among others, since the bread is still not coarse enough for R.'s taste, and return home for lunch. When I contemplate my happiness directly, realize what it is to be with him like this, undisturbed, unconcerned, then I take fright; my unworthiness threatens to destroy me, I become conscious that in all legends the divine can be seen only through a veil, and I feel like holding back every breath I take on my own so that he, and he alone, can reign supreme. And pray that the world, alas, may not cast its shadow over us! After lunch R. asks me to read a review of Jules Verne's latest book, in which the Germans are ridiculed in the most tasteless way. Toward 4 o'clock our friend [Mimi] Schleinitz pays us a visit, which R. finds very agreeable. We take her back to the P. Malipiero in a gondola, Siegf. rowing, and from there we return home, are caught in the rain, take a gondola at the Rialto, and arrive home virtually unscathed. In the evening we are visited by Dr. Thode; R. reads to us a letter in which Bismarck completely deserts his friend Puttkamer in the matter of the new orthography and comes out against Roman type. This provides an opportunity for a discussion about our present political world. The sounds of the "Pilgrims' Chorus" then come to us—after we have moved into the smoking niche on account of an accident with a lamp—as a salvation! — (When, having returned from our afternoon outing, I go to write in my diary, I find in my little notebook R.'s joke about *Les Huguenots;* I ask him to write it down, which he kindly does.) — At supper we have to laugh heartily about what R. tells us. Siegfried asked him, "Papa, what does 'colic' mean?" R.: "Tummyache. Where did you find it?" Siegfr.: "In *Coriolanus*"! . . . When, beneath the Rialto, we were talking about the "thing-in-itself," as R. puts it, R. says how well the Buddhists defined the sufferings of the world: "To part from those one loves, to live with those one hates." — Here it occurs to me that R. recently remarked that he would not compose anything on the subject of Buddha, since he is unfamiliar with the images—mango tree, lotus flower, etc.—and in consequence the text would be bound to sound artificial. — In the evening he talks to Stein and me about race and loveless marriages, and asked what could possibly come of a marriage between the German Emperor and his wife, who, though she is handsome and blooming, he did not love; this point is always ignored in any discussion of race, he says.

Sunday, October 15 R. had a good night, but the wet weather is worse than ever before. We say goodbye to our poor friend Stein, who takes his departure so sadly. But R. feels oppressed all day long, and he is thinking of moving permanently to warmer climes, "so as to live to see Siegfried's maturity!" — At breakfast we talked again about the droll *Coriolanus* anecdote, and when I say I can understand S.'s sympathy for Caius Marcius [Coriolanus], R. replies that in his youth he was put off by his conceit. Yesterday, when we were discussing Sicily with Dr. Thode, he was led to the subject of the Romans and their terrible treatment of this country, in the interior of which no tree was permitted to grow. This evening we play whist; R., continually restless and oppressed by the weather, cannot work, though he would much like to start writing his "To All of You" (the artists), since his recollections of the performances always give him pleasure, unlike anything else in the outside world. And indeed he has come to loathe the world of fine arts and the world which is content with the fine arts. W. Scott's novel *The Pirate* bores him with its longwindedness, but he quoted to me a passage from it which made an impression on him—in which a crank who drinks only water decides, with the help of brandy, to go to the rescue of his son. I jokingly tell him that, if he wants to know why this novel bores him, he should read the definition of a novel in *Opera and Drama*.

Monday, October 16 R. had a good night's rest, and we have some sunshine, albeit deceptive, for the sirocco is still blowing. Talking of our good Stein, R. regrets that he said so little about himself and his father, and, generalizing on this subject, he remarks to me how little value silence has, what much greater evidence of pride and tranquillity is shown when one talks openly to confidential friends about oneself and one's relationships. We come back to the subject of race, wondering which theory is right, Schop.'s or Gobineau's. R. feels they can be reconciled: a human being who is born black, urged toward the heights, becomes white and at the same time a different creature. At 12:30 we go by gondola—rowed by Fidi—in the direction of La Giudecca, for which R. does not much care, and get out not far from the Belle Arti; we meet the Gravinas and return home via the Piazza Manin, from which we turn off into a narrow lane to see the lovely steps which R. so likes—they remind him of Pavia, of the Hohenstaufens. It was a pleasant walk, yet R. had a spasm on our return. . . . He has lunch somewhat later than usual, and a letter from Frau Lucca —unfortunately delivered directly to him—upsets him again! The two of us go to the Piazzetta and walk a little on the Riva, but he soon sits down with me beneath the arch of the Doge's Palace; the bricks and the very low tide present him with not a very pleasing view! We then sit down again beneath the portal between the columns, and, gazing at the tower, from which a young foreigner was said to have thrown himself this morning, R. says, "He did the right thing!" The children meet us, their attention attracted by R.'s whistling the 8th Symph. At lunchtime today, when we returned home, Lusch was playing [Beethoven's] E Minor Sonata; R. remarked how many ornaments it contains, regrettable after such a theme. In the evening he sees Mendelssohn's *Lieder ohne Worte* lying on the piano (left there by Herr Hausburg); he shows me the "*Venezianisches Gondellied*," in which Mendels., leaving out the main part, uses the refrain of the *Otello* barcarole and passes it off as a folk song. Then R. tells me that, when he first heard the Scherzo of the 9th, it reminded him of Auber's tarantella. In the morning he remarked to me that rhythm is a completely new discovery, a Luther chorale contains hardly any rhythm, though it is splendidly declaimed; and he reminds me of the tarantella we saw danced in Capri, how unrhythmic and unclear the music was. — He dictates to me his letter to Frau Lucca in French, in order to put an end to the nuisance.

Tuesday, October 17 The weather is grayer than ever, and R. com-

plains bitterly about the state of his health—also about the things which
never cease to importune him, such as Frau Lucca. — Regarding his
present reading (*The Pirate*), he complains that one can easily see from
its verbosity that it was written for the world of elegant ladies. After
looking at several things with Siegfried, at 12:30 I go to fetch R. for a
gondola trip; he complains how difficult his morning was, how long
and laborious his efforts to settle down, and he was unable to do any
work. We ride along the Cannaregio and then down as far as the railroad station, where we get out to return home on foot. At lunch our
conversation turns to the housekeeping, and R. cannot help being
surprised by the total of our expenditures. (A delivery for Dan. from
Milan contained among other things a green velvet jacket, called
Rembrandt, which he put on and in which he looked exactly like
Figaro.) In the afternoon, in pouring rain he goes to the bank. But in
the evening the 3rd act of *Siegfried*, very well played by Herr Rubinstein,
pleases both him and us. "That is Gobineau music," R. says as he
comes in, "that is race. Where else will you find two beings who burst
into rejoicing when merely looking at each other? The whole world
exists just to ensure that two such beings look at each other!" "Here is
just forest and rocks and water and nothing rotten in it." "Here is a
couple who rejoice in their happiness, immerse themselves in the
happiness of being together—how different from *Tristan!*" He deplores
the foolishness of the public, which cares only for *Die Walküre,* but
praises Herr Neumann, who is disseminating the whole work abroad.
"How curious that it should have to be a Jew!" he says. —

Wednesday, October 18 R. had expressed the wish to get up earlier, in
order to gain extra time for work in the morning, but his early morning
is difficult, and when I go to fetch him for a gondola trip at 12:30, he is
feeling quite languid! But the weather is fine, the sirocco had died down,
and though we do dawdle very, very slowly from the Rialto to Saint
Mark's Square, the walk and the gondola ride seem to do him good.
He thanks me for having come to fetch him and tells me of a remark
made by W. Scott in *The Pirate* which pleased him: taken from natural
history, it is to the effect that, when shoots from trees are transplanted,
they carry on in the soil the life of the original trunk and die with it,
undergo no rejuvenation—and it is the same with nations. R. observes
that this gives cause for reflection regarding the possibility of a new
life for mankind; but he himself, he says, places his reliance, as far as
this idea is concerned, on religion. Still, W. Scott's remark pleases him,
and he can understand the delight men such as Schop. and Gob. took
in this intelligent writer. On our return home, the unexpected arrival
of the piano, as well as the question of where to put it, makes R. cross.
And when the whole large family is not yet assembled at around

4:30, he also feels vexed. But this soon vanishes, and we have a very merry walk as well as a rest in Saint Mark's Square with our friends the Schleinitzes. In the evening, since the children are all at the Pal. Malipiero, we spend the hours tranquilly together, occupying ourselves first with Siegfried's study timetable, then with a modern play, *Väter und Söhne,* which we come upon by chance and find most curious. An Indian saying from the *Hitopadesa* collection about the immutability of character, as shown by the crooked tail of a dog, amuses R. greatly.

Thursday, October 19 Splendid weather, R. arranges the outing to Torcello, we leave at 10:30 and are back at 4:30; not greatly rewarded for the expenditure of time and energy, even if much of it proved very stimulating and the stop at the Church of S. Michele pleased R., too. But he is still not feeling well; he had a spasm in Torcello, and everything is a strain on him. In the evening the arrival (for Lusch) of the 6-volume history of Venice leads to our looking through it and discussing this history in detail. Then Buddhism is also discussed, and indeed the character of animals, the instincts of the species, which help preserve animals on a stable level, whereas human beings degenerate; from this one might assume that the origin of man was a fleeting parenthesis which would lead to a return to animality "until man reveals some new quality." — "Not why, nor whence nor whither"— this wise saying of Buddha's he quotes frequently. Before this we were with Bonichen, who pleases R. greatly with her good and modest character, which, combined with her genuine beauty, makes a remarkable impression.

Friday, October 20 R. had a good night, though he got up once. He is now reading *Count Robert of Paris* and enjoying it. At around 12:30 we meet in Saint Mark's Square, I with Siegfried, he alone, and I notice at once that he is irritable and feeling ill at ease. Our lunch goes off quite well, though he soon withdraws, and at about 4:30 we go out with Eva, again to St. M.'s Square, where we meet the rest of the family. Since R. is feeling run down, we sit under the archway of the Doge's Palace and talk about W. Scott, whom he greatly esteems, even though he admits that one never exactly warms to his characters, and that Carlyle was right when he said they act their characters and do not live them. R. says, "He is the theater director who sets it all in motion; he himself is always interesting, but his characters much less so." He also remarks once again that the language is what always catches his attention, and it disturbs him to see Vareger using the word "metaphysics." He adds that this has to do with what a mixture the English language is, in which "metaphysics" is just a word like any other. He points out with amusement that W. Scott always has some Scotsman or Anglo-Saxon present—rather like W[ilhelm] Meister. We then walk back and forth along the garden and the palace, and R. is very pleased to be here; we go to Lavena's and meet our friends the Schl.'s, with whom we stroll about a little. In lovely moonlight we ride home, magically breathed upon by the buildings of the Gr. Canal. And in the evening we chat together. R. plays several of Mendelssohn's *Lieder ohne Worte,* which truly astonish us with their poverty of invention and their Italianisms. Then he talks of Mozart, compares him to the Italians, can understand why Schop. preferred the latter, since Mozart's flight was toward completely different regions, as various things show (the Donna's recitative and the entrance of the Commendatore), and he was held back by a wretched tradition. Before this he asked Herr Hausburg some questions about Siegfried's musical education.

Saturday, October 21 R. had a good night's rest. At breakfast he is delighted by a canary across from us: "What a sound that is from such a tiny body, the little fellow is nothing but sound!" Then we talk again about W. Scott, but he ends up being annoyed since no news has come from Voltz and Batz, and he gets me to send off a telegram. Around midday he suggests a visit to S. Rocco; we go there and spend a long time looking at the Crucifixion and also Christ before Pilate. From there we go to the Rialto and then ride home in good spirits. But as we are going in to lunch, R. begs to be excused; he comes to the table only later, after getting over his spasm! . . . We meet again in St. M.'s Square around 6:30, he had gone there earlier with the children, and we then ride home. In the evening we have music from *Die Msinger,* R. takes great delight in it, also in memories of the first performance (1868). Daniela's behavior causes us some concern, but R. feels that, if she were to find the right husband, everything inside her would be smoothed out, as in Blandine's case.

Sunday, October 22 Gray weather again! And various woes. But R. begins his article for the *Blätter.* Also, there was one thing which pleased him: Siegfried's whistling (something from *Der Fl. Holl.*) very early in the morning. When I go in to him at 12:30, he shows me the sheet of paper and says, "My tears gush forth; once more the pencil claims me!" Toward one o'clock we go off to the Belle Arti; R. looks at many things with great calmness and concentration, among them the Carpaccios; he prefers the Saint John in Tintoretto's *Crucifixion* to the Saint John in the *Assunta,* and in respect of his appreciation of this great work, I see to my joy that he is increasingly coming around to my feeling about it. Only the luxurious clothing of the bowed women disturbs him somewhat, as well as the excessive number of people. On our return home, we discuss the difficulties of painting Christ, and R. agrees with me when I observe that it is impossible, and that the painters sought a solution either by typifying him or by making a portrait. Lunch with friend Rubinstein, a toast to my father, departure of Rub. The rose cup. No outing for R. in the afternoon, since it begins to rain! I pay him a visit and find him quite cheerful, reading the *Fl. Blätter*. However, a letter from Dr. Strecker, which R. asks me to answer, obliges me to tell him that a reply from Frau Lucca has indeed arrived; he does not wish to read it, but all the same it leads to discussions! The elder children have gone off to bed, I visit them, and in the meantime R. plays to the younger ones. By the time they leave us the difficulties have been more or less forgotten, and R. begins, "One cannot paint Christ, but one can portray him in music." — I say that I see it as evidence of his great and so significant artistic sagacity that he abandoned the figure of Christ and created Parsifal instead: "To have Chr. sung by a tenor—what a disgusting idea!" he says. From this we go on to painting—that it was able to depict the Mother of God. But R. denies that the *Assunta* is the Mother of God; it is Isolde, he says, in the apotheosis of love, whereas in the *Sistine Madonna,* "this wonderful inspiration," one sees, for all the consummate beauty, her utter unapproachability: "Good Lord, to have any ideas about her!" "So transfigured that it takes one's breath away." "And that gaze, so sublime, even in her!" "And at the same time everything so graceful and beautiful." — Thus calmed and raised above reality by the images of art, we go off to rest. However, it was not a good night. At 4 in the morning of

Monday, October 23 R. writes down some sentences for Frau Lucca. And at breakfast he complains about life, recalling all his relationships with publishers, with V. and Batz, and comparing these people to vermin which keep crawling out of one's bed. When I have to laugh at that, he laughs, too, and we then go on to enjoy with a kind of amusement the phrases Frau Lucca uses to win him around. He recalls A. Meissner, who used to say of publishers that they were the worst, because they counted on the vanity of authors and understood it so well. They look on R.'s magnanimity as foolishness and think they can easily have their way with him! "Who imagined I would ever make my fortune? In my early days I was a sort of beggar, was pleased when someone gave me something! Now everyone attaches himself to me in order to suck me dry." . . . I translate what R. wrote at 4 in the morning and arrange the documents. Around 12:30 R. comes to fetch me, after having worked on his article, and we ride as far as the Rialto, where we buy some cheese, and then go on foot in the best and merriest of spirits as far as the railroad bridge, where we find our gondola. We meet a friendly woman who shows us the way when we go wrong. R. says, "We ought to have invited her for coffee immediately—she would have some interesting things to tell." At lunch the story of a child's being rescued by a cat and a soldier causes R. to exclaim: "Yes, danger! That is the only thing which shows what humans are capable of. And yet they can still learn from animals." — He then tells his favorite animal stories and is pleased that the people here arranged a kind of triumphal procession yesterday for the doughty soldier! — Around 5:30 we all meet in Saint Mark's Square, but soon return home, since it is cold. In the evening R. reads a few scenes from *Twelfth Night* (Malvolio) to us, to his and our very great delight. R. prefers *Twelfth Night* to *As You Like It,* in which he finds the characters too varied and too loosely connected; when I tell him that in performance this is soon corrected by the woodland scenery, he recalls the dismal performance we saw in Munich and deplores the Jewish influence on our art.

Tuesday, October 24   R. dreamed of a shining night sky in which he discovered three planets. The news that a comet can be seen in the sky has frequently woken him up in the night, but never at the right time (4 o'clock). Instead he was given his dream. At breakfast we come back to what we read yesterday, and R. says this successful ruse committed against a decent man by means of his vanity shows how close to madness a human being always is—Malv. through vanity, Othello through jealousy. R. works on his article, reads *Count Robert of Paris,* which he calls a childish piece of hack work. I fetch him around 12:30. We go by gondola, rowed by S., as far as the Rialto, get out there, and continue on foot to Saint Mark's; we enter, go as far as the ancient horses, and ride home from the Bacino. A consultation I had before this concerning Blandine, and for R. preoccupation with the nonpaying Voltz and Batz, give the day an unpleasant flavor, which, however, is as always overcome by our being together. A discussion of the comet, which the children have seen, brings us to a similar appearance in 1858, seen here then by R., and the conjectures surrounding it. In the afternoon R. and I walk to the Rialto; the wide path from our house to the Church of S. Felice pleases him enormously, and he resolves to take frequent walks along it. We then ride to the Piazzetta; in the moonlit haze the whole place looks glorious, and our homeward journey through the narrow canals gives us a dreamlike joy. In the evening I begin Daru's history of V[enice] with the children, and R. also enjoys listening. Then he plays to Biagino some themes from Beeth. symphonies (A Major, C Minor Symph., andante movements) to show him what kind of melody it is which speaks to us "like the greatest, most clearly defined thoughts of a poet." — But once we are alone Voltz and Batz crop up again, R. talks of the spirit in trade today, which consists simply in trying to buy up cheap something one thinks valuable, then selling it dear; all business people, he says, are in fact united in their adherence to this principle. During our walk R. told me the Hungarian minister has declared that the Jews' struggle is that of the have-nots against the haves, and thus there is everything to be said for it. "And that struggle is of course the most justified of all," says R. — Yesterday I mentioned to R. that the Indians regarded intelligence as the sixth sense, a concept by which the ideality of the world is so finely revealed, and I ask R. why this is not so with us. "Because we are blockheads and have taken everything over from the Jews!" As we are riding home in the moonlight, he thinks with pleasure of Fritz Brandt, who is fighting sturdily on all fronts, here against the iron curtain in theaters, there against a new Asphalia Theater. With regard to the latter, R. says, "I agree with him, without knowing what it is all about," and he is of the opinion that these days the only person that matters is the technician. — Yesterday we talked about Semper's buildings, agreed that in most of them the motive was taken from Italy, and that he was not very skilful with his decorations: "A man like that sees straight lines and nothing else." Then he states his feeling that the true sphere of architecture is the church and the theater—hardly palaces.

Wednesday, October 25 R. had a somewhat restless night. I dreamed about a garden in which I was strolling behind R. and saw two lovely big butterflies, which I wanted to show him. R. gets up in somewhat low spirits, we talk about life, and I ask him if he does not also feel that, if Kleist had known the teachings of Buddha and Schopenhauer, he would have lost his leanings toward suicide. He replies, "Yes." At breakfast R. talks about a shot of some kind, I mention the scene in *Tell:* "That is what one can point out to Gobineau as Germanic, this Swiss self-sufficiency; everything else—imperial, royal pomp—is not." We part; shortly afterward the mail arrives, R. comes in to find out if there is news from V. and Batz, discovers me reading, I am unable to conceal from him that our friend [Gobineau], the dearest of them all, has died. . . . This dominates our day—we would find it impossible to talk to others about it. . . . I go out with Siegfr.; some time after one o'clock I come upon him on the path outside our house. "When one has at last encountered something, it slips like water through one's fingers" is what he says after a while, and we retrace together the signs which pointed toward this death, the restlessness, the haste, wherever he might be, to get away, and in the end this utterly solitary death. When we met R. on the broad path, R.'s nerves were so on edge, probably because of the news, that he was quite unable to bear the tapping of the women's clogs, which he compared to castanets. He also dislikes the sirocco air. . . . At lunch R. suddenly strokes his nose, in the way our friend did when he was enjoying a private joke! In the afternoon he brings home for me a lovely promenade fan and a note-book with a swallow. The day is spent in efforts to bear up against the blow. "One feels so useless, so superfluous!" R. exclaims as we are talking of Gob.'s indifference toward his works. . . . And again and again during the day we keep coming back to this incomparable man, until in the evening R. plays the first bars of "Siegfr.'s Funeral March"! . . . Then R. reads Palest[rina]'s Mass for Pope Marcellus, finds it lacking in invention, and says that anyway he hates this version of the Mass, this credo in which all the stanzas (and what stanzas!) are com-posed with the fear of Hell always firmly in mind!

Thursday, October 26 R. dreamed of Gob., that he was telling many anecdotes, as was his way, then of Herwegh—that he went skating with him. At breakfast we talk about our deceased friend. R. goes out by himself in the morning and tells of a meeting with a very lovely girl of about 12. I begin writing the piece about G. which R. wants me to do for the *Blätter*. Over coffee I read to R. a lively letter from Wolz. and a report from Malwida about the performance of the *Pars*. Prelude in Paris. We then meet R. in St. M.'s Square, where he gives me a second notebook. He had gone there with Loldi and told her of Gob.'s death. At the whist table he says to me: "How silent you can be! It is enough to drive one mad." — And indeed I find talking impossible, and when the children, having been told the news, come to me to talk about it, I have to leave the room. In my room I pace up and down, then hear that R. is in his, and some time later I find him there, sitting in silence. Our thoughts are without a doubt on the same thing. After a while he wonders where Nietzsche is now—Wolz. told me about his latest book, *Die fröhliche Wissenschaft*. "The terrible thing is," he adds, "that the people who reply to these absurdities also seem to be fools." — In Saint Mark's Square he drank some black coffee, which did not agree with him, but he, too, is entranced by the moonlit night, and he pointed out to me our garden bathed in its beams. After the whist he suggested a game of lansquenet, but it all ends dismally! At lansquenet Lusch takes a lucky coin from her father and says she will have a bracelet made of all the things he has already given her. "You will soon be getting other things from me, dear girl," he replies to her sadly. He also complains of the fact that we cannot be alone: "Sublime Spirit, thou gav'st me everything—gav'st me Cosima—and we cannot be by ourselves." He says he never feels the desire to visit anyone, but I do have contacts outside; declares that there is something of my father in me. I tell him that, if now and again I do pay a visit, I do it for the children's sake. — He plays the funeral music from *Euryanthe* and then the conclusion of the *Egmont* Overture—in sorrow the soul is perhaps most vulnerable to music, today I feel close to bursting! When I say,

"That is heroic," he replies, "Dutch." — It is very characteristic of him to smile at Malw. for being unable, after *Parsifal,* to appreciate even Beeth. any longer, and to be not at all pleased by it.

Friday, October 27 R. slept well in spite of the black coffee, about which he is still complaining, since he drank it in the excitement of a lively conversation with our friend [Mimi]. At breakfast we discuss the idle way professors go on about a merciful or an unwilling God, while the Catholic church continues to exert its power as before. R. vehemently repeats that in these matters we are barbarians compared to the Indians. He comes to my room to fetch his mail, receives some business letters, and, though they give him no satisfaction, remains cheerful, pulls a jokingly imposing face, as he often does. "Moltke," he says, "the expression of a belligerent sheep." At one o'clock we go out together for a walk and get lost, which greatly amuses us, particularly when the Church of S. M. Miracoli suddenly appears in front of us—"the jewel box," as R. calls it. But at the start of our walk he complained about his work, saying that in fact he has no subject, nothing to say to anybody, and so it is all a form of vanity, though there is a certain artistic pleasure to be derived from the way one puts things. The weather turns bad, but we ride to Saint Mark's Square all the same. R. strolls around in a disgruntled way. — The only thing that pleases him is the lovely flower girl in her Roman costume; she is gracious and well mannered, and he would like to know something about her life—he feels she must have been an artist's model; and so she once was, as we discover at Lavena's. When we are again strolling beneath the arcades, we see her surrounded, perhaps inconvenienced: "The thought of possibly hearing some vulgar joke being made there is heartbreaking," says R. as we pass by. — Pouring rain greets us as we ride home! . . . In the evening R. arranges a game of faro, which causes much excitement among the children. — (In the morning he wrote to friend Gross.) — He kisses and greets me tenderly as he goes to and fro, making me happy, since for me this is the cherished sign that he is not feeling too indisposed. Over coffee he talks about social problems of which he has heard something here and there, and he says that, were it not for all this absurd chatter, he would begin to feel the world had ceased to exist.

Saturday, October 28 R. is melancholy in his sleep, I hear him call out something I sense rather than understand, then finally, "Poor dear wife!" Then he talks about some boats which Biagino is taking out of Genoa. He wakes up and tells me that in his dream B. had been engaged in smuggling. At last Georg comes in and tells him that people are riding in gondolas over Saint Mark's Square. During the night there was heavy thunder, and as we are sitting over breakfast, lightning strikes in La Giudecca, and all day long there is a downpour of warm rain. — Before lunch he attended S.'s music lesson, and at lunch he talks to Herr Hausburg about the utter uselessness of the conservatoires: "What one is unable to teach oneself can certainly never be learned, least of all there!" He recalls the swimming lessons and how Fidi tried in vain in Bayreuth, whereas in Naples he succeeded right away, because the teacher was standing in the water. "But to teach it from outside with a rope—that is like grammar books for languages, methods in music." — In the afternoon he is delighted by the shrill, folklike singing of a boy rowing a gondola through storm and rain, and, hearing the dismal news of the bad weather in the surrounding countryside, he says, "One feels justly punished for having sought something better in this world than one was allotted." — Our very charming friends (Frau Hatzfeldt and Countess Schleinitz) visit us, the pleasantest of diversions. Before supper R. improvises for a while, then, to amuse me, plays something *à la* Verdi and *à la* Chopin. — At table he tells me that Minna once threatened to take to drink. "To be united with those one hates, separated from those one loves—that is in fact what the world means, and all these palaces and this pomp have been provided just as a means of deceiving ourselves." — He organizes a game of faro; late in the evening we are at last alone, and glad of it; we discuss a matter with Eva, wholly in her favor, and go to bed in a peaceable mood.

Sunday, October 29 R. dreamed about Minna, and in consequence recalls her behavior in Königsberg and the dreadfully harsh treatment —reproaches—he received at the hands of Minna's mother in Dresden. He says it was the first time he had ever experienced anything so brutal, and it was terrible. He works and is satisfied with his work. Then together we go to the Correr Museum opposite, and it pleases him very much. Lunch is for him always somewhat embarrassing, on account of the many different languages which have to be used, but the most important thing for him is that the children, the Gravinas, should not notice. In the afternoon he is greatly vexed by a letter from friend Feustel, who, it seems, tells him rather carelessly that V. and Batz have submitted their accounts, but without the earnings from *Tristan*. Fundamentally, he feels, all businessmen are the same. Quite beside himself with rage, he goes with me to the post office and sends off a telegram to Herr Voltz saying that he will withhold his signature if the money from *Tristan* is not paid to him. We then take a short stroll in Saint Mark's Square, which is still fairly damp; most of all he enjoys sitting under the portal between the columns, he says he would like to be painted there. Gradually he calms down; at home he finds news of good receipts in Vienna, he writes to Feustel and, now calmed down, goes with us in the evening to our friends at the Pal. Malipiero. At supper Ada Pinelli tells us about the spiritualist *soirées* at Prince Liechtenstein's (Neulengbach), and afterward R. plays Bach's C-sharp Minor Prelude, then, accompanied by friend Mimi, Marke's speech and Tristan's farewell; finally he plays us I.'s apotheosis. He then says of his piano playing that he plays the same way that Count Sándor used to drive—throwing the reins over the horses' necks and hurtling through the countryside, crying, "This is how we drive in Hungary!" —

Monday, October 30 In the morning we say goodbye to our children the Gravinas. In spite of the persistent rain R. is in good spirits. He gazes at the palaces opposite and exclaims, "What things like that have to tell about history and events!" And later he returns to the theme, admiring the building of these massive, elegant things in the middle of the sea. His work is soon finished; since I am not feeling very well, he goes out with Eva and is pleased to encounter the flower woman. Because Lusch is in bed, we have only the three children at table for lunch and supper. A large pile of newspapers has arrived; R. is pleased that Herr Herrig describes *Siegfried* and *Die Meistersinger* as the blossoms of R.'s spirit. — R. shows me the new Dresden barracks in the *Ill. Zeitung*. . . . "How should a city be built? — If anyone were to ask that: No city should ever be built," he says. Alone in the evening, we become involved in a deep and far-ranging conversation. I admit to him that, when I read books like the one about Buddha, I then find it difficult to recapture the right mood for *Elective Affinities,* which I have just taken up; though I find every feature of it masterly and admirable, I fail to be moved as before. R., though remarking that Eduard's letter, which he has just looked at, pleases him greatly, agrees with me; he says Goethe took refuge in things like that because of a deep ennui with his surroundings. When I say that his works and Shakespeare will always remain impressive, he replies, "They are the exemplars," as it were, of the doctrines, and he remarks that there was something in this portrayal of Buddha which had been new to him— his terrible strictness. While we are engaged in this talk, a telegram arrives from Voltz, so pitiful and so curiously in line with our conversation that we burst out laughing. R. replies, "Demand my money, infamously withheld; period."

Tuesday, October 31 Early in the night R. had a frightening dream in which someone was trying to kill me and he could not come to my defense. He then wakes me at 4 o'clock to see the comet—a dream night, the comet, the Wain, Orion, full moon, the mildest air, and motionless silence! R. also sees a shooting star, and we then return to bed. In the morning everything we saw seems to me like a glorious dream, as if I had been hovering with R. in the distant vaults of

Heaven, and I start the day newly steeled. Unfortunately R. is not very well and is not entirely satisfied with his work. He has also fallen behind in his reading of the little book about Bismarck, which interests him, and in which he recognizes B. as an honest Prussian who succeeded in carrying out a diplomatic coup: "At that time he still knew nothing about the German swindle, he was a complete Prussian." — At midday we take a little walk in splendid weather, meet the gondola at the rail-road bridge, and ride on, unfortunately past the slaughterhouse, where we hear the moaning of the animals! — Once again we are with the 3 children at table. In the afternoon a telegram arrives from Biagino, the Frau Lucca relationship not so bad as we thought. We ride to Saint Mark's Square, where a splendid sunset delights us; the journey home, beneath glittering stars with the bells tolling, is wonderful. And in the evening R. brings our day to an end by reading to us several scenes from *Romeo and Juliet* (balcony scene, T[ybalt]'s death, the marriage, the parting), deeply affecting us all, he himself in tears. But who could ever describe or indeed paint him during readings of this kind? His countenance illumined, his eyes far away yet gleaming like stars, his hand magical both in movement and at rest, his voice gentle and girlish, all soul, but then plunging to the depths and soaring to the heights. May the star which today shot down as we returned home hear my wish! — Before the reading we talked about Wahnfried, Venice. I vote—and in the end R. agrees—against traveling and in favor of remaining as long as possible in Bayreuth and visiting Venice regularly.

Wednesday, November 1 R. did not have a good night, and I am so low in energy that when he jokes somewhat dryly that I never find anything for him, I cannot restrain my tears! The little bell opposite also vexes him; but his work goes well, and he helps me in my own so sorrowful task. We ride as far as the Miracoli and walk home from there. In the afternoon we meet in Saint Mark's Square, which is once again teeming with people. His chest spasm forces him to sit down again beneath the portal. We meet our old friend, who tells us very amusing things about Frau Lucca—how every month she falls in love with some young opera composer. We sit with the children under the arcades and then have a lovely homeward journey beneath a starry sky. In the evening we discuss the Glasenapps' move to Bayreuth, which seems to us urgently necessary. Then R. talks about the 1st movement of [Beethoven's] E-flat Major Symph., its perfection, and the fact that it never makes much of an impression on the audience. When he mentions the great difference between the 4th Symph. and the *Eroica*, I tell him I have the feeling that the former was written before but did not appear until after the latter; he agrees with my hypothesis, saying the 4th follows quite naturally from the Second Symphony. (Lovely bells! And boats full of people sail past to the churchyard of S. Michele.) —

Thursday, November 2 All Souls' Day! . . . R. is not well, he has frequent spasms and intends, among other things, to give up black coffee after lunch. Various grievous impressions sadden us, among others the condition of my father, and do not allow us to enjoy the fine weather; we visit Herr v. Volk., to see his water colors of Venice, and R. is in good spirits during the visit. Since I am not entirely well, R. goes out alone, and I receive friend Mimi, with whom I talk about our loss, feeling shattered by it anew. R. takes out *Elective Affinities* and reads to me the conversation between Mittler and Eduard, and the ensuing discussion restores us to our wonted path! R. remarks how various things have their hour—Calderón, for example, who no longer gives him pleasure, and even this touching *Elective Affinities*. We joke about the renunciation of Charlotte and the captain, since the others love each other simply; but here, too, R. rather misses that natural language which makes Goethe so outstanding in *Werther*, in *Götz*, in *Faust*.

Friday, November 3 A good night, good work, very fine weather! We ride to the Riva, R. and I, and go for a walk in the sun, in good spirits. Even the fact that he does not care for his new barber—chosen for reasons of economy—makes us laugh. At lunch we discuss all sorts of things with the children, including the different forms of burial. Unfortunately he is beset by a spasm in the afternoon. He stays at home. But in the evening, for Siegfr.'s sake, we go to the Malibran Theater; a horror play, *Giani Lupo,* finally proves very boring, although R. entered the theater in high spirits and looked forward eagerly to being entertained. — On our return home, the impropriety of the manservant puts the finishing touches to our feelings of revulsion!

Saturday, November 4 R. had quite a tolerable night, though the disagreeable episode hangs over us and also comes up for discussion at breakfast. We incline toward tolerance, since a character like that can scarcely be regarded as moral. — R. completes his work, and we then ride—unfortunately in fog—to S. Giovanni Crisostomo, where he attentively studies the Bellini as well as the Sebast[iano] del Piombo. Recently he teased me about my love for saints "caparisoned like bishops," I spoke in their defense, and today he yields to me and to some extent exonerates me through the interest he shows in these pictures. — Over coffee we discuss the little book about Bismarck, and then we move on to America, which R. expects one day to become the dominating world power. In the evening we visit our friends the Schl.'s in Malipiero, to say goodbye to them. R. is very tired out by this visit, for he finds contact even with the people most dear to him a heavy burden.

Sunday, November 5 [*Enclosed in the Diaries a report dealing with the causes of Gobineau's death; see notes.*] R. slept well, and at breakfast we talk about Romeo; I compare his second parting from Juliet, when he sees her in the tomb and at the same time sees day breaking, with Tristan's "dreary day, the final time." R. says that this daybreak in the 2nd act does in a curious way typify the falsehood and deceit of the world—also the world of morals, I add (through Marke). R.: "But only because he behaves kindly through all the falsehood and deceit—a force of Nature restrained by convention." This reminds me that it is precisely at this point that he so frequently has the feeling that I should have fled to him in 1858 and started my life with him then! — Since he wishes me to complete my obituary [for Gobineau], he goes to the Piazzetta by himself in the morning and meets the children there. In the afternoon we arrange to meet in Saint Mark's Square, but I find him in Lavena's shop, having had a spasm. Riding in the gondola, he and the girls had heard strains of *Lohengrin,* he then tried to hurry, and that brought on the trouble! . . . Hardly is the spasm over, however, when he beckons Tesarini and invites him and the music director to our house in the evening on account of the wrong tempi! . . . But he then says to me, "I ought to forget who I am, make no sudden movements, and turn into a boring donkey!" Not even this mood can prevent his enjoying the beauty of this place and drawing our attention to it. "This is a theater," he says, stopping in front of the twin columns, and he indicates both stage and auditorium. Then, gazing at the Doge's Palace, he praises medieval architecture and says that with its passing all imagination, life, and invention were lost; the whole Renaissance leaves him cold. He declares the place where the gondolas put in to be the loveliest urban spot anywhere. At home he reads the obituary and tells me he will copy it out for the printers! — After supper (at which he eats almost nothing) he discusses the tempi with the musicians, and then I read to him some things from the *Musik. Zeitung*—unfortunately not at all pleasing, neither the report on Berlin nor the article by friend Pohl, who is hoping for a *Jesus of Nazareth,* nor friend Wolz.'s "For and Against." — His work, on the other hand, I find refreshing.

Monday, November 6 In the morning, when we hear Siegfried and Herr Hausburg chatting in the next room, R. says: "Fidi is with his court jester," a statement which makes us laugh heartily. At breakfast he reads to me a letter by Schop. printed in the newspaper [*enclosed; see notes*]. It entertains us greatly with its precision and the introductory response to stupid objections. Then we come to Carlyle's memorial; I ask R. whom he considers the more significant, Carlyle or Gobineau;

he replies at once, Gobineau, since in Carlyle, even in his *Frederick the Great,* there are so many things which one can regard only as eccentricities. — In the morning he revises my article. — Recently he remarked to me in connection with style how much time one would need for even the most trivial piece of work if one were to try to select and pin down the images exactly; but these pieces would then lack life. Around 1 o'clock I suggest to R. a visit to S. Maria Formosa; both church and picture rouse his interest, the former on account of its intimacy, the latter its magnificence. He also feels very strongly the beauty of the coloring. But he will not admit the terror of martyrdom, which I detect in the eyes; he says it could just as well be a queen of Palmyra as a martyr. We walk to the Rialto and then take a gondola home. On the journey, laughing about my nose being blocked by my veil, he tells me about his mother, how she had gone to put on her bonnet and this got caught on her nose; everybody laughed, which at first vexed her, but then she was amused. This reminds me that recently at lunch he told us about the Klepperbeins, how they took him to the Grosser Garten, how he again told them that his father said their name meant death, and how he once screamed in order to get them to take him home in their carriage, and how he ran after the carriage. Then he also told us of a parcel from his godfather with the inscription "Fresh magpies' eggs for little Richard Geyer" (R. had a collection of eggs). — But I have to wait a long time in Saint Mark's Square for him, and when he arrives with the children, he tells me he had a very severe spasm (I wrote this morning to Standhartner). But he quickly recovers. He is particularly pleased by Fidi's rowing, amused by the gondolier's cries he hears from him. In the evening we read various things in the *I. Zeitung.* R. says that Italian newspapers always have the effect on him of bad chocolate. R. walks up and down a lot.

Tuesday, November 7 R. had a very wild night, and at the end of it he again had a nasty dream about me: "Howling, I told you that I knew you wanted to get rid of me, you wanted to leave." — But he soon recovers, tells me of his sufferings, calls his character "ill-mannered," and feels that imagination plays an undue part in all his sufferings. He reads on the calendar that today is the anniversary of the Battle of Rossbach; Fr. the Great's poem following it reminds R. of Odysseus's outburst against Polyphemus. Then we talk of the simple way in which the French of that time allowed themselves to be conquered in comparison to now, and in the course of this come to speak of Gobineau. R. reads Stein's article in the *B. Bl.* with satisfaction. Toward 1 o'clock we go to the baths, and R.'s mood throughout is very cheerful; he delights in Venice, points out to me a church with a fine portal and window beside the bathhouse, glances gaily into the

Calle [S. Moisè] and declares Venice to be the true Southern town, Palermo reminding him much more of our German towns; it is true that Naples has an African character, but Venice is Italian-Oriental. — In the afternoon he thinks of Bayreuth and says it would probably be a good thing if he were to stage all his works there, and they should also be staged there after his death, for they still survive, and the way in which they are done elsewhere is appalling. — Over coffee we talked about the Renaissance—whether the excavation of classical art had been an unmixed blessing, or had it not perhaps restricted the imagination, put an end to naïveté? The arguments for and against are mentioned, R. says, "It shows that this art was not meant to be the last word." — The Ibach grand piano arrives and pleases R. with its gentle tone, he writes to Herr I. that from now on he will write only soft music. — One can see how bad the modern world is, says R., from the fact that promising people like Nietzsche so swiftly go to the bad in it. In the evening he improvises, and *"Der Jüngling von Elvershöh"* slips in; we like to think of this ballade, which, with its pleasing ending, seems so truly German. As the evening ends, however, our conversation turns to Hans, R. taking the lead in very animated fashion! Each of us has the sickness he deserves, he says: "I, too—I have the sickness of my lack of breeding." —

Wednesday, November 8 R. took medicine today, but it puts a strain on him. In the morning he talks to me at length about his complaint and explains to me what an unduly active part the imagination plays in it. Then, at breakfast, he talks again about Hans; he deplores my marriage, then says Nature had never given him anything completely his own, he had always taken things over from someone else, and he mentions Minna and myself! Oh, how I wish from the very depths of my soul that a being without taint had devoted herself to him! — Hurt as I of course am by such a statement, my dominant feeling is happiness that he can make it, that he feels so free, is so certain of me, that he can let it all pour out, and everything that emanates from him is good! — We talk about his productions, his art, how necessary to it a fine voice and relaxed and unexaggerated gestures. Then we talk about the situation in France, the stupid misunderstandings arising from obtuseness: in Lyons a man took up the chalice during Mass and emptied out its contents, instead of ousting the priest and respecting the symbol. — He reads Stein's dialogues with enjoyment. At 1 o'clock we go for a walk together in the direction of the Ghetto Vecchio and to our astonishment emerge near S. Marciliano! These outings always raise R.'s spirits. But all the same he does not feel well, and when we come to Saint Mark's Square, he has to sit down (under the portal). Once we are in the gondola he feels better. We are constantly discussing what can be done about it! I believe he is demanding too much of his stomach with such a variety of things. — In the evening we are visited by Ada Pinelli, whom R. finds very pleasant. Her memories of Princess Wittg. bring this horrible product of Jewish Catholicism home to R. and me in a most sinister way.

Thursday, November 9   This morning R. had his spasm while still in bed; but he soon recovers, and at breakfast we chat about Ada P., whose appearance pleases R.; he says we have not come to know any man of this pleasant nature. Then "the witch" again. How can people (like Gobineau, for instance) go on visiting her? R. asks. I reply: Probably on account of Countess La Tour. And when we agree that it never occurs to anybody to show consideration toward such chivalrous characters as himself and my father, R. says they cut a sad figure in life—a man must demand obedience from a woman and allow her to influence him only within limits. He looks through my work, laughingly crosses out the "too much" said about himself. Then I suggest a visit to Madonna dell'Orto, and the little walk pleases him greatly, despite the rain and our losing our way slightly, thereby reaching the corner from which the open sea and Murano can be seen. The decorative church also surprises him greatly, and later he reproaches me for not allowing him to look longer at the Cima! At lunch he relates all the encounters we made as far as M. dell'Orto and says he always wishes he could give some practical help—first a pale-faced retired official, who showed us the way and was very grateful for a lira; then the beggar at the door, who went barefoot laboriously to summon the custodian and, when asked by R. why he had taken off his shoes, showed us that they were worn through. R. says, "It would be no use giving him money for new shoes—he wouldn't buy any, and to summon him and the shoemaker to Vendramin would be impossible, as Mama saw immediately, so we gave him something toward them." — "But then we were accompanied by a man who was carrying a kind of cheese in a bowl and offering it for sale so loudly that it cut through one like lightning. When I told Mama that we should let him get ahead, he also stopped on the bridge and cried his wares. We should have bought his cheese and asked him to wait a little; but to do that one would have had to master the language." — In the afternoon we ride to St. M.'s Sq. The view to the right from our palazzo delights R.; later he points out to me the Salute, looking in the mist "like a ghostly dream," also S. Giorgio [Maggiore], everything, and a walk through the arcades gives him much pleasure. On our journey home he tells me he feels a great longing to read something by Edgar [Allan] Poe again, and he recalls the story of the Fl. Dutchman. He visualizes the American imagination, stimulated by the worlds through which they have to wander and destined to perform great deeds, "if everything is not already spoiled." — Fidi's gondolier calls provide us with a pleasant distraction on the journey. In the evening R. sits down at the piano, plays *Preciosa,* recalls youthful impressions, above all of *Der Freischütz,* its "harmonic thrills, which are also a feature of my own music," its daemonism, without which he would have found the music abhorrent: "Nothing but fine form, that didn't appeal to me at all." And he adds, "For me everything else was hard put to it to stand up against the opening of the *Freischütz* Overture." Earlier, at supper, he talked about Riga and Holtei's *Lenore.* Later he reads out the *Venezianische Epigramme* to me, and the evening ends with irrepressible laughter from him and the children (particularly Isolde), when he told them that his mother received from her husband Geyer a cake on which a little man stood passing a ducat. — In bed he expresses his disgust with the *Epigrams.* "I don't in fact believe he lived quite such a wicked life: rather, it is an imitation of Propertius, Catullus, and Tibullus, which makes it all the more repulsive." During the reading I had the impression he was enjoying them.

Friday, November 10 R. had a tolerable night, but in the morning he has a spasm in bed, and today he has 4 in all! . . . We visit the island of Cimitero, where there is not much to delight us, though R. is attracted by a monument to Morosini, which fascinates R. on account of the vivid portrayal and the apparent good likeness of the face; the two busts of both the other Morosinis opposite also interest him. — He comes to lunch late and leaves the table very shortly. He spends the afternoon at home, and so do I; in the evening, too, he appears only for a moment. A day for reflection and sorrow! The cup of tea he drinks does not taste good to him; he says tea is "nothingness made nervous" and is convinced that we are being supplied with tea already used— that is to say, the Chinese had already brewed their own tea with the leaves. (He comes back to his idea of staging all his works in Bayreuth.)

Saturday, November 11 [*Added in margin:* "I amuse R. with the information that Tintoretto had the Golden Calf borne by the 4 greatest painters, which fits in very well with R.'s conception of the Renaissance."] R. had a tolerable night and resolves to spend the day very quietly. At breakfast we talk about Stein's dialogues, and R. criticizes them for a certain affectation and lack of clarity—"this may have told them that," for example. He also finds those set in modern times— particularly Bruno and Shakespeare—less good. But Gobineau's history of the Persians—that interests him greatly. We talk a lot about our friend, and he continues writing out my article in the morning and afternoon, also praising me for it! . . . At 1 o'clock he goes for a little walk by himself and is very cheerful at lunch. We spend the afternoon at home, I finish *Elective Affinities* in tears, and R. says to me: "You must have read the meeting in the inn. That is wonderful, and it was for that he wrote the book; the life together came afterward—when he also made some boring additions." In the evening, seeing the volume on the table beside me, he glances into it, finds it also contains [*Wilhelm Meister's*] *Lehrjahre,* and reads to me all the passages concerning Mignon, with unstinted admiration. He does not much care for the old harpist, maintains that G. made him Mignon's father as an afterthought. He says it is curious to represent him as a German poet (singer), since Mignon is given only broken language to speak. During this discussion I show him the recollection of the *tableau vivant* of Belisar which comes to the architect as he is standing beside Ottilie's coffin; this had puzzled me, too. He says it was attributable to the desire to make everything, even the tragic elements, appear beautiful, as it were—playing around with the material in a manner he himself cannot stand; in fact everything about the architect, along with the vault and the angels, he cannot stand. "And Schiller would surely never have let him get away with Belisar." — Before supper he called me from my reading with the children to listen to Fidi, who, accompanying himself on the piano, was whistling all kinds of themes and variations. After supper he has to repeat the performance to us. R. says this is just the way he himself treated music in his youth. — Before the *W. Meister* reading R. gets me to read from the newspaper the report about the Mahdi, and the idea of the Prophet's emerging from a black race seems to him just as unthinkable as a member of the Hohenzollern family's doing so. According to this report things in Egypt are by no means settled yet.

Sunday, November 12 R. slept well. A letter from Tesarini, asking for a loan, vexes him; he remarks that he is hoarse, something one should not be, and that reminds him of Falstaff's reply to the Lord Chief Justice and he bursts out laughing. But then he says, "I should never dare to make Shakespeare speak, or even Luther—in fact no historical figure." We come back to Stein's dialogues, he finds the invention of the game in G. Bruno good, but then again not. Then he talks once more about the article on Gobineau, as always with praise. As we take our seats in the gondola he says, "You must write an obituary for me too!" and before that he tells me I ought to write the *Bayr. Blätter* entirely by myself—and other friendly jests of that sort. He also comes to me before working to discuss and correct "premonition of decay." Around 1 o'clock we ride to the Papadopoli gardens, in which R. is pleased by the parrots and the pretty borders, although he says one feels no need for gardens in Venice. At lunch he sings something from the E-flat Major Quartet, asks Herr Hausburg whether he recognizes it, and, when the latter says yes and observes that it is difficult to understand:

"Not to understand, for it is all melody, but to listen to precisely, since it is all so concentrated; it is like losing the whole sense of a written passage by failing to hear one word." In the Scherzo of the 9th he finds a turn which reminds him of one in the Scherzo of this quartet. But he does not wish to hear it played, and particularly not by Germans, who always get the tempi wrong. In the afternoon he goes to bed, since he is feeling rheumatic pains; he reads the history of the Persians, which he finds very absorbing. I am with him, and, knowing that his condition is not serious, I am happy. Then I read 2 acts of *Macbeth* to Siegfried.

Monday, November 13 [*Enclosed in the Diaries a telegram from Eduard Strauss in Vienna; see notes.*] R. tells me in the morning that he has again been thinking of his three nightmares: Voltz and Batz, Lucca-Strecker, and Fürstner; the last of these will not, for example, release the score of *Tannhäuser:* "If I now want to revise *Tannhäuser,* I shall have no score." This brings him to business relationships, and he says it is the Jews who have introduced all these sharp practices. He says it is curious that such Jewish operas as [Goldmark's] *Die Königin von Saba* and [Rubinstein's] *Die Makkabäer* have established themselves, a clear sign of the change in public taste. — When, at about 2 o'clock, I return from a long walk with Siegfried, R. hands me the copy he has made of my "reminiscence"; he says he enjoyed occupying himself with it. At lunch he talks about the history of the Persians and regrets—as if it were a crime—not having told our friend how much he admires this work. Since before the end Fidi leaves with Hausburg on a trip to Murano, I relate a few things he said to me about this new companion, to R.'s great amusement. But toward evening he is greatly annoyed by the music lesson, when he hears Herr H[ausburg] playing to Siegfried a melody from *Lucia* [*di Lammermoor*]. R. at once writes to Fritzsch asking for another collection of melodies besides the Köhler one, the choice, arrangement, and connecting material of which he greatly dislikes. In the evening he is still very agitated over this incident, also over a stubborn and silly reply from Fidi (about Murano). That is how touchy he is nowadays, he tells me. He withdraws for a while, then comes to me and plays the melodies. When I say to him in connection with the "Slumber Song" from *La Muette* that something as charming and natural as this surely places Auber above Berlioz, R. replies: "I should think so. Berlioz searched for such things, but with him it sounds artificial." — He tells me he has written to Wolzogen and told him to reply, if someone asks who is the author of the article, "Wahnfried" (*Fuente ovejuna*)! He has also told him to think of the *Blätter* in the broadest terms, free of all limitations, and expressed his regrets that he is left so much alone in Bayreuth. (At supper he returned once more to the subject of his feelings of guilt for not having read the history of the Persians during Gobineau's lifetime and talking to him about it.) We chat together until nearly half past eleven and have to laugh over the way we converse as if we had just met! — R. also talks about our stay in Venice, the painful desertion of Wahnfried. We still do not know what our life is to be! We regret spending so little time in our lovely house, but the thought of the climate and much else besides makes R. shudder. Talking of his health, he says today that he has found a good balance.

Tuesday, November 14 R. slept well; in the morning, our desire to accept the invitation to go to Bologna, combined with uncertainty about my father's arrival, leads us to the latter's life, his attitude toward us: it is not satisfactory. Quite different our review of our good friend Gobineau's life! R. is reading the history of the Persians with great interest, and he tells me something from it which he feels explains everything: that once upon a time the Persians regarded everything as sacred—water, stone, everything; that, as time went on, they no longer worked themselves, yet despised those they had enslaved all the more for working for them and doing work—such as splitting stones— which they themselves were unwilling to do. He goes out to get some money, but finds the air unpleasant. In the afternoon he was much annoyed about the wine bill from Bordeaux which has been shown him, and much of the evening is taken up with the ensuing confusion. (At lunch we talked a lot about the history of Venice, which I am reading with the children.) — But gradually we turn to other subjects; I say something about my reading of *Macbeth*—for example, the reasons the murderers give for being prepared to perform such deeds. R. says: "Yes, no attention is ever given to the degeneration need gives rise to. People just say, 'He is a rogue,' but how he became one, what despair can lead to—that is not investigated at all." — At supper the Jewish problem is also discussed once more, the dispossession of the peasants, the rampant usury. Then R. reads to me from the newspaper a cry of woe about Transvaal, and he exclaims, "That is why I curse Bismarck— for dealing with all these very important problems like a Pomeranian *Junker*." [*In the foregoing sentence the word* "curse" *obliterated in ink by an unknown hand and replaced by* "deplore."] — And we pass on to music! R. plays some of the A Major Sonata and expresses his amazement at the nondescript character of the canon (in the trio of the march), whereas the march itself is so splendidly brimful of ideas; when I ask him what led to this sudden "drying up," he replies with a laugh, "Just that nothing else occurred to him." After we have gone up to bed, he begins: "The first movement of this A Major Sonata is an excellent example of what I mean by unending melody—what music really is.

The change—four bars here, boom-boom, then another four bars—is extremely clumsy. But Beethoven is unique in that respect." As an example of unendingness I cite Bach. "Yes," says R., "and what is all the more curious is that it is actually done without melody. Indeed, one can even say that compared with it the square melody is a decline. And these miracles on the clavicembalo from that poor fellow in a wig—it's incredible." He ends with a joke: "Luther held table conversations, we hold bed conversations."

Wednesday, November 15 R. got up once, and for quite a long time, and my night was very agitated. But R. is well in the morning; he talks first of all about Fidi's profile, which is becoming so handsome. I say like his, but he thinks no, he has got his figure. At breakfast we are amused by an article by Herr Schäffer, waxing enthusiastic about Frau R[eicher]-Kindermann [*enclosed in Diaries; see notes*]. R. immediately decides to dictate to me a letter to Herr Schäffer. Before that he asked himself how the Jews had ever come to assume such importance in our country, where there are still some tough and talented tribes to be found! R. answers himself: Because of the Old Testament, because we have accepted it. Toward 1 o'clock R. goes out for a while, is not pleased, however, since it is raining heavily. Venetian history, which I am reading with the children, provides the basis for our conversation. But the news of the impending arrival of the Duke of Bordeaux causes some alarm, since this is bound to mean some alterations in the palazzo. The expected arrival of my father and of Joukowsky also keeps us busy. Toward 4 o'clock we go out, R., Fidi, and I; it cheers R. up to stroll through the arcades, and our short stop at Lavena's he also finds entertaining. There his attention is caught by a handsome tomcat, who sits motionless on the sweets counter watching the movement made by the gas flame on the ceiling. R. then talks about the goats he has just seen mentioned in the history of Persia—how perfect such an animal is! "And then to turn it into a human being! It is a step backward, so to speak: how ugly the ape is, until the stage of genius is reached!" We ride home through the narrow canals, Fidi rows and calls while Luigi prompts him—"like Mephisto the astrologer," says R.; but it makes us laugh heartily to see that, when it really matters, Luigi always calls out himself. — In the evening we discuss Gobineau's life, then R. tells me some things about Persian history, among others the Persian historian's admission that it contains many lies, and only God can know the real truth about it. Later still, I hear R. laughing about this in his room as he is undressing, he opens the door and laughingly quotes to me the words "*Il y a beaucoup de mensonges*" ["There are plenty of lies"]. — In the *salon* he talked to me about character and said it was foolish to praise it, for either it was meaningless, or a person could not act otherwise than he had done. ("For example, when I did not wish to compose a ballet for *Tannhäuser:* I could not have acted differently.") I ask him whether he does not admit struggles inside a noble person. "Yes, but the decision is preordained. And the actions are what matter." . . . At supper he recalled and related his dream. He had a strange, big hat on his head, with tassels hanging from it which were very annoying; he was trying to adjust them when a giant grasshopper looked at him and thoroughly frightened him. Recently he called me in to look at a grasshopper, which, strangely enough, was looking in with huge eyes! As we were coming home in the gondola he thought of Walther von Stolzing and said he ought to have pleased Gobineau, a true knight, full of defiance until Hans Sachs comes along and guides him wisely. Then he recalls childhood memories, above all of Prague and the flea market, which he so much loved—and the journey on foot.

Thursday, November 16 R. slept well; at breakfast we discuss Lusch's projected stay in Berlin and decide against it. We arrange a rendezvous on the Piazzetta and meet there on the stroke of 1, after I have visited the palace and the library with Fidichen. The fine weather puts R. in a good mood, he has also started a letter to the King and is satisfied with it, even though he admits that he finds hyperbole rather difficult at his age. The glass of his watch is broken, we seek out a watchmaker and, while it is being replaced, go into Saint Mark's through the canal under the Bridge of Sighs, a newly discovered entrance the darkness of which Fidi at first finds frightening. As ever we are overcome by feelings of well-being inside its space, and R. also finds pleasing the thought that it is open to the poor. Fidi rows us home. At the entrance to the palazzo we find R.'s former commissionaire, Zuski, along with a Turk offering Oriental covers; and this is in fact the same man who caught R.'s attention the previous evening in the café under the arcades, on account of his striking facial features. R. tells me a very droll story about Susky: how, when R.'s rent was due at the Palazzo Giustiniani, he had no money with which to pay it; he asked Suski to borrow it for him with interest; the latter soon brought it to him and told him he had got it from the landlord himself, who lent out money on interest! This brings us, laughing, to Giustiniani. Then he gives Lusch a postcard [*enclosed in the Diaries; see notes*], to be answered with the remark that one should not bet. We then talk about Tegnér's watering down of *Frithiof's Saga* and the stupidity of such inquiries. Over coffee (drunk today for the first time for several days) he looks at the fabrics, but Byzantine things have no appeal for him, nor do secondhand goods. He rests in the afternoon; struggles with the geographical minutiae of the Persian history and decides that our friend has overtaxed his powers; with him, he says, it was not a case of "grinding" like some dry academic, since he was after all a poet, but, rather, the result of excitement and the urge to prove that he was no amateur, also his desire to clear up the matter of the races. Today he did not have a spasm! In the evening we talk about our various letters, his from the Chiemsee district, containing a long history of a convent, mine from Jouk. and Liechtenstein; the former enclosed a sonnet by M[ichel]angelo, which pleases R., too: "He had an idea there," he says. Then from *Lohengrin* (3rd act) he plays me the march and sings the final narration, and when I hear that and see him, I am almost frightened by my feelings of happiness! Why should *I* be so happy? And in such a way, in such measure! How to prove worthy of it? . . . This moves me to a prayer; I call upon the power that granted me all this, and bless both it and every suffering I have ever known or will know—a small return for my glorious fate! . . . We talk about Lohengrin, his naïveté: "Since it is never in doubt that he will have to leave, it is possible for him to be so naïve and simple." We remark how few people understand this commandment or even recognize its necessity; and now they talk about the loving woman, for whose sake he should have been permitted to reveal his secret, stay with her, and possibly even have children. But the folk tale accepts without question that he will have to depart. — (As we were leaving Saint Mark's today, R. said he would like to stage all his works in Bayreuth, then bring Siegfried to the point where he could assume control; that would mean living another 10 years, "for at the age of 23 a man already shows what he has in him.")

Friday, November 17   R. got up once but otherwise had a good night. In the morning he talks about male and female and is decidedly in favor of the latter: "For example, your introductory words to the reminiscence—coming from a man, they would sound affected and sentimental; a man must always behave as if he has no feeling, must avoid warmth, and then it is not worth having." — At the end of the evening yesterday he was talking about women, the thoughtlessness of various ladies and my father's courtesy; he recalled the impossible situations they got themselves into, which made them arrogant; I remark how beautifully Goethe portrayed humble subservience as a part of idealism, right up to the figure of Ottilie, and he says I am right. I went out with Lusch to see about the little rabbit. On our way home we meet R. on the canal with Evi and get into his gondola. He talks first about the King, to whom he has just been writing; he mentions that the latter did not behave well toward Ponsch [Blandine], expresses his dislike of the aping of Versailles, and concludes, "In all this one must acknowledge Fate, as Mary Stuart acknowledged divinity with regard to Elizabeth." We get out at the Piazza Manin and walk home. R. tells me about Persian history, saying how curious it is that a tragic fate was always assigned to the father of the chosen hero. He then talks about civilization and says its greatness can be measured by the immediacy of the ensuing decline. How swiftly Greek tragedy met its end—Spanish, too (Calderón)! How soon Shakespeare was forgotten, and even though the impression Shakespeare makes—on him, for example—is greater than on the public of his own time, it is nevertheless no longer a living thing. "But with you one thing always seems to lead to another," he says, after telling me he is sure the same thing will happen with him. — He then talks of Wolz. [*the name erased by an unknown hand*] and says, "We will have difficulty in raising him off the ground floor," using an expression of Baron Hofmann's in Vienna in relation to Jauner, and thus astonishing me with his memory! — At lunch Fidi tells us about the [Goldoni] play he saw yesterday. [*A sentence based on untranslatable word play omitted.*] R. goes to Saint Mark's Square with the children, returns home, and talks of the northern lights they saw from there. News about *Lohengrin* arouses the wish to go to Bologna; the fact that we are expecting my father makes R. cross, as obstacles always do; he enlarges upon my father's character, how he is not one of us, how to him we are just a cipher like so many others [*the last nineteen words obliterated in ink by an unknown hand*]. He is indignant with him for visiting Frl. Ramann at this time. To console him, I suggest that *Lohengrin* in Bologna would certainly tire him and cause him vexation. He agrees with that and contemplates my father's great aspects. We play whist. Lusch joins us; our good Princess H[atzfeldt] is mentioned, R. recalls that she did not take him in at Trachenberg, and that if the King had not come along, he would have been completely deserted. And in bed he says, "First came your father, then the King, then you—you set things right, you combined them both." This morning we went through all the characters of the R. *des Nibelungen* from the point of view of race: the gods white; the dwarfs yellow (Mongols); the blacks the Ethiopians; Loge the half-caste. — (Yesterday R. recalls an expression his mother heard used by a workman in connection with cholera, "There are always such *blights*.")

Saturday, November 18 R. slept well. I dreamed about our friend Gobineau, that he had our children (Fidi still very small) shown to Countess La Tour in her home, then asked me please to see to it that if his right leg became stiff he was not dragged any farther, whereupon I told him there was nobody we cared for as much as him. At breakfast R. exclaims, "*Muse des Parnass* [muse of Parnassus]! — how foolish, how very un-German!" I observe that nobody had ever made such a criticism, and he says, "Oh, yes—Weissheimer, who was upset by the agenda." We talk of W., and through him come to the many relationships in which one squandered one's emotions by ignoring one's instincts and natural feelings, which advised one to hold aloof, and by laboriously manufacturing a thousand reasons to the contrary in order to set everything right. — I do not remember how this led us to Stein's dialogues, but when I express regret that he has not included Ludwig Sand, R. says I should write to him about it and also mention Bernh[ard] v. W[eimar] with Richelieu, and Lessing with Fr. the Gr. at Tauentzien's (Breslau). — A violent clap of thunder startles us, followed by hail! R. finishes his letter to the King and tells me that in it he has spoken about the necessity of staging nothing but *Pars.* during the next two years, in order to keep down expenses. — [*Two sentences based on untranslatable word play omitted.*] When we quote A[dolf] Wagner's little poem "*Irren und Leiden*" ["Straying and Suffering"], R. jokes, "My mother thought him a bad fellow." Over coffee he speaks of past times: "dreamily sad"; Munich, where I visited him every day at noon! Nobody had any sympathy with me, he says. He returns to his idea that we should have been united in 1858: "But you were too young, and I too upset." "The native hue of resolution was sicklied o'er with the pale cast of thought." The quotation brings us to Shakesp. and he says one can actually see the green and red fruits of resolution. I say how much the scene between Malcolm and Macduff pleased me this time, though my memories of it had not been favorable; R. does not much care for the little comedy enacted in it, but he agrees with me that in this scene, taken from the legend, Shakesp. shows what a dramatic artist he is. He reads to me a sentence from Gobineau's history of the Persians, "*Il vaut mieux de méprendre que ne pas voir*" ["It is better to misunderstand than not to see"]. R. is worried about Boni, because she has not written for a long time. In the afternoon we go to Saint Mark's Square; to the Merceria, which he calls Peking. He delights in the tower, the view of Saint Mark's, the horses, and that brings us to the capture of Constantinople. Then we go into Lavena's, with whose proprietor R. enjoys conversing. An eclipse of the sun is being talked about. In the evening I read aloud my letters from Rub. and Humperdinck; R. remarks on how extraordinarily cultured the former is; the latter, which pleases him greatly, makes him reflective. What Bayreuth could be if we were there! How gladly he would stay there if the town itself, and not only the weather, had somewhat more to offer! Then he concludes, "I can already see myself strolling under the arcades"—"We could be happy there even without the arcades." At this he says I have a look in my eyes like Ed. Devrient; since I make no reply, he thinks he has offended me, and at whist and in our room is unremitting with his tenderness! — He goes through *Siegfried* and says he is glad some people have noticed that there is music in the first act.

Sunday, November 19   R. got up once during the night, but he did not have a bad night. In the morning, while still in bed, he talks about the "covetous nothing," the will which is nothing when it does not covet, and about the theory of property, the most untenable of all, since people can hardly call even their thoughts their own, so afflicted are they by the outside world. Then he turns to the article on Gob. and says it could only have been written by a woman—if a man wrote like that, it would be the feminine side of him speaking. Then he tells me some things from Gob.'s chapter on historians, which he finds most ingenious. At breakfast he recalls the Jewish problem, explaining it to himself roughly along the lines that the threat of socialism (Stoecker in alliance with Bismarck) is being turned against the Jews. — At 10 o'clock we receive news from my father that he is arriving this evening. Sincere delight on R.'s part. Around 1 o'clock—after he has written to Feustel about Voltz and Batz matters—we go out; he somewhat circumspectly, fearing a spasm. We stop at Giovanelli, and inspecting the palazzo gives him pleasure; he comes to a halt in front of the sketch for *The Tribute Money* in particular: "Then his gaze fell upon me," he says, and recalls the other picture; would like to possess such things— unusual with him. Then he is attracted by the ballroom, says he would like to build something in this style. From there we go to S. Apostoli, where religious instruction presents a cheerful sight. We return home; R. has a chest attack, but slight, thank God. In the afternoon we meet in Saint Mark's Square (at Lavena's, where he makes arrangements about quartets with a violinist; the latter asks him about Brahms and Dvořák! . . .) We ride home, R. stays in the palazzo while we go to meet my father, whom he welcomes on the steps of Vendramin. He would dearly have liked to have lighted torches, but in the absence of these, many gas lamps are burning. My father is somewhat tired but better in health than we feared. Yet, for all the cordiality on both sides, it is hard to get a conversation going.

Monday, November 20   R. had a wretched night and a very wretched morning; not until nearly midday does he reach the point of eating a little breakfast with me. He spends the whole day by himself, reading newspapers and the history of the Persians. Among the former are two copies of the *A[llgemeine] Zeitung,* brought by my father, which contain a review of "Religion and Art" by a Herr Köstlin. R. comments to me about it: According to this, one is understood only by the people who take one's part, and objectivity is an absurdity. "This gentleman thinks I am a vegetarian and that this explains my article. On the other hand, people who do nothing but echo one's views are offensive. The right ones are those who have convinced themselves that one never says anything out of mere willfulness, whereas in all the others it is always the will speaking. Stein, for example, is one who has convinced himself about me." — Later in the evening, when I go to him, he reads to me the passage in Gobineau's book about chronology, taking great delight in his intellect, but excitement is bad for him, and his spasm returns. . . .

Tuesday, November 21   R. got up once, but he is feeling better. Of people like Herr Köstlin, *A. Zeitung,* he says they give him the impression of having just come from their villages, where their fathers are still sitting in their windmills. Unfortunately R. is much vexed around lunchtime by overly strong heating, rudeness of the servant, intimidation of the children. In very bad weather we ride to the bathhouse, but it is inhospitable there, too, and we turn back. Gradually, with the help of time, I manage to raise his spirits, and when we arrive at the Pal. Vendramin, he himself suggests a visit to my father. There he is delighted with the second window, which offers such a pleasant view over the canal. Our lunch is accompanied by some inner agitation. In the afternoon I pay calls with my father; R., in St. M.'s Square with the children, returns home in annoyance. But he gradually calms down, I find him in a tranquil mood, reading the history of the Persians, which he would like to see more widely known. In the evening we play whist.

Wednesday, November 22   R. tells me in the morning that during the night he mixed up his pills and took 5 of a sort of which he should only take 1! To counter it, he is now taking opium drops again! At lunch, however, after our walk together to the Piazzetta, he is very cheerful, his defense of Tesarini and his character sketch of G. Schönaich arouse much laughter, as also his attitude toward the Societies. But in the afternoon his agitation becomes more and more pronounced, and I await the day's ending with trepidation. However, it does come to an end, and allows me to hope for a less worrisome tomorrow!

Thursday, November 23   R. had a tolerable night. He is pleased by Gob.'s assertion that history has often been written by half-castes, who never allowed a hero to predominate, but always gave him an adviser who did everything. But an article by Dr. Herrig in the *Deutsches Tagblatt* about Gust[avus] Ad[olphus], the failure, for reasons of Prussian patriotism, to acknowledge this great King's significance for Germany, the view that Wallenstein was the true German hero—all this makes him indignant, and he resolves to write an open letter to Dr. H. He also says that, if anything were to be gained by making things known more widely, he would be very glad to see Gob.'s works translated. — At around 12:30 we go out in glorious sunshine, see the children on a bridge near S. Moisè, direct them to the Piazzetta, and there stroll up and down enjoyably with them. The rest of the day belongs to the house, R. visits my father upstairs, and relations between them seem to become easier, rather than more difficult. Since the paper hanger is working in his room, R. occupies himself with pastimes which distract him, and in consequence he spends most of his time in the anterooms, reading, listening to the children, even playing on the piano some arias from the new collection. In connection with this, he is truly horrified by the Italian music of the 18th century, Corelli, Boccherini, and the comparison of one of Mendelssohn's *Lieder ohne Worte* with one of the songs from [Schubert's] *An die Entfernte* provides an opportunity to demonstrate what melody and feelings really are, in contrast to "Semitic excitability." — Schubert's "*Ständchen*" arouses great feelings of warmth in us; R. finds this uniquely beautiful song full of invention, and indeed dramatic (somewhat like the turn in the *Walküre* "Spring Song" at the words "*mit leichten Waffen bezwingt er die Welt*"). — As we are chatting together, talking of Fidi and his studies, R. asks himself if he had ever been diligent. He thinks he was at times, but he cannot remember ever having put anything he had learned to any use. Things just came into his head. The "Sailors' Song" in *Tristan,* for example—that just came into his head; he never pondered or said to himself he must do this or that, and this is probably what gives his things their naïveté and will keep them alive. — From the *Nouvelle Revue,* which Malwida has sent me, I read to him an account of the life of a Russian scholar among the Papuans of New Guinea. R. finds it very interesting. Then, awaiting father and daughter, we look out of the window, bright moonlight, gondolas gliding past "like swans," black swans, and the moon, a dancing star, rocking in the waves. "*Rheingold,*" says R. We hear the voice of our old janitor, who once served in the Austrian army, he is singing "*Ständchen*"! R. sits down at the piano and plays it again. But then we open *Tristan,* and from the 2nd act he plays the ardent reproaches of the lovers! Daniela returns, and we say good night. As R. takes out his watch as usual before undressing, he says jokingly, "A half-caste affair like that—of course it pleases you more than a genuinely Aryan work like *Siegfried.*" I reply that I had just been reflecting that *T. und Is.,* even if also thoroughly Aryan, is capable of being understood by everybody, just as the humanity of the Russians is acknowledged by the Papuans. "Yes," he says, "half-castes will understand it in their own sensual way, not transcendentally. It (*T. und I.*) contains what Hafiz has expressed: 'To sin as a sinner, how wretched, how vulgar! Learn through sin to be a saint, a god!' Faust also expresses that once: finding salvation by hurling himself in and becoming engulfed." — Today I was awakened by a theme from *Tristan,* and the day ends in the same way; as we were riding in the gondola, he recalled how easily we came to love each other, but how difficult uniting us proved to be; and the evening provides such a rich outpouring that even if I had not existed before, I could die with the feeling of having lived entirely and forever! Whereas all other contacts seem to suck me dry, here I find complete fulfillment! I feel a great urge to tell him this, but what are words? I dedicate my thoughts to silence, with the wish that it may descend on him as night's blessing!

Friday, November 24   The night was good, and breakfast passes merrily with Lusch's accounts of the previous evening. Then, since the sun does not come out, R. proposes a visit to the Palazzo Giustiniani, to show it to the children, and this we do. It brings back memories of the dismal years, "when I was standing still." — In the gondola he asks what day it is, then says, "On the 26th something stupid happened, then afterward something strange." He remembers how at that time he was just living from day to day, as if he had only a few more years to live, "and I could think of nothing at all which would not lead to some horrible disappointment." — In the afternoon we walk to Saint Mark's Square, which R. enjoys. At around 7 o'clock my father plays various things to us, the E Major Sonata and Schubert's "*Ständchen*," the latter so wonderfully that it affords R. the very greatest delight. In the evening we play whist, and during a pause R.—who has the dummy hand—plays his "Porrazzi Melody"; after only the first two bars my father stops to listen and says, "That is beautiful." This so surprises R. that he feels I must already have acquainted my father with it. When we deny it, he is very pleased and praises my father's acuteness of perception.

Saturday, November 25   R. had a good night and is considering his preface to the Stein dialogues. It is rather misty, but we go for a walk anyway, exploring the district around M. dell'Orto, and return home in good spirits. At lunch R. describes his impressions of Weber, of *Leeyr und Schwert, Freischütz*. Then, amid great laughter, he comes back to the story of my father's "Saint Moderato"—he finds it priceless! In the afternoon we stroll in Saint Mark's Square. When I remark happily that he is walking in a much livelier way, he says he ought to apostrophize his stomach in the same manner as H. IV.: *vieux paresseux* [old sluggard]. This brings him to Gobineau's failure to appreciate the French Protestants. In the evening we are visited by Herr Passini and Herr Ruben; R. finds them quite pleasant.

Sunday, November 26   R.'s night somewhat restless. But at breakfast he is cheerful, jokes (I cannot remember with what instigation) about my love for Frau v. Stein and Frau v. Kalb, and when I set out to defend the former, observing that one cannot blame her for not liking the *Venezianische Epigramme*, for example, R. replies: "Goethe had had quite enough of a relationship in which the woman gave nothing and yet wanted to be the one and only. How calmly he judged things, when he realized that all the charm of this relationship was provided by him, one can see from the letter about coffee." After various comings and goings we stroll to Saint Mark's Square, where Passini is awaiting us in order to show us the restored *Madonna dei Frari* in the Doge's Palace. R., like me, is pleased by it, and he says the flag adds something fanatical to the picture. But when we are shown other things, he becomes annoyed, and at home jokingly accuses me of a preference for the visual arts. At lunch he tells me Gob.'s views on Cyrus's significance and death, says that in this history he finds Gob. even more interesting than the Persians themselves. In the evening he plays whist with my father and Loldi, while I entertain a little violinist whom R., in order to get rid of him at Lavena's, invited to come along in the evening! This leads to many jokes! I forget in what connection R. quoted the line, "We've made him rich; 'tis now expected that we amuse his idle hours." He shows it to me in *Faust* in our room and agrees with me when I say that it expresses Schopenhauer's view on life, "Either misery or boredom."

Monday, November 27 R. slept well, got up only once. At breakfast he tells me his dream about a lovely garden belonging to the Wesendoncks, one—always the same—which he often saw in his sleep but which they had acquired after their friendship with him; this time the lady invited us to come and look at it. He then jokes with me for having referred to this lady as his *"poétique amie"* ["poetical friend"] in a letter to him in Venice. I joke back that this was the least I could do, since he had always represented her to me as a saint—he says he cannot believe this. The mail brings, via Dr. Muncker, an offer from the publishing house of Cotta! Then a proposal from Voltz-Batz! . . . At lunch I relate various things about the *Msinger* performance in Munich at which the late Empress of Russia was present. Then there is talk of the *tombola* [lottery], and R. sings the word to the scherzo of the 9th: *tom-bolà!* Then he mentions the one sentimental passage in this Scherzo, which cannot be played too sentimentally if it is not to pass quite unnoticed in the lively ending. He says this quality of "tender passion" is exclusively Beethoven's own—others either "picked up a guitar" or were too clumsy. Continuing to speak about it, R. says that Beeth. did not design symphonies with the idea of showing others after him how to do it: "He just opened up possibilities." — In the afternoon, in spite of the mist and dampness, he walks in Saint Mark's Square, buys lottery tickets with the children, and very much enjoys life, as he tells me, particularly the children's pleasure and excitement. When he tells about this at supper, he adds for my benefit, "I remembered, Brünnhilde, you!" . . . Unfortunately the evening brings him much vexation; my father wishes to keep Lusch company—she is in bed; this makes R. thoroughly indignant, and he breaks out in a rage. I remain silent, and later, too, when alone with him, sad from the depths of my heart at being unable to respond to his usual tendernesses, assuring him that I am not at all angry, yet able only to wish him a sorrowful good night.

Tuesday, November 28 R.'s night was plagued with thoughts of Voltz and Batz. And at breakfast he comes back to the previous evening. I try to explain to him that, besides wishing to keep Lusch company, my father's only thought was certainly that we ourselves might be pleased to have an evening by ourselves. But R. is quite unable to understand this. However, the little rabbit, which he then finds on his desk, amuses him. [*A dedicatory poem enclosed in the Diaries.*] The sun is shining brilliantly, and even his dictation to me of a letter to Holtzendorff for Voltz and Batz becomes a cheerful and stimulating task. At lunch, yesterday evening is referred to gaily, and then we chat about various subjects, such as Dr. Wille, etc. In the afternoon R. goes to Saint Mark's Square with the children; he brings the little hare to supper and shows it to the children. Before that my father played, together with Lusch, Beeth.'s F Major Quartet, a work for which R. frankly expresses his dislike (also for the Scherzo); then we play whist. — Late in the evening, when we are alone, R. talks about my father's latest compositions, which he finds completely meaningless, and he expresses his opinion sharply and in much detail. I ask him to talk to my father about them in the hope of preventing his going astray, but I do not think R. will do this. I go to bed with painful feelings, and I cannot stop thinking of the letter R. might perhaps write to my father— I compose it in my mind.

Wednesday, November 29 A lovely sun is shining on us, and R., coming to breakfast, shows me the little hare in his arms; soon afterward he gets up and writes the verse about Dr. Luther in my little swallow-Ricardo notebook! [*Enclosed a piece of paper bearing in Wagner's handwriting the words* "I and Dr. Luther, each one sang of a little hare."] Around 1 o'clock we ride to the Piazzetta, the weather is splendid, we catch sight of Siegfried, and we spend a merry and amiable time there together. But, home again, R. has a chest spasm, he comes to lunch rather late and is rather silent throughout; but he does then show the children his little hare, for which he has ordered a chain. In the evening R. is worn out—he has a cold; Eva made a nice copy of our dictation, he looked through it and has now sent it to friend Gross with a request to consult Herr Holtzendorff. This also proves a strain on him. He sends a telegram to Herr Neumann, telling him not to make any agreements with V. & Batz. At supper he tells us about Halévy and *La Reine de Chypre*, he has fond memories of Halévy and his ways.

Then he disappears and does not join us until later, at whist, soon withdrawing again. I follow him out. — (He read to us a telegram from Seidl which had amused him, he came to our whist table singing, "You robbers, you thieves," etc., and was annoyed that my father, serious and immersed in the game, did not join in the laughter.) — Today he begins to talk about my father again, very blunt in his truthfulness; he describes his new works as "budding insanity" and finds it impossible to develop a taste for their dissonances [*the foregoing sentence obliterated in ink by an unknown hand; an additional twelve words in it illegible.*] He keeps talking about it to me, while I remain silent, sorry that there is nothing I can say in reply! (I am also depressed today by the news, conveyed to me by my father, that Hans's health is deteriorating.) I read Prof. Haeckel's lecture on Goethe, Darwin, Lamarck, and praise it, but R. points out to us the absurdity of going from effect to cause back as far as the monad, thus always remaining trapped in the idea of time, space, and causality.

Thursday, November 30 R. had a restless night, the V. and Batz affair torments him and causes him anxiety—for how long now? Years! But in bed in the morning he gives me instructions to prepare a nice Christmas for the children. Then he observes that my father was not looking well yesterday. I: "He isn't well." He wonders whether we should not consult a doctor. I say he has consulted Brehm and is living according to his instructions, whereupon R. disputes that very violently. When I tell him that I saw him drinking only Marsala and water, R. reproaches me for contradicting him; that arouses great annoyance in me, I angrily declare to R. that my entire efforts are always directed at not opposing him in anything, whereupon he jumps angrily out of bed with the remark that I obviously think I am virtue itself. Hardly has he gone when I sorrowfully tell myself that I should have kept silent after he contradicted my statement that my father is living according to doctor's orders; his remark about my opinion of myself seemed at first a bitter and painful punishment, but in the very next moment, though still in tears, I accept it with all my heart—if it is just, as a salutary punishment, if unjust (I am not aware of having any good opinion of myself, for I have never felt myself to be above anyone else), then as a blessing! May the blessings of suffering prevail! Certainly I have deserved my sorrow on account of my anger. — R. comes to breakfast; a nice letter has arrived from the King, we talk amicably about it. Before he goes, he tells me that it is unfair of him to talk to me so freely about my father, he realizes that and regrets it. Certainly it is not that; I keep silent, however, in the way I know he prefers when he has explained something, and I kiss him with a heart wholly free of rancor; but the fact that he returns my kiss without warmth pains the violently trembling self within me; however, I have no love for this self, and I know that the present flood of tears will give way to happiness. (As I am writing this, still under the immediate influence of it all, the sun shines silver and gold and smiles on me for a moment; otherwise it is a gray day.) R. walks to the Church of I Gesuiti via S. Apostoli, guided by Siegf. Before lunch he reads to S. what the King says about him. At lunch he tells us his latest impressions of Goethe, saying that "in our threefold copy" of *Faust* he has been reading about the beating of the fur coat; he says such things can be compared with nothing else, they belong solely to Goethe. "This new creation delights me"—he laughs heartily over this. Yesterday it was the "grinning masks of life" which came into his mind in connection with Voltz and Batz. He invites me to go with him to Saint Mark's Square in spite of the gray weather; in the gondola he says how curious it is that with Caesar, Alexander, Cyrus, Napoleon, etc., the line dies out—it is as if Nature has no wish to have such excessive personalities. We stroll in Saint Mark's Square, then walk as far as the Rialto, R. in cheerful spirits throughout: "Palermo the finest climate, Venice the finest city." — In the evening he writes to Voltz; Eva copies it (as she so nicely copied out the exposé yesterday), I send it to friend Gross. Unfortunately this subject gives R. no respite. A telegram from Adolf [Gross] adds to the uneasiness. [*Enclosed in the Diaries Gross's telegram,* "Intend travel Sunday Munich Monday," *and a remark on it in Wagner's handwriting:* "Silly fellow!"] The only distraction is provided by Siegfried, who is writing a play, *Catilina!* Yesterday he delighted us with his first piano production (theme from the Andante of the A Major Symphony). The fact that the King wants to see *Pars.* in Munich also disturbs R.! . . .

Friday, December 1 R. slept well; we talk about all sorts of things at breakfast, and R. is in a good mood. Unfortunately the missing pages in the proofs sent to him cause him great vexation, he sends friend Wolzogen a telegram. The day passes peacefully, despite the bad weather; in the afternoon we go out in the gondola. R. drops me at the P. Malipiero and then goes on to St. M.'s Square with the children. In the evening games of whist alternate with talking to Herr von Volkoff. At the end of the evening, when the latter praises Gambetta, R. becomes very animated and declares G. to be a clown.

Saturday, December 2 Bad weather again, wind and snow. But R. slept well, and at breakfast we talk gaily of Fidi's *Catilina,* his inclinations toward the theater. Then he tells me about an article in the newspaper concerning a complete production of Goethe's *Faust* in Paris—a French actor wanted to attempt it, but it proved impossible. R. talks about productions of this play in general and feels it is impossible to do, though he remembers having once, in his youth in Dresden, seen Mephisto played very impressively by an actor named Pauli. He feels that, even when one is just reading it, one must take the greatest care to avoid any hint of declamation, and just allow the thoughts to make their effect by speaking them simply. — He begins his work, is somewhat annoyed by interruptions of various sorts. At lunch he displays a mixture of amiability and uneasiness. Fidi tells us about the play *Hannibal* which he saw yesterday. R. again expresses his antipathy toward the Romans, "who introduced no new principles to the world." (At lunch yesterday he told Fidi about Alexander's storming of a wall and quoted the soldier in Aeschylus: "Oh, King, he who acts must suffer.") — We do not go out, and today it is somewhat cold, even in the house. All the same, we have a peaceful evening, and the whist game becomes quite merry (R., Loldi, Father, and I). — (Before supper R. went through a little composition in my father's *Weihnachtsbaum,* and when I ask him to address his remarks about it to my father himself, he says, "That would be cruel.")

Sunday, December 3 R. had a restless night and feels he has caught a chill. While still in bed he spoke of the world's monotony, saying that what change there is is due only to the fact that people are born and die—the idea of living forever is a terrible one! He makes this remark in connection with Fidi's *Catilina,* which reminds him of his own dramatic work. Unfortunately a letter arrives at breakfast from Dr. Strecker, who, it seems, has utterly failed to understand his point of view in the Lucca affair. I shall probably reply to Dr. Strecker, but R. is annoyed all the same, continues to think about it, and summarizes his feelings toward other people by saying that those who are well disposed have no energy—only the hostile ones are energetic. We attempt an outing, since the weather is fine, but he finds it too cold, and we soon turn back. He complains of the varying temperature in each room and wishes to take his meal alone. Around five o'clock he goes to bed, then gets up again and reads with interest some of Tolstoy's Russian novel *War and Peace,* which I have recommended to him, starting at the point I myself have reached. He is pleased by the observations on the art of war, saying that he, too, regards the warrior genius simply as a schoolmaster, like Moltke, for instance. One cannot ascribe such deeds as the siege of Metz to a single warrior genius but, rather, to the disciplined character and intelligence of officers and men. — Each time I visit him he is feeling either contentment or extreme irritation, the latter provoking him into expressions of a hatred for life. (In the morning he showed me in the newspaper a quotation from Machiavelli in praise of the Germans and their religious feelings. — Reminded of the Jews, R. says, "Now all of us are confederates!")

Monday, December 4 At breakfast we talk about yesterday's rehearsal of [Goethe's] *Die Geschwister,* and I tell him my father's remark to the effect that he has no feeling for drama, and even in Shakespeare is interested only in the ideas. R. thinks, as do I, that this is the result of a French upbringing. R. goes on to say that he had been thinking previously about the F Major Symphony; one cannot really say that such a work touches one's heart, so what is it that gives one such satisfaction? It is this joyfulness, like Brahma making sport with himself. This, he says, is a very German quality. Making joyful sport with oneself in this way does not lead to laughter, for there is nothing in the least ironic about it (like the humor of Cervantes, for example)— it is entirely positive. And it is this same spirit which prevails in *Faust.* — R. then says he intends to make another attempt to read Ariosto, since such eminent minds as Schop., Goethe, Gob. held him in such high esteem. — Lusch joins us, is praised for her acting yesterday, R. jokingly offers himself for the part of Fabrice, whom he calls a second Brackenburg: "After Klärchen's death he tried again." — The conversation at lunch is very cheerful; R. is continuing to read the Russian novel with great interest and relates several things from it, how, for example, in his naïveté Napoleon wished to receive the Boyars in Moscow! . . . R. stays at home today. In the evening my father plays to us three preludes from the *48 Preludes and Fugues,* among them the "Magister"—or "Magister as Jupiter *tonans,*" as R. remarks. Then the first movement of Weber's A Major Sonata; R. says one can certainly appreciate its charm, but it is music for an audience, not the kind one makes for oneself like the Beeth. sonatas, and remembering *Preciosa* and *Euryanthe* always make one see that Weber's true sphere was the theater. One is also conscious of a certain superficiality, he says; it follows, not on Beeth., but on Hummel and Kalkbrenner. — We then play whist, in which R. has to endure much vexation over his strikingly bad cards!

Tuesday, December 5 R. did not have a very good night, and the dull weather oppresses him. He thinks of leaving here, speaks of Spain. He does not go out today, but reads Tolstoy's novel with interest. — Our life with my father is becoming easier, and this evening our game of whist, for example, was a very merry one. R. tells Jewish anecdotes, and when he makes several plays on words, my father says the lagoons are adding to his wit. [*A sentence dealing with a point of German spelling omitted.*] — Siegfried's *Hermann der Befreier* puts him in good spirits. —

Wednesday, December 6 R. had a wretched night, complains of great heaviness. But as usual our conversation at breakfast follows a smooth course, even though we begin with such difficult subjects as Hans's situation and behavior, and after that his personality. I do not remember what led R. to his flight to my father (in '49), the parting from Minna; he tells me how sorry he felt for her, until she herself forfeited it through her hardness. Elaborating on this subject, I tell him that I myself know what it is to enjoy the discomfiture of others—when people were unjust toward me, I was always overtaken by a cheerful, superior, indeed superstitious feeling that this would bring me luck. I am unable to remember why he sings Loge's *"Weibes [Wonne] und Wert,"* but he follows it by remarking how little appreciation has been shown for *Das Rheingold,* which he feels he "brought off fairly well." He says Schopenhauer appears to have appreciated it; I express my disgust with the great philosopher for having so misunderstood the *Ring;* R. says he is convinced that a single visit would have been enough to put him to shame. Then he says, "Things like Herrig's understanding of *Siegfried* give me pleasure and enable me to overlook a lot." — Around midday our dear friends the Grosses appear on the doorstep! Several things: the King is eager to have *Parsifal* staged for him with our scenery; Holtzendorff is giving good and encouraging advice about how to deal with V. & B. Friend Gr. tells me there are reports that Neumann is going bankrupt (we keep this from R.). We arrange to meet our friends in the afternoon in the Piazzetta, but R. is beset by a spasm. We go to Lavena's, where he soon recovers and jokes gaily with our friend about Venus, eclipses of the sun, etc.! In the evening R. discusses with friend Gross the price of seats, advertising the performances, etc.

Thursday, December 7   R. is vexed to see the sky still heavily overcast, and it brings further bitter complaints from him but does not prevent him from making witty remarks at breakfast, including one about the "Wittgenstand" (for *Witwenstand* [widowerhood]) of my father. He sings a phrase from the role of Amazily [in *Fernand Cortez*] and says that Spontini was the first to make use of certain accents and lines—there are hints of them in Mozart, but all rather trifling [*the last four words obliterated in ink by an unknown hand*]. We then talk about the singers Materna and Malten; he praises the former's free emission of tone, the childlike sound which does not actually convey very much to one, whereas [Therese] Malten possesses a dark timbre which is capable of tragic accents. — The sun comes out, R. goes out around lunchtime and returns cheerful and contented from his visit to "the one and only town." Lunch with our friends the Grosses. Toward 6 o'clock, after meeting in Saint Mark's Square, R. discusses with friend Adolf the performances, our attitude toward the King, who is insisting on having a performance given in Munich; R. is at first violently against it but then accepts my suggestion of offering the King our decorations and costumes in the fall instead of the spring, since there is work to be done on them, and there will have to be rehearsals in the spring. The conversation then turns to Holtzendorff, Batz, and Voltz, and it turns out that much correspondence and much time will still be needed; R. becomes very agitated and leaves the room. We have supper without him (Father and children at Princess Hatzfeldt's). But he then returns, and a friendly conversation develops after all.

Friday, December 8 R. had a wretched night, and our breakfast time is not as amicable as usual—complaints about life gain the upper hand, and even the thought of the children does not cheer R. up, their merriness seems to him like triviality. The weather is unfavorable, R. does not go out, he discusses the performances, etc., with friend Gross. Friend Jouk. arrives around 8 o'clock, received by R. with a mixture of gaiety and gruffness; he tells him his greeting must take this form if he is to avoid looking like the biggest of hypocrites. — His humor keeps on breaking through his vexation, he shows his rabbit and sings, "Stiefel must perish, though still so young!"

Saturday, December 9 This morning was very bad indeed; the fact that Feustel lost the contract and then made no copy of it when it was recovered upsets R. so much that I become extremely worried. R. sends a telegram to the lawyer. But around midday he suggests an outing and is in good spirits; he interprets the Stiefel song as being about a young recruit who suddenly feels a longing for his mother and deserts; for that he is hanged—and quite legally; he says one is ashamed of having anything to do with these robbers who organize the world. We stroll in Saint Mark's Square, which always puts him in very good spirits; but the rain vexes him, and above all the fact that our friends the Grosses see hardly anything of the town in all its beauty. Lunch is somewhat disordered by the new seating arrangements. And in the afternoon the lawyer's reply is received: Batz refuses to produce the contract, which deprives us of any chance of making headway in court! . . . R. quite beside himself; he also says that on account of all this he finds it impossible to work. (In St. M.'s Square he told me he had inquiries made of Herr Wolk. whether he would fulfill the wish I had expressed for a portrait of R. beneath the portal of St. M.'s, but Wolkoff has refused.) However, to my surprise, he disciplines himself in the evening to be friendly, spending part of the time playing whist with my father and part talking to Jouk., Marie Gr., and me, mainly about Tolstoy's novel, in which he particularly praises old Kutusov.

Sunday, December 10 To my surprise and delight, R. slept well, and our breakfast is cheerful, despite news of floods. "Stiefel must perish" comes up frequently, and when we hear friend Gross whistling Siegfried's call through the window, he becomes very high-spirited and goes for a little walk with him, during which, however, he is again beset by a chest spasm. At lunch we chat about all sorts of things, and in the afternoon the final details concerning the performances are written down for the record, the question of Glasenapp also discussed. At supper R. becomes excited in condemning the French Academy during a discussion with my father, who, according to R., has a high opinion of it. In the evening we are at Princess Hatzf.'s, where Lusch plays Marianne in *Die Geschwister.* The play itself once again moves R. to tears, but he feels that Lulu's portrayal should have been more naïve. The rest of the *soirée,* however, the introductions, etc., R. finds more than ever unbearable, though he very patiently takes it in good part. The presence of our dear Grosses is of help to him in this; we say goodbye to one another, and R. allows me to give Marie the fan I got from him.

Monday, December 11 R. had a good night; we discuss the party yesterday, and when R. compares the painter Passini to the casing of a Black Forest clock, I have to laugh so much that I at once tell the children why. Also his various replies—for example, to a painter who introduced himself, "Well, there are enough painters here," and to the Austrian consul, "If I have any big business deals, I shall come to you"—make us laugh, and they also show me the pleasure he feels now whenever he comes into contact with people. At lunch he also very comically expresses his pleasure in the consul's young son, who played Fabrice so soberly that we had to laugh heartily. — Before lunch R. and I took a ride to the square, through the Merceria on foot as far as the Rialto, with enjoyment in spite of the weather! — In the afternoon R. receives Count Contin, founder and president of the Conservatoire, R. describes correctness of tempo as the alpha and omega of what should · be taught. (My father is very, very unwell, has to take to his bed!) — In the evening R. shows me the picture in the *I. Zeitung* of Frl. Brandt as Lea in *Die Makkabäer;* he wonders how the audience can put up with something as horrible as this Jewish stuff on the stage! — We play whist, and to end the evening, R. reads to me from Tolstoy's novel the episodes of the innocent man condemned to death and the poor dog howling when its master, the soldier, is shot dead!

Tuesday, December 12 R. slept well; at breakfast (doubtless because of the Goethe mask which Countess L[a] T[our] has sent him in the name of our friend) he turns to the subject of our friend Gob.'s poem "Amadis" and says he is surprised that he chose the magicians' tales and things of that sort, since they belong quite definitely to Provence and its "Moorish population," whose trivial and gaudy images stifled the genuine features of Nordic legend. Of the history of the Persians, on the other hand, R. says this should have altered the entire course of historiography, and he says he remembers that friend Sulzer once expressed to him an opinion concerning the Greeks and Persians (mainly with reference to Alexander) which suggests that he knew G.'s book. At lunch conversation turns to various friends of ours: R. says there are bad and good people, but for each one there comes a moment when he must decide whether he is capable of sacrificing another for his own sake or not. When this theory is felt to be rather harsh, particularly in relation to the one friend, R. says, "There are certain feebly good talents which express themselves at most in bad music." — Before lunch R. visited the Conservatoire and its president. To my father, who is somewhat better but still very run down, R. gives various words of advice, and he also wishes that he would remain with us. In the afternoon he goes out with Fidi to Saint Mark's Square, comes home cheerful. He prescribes a quinine powder for Evchen, who has had to go to bed with a chill. Dr. Keppler, summoned by us, comes in the evening, alarms me by saying that one cannot yet tell whether it will develop into an infectious fever. We play whist and then chat a little, but unfortunately R. keeps coming back to his Voltz-Batz-Feustel experiences. At supper he tells us about a letter to Herr v. Holtzendorff and says he can no longer write letters, he is always making mistakes. Before whist the singers came around, and R. (who no longer cares for them) remarked, "On the other hand, they are a part of Venice." — He finds the mask of Goethe Roman. R. glances through the poems of M[ichel]angelo, which Jouk. brought with him, and significantly he gives me one sonnet to read, "The slave, held captive by a strict master . . ."

Wednesday, December 13 R. had a restless night, and he tells us that his anxious dreams brought him Voltz and Batz, but also Eva with a glass of milk (doctor's prescription). He takes medicine and in consequence remains at home in the morning. He is in a good humor at lunch, if not very talkative. He complains of never being able to get down to his work. But he is more and more absorbed by Gobineau's book, he says it is downright uncanny how much at home this man is everywhere—even in the Old Testament, for example. When I tell him that I read a song by Luther early in the morning and quote to him the drastic expression "When death gobbled up death," he says one could not expect Empress Augusta to approve of such things. He mentions a very amusing witticism in the *Bl. Blätter,* in which a corporal says, "Lieutenant, you call yourself an educated man and you can't jump over a palisade!" and adapts it as follows: "The Emperor would say to him, 'You call yourself an educated man and you can't distinguish a chassepot from a needle gun!'" — Today is payday, and our expenses are always very, very great, but R. will not hear of economizing! . . . We also talk about actors in connection with the gracefulness of old Lang, and R.

says that if they do not have sensitive and supple joints, they will also lack the right voice and the right gestures—these things go together. R. expresses his aversion for women's playing male roles; only once has that succeeded, he says: [Wilhelmine] Schröder-Devrient's Romeo, which permitted acting of an uncommonly intimate kind. In the afternoon we walk to St. M.'s Square and then through the Merceria to the Rialto. R. in good spirits. At supper Kundry's costume is discussed, with some annoyance on R.'s part on account of the money which has been wasted. In the evening whist, and with it Dr. Keppler —a source of vexation for R., since my father remains at the gaming table with his partners, leaving us to entertain the somewhat phlegmatic doctor. But it leads to much joking afterward.

Thursday, December 14 R. slept well, and we are soon in conversation about a wide variety of subjects. Among other things, he says he will never again speak about religion, explain his ideas, for instance, regarding the blood of Christ; these are things one all of a sudden grasps—let those who can understand them, one cannot explain them. — Suddenly he smiles to himself, and I ask why; he feels he should not tell me, but then he talks about the little grace note my father occasionally adds, on the same note, to make the melody sound more expressive; he says this reminds him of the wrong way certain singers sing. Then he criticizes the playing of the minuet from *Don Giovanni* yesterday and the lack of simplicity in the barcarole. I tell him that my father spoke favorably of *La Muette,* it is only "*l'amour sacré de la patrie*" which he does not like; whereupon R. says: "That is unjust, for then he is condemning a whole branch of literature, of which that is by no means the worst example. Rossini used it often enough, and one must take the duet as a whole, not just these isolated passages." We continue talking about interpretation, how in the first act of *La Juive* Duprez did not sing Eleazar's and Recha's cries at the end in strict tempo, but shouted them with broad pathos directly to the audience. R. says he saw Halévy in the wings, giving instructions for it himself, and when R. remarked on it to him, he said, "The singers want it like that, and it does make an effect." — Coming back to *La Muette* and to Th. Gautier's book on Italy, in which at my recommendation he read the description of Saint Mark's and enjoyed it, he says: "Italy had a good effect on the French—they found in it all the things they themselves had been looking for in vain." — Unfortunately our lunch is somewhat delayed by my father, R. very vexed about it, since he had promised to go with my father to the Lyceo. At supper he tells me that he had some spasms there. But when he says he must go again tomorrow, since they have no conductor, and notes my slight surprise, it bursts out of him that on my birthday he is going to play his symphony to me! . . . Great laughter from Loldi and Fidi (Eva in bed, Lusch with her grandpa at Princess Hatzfeldt's). He tells me all the difficulties he has been having at rehearsals, with missing parts, with Seidl's absence; now he has sent a telegram to Humperdinck in Paris, hoping to get him here for the occasion. It moves me to complete silence! . . . We spend a quiet evening by ourselves, he plays to me something from *Siegfried*. I then read to him from the sonnets of M[ichel]angelo, which impress him. — Luther's letter about floods in Halle a/Saale [*clipping from the* Bayreuther Tagblatt *containing the letter enclosed*] pleases us greatly with its humor and vigorous high spirits. (To his inquiry about the money, R. has received from Herr Neumann the reply "Within a month," which makes R. suspect things are in a bad way.) But, on the other hand, news that a copy of the contract is now available has an agreeable effect [*a telegram from Gross in Bayreuth announcing this enclosed*]; R. observes jokingly that I am easily pleased; hearing such things is not enough to restore him. As he goes off to bed, he says: "Oh, if only all these aches would go away! This constant joking is an ache, the muscles of my face are always aching!" —

Friday, December 15   During the night R. laughs aloud, thinking of Stiefel, then he dreams about my having to break out of a tower. These images provide us with conversation; he visualizes Lessing's and Tauentzien's reactions to Stiefel when the poor, fleeing boy is caught, Tauentzien upholding the position of "civilization," law and order, Lessing describing the terrible situation which led to this incident. — The recruit is hanged, his comrades sing a song to him; I feel that Fr. the Gr. should intervene to rescue him, but R. says no. And he goes on to say that his opinion of such rulers is sinking lower and lower, there is not much to choose between them (e.g., Fr. the Gr.) and Napol., Tamburlaine, the kings of the Huns, and there is after all a great difference between acknowledging that life is suffering and using this knowledge for cruel and selfish ends. R. goes for a short outing with Fidi before lunch. We eat early, since he is going to the rehearsal; the open secret of the "surprise" provides table conversation of the merriest kind. My mood remains subdued throughout, since the doctor is not satisfied with Eva's condition, but he does not say precisely what it is! — Around 4 o'clock R. goes to the rehearsal (yesterday Frontali, the 1st violinist, told Lusch that the players were all enraptured with R.). He returns home very content, saying it all went well! He told the players that it was an old piece, written 50 years ago, and they would find nothing new in it—if they wanted something new they had better choose a symphony by Beethoven or Haydn. — The French opera edition mentioned by my father leads R. to talk about the prolificness of the 18th century and the foolishness of publishing it all. Then he grows heated about laurel wreaths and the custom of presenting them to artists; I strive in vain to defend this symbol, and I quote to him *"das Reis"* and the muse of Parnassus! — We play whist, which does not put R. into the best of moods! — Talking to me about his symphony, R. says contentedly that it is not at all sentimental, striving throughout toward nobility.

Saturday, December 16 The night was a good one, R. is in good spirits, I try as much as possible to play down Eva's illness. At lunch a lot of anecdotes are told about Cherubini and Spontini, among them how the former said to Hiller after having heard one of his symphonies, *"On voit que vous n'avez rien de mieux à faire"* ["One can see that you have nothing better to do"]. Spontini, R. says, was a monument of maliciousness. Of Mozart he said yesterday that one had only to compare him with his contemporaries to see what a cornucopia of ideas he was. In the afternoon we go the children's *salon,* R. and I, and he then goes to rehearsal; the children go there, too, and return home in raptures, R. also pleased and excited: he recalls the performance 50 years ago, after only one rehearsal, and says the present one will be much better. Since I am not allowed to attend the rehearsals, I find it only a melancholy consolation that I cannot in any case leave Eva's bedroom at present! . . . The whist played again today arouses R.'s utter disgust! He complains that he and my father are now such strangers to each other. . . . For quite a while he continues to talk aloud about this in his room, bursting into exclamations! I go to him, and this conversation, too, though a painful one for me, is peaceable! (Fidi wrote a hymn today, R. sat correcting it for him in the smoking niche, having gone there, first, because he had been dealt very bad cards, and then because my father played with such seriousness, not allowing himself to be distracted. I soon followed R. and left Loldi to take my place.) — When R. returned from the rehearsal I went to him from Eva's room and found him, having already changed his clothes, reading *Faust*—the masquerade, which, out of context, gives him very great pleasure; he quotes to me Avarice's speech and the old woman's reply, "They're troublesome enough" makes him laugh a lot.

Sunday, December 17 R. had a somewhat restless night. At breakfast he comes back to his impressions of the whist game, we mention Gobineau, who never touched a playing card, then Semper, and R. recalls his failure to visit Tribschen after his long letter. This causes me to observe that there is something curious about forgiving: one may see these disloyal people again, but how can one have the same feelings of affection toward them? R. says, "Yes, all sympathy for what they say or do, their gestures and expressions, has been lost." — At lunch my father says jokingly that he feels humiliated—he has been told that all he is now good for is playing whist! When R. hears that, he greatly regrets what he has been saying, and he tries in every conceivable way to make up for it, just as he is wonderfully kind toward Jouk., having been somewhat curt with him on the previous day. At lunch there was talk of ancient Greek music, toward which my father shows himself cool, if not actually hostile. R. then says that he read a piece about Arabian music which could frighten one out of one's wits. "The simplicity of our music is truly godlike, as simple as Christianity; all this wealth of tones and half-tones strikes me as idol worship." Over coffee he tells my father many stories from the *Fl. Blätter,* which make him laugh heartily. Since the doctor has ordered Eva to be kept very quiet, I remain alone with her; R. goes out with the children, and they tell me he was very cheerful and sprightly and walked along swiftly and briskly; he himself is conscious of it and says it does him good to be back in his *métier* (conducting). At supper he repeats the declaration he made at lunch: he is looking forward to a splendid game of whist; yesterday the rehearsal had left him feeling agitated, then his bad cards on top of that, along with my father's solemnity—it had all been too much for him. — There is talk of Princess H. and the difficulties she is having with her house; R. says that a widow should not run a household of her own, she should either live with her children or go into a convent. Widowers, too, he says to my father. We play whist with much merriment, R. has good cards, and he also tells my father that the game is nothing if one does not take it seriously. But in the end, when R. tries to explain cadential form with examples from *Die Schweizerfamilie* or *Das unterbrochene Opferfest,* and my father, after comparing the beginning with the "*Marseillaise,*" stops listening, a comical situation arises which at first causes great laughter, but then R. becomes extremely annoyed; my father goes off, still amid laughter, but when R. finds a letter from Hedwig L[iechtenstein] to Lusch on the table, he loses his temper. We go to bed, but R. continues for a long time talking to himself in his room, severely criticizing my father. I go to him; when he assures me that it is not meant against me, I attempt to make a joke of it, telling him that it was like the cuff on Meyer's ears—"it has got nothing to do with you." However, he continues to complain about my father's character. I try to make him see that my father is very tired and not fully aware of what is going on, but he will only half accept it. I go off to bed; it is a long time before he follows me; he comes in quietly, looks to see if I am asleep; when I say good night to him, he exclaims, "You best of all creatures!" and a very tender embrace delivers us lovingly into the arms of the friendliest of gods! — During whist R. talks about his symphony and says that it could be placed between Beeth.'s 2nd and 3rd, and it sounds very droll when he adds, "If one really thought that, one would be surprised at the advanced state of preparations for the *Eroica!*" — Then to my father: "If we write symphonies, Franz, then let us stop contrasting one theme with another, a method Beeth. has exhausted. We should just spin a melodic line until it can be spun no farther; but on no account drama!" — At lunch R. told the story of a woman who threw her children to the wolves; I observed that a mother dog would have sacrificed herself first, and R. says, "Yes, because she has no reasoning power." — R. tells us that he received a complaining letter from Herr Neumann.

Monday, December 18 At breakfast R. tells me that he spoke to the children yesterday about *"gondola-tombola,"* telling them that *"gondola"* is the theme of the Scherzo in the 9th when it is played softly on the strings, *"tombola"* when it is played by the timpani. In the morning we talk to R. about Goethe's saying that mysticism should have no place in Christianity, and at lunch we continue to discuss this curious saying. At lunch he also tells us his dream. [*Sentence based on untranslatable word play omitted.*] . . . Herr Humperdinck has arrived. R. explains several things to him, and in the middle of the conversation Jouk. comes in to greet H. This so annoys R. that he packs J. off home. After a while he appears at Jouk.'s and kneels down in the middle of the room! Rehearsal in the afternoon, unfortunately very upsetting for R. First, he does not care for his Scherzo, second, a number of gentlemen staying with Herr Bassani, invited along on my father's account, have to leave early, and then he is angry with me for allowing Daniela to dine at Bassani's with her grandfather. At lunch he spoke critically of the scherzo form, saying he has no liking for it, and even in Beethoven the scherzi are always the movements which least please him; in the *Eroica,* for instance, beautiful as it is, he does not care for it after the "Funeral March"; in the 8th it is somewhat different, since there B. has no andante; in the C Minor he runs it into the last movement; and in the 9th he puts it before the Adagio. He says they have always caused him problems, and, however wittily evocative the Scherzo of the A Major, he is not very fond of it. In the evening we talk to Humperdinck about Paris and what he saw there. But then, since by nearly 10 o'clock my father has not returned, R. becomes very, very annoyed, saying that this dinner ruined his rehearsal, that if Lusch joins in such things, she no longer belongs to him, his star, in which I put my trust, cannot exert its influence. — He says all this in the angriest of tones, pacing up and down! — Then he returns and loudly throws out the news which even now, after its harshness has been softened, I cannot bring myself to write down! I cannot stay with him any longer, I flee to my room and see Hans before me, alone in that institution, and I feel like screaming, screaming to some god to help me! R. does not come to bed. I go to him, find him asleep, he wakes up, I ask his pardon, and he—he replies that I have done him a favor by waking him up. We go off to bed, but not for a moment does the picture leave me, I go through my whole life and get up in great misery. I do not believe that I shall ever have, or deserve to have, another happy moment.

Tuesday, December 19 What we talked about at breakfast I do not know—oh, God, God, always this picture in my soul! I do not wish to wipe it out—what help is there in such misery? . . . That I can sit beside Eva's sickbed, that is a great help to me. But lunch—I see my daughter and ask myself how to tell her, how to plunge the knife into her youthful happiness. . . . The sun is shining, R. wishes me to go out with him, I beg to be allowed to remain at home, this arouses his anger (at lunch he talked about his youth, his grandmother and the robin), we go out. He then goes to rehearsal, I return home to Eva, my gentle support, but I struggle to find comfort, to find God—oh, children, may you never go through hours such as these! — R. and the children return from the rehearsal, say it went very well. Shortly before supper R. comes to me in Eva's room with moist eyes; I have not the strength to respond to his expansive words, and I fear the effect his agitation may have on Eva; he goes off—in an ill-humor, it seems to me. At table he says, and I feel only partly in fun, that I hate him; when I pick up his napkin, he says I do it only out of hate. [*The whole foregoing sentence obliterated in ink by an unknown hand.*] I can scarcely look at Lusch, and in my heart sits the constant companion of all feeling. R. says that Goethe is the greatest of all poets and that he had wished to say something about him to me, but I had not been in the right mood to listen. Supper is spent in talk about the rehearsal, afterward R. is vexed by conversations with Herr Hausburg and Hump.; he is also annoyed that the matter of the engagement has not been taken up by the gentlemen of the Conservatoire. He leaves the room, I follow him and ask him to tell me now what he wished to say to me; at first he refuses, then he says he has been reading the end of the first and the second part of *Faust*. — Then he talks about "The Singer's Curse," which he saw in an illustrated supplement belonging to Georg; he calls it the silliest poem imaginable. I leave him and say good night to my father, and we go to bed, after R. has made further complaints about the rehearsal (though his final movement pleased him, and he talks of the good combination in it). I do not know why—I should have to ask life's daemons—but bitterness impelled me to say that no poet now means anything at all to me, that poetry seems to me like some wretched plaything. R. is very angry, accuses me of not understanding him; I immediately follow him into his room and beg his pardon, saying that perhaps, if he were to see inside my heart, he would excuse me. Very emotionally he tells me that I mean everything to him, that without me he is nothing. He says he came home from the rehearsal worn out, forced himself to read these two scenes in order to shut out everything, all feeling, all suffering, and tell himself that the highest being is one transfigured through suffering, is myself! He asked himself, he says, whether he is a bad person, but he is not, and for several days he had kept this news to himself. I beg him for forgiveness and God for mercy! He calms down, goes to bed, falls asleep, while I lie and lie there with this dreadful picture which has haunted me ever since yesterday; at last sleep comes to me, too!

Wednesday, December 20 We get up late, and at breakfast I pluck up courage to speak to R. about Hans's condition. R. observes that it was after all to be expected. But not by me—not that! And, even if feared, the advent of what one fears still splits open a precipice which nothing can hide! — R. is much more resigned than I am. However, I make the resolve, whatever my inner feelings, to regain my self-control. I embrace R. with all my heart and tell myself that God will have mercy, He will! — I ask Jouk., who was present when the news arrived, to write to Frau Ritter. Lusch asks me whether she should not send her father something for Christmas. . . . At lunch there is talk about legitimacy, the present legitimate princes, and R. is very bitter. Before lunch R. went out with Lusch and Jouk., walked as far as the corner from which one can see the sea and S. Michele. After coffee and his afternoon rest R. brings me the news, which is better! . . . He had already told me in the morning that the dreadful name of the illness had not been mentioned in the report, he had just deduced it from the description. And I feel as if I have been restored to life as I set out with R. on this afternoon walk. The light outside is glorious, and the sunshine in my heart matches it. R. gazes at the sea and describes the ebb and flow as its breathing in and out. Then he goes off to rehearsal; on his return I go to see him, and he tells me—after saying that I should ask the children to tell me about it—that the rehearsal began very stormily because two players were absent and the others tried to make excuses for them! R. made a speech in French which had a great effect; after that, apparently, they played excellently, and altogether the players seem to be full of enthusiasm for R., they repeat his jokes to one another and understand him quite well. R. feels very happy in his *métier*, and it is only the things coming from outside that he finds disagreeable—such as Herr Filippi from Milan, for example. This journalist was made to pay for it, and R. says he finds this type of person particularly repugnant, for they always feel they must write wittily, "and it looks very odd when witty things are written about people like us!" Of the fugue, he says that fugal themes like this are not worth a jot, since one chooses them always with an eye toward the execution. Of the symphony as a whole he says one discerns in it the pupil of Mozart and Beethoven, one can see their influence everywhere, though nothing is directly copied. — At supper R. praises my father's letters, saying that everything he writes is beautifully expressed. "I can't do that," he adds. "For that you need *noblesse,* good breeding, which I don't have." — He jokingly demonstrates to us how dogs howl, the telegram in which Herr Neumann declines on behalf of himself and Seidl (R. had sent them an invitation). In the evening we talk about folk singing; R. plays the melancholy fandango to which he had once seen a tightrope walker dance, accompanied by a forlorn violin. Later he reads to us from *King Lear* the scene with Kent in disguise and the Fool, then the one with Goneril, and the amazing scene in which the Fool is waiting for the horses. R. points out that Lear's first experience with Goneril arouses only anger, indignation in him; with Regan, however, he becomes humble, talks about his fear of going mad. — R. reports in the evening that Hans has indeed been put in an institution, but there are hopes of an improvement. R. adds that Hans will outlive us all! — I feel that God has had mercy on me. . . . (At the start of the terrible night of Monday R. cried out from his bed, "I hate all pianists—they are my Antichrist!")

Thursday, December 21   R. talked a little in his sleep (during the night from Monday to Tuesday he talked a lot!). At breakfast, in talking of Gob.'s attitude toward Christianity, R. says it is wrong not to feel everything that lies in the simple words "Come unto me, all ye that are heavy laden"—that is to say, all who because of the burden of poverty cannot attain to freedom through intelligence. — R. remarks how splendidly Luther's language suits the Gospels. — The *B. Blätter* arrives, R. gets it first, opens the door to the *salon,* where I am talking with the children, and cries that he knows what he will read to begin with. And around lunchtime he again praises my modest lines, adding, "Only a woman could have done it like that; a man would have made it look pedantic!" — Unfortunately a letter from friend Gross causes him vexation, since it concerns V. & B.; I advise him to send a telegram, which does him good—though, when he rejoins me in Saint Mark's, he jokingly chides himself for not having been ruder in his telegram. In Saint Mark's we visit the Baptisterio, then walk via "Peking" to the Rialto (which R. always calls the Lido). My father's *soirée* with Don Carlos, his presentation to the Prince upstairs, give rise to many jokes. But to one thing R. holds firm—that my father does not care for assertions of any kind; when yesterday he, R., claimed Rossini as the instigator of the stretta, my father named a predecessor for it—Mosca.

However, many things in my father's character please R. greatly. (I remind you children of "moved"!) — In the afternoon he shows me two extra bars which he has composed for the Scherzo, and he says he is curious to see whether the children will spot them. In the evening our circle is much reduced—Father, Lusch, Loldi, Jouk. with the Princess, Eva still in bed. Soon we are alone together and very pleased to be so. Our discussion of the *B. Blätter* provokes R. into some hot words to start with; he feels the article on luxury would look better in *Über Land und Meer,* and he would have preferred the obituary of Prof. Zöllner to be left out altogether. — I ask friend Humperdinck to play *something* to me, and he chooses the funeral music from *G.-Däm.* R. then shows him which of the themes should dominate and which give way, and he goes on to reflect on the path which leads from the symphony to this music, "which one might be permitted to call one's own." He relates how he once advised Tausig to improvise, and then to remember what came into his mind; the latter replied, "But how can I be sure it is my own?" — When we are alone, we once more discuss the question of dependents, then the appointment of Glasenapp. Finally R. tells me, and this with tears in his eyes, that he has sent Boni 1,000 francs for Christmas, so that she can buy something nice for her husband and herself! — I acknowledge this birthday gift to me in silence, and only much later am able to thank him for it.

Friday, December 22   I dreamed about Boni, that the dress I sent her for Christmas was too tight for her. At breakfast R. and I talk about being in the grip of a passion, no longer oneself, as in *Tristan,* in *Macbeth.* This is what makes a hero, a tragedy. Today Eva gets up. R. brings her to the lunch table, where she is greeted! In the afternoon she returns to bed, and around 4 o'clock we go to the rehearsal, which I am allowed to attend, hidden from sight! First we stroll in Saint Mark's Square, then enter the Teatro La Fenice. It is very cold! R. has a spasm, but he conducts the first movement, then, after quite a long pause, the others. I sit in concealment far away from him and am touched to think that 50 years ago he performed this work for his mother, now for me. Then I take delight in the straightforward, courageous work, and I tell R., "That was written by someone who knew no fear." We ride home, R. and I, in the moonlight with Loldi, forbearing to speak. He spends the evening by himself, and unfortunately has a very restless night.

Saturday, December 23 [*Enclosed in the Diaries a note in Wagner's handwriting:* "Dec. 23, final rehearsal."] Up late, since R. had a very bad night. We talk about yesterday's rehearsal. [*Four lines omitted, most of the passage having been obliterated in ink by an unknown hand and several words remaining indecipherable.*] I tell him of my conversation with Dr.

Keppler in praise of Luther! He tells me of Eva's grateful look as he accompanied her into the room and then looked after her. R. takes a bath, feels well after it, is cheerful at lunch; makes jokes about old-fashioned juvenile works, for which the only substitute is newfangled Jewish works, then about "numskull" painters! — My father shames us by mentioning my article—we had assumed he would not even notice it. R. goes out with the children in the afternoon, then returns and comes to my room in very good spirits. My father dines out. The evening passes in conversation; R. says of the interval in the theme of the *Leonore* Overture that it marked the beginning of a new world, something passionately sublime. [*Added on the following page, but referred back to this point:* "My father observes that the third in the Adagio reminds him of the third in the Andante of Beeth.'s Op. 106. R. says he always found this third ghostly, in his childhood he used to shout to his sister: '*Cilie!* There's a big mask-thing in your bed!' — 'Cilie' intoned to the third. — In the evening he sings Belmonte's aria from *Die Entführung* and the splendid Moorish serenade."] When we are talking about Schumann and I point out some significant things in him, R. says, "I cannot be fair—to be that one must be nothing oneself, must have nothing in one's head except weighing pros and cons." He then plays to us the "Bridal Song" from *Lohengrin* and the *Tristan* Prelude. He feels that no attention has yet been paid to the thematic working of the latter—for example, when at the end of the 1st act Isolde breaks into declarations of love. — When I sing a theme to R. with our last good-night kiss, he says these are the anxious looks which are both inquiring and eloquent. "Why is it that love reveals itself in this highest form only through suffering?" I observe that the happy love of a youthful couple also has an air of melancholy about it. He says, "Yes, that is the yearning to lose one's being and to live only in the other."

Sunday, December 24 R. slept well. — The morning is spent in preparations; R. says my face so often wears an expression of delicate sorrow, and that is why he is so pleased to hear me "singing like a lark." — He brings me better news of Hans. The doctor is allowing Eva to go to the "concert." — And so this book can be concluded with a fervent prayer of thanksgiving! And blessings beseeched for all the dear, dear beings I can call my own!

[*End of the twentieth book of the Diaries.*]

Toward 6 o'clock the tree is lit in the *sala,* and there is a very merry presentation of gifts in which our Italian servants join with great delight. My father, too, whom we imagined to be quite above such things, is with us heart and soul. Around 7:30 we set off in three gondolas, with the moon shining and bells chiming, for La Fenice. Eva is allowed to come with us! The hall festively lit; my father, the children, and I go in first, a friendly reception. Somewhat later R., received with cheers. The two first movements are played fairly quickly in succession, then there is a pause; R. comes to me and my father, talks to me very gaily. I send thanks to the orchestra players, which earns me an "*evviva.*" At the end the players come to join us, and my health is toasted. Then R. murmurs in my father's ear, "Do you love your daughter?" My father looks startled. "Then sit down at the piano and play." My father does so at once, to everybody's cheering delight. Then in French R. relates the history of his symphony. Toward 11 o'clock we ride home, Venice transfigured in a blue light. The children enchanted with the evening, R. very content!

Monday, December 25 We had a somewhat restless night; R. badly wanted to read the *Idyll,* but he gets tired all the same—I call him several times, at last he goes to bed, after admiring the most glorious of nights. Toward 9 o'clock I am given my presents, R. has his "dear God" robe on—everything very touching and harmonious! There is no toast to me at lunch, since nothing was prepared, but R. gets up and plays to me from the *salon* "Who has found so good a wife." — Before whist in the evening, I am telling my father about Gob. when R. sticks a notice on the door: "*Ici on parle français*" ["French spoken here"]. [*The piece of paper containing this inscription in Wagner's handwriting enclosed.*]

Tuesday, December 26 R. had a good night's rest, but he is upset by not receiving an answer from Boni, even after my inquiry—he wonders whether his gift has arrived. Also the nonarrival of a Worth gown for me annoys him, and his overhastiness in summoning Humperdinck here (he is not to be engaged because of patriotic indignation in connection with Oberdank) embarrasses him. Whist in the evening.

Wednesday, December 27 Blandine's inexplicable silence causes very embarrassing upset. But at last, as around lunchtime I am attending my father's sitting for Herr Wolkoff, Fidi comes to tell me that Bl. has received everything, but the telegraph lines were cut. R. came in at first, but when he saw that my father was at the piano and being drawn at the same time, he went away at once, and later told me how disagreeable he found this sight [*the last ten words obliterated in ink by an unknown hand*]. In the afternoon we go out and experience a sunset such as can only be seen here. Count Contin visits us, I receive him, the engagement of friend Humperdinck turns out to be quite impossible! — In the evening R. does not feel well, he has been drinking beer and champagne. I think that all the disturbance of the moving—

we have installed my father on this side of the house—upset him, too. In the evening Ada Pinelli visits us, but not until somewhat later does R. take some part in the conversation.

Thursday, December 28 R. had a good night's rest, but we rise late. Around lunchtime we stroll on the Piazzetta in the most glorious sunshine. R. is also in a particularly good mood, since he was able to begin his work—a report on the symphony. That always washes away all his irritation. Venice pleases him, and, thinking of his symphony, he goes on to his life, to our union, and he says with tremendous gaiety that we were quite right not to wait for the cotton gloves. (This reminds him of the bishop's blessing which Ed. Devrient introduced into the 2nd act of *Lohengrin!*) — At lunch my recollections of Mrs. Lewes (George Eliot) come up, and I relate that people said she looked like Savonarola; R. then starts to talk of the latter's personality, recalls Gob.'s description and observes that if S. had been cleverer, he would have provided a subject for the fine arts, but through the influence he exerted one can see to what extent aesthetic considerations pale when the world of morals makes itself felt. — My second Christmas gown has arrived, I put it on in the evening for R. and the children. But the day ends dismally: R. tells me that he gave Georg 100 francs as a reward for 6 years in his service; since Christmas has just gone by and there seems no real justification for it, and also our expenses are not matched by our income, I am stupid enough to make a remark about it to R. This annoys him extremely, and it takes me a long time and many confessions of remorse to pacify him.

Friday, December 29 All the same, R. had a good night, and in the morning I tell him that yesterday, after he had left the room, I stayed behind with Eva and Loldi and, so that they would not notice anything, chatted cozily with them; Eva gave me evidence of her talent for mimicry by portraying the house tutor. He is equally amused by her incredibly good imitation! Then he writes some more of his letter, while I have a little rehearsal with the children for the New Year greetings. At lunch R. is in something of an ill-humor; first, he has had a letter from Prof. Holtzendorff which gives him very little satisfaction; and second, the accounts of Princess H.'s Thursdays upset him. He does not like anyone from his circle to go elsewhere. In the afternoon we ride to the Piazzetta; recalling the fact that he has used the French word *"accessible"* in his article, he says these French words really are indispensable, since the German language is too lofty and significant to convey the irony that is usually required when one is talking about modern things. — In the evening Lusch's agitation arouses our concern! I have to speak very earnestly to her—she is probably pining for someone! R. infinitely kind in his understanding of my concern, and sharing it with me.

Saturday, December 30 R. had a melancholy night, he dreamed a lot aloud, and he tells me he dreamed that Hans was dead! — He finishes his article, and we meet in the Piazzetta after I have held another little rehearsal. At lunch there is upset over switching the places at table, I myself am much exhausted and upset by my talk with Lusch; the restriction of our accommodations due to my father's move also irritates R., who needs a lot of space. In the afternoon R. and I walk to the Piazza, where we meet Fidi, Hausburg, Humperdinck, the latter very embarrassing to R. because the appointment has fallen through. In the evening the children are very subdued, since I had to speak to them severely about their all-too-independent behavior, and I also must take Lusch in hand again! (After the rehearsal today Moretto's picture made a very strong impression on me, and I tell R. about it.)

Sunday, December 31 R. had a good night, but he is not feeling well. At breakfast we talk a lot about Lusch; he feels she should accompany her grandfather to Hungary, there would be prospects of marriage there. Final rehearsal for me; then with Fidchen to the woodcarver Besarel, finally met R. in the Piazzetta (after having bought a photograph of the Moretto for Lusch and looked briefly with Jouk. at the *Madonna Pesaro* in the Doge's Palace.) [*Added in margin:* "Both yesterday, and my inspection of the Moretto the day before."] At lunch he is in turn irritable and full of fun. When it is pointed out that the New Year starts on a Monday, he says, "Then it is beginning well again," and he tells of a man being led to execution who asked, "What day is it today?" "Monday." "Ah, the week is starting well." — He has sent off his article (he read it to me yesterday afternoon, to my great delight). In the afternoon we receive some calls, among them Herr Passini, whom we find quite pleasant. A grateful letter from a chorister in Darmstadt pleases R., and a curious one from Seidl amuses him. He writes out a telegram to the King, and Lusch takes it in the evening to the post office. We have a New Year's Eve whist party and are all very merry, the children melt wax. (The photograph of the Moretto makes a great impression on R., and he reproaches me for having doubted whether it would.)

1883

Monday, January 1 R. felt yesterday that one should not exchange good wishes at the New Year but only on birthdays, but he is not against our little ceremony at the Princess's house, and although he has spasms, he comes there himself later. At lunch he is somewhat vexed: he wants to go to the theater, where [Goldoni's] *Le Baruffe Chiozzotte* is being done, a play about which he has often talked; my father asks to be allowed to stay at home, where Lusch and Jouk. can keep him company. R. is annoyed that we do not all go, but the theater soon cheers him up, and we return home thoroughly pleased. Both play and acting delighted us. Afterward we read Goethe's description of the play in his *Italian Journey* and find it rather trivial.

Tuesday, January 2 R. had a good night; bright sunshine, I write some letters, my right eye suddenly develops a black ring, and I have to give up writing and reading. I go out with R.; he tells me a lot about the history of the Persians, with unstinted admiration. I show him the Moretto picture, which he thinks is one of the finest ever painted. — We return home in very good spirits. At lunch, accusing himself of possessing a bad character, he says, "With me one has to show foresight and forbearance." — Then he makes a lot of jokes about civil marriages and says to my father, "You mean several marriages." The news that friend Feustel's eldest son has shot himself leads to solemn conversations. In the evening the two of us are alone with Jouk. — R. talks about the Renaissance and reads various things about Venice in Goethe's *Italian Journey,* for which he does not much care. Before that he read to us from the newspaper a court case involving Jews, expressing astonishment that such language can be spoken in our country.

Wednesday, January 3 R. had quite a good night, and he writes some letters, to Fritz Brandt and various singers; yesterday he wrote to Levi. Today he receives from the latter a deeply serious letter which makes the best of impressions on him. But unfortunately the impression my father makes on him, when R. visits him in the morning, is a very bad one! And there is much confusion at lunch; my father also believes for a moment that we are smiling at his expense, which greatly pains me. R. and I go out in the afternoon, he is worried about his health that his spasms do not let up. Then we pay a call on our landlords (the Della Grazias), who look exactly like Styrian aristocrats; R. views this as proof that the aristocracy everywhere is of Germanic origin. Chat in the evening, my father is not there, he joins us later, calls for beer [*the last three words obliterated in ink by an unknown hand*], and R.'s indignation over this leads, alas, to a little argument between us!

Thursday, January 4 R. slept well; and my consultation with the eye specialist is reassuring, which I tell R. with relief. He frequently calls me into his room to tell me various things from the history of the Persians, the intellectual quality of which he finds incomparable. He writes splendidly to Feustel (I have his letter copied), and at lunch— since news of the suicide of Count Wimpfen has also been received— we discuss this subject. R. cites the case of Nerva (I think he means Otho) as a suicide committed for the sake of others; my father will not accept this, and this greatly annoys R., who complains of what he calls my father's "turbulent somnolence" [*the last ten words obliterated in ink by an unknown hand*]. On top of this, he feels constricted by the reduction in our living space, and this makes everything seem disagreeable to him! In the meantime Marie Dönhoff puts in an appearance, charming and friendly; even R. finds her pleasant, though he is usually harsh in his judgment against her, and he recently said, "What sort of a human being is that, who thinks society more important than anything else?" She wins him over by talking very earnestly about Malwida's influence on her mother in persuading her to regard things from the standpoint of ideals. In the evening R. and I are alone together, all the rest at Princess H.'s. We talk as we always do when we are alone. Gob.'s ideas—on the (artificial) scholars' conception of the 2nd Jerusalem, his statement about the Greek philosophers ("they were artists")—provide plenty of material. Then R. comes back to Carlyle's idea about colonies and answers it to the effect that things which have not yet discovered their roots cannot perhaps be described as old. Then he tells me that he does not intend to write his article about male and female, at the most he will indicate his thoughts on the subject as opportunity arises. . . . Unfortunately, however, his attitude toward my father is becoming increasingly difficult and incensed!

Friday, January 5 R. had a good night, he talked about me in his sleep. In the morning he is still upset about my father [*this sentence obliterated in ink by an unknown hand*]. Lusch tells us about a recitation of [Bürger's] "Lenore." Yesterday R. said how repugnant he finds entertainments of this sort; one cannot help being appalled by some other person, and yet one can say nothing. We ride together to the Rialto, then walk to Saint Mark's Square. R. has a spasm, and we go home. Makart's portrait of the Countess [Dönhoff] has been put on display in our apartment—something R. finds distasteful. But our friend herself is received by him in a very friendly fashion; he exclaims to the children at lunch that, since they always imitate everybody, they should imitate the Countess! — He speaks very earnestly to Herr Hausb. about curing himself of the habit of grinning. In the evening, while the others are playing whist, we are alone with Marie; she tells us her situation, R. responds by describing our fate to her. He speaks the following beautiful words: "It took Nature a very long time to produce passion; this is what can lead one to the heights; music is its transfiguration, is, alone among all the arts, directly connected with it." After and during this expansive conversation R. is infinitely kind toward me, lovingly animated. At supper, sitting opposite me, he cries out, "I love you!" — Today he was not at all pleased by having a number of society people come to our home at my father's invitation to inspect Makart's picture. (He reads to me a report of floods on the Rhine; the appeal ends with the statement that there is a shortage of money, which he finds terrible—money to rescue the victims of the flooding!)

Saturday, January 6 R. slept well, at breakfast the presence of our friend leads the conversation to all kinds of worldly matters, our friend Mimi, etc. — Around lunchtime we go out for a walk, but the weather is raw; R. takes me to see a relief which he has discovered on a *traghetto,* there we take a gondola and return home, laughing at this absurdity. — A very understanding letter from Herr Scaria, advising him to engage Siehr, gives him pleasure. (Yesterday a telegram from Herr Neumann came, announcing that he is sending 10,000 francs.) But at lunch R. is very serious, I think his sympathy for our friend is somewhat exhausted; he is taciturn, and it falls to me to keep the conversation going. In the afternoon and evening he is indisposed. My father's manners and customs offend him, he says he is just like King Lear, his acquaintances the 100 knights, and his arrangements the Learisms [*this sentence obliterated in ink by an unknown hand*]. This evening we are alone together, we talk first about Gambetta's death, which R. holds to be France's good fortune rather than otherwise, then about the history of the Persians, which reflects R.'s presentiments. Finally—since Eva has started it—he reads parts of [Shakespeare's] *All's Well That Ends Well* to me. During the night I hear him say, half-asleep, half-awake, "King Lear, horrible man," but to me, "I care about you, you are the best of all." (In our evening conversation yesterday the Countess spoke about the performances of the *Ring* in Vienna and praised them very highly, particularly Winkelm., Scaria, Materna. R. then talks about the subjects of his works, calling *Lohengrin* the saddest of them all; he also tells us about Lüttichau's suggestion that Tannhäuser should be pardoned in Rome and should marry Elisabeth.)

Sunday, January 7 In the morning we come—I cannot remember how —to Gambetta; we recall *Die Kapitulation* and the fact that Nietzsche, for instance, had no understanding of it at all. R. says it is a complete lack of imagination which hinders understanding. Lusch comes to breakfast and tells us about the *soirée.* Around lunchtime I go with R. to Reithmeyer's bank, where R. happily collects some money from his Königsberg royalties. Our friend Marie eats with us; R. more taciturn than otherwise and in the afternoon in an ill-humor. But by the evening he is cheerful again, bubbling over with wit; when someone mentions the Jews, he says, "Oh, yes, our German culture would be completely icebound if it were not for this *Schmierocco!*" And many similar things. Since my father goes out, we decide on a reading, and R. reads *Twelfth Night* to us in his splendid manner.

Monday, January 8 Hans's birthday—on which day it is given to me to learn that he has been holding a rehearsal! . . . R. had a good night, he is cheerful and comes frequently to my room during the morning to read me bits of his letter to Levi. Our lunch passes without the little Countess, who is indisposed. We visit her, first I alone, then R. comes to fetch me, and, friendly though he is toward the charming lady, the impression all her elegance in bed makes on him is a very dismal one! And so these days bear the stamp of sadness! — While my father is playing whist, R. reads *Lear* to me and Eva, the scene in which Kent is put in the stocks, and we come to the conclusion that one ought to read Shakespeare scene by scene, for otherwise one never really gets to know him. My father and the others come in unnoticed to listen, which surprises and pleases R. — In recent days R.'s face has had a wonderful radiance, and when his eyes fell on me, I felt "gladness and woe in one." Today I felt it indescribably! . . .

Tuesday, January 9 R. slept well, but he is in a disturbed state of mind, and I must feel glad that our friend stays away! Everything upsets him. He has a spasm in the morning and at lunch is all but silent. He starts a letter to the King. In the afternoon he goes out, I wait in the antechamber to greet him, but he is in an ill-humor, and in the evening this turns into anger. My father's manners and customs, the whist table, the constriction of our living space, all the disturbance arising from his visit—this makes him furious, and long, long after it is past he gives way to his anger, which I can only assuage by suffering with him in silence! — As a curiosity I might note down that R. considers the black eyes and hair of our friend to be unwomanly.

Wednesday, January 10 R. slept tolerably well and is very kind toward me; he thinks I am looking worn out and says it is impossible for me to regain my strength as long as he is the way he is. When I tell him that even to suffer with him is happiness, and if in words and manners he prefers me to others, this is something I owe entirely to him, such lovely feelings take possession of us that they give me wings to surmount the day's troubles! These consist of R.'s health, his spasms, then his vexation—about the various things from which he has to dissuade the King, for instance; he says that in his rage he has added only one sentence to the letter during the whole afternoon. He is also oppressed by the smallness of the rooms, he misses books and music, but when I suggest we return to Wahnfried, he cannot make up his mind to do so. Around 6 o'clock my father plays to us the Andante from the A Major Symph. and the Scherzo Allegretto from the F Major; twice during the latter R. comes in dancing, which makes Fidi laugh a lot. At supper afterward he is in very good spirits, and when there is talk of Oberdank and bomb throwing, he reproaches our friend with also having thrown bombs; when she protests, he says to her, "Oh, yes, you did, you are a *bombonnière!*" Dr. Kurz, recommended by Jouk., comes in the evening, he describes R.'s complaint as a stomach neuralgia and says it is a good sign that his spasms take place mainly before and not after mealtimes. — When we are alone, R. criticizes the broad tempo in which my father took the Andante of the A Major, he calls this a failure to appreciate the character of the piece. He then tells me he has a number of themes and would like to write a symphony, but how will he find the tranquillity for it? (A few evenings ago, while in bed, he sang to me the theme of a "vigorous and warlike funeral march.") — Today we thought lovingly of Friederike Meyer.

Thursday, January 11 I hear R. saying in his dreams: "If He created me, who asked Him to? And if I am made in His image, the question remains whether I am pleased about that." — Today R. finishes his letter to the King, I take our friend to the station. On my return home, I find R. very annoyed by news of a visit from friend Gross; he sends a telegram asking him to wait to see what effect his letter has. Lunch is lively and cheerful; among other things, we talk of Mme Viardot, and R. relates his experiences with this singer. — R. has had a nice letter from Herr Siehr, to whom he sent the very understanding one from Herr Scaria. In the afternoon he pays a visit to my father, and proposes to him that he remain with us. There was a report in a newspaper to the effect that we were living in a sumptuously furnished 1st-floor apartment, whereas my father had only a modestly equipped one on the mezzanine floor; this annoys R. In the evening we are alone, R. and I; before going off with the younger girls to Malip., Siegfried reads to us the first scenes of his comedy, *Die Lügner!* . . . We take delight in the boy, he is good-looking and talented, and R. observes that the Gotthard was good for him. — Talking of earlier attachments, R. says he is ashamed of them all. When I tell him that one should never be ashamed of such generous illusions, he says, "I seldom allowed any free speaking —if there had been free speaking, it would certainly not have been very nice." When we are alone together, we read *Hamlet* (the scene with Polonius, the King, and the Queen, then Hamlet and Ophelia, H. with Guildenstern & Rosen[crantz], etc., up to the players' prologue) with ever-increasing astonishment and emotion; we are indeed carried right out of ourselves, and I feel as if Richard, Hamlet, Shakespeare have become one, as if I can comprehend the one only through the other, as if Hamlet could never be understood except with R.'s voice, R.'s character except with Shakespeare's genius, and neither except through this creation of Hamlet. The goodness of Hamlet's veracity— how could I feel this so deeply if I had not experienced it through R.?

Friday, January 12 R.'s spasms start today first thing in the morning and last for more than 2 hours! He does not eat with us—in fact not at all. Dr. Keppler comes at last at 5 o'clock and proposes massage, which he begins at once, promising R. alleviation within a month! R. is greatly encouraged by this, whereas I, alas...! He tells me that when I go to see him he has to ask me to leave, yet when I am gone he is sorry that I am not there! — In the evening whist is played, but there is also a discussion about our friend Jouk.'s impending departure to attend the centennial celebrations for his father. We persuade him— though sorrowfully—to undertake the journey. . . .

Saturday, January 13 R.'s night was a good one, and today he is massaged twice. Much else besides. Above all, the arrival of our friend Gross, who did not receive R.'s telegram until Kufstein. A request has come from Munich (on account of the exposition) that we give only 10 performances this year, and these in July. R. is at first very annoyed, but then he gives way, though not before saying that the best thing would be to give it up entirely—though he then thinks of the children and feels one ought to set them an example of constancy. At 2 o'clock my father takes his departure—R. claims frequently to have discerned in him a mood of sadness about himself. In connection with my father's life, R. wonders what would have become of him if things had continued as they were in Vienna (1863). Impossible to imagine. Earlier we celebrated the birthday of our good Paul [Joukowsky], R. makes a speech, and in the evening he plays a march theme, which he then writes down for him. When we are left alone, he talks of Gobineau's interpretation of Alexander's personality, which exactly matches his own (R.'s). — And then later, when he is in his room, I hear him playing softly on the piano, the hovering forms draw close again;

yesterday he said that his symphonies would be a melody spun out in a single movement, and today he frequently plays a melody of his own which has come into his mind, in the manner of an English folk song.

Sunday, January 14 R. had a good night, and I believe that massage is really doing him good, even if it causes a little disruption, e.g., a very late breakfast. He writes letters to singers (Materna) and to Heckel. A letter from Lenbach announcing a visit causes R. to pull my leg about my enthusiasm for this artist, and when I protest he says, "When one has someone like you to tease, one doesn't often let the chance slip." Sirocco storm, no outing possible. Chat in the evening, comically enlivened by a little incident: R., feeling prejudiced against Dr. Keppler, engaged a Dr. Kurz, whose prescriptions did not, however, appeal to him, and he then sent for Dr. Keppler. Now the doctor, who was engaged to come 3 times a week, turns up, and R. falls, as he puts it, "into his jaws." — We extricate him, and have to laugh a lot over these complications! — R. sits down at the piano and improvises, lovely melodies which, as he tells us, are always piling up inside him. I tell him the fact that these blossoms are now sprouting within him is the reward for his collected outlook! "This is how we shall be," he says after playing. "Yes, this is how we shall sound," I reply to him. — I do not remember how we came to speak of the practice of summoning a priest to one's deathbed; I said that, though I can well see how life might drive us to seek this aid, I cannot understand why dying people are so reluctant to be absolutely on their own—even someone like Marie Much[anoff], for example, who died with such dignity, admitted a priest to her bedside. R. feels that the fear of Hell-fire is responsible.

Monday, January 15 More massage for R., and afterward unpleasant feelings arising from a letter to me from Countess La Tour; we feel, R. and I, that even she did not really understand her friend. . . . For the first time in many days we go for a walk; I go into Saint Mark's while R. does some shopping, then we meet at Lavena's. At lunch we resume our familiar conversations—today, for example, about Italian church music, and we seek to explain why my father has entirely lost his appreciation for it. R. recalls the fine impression Leo's *Miserere* made on him (Naples), and he deplores the simplicity—of a completely different kind—of church compositions today. In the afternoon we take a 2nd walk to the Square. I call on Princess H. with Lusch, we miss each other and do not arrive home until 8 o'clock. R. worried and therefore justifiably cross with us; my sincere apologies pacify him, but unfortunately Lusch takes a lightheartedly defiant attitude, which causes me great concern. Then there is talk of the family, of the discovery. I ask what that is, and R. plays a pompous, funereal intrada, followed by "Harlequin, thou must perish," then returns to the solemn sounds. This performance inevitably arouses hearty laughter. In the evening our conversation primarily concerns fame, whether it is desirable; friend Jouk. observes that it gives people absolute freedom, but R. and I cannot bring ourselves to see any great value in it. Then we talk about my father, what his real inner feelings may be. R. says he cannot understand why, when he got to know my brother, he did not give up everything in order to live with him. Much about my brother and my sister . . . (Today R. read friend Wolz.'s lecture and was very pleased with it.)

Tuesday, January 16 R. dreamed his old dream—that he had offended me, that I wished to leave him, that he then wanted to starve himself to death. — A consultation with Dr. Keppler reveals that my heartbeat is the strongest imaginable, and since he is also completely satisfied with R.'s condition, we joke at breakfast that neither of us will ever die! It is raining again, consequently no outing. R. reads Dr. Förster's pamphlet, in order, as he says, to steel himself for his preface to Stein's book. At lunch he talks about Wolz.'s lecture and says he would have more doubts about its value if he saw anything of significance on the other—the enemy—side; but there is nothing there, and so he is pleased with these announcements and with these supporters of his side. — As I am playing with Stiefel, his little hare, he says, "He is splendid, the symbol of everything which should arouse our pity; and that's what the German Emperor shoots at!" In the course of the day he observes what a terrible thing this military setup is—nowhere in the world has there been anything like it before. — Since I am slowly getting on with Tolstoy's novel, we talk about Nap. and the strange admiration he inspired in his contemporaries. — I cannot remember how we came to talk about the Reformation and the ensuing state of the Catholic church. When I mention Saint Francis of Sales, R. says he has no confidence in these latter-day French saints with their elegant robes—at any rate, he cannot imagine them. He writes today to friend Sulzer about the history of the Persians, having recalled that Sulzer expressed views about the Persians similar to Gob.'s. In the evening he plays the very detailed "Harlequin" improvisation, with "*Du lieber Augustin*" at the end! Death is now dancing with Harlequin! . . . And late in the evening he reads the first two conversations between Faust and Mephisto with unutterable admiration, joy, and delight: "That is German," he says. Shakespeare shows us the world as it is, Goethe shows a free spirit's playfulness with it.

Wednesday, January 17 R. tells me that when he woke up during the night, he thought once more about the conjuration of the poodle (*Faust*), with increased admiration. Today he reads B. Förster's little pamphlet, critical of certain things (for instance, he says, "One should just throw out ideas, as I do about Bach and the German language, but they make something firm and inalienable out of it—now we know"), but also pleased with some others, e.g., that the stronghold of Valhalla has turned into the Temple of the Grail. Since the sun is shining, we ride in an open gondola via the Cannaregio into the open sea, and from there to the Rialto, where we get out. Since R. was on the verge of a spasm, he would have found the walk home difficult if he had not been distracted by everything he saw along the way—two men, for example, talking to each other, one of them standing motionless wearing a large round hat, a cycling cape, around his waist an apron of blue rags stitched together, black-bearded; the other gray, beardless, with a yellow-brown jacket, trousers, and cap, violently gesticulating. Animals form the main topic of our lunchtime conversation. — As we turned into the Cannaregio in our gondola, we wondered why the Germans made the sun feminine. "That is a tremendous compliment to the female character," R. says. "They regarded the moon as a footpad, stealing around all night by himself." — He is indisposed today and has no massage. Dr. Keppler provides him with food for thought; he finds him quite pleasant but feels he has no eyes in his head; there are people who are just specialists, he says, otherwise not human beings at all. Jouk. has brought me his father's biography in connection with the jubilee, I get Loldi to read it to me, R. comes in and says he could have spent a long time watching us both, mother and daughter. Over coffee we listen to Lusch and Jouk. telling various stories about society life. R. exclaims: "Why is it always women who get talked about? Never men!" He plays the piano in the evening (yesterday something from *Die Walküre* and the introduction to the 3rd àct of *Die Msinger,* vexed with both the piano and his own clumsiness). I recall that music usually seems to produce ill-humor or irritability in him, and I speak to him about it, pointing out how much more tranquil his mood is when he has been occupying himself with books. He says I am talking in a casual tone about something of great importance, but I am right; then he pleases me by declaring that he will be quite satisfied with the 10 performances. Today he goes so far as to ask himself whether the whole thing should not be given up entirely and he should instead try to make as much money as possible, so that we could live independently! . . . (He feels that Herr Neum. will probably be obliged to give up, too, and he wonders whether in the present circumstances V. & B. will pay him.) Then he goes through our disloyal friendships—Nietzsche, Gersdorff—and feels we should be downright ashamed of not having been able to keep a better grip on them. And, no doubt telling himself inwardly that they were not people of his sort anyway, he sings, "Cilie! There's a huge mask-thing in your bed!" At the recent concert in which the *T[annhäuser]* Overture was played, the program compared it—as a mark of the highest praise—to the *Guillaume Tell* Overture; this produces from R. the remark that everything the Italians, Rossini in particular, provide in the way of ensembles, choruses, etc., is terribly vulgar, but that is not so with the French, and he agrees with me when I say that the French are more civilized. We end the evening with scenes from [Schiller's] *Don Carlos,* the end of the 1st and beginning of the 2nd acts, and R. says it is a joy to observe all the subtleties and master strokes in these youthful works.

Thursday, January 18 R. dreamed that Minna saw him weeping and that she was overjoyed—thinking it was on her account—and made such a clatter with the coffee machine that he thought she had gone mad. — Then that we were both climbing a snow-covered mountain and had Rus with us on a lead! . . . The massage today is very late, with it sunshine, so that R. thinks it is warm and has all the fur skins removed; we all feel frozen. Our mood at lunch is as a result full of vexation, and more than once tears come to my eyes! R. is restored by quite a long sleep in the afternoon, and we stroll happily through our large suite, which he is delighted to have got back again. In the evening he has another massage, and it really does seem to do him good. After supper he continues reading *D. Carlos* to us; he says that formerly he had overestimated its maturity, now he takes delight in its splendid features. He describes King Ph[ilip]'s soliloquy as Shakespearean, and finds D. Carlos's excitement when he thinks the Queen has sent for him quite unique. — Then he plays the opening theme (horns) of the *Freischütz* Overture; when we express our pleasure, he says, "Yes, what that meant to me!"

Friday, January 19 He slept well and is in such a merry mood that the doctor is unable to massage him for a while. He told him that the stomach tube was an invasion of his personal rights! At lunch we chat contentedly, memories of Prince Georg. Around 1 o'clock he goes to call on "the princes." — This stems from our meeting Count Bardi yesterday and not recognizing him; R. went after him to apologize and then announced his visit. He finds, as he tells me, two charming Austrians, with whom he jokes. We then take our walk in the botanical gardens. Over coffee *L'Italie* brings us, to our astonishment, all kinds of news from France, Prince Nap. arrested in consequence of a manifesto; this evokes a lively response in us, since we had just been talking at lunch about that terrible December 2 and the admiration for N. III it aroused in the kings of the world. — (The fact that hunts are preceded by hymn singing is also discussed.) R. talks to the doctor about vegetarianism and deplores the stupidity of vegetarians who despise milk, which is after all the food Nature gave us. — In the afternoon we ride to the Piazzetta, R. and I, and delight in Venice in the moonlight. In the evening he continues reading *D. Carlos* to us, we end with the scene between Marquis Posa and Carlos in the 4th act. R. is delighted with the *slim* and free figure of the Marquis, and, when I say to him that I believe these things, now all but ridiculed, will still grow in people's estimation, he says: "Of course. It is Aryan ideality, and it is we who have produced it." Then he plays the beginning of the 9th! He compares it to an improvisation and says: "Such sublime naïveté! How long it takes for one to reach this stage! In the early symphonies he still has scaffolding around him."

Saturday, January 20   Our breakfast brings up the subject of the children's life, whether one can and should cut them right off from the community, whether we are not asking too much of them in our isolation. Eva, for example, is curiously irritable, and the doctor has forbidden reading material such as *D. Carlos*. A difficulty which I leave to my good star! We go out, R. feels run down, he goes into Lavena's, while I enter Saint Mark's and feel as if I am swimming in gold. On our way home he tells me his dream: he was climbing a high mountain with me and thought that he was leading me, until he noticed that I was supporting him, and as the path got anguishingly narrower and narrower, he realized that I was exerting myself unreasonably to support him; then he woke up. R. is in a very gentle mood, and he tells us at lunch that we must not take his vexed remarks, such as he made last night, so seriously. He tells us some very droll things from the *Fl. Blätter* (such as Tirolean Jewish masked ball, violets optional) and declares that he prefers these illustrators to all our modern painters. In the afternoon he goes on foot to the Cannaregio (I at the antique shop). When I arrive home, I go to see him, he shows me what he has written down as the result of his walk: "Too much talking and listening gets in the way of seeing." "Profitable seeing: all the things one's gaze takes in when one is glancing across a bridge." In the evening we talk about Schiller's *Don Carlos*: the Queen's words "Never more shall I respect a man," which I have always taken to mean "since you are to die," R. interprets as love's bitter reproach to Posa for sacrificing himself. We talk of the great and deep delicacy of these turns of phrase, and when I remark how touching it is to imagine these delicate images of the soul sharing Schiller's miserable existence in Loschwitz, R. replies in a gruff but friendly tone: "Where should they come from, then? The Spanish Court, maybe?" He does not read to us this evening.

Sunday, January 21   R. is skipping the massage on Sundays, and I beg him to give up the stomach tube entirely, believing that it must upset his nerves. He has arranged an outing for today, we are to have lunch in Saint Mark's Square, and, sure enough, Venice is enveloped in fog! Today he started his preface for Stein's book, and that puts him in a good mood. But it is cold, the meal is not ready in the Cappello Nero; I read aloud a nice letter from our dear Ponsch, and that helps, but the mood almost threatens to turn sour; however, since we are entirely by ourselves except for Jouk., R. does not become irritable, and gradually a very good atmosphere is achieved. We wish to go home but are forced back by the crush, and from the restaurant we watch the masked procession, in which a cook keeps greeting R.; and R. replies. It is estimated that there are 20,000 people in the square; the children—who went off at R.'s bidding but then returned—watch the seething crowds with us, "a black mass in which patches of flesh color emerge," a strange, uncanny impression. As R. and I are riding home together, he talks about the sight and the impression, both so sad. "And yet," he says, "a person who does not try to make closer contact with the masses is not worth much!" He goes to take a rest, I pay a call; when I go into his room on my return, he wakes up. In the evening he plays things by Weber, from *Euryanthe* and again, at my request, from *Der Freischütz*. We are pleased that after Beethoven such utterly new things should have been written, which in no way detract from Beeth.'s greatness. Herr v. Wolkoff visits us, quite a pleasure for R., and since he makes an apt remark about singers and orchestra (observing that voices and instruments do not mix), R. praises his accurate discernment and says that the orchestra should be the ground, as it were, on which the singer walks; tempted into it by this conversation, he sits down at the piano and plays and sings the scene in which Fafner confronts Siegfried, the awakening of Brünnhilde, then at my request the introduction to the 3rd act of *Tristan*. But all of this upsets him; he talks in an absent-minded way and, meaning to tell us something about Dr. Rahn, forgets what he was about to say. [*Added in margin:* "R. has severely apostrophized Herr Hausburg about his conduct, which he finds lamentable!"]

Monday, January 22 And he talks and is restless almost throughout the night, is also unable to work. Yesterday was too much for him. We ride to the Square, he sits down under the portal but spends only a little time there. I receive a letter from Herr v. Bürkel, but I refrain from telling him about it; he says that the King is holding to his order for a performance of *Parsifal* in May (in Munich). — He feels the outing yesterday was a success, and he says we should always just let him grouse properly—in him imprecations are the heralds of a good mood. Two telegrams from Rubinstein's father greatly touch us and make us deplore his son's harshness. — No massage in the evening, since the doctor has a serious operation to perform. A letter from Dr. Landgraf to Dr. Kurz (!) pleases R. greatly, he says we can consider Landgraf one of our best friends. In the evening there are just the three of us, R., Jouk., and I, and R. enjoys this, he feels a need for quiet, with nothing to provoke him into lively speech. He complains about his memory—today he thought he had had a letter from Jos. Rub. I believe the reason for this is what he is now preparing for Stein's book. We come to the curious situation in France, and R. says, "They no longer have a flag." Then to Russia—he says they ought to take heed there of Gob.'s ideas. — (Recently, in connection with the question whether Jouk. should attend his father's jubilee, R. remarked how painful he would find it, were he obliged to tell himself that his fame put obstacles in Fidi's way. One's main concern is that one's children should be entirely individual and free.) Since the weather is again glorious today, we have to laugh over yesterday's fog, which looks like a spiteful parenthesis designed to spoil R.'s pleasure. — In the evening R. played the trio from the minuet of [Mozart's] G Minor Symphony, delighting in its gracefulness, but he observes that he does not believe such things make their effect in public performances; I observe that I have the feeling that both Mozart's symphonies and Schiller's dramas will vanish from the public repertoire, but that their content will come to be increasingly esteemed by all the people who matter. Agreeing with me, R. ponders on what in art might be regarded as perfect; he says, "An ancient Greek statue."

Tuesday, January 23   R. slept well and has decided to have a massage only once a day. At breakfast we chat quietly together, and I make a firm resolve to tell him as little as I possibly can, in order not to thwart or overburden the cherished workings of his mind. He does a little work, and at 12:30 we ride to the Piazzetta in glorious weather, walk almost as far as the arsenal, sit down for a while in the Giardinetto, and return at 3 o'clock. On the trip out R. mentioned Bach's fugues— "In these, chaos is turned into harmony"—he finds all other forms trivial in comparison, and yesterday he expressed his regret that music is so much the slave of its time, except perhaps only in its use of drama. On the homeward journey I sing the first movement of the C Minor Symphony, which amuses R. Our lunch is cheerful, and our receiving two calls (from Count Bardi and Princess Hatzfeldt) does not displease R. — He continues reading Gob.'s book, increasingly astonished by the author's studies. Chat in the evening, brought to an end by R. with the "Shepherd's Song" and "Pilgrims' Chorus" from *Tannhäuser*. He says he still owes the world *Tannhäuser*. Yesterday, recalling Blandine's wedding, we discussed what a catastrophe it is in these days to be born a Catholic, and R. argues that the tendency of this church is to condemn intelligence and a feeling for beauty and to rely on the common people, at the same time keeping them in a state of ignorance. During our walk today he told me about an elephant in Siam which went wild with rage, whereupon first its eyes were torn out and then it was left to starve. "Humans are the stupidest animals of all," he continues sorrowfully. I take Spontini's remark about *Rienzi* and apply it to Nature, saying that it really does appear to have done more than it can do, whereupon R. says, "Until the appearance of the Saviour on the cross." — I observe, "As recompense for all the disasters." He: "In the urge to put an end to the whole of Nature's will to live."

Wednesday, January 24 Our conversation leads us to Neumann's suggestion of performing the *Nibelungen* here in Venice. R. advises against it. He then goes to work on his preface; last night, before undressing, he came to me to say how beautiful he finds the ending to [Stein's] "Cornelia." Around lunchtime he calls me and reads to me the beginning of his letter to Stein, which moves me to tears. Since I say jokingly, "You must always put it all into words," he jokes back, saying I am never content with what he does. In the gondola he recalls Falstaff's "Tell him I am deaf," laughs, and observes that this is what he always feels like saying when someone speaks to him; then actors, who put everything into words, and he thinks of the terrible meaning this free speaking acquires in the figure of Hamlet. Yesterday he remarked how foolish it was to ascribe a general philosophical meaning to his "To be or not to be"—it was just Hamlet speaking. — It is very cold, a north wind, R. looks for a buckle for the fur he has given me; we cannot find one, and we freeze terribly. On our return home, we are much concerned about Lusch's condition, she is in bed. I consult Dr. Keppler. In consequence, a conversation with him about the present position of women, which R. describes as an unnatural one. Many, many great worries, alas! — R. tells me about a young couple who committed suicide for love, and he adds, "This is still the main tragedy of life." He recalls how the subject is dealt with by Lise and Bärbel in *Faust,* the relentlessness of common people. We are diverted from these dismal thoughts by my remarking how pretty his room (blue grotto) is, and this leads us to his desire for colors, for perfumes, the latter having to be very strong, since he takes snuff. "Taking snuff is really my soul," he says very drolly. At the start, he describes how gently glowing colors influence his mood, but later in the conversation he denies any connection and says very emphatically, "These are weaknesses." — Then we recall the roof-raising ceremony in Bayreuth (1873), and he expresses his amazement about the theater, "that it is there, that I brought it into being with my scores!" In connection with the roof-raising ceremony and the dizziness caused by heights, R. tells of a mountain-climbing expedition in which K.

Ritter got into an indescribable state. "I already saw him lying at the bottom of the ravine, thought to myself, 'Now you've got his mother to deal with,' started writing the letter"—which amuses us enormously!

Thursday, January 25 During the night R. read the scene between Valentine and Gretchen and says what a pitiful role Faust plays in it all, even in the illustrations, however handsome he may be made to look. I observe that in matters of love the women are always the more absorbing figures, with the single exception of Tristan. In the morning a telegram from Neumann, for whom R. feels sympathy, going through all his difficulties "with Semitic earnestness." — R. has caught a cold, and the thought of erysipelas worries me. The cold outside is said to be extreme today, we do not go out, R. works on his preface. At lunch there is talk about the personal participation of royal generals in battles; R. observes that it does not amount to much, they just use a telescope to assure themselves of how things are progressing; but people like Fr. the Great and G. Adolphus could not leave it at that— they had to go and see for themselves how it was getting on. Sitting in Lusch's room in the afternoon, I dictate a letter to Boni, R. comes in, takes the pen from Eva, and writes a sentence. The visit of the *gettatore* Count Vesuce gives him the chance to play another joke: he puts on the Count's coat in the antechamber and goes into Lusch's room to ask for her hand in marriage! — He has a massage and seems to be well, but he complains that life is an eternal winter, the short days are a torment to him. — In the evening I have at last to tell him the contents of Bürkel's letter; he is very agitated by it, though he shows no anger, decides to engage an orchestra of his own, and tells me I should write and say that the state of his health does not permit such communications to be sent to him. — Then he wishes to talk of other things, he brings up "To be or not to be" and says it cannot be spoken too morbidly, indeed even sentimentally—it is a brooding, an outpouring, to which it is foolish to ascribe any philosophical meaning. — But then, in our bedroom, he comes back to the King's order and says impulsively that we should give it all up: "My works are there!"

Friday, January 26 R. has calmed down, and at breakfast he tells me he does not know whether to call his future article "The Feminine in Human Life" or "The Eternal in the Feminine." Then he tells me about one of the Arsacidae, to whom a woman given him by Augustus meant more than anything else. He then goes to his work and is satisfied with what he does. But around lunchtime, when I have to inform him of the passage in Herr v. B.'s letter (he did not wish to read the letter yesterday), he gets very upset, even though the prospect of not having to do the performance until the spring of '84 is a welcome one. We then ride to the Square in nice sunshine, but he feels indisposed, and even after our return home his "heaviness" does not vanish; he comes to our meal late, having abandoned it earlier. — A letter from friend Stein raises the question whether we should not advise him to break with his family and take refuge with us. The question is: Glasenapp or Stein for Siegfried? The evening is spent quietly and cozily in chat about all sorts of things, R. somewhat taciturn but listening with enjoyment. Just now and again he flares up like a half-extinguished fire about what the King is doing to him in ordering this separate performance.

Saturday, January 27 R. told me his dream; wearing the mauve nightgown which he has on now, he went with me into a box in a theater; there people behaved improperly toward him, but he did not wish to show himself, though he could hardly avoid it, while I became very embarrassed, whereupon he woke up. R. slept well, and he works, jokingly remarking that he is no longer capable of producing an article as long as mine was. Toward 1 o'clock we take a trip to S. Moisè; but R. is somewhat agitated and remains so throughout the day, all the more so since the doctor does not come today. The evening conversation pleases him, except that he becomes very excited during the discussion of Peter Cornelius's remark in Munich about him (rough outside, good within). To end the evening we read Goethe's "Dedication," and once again R. remarks how little pleasure lyric poetry gives him.

Sunday, January 28 R. had a restless night, an error of diet (beer) seems to have caused it. He works, and we ride in wonderful weather to the Piazzetta, where preparations are being made for the masquerade. At lunch R. is somewhat out of humor, but when he declares, "The best society thou find'st will show thee thou art a man among donkeys," we laugh heartily, and he tells us that J. Rubinstein's letter to me put that into his mind! — A letter from Richter recommends the baritone singer Sommer; R. replies. Before that he told me that he was not at all interested in hearing about children's ailments in Richter's household. When he comes to my room in the afternoon, I tell him the subject of my conversation was the happiness he must feel when he opens a work of his own and sees its absolute perfection; he denies that this gives him pleasure, since all kinds of thoughts about staging and so on come into his mind. But the public which goes again and again to see the things—they interest him. He also finds pleasure in the very large receipts in Vienna. Unfortunately something is said in the evening about the heating in Wahnfried, and I, in the hope that something might be done about it, observe that our hot-air heating does not seem to be very good. This annoys R. He calms down, however, and at the end of the evening reads to us the final pages of Gob.'s history of the Persians.

Monday, January 29 No morning conversation today, since I have to remain in bed with a cold, but instead, at lunchtime, a reading of the fine preface to Stein's dialogues! R. goes out, meets the children in Saint Mark's Square, and returns in good spirits with Lusch. Much joking at lunch about a letter to me from Herr Levi, and it comes out that, whereas I dictated my letter to him, I wrote to Lenbach in my own hand. In the afternoon R. has a massage, and it seems to me that this treatment is certainly doing him good. At supper we talked a lot about Raimund's plays, which R. praised highly. In the evening we read the 4th act and the first scene of the 5th act of *D. Carlos,* with warm inner feelings over the power of ideality revealed in it, something which is completely Schiller's own. Before that we found pleasure in some melodies discovered by friend Tappert (among them one by the singer Rizio!). And R. takes delight in the children, particularly Fidi, who is writing poetry in the lobby in a very neat handwriting—not because he feels inspired, just as a routine! (Of Loldi he said yesterday, "She lands in one's soul with a thud.") — A subject to which he frequently returns is the way women dress nowadays; recently, looking at a photograph under the arcades, he exclaimed, "If I were in charge of the state, you would all run around like that!" He says, "Women dressed like that belong in a harem at best." He talks about it again in the evening and mentions a print in the Cappello Nero showing women's clothes of the Directoire period, which he thinks very pretty.

Tuesday, January 30 R. had a tolerable night, the mail brings him a nice letter from the singer Winkelmann, which pleases him. He copies out his article and then goes for a walk by himself, since I still have a cold. He returns home much delighted with the sight of the lively lanes, and observes that it is better for him to go out without me, however silly that sounds, but he is ashamed of his attacks when he is with me, the need to walk so slowly. He is afraid of offending me with this remark, seems unaware that the only thing which pleases me is what seems right to him! He has brought me a lovely coffee service, and he returned home in high spirits in anticipation of my surprise. At lunch Jouk. argues heatedly against *vaporetti* [steamers]; R. replied that he could not feel such concern about them, since they have a place in our modern world, in which the Jew Guggenheim is also one of Venice's benefactors; and if one wished to preserve Venice in its old state, one would also have to put the old families back in the palaces! — At coffeetime we receive a visit from the two friendly painters Passini and Ruben, but they make an arid impression on R. and produce from him the merriest jokes. Otherwise he is in a subdued mood, as so often now in the hours of dusk; he regrets that our palace is so far from the Square, feels we have no luck with our arrangements (a statement he tries to take back at once, fearing that it will make me sad); he says this will probably be our last stay in Italy—in future we shall just make a long journey every year. He still thinks fondly of Naples (Villa d'Angri); recently he made the bold suggestion that Venice ought to be situated where Capri is—so that one could have the two of them combined! However, he says he will do anything which he can assume will please me. — In the evening he reads to us from the newspaper *L'Italie* an account of the situation in France. (Before that, at supper, a great disturbance was caused by the news that Herr Neumann is to bring the *Ring* to Venice after all, though R. specifically advised Count Contin against it. R. sends Neumann a very emphatic telegram of disapproval.) — R. asks Lusch to play the piano with him, but unfortunately she behaves childishly and refuses. So R. plays by himself, first the Andante from the 4th Symphony ("for us the 3rd," as he says), then "*froh, froh, wie seine Sonnen*" from the 9th. — He once again points out how significant it is that Beeth. put into his symphonies none of the sentimentality so much in evidence in his sonatas, quartets. He says they are like great epics, dramas. In the sonatas, etc., he made music himself, in the symphonies the world made music through him. R. enlarges upon the stupidity of his successors, who then introduced this kind of sentimentality. At the end of the evening he tells me that he can still imagine a type of symphonic work, like the "*Kaisermarsch,*" for example, in which themes are not contrasted, but each emerges out of another. However, he says he will make no more music—it excited him too much. (Delight in Fidi, who is now looking splendid.) — The description of the King's castle in *L'Italie* annoys R., making him feel ashamed of the whole relationship. He regrets that Rothschild did not make him a gift of a million [*the last twenty-one words obliterated in ink by an unknown hand*] . . .

Wednesday, January 31 In the morning all kinds of reflections about the children. Concern, particularly for Lusch. Loldi unwell. Then R. turns to the subject of the King of Bavaria, and we reflect on the ways of life, which has turned the relationship which appeared to solve everything into an unforeseeable source of bitterness! — I have given R. an article to read by M. Ducamp in the *Revue d[es] D[eux] M[ondes]*, about Paris after Sedan, and he finds it interesting, though he observes that the author is wrong in assuming that Bismarck wanted a war with France and cleverly worked to bring it about; rather, he had foreseen the unavoidable necessity. — R. today dispatches his letter to Herr v. Stein; he comes to my room around noon and, hearing me cough ("barks instead of bells"), calls me "Phylax, who loyally on house and yard through many a night kept watchful guard," and how happily I accept that name! He tells me what an indescribable impression the line "Phylax came to die!" made on him as a child. Since it is raining, R. does not go out today, and is quite glad about it. At lunch there is much joking with the girls, R. says he has already written to Schnappauf telling him to take them off to St. Gilgenberg! Herr Neumann cables that the performance in Venice will not take place—a relief! [*Neumann's telegram from Brussels enclosed.*] R. was very pleased today that Hoffmann's valerian drops were such a help and allowed him to get on with his work by allaying his spasms. He is also very cheerful during his indoor walk in the afternoon; before that I hear him improvising, the blessed spirit of music is stirring in him, and to "Phylax" he is also overwhelmingly kind. In the evening we are visited by Herr. v. Wolkoff and Frau Pinelli, by no means unwelcome to R., who ends the evening with "Harlequin, thou must pe-e-e-rrrr-rish!"

Thursday, February 1 Restless night for R., at any rate much talking aloud during it. He also complains of earache, and I put a few drops of tepid milk in his ear. We have both sirocco and rain, but all the same I suggest a short outing. It does not cheer R. up, however, and in the evening he eats no supper, complaining a lot about his heaviness. But he becomes more cheerful as the evening goes on and also feels somewhat better. A letter from Boni is a real balm to us; so I have really been granted the boon of seeing this child pursuing the paths to which I directed her!

Friday, February 2 R. slept well, we are in a contemplative mood at breakfast; R. talks a little about G. Sand's story *"Les Maîtres mosaïstes,"* which he finds of little interest, and he observes that the whole of French poetry reflects the Italian Renaissance. Today he drafts his letter to Glasenapp. Heavy thoughts! Will we ever return to Venice again? To Italy? He misses a lot here, but the thought of being shut up in the North makes him shudder. When at breakfast he hears the bells tolling, he says one cannot blame Faust for becoming so incensed with them. — In glorious weather we ride to the Piazzetta, but the crowds milling around on account of the festival are repugnant to him, we stroll through the Merceria to the Rialto, where we embark at the side, avoiding the butcher's shop which made such a terrible impression on R. the day before yesterday. — Over coffee R. and I discuss the utter impersonality of Shakespeare. R. had read in the *Revue* that in better circumstances Th. Gautier could have given France a further 5,000 verses: "That's what they mean by poets!" R. is convinced that all Shakesp.'s sonnets were written for others: "Silently looking on, he derived his view of the world from observing, and apart from that he took good care that his actors acted well—one sees that from *Hamlet*." — At dusk he comes to me in the *salon* with Jouk.; he complains about the long evenings and also the lack of books. A letter from Malw.

Meys. vexes him because of the remarks it contains about Gobineau. The word "society" always makes him annoyed! — R. then plays—with reference to Phylax—the *"Wilde Jagd,"* the barking of the dogs, then various things by Weber, but at last we come to *Die Msinger,* and he plays a lot of things from it, pleased with this enchanting work. "Cobble your shoes"—that had been his mood at the time, he says. As we are going to bed, he wonders whether he will ever see Marke again—he says he has the feeling that we hide various things from him. — I reassure him. Memories of Molly. Then he goes to sleep.

Saturday, February 3   R. was somewhat restless during the night, and at breakfast and during the rest of the morning he feels so unwell that he declares himself unable to write a thing. (Malwida's remarks about Gob. are still bothering him.) Around midday he goes out with Evchen, and returns home in better spirits. Peaceful meal with talk about all sorts of things, most of them provided by the *Illustr. Z.* and the *Fl. Bl.* In the afternoon he goes out again. We then stroll up and down through the long Palazzo Vendramin, for which he no longer much cares. There is an article about Nietzsche's *Fröhliche Wissenschaft* in Schmeitzner's monthly; I talk about it, and R. glances through it, only then to express his utter disgust with it. The things in it of any value, he says, have all been borrowed from Schopenhauer, and he dislikes everything about the man. Jouk. reads to us from the *I. Z.* an account of the collision of two ships near Hamburg. Quite terrible! . . . Late in the evening, as we are going to bed, R. mentions that *Fl[ick] und Flock* has been performed in Berlin for the 500th time, always in the presence of the Emperor! To this I add the King of B. with his Versailles—and there you have Germany. R. is amused by Fidi's having heard a singer's voice coming over the telephone in the Square today!

Sunday, February 4   R. tells me the nice dream he had: he was with Schopenhauer, who was extraordinarily cheerful and friendly (and completely white, causing R. to ask himself, "Who would ever think that this is the great philosopher?"). Then R. drew Sch.'s attention to a flock of nightingales, but Sch. had already noticed them. — Then R. comes back to Nietzsche, observes that the one photograph is enough to show what a fop he is, and declares him to be a complete nonentity, a true example of the inability to see. Then R. goes on to *"Les M. mosaïstes"* and observes that he finds such fictional psychological subtleties impossible to accept, legends have attuned him to thinking on far broader lines. — Toward 1 o'clock he reads to me his very detailed letter to Glasenapp. At lunch R. relates what an impression of madness the *Galop infernal* made on him when he heard it in the Grand Opera in Paris. Sirocco, R. does not go out. We are expecting Levi, he arrives toward 4 o'clock, most welcome to all of us. The evening passes in chat; "Harlequin, thou must perish" is played, and Levi tells us that Nietzsche recommended to him a "young Mozart," actually a thoroughly incompetent musician! This gives us food for thought! R. says to me eventually that Nietzsche has no ideas of his own, no blood of his own, it is all foreign blood which has been poured into him. (R. writes an addition to my letter to Malwida.) [*Added at the bottom of the page:* "Note to one of the foregoing days: I expressed my astonishment over the poem 'Lenore' and its popularity, and R. says, 'Well, of course, it is a wretched poem, rustic and clerical poetry.' "]

Monday, February 5 R. a little tired, though he slept well. His mind is still full of Klärchen's death from the *Egmont* music—played yesterday by the conductor—with its churchlike chords. How such things occur to one—it reminded him yesterday of "over Heaven's vaults must a loving father dwell." — Nietzsche's wretchedness also comes back into his mind. Around 12:30 we go to see our sick Jouk., whose new picture of the gondolier Manolo with his mother pleases R. very much; he says humorously, "At last you have painted a good picture!" We then go for a walk on the [Fondamenta delle] Zattere and from there ride to St. M.'s Square, where R. suggests going into the church to look for Zuccato's cupola, which we do not find! We look at the other mosaics, and R. observes how curious it is that people prefer the stiff, black fellows, on account of their age and authenticity, to the more recent mosaics, which are much pleasanter. In the gondola he spoke, in connection with "*Les M. mosaïstes,*" of the Piombi and how it must appear to many to be a sort of natural wisdom to treat individuals with indifference and to set all hopes on the species. "But," he says, "Nature preserves what is best and most powerful, and human beings have at all times tried to destroy it." — Reflections on Gob.'s error with regard to the Catholic church; and on the homeward journey, as I am gazing at the shuttered, unoccupied palaces, R. says: "That is property! The root of all evil. Proudhon took a far too material view of it, for property brings about marriages for its sake, and in consequence causes the degeneration of the race. This is what pleased me about Heinse's "Blessed Isles"—that he says the people there owned no property, in order to avoid the many miseries connected with it." — At lunch much with the conductor about the preparations for *Pars.* Over coffee we discuss the King's deficit, he is spending 500,000 marks annually on the theater (excluding the special performances); the army of officials needed for a theater like that is discussed, and R. thinks with pleasure of Bayreuth, our theater, where there are no officials, our friend Gross taking care of everything. In the afternoon he goes out by himself, sees gondolas with masked children passing Giovanelli, but he returns home tired, indeed languid. He has a massage. — What is bothering him today is Jouk.'s studio; he wants me to ask the Bardis for a north room in the palace for him. In the evening the casting of *Parsifal* is discussed, as well as the pleasure R. got from Materna's Kundry; he also declares his wish to do *Tannhäuser* in Bayreuth first; he says that if he can get this settled, he will have achieved more than by staging *Tristan*. — For the past two days he has been thinking of the Villa d'Angri, he would not be disinclined to rent it again, and in his mind he arranges our accommodations, saying he would like to live amid such striking surroundings. In bed he says to me, "I have got the accommodations arranged." And as I go to sleep I hear him speaking divine words to me, words I may not repeat, words which wrap me around like guardian angels and settle deep, deep in my heart like the most sacred of my treasures. "Good night, my angel," I said to him yesterday. "Good night, my dear wife—that means much more."

Tuesday, February 6   In spite of good nights, R. is always very tired in the morning. But he gradually livens up at breakfast. At the end of this he reads to me from the *Berl. Tagblatt* an account of the lecture of Renan's in which he denies the existence of a Jewish race. I go with Lusch and the conductor to see Moretto's picture; on our way home I hear amid all the crush and noise "Psst!" and I know at once that it is R.; I tell my companions, who look around, and true enough, there he is sitting on the bench beside the Doge's Palace and in very good spirits; the air is splendid, and he has been happily watching two lovely boys of 5 and 7 playing with sand on the bench; he put some money in the sand pit for them. R. tells us this at lunch, then he talks about the *Graphic,* which he looked through with enjoyment yesterday; over coffee I read Tappert's very witty article on Hagen's book, which I saw yesterday. Toward evening R. reads to us the two fine poems by Kant; and at around 9 o'clock we set out to the Square for the Shrovetide celebrations. R. does this to please the children, who reward him with their gaiety. The impression is mixed; R. finds something touching about the procession carrying carnival to the grave, with its melody which he thinks to be an old one, but after going to the podium with the children, he returns to me in the Cappello Nero looking sad. He says poor artisans were hopping around there without really understanding why. But the midnight bells and the extinguishing of the flames produce another fine effect. From the restaurant he gazed at the façade of the Procurators' Palace and said how boring, unimaginative, and uninventive he found it; in '58 he had told the painter Rahl the same thing, declaring what a different effect a Gothic cathedral had on him, compared with this imitative monotony. At that time, he says, he was busy on *Tristan,* and every tissue was alive! Then he comes to us, how enigmatic our relationship had been at that time, completely *Tristan*esque: "The work was predigested bread." — We return home toward 1 o'clock. R. not entirely dissatisfied, but as I go to sleep, I hear him say, "I am like Othello, the long day's task is done." He asked me earlier whether I still care for him—he is so difficult! At lunch we talked about Moretto's picture, R. praising it highly but finding the Christ too effeminate, too sorrowful; when Jouk. singles out the Christ of Leon. d. Vinci, R. agrees completely and says, "I can still see it."

Ash Wednesday, February 7 We get up late because of yesterday evening; R. has breakfast with Fidi, who worried me yesterday by suddenly disappearing, but R. was not disturbed by it even for a moment. Toward 1 o'clock we set out for S. Michele, but R. is not feeling well, and we return home immediately. He feels uncomfortable at lunch—he probably caught a cold yesterday. Around 5 o'clock he goes to bed, reads Suetonius's stories about the emperors; the doctor finds he has no temperature. While R. was lying in bed, I discussed the Gospel According to Saint Luke with him (in connection with the woman sinner in Moretto's picture).

Thursday, February 8 I have breakfast at R.'s bedside, since he is not feeling well. He gets up toward 10 o'clock, but he does not come to lunch, in order not to excite himself; shortly before lunch he shows me the newspaper report of our friend Dohm's death. As we are finishing our meal, we hear him loudly singing *"Don Giovanni tu m'invitasti!"* He comes in to us for a moment but soon leaves us, so as not to excite himself. Toward 4 o'clock he comes into the *salon,* and we chat about all kinds of things, though I refrain from telling him that Scaria is causing difficulties! . . . In the evening, after the doctor has given him a massage, R. has supper with us and stays with us for a while, during which time the conductor's accounts of looking after the sick during the war bring back to R.'s mind his ideas (inspired by Goethe) of Siegfried's becoming a surgeon. At the start of the evening he was in somewhat low spirits, but he gradually cheers up and is merry and unconstrained, suddenly expressing delight in my "clever face"! Much laughter over Fidi's opinion of Hausburg: "He goes into the café, I into the church."

Friday, February 9 R. tells me that we slept for 11 hours! At breakfast we discuss the emigration scheme organized by B. Förster—we hear that numerous people are going, that parents are entrusting their sons to him; this alarms R. greatly, since he has no great confidence in it. — At about 12 o'clock he plays a melody which sounds very beautiful, he then comes and shows it to me, neatly written on a nice sheet of paper; he says he found it while sorting out his musical scraps and wondered how it came to be there. . . . At last he remembers that it was to be attached to *Parsifal* as a dedication page! I joke about it, saying that I had indeed been disappointed at finding nothing! Now it lies in the book. He declares, incidentally, that he will never make any use of these musical scraps. In the gondola he tells me that he will still do his article about masculine and feminine, then write symphonies, but nothing more on the literary side, though he still intends to finish the biography. While he was arranging his papers, mine also came into his hands; they breathe upon him like a swarm of All Souls, he says! He considers his article "Herodom and Christianity," which he read again today, to be his best; this leads us to Gob., whose vision was so broad and so acute, but who did not look deep enough. We ride as far as the Bacino, then stroll beneath the arcades to S. Moisè to look at some blue satin fabric which has caught R.'s eye. Lunch with the children; the conductor is ill, Jouk. keeping him company! The subject of our conversation is a letter from Papa Rub. and some droll accounts by Lusch. In the afternoon R. joins me in the red *salon,* we chat about his reading, Suetonius, who has aroused some sympathy in him for Caesar. In the evening R. talks about his supporters—how they seem to be designed to make all the ideas he expresses look ridiculous. (He excepts Stein.) [*In the foregoing* "his supporters" *has been altered in another handwriting into* "some of his supporters," *and the words* "& W[olzogen]" *added after* "Stein."] He tells Jouk. that he never expected the *Blätter* to last more than two years; he is considering what is to become of Wolz. And finally he loudly regrets having built Wahnfried, the festivals also seem to him absurd! . . . With our friend Jouk., who comes around in the evening, we discuss the health of our poor conductor! R. observes that Jewishness is a terrible curse; no possibility, for example, of marrying a Christian woman; recently, he says, he had been thinking about Dr. Markus, an Israelite who once admitted to him amid tears that he loved R.'s sister (Cäcilie) but would never be permitted to marry her, for, were he to be baptized, he would lose his practice! R. says he told this story in front of Levi, and it must have affected him deeply—the Jews, the good ones, are "condemned to a gently resigned asceticism." . . . After Joukowsky has left, the children show us their little preparations for tomorrow (the 100th birthday of Jouk.'s father). Loldi's drawing arouses R.'s utter admiration!

Saturday, February 10 R. dreamed about his mother; he met her at the Brockhauses', but she was very pretty and young—as he could only at best recall her from her portrait—and also very elegant. — But R. is not feeling well and he is very depressed; as we are finishing breakfast he says he hates himself because he is such a nuisance to me! — I rehearse Fidi in a speech for lunch, R. thinks it too long, goes to his room, and writes a verse. We come to lunch late, since he had a spasm.

But he is in good spirits, tells us various things from the *Fl. Blätter;* then mention is made of his 100th birthday, which we will surely live to see and hope to celebrate! R. leaves the table for a moment, then returns, the champagne is poured out, Fidi rises to his feet—but he has forgotten it all! I prompt him from a distance, but it is of little help. Then the telegram is brought to R. according to his instructions, he reads the merry saying, and the effect is quite splendid—a mood of great hilarity makes its triumphant entrance! — Unfortunately it is not allowed to remain with us all day; our poor conductor is very ill, and when in the evening the doctor lets fall the words "emotional disturbance," we realize that his friendship with us must in the end make him melancholy. R. almost regrets having recently told him the story of Dr. Markus! He is overworked, the victim of intrigues in his profession—also on our account! — After a sad discussion of this case (the conductor is staying in bed with us here), R. withdraws for a while, and when he returns we talk of other things, the city of Paris, its various beauties and its boring aspects, then we come to the S[istine] Chapel, which R. calls a monstrosity; he says he would like to know if it was admired when it was first opened. I bring him M[ichel]a[ngelo]'s poem about this chapel, and it pleases him greatly.

Sunday, February 11 R. saw [Wilhelmine] Schröder-Devrient in his dreams; telling me of it, he says, "All my women are now passing before my eyes." We then talk about my father, in connection with a letter he has written excusing himself for not playing for the flood victims; we talk of my father's misfortune in always being regarded as a pianist, and about the difficulties of his career, which always caused such upsets that he could not help taking countermeasures of an extreme kind; but we end by observing that, as a person of greatness, he has risen above his difficult situation. — It is raining, the barber admires R.'s wit: *"Piova di primavera,"* he says, and R. replies: *"Di seconda vera."* — He tells me this gaily at breakfast. When, as we finish, I ask him whether he cares for me, he replies, "My world which contains only Isolde, how could it be without Isolde?" — At 12 o'clock he comes to me and reports that he has begun his work, and it is so heavily salted that not even Wolz. will be willing to print it. He reads the first page to me and observes that the motives have been set out clearly enough!

Our poor conductor is causing much concern. In R. it shows itself indeed as ill-humor, he observes that one should really have nothing to do with Israelites—either it causes them emotional disturbance, or it finds expression in arrogance, as with J. Rub. This theme is discussed over lunch, R. almost angry about it. — In the evening we are alone together, R. and I, the dear children with the Princess. We read

Undine (discovered among the papers belonging to Jouk.'s father, which we looked through), and we take pleasure in the very good portrayal of this figure. Previously, when R. played the beginning of the *Leonore* Overture, the conductor told R. that in his various sketches for "*töt' erst sein Weib*" Beethoven wrote down the note of B for "*Weib.*" R. then maintains that he frequently made writing mistakes. He vehemently expresses his dislike for these so-called boldnesses, and says, "If I were to perform the *Eroica*, I should forbid the [*left blank*] in the last movement." — Around noon he came into my room. "I have a letter from Cyriax." "Is there anything in it?" "You'll soon see." When I have dried my hands, I look: it is a scherzo theme, written down on an envelope from Cyriax—he then plays it on his piano.

Monday, February 12 R. got up once during the night and looked among his papers for his checkbook, which he did not find, and that disturbs him somewhat. He tells me gaily at breakfast that his barber has been complimenting him on his progress in Italian. R. had spoken of the rain as "*piova fruttuosa*" ["fruitful rain"]. And indeed a sirocco is blowing; we say goodbye to the poor conductor, who is still very run down. R. worked on his article. At lunch the children and Jouk. tell us all sorts of droll things about the *soirée* yesterday, which amuse R. and tempt him into relating some very drastic jokes and anecdotes. In the afternoon he goes out with Eva—since I am expecting Princess Hatzf.—and he tells me on his return that he gave Eva some chocolate. Before supper he shows me in the newspaper a letter from my father, in which he quasi justifies his attitude toward the Jewish problem; the letter is very well written, but we regret that he felt the need to write it. R. recalls that it was the Princess who landed him in all these difficulties, and he says, "Your father goes to his ruin out of pure chivalry!" At supper we discuss with the children the sea and its creatures; before that, prisons, penalties (the treadmill), all there to protect property. (Yesterday R. read to me some very fine and frank statements by Bismarck about his longing to withdraw from affairs.) He reads *Undine,* of which he prefers the first part. He makes many jokes about the fact that the copy Jouk.'s father used for his translation is full of ink blots, and he quotes the joke from the *Fl. Blätter* in which a boy made excuses for all the ink blots in his schoolbook by saying that the nose of his neighbor, a little Moor, had been bleeding. — When I am already lying in bed, I hear him talking volubly and loudly; I get up and go into his room. "I was talking to you," he says, and embraces me tenderly and long. "Once in 5,000 years it succeeds!" "I was talking about Undine, the being who longed for a soul." He goes to the piano, plays the mournful theme "*Rheingold, Rheingold,*" continues with "False and base all those who dwell up above." "Extraordinary that I saw this so clearly at that time!" — And as he is lying in bed, he says, "I feel loving toward them, these subservient creatures of the deep, with all their yearning."

[*Cosima Wagner's entries end here. On the following day Richard Wagner died. The ensuing entry, which bears no date, was made in the Diaries by Daniela, presumably immediately after Wagner's death:*

Among Papa's last remarks were those made at lunch (presumably on Monday), when he said he had read Herr v. Stein's article about the chorus in Aeschylus with great satisfaction. Regarding Aeschylus himself, he exclaimed, "My admiration for him keeps on growing, Zeus's eagle for Artemis's pregnant hare—that reminds one of the Duchess of Anhalt's royal blood for ox's blood." On the previous evening he had asked Mama's opinion on whether he should retain Die Kapitulation *in the second edition of his works, since it had been received so stupidly even in Germany, and by no means understood by his friends, either. At our last meal on his final evening he said that the best thing that could happen to one would be to be exiled to Ceylon, the short days depressed him, it seemed like a perpetual winter. To Joukowsky he said, "You laughed when I said I was the most unfortunate of men for having built my lovely house in such a foul climate, but it is true." He considered, along with Mama, how little the town of Bayreuth had offered him, although they had both made efforts in all directions, and he said he could scarcely imagine Siegfried spending his whole time there, so that he had ended up exactly as he had begun. But a picture of the countryside near Brunswick appealed to him—if only the weather were better! He said he missed his library, he would have liked to go to the theater every evening, preferably to see things like* Le Baruffe Chiozzotte. *He also spoke with warm appreciation of Stein's dialogues, of "Cornelia" and "Catherine of Siena," remarking particularly on the stumbling walk and the smile, and with it the holy intrigue.*

In the evening alone with Mama (Sunday) he said as he sat down at the piano that "The Eternal in the Feminine" would be his last work, except perhaps at most something on Italian church music and German military music. On one of his last outings with Mama he resolved to write to the Duke of Mecklenburg, expressing his regret at having perhaps offended this friendly gentleman, and very cordially remembering the Duke's heir.

One of his last expressions of disgust against affairs of state was connected with Bismarck's having himself carried into the Reichstag to announce that the Emperor was giving so-and-so-many hundred thousand marks for the victims of the floods—a sum which was to come not from his own money, but from the disposal fund, that is to say, from the people.

One of his dreams during his two last nights was that he received letters from women—one of them Frau Wesendonck, another a woman whom both Papa and Mama had forgotten [added at foot of page: "*perhaps Friederike Meyer, of whom Papa was speaking during his last days, assuming that she was probably* dead"]; *he said he did not open these two, but set them on either side of the table, saying to himself, "What if Cosima is jealous?"*

When there was talk of the studio which he wished to acquire in the Palazzo Vendramin for Joukowsky, he replied to Mama, who wanted him to sit for his portrait, that he no longer wished to be painted, he was satisfied with the one photograph showing him three-quarter face, and he wanted to hear no more talk of pictures. A joke he made to Georg while dressing, and which he told Mama during a gondola ride, was: "What is the difference between a flannel jacket and a tree? One grows long and the other short."

On one of his last journeys to the Piazzetta, as the gondola was turning into the canal beneath the Bridge of Sighs, Papa told Mama of an elephant in Siam which, taking part in a festival procession, suddenly went mad and caused some damage, whereupon the people blinded the innocent beast in the most horrible manner and tortured it to death; this brought from Papa reflections on the lamentable foolishness and wickedness of people.]

Postscript

On February 13, 1883, Wagner sent word that the family should not wait for him at lunch. In his study he did some work on his article "On the Womanly in the Human." After writing in his notes the words, "All the same, women's emancipation is proceeding only in an atmosphere of ecstatic convulsions. Love—tragedy," he suffered a heart attack. He died in Cosima's arms at around 3:30 P.M.

The report of Wagner's physician in Venice, Dr. Friedrich Keppler, on Wagner's illness and the cause of his death was as follows:

"Richard Wagner suffered from an advanced enlargement of the heart, in particular of the right ventricle, accompanied by fatty degeneration of the heart tissue. In addition to this, he suffered from a fairly extensive enlargement of the stomach and an internal hernia in the right groin. The latter was particularly difficult to keep in check and had in any case been maltreated by the use of an extremely unsuitable truss, so that the very first advice I gave him was a prescription for a suitable truss.

"The complaints from which Richard Wagner suffered during the last months of his life consisted primarily of disorders located in the stomach and intestines, in particular a high degree of meteorism,* and, along with this, though as a secondary feature, painful disturbances of the heart action, caused both by a direct mechanical restriction of the chest space as a consequence of the massive accumulation of gases from stomach and intestines, and by reflexive influence of the stomach nerves on the heart nerves; this finally led to the rupture of the right ventricle and precipitated the catastrophe. It cannot be doubted that the innumerable psychical agitations to which Wagner was daily exposed on account of his particular mental outlook, his sharply pronounced attitude toward a whole series of burning problems in the fields of art, science, and politics, and his noteworthy social position, contributed much to his unfortunate end.

"The actual attack which so abruptly terminated the master's life *must* have had a similar cause, but it is not for me to speculate on this matter.

"The medical treatment I prescribed for Wagner consisted of

---

* A gaseous distention of the abdomen. It seems clear that this is what Dr. Keppler meant, though the word is misspelt in German (*Matorismus* in place of *Meteorismus*).

massage of the abdomen and the application of a suitable truss. I avoided the use of medicaments as much as possible, since Wagner had the bad habit of taking medicines prescribed for him by various physicians whom he had consulted previously, often in great quantities all together."

Paul von Joukowsky described Wagner's death in a letter written on February 22, 1883, to Malwida von Meysenbug:

"It was as glorious as his life. We were all waiting for him to appear at table, for he had sent word to us to begin lunch without him. In the meantime he had sent for the doctor on account of his usual spasms; then at about 2:30 he sent Betty to fetch Frau Wagner. The doctor came at 3:00, which made us all feel easier; but around 4 o'clock, since nobody had come out of his room, we became worried; then suddenly Georg appeared and told us simply that it was *all over*. He died at around 3 o'clock in the arms of his wife, without suffering, falling asleep with an expression on his face of such nobility and peace that the memory of it will never leave me. She was alone with him the whole of the first day and night, but then the doctor managed to persuade her to go into another room. Since then I have not seen her, and I shall never see her again; nobody will, except for the children and Gross and his wife, since he is their legal guardian. She will live in the upper rooms of the house, existing only for his memory and for the children; everything else in life has ceased to exist for her. So write only to the children, for she will never read a letter again. Since her dearest wish, to die with him, was not fulfilled, she means at least to be dead to all others and to lead the only life fitting for her, that of a nun who will be a constant source of divine consolation to her children. That is great, and in complete accord with all else in her life. . . ."

Certainly Cosima's first intention was exactly as Joukowsky described it. In her desire for death she refused all nourishment for many hours after Wagner died, then, yielding to the inevitable, cut off her hair and laid it in Wagner's coffin. Hidden from sight in black robes, she accompanied her husband's body in the train back to Bayreuth. At Wahnfried it was carried to the grave at the bottom of the garden by Muncker, Feustel, Gross, Wolzogen, Seidl, Joukowsky, Wilhelmj, Porges, Levi, Richter, Standhartner, and Niemann. Daniela, Isolde, Eva, and Siegfried walked beside the coffin—Blandine, expecting her first child, was not present. Only after their friends had left did Cosima emerge from the house to join her children as the coffin was lowered into the grave.

Among the messages of condolence was one from Hans von Bülow which said simply, *"Soeur, il faut vivre"* ["Sister, life must go on"].

It took Cosima a long time to accept this truth, and for more than a year after Wagner's death she lived alone with her children in Wahnfried, receiving nobody. For the performances of *Parsifal* given in the festival theater in the summer of 1883 Emil Scaria (the Gurnemanz) assumed artistic control, as did Anton Fuchs (the Klingsor) in the following year.

But a warning from some of the participants, conveyed to her by her daughters, that the performances were losing the special quality Wagner himself had given them at last induced Cosima, a year after his death, to come out of her seclusion and assume active control of the festival. This was one reason; another was that trouble was threatening in connection with the inheritance. Wagner had left no will, and Cosima heard that efforts were being made by his more nationalistically minded supporters, Heckel among them, to persuade Liszt and Hans von Bülow to rescue the festivals from the Jewish influence of Levi. In fact, there was no likelihood of Liszt's or von Bülow's complying, but Cosima realized that the time had come for her to assert her authority.

Only tentatively at first: she had a curtained box constructed beside the stage, from which she could watch rehearsals unseen, and from it she dispatched notes of guidance and reproof to Levi and the various participants. In 1886 she at last assumed full control of the festival theater with the staging there of *Tristan und Isolde*.

Liszt, though far from well at the time, came to Bayreuth in 1886 to see his daughter's production; there, on July 31, he died, and his body was laid to rest in the municipal cemetery. In the same year King Ludwig of Bavaria met his end by drowning in the lake at Starnberg; his increasing isolation and mental instability had led earlier in that year to his being deposed as unfit to rule, and the circumstances of his death remain a mystery. Hans von Bülow, whose marriage in 1882 to the actress Marie Schanzer passed unnoticed in Cosima's Diaries, left Meiningen in 1885 and continued his conducting career, mainly in Berlin and Hamburg, up to his death in Cairo in 1894 at the age of sixty-four.

In this year, during which the last of the leading figures intimately connected with Richard Wagner died, Cosima was deep in her work of carrying out her husband's wish to stage all his mature works at the festival theater. No longer passing notes from behind curtains, but working directly on the stage with her singers (an unheard-of activity for a woman at that time), she followed the *Tristan und Isolde* of 1886 with *Die Meistersinger von Nürnberg* two years later, and with this production achieved a popular success which at last established the

Bayreuth Festival as a permanent part of the musical scene. The choice of that work rather than *Tannhäuser* was due to the persuasive influence of Adolf von Gross, who still continued to look after the administrative side of the festival; he reminded Cosima that in an imperfect world ideals must sometimes take second place to tactics. The first consideration was that the theater should become financially self-supporting, and that object was achieved with the *Meistersinger* production. On this secure basis Cosima was able to stage *Tannhäuser* in 1891, *Lohengrin* in 1894, *Der Ring des Nibelungen* in 1896, and *Der Fliegende Holländer* in 1901. *Parsifal* was also presented at all festivals, except that of 1896.

This last year was important for another reason besides the re-emergence of the *Ring* at Bayreuth for the first time since 1876: it also marked Siegfried's debut as a conductor, sharing the duties with Hans Richter and Felix Mottl. After flirting with the idea of adopting architecture as a career, Siegfried decided in his early twenties to devote his life to music. He studied conducting with Richter and Mottl and composition with Humperdinck. In 1899, at the age of thirty, he saw his first opera produced in Munich. *Der Bärenhäuter,* for which, like his father, he wrote the text himself, was followed by more than a dozen other operas, produced at various opera houses in Germany during his lifetime but never at Bayreuth: it was fully understood that the festival theater was to be used only for the works of Richard Wagner.

Siegfried continued to assist his mother in the festival theater, as conductor and as producer (of *Der Fliegende Holländer* in 1901), until 1906, when Cosima, not far short of her seventieth birthday, suffered a serious breakdown in health. There was no festival in 1907, but from 1908 until his death in 1930, Siegfried was in sole charge at Bayreuth.

Daniela, Isolde, and Eva also took an active part in the festivals, helping first their mother, then their brother, with costumes and with secretarial work. Only Blandine remained outside Bayreuth, devoting her attention to her husband and her growing family (three sons and one daughter were born to them between 1883 and 1896).

Three years after Wagner's death Daniela married Henry Thode, a German historian briefly mentioned in Cosima's Diaries on the occasion of his visit to Wagner in Venice on October 14, 1882. The marriage was childless and unhappy, and ended in divorce in 1914.

In 1900 Isolde married a musician, Franz Beidler, who first came to Bayreuth in 1896 as a musical assistant and in 1904 and 1906 conducted some performances of the *Ring* and *Parsifal*. Their only child, a son, was born in 1901. Unfortunately, Siegfried did not get along with his brother-in-law, and he dispensed with his services when he took over control of the festival from his mother. The ensuing estrangement became irreparable in 1913, when Isolde, no doubt in the interests of her son, sought unsuccessfully to have herself recognized legally as Wagner's daughter rather than von Bülow's. She died in 1919.

Eva was over forty years of age when, in 1908, she married the British-born writer Houston Stewart Chamberlain, a close friend and supporter of her mother's. This marriage, too, was childless, and it was anxiety for the heritage which caused Eva in 1915 to remind her 46-year-old bachelor brother that it was high time to think of marrying. Siegfried wasted no time in fulfilling her wish, for later that year he married the eighteen-year-old adoptive daughter of Wagner's old friend Karl Klindworth; Winifred, née Williams, was the daughter of an English journalist and a Danish actress, both of whom died young. Between the years 1917 and 1920 four children were born to Siegfried and his wife—Wieland, Friedelind, Wolfgang, and Verena—and the family succession was assured.

Cosima welcomed her daughter-in-law and her four grandchildren with delight. She was still living at Wahnfried, though after 1906 she no longer took any part in the running of the festival, and indeed, on doctor's orders, she did not attend any of the performances: the music had too disturbing an effect on her. Only once after Siegfried assumed control did she go to the festival theater, to hear part of a performance of *Die Meistersinger;* that was in 1924, when the theater, closed during the First World War, was reopened. Though physically still active, she required constant attendance, and these duties were shared between Daniela and Eva, while Winifred devoted her attention to her husband and children.

On April 1, 1930, Cosima died in her ninety-third year, and her ashes were laid to rest beside Richard Wagner in the grave at Wahnfried. It was a time of great sorrow for Siegfried, who throughout his life had remained deeply attached to his mother. Less than four months after her death he collapsed during a rehearsal of *Götterdämmerung,* and on August 4, while the festival was still going on, he suffered a further heart attack and died, at the age of sixty-one. He was buried, like his grandfather Liszt before him and his elder son, Wieland, after him, in the municipal cemetery at Bayreuth.

To Daniela and Eva, after a lifetime spent assisting their mother and brother at the festivals, it was a bitter blow to see control pass to their young sister-in-law, Winifred, the first person in charge of the festival theater who had never known Richard Wagner himself. As a conciliatory gesture, Winifred allowed Daniela to supervise the staging of *Parsifal* at the festival of 1933. But the break with old times was too great to be repaired, and Daniela and Eva (a widow since 1927) left Bayreuth to spend the remainder of their lives in the house in which Richard and Cosima started their married life, the Villa Tribschen near Lucerne. The three surviving sisters died in close succession, Daniela in 1940, Blandine (a widow since 1897) in 1941, and Eva in 1942.

Geoffrey Skelton

Notes

1878

JANUARY 1

• *Parsifal* just received: the text of *Parsifal,* completed in 1877. • The sinful world: play on a line from *Parsifal* ("*den sündigen Welten mit tausend Schmerzen*"), Act I, bars 1204 ff. Bar references throughout are to the score of *Parsifal* edited by Egon Voss and (Act I) Martin Geck, vol. 14 of the *Richard Wagner Gesamtausgabe,* published by Schott, Mainz. • He is working: on the composition of *Parsifal,* begun on August 2, 1877. • Feustel: Friedrich Feustel (1824–91), banker in Bayreuth, member of the management committee of the Bayreuth festival, Liberal deputy in the Reichstag. • The mayor: Theodor Muncker (1823–1900), mayor of Bayreuth from 1863 and a member of the festival management committee. The King's new secretary: Ludwig von Bürkel (died 1903).

JANUARY 2

• Count Apponyi: Count Albert Apponyi (1846–1933), Hungarian politician and friend of Liszt. • Hans [von Bülow] (1830–94): conductor, first husband of Cosima. • Herr von W[olzogen]: Hans von Wolzogen (1848–1938), German writer and editor of Wagner's periodical, *Bayreuther Blätter,* living in Bayreuth from 1877. • "*Die sündige Welt*": see note for January 1, 1878.

JANUARY 3

• "*Lützow's wilde Jagd*" ("Lützow's Wild Chase"): a work for male chorus and orchestra by Carl Maria von Weber (1786–1826) to words by Theodor Körner, in the cycle *Leyer und Schwert;* Wagner knew Weber, then conductor at Dresden, in his childhood. • The Society of Patrons: founded in September 1877, it was intended to finance a Wagner music school in Bayreuth; when this project fell through, its function became to finance festival performances in Wagner's theater; members (1,700 in the first three-year period, 1878–80) paid fifteen marks annually, for which they received a free copy of the *Bayreuther Blätter* and a seat at a festival performance; 1,400 members remained in the following two years, receiving a second seat at the festival of 1882 as a reward. • The history of the Arabs: *Histoire des Musulmans d'Espagne* (*The Moors in Spain*) by the Dutch historian Reinhart Dozy (1820–83) was published in 4 vols. in 1861; the 2-vol. German edition appeared in 1873.

JANUARY 4

• The palace gardens: the Hofgarten attached to the royal palace in Bayreuth; Wagner's house, Wahnfried, directly adjoins it. • The local Societies: the Wagner Societies, set up in various towns in support of the performances of *Der Ring des Nibelungen* in Bayreuth in 1876, still continued their existence distinct from the Society of Patrons.

JANUARY 5

• Titurel's . . . appeal: "*Mein Sohn Amfortas, bist du am Amt?*" (*Parsifal*, I, bars 1246 ff.). • "*Schmerzensblatt*": Literally this means "page of sorrow," but the word "*Blatt*" is also applied in German to a newspaper; it is possible, as the German editors suggest, that Wagner is referring to the manuscript of his song "*Schmerzen*" (one of the *Wesendonck-Lieder* composed in 1857), though it could just as well be a jocular reference to the local newspaper. • Lusch: Daniela von Bülow (1860–1940), Cosima's eldest daughter.

JANUARY 6

•Pohl: Richard Pohl (1826–96), a writer on music and friend of Wagner's. • His *"Fantasie"*: Wagner's *"Klavierfantasie"* in F-sharp minor, 1831. • His essay for the [*Bayreuther*] *Blätter*: Wagner's introductory article (*"Zur Einführung"*) for the first issue of his own periodical, which was published 1878–1938 under the editorship of Hans von Wolzogen; the article is reproduced in vol. 10 of Wagner's collected writings; see note for December 7, 1878. • Herr Hill: Karl Hill (1831–93), who sang Alberich in the Bayreuth *Ring* of 1876, was a member of the opera in Schwerin. • Schuré: Edouard Schuré (1841–1929), a French writer and musical historian who championed Wagner's cause in France. • *Fliegende Blätter*: a humorous weekly periodical founded in Munich in 1844.

JANUARY 7

•Ross or Georg: servants at Wahnfried; Georg Lang had been in Wagner's employment since 1876.

JANUARY 8

•Dr. Landgraf: Karl Landgraf, Wagner's doctor in Bayreuth and a friend of the family. • Herr Senff: Berthold Wilhelm Senff (1815–1900), German music publisher, founded in 1843 the music periodical *Signale für die musikalische Welt*.

JANUARY 9

•Rossini's *Moses: Mosè in Egitto,* opera, 1818. • My two Pharaohs: i.e., Titurel and Amfortas in *Parsifal*. • His C Major Overture: Wagner composed his concert overture in 1832; on November 16, 1877, Cosima offered the work to Schott for publication, but the offer was later withdrawn.

JANUARY 10

•*"Zu diesem Amt verdammt zu sein"*: Amfortas in *Parsifal,* I, bars 1294 ff. • The proofs of the [*Siegfried*] *Idyll:* in 1877 Wagner sold this composition, composed for Cosima's birthday in 1870, to Schott for publication, much to her distress.

JANUARY 11

• *Die Sieger:* Wagner wrote a prose sketch for this music drama on a Buddhist theme in May 1856. • Kundry's kiss: in Act II of *Parsifal*.

JANUARY 12

•Fidi: Wagner's and Cosima's son, Siegfried, born June 6, 1869. • *Jessonda:* opera by Louis Spohr, 1823.

JANUARY 13

•Vreneli: Verena Stocker, née Weidmann (died 1906), married to Jakob Stocker, Wagner's housekeeper from 1859 until his departure from Tribschen in 1872. • A mistake in his biography: Wagner's assertion in *Mein Leben* that he got the first idea for *Parsifal* in the garden of the Asyl, his home on the Wesendonck estate near Zurich, on Good Friday, 1857, has always been disputed, since in fact he did not move into the Asyl until April 28 of that year, eighteen days after Good Friday. • A nice letter . . . from the King: in his letter of January 9 from Hohenschwangau King Ludwig II of Bavaria (1845–86) thanked Wagner for sending him the text of *Parsifal*. • The Academic Society in Vienna: one of the Wagner Societies. • Herr Kürschner: Joseph Kürschner (1853–1902), German writer, published a Wagner almanac (*Richard-Wagner-Jahrbuch*) in 1886. • The latter's father: Hans von Wolzogen's father, Baron Alfred von Wolzogen (1823–83), was director of the opera in Schwerin. • The conductor Schmitt: Aloys Schmitt (1827–1902), conductor in Schwerin.

JANUARY 14

•R. inscribes the pages *"Eulalia":* meaning unclear; possibly by "pages" Cosima means the *Parsifal* sketches of the previous day, which had to be rewritten. • Payment of royalties by the Munich theater: Wagner had given King Ludwig the right to produce all his works in Munich without payment; Feustel's idea was to secure royalty payments in order to clear up the deficit left by the *Ring* production in 1876; an agreement to this effect was concluded in March 1878. • Two "songs from Hell": not identified.

JANUARY 15

•Dismay over a letter from Hans: in it Hans von Bülow expresses horror over the conclusion of Act I of *Parsifal* and accuses Wagner of a lack of taste; the episode is dealt with in detail in Du Moulin Eckart's biography of Cosima (1929–31).

JANUARY 16

•Herr Marsillach: Joaquin Marsillach (1859–83), representative of the Bayreuth Society of Patrons in Barcelona, author of an essay, "Ricardo Wagner," published 1878. • *The Spaniards:* presumably chapters dealing with Spain in Dozy's *Histoire des Musulmans d'Espagne.*

JANUARY 18

•Glasenapp: Carl Friedrich Glasenapp (1847–1915) wrote the first full biography of Wagner; originally planned in 2 vols., which appeared in 1876 and 1877, it was later extended to 6 vols., the last appearing in 1911. • Lesimple: August Lesimple, bookseller in Cologne, a leading figure in the Wagner Society there. • Herr Lindau: Paul Lindau (1839–1919), journalist, writer, and founder-editor of the periodical *Die Gegenwart;* he was critical of Wagner, who had a low opinion of him. • The prophecy: sung by boys and youths off stage in Act I of *Parsifal.* • His Sonata in A Major: written for piano in 1832, not published until 1960.

JANUARY 19

•Lulu: another nickname for Cosima's eldest daughter, Daniela.

JANUARY 20

•The Communion service: the disclosure of the Grail in Act I of *Parsifal.* • Berlioz's scores of the *Requiem* and *Te Deum:* the "*Grande Messe des Morts,*" 1837, and *Te Deum* for three choruses, orchestra, and organ, 1855.

JANUARY 21

•Angelo Neumann (1838–1910): a former singer at the Vienna opera and from 1876 opera director of the municipal theater in Leipzig; through his productions of Wagner's works there, and subsequently his "traveling theater," which introduced the *Ring* to many European countries (including the United Kingdom), he became an important figure in Wagner's later life and figures frequently in the Diaries from now on; his book *Erinnerungen an Richard Wagner* (*Personal Recollections of Richard Wagner*), third edition 1907, is an important source book.

JANUARY 22

•"*Wein und Brot des letzten Mahles*": *Parsifal,* I, bar 1493, boys' voices from above. • The old man: Titurel. • The scene with the carriers: Shakespeare's *Henry IV Part I,* Act II, Scene 1.

JANUARY 24

•"*Den Erlöser, den ihr preist*": alteration made approximately as stated here, *Parsifal,* I, bars 1517 ff. • Darwin: *On the Origin of Species* by Charles Darwin (1809–82) was published in German translation in 1863. • Scott's *The Heart of Midlothian:* novel, 1818.

JANUARY 25

•My *monsieurs:* the Knights of the Grail in *Parsifal.* • "Radetzky March": by Johann Strauss the Elder.

JANUARY 26

•"*Selig in Liebe . . .*": *Parsifal,* I, bars 1563 ff.

JANUARY 27
• Peace in the East: in their war against the Turks (begun in 1877) the Russians were now approaching Constantinople; the Turks requested an armistice, which was concluded on January 31.

JANUARY 28
• Herr v. Hülsen: Botho von Hülsen (1815–86), director of the Berlin opera from 1851, also took over responsibility for the Court opera houses of Hanover, Kassel, and Wiesbaden in 1867; Wagner regarded him as an enemy. • Standhartner: Joseph Standhartner (1818–92), a physician in Vienna, a very close friend of Wagner's from 1861. • *Rheingold* . . . in Vienna: the first performance, conducted by Hans Richter, took place on January 24.

JANUARY 29
• *"Selig im Glauben"*: words sung from above at the end of Act I of *Parsifal*, as Parsifal is turned away by Gurnemanz (bars 1660 ff.).

JANUARY 30
• Herr Pollini: Bernhard Pollini (1838–97), director of the Hamburg opera from 1874.

JANUARY 31
• Tribschen, my joining him there: Cosima joined Wagner at his home near Lucerne on November 16, 1868. • Arrival of the two elder children: Daniela and Blandine, on June 22, 1869. • Fidi's birth: Siegfried was born on June 6, 1869.

FEBRUARY 1
• Eckert: Karl Eckert (1820–79), at this time conductor at the Berlin opera, had been a friend and supporter since Wagner first met him on one of his visits to Vienna, where Eckert was a conductor before moving to Stuttgart in 1860; Wagner's refusal to allow Berlin to stage the *Ring* was due to his hostility toward von Hülsen, not Eckert. • Herr Voltz: Karl Voltz, a theater agent in Mainz; in 1872 Wagner signed an agreement with him and Karl Batz, of Wiesbaden, giving them the right to collect royalties from the performances of his earlier works on his behalf. • Abt: Franz Abt (1819–85), conductor at the opera in Brunswick from 1852.

FEBRUARY 2
• Letter to me from the King: in this letter from Linderhof, dated January 27, Ludwig thanks Cosima for approaching him personally in the matter; both her letter and his reply are published in vol. 4 of the King's correspondence with Wagner (*König Ludwig II und Richard Wagner: Briefwechsel,* ed. Otto Strobel, Karlsruhe, 5 vols., 1936–39). • *Jeanie:* in Scott's novel *The Heart of Midlothian* (1818) Jeanie Deans, a girl of quiet and resolute will, walks to London from Scotland to plead for her condemned sister's life.

FEBRUARY 3
• Turgenev's *Sportsman's Sketches:* these stories by the Russian author Ivan Turgenev (1818–83) first appeared 1847–52. • *Auto:* name given to religious plays, particularly those of Calderón. • The "gooseherd": Gurnemanz to Parsifal, I, bars 1647 ff., "Leave the swans here in peace and go seek, gooseherd, the goose!"

FEBRUARY 4
• *What Is German?:* Wagner's essay *Was ist deutsch?,* published in the *Bayreuther Blätter,* February 1878, and reprinted in vol. 10 of the collected writings.

FEBRUARY 5–6
• *The Trumpeter of Säckingen:* an epic poem by Joseph Victor von Scheffel (1826–86). • The symphony by Brahms: Symphony No. 2 in D Major, first performed on December 30, 1877, in Vienna, conducted by Hans Richter. • *The Presbyterians:* Walter Scott's novel appeared in German translation in 1878.

FEBRUARY 7
•Frau Dr. Herz: orthopedic specialist in whose remedial home in Altenburg Cosima's daughter Isolde underwent treatment in 1877. • The Pope dying: Pius IX died on February 7. • Gambetta: Léon Gambetta (1838–82), French statesman, opponent of the Second Empire, proclaimed the French Republic in September 1870 and held several ministerial posts before his resignation in February 1871, subsequently leader of the Republican party. • Roscher: presumably a mistake for Jules Roche (1841–1923), a journalist opponent of the Second Empire and from 1876 editor of *La Justice*. • Cosel: a nickname for Cosima.

FEBRUARY 9
• The President: Carl Alexander von Burchtorff, district president of Upper Franconia 1876–93. Herr Seidl: Anton Seidl (1850–98), a member of Wagner's Nibelungen Kanzlei in 1876, later conductor of Angelo Neumann's traveling company. • Herr Tappert: Wilhelm Tappert (1830–1907), musicologist in Berlin, editor of the *Allgemeine Deutsche Musikzeitung* 1878–81.

FEBRUARY 10
•His prelude: to Act II of *Parsifal*.

FEBRUARY 11
•My birthday: December 25.

FEBRUARY 12
• The grief I was fearing . . .: a reference to Cosima's discovery of Wagner's relationship with Judith Gautier (1846–1917), the daughter of one French poet, Théophile Gautier, and the former wife of another, Catulle Mendès; they first met in July 1869 at Tribschen (apart from a brief meeting in Paris in 1861, when Judith was still a child, at a rehearsal of *Tannhäuser*); following her visit to Bayreuth in 1876 to see the *Ring,* they entered into a secret correspondence, with the Bayreuth barber Bernhard Schnappauf as the go-between; on February 10 Wagner wrote to her asking her to correspond only with Cosima, and their letters ceased, though Cosima continued to write to Judith, and indeed Judith came to Bayreuth in 1881 and in 1882, and will consequently be mentioned in the Diaries again; it seems likely from this reference that Cosima discovered the secret correspondence, or that Wagner admitted it to her. • The castle of Tillietudlem: in Scott's novel *Old Mortality* (1816).

FEBRUARY 14
•He saw a spider: a popular superstition that to see a spider in the morning means bad luck. • The Dardanelles: or Strait of Gallipoli; treaties gave Turkey the right to close the strait in times of war. • Prof. Haase: Friedrich Haase (1825–1911), director of the Stadttheater in Leipzig 1870–76; Wagner waged a lawsuit against him for the payment of royalties and lost his case (see June 16, 1874, in vol. I). • Rudolphi: Adolf von Rudolphi (1825–90), director of the Hoftheater in Brunswick 1872–90.

FEBRUARY 15
•Lichtenberg: Georg Christoph Lichtenberg (1742–99), satirical essayist and philosopher. • Morton's rescue . . . the Covenanters: in Scott's novel *Old Mortality*. • The episode in Freiberg: fleeing from the Dresden rebellion which started on May 5, 1849, Wagner separated from his fellow rebels Heubner and Bakunin in Freiberg and thus avoided arrest.

FEBRUARY 16
•Gross: Adolf von Gross (1845–1931), banker in Bayreuth and son-in-law of Feustel; a leading figure in the administration of the festival theater. • Marke and Brange: Wagner's two Newfoundland dogs. • Loldi: Isolde. • Herr Glatz: Dr.

Franz Glatz, Hungarian tenor sponsored by Hans Richter, though Wagner had a low opinion of him; he took part in Wagner's concert in Budapest on March 10, 1875.

FEBRUARY 17
• The May Festival: an entertainment, with text by Hans von Wolzogen, for Wagner's sixty-fifth birthday on May 22.

FEBRUARY 19
• *"Höllenrose"*: Klingsor to Kundry, *Parsifal,* II, bar 112. • Essay on Captain Cook: *"Einige Lebensumstände von Capt. James Cook, grösstenteils aus schriftlichen Nachrichten einiger seiner Bekannten gezogen"* ("Some Circumstances in the Life of Capt. James Cook, Drawn Primarily from Accounts Written by Some of His Acquaintances"), by Georg Christoph Lichtenberg.

FEBRUARY 20
• *"Fal-parsi, Parsifal"*: *Parsifal,* II, bars 788 ff. • In his speech: Bismarck's famous speech on February 19 in the Reichstag, in which he defined the role of the German empire at the Berlin Congress as that of an honest broker wishing to conclude a bargain, rather than that of an arbitrator whose word must be obeyed.

FEBRUARY 22
• Preparations for the festival: in celebration of Wagner's birthday (see note for February 17, 1878). • Frau Materna: Amalie Materna (1844–1918), Bayreuth's first Brünnhilde and Kundry; she belonged to the company of the Vienna opera.

FEBRUARY 23
• Andrássy: Count Julius Andrássy (1823–90), Austrian foreign minister.

FEBRUARY 24
• The new Court theater in Dresden: rebuilt according to the plans (by the architect Gottfried Semper) for the previous theater, destroyed by fire in 1869; the opening was on February 2, 1878. • *Iphigenie, Tasso:* dramas by Goethe. • *Minna von Barnhelm:* comedy by Lessing. • The wedding opera in Berlin: on the occasion of the marriage of Princess Charlotte of Prussia to Prince Bernhard of Sachsen-Meiningen on February 18, Mozart's *La Clemenza di Tito* and Spontini's *Olimpie* were staged; Wagner wrote about this in his essays *What Is German?* and *On Opera Poetry and Composition in Particular,* both in vol. 10 of his collected writings. • *Dido abbandonata* by Marshal Kalb: in Schiller's play *Kabale und Liebe* (*Love and Intrigue*) the character Kalb says, "Tonight is the big opera *Dido*—the most magnificent fireworks—a whole city goes up in flames."

FEBRUARY 25
• The "duet": between Klingsor and Kundry in *Parsifal,* Act II. • *Deutsche Reichspost:* predecessor of the *Reichspost,* Christian Socialist newspaper founded in Vienna in 1893.

FEBRUARY 26
• Raff: Joseph Joachim Raff (1822–82), prolific German composer whom Wagner first met in 1862. • Beethoven's B-flat Major Symphony: the Fourth. • The F Major: Beethoven's Eighth Symphony.

FEBRUARY 27
• The wife of the Master of the Household: wife of Bernhard von Bülow.

FEBRUARY 28
• *"Teufelsbraut"*: Klingsor to Kundry, *Parsifal,* II, bars 247 ff. • In Starnberg: Haus Pellet on the Starnberg lake, where Cosima joined Wagner on June 29, 1864. • Schemann's preface: Ludwig Schemann published his anthology *Die Musik und ihre Klassiker in Aussprüchen Richard Wagners* (*Music and Its Classics in Statements by R. W.*) in Leipzig, 1878.

MARCH I
•Jauner: Franz Jauner (1832–1900), director of the Vienna opera. • R. Franz: Robert Franz (1815–92), composer of songs and director of music at the University of Halle.

MARCH 2
•Herr Kipke: Karl Kipke (1850–1923), a writer on music in Leipzig. • Herr Fritzsch: Ernst Wilhelm Fritzsch (1840–1902), Leipzig, published Wagner's collected writings and also the periodical *Das Musikalische Wochenblatt.* • Herr Strecker: Dr. Ludwig Strecker (1853–1943), head of the firm of Schott's Söhne, Mainz, Wagner's music publishers from 1859. • Herr Seitz Junior: Rudolf Seitz (1842–1910), a painter in Munich, son of Franz von Seitz, costume designer at the Munich opera. • *V[ossische] Zeitung:* a daily newspaper in Berlin.

MARCH 3
•Frau v. Schleinitz: Marie, Baroness von Schleinitz, née von Buch (1842–1912), wife of Alexander, Baron von Schleinitz (1807–85), the Prussian minister of the royal household; a close friend of both Wagner and Cosima and one of the leading lights in the founding of the Bayreuth festival. • Mimir: a giant in Nordic legend, guardian of the fountain of wisdom beneath the tree of life, Yggdrasil, not identical with the Mime of the *Ring.*

MARCH 6
•His symphony: Symphony in C Major, first performed in Leipzig in 1833; the score was lost, but in 1877 the orchestral parts were discovered in an old trunk Wagner had left behind in Dresden, and from these Anton Seidl was now putting the score together again. • The conference with the Archbishop of York: *Henry IV Part II,* Act I, Scene 3. *Plevna:* or Pleven, surrendered by Osman Pasha to the Russians in 1877 following a siege, a decisive factor in the Turkish defeat.

MARCH 7
•Lassalle's *Une Page d'amour:* presumably a joke; *Une Page d'amour* was the title of a novel by Emile Zola, published in 1878, but this has no connection with Ferdinand Lassalle, the German socialist leader; in the following year Helene von Dönniges published an account of her relationship with Lassalle, who died in 1864 in a duel fought on her account (see note, May 5, 1879); possibly Malwida von Meysenbug or Cosima knew (or had heard of) Helene von Dönniges's book before its publication. • An essay by Renan: Ernest Renan (1823–92), French writer; his essay on Celtic poetry is included in his *Essais de morale et de critique,* 1859.

MARCH 10
• The Rollwenzel tavern: on the road to the Eremitage, known today as the Rollwenzelei. • Heckel: Emil Heckel (1831–1908), music dealer in Mannheim and founder of the first Wagner Society; as a member of the management board of the Mannheim theater he ran into difficulties with the anti-Wagner faction. • The performance of *Die Msinger:* at the first performance, on June 21, 1868, in Munich, King Ludwig invited Wagner to watch from the royal box.

MARCH 11
• My maidens come rushing in: a reference to the Flower Maidens in *Parsifal,* Act II; "with wild gesticulations" is a speculative translation, the words in the German text being *"mit einer milden Gabe"* ("with a charitable gift"); I have read this as *"mit einem wilden Gehabe"* ("with a wild manner"), which corresponds to Wagner's stage directions and text. • The Nikolai-Schule: Wagner was a pupil at the Nikolai-Gymnasium in Leipzig from January 1828 to Easter 1830. • Porges: Heinrich Porges (1837–1900), chorus master, writer on music, coeditor of the *Neue Zeitschrift für Musik,* production assistant at the Bayreuth festival of 1876, and later closely

concerned with the production of *Parsifal* in 1882; Wagner's remark about being "afraid" of him is connected with the publication in the *Bayreuther Blätter* of an article by Porges about art and religion. • "Swannishnesses": The German word "*Schwanereien*" is presumably a pun on the word "*Schweinereien*" ("swinishnesses"). • "*Vivan le femmine . . .*" ("Long live women, long live good wine"): Mozart's *Don Giovanni,* Act II, Scene 22. • The border in Riga: Wagner secretly crossed the border into East Prussia with his wife Minna and his dog Robber on July 10, 1839, in order to avoid alerting his creditors by applying for a passport.

MARCH 12

• His article "*Modern*": published in the *Bayreuther Blätter,* March 1878, and reprinted in vol. 10 of the collected writings. • W[ilhelm] Meister: the hero of Goethe's two novels *Wilhelm Meister's Lehrjahre* and *Wanderjahre.*

MARCH 13

• Count Du Moulin: Count Eduard Du Moulin, representative of the Society of Patrons in Regensburg and father of Cosima's biographer, Count Richard Du Moulin-Eckart. • Don Ottavio: in Mozart's *Don Giovanni.* • Gaspérini: August de Gaspérini (died 1868), a physician and friend of Wagner's in Paris 1860–61.

MARCH 14

• Ludw. Geyer: Ludwig Geyer (1778–1821), Wagner's stepfather, artist, actor, and playwright. • Adolph Wagner: usually spelled Adolf Wagner (1774–1835), writer and translator, Wagner's uncle. • My 32,000 marks: Cosima had given all her personal property, including the legacy from her mother, to help pay off the deficit remaining from the production of the *Ring.* • The irony of Lord Chesterfield: the 4th Earl of Chesterfield (1694–1773), British politician and diplomat, is chiefly remembered for his letters to his son; Lichtenberg wrote an essay about him. • Mendelssohn tried to ignore it: Wagner sent Mendelssohn the score of his Symphony in C Major in 1836, probably hoping for another performance of it; Mendelssohn failed to return it—not surprisingly, perhaps, since Wagner's accompanying letter suggested that he was sending it as a gift. • V[ictor] Hugo (1802–85): his novel *Notre Dame de Paris* appeared in 1831, *Les Misérables* in 1862. • The *Mousquetaires:* series of novels by Alexandre Dumas *père* (1802–70), beginning with *The Three Musketeers,* 1844. • "Minna and Klara": Wagner's first wife, Minna, and his sister Klara (Wolfram) sat with him in a box at the first performance of *Rienzi,* in Dresden, October 20, 1842; both were now dead.

MARCH 15

• Magdala: a village east of Weimar; on his flight from Dresden in May 1849 Wagner met Minna there before going on to Switzerland. • Jommelli: Niccolò Jommelli (1714–74), Italian composer who wrote more than fifty operas and enjoyed great success in his lifetime; he was Court music director at Stuttgart 1753–69. • The Venus scene: in Act I of *Tannhäuser* (Paris version). • Kunersdorf: or Kunowice; at a battle there during the Seven Years' War Frederick the Great was defeated; Frederick's usual official language was French. • "From time to time . . .": Mephistopheles in Goethe's *Faust,* Part One.

MARCH 16

• Our Italian journey: September–December 1876 (see vol. I of the Diaries). • The Scaligeri: or della Scala, a noble family flourishing in Verona in the thirteenth and fourteenth centuries. • Wana: a dog, of which nothing further is known. • Reissiger: Karl Gottlieb Reissiger (1798–1859), second conductor under Wagner at Dresden and composer of operas, of which *Die Felsenmühle* is the best known; his *Schiffbruch der Medusa* appeared in 1846. • Joachim: Joseph Joachim (1831–1907), famous violinist whom Wagner much disliked.

MARCH 17

• *"Verfluchtes Weib . . ."*: correctly, *"Was frägst du das? Verfluchtes Weib!"*; Klingsor in *Parsifal*, II, bars 225 f. • Baron Bradwardine: in Scott's *Waverley*. • The Diadochi: the successors to Alexander the Great. • *Wolfdietrich:* a figure in German heroic saga; these folk tales were brought out by Karl Simrock (1802–76) in his *Deutsche Volksbücher* and his *Heldenbuch* in the period 1839–49. • J. Grimm: Jacob Grimm (1785–1863), noted philologist whose books on German grammar, mythology, and ancient law form part of the foundations of scientific folklore.

MARCH 18

• Prof. Minckwitz: Johann Minckwitz (1812–85), translator of the Greek classics in Leipzig. • The Emperor of Brazil: Dom Pedro II (1825–91), a Wagner devotee, visited Bayreuth in 1876. • J. Schmidt: Julian Schmidt (1818–86), journalist and literary historian, author of a history of German literature that was attacked by Ferdinand Lassalle and Lothar Bucher in 1862. • Gottschall: Rudolf Gottschall (1823–1909), writer of epics, historical dramas, and comedies. • Leisewitz: Johann Anton Leisewitz (1752–1806), German poet of the *Sturm und Drang* period. • Hey: Julius Hey (1831–1909), singing teacher engaged by Wagner to train Georg Unger for the part of Siegfried in the *Ring* of 1876; he was also approached to teach at Wagner's projected music school in Bayreuth. • Gwinner: Wilhelm von Gwinner (1825–1917), jurist and philosopher, published his biography of Schopenhauer in 1878 (*Schopenhauers Leben*).

MARCH 20

• *Shipka'd:* a word coined from the Shipka Pass in Bulgaria, frequently fought over during the war between Russia and Turkey. • "Then and now!": probably a reference to the dismal circumstances in which Blandine (Boni) was born, on March 20, 1863 (see vol. I, March 19, 1869). • Böcklin: Arnold Böcklin (1827–1901), the Swiss painter; he also turned down Wagner's invitation to design the scenery for the *Ring* in 1876. • Sitte: Camillo Sitte (1843–1903).

MARCH 21

• Spanish biography: Marsillach's essay (see note for January 16, 1878). • *Elective Affinities:* Goethe's novel *Die Wahlverwandtschaften*. • His appointment: Heckel's appointment as president of the Mannheim Court theater committee in summer 1877; in his March 21 letter to Heckel Wagner wrote, "At no time . . . did I *rejoice* at your decision to accept the presidency . . . and those of my family present very distinctly remember that the words you quote as mine were used by the hotelkeeper Albert, not by myself. . . ."

MARCH 22

• The March days: uprisings broke out in Vienna, Berlin, and Frankfurt am Main in 1848, in Dresden there were demonstrations in the streets, and the king granted the abolition of censorship.

MARCH 23

• Schröder-D.: Wilhelmine Schröder-Devrient (1804–60), the singer, was Wagner's great idol.

MARCH 24

• "You are—a senator": Iago to Brabantio in Shakespeare's *Othello,* Act I, Scene 1; Wagner equates "senator" with "donkey" in his article "On the Application of Music to the Drama" (vol. 10 of the collected writings). • The significant Jewish voice: as the starting point of his article *"Modern"* Wagner quotes a pamphlet recently sent him in which "a significant Jewish voice" declares that the culture of modern Germany is dominated by Jews. • The episode with the seamstress: in his biography Gwinner relates that Schopenhauer was sued in Berlin by Karoline Luise Marquet for insulting her "verbally and physically." • Bierey: Gottlob

Benedikt Bierey (1772–1840), composer and conductor in Breslau and a friend of Wagner's family; Wagner relates in *Mein Leben* that Bierey highly praised his first opera, *Die Feen,* when the manuscript was shown to him.

MARCH 27

• *"Nenn' ich Euch schön . . .":* Parsifal to the Flower Maidens in *Parsifal,* Act II. • Herr v. Perfall: Baron Karl von Perfall (1824–1907), director of the Munich opera from 1867. • Sch.'s letter to the Danish Academy: Schopenhauer's essay "The Basis of Morality" was rejected in 1840 by the Danish Royal Society of the Sciences. • His letter to Bismarck: Wagner sent Bismarck a copy of his article "The Festival Theater in Bayreuth" in June 1873 with an accompanying letter in which he called Bismarck "the great new founder of German hopes." • Pusinelli: Dr. Anton Pusinelli (1815–78), physician in Dresden and close friend of Wagner's from 1842. • Sulzer: Johann Jakob Sulzer (1821–97), a Swiss cantonal secretary with whom Wagner became friends in Zurich in 1849.

MARCH 28

• "O Pain, thou spark . . .": a reversal of the line in Schiller's "Ode to Joy" (*"Freude, schöner Götterfunken,"* etc.), which forms the text of the last movement of Beethoven's Ninth Symphony. • The Grand Duke of Meckl[enburg]: Friedrich Franz II (1823–83).

MARCH 29

• Hölderlin: Johann Christian Friedrich Hölderlin (1770–1843), German poet. • Did not pay more attention to my *Ring des Nibelungen:* Wagner relates in *Mein Leben* that he sent Schopenhauer a copy of the text of the *Ring* as soon as it was completed; Schopenhauer did not acknowledge it, but Wagner later heard from mutual friends that the philosopher "spoke favorably" about it. • Kossak: Ernst Kossak (1814–80), philologist and writer on music. • *Die Feen:* Wagner's first opera, 1833–34, was not performed or published as a whole until 1888. • De Sanctis: Francesco De Sanctis (1817–83), Italian literary historian and philosopher, translated Hegel's *Logic* into Italian.

MARCH 30

• Kügelgen: Gerhard von Kügelgen (1772–1820), a painter who lived in Dresden, murdered in Loschwitz by a robber whose name is no longer known.

MARCH 31

• Beethoven's splendid songs: six songs, Opus 48, to words by Christian Fürchtegott Gellert (1715–69). • My first Italian opera: in 1857, invited by the Emperor of Brazil, Dom Pedro II, to stage some performances of his works in Italian in Rio de Janeiro, Wagner thought seriously of writing *Tristan und Isolde* for production there; nothing came of the whole project. • *Romeo and Juliet:* Bellini's opera *I Capuleti ed i Montecchi,* 1830. • Meudon: village near Paris to which Wagner went in 1841 to write *Der Fliegende Holländer;* Jadin was his landlord there.

APRIL 1

• His fellow knight Brahms: Brahms received the Bavarian Order of Maximilian in December 1873, at the same time as Wagner, much to the latter's annoyance (see vol. I, December 31, 1873). • Voss's translation: Johann Heinrich Voss (1751–1826); his German translation of Homer's *Odyssey* appeared in 1781, the *Iliad* 1793. • Loge's conclusion: in Scene 2 of *Das Rheingold:* "In water, earth and sky, none would forego the joys of love" (Andrew Porter's translation).

APRIL 2

• The theme he wrote down some time ago: presumably the *"Komm', komm', holder Knabe"* theme of the Flower Maidens in *Parsifal,* Act II, which came to him when he was working on the "Centennial March" in 1876 (see vol. I, February 16, 1876). • Herr Stern: Professor Dr. Adolf Stern (1835–1907), literary historian;

Cosima had asked him to order wreaths for Pusinelli's funeral. • Herr Porges's article: on art and religion, in the *Bayreuther Blätter*. • Friend W. reads his article: von Wolzogen reviewed Schemann's book (see note for February 28, 1878) in the April number of the *Bayreuther Blätter*. • *Le Baruffe Chiozzotte* (translated as *The Chioggian Brawls*): a comedy by Carlo Goldoni (1707–93) set in the lagoon of Venice; it is mentioned by Goethe in his *Italian Journey*.

APRIL 3
•Brandt: Karl Brandt (1828–81), technical director of the theater in Darmstadt and in 1876 for the *Ring* production in Bayreuth. • *Histoire d'un crime:* Victor Hugo's novel (*Story of a Crime*), first published in 1877. • Herr Schmitt: Friedrich Schmitt (1812–84), a former singer whom Wagner first met in Magdeburg when they were both beginners; in 1867 Wagner invited him to teach at the music school in Munich, but his rough manners caused difficulties there, and the friendship ended in a quarrel.

APRIL 4
• *"Im Lenz . . .":* Flower Maidens in *Parsifal*, Act II. • Kastner: Emmerich Kastner (1847–1916), a member of Wagner's Nibelungen Kanzlei until January 1873. • *"L'Attente"* ("Waiting"): a song to words by Victor Hugo composed by Wagner in 1840. • *"Storch . . .":* literally translated, this means, "Stork, leave thy worms in the pond."

APRIL 5
• *"Komm', holder Knabe"*: *Parsifal*, II, bars 567 ff. • An article by R.: a review of the ballet *Gräfin Egmont* (music by Giorza and Strebinger) published under the pseudonym P. C. in the *Österreichische Zeitung*, October 8, 1861.

APRIL 6
• The Crown Prince: Friedrich Wilhelm (1831–88) became German emperor under the title Friedrich III in 1888 but reigned only ninety-nine days; his wife was Princess Victoria (1840–1901), the eldest child of Queen Victoria. • Marie D[önhoff]: Countess (1848–1929), née Princess di Camporeale, married to Count Karl Dönhoff, first secretary in the German embassy in Vienna; she was one of Wagner's most ardent supporters there. • Frl. Olden: Fanny Bertram (1855–1905), a soprano, made her debut in Leipzig and Dresden in 1877, and from 1878 was a leading singer at Frankfurt; under the name Fanny Moran-Olden she later enjoyed an international reputation (America 1888–89). • Heine: Heinrich Heine (1797–1856), German poet; *Romanzero*, a collection of romances and lyrics, appeared in 1851. • *"Mignonne"*: a song by Wagner, 1840. • Agathe's aria: from Weber's *Der Freischütz*. • Saint-Saëns: Camille Saint-Saëns (1835–1921), French composer; Wagner met him in Paris in 1860 and described him in *Mein Leben* as "an extremely talented young French musician."

APRIL 7
• "Recall the pledges . . .": a slightly altered quotation from Brünnhilde's words in *Götterdämmerung* (Prelude). • Frl. Götz: presumably Auguste Götze (1840–1908), a singer who taught at the Dresden Conservatoire. • Just in your husband's line: Wagner's sister Klara was married to Heinrich Wolfram, who was a singer before he turned businessman.

APRIL 10
• *"Jeux d'eau"* and *"Anges gardiens"*: *"Les Jeux d'eau à la Villa d'Este"* and *"Angelus— Prière aux anges gardiens,"* both piano pieces composed by Liszt in 1878.

APRIL 11
•Gutzkow: Karl Gutzkow (1811–78), German playwright and novelist.

APRIL 12
• *"Man kann nicht stets . . .":* from the scene in Auerbach's cellar (*Faust,* Part One);

Bayard Taylor's translation is: "What's foreign one can't always keep quite clear of, / For good things oft are not so near; / A German can't endure the French to see or hear of, / Yet drinks their wine with hearty cheer"; but this obscures the point Wagner is making here, as do other translations.

APRIL 13
• Baron Seydlitz: Reinhard von Seydlitz, artist and writer, president of the Munich Wagner Society from 1876.

APRIL 14
• The Students' Wood: a copse on the road to the Sophienberg (*Studentenwäldchen*).

APRIL 16
• Heyse: Paul Heyse (1830–1914), German writer, poet, and translator, recipient of the Nobel Prize for Literature in 1910. • "*Du—Tor*": the final words of the Flower Maidens, *Parsifal*, Act II. • The *Album-Sonate*: Wagner's piano sonata for Mathilde Wesendonck, 1853. • "*Albumblatt für Betty Schott*": Wagner's piano piece in E-flat major, 1875.

APRIL 18
• Bonus: another nickname for Blandine (Boni). • Tauler's sermons: Johannes Tauler (c. 1300–61), a Dominican in Strassburg and a significant representative of German mysticism, of whose sermons eighty are preserved.

APRIL 19
• "*Wein und Brot . . .*": see note for January 22, 1878.

APRIL 21
• Richter: Hans Richter (1843–1916), the conductor, had been very close to Wagner since joining him at Tribschen as a copyist for *Die Meistersinger von Nürnberg*; conducted the *Ring* at Bayreuth in 1876; at this time conductor at the Vienna opera.
• Makart: Hans Makart (1840–84), Austrian painter; Wagner and Cosima met him in Vienna in February 1875.

APRIL 22
• *Odysseus* by M. Wesendonck: Mathilde Wesendonck (1828–1902) had been writing historical dramas since 1865; the dramatic poem *Odysseus* was her latest. • All those blatherings of mine: reference to Wagner's letters to Mathilde Wesendonck during and after the composition of *Tristan und Isolde*. • Renan's *Evangiles*: published 1877 as part of Renan's *History of the Origins of Christianity*.

APRIL 23
• Major Müller: possibly Hermann Müller, Wilhelmine Schröder-Devrient's lover at the time Wagner was in Dresden. • The Ezra Apocalypse: in the Apocrypha, the Second Book of Esdras, chaps. 3–14, a vision of the Last Judgment (written after the destruction of Jerusalem in A.D. 70). • Clement of Rome's *Epistle*: Pope Clement I's *First Epistle of Clement*, written to the church at Corinth around A.D. 95, was known only in fragmentary form until 1875, when a complete manuscript discovered in Constantinople was published. • C. Frantz: Constantin Frantz (1817–91), German political writer of federalist views; Wagner, though in frequent disagreement with his opinions, held him in great respect as a person and dedicated the second edition (1868) of his *Opera and Drama* to him.

APRIL 24
• Our Jew in Ashby: a character in Scott's *Ivanhoe*.

APRIL 25
• A new book by friend Nietzsche: *Menschliches, Allzumenschliches* (*Human, All Too Human*); if Nietzsche hoped that the gesture of sending his book to Wagner (who had after all sent him the *Parsifal* text four months earlier) would bring about a reconciliation, he was mistaken; on May 31 he wrote to Peter Gast: "In Bayreuth

it seems to have come under a kind of ban, and the great excommunication has been extended at the same time to its author. . . . Wagner has left untouched a fine opportunity to show magnanimity of character." • The small theater: the eighteenth-century Markgräfliches Opernhaus in Bayreuth.

APRIL 26
•Renan's *The Apostles: Les Apôtres,* 1866, part of Renan's *History of the Origins of Christianity.*

APRIL 27
•Vogl: Heinrich Vogl (1845–1903), tenor at the Munich opera; Wagner always took a somewhat hostile attitude toward him, though he gave him the part of Loge in the *Ring* in 1876 and did in fact consider him for the role of Parsifal. • Marschner's *Templer:* Heinrich Marschner (1795–1861) brought out his opera *Der Templer und die Jüdin,* based on Scott's *Ivanhoe,* in 1829. • *La Dame Blanche:* opera by Boieldieu, 1825.

APRIL 28
•Birken: a district in Bayreuth.

APRIL 29
•Jefferson's words: in London on May 8, 1877, Wagner saw the American actor Joseph Jefferson (1829–1905) play Rip van Winkle. • The Waldhütte: a restaurant in the woods to the west of Bayreuth.

APRIL 30
•The 4th J.: after Jews, Jesuits, and journalists.

MAY 1
•His "Public and Popularity" article: "*Publikum und Popularität*" appeared, unsigned, in 3 pts. in the *Bayreuther Blätter* (April, June, August 1878); in the 3rd pt. Wagner made some references to Nietzsche's *Human, All Too Human;* reprinted in vol. 10 of the collected writings. • (Seidl) returns home from Leipzig: Wagner had sent him there with Richter to watch the final rehearsals of Angelo Neumann's production of the *Ring,* which was conducted by Josef Sucher. • Schelper: Otto Schelper (1844–1906), baritone in Leipzig; he sang Wotan in the Leipzig production.

MAY 2
•Hans Herrig (1845–92): poet, playwright, and essayist; an ardent Wagnerite, he first approached Wagner in 1870.

MAY 3
•Jäger: Ferdinand Jäger (1838–1902), a tenor who became Wagner's special protégé; he figures frequently in Cosima's Diaries in later years, both as singer and as neighbor and friend in Bayreuth. • The conclusion of his article: "Public and Popularity." • Löffler: Johann Heinrich Löffler (1833–1903), organist and composer; his article on Kundry appeared in the *Bayreuther Blätter,* April-May 1878.

MAY 5
•"Spring's behest" is by no means blessed: quotation based on Hans Sachs's lines in Act II of *Die Meistersinger* ("*Lenzes Gebot*").

MAY 6
•*Die Perlenschnur (The Pearl Necklace):* a melodrama by Karl von Holtei with music by Adolf Müller, 1839.

MAY 7
•Sagarika: probably sageretia is meant, a plant with edible black berries, found at the foot of the Himalayas and elsewhere. • His Indian project: *Die Sieger.*

MAY 8
•Herr von Loën: August Friedrich, Baron von Loën (1828–87), director of the Court theater in Weimar 1867–87. • The Grand Duke: Karl Alexander von Sachsen-Weimar-Eisenach (1818–1901).

MAY 9

•Maternal cares: meaning Kundry's account, in Act II of *Parsifal,* of what happened to Parsifal's mother, Herzeleide. • "Fight with the Dragon": von Wolzogen's article *"Drachenkampf"* appeared in the *Bayreuther Blätter,* July 1878. • Schmeitzner: Ernst Schmeitzner, Schloss-Chemnitz, looked after the production of the *Bayreuther Blätter.* • Daniel's birthday: Daniel Liszt (1839–59), Cosima's brother.

MAY 10

•*"Sie bettete dich . . ."*: Kundry's narration about Herzeleide, *Parsifal,* II, bars 813–42.

MAY 12

•Shots have been fired: Max Hödel, a twenty-one-year-old unemployed man from Saxony, made an assassination attempt on Emperor Wilhelm I on May 11; this led to Bismarck's efforts to introduce legislation aimed against the socialists.

MAY 14

•*Kladderadatsch:* a satirical political weekly periodical founded in Berlin in 1848. • *Wandsbecker Bote:* a periodical edited 1770–75 by the poet Matthias Claudius. • Renan's *Saint Paul:* first published in 1867 as part of Renan's *History of the Origins of Christianity.*

MAY 15

•Josef Rubinstein (1847–84): Russian musician of Jewish birth, first made contact with Wagner in 1872 after reading *Judaism in Music* and became his devoted, if often difficult, amanuensis; did a solo piano arrangement of the *Siegfried Idyll* and also of several excerpts from Wagner's works which Cosima usually refers to as "pictures" (*"Bilder"*); he prepared the piano score of *Parsifal,* on which his name is spelled Joseph Rubinstein.

MAY 16

•Prof. Holtzendorff: Franz von Holtzendorff (1829–89), professor of law in Berlin and Munich. • Vera Sassulich: a Russian nihilist accused of wounding a Russian official, acquitted on April 11, 1878.

MAY 18

•Sorokumovski: Paul Sorokumovski contributed 200 marks; nothing more was heard of the 10,000 marks for the patrons' fund. • Humboldt: Alexander von Humboldt (1769–1859), German naturalist and explorer. • Dr. Eiser: Otto Eiser, physician and representative of the Society of Patrons in Frankfurt am Main, made several contributions to the *Bayreuther Blätter* in 1878. • *The Antichrist:* Renan's *Antéchrist,* 1873, part of his *History of the Origins of Christianity.*

MAY 20

•The *tableau vivant:* Cosima also described this episode in her entry for January 30, 1869, there spelling the councilor's name Jeorgie.

MAY 21

•The barber: presumably Schnappauf.

MAY 22

•The day of days: Wagner's sixty-fifth birthday. • Our little festival: written by von Wolzogen with the collaboration of Adolf Gross and Anton Seidl, the May Festival made use of characters and music from Wagner's works; it was performed by the five children, each taking several roles, on a specially erected stage, complete with curtains, in the hall of Wahnfried. • The new carriage: a light family carriage to replace their hired landau. • Mrs. Cooper: the English governess.

MAY 23

•Prof. Overbeck: Franz Overbeck (1837–1905), a Protestant theologian, was a professor at Basel and a friend of Nietzsche's.

MAY 25

•The government's bill: against the socialists. • Bennigsen: Rudolf von Bennigsen (1824–1902), leader of the National Liberals in the Reichstag and supporter of Bismarck's policies.

MAY 27

•The consequences of 1869–1870: in his letter from the Hochkopf, dated May 24, King Ludwig wrote, "Many things ruin my pleasure in life, which could and should be so lovely and delightful, but my existence is embittered by the consequence of '70 and '71, which might surely have taken other forms"; the reference is to the Franco-Prussian War and the consequent founding of the German empire. • The article "Bellini": Wagner's article "Bellini: A Word on His Times" was published in *Der Zuschauer,* Riga, on December 7, 1837, and is reprinted in vol. 12 (posthumous) of the collected writings. • His article on German opera: written anonymously for Laube's periodical, *Zeitung für die elegante Welt,* in June 1834.

MAY 28

•Dr. Franz: representative of the Society of Patrons in Zabern, Alsace-Lorraine.

MAY 30

•Bliss without rest . . . : based on a quotation from Goethe's poem *"Rastlose Liebe"* ("Restless Love").

MAY 31

•*"Bon, je sais ce que c'est"* ("Good, I know what it is"): the translation of these two sentences, from "Then I said to myself" to "poultices, etc.," is highly speculative, since the punctuation in the original German is so erratic that it is impossible to establish with any certainty what belongs to the dream and what to the conversation about it.

JUNE 1

•Lenbach: Franz von Lenbach (1836–1904), the German portrait painter, lived in Munich and was a personal friend, particularly of Cosima's—Wagner himself had a very guarded attitude toward him.

JUNE 2

•Clumsy old London: Wagner's series of concerts in the Albert Hall in London, in the month of May 1877, was in fact his last public appearance as a conductor. • Another attempt . . . on the Emperor's life: the special edition of the *Bayreuther Tagblatt* enclosed in the Diaries reports that early that afternoon the emperor was shot and wounded while taking a drive in Unter den Linden, Berlin; the newspaper goes on to report that the perpetrator was said (erroneously) to have taken his own life; more about him in the note for June 3.

JUNE 3

•Nobiling: Dr. Karl Nobiling, who made the assassination attempt on Emperor Wilhelm I, came from a military family and was a student of agriculture; according to his statements he was a reader of the conservative periodical *Germania,* and newspapers reported that he had a brother who was said to have attended meetings of the Social Democrats; it was reports such as these that led to Wagner's joking remarks recorded by Cosima later in the day's entry; the "Nibelung" is of course just a pun on the name Nobiling. • The new ship *Kurfürst:* the German battleship *Grosser Kurfürst* collided with another German battleship, *König Wilhelm,* in the Straits of Dover on May 31, 1878, and sank, with the loss of 284 lives. • *The Destiny of Opera:* a lecture delivered by Wagner to the Royal Academy of Arts in Berlin on April 28, 1871. • Hödel: the man who made the previous attempt on the emperor's life (see note for May 12, 1878). • Herr Pfeufer: Baron Siegmund von Pfeufer, chief of police in Munich until his dismissal in 1866. • Herr v. Lutz: Baron Johann von Lutz (1826–90), King Ludwig's Cabinet secretary at the time about which Cosima is writing; on December 6, 1865, he brought Wagner the news that the King wished him to leave Bavaria.

JUNE 4

•Hagen: Edmund von Hagen (born 1850), philosopher and writer on Wagner, paid his first visit to Wagner on August 12, 1872. • The dedication to Feuerbach: Wagner dedicated *The Artwork of the Future* (1850) to the philosopher Ludwig Feuerbach (1804–72). • *La Juive:* opera by Halévy, 1835. • The convocation of princes: in 1864, before the joint Austro-Prussian attack on Denmark over Schleswig-Holstein. • Klindworth: Karl Klindworth (1830–1916), pianist, conductor, and composer, a friend of Wagner's from 1855; he did the piano scores for the *Ring;* he visited Tribschen on July 15, 1870. • The pages R. wrote for me: June 5–12, 1869. • *Battle of Vittoria:* Beethoven's symphony, Opus 91, written in 1813 to celebrate Wellington's victory over Napoleon.

JUNE 5

•Math[ilde] Maier (1833–1910): Wagner's former mistress, a close friend from 1862. • A. Frommann: Alwine Frommann (1800–75), reader for Queen (later Empress) Augusta, a friend and supporter of Wagner's from 1844 to her death. • M. Meysenbug: Malwida von Meysenbug (1816–1903), a German writer who championed the democratic movement and workers' and women's education; she first met Wagner in London in 1855 and remained a very close friend of the family, frequently mentioned throughout the Diaries. • "Do you want to bring down your blankets?": a reference to Cosima's actions when she felt her labor pains on June 5, 1869; entered in the Diaries on that day (in Wagner's handwriting): "in order not to awake anybody, carry my bedclothes myself in two journeys down to the lower bedroom." • The twice-won battle: the battle of Marston Moor, 1644; Voltaire describes how, after the royalists had apparently won the battle, Cromwell raised more than twelve thousand men during the night ("speaking to them in the name of God, quoting Moses, Gideon and Joshua") and led them to victory. •Wolzogen's pamphlet: *Die Sprache in Richard Wagner's Dichtungen* (*The Language in R. W.'s Texts*), Leipzig, 1878.

JUNE 6

•The *orange salon:* it was in the orange *salon* in Tribschen that Wagner awaited Siegfried's birth in 1869. • How different his birthday: King Ludwig's letter of June 3 from Linderhof was a comment on Wagner's description of his sixty-fifth birthday celebrations; in 1877 Wagner was in London on his birthday, and there were none of the usual elaborate family celebrations. • Article on the "stage-dedication festival": Wolzogen's article on *Parsifal* (the *"Bühnenweihfestspiel"*) appeared in the *Bayreuther Blätter,* October 1878. • *Völu-Spa: Volospá,* an anonymous poem contained in the Icelandic *Elder Edda.* • Schlemm: Oscar Schlemm (born 1850), author of "The Educated German," an article in the *Bayreuther Blätter,* November 1878. • "Harlequin, thou must perish" (*"Harlekin, du musst sterben"*): not identifiable for certain, but mentioned again in the Diaries on January 15, 16, and 31, 1883.

JUNE 7

•40 years ago: they are probably recalling Wagner's first sight of Bayreuth, on a journey from Karlsbad to Nuremberg in July 1835. • The newly built Wolzogen house: next door to Wahnfried; the branch on the roof was connected with the roof-topping ceremony. • That *Tristan* in Berlin: on March 20, 1876; Karl Eckert was the conductor. • Scaria: Emil Scaria (1840–86), singer in Vienna; Wagner was still smarting from Scaria's refusal to sing Hagen in the *Ring* of 1876; the quarrel was resolved in 1881, when Wagner heard him sing Wotan in Berlin, and Scaria was engaged for Gurnemanz in *Parsifal* in 1882. • O. Beta: Ottomar Beta (born 1845), a writer and journalist in Berlin. • "Things could have started happening. . . . Well, what I previously had was a pine tree": a literal translation, meaning obscure, though the pine tree is presumably a reference to Wagner's first wife, Minna.

JUNE 8

•*"Perdona Signora"*: presumably *"Contessa, perdono,"* sung by the Count in the finale of Act IV of Mozart's *Le Nozze di Figaro.* • Moltke: Baron Helmuth von Moltke (1800–91), chief of the General Staff and from 1872 member of the Upper Chamber. • "Set wigs of million curls . . .": Mephistopheles in Goethe's *Faust,* Part One (Faust's study); the lines continue (in Bayard Taylor's translation): "upon thy head to raise thee, / Wear shoes an ell in height,—the truth betrays thee, / And thou remainest—what thou art."

JUNE 9

•*"Die Liebe lerne kennen"*: Kundry to Parsifal, *Parsifal,* II, bars 965 f. • The Renz Circus: E. Renz, Breslau, applied to Wagner in writing on July 2, 1878, for permission to perform "The Ride of the Valkyries" in his circus. • Dr. Berr: district medical officer of health in Bayreuth.

JUNE 10

•Carstens: Asmus Jakob Carstens (1754–98), painter and illustrator. Gladstone: William Ewart Gladstone (1809–98), leader of the British Liberals, at that time in opposition; in 1876–77 he sharply attacked Prime Minister Disraeli for his anti-Turkish policy. • Cobden: Richard Cobden (1804–65), remembered chiefly for his campaign in the House of Commons leading to the repeal of the Corn Laws. • Mama Lehmann: Maria Theresia Lehmann, née Löw (1807–83), mother of the two singers Lilli and Marie Lehmann, who sang two of the Rhinemaidens in the *Ring* of 1876. • "As pants the hart . . .": Psalm 42.

JUNE 11

•The biography: pt. IV of *Mein Leben.* "Oh, stay a while, you are so fair!": Faust in the scene in his study (Goethe's *Faust,* Part One). • Egmont and his discussion with Alba: in Goethe's drama *Egmont.*

JUNE 12

•*Cosmos: Kosmos,* by the explorer Alexander Humboldt (1769–1859), published in 5 vols., 1845–62. • Helmholtz: Hermann von Helmholtz (1821–94), distinguished physiologist. • *History of Materialism (Geschichte des Materialismus und Kritik seiner Bedeutung in der Gegenwart)*: by Friedrich Albert Lange (1828–75). • Her relations in England: Hans von Bülow's mother, Franziska, was living in London with her daughter Isa and son-in-law Viktor von Bojanowski, consul-general there.

JUNE 13

•The King of Hanover: Georg V (1819–78) was deprived of his throne when Prussia annexed Hanover in 1866; he died in Paris.

JUNE 17

•Our meeting in Reichenhall: Wagner, on his way from Munich to Vienna, traveled with Cosima's sister, Blandine, and her husband, Emile Ollivier, as far as Reichenhall, where Cosima was taking a cure; the meeting was on August 12, 1861. • Boni . . . as Evening: reference to a scene in the May Festival on Wagner's birthday. • Our friend Dittmar: Dr. Dittmar (died 1877), dean in Bayreuth, officiated at Cosima's conversion to Protestantism on October 31, 1872, and became a close friend. • Baron Staff: he and his wife, Klara Staff-Reitzenstein, were neighbors in Bayreuth.

JUNE 18

•His impressions in 1835: date of Wagner's first sight of Bayreuth (see note for June 7, 1878).

JUNE 19

•Renan's *Caliban:* essay on Shakespeare's *The Tempest* by Ernest Renan (1878). •

Barbarossa: Frederick I (c. 1122–90), Holy Roman Emperor; Wagner began a drama about him in 1846. • Arnold of Brescia (died 1155): Italian monk who campaigned against the temporal power of the pope; delivered up to Pope Adrian IV by Frederick Barbarossa and hanged.

JUNE 20

•Bhagavad-Gita: "The Song of the Holy One," philosophical poem whose translation into English in 1785 by Charles Wilkins marked the beginning of the study of Sanskrit. • C[yriax]: Julius Cyriax (died 1892), a businessman, and his wife, Anna, were friends from London. • "*Tat tvam* asini": "*Tat tvam asi*" would mean approximately "This is you"; Wagner's pun turns it into "They are donkeys."

JUNE 21

•My arrival in Starnberg: in fact Cosima joined Wagner in Starnberg on June 29, 1864. A spider at night: "brings delight," according to the popular saying.

JUNE 22

•Belloni: Gaetano Belloni was Liszt's secretary, 1841–47. • Giacomelli: a writer on music and concert agent in Paris who acted for Liszt and Hans von Bülow. • "*Ich will nicht*": Kundry to Klingsor, *Parsifal*, II, bars 296 f. • Misquoting Falstaff: correctly, "My lord, I was born about three of the clock in the afternoon, with a white head and something a round belly!" (Shakespeare's *Henry IV Part Two*, Act I, Scene 2). • *Lilacs: Flieder,* the word used by Hans Sachs in Act II of *Die Meistersinger,* can mean either "lilac" or "elder flower." • Cosimo de Medici (1389–1464): Italian statesman to whom Florence gave the name *pater patriae* (father of his country).

JUNE 23

•"Boy with a plum in his mouth": Wagner's expression is "*Matz beim Pflaumenmus*" (literally, "little boy with plum purée"); presumably he means Georg Unger, who sang Siegfried in 1876, though his opinion of him at the time was not quite so drastic! • The Congress: the Berlin Congress, the convention of the chief European powers which assembled under the presidency of Bismarck to reconstruct the Russo-Turkish peace treaty and radically changed the face of Europe.

JUNE 24

•Herr Seligmann: not identified. • Eckhoff: Konrad Eckhoff (1720–78) is considered the father of German play acting. Rée: Dr. Paul Rée (1849–1901), a physician and writer, supporter of Schopenhauer's philosophy, close friend of Nietzsche's.

JUNE 25

•Disraeli: Benjamin Disraeli (1804–81), created earl of Beaconsfield in 1876, was the British prime minister, and he represented his country's interests at the Berlin Congress with great vigor; Wagner's opinion of him was much influenced by his Jewish origin. • *Tancredi:* opera by Rossini, 1813. • The Voltaire-Goethe *Tancred:* Voltaire's drama *Tancrède* (1760) was translated into German by Goethe in 1802. • "*Nimm den Eid*": Wotan in *Die Walküre,* Act II, Scene 1, promising Fricka to withdraw his protection from Siegmund.

JUNE 26

•Obernitz: privy councilor, friend of Bismarck; Cosima has not mentioned him before, but it is possible that she knew him through her friendship with Lothar Bucher, a close companion of Bismarck. • Princess B[ismarck]: Bismarck's wife. • Miss Cartwright: Wanda Cartwright, active in political life in London and frequently mentioned in Cosima's letters to her daughter Daniela, particularly in 1881. • Lasker: Eduard Lasker (1829–84), leader of the left wing of the National Liberals in the Reichstag.

JUNE 27

•Dr. Ernst: Moritz Ernst (1826–1900), director of the Stadttheater in Cologne; the German word "*ernst*" means "earnest." Euterpe: the name of a private music society in Leipzig; Wagner's C Major Symphony, first played in the Prague Conservatoire in November 1832, received another performance under the aegis of the Euterpe society in a Leipzig tavern around Christmas 1832 and was then publicly performed at the Gewandhaus, Leipzig, on January 10, 1833. • The death of the Queen of Spain: Marie Mercedes, wife of King Alfonso XII, died on June 26 at the age of eighteen, only a few months after her marriage; the unexpectedness of her death may have given rise at the time to rumors that it was due to unnatural causes, but these were not confirmed. • Prof. Bernays: Michael Bernays (1834–97), literary historian and professor at Munich, and a personal acquaintance.

JUNE 29

•Hanslick: Eduard Hanslick (1825–1904), Austrian music critic whom Wagner regarded as his archenemy and pilloried in the figure of Beckmesser in *Die Meistersinger.*

JUNE 30

•"Oh, gods, feast your eyes . . .": Brünnhilde in *Götterdämmerung* (Prelude); Andrew Porter's translation runs: "O heavenly rulers! Holy immortals! Turn your eyes on this true, loving pair!" • The Schiff: on Briennerstrasse in Munich, rented by Wagner on September 27, 1864. • Herwegh: Georg Herwegh (1815–75), revolutionary poet and close friend of Wagner's in the Zurich years.

JULY 1

•Levi: Hermann Levi (1839–1900), conductor of *Parsifal* in 1882, much mentioned in the Diaries; conductor at the Munich opera from 1872. • Guarding the governor's hat: Schiller's *Wilhelm Tell,* Act III, Scene 3. • "Today is Simon . . .": Schiller's *Wilhelm Tell,* Act I, Scene 1.

JULY 2

•Mr. Slade: a medium; with him Prof. Zöllner (see note for February 27, 1879) attempted in 1877 to prove his hypothesis of a fourth dimension. • A. Thierry's *Les Récits mér.:* the French historian Augustin Thierry published his *Récits des temps mérovingiens (Stories from the Merovingian Period)* in 2 vols. in 1840. • Voltaire's *Pucelle:* a political satire, 1738. • His mother-in-law and two sisters-in-law: Wolzogen's mother-in-law, Ottilie von Schoeler, a general's widow, and her daughters Auguste and Marie.

JULY 3

•Osman Pasha (1837–1900): Turkish general who stubbornly defended Plevna, taken prisoner by the Russians when it fell. • Charles V (1500–58): Holy Roman Emperor 1519–56, then abdicated; also king of Spain. • Dorn: Heinrich Dorn (1804–92), musical director in Riga when Wagner was a conductor there in 1839. • *Delila: Die neue Delila,* a satire that Ludwig Geyer wrote for his wife's birthday in 1818; Geyer and his friend Councilor Georgi played the shepherds Damoetas and Philemon. • Consent to the laws: Bismarck was at this time attempting to reorganize ministerial posts in the Reich and introduce finance reforms, including a new tax law on tobacco, playing cards, etc.

JULY 4

•*Ixora:* a shrub of the Rubiaceae family found in India. • "Thou who comest . . .": Goethe's *"Wandrers Nachtlied"* ("Wanderer's Night Song"), in E. A. Bowring's translation. • The Jägers, whose home . . .: Ferdinand Jäger had settled with his family in an apartment in a wing of the old Bayreuth palace. • *Götz:* Goethe's drama *Götz von Berlichingen.* • *Euphrosyne:* a play by Otto Franz Gensichen (1847–1933), published in 1878.

JULY 5

•Lachner: Franz Lachner (1803–90), a composer whose suites were very popular. • The newspaper article: not clear what this refers to (possibly it was originally enclosed in the Diaries). • *"O Richard, ô mon roi . . ."*: a paraphrase of Blondel's words in Act I of Grétry's 1784 opera, *Richard Coeur-de-Lion;* the final words should be "everyone is abandoning him."

JULY 6

•Feustel's speech to his supporters: Feustel was a National Liberal deputy in the Reichstag. • Herr v. Trützschler: Wilhelm Adolf von Trützschler (1818–49), a jurist in Dresden who took part in the 1849 uprising in Baden, was condemned to death and shot. • *Don Giovanni* and the new version of the text: the standard German translation by Rochlitz of Mozart's *Don Giovanni* held the stage until about 1850, after which there were several new versions; it is not clear to which of these Cosima is referring. • Semper: Gottfried Semper (1803–79), architect, a close friend of Wagner's from their Dresden days until they quarreled in 1868 following the abandonment of the plan to build a Wagner theater in Munich; a reconciliation took place in Vienna in 1875 (see vol. I).

JULY 7

•Bleichröder: Gerson von Bleichröder (1822–93), a Berlin banker closely associated with Bismarck. • Strauss: David Friedrich Strauss (1808–74), German philosopher, author of *Das Leben Jesu* (*The Life of Jesus*), which was very influential in its time. • Bakunin: Michael Bakunin (1814–76), Russian anarchist, took part in the Dresden uprising of 1849, during which time Wagner was strongly under his influence.

JULY 9

•Saint Radegunde: sixth-century Frankish queen, founder of the Convent of the Holy Cross at Poitiers.

JULY 10

•The Schlegel translations: August Wilhelm von Schlegel (1767–1845) translated Shakespeare, Dante, and Calderón into German.

JULY 11

•The American march: Wagner's "Centennial March," composed in 1876 for Philadelphia. • *"Kaisermarsch"*: composed by Wagner to celebrate the conclusion of the Franco-Prussian War in 1871.

JULY 12

•The Hödel trial: see note for May 12, 1878; Max Hödel was executed in Berlin on August 16, 1878.

JULY 13

•The travel adventures of Herr Will and Frau Vorstel: these names for Wagner and Cosima were taken from Schopenhauer's *Die Welt als Wille und Vorstellung* (*The World as Will and Idea*); Wagner noted in his *Annalen* the main points of his journey with Cosima to northern Italy and Ticino, Switzerland, between September 14 and October 6, 1868, during which they experienced bad weather and floods. • The "mandarin": a dress. • Composers . . . cosimers: Wagner's words were *"Komponisten"* and *"Cosimisten."* • The Julierberg: a pass near Graubünden, Switzerland; Wagner, traveling through it on July 16, 1853, saw it as a fitting background for Wotan and Fricka in Scene 2 of *Das Rheingold*. • Fr[anziska] Ritter (1829–95): daughter of Wagner's brother Albert and wife of Alexander Ritter (1833–96). • *"Mein Vöglein . . ."* ("My wood bird flew from my sight"): *Siegfried,* Act III, Scene 2.

JULY 14

•King Humbert: Umberto I, King of Italy; the rumor was false.

JULY 15

•Glücklich van Beethoven: instead of Ludwig. • Piloty: Karl von Piloty (1826–86), painter, director of the Kunstakademie in Munich from 1874; the story to which Wagner is referring cannot be traced.

July 17
•Kietz: Ernst Benedikt Kietz (1816–92), portraitist and lithographer in Dresden, Wagner's friend in Paris, 1840–42. • *Le Curé de village* (*The Country Parson*): Balzac himself described this novel as "a portrayal of Catholic remorse." • Farrabesche: an ex-convict living as a recluse in the woods, befriended by the saintly Véronique.

July 19
•Tieck's production of *A Midsummer Night's Dream:* Ludwig Tieck (1773–1853) staged the first production in Berlin of Shakespeare's play in 1843, treating it as a romantic fairy tale. • Reminiscences of Moscow: Wagner conducted concerts there in March and April 1863.

July 20
•"*Sangst du nicht . . .*": correctly, "*Sangst du mir nicht, dein Wissen sei das Leuchten der Liebe zu mir?*" (in Andrew Porter's translation, "You said that all your wisdom came by the light of your love to me"); these words, addressed by Siegfried to Brünnhilde in Act III of *Siegfried,* are sung to the *Leitmotiv* known variously as "Siegfried love" or "world inheritance"; according to Glasenapp, Wagner first conceived this theme in 1856 in connection with *Die Sieger.*

July 23
•Gounod's *Faust:* Gounod's opera, first produced in 1859, opens with the word "*Rien*" ("Nothing"); "*Tiens*" might be translated "Just a moment!"

July 25
•Ginnungagap: in Nordic mythology, the ice-filled chaos out of which the world was formed. • His article: pt. 3 of "Public and Popularity." • Reichensperger: August Reichensperger (1808–95), a Reichstag deputy, author of *Die christlich-germanische Baukunst* (*Christian Germanic Architecture*); he contributed an article to the *Bayreuther Blätter,* January-February 1882. • *Opera and Drama:* Wagner's main work treating his ideas, written 1850–51 and reprinted in vols. 3 and 4 of the collected writings. • Kundry's "*Ich bin müde*" ("I am weary"): *Parsifal,* I, bars 236 f. • "Salvation to the savior" ("*Erlösung dem Erlöser*"): the final words of *Parsifal.* • Plüddemann: Martin Plüddemann (1854–97), German composer and music critic, wrote *Die Bühnenfestspiele in Bayreuth, ihre Gegner und ihre Zukunft* (*The Stage Festivals in Bayreuth; Their Opponents and Their Future*), Colberg, 1877. • Fischer: Wilhelm Fischer (1789–1859), chorus master in Dresden during Wagner's time there as conductor.

July 26
•*Die Jungfrau* [*von Orleans*]: Schiller's drama about Joan of Arc. • Emperor Maximilian: Maximilian I (1459–1519), Holy Roman Emperor. • Goethe described sleep: *Egmont,* Act V, prison scene, "Sweet sleep! You come like pure happiness, unbidden," and earlier, "Sweet life, the lovely and friendly habit of life and activity." • [Marianne] Willemer: Marianne von Willemer (1784–1860), a banker's wife; meetings with her in 1814–15 provided the inspiration for several poems in Goethe's *West-Eastern Divan;* their correspondence was published in 1877. • Niemann: Albert Niemann (1831–1917), German tenor in Berlin from 1866; in 1861 he sang Tannhäuser in Paris in the first performance of the revised version and caused Wagner much trouble; however, Wagner respected him despite his difficult temperament, and he sang Siegmund in the *Ring* of 1876.

July 27
•The new scene in *Tannhäuser:* the Venusberg scene written for the production in Paris in 1861.

July 29
•"*Einsam bin ich . . .*": an aria from Weber's *Preciosa.* • Rosalie: Wagner's eldest

sister (born 1803), an actress before her marriage to the writer Oswald Marbach; she died in childbirth in 1837. • How "bad" Minna had been: Minna Wagner, née Planer (1809–66), ran away with a businessman named Dietrich shortly after her marriage to Wagner in 1836, and Wagner pursued her to Dresden in order to persuade her to return to him, which she eventually did; Nathalie was Minna's illegitimate daughter by Ernst Rudolf von Einsiedel, born when Minna was only seventeen, and she was always made out to be Minna's sister. • An article by Dr. Schemann: published in the *Bayreuther Blätter* in 1879. • Having seen the Norwegian fjords: in 1839, on his journey by ship from Pillau to London (inspiration for *Der Fliegende Holländer*).

JULY 31

•"Here is ink . . .": quotation from Act III, Scene 2, of *Die Meistersinger,* as Sachs prepares to take down Walther's "Prize Song." • Wearing a hair shirt: in Balzac's *Le Curé de village* the main character, Véronique, wears a hair shirt as a penance for her love for a young man subsequently executed for murder; on her deathbed she rejects the bishop's assurance that God's forgiveness is hers, and insists on making a public confession. • Therese: in Goethe's novel Therese, daughter of a farmer, is unable to marry the rich Lothario, whom she loves, because her supposed mother previously had an affair with him; but when it is discovered that her real mother was a maidservant, she is free to marry Lothario.

AUGUST 1

•Wilhelmj: August Wilhelmj (1845–1908), famous violinist, concertmaster of the Bayreuth festival orchestra in 1876. • Barante's *Ducs de Bourgogne:* the French historian A. G. Prosper, Baron de Barante (1782–1866), wrote his history of the dukes of Burgundy, *Histoire des ducs de Bourgogne de la maison de Valois (1364–1477)* in 1824–26. • The clarinetist: Johann Gottlieb Kotte (1797–1857), summoned to Dresden by Weber in 1817, and principal clarinetist at the opera there.

AUGUST 2

•Kellermann: Berthold Kellermann (1853–1926), pupil of Liszt, with whom he first came to Bayreuth in 1876, and piano teacher at the Stern Conservatoire in Berlin as successor to Hans von Bülow and Tausig; for his work at Wahnfried he received free board and sixty marks monthly. • R.'s article . . . Brünnhilde and Siegfried: a very speculative translation of a sentence confused by unclear punctuation and the later addition of a few words. • Palestrina's *Stabat Mater:* Wagner's edition (prepared in 1848) published in 1877.

AUGUST 4

•His article about Valhalla: published in the *Bayreuther Blätter,* August 1878.

AUGUST 5

•Letters to Senff: see January 8, 1878.

AUGUST 6

•Junger Züss: Züs Bürzlin, a character in Gottfried Keller's story "*Die drei gerechten Kammacher.*" • Glagau: Otto Glagau edited a periodical, *Der Kulturkämpfer,* which advertised in the *Bayreuther Blätter.*

AUGUST 8

•His experiences in St. Petersburg: Wagner conducted concerts there in Feburary and March 1863.

AUGUST 11

•The King comes to Lady Grey: *Richard III,* Act III, Scene 3. • The power of the language: the German text gives "*Race,*" but the context suggests that "*Rede*" was intended.

AUGUST 12

• Letter from the King: in his letter of August 9, King Ludwig writes, "I, too, am to a high degree revolted by the wretched German Reich, as it has unfortunately turned out under that *Junker* from Brandenburg, thanks to his sober and uninspired Prussianism."

AUGUST 13

•"Here, here, beloved . . .": a word play on a line from Goethe's ballad *"Mignon,"* *"Dahin! Dahin möcht' ich mit dir, o mein Geliebter, ziehn."* • *Garrick in Bristol:* a comedy about the English actor David Garrick by Johann Ludwig Deinhardstein (1794–1859).

AUGUST 14

•Those French billions: France was obliged to pay a sum of five billion francs in reparations following the Franco-Prussian War.

AUGUST 15

•Ziethen: Hans Joachim von Zieten (or Ziethen) (1699–1786), Prussian general. • Herr Sucher . . . and his wife: Joseph Sucher (1843–1908), Austrian conductor, 1876–78 in Leipzig, where he conducted the *Ring;* his wife, Rosa Sucher, née Hasselbeck (1849–1927), who sang Sieglinde in that production and Isolde and Eva in London in 1882, first appeared in Bayreuth in 1886 as Isolde. • Zumpe: Hermann Zumpe (1850–1903) was a member of Wagner's Nibelungen Kanzlei 1872–75 and became a conductor in Stuttgart, Schwerin, and Munich. • Brendel: Franz Brendel (1811–68), writer on music, from 1844 with the *Neue Zeitschrift für Musik.*

AUGUST 16

•Berlioz's *Les Troyens:* opera in two parts, written 1858–63. • Ranke's *Reformation: Deutsche Geschichte im Zeitalter der Reformation* by Leopold von Ranke (1795–1886), published in 6 vols. 1839–47. • 3rd installment of "Public and Popularity": its reference to "professors" was intended as a reply to Nietzsche (not mentioned by name) for his *Human, All Too Human.*

AUGUST 17

•Three of the Pringsheims: Rudolf Pringsheim (1821–1901), landowner in Silesia; his son, Dr. Alfred Pringsheim (1850–1941), who arranged some of Wagner's compositions for piano and wrote a book about Wagner; and third, probably, Sophie Pringsheim in Berlin, a distant relative of the above; their resignations had something to do with articles in the *Bayreuther Blätter* (possibly Frantz's).

AUGUST 18

•Thiele: not identified. • "The King in Thule": Goethe's ballad *"Der König in Thule."* • "The Song of the Swan": *"Der Schwanengesang,"* a poem by Karl Leberecht Immermann (1796–1840). • Frau Schröder's daughter: Wilhelmine Schröder-Devrient; the concert was in the Leipzig Gewandhaus on November 26, 1842. • The Brockhauses: Friedrich Brockhaus (1800–65) and his wife, Luise (1805–71), Wagner's sister.

AUGUST 19

•Luise Voss: née Countess Henckel von Donnersmarck (born 1820); Cosima met her in Venice on September 22, 1876; also known as Isa.

AUGUST 21

•Frau v. M[eyendorff]: Olga von Meyendorff, née Princess Gorchakov (1838–1926), wife of Baron Felix von Meyendorff, the Russian envoy in Weimar; she was Liszt's close companion for several years. • Herr v. Bronsart: Hans Bronsart von Schellendorf (1830–1913), director of the Hanover opera from 1867.

AUGUST 25

•Our wedding day: August 25, 1870, in Lucerne. • Frl. Schinkel: Susanne Schinkel, sister of Hans von Wolzogen's mother.

AUGUST 26

•*"Ich sah ihn . . ."* ("I saw Him—Him—and I laughed"): Kundry in *Parsifal*, II, bars 1178 ff.

AUGUST 27

•My father's *Dante* Symphony: Liszt's three-movement symphony, based on Dante, 1857; dedicated to Wagner.

AUGUST 28

• The law on the socialists: an emergency law directed against the "dangerous aims" of the Social Democrats was passed in the Reichstag in October 1878; framed to last three years, it was continually renewed and not repealed until 1890. • *Orpheus:* a symphonic poem by Liszt, 1854.

SEPTEMBER 3

•*"Bist du Erlöser"* ("Art thou redeemer"): Kundry in *Parsifal,* II, bars 1135 f. • *"Die Bergwerke von Falun"* ("The Mines of Falun"): a story by E. T. A. Hoffmann in the collection *Die Serapionsbrüder.* • Tieck's *"Runenberg":* a short story by Ludwig Tieck that appeared in 1804, before Hoffmann's.

SEPTEMBER 5

•*"Sein Blick"* ("His gaze"): Kundry in *Parsifal,* II, bar 1188. • The director in H. . . .: reference to Bernhard Pollini, director of the Hamburg opera, and the conductor Joseph Sucher. • International exposition: opened in Paris in May 1878 in the Trocadéro Palace.

SEPTEMBER 6

•The Lancastrians: the kings of England belonging to this family were Henry IV, who seized the throne from Richard II in 1399, his son Henry V, and his grandson Henry VI, who lost the throne to Edward IV in 1471. • Musiol: Robert Musiol (1846–1903), author of *Konversationslexikon der Tonkunst* (*Encyclopedia of Music*). • Dr. Wille: Dr. François Wille (1811–96), a journalist, husband of Wagner's friend Eliza Wille. • *"Und ob mich Gott . . ."* (in Alfred Forman's translation, "And e'en by God and world off-cast, in thee from sin be saved at last"): *Parsifal,* II, bars 1267 ff. • Hacker: Ludwig Hacker, author of *Erziehungsgeschichte Goethe's in pädagogischen Studien* (*Educational History of Goethe in Pedagogic Studies*), 1874–78. • Peter Kroll and Jungfer Sternickel: two eccentric figures in Dresden during the period 1820–30. • Ottilie: Wagner's sister (1811–83), married Professor Hermann Brockhaus.

SEPTEMBER 7

•Battle of Arcole: during which, in the vicinity of Verona, Napoleon repulsed the Austrian army in November 1796. • The Proudhon theories: a Utopian theory of socialism stemming from Pierre Joseph Proudhon (1809–65) which had some influence on Wagner, particularly his ideas concerning property. • "Berlioz" and "the doctor": nicknames given to two of the birds. • Frau Neumann: Hedwig Neumann, née Schröder, wife of Wilhelm Neumann, inspector of the royal buildings in Berlin, a long-standing friend of Cosima's. • "Only he who has never learned . . .": the Wanderer (Wotan) in *Siegfried,* Act I, Scene 2.

SEPTEMBER 8

•*"In Ewigkeit . . .":* correctly, *"Auf Ewigkeit . . ."* ("forevermore wouldst thou be damned with me"); Parsifal in Act II, bars 1276 ff. • *"Die Labung . . ."* ("the healing which will end thy suffering"): *ibid.,* bars 1293 ff. • *"Ein andres"* ("another"): *ibid.,* bars 1306 ff. • Frl. Hacker: not identified. • Fips: the dog Fips, a present from Mathilde Wesendonck, died in June 1861 in Paris, where Wagner was preparing the *Tannhäuser* production; in *Mein Leben* Wagner describes the effect of the dog's death on him and his wife Minna as "the last cleavage in a union that had long ago become impossible." • Papo: a gray parrot Wagner brought back as a present for

Minna after attending the production of *Rienzi* in Hamburg in 1844; he relates in
Mein Leben that it would greet him with snatches from *Rienzi*.

SEPTEMBER 10

•Lipiner: Siegfried Lipiner (1856–1911), poet and playwright. • My [step]sister
Claire: born 1830, daughter of Cosima's mother by her husband, Count Charles
d'Agoult; she married Count Guy de Charnacé in 1847 and lived in Versailles. • Our
meeting in Basel: on April 7, 1867; Wagner visited Hans von Bülow there to tell
him he (Hans) had been summoned to Munich; Wagner himself returned to
Tribschen with Cosima on April 9. • A nephew of Malwida's: Karl von Meysenbug
(born 1840).

SEPTEMBER 11

•A girl like Philine: an actress, lighthearted and good-natured, in Goethe's novel
Wilhelm Meister's Lehrjahre. • The etching: based on the portrait by Hubert von
Herkomer painted in London in May 1877. • My Polish friend: Emilie Sierz-
putowska, a friend of Marie Muchanoff whom Cosima met after Marie's death (see
vol. I, September 16, 1875).

SEPTEMBER 12

•Tsar Alexander of Russia: Alexander II (1818–81), tsar from 1855. • My Berlioz:
the cock (see September 7, 1878).

SEPTEMBER 13

•"*Les Deux Grenadiers*" ("The Two Grenadiers"): Wagner's song rendering Heine's
poem in French translation, 1839–40. • Adam Czartoryski: Prince Adam Jerzy
Czartoryski (1770–1861), who lived in the Château Montsermeil near Paris.

SEPTEMBER 14

•"A Happy Evening" ("*Ein glücklicher Abend*"): first published in French in the
Gazette Musicale, Paris, in 1841, and reprinted in vol. 1 of the collected writings;
though Cosima wrote "9th Symphony," it is in fact largely a discussion of Beethoven's Seventh.

SEPTEMBER 15

•Melisma: a group of notes sung to a single syllable. • The Genelli: a watercolor,
Dionysus Being Educated by the Muses, by Bonaventura Genelli (1798–1868), an
Italian painter who lived in Munich (see September 30, 1872, and note, in vol.
I). • R. invites R.: thus written, but presumably a slip; it is impossible to know for
certain who is meant—probably Malwida. • "The Artist and the Public" and "The
Virtuoso and the Artist" ("*Der Künstler und die Öffentlichkeit*" and "*Der Virtuos und
der Künstler*"): early articles published in the *Gazette Musicale* in 1840–41 and
reprinted in vol. 1 of the collected writings. • The new work he did in Tribschen:
presumably the editing and in some cases partial rewriting of these early pieces for
publication in his collected writings. • The conditions: presumably the artist's
feelings of isolation, the underlying theme of all Wagner's early articles.

SEPTEMBER 16

•His brother Albert: Albert Wagner (1799–1874), a singer and stage director,
1857–65 at the Court opera in Berlin. Cornelius: Peter Cornelius (1824–74), composer, one of Wagner's most devoted admirers and friends since 1852; there was in
fact no break in the friendship up to Cornelius's death—at the most a slight cooling
off. • Baumgartner: Wilhelm Baumgartner (1820–67), choral conductor and
composer, a friend during the Zurich years. • Weissheimer: Wendelin Weissheimer
(1838–1910), a composer whom Wagner got to know in Biebrich in 1862; they fell
out when Wagner refused to recommend Weissheimer's opera *Theodor Körner* to
the Munich opera in 1868. • Ritter: Karl Gottlieb Ritter (1830–91), son of Wagner's
benefactress Julie Ritter and brother of Alexander Ritter, who married Wagner's
niece Franziska; very close to Wagner during the Zurich years, when Wagner tried

to help him in his musical career, he became estranged, possibly, as Wagner himself suspected, on account of *Judaism in Music.*

SEPTEMBER 17

•His construction plans from the years around '52: in Zurich, where Wagner made some expensive alterations to his home in the Zeltweg. • The outbuildings: these already consisted of one house for the servants and another in which Seidl, and later Kellermann, lived.

SEPTEMBER 18

•"*Lass mich dich* . . ." (in A. Forman's translation, "Thee let me love in thy godhood"): Kundry in *Parsifal,* II, bars 1380 ff. • "*Ja, diese Stimme*" to "*Ha! dieser Kuss*" ("Yes, this voice" to "Ha, this kiss"): Parsifal in Act II, bars 1100–19.

SEPTEMBER 19

•Robber: Newfoundland dog Wagner acquired in Riga. • Schwarzhäupterhaus: the fifteenth-century center of the foreign merchants in Riga. • I no longer had a wife: when Wagner began his engagement at Riga in September 1837, he was alone and contemplating a divorce from Minna after her flight with Dietrich; however, she returned to him in October. • Gfrörer: August Friedrich Gfrörer (1803–61), author of *Geschichte des Urchristentums* (*History of Christian Mythology*), 1838. • The *laughter:* Kundry's words about Amfortas in *Parsifal,* Act II, "*den ich verlachte, lachte, lachte, ha-ha!*" ("whom once I laughed at, laughed, laughed, ha-ha!"). • Köhler: Louis Köhler (1820–86), pianist, conductor, and writer on music.

SEPTEMBER 20

•*Cosa stravagante* (A thing beyond believing): Dandini in Act II of Rossini's *La Cenerentola.* • Prof. Lagarde: Paul de Lagarde (1827–91), professor at Göttingen, advocated a German national church.

SEPTEMBER 21

•Prof. Dühring: Karl Eugen Dühring (1833–1921), philosopher and naturalist, opposed to religions assuming a life after death, in favor of a realistic outlook; in 1877 he was deprived of his license to teach in Berlin. • In Munich *Götterdämmerung:* first performance was on September 15.

SEPTEMBER 22

•Lüttichau: Baron August von Lüttichau (1786–1863), director of the Dresden opera 1824–62. • *Renatus:* epic poem by Siegfried Lipiner (see note for September 10, 1878). • Brahms's symphony: No. 1 in C Minor (1877). • The lean Brahms . . .: Brahms helped Tausig, Cornelius, and Weissheimer to correct instrumental parts for Wagner's concerts in Vienna, 1862–63. • Sgambati: Giovanni Sgambati (1841–1914), Italian composer; he visited Wagner in Rome on November 13, 1876, and Wagner, after hearing a quintet by him six days later, recommended his works to Schott in Mainz for publication. • Handel's *Alexander's Feast:* an ode, first performed in London, 1736.

SEPTEMBER 23

•[A letter from R. W. to Neumann]: in this, as printed in the newspaper, Wagner thanks Neumann and his codirector in Leipzig, Dr. August Förster, as well as the complete ensemble, for having applied themselves so assiduously to mastering the "tremendous difficulties" of his work; he continues: "The great assiduity of our artists surprises me less than the efficiency and courage of the director: this latter quality is something I have encountered very seldom among our theater directors, whereas the singers and musicians (if not their teachers) have always lent me support in my fight against the public attitude toward the theater. . . . And with this production may I have returned happily to my native city, from which the curious musical conditions kept me apart for so many years!"

SEPTEMBER 24

•*Le Postillon de Longjumeau:* comic opera by Adolphe Adam, 1836. • Ballades by

Loewe: Karl Loewe (1796–1869) composed about 150 ballades (dramatic narrative poems set for solo voice and piano accompaniment), also about 250 songs.

SEPTEMBER 25

•"World inheritance": Wotan's desire, first expressed to Erda in Act III, Scene 1, of *Siegfried,* to surrender his power to Siegfried. • Kulke: Eduard Kulke, a writer on music, contributed several articles about the *Ring* to the *Neue Zeitschrift für Musik* in 1878.

SEPTEMBER 26

•R. returns to Goethe: Wagner's educational ideas for his son, including his training as a surgeon, owe much to Goethe's novel *Wilhelm Meister's Wanderjahre,* in which the mysterious casket also figures; its symbolic significance is somewhat obscure, but in Wagner's mind it was perhaps connected in some way with his feelings of frustration (at the time of the Franco-Prussian War?) over his isolation from his fellow countrymen. • Letamendi: Dr. José de Letamendi, a professor of anatomy; his "Thoughts on the Significance of Richard Wagner's Artistic Aims" appeared in the *Bayreuther Blätter,* September 1878.

SEPTEMBER 28

•Bulwer [Lytton]: Edward Bulwer Lytton (1803–73), English novelist, one of whose works, *Rienzi* (1835), provided the basis for Wagner's opera; his *Eugene Aram* (1832) was based on an actual historical murder case. • *"L'homme du caveau"*: Wagner's French version of Kellermann's name, which means literally "cellar man." • Stern: Julius Stern (1820–83), founder in 1850 of the Stern Conservatoire in Berlin, at which Kellermann taught. • Completed this miracle in a hotel room: Wagner completed *Tristan und Isolde* while staying, from March 28 to August 6, 1859, in the Hotel Schweizerhof in Lucerne. • My entire audience for *Das Liebesverbot*: Wagner is here talking about the planned second performance of his opera *Das Liebesverbot,* which, under the title *Die Novize von Palermo,* was given its first performance in Magdeburg on March 29, 1836; he relates in *Mein Leben* that, fifteen minutes before the curtain was due to rise on the second performance, the only people in the auditorium were "Frau Gottschalk [his landlady] with her husband and, very conspicuously, a Polish Jew in full costume"; however, a fight broke out among the singers behind the curtain, and the performance could not be given.

SEPTEMBER 29

•Young Brandt: Fritz Brandt (1854–95), son and pupil of Karl Brandt in Darmstadt; he took over as technical director for *Parsifal* following his father's death.

SEPTEMBER 30

•Lord Chatham: William Pitt, 1st Earl of Chatham (1708–78), twice British prime minister; frequently ill, he received several visiting politicians at his bedside. • A sorrow to contend with: the reason for this outburst is unclear, but possibly it is a belated echo of the Judith Gautier incident (see February 12, 1878, and note). • *"Erlösung biete ich auch dir"*: correctly, *"Erlösung, Frevlerin, biet ich auch dir"* ("salvation, sinner, I offer thee, too"); Parsifal in Act II, bars 1374 ff.

OCTOBER 1

•Lecky: William Edward Hartpole Lecky (1838–1903), Irish historian whose main work is *The History of England in the Eighteenth Century,* publication of which began in this year; Wagner is presumably referring to his *History of European Morals from Augustus to Charlemagne* (1869), a German translation of which had just been published.

OCTOBER 2

•Anders: Gottfried Engelbert Anders (1795–1866), a close friend of Wagner's in the early years in Paris, where he worked in the National Library. • Wolff: Julius

Wolff (1834–1910); he wrote the poem "The Pied Piper of Hamelin" in 1875. • As one can see from *Faust:* Wagner is the name of Faust's amanuensis in Goethe's play. • His Beethoven story: *"Eine Pilgerfahrt zu Beethoven"* ("A Pilgrimage to Beethoven"), first published in French in the *Gazette Musicale,* 1840, and reprinted in vol. 1 of the collected writings; Wagner liked to make mystifying jokes about the narrator in the story, referred to simply as R., and the version noted down by Cosima on March 29, 1874, differs from that given here; Wagner's "Reichardt" or (in the earlier version) "Reichard" is in fact nothing but a fictional projection of Wagner himself. • The anecdote about the X: in Wagner's story an Englishman gives a composition to Beethoven with a request for an opinion; Beethoven, after glancing through it, merely writes a large X on the folder containing it. • Schindler's sister: Anton Schindler (1798–1864) was Beethoven's secretary from 1816 on and wrote a biography of the composer which is considered unreliable. • *Der Gestiefelte Kater (Puss in Boots):* Tieck's fairy play, 1797.

OCTOBER 3
•Lampe: Martin Lampe was the philosopher Kant's servant in Königsberg for more than forty years.

OCTOBER 4
•Schumann's *Nachtstücke:* four pieces for piano, Opus 23.

OCTOBER 5
•*Runa:* a maidservant. • "By the mass . . .": Polonius in Shakespeare's *Hamlet,* Act II, Scene 1. *"War es mein Kuss . . ."*: correctly, *"So war es mein Kuss, der Welthellsichtig dich machte?"* ("So it was my kiss that opened thine eyes to the world?"); Kundry in *Parsifal,* II, bars 1343 ff. • The Dresden style of Kotzebue: August von Kotzebue (1761–1819), writer of somewhat bombastic historical plays that were much performed throughout Germany.

OCTOBER 6
•Duprez: Gilbert Duprez (1806–96), tenor at the Paris opera. • The text of *La Favorita:* this opera, first produced in 1840 in Paris, has a libretto by Alphonse Royer, Gustave Vaëz, and Augustin Eugène Scribe. • The Weber ceremony in Dresden: Wagner arranged to have Weber's ashes brought from London and reburied in Dresden; he wrote some music for the funeral, which took place on December 15, 1844. • The walk: reference to the "Easter walk" in Goethe's *Faust,* Part One. • *Die Bürgschaft:* opera (1823) by F. L. August Mayer, composer and singer in Dresden. • Goldmark's *Die Königin von Saba:* opera (1875) by Karl Goldmark (1830–1915); Wagner and Cosima saw it in Vienna on November 10, 1875.

OCTOBER 7
•*"Der Glaube lebt . . ."* ("Faith lives, the dove hovers"): boys' voices in *Parsifal,* I, bars 1229 ff. • *Soirées de Vienna:* arrangements by Liszt of Schubert waltzes, 1852. • Hohenlohe and wife: Prince Konstantin zu Hohenlohe-Schillingsfürst (1828–96), master of the imperial household in Vienna, and his wife, Marie (1837–97), daughter of Princess Wittgenstein by her husband, Nikolaus von Sayn-Wittgenstein. • "Ha, I like not that": Iago in Shakespeare's *Othello,* Act III, Scene 3, on seeing Cassio leave Desdemona. • He has read the mandate: meaning, presumably, Othello, on receiving the letter ordering him back to Venice and appointing Cassio his successor; but this occurs in Act IV, some time after Iago sows the first seeds of suspicion in Othello's mind concerning Desdemona and Cassio.

OCTOBER 8
•The book of Fate: *Henry IV Part II,* Act III, Scene 1. • "Can call these delicate creatures ours": Othello's speech beginning "O, curse of marriage" (Act III, Scene 3). • R. spoke of the performances: presumably of *Tannhäuser* in Paris in

1861; his account of that catastrophic occasion ("Report on the Performance of *Tannhäuser* in Paris," vol. 7 of the collected writings) makes only a brief mention of three of the singers. • Schnorr in *Tannhäuser:* Wagner's revered tenor, Ludwig Schnorr von Carolsfeld (1836–65), sang Tannhäuser in Munich on March 3, 1865, after extensive coaching by Wagner; his death, on July 21 of that year, after singing Tristan in the first performances of *Tristan und Isolde,* was a devastating blow to Wagner. • Rüpel: Wagner's poodle in Magdeburg, 1835–36.

OCTOBER 9

•The action of Gloster: Shakespeare's *Henry VI Part II,* Act I, Scene 3. • Frau Vogl's leap: the soprano Therese Vogl (1845–1921), wife of the tenor Heinrich Vogl and also a member of the Munich opera, was a good horsewoman, and she took pride in leaping into the flames on her steed in the final scene of *Götterdämmerung,* a feat that in later years Cosima dismissed scornfully as "circus tricks."

OCTOBER 10

•Twenty-five years ago today: in Paris, where Wagner dined with Liszt and his three children. • The "litanies" (*"Litanei"*): a poem in the form of a litany, praising Wagner, with the refrain "Richard, hold me dear"; printed in full in vol. 1 of Du Moulin Eckart's biography of Cosima. • The two old governesses: Mme Patersi de Fossombroni and Mme de Saint-Mars, governesses to Blandine, Cosima, and Daniel in Paris, 1850–55. • *Siegfrieds Tod:* the first version of *Götterdämmerung;* the text was written in 1848, but only a few bars of music were composed. • Princess C[arolyne]: Princess Sayn-Wittgenstein (1819–87) left her husband, a Russian landowner and Court official, for Liszt, whom she met in 1847; they lived in Weimar, but in 1860 she settled in Rome; both Wagner and Cosima were hostile toward her. • The Horseshoe Tavern: correctly, the Hoop and Horseshoe; an inn close to the Tower of London in which Wagner and Minna stayed when they arrived in London from Riga on August 12, 1839.

OCTOBER 11

•Paer's *Camilla:* opera (1799) by Ferdinando Paer (1771–1839). • His article: Wagner's *"Das Publikum in Zeit und Raum"* ("The Public in Time and Space") was printed in the *Bayreuther Blätter,* October 1878, and reprinted in vol. 10 of the collected writings. • About immortality: "In Mozart's operas we can clearly discern that the qualities which raised them above their own times placed them in the curiously disadvantageous position of living on outside their times, when the living circumstances which led to their conception and execution no longer exist. All other works by Italian composers were spared this peculiar fate; not one of them has outlived the times which gave rise to it and to which it belonged entirely. With *Le Nozze di Figaro* and *Don Giovanni* it has been different; it was quite impossible to look on these works as being there just to satisfy the needs of a certain number of Italian opera seasons; they bore the stamp of immortality. Immortality—an ominous gift from above! To what tortures is not the soul of such a masterpiece exposed when once more pressed into service by the modern stage for the delectation of posterity!"

OCTOBER 12

•Zinzendorf: Count Nikolaus Ludwig von Zinzendorf (1700–60), founder of the pietistic colony of Herrnhut for the Moravian Brethren (who greatly influenced John Wesley).

OCTOBER 15

•His letter to the King: Wagner's letter of October 15, announcing the completion of Act II of *Parsifal,* concludes with the sentence: "In worshiping love my wife looks up with me to him whom my children in amazed humility see hovering above them as the guardian angel of their existence, and it is to him that with joyful devotion I deliver my soul to be his for all eternity." • In Eysser's: Nikolaus Eysser was a cabinet and furniture maker in Bayreuth.

OCTOBER 17

•"Death in Paris" ("*Das Ende eines Musikers in Paris*"): first published in the *Gazette Musicale,* 1840, and reprinted in vol. 1 of the collected writings.

OCTOBER 18

•Leopardi: Giacomo Leopardi (1798–1837), Italian poet; a German translation by Paul Heyse of his poems and prose works, including the ones Cosima mentions here, was published in 1878 in 2 vols. • R. declares this to be the best thing: after "declares" Cosima later inserted in the text "today, Saturday," which makes it clear that she wrote the October 18 entry on the following day.

OCTOBER 19

•The whole *Romeo and Juliet* march: a theme Wagner wrote down in his *Braunes Buch* on May 7, 1868; it was apparently connected in his mind with the death of Ludwig Schnorr von Carolsfeld. • He remembers Doré: Wagner met the French illustrator Gustave Doré (1832–83) in Paris in 1861; "the retreat of the 10,000" refers to the army collected by Cyrus of Persia and chronicled by Xenophon in his *Anabasis.* • Berlioz's "*Scène aux champs*": the second movement of the *Symphonie fantastique,* Opus 14.

OCTOBER 20

•Windthorst: Ludwig Windthorst (1812–91), a leading figure in the Center party and an opponent of Bismarck. • The uses to which the Niagara Falls are being put: presumably the production of hydroelectric power. • Ten years ago: since the first production of *Die Meistersinger,* on June 21, 1868, in Munich. • The meeting in the market place: Act III of Auber's opera *La Muette de Portici.*

OCTOBER 21

•My father's "Loreley": the setting by Liszt of Heine's poem "*Die Lorelei.*" • "*Am stillen Herd*": sung by Walther von Stolzing in Act I of *Die Meistersinger.* • His music of mourning: Wagner spoke several times of writing a symphony of mourning in memory of the soldiers who fell in the Franco-Prussian War, and of including in it his *Romeo and Juliet* theme (see note for October 19, 1878). • The "phonomotor": presumably "phonograph," this invention by Thomas Edison (1877) being much in the news at that time.

OCTOBER 22

•We drink my father's health: on Liszt's sixty-seventh birthday. • "*Magnificat . . .*" ("Our soul doth magnify our best father Franz. Richard Cosima with family."). Our meeting in Leipzig: on November 1, 1862, Hans and Cosima von Bülow attended a concert given by Wendelin Weissheimer at the Gewandhaus in Leipzig at which Wagner conducted the Prelude to *Die Meistersinger* (its first public performance) and the Overture to *Tannhäuser;* Cosima was in mourning for her sister, Blandine, who had died on September 11, 1862.

OCTOBER 23

•*The lemures:* in Act V of Goethe's *Faust,* Part Two, lemures (ghosts) start digging a moat outside the palace walls to drain a marsh.

OCTOBER 24

•Elsa Uhlig: born in 1849 or 1850, she was the daughter of Wagner's Dresden friend, violinist Theodor Uhlig (1822–53); the letters referred to here were written mainly from Zurich and were subsequently published (1888).

OCTOBER 25

•Damrosch: Leopold Damrosch (1832–85), composer and violinist, 1855–59 in the orchestra at Weimar, where he became a friend of both Liszt and Wagner; he went to New York in 1871 and became a leading figure in the musical life there; in 1884 he conducted *Die Walküre* and *Lohengrin* at the Metropolitan Opera. • These wicked feelings: it is unclear to whom this outburst refers; certainly not Glasenapp, and there seems no reason why it should be Damrosch, a loyal supporter of Wagner who was entertained at Wahnfried during the festival of 1876. • *Voltaire musicien* (*Voltaire as Musician*): a book (1876) by Edmond van der Straeten (1826–95).

OCTOBER 26
•"A wonder must it be . . ." ("*Es muss ein Wunderbares sein um das Lieben zweier Seelen*"): a poem by Oskar von Redwitz set to music by Liszt in 1857. • Mitterwurzer: Anton Mitterwurzer (1818–76), a baritone at the Dresden opera who sang Wolfram in the first performance of *Tannhäuser,* 1845.

OCTOBER 27
•Benedict: Julius Benedict (1804–85), German-born composer who became a British subject; the meeting was presumably on August 20, 1839, when Wagner visited Meyerbeer in Boulogne. • *Gants jaunes:* yellow gloves; i.e., the opera claque. • *Gants blancs:* white gloves. • *Gradus ad parnassum:* this basic textbook on counterpoint by Johann Joseph Fux (1660–1741) was published in 1725.

OCTOBER 28
• 10 years ago in October: on October 14, 1868, a decisive conversation took place between Cosima and Hans von Bülow in Munich. • Claire: Claire Charnacé, Cosima's stepsister. • Princess Auguste: Wilhelm I's wife; he was not yet king of Prussia when *Rienzi* was performed in Berlin for the first time (1847).

OCTOBER 29
•Minna von Barnhelm: the heroine of Lessing's comedy of the same name. • R.'s wedding house: in Königsberg-Tragheim; his marriage to Minna Planer took place on November 24, 1836.

OCTOBER 30
•Nuitter: pseudonym of Charles Louis Etienne Truinet (1828–99), French translator of Wagner's earlier works and archivist at the Paris opera. • The [Good Friday] meadow: in *Parsifal,* Act III. • The greeting to the King of S[axony]: "*Gruss seiner Treuen an Friedrich August den Geliebten,*" chorus for male voices by Wagner, performed on August 12, 1844. • "*Mignonne*" and "*Dors*" ("*Dors, mon enfant*"): French songs by Wagner, 1840. • [Pauline] Viardot (1821–1910): née Garcia; she was at the beginning of her distinguished career in Paris at the time of which Wagner is speaking.

OCTOBER 31
•"*Ach, du lieber Augustin*": a well-known German folk song. • The *Leonore* Overtures: Beethoven wrote three overtures for his opera *Leonore* (later revised and renamed *Fidelio,* with yet another overture).

NOVEMBER 1
•The Knevels house: in Magdeburg. • Friederike Meyer: an actress with whom Wagner was intimate in 1862 in Biebrich; his visit with her later that year to Vienna upset her sister, Luise Meyer-Dustmann, who was then studying the role of Isolde, and may have been a contributory factor in the abandonment of the proposed production of *Tristan und Isolde.* • Sperl: an amusement center in Vienna at that time. • Old Strauss: Johann Strauss the Elder (1804–49), the first of the family of "waltz kings." • That wheelbarrow in Frankfurt: in which, in August 1862, Wagner offered to wheel Cosima to her hotel, much to Hans von Bülow's disapproval; the full story is told in the introduction to vol. I of the Diaries (p. 12). • The celestial Wain: another name for the constellation of the Plow or the Big Dipper, called in German *der Wagen* (cart). • Kirchner: Theodor Kirchner (1823–1903), composer and director of the music school in Würzburg until 1875; he was a

disciple of Schumann, and therefore suspect in Wagner's eyes. • The "excise": the German word for "excise" (*"Akzise"*) is very similar to the word for "asceticism" (*"Askese"*).

NOVEMBER 2

•*In front of Grant:* Ulysses Simpson Grant (1822–85) was president of the United States at the time of the centennial celebrations for which Wagner's march was composed. • "You match the spirit . . .": Mephistopheles in Goethe's *Faust,* Part One, scene in Faust's study (Philip Wayne's translation).

NOVEMBER 3

•Frl. Chiorni: Glasenapp spells the name "Chiomi" in his biography of Wagner; not identified. • Susanna's aria: presumably *"Deh vieni"* (Act IV of *Le Nozze di Figaro*).

NOVEMBER 4

•Kraussold: Dr. Lorenz Kraussold, a friend in Bayreuth. • The Trocadéro: the building erected in Paris for the international exposition of 1878 contained a gigantic festival hall with a capacity of 6,000 people. • Schnorr: Julius Schnorr von Carolsfeld (1794–1872), historical painter, father of the tenor Ludwig Schnorr von Carolsfeld. • Kaulbach: Wilhelm von Kaulbach (1805–74), Munich. • Cornelius: Peter Cornelius (1783–1867), Munich (not to be confused with the composer Peter Cornelius). • Pecht: Friedrich Pecht (1814–1903), writer and painter, Munich.

NOVEMBER 5

•The "Knights of the Grail" (*"Gralsritter"*): a group of young Wagner supporters. • The Orlando: a well-known artists' tavern in Munich (referred to as Orlando Lasso on November 14, 1881). • *Fernand Cortez:* opera by Spontini, 1809. • The present crisis in England: presumably a reference to riots in Lancashire in the course of a strike by cotton operatives.

NOVEMBER 6

•*Nulla dies sine linea:* proverbial saying derived from the remark of Pliny the Elder (*Natural History,* XXXV, 36:12) that Apelles let no day go by without drawing a line. • Mme Christiani: not identified. • Gaillard: Karl Gaillard (1813–51), editor on the staff of the Berlin *Musikzeitung* 1844–47; an admirer of Wagner since seeing *Der Fliegende Holländer* in Berlin in 1844. • Redern: Count Friedrich Wilhelm von Redern (1802–83), director of the Court opera in Berlin 1828–42, then nominal director of Court music.

NOVEMBER 7

•Funeral marches for ladies: presumably the ladies who were making life difficult for Liszt; "ecclesiastical" is clearly a reference to Princess Wittgenstein, but "subaltern" remains obscure. • The passage on animals: Shakespeare's *As You Like it,* Act II, Scene 1. • Betz: Franz Betz (1835–1900), baritone singer at the Vienna opera, the first Hans Sachs in *Die Meistersinger* (Munich, 1868) and Wotan in Bayreuth (1876). • Otto Wesendonck (1815–96): Mathilde's husband.

NOVEMBER 8

•The dress rehearsal: the first performance of *Siegfried* in Vienna took place on November 9, 1878; *Götterdämmerung* followed on February 14, 1879. • *Der Sammler:* a periodical founded in 1832.

NOVEMBER 9

•The Munich painters: Heinrich Döll (1824–92), scene painter at the Munich opera from 1854, responsible for several Wagner productions; Christian Jank (1833–88), landscape painter and theater designer, appointed a Court painter by Ludwig II. • Dr. Busch: Moritz Busch (1821–99), a journalist and, from 1870, Bismarck's assistant for press relations; his book *Graf Bismarck und seine Leute während des Krieges mit Frankreich* (*Count B. and His Staff During the War with France*) appeared in 1878. • Varnhagen: Francisco Adolfo de Varnhagen (1816–78), Brazilian historian and diplomat.

NOVEMBER 10

•Les Artichauts: a villa near Geneva in which Wagner lived from December 1865 to March 1866, working on *Die Meistersinger;* Cosima spent a number of days with him there, taking down *Mein Leben* from his dictation. • Rosenfeld style: Rosenfeld was a hairdresser in Berlin. • The marriage of Helen and Faust: in Goethe's *Faust,* Part Two. • Touchstone and Audrey: in Shakespeare's *As You Like It.* • "Classical Walpurgis Night" (*"Klassische Walpurgisnacht"*): in Act II of Goethe's *Faust,* Part Two, an allegorical scene depicting ideas of classical beauty. • Fricke: Richard Fricke (1818–1903), ballet master at Dessau, engaged by Wagner to assist with movement in his *Ring* production of 1876, and again for *Parsifal* in 1882. • Thiers: Louis Adolphe Thiers (1797–1877), French statesman, prime minister twice and 1871–73 first president of the French Republic. • "Set wigs of million curls . . .": see note for June 8, 1878.

NOVEMBER 11

•Winter: Peter von Winter (1754–1825), composer, best known for his opera *Das unterbrochene Opferfest* (*The Interrupted Sacrifice*), 1796. • The *33 V.*: the Diabelli Variations. • "I have enough wit . . .": correctly, "If I had wit enough to get out of this wood, I have enough to serve my own turn"; Bottom in Shakespeare's *A Midsummer Night's Dream,* Act III, Scene 1. • *Der Dorfbarbier:* a comic opera by Johann Schenk, 1796. • *"Stehe still"* ("Stand Still"): the second of Wagner's *Wesendonck Lieder,* 1857–58. • *"Der Tannenbaum"* ("The Fir Tree"): song by Wagner to a text by Georg Scheurlin, composed in Riga, 1838.

NOVEMBER 12

•Tausig: Karl Tausig (1841–71), pianist; both he and Peter Cornelius became friends of Wagner's during the years in Zurich, and both were now dead. • His "ABEGG Variations": Schumann's Opus 1, 1820. • C Major Overture: it is not clear whose overture is meant; Wagner himself wrote two in C Major (1830 and 1832), but the context suggests he is speaking of the work of another composer (perhaps one of Beethoven's *Leonore* Overtures). • Gurnemanz's herbs and roots: in *Parsifal,* III, Gurnemanz tells Kundry that there is no longer any work for her to do, since each now seeks herbs and roots for himself (*"Kräuter und Wurzeln findet ein Jeder sich selbst"*). • "Foolish hanging of thy nether lip": Falstaff in Shakespeare's *Henry IV Part I,* Act II, Scene 4. • *"Du wirst mir . . ."* ("Thou wilt rob me of my rest"): Leonore in Beethoven's *Fidelio,* Act I (trio). • Donna Anna's aria: in Mozart's *Don Giovanni.* • Replies to Goeze: *Anti-Goeze* (1778), a series of eleven essays by Lessing replying to the chief pastor of Hamburg, J. M. Goeze, who attacked him on theological grounds.

NOVEMBER 15

•The "butterfly": presumably a reference to Wagner's butterfly collection, brought from Paris.

NOVEMBER 16

•Ten years ago today: Cosima's arrival at Tribschen with Isolde and Eva. • In '55: though Cosima wrote '54, this clearly refers to Wagner's eight concerts in London in 1855; Cherubini's *Water Carrier* Overture was one of the works he conducted on April 16. • *"Drei Knäblein . . .":* Mozart's *Die Zauberflöte,* Act I, Scene 1.

NOVEMBER 17

•*"Kar-Freitag":* Wagner puts the stress on the first syllable instead of the second; the *"Klag"* idea was not incorporated in the score of *Parsifal.* • Geneviève of Brabant: a legendary figure, wife of the palatine Siegfried, accused of adultery by his retainer Golo and condemned to be abandoned in a forest. • The modern writers: Ludwig Tieck and Christian Friedrich Hebbel wrote dramas on the Geneviève theme, and Schumann used both as the basis of his opera *Genoveva*.

NOVEMBER 19

•*Phryne:* a play (1878) by Otto Franz Gensichen (1847–1933). • Viaresi: director of the theater in Trieste. • "Shall We Hope?" ("*Wollen wir hoffen?*"): title of an article by Wagner published in the *Bayreuther Blätter,* May 1879.

NOVEMBER 20

•The Pontine Marshes: a marshy district south of Rome; efforts to drain it date back as far as 312 B.C., but success was not achieved until this century. • *Via crucis:* Liszt's "*Les 14 Stations de la croix,*" 1879. • *Seven Sacraments:* Liszt's *Septem Sakramenta,* 1878. • Lola Montez (1818–61): Spanish dancer whom Liszt first met in Dresden; she moved to Munich in 1846, and her liaison with King Ludwig I led to his abdication in 1848. • Frl. Lango: not identified, the name not clearly decipherable in the original text. • His Starnberg poem: "*An Dich*" ("To Thee"), a poem to Cosima written by Wagner on October 1, 1864.

NOVEMBER 21

•Lauermann: identified by the German editors as August Lauermann (1838–97), actor and stage director, but it is not clear why Cosima picked him out as an example of bad singing.

NOVEMBER 22

•My father's *Chopin:* Liszt's biography *Frédéric Chopin,* first published in 1852; the revised version was dated 1879. • An Orsini-like bomb incident: an attack by Italian Irredentists as a protest against Italy's failure to gain anything from the Berlin Congress; Orsini was an Italian conspirator who, with Italian accomplices, threw bombs at Napoleon III's carriage in Paris in 1858; the emperor went unharmed, but ten people were killed. • *Rise of the Moon of Intellect* (*Prabodha-chandro-daya*): a six-act play by Krishnamishra.

NOVEMBER 25

•If Bardolph saved Falstaff . . .: "Thou hast saved me a thousand marks in links and torches, walking with thee in the night betwixt tavern and tavern"; Falstaff in Shakespeare's *Henry IV Part I,* Act III, Scene 3. • Freytag: Gustav Freytag (1816–95), German writer; his 5-vol. *Bilder aus der deutschen Vergangenheit,* 1859–67, appeared in a 2-vol. English translation, 1862–63, under the title *Pictures of German Life.* • *Tancred:* novel by Benjamin Disraeli, 1847.

NOVEMBER 26

•Champfleury: Jules Fleury-Husson, called Champfleury (1821–89), French novelist who wrote a brochure on Wagner and his music in 1860 in connection with the impending *Tannhäuser* production; Wagner met him then. • Volkmann: Friedrich Robert Volkmann (1815–83), composer. • König's *Die hohe Braut:* the editor of the *Zeitung für die elegante Welt,* Heinrich Laube, championed the 2-vol. novel *Die hohe Braut* (*The Noble Bride*) by Heinrich Joseph König, which appeared in 1833; Wagner worked out a dramatization of the novel in 1836 and six years later completed it as an opera libretto for Reissiger. • Curtius: Ernst Curtius (1814–96), leader of the excavations at Olympia, 1875–81. • Heinse's *Die seligen Inseln:* correctly, *Ardinghello und die glückseligen Inseln* (*A. and the Blessed Isles*), an influential novel of the *Sturm und Drang* period by Johann Jakob Wilhelm Heinse (1749–1803).

NOVEMBER 27

•Lord Melbourne: British prime minister at the time Wagner saw him on a visit to the House of Lords in 1839. • Rudolstadt: Wagner was there in August 1834 with the Bethmann company from Magdeburg, giving guest performances. • A minuet from *Armide:* opera by Gluck (1777); presumably the minuet was played for the children's dancing lessons.

NOVEMBER 28

•Smiling meadows ("*Lachende Aue*"): a reference to the Good Friday music in *Parsifal;* Wagner's first idea for *Parsifal* came from the sight of meadows in April 1857 (see note for January 13, 1878); it was in September of the same year that Hans and Cosima visited Wagner in Zurich on their honeymoon; hence Wagner reckons his love for Cosima from that date, she from November 28, 1863 (this date, fifteen years earlier), when he first declared his love; the "smiling meadow" spread across his piano is presumably a patterned coverlet. • The *Faust* Overture: written by Wagner in 1840, revised in 1855. • A symphony in E: Wagner composed the first movement in 1834, then abandoned it. • "*Der mir in's Herz . . .*": correctly, "*Der diese Liebe mir ins Herz gehaucht*"; Brünnhilde in *Die Walküre,* Act III, Scene 3. • "*Wie/aus der Ferne . . .*": The Dutchman in *Der Fliegende Holländer,* Act II. • Frau Dustmann: Luise Meyer-Dustmann (1831–99), soprano in Vienna. • Catalani: Angelica Catalani (1780–1849), famous Italian coloratura soprano.

NOVEMBER 29

•Mazzini: Giuseppe Mazzini (1805–72), champion of Italian freedom. • When I left Zurich: on August 17, 1858.

NOVEMBER 30

•Walter Scott's *Life of Napoleon:* published in 1827. • "*Scheint mir nicht der Rechte*" ("Doesn't seem the right one"): sung by the chorus when Beckmesser rises to sing on the festival meadow, *Die Meistersinger von Nürnberg,* Act III, Scene 5. • One of my most remarkable inspirations: Wagner claimed to have "heard" the Overture to *Die Meistersinger* complete in his mind before any of the words were written.

DECEMBER 1

•Prince Pückler: Prince Hermann Pückler-Muskau (1785–1871), landscape gardener and writer of travel books. • Friedel: another nickname for Siegfried.

DECEMBER 2

•General Muck: presumably the departing garrison commander in Bayreuth, for his successor is mentioned on January 28, 1879. • Bredow's history book: the historian Gottfried Gabriel Bredow (1773–1814) wrote several books on world history.

DECEMBER 4

•The breach with Mme Sand: the writer George Sand was intimately connected with Chopin from 1837 to 1847. • *Hungaria:* a symphonic poem by Liszt. • "*Ich grolle nicht*": a poem by Heine. • "*Zueignung*": a poem printed at the beginning of Goethe's *Faust.*

DECEMBER 5

•*Virgin Soil:* a novel by Ivan Turgenev (1818–83), published in 1877. • "Ideals" ("*Die Ideale*"): a poem by Schiller.

DECEMBER 7

•"Yes, who in his heart's . . .": quotation from Schiller's "Ode to Joy" (Beethoven's Ninth Symphony). • His collected writings: *Gesammelte Schriften und Dichtungen,* published by Fritzsch in 9 vols., 1871–73; a 10th vol. was added in 1883, after Wagner's death, and two further vols. in 1911. • Cotta: Johann Friedrich Cotta (1764–1832), Goethe's publisher.

DECEMBER 8

•Turg[enev]'s tender consideration for Mme Viardot: Turgenev had a lifelong attachment to the singer Pauline Viardot-Garcia, who was not, incidentally, Jewish, though Wagner thought she was. • My Jewish pamphlet: *Judaism in Music* (Pauline Viardot's reaction is mentioned on March 16, 1869, in vol. I).

DECEMBER 10

•His *Faust* Symphony: obviously Berlioz's "dramatic legend," *La Damnation de*

Faust (1846) is meant; only very loosely based on Goethe's drama, the work does not include a Walpurgis Night scene. • *Roméo et Juliette:* Berlioz's "dramatic symphony," 1839.

DECEMBER 11

•Putz: a poodle. • Robber: the Newfoundland dog Wagner took with him from Riga in 1839. • His "Retrospect": *"Ein Rückblick auf die Bühnenfestspiele des Jahres 1876,"* published in the *Bayreuther Blätter,* December 1878, and reprinted in vol. 10 of the collected writings.

DECEMBER 12

•Hellmesberger: Joseph Hellmesberger (1828–93), Austrian violinist and conductor in Vienna.

DECEMBER 13

•Biarritz: in this French watering place, made fashionable by Empress Eugénie, Napoleon III and Bismarck met in 1862 and 1865. • Solomin . . . Nezhdanov: revolutionaries in Turgenev's *Virgin Soil,* practical man and romantic idealist respectively.

DECEMBER 14

•Count Magnis: Count Magnis Ullersdorf, mentioned in vol. I (on July 4, 1877) as having contributed 5,000 marks toward paying off the deficit on the 1876 festival. • Prince Liechtenstein: Rudolph Liechtenstein (born 1838), a friend since Wagner met him in Vienna in 1861, later head chamberlain (*Oberhofmeister*) at the Austrian Imperial Court. • "Oh, sink down . . ." (*"O sink hernieder"*): from the love duet in *Tristan und Isolde,* Act II.

DECEMBER 15

•Laertes: Odysseus's father. • *Odysseus, the God of Spring* (*Odysseus als Frühlingsgott*): not identified. • A sigh of relief: a reference to the revolt that broke out in Brussels after the performance of Auber's *La Muette de Portici* on August 25, 1830. • The Grand Duchess of Baden: Luise, daughter of Emperor Wilhelm I and wife of Grand Duke Friedrich of Baden from 1856; Wagner had once had high hopes of gaining the patronage of the grand duke and his wife, particularly in connection with staging *Tristan und Isolde* in 1859. • The "Rheingold": presumably a Rhine wine; Herr Albert was a hotelier from Mannheim, later in charge of catering at the Bayreuth festival. • The Mrazécks: Franz and Anna Mrazéck, Wagner's servants in Vienna and Munich, 1863–67.

DECEMBER 16

•A. Müller's house: Wagner stayed at the house of Alexander Müller (1808–63) in Zurich from July to September 1849 following his flight from Dresden; Müller was a music teacher and choral conductor.

DECEMBER 17

• *Actors and Singers* (*Über Schauspieler und Sänger*): first published by Fritzsch in 1872 and reprinted in vol. 9 of the collected writings. • Karpeles: a music teacher in Bayreuth. • Börne: Ludwig Börne (1786–1837), German political writer. • His smokers' gatherings: the *Tabak-Kollegium,* which King Friedrich Wilhelm I of Prussia held almost daily in his palaces. • His wife already dead and buried: Maria Barbara, Johann Sebastian Bach's first wife, died in 1720 while he was on a visit to Karlsbad. • Rancé: Dominique Armand Jean le Bouthillier de Rancé (1626–1700), a worldly priest until he was thirty-four, founded the very strict Trappist order in 1660, after a sudden change in his life. • The *complete Passion:* Bach's *Saint Matthew Passion.* • The Richter episodes: Hans Richter first joined Wagner at Tribschen in October 1866 to help with the copying of *Die Meistersinger,* and he soon was like a member of the family.

DECEMBER 19
•The idea of the tablet: Wagner had the names of all the participants in the *Ring* of 1876 inscribed on a tablet, which can still be seen in the foyer of the festival theater. • Frl. Steinbach: possibly S. Steinbach, then a singer in Prague. • *"Träume"* ("Dreams"): one of the *Wesendonck Lieder.* • *Alexa:* presumably the heroine of the serial in the *Bayreuther Tagblatt.*

DECEMBER 20
•Bonfantini: printer in Basel, Switzerland, to whom the first private printing of Wagner's *Mein Leben* was entrusted in 1870. • Weinlig: Theodor Weinlig (1780–1842): Wagner's composition teacher in Leipzig.

DECEMBER 21
•"Oh, were I but rid . . .": from Goethe's *Zahme Xenien* II, beginning *"Auf ewig hab ich sie vertrieben"* ("I have banished them forever").

DECEMBER 22
•The Robber and the Little Doll: nicknames for the two violinists who played for the children's dancing lessons (see December 24, 1878).

DECEMBER 23
•Proch: Heinrich Proch (1809–78), conductor in Vienna, died on December 19. • The *Pommerania:* this German mail boat collided with a barque, the *Moel Eilian,* ten miles off Dover on November 25, 1878, and sank, with the loss of forty-eight lives. • *Grosser Kurfürst:* see note for June 3, 1878. • The overture in celebration of victory: the German writer E. T. A. Hoffmann (1776–1822) was also a composer; in 1814, under the pseudonym Arnulph Vollweiler, he wrote a piano fantasy entitled *"Deutschlands Triumph in der Schlacht bei Leipzig"* ("Germany's Triumph at the Battle of Leipzig").

DECEMBER 24
•His niece Johanna: Johanna Jachmann-Wagner (1826–94): adopted by Wagner's brother Albert after her mother became Albert's wife in 1828; was the first Elisabeth in *Tannhäuser,* 1845, and sang in Beethoven's Ninth Symphony at the Bayreuth foundation-laying ceremony and also in the 1876 *Ring* (First Norn, Valkyrie). • A Serapion Pact: a reference to E. T. A. Hoffmann's book *Die Serapionsbrüder.*

DECEMBER 25
•Fugal Overture: Beethoven's Overture *"Zur Weihe des Hauses,"* Opus 124; it was written in 1822 for the opening of the Josefstädter Theater, which is situated in the Piaristen Gasse, near the city center of Vienna. • Fr.'s magic violin: presumably a reference to Friedhold Fleischhauer, the concertmaster of the Meiningen orchestra.

DECEMBER 26
•Schäffer: correctly, Hermann Scheffer, commanding officer of the Bayreuth garrison.

DECEMBER 27
•Förster: August Förster (1828–89), director of the Stadttheater in Leipzig, 1857–82. • *"Lass mich sterben":* Tristan to Isolde in Act II, Scene 2. • Banquo's descendants: revealed to Macbeth by the witches in Shakespeare's *Macbeth,* Act IV, Scene 1.

DECEMBER 28
•Pohl about his wife: Wagner's friend Richard Pohl (1826–96), a writer on music, wrote a book about his wife, Johanna, after her death in 1870. • Our Nibelungen copyist: Franz Fischer (1849–1918), a member of the Nibelungen Kanzlei during the 1876 festival and conductor at Mannheim from 1877.

NOTES
•*Tuesday the 24th* MacMahon: Maurice, Marquis de MacMahon (1808–93), French field marshal and president of the French Republic, 1873–79. • *Wednesday the 25th*

Miss Murchison: the governess. • *Friday the 27th* Ludwig Devrient (1784–1832): the eldest of the famous family of actors; in his essay *Actors and Singers* Wagner relates that after a performance of Shakespeare's *King Lear* in Berlin, in which Ludwig Devrient played the title role, the audience was so moved that it remained seated in silence—the highest form of tribute.

DECEMBER 29

•Paraphrase of Mephisto's words: in Goethe's *Faust,* Part One (Faust's study); the words (in Bayard Taylor's translation) are: "*He* [God] dwells in splendor single and eternal, / But *us* he thrusts in darkness, out of sight, / And *you* he dowers with Day and Night." • The geologist Murchison: Roderick Impey Murchison (1792–1871), who established the Silurian system; a biography by A. Geikie was published in 1875. • Calderón's *El verdadero dios Pan* (*The True God Pan*).

DECEMBER 31

•His "introduction": to Hans von Wolzogen's essay "On the Decay and Rehabilitation of the German Language," *Bayreuther Blätter,* February and November 1879; the introduction is reprinted in the collected writings, vol. 10. • Casting lead: dropping molten lead into cold water and "interpreting" the form it assumes, a favorite Christmas pastime of Cosima's children.

1879

JANUARY 1

•The "octave" of the concert: i.e., a week since it took place. • That time in Zurich: from July 21 to August 16, 1858, Hans and Cosima von Bülow were again in the Asyl in Zurich, while Wagner was breaking up his home and parting from his wife Minna; during the same period his final breach with Karl Ritter occurred.

JANUARY 2

•Dionysius the Younger: the tyrant of Syracuse in the fourth century B.C. was the nephew of Dion of Syracuse, of whom Plutarch wrote a biography; Dion summoned Plato to Syracuse. • "*Wirkte dies der heilige Tag*" ("Is this the effect of the holy day?"): Gurnemanz in *Parsifal,* III, bars 148 ff. • Dupont: Pierre Dupont (1821–70), singer and song writer. • Droysen: Johann Gustav Droysen (1808–84), German historian whose *Geschichte des Hellenismus* appeared 1836–43 in 2 vols.

JANUARY 5

•Agesilaus's reply: in Plutarch's biography, chap. 23, the words are actually, "If everyone were just, one would have no need of courage."

JANUARY 8

•Herr Müller: Hermann Müller, Wilhelmine Schröder-Devrient's lover, who went to Switzerland after the Dresden uprising in 1849; he met Wagner and Cosima in Lucerne on April 8, 1870 (see that date in vol. I). • His "Stabat Mater": "*Stabat Mater de Pergolèse,*" article written for the *Gazette Musicale* in 1840, reprinted in the appendix to vol. 12 of the collected writings. • Hans's birthday: Hans von Bülow was born January 8, 1830; see also entry and note for February 27, 1881. • My father's visit: to Tribschen, October 9–10, 1867, to discuss Wagner's relationship with Cosima; Wagner noted in his *Annalen,* "Liszt's visit: feared, but pleasant." • E[lisabeth] Nietzsche (1846–1935): married Dr. Bernhard Förster in 1885; she had been a welcome guest at Tribschen (see vol. I).

JANUARY 9

•Sudden departure for Paris: on January 15, 1858, Wagner left the Asyl, to get away from Minna and the Wesendoncks for a while, as he relates in *Mein Leben;* he went to Paris, where he saw a lot of Cosima's sister, Blandine, and her husband, Emile Ollivier, and also visited Berlioz; he returned to Zurich on February 6.

JANUARY 11

•"But I will": Goethe's *Faust,* Part One (scene in Faust's study); with these words Faust expresses his desire to conclude a pact with Mephistopheles. • "A human being must acknowledge necessity": a reversal of Lessing's sentence in *Nathan der Weise,* Act I, Scene 3, which runs: *"Kein Mensch muss müssen"* ("No human being is bound by necessity").

JANUARY 12

•"Wherever Tristan goes . . ." (*"Wohin nun Tristan scheidet, willst du, Isold', ihm folgen?"*): *Tristan und Isolde,* Act II, Scene 3. • *Médée:* opera by Cherubini, 1797. • His article "On the Overture" (*"Über die Ouvertüre"*): written for the *Gazette Musicale,* 1841, and reprinted in vol. 1 of the collected writings. • *The Water Carrier (Les Deux Journées), Les Abencérrages, Anacréon:* operas by Cherubini. • *La Vestale:* opera by Spontini, 1807.

JANUARY 13

•*"Wahnlos hold bewusste Wunsch"*: *Tristan und Isolde,* Act II, Scene 2. • Rietz: Julius Rietz (1812–77), conductor in Leipzig and Dresden. • His father is a rabbi: Dr. Levi was chief rabbi in Giessen, Germany.

JANUARY 14

•*"Er starb . . ."* ("He died, a man as all are"): *Parsifal,* III, bars 416 ff.

JANUARY 16

•The (Zurich) stories of G[ottfried] Keller: *Züricher Novellen,* a collection of stories published in 1876; the Swiss writer Gottfried Keller (1819–90) was a friend of Wagner's in the Zurich years. • The last story: "Ursula."

JANUARY 17

•*"Nicht so"*: correctly, *"Nicht doch"*; *Parsifal,* III, bars 459–540. • His quarrelsomeness: the Swiss religious reformer Huldreich (or Ulrich) Zwingli (1484–1531) believed in employing violent methods and took an active part in the war between Zurich and the Swiss Catholic cantons; he was killed in the Battle of Kappel.

JANUARY 18

•*Saint Paul:* oratorio by Felix Mendelssohn-Bartholdy, 1836.

JANUARY 19

•Siegfried and the Norns: there is, of course, no such scene in the *Ring;* presumably Cosima meant to write "the Rhinemaidens" (*Götterdämmerung,* Act III, Scene 1).

JANUARY 20

•Mendelssohn's *Antigone:* incidental music for Sophocles's drama, 1841. • Our opera house here: the eighteenth-century Markgräfliches Opernhaus in Bayreuth. • Patti: Adelina Patti (1843–1919), celebrated Italian-Spanish soprano. • Nicolini: Ernest Nicolini (1834–98), French tenor, Patti's usual partner (and later husband); he was London's first Lohengrin.

JANUARY 21

•*Die Wibelungen:* a sketch in essay form of Wagner's proposed drama about Frederick Barbarossa, 1848; reprinted in vol. 2 of the collected writings.

JANUARY 22

•A nice letter to him from the King: not in the published correspondence, presumably lost. • *"Augentrost"*: literally, "solace to the eyes"; the word is found in German songs of the fourteenth century.

JANUARY 23

•"The Nibelung Myth": *"Der Nibelungen-Mythus als Entwurf zu einem Drama,"* 1848, the first prose sketch of the drama that developed into *Der Ring des Nibelungen:*

both it and *Siegfried's Tod* are in vol. 2 of the collected writings. • The Valkyries' scene: in *Siegfried's Tod* Brünnhilde on her rock is visited by eight Valkyries—not just one (Waltraute), as in *Götterdämmerung;* the Valkyries' theme employed in *Die Walküre* is the oldest in the entire *Ring,* dating back to 1850.

JANUARY 24
•Dr. Jenkins: Newell Sill Jenkins, American dentist practicing in Dresden.

JANUARY 25
•Comparison with the golden bucket: "Passing gold buckets to each other, how heavenly powers ascend, descend!"; Louis MacNeice's translation of the lines from Faust's opening soliloquy in Goethe's *Faust,* Part One.

JANUARY 26
•*"Dass heute noch . . ."* ("That today he will greet me as king"): *Parsifal,* III, bars 566 ff.

JANUARY 27
•"Plan for a German National Theater", *"Entwurf zur Organisation eines deutschen Nationaltheaters für das Königreich Sachsen"*): a detailed plan drawn up by Wagner in 1849 for the reform of the theater in Saxony, reprinted in vol. 2 of the collected writings; it contains several ideas he later attempted to put into practice in Munich and Bayreuth, but was of course rejected in Dresden.

JANUARY 28
•The new general: presumably the new commander of the Bayreuth garrison. • Like Walther von Stolzing: in Act III, Scene 1, of *Die Meistersinger,* Walther sees Eva, his beloved, standing in Sachs's workroom, and they gaze at each other, speechless.

JANUARY 30
•*Rienzi* in London: the first performance (sung in English) was at Her Majesty's Theater on January 27.

JANUARY 31
•Minna in Brestenberg: where she went to take a cure in the summer of 1858; Wagner visited her weekly, accompanied sometimes by the sixteen-year-old Karl Tausig, who was staying with him in Zurich. • Introduction to the 3rd and 4th volumes: dealing with his "revolutionary" works (*Art and Revolution, The Artwork of the Future, Opera and Drama*). • Grévy: Jules Grévy (1807–91), French politician, elected third president of France in 1879. • *Leitmotive:* a term invented by F. W. Jähns to describe musical figures used repeatedly (particularly by Weber) in association with a figure or a dramatic idea in opera; Wagner, who greatly developed this technique, usually objected to the use of the word "*Leitmotive*" in connection with his own work, so here he is perhaps employing it ironically. • *"Salve Regina":* in the nuns' chorus of *Das Liebesverbot,* Act I, Scene 2, Wagner makes use of the "*Dresdner Amen,*" which he used again in *Tannhäuser.*

FEBRUARY 1
•"Leave me the veil . . ." ("*Lasst den Schleier mir, ich bitte*"): in the finale of Act II of Marschner's *Der Templer und die Jüdin.* • "Nothing is so dear to me . . .": lines, possibly from a musical play, that Wagner quoted to Cosima, in a slightly different form, on November 27, 1870 (see vol. I). • "But nothing compared with their contentment": a quotation from Goethe's novel *Elective Affinities* (*Die Wahlverwandschaften*), which Wagner and Cosima once came upon simultaneously while separated, according to her account on March 14, 1873 (see vol. I). • *Minna von Barnhelm:* Lessing's comedy, over which Cosima wept on March 14, 1869 (see vol. I). • Two legends by Keller: from *Sieben Legenden* by Gottfried Keller, "*Das Tanzlegendchen*" and "*Die Jungfrau und die Nonne.*"

FEBRUARY 2

•His *Braunes Buch* (*Brown Book*): a leather-bound notebook given to Wagner by Cosima in 1865 so that he could write down his replies to her letters during a period in which they were forbidden to correspond; Wagner later used it for notes, sketches, and annals; first published in full in 1975; here Cosima is presumably referring to the sketch of a poem to King Ludwig for his birthday in 1873, which refers to the "lap of Fate" ("*Schicksalsschoos*"). • "Laughing death" ("*Lachender Tod*"): the final words of *Siegfried.*

FEBRUARY 3

•The entry of the kettledrum: *Parsifal,* III, bars 623 ff.; however, Wagner's remark refers to the orchestral sketch, for in the full orchestral score he omits the kettledrum and substitutes cello and double bass. • The anointment of Parsifal by Gurnemanz: Cosima wrote "by Titurel," an obvious slip, no doubt arising from Parsifal's reference to Gurnemanz as "Titurel's companion" ("*Titurel's Genoss*"). • A Brahms symphony: No. 2.

FEBRUARY 5–15

•*Il Barbiere:* Rossini's *Il Barbiere di Siviglia;* the quotation comes from the sextet in the finale of Act I, "*Mi par d'esser colla testa in un orrida fucina.*" • Gogol's *Hetman:* a story about a landowner in the collection *Mirgorod* (1835).

FEBRUARY 16

•How do we regard Wolfram von Eschenbach?: this German poet flourished around 1200, i.e., 600 years before Wagner's own time.

FEBRUARY 17

•"*Der liess sie so gedeihen*" ("that has made them grow thus"): Gurnemanz in *Parsifal,* III, bars 692 ff. • "The three lansquenets": probably a joking reference to Dumas's *The Three Musketeers*—a lansquenet is a mercenary soldier and also the name of a card game (German: *Landsknecht*).

FEBRUARY 18

•A transition: *Parsifal,* III, bars 702–5.

FEBRUARY 19

•*Theologia Germanica:* or *Theologia Deutsch* (*German Theology*), mystical text written c. 1400 by a priest ("*Der Frankfurter*"); Luther edited it in 1516.

FEBRUARY 20

•Letter to R. from the King: not in the published correspondence, presumably lost.

FEBRUARY 26

•Frau Jäger: Aurelia, née Wilczek, a singer and singing teacher, married to the tenor Ferdinand Jäger. • A[nton] Rubinstein (1829–94), Russian composer; the episode with von Hülsen, director of the Berlin opera, is not known, but Rubinstein would have been in contact with him in connection with the Berlin production of his operas *Die Maccabäer* in 1875 and *Nero* in 1880. • The "swan": one of Cosima's dresses.

FEBRUARY 27

•Marr: Wilhelm Marr, author of *Der Sieg des Judentums über das Germanentum* (*The Victory of Judaism over Germanic Civilization*), 1879, and other anti-Semitic writings. • Prof. Zöllner: Friedrich Zöllner (1834–82), professor of astrophysics at Leipzig, much interested in spiritualism.

FEBRUARY 28

•Serov: Alexander Serov (1820–71), Russian composer and writer and Wagner's champion in Russia; he visited Wagner and Cosima at Tribschen not long before his death (see vol. I). • Grand Duchess Helene: Helene Pavlovna (1807–73), daughter of Prince Paul of Württemberg.

MARCH 1

•*"Du weinest . . ."* ("Thou weepest—see, the meadow smiles"): *Parsifal*, III, bars 783 ff. • Songs by R. Franz: Robert Franz (1815–92), texts by Heinrich Heine. • *"Sei mir gegrüsst"*: setting of a poem by Friedrich Rückert, 1822. • Raimund: Ferdinand Raimund (1790–1836), actor and author of plays in the Viennese *Volkstheater* tradition.

MARCH 2

•"Please do not be angry . . .": Wagner's actual words are *"Sei mir nicht mehr böse, sei mir wieder gut."* • Entrance of the Flying Dutchman: arrival of the phantom ship and the Dutchman's aria *"Die Frist ist um"* ("The term is past"), in Act I of *Der Fliegende Holländer*.

MARCH 5

•Hans's flight to him: Hans von Bülow's parents wished him to adopt law, not music, as a career; in October 1850 the twenty-year-old Hans appealed to Wagner; Karl Ritter took Wagner's reply, advising him to stick to his ideals, to Hans at his father's home near St. Gallen, Switzerland; Hans left immediately with Karl, and the two penniless young men arrived at Wagner's home in Zurich two days later, on October 7, having walked all the way; Wagner got Hans a job at the Zurich theater, where he had already installed Karl.

MARCH 6

•Villa d'Angri: a house in Naples that Wagner was contemplating renting. • Daudet: Alphonse Daudet (1840–97), French writer; by this time the first of his Tartarin stories had appeared, as well as the work some consider his masterpiece, *Fromont jeune et Risler aîné* (1874).

MARCH 7

•The bells: accompanying the transformation scene, *Parsifal,* Act III; written throughout in common time, except for two bars in $\frac{6}{4}$ time at the start.

MARCH 11

• *"Die Wacht am Rhein"*: it is unclear whether Cosima is referring to the song of that name, which achieved great popularity during the Franco-Prussian War, or to the painting by the German artist Lorenz Clasen (1812–99). • Hans's *Nirwana*: symphonic poem, Opus 20, by Hans von Bülow, Leipzig, 1866.

MARCH 13

•A Piccolomini banquet: a reference to the banquet scene in Act IV of Schiller's drama *Die Piccolomini* (second part of the *Wallenstein* trilogy).

MARCH 14

•"Poets alone . . .": Wagner slightly misquotes Goethe's verse, "*Wer den Dichter will verstehen muss in Dichters Lande gehen,*" in *Noten und Abhandlungen zu besserem Verständnis des Westöstlichen Diwans* (*Notes Leading to a Better Understanding of The West-Eastern Divan*), 1819.

MARCH 16

•Titurel is carried in: *Parsifal*, III, transformation to Scene 2, bars 856 ff.

MARCH 18

•"Stirbt der Fuchs . . ." Goethe's poem is translated by E. A. Bowring under the title "When the Fox Dies, His Skin Counts," and it begins: "We young people in the shade / Sat one sultry day; / Cupid came, and 'Dies the Fox' / With us sought to play." Bowring appends to his translation a note explaining that the game "Dies the Fox" is known in England as "Jack's Alight."

MARCH 20

•*Die Schweizerfamilie* (*The Swiss Family*): opera, 1809, by Joseph Weigl (1766–1846). • A toast to Boni: Blandine's sixteenth birthday. • The meeting in Reichenhall: see note for June 17, 1878. • The Szegedin catastrophe: this old town in

Hungary was almost completely destroyed by floods. • The "elegy": the passage
"Du weinest, sieh! es lacht die Aue"; Parsifal, III, bars 783 ff.

MARCH 21

•The Battle of Torgau: presumably the dream concerned a magic-lantern slide
depicting the battle (in which Frederick the Great defeated the Austrians in 1760),
rather than the battle itself! • Bach's birthday: March 21, 1685.

MARCH 22

•The Sistine Chapel: in the Vatican, renowned for its Michelangelo frescoes. •
Doepler: Carl Emil Doepler (1824–1905) designed the costumes for the 1876
Ring production. • The King of the Zulus: Cetewayo; see note for September 24,
1879. • Steinbach: Emil Steinbach (1849–1919), conductor in Mainz. • Herr
Lindau: Paul Lindau, see note for January 18, 1878.

MARCH 23

•"For all guilt . . ." (*"Denn alle Schuld rächt sich auf Erden"*): concluding line of the
Harpist's song in Goethe's novel *Wilhelm Meister's Lehrjahre.*

MARCH 24

•*"Pulsator":* according to information kindly supplied by Mr. John H. Steinway,
Senior Vice President of Steinway and Sons, New York, the "pulsator" was an
invention made in 1878 by C. F. Theodor Steinway; it consisted of extra sustaining
bars over the pianoforte's sounding board, for the dual purpose of preventing the
sounding board from warping, and increasing the duration and strength of the
sound; Mr. Steinway remarks: "All that extra weight did not improve the vibrations,
but rather hindered them, so we abandoned the whole idea." • Wallace: William
Vincent Wallace (1813–65), Irish-born composer whose opera *Maritana* (1845) is
still occasionally revived; in his youth he spent several months in New Zealand, and
Berlioz gives an account in the second epilogue of his book *Les Soirées de l'orchestre*
(*Evenings with the Orchestra*) of Wallace's adventures among the "savages" there, as
told him by Wallace himself. • Roon: Count Albrecht von Roon (1803–79), former
Prussian minister of war.

MARCH 26

•Phocion: Athenian general of the fourth century B.C. who attempted to modify his
country's aggressive policies. • *Peabody:* George Peabody (1795–1869), American
merchant and philanthropist, founded and endowed the Peabody Institutes in
Baltimore, Md., and Peabody, Mass., and the Peabody Museums at Yale and
Harvard Universities.

MARCH 27

•He writes to the King: about *Parsifal* and travel plans. • Carlyle: Thomas Carlyle
(1795–1881), one of Wagner's favorite British authors. • Carlyle's essay on
Cagliostro: *Fraser's Magazine,* July-August 1833, reprinted in *Critical and Miscellaneous Essays.*

MARCH 28

•[*German*] *Art and* [*German*] *Politics* (*Deutsche Kunst und deutsche Politik*): a series of
articles written by Wagner in 1867 and published as a book in 1868, reprinted in
vol. 8 of the collected writings. • Dr. Schemann's article: "The Stage Dedication
Festival Play *Parsifal,*" *Bayreuther Blätter,* March 1879.

APRIL 2

•His next article: "*Wollen wir hoffen?*" ("Shall We Hope?"). • *La dame blanche:* in
Boieldieu's opera a girl named Anna appears as a phantom nurse (*Pflegerin*);
Wagner turns this word into *Fegerin* (female sweeper) for the purposes of his joke.

APRIL 3

•Carlyle's "Voltaire": *Foreign Review,* April 1829, reprinted in *Critical and Miscellaneous Essays.* • The French Restoration: the reinstatement of the Bourbon monarchy in 1814. • *Nuppler:* not a known German word, but its meaning can perhaps be inferred!

APRIL 4

•The A-flat major from *Tristan:* the *Liebestod* motive. • Ännchen's aria: Act II, Scene 1, of Weber's *Der Freischütz;* the words cited by Wagner should correctly be *"Blickchen hin und Blick herüber."* • Kummer: Friedrich August Kummer (1797–1879), oboist and cellist in the Dresden Court orchestra. • Julie Zucker: Julie Zucker-Haase (1800–26), soubrette at the Dresden Court theater.

APRIL 5

•Charlotte v. Kalb (1761–1843): German writer, a friend of Schiller; a new edition of her memoirs, entitled *Charlotte,* was published in 1879. • *Der Vampyr:* opera by Marschner, 1828.

APRIL 6

•*Nathan der Weise (Nathan the Wise):* Lessing's play about religious tolerance. • Shepherd's scene: Shakespeare's *The Winter's Tale,* Act III, Scene 3.

APRIL 8

•Apel: Theodor Apel (1811–67), writer and friend of Wagner's during their youth.

APRIL 9

•Carlyle's "Diderot": *Foreign Quarterly Review,* April 1833, reprinted in *Critical and Miscellaneous Essays.* • Grote: George Grote (1794–1871), English politician and historian, author of the 8-vol. *History of Greece,* 1845–56; Grote actually gave up banking in 1843 to devote himself to his writing.

APRIL 12

•R. replies by telegram: the poem is printed in vol. 3 of the Ludwig-Wagner correspondence; the King's words accompanying the flowers have not been preserved.

APRIL 13

•Struensee: Count Johann Friedrich von Struensee (1737–72), physician to King Christian VII of Denmark; accused of having an affair with Queen Caroline Matilda.

APRIL 14

•Auber's *Lestocq:* opera, 1834.

APRIL 16

•Carlyle's "Novalis": an essay on the German poet and philosopher, *Foreign Review,* July 1829, reprinted in *Critical and Miscellaneous Essays.* • Renunciation is not the aim: "The great doctrine of *Entsagen,* of 'Renunciation,' by which alone, as a wise man . . . has observed, can the real experience of life be properly said to begin" (Carlyle's "Novalis").

APRIL 17

•B-flat Major Fugue: for string quartet, Beethoven's Opus 133. • He dedicated that to Countess Erdödy: Beethoven in fact dedicated the Sonata in A Major, Opus 101, to Baroness Dorothea Ertmann; it was his Opus 102 (sonatas for cello and piano) that he dedicated to Countess Erdödy.

APRIL 18

•Klopstock: Friedrich Gottlieb Klopstock (1724–1803), German poet.

APRIL 19

•His sketch for a New Year farce: entitled merely *"Ein Lustspiel in 1 Akt"* ("A Comedy in 1 Act"), it is written down in Wagner's *Braunes Buch,* dated September 1, 1868. • My father's *Tasso:* a symphonic poem, 1849.

APRIL 20

•The May Festival: celebration of Wagner's birthday (May 22). • *Rameau's Nephew (Le Neveau de Rameau):* by Denis Diderot (1713–84), translated into German by Goethe in 1805.

April 21
•The study of Jean Paul: "J. P. F. Richter" by Thomas Carlyle, *Edinburgh Review*, June 1827, reprinted in *Critical and Miscellaneous Essays*.

April 22
•Carlyle (on W. Scott): "Sir Walter Scott," *London and Westminster Review*, January 1838, reprinted in *Critical and Miscellaneous Essays*.

April 24
•Essay on Dr. Francia: *Foreign Quarterly Review*, July 1843, reprinted in *Critical and Miscellaneous Essays*.

April 26
•The completion of *Parsifal:* the orchestral sketch of Act III bears the date April 26, 1879.

April 27
•Malwida's book: *Stimmungsbilder (Impressions),* by Malwida von Meysenbug, 1879.

April 28
•The King of Saxony: Albert (1828–1902), who succeeded his father, Johann, in 1873. • Eva in Paradise: a quotation from Walther's "Prize Song" in *Die Meistersinger,* Act III. • Some Carlyle . . . about the French Revolution," *London and Westminster Review,* September 1837, reprinted in *Critical and Miscellaneous Essays*.

April 29
•The middle part in the *Faust* Overture: Wagner considerably extended the middle section (second subject) when he revised his overture (written 1840) in 1855. • "Triviality run distracted": from Carlyle's essay "Mirabeau," *London and Westminster Review,* January 1837, reprinted in *Critical and Miscellaneous Essays*.

May 1
•A Wolz. manuscript for America: "The Work and Mission of My Life," *North American Review,* August 1879; published in German under the title *"Das Werk und die Aufgabe meines Lebens"* in *Mehr Licht,* Berlin, August-September 1879, after which Wagner forbade further publication of it. • My father's *Hamlet:* symphonic poem, 1858. • Carlyle's "Playwrights": "German Playwrights," *Foreign Review,* January 1829, reprinted in *Critical and Miscellaneous Essays*.

May 2
•His work for the *Bayr. Bl.: "Über das Dichten und Komponieren"* ("On Poetry and Composition"), *B. B.,* July 1879. • Caspar sang: for the production of Weber's *Der Freischütz* in Paris in 1841, Berlioz supplied sung recitatives to replace the original spoken dialogue. • Carlyle's essay on Burns: *Edinburgh Review,* December 1828, reprinted in *Critical and Miscellaneous Essays*.

May 3
•Their first meeting: though Wagner sent his telegram on May 3 and referred to this date in his rhymed greeting, it was in fact on May 4, 1864, that King Ludwig received him for the first time; May 3 was the date of Wagner's arrival in Munich at the king's summons.

May 4
•Father Felix: presumably Felix Korum (1840–1921), later bishop of Trier.

May 5
•A book about Helene Dönniges and Lassalle: Helene von Dönniges, née Ritter (1845–1911), published in 1879 *Meine Beziehungen zu Ferdinand Lassalle (My Relations with F. L.),* an account of her love affair with the leader of the German socialists, culminating in his death in a duel in 1864.

May 6
•Letters . . . from him to me: Wagner's daughter Eva (Chamberlain) revealed in a written statement dated November 9, 1934, that she had burned all her father's

May 1879

letters to her mother shortly after the death (on August 4, 1930) of her brother, Siegfried, at his express wish. • A letter arrived from the King: not in the published correspondence, presumably lost. • Schön: Friedrich Schön (born 1850), a factory owner in Worms, is regarded as the founder of the Bayreuth Festival Scholarship Fund (*Stipendienstiftung*), established in May 1882; he contributed 10,000 marks to it; in a letter to Daniela dated September 12, 1879, Cosima describes Schön as a young man with blue eyes "full of candor" and says his factory employs 1,100 workers. • "Of all else . . ." ("*Il resto nol dico*"): from Figaro's aria "*Aprite un po'* " in Act IV of Mozart's *Le Nozze di Figaro*.

MAY 7

•Rohde: Erwin Rohde (1845–98), philologist and friend of Nietzsche, a frequent guest at Bayreuth until 1876. • "Midas": *Past and Present,* bk. I, chap. 1, 1843.

MAY 9

•Wagner Concerts in London: at the Saint James's Hall, conducted by Hans Richter; see also July 17, 1879, and note. • "*Einsam in trüben Tagen*"*:* Elsa in *Lohengrin,* Act I, Scene 2.

MAY 10

•His sister: Klara Wolfram, who lived in Chemnitz. • Cromwell had already embarked for America: the incident is reputed to have occurred in 1638 on an emigration ship in the Thames; however, it is of doubtful authenticity. • Reminiscences of Frankfurt: Wagner conducted *Lohengrin* there on September 12, 1862; Cosima was not present. • Report of the General Staff: on the Franco-Prussian War. • Princess Metternich: Pauline (1836–1919), wife of the Austrian ambassador in Paris, largely instrumental in persuading Napoleon III to command the performance of *Tannhäuser* in Paris in 1861. • Wilhelm I for Mimi: Emperor Wilhelm I, who attended the Bayreuth festival in 1876 (see August 7, 1876, in vol. I), commanded the first performance of *Tristan und Isolde* in Berlin on March 20, 1876, and no doubt Frau von Schleinitz (Mimi) played a part in that decision.

MAY 13

•He finishes his article: "Shall We Hope?" • Seignobos: Charles Seignobos (1854–1942), French historian, commissioned by the French government to study teaching methods in German universities, 1877–79. • An unexpected meeting: Cosima had invited Fricke to Bayreuth to help with the approaching birthday festivities, and Wagner was not supposed to know he was there. • Rosalie as *La Muette:* Wagner's sister Rosalie played the part of the dumb girl in Auber's *La Muette de Portici* in Leipzig in 1829. • A ballet for the 2nd act of *Tannhäuser:* for the Paris production in 1861; it was Wagner's insistence on putting the—for French tastes obligatory—ballet into the first act (Venusberg music) that was the chief cause of its disastrous reception.

MAY 14

•Carlyle's history of the Abbey of St. Edmundsbury: *Past and Present,* bk. II, "The Ancient Monk," 1843; King Henry II of England is portrayed briefly in it, in connection with the election of Abbot Samson (chap. IX).

MAY 15

•Herr Wiener in Prague: not identified. • Dr. Adler: Guido Adler (1855–1941), Austrian musicologist. • Herr Marsano: son of the Austrian poet Wilhelm von Marsano. • "A defect of telescopes": in chap. IX of Carlyle's "The Ancient Monk": "The defect . . . is less a defect of telescopes than of some eyesight. Those superstitious blockheads of the Twelfth Century had no telescopes, but they still had an eye."

MAY 16

•A manuscript of his: a music shop in Würzburg (C. Roeser) advertised in the

Musikalisches Wochenblatt of May 16, 1879, "an unquestionably genuine manuscript by Richard Wagner, dated March 1, 1833"; this consisted of the 36-p. score of the uncompleted opera *Die Hochzeit (The Wedding)*; Wagner sued to recover the manuscript but was unsuccessful (see May 18 and July 20, 1879, and February 16, 1881).

MAY 17

•Fürstenau: Moritz Fürstenau (1824–89), composer in Dresden through whom Wagner eventually recovered the letters he had written from Switzerland to Theodor Uhlig. • Kahnt's periodical: Christian Friedrich Kahnt (1823–97), editor of the *Neue Zeitschrift für Musik* from 1868. • Offenbach's *Orpheus: Orphée aux enfers (Orpheus in the Underworld)*, comic opera first produced in Paris in 1859.

MAY 18

•Religion, the Pope, the London hatter: Carlyle's *Past and Present,* bk. III, chap. 1. • The Würzburg publisher: Roeser; see note for May 16, 1879. • Giulia: presumably meaning Giulietta Guicciardi, once believed to have been Beethoven's "immortal beloved." • Frau Tichatschek: Pauline, second wife of the tenor Joseph Tichatschek, Wagner's Rienzi and Tannhäuser in Dresden. • His Wotan: Friedrich (Fritz) Plank (1848–1900) sang Wotan in Mannheim; he sang at Bayreuth from 1884 on (Klingsor, Kurwenal, Sachs, Pogner).

MAY 19

•Semper's death: Gottfried Semper died on May 15. • Herr v. Birk: not identified. • Novalis's remark: " 'Bending before men,' says Novalis, 'is a reverence done to this Revelation in the Flesh. We touch Heaven when we lay our hand on a human Body' " (from chap. 16 of Carlyle's "The Ancient Monk").

MAY 20

•Regarding overproduction: Carlyle's *Past and Present,* bk. III, chap. 7.

MAY 21

•Donner: the Nordic thunder god; it is he who in *Das Rheingold* prepares the rainbow bridge by which the gods enter Valhalla. • Frau v. Wöhrmann: Baroness Emma Wöhrmann, Berlin, a friend of Marie von Schleinitz.

MAY 22

•The Pilgrim: a character (played by one of the children) in the little birthday play written by the Wolzogen family; other characters in it (mentioned later) are Webia and Michel. • My picture: Lenbach's new portrait of Cosima. • The Bayreuth colony: the friends who had settled in Bayreuth (the Wolzogens, the Jägers, Rubinstein). • *"An den Geliebten"*: possibly the fifth (*"An den fernen Geliebten"*) of Beethoven's songs, Opus 75. • *"Wer ein holdes Weib errungen"* ("who has won a noble wife"): Beethoven's *Fidelio,* Act II finale. • Our pantomime: choreographed by Fricke, this depicted a schoolroom in which, after the teacher (played by Fricke) has left, the children throw books around and dance a tarantella; the teacher returns and threatens the children, but Columbine (played by Daniela) enters and persuades him to join in the dance; the music was provided by Rubinstein at the piano. • "Ah, there is happiness . . ." (*"Es gibt ein Glück, das ohne Reu"*): Elsa in *Lohengrin,* Act II, Scene 2.

MAY 25

•Gedon: Lorenz Gedon (1843–83), architect and sculptor in Munich.

MAY 26

•Webia's and Michel's gifts: see note for May 22, 1879.

MAY 27

•Expressed this idea somewhere: in *The Artwork of the Future* melody and rhythm are described as the "riverbanks" of music; in *Beethoven* Wagner describes melody as the "principal form" of music. • Section on Cromwell: lecture VI ("The Hero as King") in Carlyle's *Heroes and Hero-Worship,* 1841, translated into German 1853.

May 29

•Doepler, whom he did not mention: in his "Retrospect of the Stage Festivals of 1876," presumably because he had not been satisfied with Doepler's costumes for the *Ring*.

May 30

•*History of the* [French] *Revolution:* by Thomas Carlyle, 1837. • Riedelsberg: home of the Feustels.

May 31

•Geier: Wilhelm Geier, sculptor in Bayreuth. • Carlyle's first lecture: in *Heroes and Hero-Worship,* "The Hero as Divinity: Odin, Paganism, Scandinavian Mythology."

June 1

•*"Sei standhaft"* ("Be steadfast"): the Three Boys to Tamino in Mozart's *Die Zauberflöte,* Act I, Scene 15. • "Mohammed": lecture II in *Heroes and Hero-Worship,* "The Hero as Prophet: Mahomet, Islam."

June 2

•"Theater Reform": Wagner's article entitled *"Theaterreform,"* published in the *Dresdner Anzeiger,* January 16, 1849, under the pseudonym "J. P.—F. R., actors without an engagement"; reprinted in vol. 12 of the collected writings.

June 3

•Herr Mosely: there is a letter from a Dr. L. Mosely in the Wagner archives at Wahnfried. • Mommsen: Theodor Mommsen (1817–1903), German historian and politician, at this time a National Liberal; his *Römische Geschichte* (*Roman History*) appeared in 3 vols., 1854–56. • Putbus: a village on the Baltic island of Rügen.

June 4

•My secret visit to him in Munich: the summer of 1867 at the earliest. • My journey to southern France: Cosima accompanied Liszt to Toulon and Marseilles in October 1864 and on the return journey to Berlin met Wagner in Munich. • The Symphony in C Major: Schumann's Second Symphony, Opus 61. • *Rosalia* devices: raising the pitch at each repetition of a phrase. • The women's uprising: Stanislas Maillard, Marat's henchman in the September massacres of 1792, led a column of several thousand women to Versailles to storm the palace; the incident is described at length by Carlyle in *The French Revolution,* 3 vols., 1837.

June 7

•"Franconian Switzerland": the wooded, hilly country around Bayreuth is known as *"die fränkische Schweiz."*

June 8

•I tell him about the church. . . . Yet to how many people is it a comfort!: because of faulty grammar and a missing word (or words), the translation of this whole passage is largely speculative; it has been assumed that by *Die Nachahmung Christi* Cosima means Thomas à Kempis's *De imitatione Christi,* though its usual German title is *Die Nachfolge Christi;* and there may be some connection in her mind between Thomas à Kempis himself, who came from peasant stock, and the peasant girl who belonged to the Hummelbauers, a rather gypsylike community living in the vicinity of Bayreuth; but Wagner's remark suggests that several vital strands are missing from Cosima's account.

June 9

•"When my master . . .": Oliver's aria in Act I of Boieldieu's opera *Jean de Paris,* 1812.

June 10

•*Camöne* (the Camenae): nymphs in a grove outside the Porta Capena in Rome, identified by Roman poets with the Greek Muses.

JUNE 11
•The Emperor's golden wedding anniversary: of Emperor Wilhelm I of Germany
and Empress Augusta.

JUNE 12
•*Alexander:* a fragment by the twelfth-century German priest and poet Pfaffe
Lamprecht, based on the poem by Albéric de Besançon. • Förster: Dr. Bernhard
Förster (1843–89), schoolteacher, anti-Semitic agitator, married Nietzsche's sister,
Elisabeth, in 1885.

JUNE 13
•He starts on his article: *"Über das Dichten und Komponieren"* ("On Poetry and
Composition").

JUNE 14
•August 10: on August 10, 1792, in Paris the royal palace was stormed and the
monarchy overthrown.

JUNE 15
•"Apostles of freedom . . .": from Goethe's *Venezianische Epigramme,* quoted in
German as a motto in Carlyle's *The French Revolution* (*"Alle Freiheits-Apostel, sie
waren mir immer zuwider"*).

JUNE 16
•*Isidor und Olga:* play (1826) by Ernst Raupach (1784–1852). • "Greeting to the
Beloved": presumably the Beethoven song sung on Wagner's birthday. • "You
are a full thirty years old": from the comic opera *Lenore* by Karl von Holtei (1798–
1880).

JUNE 17
•*Fingal's Cave* Overture: another name for Mendelssohn's *Hebrides* Overture. • [*Das*]
Liebesmahl der Apostel: The Apostles' Love Feast, choral work by Wagner, performed
on July 6, 1843, by 1,200 singers and 100 instrumentalists in the Frauenkirche
in Dresden. • Oberammergau play: a reference to the famous Passion play, performed in the Bavarian village of Oberammergau every ten years since 1633. • His
Columbus Overture: written 1835 to precede Theodor Apel's play of the same
name; Mendelssohn's *Calm Sea and Prosperous Voyage* Overture appeared two years
earlier.

JUNE 18
•He has finished his article: "On Poetry and Composition," finally completed on
July 1 after extensive revision, and published in the *Bayreuther Blätter* of that
month (vol. 10 of the collected writings). • Charlotte Corday: who during the
French Revolution stabbed the Jacobin leader Marat to death and was executed. •
"*Homer blind . . .":* this is brought into "On Poetry and Composition."

JUNE 19
•Frau Müller: wife of Wagner's friend Alexander Müller, with whom he first
stayed in Zurich on his flight from Dresden; he relates in *Mein Leben* Frau Müller's
reply to Minna's complaints about his ruining his conducting career in Dresden.
 • Tschudi: Aegidius or Gilg von Tschudi (1505–72), Swiss historian to whom the
later version of the William Tell legend is attributed.

JUNE 20
•Nap. III's son: Prince Louis Napoleon (born 1856), only son of Napoleon III and
Empress Eugénie, fell on June 1 while fighting for the British in the Zulu War. •
"There is no sure foundation . . .": Cosima quotes this in English; not identi-
fied. • "Inventor of wild tales": epithet applied by the thirteenth-century German
poet Gottfried von Strassburg to the writer of *Parzival* (Chrétien de Troyes). •
Grimm and Behn: Jacob Grimm; "Behn" not identifiable.

JUNE 22

•Sadowa: name of the battle in which Prussia defeated Austria on July 3, 1866.

JUNE 24

•The Midsummer Day melody: Pogner's speech in Act I of *Die Meistersinger.*

JUNE 26

•The way Nature rewards the poet: Carlyle's *On Heroes and Hero-Worship,* lecture III, "The Hero as Poet": "Nature at her own time . . . sent him forth. . . . What Act of Parliament . . . was it that brought this Shakespeare into being? . . . Priceless Shakespeare was the free gift of Nature, given altogether silently. . . ." • The Catholic church will last . . .: *ibid.,* lecture IV, "The Hero as Priest": "While a good work remains capable of being done by the Romish form; or, what is inclusive of all, while a *pious life* remains capable of being led by it, just so long, if we consider, will this or the other human soul adopt it, go about as a living witness of it." • This month, 15 years ago: Cosima joined Wagner at Haus Pellet, Kempfenhausen, on June 29, 1864.

JUNE 30

•C. Frantz's latest book: *Der Föderalismus* (*Federalism*) by Constantin Frantz, 1879.

JULY 1

•Like Beckmesser: in Act I of *Die Meistersinger,* Beckmesser, as Marker, withdraws into a cubicle and closes the curtains to judge Walther's trial song. • "Adelaïde": Beethoven's setting of a poem by Friedrich von Matthisson, Opus 64.

JULY 2

•"In laughter die" (*Lachend zu Grunde gehn*"): *Siegfried,* Act III. • "*Alles nach Gefallen . . .*" ("Just as you please, how happy will you be with wreath and zither!"): Lysiart to Adolar in Act I of Weber's *Euryanthe* (trio). • "For thee, beloved . . .": adaptation of Walther's words ("*Für dich, Geliebte, sei's getan!*") before starting his trial song in *Die Meistersinger,* Act I, Scene 3. • M. Muchanoff: Marie Muchanoff, née Nesselrode (1823–74), married first to a Greek diplomat named Kalergis, then to a Russian named Muchanoff; a loyal friend of Wagner's from 1845 until her death; see vol. I. • Miss Parry: a governess. • The composer of Weber's last idea: a waltz by Karl Gottlieb Reissiger (1798–1859), conductor under Wagner in Dresden; he is mentioned in "On Poetry and Composition."

JULY 3

•Herr Glagau's *Des Reiches Not:* Otto Glagau (see note for August 6, 1878); *Des Reiches Not und der neue Kulturkampf* (*The Peril of the Reich and the New Cultural Struggle*). • "Found? Where?": Weber's *Oberon,* Act I, Scene 13.

JULY 5

•Berlioz's "Queen Mab" and parts of the love scene: in the dramatic symphony *Roméo et Juliette.*

JULY 7

•Dr. Schrön: Prof. Dr. Otto von Schrön (1837–1917), director of the Pathological Institute at the University of Naples from 1865. • Prof. Fries: Carl Fries, a teacher at the boys' school in Bayreuth. • K. Kolb: Karl Heinrich Sofian Kolb (1824–95), director of the cotton mills in Bayreuth. • "Each seventh year . . .": a reference to *Der Fliegende Holländer.*

JULY 8

•The acquittal of Cassagnac: Paul Adolphe de Cassagnac (1843–1904) was tried in Paris for exciting hatred and contempt for the French Republican government with the violent language used in his newspaper, *Le Pays;* he was acquitted on July 3, 1879. • I quickly write down a few lines: these appear in vol. 10 of the collected writings under the title "*Erklärung an die Mitglieder des Patronatvereines*"

("Announcement to the Members of the Society of Patrons"), dated July 15, 1879. • A new composition by my father: the piano piece "in memory of Petöfy" (the Hungarian poet and national hero) had in fact appeared in 1877. • *"War es so niedrig"* ("Was it disgraceful"): Brünnhilde in *Die Walküre,* Act III, Scene 3.

JULY 9

•Huth: Waldemar Huth, clarinetist in Berlin. • Friedrich Wilhelm IV: King of Prussia from 1840 until his death in 1861, when he was succeeded by his brother, Wilhelm I.

JULY 10

•A continuation of his article: *"Über das Opern-Dichten und Komponieren im Besonderen"* ("On Opera Poetry and Composition in Particular"), *Bayreuther Blätter,* September 1879, and vol. 10 of the collected writings. • The church concert: on the program enclosed in the Diaries Cosima made the following notes. "Responsorium" by Palestrina: "Here genius"; Motet by Jacobus Gallus (1591): "Here convention"; "Shall I in Mamre's fertile plain," bass aria from Handel's *Joshua:* "Simply boring, trivial"; "God, show thou mercy," aria from Mendelssohn's *Saint Paul:* "Insipid accompaniment and clumsy declamation"; "Jubilate" by H. Moore (18th century): "Well sung"; 8-part Motet by Eduard Grell (1800–1886): "Insipid; bombastic accompaniment," and beneath this: " 'Bad and modern,' says R."

JULY 11

•His announcement: see note for July 8, 1879. • General Manteuffel: Baron Edwin von Manteuffel (1809–85), Prussian general who figured prominently in the Franco-Prussian War. • Lionel Rothschild (1808–79): London banker involved with Disraeli in the purchase of Suez Canal shares.

JULY 15

•K. Moor: Karl Moor in Schiller's play *Die Räuber.* • One of the "Pictures": piano arrangements by Josef Rubinstein.

July 17

•Richter's "triumphs": following his visit to London with Wagner in 1877, Hans Richter became a regular visitor, conducting an annual series known as the "Richter Concerts" until 1897. • The house in which R. stayed in Boulogne: during his visit to Meyerbeer in August 1839, a wine merchant's villa.

JULY 18

•*De imitatione Christi:* see note for June 8, 1879.

JULY 19

•Dommayer: landlord of the Fantaisie.

JULY 20

•Sascha Ritter: Alexander Ritter (1833–96), husband of Wagner's niece Franziska. • Herr Roeser: see note for May 16, 1879. • Rühlmann: a son of the conductor Adolf Julius Rühlmann (1816–77), whose edited version of Gluck's *Iphigénie en Aulide* Wagner staged in Dresden in 1847. • Gogol's *The Government Inspector:* play (1836) by the Russian dramatist Nikolai Gogol, also known in English as *The Inspector General.*

JULY 22

•An opera by Hiller: *Romilda* by Ferdinand Hiller (1811–85), mentioned in Wagner's article "On Opera Poetry and Composition in Particular." • A miners' revolt in Silesia: there is no evidence of a "revolt," though isolated strikes did occur around this time.

JULY 23

•*Die Folkunger:* opera (1874) by Edmund Kretschmer (1830–1908). • The municipal gardener: the enclosed clipping from the *Bayreuther Tagblatt* of July 24 reports, "The municipal gardener Helmrich, a very able man in his best years, shot himself in the large restaurant in front of the Richard Wagner Theater. The motive is not yet known."

JULY 24

•Sonata in F-sharp Minor: by Robert Schumann, Opus 11. • *Maitrank:* or *Maibowle,* wine and champagne flavored with woodruff and frequently served with fruit.

JULY 25

•The high-minded Tithonus: consort of Eos, in Homer's *Odyssey* (beginning of bk. V). • Schiller's "*Die Götter Griechenlands*" ("The Gods of Greece"): a philosophical poem (1788) contrasting Classicism and Christianity.

JULY 26

•Funny remark (about Brahman marriages): in his article "On Opera Poetry and Composition in Particular" Wagner equates Weber's triumph over the bad libretto of *Euryanthe* (written by Helmina von Chézy) with the Hindu belief that a marriage between a Brahman and a lowly Chandala woman may produce a quite acceptable child, whereas the child of a lowly Chandala and a Brahman woman is worthless; in the conception of *Euryanthe,* Wagner says, the situation is complicated by the fact that the poet-father was a woman and the composer-mother a man!

JULY 27

•*Armin:* opera (1877) by Heinrich Hofmann (1842–1902). • *Königin von Saba:* opera by Karl Goldmark (see note for October 6, 1878).

JULY 28

•Schloemp: Edwin Schloemp, Leipzig publisher, mainly of works on Wagner.

JULY 30

•*Kladderadatsch:* a satirical political periodical published from 1848 in Berlin. • "It is decreed . . .": a parody of the well-known poem by Ernst von Feuchtersleben (1806–49), "*Es ist bestimmt in Gottes Rat,*" of which the first lines might be translated: "It is decreed in God's great plan / That what he loves must every man / Once part from"; the best-known musical setting of the poem is by Mendelssohn (Opus 47, No. 4).

AUGUST 1

•Herr v. Schlör: presumably an officer in the Bavarian administration. • Buonamici: Giuseppe Buonamici (1846–1914), Italian pianist and composer, pupil of Hans von Bülow, from 1868 a teacher at the music school in Munich. • Beeth.'s Variations in F: Opus 34.

AUGUST 2

•Markings for . . . the Ninth: see note for September 26, 1879. • That time in '59: during his visit to Paris in 1859 Wagner was frequently with Cosima's sister, Blandine, and her husband, Emile Ollivier.

AUGUST 3

•"Dark's the time for sparks": word-play on the German proverb "*Im Dunkeln ist gut munkeln,*" which could be translated, "Dark's the time for secret larks." • "Leave me the veil . . .": see note for February 1, 1879.

AUGUST 4

•*La Dame Blanche* (the auction): Act II, Scenes 11 and 12, of Boieldieu's opera. • I again got Minna to come: Wagner's last attempt to rescue his marriage; Minna joined him in Paris, Rue Newton, on November 17, 1859.

AUGUST 5

•*Marie Tudor . . . Angelo:* two plays by Victor Hugo, 1833 and 1835 respectively.

AUGUST 6

•*Hernani:* play by Victor Hugo, 1830. • His article on Schumann: "*Über die Schumann'sche Musik*" ("On Schumann's Music") by Josef Rubinstein, *Bayreuther Blätter,* August 1879.

AUGUST 8
•Prince Napoleon: Napoleon II (1811–32), son of Napoleon I and Marie Louise of Austria. • Elisabeth: in *Tannhäuser*.

AUGUST 9
•Kohlhaas: a historical character, portrayed in Heinrich von Kleist's story "Michael Kohlhaas," who attempted to gain justice for himself through private warfare and was executed. • *Käthchen von Heilbronn:* play by Kleist.

AUGUST 10
•*L[ucrèce] Borgia:* play by Victor Hugo, 1833. • Herr Löffler (Kundry): see note for May 3, 1878. • Dr. Kienzl: Wilhelm Kienzl (1857–1941), composer of the opera *Der Evangelimann* (1895) and author of a biography of Wagner (1904).

AUGUST 11
•Letter from the King: not in the published correspondence, presumably lost.

AUGUST 12
•Prof. Nohl: Ludwig Nohl (1831–85), a writer on music and an authority on Beethoven. • Leuckert: probably the former Berlin music-publishing house, Luckhardt; its successors, Raabe und Plothoco, published the *Allgemeine Deutsche Musik-Zeitung.*

AUGUST 13
•To present to R. on the 25th: probably ideas for a poem (August 25 was their wedding anniversary).

AUGUST 14
•Herr v. Weber: Ernst von Weber (1830–1902), naturalist and founder of an international society against vivisection, author of the pamphlet "*Die Folter-kammern der Wissenschaft*" ("The Torture Chambers of Science"), 1879; Wagner's letter to him was later enlarged into an article attacking vivisection, which appeared in the *Bayreuther Blätter,* October 1879, under the title "*Offenes Schreiben an Herrn Ernst von Weber*" ("Open Letter to E. v. W."), reprinted in vol. 10 of the collected writings.

AUGUST 16
•Claude Bernard (1813–78): French physiologist.

AUGUST 17
•R. has a bridge put up: across a wide ditch in the meadows lying between the two houses. • *Ruy Blas:* play by Victor Hugo, 1838.

AUGUST 18
•"*Selig, wie die Sonne . . .*": Eva in the quintet in *Die Meistersinger von Nürnberg,* Act III, Scene 4. • *The Old Testament:* transcription by H. Haug "to make the O. T. understandable for the first time to all lovers of the truth" (*Das Alte Testament* "*Der-von-Schiloh,*" Berlin, 1872).

AUGUST 19
•The Christ of the tribute money: in Titian's picture *Christ and the Tribute Money* (Dresden). • Madonna Gloriosa: correctly, Mater Gloriosa, who appears at the conclusion of Goethe's *Faust,* Part Two; the Gretchen of Part One also appears in this scene as a penitent. • Prof. Moleschott: Jakob Moleschott (1812–93), Dutch psychologist and materialistic philosopher. • My wedding day: marriage to Hans von Bülow in 1857 (actually on August 18).

AUGUST 21–31
•Letter from the King: not in the published correspondence, presumably lost. • The Bassenheims: Count Waldbott and Countess Caroline von Bassenheim, friends and neighbors in Lucerne during the Tribschen years, frequently mentioned in vol. I of the Diaries.

SEPTEMBER 6
•Cromwell: Oliver Cromwell (1599–1658) took the title of lord protector of England, Scotland, and Ireland in 1653, two years after defeating King Charles II (1630–85) at the Battle of Worcester. • The scene in *Coriolanus*: Act IV, Scene 5, of Shakespeare's play.

SEPTEMBER 8
•*Die Kapitulation (A Capitulation, Comedy in the Ancient Style)*: a one-act farce written by Wagner in November 1870 that pokes fun at the French during the Franco-Prussian War (vol. 9 of the collected writings); in the draft Wagner signed it with the pseudonym "Aristop Hanes." • L. Bucher: Lothar Bucher (1817–92), German diplomat and close companion of Bismarck; he was a friend of Cosima and Hans von Bülow in Berlin. • *"Wagschaft"*: meaning unclear. • The story of the ring: story in the tale in Boccaccio's *Decameron* on which Lessing based his play *Nathan der Weise,* concerning a Jew who, when asked to state which religion is the true one—Jewish, Christian, or Mohammedan—tells of a sultan who had three sons whom he loved equally, but only one family ring to bequeath on his death; he therefore had two replicas made; this led to arguments among the sons, since no one could decide which of the three rings was the genuine one. • Moses Mendelssohn (1729–86): Jewish philosopher and emancipator, a close friend of Lessing, who portrayed him in the character of Nathan.

SEPTEMBER 10
•Von Einem: Karl von Einem (1853–1934), in later years Prussian minister of war and commander in chief of the German army. • "The Work and Mission of My Life": see note for May 1, 1879. • L[ouis] Lambert: novel by Balzac, 1832–33. • Plays a concerto: presumably Brahms's Piano Concerto No. 1 in D Minor (1861).

SEPTEMBER 11
•Two more articles: *"Über die Anwendung der Musik auf das Drama"* ("On the Application of Music to the Drama"), *Bayreuther Blätter,* November 1879, and *"Religion und Kunst"* ("Religion and Art"), *Bayreuther Blätter,* October 1880, both in vol. 10 of the collected writings. • *"Nun such' ich ihn . . ."* ("I seek him now from world to world"): Kundry in *Parsifal,* II, bars 1198 ff. • Lascoux: Antoine Lascoux (died 1906), a Wagner supporter in Paris, an examining magistrate.

SEPTEMBER 13
•The Boers: in 1877 the British claimed the South African province of Transvaal as their colony, a claim resisted by the white settlers of Dutch descent (Boers) who had founded it in 1856.

SEPTEMBER 14
•The three weeks in Zurich: after fleeing from his creditors in Vienna in March 1864, Wagner took refuge in Mariafeld, near Zurich, the home of his friend Eliza Wille.

SEPTEMBER 15
•His article for the November issue: "On the Application of Music to the Drama."
 • Wolzogen's article: 2nd pt. of "On the Decay and Rehabilitation of the German Language," *Bayreuther Blätter,* October-November 1879 (1st pt. mentioned December 31, 1878). • Dr. Hammer: pseudonym for Ernst Grysanowski (died 1888), author of *"Die Verteidiger der Vivisektion und das Laienpublikum"* ("Champions of Vivisection and the Ordinary Public").

SEPTEMBER 18
•Emil Devrient (1803–72): actor in Dresden. • Prince Hal's "hanging nether lip": in Shakespeare's *Henry IV Part I,* Act II, Scene 4, Falstaff, impersonating the king, tells Prince Henry, "That thou art my son, I have partly thy mother's word, partly

my own opinion; but chiefly a villainous trick of thine eye, and a foolish hanging of thy nether lip, that doth warrant me."

SEPTEMBER 19

•Sgambati's quintet: Sgambati wrote two quintets, both published by Schott at Wagner's recommendation. • "King's fisher": written thus in English by Cosima.

• Gfrörer's *Philo of Alexandria:* in his *Geschichte des Urchristentums.*

SEPTEMBER 20

•His letter to Herr von Weber: see note for August 14, 1879.

SEPTEMBER 23

•The Berlin peace treaty: concluded at the Berlin Congress on July 13, 1878, setting up independent states in the Balkans. • Faf: a Newfoundland dog. • Impressive entrance to the town: at that time the festival theater in Bayreuth was visible from the railroad station, for the intervening buildings were all erected later. • Carlyle's essay on conditions in England: presumably *Past and Present,* bk. III, "The Modern Worker."

SEPTEMBER 24

•Cetewayo: king of the Zulus in South Africa, defeated by the British at Ulundi in 1879 and taken prisoner, restored to his throne in 1883. • My father: Wagner's stepfather, Ludwig Geyer.

SEPTEMBER 25

•English translation of *Parsifal:* by Frederick and Henrietta Louisa Corder, published in 1879 by Schott.

SEPTEMBER 26

•His, based on *Faust:* Wagner conducted Beethoven's Ninth Symphony in Dresden on April 5, 1846; for the performance he wrote a program note in which he used quotations from Goethe's *Faust;* it is contained in *Mein Leben* and also reprinted separately in vol. 2 of the collected writings. • Saint Cosmas: Saints Cosmas and Damian, brothers martyred in the fourth century, patron saints of medicine; their feast is on September 27.

SEPTEMBER 27

•*Alexander and Darius:* a tragedy (1827) by Friedrich von Uechtritz (1800–75). • Beethoven's first quartet: in F Major, Opus 18, No. 1.

SEPTEMBER 28

•The "Cosmos-Eos": presumably a lambrequin designed by Cosima; mentioned again on September 29.

SEPTEMBER 29

•News from Wiesbaden: enclosed is a telegram dated September 28 and signed by Wilhelmj: "*Meistersinger* enjoyed unprecedented success under Jahn's incomparable direction without cuts. Jahn and singers demonstratively applauded at all breaks. Various things encored"; Wilhelm Jahn (1834–1900), was conductor at Wiesbaden 1864–81, subsequently in Vienna.

SEPTEMBER 30

•"The Storm Breaks Out": from the song "*Männer und Buben*" by Theodor Körner (1791–1813). • The Queen of the Night's aria: in Mozart's *Die Zauberflöte.* • The play: Uechtritz's *Alexander and Darius.* • Herr von Stein: Heinrich von Stein (1857–87), from Coburg, came to Wahnfried as Siegfried's tutor after completing his philosophical studies in Halle; he became a great favorite of both Wagner and Cosima and figures frequently in the Diaries from now on, both as a person and as a writer. • Dingelstedt: Baron Franz von Dingelstedt (1814–81), director successively of the Court theaters in Munich (from 1851), Weimar (from 1857), and Vienna (from 1867); the reference is presumably to his book *Münchener Bilderbogen*

(*Munich in Pictures*), 1879. • "Palla*sch* Athena": ɛ pun on the name Pallas Athena, *Pallasch* in German meaning a heavy sword. • "It is common": in Shakespeare's *Hamlet,* Act I, Scene 2; "Queen: Thou know'st 'tis common,—all that live must die, / Passing through nature to eternity. Hamlet: Ay, madam, it is common."

OCTOBER 1

• Jaques: in Shakespeare's *As You Like It.* • Prospero: in Shakespeare's *The Tempest.*

OCTOBER 4

• This little expedition: Daniela went to Munich with Liszt on August 31, then to the Bassenheims' at Buxheim; their daughter Marie had been a close friend of Daniela's since the Tribschen years.

OCTOBER 5

• Mottl: Felix Mottl (1856–1911), Austrian conductor, a member of Wagner's Nibelungen Kanzlei in 1876, from 1881 principal conductor in Karlsruhe. • Frau Lucca: Giovanna Lucca, who continued to run her husband's music-publishing business in Milan after Francesco Lucca's death in 1872; the firm was taken over by Ricordi in 1888.

OCTOBER 6

• Hildebrandt: Eduard Hildebrandt (1818–68), German landscape painter; Wagner had some of his water colors at Wahnfried. • Hillebrand: Karl Hillebrand (1829–84), German historian living in Florence.

OCTOBER 8

• E. v. Hagen on . . . *Rheingold: Richard Wagner als Dichter in der zweiten Szene des "Rheingold"* (R. W. *as Poet in the Second Scene of* Das Rheingold) by Edmund von Hagen, Munich, 1879 (266 pp. long!). • "The end of the eternal gods": "*So ist es denn aus mit den ewigen Göttern,*" Fricka in *Die Walküre,* Act II, Scene 1.

OCTOBER 10

• To celebrate the 10th: Wagner's first meeting with Cosima, on October 10, 1853, while he was in Paris with Liszt. • Herr Angelo: Angelo Neumann. • Dannreuther: Edward Dannreuther (1844–1905), founder of the Wagner Society in London and a friend, frequently mentioned in vol. I.

OCTOBER 11

• *Agamemnon:* by Aeschylus. • The Princess of Rudolstadt: Schiller tells in his anecdote "Duke Alba at a Breakfast in the Castle of Rudolstadt in 1547" that the Duke was deterred from committing further acts of violence against the peasants and the Protestants by the resolute behavior of Countess Katharina of Schwarzburg. • He writes to the King: it is in this letter, dated October 11, that Wagner tells King Ludwig that Cosima "is writing for our son a remarkably exact diary, in which there are entries for every day regarding my state of health, my work, and my occasional sayings, etc." • The preacher Stoecker: Adolf Stoecker (1837–1909), a Protestant clergyman, was Court preacher in Berlin and, 1879–98, a deputy in the Prussian Parliament (1881–93 also a member of the Reichstag); in 1878 he founded the Christian Social party and introduced anti-Semitism into German politics.

OCTOBER 12

• The "Spinning Chorus": in Act II of *Der Fliegende Holländer,* which was written at Meudon, near Paris; Bellevue was close by. • The Quai Voltaire: there, at the Hotel Voltaire, in the center of Paris, Wagner wrote the text of *Die Meistersinger von Nürnberg* in January 1862.

OCTOBER 13

• Merz: Oscar Merz, member of the Society of Patrons, a musical assistant at the *Parsifal* performances of 1882. • Jäger's attitude toward the school: Ferdinand Jäger was the only singer to apply for admission to Wagner's music school. • The house in which he was born: in Leipzig, named "Roth und Weisse Löwe" ("Red and White Lion"). • Going on with the biography: *Mein Leben.*

OCTOBER 14

•*Orbis Pictus:* illustrated periodical. • The poem of "Alexander's Feast": the text of Handel's ode (1736) was based on a poem by Dryden.

OCTOBER 15

•All the theological subtleties stem from him: Philo Judaeus (fl. late 1st century B.C. and early 1st century A.D.), a Jew living in Alexandria, is known for his attempt to reconcile Platonic philosophy with the doctrines of the Pentateuch.

OCTOBER 16

•The remarkable passage in Carlyle's *Heroes and Hero-Worship:* in lecture III, "The Hero as Poet": "A *musical* thought is one spoken by a mind that has penetrated into the inmost heart of the thing; detected the inmost mystery of it, namely, the *melody* that lies hidden in it. . . . [Music] . . . a kind of inarticulate unfathomable speech, which leads us to the edge of the Infinite, and lets us for moments gaze into that!"

OCTOBER 17

•Lenbach's pastel drawing: of Cosima, 1879.

OCTOBER 20

•"A black one and a white one": Wolzogen being dark-haired, Stein fair-haired. • Dühring: see note for September 21, 1878.

OCTOBER 22

•In separate copies: through the Court bookseller H. Voigt in Leipzig. • *Die deutsche Wacht:* a periodical published in Dresden and Berlin. • *Apprentice Years* and *Travels:* Goethe's novel *Wilhelm Meister* is much concerned with idealistic teaching methods; Cosima's hope is that Stein will be inspired by Goethe rather than the materialistic Dühring.

OCTOBER 23

•He forbids any *Ottilie:* a character in Goethe's novel *Elective Affinities* who commits suicide by refusing all nourishment. • Frau Helmholtz: wife of Professor Hermann von Helmholtz, a physiologist in Berlin. Eckert: Karl Eckert (born 1820), conductor of the Berlin opera and a friend of Wagner's.

OCTOBER 24

•He works on his article: "On the Application of Music to the Drama."

OCTOBER 25

•Prof. Oncken: Wilhelm Oncken (1838–1905), historian and member of the Reichstag 1873–76. • The Wagner lexicon: *Hauptbegriffe der Kunst- und Weltanschauung Richard Wagners* (*The Main Concepts in R. W.'s Ideas on Art and Philosophy*), an anthology culled from Wagner's writings by Carl Friedrich Glasenapp and Heinrich von Stein and published in Stuttgart in 1883.

OCTOBER 26

•The Battle of Näfels: in which, on April 9, 1388, Swiss confederates defeated an Austrian army. • Nietzsche's health: Nietzsche was suffering at this time from almost constant headaches and vomiting; he wrote to Frau Baumgartner on December 29, 1878, "Half dead with pain and exhaustion." • Tischbein's portrait: Johann Friedrich August Tischbein (1750–1812) painted his portrait of Schiller in 1805. • Bernhard von Weimar (1604–39): Bernhard, the Duke of Sachsen-Weimar, served under King Gustavus Adolphus of Sweden during the Thirty Years' War; Wagner also thought of writing a drama about him. • [Schiller's] essay on the naïve and the sentimental: "*Über naive und sentimentalische Dichtung,*" 1795.

OCTOBER 27

•Herr v. W[eber]'s account of his African journey: Ernst von Weber spent 4 years in Africa with Count Krockow, searching for diamonds. • Busch's *"M[ax] und Moritz"*: Wilhelm Busch (1832–1908), the humorous writer and illustrator, published this, his most famous work, in 1865. • Dr. Gide: a physician, not further identified.

OCTOBER 28
•His uncle: Adolf Wagner.

OCTOBER 29
•Herr v. Puttkamer: Robert von Puttkamer (1828–1900), Prussian minister of education 1879–81. • That daemonic night: possibly a reference to Cosima's discovery of Wagner's secret correspondence with Judith Gautier, though her cryptic reference to that in the Diaries was not in January, but on February 12, 1878. • M. de Fourcaud: Count Louis de Fourcaud; the *Gaulois* was a newspaper founded in Paris in 1867.

OCTOBER 30
•Dr. Dühring's book about R. Mayer: *Robert Mayer, der Galilei des neunzehnten Jahrhunderts* (*R. M., the Galileo of the Nineteenth Century*), Chemnitz, 1880 (predated); Mayer made significant discoveries in the field of energy.

OCTOBER 31
•An act of harshness toward a friend: Wagner met with Saint-Saëns in Paris in 1860 and 1861 and in Bayreuth in 1876, when Saint-Saëns played the piano at a reception in Wahnfried. • Prof. Oken: Lorenz Oken (1779–1851), German naturalist and philosopher. • Fichte: Johann Gottlieb Fichte (1762–1814), German philosopher. • The Communards: participants in the 1871 uprising in Paris.

NOVEMBER 1
•"Dietegen": a story in Gottfried Keller's collection of sketches about Swiss provincial life, *Die Leute von Seldwyla*, 1856.

NOVEMBER 2
•*Webia*: see note for May 22, 1879. • *"Urlögtrygia"*: an invented word based on the Norns' saga, meaning approximately "goddess of Fate." • Keller's *"Das verlorene Lachen"*: story in *Die Leute von Seldwyla*.

NOVEMBER 3
•Wölffel: Carl Wölffel (1833–93), architect in Bayreuth.

NOVEMBER 4
•A certain feature of his nether lip: see note for September 18, 1879. • Grétry's *Raoul Barbe-Bleue*: opera, 1879. • *"Kleider machen Leute"*: story in Keller's *Die Leute von Seldwyla*. • His conducting position in Hanover: Hans von Bülow took over this position in 1877; at the beginning of 1880 he became conductor of the Court orchestra in Meiningen. • The tenor Herr Schott: Anton Schott (1846–1913).

NOVEMBER 5
•Gersdorff: Karl von Gersdorff (1844–1904), a close friend of Nietzsche and, through him, of Wagner and Cosima from the Tribschen years on.

NOVEMBER 8
•Héloïse: presumably the lover of Peter Abelard. • The last sentence is excellent: "But in Seldwyla he did not leave a single cent behind: was it ingratitude or revenge?"

NOVEMBER 10
•Prof. Zöllner: Friedrich Zöllner (see note, February 27, 1879); the book he sent Wagner was the 3rd vol. of his *Wissenschaftliche Abhandlungen* (*Scientific Studies*). • Baudelaire: Charles Baudelaire (1821–67), the French poet, was a fervent champion of Wagner in France, and they met in Paris in 1860. • *"Die missbrauchten Liebesbriefe"*: in Keller's *Die Leute von Seldwyla*.

NOVEMBER 11

•"For all have sinned . . .": Cosima quotes this sentence from the Epistle of Paul to the Romans (iii, 23) incompletely, leaving a blank space at the beginning.

NOVEMBER 12

•Salvini: Tommaso Salvini (1829–1915), Italian actor famed for his Othello. • "O, these men . . .": *Othello,* Act IV, Scene 3.

NOVEMBER 13

•A brute like Shakespeare: in the Diaries the word *"Vieh"* ("brute") has been altered by an unknown hand into *"Dichter"* ("poet").

NOVEMBER 14

•The Elector Friedrich . . . Charles V: the Elector Johann Friedrich of Saxony (1503–54) was defeated in 1547 by Charles V (1500–58), King of Spain and Holy Roman Emperor; Charles endeavored to uphold Roman Catholicism against Luther and the Protestant Reformation.

NOVEMBER 15

•The Goethe verse: the enclosed clipping from the *Halle'sche Zeitung* contains a hitherto unknown anecdote about the aged Goethe, who in a tavern was scoffed at by a drunken student for diluting his wine with water; Goethe replied with a little verse pointing out that water alone produces dumbness, wine alone foolishness, and, since he wished to be neither dumb nor foolish, he mixed the two. • His ruled score: in the orchestral sketch of *Parsifal,* most of it written out on two or three staves (occasionally more), Wagner indicated the instrumentation and noted down other private instructions to himself relating to the full score; with these aids he was able to lay out the whole full score in advance, marking the staves for the various instruments, putting in the bar divisions, etc., thus leaving only the notes to be filled in; the preparatory work took considerable time, and there are frequent references in Cosima's future entries to the task of ruling the score.

NOVEMBER 16

•The *Gartenlaube:* a periodical, founded in Leipzig in 1853. • The postcard from Leipzig: signed by three medical students, "enthusiastic supporters of the music of the future," it thanks Wagner for his latest "revelation" (the "Open Letter to Herr von Weber" on the subject of vivisection) and begs him to continue pointing out the way to the younger generation, "which will follow the flaming comet enthusiastically." • Goethe's saying: as printed in the newspaper clipping: "Particles of gold. In the world every man is taken for what he professes to be; but something he must also be. One can put up with the uncongenial more easily than one can tolerate the insignificant." • Sismondi: Jean Charles Léonard Simonde de Sismondi (1773–1842), Swiss historian whose works include *Histoire des républiques italiennes du moyen âge* (*History of the Italian Republics During the Middle Ages*), 16 vols., 1807–24. • Herr Gützlaff: Dr. von Gützlaff, *Schopenhauer über die Tiere und den Tierschutz* (*S. on Animals and Animal Protection*).

NOVEMBER 17

•Frau Heim: Emilie Heim, singer and wife of Ignaz Heim, musical director in Zurich. • The Green Vault: the royal treasure chamber (1560) in Dresden.

NOVEMBER 18

•A pamphlet: Gützlaff's; see note for November 16, 1879. • Herr Schön's appeal: addressed to representatives and members of the Bayreuth Society of Patrons by the Society's committee, and headed "Bayreuth, October 1879." • The anecdote about the courtier: Wagner mentions this episode again on March 26, 1882 (*q.v.*), when it becomes clearer that what most impressed him was the idea that every word of a monarch, however unorthodox, must be obeyed as a command; Louis II (*deux*) is clearly King Ludwig of Bavaria.

NOVEMBER 19

•Littré: Maximilien Paul Emile Littré (1808–81), French lexicographer and philosopher, published his *Dictionnaire de la langue française* (*Dictionary of the French Language*) 1863–72.

NOVEMBER 20

•Nietzsche's "Appeal to the Germans" ("*Mahnruf an die Deutschen*"): this appeal for support for the Bayreuth enterprise, written in October 1873, was not in fact used (see October 31, 1873, in vol. I). • R[iedel]: Professor Karl Riedel (1827–88), Leipzig, who wrote the appeal that was used in 1873 instead of Nietzsche's; he was president of the Leipzig Wagner Society. • His first father-in-law: Gotthelf Planer (1770–1855), father of Wagner's first wife, Minna, had been an army bugler before becoming a mechanic. • How much he learned from the former: Cosima in fact wrote "latter," but the sense suggests that Wagner meant Planer and not Liszt. • The poor Archbishop: Georges Darboy (1813–71), archbishop of Paris from 1863, was held by the Paris Commune as a hostage in 1871 and, when Thiers refused to negotiate, shot along with five other hostages.

NOVEMBER 21

•Letter from the King: not in the published correspondence, presumably lost.

NOVEMBER 22

•The vivisectionist Schiff: professor of physiology in Florence; according to a tract by Richard Nagel issued with the *Bayreuther Blätter* of February 1881, "Prof. Schiff has dissected 700 dogs annually in the past 20 years—that makes a total of 14,000 dogs." • König's book on literature: *Deutsche Literaturgeschichte* by Robert König (1828–1900), 1879.

NOVEMBER 24

•Magister Sillig: Wagner's teacher at the Kreuzschule in Dresden. • "I like that not": written in English by Cosima; correctly, "I like not that," spoken by Iago in Shakespeare's *Othello*, Act III, Scene 3.

NOVEMBER 25

•"I set you an example": Egmont's final words before his death, in Act V of Goethe's drama. • Once before extended a hand to Baron Perfall: Wagner visited the much-despised director of the Munich opera on July 21, 1877, in the hope of finding some way to clear up the deficit left by the *Ring* production of 1876 in Bayreuth (see entry for that date in vol. I). • "*Durch die Wälder . . .*": Max's aria in Weber's *Der Freischütz*, Act I, Scene 4.

NOVEMBER 26

•*The Great Passion:* Albrecht Dürer's series of twelve woodcuts, 1511. • *Maximilian's Prayer Book:* printed in 1513, it contains illustrations drawn by Dürer while he was in the service of the Holy Roman Emperor Maximilian I.

NOVEMBER 27

•With Munich . . . he would deal very briefly: Wagner never actually took *Mein Leben* beyond 1864, the date of his summons to Munich. • A book by Karl Ritter on the theory of tragedy: *Theorie des Deutschen Trauerspiels,* Leipzig, 1880. • Schlagintweit: Hermann von Schlagintweit (1826–82), German naturalist and author of *Reisen in Indien und Hochasien* (*Travels in India and High Asia*), 4 vols., 1869–80. • Tears gush forth . . .: a reversal of Faust's lines in Goethe's *Faust,* Part One (night scene); in Bayard Taylor's translation, "My tears gush forth: the Earth takes back her child"; in Philip Wayne's, "Tears dim my eyes: earth's child I am again."

NOVEMBER 28

•The "musical Jew": Ferdinand Hiller had been director of music in Cologne since 1850. • *La guarda cuidadosa* (*The Alert Sentry*): interlude by Cervantes. • My father's *Tasso:* symphonic poem by Liszt. • Goethe's poem on brooms and boys:

"Johannis-Feuer sei unverwehrt," in *Zahme Xenien.* • The *"Pustkuchen"*: *"Goethe und Pustkuchen,"* from *Invectiven.* • *Die Hexe:* play (1878) by Arthur Fitger (1840–1909).

NOVEMBER 29

•The Bayreuth factotum: probably Bernhard Schnappauf.

NOVEMBER 30

• *Anti-Stoecker:* title of a book by E. Lefson (Berlin, 1879) attacking Adolf Stoecker; see note for October 11, 1879. • Jean Paul: German writer (full name Johann Paul Friedrich Richter) who was Bayreuth's most distinguished citizen before Wagner.

DECEMBER 1

•Pfau: Hermann Pfau, a ne'er-do-well from Leipzig who lived in Paris as a vagabond, 1840–41; mentioned in *Mein Leben.* • His visit to the 1867 world exposition: when staying at the Grand Hotel in Paris, October 28 to November 4 of that year. • The Duke of Brunswick: Karl, Duke of Brunswick, abdicated in 1831 in favor of his brother Wilhelm and went to live in the Swiss city of Geneva, to which he bequeathed all his property. • The King of Denmark: Christian IX. • The Guelph fund: moneys sequestrated when Hanover was annexed by Prussia in 1866; an official announcement of its ultimate destination was made in Berlin in November 1879. • Josephine Gallmeyer (1838–84)]: a soubrette singer in Vienna.

DECEMBER 3

•Thénardier-type manifestations: Louis Jacques Thénardier (1777–1857) was a specialist for complaints of the gall bladder.

DECEMBER 4

•The Duke of Cumberland: Ernst August, Duke of Cumberland and Brunswick-Lüneburg (1845–1923), only son of the deposed King Georg V of Hanover.

DECEMBER 5

•*"Der goldene Topf":* a story by E. T. A. Hoffmann. • Councilor Carus: Carl Gustav Carus (1789–1869), German writer and Court physician in Dresden.

DECEMBER 8

•" 'Tis there, 'tis there": the nostalgic words of Mignon as she longs for Italy in Goethe's ballad "Mignon" ("Know'st thou the land where the citrons bloom?"), set to music by several composers, including Beethoven (1809), Schubert (1815), Liszt (1842), and Schumann (1849). • "Have you seen Bosco?": Bosco was a celebrated magician. • Andolosia: a son of the legendary Fortunatus, possessor of wishing caps and inexhaustible purses.

DECEMBER 9

•The debate: the newspaper clipping contains a report on the debate in the Prussian Parliament on the state of emergency in Silesia, protective tariffs, etc. • *Charivari:* humorous political periodical in Paris.

DECEMBER 10

•Titania and Bottom: in Shakespeare's *A Midsummer Night's Dream* Titania, the queen of the fairies, falls in love with the weaver Bottom, although his head has been transformed into that of an ass.

DECEMBER 11

•Zanzibar: island off the east coast of Africa, at that time a British protectorate, now a part of Tanzania; the human cruelty to which Cosima refers was probably connected with the slave trade, not finally declared illegal until 1875.

DECEMBER 14

•*"Die Macht der Musik":* correctly, *"Die heilige Cäcilie oder die Gewalt der Musik"* ("Saint Cecilia, or the Power of Music"), a story by Heinrich von Kleist, 1810.

DECEMBER 15

•Dr. Reuter: Johann Konrad Reuter, an eye specialist in Bayreuth. • Our young friend: Heinrich von Stein. • The conductor Fischer: Franz Fischer.

DECEMBER 16
• *Virginia:* a tragedy by Karl Ritter.
DECEMBER 18
•Fotheringhay: castle in the county of Northamptonshire where Mary, Queen of Scots, was held prisoner and finally executed in 1587.
DECEMBER 19
• The news from Italy: Irredentist attacks in protest against the Berlin Treaty.
DECEMBER 20
•Flachs: an eccentric with whom the sixteen-year-old Wagner made friends in Dresden after seeing him at open-air concerts; in *Mein Leben* Wagner describes him as tall and very lean, with a particularly narrow head and a curious way of walking and speaking; when listening to the music, Wagner relates, he would nod his head and puff out his cheeks, "actions which I interpreted as signs of daemonic ecstasy."
DECEMBER 22
•Gedon's letter: presumably Wagner had ordered something from the artist Gedon for Cosima's birthday, on December 25.
DECEMBER 23
•Frau v. Aufsess: Charlotte von Aufsess (1804–82), widow of Baron Hans Aufsess, founder of the Germanic Museum in Nuremberg. • "Sing, heigh-ho . . .": from the song "Blow, Blow, Thou Winter Wind," sung by Amiens in Shakespeare's *As You Like It,* Act II, Scene 7. • Suit-ruin-matism: hardly more excruciating than Wagner's own pun, which is *"Kleidreiss-matismus"* (in contrast to Eva's *"Gelenk-Rheumatismus"*). • Frau v. Stein's 46 years: Charlotte von Stein (1742–1827), the wife of the ducal equerry in Weimar, was six years older than Goethe; their relationship, which began in 1775, was broken off by Goethe on his return from Italy in 1788; Frau v. Stein was then forty-six years old.
DECEMBER 24
• The newspaper reports enclosed: the first clipping concerns the birth of a child in a Munich street, the second an executioner who was so affected by the repentance shown by a murderer as he died that he talked of giving up his post. • "Armand Pensier": Heinrich von Stein, who had used this pseudonym for his *Die Ideale des Materialismus* (*The Ideals of Materialism*), published in Cologne in 1878, retained it for his translation of a chorus from Aeschylus's *Agamemnon,* published in the *Bayreuther Blätter* of December 1879. • When I went off to Venice: on August 17, 1858, to work on *Tristan und Isolde;* on the day before his departure Hans and Cosima von Bülow visited him in Zurich.
DECEMBER 26
•Rubinstein's article: "Some Reflections on Musical Style in Modern Germany" by Josef Rubinstein, *Bayreuther Blätter,* March 1880. • "I see him still": neither this nor "We see him" are actual quotations from the German translation of *Hamlet,* but they obviously refer to the appearance of the ghost of Hamlet's father in Act I, Scene 1.
DECEMBER 28
•[A story by Friedrich Axmann]: *"Des Todfeindes Rache";* no further details available. • Nietzsche's new book: *Der Wanderer und sein Schatten* (*The Wanderer and His Shadow*) appeared a few weeks earlier. • His article for the New Year: *"Zur Einführung in das Jahr 1880,"* *Bayreuther Blätter,* Jan.-Feb. 1880, and vol. 10 of the collected writings.
DECEMBER 31
•Remarkable New Year's Eve: during it Cosima discussed with Herr von Bürkel the idea of persuading King Ludwig to assume a "protectorate" over the Bayreuth undertaking.

1880

JANUARY I
•Dr. Bezold: an eye specialist in Munich.

JANUARY 5
•An indescribable view: the Villa d'Angri, a substantial house in a large garden on the slopes of the Posilipo just outside Naples, commanded a wide view of the bay.

JANUARY 6
•Chancellor Müller's *Goethe:* the lawyer Friedrich von Müller (1779–1849) became chancellor in Weimar in 1815; he wrote an account of his conversations with Goethe which was published by C. A. H. Burkhardt in 1870 under the title *Goethes Unterhaltungen mit dem Kanzler von Müller.*

JANUARY 7
•On the Seifengasse: Goethe in his conversation with Müller on January 27, 1830: "One reads folios and quartos and becomes no wiser than if one spent all day reading the Bible; all one learns is that the world is stupid, and that one can also put to the test here on the Seifengasse."

JANUARY 8
•The melody of the three graces: in Act I, Scene 1, of the Paris version of *Tannhäuser* (Venusberg). • Gleizès: Jean Antoine Gleizès (1773–1843), French vegetarian; his book *Thalysia,* first published in 1821, was translated into German in 1872.

JANUARY II
•Poerio: Alessandro Poerio (1802–48), Italian patriot who took part in the Neapolitan revolution of 1820 and fought in defense of Venice against the Austrians in 1848, during which action he was mortally wounded; his patriotic songs exerted a great influence in Italy.

JANUARY 12
•The Camorra: a secret society founded around 1820 that attained great power in Naples, and in the '60s was carrying on a reign of terror in southern Italy; its power was ostensibly broken by the government in 1877, but it continued an effective underground existence for several years after that. • Düntzer's life of Goethe: Heinrich Düntzer (1813–1901) had thus far published two books about Goethe, *Goethe und Karl August* (2 vols., 1860–61) and *Aus Goethes Freundeskreise* (1868).

JANUARY 13
•Max Weber: Max Maria von Weber (1822–81), son of the composer; he was present at the first performance of *Tannhäuser,* in Dresden in 1845.

JANUARY 14
•The palm tree: at the highest point of the sloping garden behind the Villa d'Angri.

JANUARY 15
•Mattei: probably Ernst Matthäi (1779–1842), German sculptor and inspector of plaster casts at the Dresden museum. • Empress Eugénie (1826–1920): widow of Napoleon III; in 1880 she paid a visit to South Africa, where her son, Prince Louis Napoleon, had died the previous year fighting in the Zulu War (see June 20, 1879, and note). • To fall from grace: Cromwell's question on his deathbed. • Julian: Flavius Claudius Julianus (331–63), named the Apostate, Roman emperor who renounced Christianity but proclaimed religious toleration within his realm. • Fröbel: Friedrich Fröbel (1782–1852), German educator, founder of the kindergarten system.

JANUARY 16
•[Christiane] Vulpius (1765–1816): sister of the writer Christian August Vulpius in

Weimar; she lived with Goethe from 1788 on and bore him five children, but he did not marry her until 1806.

JANUARY 17

•About the physiognomy: Schopenhauer's *Parerga und Paralipomena,* vol. 2, chap. XXIX ("*Zur Physiognomik*"). • *Notre Dame de Paris:* novel by Victor Hugo, 1831; Halévy's opera *La Juive* was first produced in Paris in 1835; Wagner got to know the composer during his early years in Paris. • Brangäne's theme: in *Tristan und Isolde.*

JANUARY 18

•Karl August (1757–1828): Duke (1815 Grand Duke) of Sachsen-Weimar-Eisenach, Goethe's patron, brought the poet Herder and later Schiller to Weimar, where he founded the Court theater in 1791. • The Queen: Queen Victoria (1819–1901) reigned until her death, and her eldest son, the prince of Wales, was already sixty when he succeeded her as King Edward VII. • Herr v. Joukowsky: Paul von Joukowsky (1845–1912) had a Russian father (a poet) and a mother of German extraction; he himself was a painter; he first met Cosima in Munich and visited her again in Bayreuth during the *Ring* festival of 1876, but was not introduced to Wagner then; having a studio in Naples within a short distance of the Villa d'Angri, he called on Cosima again, and this time met Wagner, as here noted; he quickly became a friend to both (one of his assets in Wagner's eyes being the ability to speak German fluently!) and figures prominently in the Diaries from now on.

JANUARY 19

•J[ohanna] Schopenhauer (1766–1838): mother of the philosopher and herself a writer living in Weimar. • Princess Ouroussoff: Monia Ouroussoff, wife of a Russian provincial governor.

JANUARY 20

•*Pungolo:* an Italian periodical. • Unrest in Hungary: a rebellion of the Croats, at that time under Hungarian rule.

JANUARY 21

•A. Dumas the younger: Alexandre Dumas *fils* (1824–95), son of the author of *The Three Musketeers;* his best-known work is *La Dame aux Camélias,* published as a novel in 1848 and adapted for the stage in 1852.

JANUARY 22

•U[lrike von] Lev[etzow] (1804–99): Goethe met her in Marienbad in 1821, proposed to her, and was rejected. • Unrest in Ireland: Charles Stewart Parnell (1846–91) was leading the struggle in Ireland for a national identity, having become leader of the Home Rule party in 1879.

JANUARY 23

•*Thalysia:* by Gleizès; see note for January 8, 1880. • Renan's *Les Eglises: L'Eglise chrétienne,* 1878, part of Renan's *History of the Origins of Christianity.*

JANUARY 24

•*Norma:* opera by Bellini, 1831.

JANUARY 29

•Bajazet: the play about him was by Racine, not Corneille (1672). • His illness in Paris: Wagner fell ill with typhoid fever during the *Tannhäuser* rehearsals and was absent from the theater from October 27 to November 20, 1860. • Royer: Alphonse Royer (1803–75), director of the Grand Opera in Paris at the time of the *Tannhäuser* production there.

JANUARY 31

•Our stay in Heidelberg: July 5–18, 1877. • "My Kingdom . . .": The Gospel According to Saint John, 18:36.

FEBRUARY 3

•Countess Schulenburg: wife of Count Dietrich von der Schulenburg, hereditary member of the Upper House of the German Parliament. • Count Arnim: Harry, Count von Arnim (1824–81), German ambassador in Paris from 1872, was recalled in 1874 by Bismarck for showing favor to certain Court circles and then arrested for refusing to surrender documents connected with his diplomatic activities; he fled abroad and in 1876 published a pamphlet in Zurich entitled *Pro Nihilo,* in which he made use of secret documents to attack Bismarck.

FEBRUARY 6

•The *B. Blätter* with his article: *"Zur Einführung in das Jahr 1880."* • Dr. Kirchner: Friedrich Kirchner (1848–1900), author of "The Present Time and 'The Artwork of the Future,' " *Bayreuther Blätter,* Jan.-Feb. 1880.

FEBRUARY 10

•Spichern . . . Wörth . . . Mars-la-Tour: battles in the Franco-Prussian War, 1870–71.

FEBRUARY 11

•The Grand Duke of Weimar: Karl Alexander of Sachsen-Weimar-Eisenach (1818–1901), grand duke from 1853.

FEBRUARY 12

•Old Tiefenbach: one of Wallenstein's generals, figures in Schiller's drama *Die Piccolomini.* • Hübsch: Anton Hübsch (1801–50), director of the theater in Königsberg 1836–37; Wagner relates in *Mein Leben* that he persuaded Hübsch to keep the theater open during the summer months, but this meant cuts in salary for the whole company, including Wagner, the conductor; the resulting poverty, coupled with the hostility of both company and public toward him, made this a difficult time for him and led additionally to bitter quarrels with Minna.

FEBRUARY 19

•Another attempt on the Emperor's life: Alexander II of Russia, on whose life several attempts were made before his assassination in 1881. • Count Tolstoy: Count Dmitri Alexandrovich Tolstoy (1823–89), Russian minister of public instruction 1866–80 and much disliked for his measures against universities and students. • The Vienna period: November 14, 1861, to March 23, 1864, with some interruptions. • The work we are bequeathing to our Siegfried: *Mein Leben.*

FEBRUARY 21

•Hans's concert in Bayreuth: Hans von Bülow gave two piano recitals in Bayreuth at this time, part of his self-imposed effort to raise 40,000 marks for the benefit of Wagner's cause.

FEBRUARY 22

•"Some wild dream . . .": from the scene in Faust's study in Goethe's *Faust,* Part One; the lines that follow are (in Bayard Taylor's translation): "The God that in my breast is owned / Can deeply stir the inner sources; / The God above my powers enthroned, / He cannot change external forces"; Cosima also refers to this passage on November 27, 1877 (see vol. I). • *Cain:* a mystery (play) by Byron, 1821.

FEBRUARY 23

•*Totten:* not an identifiable German word; it may conceivably be associated with the French word *"toton"* ("teetotum"), and imply "spinning like a top." • G. Bruno: Giordano Bruno (1548–1600), Italian philosopher of pantheistic views who perished on the stake, a victim of the Inquisition.

FEBRUARY 26

•The brewery: Dreher, on the Via di Roma, brewed Viennese beer.

February 27
•His life in Biebrich: working on *Die Meistersinger,* February 8 to November 13, 1861.

March 1–5
•Wagner's interruption: Wagner is Faust's amanuensis in Goethe's *Faust,* Part One. • Ravesteijn: Jan van Ravesteijn (c. 1572–1657), Flemish painter. • Goethe's *Campaign in France (Kampagne in Frankreich* 1792): Goethe accompanied the duke of Weimar on an invasion of France in the year 1792. • Frau Schwab: not identified. • The Wöhrmann family: Joukowsky's sister, Baroness Alexandra (Sascha) Wöhrmann, with her husband and son; they were staying with Joukowsky in the Villa Postiglione.

March 6
•His *Annalen:* Richard Wagner's annals covering his period in Munich (May 4, 1864, to December 10, 1865) have been published in the correspondence with King Ludwig (*König Ludwig II und Richard Wagner, Briefwechsel,* vol. 1, Karlsruhe, 1936), *Mein Leben* (Munich, 1963), and *Das braune Buch* (Zurich, 1975).

March 7
•Frl. Hauk: Minnie Hauk (1851–1929), American soprano, by 1880 internationally known as a singer, mainly of soubrette roles.

March 9
•Frl. Pauschwitz: not identified.

March 12
•The Count of Schlabrendorf begs to be excused: a reference to Count Gustav von Schlabrendorf (1750–1824), who devoted his life to good works, escaped the guillotine during the French Revolution, and spent his last ten years in almost complete seclusion.

March 13
•Joachim: Joseph Joachim (1831–1907), famous violinist whom Wagner disliked intensely; Joachim had been head of the Hochschule für Musik in Berlin since 1868; his rival Wilhelmj was at this time running a violin school at Biebrich in the Rhineland.

March 14
•Loris-Melikov: Mikhail Tarielovich, Count Loris-Melikov (1826–88), Russian general and minister of the interior 1880–81; on March 3, 1880, he escaped an attempt on his life. • The King of Saxony: King Albert, who succeeded his father, Johann, in 1873. • The Gotthard tunnel: the digging of the Gotthard tunnel in Switzerland, creating a rail link between northern Europe and Italy, was completed in February 1880.

March 17
•*"Durch des Mitleides"*: *"Durch Mitleid wissend"* ("Through compassion knowing"); sung by boys and youths from above, *Parsifal,* I, bars 1404 ff. • The Riedel choir: the Riedel-Verein, founded 1854, was led by Karl Riedel, chairman of the Leipzig Wagner Society, from its inception until Riedel's death in 1888. • The quotations from Carlyle: included in an anthology, *"Stimmen aus der Vergangenheit"* ("Voices from the Past"), published in the *Bayreuther Blätter,* March 1880. • R. criticizes the many underlined words: Cosima wrote *rühmt* (praises), but the context suggests that she meant to write *rügt* (criticizes).

March 18
•Who would be prepared to give 300 marks: the idea of establishing the Bayreuth festival came to a head shortly after the conclusion of the Franco-Prussian War, when Wagner was working on *Götterdämmerung;* originally he hoped to finance it

by selling 1,000 certificates of patronage at 300 marks each; this goal was not reached. • The "Jockeys": members of the Jockey Club in Paris, mainly men of fashion; it was above all their displeasure over Wagner's refusal to provide a ballet in Act II of *Tannhäuser* that led to the demonstrations in the auditorium of the Paris opera in March 1861.

MARCH 19

•His work on the affinities of art and religion: the first draft of *"Religion und Kunst"* was written in 1880. • Lo Piccolo: owner of the Villa d'Angri. • Parliament has been dissolved: Disraeli's administration; in April 1880 the Liberals came into office under Gladstone.

MARCH 20

•The resumption of the biography: Wagner took up work again on *Mein Leben* with an account of rehearsals for a concert he had conducted in Vienna on December 26, 1862. • To see Marie Muchanoff exonerated: Wagner relates in *Mein Leben* that Marie Muchanoff (at that time Madame Kalergis) used her influence to persuade Edward Robert Bulwer Lytton (1831–91, from 1877 earl of Lytton), then an attaché at the British embassy in Vienna, to loan his Vienna apartment to Wagner during his absence; she arranged a meeting in the apartment, to which Wagner went with Peter Cornelius; his attempt to read aloud the text of *Götterdämmerung* proved heavy going, and he broke off and left with Cornelius, while Marie stayed behind with Bulwer Lytton; Wagner, inclined at the time to regard this as proof of an affair between Marie and the young attaché, declares in *Mein Leben* that his suspicions were unfounded and that Marie's efforts with Bulwer Lytton were entirely in his behalf (he was allowed to take over the apartment). • Herr Vitari: not identified. • *"Wunschmaid warst du mir"* ("My handmaiden wert thou"): Wotan to Brünnhilde, *Die Walküre*, Act III, Scene 2. • The Neapolitan stories: *Nouvelles napolitaines* (1879) by Marc Monnier (1829–85). • "You are the God . . .": see note for February 22, 1880.

MARCH 21

•The King of Saxony's translation of Dante: King Johann of Saxony (1801–73, reigned from 1854) was a Dante scholar, and he translated the *Divina commedia* into German, 1839–49, under the pseudonym Philaletes. • Prof. Witte the *Wunderkind:* Karl Witte (1800–83), a Dante scholar who gained a reputation as a child prodigy through his early talent for learning foreign languages.

MARCH 22

•*I Puritani:* opera by Bellini, 1835. • The Körner songs: Weber set a number of Theodor Körner's poems in the collection *Leyer und Schwert,* including *"Jägerlied"* ("Hunter's Song") and *"Lied des schwarzen Jägers"* ("Song of the Black Hunter"), to music for chorus. • Miss Tilton: an American friend of Dr. Jenkins, Wagner's dentist, who lived in Dresden and Florence. • Schurz: Carl Schurz (1829–1906) took part in the democratic uprisings in Germany in 1848 and fled to Switzerland (where he met Wagner), then emigrated to the United States in 1852; there he rose to be a brigadier general on the Union side during the Civil War, later minister to Spain, senator (from Missouri), and secretary of the interior. • The cantor in Zittau: the musical director W. Fischer, representative of the Society of Patrons in Zittau.

MARCH 23

•Alfonso: Alfonso V, the Magnanimous (1416–58), King of Aragon, Sicily, and Naples; in 1435 he conquered Gaeta and united it with Naples.

MARCH 24

•Beethoven's *"Herz, mein Herz"* ("Heart, My Heart"): poem by Goethe; Opus

75, No. 2. • Reisenauer: Alfred Reisenauer (1863–1907), a pupil of Liszt; he made his public debut as a pianist in Rome in 1881.

MARCH 25

•Cossa: Pietro Cossa (1830–81), Italian dramatist. • The Duchess of Bagnara: wife of the president of the Conservatorio di Musica in Naples. • Leo: Leonardo Leo (1694–1744), Italian composer; his *Miserere* (1739) is an 8-pt. *a cappella* oratorio.

MARCH 26

•Certain days set aside: March 26 was Good Friday.

MARCH 27

•Schopenhauer on the subject of language: *Parerga und Paralipomena,* vol. 2, chap. XXV, *"Über Sprache und Worte"* ("On Language and Words"). • Herr Tachard: not identified; Wagner wrote humorously to Daniela on March 30, "Here there has recently been much yelling that Mr. Tachard has ruined me personally."

MARCH 30

•A telegram from Wiesbaden: from the meeting of the Society of Patrons, March 29–30. • Alba: a character in Schiller's drama *Don Carlos.*

APRIL 1

•Our second meeting in Berlin: on Wagner's return from a conducting trip to St. Petersburg, April 23–24, 1863.

APRIL 2

•Liphart: Baron Karl Eduard von Liphart, whom Wagner and Cosima met in Florence in December 1876 (see December 7, 1876, in vol. I).

APRIL 3

•Hafiz: pseudonym of Shams ud-din Mohammed (1327–90), Persian poet whose *Divan,* translated into German in 1812, influenced Goethe. • "The moment one starts to speak . . .": from Goethe's *Poems, Epigrammatic.*

APRIL 4

•Glendower, Percy, etc.: in Shakespeare's *Henry IV.* • The courtship scene in *H[enry] V:* Act V, Scene 2. • The epitaph . . . mentioned in *Heroes and Hero-Worship:* in lecture III, "The Hero as Poet," Carlyle writes with reference to Shakespeare: " 'We are such stuff as Dreams are made of!' That scroll in Westminster Abbey, which few read with understanding, is of the depth of any seer. But the man sang; did not preach, except musically." (The quotation comes from *The Tempest,* Act IV, Scene 1.) • *Kvasir* and *Odhrerir:* in Norse mythology Odhrerir was a cauldron containing a magic potion, an ingredient of which was the blood of Kvasir, the wisest of men; for "Oh, were I but rid . . ." see note for December 21, 1878. • Queen Luise (1776–1810), wife of King Friedrich Wilhelm III of Prussia; her monument is in the Tiergarten in Berlin. • "Togs": the German word for the uniform worn by students on festive occasions is *"Wichs"*; Cosima's surprise at finding this word printed in a newspaper was probably due to its having become a slang expression for festive garb in general.

APRIL 5

•Cottran: not identified.

APRIL 7

•The Duke of Meiningen: Duke Georg II of Saxe-Meiningen (1826–1914) formed the theatrical company in Meiningen, which had a powerful influence on stagecraft throughout Germany; Wagner, who had considerable respect for him, visited Meiningen with Cosima in March 1877 (see March 9–12, 1877, in vol. I). • The horn player Levy: since Cosima spelled this name incorrectly (she wrote "Levi"), it could be either Lewy, horn player in Dresden during Wagner's period there as conductor, or Richard Levy, horn player in Vienna and 1870–79 chief inspector of music at the Vienna Court opera.

APRIL 9
• The most moving dictation: this is the passage in *Mein Leben* in which Wagner tells of his meeting with Cosima in Berlin on November 28, 1863, during which, while driving to a concert to be conducted by Hans von Bülow, "amid tears and sobs we sealed our vow to belong entirely to each other"; the passage was suppressed in all editions of *Mein Leben* up to 1963.

APRIL 10
• [A poem by Wagner on Isolde's birthday]: this poem, written for Isolde's fifteenth birthday, removes all doubt that Wagner considered Isolde to be his natural daughter; it runs: "*Vor fünfzehn Jahren wurdest du geboren: | Da spitzte alle Welt die Ohren; | Man wollte 'Tristan und Isolde'— | doch was ich einzig wünscht' und wollte, | Das war ein Töchterchen: Isolde! | Nun mag sie tausend Jahre leben, | Und 'Tristan und Isolde' auch daneben! | Vivat hoch! — R. W.*" ("Fifteen years ago you were born: | The whole world pricked up its ears; | Others wanted *Tristan und Isolde*— | but all I wished for and wanted | Was a little daughter: Isolde! | May she now live a thousand years, | And *Tristan und Isolde* also!")

APRIL 11
• The death of our dear Brange: the news was sent to Cosima by Muncker, the mayor of Bayreuth; the dog died suddenly on April 7 of an apoplectic fit.

APRIL 12
• "Is that any thing now?": Antonio in Shakespeare's *The Merchant of Venice,* Act I, Scene 1.

APRIL 14
• Much Bissing nonsense: Henriette von Bissing, née Sloman (1798–1879), novelist and sister of Wagner's friend Eliza Wille; when she met Wagner again in 1863 at concerts he conducted in Löwenberg and Breslau, she offered to help him financially, but did not keep her promise; Wagner suggests in *Mein Leben* that her reason for withdrawing was jealousy of Mathilde Wesendonck. • The "Strömkarl": a water sprite that figures in the *Tannhäuser* "Bacchanale."

APRIL 15
• Baron Hofmann: Baron Leopold Friedrich von Hofmann, Austrian minister of finance from 1876, previously closely concerned with the administration of the Austrian state theaters. • Dr. Förster's lecture: Bernhard Förster's "*Richard Wagner als Begründer eines deutschen Nationalstils mit vergleichenden Blicken auf die Kulturen anderer indogermanischer Nationen*" ("R. W. as Initiator of a National German Style and Comparisons with the Cultures of Other Indo-Germanic Nations"), *Bayreuther Blätter,* April 1880.

APRIL 16
• Baron Hirsch: Baron Moritz von Hirsch (1831–96), financier and philanthropist.
• Count Schönfeld: Baron Casimir von Schönfeld; in 1883 he was the official representative of Concordia, the firm of undertakers that transported the coffin for Wagner's remains from Vienna to Venice.

APRIL 18
• The stay in Munich: Wagner describes in *Mein Leben* how, on his flight from his Viennese creditors, he passed through Munich on March 25, 1864, and saw in a shop window a picture of the handsome young prince who had just become King Ludwig II of Bavaria. • The Duke of Meiningen and his wife: for the duke, see note for April 7, 1880; his third, and morganatic, wife, Baroness Ellen von Heldburg (1839–1923), had been an actress, Ellen Franz, in Mannheim and Meiningen.
• Our sweet secrets: a literal translation of Cosima's "*süsse Geheimnisse*"; in his biography of Wagner, Glasenapp transcribed (or interpreted) this as "*religiöse Geheimnisse,*" which might be translated as "religious mysteries."

APRIL 21

•The operetta: a reference to *La Bataille de Marignan,* a parody of the Mass by the French composer Clément Janequin (c. 1480–1560).

APRIL 23

•A letter . . . to the Duke of Bagnara: containing a plan for an opera school at the Naples Conservatoire, recommending intensive study of a work by Mozart (for instance, *Le Nozze di Figaro*) for vocal and dramatic composition, and of Gluck's two *Iphigénie* operas and Spontini's *La Vestale* for tragic opera. • He intends for the time being to conclude: in fact, this marks the conclusion of *Mein Leben;* Wagner never took it further.

APRIL 24

•Changing the theater director: in his letter of April 20, Ludwig von Bürkel writes: "His Majesty has condescended to tell me that I am so indispensable as Cabinet secretary—I blush as I write this—that some other suitable person should be suggested as theater director. I therefore request you most urgently to reflect on another candidate and to let me know your suggestion as soon as possible in order to forestall some mistaken choice." • The Vienna pamphlet: *Das Wiener Hof-Opernntheater* ("The Vienna Opera-house"), first published as a brochure in 1863 and reprinted in vol. 7 of the collected writings. • Portrait of Paul III: the portrait of Pope Paul III in Naples was painted by Titian (1545).

APRIL 27

•The Waldenses: also known as Vaudois, a religious movement founded around 1176 by Peter Waldes, a merchant from Lyons, France; they were persecuted for certain unorthodox doctrines throughout the centuries.

APRIL 28

•The Jamnitzer centerpiece: a centerpiece one meter high by the goldsmith Wenzel Jamnitzer (1508–85), bought by Henri de Rothschild in Paris.

APRIL 30

•Sitting for the picture: portrait of Cosima by Paul Joukowsky.

MAY 5

•The question of vivisection: the undated newspaper clipping, headed "From the Commission on Petitions," reports a speech in the Reichstag debate by Professor Rudolf Virchow arguing that without vivisection science could not have advanced as far as it had, and that there were police powers to guard against abuses; on the Commission, the newspaper adds, there was a general feeling against the anti-vivisection movement; readers of the *Bayreuther Blätter* had been urged in the April issue to sign the petition against vivisection.

MAY 6

•Sends the biography off to the printers: the fourth and final vol. of the private printing of *Mein Leben* was done by T. Burger in Bayreuth, but it was not ready until August 1880; see July 26, 1880.

MAY 9

•This is what has made him so cold: in this obscure sentence the "him" appears to refer to Wagner; it probably reflects his disapproval of Liszt and Countess Wittgenstein for their treatment of Cosima's brother. • A Duchess Ravaschieri: not identified.

MAY 15

•The *"Urbild"*: literally, "original picture"; it refers to Joukowsky's portrait of Cosima. • Delaroche's picture: Paul Delaroche (1797–1856), French painter, specialized in historical subjects. • His cousin Kühnlein: the reference is presumably to the German composer Johann Christoph Kienlen (1784–1830), whom Wagner met in Dresden in his childhood and of whom he writes in *Mein Leben;* they were not actually cousins—the word is used in a familiar sense, probably because Kienlen was an eccentric character.

MAY 16

•A little poem: This reads, *"Es ist nun einmal so, wie möcht' es anders sein, ob davon trüb' ob froh, wir liessen uns drauf ein"* ("So it is, how could it be different, whether glad or sorry about it, we let ourselves in for it").

MAY 17

•The Knights of the Grail: in this case Humperdinck, Plüddemann, Rubinstein, and Dr. Hartmann from Munich.

MAY 19

•"Wit has returned . . .": a parody on Faust's lines, "My tears gush forth: the Earth takes back her child," in Goethe's *Faust,* Part One (night scene). • Only 4 more years to write down: Wagner kept annals for the years 1864–68 (until Cosima joined him at Tribschen), intending to continue *Mein Leben* up to that point.

MAY 20

•Schopenhauer . . . on the subject of professors: *Parerga und Paralipomena,* vol 1, *"Über die Universitäts-Philosophie"* ("On Philosophy at Universities"). • Mme Hartwig: Friederike Wilhelmine Hartwig, née Worthon (1777–1849), actress in Leipzig. • Stella Bonheur (1855–1901): French mezzo-soprano. • *Timon [of Athens]:* by Shakespeare. • Our journey through the floods in Ticino: September 14 to October 6, 1868.

MAY 21

•Schopenhauer on beards: *Parerga und Paralipomena, Aphorismen zur Lebensweisheit* (*The Wisdom of Life*). The "Apparent Deliberateness" chapter: *ibid.*

MAY 22

•Loldi's drawings: for Wagner's sixty-seventh birthday sixty-seven flowerpots containing roses had been wrapped in paper on which Isolde had made drawings, each depicting an event in one of the years of Wagner's life. • To which I had linked . . . *Parsifal:* as Wagner's thirteenth opera (starting from *Die Feen*). • The suns: a reference to Wagner's dream (see April 11, 1880). • The year '13 of this century: in which Wagner was born. Wagner, describing the birthday celebrations in his May 31 letter to King Ludwig, explained that he was opposed to having 13 people at table, "since a person to whom the stars have been so kind as they have to me has a right to be a little superstitious"; the fourteenth guest invited was Heinrich von Stein. • Humperdinck: Engelbert Humperdinck (1854–1921), composer of the opera *Hänsel und Gretel* (1893) and others; he appears quite frequently in the Diaries later, since he was engaged as a musical assistant for the *Parsifal* production of 1882.

MAY 23

•Mme Minghetti: Donna Laura Minghetti (1829–1915), wife of the Italian states-man Marco Minghetti; Marie Dönhoff was her daughter by her first marriage, to the Prince of Camporeale; Wagner had known her since 1861, when she impressed him by singing Isolde's *Liebestod* with "a surprising sureness of intonation" at a private gathering in Paris (*Mein Leben*).

MAY 25

•"When my master . . .": Oliver's aria in Act I of Boieldieu's *Jean de Paris.*

MAY 26

•Discovered Klingsor's garden: after visiting the park of the Palazzo Rufalo in Ravello, Wagner wrote in the visitor's book, "Klingsor's Magic Garden is found!" (see Cosima's account at the conclusion of the day's entry). • Mr. Reed: Neville Reed (spelled "Read" in Ernest Newman's biography of Wagner), an Englishman, owner of the Palazzo Rufalo.

MAY 30

• A letter to the King: in which, among other things, Wagner thanks King Ludwig for his birthday gift, an offer to pay the rent of the Villa d'Angri out of his own personal funds for a further five months (a total of 5,200 lire), thus enabling Wagner to prolong his stay in Italy for the benefit of his health.

MAY 31

•*La Tentation de Saint Antoine* (*The Temptation of Saint Anthony*): novel (1874) by Gustave Flaubert (1821–80). • Spohr and his last . . . opera: *Die Kreuzfahrer* (*The Crusaders*), first performed in 1845 in Kassel and also staged later that year in Berlin, but rejected by Dresden, where Wagner was then conductor; Wagner writes about the incident in *Mein Leben*.

JUNE 1

•Photographer and painter: the firm of P. Biondi e Figlio photographed Wagner with Siegfried, and Edmond Jean de Pury (1845–1911) painted a portrait of him in oils.

JUNE 4

•The bass singer Kneisel: Wilhelm Kneisel (died 1885), a member of Bethmann's company, for which Wagner was the conductor in Bad Lauchstädt and Magdeburg; Matteo is a character in Auber's *Fra Diavolo*.

JUNE 6

•"*Jungfernkranz*": bridal chorus in Weber's *Der Freischütz*, Act III. • Fetching my blankets: see note for June 5, 1878.

JUNE 7

•[Wagner's points]: set down in telegraphic style in Wagner's handwriting as follows: "Protectorate—royal decision acceptable to us, German Reich idea of friends rejected, unfruitful. *Earlier:* Only raised because of difficulties in Bavaria. Therefore director question so important. No candidate yet, Bürkel in better position to find one. Perhaps take up my Vienna plan with economic control (Bürkel, remaining secretary). Difficult, not impossible to find right way. Desired goal regular festivals in Bayreuth, to provide at same time model productions of all works for Munich and for German audiences everywhere in a German location (outside theater framework), Society of Patrons always covering extra costs. Start with *Parsifal* 1882. Consequently no unduly heavy expenditure for the King." • Baggesen: Jens Baggesen (1764–1826), Danish satirist and theater director; the *Musen-Almanach* was a periodical published by Schiller, 1796–1801.

JUNE 8

•Writing about Raphael: on the *Sistine Madonna* in "*Religion und Kunst*" ("Religion and Art"), *Bayreuther Blätter,* October 1880; see also June 10, 1880.

JUNE 9

•*Die Horen:* a periodical published by Schiller, 1795–97. • The heir's accession to the throne: this was looking ahead, since Tsar Alexander II was still alive; he was assassinated on March 13, 1881, and succeeded by his son, Alexander III.

JUNE 10

•"A man among the rest": Mephistopheles in Goethe's *Faust,* Part One (Faust's study); in Bayard Taylor's translation, "The worst society thou find'st will show thee / Thou art a man among the rest." • The Chiaia: the main coastal thoroughfare in Naples.

JUNE 11

 Lübke: Wilhelm Lübke (1826–93), an art historian, published in 1869, with the Austrian critic Eduard Hanslick, a pamphlet, "*Über Richard Wagner.*" • The 1864 album leaf: written by Wagner for Frau von Schleinitz (at that time—before her marriage—Marie von Buch) at the beginning of 1864 in Vienna, after his return from conducting a concert at Breslau (December 1863) at which she was present; a copy of the album leaf was discovered in the Diaries beside the entry for October 9, 1880; see note for that date.

JUNE 14
•Schopenhauer's dialogue about death and life after death: *Parerga und Paralipomena,* vol. 2, chap. X.

JUNE 15
•Fidi's *Kurwenal:* Kurwenal is Tristan's faithful companion in *Tristan und Isolde.* • Mme Mennikoffer: not identified.

JUNE 16
•The unveiling of the Goethe monument: on June 2, 1880, in Berlin, monument by Fritz Schaper.

JUNE 17
•The Order of Maximilian: Wagner, who reluctantly accepted this Bavarian decoration in 1873, was subsequently annoyed to discover that it had been awarded to Brahms at the same time (see December 31, 1873, in vol. I). • Kleist's *"Das Erdbeben in Chile"* ("Earthquake in Chile"): short story.

JUNE 20
•The subject in the history of Siena: at a meeting in Rome on November 30, 1876, Wagner advised Sgambati and the poet Cossa to undertake something together, suggesting a story about Siena in Sismondi's *History of the Italian Republics* (see vol. I).

JUNE 21
•Darwin's poem: the letter (January 1798) concerned the poem "The Botanic Garden" by Erasmus Darwin (1731–1802). • *"Steh nur auf"* ("Now Get Up"): a folk song from Silesia. • *Moses:* Rossini's opera *Mosè in Egitto,* 1818.

JUNE 22
•*"Die Kraniche des Ibykus"* ("The Cranes of Ibycus"): ballad by Schiller in which the murderers of the poet Ibycus are subsequently revealed by a flock of cranes that saw the crime committed.

JUNE 23
•Goethe's poem: presumably one of those about the moon, such as *"An Luna"* or *"An den Mond."* • "Urworte" ("Ancient words"): a poem by Goethe. • "Lovely moon . . .": from a German folk song of unknown authorship (*"Guter Mond, du gehst so stille | in den Abendwolken hin"*). • *"Der Schweizerbub"* ("The Swiss Boy"): a Swiss folk song.

JUNE 24
•Mendelssohn's *"Vieles Gewaltige lebt"* chorus: "Much that is mighty lives"; from the incidental music to Sophocles's *Antigone,* Opus 55. • *The Suppliants:* drama by Aeschylus.

JUNE 25
•A model for the diver and the maelstrom: in Schiller's ballad *"Der Taucher"* ("The Diver") a pageboy dives into a raging sea to recover a gold goblet thrown down by the king. • Dr. Schlemm: in 1880 Oscar Schlemm (see note for June 6, 1878) published *Drei Dramen, zur Komposition geeignet* (*Three Dramas, Designed to be Set to Music*).

JUNE 26
•*"Da sah ich ihn"* ("Then saw I' him"): from Tannhäuser's "Rome Narration," *Tannhäuser,* Act III, Scene 3.

JUNE 27
•King John's demands for money: a reference to the signing of the Magna Carta at Runnymede, England, in 1215. • Hegel: Georg Wilhelm Friedrich Hegel (1770–

1831), German philosopher. • Droysen: in his Dresden library Wagner had Johann Gustav Droysen's translations of Aeschylus, published 1832 in 2 vols. • Otfried Müller (1797–1840): author of a history of ancient Greek peoples (*Geschichte der hellenischen Stämme*), of which the 2nd vol., dealing with the Dorians, was in Wagner's Dresden library. • *Apollo Belvedere:* a statue in the Vatican. • Hermann: Gottfried Hermann (1772–1848), German classical philologist noted for his critical editions of Homer (the "famous" Hermann is presumably the chief of the Cherusci, Arminius, who defeated the Romans and became a German national hero).

JUNE 28
• "Pygmalion": a monodrama by Georg Benda, based on Rousseau; first produced in 1779, it was revived in Weimar in April 1798, and was discussed by Goethe and Schiller in their correspondence at that time. • The Gendarmen-Markt: square in Berlin; Karl Begas's statue of Schiller was erected there. • The *Kreuz-Zeitung; Neue Preussische Zeitung,* a conservative newspaper.

JUNE 29
•Miss Ouragan: not identified. • My two "ladies": Daniela and Blandine, with whom Cosima arrived in Starnberg on June 29, 1864.

JUNE 30
•Anecdote about Frau Beer with Frau Schröder-Devrient: not known; Frau Beer unidentifiable.

JULY 1
•"When menials build . . .": a reversal of Goethe's *Xenia* about Kant and his interpreters ("When monarchs build, menials have their hands full"). • *La Sonnambula:* opera by Bellini, 1831. • Gräfe: Konrad Gräfe, builder in Bayreuth; in fact, he survived his fall.

JULY 2
•Lusch, who was not with us: Daniela was at boarding school when the family stayed in Sorrento, October 5 to November 7, 1876. • Hummel's septet: in D Minor, Opus 74, by Johann Nepomuk Hummel (1778–1837). • Ercole: a dog. • *Hermann und Dorothea:* Goethe's epic idyll, 1798.

JULY 3
•Stein's work on G. Bruno: either the paper he wrote to qualify as a university lecturer, "On the Significance of the Poetical Element in the Philosophy of Giordano Bruno" (1881), or *"Der Wahn eines Helden"* ("A Hero's Madness"), published in Schmeitzner's *Internationale Monatsschrift,* January-February 1882. • "Sect for good": in his correspondence with Schiller, Goethe remarked on the many religious sects in existence but said there was still no "sect for good" (*"Sekte für das Gute"*). • Hähnel: Ernst Hähnel (1811–91), German sculptor whom Wagner met in Dresden in 1845; Wagner says in *Mein Leben* that he considered him affected.

JULY 5
•The Princess of Meiningen: Maria Elisabeth (1853–1923), daughter of the Duke of Meiningen by his first wife, Princess Charlotte of Prussia. • The scene from *As You Like It:* Jaques's attachment to deer is mentioned in Act II, Scene 1; his words on being confronted with a dead deer, Act IV, Scene 2.

JULY 6
•The regulation of the Greek border: at the second Berlin Congress, 1880. • The Goethe-Meyer classification of painters: the Swiss painter and writer Hans Heinrich Meyer (1760–1832), whom Goethe met in Italy, was called to the Academy of Design in Weimar in 1792 and became director in 1806; he was Goethe's adviser in matters of art.

JULY 7
•The *"Wilde Jagd"*: *"Lützow's Wilde Jagd"*; see note for January 3, 1878; the line quoted by Wagner ("That was Lützow's wild and daring chase") is the last, and the joke lies in the addition of the word *"jewesen,"* the Berlin dialect form of *"gewesen"* ("been") at the end.

JULY 9
•Stein's departure: he had been summoned back to the family estate by his father.
• What he has written . . . about Moltke: in *"Religion und Kunst."* • *Götz von Berlichingen:* Goethe's first drama, published 1773.

JULY 10
•The bishop in Belgium: possibly a reference to Joseph Hubert Reinkens, who became bishop of the Old Catholics in 1873 after having been excommunicated for opposing the doctrine of papal infallibility.

JULY 11
•Papageno: the simple birdcatcher in Mozart's *Die Zauberflöte.*

JULY 12
•His *"peau de chagrin"* walk: on a subsequent occasion Wagner uses the expression *"peau de chagrin"* ("shagreen") in the sense of a material shrinking the more it is worked on, and it seems feasible that he means something similar here, i.e., that each time he takes a certain walk it seems to become shorter; equally, the expression might derive from Balzac's novel *Peau de Chagrin* (translated as *The Fatal Skin* and *The Wild Ass's Skin*), which is based on the legend that the possessor of the skin sees it shrink every time a wish is fulfilled; in this case, Wagner might have thought that in his present state of health, any exertion (such as the walks he loved to take) might shorten his life.

JULY 13
•"One impulse . . .": Faust in Goethe's *Faust,* Part One (scene outside the city gates), Bayard Taylor's translation.

JULY 14
•The dispute between Russia and China: border encroachments in Ili, a constant source of trouble.

JULY 15
•*Via Crucis:* a work by Liszt, subtitled *"Les 14 Stations de la Croix"* ("The 14 Stations of the Cross"), for chorus and soloists with organ (or piano) accompaniment; written 1878–79, but not performed in public until 1929. • Frau Helbig: Nadine, née Princess Schahawski (1847–1915), wife of Wolfgang Helbig, a German archaeologist living in Rome, and a former pupil of Liszt. • Herr v. Keudell: Robert von Keudell (1824–1903), Prussian diplomat and ambassador in Rome at the time of Wagner's stay there, November 9 to December 3, 1876, during which Wagner saw both him and the Helbigs.

JULY 16
•*Die Hermannsschlacht:* drama by Kleist, published posthumously in 1821. • Wetter von Strahl: a character in Kleist's drama *Das Käthchen von Heilbronn.* • The Hohenstaufens: members of this German dynasty were holy Roman emperors during the years 1138–1254, the most renowned being Friedrich Barbarossa; the male line became extinct in 1268. • Friedrich II: Holy Roman Emperor from 1220, excommunicated by Pope Gregory IX in 1239 and declared deposed in 1245 by Pope Innocent IV.

JULY 19
•Malchen Lehmann: in 1826–27 the young Richard Wagner was a boarder in the home of a Dr. Böhme in Dresden, but he makes no mention of Malchen Lehmann

in *Mein Leben.* • My words about the Wittelsbach celebration: *"Zur Feier des 25. Augusts und zur Nachfeier des Wittelsbacher Festes"* ("In Celebration of August 25 and Belatedly of the Wittelsbach Festival"), published anonymously in the *Bayreuther Blätter,* August 1880; in it Cosima reproduces Goethe's letter to King Ludwig I of Bavaria (see note for July 12, 1880). • *"Wahnlos hold bewusst":* quotation from the love duet in Act II of *Tristan und Isolde.*

JULY 20
•Lothario: a character in Goethe's novel *Wilhelm Meister.* • December 2: date of Napoleon III's *coup d'état* in Paris in 1851.

JULY 22
•The E-flat Major Quartet . . . in Paris: a performance by the Morin-Chevillard Quartet that Wagner and Liszt heard in 1853.

JULY 23
•As a motto for his article: *"Religion und Kunst"* is prefaced by the following quotation: "In the Christian religion I find virtually everything which tends toward the highest and noblest, and the various forms it has taken in life seem to me repugnant and inept only because they are garbled representations of this highest. — Schiller to Goethe."

JULY 24
•Goethe's *"Der Sänger"* ("The Singer"): ballad, 1783. • Böcklin: Arnold Böcklin (1827–1901), Swiss painter best known for his painting *The Isle of the Dead.*

JULY 26
•"All you are fit for . . .": Mephistopheles in Goethe's *Faust,* Part One (Faust's study), the idea being that, whereas God can dwell in eternal light and the Devil in eternal darkness, the frailer human being requires constant change; for Bayard Taylor's translation of the whole passage see note for December 29, 1878. • Printing delays: in the preparation of the 4th vol. of *Mein Leben.*

JULY 27
•Herr Oelten: not identified. • A glass of beer at Dreher's: Cosima wrote "at Angermann's" by mistake. • Gräfenberg: a holiday resort in Silesia, Germany.

AUGUST 6
•Hawthorne: Nathaniel Hawthorne (1804–64), American novelist; *The Scarlet Letter* (1850) was translated into German in 1851.

AUGUST 7
•Poem to Prof. Schrön: a playful rhyme in praise of Naples and of Schrön (*"Was man als Wonn' und Wunder preist, | wie wär Neapel selbst so schön, | behütet uns so Leib als Geist | ein Freund nicht wie Professor Schrön? | Will ich Neapel's Pracht ermessen, | wie sollt' ich dieses Freund's vergessen?"*).

AUGUST 9
•Old Beppa: a flower seller encountered on a previous visit to Florence (see December 6, 1876, in vol. I).

AUGUST 10
•Ghibellines: since the thirteenth century the supporters of the holy Roman emperor against the Guelphs, supporters of the pope. • Magdala: village near Weimar in which Wagner stayed May 20–23, 1849, on his flight from Dresden.

AUGUST 11
•*Causes célèbres: Causes célèbres et intéressantes,* a 20-vol. series of famous criminal cases collected by François Gayot de Pitaval, published in Paris from 1734 on. • In such a h——: "*L*——" in German, presumably meaning *"Loch"* ("hole").

AUGUST 13
•The nut-brown maid: a figure in Goethe's novel *Wilhelm Meister* (*Wanderjahre*). • Morlacchi's successor: Francesco Morlacchi (1784–1841) was conductor of Italian

opera in Dresden from 1810 until his death; Wagner, who came to Dresden as a conductor in 1842, was not, however, precisely his successor, since he was engaged to conduct German operas.

AUGUST 15

•Helena's "significant group": in Act III of Goethe's *Faust,* Part Two, a stage direction reads, "Helena and the Chorus stand amazed and alarmed, in a significant group, well prepared in advance." • The burning down of the library: on July 12 the house of the historian Theodor Mommsen (1817–1903) in Berlin had been burned to the ground, with the loss of his own library and other valuable books from outside libraries. • Fragments by Schop. about intellect: Schopenhauer's *Parerga und Paralipomena,* vol. 2, chap. III.

AUGUST 16

•Graves of the Volumni: Etruscan remains near Perugia.

AUGUST 20

•Vaillant: physician whose water-cure sanatorium in Mornex, Switzerland, Wagner visited from June to August 1856, in the hope of curing his erysipelas.

AUGUST 21

•A visit to the cathedral: the interior of the cathedral in Siena was used as a model for the Temple of the Grail in the 1882 production of *Parsifal.* • Many things about medicine and physicians: Schopenhauer's *Parerga und Paralipomena,* vol. 2, chap. VI.

AUGUST 23

•Rental terms: the rent for the villa was 800 lire a month.

AUGUST 24

•Telegram to the King: enclosed in the Diaries a draft in Wagner's handwriting, sending birthday greetings and referring to his birthday gift—the final volume of *Mein Leben,* to be dispatched directly from the printers' in Bayreuth.

AUGUST 26

•The sight of this on a bottle: presumably the emperor's uniform.

AUGUST 28

•"Mozartiana": article by Ludwig Nohl published in the *Allgemeine Deutsche Musikzeitung,* August 13–20, 1880. • Burckhardt: Jacob Burckhardt (1818–97), Swiss art historian, author of *Geschichte der Renaissance in Italien* (*History of the Renaissance in Italy*); a professor at Basel University at the same time as Nietzsche. • *Numancia: El cerco de Numancia* (*The Siege of Numancia*), an intermezzo by Cervantes. • [A postcard]: addressed to Wagner at Bayreuth from Hamburg and dated August 17, 1880, it reads: "I am president of a dramatic club in Chicago and would be able to stage your earlier works there; but I have no fair-haired singers for the roles, but for the most part just dark-haired Jews, who are nonetheless enthusiastic admirers of your art. Would you advise me to risk it with such people in front of a Germanic audience? Request courtesy of an answer to Chicago and am yours respectfully, H. v. Leesen, president, Club 'Freundschaft,' corner of La Salle & Randolph Sts."

AUGUST 30

•Peruzzi: Baldassare Peruzzi (1481–1536), Italian painter and architect. • Prokrok: possibly August Prokop, author of "*Die Sicherheit der Person im Theater nebst Vorschlägen zur Reform des Theaterbaues*" ("Personal Safety in the Theater and Proposals for Theater Building Reforms"), published in Vienna in 1882 after the disastrous theater fire there; in it the Bayreuth festival theater is mentioned. • E. von Hagen: in an article in *Die Tonkunst,* vol. IX, 1880.

AUGUST 31

• The Wittelsbach jubilee: the seventh centennial of the Wittelsbach dynasty was celebrated in Bavaria on August 25, the birthday of the reigning Wittelsbach, Ludwig II.

SEPTEMBER 2

•Herr Schletterer: this undoubtedly refers to Heinrich Schletter, a rich Leipzig merchant and art patron, from whom Wagner borrowed money in 1840 during his first stay in Paris.

SEPTEMBER 3

•Ritter Toggenburg: in the ballad of the same name by Schiller, 1797.

SEPTEMBER 5

•The Strozzis: a noble family in Florence.

SEPTEMBER 6

•The papal bed: Pope Pius VI was said to have spent a night at the Villa Torre Fiorentina in 1775; see also September 28, 1880. • A poem by E. Geibel: "*Am 3. September 1870*" by Emanuel Geibel (1815–84); it was published in the *Illustrirte Zeitung* on the tenth anniversary of the Battle of Sedan. • For the ballet: a reference to the emperor's well-known affection for the ballet *Flick und Flock* or, correctly, *Flick und Flocks Abenteuer* (*The Adventures of F. and F.*), performed 419 times in Berlin alone between 1858 and 1885. • Bismarck has now become minister of commerce: he assumed this post in the Prussian government additionally in 1880, in order to facilitate the change-over from free trade to protective tariffs.

SEPTEMBER 7

•His brother Albert's debut: in *Mein Leben* Wagner relates that his eldest brother, fourteen years older than himself, made his debut as a tenor in Breslau, but he does not say exactly when or in what work; Albert, originally destined for a medical career, became a singer on the advice of Weber, who praised his voice. • Schrenck: Baron Karl von Schrenck (1806–84), Bavarian statesman. • *The Sorrows of Werther* (*Die Leiden des jungen Werthers*): Goethe's first novel (1774), a leading example of the *Sturm und Drang* movement.

SEPTEMBER 9

•"*An Werther*" ("To Werther"): the first poem in Goethe's "*Trilogie der Leidenschaft*" ("Trilogy of Passion"), 1824; the line "A fearful death . . ." ("*Ein grässlich Scheiden machte dich berühmt*") occurs in the last verse; "Elegy" ("*Elegie*") is the 2nd poem in the trilogy.

SEPTEMBER 10

•Albert: Lotte's husband in *Die Leiden des jungen Werthers*. • His "Nikolai" hymn: composed 1837.

SEPTEMBER 11

•The two women in *Tasso:* Leonore von Este and Leonore Sanvitale in Goethe's drama *Torquato Tasso*. • *Tancred:* here presumably *Tancrède*, Voltaire's drama, translated into German by Goethe.

SEPTEMBER 12

•"A Man's Place in the Estimation of Others": chap. 4 of Schopenhauer's *Aphorismen zur Lebensweisheit* (*The Wisdom of Life*).

SEPTEMBER 13

•[Goethe's] *Die Geschwister* (*Brother and Sister*): a play in one act, 1787.

SEPTEMBER 14

•The Franco-Russian War: Napoleon I's campaign in Russia, 1812–13. • A mass emigration of Englishmen from two provinces: Cosima is presumably using "Englishmen," in the usual German way, to describe all the inhabitants of the British Isles; the total number of emigrants to America from these was 145,000 in 1880, of whom 72,000 came from Ireland, and 13,000 from Scotland; the total from Germany in the same year was 85,000.

SEPTEMBER 18

•*Le Faux Démétrius* (*The False Demetrius*): account by the French writer Prosper Mérimée (1803–70) of an impostor who laid claim to the Russian throne in the early seventeenth century.

SEPTEMBER 20

•Three Petrarch sonnets: songs by Liszt, first published (with Italian text) 1846–47; arranged for piano, 1857; German texts added, 1880; the title of the third, omitted by Cosima, is "*Io vidi in terra angelici costumi.*"

SEPTEMBER 21

•*Smaller Catechism:* by Luther.

SEPTEMBER 23

•Prof. Volkelt: Johannes Immanuel Volkelt (1848–1930), German philosopher, professor in Jena.

SEPTEMBER 25

•"Tasso to the Princess": in Goethe's *Torquato Tasso* (Act I, Scene 3) Tasso comes to Princess Leonore with a book, saying, "I come slowly to bring you a work, and hesitate to give it to you. . . ." • The artist's imitation of Nature: Schopenhauer's *Parerga und Paralipomena,* vol. 2, chap. XIX.

SEPTEMBER 27

•The letter C: standing for ,Cosmas; drawn and decorated by Isolde. • Ferry: Jules Ferry (1832–93), French politician, Republican; prime minister 1880–81 and 1883–85; Wagner became friends with him in Paris in 1859, when Ferry was working as a journalist, and he included him among the figures in his play *Eine Kapitulation.*

SEPTEMBER 28

•Quaglio: Angelo Quaglio (1829–90), head of the scenery department of the Munich Court theaters from 1849. • Morosini: Francesco Morosini (1618–94), a sea captain who became doge of Venice in 1688. • Schulenburg: Count Johann Matthias von der Schulenburg (1661–1747), Saxon and Venetian general, defended Corfu against the Turks in 1716. • A minister of education: Ferry held this position and then that of minister for foreign affairs in the French Republican government of 1879.

SEPTEMBER 29

•As previously in Corinth: a reference to Saint Paul's stay there.

OCTOBER 3

•"*Der Geisterseher*" ("The Man Who Saw Ghosts"): unfinished story by Schiller (1788) about the charlatan Cagliostro; it is set in Venice.

OCTOBER 6

•Tesarini: Luigi Tesarini, an Italian supporter of Wagner and a piano teacher in Venice, where Wagner first met him in 1858.

OCTOBER 7

•The first "Picture" from *Tristan:* one of Josef Rubinstein's piano arrangements. • "She who kept silent . . .": Tristan in Act I, Scene 5, of *Tristan und Isolde* ("*Des Schweigens Herrin heisst mich schweigen*").

OCTOBER 9

•Reunion with Mimi: Frau von Schleinitz; enclosed beside this entry is a sheet of paper inscribed in Cosima's handwriting, "Appendix to the biography / album leaf for Frl. von Buch (in text of biography slight correction, addition, to be made)"; on the reverse side are a few bars from *Tristan und Isolde* and a written dedication, "*Was ich liebe, was ich hasse | Wär' zu sagen viel gewagt: | Was als höchstes Glück ich fasse | Sei in Tönen hier geklagt. | Richard Wagner*" ("To say what I love and what I hate would be too bold; let what I see as the greatest happiness be here bewailed in music"); also written down is a variant for the two last lines, "*Was ich lieber raten lasse | Sei in Tönen hier gesagt"* ("Let what I prefer to advise be here expressed in music"); the projected appendix to *Mein Leben* was never carried out by Wagner and Cosima; for an earlier reference to this album leaf, see note for June 11, 1880.

OCTOBER 10

•My salute to the 10th: anniversary of Wagner's first meeting with Cosima, in Paris, 1853.

OCTOBER 13

•Paesiello's *Barbiere di Siviglia:* opera (1782) by the Italian composer Giovanni Paesiello (1740–1816).

OCTOBER 14

•Bellini's picture: a Madonna with saints and angels, also containing a representation of the Doge Barbarigo; it is not, however, in the cathedral at Murano, but in the Church of S. Pietro Martire. • "The Children Next Door" ("*Die wunderlichen Nachbarskinder"*): a short story within the framework of Goethe's novel *Elective Affinities* (*Die Wahlverwandtschaften*).

OCTOBER 15

•Princess Hatzfeldt: Marie, née von Nimptsch (1820–97), widow of Prince Friedrich von Hatzfeldt-Trachenberg (1808–74); he was her second husband; Marie von Schleinitz was the daughter of her first marriage.

OCTOBER 16

•Our matter is now settled: on October 15 Ludwig II sanctioned the use of orchestra and chorus from the Munich opera at the Bayreuth festival of 1882.

OCTOBER 18

•"What Boots This Knowledge?" ("*Was nützt diese Erkenntnis?"*): a supplement to "*Religion and Art,*" *Bayreuther Blätter,* December 1880, and collected writings, vol. 10. • The Manin monument: a bronze statue, close to the Teatro Rossini, commemorating the Venetian freedom fighter Daniele Manin (1804–57).

OCTOBER 19

•"*Wohin Tristan geht*": correctly, "*Wohin nun Tristan scheidet, willst du, Isold', ihm folgen?*" ("Wherever Tristan may go, wilt thou, Isolde, follow?"); *Tristan und Isolde,* Act II, Scene 3.

OCTOBER 21

•The cardinal virtues: meant here are not those of the ancients (prudence, justice, temperance, and fortitude) but, rather, the Christian virtues mentioned in "What Boots This Knowledge?"—faith, hope, and charity. • The Cologne Cathedral festivities: the famous cathedral, begun in 1248, was not completed until 1880, when the inauguration took place in the presence of Emperor Wilhelm I. • Herr Oppenheim: the Cologne banker Baron Abraham von Oppenheim (1804–78) was very active in facilitating the completion of the cathedral; Cosima's reference could be to him or to one of his brothers, Simon and Dagobert.

OCTOBER 22

•Count Gobineau: Count Joseph Arthur de Gobineau (1816–82), a widely traveled French writer and diplomat, chiefly remembered for his racial theories, an influence on Nietzsche, Houston Stewart Chamberlain, and subsequently Adolf Hitler; his 4-vol. work, *Essai sur l'inégalité des races humaines* (*The Inequality of the Human Races*), 1853–55, was translated by Schemann into German; he also wrote a history of the Persians (*Histoire des Perses,* 1869), a long poem, *Amadis* (1876), a series of stories on Asian themes (*Nouvelles asiatiques,* 1876), and a series of dialogues involving figures from the Renaissance period (*La Renaissance: Scènes historiques,* 1877); he became a very close friend of the Wagners, and he and his works figure frequently in future entries in the Diaries.

OCTOBER 26

•Frau v. W[öhrmann]: Baroness Emma von Wöhrmann; actually, she became ill and remained in Venice.

OCTOBER 27

•A letter from the King . . . causes dejection: Wagner, in his September 28 letter to King Ludwig from Siena, had asked the King to arrange performances of *Lohengrin* and *Die Meistersinger* in Munich in the first two weeks of November, when he intended to be there, so that the children could see them; Ludwig, replying on October 24 from Linderhof, agreed to arrange the performances but added that it would cause less difficulty if these could be in the second half of November, rather than the first. • His private performances: King Ludwig had many plays, frequently on French historical themes, specially written and performed for him alone in the Residenztheater in Munich during the years 1876–85; Verdi's opera *Aida* was, of course, not among these; since its first production in Cairo in 1871 it had rapidly spread throughout Europe and would have been in the normal repertoire of the Munich opera.

OCTOBER 30

•"Then goes he . . .": a paraphrase of Sarastro's words in Act II, Scene 12, of Mozart's *Die Zauberflöte* ("Then goes he, led by a friendly hand, pleased and gay to a better land").

OCTOBER 31

•Brockhaus: Friedrich Brockhaus, husband of Wagner's sister Luise. • From Magdeburg to Königsberg: in the summer of 1836. • Briennerstrasse 8c: close to Briennerstrasse 21, Wagner's first house in Munich, to which he came in September 1864.

NOVEMBER 2

•[Méhul's] *Joseph:* opera, 1807.

NOVEMBER 3

•Jacolliot's book: *Voyage aux pays des éléphants* (*Voyage to the Land of Elephants*) by Louis Jacolliot (1839–90), Paris 1876.

NOVEMBER 4

•Sitting with the photographer: Joseph Albert, Munich. • Herr v. Ziegler: Friedrich von Ziegler (1839–97): King Ludwig's Cabinet secretary.

NOVEMBER 7

•Young Muncker: Franz Muncker (1855–1926), son of the mayor of Bayreuth.

NOVEMBER 8

•Charge admission for the performances: it had always been an integral part of Wagner's Bayreuth festival idea that there should be no direct charge for admission to performances—an ideal he was obliged to abandon if *Parsifal* was to be staged at all, owing to lack of funds.

NOVEMBER 9

•A sitting for him with Gedon: for a bronze bust that was not cast until 1883, after Wagner's death. • *Coppélia:* ballet (1870) by Léo Delibes (1836–91).

NOVEMBER 11

•The program for *Parsifal:* a description of the Prelude to *Parsifal,* written for the King, to accompany the performance of the Prelude on the following day; reprinted in the correspondence between Wagner and King Ludwig and in vol. 12 of the collected writings.

NOVEMBER 12

•The King demands the Prelude to *Lohengrin:* for this Wagner handed over the baton to Levi. • Kings having curious humors: Nym in Shakespeare's *Henry V*

(Act II, Scene 1), "The king hath run bad humors on the knight," and "The king is a good king: but it must be as it may; he passes some humors and careers."

NOVEMBER 13

•*Staberl's Abenteuer:* correctly, *Staberl's Reiseabenteuer* (*Staberl's Adventurous Travels*), a popular Viennese farce (1822) by Adolf Bäuerle (1786–1859). • The actor Lang: Ferdinand Lang (1810–82), in Munich since 1834, was famous for roles such as Staberl. • Gobineau's *La Renaissance:* see note for October 22, 1880.

NOVEMBER 14

•The Orlando Lasso: a restaurant in Munich much frequented by the artistic community. • Possart: Ernst Ritter von Possart (1841–1921), actor and stage director at the Munich Court theater from 1864; subsequently became theater director and was responsible for the model productions of Wagner's works in the Munich Prinzregententheater (a replica of the Bayreuth festival theater) from 1901.

NOVEMBER 17

•Moritz and Fuchs: Jacob Moritz and Konrad Fuchs, inspector and janitor respectively at the festival theater.

NOVEMBER 18

•Irwine: David Irwine, a moneyed Scotsman living in Leipzig and a generous contributor to the Society of Patrons; he wrote several books about Wagner, including *A Wagnerian's Midsummer Madness, Being Essays on the Wagner Question* (H. Grevel & Co., London). • Rosenlehner: Rudolph Rosenlehner, Munich, a life member of the Society of Patrons; he was in fact cited in the *Bayreuther Blätter* in 1880 for making a special contribution of 400 marks to the festival funds, on top of his life membership of 1,000 marks.

NOVEMBER 19

•The sad tune: played by the shepherd in Act III of *Tristan und Isolde.* • A lady called Ramann: Lina Ramann, a piano teacher who ran a music school in Nuremberg; the first volume of her well-known biography of Liszt, covering the years 1811–40, appeared in 1880; two further volumes followed. • Bellagio: the village on Lake Como in which Cosima was born.

NOVEMBER 20

•Count G.'s book: Gobineau's *La Renaissance;* the two scenes mentioned occur in the chapter titled "Michelangelo."

NOVEMBER 21

•"Moving with me . . .": based on the final words of the theater manager in the "Prelude on the Stage" to Goethe's *Faust,* Part One. • V[ittoria] Colonna (1492–1547): Italian poet.

NOVEMBER 22

•The banner of love: a yellow silk embroidered coverlet presented to Wagner on his most recent birthday. • Good news of Boni: Blandine was in Munich. • Our first journey to Italy: September-October 1868.

NOVEMBER 23

•*Der Bauer als Millionär* (*The Millionaire Peasant*): play by Ferdinand Raimund, 1826.

NOVEMBER 24

•The old opera house: the Markgräfliches Opernhaus in Bayreuth. • Schelling: Friedrich Wilhelm Joseph von Schelling (1775–1854), German idealist philosopher; Constantin Frantz's book about him, *Schellings positive Philosophie,* appeared in 3 pts., 1879–80, and was dedicated to Wagner.

NOVEMBER 28

•Festive day: anniversary of Wagner and Cosima's vow in 1863 "to belong entirely to each other." • The theater director asks for a certificate: Angelo Neumann requested Wagner to give him written authority to produce the *Ring* in Berlin.

NOVEMBER 29

•The Reichsadler: a hotel in Bayreuth. • Melanchthon: Philipp Melanchthon (1497–1560), Luther's friend and assistant. • Michael Servetus: correctly, Miguel Serveto (1511–53), scholar, physician, and anti-Trinitarian, condemned to death by the town council of Geneva and burned at the stake.

NOVEMBER 30

•Set the ball rolling in the Emperor's Court: "Such paper, stead of gold and jewelry, / so handy is—one knows one's property"; Mephistopheles in Act I of Goethe's *Faust,* Part Two (Bayard Taylor's translation). • Publishing these letters: the letters to Theodor Uhlig, Wilhelm Fischer, and Ferdinand Heine first published together in Leipzig, 1888; those to his first wife, Minna, in 2 vols., Berlin and Leipzig, 1908; to Alwine Fromann, in the *Bayreuther Blätter,* 1912; the correspondence with Liszt in 2 vols., Leipzig, 1887 (third, much-enlarged, edition, 1910); the letters between Wagner and Cosima were destroyed, apart from a few (see note for May 6, 1879).

DECEMBER 1

•New Zealand: although Cosima wrote "Seeland," the context suggests that she meant "Neuseeland" (New Zealand), not the Dutch province of Zeeland. • A compulsory savings bank: the beginning of social insurance in Germany, initiated by an imperial proclamation on November 17, 1881. • The eternal feminine drags one downward: a reversal of the final line of Goethe's *Faust,* Part Two, "*Das Ewig-Weibliche zieht uns hinan*" ("The eternal feminine leads us on"). • "Brooms, oh, brooms . . .": from Goethe's poem "*Der Zauberlehrling*" ("The Sorcerer's Apprentice"). • Creuzer: Friedrich Creuzer (1771–1858), German philologist, author of *Symbolik und Mythologie der alten Völker, besonders der Griechen* (*The Symbolism and Mythology of Ancient Peoples, Particularly the Greeks*), 4 vols., 1810–12, in Wagner's library.

DECEMBER 2

•His reply to the King: the gesture King Ludwig inquired about in his letter of November 17 was made by Wagner during the private performance of *Lohengrin* in Munich on November 10 (incidentally, his last meeting with the King); in his reply, dated December 2, Wagner said that he had been conducting a soliloquy in his mind about the nature of music and had resolved to stage all his works "perfectly" in Bayreuth: "*Parsifal* shall prepare the way for it, and he—your fair King— will help you without fail!" • *Joseph:* Méhul's opera.

DECEMBER 3

•"But nothing compared . . .": quotation from Goethe's novel *Elective Affinities;* see March 14, 1873, in vol. I.

DECEMBER 4

•Fr[itzsch]'s music periodical: *Musikalisches Wochenblatt.* • Ehlert: Louis Ehlert (1825–84), German composer and writer on music.

DECEMBER 5

•A telegram from Herr v. Hülsen: "Dear Master, does joint performance with director Neumann in opera house of *Ring* cycle give me subsequent right to include *Die Walküre* in permanent repertoire against usual royalties? Reply paid, v. Hülsen." • *Preciosa:* play by P. A. Wolff based on Cervantes's story "*La Gitanella*" ("The Gypsy Girl"), with music by Weber (1821); but see note for December 12, 1880.

DECEMBER 9

•Fischer's appointment: Franz Fischer, hitherto in Mannheim. • Robert Springer: a Berlin vegetarian and translator of Gleizès's *Thalysia* into German; contributed an article ("Richard Wagner's Regenerative Idea") to the *Bayreuther Blätter,* February

1881. • Röckel's misdeed: August Röckel (1814–76), a fellow conductor and close friend of Wagner in Dresden in the 1840's; after spending several years in prison for his role in the Dresden uprising of 1849, he settled in Munich, and the friendship was resumed; however, in 1868 Wagner suspected him of having spread gossip about his relationship with Cosima, and the friendship ended; this was presumably the "misdeed," greeted by Wagner as "a salvation" since it brought the matter out into the open and contributed to Cosima's decision to give up Hans von Bülow and join Wagner permanently. • The General Staff's report: on the Franco-Prussian War; publication by the historical section of the German General Staff began in 1772 (*Der deutsch-französische Krieg 1870–71, redigiert von der Kriegsgeschichtlichen Abteilung des grossen Generalstabs,* Berlin). • *Gnautis auton:* Cosima's spelling of the inscription ("Know thyself") in the temple of Delphi. • Antonio: the state secretary in Goethe's play *Torquato Tasso.*

DECEMBER 10
• Performance of an opera in the presence of "the master": a caricature by Adolf Oberländer in the *Fliegende Blätter.*

DECEMBER 11
• Freytag's *Die Ahnen (The Ancestors)*: a series of six historical novels dealing with a German family from early to modern times, by Gustav Freytag, published 1872–80. • Ossian: a semimythical Gaelic bard whose works James Macpherson claimed, in the eighteenth century, to have discovered and translated; they had a great influence in Germany, though at home there was always doubt about their authenticity. • *"Sterbe, höchste Gnade": * correctly, *"Sterben . . . Einz'ge Gnade"* ("To die . . . the only mercy"); Amfortas in *Parsifal,* III, bars 977 ff. • Jn. Pérès: Jean-Baptiste Pérès (1752–1840), a French librarian who attempted in 1835 to prove that Napoleon I had never lived. • A mood such as I can well imagine him to have had: in his *Beethoven* Wagner likens the first movement to an awakening on the morning of a day "which in its long course will not fulfill a single wish—not one"; Cosima refers more explicitly to this passage on December 12.

DECEMBER 12
• The day would not fulfill any wish: a reference to Wagner's *Beethoven;* see note for December 11, 1880. • Cervantes's story: presumably *"La Gitanella"* ("The Gypsy Girl"); this suggests that Cosima, when referring to *Preciosa* (see entry and note for December 5, 1880), meant Cervantes's original story and not Wolff's dramatic adaptation of it.

DECEMBER 13
• The revolutionaries: the German editors state that the word used here can only be read as *"Reaktionäre"* (reactionaries), but they conclude that Cosima must have meant *"Revolutionäre."*

DECEMBER 15
• R[ichard] III and his soliloquy: Shakespeare's *Richard III,* Act I, Scene 1 ("Now is the winter of our discontent . . .").

DECEMBER 17
• The American march: the "Centennial March." • Beethoven's birthday: December 17, 1770 (actually the date of his christening). • Louis Schlösser (1800–86): composer, conductor, and music critic who wrote reminiscences of Beethoven for the *Allgemeine Musikzeitung.* • R.'s short story: "A Pilgrimage to Beethoven."

DECEMBER 18
• *Amadis:* Gobineau's poem was written in 1876 but not published until 1887, posthumously, so Wagner must have read it in manuscript. • Vogler: Heinrich Vogler, head teacher in Bayreuth. • Hans's cousin Frege: Arnold Frege, son of Hans von Bülow's uncle and aunt Woldemar and Livia Frege. • The Bülow fund:

the proceeds (40,000 marks) of a concert tour undertaken by Hans von Bülow in support of the Bayreuth festival (see February 21, 1880, and note, and September 3, 1880). • Frau D[egele]: wife of the singer Eugen Degele (1834–86), at Dresden from 1861; his roles included the Flying Dutchman and Wolfram in *Tannhäuser*.

DECEMBER 19
•Busch: Dr. Moritz Busch; see note for November 9, 1878.

DECEMBER 20
•His son-in-law: Adolf von Gross.

DECEMBER 21
•Ailinos: a cry of anguish (Greek). • Our friends stay to supper: Feustel, Gross, and Muncker. • *"Am stillen Herd"*: Walther von Stolzing's song in Act I of *Die Meistersinger*.

DECEMBER 22
•Wehwalt: the name Siegmund (sung in Bayreuth in 1876 by Niemann) calls himself in *Die Walküre*, Act I.

DECEMBER 23
•*"Schon nah' dem Schlosse . . ."*: Gurnemanz in *Parsifal*, I, bars 518 ff.

DECEMBER 24
•The *Christkind*: the infant Jesus, whom children in South Germany and Austria traditionally believe to bring the Christmas presents. • He wants Joukowsky to paint it: the *tableau vivant* of the Holy Family, as painted by Joukowsky, shows the artist as Joseph, Daniela as Mary, Blandine as an angel with a lute, Isolde as an angel with a violin, Eva as an angel with a shawm, and Siegfried as the boy Jesus; at this first showing Joseph was depicted by Pepino, not Joukowsky.

DECEMBER 25
•*"Geschreibsel, Gebleibsel!"*: as a birthday present, Wagner gave Cosima a little casket, on which he had had inscribed the words, *"Geschreibsel, Gebleibsel für lieb' gut' Weibsel"* ("Scribbles and scraps for my good little wife"); it was accompanied by an "Antique Choral Song," which the children sang; the music for this does not appear to have been preserved. • The 9th Symphony, copied out by R.: the complete orchestral score of Beethoven's Ninth Symphony, copied by Wagner in 1830; when he left Dresden in 1849, Wagner gave it to his friend Theodor Uhlig. • Sending birthday bliss to the sun: Wagner's telegram to the King reads, *"Und abermals strahlte die Sonne, / Es dankt Geburtstag Wonne"* ("And once more the sun shone, to be thanked by birthday bliss"). • "When thou appearest": ". . . the wilderness grows bright" (*"Wo du erscheinst, da wird die Wildnis helle"*); Weber's *Euryanthe*, Act I, Scene 7. • The C Major Overture: all three of Beethoven's *Leonore* Overtures are in C Major, so this could refer to either No. 1 or No. 2 (the "great" one being No. 3).

DECEMBER 26
•Faf on the hill: the Newfoundland dog at the festival theater.

DECEMBER 27
•His new castle: Neuschwanstein, built on the top of a hill west of Hohenschwangau, Bavaria; begun in 1869, it was not completed until the year King Ludwig died, 1886.

DECEMBER 28
•*A Voyage to the Land of Elephants*: Jacolliot's book; see note for November 3, 1880. • A scientific encyclopedia by Hederich: *Realschullexikon*, by Benjamin Hederich (1675–1748).

DECEMBER 29
•Gobineau's *Nouvelles asiatiques*: see note for October 22, 1880. • Krupp: Alfred Krupp (1812–87), son of Friedrich Krupp, who founded the famous steelworks in

Essen, Germany, in 1811. • Talk of Meiningen: where in 1880 Hans von Bülow had become music director, a post he held until 1885.

DECEMBER 31

•The Giessels: Carl Giessel (1824–1907) was a Bayreuth bookseller and publisher of the newspaper *Bayreuther Tagblatt*. • The A Major Symphony: both here and on January 1, 1881, Cosima in fact wrote "E-flat Major Symphony," but the context makes it clear that she was referring, not to Beethoven's *Eroica* Symphony, but to the Seventh (see note for January 1, 1881). • We experienced it yesterday: i.e., New Year's Eve—presumably the sight of Lenbach's picture reminded them of the previous New Year's Eve, spent in Munich with Lenbach and others (see December 31, 1879). • Helm: Theodor Otto Helm (1843–1920), Austrian musicologist; his books include *Beethovens Letzte Quartette* (*Beethoven's Last Quartets*), 1868, and *Beethovens Streichquartette. Versuch einer technischen Analyse* (*Beethoven's String Quartets: An Essay in Technical Analysis*), 1873.

1881

JANUARY 1

•In Mannheim: at a concert there on December 20, 1871, Wagner conducted Beethoven's Seventh Symphony in A Major. • Tausig once said to me about the *Freischütz* Overture: Wagner conducted this work in a concert in Vienna, organized by Karl Tausig, on December 27, 1863. • Dr. Schanzenbach: Oskar Schanzenbach, personal physician to the Bavarian prime minister, Prince Chlodwig zu Hohenlohe-Schillingsfürst, when Wagner was obliged (in 1867) to leave Munich at King Ludwig's request; Schanzenbach worked as an intermediary in efforts to secure Wagner's return to Munich. • Elvira's lament: Elvira is Don Giovanni's discarded sweetheart, whom he mocks when she continues to pursue him. • The wedding of the Crown Prince: Rudolf (1858–89), only son of Emperor Franz Joseph of Austria, who married Princess Stephanie of Belgium. • But for the boors: Wagner used this word in English to make his pun.

JANUARY 2

•"*La Española inglessa*" ("The Spanish-English Lady"): one of Cervantes's *Novelas exemplares* (*Exemplary Tales*).

JANUARY 3

•Phidias's *Athena:* the Greek sculptor Phidias, or Pheidias (born c.500 B.C.), produced many statues of the goddess Athena (in the Propylaea, the Parthenon, etc.), though none of them can be claimed as his work with absolute certainty; the find recorded by Cosima was probably connected with the excavations at Pergamus, made by Prussian archaeologists in 1880.

JANUARY 4

•Councilor Tusmann: character in E. T. A. Hoffmann's story "*Die Brautwahl.*"

JANUARY 5

•"*In heilig ernster Nacht . . .*": correctly, "*Ihm neigten sich, in heilig ernster Nacht, dereinst des Heilands selige Boten*" ("Once, on a solemn, holy night, the blessed heralds of the Saviour bowed before him"); *Parsifal,* I, bars 575 ff. ("*Heiland*" means "Saviour"). • "*Die Brautschau*": correctly, "*Die Brautwahl,*" the E. T. A. Hoffmann story alluded to on the previous day.

JANUARY 6

•Countess La Tour: Marie Mathilde Ruinart de Brimont (born c.1842), wife of Count Victor de La Tour, Italian ambassador in Stockholm; there, in 1872, she met Gobineau, with whom she formed an intimate relationship; she was an artist and painted a portrait of Count Gobineau. • The [Opus] 133 Fugue: Beethoven's

Grosse Fuge in B-flat Major for String Quartet. • The philosopher Hartmann: Eduard von Hartmann (1842–1906), who attempted to combine the basic principles of Schelling, Hegel, and Schopenhauer; his book *Philosophie des Unbewussten* (*The Philosophy of the Unconscious*), 1869, attracted much attention.

JANUARY 7
•*Ottar Jarl: Histoire d'Ottar Jarl, pirate norvégien* (*Biography of Ottar Jarl, Norwegian Pirate*), 1879.

JANUARY 9
•Marius: Gaius Marius (156–86 B.C.), Roman general and consul, subject of a biography by Plutarch.

JANUARY 10
•Molle: a Newfoundland bitch; her name was soon changed to Molly. • The Magic Garden: the setting for Act II of *Parsifal*.

JANUARY 11
•The Chileans, who are now outside Lima: in the war with Peru over the nitrate fields of Tarapacá (1879–83), Chile captured Lima on January 17, 1881, and occupied Peru. • *"L'Illustre magicien"*: a story in Gobineau's *Nouvelles asiatiques*.

JANUARY 12
•Wilhelmj's new wine: the violinist August Wilhelmj owned a vineyard on the Rhine. • Humperdinck: Engelbert Humperdinck came to Bayreuth on January 8 to start work on a fair copy of the *Parsifal* score. • Dorfbarbier: *Der Dorfbarbier* (*The Village Barber*), a comic opera (1796) by Johann Schenk (1753–1836). • *Donau-Weibchen: Das Donauweibchen* (*The Danube Nymph*), a comic opera (1798) by Ferdinand Kauer (1751–1831). • Marsillach: see note for January 16, 1878. • *Ich-Neumann:* literally, "I-Neumann"; in German it would sound like "ichneumon" (the generic name for wasplike insects). • A pamphlet against the Jews: *Die Judenfrage als Racen-, Sitten- und Kulturfrage* (*The Jewish Problem from Its Racial, Moral, and Cultural Aspects*), by Karl Eugen Dühring, 1881; Dühring was one of the main instigators of political anti-Semitism, along with Bernhard Förster and Adolf Stoecker.

JANUARY 13
•Karl Brandt (1828–81): technical director of the theater in Darmstadt; he took a leading part in the building of the festival theater in Bayreuth and in the 1876 production of the *Ring;* Feustel's objection to him was probably that he was not always very easy to get along with, but Wagner had a high opinion of him.

JANUARY 14
•The lighting for the dove: at the end of *Parsifal* a white dove appears from the cupola of the Temple and hovers over Parsifal's head.

JANUARY 15
•*"Gamber-Ali"*: story in Gobineau's *Nouvelles asiatiques*.

JANUARY 16
•The poem by Emperor Heinrich: the Hohenstaufen Holy Roman Emperor Heinrich IV (1165–97) was also one of the minnesinger poets; three of his poems are preserved.

JANUARY 17
•The Berrs: Dr. Berr, the district medical officer in Bayreuth, and his wife, Amalie. • The Crown Prince: Friedrich Wilhelm, later Emperor Friedrich III; his wife was Princess Victoria, daughter of Queen Victoria. • Magnus: Magnus Schwantje, president of the world federation against vivisection. • The confirmation of the two girls: Isolde and Eva; since both were born while Cosima was married to Hans von Bülow, they were still legally his daughters. • The [Opus] 106 Sonata: Bee-

thoven's *Hammerklavier* Sonata. • Living together for 17 years: Cosima joined Wagner at Starnberg in June 1864.

JANUARY 18

•His book on style: *Der Stil in den technischen und tektonischen Künsten* (*Style in the Technical and Tectonic Arts*), by Gottfried Semper, 2 vols., 1860–63.

JANUARY 20

•"*Les Amants de Kandahar*": a story in Gobineau's *Nouvelles asiatiques.* • "*Ich sank in süssen Schlaf*" ("I sank into a sweet sleep"): Elsa in *Lohengrin,* Act I, Scene 1 (conclusion of "*Einsam in trüben Tagen*").

JANUARY 21

•Rossi: Ernesto Rossi (1827–96), an Italian actor. • Delitzsch: Franz Delitzsch (1813–90), a Protestant theologian from Leipzig, active in missionary work among the Jews. • "*La Guerre des Turcomans*": a story in Gobineau's *Nouvelles asiatiques.*

JANUARY 22

•A pamphlet by Paul de Lagarde: probably *Semitica,* 1879. • The guarantee certificates: one of the measures decided on at the meeting of the Society of Patrons earlier in the month—a call for guarantees ranging from 100 to 10,000 marks to ensure yearly festivals, 1882–84. • Lilli Lehmann (1848–1929): sang Woglinde, Helmwige, and the Wood Bird in the 1876 *Ring* production; at this time she was singing in Berlin and also in London.

JANUARY 23

•The old clog-maker: a reference to Dürer's portrait of Hieronymus Holzschuher.

JANUARY 25

•His French text of *Der Fl. Holländer:* Wagner submitted his prose sketch for *Der Fliegende Holländer* (based in part on a tale by Heine, who lived in Paris) to the Grand Opera in Paris in the summer of 1840, in the hope of being commissioned to write the work; the opera offered him 500 francs for the sketch, which Wagner, being short of money, accepted, and Pierre Dietsch wrote an opera based on it entitled *Le Vaisseau Fantôme;* this work, staged in Paris in 1842, had only eleven performances.

JANUARY 26

•"*Vidriera*": "*El licenciado vidriera*" ("The Licentiate of Glass"); one of Cervantes's *Novelas exemplares.* • Episode of Duplessis-Mornay and H[enri] IV: the French statesman Philippe de Mornay, Seigneur Duplessis-Marly (1549–1623), was converted to Protestantism and in 1576 entered the service of Henri IV, King of Navarre and France, for many years the leader of the Protestant cause.

JANUARY 28

•The puppet theater in Heidelberg: Cosima gives an account of their visit to it on May 14, 1871 (see vol. I). • St. Gallen: Wagner and Liszt both conducted at a concert there on November 23, 1856; probably Liszt played Beethoven's *Hammerklavier* Sonata privately while they were there.

JANUARY 29

•A poor neighbor: Frau Amalie Berr. • Dr. Falko's institute: Dr. Falko practiced in the mental hospital at St. Gilgenberg, near Bayreuth. • "*La Danseuse de Samakha*": a story in Gobineau's *Nouvelles asiatiques;* it deals with the Lezghians, one of the Caucasian peoples of Daghestan. • He jests at scars: Cosima slightly misquotes Romeo in Shakespeare's *Romeo and Juliet,* Act II, Scene 2; it should be "that never felt a wound."

JANUARY 30

•R.'s program note: see note for September 26, 1879. • It was a German who revived the memory of this being: Schiller, in his play about Joan of Arc, *Die Jungfrau von Orleans.*

JANUARY 31
•Stein's article: a review by Heinrich von Stein of Gobineau's *La Renaissance, Bayreuther Blätter,* January 1881.

FEBRUARY 1
•Prof. Dühring's essay: the pamphlet *Die Judenfrage;* see note for January 12, 1881.
• *"Vie en voyage"*: correctly, *"La vie de voyage,"* the final story in Gobineau's *Nouvelles asiatiques.* • Our journey across the Brünig: on March 30, 1866, coming from Geneva, Wagner and Cosima reached the Lake of Lucerne and saw Tribschen for the first time. • *Schwendi Fluh:* a steep cliff in Obwalden, part of the Swiss canton of Unterwalden.

FEBRUARY 2
•He got down to his article: *"Erkenne dich selbst"* ("Know Thyself"), a supplement to "Religion and Art," *Bayreuther Blätter,* February–March 1881, and vol. 10 of the collected writings. • An anecdote told in Vienna: not identified.

FEBRUARY 3
•To choose between *l'attrape* . . . and La Trappe: *"l'attrape"* means "hoax," La Trappe is the Cistercian abbey in France in which the austere Trappist branch of the order originated in the seventeenth century. • Epaminondas: a general in Thebes in the fourth century B.C. • *"La fuerça de la sangre"* ("The Force of Blood"): one of Cervantes's *Novelas exemplares.*

FEBRUARY 4
•Dean C[aselmann]: Wilhelm Caselmann, Bayreuth. • Beeth.'s last quartet—ours: Cosima usually describes as "ours" the C-sharp Minor Quartet, Opus 131; Beethoven's last was actually the Quartet in F Major, Opus 135.

FEBRUARY 5
•Gob.'s *Les Pléiades:* novel, 1874. • Lais and Thais: courtesans in ancient Greece.
• Count Tyszkiewicz: this could be either Count Thaddäus Tyszkiewicz of Posen, a writer on music whom Wagner describes in *Mein Leben* as "a formerly much-respected friend," or his son, Count Vincenz Tyszkiewicz, whom Wagner met in Paris in 1850. • The 7 Montagnards: members of a radical party in the French Assembly of 1848–49.

FEBRUARY 6
•That scene with the swan: shot down by Parsifal in Act I. • The hunt in *Tristan:* Tristan and Isolde meet in Act II while King Marke is away on a hunt, sounds of which are heard in the orchestra. • [Calderón's] *El mayor monstruo los zelos (Jealousy, the Greatest of Calamities); Muger, llora, y vencerás (Weep, Woman, and You Shall Triumph).*

FEBRUARY 7
•[Hebbel's] *Herodes und Mariamne:* tragedy, 1850. He introduced his hermit: in Act III of *Der Freischütz.* • The Reichskanzler's speech: on the treaty of neutrality, renewing the 1872 agreement between the German Reich, Austria, and Russia.

FEBRUARY 8
•*"Herr Oluf"* and *"Der Wirtin Töchterlein"*: two ballades by Karl Loewe. • An idea written down in his *Braunes Buch:* a passage concerning the importance of family feeling in learning to love one's fellow men—used almost word for word in "Know Thyself."

FEBRUARY 9
• "The worst weather . . . .": parody of Mephistopheles's line in Goethe's *Faust,* Part One (Faust's study), "The worst society thou find'st will show thee thou art a man among the rest" (Bayard Taylor's translation). • Grisi: Giulia Grisi (1811–69), Italian soprano; Wagner expressed great appreciation for her Donna Anna in Mozart's *Don Giovanni* in his article *"Der Virtuos und der Künstler"* ("The Virtuoso

and the Artist"), written in Paris in 1840. • Judith: Judith Gautier, whose mother was Giulia Grisi's sister.

FEBRUARY 10

•Senfft: the bookbinder in Bayreuth, Christian Senfft, bound most of the books contained in the Wahnfried library. • *Deutsche Reform:* periodical of the Deutscher Reformverein (German Reform Society), a nationalistic and anti-Semitic group. • "The Wagnerite as Writer" ("*Der Wagnerianer als Schriftsteller*"): appeared in the *Musikalisches Wochenblatt,* Leipzig, 1881.

FEBRUARY 11

•The president: the district president in Bayreuth, von Burchtorff. • [Bakker Korff]: Alexander Hugo Bakker Korff (1824–82), Dutch artist; his best-known work, *The Romance,* is the one described here by Cosima. • Beethoven's *33 Variations:* the *Diabelli* Variations, Opus 120. • The Freemasons' new building: built 1880 by Carl Wölffel, now a museum in Bayreuth. • "*O sink hernieder*": *Tristan und Isolde,* Act II (love duet). • Br[uno] Bauer (1809–82): German philosopher and theologian, friend of the von Bülows in Berlin in the 1850's.

FEBRUARY 13

•Colonel Schäffer: correctly, Hermann Scheffer, lieutenant colonel. • "*El zeloso estremeño*" ("The Jealous Estremaduran"): one of Cervantes's *Novelas exemplares.* • Pott: August Friedrich Pott (1802–87), philologist, author of *Etymologische Forschungen* (*Etymological Studies*), 6 vols., 1859–76, in which reference is made to Gobineau's *Essai sur l'inégalité des races humaines.*

FEBRUARY 14

•The "Order of the Holy Grail": this group of admirers, formed 1877 in Munich under the name "Der Orden vom heiligen Gral," sent Wagner a velvet hat with a punning inscription, "*Der Meister in des Ordens Hut, der Orden in des Meisters 'Hut'!*" ("The master in the order's hat, the order in the master's care!"). • "Herodom and Christianity" ("*Heldentum und Christentum*"): 2nd supplement to "*Religion und Kunst,*" begun on August 23, completed September 4, *Bayreuther Blätter,* September 1881, and vol. 10 of the collected writings; the curious word "Herodom" seems to be the invention of the English translator of Wagner's collected writings, W. Ashton Ellis, whose titles are retained throughout this book for ease of reference.

FEBRUARY 15

•"Bitz*barkeit*": there is no such word in German—Wagner had obviously made a slip of the pen. • Marschall: Hermann Marschall von Bieberstein, aristocrat and lawyer in Dresden who took part in the 1849 uprising and also fled to Zurich, where he worked as an insurance agent and a journalist until his death in the mid-'70s. • The specks of dust: in a description of the introduction to Act III of *Die Meistersinger,* contained in his letter of November 22, 1866, to King Ludwig, Wagner talks of the first entry of the "*Wach' auf*" melody: "After the first bars of this melody, the string instruments come in again, as if with their tender touch raising the eyes of the meditating cobbler to the sun, which is shining companionably through the window above his head and setting the dust dancing in its golden beam."

FEBRUARY 16

•His godfather, Träger: Adolf Träger, a Leipzig businessman. • The loss of our lawsuit: see note for May 16, 1879. • "*La illustre fregona*" ("The Illustrious Kitchenmaid"): one of Cervantes's *Novelas exemplares.*

FEBRUARY 17

•Eva was born today: on February 17, 1867, at Tribschen; while Cosima was in labor, Wagner sat in an adjoining room playing the "Prize Song" melodies from *Die Meistersinger,* the composition sketch of which he had completed ten days earlier. • The two Vidrieras: a reference to Cervantes's story *"El licenciado vidriera"* (see note for January 26, 1881). • We end the story: Cervantes's *"La illustre fregona."*

• His gambling night: in *Mein Leben* Wagner vividly describes the 3-month gambling phase he went through at the age of 18 as a student in Leipzig; it culminated in his staking his mother's widow's pension in August 1831, losing all but the last thaler, then, with that, winning enough to recover the pension sum and settle all his other debts; after that experience, he never gambled again. • His misunderstood remark to Dr. Förster: Wagner refused to sign an anti-Jewish petition initiated by Dr. Bernhard Förster.

FEBRUARY 18

•W. v. Humboldt: Baron Wilhelm von Humboldt (1767–1835), philologist, historian, and diplomat. • George Eliot: Wagner and Cosima met the English novelist, whose real name was Mary Ann Evans (1819–80), in London in April 1877 (see vol. I).

FEBRUARY 19

•Cervantes's *"El casamiento engañoso"* ("The Deceitful Marriage"): one of the *Novelas exemplares;* it contains a dialogue between Cipion and Bergança, dogs at the Hospital of the Resurrection in the city of Valladolid.

FEBRUARY 20

•*Numancia:* see note for August 28, 1880. • Disraeli's *Tancred:* a novel, 1847. • Dr. Hess: Otto Hess, physician in Bayreuth. • Krug: Heinrich Krug, a day laborer in Bayreuth. • Count Hatzfeldt's daughter: Helene, daughter of Count Paul von Hatzfeldt-Wildenburg, a member of the Upper House of Parliament; it was reported in the German press that she was about to marry one of the sons of the Berlin banker Gerson von Bleichröder, but she never did. • *"Waren die Menschen..."*: correctly, *"Die mich bedrohten, waren sie bös'?"* ("Those who threatened me, were they evil?"), Parsifal in Act I, bars 990–92. • Louise Michel (1833–1905): a French teacher and anarchist deported for her role in the Paris Commune of 1871, amnestied, returned to France in 1880, continually held in prisons and mental hospitals, wrote dramas and novels. • *"Wer ist gut"* ("Who is good"): Parsifal after Gurnemanz's laughter, *Parsifal,* I, bars 993 f.

FEBRUARY 21

•Assertions by Herr v. Hülsen: see note for March 1, 1881.

FEBRUARY 23

•A growing danger of the Jews' staying away: on account of the recent anti-Jewish petition instigated by Förster; Wagner replied to Neumann, "I have nothing at all to do with the present 'anti-Semitic' movement: an article by me which will shortly appear in the *Bayreuther Blätter* will make this so abundantly clear that intelligent people will find it completely impossible to connect me with that movement." • Hoffmann's continuation: *"Nachricht von den neuesten Schicksalen des Hundes Berganza"* ("News of the Recent Destinies of the Dog Bergança"), in E. T. A. Hoffmann's collection, *Phantasiestücke in Callot's Manier;* it is a sequel to Cervantes's *"El casamiento engañoso"* (see note, February 19, 1881).

FEBRUARY 27

•Prof. Toussaint: Maximilian Toussaint, teacher at the Lateinschule (Latin school) in Bayreuth. • Queroy: a restaurant in Munich in which Hans von Bülow's birthday was celebrated on January 8, 1868, Wagner proposing the toast.

FEBRUARY 28

•A letter from the King: not in the published correspondence, presumably lost. • J. Rub.'s article: *"Symphonie und Drama," Bayreuther Blätter,* February-March 1881.

• The prison governor: Ignaz Herzinger, governor of the St. Georgen prison, Bayreuth.

MARCH 1

•The letter from "more Wagnerites": the "Open Letter to the General Director of the Prussian Court Theaters, Herr von Hülsen" was signed *"mehre Wagnerianer"* ("more Wagnerites"), but was in fact written by Cosima alone; it appeared in the *Bayreuther Blätter,* February-March 1881. • Herr Köhler: a schoolteacher from Cologne.

MARCH 2

•The wedding celebrations: Wilhelm (1859–1941), son of Crown Prince Friedrich Wilhelm and German emperor 1888–1918 (Wilhelm II), married Princess Auguste Viktoria von Schleswig-Holstein-Sonderburg-Augustenburg (1858–1921) on February 27, 1881. • [Calderón's] *La dama duende* (*The Phantom Lady*).

MARCH 3

•Music for the scene painters: the music written for the transformation scene in *Parsifal,* Act I, did not allow sufficient time for the scenery to be changed; there is more about this problem later. • They were beaten by the Boers: war broke out between the Boers of Transvaal (South Africa) and the British in 1880, after the Boers proclaimed Transvaal an independent republic; at the battle of Majuba Hill on February 27, 1881, the Boers defeated the British; on August 3, 1881, Gladstone acknowledged the independence of Transvaal.

MARCH 4

•Prof. Ihering: Rudolf von Ihering (1818–92), German jurist and professor at Göttingen, author of several works on jurisprudence.

MARCH 6

•Additional music for *Parsifal:* for the transformation scene in Act I. • The Kolbs: two brothers in Bayreuth, Johann Ludwig Georg Kolb, head of the local flax mills, and Karl Heinrich Sofian Kolb, director of the cotton mills.

MARCH 8

•Captain Darmer's letter: Darmer, like Wagner, was a member of the committee formed to assist the wounded Boers in Transvaal; an appeal by the committee was published in the *Bayreuther Blätter* in 1881. • The *Intermeses:* Calderón's *Intermezzos.*

MARCH 9

•Gutmann: Friedrich Gutmann, teacher at the girls' school in Bayreuth.

MARCH 11

•H. Burgkmair: Hans Burgkmair (1473–1531), German painter and engraver; the original of *Der Weisskunig,* done for Emperor Maximilian I, is in Graz, Austria. • *"Gruss seiner Treuen"*: full title, *"Gruss seiner Treuen an Friedrich August den Geliebten"* ("Greeting to the Beloved Friedrich August from His Loyal Subjects"), a work for male chorus and orchestra composed by Wagner for the King of Saxony and performed in Pillnitz on August 12, 1844.

MARCH 12

•His 3-minute music: for *Parsifal,* Act I (transformation scene).

MARCH 13

•Löher: Franz von Löher (1818–92), director of the Bavarian state archives 1865–88. • Bovet: Alfred Bovet (died 1900), from Valentigney, France, bought the manuscript of Wagner's piano *"Fantasie"* (1831) and presented it to Wagner in 1876.

MARCH 14

•The assassination of the Tsar: the enclosed special edition of the *Oberfränkische Zeitung* contains a dispatch from St. Petersburg dated March 14 stating that two bombs were thrown at Tsar Alexander II when he was returning to the Winter Palace; the tsar was wounded in the legs, and an officer and two Cossacks accompanying him were killed; the final sentence reads, "The tsar died yesterday afternoon at 3:30 as a result of his injuries." • Cervantes's *El retable de las maravillas* (*The Marvelous Pageant*): an intermezzo about two showmen who trick a whole village by pretending to perform feats of magic that are visible only to persons of respectable birth; since nobody is willing to admit being otherwise, all claim to see the nonexistent feats.

MARCH 15
•An actor called Stein: Eduard Franz Stein, real name Baron Franz Matthias von Treuenfels (1794–1828), actor in Leipzig.

MARCH 16
•*La femme de trente ans:* a reference to the title of a novel by Balzac, 1831.

MARCH 17
•The "Open Letter": to von Hülsen; see note for March 1, 1881.

MARCH 18
•S[ain]t-Saëns's remarks: in an article in the French newspaper *Renaissance Musicale* Saint-Saëns remarked that Gounod was being ignored in favor of Wagner; some German newspapers published reports on this. • A supplement to the *B. Bl.:* "The Scientific Worthlessness of Vivisection in All Its Forms," by Dr. Richard Nagel, issued with the *Bayreuther Blätter,* February-March 1881. • Springer's article: see note for December 9, 1880.

MARCH 19
•Calderón's *El medico de su honra* (*The Physician of His Own Honor*): one of Calderón's best-known plays.

MARCH 20
•Donna Mencia: character in Calderón's *El medico de su honra.* Elisabeth's theme: from *Tannhäuser.*

MARCH 22
•"Not so, neither": Bottom's reply to Titania's "Thou art as wise as thou art beautiful" in Shakespeare's *A Midsummer Night's Dream,* Act III, Scene 1—the scene in which Bottom's head is turned into that of an ass. • The Brückner brothers: Max (1836–1919) and Gotthold (1844–92), scene designers and painters in Coburg; they prepared the scenery at Bayreuth, both for the *Ring* in 1876 and for *Parsifal* in 1882.

MARCH 23
•The serpent without a neck: the neck for the serpent in *Siegfried* did not arrive in time for the first performance (in 1876), having been mistakenly dispatched from London to Beirut (Lebanon) instead of to Bayreuth (Germany).

MARCH 24
•His brother-in-law General Meck: the Russian general Carl von Meck was married to Minna's sister Amalie. • The first Oupnekhat (Colebrooke): presumably in *Essay on the Vedas* by Henry Thomas Colebrooke (1765–1837), first mentioned by Cosima on January 13, 1874 (see vol. I); Oupnekhat is the French title of the Upanishads in the translation by Anquetil-Duperron.

MARCH 26
•[Schopenhauer's] *Will in Nature: Über den Willen in der Natur,* 1836.

MARCH 28
• Herwegh's poem to me: in 1857 the poet Georg Herwegh wrote a verse in Cosima's album, concluding with the lines: "The genius of harmony/will surround thee with its wondrous sounds,/and never wilt thou be/content with the discordant world." • "How cold were I . . ." ("*Wie wär ich kalt, mich glücklich nur zu nennen*"): Elsa in *Lohengrin,* Act III, Scene 2.

MARCH 29
•He went to a lot of trouble with it in Zurich: at a concert for the Zurich Musical

Society on December 13, 1853, Wagner conducted Beethoven's *Egmont* Overture and some of the incidental music; he writes in *Mein Leben,* "It gave me great pleasure to have Beethoven's music for *Egmont* played for once." • Kummer: Friedrich August Kummer (1797–1879), oboist and cellist in the Dresden Court orchestra. • The account of this concert: in Zur Stadt London, a restaurant in Leipzig, in 1835; Wagner relates in *Mein Leben* that the noise the reinforced orchestra made performing Beethoven's *Battle* Symphony in the confined space was so appalling that the audience literally fled.

MARCH 30
•The theater director in Cologne: Moritz Ernst (1826–1900), director of the Stadttheater from 1875.

MARCH 31
•Racinet: Albert Charles Auguste Racinet (1825–93), a graphic artist in Paris.

APRIL 1
•His German novel: *Wilhelm Meister.*

APRIL 2
•*"Mein Sohn Amfortas"*: Titurel in *Parsifal,* I, bars 1246 f.

APRIL 3
•Count G.'s book: the reference to "long books" suggests that Wagner must have meant Gobineau's *Essai sur l'inégalité des races humaines,* published 1853–55 in 4 vols. • Grote's history: see note for April 8, 1879. • O. Müller's work on the Dorians: see note for June 27, 1880. • E. v. Weber's lecture on the Boers: *Der Unabhängigkeits-kampf der Boers in Südafrika (The Boers' War of Independence in South Africa),* published as a brochure in Berlin in 1881; half of the proceeds of its sale went to aid the Boer wounded. • Canning: George Canning (1770–1827), British prime minister in 1827. • "Oh, grant that with rapture . . ." (*"O gönne mir, dass mit Entzücken ich deinen Atem sauge ein"*): Lohengrin to Elsa in *Lohengrin,* Act III, Scene 2. • The nation has also recognized it: *Lohengrin* and *Tannhäuser* were Wagner's most frequently performed works during his lifetime.

APRIL 4
•Wanner: Wilhelm Wanner (1837–94), German actor.

APRIL 5
•[Calderón's] *Hombre pobre todo es trazas (Contrivance Is the Poor Man's Lot).*

APRIL 7
•Francke: Hermann Francke, violinist and concert promoter in London, who was planning with Bernhard Pollini of Hamburg to stage *Tristan und Isolde* and *Die Meistersinger* at the Drury Lane Theater in London. • My grandfather: Gottlob Friedrich Wagner (1736–95) was an excise officer in Leipzig.

APRIL 9
•Isolde's birth: on April 10, 1865, in Hans von Bülow's house in Munich; on the same day Hans conducted the first orchestra rehearsal of *Tristan und Isolde.*

APRIL 10
•Kniese: Julius Kniese (1848–1905), a German conductor who served as a musical assistant at the Bayreuth performances of *Parsifal* in 1882 and 1883; from 1888 to 1904 he was chorus master of the Bayreuth festival theater. • Telegrams from Herr Neumann: Angelo Neumann was alarmed by the prospect that his *Ring* productions in London (Her Majesty's Theater) might coincide with the Francke-Pollini productions at the Drury Lane (see note for April 7, 1881); the overlapping did in fact occur. • Letter to Kotzebue from Beeth.: in a letter to the dramatist August von Kotzebue dated January 28, 1812, Beethoven expressed the desire for "an opera of your unique dramatic genius, whether romantic, wholly serious, heroic, comic, or sentimental"; Wagner was no doubt amused that a composer of Beethoven's

quality addressed such a letter to the bombastic (though at that time celebrated) dramatist.

APRIL 12

•Thrasybulus: Athenian general and statesman in the 4th century B.C. who, banished by the so-called Thirty Tyrants, returned to Athens with other exiles to defeat them and restore democracy; he was killed in action in 388 B.C.

APRIL 17

•The bust in Leipzig: a bust of Wagner in the foyer of the Leipzig Stadttheater by Melchior zur Strassen (1832–96); various replicas of it were advertised for sale in the *Bayreuther Blätter*.

APRIL 20

•*Auteurs:* the Société d'Auteurs et Compositeurs in Paris; as translator into French of Wagner's earlier works, Nuitter (Truinet; see note for October 30, 1878) would have an interest in royalties on their performances.

APRIL 22

•The composer Bruckner: Anton Bruckner (1824–96) visited Wagner in Bayreuth on September 13 and 14, 1873. • His introduction to Count Gobineau's work: Gobineau's article *"Ein Urteil über die jetzige Weltlage"* ("A Judgment of the Present World Situation") appeared in the *Bayreuther Blätter* of May-June 1881 with an introduction by Wagner.

APRIL 23

•Benedix: Roderich Benedix (1811–73), a popular German playwright whose *Collected Plays,* published 1862–68, ran to 21 vols.; his bust was also in the Leipzig Stadttheater. • The Giorgione: there is no evidence of a Giorgione picture in Brunswick fitting this description.

APRIL 25

•The picture (a surprise): for Wagner's birthday Joukowsky painted a picture entitled *The Holy Family,* based on the *tableau vivant* of the previous Christmas (see entry and note for December 24, 1880).

APRIL 27

•Today's reunion: Daniela's meeting with Hans von Bülow (see April 10, 1881).

APRIL 29

•Of whistling: in some European countries a theater audience conveys its disapproval, not by hissing, but by whistling.

MAY 1

•The waxwork figure of Beaconsfield: Benjamin Disraeli, 1st Earl of Beaconsfield, died on April 19, 1881; the waxwork figure was possibly a replica of the bust by Christian Rauch.

MAY 2

•Scheibe: the stage prompter.

MAY 3

•Pollini, preparing a cycle: Bernhard Pollini intended to produce the *Ring* in Hamburg with Joseph Sucher as conductor, rather than take over Angelo Neumann's production. • Mime "a Jewish dwarf": the role was played in Neumann's traveling theater by Julius Lieban (1857–1940), son of a Jewish cantor. • Seidl: Anton Seidl conducted this and all other performances by Neumann's company. • The scene with the Wala: *Siegfried,* Act III, Scene 1. • *"Dort sehe ich Grane"* ("And there is Grane"): Brünnhilde in Act III, Scene 3.

MAY 6

•The fight in *Walküre:* between Siegmund and Hunding, Act II, Scene 5. • "Today is Simon and Judah . . .": quotation from Schiller's *Wilhelm Tell*.

MAY 7

•Dr. Zwingenberg: a physician in Berlin. • *Opera and Drama* in 1851: Wagner's book *Oper und Drama* was first published by Weber in Leipzig in November 1851, in an edition of 500 copies; the second edition appeared in 1868–69. • Frau v. Heldburg: see note for April 18, 1880.

MAY 9

•My grandmother's and my brother's birthday: Liszt's mother, Anna Liszt, née Lager (1788–1866), and his son, Daniel (1839–59). • The Crown Prince wished to see . . .: the sentence enclosed in parentheses seems to have been added later, to judge by the color of the ink; the Crown Prince's invitation, conveyed to Wagner in the second intermission of *Götterdämmerung,* was refused by him with the excuse that he was feeling overtired and was always in an agitated mood during the performance of his works; more will be heard of this incident later.

MAY 10

•Prof. Werder: Karl Friedrich Werder (1806–93), poet and dramatist; Wagner was grateful to him for his encouragement after the second performance of *Der Fliegende Holländer* in Berlin was hissed in 1844.

MAY 18

•Herr Heim: his Zurich friend Ignaz Heim (born 1813) had died in 1880.

MAY 19

•His score *de race mélanésienne:* presumably Wagner's reference to the score of *Parsifal* as "of Melanesian race" (i.e., primitive) was based on a private joke arising out of Gobineau's book.

MAY 20

•The Eyssers: decorators who painted the coats of arms of all towns possessing Wagner Societies on the moldings of the ceiling in the Wahnfried *salon,* a surprise for Wagner's birthday.

MAY 22

•The Flower Greeting: a piece written by Wolzogen for Wagner's 68th birthday, in which Siegfried was dressed up as Parsifal and the girls as Flower Maidens. • Gustav: Gustav Schönaich (1840–1906), a journalist, Standhartner's stepson. • Ferdi Jäger: son (born 1874) of the singer Ferdinand Jäger. • Julchen and Elsa: daughters of Alexander and Franziska Ritter. • "*Nicht Gut noch Pracht,*" etc. ("Not goods nor pomp," etc.): Brünnhilde's concluding words in *Götterdämmerung,* omitted from the music drama, but composed at King Ludwig's request (with piano accompaniment) and given to him as a birthday present in 1876. • Farces by Lope and Sachs: *Del degollado* (*The Man with His Throat Cut*) by Lope de Vega and *Der Rossdieb von Fünsing* (*The Horse Thief from Fünsing*) by Hans Sachs. • The military band: according to the account in Glasenapp's biography of Wagner, it outstayed its welcome by playing for a full hour and a half in the palace gardens. • "All transient things . . .": quotation from Goethe's *Faust,* Part Two.

MAY 26

Frau Overbeck: Baroness Romaine Overbeck, a friend of Hans von Bülow. • Frau Hofmeister: Anna Sachse-Hofmeister (1852–1904), soprano at the Berlin opera 1882–89.

MAY 29

•Kathi Eckert: widow of the conductor Karl Eckert. • When Herr Neumann starts an ovation: by inviting Wagner to join the singers on the stage at the end and from there making a speech of thanks, during which Wagner left the stage, afterward taking a bow from his box; to Neumann, who was greatly offended by this act, he later made the excuse that he felt one of his "chest spasms" coming on, but it is significant that Cosima makes no mention of that in her entry.

MAY 30
•Herr Neumann's letter: declaring that, in view of Wagner's behavior in the theater on the previous evening, all personal contact between them should cease; Wagner replied as indicated in the note for May 29. • *Dogme et philosophie:* correctly, *Religions et philosophies dans l'Asie centrale* (*Religions and philosophies in Central Asia*), presented by the author to Wagner on the previous day with the inscription "A souvenir of the sincerest admiration and most affectionate friendship."

JUNE 2
•My green stone: Wagner wrote in his *Annalen* on January 1, 1868: "First hour of the New Year. Significant omens. Cosima's ring lost and found again. Great apprehensions."

JUNE 4
•With a dedication: "*Normann und Sachse, das ist der rechte Bund, was noch frisch und gesund, dass das blühe und wachse*" ("Norman and Saxon, that is the proper bond, still fresh and healthy, may it blossom and grow"). • [Ernst Dohm] (1819–83): German writer and satirist, president of the Berlin Wagner Society and a close friend of Cosima.

JUNE 5
•Rausch: Konrad Rausch, the gardener at Wahnfried.

JUNE 7
•Herr Lindau's article: Lindau wrote two articles about the *Ring* production in Berlin, one in *Nord und Süd,* Berlin, June 1881, and one in the *Kölnische Zeitung* of May 30, 1881. • His behavior during Neumann's speech: see note for May 29, 1881. • "Vanish, you arches": song of the spirits in Goethe's *Faust,* Part One (scene in Faust's study).

JUNE 8
•An anonymous letter: in connection with Wagner's rejection of the Crown Prince's invitation on May 9 (see entry and note for that day); according to Glasenapp, the letter reads: "Herr Wagner, Did you consider well the reply you gave our Crown Prince in response to his kind and even *for you* very honorable invitation? Take care lest, when people later write about your works, they do not say too much about your character!"

JUNE 9
•The "Nutcracker": presumably a reference to E. T. A. Hoffmann's tale ("*Nussknacker und Mausekönig*") about a nutcracker that, after a fight with the king of the mice, turns into a prince.

JUNE 10
•"Sonfi": meaning unknown: perhaps a writing mistake. • Seidl's telegram: see June 12, 1881.

JUNE 11
•Quarreling over Littré's body: the French lexicographer and philosopher Maximilien Paul Emile Littré died on June 2, 1881.

JUNE 12
•R. writes to Herr Förster: August Förster, director of the Stadttheater in Leipzig. • The neighboring house: Wolzogen's.

JUNE 13
•"Further, further!" ("*Weiter, weiter!*"): Sieglinde in *Die Walküre,* Act II, Scene 3, urging Siegmund to escape with her from the pursuing Hunding. • Quivers and qualms: "*Langen und bangen,*" a quotation from Goethe's *Egmont.*

JUNE 15
•Hyderabad: at that time one of the princely states in India.

JUNE 17
•The Bahais: or Babis, a sect founded in 1844 by a Persian, Ali Mohammed of Shiraz; combining Mohammedan, Christian, Jewish, and Zoroastrian elements in its doctrines, it was much persecuted, and its founder was executed in 1850.

JUNE 18
•Egusquiza: Rogelio Egusquiza (1845–1915), Spanish painter who visited Bayreuth and Venice several times between 1877 and 1882; his portrait of Wagner was exhibited at the world exposition in Paris in 1900.

JUNE 20
•"Heavy weigh my weapons" (*"Schwer wiegt mir der Waffen Wucht"*): Brünnhilde in *Die Walküre,* Act II, Scene 2.

JUNE 24
•Count and Countess Nako: Count Coloman Nako and his wife, Bertha, Hungarian-born landowners at Schwarzau, near Vienna, acquaintances of Wagner from 1861. • Mozart's "Lacrimosa": from the unfinished *Requiem.* • Our "flowers and ribbons": a reference to the final scene of *Die Meistersinger* (Festival Meadow), in which girls carry staves decorated with flowers and ribbons to celebrate Mid-summer's Day.

JUNE 25
•Herr Staudt: the firm of Emil Staudt, Frankfurt, installed the gas in the festival theater.

JUNE 29
•A nice letter: an anonymous letter in which, as Cosima wrote to Daniela on July 1, "poor Levi was so scandalously accused (and in connection with me!) that he could not get over it"; in the letter Wagner is also exhorted not to allow his work to be conducted by a Jew; Cosima's account in the Diaries of this incident and Levi's reaction to it corrects previous accounts in some details: Levi did not leave Wahn-fried at once, but on the following day, and remained away for only two days (see July 2). • Marianne Brandt (1841–1921): distinguished mezzo-soprano (Berlin, 1868–86) with whom Wagner's relations were always rather strained; he had wanted her to sing Sieglinde in the *Ring* in 1876 but allowed himself to be persuaded by others that she was "too ugly" for the role; now he offered her the role of Kundry, which she in fact sang (though sharing it with two other singers) in the *Parsifal* of 1882, and Wagner seemed to value her performance least of all; she appears fre-quently in the Diaries from now on.

JUNE 30
•Levi . . . to take leave of: he went to Bamberg, Bavaria. • The new Venusberg music in London: at the so-called Richter concerts in the Saint James's Hall (see note for July 17, 1879). • The theatrical venture: the Francke-Pollini performances of *Tristan und Isolde* and *Die Meistersinger* in London, which Richter was to conduct.

JULY 1
•R. writes to him: "For God's sake, come back at once and get to know us properly! Lose nothing of your faith, but find some courage and strength for it! Perhaps there will be a great turning in your life—but in any case, you are my *Parsifal* conductor!" Levi returned on the following day.

JULY 5
•A telegram . . . about my father: Liszt fell down a flight of steps on July 2.

JULY 11
•"What couldst thou do else" (*"Was könntest du wehren"*): Brünnhilde in *Götter-dämmerung,* conclusion of Act I. • *"Auf eigner Weid und Wonne"* ("On thy own blissful pastures"): Kurwenal to Tristan, *Tristan und Isolde,* Act III, Scene 1. • *Die Schweizer-familie:* the Weigl opera.

JULY 13
•The Magdeburg Festival: 250th anniversary of the siege and destruction of the town in 1631.
JULY 14
•*Revue Nouvelle:* correctly, *La Nouvelle Revue,* a political and literary fortnightly periodical founded in Paris in 1879. • *Sappho:* tragedy (1819) by the Austrian dramatist Franz Grillparzer.
JULY 15
•How many Sibyls there were: here Wagner is thinking of Michelangelo's painting on the ceiling of the Sistine Chapel in the Vatican, in which the Libyan, Cumaean, Erythraean, and Delphian Sibyls are depicted. • His father Geyer's parody: there is no complete record of Ludwig Geyer's dramatic compositions, many of which were written for private or family occasions.
JULY 16
•The *Bullrich: "Bullrichsalz"* is the German word for "bicarbonate of soda," and Wagner was apparently using the word as a euphemism for the breaking of wind that is the outcome of taking it—though it is not clear to which passage in the *Egmont* Overture he was referring! • The purchase of a tom-tom: for the temple bells in *Parsifal* Wagner first made use of tom-toms (gongs), which he ordered in London through Dannreuther.
JULY 17
•His letter to Feustel: Feustel was in charge of the finances of the Society of Patrons and was administrator of Wagner's own estate; the letter, dated July 18, deals with Wagner's contractual relationships with the firm of Schott, particularly in connection with the publication of *Parsifal;* on August 30, 1881, Wagner demanded 100,000 marks for the piano arrangement and score, and this was agreed upon. The rabbi's curious statement: presumably something said by Dr. Salamon Kusznitzki, the rabbi in Bayreuth. • Hammerstein: correctly, Heinrich Hammermeister (1799–1860), a well-known exponent of the role of Bois-Guilbert in Marschner's opera. • Frau Hartwig: Friederike Wilhelmine Hartwig (1774–1849), actress in Leipzig and godmother to several of the Wagner children. • Platen's article: probably *"Das Theater als ein Nationalinstitut"* ("The Theater as a National Institution") by the German poet Count August von Platen (1796–1835).
JULY 18
•The stupid legacies of Schott of blessed memory (*"Die albernen Legate von Schott selig"*): in his will of February 8, 1874, Franz Schott left property worth 280,000 florins to the city of Mainz to establish a foundation for the promotion of music in the city.
JULY 19
•Camões: Luiz Vaz de Camões (1525–80), Portuguese poet.
JULY 20
•The Indescribable . . .": a play on the concluding lines of Goethe's *Faust,* Part Two, which are (in Bayard Taylor's translation), "The Indescribable, / Here it is done: / The Woman-Soul leadeth us / Upward and on!"
JULY 21
•*Fiesco:* Schiller's tragedy *Die Verschwörung des Fiesco zu Genua* (1783) ends with the conspirator Verrina pulling off Fiesco's coat and then hurling him over a cliff to his death; Wagner's facetious alternative comes from the "Coat Song" in Karl Holtei's comic opera *Lenore* (1827). • Frl. Wülfinghoff: singer in Regensburg who sang the roles of Waltraute and Gutrune in the 1878 *Ring* production in Munich.
JULY 22
•A pariah fable: in Jacolliot's book about India.

JULY 23

•*Die Ruinen von Athen* (*The Ruins of Athens*): in 1812 Beethoven wrote an overture and incidental music to the play by Kotzebue.

JULY 25

•"His line fell to me" ("*Sein Stamm verfiel mir*"): Klingsor in *Parsifal,* II, bars 258 f.; Wolzogen's mistake occurred in pt. 4 of his article "*Zur Kritik des 'Parsifal'* " ("On the Criticisms of *Parsifal*"), *Bayreuther Blätter,* August 1881.

JULY 26

•Kranich: Friedrich Kranich, Sr. (1857–1924), a pupil of Karl Brandt, was technical director of the Bayreuth festival 1886–1914. • "Thou know'st where . . ." ("*Du weisst, wo du mich wieder finden kannst*"): Parsifal's final words in Act II. • Calderón's *El mayor encanto amor* (*Love, the Greatest Enchanter*).

JULY 27

•Nathalie: Nathalie Bilz, née Planer, Minna's illegitimate daughter.

JULY 28

•"Not a word of me": Act IV, Scene 2. • Agathe's . . . aria: Act II, Scene 2.

AUGUST 1

•"Now Get Up": Silesian folk song; see note for June 21, 1880. • "Art and Climate" ("*Kunst und Klima*"): written in Paris in February 1850, in vol. 3 of the collected writings.

AUGUST 2

•The Suleika songs: from Goethe's *West-Eastern Divan,* set to music by Schubert (also Mendelssohn). • Tichatschek: Joseph Aloys Tichatschek (1807–86), tenor at the Dresden opera and Wagner's first Rienzi and Tannhäuser. • "*Wer nie sein Brot*": song of the Harpist in Goethe's novel *Wilhelm Meister,* set to music by Schubert (also Schumann). • "*Die Forelle*": poem by C. F. D. Schubart, set to music by Schubert.

AUGUST 5

•Carrie Pringle: an English singer who sang one of the solo Flower Maidens in *Parsifal,* 1882; an article by Herbert Conrad, published in a supplement to the *Nordbayerischer Kurier* (No. 8, 1978), suggests, though on somewhat flimsy evidence, that Wagner might have been in love with her.

AUGUST 6

•"If she is called Caroline": Queen Caroline, consort of George II of England, plays a significant part in Scott's *The Heart of Midlothian,* since she is responsible for securing a pardon for Effie Deans, unjustly condemned to death, after listening to a plea from Effie's sister Jeanie. • Their resort to arms in '52: in 1852 there was trouble between Switzerland and Austria following an incident in the canton of Ticino, but it could scarcely be called a "resort to arms," a description that would, however, fit the clash between republicans and royalists in 1856 over Neuchâtel, which nominally belonged to Prussia; since Wagner was living in Zurich at the time of both incidents, he may have confused the dates. • The Meyerbeer Prize: Meyerbeer bequeathed a sum of money to set up a scholarship enabling German students trained in Berlin (Hochschule and Stern Conservatoire) and Cologne to spend eighteen months studying in Italy, Paris, Vienna, Munich, and Dresden; Humperdinck, who was trained in Cologne, was awarded the scholarship in 1881.

AUGUST 7

•August 25: King Ludwig's birthday.

AUGUST 8

•All these prize-winnings: Humperdinck had also been awarded the Mendelssohn Prize in 1879. • The Westphalians: Humperdinck was born in Siegburg, at that time in the province of Westphalia. • Du Bois-Reymond: Emil Du Bois-Reymond (1818–96), professor of physiology in Berlin. • Zante: the Italian name for the Greek island of Zacynthus. • The "bell piano": the special keyboard instrument devised for the temple bells in *Parsifal* took some time to develop, and in 1882 Wagner had to make do with his tom-toms (see July 16, 1881, and note); on July 12, 1882, he sent a telegram to Dannreuther in London, "A Kingdom for a Tamtam! *mit richtigem C-Diapason normal*" ("with proper standard C-diapason").

AUGUST 9
•R. starts a reply: the letter, dated August 11, begins, "That you are not Croesuses displeases me immensely!"

AUGUST 10
•Jungfer Züss: correctly Züs, a character in Gottfried Keller's story *"Die drei gerechten Kammacher."* • "Jouk., who did not educate Tsar Alexander III": a joking reference to the fact that Joukowsky's father had been tutor to Alexander II.

AUGUST 11
•Letters from R. to Herbeck: Johann Herbeck (1831–77) was conductor in Vienna 1869–75; Wagner's letters to him were published in the *Neue Freie Presse,* Vienna, on June 29 and July 6 and 13, 1881; Tappert's article appeared in the *Deutsches Tageblatt,* Berlin, August 10, 1881. • *"Brüderlein fein":* famous song in Raimund's *Der Bauer als Millionär* (*The Millionaire Peasant*) in which the spirit of Youth takes leave of the aging peasant.

AUGUST 12
•Abu Hema: emissary of Sheikh El Haddad in the rebellions of the Kabylia in the then French protectorate of Algeria. • Körner with Friesen, Lützow, and some others: during the struggles against Napoleon I, Baron Adolf von Lützow (1782–1834), a Prussian cavalry officer, formed a volunteer corps; it was commanded by Karl Friedrich Friesen (1784–1814), and the poet Theodor Körner (1791–1813) belonged to it; Körner was killed at Gadebusch while fighting with the corps. • Briseïs: the slave girl of Achilles who is taken from him by Agamemnon at the beginning of Homer's *Iliad.* • *"Es waren hochbedürftige Meister . . ."* (correctly, *"Das waren . . ."*): Hans Sachs in *Die Meistersinger,* Act III, Scene 2. • *Actors and Singers* (*Über Schauspieler und Sänger*): an essay written by Wagner in 1872, in vol. 9 of the collected writings.

AUGUST 13
•He quotes Polonius: in Shakespeare's *Hamlet,* Act II, Scene 2.

AUGUST 16
•Egill: Egil, the hero poet of the *Egilsaga,* one of the Icelandic family sagas (870–980). • "The Metamorphosis of the Animals" (*"Metamorphose der Tiere"*).

AUGUST 17
•Stein's article: *Bayreuther Blätter,* August 1881.

AUGUST 18
•The costume designer: the firm of Schwab und Plettung prepared the costumes and props for *Parsifal;* Johann Georg Plettung (1833–90) was head costume designer at Frankfurt. • His visit to Eisleben: on April 27, 1873, Wagner and Cosima visited Eisleben, in Saxony (birthplace of Martin Luther), where as a child Wagner had spent a year following Ludwig Geyer's death, at the home of Geyer's brother; see that date and May 3, 1873, in vol. I.

AUGUST 19
•Kyffhäuser: the *Kyffhäuserbund* was an ex-servicemen's association. • *"An die entfernte Geliebte"* ("To the Absent Sweetheart"): this could refer either to Beethoven's song cycle *"An die ferne Geliebte"* or to Schubert's song *"An die Entfernte."*

AUGUST 20

•To the King for the 25th: Ludwig's thirty-sixth birthday; the poem is published in the correspondence between Wagner and King Ludwig.

AUGUST 21

•A nice letter written . . . about R.: Liszt's letter of May 14, 1849, to Belloni, reprinted in the *Bayreuther Tagblatt*. • Winkelmann: Hermann Winkelmann (1849–1912), recommended to Wagner by Richter after he had sung Tannhäuser and Lohengrin in Vienna; he sang Parsifal in Bayreuth in 1882 and at every festival until 1888, also Tannhäuser in 1891. • Osmin: the Pasha's steward in Mozart's *Die Entführung aus dem Serail*.

AUGUST 22

•The last verse: of the poem for King Ludwig's birthday; it contains a tribute to Cosima for her devoted care, which enables Wagner to continue working by the light of the King's "summer moon." • The royal box: the so-called royal annex (*Königsbau*) added to the front of the Bayreuth festival theater. • *"Braut von Corinth"*: Loewe did indeed set this Goethe ballad to music (Opus 29).

AUGUST 23

•He begins his article: *"Heldentum und Christentum"* ("Herodom and Christianity"). • Frau [Reicher-]Kindermann: Hedwig Reicher-Kindermann (1853–83) sang Grimgerde and Erda (for one cycle when Luise Jaide was indisposed) in the Bayreuth *Ring* of 1876, and Brünnhilde in Angelo Neumann's traveling company; her early death during that tour was generally considered to have deprived the world of one of its finest dramatic sopranos. • The Schweizerei: a restaurant. • *"Fanget an"* and *"Am stillen Herd"*: sung by Walther von Stolzing in Act I of *Die Meistersinger*.

AUGUST 25

•Ludwig Day: the king's birthday, and also the Wagners' wedding day. • The "Forging Songs": *Siegfried*, Act I. • "Hurrying clouds . . ." (*"Eilende Wolken, Segler der Lüfte"*): Schiller's *Maria Stuart*, Act III, Scene 1.

AUGUST 26

•The Sachse-Hofmeister couple: Anna Sachse-Hofmeister (1852–1904), a soprano in Berlin who later had a distinguished career as a Wagnerian singer, and her husband (Sachse), also a singer.

AUGUST 27

•*Otello*: opera by Rossini, 1816. • Letters to the other artists: i.e., to the singers he wished to engage for *Parsifal*.

AUGUST 30

•*Fortunatus' Abenteuer*: no play with this title (*The Adventures of Fortunatus*) is traceable, but it is possible that Cosima is referring to Raimund's *Der Bauer als Millionär*, in which the main character is named Fortunatus Wurzel.

AUGUST 31

•The palace of the Office of the Royal Household: the Berlin home of Count and Countess Schleinitz, who were no favorites of Bismarck. • "Hagen's Watch": in Act I, Scene 2, of *Götterdämmerung*; in the music drama it is actually linked to Waltraute's scene (Scene 3). • "That is a seignorial right . . .": Schiller's *Die Jungfrau von Orleans*, Act III, Scene 3. • I look like a flea: a reference to "The Song of the Flea," sung by Mephistopheles in Goethe's *Faust*, Part One (scene in Auerbach's cellar); it is about a king who loved a flea and showered favors on it.

SEPTEMBER 1

•Fould: Achille Fould (1800–67), French financier and minister of finance; though Wagner mentions him a few times in *Mein Leben* as being opposed to producing

Tannhäuser in Paris in 1861, he does not mention visiting Fould's house. • "Marble statues stand . . .": paraphrase of a line in Goethe's poem "*Mignon*."

SEPTEMBER 2

•Dr. Korum: Michael Felix Korum (1840–1921), appointed bishop of Trier in 1881 (see also May 4, 1879, and note). • President Garfield: James Abram Garfield (1831–81), twentieth president of the United States of America, was shot by a fanatic on July 2, 1881, only five months after taking office, and died of his wounds on September 19.

SEPTEMBER 6

•[Therese] Malten (1855–1930): soprano at the Dresden opera throughout her singing career (1873–1903); she sang Kundry at Bayreuth in 1882 and in subsequent festivals until 1894, also Isolde and Eva.

SEPTEMBER 7

•Schuch: Ernst von Schuch (1846–1914), conductor at Dresden from 1873; his visit concerned the tempi in *Der Fliegende Holländer*. • Augustus the Strong: Augustus II (1670–1733), King of Saxony. • The Stille Musik: a narrow corner in Dresden, described by Cosima on April 24, 1871, as "gruesome." • Kietz: Gustav Adolf Kietz (1824–1908), a sculptor in Dresden and brother of Ernst Benedikt Kietz, Wagner's friend in Paris; he visited Bayreuth in May 1873 to make busts of both Wagner and Cosima.

SEPTEMBER 8

•Wüllner: Franz Wüllner (1832–1902), conductor at Munich; he earned Wagner's disfavor by conducting the first performances of *Das Rheingold* and *Die Walküre* in Munich, in 1869 and 1870 respectively. • The music for the returning King: his "*Gruss seiner Treuen an Friedrich August den Geliebten*," on the king's return from a visit to England in 1844 (see note for October 30, 1878). • Councilor Braun: Hofrat Braun, not further identified. • Gross-Graupen: a village near Pillnitz where Wagner began work on the composition sketch of *Lohengrin,* on May 15, 1846.

SEPTEMBER 9

•Dr. Hartmann: Ludwig Hartmann (1836–1910), music critic and composer, a pupil of Liszt; Hartmann wrote a report for the *Dresdner Nachrichten* on Wagner's visit to Dresden.

SEPTEMBER 10

•The Marcolini: Wagner lived in an apartment in the former Marcolini palace in Dresden in 1847. • Weber's funeral procession: the composer's ashes, brought back from London at Wagner's instigation, were buried in Dresden on December 15, 1844.

SEPTEMBER 11

•The Schlesingers: Maximilian Schlesinger (died 1881), a Hungarian emigrant working in London as a journalist, had looked after the financial side of Wagner's London concerts in 1877; he had since moved to Dresden with his wife, Kathleen, and family. • Frl. von Zettwitz: Countess Marie von Zettwitz, a lady in waiting at the Saxon Court.

SEPTEMBER 12

•The Kreuzschule: school in Dresden that Wagner attended as a child.

SEPTEMBER 18

•The sketches: in his letter to King Ludwig (dated September 19) Wagner answers the king's request to see the sketches of the *Parsifal* scenery with the excuse that these are incomplete and not revealing enough; he expresses the wish (which he himself describes as impossible) that the king might visit Bayreuth incognito and see the scenery (now ready) for himself.

SEPTEMBER 19

•Thomas More's *Utopia:* it is not clear why Thomas More's book, first published in 1515 and translated into German in 1753, should have been talked about in the newspapers at this time, unless it was perhaps in connection with ideas of building a new community in emigration. • His letter for the *B. Blätter:* Heinrich von Stein wrote an "Open Letter to the Publisher of the *Bayreuther Blätter*" to celebrate the fifth year of the paper's publication; it appeared in the October-November 1881 issue. • "Let the ghost . . .": quotation from Goethe's *Faust,* Part Two.

SEPTEMBER 20

•*"Strapontin":* a coach with collapsible seats.

SEPTEMBER 23

•Fürstner: the Berlin music publisher Adolph Fürstner (1833–1908) acquired rights in *Rienzi, Der Fliegende Holländer,* and *Tannhäuser* when he bought out the firm of C. F. Meser, their original publisher, in 1872; however, his rights in *Tannhäuser* did not extend to the new material written for the Paris production of 1861, which Wagner sold to another publisher (Flaxland in Paris); since in both versions (Dresden and Paris) most of the material is the same, there was a continual dispute between Fürstner and Wagner on the contractual situation.

SEPTEMBER 25

•F. Muncker: Franz Muncker, son of the mayor of Bayreuth.

SEPTEMBER 26

•Burnouf: Eugène Burnouf (1801–52), French orientalist, author of *An Introduction to the History of Buddhism; Die Sieger* was Wagner's projected music drama on a Buddhist theme.

SEPTEMBER 28

•*"So schüttelte sie die Locken":* correctly, *"So flatterten lachend die Locken"* ("Thus in laughter did her tresses fly"); *Parsifal,* II, bar 1109.

SEPTEMBER 29

Benediktus: correctly, Ludwig Benedictus, who became Judith Gautier's lifelong companion after the breakup of her marriage to Catulle Mendès; son of a Dutch diamond merchant, he was an amateur composer and an ardent Wagnerite. • Jadin: Wagner's eccentric old landlord in Meudon (see March 31, 1878, and note); in *Mein Leben* Wagner relates that the walls of M. Jadin's room were covered with very childish caricatures of animals.

OCTOBER 2

•*"Fühlst du im Herzen . . ."* ("If only in your heart you could feel the pain of others"): Kundry in *Parsifal,* Act II.

OCTOBER 3

•H[ermann] Wittig: medal maker and sculptor; his medal, a relief 9.5 centimeters in diameter, shows Wagner's head in profile (looking to the right). • *"Ich sah ihn— ihn"* ("I saw Him—Him"): Kundry in *Parsifal,* II, bars 1178 ff.; kettledrum before the second *"ihn."* • *Lumpazivagabundus:* a play (1833) by Johann Nestroy, with incidental music by Adolf Müller.

OCTOBER 9

•*"Agnus mundi . . .":* though not correct grammatically, this may perhaps have been intended as a simple reversal of the line from the Mass, *"Agnus Dei qui tollis peccata mundi,"* so that it might be translated, "Lamb of the world who takes the sins of God on thyself."

OCTOBER 10

•How she left him in Dresden: following her flight from Königsberg in 1837, Minna went to her parents' home in Dresden; there Wagner saw her and eventually persuaded her to return to him; they went to live in Blasewitz, not far from Dresden, but after a few weeks there Minna left him again.

OCTOBER 11

•A journey up the Nile: as later entries make clear, this was a holiday plan that was seriously considered. • Haymerle: Baron Heinrich Karl von Haymerle (1828–81), Austrian foreign minister from 1879; he died of heart failure on October 10. • Dr. Leube: Wilhelm Leube (1842–1922), Erlangen. • *"Mein ganzes Liebes-Umfangen"*: correctly, *"Mein volles Liebes-Umfangen"*; Kundry in *Parsifal,* II, bars 1350 ff. • Dr. Brehm: presumably Alfred Edmund Brehm (1829–84), zoologist and ornithologist.

OCTOBER 12

•Baer's *Urmensch:* presumably *Der vorgeschichtliche Mensch* (*Prehistoric Man*) by Wilhelm Baer, published 1874 and in the library at Wahnfried. • Dr. Hering: Richard Hering. • Professor Weisse: Christian Hermann Weisse (1801–66), philosopher in Leipzig whom Wagner first met as a young man at the home of his uncle Adolf, then again in 1862 in Leipzig.

OCTOBER 13

•We read in Uhland: Ludwig Uhland's *Schriften zur Geschichte der Dichtung und Sage* (*Writings on the History of Legend and Saga*) appeared in 8 vols., 1865–73.

OCTOBER 14

•Correspondence with Humboldt: Schiller's correspondence with the philosopher Wilhelm von Humboldt was published in 1830. • Alexander Humboldt: see note for June 12, 1878. • "It is all Spanish to me": the equivalent of our "all Greek (or double Dutch) to me"; Wagner's hypothesis was wrong; the German expression dates from the time of the Holy Roman Emperor Charles V (1500–58), who was also king of Spain, and whose attempts to introduce Spanish customs into Germany aroused displeasure.

OCTOBER 15

•Alfonso of Aragon (1385–1458): Alfonso V, the Magnanimous, King of Aragon, Sicily, and Naples, a patron of literature.

OCTOBER 16

•Hausburg: Ernst Hausburg, *Parsifal* copyist from August 1881, a coach and musical assistant at the festival of 1882; he made the copy of the *Parsifal* score used by the two conductors Levi and Fischer.

OCTOBER 17

•The inspector from Leipzig: Eduard Römer, technical director at the Leipzig Stadttheater; he had come to make an inventory of the *Ring* scenery, which Neumann wanted to take over for his traveling theater. • *"Frauentreue"* ("Women's Loyalty"): from *Gesammt-Abenteuer* (*Collected Adventures*), the work of an anonymous 14th-century German poet; its tales of chivalry bear some relationship to the Tristan legend and the idea of death through love, and Wagner knew the book in the 1850 edition of Friedrich Heinrich von der Hagen.

OCTOBER 20

•Stein's new dialogue: *"Solon und Croesus"* from *Helden und Welt* (*Heroes and the World*), at this time in manuscript.

OCTOBER 21

•The telegram to my father: Liszt celebrated his seventieth birthday on October 22.

OCTOBER 22

•His speech at the concert: on December 25, 1878, *q.v.*

OCTOBER 23

•Male and female in art and religion: a projected final supplement to *"Religion und Kunst"* that was never completed, though two fragments remain: *"Über das Männliche und Weibliche in Kultur und Kunst"* ("On Masculine and Feminine in Culture and Art"), written down in the *Braunes Buch* in 1882 (see March 27, 1882, in these Diaries); and *"Über das Weibliche im Menschlichen"* ("On the Womanly in the Human"), on which Wagner was working at the time of his death; the latter fragment is printed in vol. 12 of the collected writings. • *"Krummstab": * the German word for "bishop's crook"—presumably a tree of that shape. • A ghost story by Apel: in 1815 Johann August Apel (1771–1816) published a book of ghost stories, *Gespensterbuch,* with Friedrich Laun.

OCTOBER 25
• The Battle of Möckern: victory of the Prussians over the French on April 5, 1813.
OCTOBER 26
• Walks in the Sihl valley: in Switzerland, summer 1857.
OCTOBER 27
• Frau von Marenholtz: Bertha von Marenholtz-Bülow (1816–93), a kindergarten teacher.
OCTOBER 28
• Lubbock on primitive man: Sir John Lubbock, 1st Baron Avebury (1834–1913), English politician and naturalist, wrote *Prehistoric Times* (1865, translated into German 1873–74), *The Origin of Civilisation and the Primitive Condition of Man* (1870, German 1875), etc.; the former was in the Wahnfried library. • Kant's *Theory of the Heavens: Allgemeine Naturgeschichte und Theorie des Himmels (General Natural History and Theory of the Heavens),* 1755, in which Kant anticipates Laplace's theory on the origin of the solar system.
OCTOBER 29
• "And though a cloud . . .": Agathe's cavatina in Weber's *Der Freischütz,* Act III, Scene 2. • "The ball still stands . . .": a play on the second line of Agathe's cavatina, "the sun still stands in heaven's vault." • The troubadour's song: Jean's aria in the 2nd act.
OCTOBER 30
• "Werbel and Swemel": nicknames for Humperdinck and Hausburg. • *"Die Klage . . .":* correctly, *"Klage! Furchtbare Klage!"; Parsifal,* II, bars 1005 ff. • *"Unter blühenden Mandelbäumen"* ("Under blossoming almond trees"): Adolar's cavatina in Act I of Weber's *Euryanthe.* • The scene with Pointz: Shakespeare's *Henry IV Part II,* Act II, Scene 2. • With the King: Act IV, Scene 4.
NOVEMBER 1
• *Das unterbrochene Opferfest (The Interrupted Sacrifice):* opera by Peter Winter, 1796. • In Frankfurt (1862): when Hans and Cosima concluded their visit to Biebrich in August 1862, Wagner accompanied them as far as Frankfurt, where they all saw a performance of Goethe's *Torquato Tasso* in which Friederike Meyer played the princess.
NOVEMBER 2
• Parricida: Johannes Parricida, Duke of Swabia, who murdered his uncle and, as a character in Act V of Schiller's *Wilhelm Tell,* says of himself, "I wander through the mountains, a terror to myself."
NOVEMBER 3
• In front of Rossini: Rossini was born in Pesaro, where there is a statue of him.
NOVEMBER 8
• Nestor, Hector: in Shakespeare's *Troilus and Cressida.*
NOVEMBER 9
• The trial in Pizzo: presumably a newspaper report of a recent court case; Pizzo is a town in the toe of Italy. • Herr Türk: Siegfried's tutor, engaged in Bayreuth just before the departure for Palermo.

NOVEMBER 11

•"Believe me," etc.: Mephistopheles in *Faust,* Part One (Faust's study), "Believe me, who for many a thousand year / The same tough meat have chewed and tested" (Bayard Taylor's translation). • "So to the actively eternal": continues (in Bayard Taylor's translation), "Creative force, in cold disdain / You now oppose the fist infernal, / Whose wicked clench is all in vain!"

NOVEMBER 12

•Joan La Pucelle: Joan of Arc. • Dr. Berlin: physician in Palermo.

NOVEMBER 14

•My next article: clearly the projected supplement to "Religion and Art" (see note for October 23, 1881); the German word for "sun" (*Sonne*) is of feminine gender. • "*Kalt und starr*": Gurnemanz, *Parsifal,* III, bars 78 ff., muted horns at bars 82 f. • "*Notte e giorno faticar*" ("to plague oneself night and day"): quotation from Mozart's *Don Giovanni,* libretto by Lorenzo da Ponte; its significance here is not very clear. • The two lines about the miracle: presumably the words of Shakespeare's King Henry VI (*Part II,* Act II, Scene 1) on hearing that a blind man at Saint Alban's shrine had his sight restored, "Now, God be praised, that to believing souls / Gives light in darkness, comfort in despair."

NOVEMBER 16

•"The hand that wields the broom . . .": First Student in Goethe's *Faust,* Part One, scene before the city gate (Bayard Taylor's translation).

NOVEMBER 18

•*Die Sarazenin* (*The Saracen Woman*): Wagner sketched out a text for this opera in Paris, 1841–42, and completed the text in Dresden in 1843, though he did not set it to music; Manfred, the son of Friedrich II, is a character in it.

NOVEMBER 19

•The prefect: Count Bardessone; Wagner's letter of November 22, 1881, to King Ludwig shows that the king had requested that Wagner be given the prefect's especial protection.

NOVEMBER 20

•Ignaz Denner: the main character of E. T. A. Hoffmann's story of that name, in which Trabacchio also appears.

NOVEMBER 21

•*Marc Aurèle* (*Marcus Aurelius*): the final volume of Renan's *History of the Origins of Christianity,* 1880.

NOVEMBER 22

•He has dealt particularly with the subject of the Jews: what Wagner has to say on the subject in his letter of November 22 to King Ludwig bears no resemblance to what Cosima reports; after attributing the king's liberal attitude toward the Jews to lack of experience with them, Wagner declares that, though he has friendly and sympathetic relations with several of these people, he considers the Jewish race to be the born enemy of pure humanity and all that is noble in it. • Traces of great ancestors: in his letter to the king Wagner refers to the Hohenstaufen Emperor Friedrich II, who became king of Sicily through his Sicilian mother in 1198, and his son Manfred; also to King Ludwig I of Bavaria, who restored the damaged parts of Monreale Cathedral. • Count Tasca: Count Almerita-Tasca.

NOVEMBER 23

•It is found difficult to get rid of Gloster: in Shakespeare's *Henry VI* the young king's protector and uncle, the Duke of Gloster, is surrounded by enemies, but his murder is not achieved until Act III of *Part II;* the king himself is killed (by another Gloster, later King Richard III) in *Part III* (Act V, Scene 6), and immediately after his death his successor, Edward IV, says, "And now what rests, but that we spend the time / With stately triumphs, mirthful comic shows, / Such as befits the pleasure of the court?"

NOVEMBER 24

•J. Gallmeyer: the Viennese soubrette Josephine Gallmeyer, who, as Cosima reports on May 10, 1872 (see vol. I), sat in a corner during a concert rehearsal in Vienna, listening to Wagner's music "with tears in her eyes."

NOVEMBER 26

•"Retrospect of the Stage Festivals" ("*Ein Rückblick auf die Bühnenfestspiele des Jahres 1876*"): Wagner's own account of the first *Ring* production; in the *Bayreuther Blätter,* December 1878, and vol. 10 of the collected writings. • "The Guadalquivir": a river in southern Spain.

NOVEMBER 27

•All he has encountered in the way of assistance and understanding: Wagner seems to have been dissatisfied with the articles in the *Bayreuther Blätter;* in a letter to Daniela dated November 21, Cosima comments on the October-November 1881 issue, calling Porges's article on Liszt "well meant and also well considered, but badly constructed," Bruno Bauer's on Luther "good except for the passage on Christianity," Stein's on the fifth anniversary of the periodical "a bit affected," and Fritz Lemmermeyer's on tragedy "superfluous."

NOVEMBER 28

•Kant's remarks . . . about life: quoted in Bauer's article as follows: "One must have a very poor understanding of the value of life if one can wish it to last longer than it does in reality, for that would only mean the prolongation of a laborious wrestling match." • *Tristan* today: in Berlin; see also December 7, 1881.

NOVEMBER 29

•B. Bauer's article: in the *Bayreuther Blätter,* October-November 1881 (see note for November 27, 1881). • The quartet in Paris: the Morin-Chevillard String Quartet, heard by Liszt and Wagner in Paris in 1853 (see July 22, 1880) and invited to Tribschen by Cosima in 1869 to play Beethoven quartets on Wagner's birthday (see vol. I). • *Des Bohémiens:* Liszt's book *Des Bohémiens et de leur musique en Hongrie* (in German *Die Zigeuner und ihre Musik in Ungarn,* and translated into English as *The Gypsy in Music*) appeared in a second edition in 1881, and certain passages were severely criticized, particularly those in which Liszt compares gypsies favorably with Jews, whom he describes as sullen, servile, cruel, and avaricious. • *Princess Narischkin's Wig* (*Die Perücke der Prinzessin Narischkin*): a novel by Fedor von Zobeltitz (1857–1934) that was serialized in 1881 in the Berlin newspaper *Deutsches Tageblatt* (which Wagner read regularly) before being published in 2 vols. in 1882.

NOVEMBER 30

•"Deliver them . . .": Falstaff to Pistol in *Henry IV Part II,* Act V, Scene 3. • The poem by Walther v. der Vogelw[eide]: in his *"Mailied"* ("May Song") the fourteenth-century minnesinger poet tells of flowers and clover quarreling in the meadow ("I am shorter, thou art longer"); Wagner, in his *Parsifal* Meadow (the Good Friday scene in Act III), several times gives the "Flower Meadow motive" to the oboe ("shorter") above a sustained pedal point on the horns ("longer"). • *Pirata, Lucia, Sonnambula:* the first and last by Bellini, the second by Donizetti.

DECEMBER 2

•"*Durch sie ging . . .*" ("Through them all my happiness was lost"): Queen of the Night in Mozart's *Die Zauberflöte,* Act I, Scene 6.

DECEMBER 3

•The Berlin *Tage-Blatt: Deutsches Tageblatt.*

DECEMBER 4

•Kant's book about the human races: *Von den verschiedenen Rassen der Menschen,*

1775. • The Beeth. symphonies in Zurich: in the concerts he conducted between 1850 and 1855 for the Musical Society of Zurich, Wagner performed all the Beethoven symphonies from the Third to the Eighth, some of them more than once. • R. W. calendar: presumably an advance proof of the *Richard-Wagner-Kalender,* which was published by Fromme in Vienna in 1882 and contained the dates of rehearsals and performances at the Bayreuth theater in that year.

DECEMBER 5

•Eduard Dev[rient] (1801–77): German stage and theater director with whom Wagner fell out when the projected first performance of *Tristan und Isolde* (in Karlsruhe in 1859) failed to materialize; in 1869 he published a book, *Meine Erinnerungen an Felix Mendelssohn-Bartholdy und seine Briefe an mich* (*My Reminiscences of F. M.-B. and His Letters to Me*). • Just think of *Tristan:* since its first production in Munich in 1865, *Tristan und Isolde* had so far been done on only two other stages, Weimar in 1874 and Berlin in 1876, but this was largely because of Wagner's unwillingness to allow unsupervised productions of it. • A letter to Wolz.: not published in the *Bayreuther Blätter.*

DECEMBER 6

•He wrote in his *Braunes Buch:* Wagner's actual words are, "The isolation of a genius in this world can be very well measured by the stupid questions put to him."

DECEMBER 8

•The Battle of Meloria: a naval battle in 1284 between Pisa and Genoa which led to Pisa's loss of Corsica. • "The Diver": Schiller's ballad *"Der Taucher"* tells about a page who dived into a raging sea to recover a goblet thrown into it by the king. • To build a dam against that: in Goethe's *Faust,* Part Two, Acts IV and V.

DECEMBER 10

•The theater fire in Vienna: on December 8, 1881, a fire broke out in the Ringtheater in Vienna just before the curtain was due to rise on Offenbach's *The Tales of Hoffmann,* and more than 400 people lost their lives. • Spichern: a battle in the Franco-Prussian War in which the Germans gained a victory over the French. • "The Hostage": Schiller's ballad *"Die Bürgschaft"* deals with the story of Damon (whom Schiller named Meros in the first version of his poem) and Pythias; Pythias (Phintias), condemned to death for plotting against the tyrant Dionysius I of Syracuse, leaves his friend Damon behind as a hostage and goes to settle some family affairs, returning just in time to prevent Damon's being put to death (by crucifixion, according to Schiller); the tyrant, impressed, frees them both. • "The Journey to the Forge": Schiller's ballad *"Der Gang nach dem Eisenhammer"*; in this the count is told by Robert, a hunter, that Fridolin, a page, is showing too much attention to the count's wife; he gives secret orders that the first person to arrive at a forest forge be thrown into the fire, then sends Fridolin there; however, Fridolin goes to a Mass at his mistress's request, to pray for her dying son, and when he eventually arrives at the forge, the count's orders have already been carried out, the victim being Robert.

DECEMBER 11

•The 2nd *Tristan* performance: this could refer to the revival of *Tristan und Isolde* in Berlin (see November 28 and December 7, 1881), but seems more likely to be connected with the production in Königsberg on December 10; Wagner's astonishment at its success, puzzling with regard to Berlin, is less so in relation to Königsberg, where "things must really have changed a lot" since he himself was conductor there in 1836 (see references to this production on December 16 and 17).

DECEMBER 12

•Wusstlich: not identified. • Mendel.'s performance of the Bach Passion: the famous performance of Bach's *Saint Matthew Passion* conducted by Mendelssohn in

Berlin on March 11, 1829, which marked a revival of interest in Bach's music.

DECEMBER 14

•*Le Serment:* opera by Auber, 1832. • *La Fiancée:* full title *La Fiancée du Roi des Garbes,* opera by Auber, 1864.

DECEMBER 16

•*Trist. und Is.* has now come to Königsberg: see note for December 11, 1881. • *Baron Marx:* Wilhelm Marx, Baron von Marxberg (1815–97), chief of police in Vienna.

DECEMBER 17

•An article by Dr. Herrig: in an article in the *Deutsches Tageblatt* Hans Herrig drew attention, in connection with the disastrous fire in the Ringtheater in Vienna (see note for December 10, 1881), to the safe conditions of the Bayreuth festival theater.
• The Albert Hall: the hall in London in which Wagner conducted concerts of his music in 1877 (see vol. I).

DECEMBER 18

•Friedrich III: fifteenth-century Habsburg Holy Roman Emperor. • Holtzmann: Adolf Holtzmann (1810–70), Indian and German philologist. • *La devoción de la cruz* (*Devotion at the Cross*): a play by Calderón. • An article on Kleist by Wolz.: *Bayreuther Blätter,* October-November 1881. • The statement concerning the performance of *Pars.:* Wolzogen's announcement that *Parsifal* would be presented exclusively in Bayreuth, *Bayreuther Blätter,* October-November 1881. • Parsifal's entrance: III, bar 1030 (horns and trumpets).

DECEMBER 19

•During the floods (1868): in Ticino, Switzerland; Wagner noted in his *Annalen* under October 1, "Lavorno—walk through mud. Lamp! Wrecked bridge: through the water."

DECEMBER 20

•Princess Butera: or Buttera; Count Tasca's sister-in-law. • Gambetta's *coup d'état:* elected temporary president of the Chamber by left-wing parties in October 1881, Gambetta forced the resignation of Ferry's administration and, in November, formed his own ministry.

DECEMBER 21

•Mme Rémusat: Countess Claire Elisabeth Jeanne de Rémusat (1780–1821), lady in waiting to Empress Josephine; her *Mémoires* appeared in 3 vols. (1879–80), her *Lettres* in 2 vols. (1881).

DECEMBER 23

•Berthier: Alexandre Berthier (1753–1815), Prince of Wagram, Napoleon's minister of war and chief of staff, deserted to the Bourbons in 1814.

DECEMBER 25

•*Polonia:* overture by Wagner, 1836; thought to have been lost, it was recovered and returned to him in 1869 through the French conductor Jules Pasdeloup. • The completed score: actually not quite complete; in order to be able to present it to Cosima as a birthday present, Wagner completed the final page and left the preceding pages temporarily blank; the orchestration of *Parsifal* was in fact completed on January 13, 1882 (*q.v.*). • The episode of *La Favorita:* in 1840 in Paris the French publisher Maurice Schlesinger commissioned Wagner to prepare some arrangements from the Donizetti opera, first produced that year in Paris. • Klepperbein . . . that means death: the German word for "skeleton," as a medieval symbol for death, is "*Klapperbein.*"

DECEMBER 26

•The Palazzo Gangi: home of Prince and Princess Gangi, he being a member of the

Sicilian aristocracy, she the daughter of Countess Tasca.

DECEMBER 28

•My father confessor: Abbé Bucquet in Paris.

DECEMBER 29

•*Schleppcour:* a ceremony at the Bavarian Court which Napoleon witnessed in Munich and introduced into his own Court; it consisted of all the courtiers passing before the monarch on his throne and making a deep bow or curtsey.

•Ragusa: manager of the Hôtel des Palmes in Palermo. • [Death of Karl Brandt]: of pneumonia on December 27 in Darmstadt, at the age of fifty-three. • The same grave as Offenbach: the French composer died in October 1880.

DECEMBER 30

•Countess Mazzarino: a member of the Sicilian aristocracy.

DECEMBER 31

•Princess Filangieri: another member of the Sicilian aristocracy, related to the Tascas.

1882

JANUARY 2

•[Schiller's] ballad "The Glove" ("*Der Handschuh*"): about a knight who, on a lady's command, ventures into an arena of raging lions, tigers, and leopards to recover her glove, which he then returns to her with an expression of contempt. • A quarter of a page: Cosima wrote "*eine 4 Seite*" ("one 4 page"), the meaning of which is doubtful. • The scene between the two queens: in his play Schiller invents a meeting between Mary, Queen of Scots, and Queen Elizabeth I of England. • The scene with the two carriers: Shakespeare's *Henry IV Part I,* Act II, Scene 1.

JANUARY 3

•He hears the message: a quotation from Goethe's *Faust,* expressive of skepticism; *Tristan und Isolde* was given its first performance in Leipzig on January 2, 1882, conducted by Anton Seidl and produced by Angelo Neumann. • Linderhof: a castle in Upper Bavaria, built for King Ludwig 1869–78.

JANUARY 5

•The saltcellar of Benvenuto Cellini: in the Kunsthistorisches Museum in Vienna. • Kalkbrenner: Friedrich Wilhelm Michael Kalkbrenner (1788–1849), a German pianist who wrote many works for piano, very popular in their time. • The *Tristan* night: Act II (love duet). • The *Walküre* night: Act I (Siegmund-Sieglinde), in which moonlight certainly does figure, though the moon itself is not seen.

JANUARY 6

•Cherubini: an article by Ludwig Schemann about Cherubini appeared in the *Bayreuther Blätter,* January-February 1882. • "Man should not visit the gods": Wagner's play on a line from Schiller's ballad "*Der Taucher*" ("The Diver"), in which he substitutes "*besuchen*" ("visit") for "*versuchen*" ("tempt"). • The Pope's new position: at this time feelings were running high in Italy about the status of Rome in relation to the state and the papacy; Prussia, which had withdrawn its embassy at the Vatican in 1874 in connection with the so-called *Kulturkampf,* was now about to reopen it, and presumably Lothar Bucher was concerned in the new arrangements. • The story of Salome: "*Das Tanzlegendchen,*" the last story in Gottfried Keller's collection *Sieben Legenden (Seven Legends).*

JANUARY 8

•Memling's charming and masterly picture: the Palermo museum contains a

Madonna attributed to Hans Memling. • The Greek ram: a bronze figure discovered in Syracuse. • The dinner in Munich in 1868: Hans von Bülow's thirty-eighth birthday; see February 27, 1881.

JANUARY 9
•How he puts jackets on madmen: the Bayreuth factotum Schnappauf included working at the mental institute of St. Gilgenberg among his many tasks. • "*Die arme Baronin*": by Gottfried Keller (in *Das Sinngedicht*).

JANUARY 10
•"Correa": "Don Correa" in Keller's *Das Sinngedicht*.

JANUARY 11
•"*Die Berlocken*": in Keller's *Das Sinngedicht*.

JANUARY 12
•The story about Lucie: in Keller's *Das Sinngedicht*.

JANUARY 13
•All is completed: i.e., the full orchestral score of *Parsifal* (see also December 25, 1881, and note). *Martha*: opera by Friedrich von Flotow, 1847.

JANUARY 14
•Berlioz's *Harold* Symphony: *Harold en Italie*, 1834.

JANUARY 15
•Renoir: the French Impressionist painter Auguste Renoir (1841–1919) made a portrait sketch of Wagner in Palermo, which he later completed in full color; in her diary Cosima spelled his name "Renouard." • Victor Noir: a French journalist shot dead by Prince Pierre Napoléon Bonaparte in 1870.

JANUARY 18
•"To see where Barthel gets his cider": this phrase, here translated literally, is actually a German idiom meaning "to be in the know." • Herr von Lutz: Baron Johann von Lutz (1826–90), in 1865 King Ludwig's Cabinet secretary, from 1880 Bavarian prime minister.

JANUARY 19
•Saint Blandine: Blandina, a slave girl in Lyons, was crucified in the year 177; she was patron saint of maidservants.

JANUARY 21
•Her father confessor: identity not known. • A. Springer: Anton Springer (1825–91), German historian and art historian.

JANUARY 22
•Prof. Salinas: an art historian. • Her infidelity: presumably a reference to Minna's flight with Dietrich from Königsberg in 1837.

JANUARY 23
•The former's villa in the country: the Villa del Principe Gangi, Piazza dei Porrazzi, was situated on the road to Monreale; it was a summer residence, with a terrace and a large garden.

JANUARY 25
•Moleschott: see note for August 19, 1879.

JANUARY 27
•Schnappauf and his decorations: the *Bayreuther Tagblatt* of January 21, 1882, quoted a report from the *Berliner Börsen-Courier* about Wagner's style of living in Palermo; according to this, "the master's courier," dressed in a black frock coat and wearing all his decorations and war medals, stood on the steps of the hotel to receive the prefect when he came to visit Wagner; the prefect mistook the courier for Wagner himself and was overwhelmed by the courtesy extended to him by the "*illustrissimo maestro tedesco*"; commenting on this report, the *Bayreuther Tagblatt*

adds, "The master's courier is obviously our fellow citizen Herr Schnappauf, whom the correspondent of the Berlin newspaper has incidentally somewhat over-embellished, since Herr Schnappauf possesses no decorations or war medals, except the medal for noncombatants."

JANUARY 28
•Claar: Emil Claar (1842–1930), director of the Stadttheater in Frankfurt am Main from 1879.

JANUARY 29
•A letter he would not know what to do with: "Letter to Herr v. Wolzogen," *Bayreuther Blätter,* April 1882; see also March 11 and 13, 1882. • In the style of Abelard: this presumably refers to *Abélard, drame philosophique,* a dialogue written by the French writer François Marie Charles de Rémusat (1797–1875), published posthumously in 1877.

JANUARY 30
•Kant on earthquakes: following the earthquake in Lisbon on November 1, 1755, Kant wrote three articles on the causes of earthquakes. • Stein's article on Rousseau: "*Über Werke und Wirkungen Rousseau's,*" *Bayreuther Blätter,* December 1881. • Cavaliere Guccia: Wagner wrote to King Ludwig on March 1, 1882: "Sicily is the poorest part of Italy as regards music, and there is very little opera-going here, but it so happens that quite a few among the upper classes have attended performances of my works—last year in Munich, for example; among these a young Marquis Guccia introduced himself to me, and through him we have gradually become acquainted with almost the entire aristocracy of Palermo, some of them now firm friends."

FEBRUARY 2
•Rue de la Tonnellerie: in Paris; in 1839 Wagner and Minna lived in number 3 (said to be the birthplace of Molière).

FEBRUARY 4
•"Call to My People": delivered by King Friedrich Wilhelm III of Prussia in Breslau on March 17, 1813. • [George Sand's] *Le Piccinino:* novel in 5 vols., 1847.

FEBRUARY 7
•Humboldt's *Kawi-Sprache: Über die Kawisprache* (*On the Kawi Language*) by Wilhelm von Humboldt, 1836–40; Kawi is the literary language of Java. • *Ruhe ist die erste B[ürger]pflicht* (*The First Duty of a Citizen Is to Keep Calm*): novel (1852) by Willibald Alexis (1798–1871).

FEBRUARY 8
•Dinner with the Cardinal: Prince Gustav Adolf zu Hohenlohe-Schillingsfürst (1823–96), a cardinal from 1866, brother of the princes Chlodwig and Konstantin and a friend of Princess Wittgenstein.

FEBRUARY 9
•Herr Hiller: Ferdinand Hiller, conductor and composer. • His preface to Stein: Wagner's preface to the book of Stein's dialogues, *Helden und Welt,* appeared in the form of a correspondence, published in the *Bayreuther Blätter* in 1883.

FEBRUARY 10
•Eteocles: a son of Oedipus.

FEBRUARY 12
•The imminent flight of the Pope: Leo XIII, striving to restore a church state, was in conflict with the Italian government; however, he was not obliged to take flight.

FEBRUARY 20
•The Duke of Augustenburg: Duke Friedrich VIII zu Schleswig-Holstein-Sonder-

burg-Augustenburg (1829–80) laid claim to the Danish throne, and presumably the claim was being restated by his son Ernst Günther.

FEBRUARY 21

•The "Pilgrims' March": in Berlioz's *Harold en Italie.* • Wolz.'s article: *"Heutiges für Künftiges"* ("Present Things for Future Things"), *Bayreuther Blätter,* January-February 1882. • A vegetarian menu: announcement of the availability of a vegetarian diet during the festival of 1882.

FEBRUARY 23

•Turgenev's *Fathers and Sons:* novel, 1862. • Quotations in the *B. Blätter:* selected by Ernst Ludwig, January-February 1882; *Le Neveu de Rameau (Rameau's Nephew)* is a novel by Denis Diderot. • Jommelli: Niccolò Jommelli (1714–74), Italian composer and Court conductor in Stuttgart who wrote many operas. • Durante: Francesco Durante (1684–1755), Italian composer, mainly of church music (no operas).

FEBRUARY 25

•Count Basewitz's family: possible misspelling of Bassewitz, Prussian aristocrats and statesmen. • The Grand Duke's heir: Friedrich Franz (1851–97), who became grand duke of Mecklenburg-Schwerin in 1883, was forced by ill health to spend most of his time in the South. • "When for six stallions . . .": Mephistopheles in Goethe's *Faust,* Part One (Faust's study); Bayard Taylor's translation of the passage is: "If I've six stallions in my stall, / Are not their forces also lent me? / I speed along, completest man of all, / As though my legs were four-and-twenty."

FEBRUARY 26

•The Scherzo (butterfly!): in Beethoven's Quartet in E Minor, Opus 59, No. 2.

FEBRUARY 27

•Carlyle, whose biography he is reading: Thomas Carlyle died in February 1881; his *Reminiscences,* edited by J. A. Froude, were first published later that year.

FEBRUARY 28

•Friedrich Schlegel's conversion: Karl Wilhelm Friedrich von Schlegel (1772–1829), the historian and literary critic who with his brother August led the Romantic movement in German literature, was converted to Roman Catholicism in 1803. • General Skobeleff: Mikhail Dmitrievich Skobelev (1843–82), a Russian general who distinguished himself in the Russo-Turkish War. • The supplement to the *B. Blätter:* advertisement of a lecture by Otto Rabe, "Protection of Animals from the Point of View of a Vegetarian." • Kietz's bust: done by Gustav Adolf Kietz in 1873.

MARCH 1

•Only the three of us: i.e., Wagner, Cosima, and Siegfried.

MARCH 2

•*A House of Gentlefolk:* novel by Turgenev, 1859. • A melody: the "Porrazzi Melody," rounding off an idea that came to Wagner while he was composing Act II of *Tristan und Isolde.*

MARCH 3

•Baza[rov]: a character in Turgenev's *Fathers and Sons.* • [Goethe's] *"Reineke Fuchs":* a long poem. • Mme Odintzov: a character in Turgenev's *Fathers and Sons.* • Her first appearance in R.'s life: Marie Muchanoff, then Mme Kalergis, was sent by Liszt, with whom she was intimately involved, to Dresden in 1845 to attend the first performance of *Tannhäuser.*

MARCH 4

•Kant's physical geography: *Allgemeine Naturgeschichte und Theorie des Himmels.* • His idea concerning poets and scholars: Wagner wrote in his *Braunes Buch* on this day: "The difference between us and you lies in the fact that your knowledge of the world is governed only by a physiological interest, ours, however, by a moral interest. The poet sees the world from its moral aspect, the scientist from its mechanical one." • The defeat of Varus: Quintilius Varus, the Roman governor in Germany, was defeated by Arminius in the Teutoburger Wald in A.D. 9. • The assassination attempt on the Queen of England: Queen Victoria was fired at when about to enter her carriage at Windsor station on March 2, 1882, but was not injured; the perpetrator was Roderick Maclean, described as a man of respectable family fallen on bad times.

MARCH 5
•The Treaty of Passarowitz: or Požarevac; signed 1718 between Austria and Turkey, it restored Belgrade and part of Bosnia and Wallachia to Austria. • Forman: Alfred Forman (1840–1925); his translation of *Der Ring des Nibelungen* was published in 1877. • Dr. Keppler: Friedrich Keppler, surgeon and physician in Venice, later became Wagner's personal doctor there. • I permitted myself that in Lucerne: Wagner spent nearly six months in Lucerne (Hotel Schweizerhof) in 1859, working on Act III of *Tristan und Isolde;* Act II was in fact completed in Venice, before he went to Lucerne.

MARCH 6
•Cassander: actually the son of Antipater. • Grube's historical studies: *Charakter-bilder aus der Geschichte und Sage (Character Portraits from History and Legend)* by the educational writer August Wilhelm Grube (1816–84), published in 3 vols., 1852. • Bruckmann: Friedrich Bruckmann (1814–98), owner of an art and book publishing firm in Munich.

MARCH 7
•*"Bon, je sais ce que c'est"*: quotation from Victor Hugo's *Histoire d'un crime* (see May 31, 1878). • *"Die Trommel gerühret"* ("Sound the drum"): set to music by Beethoven in his incidental music to Goethe's *Egmont.* • *"Freudvoll und leidvoll"* ("Joyful and sorrowful"): ditto. • Dumas's *Les Garibaldiens:* a history of the revolution in Sicily and Naples by Alexandre Dumas *père* (1861). • The entry into Palermo: Giuseppe Garibaldi (1807–82), the Italian liberator, entered Palermo in 1860 after defeating the Neapolitan troops, thus ending the Bourbon rule there. • "Who can know the pangs of woe": Gretchen in Goethe's *Faust,* Part One (prison scene). • The performance of *Egmont* in Zurich: see note for March 29, 1881. • Gladstone's resignation: the British prime minister did not in fact resign at this time, but remained in office until 1885.

MARCH 8
•The 1,000: the "thousand volunteers" with whom Garibaldi took Sicily in 1860. • Springer: Anton Springer; see note for January 21, 1882. • Brunn: Heinrich von Brunn (1822–94), German archaeologist, professor in Munich from 1865.

MARCH 9
•[Goethe's] *Clavigo:* a play, 1774.

MARCH 10
•*"Güllverständnis"* ... *"Mis-t-verständnis"*: the German word for "misunderstanding" is *"Missverständnis"; "Güll"* and *"Mist"* both mean "manure."

MARCH 12
•A "black sail": a reference to the legend of Tristan and Iseult. • Her Imperial Highness: the wife of Friedrich Franz, heir to the grand duke of Mecklenburg-Schwerin, was formerly Grand Duchess Anastasia Michailovna (born 1860). • *"Wisst ihr, Kinder"*: correctly, *"Sagt mir, Kinder";* from *Kinderkatechismus (A Children's Catechism)*, written for Cosima's birthday on December 25, 1873 (see vol. I).

MARCH 13
•His brother Julius: Julius Wagner (1804–62), Wagner's elder brother, a goldsmith. • Ottilie: Wagner's sister Ottilie Brockhaus (1811–83) lost both her husband, Professor Dr. Hermann Brockhaus (1806–77), and her son Clemens (1837–77) in the same year.

MARCH 15
•Count Gravina: Count Biagio Gravina (1850–97), second son of the prince of Ramacca, an aristocratic family from Catania, Sicily. • Grand Duke Konstantin: Konstantin Konstantinovich (1858–1915), a member of the Russian nobility, poet and translator and later president of the academy of sciences.

MARCH 17
•The marches for King and Emperor: Wagner's *"Huldigungsmarsch"* and *"Kaisermarsch."*

MARCH 20
•Acireale: a spa on the slopes of Mount Etna.

MARCH 21
•Molière's *Les Femmes savantes* (*The Learned Ladies*): a play, 1672. • The Turgenev novel: *A House of Gentlefolk.*

MARCH 22
•*What Is German?* (*Was ist deutsch?*): a series of observations written by Wagner for King Ludwig in 1865 and first published in the *Bayreuther Blätter* in 1878; in vol. 10 of the collected writings.

MARCH 24
•The "children's friend": Cosima herself supplies an explanation of this name (*"Kinderfreund"*) at the end of her entry for March 25.

MARCH 26
•Balder: the Norse god of light. • Prince Scalea: not identified. • Anecdote of the courtier: see note for November 18, 1879.

MARCH 27
•Work on the subject of male and female: a two-page draft headed *"Über das Männliche u. Weibliche in Kultur und Kunst"* ("Male and Female in Culture and Art"), the final entry in Wagner's *Braunes Buch.* • Palmerston: Henry John Temple, 3rd Viscount Palmerston (1784–1865), at that time British foreign secretary, supported Napoleon III's assumption of power in France in 1851 without consulting his colleagues and was dismissed from office; but in 1855 he was back in power as prime minister; his actions as both foreign secretary and prime minister did much to further the cause of Italian unity. • Capua: the main seat of Neapolitan resistance to Garibaldi in 1860.

MARCH 28
•Baron Pennisi: Baron Pasquale Pennisi, who owned a large collection of coins, was possibly expected to call on Wagner on this day; Wagner and Cosima visited him on March 31 (*q.v.*). • Laube: Heinrich Laube (1806–84), journalist, dramatist, and subsequently theater director, was a close friend of Wagner in earlier years, but they fell out in 1867, when Wagner failed to support Laube in his desire to become director of the Munich opera.

MARCH 29
•Einsiedeln: a place of pilgrimage in Switzerland; its Benedictine abbey was founded in the tenth century, and it has a famous library. • Frau Dietz: possibly Sophie Dietz (1820–87), who sang Magdalene in the first performance of *Die Meistersinger* in Munich in 1868; another possibility (since Cosima wrote "Fr. Dietz") is Friedrich Christian Diez, author of a grammar of Romance languages

published in 3 vols., 1858–70, copies of which were in the Wahnfried library. • The
Album-Sonate: Wagner's Piano Sonata in A-flat Major, written in 1853 for Mathilde
Wesendonck (*Sonate für das Album von Frau M. W.*).

APRIL 1
•Marquis S. Giuliano: Antonio Marchese Paternò Castelli di San Giuliano (1852–
1914), mayor of Catania from 1879, later Italian minister of foreign affairs.

APRIL 2
•*Bund: Der Bund,* a periodical founded in Berne, Switzerland, in 1850.

APRIL 3
•In Schreckenstein: June-July 1842, while Wagner was working on the prose sketch
of *Tannhäuser.* • This theater: the main attraction in Taormina is an ancient theater,
built by the Greeks and restored by the Romans.

APRIL 4
•Gerber: Karl Friedrich Wilhelm von Gerber (1823–91), Saxon minister of public
education; his edict was concerned, among other things, with school homework.

APRIL 5
•Nadar: pseudonym of Félix Tournachon (1820–1910), French writer and caricatur-
ist, constructor and navigator of air balloons. • *Carmen* is providing him with
competition: Bizet's opera, a failure when first performed in Paris in 1875, had
by this time established itself in opera houses throughout the world (London and
New York 1878, Melbourne 1879, Hamburg and Berlin 1880, Rio de Janeiro and
Madrid 1881, etc.).

APRIL 7
•"Present and Future": Hans von Wolzogen's *"Heutiges für Künftiges,"* Bayreuther
Blätter, January-February 1882. • The scene of the griffins and sphinxes: in Goethe's
Faust, Part Two. • The first thoughts of *Parsifal:* see note for January 13, 1878.
• L. Lehmann has declined to take part: in *Parsifal* at Bayreuth in 1882, because of
her reluctance to come into contact again with Fritz Brandt, with whom she had had
an unhappy love affair.

APRIL 9
•Wagner's words about ten-pin rolling: in Goethe's *Faust,* Part One (before the
city gate); Wagner is Faust's amanuensis. • Pasquino: leader of a company of
Sicilian folk players whom Gravina engaged to give a performance in the hotel.

APRIL 10
•Our departure for Messina: seaport in Sicily where they remained until leaving for
Naples on April 13.

APRIL 11
•The Antonellos: pictures in the national museum of Messina painted by Antonello
da Messina (1444–93). • [Schiller's] *Die Braut von Messina:* a play in the ancient
Greek manner, 1803.

APRIL 12
•The ex-Khedive: Ismail Pasha (1830–95), who abdicated as khedive of Egypt in
1879 and spent the rest of his life in exile.

APRIL 16
•Strakosch: Maurice (Moritz) Strakosch (1825–87), pianist and impresario from
Galicia, active 1848–60 in America, then mainly in Europe.

APRIL 17
• Schulz-Curtius: a Wagner supporter active in London musical life; in a letter from
him, preserved in the Wahnfried archives, he suggested building a special Wagner
theater in London. • His "Gondolier's Song": see note for "the melody" in the next
entry.

APRIL 18

• His remarks on "Hunger": enclosed is a sheet of notepaper from the Grand Hôtel des Bains in Acireale, on which is written in Wagner's handwriting, "Hunger and love keep the world going—now only hunger—soon it will be just thirst." • The melody: enclosed is a sheet of paper with four musical staves, a copy by Cosima of Wagner's Italian poem to Peter Cornelius of November 13, 1861, and a melody in the style of Italian recitative, above which is written, "*Canto anticchio italiano*" ("ancient Italian song").

APRIL 19

•Scribe's *Bataille des dames* (*The Women's Battle*): play (1851) by Eugène Scribe (1791–1861).

APRIL 20

•"She is not the first": in Goethe's *Faust*, Part One, Mephistopheles's reply to Faust when he learns of Gretchen's imprisonment (scene in a field, dreary day).

APRIL 22

•Hans's engagement: Hans von Bülow had become engaged to the actress Marie Schanzer (1857–1941), whom he married later in the year.

APRIL 23

•Fafner and Fasolt: the two giants in *Der Ring des Nibelungen*. • "Signor Formica": a story in E. T. A. Hoffmann's *Serapionsbrüder,* and a possible influence on *Die Meistersinger* (it concerns an elderly man who serenades a young girl).

APRIL 24

•The report in the *B. Bl.* about vivisection: "*Die Frage der Vivisektion im Deutschen Reichstage,*" by Bernhard Förster, March 1882. • Darwin's death: Charles Darwin died on April 19.

APRIL 25

•The old altarpiece: Francesco Bissolo's *Assunta,* 1358. • His future work: the proposed article on male and female.

APRIL 26

•The awesome quotation from Father Molinos: the words of the Spanish mystic Miguel de Molinos (1640–97), quoted by E. T. A. Hoffmann in the conversation in *Die Serapionsbrüder* entitled "Zacharias Werner," are: "It is not necessary to be concerned about temptation, or to offer any resistance to it. If Nature stirs, it should be allowed its way; it is only Nature."

APRIL 27

•*Smoke:* novel by Turgenev, 1867; the French edition (*Fumée*) of 1874 had a foreword by Prosper Mérimée. • Rachel: Elisa Rachel Félix (1820–58), French actress who excelled in tragic roles.

APRIL 28

•A fine article by Dr. Schem.: an appreciation by Schemann of Goethe on the fiftieth anniversary of his death, *Bayreuther Blätter,* March 1882.

APRIL 30

•*Around the World in 80 Days:* a stage adaptation of the novel *Le Tour du monde en quatre-vingt jours* by Jules Verne (1828–1905), made by the author in collaboration with Adolphe Philippe d'Ennery (1811–99).

MAY 3

•The new façade: resulting from the erection of the royal box.

MAY 5–6

•Start of rehearsals: for Wagner's birthday celebrations.

MAY 8

•Merz: Oscar Merz, Munich; coach and musical assistant for the Bayreuth festival of 1882.

MAY 9

•*Siegfried* [in London]: the complete *Ring* cycle was performed four times in London in May and June 1882 by Angelo Neumann's traveling company; it was conducted by Anton Seidl, and the singers included Therese Vogl and Hedwig Reicher-Kindermann as Brünnhilde, Heinrich Vogl and Georg Unger as Siegfried, Albert Niemann as Siegmund, and Karl Hill as Alberich; in the first cycle Emil Scaria, playing Wotan, suffered a mental breakdown and had to be helped through *Siegfried* by the prompter and his fellow singers.

MAY 10

•"Vanish, you dark arches . . .": from Goethe's *Faust,* Part One. • *Ottar Jarl:* by Gobineau.

MAY 18

•Very favorable to Richter: Hans Richter was the conductor of the Francke-Pollini performances of *Tannhäuser, Lohengrin, Die Meistersinger,* and *Tristan und Isolde* at the Drury Lane Theater in London, which were running concurrently with Neumann's *Ring* performances there at Her Majesty's Theater; Richter's singers included Rosa Sucher as Eva and Isolde, Hermann Winkelmann as Stolzing and Tristan, Marianne Brandt as Brangäne, and Eugen Gura as Hans Sachs and King Marke. • Else Ritter: daughter of Alexander Ritter.

MAY 22

•The "Thespis Cart": an introductory *tableau* devised by the children, depicting the beginnings of art. • The hangings: fifty meters of a light-blue satin material, three meters wide, on which Joukowsky had painted an old Chinese pattern of trees, flowers, and birds. • Blandine . . . speaks her toast: the text, enclosed in full in Blandine's handwriting, pays tribute to Wagner for having taken her into his home and brought her up, and thanks him for his loving care; it ends, "He who gave me hope, he who gave me faith, who showed me love—long may he live!" • The choir starts to sing: the boys' chorus from *Parsifal, "Der Glaube lebt,"* rehearsed by Humperdinck. • The black swans: a present from King Ludwig; Wagner named them Parsifal and Kundry. • The first play: *Los habladores* (*The Gossips*), an intermezzo by Cervantes. • *Liebes-Not* (*Love's Distress*): a play written by Cosima herself, in which Daniela played the leading role.

MAY 23

•Herr Albert: manager of the Schlosshotel in Heidelberg, he had come to Bayreuth to look after the theater restaurant during the festival of 1882. • The hangings from the King: richly embroidered silk hangings, a present from King Ludwig. • Roldan: a character in the Cervantes play. • The "Mephisto" movement: the third and last movement in Liszt's *Faust* Symphony.

MAY 24

•Els'chen: Else Ritter. My *West-Eastern Divan:* a humorous reference to the hangings presented to Wagner by King Ludwig; they presumably reminded him of Goethe's poems in the manner of the Persian poet Hafiz, the *West-Eastern Divan.*

MAY 25

•*Die Kawi-Sprache:* see note for February 7, 1882.

MAY 26

•"I am like a flower": a parody of Heine's poem *"Du bist wie eine Blume"* ("Thou art like a flower").

MAY 28

•A letter to Herr Schön: it includes the sentence, "It would be in line with my outlook if you were to establish a foundation enabling people of scant means to attend the performances"—the first expression of this idea (see May 18, 1882).

MAY 30
•Greeting in music:

It is truly sultry—but I am violet

• "Frl. I. von Bülow": Wagner was annoyed by this form of address for his elder daughter; in the first years after Isolde's birth Cosima was wont to deny to others that she was Wagner's child, and when Isolde laid claim to a share of the Wagner inheritance in 1913, Cosima allowed the case to go to court; Isolde's failure to establish her claim led to a final breach between mother and daughter.
JUNE 1
•The music festival: in Aachen; Hans von Bülow was among the participants, and Daniela had gone there to hear him conduct.
JUNE 3
•The encoring of *Tr. und Isolde:* i.e., the Prelude. • Garibaldi's death: Garibaldi died at his home on the island of Caprera on June 2.
JUNE 5
•The best German opera after his: Saint-Saëns's opera *Samson et Dalila,* given its first performance in Weimar in 1877 at Liszt's instigation, was still unknown outside Germany.
JUNE 7
•A letter from Daniela: in Nuremberg Daniela had met for the first time the actress Marie Schanzer, who was to become Hans von Bülow's second wife; she was taking part in a performance given there by the Meiningen company. • *State and Religion* (*Über Staat und Religion*): written by Wagner in 1864, in vol. 8 of the collected writings. • His poem to the King: "*Dem königlichen Freunde*" ("To My Royal Friend"), written in summer 1864, in vol. 8 of the collected writings.
JUNE 8
•Herr Vogl's final decision: not to sing the role of Parsifal.
JUNE 9
•The lines in *Faust:* Part One, Prologue in Heaven. • Tyler's Rebellion: in 1381, rebels led by Wat Tyler marched on London, broke into the Tower, and killed the archbishop of Canterbury; they met King Richard II at Smithfield, where Tyler was killed by the lord mayor of London.
JUNE 10
•Duplicate weddings: ceremonies in both Catholic and Protestant churches. • Hume's *History of England:* David Hume (1711–76), the Scottish philosopher and

historian, published his *History of England* in 5 vols., 1754–61; a German translation was published in 6 vols., 1767–71. • Lachmann: Karl Lachmann (1793–1851), German philologist; his translation of the sagas, *Saga-Bibliothek,* was known to Wagner before 1848.

JUNE 11

•His school idea: in his *"Offenes Schreiben an Herrn Friedrich Schön in Worms"* ("Open Letter to F. S. in Worms"), published in the *Bayreuther Blätter,* July 1882, and in vol. 10 of the collected writings, Wagner puts forth his original idea of a music school in Bayreuth only to dismiss it as no longer valid, first, because he no longer believes in German music, and second, because he remembers Gobineau's prophecy that within ten years Europe will be swamped by Asiatic hordes (he is referring to this in his subsequent remark to Cosima about the Bashkirs); he now puts his faith, not in music schools, but in the German public, and the best possible school would be an organization that would enable supporters without means of their own to attend performances at Bayreuth free of charge; he recommends that the Society of Patrons turn its thoughts in this direction. • Falstaff and the Lord Chief Justice: Shakespeare's *Henry IV Part II,* Act I, Scene 2. • His 50th birthday: correctly, his fifty-first birthday, in 1864, which he spent in Starnberg with Franz Seraph von Pfistermeister (1820–1912), King Ludwig II's Cabinet secretary; Wagner spent his fiftieth birthday in Vienna with Standhartner, and it was only in the following year, on May 3, 1864, that he met Pfistermeister, sent by the new Bavarian king to Stuttgart to seek out Wagner and bring him to Munich.

JUNE 12

•The Grand Duke of Schwerin: Friedrich Franz II von Mecklenburg-Schwerin (1823–83).

JUNE 13

•The *Parsifal* reading by actors in Brunswick: this had happened on April 2, 1882, and Ludwig Schemann reported on it in the *Bayreuther Blätter,* May-June 1882.

JUNE 14

•Things from his letter: the "Open Letter to Friedrich Schön in Worms" (see note for June 11, 1882). • An article against eating meat: *"Die Epidemien als Kultur- krankheiten"* ("Epidemics as Sicknesses of Civilization"), by Ernst Grysanowsky, *Bayreuther Blätter,* May-June 1882. • His Bach prelude: presumably the E-flat Minor from bk. I of Bach's *48 Preludes and Fugues.* • A cantata: *"Gleichwie der Regen und Schnee vom Himmel fällt"* ("Just As the Rain and Snow from Heaven Fall") by Johann Sebastian Bach, BWV 18 (c.1715).

JUNE 15

•*"Prinzessin Brambilla"*: a story by E. T. A. Hoffmann.

JUNE 16

•Before giving up his directorship in Leipzig: both Angelo Neumann and August Förster left Leipzig in August 1882 on the expiry of their contracts there.

JUNE 17

•To refuse the imperial crown: at the Congress of Vienna (1814) the Prussian statesman Baron Heinrich von Stein unsuccessfully pleaded for the establishment of a united Germany. • "Excellent!": this presumably refers to the tom-toms that Dannreuther had procured for Wagner in London. • "Creating" the roles: in his "Open Letter to Friedrich Schön in Worms" Wagner deplored the new tendency among singers, which originated in Italy and France and was now spreading to Germany, of competing for the privilege of being the first to sing a particular role; he ascribed the desire to personal vanity—not to any concern about the composer's work.

JUNE 18

•The *"Adam-Dam"*: the German word for "tom-tom" is *"Tamtam."*

JUNE 19

•Anecdote of the conductor Proch: Heinrich Proch, Vienna (see entry and note for December 23, 1878); the work is Weber's *Der Freischütz*. • "If I did it right . . .": a paraphrase of the quotation from Schiller's *Wilhelm Tell* ("If I were prudent, I should not be Tell"). • Cramer's music encyclopedia: Carl Friedrich Cramer (1752–1807) published his *Magazin der Musik* 1783–87.

JUNE 20

•The script of the play: Cosima's *Liebes-Not,* written for Wagner's birthday (see May 22, 1882, and note). • Streicher's little book about [Schiller's] flight: Andreas Streicher (1761–1833), a piano builder, fled with Schiller from Mannheim in 1782 after Schiller's first play, *Die Räuber,* aroused the Duke of Württemberg's displeasure; his account of the flight, *Schillers Flucht,* was published in 1836. • *Ariadne auf Naxos:* opera by Georg Benda, 1775. • "To kick against the pricks": Acts of the Apostles 26:14.

JUNE 24

•A Herr Strauss: Franz Strauss (1822–1905), horn player at the Munich opera and father of the composer Richard Strauss; a man of some wealth, having married into the family that owned one of the large Munich breweries, he was inclined to behave in a boorish way at rehearsals, and was apparently particularly trying to both Wagner and Hans von Bülow during the *Meistersinger* rehearsals of 1868; Strauss did in fact play in the Bayreuth festival orchestra in 1882. • Froh: a Saint Bernard dog.

JUNE 26

•*The Destiny of Opera* (*Über die Bestimmung der Oper*): a lecture given by Wagner at the Academy of Arts in Berlin on April 28, 1871; published in vol. 9 of the collected writings. • [Lessing's] *Laokoon:* first published in 1766, it is still regarded as a masterpiece of aesthetic criticism. • The break with the Duke: the duke of Württemberg (see note for June 20, 1882). • Old Bierey: see note for March 24, 1878.

JUNE 28

•A suggestion made by Humperdinck: this presumably refers to the bars of connecting music that Humperdinck wrote of his own accord and showed to Wagner (according to Humperdinck's own reminiscences) on June 22; Wagner approved them, and they were incorporated in the score for the 1882 performances, then dropped in succeeding years, when ways were found of changing the scenery more swiftly. • Gudehus: Heinrich Gudehus (1845–1909), tenor in Dresden from 1880; he was one of the three Parsifals in 1882, and in subsequent Bayreuth festivals also sang Tristan and Walther von Stolzing.

JUNE 29

•The lawyer Simson: August Simson (1837–1927); before representing Wagner in the Fürstner suit, he represented Hans von Bülow in the divorce proceedings (see vol. I).

JUNE 30

•Lucian's story about the ass: "Lucius or the Ass" by the Greek satirist Lucian (c.120–180).

JULY 1

•The execution of the President's assassin: Charles Jules Guiteau, assassin of President Garfield in 1881, was hanged in Washington, D.C., on June 30, 1882.

JULY 2

•The orchestra: from the Munich opera, reinforced by instrumentalists from Berlin, Meiningen, Karlsruhe, Darmstadt, etc. (107 players in all). • The exhibition in Nuremberg: the Bavarian industrial, trade, and art exhibition had been opened on May 15 by Prince Luitpold, representing King Ludwig; presumably Wagner felt that the king, having missed this important event, had qualms about coming to Bayreuth in person. • Reichmann: Theodor Reichmann (1849–1903) made his debut in Magdeburg in 1869 and appeared in Hamburg and Berlin before joining the Vienna opera in 1882; he sang Amfortas at Bayreuth in 1882 and in subsequent festivals until 1902, and also sang Hans Sachs and Wolfram (*Tannhäuser*) there. • The "Blue Moor": Angermann's.

JULY 3
•The two Kundrys: Amalie Materna and Marianne Brandt. • Herr Winkelmann's letter: he was threatening to leave Bayreuth at once, having learned that Gudehus was to sing Parsifal at the first performance.

JULY 4
•At that time (1858): Cosima and Hans von Bülow stayed with Wagner at the Asyl in Zurich during July and August. • Tante Schinkel: Susanne Schinkel, sister of Hans von Wolzogen's mother.

JULY 7
•Betty Braun: a friend of Cosima. • Siehr: Gustav Siehr (1837–96), a singer in Wiesbaden, was engaged at the last moment to sing Hagen in the Bayreuth *Ring* of 1876 and made a great impression on Wagner; he sang at Bayreuth until 1889 (Gurnemanz and King Marke).

JULY 8
•He writes to the King: "I could not have received a bitterer blow than the news that my noble benefactor had decided to attend none of the performances of my stage dedication play. . . . It is the last thing I shall write. The tremendous over-exertion, which leaves me only enough strength for these few lines today, tells me how things stand with my powers. From me *nothing* more can be expected. . . ."

JULY 9
•"*So war es mein Kuss . . .*" ("So it was my kiss that gave thee understanding"): Kundry to Parsifal, II, bars 1343 ff. • "*Die Marquise de la Pivardière*": one of E. T. A. Hoffmann's final stories. • Arabi Pasha (1840–1911): Ahmed Arabi, not khedive of Egypt, but leader of an insurrectionary party, whose acts led to a war with Great Britain; he was defeated on September 13, 1882, and expelled. • Penzing (Dommayer): Penzing was the part of Vienna in which Wagner lived 1863–64; Dommayer was the name of a restaurant in Vienna in which the Strauss family played.

JULY 10
•Lessmann: Otto Lessmann (1844–1918), editor of the *Allgemeine Musikzeitung* 1881–1907. • Frl. Dompierre: sang the alto solo role in *Parsifal* in 1882. • Fuchs: Anton Fuchs (1849–1925), singer in Munich, in addition to singing a Knight, did four performances as Klingsor in the *Parsifal* of 1882; in subsequent years (until 1899) he was Cosima's chief assistant on the production side of the festival, and also sang Amfortas, Kurwenal, King Marke, and Titurel.

JULY 11
•Stein's draft: "*Das Bayreuther Patronat, ein neuer Ruf an unsere alten Freunde*" ("The Bayreuth Patrons, a New Appeal to Our Old Friends"), published without signature in the *Bayreuther Blätter,* August 1882. • Oesterlein: Nikolaus Oesterlein (1842–98) published his *Katalog einer Wagner-Bibliothek* (*Catalogue of a Wagner Library*) in 4 vols., 1882–95.

JULY 15
•"*Die Mutter!*" ("My mother!"): Parsifal's exclamation on hearing from Kundry in Act II how his mother, Herzeleide, died.

JULY 16
•Killing of the Europeans in Alexandria: in the course of the uprising of Ahmed Arabi in Egypt.
JULY 19
•"He is my father" ("*Quello è mio padre*"): Figaro in Act III of Mozart's *Le Nozze di Figaro.*
JULY 21
•The carnage in Alexandria: in the uprising of Ahmed Arabi, part of the European quarter of Alexandria was burned to the ground.
JULY 23
•An imagined slight: according to Glasenapp, Marianne Brandt was unwilling to do more than kneel after Kundry's baptism by Parsifal, and Wagner physically pushed her head down to the floor! • The *Almanach de Gotha:* beginning as a court calendar in 1763, it had by now extended its coverage to ducal and baronial families.
JULY 26
•The first act goes more or less according to his wishes: this was the first performance of *Parsifal,* of which sixteen performances were given, the first two being for members of the Society of Patrons, the remainder for the general public; the chief conductor was Hermann Levi, though some performances were conducted by Franz Fischer; the role of Parsifal was sung by Hermann Winkelmann (nine, including first and last performances), Heinrich Gudehus (five), and Ferdinand Jäger (two); Kundry by Amalie Materna (eight, including first and last), Marianne Brandt (five), and Therese Malten (three); Gurnemanz by Emil Scaria (ten, including first and last) and Gustav Siehr (six); Amfortas by Theodor Reichmann; Klingsor by Karl Hill (twelve, including first and last) and Anton Fuchs (four); Titurel by August Kindermann; there were twenty-nine Flower Maidens (six solo, twenty-three chorus), thirty-one Knights of the Grail, twenty-nine singers behind the scenes (twelve female, seventeen male), and fifty boys' voices.
JULY 30
•Mihalovich: Edmund von Mihalovich (1842–1929), a Hungarian composer and a pupil of Hans von Bülow. • Apponyi: Count Albert Apponyi (1846–1933), a Hungarian politician and a friend of Liszt.
JULY 31
•[A newspaper clipping enclosed]: from an unidentified paper, reviewing the third performance of *Parsifal* (on July 30), about which it says, "brilliant; the orchestra sounded wonderful, and the choruses, too"; the review praises in particular Reichmann (Amfortas), Scaria (Gurnemanz), Amalie Materna (Kundry), and Winkelmann (Parsifal), and reports storms of applause after Acts II and III. At the end of the performance Wagner, visibly moved, thanked the audience for the applause given to his singers: "It proves to me that you were satisfied with their achievements." This brought more applause, and the curtains parted to reveal the participants in their positions from the final scene. On the clipping, beside the remarks about the performance, is written in Wagner's hand, "Excellent, RW."
AUGUST 1
•"I am tired": a reference to Kundry's "*Ich bin müde*" in Act I of *Parsifal.*
AUGUST 2
•The former directors of the Leipzig theater: August Förster and Angelo Neumann. • Countess Voss: presumably Luise Voss (see note for August 19, 1878).
AUGUST 3
•A tutor for Siegf.: presumably the Austrian Dr. Dorda (see September 3, 1882, and note).

AUGUST 7
•The *Indépendance: Indépendance Belge,* a newspaper in Brussels.

AUGUST 9
•Passini: Ludwig Johann Passini (1832–1903), German painter and engraver.

AUGUST 10
•*"Mademoiselle de Scudéry"*: correctly, *"Das Fräulein von Scuderi"; in* E. T. A. Hoffmann's *Die Serapionsbrüder.*

AUGUST 12
•Fritz Brockhaus: Friedrich Arnold Brockhaus (1838–95), a jurist, son of Hermann Brockhaus and Wagner's sister Ottilie; Fritz's sister was Doris von Berckefeld.

AUGUST 14
•Emilie Sierz[putowska]: see note for September 11, 1878. • Alex[andra] Schl[einitz]: a niece of Count and Countess Schleinitz. • Who never saw his dearest suffer . . .: Cosima's adaptation of Goethe's poem *"Wer nie sein Brot mit Tränen ass"* (in E. A. Bowring's translation, "Who never ate with tears his bread, who never through night's heavy hours sat weeping on his lonely bed, *he* knows you not, ye heavenly powers!").

AUGUST 15
•*"Habt Dank"* ("My thanks"): Amfortas in *Parsifal,* I, bars 259 ff.

AUGUST 16
•Unzelmann, Gerlach . . . now Levi: Unzelmann may be the famous actor Karl Wolfgang Unzelmann, who performed in Dresden in Wagner's youth; but Gerlach is not identifiable, and the connection with Levi is unclear.

AUGUST 17
•*"So flatterten die Locken"*: Parsifal describing Kundry's seduction of Amfortas, II, bar 1109.

AUGUST 19
•The contract with Venice: the lease for the Palazzo Vendramin.

AUGUST 21
•*"So, too, thy tear . . ."*: Parsifal's words to Kundry in Act III (*"Auch deine Träne ward zum Segenstaue"*). • Calderón's *La sibila del oriente (The Prophetess of the East).*

AUGUST 23
•Francke's bankruptcy: Francke got into financial difficulties as a result of the performances of Wagner's works at the Drury Lane Theater in London in 1882; Angelo Neumann writes in his *Personal Recollections of Wagner:* "The Francke-Pollini venture ended in most dismal failure. . . . At the close of the season their chorus and orchestra could not be paid, and their sad adventures were long a scandal in the theatrical world."

AUGUST 24
•A telegram to the King: sending greetings for the king's birthday on August 25, Wagner reproaches him in verse for having "spurned" *Parsifal;* this brought explanations from both von Bürkel (see September 3) and von Ziegler (see September 4) that the king's failure to come to Bayreuth was due solely to ill health.

AUGUST 25
•Prince Castelcicala: Don Fabrizio Ruffo, Prince of Castelcicala (1755–1832), a Neapolitan diplomat.

AUGUST 26
•The church wedding: in the Roman Catholic Schlosskirche in Bayreuth.

AUGUST 28
•The Grand Duke of Weimar: Karl Alexander von Sachsen-Weimar-Eisenach

(1818–1901), grand duke from 1853. • The Princess of Meiningen: Princess Maria Elisabeth (1853–1923), daughter of Georg II, Duke of Sachsen-Meiningen, and Princess Charlotte of Prussia; Maria Elisabeth had accompanied the crown prince to the performance on the previous day.

AUGUST 29

•He takes the baton himself: Wagner conducted the final scene, from the twenty-third bar of the transformation music in Act III to the end; according to Glasenapp, he did this because he noticed that Levi was indisposed; Levi, however, remained standing beside him, and 2 days later he wrote as follows to his father: "At the conclusion of the work the audience broke into cheers which defy all description. But the master did not show himself, remaining seated below among the musicians, making bad jokes; when after 10 minutes there was no sign of the noise in the auditorium ceasing, I cried out from the bottom of my lungs, 'Quiet! Quiet!' That was heard up above, silence really was achieved, and then the master began to speak (still from the conductor's podium), at first to me and the orchestra; then the curtains were opened, disclosing all the singers and technical assistants assembled on the stage. The master spoke with such warmth that everyone began to weep— it was an unforgettable moment." • "*Sterben, einz'ge Gnade*" ("Dying, final solace"): Amfortas, *Parsifal,* III, bars 977 ff.

AUGUST 30

•Frl. Galfy: Hermine Galfy (1848–1933), Vienna; sang 1st Squire and a solo Flower Maiden in *Parsifal,* 1882. • Count Wolkenstein: Count Anton Karl Simon Wolkenstein-Trostburg (1832–1913), Austrian diplomat, in 1882 ambassador in St. Petersburg; Marie von Schleinitz, who became a widow in 1885, married him the following year. • Levi's concern that he might upset the performance: when Wagner took the baton from him on August 29.

SEPTEMBER 2

•The historic Thursday gathering: a group of prominent Bayreuth citizens who met every Thursday in one another's houses to discuss political and other questions; it was founded in 1861, and Wagner frequently took part during the years immediately after his arrival in Bayreuth (see vol. I).

SEPTEMBER 3

•A letter from Herr von Bürkel: see note for August 24, 1882. • Dr. Dorda: the tutor mentioned on August 3, 1882. • The Amen of the Dresden Mass: the so-called Dresden Amen, which Wagner used in *Das Liebesverbot* and *Tannhäuser* as well as in *Parsifal.* • Johann Gottlieb Naumann (1741–1801): a very prolific composer in Dresden whose output included twenty-one masses, twenty-three operas, and eighteen symphonies.

SEPTEMBER 4

•Herr von Ziegler (secretary) writes to me: see note for August 24, 1882. • R.'s word of thanks: appearing in the *Bayreuther Tagblatt* on September 5, this thanks "my friendly fellow citizens" for their willing participation, which helped to make such a success of the *Parsifal* performances. • The "Maid of Orleans": Joan of Arc, who figures in Shakespeare's *Henry VI Part I* as Joan La Pucelle. • Accounts of the festival performances: these, in Feustel's handwriting, show receipts of 244,805 marks from the sale of tickets, 141,220.66 marks from the Society of Patrons' contributions, and 52,000 marks from the sale of the *Ring* scenery, making total receipts of 438,025.66 marks; the expenditures were 44,000 marks for scenery and sketches, 80,000 marks for singers and orchestra, 13,000 marks for Karl Brandt's machinery, 40,000 marks for Fritz Brandt, 32,000 marks for the royal box and structural repairs, 6,000 marks for musical assistance (Humperdinck, Hausburg, Jäger), 12,000 marks for advertising, 12,000 marks for the *Bayreuther Blätter* in

1881 (including an honorarium for Wolzogen), 7,000 marks for fire insurance, 15,000 marks for gas, 27,000 marks for costumes, 6,000 marks for sundries (and 885.88 marks not entered), making total expenditures of 294,885.88 marks, leaving a surplus of 143,139.78 marks.

SEPTEMBER 5
•The "Goethe-Philistines": correctly, *"Die Goethe-Pedanten"*; sonnet by Gottfried Keller, 1845.

SEPTEMBER 6
•Sulzer's . . . article about *Parsifal: "Das Bühnenweihfestspiel in Bayreuth,"* published in *Der Bund,* Bern, September 5, 1882.

SEPTEMBER 8
•Dr. Meyer: Gustav Meyer, lawyer in Bayreuth.

SEPTEMBER 9
•Cooper's *The Bravo:* novel (1831) by James Fenimore Cooper (1789–1851).

SEPTEMBER 11
•*Fuente ovejuna:* a drama by Lope de Vega.

SEPTEMBER 12
•Zeisel: Jakob Zeisel, barber-surgeon in Bayreuth. • *"Nicht so":* correctly, *"Nicht doch";* Gurnemanz to Kundry in Act III of *Parsifal.* • Schack: Count Adolf Friedrich von Schack (1815–94), translator of Lope de Vega and author of a 3-vol. history of dramatic literature and art in Spain (1845–46). • His ultimatum: an announcement, published "on Richard Wagner's instructions" in the *Bayreuther Blätter,* September-October 1882, inviting former members of the Society of Patrons to subscribe to the periodical at an annual cost of twenty marks, thus giving them the right to a seat at the festivals and supporting the scholarship fund.

SEPTEMBER 13
•Part of Max's aria: *"Durch die Wälder, durch die Auen"* ("Through the woods and through the meadows") from Weber's *Der Freischütz,* Act I, Scene 4. • Elsa would not have the right: in Act I Elsa offers to give Lohengrin her hand in marriage and the throne of Brabant if he successfully defends her honor against Telramund.

SEPTEMBER 15
•"Abellino, the great bandit": *Abellino, der grosse Bandit* was the title of a popular novel published anonymously in 1793; the author was the Swiss writer Heinrich Zschokke (1771–1848).

SEPTEMBER 16
•*"Dich teure Halle . . ."*: Elisabeth in *Tannhäuser,* Act II. • Wallace: Alfred Russell Wallace (1823–1913), the naturalist whose views on natural selection, reached independently, closely resembled those of Charles Darwin. • The P[alazzo] Vendramin: in this house on the Grand Canal the Wagner family occupied an apartment of fifteen to eighteen rooms on the mezzanine floor. • *Über Land und Meer:* an illustrated periodical devoted to natural history, founded in Stuttgart in 1858.

SEPTEMBER 17
•*Balzac chez lui (Balzac at Home):* by Léon Gozlan (1803–66), first published 1862.
• Staegemann: Max Staegemann (1843–1905), the newly appointed director of the Stadttheater in Leipzig.

SEPTEMBER 18
•The book on Buddha: *Buddha, sein Leben, seine Lehre, seine Gemeinde (Buddha, His Life, Teaching, and Community)* by Hermann Oldenberg (1854-1920), first published 1881.

SEPTEMBER 19–20
•[Telegram enclosed]: Glasenapp was accepting Wagner's invitation to take over the education of Siegfried; his telegram reads, "All doubt regarding my ability

dispelled by trust put in me, we can make ourselves available within few weeks and await more detailed instructions, our feelings beyond expression."

SEPTEMBER 23

•The Arch-Chamberlain's words: in Act IV of Goethe's *Faust,* Part Two (Bayard Taylor's translation).

SEPTEMBER 25

•Bernhard von Weimar: see note for October 26, 1879. • Prince Biron: Calixt Biron, Prince of Curland (1817–82).

SEPTEMBER 28

•He writes to Wolz.: concerning the "ultimatum" (see note for September 12, 1882); Wagner expresses his dislike of societies and adds, "A committee being formed after my death, or perhaps even telling me what to do in the last years of my life—that I do not want!" • Fénelon: François de Salignac de la Mothe-Fénelon (1651–1715), French archbishop, theologian, and writer. • *Phantasus:* a collection of old folk tales and legends by Johann Ludwig Tieck (1773–1853), published in 3 vols., 1812–16. • Calderón's *Amor, honor y poder* (*Love, Honor, and Power*).

SEPTEMBER 29

•Wolkoff: presumably Vassili Alexeivich Volkov (born 1842), a Russian portrait painter. • [Joseph Schroeder]: not identified; "founder of idealism" meant as a joke.

SEPTEMBER 30

•Riemer: Friedrich Wilhelm Riemer (1774–1845), German literary historian, literary assistant to Goethe and coeditor of the last edition of his works. • Falk: Johannes Daniel Falk (1768–1826), German writer, author of reminiscences of Goethe (published 1832). • Meyer: see note for July 6, 1880. • Our two North German friends: presumably Wolzogen and Stein. • *Les Deux Frères Corses:* the French dramatization of the novel by A. Dumas *père* was adapted into English for Charles Kean in 1852 by Dion Boucicault under the title *The Corsican Brothers;* however, there were also several other adaptations being presented in London at the time Wagner saw the play (1855). • Conversation with Meph. before the battle: in Goethe's *Faust,* Part Two, Act IV. • "And how he did enjoy it . . .": Mephistopheles's reply to Faust when the latter asserts that a military commander gives his orders for higher reasons than mere enjoyment. • Bellini's painting: *Madonna Enthroned and Four Saints.*

OCTOBER 1

•"For all guilt . . .": Wagner's parody of the Harpist's song in Goethe's *Wilhelm Meister* ("*Denn alle Schuld rächt sich auf Erden*"). • Hagen on the Wasgenstein: a reference to Act II of *Götterdämmerung.* • More significant than Köppen's: *Die Religion des Buddha und ihre Entstehung* (*The Buddhist Religion and Its Origin*) by F. Köppen, 2 vols., Berlin, 1857–59.

OCTOBER 2

•*Lohengrin*'s success in Vienna: the first performance took place on August 19, 1858.

OCTOBER 3

•Gob.'s article with his preface: *Bayreuther Blätter,* May-June 1881. • Atman: in Indian philosophy, the universal soul.

OCTOBER 4

•*Fermata:* in musical notation, a rest of unspecified length; the passage is so marked in Act III of *Parsifal.* • Frau v. Uexküll: probably the actress Ida Aalborg-Uexküll. • The Andante: presumably the andante variation in the final movement of Beethoven's *Eroica* Symphony.

OCTOBER 6

•His favorite scene: in Shakespeare's *Twelfth Night.*

OCTOBER 7

•He reads Wolz.'s article: see note for October 8, 1882. • The error of the 9 volumes: at that time ten works by Gobineau (in fourteen volumes) had been published. • The phonograph: invented by Thomas Edison in 1877. • Lassalle . . . and his visit to Starnberg: Ferdinand Lassalle visited Wagner at the Haus Pellet in Kempfen-hausen in August 1864, just before fighting the duel in Geneva on August 28 which caused his death. • Frl. v. D[önniges]: Helene von Dönniges: see note for May 5, 1879. • In front of Messala: in Shakespeare's *Julius Caesar,* Act IV, Scene 3; Cosima mistakenly wrote "Metullus" instead of "Messala."

OCTOBER 8

•Frl. Belce: Luise Belce (1862–1945), who, like Frl. Galfy, sang one of the solo Flower Maidens in the *Parsifal* of 1882; later, under her married name of Reuss-Belce, she became one of the main figures at Bayreuth, singing Eva and Fricka as well as smaller roles up to 1912, then acting as dramatic coach until 1933. • Wolz.'s article on Gobineau's book: "*Die Ungleichheit der menschlichen Rassen. Nach des Grafen Gobineau Hauptwerke*" ("The Inequality of Human Races. Based on Count Gobineau's Main Work"), *Bayreuther Blätter,* September-October 1882; in this article Hans von Wolzogen quotes extensively from a book by the Austrian orientalist Adolf Wahrmund (*Babyloniertum, Judentum und Christentum*) and an essay by the German Egyptologist Georg Moritz Ebers ("*Ursprung und Entwicklung der altägyptischen Religion*," published in *Die Gegenwart,* 1882). • *Lari Fari:* a German expression meaning "stuff and nonsense," used jocularly by Wagner as an epithet for the Church of S. Maria Gloriosa dei Frari; the Bellini picture there is *Madonna with Saints.* • Schumann's *Manfred:* overture and incidental music to Byron's dramatic poem *Manfred.* • Mme Beecher Stowe: Harriet Beecher Stowe (1811–96), American novelist; her best-known novel, *Uncle Tom's Cabin* (1852), enjoyed an enormous success, being translated into 22 foreign languages and influencing opinion on the subject of slavery. • He no longer wishes to read this newspaper: the *Deutsches Tageblatt,* Berlin, of which Herrig became editor in 1881.

OCTOBER 10

•Today is the 10th: anniversary of their first meeting, in 1853. • Glasenapp's chronicle: in vol. 6 of his biography of Wagner, Glasenapp refers to "an un-satisfactory chronicle of the festival," written by a contributor to the *Bayreuther Blätter.* • The Palazzo Malipiero: where the Schleinitzes were staying with Princess Hatzfeldt. • Herr von Glümer: a former Prussian lieutenant, sent to the same prison as August Röckel after the Dresden uprising of 1849.

OCTOBER 11

•The *Maria Aegyptiaca:* painting by Tintoretto in the Scuola di S. Rocco, Venice. • The three gods of Lithuania: in Lithuanian mythology Dievas, the earth goddess Zemyna, and the goddess of fate Laima. • Charlotte von Hagn (1809–91): German actress.

OCTOBER 12

•"How perceive it . . .": quotation from Act II of *Tristan und Isolde* ("*Wie sie fassen, wie sie lassen, diese Wonne*"). • "*Du bist der Lenz*" ("You are the spring"): Sieglinde in *Die Walküre,* Act I, Scene 3. • Katharina von Bora: Luther's wife; the joke lies in the fact that "*Bora*" is the Italian name for the northeast wind that blows in the Adriatic in winter.

OCTOBER 13

•Hugo's curious play: *Torquemada,* 1882, about the Spanish inquisitor Tomás de Torquemada (1420–98). • Zanipolo: local name for the Church of SS. Giovanni e Paolo.

OCTOBER 14
• The duet between Valentine and Marcel: in Act III of Meyerbeer's *Les Huguenots*.
• Jules Verne's latest book: presumably *L'Ecole des Robinsons* (*The School for Robinsons*). • Dr. Thode: Henry Thode (1857–1920), German art historian, professor in Heidelberg, and until 1891 director of the Städelsche Art Institute in Frankfurt am Main; in 1886 he married Cosima's daughter Daniela. • My little notebook: some of Cosima's small notebooks, in which she jotted down reminders for the Diaries, are preserved in the Richard-Wagner-Museum in Wahnfried; the final notebook contains two drawings of Wagner, one in profile, one full face, made by Joukowsky on February 12, 1883, the day before Wagner's death; the joke about *Les Huguenots* is not preserved, however.

OCTOBER 15
• We say goodbye to . . . Stein: he left Venice to take up residence and qualify at the University of Halle. • "To All of You" ("*An Euch*"): the original title for Wagner's retrospect of the *Parsifal* production (see note for October 22, 1882).

OCTOBER 16
• Mendelssohn's *Lieder ohne Worte* (*Songs Without Words*): a collection of piano pieces.

OCTOBER 18
• *Väter und Söhne* (*Fathers and Sons*): a play (1882) by Ernst von Wildenbruch (1845–1909). • The *Hitopadesa* collection: Sanskrit *Book of Useful Counsels,* a 10th-century reworking of the *Pañcha Tantra* (*The Fables of Pilpay*).

OCTOBER 19
• The . . . history of Venice: *Histoire de la république de Venise,* by Pierre Bruno Daru (1767–1829).

OCTOBER 20
• *Count Robert of Paris:* novel (1832) by Walter Scott. • Vareger: a character in Scott's novel *The Pirate*.

OCTOBER 21
• A visit to S. Rocco: the pictures mentioned by Cosima (both by Tintoretto) are not in the church, but in the adjoining Scuola di S. Rocco.

OCTOBER 22
• R. begins his article: "*Das Bühnenweihfestspiel in Bayreuth 1882*" ("The Stage Dedication Festival in Bayreuth, 1882"), *Bayreuther Blätter,* November-December 1882, and vol. 10 of the collected writings. • "My tears gush forth . . .": parody of Faust's line in Goethe's *Faust,* Part One (in Bayard Taylor's translation, "My tears gush forth: The Earth takes back her child").

OCTOBER 23
• A. Meissner: Alfred Meissner (1822–85), a physician and writer; a friend of Cosima in Berlin, he visited her and Wagner at Tribschen in November 1870 (see vol. I).

OCTOBER 24
• The nonpaying Voltz and Batz: as later entries show (October 29 onward), Wagner's agents were withholding payments to him because of a dispute concerning *Tristan und Isolde,* for which Wagner claimed the right to sanction or veto all performances.

OCTOBER 25
• Our friend . . . has died: Gobineau died of heart failure in Turin on October 13. • Palest[rina]'s Mass for Pope Marcellus: *Missa Marcelli,* 1555.

OCTOBER 26
• The piece about G.: Cosima's obituary of Gobineau, mentioned frequently in subsequent pages of the Diaries, appeared in the *Bayreuther Blätter,* November-

December 1882, under the title *"Graf Arthur Gobineau. Ein Erinnerungsbild aus Wahnfried"* ("Count A. G. A Reminiscence from Wahnfried"); it is signed "Wahnfried." • *Die fröhliche Wissenschaft* (translated as *The Joyful Wisdom*), published by Schmeitzner in Chemnitz on August 30, 1882.

OCTOBER 28
•Frau Hatzfeldt: Princess Hatzfeldt, Countess Schleinitz's mother.

OCTOBER 29
•Her behavior in Königsberg: in 1837 Minna's familiarity with the merchant Dietrich led to bitter quarrels; when she fled with Dietrich and went to Dresden, Wagner, seeking her at her parents' home there, was blamed by them for causing their daughter such unhappiness. • The Correr Museum: part of the Museo Civico, situated in the former Fondaco dei Turchi, immediately opposite the Palazzo Vendramin. • Ada Pinelli (1840 to after 1916): née Treskow, daughter of a Prussian army officer, married an Italian official, J. Pinelli, in 1866; from 1881 companion to Princess Hatzfeldt in Venice; wrote novels under the pseudonym Günther von Freiberg. • Neulengbach: Prince Liechtenstein's estate near Vienna. • Count Sándor: probably Maurice Sándor, father of Wagner's Austrian patroness, Princess Pauline Metternich; Ernest Newman describes him in his biography of Wagner as "mentally unhinged and almost ungovernable."

OCTOBER 31
• The little book about Bismarck: this cannot be identified with certainty, but was probably one of Moritz Busch's publications (see note for November 9, 1878).

NOVEMBER 1
•Our old friend: presumably Tesarini.

NOVEMBER 3
•*Giani Lupo:* not identified.

NOVEMBER 4
•R. completes his work: the article *"Das Bühnenweihfestspiel in Bayreuth 1882."* • The Bellini: *Three Saints,* Bellini's last signed work. • The Sebast[iano] del Piombo: *Saint Chrysostom with Saints.*

NOVEMBER 5
•[The causes of Gobineau's death]: a handwritten list of disorders identified at the post-mortem, ending with "Probable cause of death: heart failure." • Pohl, who is hoping for a *Jesus of Nazareth:* Richard Pohl concluded his *"Bayreuther Briefe"* ("Bayreuth Letters") in the *Musikalisches Wochenblatt* with the hope that Wagner would write another work and suggested it could deal only "with the sublimest subject of all—the human Jesus of Nazareth"; Pohl may or may not have known about Wagner's sketch for a "Jesus of Nazareth," written in 1848 but not published until 1888, in vol. 11 of the collected writings. • Wolz.'s "For and Against": a reply by Hans von Wolzogen in the *Musikalisches Wochenblatt* to an anthology of reviews of the *Parsifal* performances, selected by Wilhelm Tappert.

NOVEMBER 6
•A letter by Schop.: reprint of a letter from Schopenhauer to the conductor of the Frankfurt Stadttheater, first published in the *Frankfurter Zeitung,* November 5, 1844; it complained about disturbing noises in the auditorium. • Both church and picture: probably Palma Il Vecchio's *Saint Barbara and Four Saints,* in the Church of Santa Maria Formosa. • His godfather: Adolf Träger, a Leipzig merchant. • Richard Geyer: Wagner bore the name of his stepfather until his fourteenth year; the German word for "eggs" (*Eier*) rhymes with "Geyer."

NOVEMBER 7
•The Battle of Rossbach: in which Frederick the Great defeated the French, in 1757. • Stein's article in the *B. Bl.*: a review of Renan's *Marc Aurèle,* September-

October 1882. • The Ibach grand piano: Rudolf Ibach, the pianoforte manufacturer, was also the representative of the Society of Patrons in Barmen, where his
factory was situated; the piano is now in the Richard-Wagner-Museum at Wahnfried. • *"Der Jüngling von Elvershöh"*: ballade by Karl Loewe.

NOVEMBER 9
•"The witch": Princess Wittgenstein. • The Cima: the picture by Cima da Conegliano
in the Church of Madonna dell'Orto is *Saint John the Baptist with Saints*. • Edgar
[Allan] Poe (1809–49): American author and poet.

NOVEMBER 10
•A monument to Morosini: a prominent Venetian family; Francesco Morosini
(1618–94), sea captain and doge, is the best known, but at least three other Morosinis
were also doges.

NOVEMBER 11
•Gobineau's history of the Persians: *Histoire des Perses,* 2 vols., 1869. • The Mahdi:
Mohammed Ahmed (1843–85), rebel leader in the Sudan, claimed to be the Mahdi
(the spiritual and temporal leader expected by the Mohammedans) and overthrew
the Egyptians in the Sudan in the period 1881–83.

NOVEMBER 12
•Falstaff's reply to the Lord Chief Justice: in Shakespeare's *Henry IV Part II,*
Act I, Scene 2, Falstaff tells the Lord Chief Justice, "For my voice—, I have lost it
with hallooing, and singing of anthems."

NOVEMBER 13
•[A telegram from Eduard Strauss]: "In my concert yesterday played *Parsifal*
Prelude, tremendous reception, brilliant success, had to give encore. Warmest
congratulations"; Eduard Strauss (1835–1916), younger son of Johann Strauss the
Elder, and himself a composer, took over the direction of the Strauss orchestra in
Vienna in 1870. • "Wahnfried" (*Fuente ovejuna*): the connection between the name
of Wagner's house and that of Lope de Vega's play is unclear.

NOVEMBER 14
•Square melody: Wagner's name for a periodically constructed melody.

NOVEMBER 15
•An article by Herr Schäffer: the article is signed Carl Schäffer, but his correct name
was Carl Schäfer, and he was a member of the committee of the Society of Patrons
in Berlin; his article is about Angelo Neumann's traveling production of the *Ring,*
of which he is critical (though not of the singer Hedwig Reicher-Kindermann!). •
The Duke of Bordeaux: Henri de Bourbon, Duc de Bordeaux (1820–23) and
Comte de Chambord, pretender to the throne of France; the news Cosima reports
was false, and he did not take up residence in the Palazzo Vendramin, which in fact
belonged to him. • The journey on foot: in the spring of 1827 Wagner walked with
his friend Rudolf Böhme from Dresden to Prague.

NOVEMBER 16
•Palazzo Giustiniani: on the Grand Canal; Wagner lived there in 1858; the story
of the commissionaire is not told in *Mein Leben,* and it is thus not possible to check
Cosima's various spellings of his name (Zuski, Susky, Suski). • A postcard: this,
from Breslau, reads: "On the centennial of Esaias Tegnér's birth. Please, NOBLE
MASTER, tell me (it is in connection with a bet) whether YOUR soul has ever been
touched by the thought of celebrating Frithiof and Ingeborg's love in music drama,
whether the Germanic world can hope for such a splendid work. — Marianne,
daughter of the head teacher Neide." • Tegnér: Esaias Tegnér (1782–1846),
Swedish poet, wrote a poem based on the Icelandic *Frithiof's Saga* in 1825, which
was translated into German in 1826.

NOVEMBER 17

•The little hare: as a reminder of the legend that Buddha was reborn as a rabbit (see September 28, 1882), Cosima gave Wagner a gold pendant in the form of a hare for his watch chain, and it is frequently mentioned in subsequent entries. • Did not behave well toward Ponsch: perhaps in connection with Blandine's marriage to Gravina. • She did not take him in at Trachenberg: though in *Mein Leben* Wagner is very reticent about the steps he took and the friends he appealed to when he fled from Vienna in 1864 to escape his creditors, this suggests that Princess Hatzfeldt may have been among those he approached; Trachenberg was her husband's estate. • The blacks the Ethiopians: presumably Cosima meant the giants.

NOVEMBER 18

•*Muse des Parnass:* expression used by Walther in his "Prize Song" in Act III of *Die Meistersinger.* • Weissheimer, who was upset by the agenda: Wendelin Weissheimer, who was close to Wagner in Biebrich during the composition of Act I of *Die Meistersinger,* objected to the way the mastersingers were shown to conduct their meetings. • Ludwig Sand: Karl Ludwig Sand, who in 1819 killed the dramatist August von Kotzebue, suspecting him of being a Russian spy. • Tauentzien: Friedrich Bogislaw von Tauentzien, a Prussian general and governor of Silesia who defended Breslau in 1760; Lessing was his secretary at the time. • A[dolf] Wagner: Wagner's uncle. • "The native hue . . .": *Hamlet,* Act III, Scene 1. • The scene between Malcolm and Macduff: in Shakespeare's *Macbeth* (Act IV, Scene 3); Malcolm, son of the murdered King Duncan, pretends to Macduff that he himself is more wicked than Macbeth, in order to test Macduff's integrity. • The Merceria: the main shopping street in Venice.

NOVEMBER 19

•Giovanelli: the sumptuous ballroom of the fifteenth-century Palazzo Giovanelli contains pictures by Titian and Tintoretto. • "Then his gaze . . ." ("*Da traf mich sein Blick*"): Kundry in *Parsifal,* Act II.

NOVEMBER 20

•Köstlin: Heinrich Adolf Köstlin (1846–1907), theologian and musicologist; the review appeared in the supplement to the *Allgemeine Zeitung,* Munich, on November 15, 16, and 17, 1882, under the title "*Die religiösen Anschauungen Richard Wagners*" ("The Religious Views of R. W.").

NOVEMBER 23

•An open letter to Dr. H.: not written. • Schubert's "*Ständchen*": the famous "Serenade" ("*Leise flehen meine Lieder*") from the posthumous *Schwanengesang.* • "*Mit leichten Waffen . . .*": correctly, "*Mit zarter Waffen Zier bezwingt er die Welt*" (freely translated by Andrew Porter as "He waves his wand of magic over the world"); Siegmund in *Die Walküre,* Act I, Scene 3.

NOVEMBER 25

•His preface to the Stein dialogues: written in the form of a "Letter to Herr v. Stein" and published in the *Bayreuther Blätter,* 1883, and vol. 10 of the collected writings; Stein's book was entitled *Helden und Welt (Heroes and the World).* • "*Leyer und Schwert*" ("Lyre and Sword"): Weber's song cycle for men's chorus to texts by Theodor Körner (including the famous "*Lützows wilde Jagd*"), 1814. • H. IV: not the English king, but Henry IV of France (1553–1610), who was a Protestant until the age of forty. • Ruben: Franz Leo Ruben (1842–1920), German painter who lived in Venice; his works include the Lohengrin paintings in King Ludwig's castle at Hohenschwangau.

NOVEMBER 26

•The letter about coffee: from Goethe to Frau von Stein, June 1, 1789. • The restored *Madonna dei Frari:* though Cosima puts it in the Doge's Palace, the Titian painting she describes is an altarpiece in the Church of S. Maria Gloriosa dei Frari, where it is known as the *Madonna of the Pesaro Family.* • Cyrus: Cyrus the Great (died 530 B.C.), founder of the Persian Empire. • "We've made him rich . . .": Faust in Goethe's *Faust,* Part Two (Act I, Scene 5), talking to Mephistopheles about the Emperor (Bayard Taylor's translation).

NOVEMBER 27

•"I remembered, Brünnhilde, you": paraphrase of Waltraute telling Brünnhilde about Wotan in *Götterdämmerung,* Act I, Scene 3, *"Er gedachte, Brünnhilde, dein."*

NOVEMBER 28

•The little rabbit: see note for November 17, 1882. • Beeth.'s F Major Quartet: Opus 135.

NOVEMBER 29

•"I and Dr. Luther . . .": the final version of this verse, *"Das Häs'chen"* ("The Little Rabbit"), is: *"Ich und der Doktor Luther, | trug Jeder ein Häs'chen klein! | Ihm beschmutzt' es das Ärmel-Futter, | Das meinige liess es rein, | wie mag das sein?"* ("I and Dr. Luther, | each had a little rabbit! | His dirtied the lining of his sleeve, | mine left it clean. | Why was that?"). • A request to consult Herr Holtzendorff: Gross was instructed to ask the professor of law (see note for May 16, 1878) for an opinion on the dispute with Voltz and Batz after considering Wagner's *exposé.* • Halévy and *La Reine de Chypre:* Wagner saw the first performance of this opera by Halévy in Paris in December 1841 and wrote a long report on it for the Dresden *Abendzeitung* (reprinted in vol. 1 of the collected writings); he also arranged the vocal score.

NOVEMBER 30

•A nice letter has arrived from the King: King Ludwig's last letter to Wagner, headed Hohenschwangau, November 26. • What the King says about him: Ludwig writes in his letter: "I should be so pleased to hear once more detailed news of your son, Siegfried. Is he developing well and flourishing? Is his education still proceeding along the lines of *Wilhelm Meister,* as you intended? I very much hope that the Italian climate will be more favorable to him than last year."

DECEMBER 2

•Pauli: Ludwig Ferdinand Pauli (1793–1841), actor at the Dresden Court theater from 1819; his main roles were Iago, Falstaff, and Mephistopheles. • He begins his work: the letter to Stein. • *Hannibal:* author not identified; there were several plays about Hannibal. • *Weihnachtsbaum (Christmas Tree):* 12 pieces for piano by Liszt, 1874–76.

DECEMBER 3

•*War and Peace:* Tolstoy's novel was first published 1863–69; since Cosima gives the title in French, they were presumably reading it in that language.

DECEMBER 4

•[Goethe's] *Die Geschwister (Brother and Sister):* Goethe's play was being rehearsed for an amateur production at the Palazzo Malipiero. • Fabrice: a character in Goethe's *Die Geschwister.* • Brackenburg: a character in Goethe's *Egmont.* • The "Magister": it is unclear to which of Bach's *48 Preludes and Fugues* this title refers. • Weber's A Major Sonata: presumably the A-flat Major Sonata, Opus 39.

DECEMBER 5

•Siegfried's *Hermann der Befreier (Hermann the Liberator):* title of a play about Arminius by Siegfried Wagner; in his *Reminiscences (Erinnerungen)* Siegfried later wrote about this period in Venice: "I wrote a series of exciting pieces about knights of old; Catilina was another victim. As he passed by, my father would peer into my notebook and call out, 'Quiet, children, don't disturb Fidi, or he'll tumble from his Pegasus!' "

DECEMBER 6
• His flight to my father: Wagner first went to Liszt in Weimar on his flight from Dresden in 1849; he parted from Minna in Magdala before going on to Zurich. • *"Weibes [Wonne] und Wert"*: in Andrew Porter's translation, "Woman's beauty and love"; Loge in *Das Rheingold,* Scene 2.

DECEMBER 8
• "Stiefel must perish . . ." (*"Stiefel muss sterben"*): a folk song from the Seven Years' War; as will be seen later, Wagner connects his rabbit pendant with the boy Stiefel.

DECEMBER 11
• The pleasure he feels now whenever he comes into contact with people: the German editors state in a footnote that the word "pleasure" (*"Behagen"*) is correct, however surprising; but, since Cosima uses this word again in the following sentence, it is possible that the first use of it was a slip of the pen. • Count Contin: Count Giuseppe Contin di Castelsepio founded the Società Benedetto Marcello in 1877 to perform music both old and new.

DECEMBER 14
•Duprez: Gilbert Duprez (1806–96), tenor at the Paris opera. • Th. Gautier's book on Italy: *Voyage en Italie* (1852) by the French writer Théophile Gautier (1811–72); he was Judith Gautier's father. • His symphony: the Symphony in C Major, 1832; the score was lost, but in 1877 the instrumental parts were discovered in an old trunk in Dresden, and the score was reassembled from these by Anton Seidl.

DECEMBER 15
•Frontali: Raffaele Frontali (1849–1916), Italian violinist and teacher. • *"Das Reis"*: the meaning here is "the palm branch of victory"; Wagner uses it in the final scene of *Die Meistersinger,* when Eva urges the assembled people to award it to Walther von Stolzing after he has sung his "Prize Song."

DECEMBER 16
•The performance 50 years ago: probably Wagner is referring to the performance of his symphony at the Leipzig Gewandhaus on January 10, 1833; it had in fact been performed twice previously, in Prague (a private performance at the Conservatoire) and in a semiprivate performance by the Euterpe Society in Leipzig. • Avarice's speech: in Act I of Goethe's *Faust,* Part Two, spoken by *"Der Abgemagerte"* ("The Starveling" in Bayard Taylor's translation); in reply to his defense of avarice, the "Leader of the Women" replies (in Bayard Taylor's translation), "He comes, the men to spur and egg on, / And now they're troublesome enough."

DECEMBER 17
•The cuff on Meyer's ears: presumably for the Bayreuth lawyer Gustav Meyer, in a dispute with Voltz and Batz, since in Cosima's little notebook the name "Meyer" is written directly beside the names "Voltz and Batz."

DECEMBER 18
•Bassani: a Jewish agent. • The news . . . which I cannot bring myself to write down: Wagner and Cosima seem to have assumed—probably because of the institution to which he was admitted—that von Bülow had gone insane; actually, he had injured his head in a fall and sustained a concussion.

DECEMBER 19
•The matter of the engagement: of Humperdinck as a conductor in Venice. • "The Singer's Curse" (*"Des Sängers Fluch"*): a ballad by Uhland.

DECEMBER 20
•Filippi: Filippo Filippi, a critic from Milan.

DECEMBER 21
•My father's *soirée* with Don Carlos: at a reception in Paul Metternich's house Liszt was presented to the pretender to the Spanish throne, Don Carlos Maria de

los Dolores de Borbón (1848–1909). • Stretta: the final part of an aria, taken at a faster tempo. • Mosca: Luigi Mosca (1775–1824), Italian operatic composer. • "Moved": meaning unclear (the German word is *"ergriffen"*). • The article on luxury: *"Die Härte des Luxus"* by Meta Wellmer, *Bayreuther Blätter,* November-December 1882. • The obituary of Prof. Zöllner: in the same issue of the *Bayreuther Blätter* Bernhard Förster wrote an obituary of Friedrich Zöllner, who had died on April 25, 1882.

DECEMBER 23
•Cilie: Wagner's stepsister, Cäcilie Geyer (1815–93), married the bookseller Eduard Avenarius in 1840.

DECEMBER 24
•My father, the children, and I: besides these, the audience consisted only of Count Contin, Joukowsky, Hausburg, and the governess; public and press were rigidly excluded.

DECEMBER 25
•"Who has found so good a wife" (*"Wer ein holdes Weib errungen"*): both in Schiller's *"An die Freude"* (Beethoven's Ninth Symphony) and in the Act II finale of *Fidelio.*

DECEMBER 26
•Worth: a famous fashion house in Paris. • Oberdank: Wilhelm Oberdank, also known as Guglielmo Oberdan (1858–82), an Italian Irredentist who led a conspiracy to assassinate Emperor Franz Joseph of Austria during his visit to Trieste in August 1882; the plot was discovered on the day preceding the emperor's visit, and Oberdank was arrested; he was hanged on December 20.

DECEMBER 28
•A report on the symphony: *"Bericht über die Wiederaufführung eines Jugendwerkes"* ("A Youthful Symphony"), first published in the *Musikalisches Wochenblatt* and reprinted in vol. 10 of the collected writings. • Mrs. Lewes (George Eliot): the English novelist George Eliot was known as Mrs. Lewes, though in fact she was not married to George Henry Lewes; the Wagners met them both in London in 1877 (see vol. I).

DECEMBER 30
•He finishes his article: on the performance of his C Major Symphony (see note for December 28, 1882). • Moretto's picture: *Christ in the House of the Pharisee,* by Moretto da Brescia (1498–1555), is in the Church of S. Maria della Pietà.

DECEMBER 31
•Besarel: Valentino Besarel (1829–1902), sculptor and woodcarver in Venice.

1883

JANUARY 1
•*Le Baruffe Chiozzotte:* see note for April 2, 1878.

JANUARY 3
• The Della Grazias: the actual owner of the Palazzo Vendramin was the Comte de Chambord, Duc de Bordeaux, a stepson of the Duke della Grazia, Marchese Luchesi Pally.

JANUARY 4
•Count Wimpfen: Count Felix von Wimpfen, or Wimpffen (born 1827), Austrian envoy in Rome, committed suicide on December 30, 1882. • Nerva: Marcus Cocceius Nerva (A.D. 30–98), Roman emperor. • Otho: Marcus Salvius Otho (A.D. 32–69), Roman emperor who committed suicide after being defeated by

Vitellius. • The 2nd Jerusalem: an early Christian concept of an ideal Jerusalem in the heavens.

JANUARY 6
•His acquaintances the 100 knights: in Shakespeare's *King Lear,* the king insists on having a retinue of 100 knights of his own when he is staying with his daughters Goneril and Regan. • Gambetta's death: the French statesman died on December 31, 1882.

JANUARY 7
•We recall *Die Kapitulation:* Gambetta appears as a character in Wagner's farce, *Eine Kapitulation,* written at the time of the Franco-Prussian War (vol. 9 of the collected writings). • "*Schmierocco*": a pun on "sirocco," the warm wind of the Mediterranean; the German word "*Schmiere*" has a derogative meaning, which might be translated as "rabble."

JANUARY 8
•"Gladness and woe in one": presumably a running together of two quotations from Act I of *Die Walküre*—Siegmund's "*gehrt' ich nach Wonne, weckt' ich nur Weh*" ("striving for gladness, I found only woe") and Sieglinde's "*Tränen und Trost zugleich*" ("sorrow and solace in one").

JANUARY 10
•Dr. Kurz: A. Kurz, physician in Venice.

JANUARY 11
•His letter to the King: Wagner's last letter to King Ludwig; it deals mainly with domestic matters (reflecting the events described by Cosima in her Diaries) but also contains an offer to give three or more private performances of *Parsifal* for the king in the Bayreuth theater, at the conclusion of the 1883 festival. • The Gotthard is good for him: presumably a reference to Siegfried's conception; in September 1868 Wagner and Cosima journeyed together to Italy via the St. Gotthard pass in Switzerland.

JANUARY 12
•The centennial celebrations for his father: Vasili Andreievich Joukowsky, or Zhukovski (1783–1852), tutor to the future Tsar Alexander II, was also a poet and a translator of Homer, Goethe, Schiller, Byron, etc., into Russian.

JANUARY 13
•The exposition: a Bavarian national exposition in Munich. • The hovering forms: "*Ihr naht euch wieder, schwankende Gestalten,*" opening line of the "*Zueignung*" ("Dedication") of Goethe's *Faust,* Part One ("Again ye come, ye hovering forms," in Bayard Taylor's translation).

JANUARY 15
•"Harlequin, thou must perish" ("*Harlekin, du musst sterben*"): not identifiable for certain, though Bierey (see note for March 24, 1878) and Ferdinand Kauer both wrote Harlequin pantomimes; the song is also mentioned on June 6, 1878.

JANUARY 16
•Dr. Förster's pamphlet: *Parsifal-Nachklänge* (*Echoes of Parsifal*) by Bernhard Förster, Leipzig, 1883. • "*Du lieber Augustin*": a popular German folk song.

JANUARY 18
•Rus: Wagner's Newfoundland dog during the Tribschen and early Bayreuth years; Russ (as the name was generally spelled) died on May 2, 1875.

JANUARY 19
•Prince Georg (1826–1902): of Prussia; son of Wilhelm I's nephew, Prince Friedrich; a Prussian general, he wrote plays under the pseudonym G. Conrad; he visited the Wagners at both Tribschen and Bayreuth (see vol. I). • Count Bardi: son and

heir of the Duke of Parma (his mother was a daughter of the Duke of Berry), he lived in the Palazzo Vendramin with his wife, Adelgunde. • Prince Nap.: Napoleon Joseph Charles Paul (1822–91), youngest son of Napoleon I's brother Jérôme, commonly known as "Plon-Plon"; on January 15, 1882, he published a manifesto announcing his readiness, as the heir of the Napoleons, to assume power in France; he was arrested on the day of publication and brought to trial on January 31, when he was acquitted.

JANUARY 21
•Dr. Rahn: correctly, Rahn-Escher, Wagner's doctor in Zurich from 1852.

JANUARY 22
•A letter from Herr v. Bürkel: in this letter dated January 20, the Cabinet secretary said that King Ludwig was holding to his wish for performances of *Parsifal* in Munich, but was willing to have them postponed until the spring of 1884; Cosima replied to this letter on January 29; the performances in Munich were in fact given in May and November 1884 and again in April 1885.

JANUARY 23
•To have done more than it can do: in *Mein Leben* Wagner relates that Spontini, on a visit to Dresden in 1844, said to him: "*Quand j'ai entendu votre* Rienzi, *j'ai dit, c'est un homme de génie, mais déjà il a plus fait qu'il ne peut faire*" ("When I heard your *Rienzi* I said, 'The man is a genius, but already he has done more than he can do' "). Asked by Wagner to explain this paradox, Spontini replied that he himself had already made all the improvements that could be made in opera, so how could anyone else do better? Since *La Vestale* not a note had been written that was not stolen from his scores.

JANUARY 24
•His letter to Stein: the foreword to Stein's book. • "Tell him I am deaf": Shakespeare's *Henry IV Part II,* Act I, Scene 2. • Lise and Bärbel in *Faust:* Part One, scene at the fountain, in which the two girls gossip about Gretchen's love affair with Faust. • The roof-raising ceremony in Bayreuth: on August 2, 1873 (see vol. I). • A mountain-climbing expedition: on the Hoher Säntis in Switzerland in July 1851, with Karl Ritter and Theodor Uhlig; the incident is described in *Mein Leben*.

JANUARY 25
•Count Vesuce: not identified; the name was all but indecipherable; *gettatore* is a term used to apply to people said to possess "the Evil Eye."

JANUARY 27
•Goethe's "Dedication" ("*Zueignung*"): *Faust,* Part One.

JANUARY 28
•"The best society . . .": a parody of Mephistopheles's lines in Goethe's *Faust,* Part One (Faust's study); in Bayard Taylor's translation, "The worst society thou find'st will show thee / Thou art a man among the rest." • Sommer: Karl Sommer, baritone at the Vienna opera, sang Telramund in *Lohengrin* in 1881.

JANUARY 29
•The singer Rizio: the name is not clearly written, but probably David Rizzio, or Riccio, is meant—the Italian musician whom Mary, Queen of Scots, made her secretary and who was murdered in 1566 on suspicion of being the queen's lover; Tappert published various collections of old melodies. • The Directoire period: end of the eighteenth century, costumes based on Greek and Roman styles.

JANUARY 30
•The Jew Guggenheim: Meyer Guggenheim (1828–1905), who emigrated to the United States from Switzerland, and his son Daniel (1856–1930) were generous patrons of the arts. • For us the 3rd: a reference to Cosima's conviction that Beethoven must have written his Fourth Symphony before the Third (the *Eroica*).

JANUARY 31

•Ducamp: Maxime Ducamp (1822–94), French writer. • *Revue d[es] d[eux] M[ondes]*: French fortnightly periodical, founded in Paris in 1829. • "Phylax, who loyally . . .": from the poem *"Der Hund"* ("The Dog") by Christian Fürchtegott Gellert. • St. Gilgenberg: the mental institution in Bayreuth.

FEBRUARY 2

•*"Les Maîtres mosaïstes"* ("The Masters of Mosaic"), novel by George Sand, 1842. • The *"Wilde Jagd"*: Weber's *"Lützow's wilde Jagd."* • "Cobble your shoes" (*"Mach deinen Schuh"*): Hans Sachs in *Die Meistersinger,* Act III, Scene 4, deciding resignedly that a cobbler should stick to his last.

FEBRUARY 3

•Schmeitzner's monthly: *Internationale Monatsschrift,* Chemnitz. • The collision of two ships: the German mail boat *Cimbria* collided with a British ship, the *Sultan,* near the mouth of the river Elbe and sank, with the loss of more than 400 lives, many of them emigrants bound for New York.

FEBRUARY 4

•A "young Mozart": Peter Gast, real name Heinrich Köselitz (1854–1918), a friend of Nietzsche, who became infatuated with his music. • *"Lenore"*: ballad by Gottfried August Bürger.

FEBRUARY 5

•"Over Heaven's vaults . . .": free quotation from Schiller's *"An die Freude"* ("Ode to Joy"); correctly, *"Ahnest du den Schöpfer, Welt? | Such ihn überm Sternenzelt! | Über Sternen muss er wohnen."* • The Piombi: prisons under the lead roof of the Doge's Palace. • Proudhon: see note for September 7, 1878. • Heinse's "Blessed Isles": in the novel *Ardinghello* (see note for November 26, 1878).

FEBRUARY 6

•The *Graphic:* an illustrated weekly periodical founded in London in 1869. • Hagen's book: *Beiträge zur Einsicht in das Wesen der Wagner'schen Kunst* (*Insights into the Nature of Wagner's Art*) by Edmund von Hagen, reviewed by Wilhelm Tappert in the *Musikalisches Wochenblatt.* • Rahl: Carl Rahl (1812–65), an Austrian painter whom Wagner met in Venice in 1858. • "The long day's task is done" (*"Mein Tagwerk ist vorbei"*): a quotation from Shakespeare's *Antony and Cleopatra* (Act IV, Scene 12), not *Othello.*

FEBRUARY 8

•Our friend Dohm's death: Ernst Dohm died on February 5, 1883. • *"Don Giovanni tu m'invitasti"* ("Don Giovanni, thou hast invited me"): the Commendatore in Mozart's *Don Giovanni,* Act II, Scene 24.

FEBRUARY 9

•The emigration scheme: Bernhard Förster founded a colony called Nueva Germania in San Bernardino, Paraguay; he died there in 1889.

FEBRUARY 10

•M[ichel]a[ngelo]'s poem: "To Giovanni di Pistoia."

FEBRUARY 11

•*"Piova di primavera"*: Italian for "spring rain"; Wagner's pun on *"prima"* ("first") and *"seconda"* ("second") defies translation. • "My world which contains . . ." (*"Die mir Isolden einzig enthält, wie wär Isolde mir aus der Welt"*): Tristan in *Tristan und Isolde,* Act III, Scene 1. • He has begun his work: on the article *"Über das Weibliche im Menschlichen"* ("On the Womanly in the Human"). • *Undine:* a novel by Friedrich de la Motte-Fouqué (1777–1843); Wagner read it in a copy in which Joukowsky's father had written out his Russian translation. • *"Töt' erst sein Weib"* ("First kill his wife"): Leonore in Act II of Beethoven's opera *Fidelio* as she shields her husband, Florestan, from Pizarro's dagger. • "If I were to perform the *Eroica"*:

according to Levi, he would have altered an A flat in the 2nd violins to a G.

FEBRUARY 12

•He reads *Undine:* while he was doing so, Joukowsky drew the two last sketches of him in Cosima's notebook. • *"Rheingold, Rheingold":* the Rhinemaidens at the conclusion of *Das Rheingold.* • "False and base . . ." (*"Falsch und feig ist, was dort oben sich freut"*): the final words of the "Rhinemaidens' Song."

DANIELA'S ENTRY

•The Duchess of Anhalt: either Wagner or Daniela erred in attributing to her the remark "Royal blood for ox's blood"; it was Countess Katharina of Schwarzburg who, in the 16th century, saved her subjects in Rudolstadt from further plunder by placing herself at their head with these words; the story is told by Schiller in his story *"Herzog Alba bei einem Frühstück auf dem Schlosse zu Rudolstadt im Jahr 1547"* ("Duke Alba at a Breakfast in the Castle of Rudolstadt in the Year 1547"). • "The Eternal in the Feminine": a reference to the fragment *"Über das Weibliche im Menschlichen"* ("On the Womanly in the Human"), published in vol. 12 of the collected writings.

Chronology

1869

JANUARY   R. W. working on full orchestral score of *Siegfried*, II.   3: second edition of *Judaism in Music* completed.   10: dictation of *Mein Leben* resumed.   21: *Die Meistersinger* in Dresden.

FEBRUARY   10 (to 15): R. W. working on article "Herr Eduard Devrient and His Style."   23: full orchestral score of *Siegfried*, II, completed.

MARCH   1: composition sketch of *Siegfried*, III, begun.   8: death of Berlioz.   10: King Ludwig II commands performance of *Das Rheingold* in Munich in August.

APRIL   2 (to 5): Hans Richter at Tribschen to discuss Munich production of *Das Rheingold*.   8: C.'s daughters Daniela and Blandine arrive at Tribschen.

MAY   17: Nietzsche's first visit to Tribschen.

JUNE   5 (to 6): Nietzsche at Tribschen.   6: Siegfried Wagner born.   14: composition sketch of *Siegfried*, III, completed.   15: C. asks von Bülow for divorce.   20: von Bülow conducts *Tristan und Isolde* in Munich.   25: orchestral sketch of *Siegfried*, III, begun.

JULY   4 (to 8): Richter at Tribschen.   9: Serov at Tribschen for first time.   16: Catulle Mendès and wife Judith (Gautier) at Tribschen for first time.   31: von Bülow consents to divorce.   31 (to August 1): Nietzsche at Tribschen.

AUGUST   4: orchestral sketch of *Siegfried*, III, completed.   7: von Bülow submits resignation in Munich.   21 (to 22), 28 (to 29): Nietzsche at Tribschen.   25: full orchestral score of *Siegfried*, III, begun.   29: Richter dismissed as conductor in Munich.

SEPTEMBER   1 (to 2): R. W. in Munich in connection with *Das Rheingold* production.   11: Marie Muchanoff at Tribschen.   12: von Bülow's resignation accepted in Munich.   18 (to 19): Nietzsche at Tribschen.   22: *Das Rheingold* performed in Munich.

OCTOBER   2: composition sketch of *Götterdämmerung* Prelude begun (with Norns' scene).   31: essay "On Conducting" begun.

NOVEMBER   13 (to 15): Nietzsche at Tribschen.

DECEMBER   12: composition sketch of *Götterdämmerung* Prelude completed.   16: composition sketch of "Siegfried's Journey to the Rhine" begun.   24 (to January 2): Nietzsche at Tribschen.

1870

JANUARY   9: orchestral sketch of *Götterdämmerung* Prelude begun (with orchestral opening).   12: King Ludwig commands performance of *Die Walküre* in Munich.

FEBRUARY   12 (to 13): Nietzsche at Tribschen.   27 (to March 10): Heinrich Porges at Tribschen.   27: *Die Meistersinger* in Vienna.

MARCH   5: R. W. first thinks of Bayreuth as the place for his festival theater.   23: *Lohengrin* in Brussels (Richter conducting).   31 (to April 2): Richter at Tribschen.

APRIL   1: *Die Meistersinger* in Berlin.

JUNE   5: composition sketch of *Götterdämmerung*, I, completed.   11 (to 12):

Nietzsche at Tribschen. 26 (to April 1871): Richter at Tribschen. 26: *Die Walküre* performed in Munich.

JULY 2: orchestral sketch of *Götterdämmerung*, I, completed 15 (to 17): Karl Klindworth at Tribschen. 18: C.'s divorce from von Bülow granted (news received on 27). 19: outbreak of Franco-Prussian War; Catulle and Judith Mendès in Lucerne. 20: work begun on *Beethoven and the German Nation*. 29: Nietzsche and sister, Elisabeth, at Tribschen. 30: visitors (including Mendèses) depart.

AUGUST 3: Malwida von Meysenbug at Tribschen for first time. 25: R. W. and C. married at Protestant church in Lucerne. 28 (to 29): they visit Frau Wille at Mariafeld.

SEPTEMBER 2: Battle of Sedan. 4: Siegfried baptized. 7: *Beethoven and the German Nation* completed.

OCTOBER 2: "Proclamation" concerning Bayreuth drafted. 26 (to 27): R. and C. W. visit Sulzer and other friends in Zurich (C. W. visits Mathilde Wesendonck). 29: R. W. "orchestrates" (in fact working secretly on *Siegfried Idyll*).

NOVEMBER 8 (to 16): R. W. working on *Eine Kapitulation*. 26 (to 27): Nietzsche at Tribschen.

DECEMBER 4: C. W. believes she is pregnant. 7: tells R. W. she is wrong. 16: Richter plays his music for *Eine Kapitulation*. 24 (to January 1): Nietzsche at Tribschen. 25: *Siegfried Idyll* performed at Tribschen in honor of C. W.'s birthday.

1871

JANUARY 18: Wilhelm I proclaimed German Emperor.

FEBRUARY 5: full orchestral score of *Siegfried*, III, completed. 9: news of Serov's death. 13: "clear first draft" of "*Kaisermarsch*." 17 (to 18): R. and C. W. visit Zurich (Wesendoncks and Willes). 25: orchestral sketch of "*Kaisermarsch*" completed.

MARCH 5: work begun on "The Destiny of Opera." 15: full orchestral score of "*Kaisermarsch*" completed. 16: R. W. works on his "*Kaiserlied*." 24 (to April 2): Countess d'Agoult at Tribschen.

APRIL 3 (to 8): Nietzsche at Tribschen. 17: R. and C. W. arrive in Bayreuth on tour of inspection. 19: decision to settle in Bayreuth and build theater there. 20: they leave Bayreuth for Leipzig. 22 (to 25): in Dresden. 25: to Berlin. 28: R. W. gives lecture ("The Destiny of Opera") in Berlin.

MAY 3: R. W. meets Bismarck. 5: R. W. conducts concert in Berlin. 8: R. and C. W. in Leipzig, where R. W. announces plan to stage the *Ring* in Bayreuth. 10: end of Franco-Prussian War. 13: R. and C. W. in Darmstadt, discussion with Brandt on stage of festival theater. 14 (to 15): in Heidelberg. 16: return to Tribschen. 19: Heckel proposes establishment of Wagner Society in Mannheim. 24: work begun on collected edition of R. W.'s writings; Nietzsche at Tribschen (also 28 to 29).

JUNE 24: composition sketch of *Götterdämmerung*, II, begun.

JULY 5: orchestral sketch of *Götterdämmerung*, II, begun. 13: Franz and Betty Schott at Tribschen. 17: death of Karl Tausig. 31 (to August 3): Nietzsche at Tribschen.

AUGUST 21: Frau von Schleinitz (to 27) and Baron Loën (Tausig's successor) at Tribschen.

SEPTEMBER 1: Julius Hey at Tribschen. 14: first plans for foundation stone ceremony in Bayreuth (see also 20, October 6). 29: R. W. composes "Siegfried's Funeral March."

OCTOBER 25: composition sketch of *Götterdämmerung*, II, completed. 27 (to 28): Nietzsche at Tribschen. 31: *Reminiscences of Auber* completed.

NOVEMBER 1: *Lohengrin* in Bologna; R. W. informs Feustel officially of his wish to build a festival theater in Bayreuth. 7: Bayreuth offers site for theater. 19: orchestral sketch of *Götterdämmerung*, II, completed. 21: Heckel submits his plan for Wagner Societies.

DECEMBER 14: R. W. arrives in Bayreuth to choose a site for his theater. 16: R. W. to Mannheim, where C. W. joins him. 20: R. W. conducts concert in Mannheim, "*Kaisermarsch*" performed.

1872

JANUARY 4: composition sketch of *Götterdämmerung*, III, begun. 8: Feustel and Muncker at Tribschen; decision to move to Bayreuth in summer. 10: decision to perform Beethoven's Ninth Symphony at laying of foundation stone. 24 (to February 5): R. W. in Berlin, Weimar, Bayreuth, and Munich on business connected with the Bayreuth plan.

FEBRUARY 9: orchestral sketch of *Götterdämmerung*, III, begun. 18: Nietzsche at Tribschen.

MARCH 4: news of establishment of a Wagner Society in London. 26: news of King Ludwig's opposition to the Bayreuth plan. 28 (to April 1): Nietzsche at Tribschen.

APRIL 10: composition sketch of *Götterdämmerung*, III, completed. 21: Josef Rubinstein's first visit. 22: R. W. leaves Tribschen for Bayreuth. 25 (to 27): Nietzsche at Tribschen. 29: C. W. leaves Tribschen with children to join R. W. at Hotel Fantaisie, Bayreuth.

MAY 6 (to 14): R. and C. W. in Vienna. 12: R. W. conducts concert in Vienna. 18: Nietzsche and other friends arrive in Bayreuth. 22: foundation stone of Bayreuth festival theater laid; R. W. conducts Beethoven's Ninth Symphony.

JULY 4 (to 8): Marie Muchanoff in Bayreuth. 13 (to September 27): J. Rubinstein in Bayreuth. 18: contract for building of Wahnfried received. 22: orchestral sketch of *Götterdämmerung*, III, completed. 30 (to August 28): R. W. working on *Actors and Singers*.

AUGUST 1: work on *Mein Leben* resumed. 6 (to 8): Richter in Bayreuth. 17 (to 18): Niemann and Levi in Bayreuth.

SEPTEMBER 2 (to 6): R. and C. W. visit Liszt in Weimar. 21: move to Dammallee 7 in Bayreuth. 28: Anton Seidl comes to Bayreuth as copyist.

OCTOBER 15 (to 21): Liszt in Bayreuth. 26: R. W. working on article "On the Term 'Music Drama.' " 31: C. W. converted to Protestantism.

NOVEMBER 1 (to 2): Marie Muchanoff in Bayreuth. 10: R. and C. W. leave Bayreuth to gain support and find singers for the festival. 10 (to 12): Würzburg. 12 (to 14): Frankfurt. 14 (to 15): Darmstadt. 15 (to 19): Mannheim. 19 (to 20): Darmstadt again. 21 (to 22): Stuttgart. 22 (to 24): Strassburg. 24 (to 26): Karlsruhe. 26 (to 30): Mainz, Wiesbaden. 30 (to December 5): Cologne, Bonn.

DECEMBER 5: Düsseldorf. 6 (to 7): Hanover. 7 (to 10): Bremen. 10 (to 11): Magdeburg. 11 (to 12): Dessau. 12 (to 15): Leipzig. 23: R. W. starts work on "A Glance at the German Operatic Stage of Today."

1873

JANUARY   12: R. and C. W. in Dresden, where on 13 they see *Rienzi*.   16: in Berlin, where on 17 R. W. gives a reading of the *Götterdämmerung* text.   18: in Hamburg, where R. W. conducts concerts on 21 and 23.   25: in Schwerin, where they see *Der Fliegende Holländer*.   27: in Berlin.
FEBRUARY   4: R. W. conducts concert in Berlin in presence of Emperor (own works, including *"Kaisermarsch"*).   6: in Dresden, where they see *Lohengrin*.   8: return to Bayreuth.
MARCH   R. W. working on article "On Beethoven's Ninth Symphony" (completed on 10).   8: Brandt and Brückwald (architect) visit R. W. to discuss building of stage; decision to put off festival for a year.   25: R. W. starts article "The Festival Theater in Bayreuth."
APRIL   6 (to 12): Nietzsche in Bayreuth.   20: R. and C. W. in Würzburg.   21: in Cologne, where R. W. conducts concert on 24.   26: in Kassel.   27: in Eisleben and Leipzig, where on 28 they meet Liszt.   28: return to Bayreuth.
MAY   2: work resumed on *Götterdämmerung*.   28: R. and C. W. and Daniela go to Weimar to attend performance on 29 of Liszt's *Christus*.   30: return to Bayreuth.
JULY   25 (to August 5): Liszt in Bayreuth.
AUGUST   2: roof-raising ceremony at festival theater.   11: R. W. asks King Ludwig for a financial guarantee for completion of theater.
SEPTEMBER   13: German Crown Prince in Bayreuth.
OCTOBER   1: Schott pays an advance of 10,000 marks on *Götterdämmerung*.   12 (to 14): Frau von Schleinitz in Bayreuth.   30 (to November 2): Nietzsche in Bayreuth.
NOVEMBER   11: celebrations in Pest for Liszt's 50th anniversary as professional musician (R. and C. W. not present).   20: R. W. and Feustel in Munich to discuss guarantee.   28: arrival of Hoffmann's sketches for *Ring* scenery.
DECEMBER   6: King Ludwig offers R. W. Order of Maximilian, which he accepts.   25: C. W. receives final score of *Götterdämmerung*, I, as birthday present, also the *"Kinderkatechismus."*

1874

JANUARY   6: King Ludwig refuses guarantee.   15: appeal for help to Grand Duke of Baden.   24: R. W. offers six overtures to Schott in order to earn money.   27: King Ludwig vows not to abandon R. W.
FEBRUARY   9: R. W. signs agreement with Schott for six overtures; King Ludwig asks Feustel to formulate proposals for guarantee.   20: agreement reached with King Ludwig for a loan.
APRIL   28: Wagner family moves into Wahnfried.
MAY   20 (to July 25): Richter at Wahnfried.   22: death of Marie Muchanoff.   27: C. W. gives her savings to pay debts on house.   31: Daniela confirmed.
JUNE   (to August): casting the *Ring;* various singers in Bayreuth for auditions and study.
JULY   10: work begun on full orchestral score of *Götterdämmerung*, III.
AUGUST   5 (to 15): Nietzsche in Bayreuth.
OCTOBER   26: death of Peter Cornelius.
NOVEMBER   21: full orchestral score of *Götterdämmerung* completed.
DECEMBER   19 (to 21): R. W. in Leipzig in search of singers.

1875

JANUARY 27: marriage of Hans Richter. 30: R. W. working on *"Albumblatt"* for Betty Schott.

FEBRUARY 5 (to 7): Richter and wife in Bayreuth. 15 (to March 25): Elisabeth Nietzsche at Wahnfried to look after children in R. and C. W.'s absence. 21: R. and C. W. in Vienna.

MARCH 1: R. W. conducts concert in Vienna (*"Kaisermarsch"* and extracts from *Götterdämmerung*). 3: meeting and reconciliation with Gottfried Semper. 6: R. and C. W. to Pest, where Liszt meets them. 10: concert, in which R. W. conducts and Liszt plays Beethoven's *Emperor* Concerto. 11: R. and C. W. return to Vienna, where on 14 R. W. conducts concert. 16: return to Bayreuth. 17: death of Klara Wolfram (R. W.'s sister).

APRIL 5: death of Betty Schott. 10: R. and C. W. in Leipzig to resume search for singers. 11: in Hanover. 13: in Brunswick. 15: in Berlin, where R. W. conducts concerts on 24 and 25. 27: return to Bayreuth.

MAY 3 (to 8): R. and C. W. in Vienna, where R. W. conducts concert on 6.

JUNE (to August): rehearsals with singers and orchestra in Bayreuth. 16 (to 19): C. W. in Weimar to visit Liszt.

SEPTEMBER 12 (to 19): family holiday in Bohemia.

OCTOBER 30: R. and C. W. leave for Vienna via Munich.

NOVEMBER 3: start of rehearsals for *Tannhäuser* (Paris version) in Vienna. 18: meeting with Brahms. 22: first performance of *Tannhäuser*. 26: start of rehearsals for *Lohengrin*.

DECEMBER 15: first performance of new *Lohengrin* production in Vienna. 17: return to Bayreuth.

1876

JANUARY 10: work resumed on *Mein Leben*.

FEBRUARY 5: R. W. expresses desire to start work on *Parsifal*. 9: work begun on "Centennial March." 29: R. and C. W. leave Bayreuth for Vienna.

MARCH 2: R. W. conducts *Lohengrin* in Vienna. 4: R. and C. W. arrive in Berlin. 5: death of Marie d'Agoult. 6: start of rehearsals for *Tristan und Isolde* in Berlin. 17: "Centennial March" completed. 20: first performance of *Tristan und Isolde* in Berlin. 24: return to Bayreuth.

APRIL Last-minute difficulties with casting (Sieglinde), rehearsals with Unger (Siegfried).

MAY Preliminary rehearsals with individual singers.

JUNE 1 (to 11): rehearsals of *Das Rheingold*. 12 (to 21): rehearsals of *Die Walküre*. 22 (to 30): rehearsals of *Siegfried*.

JULY 1 (to 11): rehearsals of *Götterdämmerung*. 14 (to 15): final rehearsals of *Das Rheingold*. 17 (to 19): final rehearsals of *Die Walküre*. 20 (to 22): final rehearsals of *Siegfried*. 23: Act II of *Götterdämmerung* performed before an audience to test theater acoustics. 24 (to 25): final rehearsals of *Götterdämmerung*. 24 (to August 2 or 3): Nietzsche in Bayreuth. 26 (to 31): various costume trials.

AUGUST 1: arrival of Liszt. 5: arrival of King Ludwig. 6 (to 9): dress rehearsals of *Ring* in presence of King Ludwig, who departs on 10. 12: arrival of Emperor Wilhelm I. 13 (to 17): first cycle of the *Ring*. 20 (to 23): second cycle. 27: King Ludwig returns for third and last cycle (27 to 30). 30: King Ludwig departs.

SEPTEMBER   2: Liszt departs.   14: R. and C. W. leave Bayreuth with family for Italy.   16: Verona.   19: Venice.   26: Bologna.   29: Naples.
OCTOBER   5: Sorrento.   27: Nietzsche visits R. and C. W. in Sorrento.
NOVEMBER   2: last meeting with Nietzsche.   7: Wagner family leaves Sorrento for Naples.   9: Rome.   11: meeting with Princess Wittgenstein.
DECEMBER   3: Florence.   6: meeting with Jessie Laussot.   18: Munich.   20: return to Bayreuth.

1877

JANUARY   8: R. W. calls for establishment of a Society of Patrons to promote a music school in Bayreuth.   14: Hans von Wolzogen in Bayreuth to discuss starting *Bayreuther Blätter* (periodical).   21 (to 23): Düfflipp (King Ludwig's Cabinet secretary) in Bayreuth to discuss future of festival.   25: work begun on *Parsifal* text.
FEBRUARY   28: *Parsifal* text completed in prose dialogue.
MARCH   9 (to 12): R. and C. W. visit Meiningen.   24 (to April 3): Liszt at Wahnfried.   30: text of Act I of *Parsifal* completed.
APRIL   13: text of Act II of *Parsifal* completed.   19: text of Act III of *Parsifal* completed.   29: R. and C. W. leave Bayreuth for London.
MAY   1: arrival in London.   6: meeting with George Eliot.   7: R. W. conducts first concert at the Albert Hall.   12: R. W. received by Prince of Wales.   17: R. W. received by Queen Victoria at Windsor.   29: R. W. conducts final concert at the Albert Hall.
JUNE   4: R. and C. W. leave London.   5: arrival in Ems (Germany), where the children join them.
JULY   5: family in Heidelberg.   18: in Lucerne.   19: visit to Tribschen.   20: in Munich, where on 21 R. W. discusses future of festival with Düfflipp and Perfall.   23: in Weimar with Liszt.   28: R. W. and children return to Bayreuth.
AUGUST   1: C. W. returns to Bayreuth.   2: first notes of music for *Parsifal*.   12 (to 15): Liszt at Wahnfried.
SEPTEMBER   14 (to 15): Wagner Society delegates meet in Bayreuth to discuss future of festival and founding of music school; Society of Patrons formed.   26: orchestral sketch of *Parsifal* Prelude completed.
OCTOBER   (to December): R. W. working on composition sketch of *Parsifal,* I.   29: C. W. starts translating *Parsifal* text into French.
DECEMBER   4: decision to publish *Bayreuther Blätter.*

1878

JANUARY   R. W. working on orchestral sketch of *Parsifal,* I.   21: Angelo Neumann visits Bayreuth.   24: first performance of *Das Rheingold* in Vienna.
FEBRUARY   R. W. working on orchestral sketch of *Parsifal,* II (to October 13), and article *What Is German?*   7: first issue of *Bayreuther Blätter* published.
MARCH   3 (to 8): Frau von Schleinitz in Bayreuth.
APRIL   2: news of Anton Pusinelli's death.   8 (to 17): Liszt in Bayreuth.   19 (to 22): Amalie Materna in Bayreuth.   25: Nietzsche sends his new book, *Menschliches, Allzumenschliches.*   28 and 29: *Das Rheingold* and *Die Walküre* in Leipzig (Neumann).
MAY   (to July): R. W. working on article "Public and Popularity."
JUNE   23: opening of Berlin Congress.

JULY 1 (to 2): Levi in Bayreuth. 13: Berlin peace treaty signed.
AUGUST 1 (to 2): Levi in Bayreuth. 2: Kellermann comes to Bayreuth as copyist.
5 (to 10): Klindworth in Bayreuth. 20 (to 31): Liszt in Bayreuth. 27 (to October
14): Malwida von Meysenbug staying in Bayreuth.
SEPTEMBER 15: first performance of *Götterdämmerung* in Munich. 16 (to 17):
Standhartner in Bayreuth. 21 and 22: *Siegfried* and *Götterdämmerung* in Leipzig
(Neumann).
OCTOBER 13: orchestral sketch of *Parsifal,* II, completed. 31: R. W. plays Prelude
to *Parsifal,* III, to Cosima.
NOVEMBER R. W. working on orchestral sketch of *Parsifal,* III (to April 26,
1879). 9: *Siegfried* in Vienna.
DECEMBER 11 (to 19): R. W. working on his article "Retrospect of the Stage
Festivals of 1876." 25: *Parsifal* Prelude played at Wahnfried by Meiningen
orchestra as birthday gift for Cosima; concert of Beethoven works at Wahnfried,
conducted by R. W.

1879

JANUARY 13: Levi in Bayreuth. 28: first performance of *Rienzi* in London.
FEBRUARY 14: *Götterdämmerung* in Vienna. 22 (to 25): C. W. in Munich (alone).
APRIL 2 (to May 13): R. W. working on article "Shall We Hope?" 10: Levi in
Bayreuth. 26: orchestral sketch of *Parsifal* completed.
MAY 15: death of Gottfried Semper. 21: Frau von Schleinitz, Levi, and Lenbach
in Bayreuth for R. W.'s birthday.
JUNE 13 (to 18): R. W. working on article "On Poetry and Composition."
JULY 6: decision to postpone production of *Parsifal* (originally promised for 1880).
10 (to 29): R. W. working on article "On Opera Poetry and Composition in
Particular."
AUGUST 7: beginning of R. W.'s active interest in problem of vivisection. 21
(to 31): Liszt in Bayreuth. 23: R. W. begins work on full orchestral score of
Parsifal.
SEPTEMBER 12 (to 13): Ernst von Weber in Bayreuth. 15 (to November 11):
R. W. working on article "On the Application of Music to the Drama." 20 (to
29): R. W. working on his "Open Letter to E. v. W." (article on vivisection). 22
(to 24): Friedrich Schön in Bayreuth.
OCTOBER 15 (to 18): Levi in Bayreuth. 20: Stein comes to Bayreuth as Siegfried's
tutor.
NOVEMBER 5 (to 6): Richter in Bayreuth. 5 (to December 4): Gersdorff in
Bayreuth.
DECEMBER 5 (to 20): R. W. ill with erysipelas. 31: R. W. and family depart for
Italy.

1880

JANUARY 1 (to 2): in Munich, meetings with Levi, Lenbach, and Gedon. 4:
arrival at Villa d'Angri, Naples, met by Gersdorff. 6 (to 13): recurrence of erysipelas. 12: arrival of Stein. 16: departure of Gersdorff. 18: Joukowsky's first
visit. 27 (to February 9): recurrence of R. W.'s erysipelas.
FEBRUARY 19 (to April 23): working on *Mein Leben.* 20: Joukowsky begins
portrait of C. W.

MARCH   10 (and 25): Giovanna Lucca at Villa d'Angri.

APRIL   4: *Lohengrin* performed in Rome.

MAY   17 (to June 21): Malwida von Meysenbug in Naples.   17: visit to Villa d'Angri of Hartmann, Humperdinck, and Plüddemann.   22: *Parsifal* choruses sung for R. W.'s birthday; as a birthday gift King Ludwig undertakes to pay rent of villa in Naples for a further five months.   26: visit to Ravello, "discovered Klingsor's garden."

JUNE   R. W. working on article "Religion and Art" (to July 25).   7: plans for making the Bayreuth festival a "protectorate" of the King of Bavaria.

JULY   10: departure of Stein.

AUGUST   6: decision to leave Naples because of recurrence of erysipelas.   8: R. and C. W. in Rome.   9 (to 12): in Pistoia.   13 (to 20): in Perugia.   21: in Siena, visit to Siena cathedral.   22: rejoined by children (and Joukowsky) in Siena (Villa Torre Fiorentina).

SEPTEMBER   16 (to 25): Liszt in Siena.   24: R. W. finishes ruling lines for full orchestral score of *Parsifal*.

OCTOBER   1: R. W. and family (and Joukowsky) leave Siena for Florence.   4: arrival in Venice.   6 (to 8): Wolzogen in Venice.   18 (to 25): R. W. working on article "What Boots This Knowledge?"   22: R. W.'s first meeting with Gobineau.   30: departure from Venice.   31: arrival in Munich.

NOVEMBER   4: R. W. at performance of *Der Fliegende Holländer*.   7: *Tristan und Isolde*.   10: meeting with King Ludwig and performance of *Lohengrin*.   12: R. W. conducts private performance of *Parsifal* Prelude for King Ludwig.   17: return to Bayreuth.   23: R. W. resumes work on full orchestral score of *Parsifal*.   28: Neumann in Bayreuth.

DECEMBER   6 (to 15): Stein in Bayreuth.

1881

JANUARY   7 (to 10): Heckel, Schön, and Pohl in Bayreuth for conference of Society of Patrons.   8: Humperdinck arrives in Bayreuth to prepare a fair copy of *Parsifal* score.   13 (to 14): Karl Brandt in Bayreuth to discuss staging of *Parsifal*.   31: Levi in Bayreuth.

FEBRUARY   2 (to 10): R. W. working on article "Know Thyself."

MARCH   6 (to 12): R. W. composing extra music for transformation scene in *Parsifal*, I.   14: assassination of Tsar Alexander II.   22 (to 23): Brandt and Brückner brothers in Bayreuth to discuss *Parsifal* scenery.   27: R. W. accepts Joukowsky's costume designs for *Parsifal*.

APRIL   7 (to 8): Francke in Bayreuth to discuss plans for staging Wagner works in London.   12 (to 13): Levi in Bayreuth.   27: Daniela reunited with Hans von Bülow in Berlin.   29: R. and C. W. arrive in Berlin for *Ring* performances (Neumann).

MAY   1 (to 4): R. W. at *Ring* rehearsals.   5: *Das Rheingold*.   6: *Die Walküre*.   8: *Siegfried*.   9: *Götterdämmerung;* R. W. refuses invitation to meet the German Crown Prince.   11: return to Bayreuth, met by Gobineau, who was visiting Wahnfried (to June 7).   25: R. and C. W. return to Berlin with children, Gobineau, and Joukowsky to see the *Ring*.   29: R. W. offends Neumann by leaving stage during speech of thanks.   30: return to Bayreuth.

JUNE   26: Levi arrives in Bayreuth.   29: anonymous letter upsets Levi.   29 (to July 2): Marianne Brandt in Bayreuth, R. W. offers her role of Kundry.   30: Levi departs for Bamberg.

JULY 1 (to 4): Levi again in Bayreuth. 6 (to 7): Frau von Schleinitz in Bayreuth. 10 (to 11): C. W. in Nuremberg, where she meets Hans von Bülow. 19: Neumann in Bayreuth, reconciliation. 26: scenery for Magic Garden in *Parsifal* ready for inspection.

AUGUST 3 (to October 22): Stein in Bayreuth. 5: Carrie Pringle sings at Wahnfried. 7 (to 8): Francke in Bayreuth, contract signed for London performances. 8 (to 9): Weber in Bayreuth. 21: Winkelmann sings at Bayreuth. 23 (to September 17): R. W. working on article "Herodom and Christianity." 26: Marianne Brandt in Bayreuth; rehearsals with Winkelmann.

SEPTEMBER 5 (to 14): R. and C. W. in Dresden. 6: Therese Malten in *Der Fliegende Holländer.* 22 (to October 10): Liszt in Bayreuth. 26 (to 29): Judith Gautier in Bayreuth.

OCTOBER 19: orchestration of *Parsifal,* II, completed. 23 (to 25): R. W. starts work on article "On the Womanly in the Human" but breaks off.

NOVEMBER 1 (to 5): R. W. and family journey to Palermo (Hôtel des Palmes) via Munich, Verona, and Naples. 8: R. W. starts work on full orchestral score of *Parsifal,* III.

DECEMBER 24: Joukowsky rejoins the family. 29: news of Karl Brandt's death.

1882

JANUARY 13: completion of full orchestral score of *Parsifal.* 15: Renoir paints portrait sketch of R. W. 22: Joukowsky departs.

FEBRUARY 2: move into Villa del Principe Gangi, Piazza dei Porrazzi.

MARCH 2: R. W. composes "Porrazzi Melody." 15: Count Gravina asks for Blandine's hand in marriage. 18: R. W. gives concert, conducting local military band in his own works. 20: R. W. and family move to Acireale with Gravina. 28: R. W. has severe heart attack.

APRIL 10: R. W. and family leave Acireale for Messina with Gravina. 14: parting from Gravina in Naples. 15: arrival in Venice. 22: news of Hans von Bülow's engagement to Marie Schanzer. 29: R. W. attempts to visit Karl Ritter; departure from Venice. 30: in Munich.

MAY 1: arrival in Bayreuth. 5 (to 6): Levi in Bayreuth, preparations for *Parsifal* production. 9: Fritz Brandt in Bayreuth, news of *Ring* in London (Neumann). 11 (to June 17): Gobineau in Bayreuth. 18: news of Francke-Pollini season in London. 22 (to June 7): Gravina in Bayreuth.

JUNE 11 (to 17): R. W. working on his "Open Letter to Friedrich Schön in Worms" (school plans). 14: Levi in Bayreuth. 22: arrival of Stein in Bayreuth. 28: R. W. accepts Humperdinck's music for *Parsifal* transformation scene.

JULY 2: start of rehearsals with full company. 15 (to August 30): Liszt in Bayreuth. 18 (to September 2): Malwida von Meysenbug in Bayreuth. 24 on: guests arrive for festival, including Frau von Schleinitz, Judith Gautier, and Mathilde Maier. 26: first performance of *Parsifal.*

AUGUST 9: Gravina arrives in Bayreuth. 25: Gravina and Blandine married (church ceremony on 26). 29: last performance of *Parsifal,* R. W. conducts final part.

SEPTEMBER 14: R. W. and family, accompanied by Stein and Rubinstein, leave for Venice via Munich and Verona. 18: move into Palazzo Vendramin.

OCTOBER 3 (to 8): Levi in Venice. 8: Schleinitzes in Venice. 15: departure of Stein. 22 (to November 4): R. W. working on article "The Stage Dedication Festival in Bayreuth 1882." 25: news of Gobineau's death.

NOVEMBER   19 (to January 13, 1883): Liszt at Palazzo Vendramin.
DECEMBER   6 (to 10): Gross in Venice to discuss King Ludwig's insistence on
Parsifal in Munich.   8: arrival of Joukowsky.   18: Humperdinck in Venice.   18:
news of Hans von Bülow's serious illness.   24: R. W. conducts his youthful
Symphony in C Major at the Teatro La Fenice.   28 (to 30): R. W. working on his
article "A Youthful Symphony."

1883

JANUARY   4 (to 11): Marie Dönhoff in Venice.   13: Gross in Venice to discuss
Parsifal performances in 1883.   21 (to 29): R. W. working on his "Letter to Herr
von Stein" (preface to volume of Stein's works).
FEBRUARY   4: Levi arrives in Venice.   11: R. W. starts work on his article "On the
Womanly in the Human."   13: R. W.'s death.

Index

R. W.'s Musical Compositions

Index of R. W.'s Writings

General Index